In the Ring

With

Jack Johnson

Part II: The Reign

Adam J. Pollack

**WIN BY
KO**

Win By KO Publications

Iowa City

In the Ring With Jack Johnson
Part II: The Reign

Adam J. Pollack

(ISBN-13): 978-0-9903703-4-5

(hardcover: 50# acid-free alkaline paper)

Includes footnotes, appendix, bibliography, and index.

Cover design by Gwyn Snider ©

Front cover photo colorization by Corey Parker ©

Manufactured in the United States of America.

Win By KO Publications

Iowa City, Iowa

winbykopublications.com

Contents

CHAPTER 1

The Return

On December 26, 1908 in Sydney, Australia, Jack Johnson became the first black man to win the world heavyweight championship when the police stopped his fight with Tommy Burns in the 14th round and referee and promoter Hugh McIntosh awarded the decision to Johnson.

Ordinarily in this series, the focus has been primarily on a fighter's boxing life, usually referencing his outside-the-ring life if it had an impact upon his boxing career. In no other career has a fighter's life outside of boxing been as relevant to the analysis of his ring life as with the case of Jack Johnson. Sociology and race politics are critically important to understanding Johnson's ring career. The impediments and restrictions he faced, as well as some of the analysis of him as a fighter and person are directly intertwined with race.

Jack Johnson was an anomaly. Prior to Tommy Burns, no other heavyweight champion had given a black man the opportunity to win boxing's top crown. This was in part because it was believed that the social order was threatened if a black man was able to compete for or represent supremacy in anything. To many, a black man never should have been given the opportunity to win the title.

Immediately after Jack Johnson won the world heavyweight championship, much of the white press and public began seeking a white challenger to regain the championship for the white race, so that the color line could once again be drawn firmly. Thus began the start of the "white hope" era.

The public and press were so obsessed with Johnson that probably no other human being received as much press as he did during his reign. Johnson wore white hatred and the desire to unseat him from the championship like a badge of honor. His success was a symbol of hope to oppressed black Americans.

"BLACK MAN'S BURDENS."

Washington Bee, January 2, 1909

The fight that the press and public most wanted was Johnson vs. retired undefeated former champion James J. Jeffries, because many believed that the invincible Jeffries could return the championship to the white race.

Initially, Jeffries balked at the idea of a comeback and insisted that he would not return to the ring if Johnson won. However, soon after the fight, in January 1909, in response to public pressure, Jeffries said that he would do some training and exhibiting and see how his body responded. If he felt that he could get back into form, he might consider fighting Johnson.

Reports oscillated back and forth about whether Jeff really intended to return again. Jeffries put up his alfalfa farm for sale, which made some believe that he intended to return to his old boxing life. During January, Jeff began making very good money giving short sparring exhibitions with heavyweight Sam Berger throughout the country, for the public turned out in droves to see whether Jeff could come back. A potential Jeffries comeback was a running theme which newspapers and the public obsessed about for some time to come. The amount of ink devoted to both Johnson and Jeffries was tremendous, omnipresent, and continuous.

While black newspapers often printed opinions of those who thought Jeff would lose such a bout, white newspapers were more inclined to print the opinions of those who believed that Jeffries would restore the honor of the white race. As time progressed, it practically was considered sacrilege and disloyal to the white race to give an opinion otherwise. Although there were those who wondered whether Jeffries could come back, most wanted him to try, feeling that he could defeat Johnson if he got back into shape.

Once Jack Johnson became champion, the white press began scrutinizing his every move, and increasingly focused on his personal life, which previously had been given little mention in the newspapers. This shift became quite palpable as the years progressed.

Unlike whites, most blacks rejoiced at the fact that a black man now occupied the esteemed position of world heavyweight champion. It had a psychologically uplifting effect. This was important, given that this was a time when blacks were held back by Jim Crow laws and told that they were inferior to whites. Of course, this also explains why many white folks felt the need to tear down Johnson personally and hope to see him defeated.[1]

Throughout January and the first half of February 1909, under Harry Rickards' management, champion Jack Johnson spent time in each of the various Australian states making easy money participating in exhibitions.

Johnson said he was willing to meet Jeffries, Burns, or any other man alive if sufficient financial inducements were offered. Jack planned to go to Vancouver, Chicago, and then Galveston to visit his mother. He intended to return to London in April to commence music hall engagements before fighting Sam Langford at the National Sporting Club.[2]

Johnson's mother Tiny Johnson said Jack helped his family, often sending money to her and his sisters. He had purchased a home in Galveston for his mother. Before the championship fight, he had told his family that he could not lose to Burns, and advised them to sell the furniture and bet it all on him.[3]

On Monday February 15, 1909, Jack Johnson left Sydney, Australia on the steamer *Makura*, headed towards Vancouver, Ontario, Canada.[4]

The *Sydney Bulletin* opined as to why blacks were successful in the ring.

> The Yankee is becoming perturbed over the success of the negro in the square 'ring.' There are 72 millions of white men, and only eight millions of blacks, in the U.S.A., and yet the number of clever colored boxers is out of all proportion to their population basis. Why? … The general impression seems to be that the white bruiser gets a swelled head before the colored one. In fact, he gets it before he has learned his business thoroughly, whereas it is only when he has become 'a scientist,' like Jack Johnson and other great men, that the negro begins to inquire for 9 ½ inch hats. … But, all the same, writer's opinion is quite different. The black man is still the child of Nature,

---

[1] *Washington Times*, January 14, 1909; *Nashville Globe*, July 9, 1909.
On January 14, 1909 in Philadelphia, top black lightweight/welterweight Jack Blackburn (who once had sparred with Johnson) shot Alonzo Polk and both of their respective wives. Blackburn's wife had attempted to stab Alonzo Polk's wife. Mr. Polk joined the fight, and then Blackburn. Eventually Blackburn started shooting, hitting all three, one bullet unintentionally striking his own wife. Alonzo Polk later died from his injuries and Blackburn was charged with murder. In July, Blackburn, pled guilty to second degree murder and was sentenced to 15 years in prison. About two weeks earlier, Blackburn's own brother had slashed and badly cut his face with a razor. Years later, Blackburn would train Joe Louis.
[2] *New York World*, February 13, 15, 1909.
[3] *Los Angeles Times*, December 27, 28, 1908.
[4] *Sydney Bulletin*, February 18, 1909.

closer to the earth. He is handier to the period when man had to rely for his defence upon his own physical powers. The white man has passed that stage. He slays his enemies with projectiles. … Boxing is, after all, a barbaric business, inasmuch as it is the art of pounding an opponent into submission by brute force. Brute force, scientifically applied, if you like; but, nevertheless, brute force. And in the white man's blood the idea is to apply not physical force, but mechanical power. Therein lies the difference between the two races, and naturally the race that is closest to the stage in which man fought for his life with his hands, feet, and teeth, will produce the larger proportion of boxers.[5]

Although Jim Jeffries was still telling his friends that he had no intention of fighting Johnson, the training he was doing as part of his theatrical show, which contained some brief sparring, caused many to suspect that he was considering something more. The *Sydney Bulletin* wrote,

Among fight-followers it is whispered that James is really testing himself. He is deplorably out of condition, has got fat inside, and knows it. But if, after six weeks or so of training, he feels that he is getting good, and his progress indicates that he can get back to his former state of toughness, he will one day emerge from his shell. … The general opinion among pugs of all sorts is if Jeff can get back to condition Massa Johnson will climb between the ropes before 10 rounds are through. The *Bulletin* doesn't think so. Johnson may not be a heroic fighter, but he knows enough to keep the ex-boilermaker at bay for 10 rounds. It is after the 10th that he will probably begin to go to pieces.[6]

Some said that world middleweight champion Stanley Ketchel was adding weight, and at 170 pounds would prove dangerous for anyone. He was game and one of the hardest punchers in the world. Although previously he had drawn the color line, Ketchel said he was willing to cross the line to win the heavyweight championship back for the white race.[7]

On February 20, 1909 in Paris, France, Sam McVey (sometimes called McVea) won a 20-round decision over Joe Jeannette.

When he arrived in Chicago on March 1, 1909, Jim Jeffries proved that he was still the most popular fighter in the U.S., for the police had to be summoned to clear the streets. Interviewers anxious to learn if he would enter the ring again to fight Jack Johnson besieged him. The former champion said,

---

[5] *Sydney Bulletin*, February 25, 1909. It should be noted that Australians were not exactly thrilled themselves that a black man had defeated a white man for the championship.
[6] *Sydney Bulletin*, February 25, 1909.
[7] *Richmond Planet*, February 20, 1909.

The interview in which I am represented as saying that I had decided to meet Jack Johnson and that I thought it was up to me to retrieve the honor of the white race and all that rot was a simple fabrication. I never said anything of the sort.

It would be foolish of me to make any such assertion until I know just what my actual condition is and whether I can be the fighter of the past once more. I am now trying to learn just how far I can go and what shape I can train into. Not till that is definitely settled to my own satisfaction one way or the other will I make a definite authorized statement as to my boxing plans.

During subsequent days, Jeff further explained why he did not want to announce his comeback or confirm that he was going to fight Johnson:

I weigh just 245 pounds. I haven't smoked cigarettes and I haven't dissipated. I can go along nicely for some time on the route I am now going and I can keep conditioned. I may not need to meet this nigger. I want to say that if I should announce right now that I would go in the ring with him and then fail to reach the training condition that would make me feel I was right the public would put me down as a faker. I would rather go in the ring and take a chance to be knocked out than be considered a confidence man.

Jeffries consistently maintained that before deciding whether or not he would fight Johnson, he needed time to get into condition and see whether he felt that he could get back to his old form again. Regardless, everywhere he went, he was given a great reception and hounded with questions of whether and when he would return the title to the white race. He was advertised as the undefeated heavyweight champion.

The *New York World* said that when Jeffries arrived in New York, the throng of humanity that came to see him far exceeded that which came to greet the President-elect of the United States, William H. Taft.

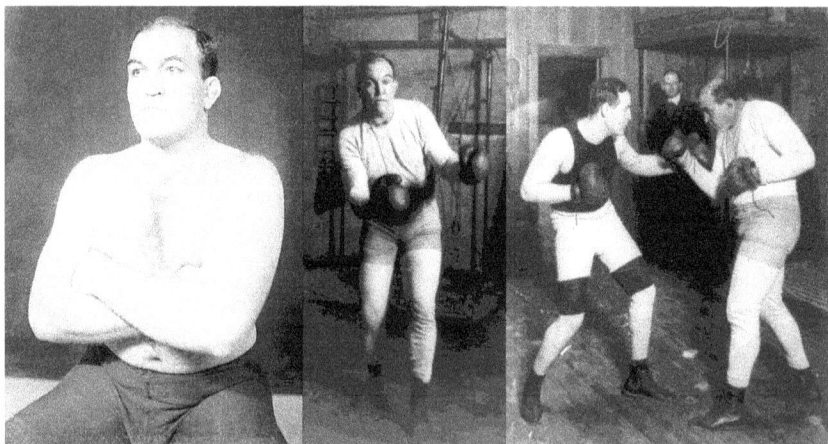

Jim Jeffries as of March 1909, sparring Sam Berger

Jeffries was a big hit on the New York vaudeville stage. Large crowds watched him train - skipping rope, throwing the medicine ball, pulling levers, pushing springs, working his stomach muscles, and sparring. For his abdominal work, while seated on a stool, Jeff reached backward, touched the stage with his massive head, and raised himself at will by sheer force of the abdominal muscles, doing this several times. He then boxed 4 shortened rounds with big Sam Berger in tame and friendly fashion. Still, observers were surprised at Jeff's speed and agility. "Jeffries now is the repository of a yearning of a race which longs to assert its supremacy. So it is that he is the magnet of the hour, drawing an enormous salary for an extraordinary period for spending about ten minutes a night on the stage."[8]

Jack Johnson was traveling with a white woman who purportedly was his wife. There was some mystery surrounding how he had met her, when or if he had married her, and who she was. One newspaper said that apparently, without divorcing his first wife, who had sued him for nonsupport, Johnson had married a white English barmaid while he had been in England.[9]

Another newspaper said Johnson was accompanied by his white wife, Nellie O'Brien (who others called Hattie Smith, Hattie McLay, Anna McClay, or Hattie Watson), "who married him after his victory over Burns." It said he had met her in Philadelphia. Some said he had married her in Philly several years ago, while others claimed he married her in England or Australia. No one really knew. More would be revealed later. Quite frankly, Johnson had a habit of often calling a current girlfriend his "wife." "She says she is very proud of her dark husband and thinks he is the greatest man in the world. She was very much disappointed at not being permitted to see the fight at Sydney, but contented herself with the statement that, anyhow, Mrs. Burns did not see it either." In his autobiography, Johnson called her Hattie McClay and said she was a New York Irish gal whom he had met before his trip to Europe to chase after Burns.

While on board the ship on his return journey, Johnson participated in a couple of concerts, playing the bass violin. Mrs. Johnson played the piano and accompanied Jack, and they were well received.

---

[8] *New York World*, March 2 - 4, 9, 1909.
[9] *San Francisco Call*, January 24, 1909. When Johnson had been in Australia, an Australian paper printed a story about his intended marriage with a white Oakland woman named Lola Toy. She entered a libel suit against the newspaper and secured a verdict for $7,500.

Johnson said that he was a bad sailor, and often felt sick to his stomach at sea. However, he was quite popular on the ship. A score of ladies clustered about him to say good-bye when he eventually left.

Johnson decided to part ways with his manager, Australian Sam Fitzpatrick. Jack had a reputation for jilting managers. He had many in his time, and sporting men said Fitzpatrick was lucky to hold on to him for so long. When Alex McLean managed his 1907 Australian tour, Johnson not only left him but gave him a beating as well.

Johnson said he had no trouble with Fitzpatrick or any ill will. It just was a matter of economics. He felt that he no longer needed a manager. Jack said, "His contract was up, and it was not renewed."

Regarding their split, Fitzpatrick shrugged his shoulders and said it was impossible for any man to handle Johnson after he won the title, for Jack had a "bad case of a swelled head." "Johnson was a different man before the fight. He would feed out of the hand then, but he is a hard man to handle now. We decided to split up soon after the Makura left. Anyhow, he don't want a manager now. He has got Mrs. Johnson as his manager." Another newspaper said they had split "owing to the woman in the case."

Despite the separation, Sam Fitzpatrick bore him no ill will, and still was quite high on Johnson as a fighter. He said,

> I can see nothing to it but that Johnson will be champion for as many years as Jeffries held the title. … You may take it from me that Johnson is not afraid to meet Jeffries. The colored man says that he will meet any man and literally that includes Jeffries, and he means it that way. In their fight in Sydney Burns was never in it for a moment. He had no chance at all. I believe fully that Johnson is the greatest fighter now in sight, white or black. He has great courage and endurance and his science is unquestioned. He is as quick and as agile and hard as a big tiger.

Fitzpatrick felt that Jeffries and others were underrating Johnson. Sam said Jeffries was the only white fighter who had any chance with Johnson.

> But I don't think that even Jeffries could beat the black. Jeff is a long way from being in shape, and even if he got in good condition, I sincerely believe, knowing both well, that the black man would have the better of it. For Corbett to fight Johnson would be ridiculous. Ketchel is altogether too small. It would be a shame to match them. … Johnson is destined to hold the championship for some time to my way of thinking.

Johnson was irritated by the treatment that he had received in Australia. Not only did sportswriters and the sporting element criticize him, but the general public did as well. They were Burns fans, and preferred the white man. They criticized Johnson for his playful taunts directed at Burns, but failed to note how Burns had insulted Johnson. Jack did not feel that he had received the treatment that was due him as champion in Australia, though the better class treated him very well.

Although race was a factor, Johnson did not think his race was the only factor that counted against him with Australians. Burns had been there longer and had more opportunity to square himself with the masses. Also, religion had an impact. A large percentage of the population was Roman Catholic, which was Burns' faith, which made him popular. Johnson was a Methodist, and therefore, "outside the pale." Further, Burns was the betting favorite; a lot of people had their money on him, and therefore were rooting for him. They did not think Johnson had trained properly. They blamed Johnson for their having lost money. Jack said,

> They didn't understand my method of training. I used to get up at 6 o'clock in the morning, eat an orange or some other fruit, and then go on the road. By 9 o'clock I had done all my work, and the rest of the day I would spend driving about in my car. As the people did not see me do my training, they thought I wasn't doing any. Then a couple of days before the fight, I went out with a party of friends and had a glass of wine, and the report was circulated that I was drunk. Why I never drink to excess at any time, and least of all when training, but it just goes to show how I got in bad.[10]

Johnson noted that while in Australia, despite being a Methodist, the churches there drew the color line on him, for "they did not seem to have much use for a colored man in the Methodist churches of that white Australia."

Still, he said that overall, Australians were good sports. "They treated me fine and I've got no kick coming. But, on the square, they seemed to think more of Tommy Burns after I had licked him – giving him such a licking as anybody ever had – than they did of me, and me the champion." To him, this defied logic. "Australia has no reason to complain about me though. I paid my income tax all the time and I raised a good deal of money for various charities while in Sydney." On a personal note, Johnson said he liked to read Shakespeare for comfort.

When Johnson's attention was called to a Galveston dispatch announcing that committees had been formed to arrange a parade for him in Galveston, where he grew up, his eyes sparkled, he showed his gold-tipped teeth with a grin, and said, "Tell them I'll be there."

On the morning of March 9, 1909, after three weeks at sea, Johnson arrived in Victoria, Canada. The big crowd of fight fans who congregated at the dock gave him a great reception. Everyone wanted to shake his hand. The reception tickled the smiling Johnson. George Paris, the Vancouver Athletic Club's boxing instructor, met Johnson there and came with him on the boat from Victoria to Vancouver.

Before leaving Victoria, Johnson said,

---

[10] *Daily Province, Ogden Standard, San Francisco Call, New York World*, March 10, 1909.

I am willing to meet Jeffries. I am willing to meet any man in the world, and I don't think anyone can get a decision over me much less put me out. It amuses me to hear this talk of Jeffries claiming the championship. Why when a mayor leaves office he's an ex-mayor, isn't he? When a champion leaves the ring he's an ex-champion. Well that's Jeff. If he wants to try to get the championship back I'm willing to take him on. … In all the notices I have seen, it's all what Jeffries will take. What's the matter with what Johnson will take. I'm the champion, ain't I? I want a winner and loser's end; I don't care what it is, 60 and 40, or 75 and 25, but there's got to be a winner and loser's end. … If Jeffries wants a go, as the papers say, he's got to see me, and there's got to be a winner and loser's end.[11]

Some said that Jeffries wanted a small ring if they were to fight. Johnson said that kind of talk did not scare him. "I will fight him in a 16, 12, or even a 10-foot ring if he wants to have it that way."

A delegation of colored sports, including Denver Ed Martin (with whom Jack was set to spar at the Vancouver Athletic Club), met Johnson in Vancouver and gave him a mighty cheer. Beautifully attired in white pants, red necktie, and lavender shirt, Johnson received the adulation of scores of "dusky skinned admirers" who had flocked to Vancouver from the U.S. He attracted more attention than "an Indian potentate."

George Paris tried to help Johnson secure lodging at a Vancouver hotel. However, despite application at a half dozen downtown hotels, including the St. Francis, the Rainier, the Irving, the Metropole, and the Astor, all of them essentially drew the color line. They did not do so explicitly, all saying that there was no room and they were filled up, but it was obvious what they were doing. Finally, a frustrated Mr. Paris had Johnson and his wife stay at his home.[12]

Johnson said he would not be defending his title against Sam Langford in May in London, as had been reported. Negotiations had fallen through. The National Sporting Club had offered a total purse of only 1,000 pounds ($5,000), a paltry amount for a world heavyweight title fight, particularly one against a well-regarded contender. Johnson said, "I wouldn't fight for that." Now that he was champion, Jack realized his economic value and power. The days of being paid a fraction of his true value were over. He wanted fair compensation, and was not about to allow either opponents or promoters to obtain the lion's share of the money.

---

[11] *Daily Province* (Vancouver, British Columbia, Canada), March 9, 1909. Johnson said he would fight Jeffries anytime, and even on as little as three weeks' notice. He would drop any and all theatrical engagements to make the fight happen.
[12] *Daily Province, Tacoma Times*, March 10, 1909. On the afternoon of the 9th, Johnson gave a talk to the juvenile class at the Vancouver Athletic Club, offering his advice. That evening in Vancouver, Johnson was the guest of the Railway Porters' club, where he entertained members with ring stories.

Johnson felt that it was time for him to reap the financial rewards that other champions had. "I think I should be given a chance to cut the melon. I went to Australia and gave Burns everything he asked in the way of money just to get at him, and now that I am the champion I think I should be allowed to reap the profits." He would make easy money with theatrical engagements for a while. This made perfect sense. "Johnson got all the glory and very little of the money in the Burns battle, and it is apparent from his demeanor that he intends to get the money as well as the glory next time."

Following his theatrical engagements, Johnson was willing to meet anybody in the world, as long as there was a winner's and loser's end. At that time, he believed that the amount earned should be based upon success in the fight. "It must be admitted that he is asking for the fairest sort of a shake at that. Other champions of the day are prone to demand a guarantee win or lose, but Johnson admits that he will be content to split the purse with any man in the world on a winning and losing percentage basis." Jack further said, "I will fight Ketchel, Jeffries or anybody else when the time comes. The public seems to demand a fight between me and Ketchel, and I think that he should be the first one."[13]

The *San Francisco Call* printed a poem entitled "The Color Question."

> Says Mistah Johnsing to Mistah Jeffries:
>
> Come, now tell us, Mistah Jeffries, is yo' re'lly gwinter fight,
> Is yo' gwinter take your chance wif de culled man's delight,
> Is yo' game to face de moosic when de coon begins to play.
> Or does de whisper frum yo' hea't say, "Honey, keep away"?
> Yah! Yo' mahty gran' an' haughty as yo' walk upon de stage,
> An' puff yo' chest an' show yo' ahms an' jes' be all de rage;
> But dere's de white man's burden – which de white men couldn't pack –
> Now, is y' gwinter pick it up, or is yo' turnin' back?
> Is yo' gwinter quit yo' bluffin', is yo' comin' to de scratch,
> Is yo' gwinter quit yo' talk, is yo' gwinter to make a match,
> Is yo' hank'ring fer to step in where de udders have not dared,
> Come, tell us, Mistah Jeffries, will yo' fight – or are yo' scared?[14]

On Wednesday March 10, 1909 at the Vancouver Athletic Club in Vancouver, British Columbia, Canada, the day after his arrival in Canada, world heavyweight champion Jack Johnson boxed a scheduled 6-round exhibition bout against a Tacoma-based fighter named Victor McLaglen (also spelled McLaglan), who was of Scottish ancestry.

McLaglen was a substitute for Denver Ed Martin, who was supposed to be boxing Johnson that evening, but allegedly unexpectedly was called away

---

[13] *Daily Province, Tacoma Times*, March 10, 1909.
[14] *San Francisco Call*, March 10, 1909.

to Seattle. Perhaps he got intimidated. Upon seeing Martin earlier on the 10th, Johnson said, "Better look out for yourself, Ed. I am feeling pretty fine now that I have gotten rid of my sea legs and I feel just like eating up some large man, black or white, I don't care much which." Denver Ed smiled and assured the champion that he would be able to "step lively." Yet, Martin pulled out of the exhibition.[15]

So McLaglen actually was a last-minute fill-in. The 25-year-old McLaglen's record included: 1908 W20 Emil Schock, KO6 Curley Carr, KO2 Fred Russell, and LKOby3 Denver Ed Martin.

Victor McLaglen and Jack Johnson before their 6-round exhibition bout

According to the local *Daily Province*, when the show commenced, Johnson appeared in the ring resplendent in his formal evening tuxedo. After the club president introduced him, the crowd cheered Johnson, who responded with a speech. This was his first exhibition as champion in North America, and he complimented the people of Vancouver for being fair-minded and good sports. He called Burns "that great, game little fellow." He concluded by saying that he was ready and willing to meet Jeffries at any time or place. Johnson left to change and prepare himself.

Before the bout began, it was announced that McLaglen weighed 198 pounds, while Johnson weighed 211 pounds. Secondary sources say Victor stood 6'3".

In terms of physical appearance, McLaglen shaped up well to the champion. However, in the clinches, Johnson was far stronger, handling Mac "as though he were a child. He threw McLaglan around at will, and made the Tacoma man look foolish most of the time." Victor tried hard to do something, but could not.

---

[15] *Daily Province, Tacoma Times*, March 10, 1909.

The bout almost terminated in the first minute of the 1st round. Johnson had McLaglen's arms locked, when Jack suddenly broke away his left from the clinch and shot it hard into the body. It was the wallop that Fitzsimmons made famous, a left into the solar plexus. McLaglen was smiling at the time, but the smile changed to a look of agony as he backed away slowly. He remained on his feet for a few seconds, but then in a delayed reaction, sank to his knees and doubled up on the floor.

Even after rising, McLaglen was very weak and all-in for about 30 seconds. However, because it was only an exhibition, Johnson did not try to finish him. "As McLaglan had no business in the ring in the first place, not having the speed to cope with the shifty black, he made but a sorry showing thereafter. Johnson had to take the best of care not to do any damage, and it must be admitted he succeeded admirably." Johnson carried the hopelessly outclassed McLaglen, toying with him for 6 rounds.

Between rounds, Johnson did not even bother to sit on his stool. He stood up against the ropes and carried on an animated conversation with George Paris about the latest fashions in diamonds in London. Conversely, Victor's seconds fanned and watered him.

The champ took things coolly and never extended himself.

> Johnson just did enough work during the bout to demonstrate his marvelous speed and skill. He did not cover much territory in boxing, moving but little, but his defensive work was great. He is probably the fastest big man in the ring today. At long range he hit McLaglan whenever he felt inclined, while in the clinches he was supreme, holding McLaglan powerless, while he was always free to slam away with either mit. His work made an impression on the many fight fans present.

Many years later, in 1935, the film industry's Academy Awards bestowed upon Victor McLaglen the Best Actor Oscar for his role in the film *The Informer*.

After the exhibition, later that same evening, a number of his colored admirers hosted a banquet for Johnson at the Bismark café. Johnson gave a speech, saying that he was glad to see the two races sitting together around the festive board. He also gave Burns credit for fighting him.

> Let me say of Mr. Burns, a Canadian and one of yourselves, that he has done what no one else ever done; he gave a black man a chance for the championship. He was beaten, but he was game. Of course, he got the money for doing it, but just the same he did what nobody else has ever done.

The next day, Johnson left on the Canadian Pacific Railroad, headed east for Chicago. To see the new champion off at the depot was a big delegation of both colored citizens and a great many white folk as well.[16]

---

[16] *Daily Province*, March 11, 1909.

Johnson said,

> I don't see why Jeffries should not fight me. I fought Jeffries' brother, the same flesh and blood, and why shouldn't he fight me? He is no better than I am. I want to fight Jeffries above every one else. Just let them know that Jeffries need not be afraid about me being hard to come to terms with. I will listen to anything in reason.

At that time, John L. Sullivan opined, "I don't believe that Jeffries will meet Johnson, for I don't think that Jeff can ever get back into condition again. Jeff has been out of the game for four years. He has been a good liver, too. Men of Jeff's age, 34 years, don't come back after that length of inactivity." Sullivan also said that he did not think Johnson was champion, because Burns was not a first-rate heavyweight.[17]

The *Sydney Bulletin* said,

> Just at present half the white man's world has one eye fixed on a big, bull-necked man in New York, wondering what he will do. Will Jeffries challenge Johnson? That is the question. Till he started training recently, Jeffries had not had a glove on for four years. Also, it is said that he had given up practically all athletic exercise, and never walked where he could drive, and that from taking a size 18 collar, he had to resort to made-to-order neck gear that went about 22. These are serious considerations in the progress of a bruiser. They all indicated that he had got 'fat inside'; that is to say, had developed throughout his innards a vast mass of soft adipose tissue which could not be worked out or hardened up except by about two years' hard graft on plain, solid food.

Yet, Jeff had been training. He hit the punching ball and was sparring Sam Berger and Al Kaufman. "Kaufman had a rough time of it, and Sammy Berger fared but little better. Seen afterward, Berger, with his mouth in a sling, explained that Jeffries was as formidable as ever."

When Jeffries appeared in New York, the city "demanded what he was doing in the matter of that nigger. Was he going to wipe him out!"[18]

Al Kaufman challenged Jeffries to fight, but Jeffries said that if he was to come back, it would be solely to re-acquire the championship for the white race from Johnson, not because he wanted to be a fighter in general. "If I ever fight again it will be with the negro and then only to win back the championship to the white race." His motivation was racial. "If Johnson had been a white man, I never would have thought of fighting again; I would have stayed in retirement for the rest of my life."[19]

---

[17] *Tacoma Times*, March 11, 1909.
[18] *Sydney Bulletin*, March 11, 1908. Jeffries again explained that if after doing some training he felt convinced that he could recover his old condition, he would fight Johnson.
[19] *Tacoma Times*, March 11, 1909; *Daily Province*, March 12, 1909.

Upon his arrival in Chicago, Johnson received a cordial welcome. He said,

> I beat Burns easily, but he was game to the core. That's all the good one can say for him. He was too small to begin with; he could not reach me, and in cleverness I had it on him. I really don't feel like I deserve any credit for my victory over Burns, but the world will never know the great satisfaction it afforded me to slash down the man who for two years continuously vilified me, belittled me, and finally proved his unsportsmanship by forcing me to accept unheard-of terms in order to get the match.
>
> However, when he dictated the impossible terms, he did so to avoid me, and I fooled him and cornered him, forcing him to fight me.
>
> Now that I have beaten him, I want to go on record as saying that I never will give him a chance to earn a dollar off me.
>
> Jim Jeffries? The sooner he announces his willingness to fight me, the better I like. I will cancel all engagements to take him on any time.
>
> It stands to reason that I can go over a longer route more easily than can Jeffries. I am in the grandest shape of my career right now, and can fight all day and night, if necessary. In the bout with Burns I hardly got a sweat up, and Jeffries cannot carry me any faster than Tommy did. I was just getting down to work when Referee McIntosh stopped the fight. I feel sure that Jeff's wind has been somewhat impaired, and think it would be mighty difficult for him to fight over twenty rounds, if indeed he could go that far. And most surely he can't stop me in twenty rounds. ...
>
> I don't believe I shall go to England to fight Sam Langford in May, as was my original intention. I would only get $5,000 for the fight, and think there is more money to be had in the United States. And believe me, I am out for the money. I am a champion who fought his way to the top by taking the small end of purses in order to get matches, and have little to show for all my trouble. Now that I am at the top, I intend to go out hard after the coin. Langford is a good fighter, and would give me an interesting contest, but would have no chance to win. I beat him once, really knocked him out two or three times, the kindness of the referee only permitting him to stay the limit.
>
> Right now I want to brand as a lie the story that credited me with saying that I would insist on a colored referee in the event that I met Jeffries. ... There is one referee, a white man, whom I believe capable and honest enough to referee any ring contest. ... The man is Jack Welch of San Francisco. ... I have been outrageously treated by

referees times without number, but do not think I would be taking chances of unfair usage with Welch as judge of the bout.[20]

On March 12, 1909 in New Orleans, Louisiana, Tony Ross was in the process of beating Marvin Hart. During the 13th round, Ross dropped Hart. However, Tony struck Marvin while he was down, and as a result was disqualified. Still, the bout greatly raised Ross' stock, owing to his strong and likely winning performance but for the foul.

Hugh McIntosh arrived in New York on March 12 with 15,000 feet of Johnson-Burns fight films. McIntosh said that on the day of the big fight, Burns was a physical wreck from nervousness. Johnson dropped him in the 1st round and had him groggy. From that time on, Burns had no chance. Tom was game and kept trying, but Johnson's ring tactics were too superb.

McIntosh said that if he could be convinced that Jeffries could get into top condition again, he would offer a $50,000 purse for a fight with Johnson. In his estimation, Jeff would need to be sharp to be competitive against the new champion. "Johnson should not be underestimated. He is one of the greatest fighters that ever put on a glove. He is the coolest proposition in the ring I've ever seen. He has no yellow streak. In fact he is a man of much bravery, big, strong, fast, and a phenomenal boxer, particularly on the defense." Johnson had told Hugh that he would jump at a chance to fight Jeffries, feeling sure that he could stop him, but did not think Jeffries wanted to fight him.

When told about McIntosh's statement, Jeffries responded sneeringly,

> So he offers $50,000, eh? Why, that's a piker's offer. A syndicate in Seattle has made a bona fide offer of a purse of $150,000 for the contest to be fought at the Seattle Exposition, and that offer is, I am confident, on the level. I have never met Mr. McIntosh and he has never met me. I see he says he wouldn't think of offering a purse unless he was personally convinced I was in condition. I am not asking Mr. McIntosh to judge whether I shall enter the ring again or not.

McIntosh replied that it was not his intention to belittle Jeffries, saying Jeff took his comments in the wrong spirit. Hugh said Jeff was the greatest fighter who had ever lived. Further, "My anxiety is not an overweening one to make money out of this contest, but a worthy ambition to recover the championship of the world for the white race, as I was perhaps, one of the humble instruments in the white race losing it."[21]

---

[20] *Freeman*, March 27, 1909; *Honolulu Evening Bulletin*, April 2, 1909.

[21] *New York Sun*, March 13, 1909; *New York World*, March 13, 15, 1909.
McIntosh marveled at Burns' popularity in Australia, even in defeat. "His popularity after the defeat was one of the most remarkable features. When he went back to Melbourne the correspondents telegraphed: 'Burns has returned and is a popular idol.' Wherever he went he was followed by thousands. He drove in his motor car about the streets which became blocked with people."

Despite wanting to visit his family, it appeared that Johnson and his wife would have to abandon their planned trip to Galveston, Texas. That state had a statute forbidding intermarriage between whites and blacks. The law did not allow mixed-race couples to live together inside the state even if they were married in another state which permitted such a union. Texas did not give full faith and credit to mixed-race marriages. The U.S. Supreme Court had upheld such laws as constitutional. Texas authorities said they would prosecute Johnson if he brought his white wife there. Hence, he could face imprisonment for co-habiting with his own wife in his home state of Texas.

Adding to the trouble, Johnson's first wife, Mary Austin, a colored woman, declared that Johnson was a bigamist and still was legally married to her, for he had not obtained a divorce from her. She was seeking money from Johnson.[22]

Johnson denied that his wife was white. He said, "Mrs. Johnson is three-quarters colored blooded, and I did not marry her in Australia. Her maiden name was Hattie Smith, and we were married in Mississippi about two and a half years ago. She went to Australia from London with me."

Johnson offered to bet $1,000 that his wife was not white. However, Mrs. Johnson decided that they would not go to Texas, for she feared that she would be forced to permit the "white Christian gentlemen" to examine her carefully in every way to see whether she really was white or a "nigger," and then after they had settled themselves on that point, they might rape her. She refused to submit to such indignities.[23]

While Johnson was in Chicago, on March 15 his admirers in Chicago's "darktown" followed him around. "His every word and move spoke of self-reliance and a firm belief in his ability to master any other boxer in the world." Jack said that he was the world's best boxer and could lick Jeffries, who never beat a young man. "I am going to New York to make him fight or shut up. ... I know I can outbox Jeffries; I think I can hit as hard as he can, and I believe I am just as strong." Jack wanted Jeff to be in top shape before they fought, so that no one would say that Jeff was too old and fat to do himself justice.[24]

The *Sydney Bulletin* did not feel that Jeffries was a coward for having refused to defend the title against Johnson owing to the color line, which it understood. However, now that Johnson was champion, folks wanted and expected Jeff to recover the title for the white race.

> When Jeffries fought niggers he wasn't champion of the world. When he became champion he declined to allow any nigger to have a chance of winning the fighting supremacy from the white race. And in the light of the strong racial feeling in the States this is quite

---

[22] *New York World*, March 13, 1909; *Freeman*, March 20, 1909.

[23] *Chicago Broad Ax*, March 20, 1909. *Freeman*, March 27, 1909.

[24] *Honolulu Evening Bulletin*, April 2, 1909.

understandable without any suggestion of fear to account for it. That the pressure which is being brought to bear to induce Jeffries to come out and fight Johnson is tremendous is evident enough even in this corner of the globe. From all over the world handsome purses – record swags of cash are being offered for the fight.

Jeffries was being badgered by the press and public on a daily basis.

However, the *Bulletin* was not so sure that Jeff should come back. "There are a dozen excellent reasons for believing that the second edition of Jeffries must be very inferior to the first, and it's quite likely that J. Johnson could easily account for a mere inferior reprint of the original Jim." Yet, the public pressure on Jeff was great, because most thought that he was the only one with a chance to beat Johnson.[25]

The black-owned *New York Age* said Jeffries was lucky that Johnson defeated Burns, because as a result, Jeff was able to make several thousand dollars weekly in variety houses posing as the undefeated champion, for folks would pay to see him with the hope that he would fight Johnson.

> As it is, he is looked upon by our white fellow citizens as the Moses who will lead the race out of the embarrassing position Tommy Burns allowed Johnson to put it in. There are few white writers who really believe that Jeffries will be able to get in condition to fight Johnson, and they are secretly casting their eye around for another Moses.[26]

Johnson and middleweight champion Stanley Ketchel tentatively agreed to fight, the date and location to be determined. If Ketchel were to win, it "would release Jeffries from the White Man's Burden."[27]

Although one black-owned newspaper in Tennessee opined that the negro press should not boast too exultantly over Johnson's success, the black-owned *Freeman* disagreed, saying that the negro should be proud of Johnson and the fact that a member of their race was at the top of the ladder of pugilistic fame. "Our white papers all laud James J. Jeffries. Why should not we say a few words about Mr. Johnson? Shall we keep mum? Should we not feel honored to have the world recognize us as having the best, even though it be in athletic or boxing circles?" This newspaper took racial pride in Johnson and appreciated his skilled science. It noted that even white papers had said the negro should be proud of him. "Not only should we be proud, but openly express the pride we have in him."[28]

Talk about a potential Burns-Johnson rematch had died out. Although Johnson likely would be willing to fight for a 75/25% split based on winner/loser, it probably would not be a sufficient inducement for Burns, who was not "game to buy another defeat at the price." Furthermore, the

---

[25] *Sydney Bulletin*, March 18, 1909.
[26] *New York Age*, March 18, 1909.
[27] *New York World*, March 19, 1909.
[28] *Freeman*, March 20, 1909. The weekly *Freeman* only cost $1 for a year's subscription.

Australian authorities had said they would prevent a rematch. Clearly, they did not want to see their white idol badly beaten again.[29]

On March 26, 1909 in New York, Stanley Ketchel unofficially won a 10-round no-decision bout against former middleweight and light-heavyweight champion Philadelphia Jack O'Brien, who had fought Tommy Burns three times, twice for the heavyweight championship (W6, D20, and L20). O'Brien boxed very well early, outpointing Ketchel through the first 6 rounds, just as he had done with virtually all of his opponents. However, Ketchel came on, wore him down, and badly hurt O'Brien late. In fact, O'Brien was knocked out cold at the end of the 10th round, but was saved by the bell. The bout further boosted Ketchel's stock. The feeling was that if he could catch up with a fleet-footed master like O'Brien, then Ketchel could do so with Johnson as well. Many believed that Stan hit hard enough to hurt anyone.

Ketchel drew the color line on Sam Langford, refusing to give a black man a chance at the middleweight title. But when it came to recovering the heavyweight crown for the white race, Ketchel was willing to cross the line. If he lost to Johnson, he still would be middleweight champion. However, if he lost the middleweight title to Langford, it "would be too much for our neighbors," meaning whites. The *Freeman* opined, "In our opinion Langford is Stanley's master, and can take his measure on short notice."

Jim Corbett said, "Stanley is a good little man, but the same was true of Burns. And then I don't think the Michigan boxer is fast enough for Johnson. He is a stiff puncher, but I hardly think he is in Johnson's class."

The *Freeman* noted,

> Jeffries thinks that he can defeat Jack Johnson. … He says that Johnson is a quitter; if so, then why take so much time and pains to get back in condition to meet a quitter? Jeffries realizes that when he meets Johnson he will be up against the real thing, and that he must take no chances.

The *Freeman* also printed a poem about Johnson:

> He and Choynski fought a twenty-round bout;
> Choynski was at his best, and knocked poor Jack out.
> He can't do it again, I'll bet ten thousand on the side;
> If Jack looks at Choynski now he'll run off and hide.
> Fitz says, "Jack's a fighter – pretty good one, too."
> All you pugs come in and give the champ what's due!
> Corbett was scientific – got nick-named 'Fancy Dick.'

<hr />

[29] *Sydney Bulletin*, March 25, 1909.

He never won many battles – always got licked.
Sullivan, ex-American champ, was called 'Dad Bud';
Had he fought Peter Jackson, his name would been mud.
Out of the ring Burns is a dodger with vim;
He couldn't duck those rights and lefts Jack shot at him.[30]

Johnson said he was so confident of defeating Jeffries that he even would agree to an 85/15 or 90/10 winner/loser apportionment of the proceeds. "All I want if I lose is enough to pay my training expenses. But I won't lose. And I'm not going to ask anything unreasonable of any man."

I am keeping myself in the best of trim. … Why, if I made a break into bad habits there would be a thousand to shove me down, and once down, you know, a champion doesn't come back.

Don't let anybody have any foolish notion about this theatrical life spoiling me. I do my daily stunt at exercise and will continue to do so, and I guess I'm doing nearly as much as Jeffries does, though he needs it a lot more than I do.

I am living regularly, pretty nearly as regularly as I lived up to within a month of my fight with that young person out in Australia. I could get in trim in six weeks for a championship battle. I don't bar anybody, but of course, there would be more money and more glory in defeating Jeffries than anybody else, and that's why I'm so anxious to meet him. I believe I can beat him, sure, and am willing to try. If he wants my title he knows he can try to get it.[31]

On the morning of March 29, 1909, Johnson arrived in New York from Chicago. A large black crowd greeted him at the Grand Central Depot. One writer said, "Looking along 42nd Street west there was a streak of black such as I have never seen accentuate a crowd in New York City since the old Ninth Ward Republican Club used to parade for Blaine and Logan. … Darktown was everywhere. And why shouldn't the colored brother laud the champion heavyweight of the world?" Jack was taken to Barron Wilkins' hotel and compelled to make a speech.

That week, the hotel would attract large crowds seeking to get a look at the new champion. Whenever Jack visited a colored club, they asked him to make a speech.

Johnson exhibited twice that day at Hammerstein's Victoria Theater on 42nd Street. He would do business there for 2 weeks at $2,000 a week. When introduced to the mixed-race crowd, he was both cheered and hissed.

Johnson hit the punching bag (known today as the speed bag), which

[30] *Freeman*, March 27, 1909.
[31] *New York World*, March 29, 1909. In Johnson's party were his wife ("she is white O.K."), George Little (who either was or would become Johnson's manager), Little's wife, former opponent Charles "Kid" Cutler (Jack's current sparring partner), Cutler's wife, and manager Abe Arends.

was bordered by red, white, and blue electric lights. At one point, Jack made the bag fly into the first balcony, just as Fitzsimmons used to do.

Next, a 247-pound 5'7" Kid Cutler sparred 3 rounds with the 210-pound Johnson. Jack just played with him, jabbing whenever he pleased, not trying to hurt Cutler. One *World* reporter thought they were faking. Another said,

> I saw Johnson work yesterday afternoon. He is not and never can be a genuine heavyweight champion. He lacks the punch. He hasn't any ring sense. How such a man got away with poor but plucky little Tommy Burns is a mystery to me. He showed nothing yesterday, and I don't believe he ever had anything to show.

Of course, what the writer failed to realize was that when Johnson fought Cutler in a real fight, not an exhibition, he stopped him in 1 round.

Regardless, blinded by prejudice, *World* writer William McLoughlin said the fans agreed with him that "Johnson won't do as the heavyweight champion of the world. … I know that Jeffries has his heart set on getting back that heavyweight title for the white men."

> And atop of all this, the law is after Johnson. It seems that last year, about this time, he was circulating in the Tenderloin and lost some jewelry. He caused the arrest of two women. They, in turn, caused his arrest on a charge of indecent conduct. Johnson has been out on $1,000 bail since his arrest.

The black-owned *New York Age* noted the press' hypocrisy. It countered that Jeffries was sparring tame rounds, making easy money by posing as the only man who can give Johnson an interesting argument. Therefore, Johnson also was entitled to earn easy money with tame exhibitions as well.

Johnson said,

> Ah doesn't mind what the papers say about myself, Ah'm a prizefighter. But I do object to them going into my private affairs and talking about the color of – well I will stand for anything that is said about me.

> Ah want to meet anybody that comes along – Jeffries, of course, preferred, but I bar no fighter.[32]

On April 1, 1909 in New York, Johnson appeared in court to answer a long standing charge against him made by Aimee Douglas, a 17-year-old light-skinned negress. Most said the charge was attempted statutory assault. Another newspaper said it was a charge of adultery, which had been pending since March 1908.

Interestingly enough, before Johnson's appearance, Joseph Netherland, a negro porter, was arrested and charged with attempting to bribe Miss

---

[32] *New York World*, March 30, 1909; *New York Age*, April 1, 1909.

Douglas $75 to get her to stay away and not show up to court, which in today's terms is called witness tampering.

At the hearing, Johnson entered no defense, was convicted, and the court imposed a $200 fine, which Jack immediately paid in cash. As he left the courtroom, Douglas and her friend Katie Madison, who was a witness concerning the charge, taunted him and asked, "Now will you be good?" As his car started, Jack called back, "I certainly got off cheap. Why, girls, dat was just cigarette money." His car whirled away amid jeers and hoots from the crowd.

Douglas later intimated that Johnson's offense might have gone unnoticed had he not had them arrested two days after the incident and charged with having stolen two of his rings. His case was dropped for lack of corroborative evidence, but Douglas then filed a counter charge.[33]

The *Freeman's* writer opined about Johnson's chances with Jeffries:

> After reviewing Jeff's record I find nowhere in the records of pugilism where he has defeated a young man of class. ... Johnson's chances of victory over Jeffries look exceedingly rosy. Johnson is a boxer and fighter, and Jeffries' great strength will count for naught when opposed to Johnson's exceptional cleverness and great speed, and before the battle has gone many rounds Jeff will wish he was back on his alfalfa farm in Los Angeles, Cal. ... It won't be Jack Johnson, but one James J. Jeffries, groveling on the canvas in defeat, and the advocates of white supremacy will be in deep mourning. Jack Johnson will be recorded in pugilistic history not one of the greatest, but the greatest of all heavyweight champions, modern or ancient, that ever graced the squared circle. Watch the calendar and see if I'm right.

Johnson claimed that he had never signed articles for a fight with Langford, but rather his former manager had done so. Johnson repudiated any such agreement.

> I know of no reason why I should go to London to fight Langford for $5,000. I can get so much more in this country with any of the men that have been proposed. ... The money comes easily to a man in my position for a short period only, and I make no bones in saying that I want to make all the money I can while I can.

Like Burns, Johnson was a businessman out to make the most coin.[34]

On April 5, Sam Fitzpatrick wrote the *World* to challenge some of Johnson's statements.

> I read in The World of Jack Johnson's arrival in the 'big city.' I had decided not to bother much with his name again, but as he saw fit to

---

[33] *Tacoma Times*, April 1, 1909; *Alexandria Gazette*, April 1, 1909; *New York Sun*, April 2, 1909; *Billings Gazette*, April 2, 1909.
[34] *Freeman*, April 3, 1909.

criticize me for giving Burns all the best of the arrangements in the fight in Australia and saw that he was going to repudiate the Langford match in London, I thought a little inside 'dope' would not be out of place at this time.

My experience with Johnson the last couple of years has taught me that repudiating is one of Arthur's long suits. He could not see where he should come through with the money I loaned him some time before, which he wanted, as he said 'to keep up appearances.'

Negotiations for the Langford match at the National Sporting Club of London were well under way when an offer came from Hugh D. McIntosh for a fight with Burns in Australia; but nothing definite was done until a few days after Johnson agreed to meet Langford. In fact, the representative of the National Sporting Club in New York cabled to Mr. Bettinson that Langford had decided on that day for sailing. When the offer came from Australia for Burns, Mr. Bettinson acted in a very sportsman-like manner and said he would not stand in the way of Johnson meeting Burns first, as he might not get another chance. Johnson said in my presence to the manager of the National Sporting Club that he was very thankful to him for many favors he had done for him while in London and that he would return immediately after the Burns fight and meet Langford on condition that it went win or lose with Burns. To this Mr. Bettinson agreed.

Johnson talks about me letting Burns have all 'the best of the arrangements' – that I admit. Had I not done so, the chances are Langford would be the 'big noise' in London today and Johnson would be matched with Sam McVey, 'Black Bill' or Joe Jeannette, and then possibly 'back to Philadelphia to an obscure thoroughfare,' where I found him.

Yours very truly,
Sam Fitzpatrick[35]

Once he was champion, Johnson realized his economic value, and like Burns, wanted to be paid well for tough title defenses. He believed he could get a lot more money for Langford than what the English offered.

Johnson said he wanted to fight Jeffries because it would be the most valuable fight to him financially.

You understand, I ain't mean or ugly about this Jeffries thing. I want to fight him as a business matter. Otherwise I – well, you know, I kind of like him. He's a fine big fellow. ...

An' I'll tell you one thing mo'. If I fight him an' he whips me, Jack Johnson is going to be the first man to shake his hand when it's over.

---

[35] *New York World*, April 11, 1909.

I'd know then that he was a better man than me. I'd have done the same thing with Tommy Burns, mean as he treated me. My gracious, there is surely one mean man! He used language to me I wouldn't repeat. An' I was fighting him as nice an' careful as I could. Never let to with a punch that could be called a foul. His best friend was refereein', you understand. ...

Could have got twenty thousand bones for fightin' McVey in Paris. I offered him eight thousand for his losin' end, but he said he was too strong over there to risk it.[36]

Regardless of all the talk, although willing to fight Johnson, the 160-pound Langford was most interested in fighting Stanley Ketchel for the middleweight championship. However, Ketchel wanted to fight Johnson and refused to box Langford. Johnson had fought Langford once before and had pummeled him badly. Sam's own manager Joe Woodman said he did not want Sam to fight Johnson more than 12 rounds, fearing that Jack's superior weight would tell in a long bout.

While in Boston, a Harvard doctor told Jeffries that he could get in shape again, but needed to do it slowly, for removing fat too quickly would adversely affect his heart. Reporters estimated Jeff's weight to be about 251 pounds.[37]

On April 13, 1909 in New York, Al Kaufman gave Tony Ross a severe beating en route to an unofficial 10-round no-decision victory. With the exception of the 5th round, when Ross nailed him with a right on the jaw, hurting Al briefly, Kaufman won all the way. Kaufman had Ross's eyes cut and swollen, and his mouth bleeding. In the 9th round, Kaufman dropped Tony with a left, but Ross showed grit, toughness, and defense, and lasted the full 10 rounds.[38]

Johnson was at ringside to see Kaufman-Ross, and allegedly laughed. Promoter Jim Coffroth was a spectator, and said he was more interested in securing a Johnson-Ketchel match.

On April 15, Jim Coffroth officially announced that Johnson had been matched to fight Stanley Ketchel 20 rounds for the heavyweight championship at Colma, California on October 12. The fighters would receive 50% or 60% of the gate receipts (depending on the source), divided 65% to the winner and 35% to the loser, with an additional $5,000 side bet.

Coffroth and Johnson believed that a bout with the wonderful "Michigan Lion" Ketchel would draw more money than a battle with Kaufman or Langford. Coffroth was banking on the fact that Ketchel had an army of followers on the West Coast. Kaufman was a much bigger man, and a true heavyweight, but Ketchel was the much better drawing card. Jack Sullivan and Al Kaufman drew less than $4,000 for their 25-round bout at

36 *Freeman*, April 10, 1909.
37 *Washington Times*, April 5, 1909; *San Francisco Examiner*, December 22, 23, 30, 1909.
38 *New York Journal*, April 14, 1909.

Colma, whereas Sullivan and Ketchel drew more than $12,000. Hence, it was a matter of economics. Plus, Ketchel argued that he had stopped O'Brien, who had stopped Kaufman several years ago.

Both Johnson and Ketchel agreed to be in San Francisco a month before the bout. They agreed that they could wear soft bandages or fingerless kid gloves under the mitts.

Ketchel said,

> I'll beat him, sure. I know he can't hurt me, and furthermore he can't keep away from me like O'Brien. All I want is to get home a few smashes in the body, and I will bring Johnson down so I can knock his head off. When I get into the ring I'll scale at 175, or perhaps 180, for I'll have more than five months in which to build up. I'm a heavyweight now, for that matter, and find it a handicap to reduce to the middleweight limit.

Johnson simply declared that Ketchel would be as easy a mark as Burns.[39]

On April 17, 1909 in Paris, France, Joe Jeannette and Sam McVey engaged in an epic battle, won by Jeannette at the start of the 49th round, when McVey was unable to continue and retired in the corner. Jeannette had been dropped and badly hurt several times throughout the bout, but proved his toughness, resilience, condition, and determination, and eventually won, despite having suffered a bad beating.[40]

While in Philadelphia, Johnson said Jeffries could not get into condition, and no one knew that fact any better than Jeffries himself. "I have no fear of Jeffries. He never will be much good any more." Regarding Burns, Johnson said, "He was too easy."

At that point, Johnson admitted to having made a match with Langford, but "your word is one thing and money is another. The purse offered was too small. It was only $4,000, and I can make that in a week now without fighting at all." Johnson said of Sam, "I have met him, and I don't think he is so hard." He felt that Langford needed to prove himself further, just as he did, by licking everyone and creating such a great demand that the fight would be a big money-maker.

Johnson was on his way to Pittsburg, where he had a one-week sparring engagement with Yank Kenny. He would be on the stage for about 15 weeks, in Pittsburg, Chicago, Buffalo, and Rochester, before going overseas to make more money in exhibitions. Jack said he was weighing 222 pounds, and expected to fight Ketchel at about 206.[41]

---

[39] *Tacoma Times*, April 15, 1909; *Freeman*, April 24, 1909. The split of the motion picture proceeds would be negotiated at a later time.

[40] One report said that Jeannette inhaled oxygen between rounds, which revived him quickly after being on the verge of a knockout. Jeannette was said to stand 5'10" and weigh 185 pounds. *Times Dispatch*, April 18, 1909; *Tacoma Times*, April 27, 1909; *Freeman*, May 1, 1909.

[41] *Washington Times*, April 19, 1909.

During April 1909, in Pittsburg, Johnson boxed in a 4-round exhibition against Frank Moran, whom he would meet in an official title defense several years later.

On April 19 at the Gaiety Theater in Pittsburg, when he announced to the audience that Jeffries was afraid of him, the crowd practically hooted Johnson from the stage.[42]

Jim Jeffries continued calling himself the undefeated heavyweight champion of the world. On April 20 at New York's American Music Hall, before sparring Sam Berger, the audience kept asking Jeff whether and when he would fight Johnson. The public was "semi-hysterical."

HEAVYWEIGHT CHAMPION JACK JOHNSON
Whom Ex-Champion James J. Jeffries Has Consented to Fight within Two Months.

At that point, for the first time, Jeffries said that as soon as he could get into good condition, he would fight Johnson. Jeff said he needed at least ten months of work before signing articles, and Johnson needed to defeat Ketchel. Jeff wanted the fight to take place in the U.S., and he wanted a fight to the finish. Although previously he had held off making a public commitment, he felt that he was losing weight and returning to his old form in a sufficient manner such that he would be ready to fight Johnson.[43]

The Johnson-Burns films were being shown throughout America, in places like Los Angeles, Chicago, San Francisco, New York, and Salt Lake. Some theaters were also showing the best rounds of the Jeffries-Sharkey fight, so that patrons could compare Johnson with Jeffries.[44]

After a showing of the Burns-Johnson films at the Los Angeles People's Theater, the *Los Angeles Herald* wrote, "Johnson's superiority is so manifest that the match becomes a farce after the first round. But in spite of the difference there were two or three flashes when Tommy, small and handicapped as he was, actually outboxed the big black." The general feeling was that Johnson would have little chance with Jeffries, who would weigh more, have an equal reach, a far harder punch, and likely superior gameness.[45]

---

[42] *Richmond Planet*, May 1, 1909.

[43] *Tacoma Times*, April 20, 1909; *Los Angeles Herald*, April 21, 1909; *Honolulu Evening Bulletin*, May 1, 1909.

[44] *Goodwin's Weekly*, May 8, 1909; *Salt Lake Herald*, May 9, 1909.

[45] *Los Angeles Herald*, April 21, 1909.

A *Freeman* writer who saw the Johnson-Burns fight pictures said, "The first ten minutes of the pictures were devoted to the training quarters of the fighters and views around and in the stadium, which was built of two thousand tons of timber." The debate about Burns' arm bandages could be seen.

As for the fight, the 3 to 1 favorite Burns was the aggressor, but "showed nothing commendable but his gameness. ... The Texan simply toyed with him at leisure throughout the fight, seldom missing a blow. The ex-champion resorted continually to clinching, and at times the fight seemed to have been diverted into a wrestling match." At the end of the 8th round, Johnson waved his glove at Burns.

MOVING PICTURE REPRODUCTION OF THE WORLD'S CHAMPIONSHIP BATTLE

At one point, when Tom clinched, Johnson looked up at the sky, admiring the Australian summer weather. He wore his grin and talked with those seated at ringside. "Artha even dropped his guard, stood almost perfectly still, and did other stunts, giving Burns advantages, but still the French-Canadian could do no harm. In many instances the black walloper made it really laughable."

From the 10th round on, it appeared that Johnson was trying to land a knockout blow. "One could easily observe his tactics of tiring Burns before he attempted to land the big thump." In the 14th round, after Johnson had floored Burns, the chief of police interrupted and told Referee McIntosh to terminate the bout, which he did. McIntosh then announced Johnson as the winner and new heavyweight champion of the world. Johnson went over to Tom's corner and shook hands. "The whole fight looked like a boy and a man fighting."[46]

A report on a viewing of the championship fight pictures at the Salt Lake Theater said Burns was game and aggressive, but had no chance.

> In the fifth round he goes down from a smashing hook and in falling it is plainly seen how his right ankle is wrenched. Later on in the fight, when Johnson smashes him with rights and lefts, the bruised, battered and lacerated face of Burns is plainly seen. Still he continues the uneven struggle while Johnson, the big black, regards the efforts of Burns with sneers and treats the fight more as a joke than a struggle for the heavyweight championship crown.

---

[46] *Freeman*, May 1, 1909.

Johnson waited for Burns most of the time except in the thirteenth and fourteenth when he sailed in and tried for a knockout. Burns is shown to be at all times willing. ...

In the middle of the fourteenth round, after the men had clinched and indulged in several hot exchanges, the big black man's right hand, a hand as big as a ham, is seen to land with a right swing and down goes Tommy. He is not knocked out but is on hands and knees waiting and at the count of eight a police official raises his hand and stops the fight and Referee McIntosh awards the fight to Johnson.[47]

Years later, Hugh McIntosh opined that three judges should decide a fight, because one arbiter missed many of the blows scored owing to limitations which prevented one man from seeing from different angles.

McIntosh said even moving pictures had their limitations. For example, the Burns-Johnson fight pictures did not show the bout's most important blows. Eager to face the camera, Johnson backed Burns around so that his own face would be shown. Therefore, Johnson's most effective punches, short close-range right uppercuts and snappy left hooks were delivered while Burns' back was toward the camera, and Tom's head and shoulders completely hid the blows from the picture machine's view. "It was apparent from the pictures that Burns was soundly beaten, but they did not half tell how badly he was punished."[48]

The famous Philadelphia Jack O'Brien wanted a bout with Johnson. He posted $2,000 for a match with him.[49]

On April 27, 1909 in Boston, Sam Langford and Sandy Ferguson fought to a 12-round draw.

In late April, from Chicago, Johnson said of Jeffries,

[47] *Deseret Evening News*, May 11, 1909.
[48] *Freeman*, September 20, 1913.
[49] *Daily Capital Journal*, April 23, 1909.

All I want is to get in the ring with him. … Never until I beat Jeffries will I be able to demonstrate to the American people that I am in his class, I suppose. … I have had it thrown up to me that I never beat a really good man, that it took me an awful lot of rounds to beat Tommy Burns. … Let me tell the American people that I could have beaten Burns that day in six rounds.

Johnson said he would box a 6-round bout with Philadelphia Jack O'Brien in Philadelphia, "because that is easy money that I can't afford to overlook." Jack said he would not fight Ketchel unless Stan covered the $5,000 side-bet that he had posted.[50]

Jeffries confirmed that he was going to fight Johnson, eventually.

Sure, I'm going to fight. Might as well. … I never would have made this statement if I hadn't felt sure that I was able to get back into fighting trim. … My wind is getting better right along. … I'll take plenty of time. I can't afford not to. Johnson may be a tough man to whip, and he may not, but I've got to be ready for the fight of my life, because I can't take any chances on that point. You can say for me that when I get into the ring to fight Johnson I'll be the same old boy. I'm going to make it my business to be the same old boy. …

Ketchel? I do not think he can beat Johnson. … I'm going to pull for Ketchel to beat him and knock him out. If Ketchel can lick him there will not be any sense in my keeping on in training.[51]

The *Los Angeles Herald* said of Johnson, "All his life he has been faking fights. He says he had faked because he had to fake to get matches, and that now he will make his own terms and fake no more." Johnson said he would defend the title on the level.

This writer opined that Jack's "yellow streak," shown in some old fights, might be wiped out by his confidence. "And in that case, with his size and strength and speed and all-around cleverness, he may last a time. The white world is waiting for Jeffries to come back into the ring."[52]

On May 3, 1909, the *New York World* published a 1908 letter signed by Johnson to Arthur F. Bettinson of the National Sporting Club, in which he agreed to return to England to fight Langford after the Burns fight. The *World* argued that this was evidence of Jack's lack of honesty and bad faith. Bettinson said Johnson "is a nigger, and a very bad type of one."

---

[50] *Boston Post*, April 27, 1909; *Freeman*, May 1, 1909.

[51] *Freeman*, May 1, 1909.

[52] *Los Angeles Herald*, May 2, 1909.

CHAPTER 2

Philadelphia Jack O'Brien

As of May 1, 1909, Philadelphia Jack O'Brien had started hard training for a scheduled 6-round no-decision bout with Jack Johnson, set to be held at the National Athletic Club in Philadelphia on May 19. Training and residing at the King of Prussia Inn (about 19 miles from Philadelphia), O'Brien was reeling off 10 miles of roadwork per day on Chester Valley road with Jack Hagan and Jack Rowan.[53]

National Athletic Club manager Harry D. Edwards had secured the bout. Originally, he had offered Johnson $4,000, but the champion held out for a $5,000 guarantee, which was very good money for a mere 6 rounds, and "should the bout go the limit he will earn $277.77 each minute he is in action, or $4.63 each second. Financially, it pays to be a world's champion pugilist." That was the same amount of money that the English had offered Johnson to fight Langford 20 rounds.

O'Brien cut a deal for 30% of the gate receipts, feeling that the bout would draw very well. Hence, if he was correct, he stood to make more than Johnson, or less if he was wrong.[54]

Johnson started training for O'Brien in Chicago on May 3. He had been sparring lightly with Kid Cutler, Tony Caponi, and Yank Kenny. They would act as his sparring partners for the next two weeks.[55]

The *Philadelphia Public Ledger* opined that the O'Brien bout would be a supreme test of Johnson's cleverness. "O'Brien will be the first really clever man Johnson has ever met in public." O'Brien had the fastest left hand of any man in the ring, as well as the fastest feet. He was the best in the business at the 6-round distance. The champion could also prove his gameness by standing the jabbing that O'Brien was sure to give him. Ring followers thought well of the fight, for thousands of dollars' worth of seats were sold immediately.

This writer recalled a sparring session one afternoon in Philadelphia at John Henry Johnson's gymnasium, in which Johnson sparred with lightweight/welterweight Jack Blackburn, who stabbed Johnson repeatedly in the mouth with his left. "Johnson had little defense for a left-hand jab, and he has not improved since that bout." Hence, the conclusion was that Johnson would eat O'Brien's jabs.

[53] *Salt Lake Tribune*, May 2, 1909.
[54] *Philadelphia Public Ledger*, May 3, 1909.
[55] *Ogden Standard*, May 3, 1909; *Philadelphia Public Ledger*, May 4, 1909. George Little, who was managing Johnson, said that Jack also had matches tentatively scheduled with both Kaufman and Ketchel, but first Jack would sail to England on May 26 for engagements there.

Still, Johnson was slightly taller, 6' ¼" vs. 5'10 ½", and much heavier than the 170-pound O'Brien. Both were 31 years old.

Men like Corbett and Choynski classed O'Brien as the fastest man of his weight in the world. "If Johnson can stand the grueling for six rounds that Ketchel did, and succeeds in handing out as much punishment to O'Brien, no one will deny that he is the real goods."

O'Brien actually had the superior ring experience, having fought far more bouts than Johnson. "O'Brien has more than held his own with every pugilist of note in America who is in the ring today." With well over 100 bouts to his credit, O'Brien had fought the who's who of boxing. His results included: 1902 WND6 Young Peter Jackson (avenging a 1900 LKOby13), W6 Billy Stift, W6 Joe Choynski, WND6 Jim Jeffords, and DND6 Marvin Hart; 1903 W10 Jim Jeffords, WND6 Choynski, DND6 Marvin Hart, WND6 Jim Jeffords, W6 Mike Schreck, W15 Jack "Twin" Sullivan, and WND6 Jim Jeffords; 1904 WND6 Tommy Ryan, W15 Mike Schreck, KO3 Jack "Twin" Sullivan, KO3 Kid Carter, KO2 Billy Stift, W6 Tommy Burns, KO3 Jim Jeffords, WND6 Black Bill, and WND6 Morris Harris; 1905 WDQ2 and W10 Young Peter Jackson, L10 Hugo Kelly, D20 Sullivan, KO17 Al Kaufman, and KO13 Bob Fitzsimmons; 1906 D20 Tommy Burns; and 1907 L20 Burns. Since the Burns scandal (in which it was revealed that O'Brien would not take the fight unless Burns agreed to throw it), O'Brien's bouts included: 1908 WND6 Jack Bonner, WND6 Jack Blackburn, WND6 Larry Temple, and WND6 George Cole, and the recent March 26, 1909 LND10 Stanley Ketchel.

Common opponents included Billy Stift, Joe Choynski, Black Bill, Jim Jeffords, Morris Harris, Young Peter Jackson, Marvin Hart, Bob Fitzsimmons, and Tommy Burns. O'Brien held 6-round victories over men like Burns and Choynski, and knockouts over Kaufman and Fitzsimmons. "O'Brien is 31 years old and has been in the prize ring since 1896, taking part in more than 160 battles." Johnson allegedly had fought about 60 contests.[56]

O'Brien said he was leaving no stone unturned in his training, and would put up an even faster fight than he did with Ketchel. Many recalled that O'Brien had outpointed Ketchel clearly in the first 6 rounds of their contest, and noted that the upcoming bout was only 6 rounds. Since O'Brien was the world's best 6-round fighter, it was not outside the realm of possibility that he could outpoint Johnson over a short distance.

The fight would give the public a chance to get a line on the Johnson-Ketchel fight. If O'Brien did well, it would encourage Ketchel's admirers to believe that he had more than a chance with Johnson. "If O'Brien outpoints Johnson, ring experts say that there will be increased interest in the Johnson-Ketchel fight at Colma, in October."[57]

In the meantime, Jim Jeffries was exhibiting with Sam Berger twice a day, and would do so for the next 10 weeks at a salary of $2,000 per week to "amuse a sensation-loving public." Pacific coast amateur heavyweight champion Berger had won gold at the 1904 Olympic Games held at the St. Louis Exposition. He was only 21 years of age, stood 6'2", and weighed 225 pounds. Berger said,

> When a man gets to the head of his profession, I don't care whether it be the law, sculpture, street-cleaning, pants-making or fighting, he has to be a man who thinks and works. Jeffries is a thinker. Every blow he hits, even in our stage stunts, is backed by a reason. He never loses his head. He never strikes at me wild. … I get some hard ones!

Berger showed the reporter several bruises "on flesh as firm as muscle and skin can be." Still, Berger said Jeff took it easy on him in sparring and did not try to knock him out. Jeff was running, punching the bag, jumping rope, and sparring.[58]

While in Chicago on his vaudeville tour, Jeffries spoke of Johnson, who was in the same town, saying,

> If that fellow comes to see me he will get a cleaning for which he might get a lot of money later on. I don't want to see him. I don't want him to sneak any advertising at my expense. I have said I will fight him and that goes. But I won't even talk to him until I have finished my theatrical contract in July. Tell his friends to keep him out of my sight, for I'll knock his block off the first time I see him. … I could whip him on one second's notice. …
>
> Jack Johnson won an easy victory over Tommy Burns. … Just such an easy victory will I have over the negro fighter, who says he is champion of the world, but he will be a more marked fighter than

[56] *Philadelphia Public Ledger*, May 4, 19, 1909; *New York Sun*, May 19, 1909; Boxrec.com.
[57] *Washington Herald*, May 4, 1909; *Deseret Evening News*, May 14, 1909.
[58] *New York World*, May 9, 1909.

Burns was. I will batter him beyond recognition. I have harbored ill-feeling for a number of the men I met in battle, but never so bitter have I been against any other living soul. I'll batter him into such a state of helplessness that he will never fight again. I'll show no mercy.

It would not surprise me if I knocked him out in a jiffy – that is, if he'll stand up and fight. The club that offers me the best inducements will get the mill.[59]

Some speculated that Jeffries' sudden outburst of hatred for Johnson indicated a falling off in public interest in his theatrical performances, rather than any new feeling of bitterness. Such a statement could reinvigorate interest in his performances. The statement might have originated from his press agent rather than Jeffries himself. Still, it is possible that Jeff did not appreciate all of Johnson's talk. Jeffries was a sensitive man.[60]

The *Bisbee Daily Review* said that Johnson's wife, Hattie Smith, born near Biloxi, Mississippi 26 years ago, had attracted more attention than any other boxer's wife. Married for 2 ½ years, they had lived in comparative obscurity. However, once her husband won the title, a great deal of attention was paid. Although several reports said she was white, making her an international figure at once, others said she actually was black, but that reporters were misled by her extremely light color. She was of a dark olive tint and readily could pass for a white woman, "but admits a strain of colored blood." Allegedly, they were married at Las Vegas, New Mexico.[61]

Many Philadelphia fight critics felt that Jack O'Brien's experience, skill, and speed would more than overbalance Johnson's great physical advantages. O'Brien said he would weigh about 170 pounds for the bout. Johnson expected to weigh 210 pounds. Hence, there would be at least a 40-pound weight difference. Still, O'Brien expected to outpoint Johnson and not get close enough to him to get hurt.

The *Philadelphia Public Ledger* said O'Brien was the cleverest man that Johnson had met in nearly a decade. If the champion's heart was not in the right place, "he is in for a lacing." "The negro is clever and can hit, but he has always been timid about using his reach. If he exhibits the same timidity when in the ring with O'Brien, the Philadelphian should jab his head up."[62]

The *Los Angeles Herald* lamented that "faker" O'Brien was in the limelight again. It remembered how he would not fight Burns in a rematch unless Tommy agreed to throw the fight. O'Brien's history caused some to wonder whether the upcoming bout would be on the level.[63]

---

[59] *New York World*, May 11, 1909.
[60] *Philadelphia Record*, May 16, 1909.
[61] *Bisbee Daily Review* (Arizona), May 4, 1909.
[62] *Philadelphia Record*, May 9, 1909; *Philadelphia Public Ledger*, May 10, 1909; *Deseret Evening News*, May 11, 1909.
[63] *Los Angeles Herald*, May 12, 1909.

When Jack Johnson and Jack O'Brien meet at Philadelphia next week in a six-round bout it will be the first time the colored fighter has been in the ring since he beat Tommy Burns for the championship last December. Many believe that O'Brien has a chance to outpoint Johnson in six rounds.

JACK JOHNSON.   JACK O'BRIEN

The *New York Journal* also opined that O'Brien had a chance to beat Johnson. In his fight with Ketchel, he had shown wonderful cleverness, speed, blocking, and superb footwork, going at lightning speed for 7 rounds, until fatigue set in. Had he not been knocked out at the conclusion of the 10th round, O'Brien would have been given the popular decision.

As a Philadelphia fighter, O'Brien had earned his reputation in 6-round no-decision bouts, the longest distance allowed there, so he was most comfortable boxing that duration, and fatigue would not be a factor. "O'Brien is without doubt the cleverest big white man in the ring today." Johnson was the cleverest black man, and normally one of the most careful boxers, but he would be forced to go his fastest against O'Brien to win.

Furthermore, Jack McGuigan would referee, and he would insist upon clean breaks, which would help O'Brien, for Johnson liked to work on the inside. Clean breaks would reduce the inside game and limit Johnson's ability to use his weight and strength while close. It would be difficult to hit the clever O'Brien from the outside, for he was "as fast as a flash of lightning and is so shifty that he evades the force of many a hard punch by being on the 'get away' when it lands." Therefore, the "bout appears to be a close one."[64]

On May 14, five days before the fight, Johnson arrived in Philadelphia via train. A curious throng, with those of the black race in the majority, blocked the train station stairways and exits, wanting to see the champ.

Johnson was looking big and strong. He said he had been training regularly for two weeks, and the additional weight he had put on since the Burns bout would not trouble him at all in a short bout.

> I will fool this fellow O'Brien and his admirers. He is clever, but cannot hit hard, and all this talk about jabbing my head off is rot. My left hand is just as clever as his, and I will stop him inside of six rounds. I am the champion, and I propose to prove my class. I took on this bout just to redeem myself in Philadelphia. You critics have never given me credit for what I can do, and I considered O'Brien one of the best men of his weight in the world, and felt that if I beat him decisively right in his own city, you certainly must rate me as the premier heavyweight.

Johnson acknowledged, "O'Brien is a slippery fellow. I've seen him fight, he's mighty fast, but I think I can beat him down."

The champ left for nearby Merchantville, New Jersey, about 7 miles east of Philadelphia, where he would complete his training at George Cole's physical culture resort, which formerly had been an old frame church for colored folk.[65]

The National in Philadelphia, where O'Brien-Johnson would take place, was showing the Burns-Johnson films three times a day.[66]

On Saturday afternoon, May 15, Johnson trained at George Cole's before a big crowd, sparring

NATIONAL

All This Week.   Three Shows Daily.
3, 8, 9.30 O'CLOCK. POPULAR PRICES—
15c to 50c.
Animated Reproduction of the World's Championship Contest, which took place at Sydney, Australia, Dec. 26th, 1908, between

Burns vs. Johnson

with Cole, a very experienced black boxer who had over 60 pro fights under his belt. Cole had boxed O'Brien several times, most recently in 1908, having lost a 6-round no-decision.

---

[64] *New York Journal*, May 12, 17, 1909; *Deseret Evening News*, May 14, 1909.
[65] *Philadelphia Public Ledger, Philadelphia Evening Bulletin, Philadelphia Record*, May 15, 1909. At that time, just outside New York City, Stanley Ketchel was sparring with Bob Armstrong, preparing for a bout with Hugh McGann, set to take place in Pittsburgh.
[66] *Philadelphia Inquirer*, May 16, 1909.

Picture shows Champion Johnson Working Out With George Cole Soon After His Arrival Yesterday at Merchantville

The champ said he was in fairly good shape, though a trifle high in flesh. His wind was not as good as he wanted it, but he felt that it was good enough for O'Brien.[67]

That same day, Johnson drove to Philadelphia to exhibit that evening at the National Club. When Johnson was introduced, the hisses, hoots, and groans were so loud that Jack could not be heard when he tried to give a speech. Nevertheless, Jack smiled and bowed. It was clear that the local O'Brien would be the fan favorite.[68]

That day, police officers in two separate states stopped "Champeen Jack Johnsing." On his drive from Merchantville to Pennsylvania, a motorcycle officer saw that the only license displayed on his vehicle was out of Illinois,

---

[67] *Philadelphia Inquirer, Philadelphia Record*, May 16, 1909.
[68] *New York Sun*, May 17, 1909; *New York World*, May 18, 1909.

not Pennsylvania, so he stopped him. Then, when Johnson returned to New Jersey, an officer detained him there for the same reason.[69]

It would become a running theme for Johnson to be stopped and ticketed for various minor traffic offenses, most often speeding. He probably was the first black man to be stopped incessantly for "driving while black," as they say, police officers using whatever excuse they could to pull him over whenever they could.

THE JOHNSON-O'BRIEN FIGHT HOLDS THE CENTRE OF THE STAGE

Philadelphia Record, May 16, 1909

The *Philadelphia Record* said O'Brien's display of gameness against Ketchel caused many to forgive and forget his past and take him at his word when he said that he would fight Johnson on the level. His punishment for confessed faking had been banishment from big fights for nearly two years. Still, O'Brien had been active, with nine bouts since the 1907 loss to Burns, and most of those fights had taken place within the past year. He had earned great respect from the Ketchel bout, showing his usual skill and cleverness, but also gameness, taking some huge blows and absorbing great punishment late in the fight.

O'Brien was fight-sharp, for he had been training hard and steadily. Conversely, Johnson had done real work only recently, and did not appear to be taking the bout seriously. The *Ogden Standard* said the general feeling was that Johnson was taking O'Brien lightly, and taking a lot of liberties and chances with his lack of training. He was overweight. While sparring, he made no effort to lead, and merely countered. His footwork was slow and

---

[69] At that time, each state required a license be obtained to drive in that individual state. They did not honor the U.S. Constitution's full faith and credit clause the way they do today, just as today many state athletic commissions do not honor out-of-state federal boxing licenses even though the system has been federalized. Johnson was given a 48-hour temporary visitor's card, and he promised that he would obtain the proper license.

draggy and he did not display any snap in his work, although it was natural for him to hold back against smaller sparring partners. Johnson obviously had "inordinate confidence and conceit in his own ability."

The *Philadelphia Record* said, "Johnson is so big and strong that he may loaf along and chase O'Brien in a half-hearted way - just enough to make the white man work hard to avoid what he thinks is coming, and yet never really attempt to do much. This will be more likely to happen if Johnson is not in first-class condition."

If both tried their utmost, it probably would be a "wonderfully clever fight." O'Brien likely would use his footwork and defense to avoid Johnson, making the champ force matters. "A draw will be practically a victory for him, while if he can outpoint Johnson it will queer the latter's claim to the title." Ultimately, the *Record* writer opined that because Johnson had big advantages in height, reach, and weight, he would win.

Some thought O'Brien should force matters even if it risked causing his own defeat, rather than allow Johnson to get away with an easy bout just because neither man would dare to cut loose.

> If Johnson does not show a disposition to make a real fight of it, O'Brien can gain glory by forcing him to it. If the colored man, owing to lack of training, wants to cut the bout down to about two rounds of actual fighting, O'Brien's best way to beat him is to set a fast pace early in the contest and maintain it to the very last gasp.

If each waited on the other, it could be a dull bout. Johnson had a history of not minding boxing in a less than entertaining manner as long as he did not lose.

> The majority of spectators will favor O'Brien, for the white man always has the house with him when he fights a negro, so there will be no lack of encouragement for Jack to do his best. This is wrong, of course, for the white man who fights a negro is no better than the negro, and they should have a fair field, with no favors. In this case, however, the fact that O'Brien will weigh some thirty-odd pounds less than Johnson will prejudice every one in his favor.

Another local writer said Johnson might regret his overconfidence, holding O'Brien cheap. Johnson had done little training for months, mostly doing a little theatrical work and joy riding with a bunch of ladies in his automobile. O'Brien was the cleverest man in the business and had been training continuously and religiously, so much so that many were saying he was never better. Johnson was bigger, could hit hard, and was "as good, or nearly as good, a boxer as the Philadelphian." However, many were saying that O'Brien was faster than Johnson, and noted that he was more experienced than the champion. Given that O'Brien was at his best, while Johnson appeared to be less than his best, the uncertainty made the fight interesting.

The bout proved boxing's popularity. The cheapest ticket price was $2 for the furthest gallery seat, which normally sold for 50 cents at regular boxing shows. The $3 seats normally sold for 75 cents, and the $5 and $10 seats normally sold for $1. Yet, ticket sales were brisk, with nearly every seat already sold a week before the bout. At least a $20,000 house was assured. The Philadelphia 6-round bout record was $23,000 for the Battling Nelson-Terry McGovern fight. Given that O'Brien took the percentage over the fixed guarantee, he would earn more than Johnson.[70]

Philadelphia Press, **May 17, 1909**

The *Philadelphia Public Ledger* said the O'Brien-Johnson bout would pit speed and skill against strength and ruggedness, and would prove whether Johnson was a real champion. Johnson had the physical advantages, but O'Brien was the fastest man he had ever met. The regulation-size ring would give O'Brien ample opportunity to use his footwork.

> It will be up to Johnson to be the aggressor, and, unless the writer's judgment goes wrong, he is in for a good jabbing. O'Brien's left hand is faster than ever, and Johnson is sure to run into it if he undertakes to chase the wily, elusive Philadelphian. Johnson has never beaten a good, clever man decisively. In fact, O'Brien is the cleverest he ever met, and for that reason if the new champion has any latent merit the coming bout is sure to develop it.

Sporting men did not believe there was a man in the ring who could outbox O'Brien in a 6-round contest, including Johnson. It was believed that Ketchel could hit as hard as or harder than Johnson, and still O'Brien outpointed him for the first six rounds. Johnson would not have the same time to wear out O'Brien as Ketchel did.

O'Brien said,

> I will take all that the big negro can hand out, and he is sure to get a lacing. I never felt more confident in my life. It took him 14 rounds to put Burns away, a man who can be hit easily. That shows that Johnson does not possess a knockout punch. However, he will have

---

[70] *Philadelphia Record*, May 16, 1909; *Ogden Standard*, May 17, 1909.

to box faster than he ever boxed before to reach me on a vulnerable spot. Tell my friends that I will give Johnson the battle of his career and prove his real worth.

Some noted that Burns weighed no more than O'Brien, and reasoned that since Johnson had not knocked out Burns; O'Brien stood more than a good chance to last the full 6 rounds.[71]

In Pittsburg, Stanley Ketchel saw the Johnson-Burns fight films and said Johnson would need to show better form and do a lot faster work than he did against Burns to beat him. He opined that Burns was afraid, running into a clinch whenever he got the chance. He said Johnson should have knocked his head off in a few rounds. Stan was not worried about Johnson at all. "I will say frankly that I don't believe this big colored fellow is of championship caliber. Champion? Of course he's champion. So was Peter Maher – once, when Corbett handed him the belt from a theatre box."[72]

Those who saw the films had an opportunity to assess Burns' claims that Johnson's seconds had induced the police to interfere, that Jack was tiring, and that Tommy was strong enough to continue. Most felt that Burns was just making the excuses that ex-champions often did.

The pictures certainly do prove that Burns was hopelessly outclassed from the beginning, physically, scientifically and in every other way, barring gameness. He had the true courage of the fighting man, and it is marvelous to us how he continued despite the terrific battering he received. The pictures show Burns to have been the receiver-general of a successive volley of assaults that would have hammered into insensibility a less sturdy man long before the fatal fourteenth round was reached. ...

It is true that Burns was on his feet and still fighting aggressively when the contest was ended. But a minute before he was lying prone in the ring, and it was while he was in this position that the police, as the pictures show, decided it was time to cry enough. The pictures prove that Burns could have gone on further than the bout terminated, but how long? ... That he could have gone on when the bout was stopped is certain; that he could have remained a combatant to the end is most uncertain. Human nature could not stand much longer and the police interference, taken only for the sake of humanity, not only saved Burns from the inevitable knock-out, but also prevented a gallant man from receiving an unnecessary drubbing.

After another showing of the Johnson-Burns films, the *Public Ledger* said,

Johnson outpunched Burns and was the stronger in the clinches. Each blow that dropped the Canadian landed either in a clinch or

[71] *Philadelphia Public Ledger*, May 17, 1909.
[72] *Philadelphia Record*, May 17, 1909.

when the latter was breaking away. The negro's left hand was apparently useless. He made no left-hand leads, boxed flat-footed and depended on a right short-arm jolt to win the fight. In fact he dropped Burns with a right-hand uppercut in the first 15 seconds of the first round.[73]

Johnson was a 2 to 1 betting favorite to defeat O'Brien (at least unofficially). Still, many were willing to bet that O'Brien could outpoint Johnson in a short bout, for Johnson often liked to loaf early on in fights.[74]

Two days before the bout, on Monday May 17 at the King of Prussia Inn, O'Brien ran 6 miles and punched the bag. He weighed 167 pounds and appeared to be the picture of health. O'Brien's lightning jabs and quick footwork would make it difficult for Johnson to lay back and counter. With the look of one brimful with confidence, O'Brien said,

> Never in my life did I at any time feel better or more fitted to fight than I do at this moment. ... I can truthfully state that I have trained for the Johnson fight harder than I ever trained before, and that is saying a whole lot; I am certain that my many friends will have no kick coming on the result of my showing against the negro.[75]

O'Brien had seen Johnson box several times, and knew him like a book. He further said,

> I have never seen a flat-footed man in my life that I cannot beat, and Johnson will be a remarkable exception if I am wrong. I admit that Johnson is a good man, and I have seen him do things in the ring which none but a master could perform, but he has never met as speedy a boxer as myself, and perhaps I shall hand him a surprise.[76]

Those who saw O'Brien said he was in remarkable physical condition. "It is conceded on all sides that Johnson is much slower in attack and defence than O'Brien and that if he is not in the finest possible condition he may have his hands full."

The general opinion was that Johnson would be satisfied to stand flat-footed and pick off O'Brien's blows with his long reach, but would not be able to outpoint O'Brien at long range. Most thought that the native Philadelphian would use Jim Corbett tactics - speedy long-range boxing, and avoid close work, where Johnson was at his best.[77]

On May 17, Johnson sparred at George Cole's gymnasium, which was crowded to suffocation by black patrons anxious to see the champion. Even a few white followers were there.

---

[73] *Philadelphia Public Ledger*, May 17, 18, 1909.
[74] *Washington Times*, May 17, 1909.
[75] *New York World*, May 18, 1909.
[76] *Philadelphia Evening Bulletin*, May 18, 1909.
[77] *New York Sun*, May 18, 1909.

For 5 rounds, Johnson went hard at former opponent Black Bill. At the conclusion, Bill was tired and wobbly, and his face and breast covered with blood flowing from his nose and mouth.

Against Topeka heavyweight Bob Kerns, also a former opponent, Johnson mostly worked on his footwork, for had he used his hands, Kerns would have been taken out.

Johnson then sparred 2 two-minute rounds with Anthony J. Drexel Biddle, society man, author, poet, and all-around athlete and amateur boxer. Biddle enjoyed sparring with boxers of note, including Fitzsimmons, Corbett, and O'Brien. The short bout was full of action, though not rough, for Johnson mostly boxed on the defensive. Afterwards, the champ said, "Biddle is a strong kid and a fine gentleman." Jack was pleased with the attention shown him by a representative of Philly's exclusive social circles, especially in light of the hoots that had greeted him on the 15th at the National Athletic Club.

Johnson next sparred Frankie Madole and Paddy Lavin, one after the other in rapid succession. He worked fast with the little men, boxing good-naturedly and taking care not to get rough.

The champ wound up his training with a little dancing to live music supplied by a couple of wandering musicians. "Johnson's dancing pleased the colored brethren present, and it proved that, despite the fact that he is a giant in size, he is nimble and active on his feet."

Although slightly overweight, in sparring with five different men, Johnson proved that he would have no trouble going 6 rounds, and it would take all of O'Brien's cleverness to outpoint him.

That evening, Biddle sat with O'Brien in a private box at the National Theatre to watch the Johnson-Burns fight films. O'Brien was studying the champ. Johnson outclassed Burns, who despite boring in continuously was "only a child in Johnson's hands." Although Burns was still strong on his feet at the end, it was evident that he had no chance to win, for Johnson smothered nearly all of his blows and pushed and struck him as he pleased. It was more of a wrestling contest than a boxing match, owing to the fact that they were allowed to fight in the clinches. Johnson's most apparent weaknesses were that he rarely used his left, and he was flatfooted.

Still, O'Brien obviously was impressed with Johnson. He would have to be quite wary of Johnson's right, which was very dangerous at short or long range. Johnson had fearful right uppercuts and kidney punches.

As a wind-up, one round of the Jeffries-Sharkey championship fight was shown, and the contrast in style and speed was marked. "The universal verdict is that Jeffries or Fitzsimmons in their prime would have made short work of Johnson."[78]

---

[78] *Philadelphia Record, New York Times*, May 18, 1909. The lecturer who accompanied the films said Johnson weighed 203 pounds to Burns' 166 ½ pounds. Johnson wisely made Burns come to his corner, and ended rounds in his corner as well, so Burns would have to cross the ring to get to his chair. Tom usually ran to his corner, showing his condition.

The *New York Journal*'s Tad Dorgan noted that for the first six rounds of the Ketchel bout, O'Brien won by a mile, pumping lefts into the face of the hard-punching Ketchel, making Stan miss quite often, dazzling him with his speed. In the final three rounds, O'Brien caught some hard blows that changed matters, but those were rounds that O'Brien would not have to box against Johnson. He had beaten Burns in a 6-round bout, but then had drawn and lost to Burns in 20-rounders. Johnson had beaten Burns so easily and badly that the police had to interfere to save him.

Johnson was taller, heavier, and had a longer reach, but "his style is a puzzler. He is what we might term a natural born waiter. He makes the other fellow lead. He says that he can make any man in the world lead, and he can." Like most clever fellows, he was not a tearing, ripping fighter. He waited, watched his foe like a cat, and struck when the opportunity offered. He seldom if ever had been marked after a bout.

O'Brien was as shifty as or shiftier than Johnson. Since both men were careful and clever, there was "little chance of the thing ending before the limit."[79]

In Chicago on May 18, 1909, Jim Jeffries took the scales in public for the first time and tipped the beam at 243 pounds.

Also on May 18, 1909, in Pittsburg, the day before Johnson-O'Brien, Stanley Ketchel unofficially won a 6-round no-decision bout against Hugh McCann, otherwise known as Kid Hubert. McCann was down several times throughout. This had some significance, because in October 1908, McCann had fought Marvin Hart to a 12-round draw. It was opined that Johnson's blows were shorter and cleaner than Ketchel's, but that Stanley had the harder and more dangerous punch. Nearly 10,000 spectators attended, once again confirming that Stan was a big gate draw.

That same day, Johnson's final training included road work, bag punching, medicine ball, weight-pulling machine, rope skipping, shadow boxing, and footwork. Jack then took his auto for a spin.

O'Brien's day-before-the-fight workout consisted of running 3 miles, punching bag for half an hour, and tossing the medicine ball. He expected to weigh between 167 and 170 pounds for the fight.

O'Brien confidently said that he had watched the Johnson-Burns fight films and believed that if Johnson adopted the same tactics against him that there would be a different story to tell. O'Brien claimed to be much faster than Burns. "I have trained more conscientiously than I ever did in my life and I have taken on weight instead of reducing." O'Brien said he would set a hot pace and surely outpoint Johnson. "I am not predicting I will knock out Johnson, but I am sure I will outpoint him in six rounds, and he will know he has been in the ring when it is over, too."

Johnson had not trained as hard, but reasoned that it was only a 6-round bout and he had an immense weight advantage. He predicted that the fight

[79] *New York Journal*, May 18, 19, 1909.

would not go the limit unless O'Brien ran from him. "I will have no trouble in making O'Brien look like a deuce spot, and you can say for me that people will understand why I am champion when the bout is over." He also said, "I am trained to the minute and will win in a walk." Jack claimed that he would weigh about 205 pounds, but few believed him, feeling that he was much heavier.[80]

The *New York Sun* said that although O'Brien was fast and clever, he did not have a great deal of punching power, and therefore "in a fight to a finish Johnson would surely win because of his strength and endurance; and also his patience and cautiousness."

However, the *Sun* also said O'Brien's feet and hands were so fast that the normally careful Johnson would have to hustle and fight his fastest to get an even break in a mere 6 rounds. O'Brien's fast footwork would prevent Johnson from using his inside clinch-and-punch tactics.

> Johnson's strongest point is an impregnable defence. He lacks aggressiveness. He seldom rushes into slugging bees, thereby leaving himself open, and depends wholly upon his ability to block punches and hold an opponent's biceps in the clinches – a trick that few pugilists have been able to work as successfully as the big black man.[81]

Like Corbett, O'Brien knew how to stick and move and clinch and use defensive tactics. Unlike the black Johnson, whose defensive and cautious style was often criticized, O'Brien's and Corbett's defensiveness and cleverness were lauded as brilliant.

Members of the press who were on scene agreed that O'Brien was by far the better trained of the two. He had trained hard and consistently, and looked good. Conversely, Johnson appeared to have accepted too many invitations to banquets to be in the best shape. Since his return from Australia, theatrical work had taken up most of his time, and he had been living an easy life. "He was terribly fat on leaving New York, and it would take a good two months to get it off. Two weeks work is only a start when a man is fat and out of shape." Johnson was

[80] *Philadelphia Press, Marion Daily Mirror, San Francisco Call, Los Angeles Herald, New York Journal,* May 19, 1909.
[81] *New York Sun,* May 19, 1909.

overweight, soft, and blew like a porpoise when boxing with his sparring partners.

Some thought Johnson might be trying to affect the odds or increase the interest in the fight by appearing less than prepared.

> Johnson may have his faults, but he has also some of the caginess peculiar to his race. He has all at stake. If he should happen to be outpointed by O'Brien, his stock would fall immeasurably in the estimation of the sport-going public generally, and would be regarded as a vindication of the judgment of those who have maintained that he is a false alarm champion.

Of course, the other way to look at it was that Johnson would get paid either way, and still would be champion even with a poor performance, for it was a no-decision bout. A less-than-stellar performance might lead to an even more lucrative rematch in a longer bout, or make the sports think that other prospective opponents, including Ketchel, had a chance to beat him, which would make those bouts more lucrative and marketable. Further, if he did not do so well with a small man like O'Brien; maybe that would make it more likely that Jeffries would fight him for the mega payday.

Aside from such speculation, Johnson appeared to believe that he only needed limited preparation for a 6-round bout, and was in good enough shape to beat a much smaller man like O'Brien.

Owing to their supposed differences in preparation and condition, respected gamblers were wagering big money that Johnson would not knock out O'Brien. Few would risk much on a knockout proposition. Many believed that O'Brien would outpoint Johnson through his superior speed. Others felt that Johnson was too big and strong for him and that if he cut loose and tried his best to win, O'Brien would be lucky to stay the 6 rounds.

The day of the fight, nearly all of the tickets were sold, except those held by speculators. Most of the $10, $5, and $3 seats had been sold over a week prior. A record-breaking crowd was anticipated, with folks coming from Philadelphia, New York, Washington D.C., Baltimore, and Pittsburg.[82]

On Wednesday May 19, 1909 at Philadelphia's National Athletic Club on Eleventh Street, Jack Johnson and Philadelphia Jack O'Brien fought their scheduled 6-round no-decision bout.[83]

At 2 p.m., Johnson arrived at the National Athletic Club in his auto and informed club manager Harry Edwards that he needed to be paid the $5,000 guarantee at that time. Jack was backed by his manager, George

---

[82] *New York World, New York Journal, Philadelphia Inquirer, Philadelphia Press, Philadelphia Record,* May 19, 1909. Those with tickets saying "South Door" would enter at Catharine Street, while those marked "North Door" would enter at Fitzwater Street.
[83] The following account is an amalgamation of the *Philadelphia Public Ledger, Philadelphia Press, Philadelphia Inquirer, Philadelphia Record, Philadelphia Evening Bulletin,* and the *New York World* and *New York Journal,* May 20, 1909, all of which had reporters on scene.

Little. This was shocking to Edwards, for traditionally fighters were paid after their performance.

Edwards replied, "Ain't you rushing it a bit? I have heard of hold-ups by fighters before, at the last moment, but this is the first time I know of such a thing taking place ten hours before ring time." Johnson responded, "Well, I've got to have my money now." Then there was a whispered consultation between Johnson, Edwards, Little, and Jack McGuigan, who would referee that evening. The four men then drove to a bank and Johnson got his $5,000 in large bills, which he tucked away under Little's careful scrutiny.

Apparently, Johnson had been given a tip that his various creditors would attach his purse. The sheriff was waiting to execute on a debt of $850. Hence, Jack wanted to be paid before his creditors could get at the money. Jack said, "When I get it in my jeans they can whistle their attachments." Edwards acquiesced and made early payment. He later said, "I learned that Johnson had taken this step to foil an army of creditors."

There was fear that Johnson might "throw" the club and refuse to perform after receiving his money. Edwards said, "If he refuses to go on I will arrest him for grand larceny."

Three or four special trains brought several hundred sports from New York City. A big electric sign glittered on the front of City Hall, saying, "Welcome."

At noon, nearly a hundred men and boys were in line, willing to wait until 7 p.m., when the box office was opened and the final sale of tickets began. As early as 5:30 p.m., a huge crowd had gathered at the main entrance. Market Street was packed from curb to curb with fight fans.

However, most of the tickets had been sold for several days, so there was nothing to be purchased except the tickets vended by speculators at big increases on the original prices. Scalpers flourished, getting double and triple the face value of the tickets. They were selling $2 tickets for $4 and demanded $10 and $15 for the $5 tickets. An estimated 4,000 persons paid from $2 up to $50 to watch the bout. Another said there were seats for 3,700, and all of them were filled, plus 500 others choked the narrow aisles. "Had there been room to accommodate them fully 500 additional tickets could have been sold."

Yet, one source said some ticket speculators were stung badly, and had to sell $10 tickets for $2. It said scalpers actually lost money, for $603 of tickets that had been sold were not presented at the doors for admission.

By 7 p.m., the crowd had increased to such proportions that an extra police detail was necessary to preserve order. The Police Superintendent arrived on scene. The police had their hands full keeping the clubhouse doors from becoming congested. The *New York World*'s writer, William P. McLoughlin, said Philadelphia was a strange place. "They still employ coon policemen."

Regarding the venue, the *World* writer said, "The building is in the heart of a negro district. It looked as if every 'cullud pusson' in town turned out to get a peek at Johnson and to wait for the result of the fight. The street was like a mass of black soot studded with straw hats." The scene featured brick sidewalks, and the building had green shutters and white marble steps. Some of the hall doors had brass knockers.

Black residents of the Lombard Street vicinity had saved for months for a chance to see their champion in action. "For, although he is champion of the world, he is principally their champion and the colored population was more than well represented."

Still, the majority of fans were white, and they would be there to see and root for the local man, O'Brien.

Owing to the police maintaining order, those with tickets had little difficulty getting into the club, pouring into the building at 8 p.m. Still, there were almost as many people outside of the club-house as there were on the inside. People liked hanging around the scene of a fight.

The estimated and reported gate receipts included $18,300, $20,000, $20,564, $22,000, $23,000, and $25,000. The receipts were either the largest or the second largest on record for Philadelphia, with McGovern-Nelson having drawn about $23,000.

Some said O'Brien earned 30% of the gate receipts. However, others reported that O'Brien had struck a new deal, wherein he purchased the right to 75% of the gate receipts, but guaranteed to pay Johnson's purse, which would come out of his end. Reports of what O'Brien earned included $6,169.20, $6,600, $8,875, $11,000, or $12,000. Regardless of the exact amount, it was very good money for only 6 rounds of work. "Big bouts pay."

Johnson earned $5,100 (an extra $100 for expenses), while the club made $9,294.80. It turned out that Johnson would have obtained more money if he had accepted the offer of 30% of the receipts. However, Johnson feared the unknown, and was neither sure of how big the house would be nor how scrupulous the accounting would be. He preferred the guaranteed bird in the hand to two in the bush.

There was a curious absence of betting. There were all sorts of rumors floating around. Hence, the general impression was that it was a good fight to keep away from wagering hard-earned money. Jimmy DeForest said, "I hear Johnson hasn't trained. He looks it." Club co-manager and bout referee Jack McGuigan said, "O'Brien is in fine condition." With the fast and clever O'Brien being in top trim, and with Johnson having a paunch, the crowd did not want to wager, for it looked too close to call.

Early in the afternoon, O'Brien, whose real name was Joseph Hagan, told his mother that he would lick Johnson. She later said, "I believe he will do it. He never failed to keep his word with me."

O'Brien came to the arena from A. J. Drexel Biddle's home.

Shortly after 9 p.m., Johnson arrived at the venue in a big touring car.

In his dressing room, Johnson said, "No matter what is said about my condition, I am good enough to put it on O'Brien, and if I do not knock him out, I will at least give him the walloping of his life."

At 10:20 p.m., Johnson was the first to appear and enter the ring, clad in a big pearl-gray bathrobe. He received only a mild amount of applause, mostly from the several hundred black persons present, which was mixed with many moans and hisses, with the "boohs" drowning out the cheers.

Attending Johnson were manager George Little, Yank Kenny, George Cole, and Frank Madole. One writer said a "retinue of negroes" escorted the champ. Little and Kenny were white.

Johnson gave his weight as 205 or 206 pounds, but most thought he weighed a lot more. He unquestionably was carrying too much weight, but looked to be in pretty good form nevertheless.

One minute later, O'Brien entered and hopped through the ropes. He was cheered to the echo, rousingly and tremendously for several minutes. Wearing a tasteful white silk kimono, he smiled and bowed in acknowledgement. "Oh dear, but it was just too cute." The reception O'Brien received was in marked contrast to that accorded to Johnson, who had received only a perfunctory cheer.

"Jawn" O'Brien had quite an array of seconds. They included Abe Attell, Jack Egan, Joe Dougherty, Jack Hanlon, Jack Rowan, Joe Hagan, Eddie Reilly, and Frank Floyd. A. J. Drexel Biddle also entered the ring and went to O'Brien's corner, receiving a big ovation. Attell would advise O'Brien continually during the bout, and his suggestions proved valuable.

Johnson walked over and shook O'Brien's hand.

A little boy entered the ring, walked over to O'Brien's corner and tied an American flag on Jawn's waist. O'Brien kissed the child, who then exited.

O'Brien claimed to weigh 162 ½ pounds, although he was closer to 170. He looked to be trained as finely as a racehorse.

While they were adjusting their gloves, a San Francisco-based telegram was read, in which Bill Delaney challenged Johnson on behalf of Al Kaufman, offering to wager $10,000, winner-take-all. Johnson's eyes flashed and he grinned, saying, "I'll do it when I come back from Europe." O'Brien said, "I want a bit of it myself."

Boxing celebrities were introduced to the truly cosmopolitan crowd, and each received generous applause. They included Stanley Ketchel, Abe Attell, Young Corbett, Tom Sharkey, Terry McGovern, Jack McAuliffe, Al Kubiak, and Tommy Sullivan. When Ketchel was introduced, he entered the ring and received a tremendous welcome. He announced that he would be Johnson's next opponent. Stan looked very small beside Johnson.

The crowd included prominent men from all professions, including merchants, bankers, and men who ruled the town's financial and commercial destinies. Those at ringside included William Brady, George Considine, and the mayor's son.

Jack McGuigan refereed. At 10:25 p.m., he called the fighters to the ring center for instructions. McGuigan announced that they would box Philadelphia rules, which meant that they would break clean when told and not strike on the breakaways. This would help O'Brien, for Johnson was an adept infighter and had done damage to Burns in clinches and on the breakaways, using straight Queensberry rules.

Before the bout began, Johnson stood leaning on the ropes in his corner, calmly looking at O'Brien. O'Brien sat on the stool in his corner appearing composed.

1 - They mixed it from the start. Johnson rushed wildly, his speed carrying O'Brien to the ropes. There was a split of opinion regarding whether Johnson knocked O'Brien down or pushed him down, or if O'Brien slipped down, or whether it was the result of a combination of those factors.

William Rocap, the *Evening Bulletin*, and the *World* said that first Johnson pushed or threw him to the ground, and then, soon after O'Brien rose, Johnson dropped him with a left to the stomach. O'Brien rose in two seconds. The *Public Ledger* said Johnson landed rights and lefts to the body, and one right to the ribs dropped him.

The *Inquirer* version said O'Brien slipped. The *Record* said Johnson's rush carried O'Brien off his feet and he slipped to the floor. The *Journal* said they wrestled and O'Brien slipped to the floor. After O'Brien rose, Johnson landed a left to the body, and in eluding a right swing, O'Brien fell and nearly went through the ropes.

Thereafter, O'Brien mostly jabbed and dodged out of the way of vicious rushes. Despite jabbing often, O'Brien's punches had little power or effect. Johnson mostly grinned and laughed at him. The champ threw and landed the harder blows to the head and body, which led to several clinches. Johnson wrestled him around as if he were a child. The champ laughed as he held Jawn in a clinch. Johnson landed a hard overhand right to the jaw or neck.

However, Johnson slowed his attack, played defense for a while, and allowed Jawn to jab at him. The crowd cheered a couple jabs and a right from O'Brien. However, Johnson landed a right to the jaw and followed with a rush that carried him to the ropes.

The *Inquirer* said, "The round favored the champion." The *World* and *Public Ledger* agreed it was Johnson's round. The *Journal* said, "O'Brien wore a worried look, for he did not land a good blow during the round." Yet, incredibly, the *Press* called it an even round.

2 - O'Brien used feints and jabs before dancing away. He landed a left to the jaw but Johnson rushed him across the ring, hitting the body. Many of Johnson's rushing blows fell short, for O'Brien was dancing away. However, the champ landed several lefts to the stomach and a right to the jaw that caused O'Brien to blink. On the inside, Johnson landed two hard rights to the body and the referee warned him for hitting on the break. Johnson rushed Jawn to the ropes. In a clinch, the American flag that O'Brien wore around his belt slipped off, and Referee McGuigan picked it up. The crowd hooted Johnson for roughing O'Brien in the clinches.

O'Brien kept pumping and landing jabs. The local man straightened up and caught Johnson with a right to the mouth, which caused a little blood to trickle from Johnson's lips. O'Brien's clever work brought roars from the crowd. They cheered whenever he landed. He pranced up and down, in and out, and had Johnson a bit confused. By skillful feinting, he had Johnson ducking and eluding to escape bluff jabs.

The champ appeared to be slowing down, for the pace seemed to be telling on him. Still, Johnson landed his hard right to the chest and jaw. His most effective blows were to the body. He looked a bit tired at the bell.

The *Inquirer* and the *World* both said the round was even. The *Journal* said, "O'Brien made a fine showing during the round, and he fought much better than at the start." The *Public Ledger* and *Press* said it was O'Brien's round.

3 - The crowd and his advisors again cautioned O'Brien to fight carefully and to side-step Johnson's rushes. In this round, Johnson made another great effort to use his strength and rush O'Brien about the ring. Johnson landed his left full into the face. The champion rushed O'Brien to the ropes with a vicious plunge and landed a hard right to the kidneys as they came together in a clinch. Johnson followed with a left swing to the body, but after breaking, O'Brien jabbed several light lefts to the face as he danced away. Johnson landed a savage right to the body.

In general, O'Brien jabbed the face and Johnson hit the body. O'Brien kept sending his left out and clinched whenever Johnson became dangerous. He succeeded in holding him safe.

Johnson was puffing like an overworked engine. While he was trying to get his wind, O'Brien jabbed his face and had no trouble getting out of the way. The big fellow, seeing how cleverly O'Brien was eluding his wallops, started to rush matters again. Johnson rushed him to the corner and sent left and right to the head and body. He again chased O'Brien to the ropes as the bell rang.

The *Public Ledger, Inquirer,* and *Press* all said it was an even round. The *Record* said that although O'Brien was in the best shape of the two, he was nervous. Johnson perspired freely. The *World* said O'Brien won the round. He feinted and had Johnson tired and confused at the end. The *Journal* opined that O'Brien had a slight points lead after the 3rd round, having won the 2nd and 3rd, though he did no harm with his blows.

4 - Three times Johnson sent his left to the body. O'Brien continued jabbing, while Johnson only smiled after each punch. The smaller man's work set the crowd yelling. Johnson shook him off from a clinch and shot left and right to the body. O'Brien returned quickly with his left, stinging Johnson on the nose. With his quick footwork, O'Brien skipped away from Johnson's follow-up rush. Johnson missed a wicked punch for the jaw, with it glancing over the shoulder.

O'Brien gave him considerable room, but managed to land twice to the face with two light lefts. Johnson swung a heavy right to the body and put a stiff left to the face that had plenty of steam behind it. The blows seemed to have a visible effect on Jawn.

O'Brien feinted and Johnson missed his counter. The smaller man followed with a right swing that Johnson ducked, and in missing, O'Brien fell and went to his knees.

Soon thereafter, Johnson again hurt O'Brien. Rocap of the *Ledger* (same as the *Evening Bulletin* account) said Johnson shot his hard right to the heart and then staggered O'Brien with a right to the ear. The *World* agreed that a hard right on the ear made Jawn hold. The *Record* said O'Brien missed a jab and received a hard smash on the side of the head that shook him up a bit. O'Brien clinched and hung on. The *Journal* said Johnson nearly toppled O'Brien with a right swing over the heart which landed as they were coming into a clinch. O'Brien recovered relatively quickly and jabbed a left to the face. Johnson stood still, waiting for O'Brien to lead.

Before the round closed, O'Brien ran into a stiff right that caught him on the left cheek bone and caused a swelling there.

In a clinch, they wrestled, Johnson sent a hard right to the heart or ribs, and O'Brien went to the floor. Some said it was a slip, while others said it was a knockdown. He was up in a flash and they clinched again, and the bell rang.

After O'Brien returned to his corner, his second made an incision in the swelling on his left cheek bone and reduced it so that he did not suffer any disadvantage to his vision from the effects of a puffy eye.

The *Inquirer* said it was Johnson's round. The *World* said Johnson did the forcing in this round and edged it. The *Journal* said this was a clear Johnson round. However, the *Press* and *Public Ledger* said it was an even round.

5 - Johnson held back, waited, and made O'Brien come to him. O'Brien went at Johnson, but once again, O'Brien went to the floor. As usual, there was a discrepancy of opinion regarding how it happened:

The *Ledger* and *Inquirer* said Jawn aggressively jabbed the face and nose a couple times, but in the close mix-up that followed, Johnson threw him to the floor. The crowd hissed Johnson for his rough tactics.

The *World* said Johnson both wrestled and punched O'Brien to the floor. Jawn rose with a big lump under his left eye. Johnson grinned as the crowd hooted him.

The *Record* said a hard smash on the side of the head sent O'Brien to the floor.

The *Journal* version said they mixed it, Johnson landed a right to the jaw, and O'Brien slipped down again. He rose quickly.

After O'Brien rose, Johnson landed a left and powerful right to the sore eye and Jawn clinched. The blows closed or nearly closed O'Brien's left eye, which also was badly cut and bleeding freely, the blood flowing down his face.

Another version of the sequence said that after O'Brien rose, a short right staggered and dropped him to his knees, though he immediately rose without a count. The blow was terrific and it closed O'Brien's left eye and sent a stream of blood from his cheek.

O'Brien lacked steam and Johnson shot a left to the body and a right to the head as he rushed in to a clinch. O'Brien showed great ring generalship and avoided the savage rush that followed. Jawn was cheered for his gameness, each time coming back with a jab to the face.

Suddenly, Johnson stopped his aggressiveness, held back, and waited until O'Brien took up the aggressive again. The crowd was pleased that O'Brien carried the fight to his bigger opponent.

As the smaller man was coming in, a hard left uppercut to the stomach made O'Brien wince. He clinched and then slipped to the floor in his own corner. This was the fourth time that Jawn went down, and some of the crowd started to hiss him for it. Another version said Johnson rushed O'Brien into a corner, where he slipped down. He rose, then jabbed and clinched a couple times. Johnson was cool and sent his hard right to the body. They exchanged hooks to the face at the bell.

The *World*, *Inquirer*, *Public Ledger*, and *Journal* all said the round belonged to Johnson. The *Press* said it was an even round.

6 - When they shook to start the last round, their gloves barely touched the tips, each man "fearful of the other playing that time honored ring trick of hitting while shaking hands." The *Inquirer* said their half-hearted shake was like "a social greeting between two cold blooded society dames."

O'Brien continued forcing the fight. He made lead after lead but Johnson threw his head aside, ducking many of the jabs. Johnson then chased O'Brien around the ring, but missed him.

O'Brien landed a left to the face and also a good right to the body. Johnson rushed, and after sidestepping several swings, O'Brien slipped down to his knees.

After Jawn rose, Johnson landed a hard left to the body. This blow hurt, and before O'Brien could get over its effects, Johnson hooked a right to the stomach. Johnson then planted a left hook to the mouth and crossed his right to the closed eye. O'Brien's mouth started bleeding as well. Still, he slammed a right to the champ's stomach and then jabbed the nose.

Johnson jabbed the face and uppercut him with his right to the chin. In order to protect himself from Johnson's right uppercuts and body shot counters; O'Brien clinched until the referee tore him away.

Johnson missed a vicious overhand swing and received two jabs from O'Brien, who took advantage of the opening. Johnson landed a left to the face but Jawn came back quickly by jabbing the nose and following with a right to the face. O'Brien was still forcing matters. He landed a left to the mouth and was swinging with both hands even after the bell rang. Referee McGuigan had to jump between the two to stop further proceedings.

The *World*, *Inquirer*, and *Journal* gave Johnson the final round. Even the *Press* said the last round was Johnson's round. However, the *Public Ledger* gave the 6th round to O'Brien.

Johnson walked over to the ringside pressmen and asked how they gave the verdict, "and judging from the look on his face, he did not get much encouragement."

The crowd gave O'Brien a vociferous ovation, standing up and cheering thunderously when he left the ring for his dressing room. He was compelled to shake hands with dozens of his admirers.

When Johnson left, the crowd hissed him.

The *Ledger*, *Press*, and *Bulletin* called it a draw, while the *Inquirer*, *Record*, *World*, and *Journal* all said Johnson had won.

The *Philadelphia Public Ledger* said O'Brien earned a draw in an exciting bout. The Philadelphian forced the fight, did a majority of the leading, and kept Johnson on the defensive in four of the six rounds, but his blows lacked strength. Although O'Brien landed many left jabs flush to the mouth, the only harm done was to cause a little blood to trickle over Johnson's shiny gold-rimmed teeth. Johnson was a disappointment, for he allowed his lighter opponent to set the pace.

Deficient in height, reach, and weight, O'Brien took almost no chances of using his right. He frequently feinted, and Johnson made futile attempts to counter with either hand.

Johnson primarily attempted to rush his lighter opponent across the ring and then use his great strength in the clinches. Several times he wrestled O'Brien to the floor, but only once did he drop him from the force of a clean punch. This occurred in the first 30 seconds of the 1st round.

Two days later, this writer scored the rounds 2-2-2:

1 – Johnson
2 – O'Brien
3 – Even
4 – Even
5 – Johnson
6 – O'Brien

The *Philadelphia Press* agreed that they had boxed a fast and furious draw before a cosmopolitan crowd. The well-trained O'Brien used all of his old-time craftiness, and was always in the milling. Both fighters were looking to land counters, but their guarding was so near perfection that the bout was even. Although Johnson was much heavier, he was equally shifty on his feet and as able in his guarding.

O'Brien had trained earnestly for the past month, and it showed. "O'Brien was in better condition last night than ever before in his history." He came in as the fan favorite because he was the local man, white, smaller, and had shown heart against Ketchel. "Once despised for questionable dealings, O'Brien won back the hearts of the fight fans by the excellent fight he put up against Stanley Ketchel in New York."

Apparently, Johnson had been living in a luxurious way. Yet, he remained confident that he would keep the championship for some time to come.

The *Press* had nearly the exact same round-by-round description as the *Public Ledger*, though it scored the rounds differently, 1-1-4:

1 – Even
2 – O'Brien
3 – Even
4 – Even
5 – Even
6 – Johnson

The *Philadelphia Evening Bulletin* also said O'Brien was entitled to a draw. Compelled to do most of the leading, O'Brien made a fine showing. Johnson's performance was a disappointment and he lost prestige.

Johnson had height, reach, weight, and strength advantages, but he worked like a "has-been" rather than a current champ. He forced O'Brien to do nine-tenths of the leading in the hope of landing a counter, but only succeeded in landing one high on the cheekbone, which made O'Brien clinch until he recovered. It raised a nasty lump under the left eye, but O'Brien smiled and went about his task. "Had O'Brien followed Johnson's example there would have been a poor bout. The Philadelphian jeopardized his chances in doing all the leading, but it helped him to get a draw."

Johnson's magnificent physique made O'Brien look even smaller. The champion wore his usual smile of assured confidence, undisturbed by the cool reception he received compared with the rousing welcome tendered to O'Brien.

Johnson appeared altogether too big, but O'Brien was made of good material. When he found that Johnson would not do any of the leading, he forced the fighting. The champ grinned, as if O'Brien was playing right into his hands. However, as the bout progressed, Johnson found that it was not as easy to land as he thought it would be, and many of his punches went astray. When he did assume the aggressive, he found it hard to locate the elusive Philadelphian, and time after time his blows struck the air. In several rounds, O'Brien feinted him into knots.

After the 3rd round, Johnson's smile began to fade away. He realized it was not the cinch he expected, and he settled down to business and tried his hardest to land an effective punch. O'Brien was too good a ring general to be tempted into a false lead, and he made full use of the ring, moving about to avoid the punches. At times it seemed as if Johnson would land a finishing blow, but O'Brien would get out of harm's way and jab his left to the face.

O'Brien was game, but in the last two rounds he began to tire under the strain and had to call upon all of his ring skill and generalship to keep Johnson away. Luckily for him, the champ was puffing himself, and not in the best shape. Johnson once threw O'Brien to the mat, and also was warned for unsportsmanlike tactics in hitting on the breakaway. The crowd hissed him several times.

Taken altogether, Johnson made a very poor showing for a champion, and the general opinion was that Jim Jeffries in his prime would have made short work of him. His judgment of distance was poor, and while his blows had lots of steam behind them he only landed half a dozen that had any effect. O'Brien outgeneraled him at nearly every stage and his left hand leading and feinting were immeasurably superior. Notwithstanding Johnson's advantages, O'Brien went after him in earnest fashion, and had the weights been any way even there would have been only the Philadelphian in it as far as the decision was concerned.

It was an O'Brien crowd before the bout began, and after it was over he was an even bigger favorite than ever.

Johnny and Charley White, the New York referees, were on hand and were loud in their praise of O'Brien's work. "The consensus of opinion was that Johnson has not improved since his last visit here, and that he was a lucky man to hold the championship."

O'Brien not only outwitted him in the ring, but he also got the better of the financial end by taking the percentage instead of the guarantee.

Unlike the *Ledger, Press*, and *Bulletin*, which scored the bout a draw, the local *Philadelphia Inquirer* said that Johnson, with his greater weight and harder punches, had bested O'Brien in a hard bout. The local man did most of the leading and had the better of the early rounds, for his speed fooled Johnson, who seldom landed. However, Johnson's punches hurt when they connected, and therefore he deserved the verdict. It saw his work as being more effective. The *Inquirer* said the bout proved that a good little man, no matter how good, could not lick a good big man. Johnson outbulled O'Brien, though the latter was never in any serious danger.

O'Brien was in superb fettle, and gave an exhibition of footwork that made him look like a lithe cat in comparison with the slow plodding Johnson, who was not in condition.

After the 2nd round, Johnson was breathing harder, and on two occasions deliberately let up in his aggressive tactics. "In clean punches O'Brien probably landed two to the champion's one, but back of the black's punches there was a great amount of steam. He landed one punch in the fourth round – a straight left to the jaw – that was probably the hardest and best timed of the fight."

Johnson smiled throughout. O'Brien's jabs did not appear to affect him at all. Starting with the 3rd round, Johnson walked right into them in order to land one to the body or jaw.

O'Brien's worst round was the 4th. He led with a left jab to the mouth, but Johnson returned with a left and then landed a pretty stiff right to the jaw, compelling the local man to hold.

Three or four times during the mix-ups, O'Brien was roughed to the floor, and once he got tangled in the ropes.

In the 5th round, O'Brien's left eye had developed a "large-sized shanty," and his right eye seemed to be in trouble as well. Other than a little blood on his lips, Johnson had no marks at the end.

The *Inquirer's* round-by-round scoring was 4 rounds Johnson, 2 even:

1 - Johnson
2 - Even
3 - Even
4 - Johnson
5 - Johnson
6 - Its description gave the impression of a Johnson round.

Regardless of its opinion that Johnson had won, his performance left something to be desired. "Johnson's showing did not impress those about the ringside as being that of a real champion. On the form he showed last night he would not have been common amusement for Sullivan, Fitzsimmons or Jeffries."

Afterwards, when the crowd outside first heard the news that O'Brien had gone the limit and that Johnson had not made good on his threat to knock him out, a cheer spread up and down the street with the rapidity of a prairie fire. The result was a popular one.

Like the *Inquirer*, the *Philadelphia Record* agreed that Johnson was too big for O'Brien and had bested the Philadelphian, though he failed to stop him. The local man was very game and took the fight to his 43-pound larger opponent for the greater part of the bout, gaining credit for his showing. O'Brien was still strong on his feet at the end. "But in doing this O'Brien got some very hard bumps and was pretty badly hurt at times, and there is no doubt that the negro had the better of the contest." O'Brien deserved credit for going after Johnson, for the champion "seemed for the greater part of the time disposed to loaf along and make the contest as easy as possible."

On a few occasions, Johnson cut loose with great vigor, and it was then that O'Brien was punished severely. "The white man was down several times, although only once on a fair knockdown. Once O'Brien was carried through the ropes by one of Johnson's fierce rushes and had it not been for the assistance of those on the outside he would have fallen to the floor outside the ring." Ultimately, this writer opined that Johnson was the better fighter. "He is a tremendously big, powerful man, and much too good for all such fighters as O'Brien."

At the sound of the first bell they came together with considerable speed. Johnson started fiercely and aggressively, as if he was going to try to stop O'Brien. However, he ran into a punch in the face that made him slow up and fight more cautiously. Perhaps he also saw that hitting O'Brien was not all that easy, and he did not want to wear himself out trying to do so.

O'Brien tried to stab Johnson with his famous left, but to his surprise he missed the face repeatedly. Johnson's little side step and duck made the left shoot harmlessly over his shoulder time and again, and Johnson's golden smile that made him so many enemies in Australia was in evidence. The local man's admirers shouted, "Knock the gold out of his teeth."

O'Brien's chief advisor, featherweight champion Abe Attell, told his man, "Steady Jack; feint and make him lead." Jack tried to take the advice and draw Johnson out, but it was evident that the champ was not there to do much leading except at such times as he felt like cutting loose for a supreme effort.

The *Record* writer said the blow that knocked down O'Brien was delivered in the 5th round and came in the midst of a fierce Johnson rally. His lefts and rights drove O'Brien backward, and Johnson's famous short right caught O'Brien under the left eye and he went down as though kicked by a mule. He came up quickly though, without waiting for the count. The mark made by the blow was plainly visible, for blood trickled from an abrasion, and a swelling about the size of a mouse slowly appeared. O'Brien wisely tried to hold until he could gather his senses, but the burly Johnson shook him off and shot home two or three more lefts and rights which O'Brien slipped or parried.

On the occasions when he did go after O'Brien, Johnson always gave him something to remember, but then he seemed content to wait for the smaller man to come to him.

Had O'Brien fought as Johnson did, there would have been a few fierce rushes and a whole lot of waiting. This, along with the color of the two men, made O'Brien the spectators' favorite.

> But in giving O'Brien full credit for the fight he put up, it must not be forgotten that he did not hit Johnson one damaging blow, and that the lefts which he finally got home to the big man's face were little more than touches. It was a fast, clever boxer against a big, clever fighter, and while the little man did remarkably well, he never had any chance of winning.

The *New York World*, which had reporter William P. McLoughlin on scene, also said the black champion defeated O'Brien in a fast fight. He sent O'Brien through the ropes to the floor in the 1st round, and later on closed one eye with hard swings. However, O'Brien was game and clever, rose quickly after going down, and at times chased Johnson, jabbing away. The crowd hissed the champ for rough work, and the referee warned him. Although O'Brien showed extreme cleverness, did most of the leading, and landed some good stiff jabs, he was no match for Johnson, who was about 40 pounds heavier and six inches taller. "When Johnson did send over a sweep it counted, and Jack showed the effects of the big fellow's wallops."

For the most part, Johnson used waiting tactics and was hooted for it. When he did mix it up his bulk and strength soon told on O'Brien.

Up to and including the 3rd round, it was O'Brien's fight. He did all the leading and landed several good, clean blows.

However, near the end of the 4th round, Johnson landed a right that sent O'Brien to his knees, and from that time on it was "Mistah Johnsing's go. O'Brien's left eye was almost closed in this session."

Johnson showed some fatigue in the 5th and 6th rounds, but in the middle of the 6th round he hammered O'Brien with right and left, and his wallops were hot ones. "It was Johnson's go, but O'Brien deserves a good deal of credit for a game and clever battle."

The *World's* round-by-round scoring (in part from the impression given from its description) was 4 rounds Johnson, 1 O'Brien, 1 even:

1 – Johnson
2 – Round about even
3 – O'Brien
4 – Johnson edged it
5 – Johnson
6 – Johnson

This author said Johnson "shaded" O'Brien, meaning he won by a small margin.

The *New York Journal's* famous sportswriter Tad Dorgan, whom black periodicals often said was amongst the fairest of the white writers towards blacks, was present at the fight. He said Johnson had a close call with O'Brien, but won. "Jack Johnson was just a bit too big and strong for Jack O'Brien." The challenger was in the best shape, but too small for the champion. Johnson was out of shape, as "round as a baby doll," and stalled his way through the bout without hardly mussing his hair, so to speak. "His size and strength alone won out for him."

Johnson was afraid to mix too hard or long for fear that his condition would give out on him. "In condition Johnson is a dangerous fellow. He is as quick as a cat, has a ripping uppercut that is a terror and his boxing is grand, but last night he was a second-rate Johnson." O'Brien successfully feinted him out of position, jabbed him as no one else ever had, and had a slight lead in the first 3 rounds.

> O'Brien did practically all of the leading, but there wasn't one good solid punch throughout. He stabbed and grabbed all the way. He was afraid of Johnson and when he did lead he followed it up with a hug, fearing a mix or a return from the black fellow, who was vicious with his uppercuts and quite generous.

Early on, O'Brien did the "jumping jack stuff" and "had Johnson guessing." Neither man did much except stall and feint.

The 1st round was a feel out. O'Brien led and jabbed the nose two or three times and cleverly ducked returns. When danger loomed up in a mix, he flopped to the floor, and then rose. He danced and jabbed some more. When Johnson lashed out with right and left, "Jawn" slipped down again. "He didn't seem able to hold his feet at all." The suggestion was that either

Johnson was knocking him off his balance or that O'Brien was going down intentionally in order to avoid punishment.

O'Brien landed one out of every three jabs, which was more than what Johnson was doing. However, in a mix near the ropes, Johnson landed a right on the jaw and O'Brien staggered and grabbed, holding on for dear life. Johnson tried to break free, but O'Brien would not let go, and the bell came to his rescue.

In the 2nd and 3rd rounds, O'Brien feinted, danced, jumped, jabbed, and grabbed. Johnson could not get to him at all, and there was no chance for him to get going. O'Brien did the leading and landed some punches that did no damage, though they scored points.

However, after this round, O'Brien slowed down considerably. The 4th round "came near being the end of Jawn the jumper." Johnson rushed him into a corner and whaled away with both hands. Jawn grabbed around Artha's neck and tried to clinch. Johnson swung him around in the air and belted him three solid stomach blows before Jawn dropped to the ground. However, he rose, and when Johnson subsequently missed a right and Jawn smiled, the crowd howled with joy.

Johnson backed him up to the ropes again, feinting his left. Jawn ducked and the champ drove a short right to the left eye, staggering him and closing the eye. O'Brien was weak and wobbly, and Johnson rushed in to finish him, but Jawn grabbed and clung to him like a leech. The referee tried to break them, but O'Brien held on until they were on the other side of the ring. Blood streamed down from Jawn's eye. O'Brien danced away from Johnson, who followed. They mixed it in the corner, and Jawn pulled his stunt of dropping to the ground again, rising just at the bell. He dropped into his chair, weakened from the mauling. Johnson was puffing in his corner.

In the 5th round, Johnson cornered him and started to pump in both hands, and O'Brien tumbled again. He was up in a jiffy and hugged once more. Johnson landed lefts and followed with right uppercuts that jarred O'Brien. He banged the eye again, puffing it some more. Johnson's straight left sent his head back with a snap. O'Brien was slower than ever, while Johnson was anxious. Jawn jumped and belted Johnson on the mouth with a left, but took one on the stomach that "sounded as though a drum was soaked with a potato." Johnson rushed and swung both hands to the body, and O'Brien fell again. "Strangest thing the way that fellow tumbles." The bell rang just when he arose.

The 6th and last round started and they touched gloves. For a while, they stood far off from one another. Then Johnson went after him, ripping in an uppercut to the face and following with a left to the same spot. O'Brien danced away and jabbed. He jabbed again but took a left to the body, after which he hugged Johnson hard for a while. They waltzed around and Johnson waited. Jawn jabbed his nose, which angered Johnson, who rushed in. "Honest Jawn tumbled again. He was the original fall guy."

O'Brien did not take the count, but hopped up again and resumed his jumping-jack tactics, jabbing the nose. Johnson jabbed his left in return and uppercut hard on the mouth. He landed a left to the jaw and hooked it onto the ear while O'Brien danced along the ropes, seeming leg weary and bleeding. Johnson hooked his right onto the ear but took a hard left in the stomach. They landed light lefts and clinched. After breaking, Jawn led a couple times again until the bell rang.

Tad scored it 4 rounds Johnson, 2 O'Brien:

1 – Johnson
2 – O'Brien
3 – O'Brien
4 – Johnson
5 – Johnson
6 - Johnson

Another *Journal* writer said that either Ketchel or Langford could have beaten Johnson had they been in the ring with him. Johnson had been leading an easy life, "and unless he gets down to business and works faithfully for future battles he will not remain champion very long. He was never so big and fat before."

After the fight, Johnson said, "I thought I won the bout." The champ said O'Brien did no damage with his punches, whereas he had O'Brien going on several occasions, and Jawn grabbed and held in order to survive. Although disappointed that he was not able to knock him out, Jack felt that he would have done so if O'Brien had used different tactics, or if the bout had been longer.

> I am still sure that I would have [knocked him out] had he stood up and fought me. Instead of fighting the Quaker spent all his time hanging on and thus saved himself. He is clever, but cannot hit with any force. Like the bout I had with Sailor Burke, my opponent would do anything but fight, and when that happens it is mighty hard to put a man out. Burke spent all his time on the floor, while O'Brien hung on for dear life. Ketchel is not a hugger, and in the fight with him I will show what punching means.

If folks disagreed with his opinion, and the demand was sufficient, Johnson was willing to take on O'Brien in a longer fight.

Still, Johnson admitted that O'Brien was clever, fast, and a good ring general. "He is a wonderfully clever fellow and the best boxer I ever met in a ring."

Johnson said that as soon as he returned from Europe, he would accept Bill Delaney's offer of a $10,000 side-bet for a Kaufman bout. However, another reporter said the champ spoke with a Kaufman representative and told him that if Kaufman really meant business, he would postpone his European trip and box him. Jack was willing to bet $1,000 that he would win every round.

Jack O'Brien said, "I beat Johnson, and the job wasn't hard." He knew that the champ was not in the best condition, but that was not O'Brien's fault. "Fighting as he did last night he would be a cinch for Ketchel. With Jeffries he would be a joke. Johnson is a better fighter than he showed, however." He said the champion's vaunted cleverness was not in evidence. "He can hit, though, as that wallop that almost closed my left eye proves."

Stanley Ketchel was present at the fight, and was not impressed with Johnson. Ketchel hoped no one else would get Johnson before he beat him.

> Jack Johnson's showing against O'Brien didn't impress me as being of championship caliber. He is a big fellow and carries a lot of weight, but he will be soft for me, judging from the way he fought. If I had been in O'Brien's place I think I would have had a great chance to score a knockout over the big negro. He has a great defense and is very cagey in the clinches, but I would surely break through his guard with my heavy blows and only one blow would be necessary to make him hit the carpet for the count. No one has ever made him back up, but I don't think he would stand up under punishment. I don't think he was in the best condition last night, because the superfluous flesh was very much in evidence. But he showed that he is no demon for aggressiveness.
>
> O'Brien made a fine showing when he had all his speed in the early rounds, and he outpointed the big colored man two to one. He feinted at will and made him miss many hard blows that would probably have ended the battle had they landed. O'Brien tired fast in the closing chapters from forcing the battle against his heavier opponent. There must have been at least fifty pounds in weight which told on O'Brien in the end when he had to do some stalling to keep away from the heavy lunges of Johnson.
>
> I think the forceful tactics of the negro and the heavy blows he landed in the latter rounds about evened up the go. …
>
> O'Brien looked to be in grand condition, but the defense of Johnson made it difficult for him to score any effective punches. The best he got away with were a few light stabs on the face which didn't appear to feaze Johnson in the least.
>
> I will prove…that I am a far better man and more entitled to the heavyweight championship than Johnson. When we meet at San Francisco he will not neglect his training and will surely be much faster than he was.
>
> He looks to me like a man who will not stand up under much punishment, and once I connect good and hard on him there will be nothing to it.

From Chicago, upon learning of the result, James J. Jeffries said,

Nothing Jack Johnson can do in or out of the ring makes the slightest difference to me. I will be ready to talk fight to Johnson when I have finished my present engagement some time in July. Then I will be ready to sign up for a fight within five months of the date of signing. … I do not think he wants to meet me in the ring. …

The result of the fight is no surprise to me, although I expected Johnson would do better. O'Brien is a flashy man in a six-round fight and could keep almost any one off for that length of time.

Johnson, with his superior height and weight, should be able to make a better showing than he did. On the whole, the result is what might be expected, and will make no change in my plans.

Another report quoted Jeffries as saying, "In my opinion the fight was a defeat for Johnson." He greatly outweighed his foe and had claimed that he was going to stop O'Brien, but failed to do so. "A real champion of the world – mind you I never have said that Johnson was such – who is able to knock down an opponent forty pounds lighter than himself should be able to stop him." Jeff said Johnson failed to finish O'Brien because he did not have enough class to do so. "I thought little of Johnson's claims to the championship before this fight and I think less of them now."

Excerpt from Philadelphia Record cartoon, May 20, 1909

New York Journal, May 20, 1909

LIL' ARTHA'S NARROW ESCAPE---By Tad

Excerpts from *New York Journal* cartoon, May 20, 1909

A couple days after the fight, the newspapers were still discussing the bout. Some insisted that Johnson won. Others insisted that O'Brien had secured a draw. Another theme was whether Johnson had faked and carried O'Brien. There was a mix of opinion.

The *Philadelphia Record* said there would be no local demand for a rematch between Johnson and O'Brien.

> Philadelphia would hardly stand for another meeting, for the reason that the local fight followers now know that Johnson is entirely too big for O'Brien and that he in condition and so disposed, should beat O'Brien in short order. This is not to intimate that Johnson faked on Wednesday night, for there was no indication that such was the case, but he surely did not try his best in every round. Just why he loafed Johnson knows better than any one else.

Regardless, the locals gave O'Brien great credit for his splendid showing. Some even declared that he deserved the points victory. "Had it been a contest with blackened gloves, in which every touch must be counted as a point, possibly O'Brien would have figured as the winner, but it was not that kind of a contest and the mere touches counted no more than feints." Still, he was entitled to glory for fighting hard and doing relatively well. "Johnson hurt his reputation by not training carefully and going into the ring many pounds overweight."[84]

---

[84] *Philadelphia Record*, May 21, 1909.

THE JOHNSON-O'BRIEN FIGHT STILL A LIVE SPORTING TOPIC. —By McGurk.

Philadelphia Record, **May 21, 1909**

The *Philadelphia Public Ledger* said that although he was outclassed physically, O'Brien fought a courageous fight and showed-up the world's champion, who primarily was a defensive boxer.

> As in all great ring contests where the result is not decisive, where no knockout is achieved, there is always a great difference of opinion as to the relative merits of the contestants. Many were sure in their judgment that O'Brien won, others favored the negro, while a verdict of a draw was considered a just decision by another class. The writer could not see sufficient difference in the work of the two men at the end of the 18 minutes of fighting to justify either being given a clean-cut decision. An analysis of the bout showed Johnson to have a clear advantage in the first and fifth rounds, O'Brien had a good lead in the second and sixth, while honors were even in the third and fourth rounds. Each man had two rounds to his credit and two were even, and in consequence, in the writer's judgment, a draw would have been a just verdict, and would not cause any hardship to either man.

O'Brien tried to fight mostly on the outside, cognizant of the fact that Johnson was bigger and stronger and rough in the clinches. The local man was clever and elusive, but he also brought the fight to Johnson, did the bulk of the leading, and if it had not been for his aggressive tactics, "the bout would likely have developed into a disgusting exhibition."

> There are two sides to boxing – offensive and defensive. Of course, the man who is the aggressor catches the crowd. There is, however, just as much cleverness and skill on the defensive side as there is on

the other. Jack Johnson is a defensive boxer. He proved that in the O'Brien bout. The Philadelphian's jabs bothered the big negro, but they apparently did not hurt him. At the same time he showed to the crowd that he did not relish punishment. With his great physical advantage and the way he started in to annihilate O'Brien in the first round many thought the bout would scarcely last three rounds. It is therefore all the more to the credit of O'Brien that he was able to stand off his giant opponent for six rounds. He fought a courageous fight and should be 'lionized' by his friends.[85]

Philadelphia Press, May 21, 1909

Some suspected some form of a frame-up. The *New York World's* writer said the fight had some queer features. The words used gave the impression that this writer felt that Johnson had carried O'Brien to some degree. Johnson's punches seemed to lack knockout force, but whenever he did throw in a hard one for the "sake of appearances" it sent O'Brien to the floor. O'Brien was great at the tap-tap-tap game with his punches, though they did no damage.

How one scored the bout depended upon one's criteria. "Counting each tap, tap, tap, tapity-tap of that touch-and-run pugilist Philadelphia Jack O'Brien, he had it on Jack Johnson a thousand ways." However, "Counting the chug, thug, bump, smash, that send men jiggering into strange sleeps, the big black champion had it on O'Brien right from start to finish." O'Brien had landed more taps and touches, but Johnson landed the harder, more effective blows.

[85] *Philadelphia Public Ledger,* May 21, 1909.

O'Brien would dance up to Johnson, land a tap or swat, sometimes winking at his corner, and the crowd would yell with ecstasies of delight, while Johnson responded with a great mouthful of gold-filled teeth and laughed aloud, "He-yi, he-e-e!" But then Johnson would "forget himself so far as to swat O'Brien on the jaw. Sometimes hot and sometimes cold. Twice he did it real hard and O'Brien went down each time." O'Brien's left eye was banged up so badly that it had a cornice of deep black. In the 5th round, Jawn's smile vanished. He no longer could wink or else he'd be blind, for his left eye was closed completely.

This writer opined that Johnson had the best of the bout, and said,

> [While some declare that the] hit-and-get-away counts as more effective than the punch-and-get-one-that-doesn't-hurt-in-return…I beg respectfully to differ. Ruling on the idea of foot racing and shadow boxing, O'Brien had it on Johnson. But when it came to sending in a smash – tee hee - why that there Jack Johnsing he just banged O'Brien to the floor when he felt he had to do it to keep up appearances.

The writer thought the bout had a bad odor, opining that Johnson could have knocked out O'Brien if he had wanted to do so. "Could Johnson knock O'Brien out? Yes-s-s-s! With one right or left punch."

The author opined that Johnson was not about to knock out the man who was paying him. O'Brien engineered the making of the bout, and therefore was helping Johnson earn good money. O'Brien was the one who was guaranteeing Johnson's purse as well. The inference was that the smaller man perhaps had gotten the larger one to work with him to some degree so that they could make money, and Johnson had obliged him for the payday in which there was no danger of him losing his title.

Stanley Ketchel said, "I knocked the life out of O'Brien. I wonder what I could do to that nigger?" The writer responded, "So do I."[86]

The *New York Journal's* Tad also wondered whether Johnson had played possum with O'Brien and others. Some were saying, "He could have knocked the Quaker out had he tried real hard, but he took it easy." Ketchel saw the fight and said he wished that he had been inside the ropes instead of O'Brien. "Maybe that's what the champ wanted. … Some one will tell Jeff now that Johnson is a terrible joke and he may jump at an offer." The implication was that Johnson could induce others to fight him, and generate excitement surrounding other bouts if he did not look too good.

However, ultimately, Tad did not think it was a grand scheme on Johnson's part. He thought Johnson was surprised at how good O'Brien was. "After the fight he told a big Broadway sport that O'Brien was the fastest fellow he had ever met." Johnson used the words "marvelously fast." Plus, Johnson had not trained properly, so it simply was a tall order to stop a very experienced, fast, clever, in-shape, 6-round defensive master. Still,

---

[86] *New York World*, May 21, 1909.

Johnson "was the better fighter, we could all see that." The thrill was that O'Brien did better than expected. Ultimately, Tad believed that neither O'Brien nor Ketchel were big enough to beat Johnson over longer routes. "Let Al Kaufman or Jeffries fight Johnson, they are the big fellows."[87]

The *New York Sun* said nobody believed for a moment that Johnson did not do his best to put O'Brien away. His reputation was at stake. He took on O'Brien because he believed that he would be a soft mark, and before the bout was half over he realized his mistake.[88]

The *Philadelphia Record* reported that some were speculating that the Johnson-O'Brien fight was a frame up because it appeared that Johnson tried only in flashes. "It will be hard to make those who witnessed the contest believe that Johnson could not have done better work had he been so inclined." Johnson showed few flashes of his power, and when he did, O'Brien was made to look like a boy fighting a man, but then Johnson would fail to follow up advantages gained and instead loafed along. As a result, some spectators, carried away by prejudice or sympathy for the smaller local man, thought O'Brien deserved credit for victory.

These writers believed that Johnson indeed was in condition and could have done much better than he did. He was in no worse condition at the finish than at the start. Yet, he did no aggressive work in the last round. The way he backed up at times might have led one to think he was afraid of O'Brien, who forced the battle most of the time. "Johnson's cautious tactics seemed quite ridiculous under the circumstances, for O'Brien is not a knocker out."

Johnson was criticized for slipping lefts but failing to counter with his own left. Either he was very slow to react or he was not trying his best. Others said he was overcautious. He was further criticized for fighting flatfooted as well.

Others felt that Johnson only fought in spots because he didn't have the condition to do otherwise. They said he would not do as champion because he had no pride in his position and was not willing to keep himself in shape.

Yet, those who believed Johnson carried O'Brien said that even granting that Johnson was not in top condition, there was "still no good explanation for the manner in which he met O'Brien's attack. If he knows no better then he certainly is a very poor champion, and if he did not try then the bout must have been a 'frame-up.' If it was time will solve the riddle."

Also odd was the fact that "O'Brien displayed unnatural confidence in carrying the fight to an opponent so much his superior in physical power, as well as a reckless abandon foreign to his usual crafty style of fighting, in failing to take advantage of those little intervals of rest allowed him by the rules after being sent down by the burly colored man."

---

[87] *New York Journal*, May 21, 1909.
[88] *New York Sun*, May 22, 1909.

Johnson received his money in advance, so he was set up well financially regardless of the result. Since it was a no-decision, he might not have cared what happened.

The *Record* said at least one knockdown was the real thing, for a mouse appeared under O'Brien's eye. Yet, Johnson made no effort to take advantage of the fact that O'Brien quickly rose and continued. O'Brien kept after Johnson, except when the champ came after him, and then Jawn would jump about and dodge. Johnson's rallies appeared to be the real thing. Still, rumors of fake would not die down.

O'Brien proved that he was still fast and clever, with a great eye for distance. Johnson proved that he is a "tremendously strong powerful fellow, with a great kick in his right hand, a left that should be dangerous if he can only be made to remember to use it to hit with at long range as well as to block."

Many were saying that Johnson could beat smaller men, but "would have been only a plaything to such a fighter as Jeffries when 'Jeff' was at his best, if the form shown against Burns and O'Brien tell the black man's true capabilities. Bob Fitzsimmons would have beaten Johnson easier than he did Corbett." However, it was opined that Johnson probably could have beaten Sharkey, Ruhlin, or McCoy.[89]

O'Brien's past record also caused suspicion to surround the bout. Some thought that Johnson might have posted a forfeit agreeing not to knock him out. That was speculation. However, others said that such was an old O'Brien method of doing business with boxers whom he was concerned might stop him.

The *Washington Times* noted that O'Brien was a "self-confessed faker" known to take part in or attempt to take part in fixed fights. Many folks thought it bad for the sport to allow a man with a shady history to be involved in a high-profile bout. After the revelations concerning O'Brien's attempt to fix the Burns bout, O'Brien "was branded in terms that would have made a right-thinking man want to commit suicide." He was supposed to be obliterated forever under a weight of shame. However, enough time had passed, O'Brien boxed some, began to come into the limelight again, and was forgiven. However, many wondered whether Johnson had carried him intentionally pursuant to some sort of side-deal. Johnson himself had a record that "has never appealed to sportsmen."

> [C]ompetent critics at the ringside are at a complete loss to understand the tactics of Johnson on any other basis than that he was not trying his best. That he had several rallies and showed flashes in which, with his boxing ability and superior weight and reach he made O'Brien look weak is admitted, but that he absolutely failed to use his natural advantages and fought most of the time as if tied to a post is also admitted. Although not well trained, it is claimed he did not

---

89 *Philadelphia Record*, May 23, 1909.

attempt to exert himself as much as his remaining strength would have permitted, and was content to let the white man dance in and out and take desperate chances which would not have been predicted by any critic familiar with O'Brien's style.

The presumption hinted at by some of those who have considered the queer angles of the bout is that Johnson was under a heavy forfeit not to put out O'Brien, and was too much afraid of losing the money to get too gallus in the way of heavy punches. It will be remembered that O'Brien once had Tommy Ryan sewed up in just such a manner, and that there was almost exactly the same agreement when he first met Tommy Burns. … Jack McGuigan, the referee and guiding spirit of the National Athletic Club, which pulled off the affair, accompanied by Jack O'Brien, went to Pittsburg to see Johnson to arrange for the match, which does not sound well to start with. Business Manager Edwards, of the club, says the proposed financial scheme did not go through, that O'Brien got 30 per cent of this house, $6,169.20, and Johnson $5,100.

Others said Johnson simply was not that good, and was overrated.

These lofty thinkers forget that he is merely a negro prizefighter, whose head, from all accounts has been inordinately swelled by a sudden rise to prominence, and who, but for his blind luck in coming into the arena at a time when there are no real heavyweights, would never have been more than a third rate scrapper figuring in preliminaries and semi-windups, when men of class were performing.[90]

Philadelphia Press, May 22, 1909

[90] Washington Times, May 23, 1909.

Most newspapers throughout the nation, relying on dispatches, were quicker to use the "draw" result version than the several versions that said Johnson had won. They reported that O'Brien did most of the leading, and his marvelous quick shifty footwork and superior blocking and ducking saved him from damaging punishment.

The black-owned *Seattle Republican* said Johnson played a game of hide-and-go-seek with O'Brien in a show fight. Johnson demonstrated a lack of training. Its writer warned, "Be careful, Mr. Black Jack, or your 'good time' will land you in the pit of defeat."[91]

Many questioned just how long Johnson would be able to reign as champion. William Rocap opined that Johnson might soon lose his title. "Jack Johnson's future in the ring will not be all roses. American promoters are bound to get him beaten. He must meet Stanley Ketchel on October 12, or else confess that he is afraid of the Montana cowboy." Jeffries, Jeannette, and Langford also would be after him. Of course, Johnson had beaten two of those named men already, scoring all of the knockdowns in those bouts, so it might have been a case of the continued theme of folks underestimating him.

The day after the fight, both men were seen around town. O'Brien had an abrasion on his left cheek bone, but showed few other marks. Johnson had swollen lips, but was able to smile enough to show the glittering gold in his teeth.

Johnson said,

> I won. Everybody knows I did; but I must admit I never dreamed O'Brien was so fast and clever, and any one who tells you he cannot hit is crazy. He punches as hard as any man in the ring. I tried to catch him coming, but he is a little too cute to be copped in six rounds. Ten rounds would enable me to do the trick.

O'Brien said,

> I simply had to carry it to Johnson or else there would not have been any fight. He stood still and I was obliged to lead. Had I done the same the crowd would have been disgusted. They would likely have hissed. I could not stand that in my home town. So it was up to me to show up Jack Johnson, the heavyweight champion of the world – and I believe I did.

Still, O'Brien praised Johnson's strength.

> I am satisfied with the result of the bout. Johnson had fifty pounds the better of the weights, and his reach and height were against me, and still I had to force all the fighting. I was better against Johnson, because of my condition, than I was against Ketchel. … Johnson is a big, powerful fellow, with a terrific punch in either hand. He was in

---

[91] *Citizen* (Honesdale, PA), *Seattle Republican*, May 21, 1909; *Free Lance*, May 22, 1909.

good shape, and he waited for me to lead, so that he could cross me and win with a knockout. No one can realize what a proposition I had on my hands. It was the cheers which helped me.

In another interview, O'Brien said Ketchel would vanquish Johnson, for Stanley had a terrific punch, the hardest in the world, and the gameness required to win. He opined that Johnson was much overrated. He did not think Johnson could take punishment, although he admitted that he was an awkward man to hit and knew much about the art of self-defense. However, when he made Johnson back up from body blows, he realized that the champion would prove a mark for a slugger. Johnson was a big strong fellow with a good punch, but he did not know how to land except when in a flat-footed position. He was rattled easily by a shifty fighter and could not hit while in motion. "Johnson isn't in Ketchel's class when it comes to hitting and gameness, two qualities that make real champions invincible. I think that if the negro ever gets into a slugging bee with Ketchel at close quarters he will be the first to go down, for he cannot stand up under the smashes that Ketchel will hand out." He admitted that comparatively, Ketchel was easy to hit, but "Johnson cannot punch much harder than I can," and therefore Stanley would be around long enough to land a knockout wallop. Ketchel was faster on his feet than Johnson and vastly more aggressive. He could score a knockout with one good smash, and if he bulked up enough, "he will win back the world's heavyweight championship for the white race."[92]

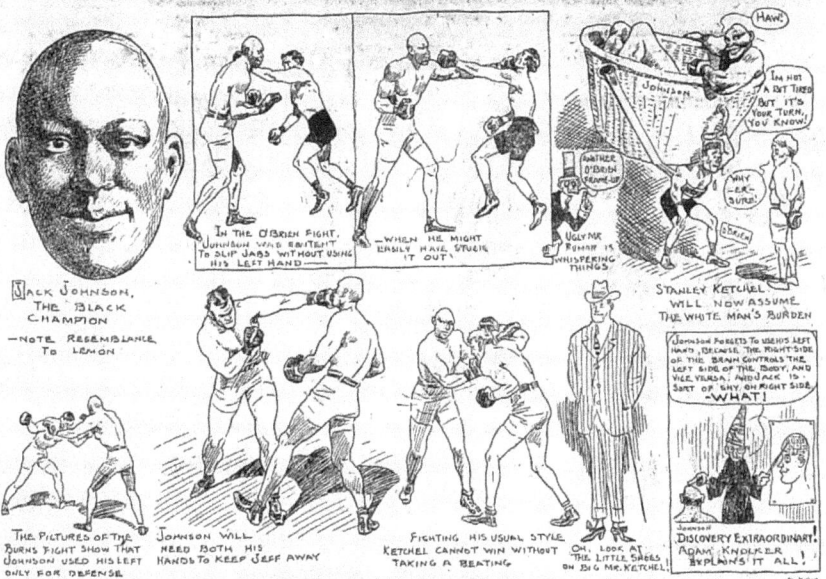

Philadelphia Record, May 23, 1909

---

[92] *Washington Herald*, May 22, 1909. On May 22, 1909 in Paris, 190-pound Joe Jeannette won a 20-round decision over 210-pound Sandy Ferguson.

Another *Record* writer said Johnson's boxing ability should not be judged by his showing against O'Brien. He was a dangerous big fellow, too clever and strong for any man in the ring. True the bout was not first-class, and if repeated, would not draw enough money to warrant serious consideration. "O'Brien could not do anything with the big black fellow, and Johnson was so lazy and indifferent that he did nothing much with O'Brien." Despite O'Brien's friends' claims that he outpointed Johnson, this writer felt that such might be true if only mere touches counted. However, the amount of punishment inflicted had to be considered.

> Granting that O'Brien landed the most blows, which would be hard to prove, as there was no means of recording them, the difference in the effectiveness of the blows would make the contest in favor of Johnson. The best friends of O'Brien would, no doubt, be willing to admit that he was knocked down and battered around, and that he received many hard blows on the head and body. The friends of O'Brien would be hard pressed to tell when the blows of O'Brien did any damage to the black champion.

O'Brien was in top shape, whereas Johnson was hog fat.

> Yet conservative observers came out of the big arena expressing the opinion that O'Brien had been lucky to stay the six rounds. With Johnson in the same condition as O'Brien and trying his best to win, which he evidently was not doing on Wednesday, it is very doubtful if any man who saw Wednesday night's contest would back O'Brien with real money to stay three rounds with the big Texan.

O'Brien was entitled to great credit for taking it to Johnson and forcing matters for the greater part of the bout, despite having all of the physical handicaps. If it had not been for his work, there would have been no contest at all. Each time that Johnson did take the aggressive – once in the 1st and again in the 5th, "it was rather bad business for the other Jack. He carried O'Brien completely off his feet and drove him from one side of the ring to the other." However, after the rushes, the champ took it easy.

Some were surprised at the high level of skill, and at times, speed, that Johnson displayed. "It developed during the bout that Johnson was as clever as O'Brien, and that there was very little difference in the speed of the two men when the black fellow was really trying, which was seldom."

This writer disagreed with the reports that said O'Brien landed many blows. Where a spectator was sitting had a considerable impact upon the opinion as to whether or not the blows landed. Many blows that appeared to land in fact did not.

> A close record, had it been kept, would have shown that O'Brien missed almost as many jabs as he landed, for there were blows which slipped by Johnson's head which from another angle of the ring would have appeared to have reached his face. No man who has ever boxed O'Brien in this city has made him miss as often as Johnson

did. … In fact, it appeared as if Johnson could make O'Brien miss whenever he wanted to. Taking into account the fact that O'Brien is one of the fastest boxers in the ring, and that he was in perfect condition…Johnson must be given credit, for his skill as a boxer ranks with that of any big man who has been seen in local rings in recent years. He put at rest the idea that he cannot use his left hand, for whenever he tried he landed it on O'Brien, and he landed it hard – not too hard, but just hard enough to show that if he desired he could do terrible execution with it. Johnson boxed flat-footed, but he was not slow on his feet, and he had no reason to get on his toes to reach O'Brien, as he could reach the latter by just stepping in and extending his arm to its full length. The flatfooted style is the one for a long fight, which Johnson is used to, and it was also the best style for a man who was lazy and not anxious to mix it up… As to Johnson's right hand, he could whip it in any time he saw fit, and that it had force behind it was demonstrated on various occasions. Even in the poor physical condition in which Johnson appeared…he was able to evade O'Brien's attack when he felt like it, and he carried the fight to the Philadelphian when he felt so disposed. Just why he did not train and get in shape for the bout, and just why he did not extend himself more while he was in the ring are best known to himself; but that he could have done better was evident to those close to the ring.

Some said that Johnson was used to taking it easy on his opponents in order to obtain matches, and old habits die hard.

It is only a short time ago since Johnson was forced, or thought he was forced to agree to go lightly with his opponents in order to get matches. But that time has passed. He is the champion of the world, even if he only beat second-raters to gain the title. Had he been of the caliber of John L. Sullivan he would have been prepared to do his best and would have gone into the ring and done it.

This writer opined that the general feeling was that Johnson would never occupy the place in the hearts of the sporting public held by other great colored boxers like Peter Jackson and George Dixon.[93]

Two days after the fight, on May 21, Johnson allegedly paid $3,000 for a special speed roadster and $1,800 for a big diamond. However, after the purchase, the auto was seized at the instance of Johnson's former black girlfriend/wife Clara S. Kerr of Philadelphia, who served Jack with an attachment on the auto to recover $405.95 on an alleged board bill for Johnson's blind brother Charles.

Although Johnson claimed that the car was not his, but belonged to his manager George Little, who confirmed the statement, the police officer

---

[93] *Philadelphia Record*, May 23, 1909.

Clara Kerr and Johnson in happier days past

insisted that the auto had to go to Camden for an authority there to decide the matter. They went before a district court judge, and Little produced a bill of sale showing that he had purchased the auto, not Johnson. The judge asked Johnson why he didn't simply go ahead and pay the bill. Jack defiantly replied, "Before I'll pay that bill I'll go to jail for ten years. It is a very unjust bill and I will never pay it. I'll fight it to the limit."[94]

Professor James De Forest, a veteran boxing instructor and trainer who claimed to have trained Johnson a decade or so ago in New York, said that Jack was a patient, defensive, cautious fighter who would not risk losing in order to administer more punishment:

He is crafty and cautious now, because he doesn't want to lose his title. He is one of those fellows who don't want to be licked, no matter how little damage they can inflict in a short bout. In short Johnson is a typical finish fighter – a man who can stay on his feet in the ring for hours, if necessary, until the other fellow is so worn out that he can be stowed away.

Johnson has never been whipped soundly and has never been severely punished. He's never knocked out a good man either. But he's so big, strong and patient that only a man of his own size can ever hope to stop him. Ketchel is a game young fellow with a terrific punch in either hand, but you'll find that Johnson will not let him land a single blow in twenty rounds at Colma that can work any harm. Ketchel is nearly four inches shorter than Johnson and will weigh all of forty pounds less. He is much easier to hit than O'Brien, and for that reason Johnson, in my opinion, will have no trouble in uppercutting him as he comes boring in. O'Brien had Ketchel groggy a greater part of seven rounds in their recent fight here, and as Johnson is a harder hitter than O'Brien I cannot believe that Ketchel will be able to stick it out more than ten or twelve rounds. Still, I must admit that from what I know of Johnson he lacks heart. He does not like to be punched in the stomach, and if Ketchel should happen to reach that spot in a hot mix up Johnson might quit, but in fighting at close quarters I think Ketchel will be overmatched and outclassed in science. I should like to see Ketchel win, but he's up against a tremendously hard proposition.

[94] New York World, May 22, 1909; Los Angeles Herald, May 23, 1909.

Jimmy Johnson, a boxing manager, said Johnson would stop Ketchel because Stanley's defense was too open. By forcing the fight he would get hit even harder than he was against O'Brien. "If Ketchel can reach the jaw or the stomach with one punch he'll make the negro quit, but I think he's too small to accomplish such a feat."[95]

However, following Johnson's performance against O'Brien, many in New York favored Ketchel's chances with Johnson. Since O'Brien had boxed both, his opinion was looked upon as high authority, and he was saying that Ketchel would have an easy time with the champ.[96]

On May 24, 1909 in London, England, Sam Langford scored a 4th round knockout over 24-year-old 189-pound British heavyweight champ Ian Iron Hague, who had won the British heavyweight crown by scoring a 1st round knockout over Gunner Moir.

Upon hearing of the result, Johnson said,

> Well, they all have iron jaws until a fellow like Langford drops one over. If Langford hits a jaw right, the man never comes back. Sam has to get them early, though. … That's a great little man, Langford. He gave me a fine run for fifteen rounds a few years ago. He's awfully short, but, like Walcott and Sharkey, he's as strong as an ox.

> Now, if they can get Ketchel and Langford in a fight you'll see the greatest slugging match that was ever held. Both can take a punch, both have hard wallops and both are as game as pebbles. I'd hate to try and pick the winner, but I believe that whoever does win will be on the floor more than once before the fight is over.[97]

Johnson decided to cancel his European trip, and instead remained in the U.S. to train for a potential bout with Al Kaufman before fighting Ketchel in October.[98]

On June 2, 1909 in New York, Stanley Ketchel scored a KO4 over Tony Caponi, who back in 1904 had fought two 6-round bouts with Tommy Burns, one a draw and another a decision loss.

Chicago's E. E. Coulon saw Jim Jeffries and said he looked much better than he did four months ago, when he was hog fat. Jeff was a different man, and had taken off at least 40 pounds. "His work is fast and snappy and his shadow boxing marvelous." Jeff told him, "I don't know when it will be, but I will lick that big smoke if it's the last thing I ever do in this life."[99]

On June 9, 1909 in Philadelphia, just three weeks after O'Brien boxed Johnson, and one week after Ketchel boxed Caponi, Stanley Ketchel fought Jack O'Brien for the second time. From the start, Ketchel rushed and tore

---

[95] *New York Sun*, May 23, 1909.

[96] *Salt Lake Herald*, May 23, 1909.

[97] *New York Journal*, May 25, 1909. Hague also held victories over Charley Wilson and Ben Taylor. The purse was $7,000, with a $1,000 side bet.

[98] *New York Journal*, May 25, 1909; *Philadelphia Record*, May 26, 1909.

[99] *Pittsburg Press*, June 7, 1909.

into him like a human tornado, viciously ripping, smashing, and hammering away with fearful punches that broke through O'Brien's defense and made him run. Stan was so aggressive that O'Brien could not keep away. In the 2nd round, Ketchel landed heart-breaking body blows and jaw-breaking rights to the jaw, sending O'Brien reeling to the ropes and decking him twice in the round. In the 3rd round, Ketchel again beat down O'Brien with sledgehammer blows. O'Brien was helpless and beaten so badly that the referee had to step in to save him. Stanley Ketchel had shattered and knocked out in 3 rounds the shifty man whom Jack Johnson could not stop in 6 rounds. Therefore, his stock further skyrocketed.

The fans loved watching Ketchel fight, which made him a marketable attraction. "He is the sort of fighter who stands the audience on their heads with excitement. He makes them yell. He makes them jump. He is tearing in viciously all the time."

The victory further heightened the demand to see Ketchel fight Johnson. "He wanted to show the fight-loving public that he was a fit opponent for Champion Jack Johnson, and he certainly did."

Afterward, Ketchel said, "I am more confident than ever that I can whip Johnson. The negro's poor showing against O'Brien convinced me of this." He also said, "I think people ought to admit that I am the man to fight Johnson and that I should have a first crack at him."

O'Brien said, "Ketchel is a great fighter. The best in the world today. He can beat Johnson or anybody else. He surprised me with his speed, while nobody could have stood up under his terrible punches." Another quoted him as saying, "Ketchel will beat Johnson to a pulp. ... He is the hardest hitter I ever met. ... I would sooner have a roof fall on me than to act as the receiver for many of Ketchel's blows."

This result ended any chance for O'Brien to secure a longer bout with Johnson, and made the Johnson-Ketchel fight even more intriguing. Ketchel had "earned the right to have first choice at Jack Johnson." This impressive victory had set "fistom mad" with delight. Stan was the reigning sensation. His punches were like thunderbolts, and many saw him as the most logical fighter to "bring back the heavy weight crown to the white man."

However, others claimed that Ketchel was just the kind of man that Johnson could trim handily. They said that Stan could not hit much harder than Burns, and Johnson would meet his rushes calmly and gradually tear him to pieces.

Referee Eddie Smith said Johnson would not be able to use his left jab on Ketchel because Stan's crouch and head movement made jabs miss. "That style of Ketchel's is so awkward, peculiar and changeable that it bothers a fast man." He believed Ketchel had enough power to drop Johnson.[100]

[100] *Boston Herald, Pittsburg Press,* June 10, 1909; *San Francisco Call,* June 13, 1909.

From Boston, where he was doing some light training at the Armory Athletic Association, Johnson was so confident that Ketchel would be easy for him that he said Stan's impressive victory over O'Brien did not change his opinion.

Johnson had been served with a writ, a complaint by his former manager Alex McLean, who claimed that Jack owed him $110 with interest on a promissory note, an amount owed for two years. Johnson said he did not owe McLean anything. Jack was arrested and released on $400 bonds. At that time, one could be arrested on civil claims.[101]

Ketchel and his manager, Willus/Willis Britt, wanted Jim Jeffries to referee the championship bout. Johnson said the only referee he would accept was Jack Welsh (or Welch) of San Francisco. Johnson was well aware of the feeling against him, and wanted a man whom he could depend upon to be fair. "When Welsh acts as the third man in the ring, it does not matter to him what men are boxing, he treats one just as fairly as the other."[102]

Jack O'Brien again said Ketchel was a wonder and the best man he ever fought, and although the Ketchel-Johnson bout was a toss-up, he would have a ticket (wager) on Stanley.

> Ketchel is a terrific puncher, his left hook to the head being his most damaging punch. Johnson can fight when right, and he is not in condition now, nor has he been of late. He has height, weight and reach on Ketchel, and in condition these will be of advantage to him, but if he underestimates this kid and takes him on out of condition, then his physical advantages will be a handicap to him. He has a knack of blocking that is marvelous. I tell you that's what made Johnson a fighter – his great defence that comes natural to him.[103]

The *Philadelphia Record* said Ketchel was very strong and fearless, with perfect confidence in his ability. He was a true knockout artist, having won most of his bouts by knockout. He only once tasted defeat, to Billy Papke (whom Ketchel had defeated previously), but avenged the loss one bout later with a knockout. He was proving his lionhearted, fearless nature by scheduling yet another bout with Papke for the middleweight crown, risking the Johnson fight with a potentially tough intermediate bout. Ketchel was only 22 years old and getting better. "Stanley Ketchel promises to become the most popular fighter of the age. He now enjoys greater popularity than any other fighter who is before the public."

Ketchel said Johnson would be no harder to defeat than O'Brien. Philadelphia Jack was notoriously fast, but seemed slow compared to Stan. Ketchel said Johnson was only a one-handed fighter, and that he only had to watch out for the champ's right. At close quarters he felt sure that he could outgame and outfight Johnson.

---

[101] *Boston Herald, Boston Globe,* June 10, 1909.
[102] *Boston Globe,* June 11, 1909.
[103] *Boston Globe,* June 12, 1909.

Many agreed with Stan. "Everyone who saw Ketchel curl O'Brien up with body blows feels confident that a few such punches would take all the fight out of the big black." Ketchel had a sleep producer in either hand. "Johnson is a great blocker, but it is doubtful if he can smother both of Ketchel's hands for any length of time." Ketchel's blows hurt no matter where they landed, and just one in the right spot would end the fight.

However, they also felt that Ketchel would not be able to get to Johnson as easily, for Johnson was a much better defensive fighter and was naturally strong and very cautious, willing to play a waiting game and force Ketchel to do most of the leading. "Ketchel's greatest danger will be in walking into a hard one from Johnson, for Stanley fights with a wide-open guard." Ketchel was a swinger, which could cause him to run into one. Johnson could punch hard when he wanted to do so. Many critics felt that Johnson did not show his best form in either the Burns or O'Brien fight, "in which the colored man now admits that he did not try."

Others said Ketchel was too small, and the fight would prove the adage that a good big man beats a good little man. Despite the fact that he was fast and a terribly hard hitter, it would take more than that to defeat Johnson. At 5'9" and 165 pounds, Ketchel was about the same size as Burns, whom the 6'1½" 204-pound Johnson completely dominated. Johnson would be much heavier and taller, could hit as hard or harder, and was a much cleverer boxer, with better defense and use of straight punches as opposed to Ketchel's swings.[104]

The *Freeman* reported that Ketchel's victory over O'Brien had made him the favorite over Johnson in Philadelphia. Those who saw the bout said Ketchel hit harder than Johnson, was very much faster, and that Johnson's flat-footed style would make him a comparatively easy mark. O'Brien said Ketchel was the hardest hitter he had ever met. He also said black fighters could not take body blows, and Ketchel had a thunderous body punch.

Upset that Johnson was not taking the Langford fight upon the original agreed-upon terms of a $5,000 purse, the National Sporting Club in England announced that it was recognizing Sam Langford as the heavyweight champion.[105]

Boxing was hot; chock full of fighters, owing to the fact that there was a great amount of money to be made in the sport. Hence, it tempted many young men to take up the calling. "The fact that there is so much money in the game proves the popular interest. All the world loves a manly man, and

[104] *Philadelphia Record*, June 13, 1909; *Ogden Standard*, June 12, 1909.
[105] *Freeman,* June 19, 1909; *Boston Herald*, June 14, 1909. Langford had caught the hearts of English boxing lovers. He was playing to crowded houses in the music halls. There was talk of him meeting Tommy Burns in the fall. Burns was quite popular in Australia, making big money giving exhibitions. Motion pictures of his Squires and Moir bouts were shown, while Burns would describe the various incidents of the fights to the audience. *Philadelphia Press*, June 29, 1909.

boxing under humane rules with padded gloves is one of the best methods of testing the courage and self-reliance of a man of muscle."

Rumors were afloat that Johnson received $3,000 for not trying to knock out O'Brien. Hence, it was said that Johnson and Ketchel's relative performances against O'Brien should not be used to gauge a bout between them. "Johnson showed very plainly that he could have stopped O'Brien in one round had he tried." Many felt this despite the fact that he did not train.

One writer said Johnson was no fool and was a very shrewd businessman. It would not make sense for him to take only $5,000 for a fight that likely would generate over $20,000. Hence, it stood to reason that he had an extra $3,000 guarantee to not stop O'Brien.

This rumor was circulating amongst blacks who lost money betting on Johnson to stop O'Brien. Hence, they were angry at the champion. "There is the most bitter prejudice against Johnson that has ever been expressed against any man who has held a boxing or fighting championship in the history of the ring, and, strange to say, the prejudice against Johnson seems to be as bitter among the men of his own race as it is among white men."

> One of the men who is telling around that Johnson got $3,000 for not knocking out O'Brien states that Johnson told the story himself and gave that as his reason for not extending himself when the men met recently in this city. Those who saw the Johnson-O'Brien contest could see that the black champion was not extending himself, for he knocked O'Brien down and almost through the ropes with one punch in the first round, and then did practically nothing for the rest of the time till the fifth, when he again hit O'Brien hard, knocking him to the floor and closing one of the white fighter's eyes completely. The fact that Johnson was in poor condition, hog fat and twenty pounds at least over weight caused some to think that it was this lack of condition which tied Johnson up, but there was abundant evidence that even as he was, he was not trying to go his best pace, for the work he did was nothing like that which he could and did do on other occasions in this city. [106]

The *Ogden Standard* opined that an Al Kaufman bout would make Johnson show his true form, and it would be a great battle. Both men were willing to fight in September in San Francisco. While Kaufman's performances had not set the pugilistic world afire, he had beaten top fighters on a consistent basis, usually by knockout, and had shown improvement in each fight. He was a big, tough, powerful, well-conditioned man who could both deliver and absorb a lot of punishment. "There is no doubt that Johnson will have the time of his life trying to defeat Kaufman – in fact, I do not think the colored man can perform the feat. The California Hercules has a sleep producing wallop in either hand and is every bit as clever as the colored man."

---

[106] *Philadelphia Record*, June 13, 1909.

Kaufman had scored both early and late knockouts. He only had one loss on his record; the 17th round knockout loss to O'Brien, when Kaufman had a mere four fights to O'Brien's over one hundred. Since then, Kaufman had been undefeated in fifteen consecutive bouts, all but three won by knockout. Kaufman was bigger and taller than Johnson, so Jack would have no size advantages.

The writer explained Johnson's style and perceived lack of knockout power.

> There is no doubt that Johnson is clever and can hit, because he's built for hard hitting, but up to date he has never shown ability in that line, and all because he bends back like the leaning tower of Pisa. The colored man is so willing to take good care of his face and stomach that he doesn't hurl himself in with his punches like Ketchel, Fitzsimmons, and all other great hitters.

This writer explained and excused Johnson's recent performance against O'Brien as being not only the result of poor condition, but because the crowd threatened him.

> When properly trained Johnson can dispose of the Quaker in a few rounds. Another cause for his poor showing was that he was threatened with personal injury if he disposed of O'Brien by the knockout route. Several times during the contest, when the colored man became the aggressor or acted on the offensive, he was hooted, jeered, and threatening remarks were heard from several sides. This unsportsmanlike method of several rowdies caused Johnson to fear for his life.[107]

Years later, Johnson said he dropped O'Brien in the 1st round with a left to the body, in the 4th round with a right to the body, and in the 5th round as well. The crowd and referee were O'Brien fans, and did not approve of the way he was hitting their esteemed fellow citizen. The crowd made it known that he was hitting their favorite too hard and threatened him if he didn't change tactics. Hence, for the most part, he and O'Brien played a gentle game. Since there would be no points decision, the result meant nothing to him.[108]

---

[107] *Ogden Standard*, June 12, 1909.
[108] *My Life and Battles* at 81-82.

CHAPTER 3

Building and Scouting the Bouts

In June 1909, from Boston, Jack Johnson said, "I know very well that Jeffries is training for me on the quiet. As for myself – well, take it from me I don't intend to be caught napping on the question of physical condition. I have an offer of a purse of $50,000 to fight Jeffries in December. I think it to our mutual benefit to accept the offer."

However, Johnson also said that most likely Jeffries was bluffing about meeting him. Jack was amongst those who believed that Jeff was using the excitement about a potential match with Johnson as a way of making easy money giving exhibitions with Sam Berger, who was Jeff's sparring partner and manager, but that ultimately Jeff would not make the match with him.

> I am ready to box every week in the year if I am given my price for my services. I bar no man who has any right to challenge. I am ready to box Jeffries, Ketchel, Kaufman, Hart, or any one else who wants to meet me. ... I regard a match with Jeffries as the surest way of proving that I am in truth the world's champion.[109]

When shown a dispatch claiming Johnson would attend the 6-round Jeffries-Berger exhibition in Pittsburg on June 15, Johnson was upset. He said it was a false story that emanated from Jeff's press agent, who wanted to draw a crowd. "I will go there if Jeff will box me instead of Berger, and I will be willing to let the box office receipts go to charity. All I want is a chance to show that I can beat Jeffries in either six rounds or to a finish."[110]

On Monday evening, June 14, 1909, Johnson appeared on the stage of Boston's Columbia Theatre, performing to a modestly-sized mostly black audience.

Boxing 3 rounds with black veteran George Byers, Johnson played a waiting game, content to counter the Bostonian's leads. The champ did not let himself out to any extent, but displayed enough skill and spirit to satisfy those present that he was a great boxer. He was a clever feinter and blocker, and had a fine left, which he used to hook and jab. He also showed science in the clinches, tying up Byers' hands so that George could not land any blows. Jack did not use his right uppercut, which was his best punch. "Johnson showed that he is a pretty fast big man, and appears to have the qualifications that go to help make a champion." He appeared a little fleshy, but otherwise was in good condition.

---

[109] *Boston Globe*, June 13, 1909.
[110] *Boston Post*, *Pittsburg Press*, June 14, 1909.

When called upon for a speech, Johnson said, "I am ready and willing to fight any man in the world, and in particular would like to meet Mr. Jeffries. I am matched to fight Kaufman and Stanley Ketchel."

Johnson had been scheduled to box Bob Armstrong at the Armory the following evening. However, Armstrong left and joined the Ketchel crew, for Bob had been hired to be Stanley's sparring partner for the upcoming Papke and Johnson bouts.

Johnson was perturbed by Armstrong's abandonment, because after Bob had told him his hard-luck story, Jack had given him $25, a hat, and paid for his hotel room and board. Some thought that Armstrong had visited Boston as a spy for Ketchel.

Also on June 14, upon his arrival in Pittsburg, a massive crowd of 20,000 greeted James J. Jeffries. He said,

> I see Mr. Johnson is talking a lot. … I want to meet that black fellow more than I ever wanted to fight any living man. I have always been afraid of my own strength in a ring for fear I would kill a man, but I will have no such fear when I get into the ring with this fellow. For the first time in my life I will then hit a man with all the force that is in me. I want to see how far I can knock him.

> It looks now as if it is up to me to whip this fellow. … Do I hope Young Ketchel beats this black? Yes, I hope for far more than that. I hope when Ketchel meets Johnson he kills him. I repeat, I hope he kills him!

Upon hearing of Jeffries' statement, Johnson challenged Jeffries to fight at once or within 2 months or hold his tongue. "I believe he is a four-flusher in the backbone. … I will not stand for his abuse and slurs any longer. If he means to fight me, why don't he come out like a man and set the time and place?"[111]

Famed New York sportswriter Tad Dorgan said Stanley Ketchel had a great chance with any living man, owing to his big punch. Johnson was bigger, cleverer, heavier, had a longer reach, and was by far the better ring general. However, Ketchel could really hit, and could hurt anyone he hit.

W. W. Naughton said Johnson was brilliant at withholding his attack until his opponent led first. "Johnson does not get ruffled, though. He will stand there all day if necessary until his opponent leads. He will feint and taunt his man into leading." In this way, he got his foes to open up and create openings for his counters. This cautious style kept him defensively sound, and also allowed him to conserve energy.

New York writer Charles Meegan opined that if Johnson followed his usual line of battle against Ketchel, there would be a new champion.

> I mean by this, if he attempts to stand still, assume the defensive and try to stop Ketchel's rushes by jabbing he's whipped sure. His yellow

---

[111] *Boston Herald, Boston Globe, Boston Post,* June 15, 1909.

streak will beat him if nothing else will in that sort of a fight. Two or three of Ketchel's terrific smashes would open the floodgates of the big negro's courage tank and he would drown himself. … I repeat, if Johnson fights Ketchel in the same manner he has fought most of his battles he's a 'gone coon' for sure.[112]

On Tuesday June 15, 1909 at Boston's Armory Athletic Association, Johnson again sparred 3 rounds with George Byers. According to the *Boston Post*, "Johnson stripped in beautiful shape. He is certainly a splendid specimen of athletic manhood, and it is hard to see what heavyweight of the present day would have a chance with him."

Afterwards, in Johnson's speech to the crowd, he reiterated his challenge to Jeffries. He noted that he had posted $5,000 for Jeffries to cover, but Jeff had not yet done so. "I am matched to fight Stanley Ketchel because the newspaper men of this country selected him, and I am also matched to fight Kaufman." The *Boston Post* said, "Considering the heat of Jeffries' reported utterances in Pittsburg Monday night, Johnson's remarks were wonderfully temperate."

Johnson was set to appear in Cambridge on Friday, sparring at a benefit concert given by the colored Methodist church. It was said to be the first instance of a fighter participating in a church charity entertainment.

That same night in Pittsburg, 5,000 spectators paid $2, $3, and $5 to watch Jeffries box Sam Berger 6 rounds. However, the rounds were short, each averaging only 50 seconds. This angered the crowd, which had paid hefty prices expecting to see three-minute rounds.

Jeffries did the leading and delivered practically all of the blows, with Berger taking the punishment. Although still heavy, Jeff appeared to have lost a great deal of weight. He was extremely fast on his feet and very quick with his hands. Still, many questioned his condition, given that he was boxing very short rounds. Regardless, Jeff said, "When the time comes I'll deliver the goods."

Harvard University's Dr. Sargent opined that Jeffries would be able to get into shape to meet Johnson. "Jeffries has made remarkable progress. Four months ago he was hog fat and weighed 300. Today he tips the scales at 230. His muscles then were flabby and the tissues soft and unresponsive – today he is one of the finest specimens of manhood extant."

However, others reported that upon weighing him, the Harvard professor found Jeff's weight to be 247.2 pounds. He was larger than what was claimed, but no bigger than he was between fights while champion. He stood 6' ¾".

Every day, newsmen were printing the epithets that Johnson and Jeffries were throwing at each other. "Jeffries declares that Johnson is not a real champion and Johnson hurls back the defiant cry that Jeffries is only stalling and is afraid to meet him. … What the sporting public wants is

[112] *Ogden Standard*, June 17-19, 1909.

action, not words." Jeff's popularity had soared when he announced that he would meet Johnson to redeem the title, but his popularity could not continue unless he signed for a fight. Regardless, all the talk helped build up interest in the fight to an unprecedented level.[113]

The *New York Sun* reported that Jeffries could not box more than 6 rounds of one minute each without blowing like a whale. He was making soft money by lightly sparring Berger, but refused to box 10 or 15 rounds with Jim Flynn for a $10,000 purse, insisting he would fight only Johnson.

Sam Langford said he would be no match for a fit Jeffries, and therefore had no intention of challenging Jeff.[114]

On June 16, Jeffries arrived in Philadelphia. He claimed to weigh 235 pounds. Jeff said of Johnson,

> So, he calls me a four-flusher. Well, I'll make him look worse than that when I get ready to talk business. I promised some weeks ago that I would be ready to make a match with the colored man when my theatrical engagement was ended, and it has only five weeks to go now. At the end of that time I shall be ready to sign articles and then he must agree or let the public estimate him for what he is worth. His great mistake was in thinking that I had no intention of re-entering the ring, but I will fool him. You can say for me that I shall be my old self when I go into the ring and I shall take a savage delight in repaying him for the many things he has said since he beat Burns. I was correctly quoted in saying that I hoped Ketchel knocks his head off, and if Stanley does not do it I will turn the trick myself. I have surprised myself with my speed and condition and in Pittsburgh last night I was as fast as ever in my life. My wind, too, is good and my friends need not worry in the slightest when I fight Johnson – that is, if he will fight me. … My personal opinion is that the colored man is four-flushing and will refuse to sign to meet me.

Sam Berger said Jeff had been working faithfully and was fit to enter the ring. Jack O'Brien said if Jeffries was anything like as good as he was when he retired that Jeff would be the only man in the fight.[115]

That evening at the National Athletic Club, before a crowd of about 2,000, Jeffries, who had lost a considerable amount of weight, skipped rope like a middleweight and boxed 3 one-minute rounds with Berger, showing remarkable hand-speed, pretty footwork, astonishing agility, well-timed ducking skill, and good judgment of distance. Jeff weaved in and out, sometimes standing erect, while at other times using his famous crouch.

The *Philadelphia Record* said everyone white had been "hoping and praying" that Jeff "would be able to get into good enough condition to knock Jack Johnson not only out, but clean out of the ring with the first

---

[113] *Boston Post, Boston Herald, Pittsburg Press,* June 16, 1909; *Philadelphia Record,* June 20, 1909.
[114] *New York Sun,* June 17, 1909.
[115] *Philadelphia Evening Bulletin,* June 16, 1909.

good punch he could land on the Texas negro." The *Record* and *Evening Bulletin* agreed that his showing had raised their hopes.

However, many who saw him were a bit doubtful as to whether he could get into the type of shape and form necessary to beat the reigning champion in a long, grueling contest. The work he did was not enough to tire out even a fat man. One said, "He is a good old man." Jeff's muscles had lost their fullness, and seemed soft and flabby. His hair was thinning. "In appearance Jeffries looks older than his years. He was 34 the 15th of last April, and has

Sam Berger spars James J. Jeffries

the appearance of a man of 40." His body had numerous boils. "He will have to be in a great deal better condition than he is in now to have any chance with the big black fellow." Hence, some felt that "the winning of the championship back for the white race will have to depend on someone else rather than Jim Jeffries."

One writer said that Jeff's "con" tactics with his short rounds had lost him some admirers. However, the crowd still gave him a tremendous ovation.

Some said that Jeff's best chance might be to try to win as quickly as possible, for the longer the battle went, the greater the physical strain would be on him, given his age and years of inactivity. Johnson's relative youth and activity would give him a great endurance advantage. Jack's usual style was to wait and never lead if he could help it, which would force Jeffries to do all the work. Johnson's style was perfect to defeat an aging fighter who might have stamina issues. "Unless Jeffries could land a knockout punch inside of the first ten or twelve rounds the chances of him getting the black fellow would be slim, as Jeffries would be tiring all the time, while Johnson could nurse his strength and take care of himself."

Jeffries' supporters said Johnson would be a plaything in his hands. They consistently said Johnson had a yellow streak and that Jeffries would find it, for he had the skill, experience, size, strength, power, and toughness required to stop him. Jeff had plenty of time to train and gradually get into great shape, which he always did for all of his fights.

Ultimately, the *Record* opined, "He will surely never be the Jeffries of old, but he still looks good enough to beat Johnson if he will continue to train for some months longer."[116]

Johnson was also matched to box either Tony Ross or Marvin Hart 6 rounds in Pittsburg on June 30.[117]

On June 19, a Boston court issued a warrant for Johnson's arrest for failing to appear on charges of speeding, operating without a license, and failing to register his vehicle in Massachusetts.[118]

Hugh Doyle Pictures What Jeff Says He Will Do to Johnson

Philadelphia Press, June 21, 1909

[116] *Philadelphia Record, Philadelphia Evening Bulletin, Boston Post,* June 17, 1909; *Philadelphia Record,* June 20, 1909; *Washington Herald,* June 22, 1909.
[117] *Philadelphia Record,* June 18, 1909.
[118] *New York Sun,* June 20, 1909.

CHAPTER 4

Tony Ross

On June 20, 1909, the *Pittsburg Press* announced that big Italian Tony Ross would fight Jack Johnson at the local Duqesne Gardens under the auspices of the National Athletic Club on June 30, ten days away. Statements made by Bill Delaney, who managed Al Kaufman, influenced matchmaker Jimmy Dime to select Ross to oppose Johnson. Ross had fought 10 furious rounds with Kaufman. Delaney said, "It is true Kaufman did not stop Ross, but that is not to his discredit. The Italian is a mighty tough customer." Delaney was willing to back his opinion with money, offering to wager $10,000 that Johnson could not stop Ross in 6 rounds. He also said Kaufman would withdraw his challenge for the championship if Johnson stopped Ross.

Tony Ross was a native Italian, originally named Antonio Rossilano. Born in 1885, he was 24 years old. He had not yet mastered English. Most reporters cleaned up his quotes, but one did not: "Me fight Johnson. Me lick Johnson. ... Me not afraid of no man in the world. ... Me lick Marvin Hart three months ago."

Dime said the experience that Ross had gained from his bouts with Hart and Kaufman had done wonders for him, for he was a much improved man. Ross would train at New Castle, Pennsylvania, where he resided.[119]

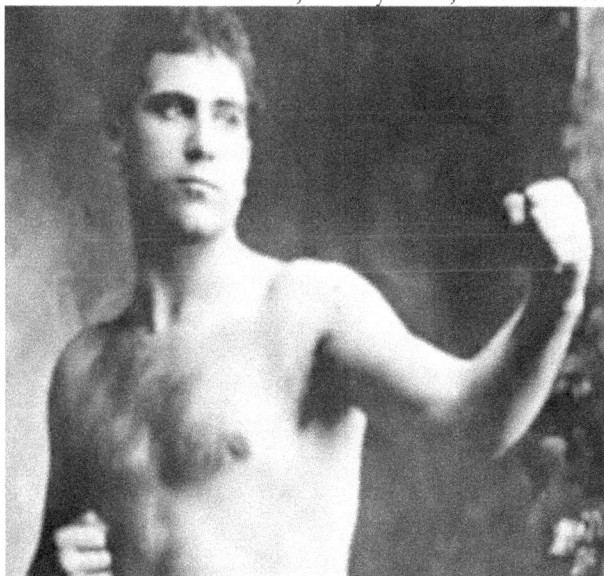

Tony Ross

[119] *Pittsburg Press*, June 20, 21, 1909.

Tony Ross's record included: 1906 LKOby6 Jim Scanlan; 1907 LKOby13 Mike Schreck, LDQby13 Jim Flynn, and LKOby2 Jim Barry; 1908 D10 Mike Schreck, KO3 Jim Jeffords, KO10 Mike Schreck, KO7 George Gardner, D12 Jim Barry, and LKOby5 Sam Langford; and 1909 LDQby13 Marvin Hart, and April 13, 1909 LND10 Al Kaufman. Knockout victories over Schreck (who had beaten Hart) and Gardner showed that Ross was a solid fighter. It appeared that Ross would have defeated Hart but for his foul of hitting Hart after decking him. Hence, in essentially beating a big, tough, hard-hitting fighter in Hart, Ross showed that he was made of good stuff. He once again had proven his toughness and durability by lasting the distance and putting up a competitive bout for 10 rounds against another big, hard-punching heavyweight in Kaufman.

In the meantime, the press could not stop talking about potential Johnson bouts with Kaufman, Ketchel, and Jeffries.

COLORED HEAVYWEIGHT CHAMPION JACK JOHNSON AND AL KAUFMAN AS THEY WILL APPEAR IN RING.

As of June 21, it was announced that Johnson would fight Al Kaufman in September at Colma for promoter Jim Coffroth. Initially, the bout was scheduled for 20 rounds. Kaufman was very strong and tough, taller than Johnson, and just as heavy, but he was not as fast as Ketchel. A veteran referee said, "Johnson will beat Kaufman on points, and will have the fight of his life with Ketchel. There may be some interest in the Kaufman-Johnson battle, but it will not begin to compare with the world-wide excitement when Johnson hooks up with Ketchel."[120]

Jim Corbett said fans saw Ketchel as being Johnson's superior, based on his knockout of O'Brien. "Through Ketchel's sudden rise in the estimation of the public the demand for a battle between Jeffries and Johnson has suddenly quieted down." Corbett said Ketchel had a puncher's chance:

I have said over and over again that Ketchel had a punch the like of which I had seldom seen. For his inches he can hit harder than any man in the world today. I have also said that he could land his punch on anyone. His deceptive way of delivering it would fool the cleverest man that ever lived.

[120] *Washington Herald*, June 22, 1909.

Still, although Corbett granted that Ketchel was a very good fighter, it was no sure thing that he would beat Johnson. To say that Johnson was inferior to Ketchel was not fair to the title-holder, "even if he is classed as a paper bag champion." Corbett noted that Johnson was in poor shape when he boxed O'Brien. "It was a case of get the money with him." Since it was a no-decision bout, he could not lose the title if he was not stopped. Corbett said Johnson should be the favorite over Ketchel, for he had every advantage over him, and if he was in the shape that he was in against Burns, he would be two or three times as good as he was against O'Brien.[121]

The *Edgefield Advertiser* wondered whether Johnson would look for a way to crawl out of the Ketchel match, for Johnson had become a "great jumper of contracts and he is somewhat fearful of Stanley." "It will take only one of Stanley's punches to make Johnson take it on the run, and then – well, it will be all off." O'Brien had the fastest footwork in the business, and even he could not escape Stan's blows. Therefore, it stood to reason that Ketchel would catch up with and land on Johnson.[122]

Johnson declared that he was taking the Ross match seriously, for he had seen him box and respected him. He wrote,

> Ross is a tough customer and nobody can make me believe anything else. I know that I am going against a far more dangerous man than Jack O'Brien. Now the people have been saying that Jeffries and myself are just hot-airing for the sake of the money we can get. … Well, I am going to show them that they are wrong as far as I am concerned. Would Jeffries take any chances on a man like Ross? No, you can bet he wouldn't. Well, I will and I'll make good with the people by showing them that I have the goods with me. I'll be in shape for this fight and won't take any chances.[123]

Johnson declared that ever since he won the championship, his enemies had formed a ring to ruin him in the public eye. He had no intention of calling off the Ross bout as rumored. He said the ring of conspirators had started the report in order to injure him with the public. Jack said,

> I'll show some of these cheap fourflushers whether I am afraid to meet Ross. I'll show them just who I can fight when I am aroused. Ross is a good man. Even those who say that I don't want to meet him admit that. Well, when I finish him in quick time it will be pretty plain that I am the real champion, won't it?[124]

---

[121] *Ogden Standard*, June 22, 1909.

[122] *Edgefield Advertiser*, June 23, 1909.

On June 22, 1909 in Boston, Sandy Ferguson scored a 1st round knockdown en-route to a 12-round decision victory over Joe Jeannette. One paper said, "Score No. 1 for the Society of White Boxers." *San Francisco Call*, June 24, 1909; *Pittsburg Dispatch*, June 27, 1909.

[123] *Pittsburg Press*, June 22, 1909.

[124] *Pittsburgh Post*, June 25, 1909.

There were rumors that there was a plot to get Johnson whipped as soon as possible. The Ross bout was the first step in a scheme by white managers. Ross was tough enough to test Johnson and make him fight hard, and that was what managers wanted to see, so they could scout him, note his strengths and weaknesses, and use the information in the future.

> I can state to you positively that Kaufman, Ketchel and several other fighters and managers will have representatives at the ringside taking careful note of everything the negro does. They will not come themselves, as they tried that in the O'Brien case, and Johnson held back purposely. He could afford to hold back with O'Brien and not risk the chance of being put out, but with a man who can hit like Ross, Johnson can take no chances. ... Ross can hit hard enough to put him away and there is a possibility of this, and then Johnson will have to show his best hand.[125]

Johnson was confident that he could stop Ross inside of 6 rounds. However, it was a task that "many ring experts say he can never perform." Reporters said the bout could show how good Johnson was against a man near his own size. Ross weighed at least 190 pounds and stood 5'9". Of course, Johnson had fought and defeated bigger men, like Fred Russell, Sam McVey, and Sandy Ferguson (who recently defeated Jeannette), but many writers conveniently forgot that.

Working steadily and seriously in New Castle, Ross was confident that he would make a good showing. He said that he knew the big smoke's weakness and would play for that spot for all he was worth. He declared that stopping Johnson was possible.

Ross had fought a majority of his battles in Pennsylvania, so he would be the local favorite. "All in all he is not a bad sort; a young man with a punishing punch. Unless Johnson is in good condition Tony will certainly prove troublesome – not dangerous perhaps, but troublesome."[126]

Allegedly, Johnson called off the match with the "lumbering" Kaufman because Al refused to concede another 5% share of the purse to him. As champion, Johnson had become a tough negotiator. This caused some in the press to roast him and claim he was afraid.

The *Philadelphia Record* said that typically, despite what the general public was told about the purse split, most scrappers were willing to split their share of the gate receipts evenly (50/50) so as not to take any chance of losing out on the money, regardless of result. For marketing purposes, many boxers talked loudly about betting large amounts on the result; when in fact they neither had any money to bet, nor willingness to bet it if they had it. They just talked to hype themselves and the fight. The *Record* said that such boxers were businessmen purely concerned about money, rather than honor and glory, lacking true sporting blood or self-confidence. "These are the

---

[125] *Pittsburg Press*, June 26, 1909.
[126] *Pittsburg Dispatch, Pittsburgh Post, Pittsburg Press,* June 27, 1909.

fellows who are willing to arrange bouts at any time to let their opponents win, if the financial consideration is arranged to their liking." This caused many patrons to turn away from the game.

However, apparently Stanley Ketchel was backing himself with $5,000 of his own money against Johnson, honestly feeling that he could beat him. He was willing to post the money to prove it.

There were a number of wealthy men, especially in the West, who thought that Ketchel could whip Johnson, particularly in a long fight. They believed that Johnson might lose as a result of overconfidence and lack of training, enjoying too many of the good things that came with pugilistic fame, for he had more money than ever before.

> Johnson has met big, strong men, who could hit hard and who could take a lot of punishment, but he never met as vicious and determined a man as the one he is booked to fight in California next October. Neither has he ever met a big man who had the speed and aggressiveness which Ketchel possesses.

If Johnson entered the ring at less than his best against Ketchel, he likely would pay dearly for it. "No man, no matter how big or how strong he may be, can stand such punching as Ketchel can give for any great number of rounds unless he is in perfect health."

Ketchel loved to train, and took the best care of himself. He had knocked out three heavyweight sparring partners in training, and was down to 160 pounds, set to make 158 for his upcoming fight with Billy Papke.[127]

Johnson said Ross would be easy. Some thought Jack was overconfident. Eastern sporting men were pulling for Ross, and "it seems to be the unanimous wish that he punch holes in every portion of the big negro's anatomy."

Jimmy Dime, who was hosting the fight, was training Ross. Pleased with his hard training, Dime said, "Ross has got a punch that will knock anybody in the world cold, I care not who he is, and if Johnson is not in better shape than he was against O'Brien, watch out."[128]

When Jack Johnson failed to appear in Atlantic City on two charges of driving without a license, his two $25 bonds were forfeited. Jack had headed to Pennsylvania for the Ross fight.

The day before the fight, on the morning of June 29, Johnson arrived at Union station in Pittsburg on a train from Atlantic City. Blacks gave him a royal welcome. They, along with the Knights of Pythias Band, formed a parade which escorted Jack from the station through the downtown streets to his hotel on Wylie Avenue. Hundreds followed and clung to him, "proving that he is the idol of the negro race."[129]

---

[127] *Philadelphia Record*, June 27, 29, 1909.
[128] *Pittsburgh Post, Pittsburg Press*, June 28, 1909.
[129] *New York Journal, Pittsburg Press*, June 30, 1909.

That afternoon, the champion trained for over two hours at Victor & Barth's gymnasium, and appeared to be in good condition.

Johnson said, "I am out to show the people that I am a champion. Ross is too dangerous a man to take any chances with. They have been calling me a side-stepper but I will show tomorrow night what made me the champion."

On the evening of the 29th, "his fellow countrymen" (meaning blacks) gave Johnson a parade in the Hill district, which was a black neighborhood.[130]

The fight would be held under the auspices of Jimmy Dime's National Athletic Club in Pittsburg. Owing to the fact that club members felt swindled and were upset that Jeffries had boxed only a few one-minute rounds with Berger, promoter Dime told the fighters that they would not be paid unless it was a real fight and not an exhibition. The public wanted no faking or stalling.

Johnson angrily responded that he wanted payment in advance of the bout, for he had arrangements to leave town on the midnight train. Allegedly, Johnson had been promised $2,000. Jack was told that he would be paid promptly once the bout was over, providing it was no fake.

Contrary to the local Pittsburg papers, which claimed that Johnson would not be paid until after the bout, the *Philadelphia Press* said Johnson sustained his reputation as a shrewd businessman, securing his $2,000 guarantee from the National Athletic Club managers during the late afternoon, prior to the fight.

Johnson was in better shape than he was against O'Brien, but still not at his best. One writer opined that it would require a good month's training before he would be in proper shape for a hard contest.

The day of the fight, Johnson said, "I will stop Ross in six rounds. I realize that the public expects something good from me and I will risk my reputation as champion on my ability to do this tonight." He also said,

---

[130] *Pittsburg Dispatch, Pittsburgh Post*, June 30, 1909. The Hill district later became a famous black cultural center in the area.

94

"There ain't a chance in the world for me to lose, cause I can't afford to be licked just now. I'm going West to the coast, where the big money is easy to be found and I'd be easy if I let this New Castle man whip me in six rounds."

Tony Ross similarly said, "I feel that I have a good chance to cop the champ and the honors as well. One punch in the right place is all I want to land and I am confident of my ability to do this." Another paper quoted Ross as saying, "I am going to stop this dusky champion inside the limit, even if he has everything on me in height and weight." Ross was never better. Hence, a grueling battle was anticipated.[131]

TONY ROSS

WHO MEETS JACK JOHNSON AT DUQUESNE GARDEN TONIGHT.

On Wednesday June 30, 1909 at Duqesne Garden in Pittsburg, the Jack Johnson vs. Tony Ross 6-round no-decision fight took place. The show was set to start at 8 p.m.

Preparing for fans to attend the bout from New York, Philadelphia, and even as far as Chicago and St. Louis, Jimmy Dime had 2,000 circus seats installed on the arena floor. To keep the arena and spectators cool during the hot summer, 50 gigantic exhaust fans would buzz continuously, and the cooling apparatus used for making ice would be used to cool the arena as well.

The local press said that despite the sweltering heat, a packed house of 4,000 was on hand. It actually was cooler inside the Garden than outside, owing to the big fans that the management had working all evening. Standing room was at a premium, for many out-of-town fans were willing to pay prohibitive prices. New Castle, Ross' home town, was well represented, with nearly 250 of his admirers in attendance.

---

[131] *Pittsburg Dispatch, Pittsburg Post*, June 30, 1909; *Philadelphia Press*, July 1, 1909.

When he entered the ring, the Pittsburg audience gave Johnson a cool reception. On the other hand, when Ross appeared, the audience rose and cheered vociferously for more than a minute. The *Pittsburg Press* wrote,

> Johnson did not get the greeting from the crowd last night that might have been accorded a champion. There were cheers, but faint ones. When Ross entered…he was received warmly and the uninitiated ones might have thought he was the champion approaching.

Johnson still carried much of the weight so noticeable in his bout with O'Brien. Sportswriters believed that he had been lax in his training.

Betting was very light. A few wagers were laid at 6 to 5, with Johnson the favorite.

Buck Connelly refereed.

According to the next-day local *Pittsburg Post* and *Pittsburg Press*, the bout nearly ended in the 1st round. In the last ten seconds of the round, Johnson dropped Ross with a series of hard rights and lefts to the head. Referee Buck Connelly was in the process of counting him out, but the ringing of the bell saved him. Ross was lying on the floor, out cold, with his face bloodied. At that time, a fighter could be saved by the bell.

According to the *Post*, from the 2nd round on, Ross covered up at every opportunity, not wanting to open up and expose himself to dangerous blows. Johnson was smiling continually from ear to ear. He obviously held his opponent cheaply. Throughout, Johnson used his left jab, hitting the nose on nearly every occasion. When he missed the nose he still landed on the lip or the eye.

Before the 3rd round was over, Ross was cut to ribbons. Some sources said he was decked in this round for a five-count.

Ross was so afraid that he was unable to lay a glove on Johnson until the 4th round, when he landed a few short-arm jolts to the chin. However, in the 5th round, once again Tony was cautious.

In the 6th round, Ross let out a bit and managed to land two blows through the champ's clever defense, though neither one did any harm.

At the conclusion of the 6th round, Ross was the happiest person in the vast auditorium, for the beating was over.

The *Post* said the champ was in good shape and gave the spectators their money's worth. Johnson started out at a fast pace, but after he saw how afraid Ross was, he let up in his aggressiveness, being satisfied to jab and swing from a distance. Still, he gave Ross a terrific beating.

Johnson was able to feint Ross into a knot whenever he pleased. Typically, Jack felt him out with the left and then shot his right to the head. Little infighting was done, as the men were seldom in a clinch.

Even when he threw, Ross rarely landed. "Johnson's defensive tactics were the best ever displayed by a fighter here, and the few blows that Ross did uncork were nearly always neatly turned away by the negro."

This writer opined that Ross should have been more aggressive, for being cautious allowed Johnson to beat him up even more. If Ross had taken more chances, he might have forced Johnson to play more defense. Of course, had Tony opened up more, he might have been brutally counterattacked. Hence Ross was cautious after the 1st round, when he learned that Johnson could hurt and deck him.

Although for the most part Johnson toyed with Tony, Ross "took one of the worst beatings that a fighter ever received in a local ring." Johnson impressed the crowd.

> Those that were present last evening are fully convinced that his right to wear the crown at present cannot be disputed, for in the short period he was in the roped arena he showed everything that a champion needs. Ross was only a plaything in his hands and it is a question whether he could not have put him away any time during the six rounds.

The general feeling expressed was that Johnson would hold the crown until he met Jeffries, at which time he would lose. Opinion was that he would defeat Ketchel.

The local *Pittsburg Press* agreed that Johnson outfought Ross from start to finish. It noted an additional knockdown that the *Post* did not, other than the one at the end of the 1st round. "Later on Ross was again knocked down, but he stayed down for the count of five." It failed to say in which round this occurred, though there is some evidence from other sources that a second knockdown occurred in the 3rd round.

> Ross performed as though he was afraid. He did not attempt to carry the battle to Johnson until late in the fight, when he made the crowd, with the exception of the colored brethren, yell lustily.

> That Johnson is a great fighter there is no doubt. He is big and fast, and while he found Ross a rather easy opponent, yet he appeared to have courage. He moves about with almost the speed of a lightweight and he gets his arms into action with speed that is surprising, but he does not have the power behind his blows to knock out a big, husky and game fighter of the championship type.

The local *Pittsburg Dispatch* had a completely different take on the bout. It had more of an anti-Johnson stance that smacked of the typical white prejudice and bias which attempted to minimize his success and denigrate Johnson's performances as much as possible. It said the bout required no round-by-round description, for each round was a repetition of clinching and breakaways. "Not one good, square, resounding lick was struck by either of the fighters, though a glance shot on the nose of Ross brought the claret."

Its writer said the fact that Ross, without any particular punishment, stood for the full 6 rounds, lent new interest in possible matches between

Johnson and Ketchel and Jeffries. "It was a general remark last evening among the thousands that Johnson is too much for Ross, but Johnson gave no great evidence of the fact." This writer claimed that amongst several sporting men, the opinion was that Johnson's championship reign would be short-lived and that the first challenger would put him out. "He has immense strength, but absolutely no good fine boxing qualities." As the unsatisfactory bout ended, the general cry was, "Oh, for one round of Jeffries!"

The *Philadelphia Record*, which offered a more detailed round-by-round description, said the Italian heavyweight took a terrible beating and the bell saved him in several of the rounds.

1 - Johnson led with his left into the stomach and repeated it with telling effect. Ross threw a right to the jaw. Johnson landed a stiff left to the chin and then landed a counter right, drawing blood from the nose. With left and right to the face Johnson staggered Ross, who went to his knees, taking a 9-count, the bell just saving him. Johnson's round.

2 - Ross led with a left to the jaw. Johnson smiled and sent a wicked left to the face and followed it with a counter to the stomach. Ross' mouth was bleeding freely. Johnson repeatedly swung a wicked left into the face, rocking Ross on his legs. They clinched. Johnson landed lefts to the face with good effect until the bell rang. Johnson's round.

3 - Ross tried to make a better showing. With a right to the stomach and left to the jaw he removed the grin from Johnson's face. Ross showed extreme nervousness though. Johnson continued using his vicious left swing.

In eluding the powerful jabs, Ross stumbled and slipped to his knees, taking an eight-count for a rest. Johnson landed a right to the stomach and the round ended with Ross hanging on. Johnson's round.

4 - Johnson came up smiling. Ross was in distress. Jack goaded him, making remarks concerning his bloody nose and mouth. Johnson led with a left to the jaw and they clinched. Ross made a vicious lunge, swinging his right to the jaw. This was the first effective blow he landed. The round ended in a clinch. Johnson's round.

5 - Ross came up appearing groggy. Johnson grinned, for it was an easy fight for him. He rocked Ross with a vicious left swing to the face. Tony bravely tried to stand him off, but there was no chance. Johnson was in and out like a flash, and Ross could not stop him. The gong saved him from further punishment. Johnson's round.

6 - Knowing that it was the last round; Ross came up willing and fired a left uppercut to the jaw. Johnson returned with a right uppercut, closing Ross' eye. They clinched. Johnson beat him unmercifully with his left hook, which he had used so effectively throughout. The gong rang with Ross hanging on. Johnson's round.

The *Philadelphia Inquirer* reported that public opinion willingly conceded that Johnson had the best of the fast fight from start to finish. The crowd shouted wildly whenever Ross landed what appeared to be a good blow, and hooted Johnson for his apparently rough work in the clinches. Jimmy Dime said Ross did remarkably well in the face of the fact that Johnson had it over him in weight and height. Johnson refused to talk afterwards.

The *Philadelphia Evening Bulletin* said Johnson did not exert himself, though he outpointed Ross and "was entitled to what frugal glory accrued from the tame exhibition." Jack wore his sardonic smile throughout, and easily handled his smaller and less skilled foe, doing what was required to get the coin.

In the 1st round, Johnson used his left continually to the jaw, and within a minute had Tony bleeding badly from the nose. A left hook and right chop to the face dropped Ross for a nine-count just before the bell rang.

In remaining rounds, Ross appeared scared to death, and kept in a defensive shell, evidently in a bad way until the end. He did a great deal of clinching and hanging on to protect himself. He only landed one good blow, a right to the jaw in the 4th round.

Despite having plenty of opportunities to end matters with a knockout in almost any round, Johnson either was unable or unwilling to finish him. Many believed it was another occasion of his "pulling" strategies to delude the public in view of coming matches. The feeling was that Johnson wanted to make the public think future opponents had a chance with him so that it would make the bouts more lucrative. Another way to look at it was that throughout his career, Johnson was content to win easily on points without taking undue risks.

The *New York World* and *New York Journal* said Ross was frisky in the 1st round, whipping in a left to the head and a hard smash to the body. The blows angered Johnson, who rushed in like a mad bull, smashing, uppercutting, and lifting Ross off his feet.

In the next two rounds, Johnson lessened his speed, and it was evident that he was holding back. Ross showed a great desire to clinch. In eluding a blow, Tony dropped his head down quite low and Johnson said, "Don't duck so low, mister man, or you surely will get hurt." Johnson straightened him up with a left hook to the face. At one point, Ross dropped to the floor to save himself. Tony also turned his back to Johnson to avoid being knocked down. Jack stood back and smiled.

The last three rounds saw Referee M. J. Connolly busy breaking them apart, as Ross was disposed to clinch to save himself.

Nationally, the black-owned *Boston Guardian* reported that the crowd's show of color prejudice did not worry the black world's champion, who grinned at the audience. Public opinion willingly conceded that Johnson bested Ross easily, winning from start to finish, for without difficulty,

Johnson hit Ross at will and was in total control throughout, while Ross kept stalling in order to save himself from being knocked out.[132]

Speaking of press bias, the black-owned *New York Age* said that often it was difficult for a white man to be fair on any question wherein members of both races were concerned. This included most white sportswriters. However, it opined that Bat Masterson of the *New York Morning Telegraph* and Tad Dorgan of the *New York Journal* were the fairest of the white reporters. In a recent issue of the *Telegraph*, Masterson accused fellow white sportswriters of clubbing Johnson over the head because he was colored.

> The writer will agree with 'Bat' Masterson and the other sporting writers that Jack Johnson has not in some instances conducted himself in a manner deserving of praise from the members of his race, but when the white writers inject their personal feelings in their articles because Johnson is colored and will not agree with them as to when and with whom he should make matches, that is a horse of another color.

This writer felt that Johnson had made many a sacrifice to win the title, and now was in a position to dictate terms. This upset many whites.

The *Age* quoted Masterson, who said,

> But in all fairness, Jack Johnson has had more bricks thrown at him than he deserves. It might be all right to slam him in the neck when he openly violates the proprieties of decent living...[or] when he attempts to slouch his way through a match by failing to properly condition himself.... But when sporting writers assume to condemn him and abuse him for refusing to be driven into matches, mostly of their own making, they go beyond the province of fair and honest criticism. Johnson is the champion; newspaper denunciation and abuse are not going to take the title from him, that is certain. ... As he has truthfully said, he won the championship by conceding about everything there was in the game to his opponent. ... Johnson has the same right to demand concessions from a prospective opponent for the title that he was forced to concede to Tommy Burns.

Masterson opined that writers were not actually expressing public sentiment, but voicing their own personal views and prejudices. And if in fact they were expressing public sentiment, "Johnson could not well be blamed for refusing to fight at all. He certainly could not expect to get a square deal in this country." Masterson went on to say,

---

[132] *Pittsburgh Post, Pittsburg Press, Pittsburg Dispatch, Philadelphia Record, Philadelphia Press, Philadelphia Inquirer, Philadelphia Evening Bulletin, New York World, New York Journal, San Francisco Call, Salt Lake Herald, Arizona Republican,* all July 1, 1909; *Boston Guardian,* July 3, 1909.

Clubbing Johnson over the head, through the newspapers, because he is a Negro, will hardly work in this country. No doubt Johnson has left himself open to criticism on account of the way he has acted with reference to some of his contracts; but no one who has taken the trouble to go over his record since he has been champion can help but realize that a good deal of the roasting he has been receiving through the papers was chiefly due to the fact that his skin was black. Johnson's conduct since he became heavyweight champion compares favorably with that of some of his white predecessors.

Johnson was being charged with sidestepping a match with Al Kaufman. However, critics conveniently overlooked the fact that when Jeffries was challenged by Kaufman and did not accept, he suffered no censure. Although many wanted Johnson to fight Kaufman and Ketchel, those same folks would demand big odds before they wagered on either man to defeat Johnson. Continuing, Masterson said,

It is all well enough to roast a man through the newspapers for the sake of filling up space, but quite another thing when it comes to putting up money to back what you say. Johnson will no doubt get in condition for a fight with a man capable of giving him an argument, and in condition the big black will come pretty near bringing home the goods. Jeffries in shape would take the Negro's measure without a doubt; but there is little hope that any of the other heavyweights now in training could turn the trick. Such fighters as Ketchel and Langford would be a little tapioca for the big black and no one knows this better than Ketchel and Langford themselves. Pounding Johnson chiefly because he happens to be a Negro will not get the money in this country.

The *Age* writer said Johnson's championship victory, combined with race prejudice, helped Jeffries earn more easy money in vaudeville exhibitions than ever before in his life. Jeffries was appealing to the white man's racial sensibilities, knowing that whites would herald him as a Moses-like figure. "The former champion is making money by working on the racial sympathies of the white brother, who is not wise enough to know it."

This writer opined that Jeff was faking the public into thinking he would fight Johnson, so that he could earn easy exhibition money, but that ultimately he would not fight. Even some white writers were suspicious that Jeff might eventually decide that he could not get into shape and would decline to fight again; though only after fulfilling lucrative vaudeville contracts. The *Age* wanted Johnson to stop paying attention to Jeffries, for challenging him only gave Jeff more advertising, which led to Jeffries capitalizing even more on race prejudice, making him more money than Johnson, the current champion.[133]

---

[133] *New York Age*, July 1, 15, 1909.

Johnson said he would be in Colma on July 5 to watch Ketchel fight Billy Papke. Nine weeks prior, Johnson had posted $5,000 for a match with Ketchel. He was surprised when Ketchel actually covered the money. Since Ketch had knocked out O'Brien, Johnson was taking him seriously.[134]

On July 5, 1909 in Colma, California, "Michigan Assassin" Stanley Ketchel successfully defended his world middleweight championship with a 20-round decision over elite middleweight Billy Papke. It was the third time that Stan had beaten him, but the second time that Ketchel had avenged an earlier knockout loss to Papke (1908 W10, LKOby12 and KO11 Papke). Papke was coming off an impressive KO1 over Hugo Kelly, another top middleweight. Ketchel later said that he was unable to stop Papke because he was weight drained in making the middleweight limit, and would be stronger as a heavyweight. Most agreed.[135]

The fight was filmed, and several rounds still exist. The footage shows Ketchel to be very aggressive, digging in short body shots and uppercuts, while Papke did a lot of clinching; only firing in spots. Ketchel even demonstrated that he could move back and box a bit at the times when Papke was the aggressor.

The *Philadelphia Evening Bulletin* quoted a *New York Sun* critic who said that Ketchel was a great slugger, but would be easy for Langford or Johnson, for he had little science, while they had the punch and science combined. Further, this critic opined that Langford would be easy for Johnson.

> If Ketchel and Johnson meet I'll predict right now that Johnson will win easily. The colored man is quick on his feet, bristles with science and can nail any man in the world that comes to him. His defensive tactics will nullify Ketchel's assault, and after he has jabbed the white boy into a state of grogginess he'll knock him out. I don't believe that Ketchel will be able to reach Johnson's head, while the colored man has the art of blocking body blows down to a science.
>
> Can Johnson beat Langford? Yes! Johnson will use the same tactics that he will employ in the bout with Ketchel. Langford will not be able to reach him and will have his face jabbed to ribbons. Johnson may be unpopular, but he can fight; at least he knows how to keep the other fellow from hurting him and that means a whole lot!

That was one man's opinion, but it did not meet with the endorsement of many ring judges or the fans, who thought their idol Ketchel was a whole lot better than that, and were excited to see Stan fight Johnson for the championship.[136]

---

[134] *Philadelphia Evening Bulletin*, July 2, 1909.
[135] Papke proved his durability in going the full 10-round distance with Jim Flynn twice, both before the Ketchel fight in March 1909, and nine days after the Ketchel fight, on July 14, 1909. In 1912, Papke would score a KO18 over Georges Carpentier.
[136] *Philadelphia Evening Bulletin*, July 9, 1909.

CHAPTER 5

Al Kaufman

In July 1909, Jack Johnson accepted promoter Jim Coffroth's offer of $10,000 guaranteed to fight Al Kaufman 20 rounds, the bout to take place on or about August 27 at Coffroth's Mission Club in San Francisco.

However, the next day, Bill Delaney said Kaufman would take his time and not be rushed into a fight. Bill would not allow Al to fight until he was in top shape, and did not think Al would be at his best by August or September. So, the Kaufman camp was looking to delay a Johnson bout. Nevertheless, Al would train in anticipation of a future big match.

From Toronto, Jim Jeffries said he would fight Johnson at the proper time. "I'll fight him, and it won't be any Tommy Burns he'll find in the ring." Jeff claimed that he had never given his title to Marvin Hart, and therefore he still was champion. He said he was down to 235 pounds, and had taken off 45 pounds since he started training.[137]

On July 13, 1909 in Pittsburg, Sam Langford fought Klondike Johnny Haynes/Haines to a 6-round no-decision in a back-and-forth battle. In the 1st round, Klondike dropped Langford with a left hook. In the 2nd, Sam came back and floored Klondike. In the 4th round, Klondike again dropped Langford with another hook. In the 5th round, Langford turned the tables and decked Klondike twice. The *Freeman* wrote, "The consensus of opinion is that Langford will have to show better form before he reaches championship timber."[138]

On July 26, 1909 in Terre Haute, Indiana, Mike Schreck stopped Marvin Hart in the 4th round. It appeared that Hart had been worn out from all of the wars and punishment that he had absorbed over the years.

After arriving in New York from Chicago, on the 28th Jeffries deposited a $5,000 forfeit with Robert Edgren as evidence of good faith of his intent to defend his championship against Jack Johnson. Jeff said, "Jack Johnson is not, and will not be, the champion until he whips me, and he never will do that." Jeff said he would be ready to fight within five months.

Johnson said he would cover Jeff's deposit. "I expected he would do something of the kind as a sort of a bluff and to make good his statement that he would fight me. I will be ready to fight almost any time. I think I am in condition now to clean up on Jeffries within fifteen rounds."

On July 29 in Detroit, a motorcycle policeman arrested Johnson on a speeding charge. Jack was taken to the police station, where he was required to deposit $25 to guarantee his court appearance. Johnson produced a

[137] *Philadelphia Evening Bulletin*, July 13-15, 1909.
[138] *Freeman*, July 24, 1909.

$1,000 bill, but they did not have change for such a large amount, so they took him to a local auto factory to obtain change.

On August 5, 1909, Jim Jeffries set sail for Carlsbad, Bohemia, near Germany, which is modern-day Czech Republic. He would train there for the next six weeks. Jeff again confirmed his intention to fight Johnson.

Sam Fitzpatrick, Johnson's former manager, predicted that Jeffries would defeat Johnson by knockout. He believed that Jeff did not have to be at his best to win. "There was never a champion so thoroughly hated as Johnson, and it is going to be a sweet menu for the fans when Jeffries hands this fellow a whaling, and he will do it sure." Jeff could hit hard, was game, durable, could throw Johnson about, and beat down his guard. Fitzpatrick thought Johnson would be surprised and his courage would diminish as soon as he got hit. "I always told Johnson to be modest and keep away from Jeffries; but he knew it all and sneered at Jeffries."[139]

On August 11, 1909 in Chicago, Johnson and Jeffries' manager Sam Berger signed preliminary articles for a Johnson-Jeffries fight, to be held within eight months for the club offering the best inducements. Johnson insisted that the articles omit any reference to Jeffries as the champion. Jeff would have the option to choose the purse split on a winner/loser percentage basis, 60/40, 75/25, or winner take all. Johnson did not care. Each would post $5,000 as a performance guarantee, with said amount also to operate as a side bet. These articles were not yet final or definite, but it showed signs that they were getting closer to making the fight.[140]

From Plymouth, England, Jeffries said that for the past five months he had been working regularly, both privately and in public sparring exhibitions. He knew nothing about the recent agreement that had been signed, for it was done without his approval. Regardless, he said the fight would happen.

On August 16, Johnson was unable to secure lodging in Salt Lake City, Utah. He had booked rooms for himself and his wife, but upon their arrival, the hotels drew the color line on him.[141]

On August 22, after Johnson arrived in San Francisco from Los Angeles, he said that he was settling down to training for the October fight with Ketchel. Manager George Little was representing him. Johnson would train at Dave Cockerill's in Emeryville, in the Oakland area. Jack said he weighed 225 pounds, but did not need a lot of work to get into the best kind of shape.

When he heard that Stanley Ketchel was planning to fight Sam Langford first, on September 15 in New York, a concerned Johnson said, "Ketchel is foolish to think of fighting anybody else before he fights me. The second fight will be the money getter for him." Johnson's logic was, "If Langford beats him he will not be the great card to send in against me in October,

---

[139] *Philadelphia Evening Bulletin*, July 27, 28, 30, 1909, August 5, 6, 1909.
[140] *San Francisco Call*, August 12, 1909.
[141] *Philadelphia Evening Bulletin*, August 13, 17, 1909.

whereas if I beat him then he can go back and fight Langford, for the reason that he can still make the middleweight limit. This is his out, and it's the best answer."

However, the confident Ketchel said, "I am right, and I know that I can beat Langford."

Johnson was willing to bet $1,000 that Jeffries would never fight him. He did not think Jeff actually wanted the fight. Since Jack did not believe the fight would happen, he was busy trying to make other matches. "I am going to start training for Ketchel, and if they dig up another opponent for me in the meantime I will take him on also. I am in this game to get the money."

Jim Coffroth was trying to find an opponent for Johnson so he could put him on his September boxing card. He was negotiating with Kaufman.

Discussing a potential Kaufman bout, wearing a brown suit, Panama hat, black tie, and patent leather shoes, Johnson said,

> Nothing would suit me better than a match with Kaufman. In fact, he is the man I am looking for. He made the announcement some months ago that he wanted to fight me, but when I agreed to come out here and meet him he quickly backed down. I don't understand his system at all. Why did he challenge me if he does not want to fight?

Johnson claimed that Kaufman had turned down several offers from Coffroth.

Jim Coffroth said the trouble in making Johnson-Kaufman was that both boxers wanted so much money that the fight would put him in debt and he'd make no money if he acquiesced to their demands. Johnson was the "guarantee kid." He liked guaranteed purses paid up front, not wanting to take any chances on a speculative gate. Negotiations were ongoing.[142]

However, on August 24, Jim Coffroth made the Johnson-Kaufman fight. It was set to be held sixteen days later, on the afternoon of September 9 at the Mission street arena. The catch was that they would box only 10 rounds in a no-decision bout. "This seems strange in a community that can stand for a finish fight, but it seemed to suit all the parties concerned. If the men are on their feet at the finish there will be no decision."

Kaufman did not want to go further than 10 rounds with the champion, although he was willing to fight Jack O'Brien 25 rounds. In order to make the match, Coffroth gave in to Morris Levy, Kaufman's then acting manager, and made it a 10-round affair. The no-decision clause was also said to have been added to help Kaufman, "for Johnson is far the more clever boxer."

The limited number of rounds was a compromise, given the limited amount of preparation time, and possibly the financial incentive being too

---

[142] *San Francisco Call*, August 22-24, 1909. There was some talk of Jack O'Brien fighting Kaufman instead.

small to justify a longer fight. With a shorter no-decision bout, the fighters would not need as much time to prepare, would not have to worry about losing a decision if it went the distance, and likely would suffer less physical damage. Hence, the incentive to sign was greater, particularly for Kaufman, who had been reluctant to do so.

Eddie Smith was selected to referee. He said that if the fighters stalled and did not fight, the moment it looked like a job, he would terminate the bout, call it a no contest, and forfeit each man's share of the purse.

Regarding the terms, the use of soft surgical bandages would be permitted. The promoter would set the time of the fight, and the contestants would be notified at least three days in advance. They had to be present at least one hour before the bout's start, and to submit to a physical exam by the club physician. Both fighters were to deposit a $1,000 forfeit to guarantee their performance.

On the morning of August 25, Johnson began training at Dave Cockerill's Emeryville quarters, across the bay. On the road bright and early, Jack went for a six-mile run. In the afternoon, at the gymnasium he boxed 4 rounds with the very clever Bob Armstrong, who had been Ketchel's sparring partner for the Papke fight. The 225-pound Johnson said he hoped to remove about 20 pounds before he fought Ketchel. He planned to box every afternoon, and was looking for more sparring partners.

For fun, Johnson liked to ride around in his red racing car with Commissioner Tom Corbett.

Johnson repeated his training routine on the 26th, doing morning roadwork and in the afternoon spending an hour in the gym, which included sparring 4 rounds with Bob Armstrong. Though Armstrong was clever, he could not lay a glove on Johnson.

On the 27th, Johnson increased his boxing to 6 rounds, going 3 with Bob Armstrong and 3 rounds with former opponent Young Peter Jackson.[143]

The *San Francisco Call* said the fact that Johnson was black detracted somewhat from his reception, although he still was receiving the notoriety and recognition that came with being champion. The Kaufman bout would be the champion's first appearance in the West since winning the title, so there was interest in seeing him. Fans wanted to see how much he had improved, and to measure how he would do against Jeffries.

It was hoped that Johnson would do more than he had in his other performances in the city, in which "Jack failed to impress anybody, with the possible exception of himself. He put up a good fight when he flattened Flynn nearly two years ago, but the others were awful." No one who saw him and Ferguson do very little for 20 rounds ever dreamed that Johnson would be champion five years later. But that "was not Johnson's last offense either. Far from it." Marvin Hart obtained a decision against him,

---

[143] *San Francisco Call*, August 25, 26, 28, 1909; *Philadelphia Evening Bulletin*, August 27, 1909.
Also on August 27, 1909 in the Bronx, New York, Joe Jeannette stopped Sandy Ferguson in the 8th round.

"not because of any class he displayed, but simply because Johnson would not do any fighting." Jack also tapped McVey for 19 rounds, until he woke up suddenly and stopped Sam in the 20th round.

Based on form and class, Johnson could keep Kaufman off, use his left jab and outbox him. However, local fans preferred fighters who tore into each other and made a fight of it. They liked boxers like Ketchel – men who walloped hard and tried for the knockout.

The *Call* felt that 10 rounds was too short for Kaufman, who previously had shown that he was a strong fellow who could take a good beating and then come back and stop his man after his opponent had spent his strength. However, if Al made a good showing, it could garner momentum for a rematch in a longer bout.

Kaufman was training at Millett's, near Colma. On August 29, the blacksmith's impressive work boosted the fans' opinion of him. He was sparring 3 rounds each with light-heavyweight Joe Willis and lightweight Jack Cordell. Weighing in the neighborhood of 216 pounds, Kaufman displayed far more speed and cleverness than in the past. He was ever ready with his left jab, shooting it into his sparring partners' faces. He was at least awkwardly clever, and appeared to be in grand shape.

That same day, Johnson sparred with Armstrong, showing his great left, right uppercut, and his right swing.

On August 30, Johnson's 45 minutes of gym work included sparring in an open-air ring; 3 rounds with Young Peter Jackson and 3 more with Dave Mills (both black). He had little trouble in buffeting Jackson around, while Peter found it almost impossible to land a clean blow. The champ was fast on his feet, masterfully moving about like a lightweight. Johnson kept him away with his left, but whenever Jackson bore in, Johnson rapped him with his famous right uppercut.

Johnson never took the initiative. He always was willing to wait for the other man to lead. It was opined that if he was in the ring with someone like himself, there would be no fight at all. Some criticized that Jack lacked the aggressiveness that the public expected from a champion.

The *Call* reported that Kaufman was training harder than Johnson. On the 30th, he sparred 4 rounds with Joe Willis and 4 rounds with Jack Cordell, working on his speed.[144]

There were plans for Johnson to meet big Jim Barry as well. Johnson said he would weigh about 215 pounds when he met Kaufman and Barry in 10-round bouts, but would reduce to about 205 for Ketchel.[145]

Up to that point, 23-year-old Al Kaufman's known record was 19-1 with 16 KOs. Many of his bouts were fights to the finish, and therefore he obtained more quality experience in one lengthy bout than most fighters do today in several years of boxing. His only loss came in his fifth pro bout -

[144] *San Francisco Call*, August 29-31, 1909.
[145] *Philadelphia Evening Bulletin*, August 31, 1909.

LKOby17 to Jack O'Brien, when he was just a novice and had never fought more than 3 rounds before that. Since then, Kaufman had been 15-0 with 12 KOs. His resume was very impressive, amongst the best of all heavyweight contenders. Important victories included: 1906 KO14 Dave Barry, KO1 Jack Sullivan, KO10 Sam Berger, and KO14 George Gardner; 1907 KO7 Mike Schreck, KO3 Dave Barry, and W25 Jack Sullivan; 1908 W6 Joe Grim, KO9 Jim Flynn, KO14 Terry Mustain, and KO39 Jim Barry; and 1909 WND10 Tony Ross. He had fought the majority of his bouts in California. Hence, the locals were quite familiar with him.

Photograph of Al Kaufman, The San Francisco heavyweight in training at Miller's. Kaufman's big reach is shown in the pose. Al has the advantage of nearly two inches in height over Johnson, according to the official measurements.'

Kaufman's 1907 KO7 victory over Schreck was very significant, owing to the fact that Schreck had stopped Marvin Hart, and had done it again even after losing to Kaufman (1906 KO21, 1909 KO4). The Sullivan victories were significant because Sullivan held a decision over Burns at middleweight, and was a vastly experienced, highly regarded fighter. Dave Barry was a known puncher (1905 L20 and LKOby20 to Tommy Burns). Knockout victim Gardner was a former light-heavyweight champion who had gone the distance with both Johnson and Fitzsimmons. Kaufman had stopped Flynn faster than either Burns or Johnson. Berger was a big man, highly touted, and a former Olympic champ. Jim Barry was a skillful, strong, experienced, well-regarded heavyweight who did not draw the color line. Al had proven his toughness and condition in stopping Barry late. Based on results, Kaufman was more deserving of a title shot than any other white contender.

However, former Kaufman manager Billy Delaney was upset about the match. He wanted Kaufman to wait for the bout to build up even more, to take his time in preparing for it, and for it to be scheduled for a great many rounds. "When I turned Kaufman over to Morris Levy it was with strict instructions that he keep him away from the negro for some little time, and that when Kaufman did fight Johnson that the match be for not less than forty-five rounds." Billy thought the 10-round distance was all wrong for Al. Kaufman's methodical style was designed for longer matches. He was slow and steady, but powerful, well-conditioned, and could take punishment and continue fighting strong. He had proven this against the cleverer Jim Barry, coming from behind on points to stop him in 39 rounds.

San Franciscans were critical of the fact that the bout was only 10 rounds, and that it would have no formal points decision. They were used to title fights of 20, 25, and even 45-rounds. "That sort of thing might go well enough in New York or Philadelphia, where they can't do better. But we want none of it here." The bout's terms were criticized continually.

In the meantime, a potential Jeffries fight continued to loom large in the fight public's minds. Sam Berger said Jim Jeffries was not only a "fighter in a million," but a "man among men." He was special, and could overcome years of inactivity and indulgence. "I expect the western people to be at least mildly surprised at his condition." Berger said that while they were sparring in Boston, he crashed a right onto Jeff's jaw with all of his 225 pounds behind it, and Jeffries took it like it was nothing.

> Whatever fat he had on his stomach is rapidly being displaced by clearly defined-muscles, and with a few months' active training, there is not the slightest doubt in my mind but that he will be as good, if not better, than when he retired. I feel sure that when Johnson and Jeffries meet, the white race will be in no danger of losing the heavyweight championship of the world.

Alarmed by news that Stanley Ketchel was a full-fledged heavyweight, because his man was a middleweight, Sam Langford's manager Joe Woodman said Ketchel had to make the middleweight limit or Langford would not fight him. Ketchel allegedly weighed about 185 pounds at that time, and probably would not be able to make the middleweight limit in the near future. Hence, the fight appeared to be in doubt. Of course, if Woodman did not want Langford to fight a heavyweight version of Ketchel, then it stood to reason that he did not want Langford to fight the even bigger Johnson either. Another potential impediment to the Ketchel-Langford fight arose when there was talk that New York Governor Charles Hughes might intervene and prevent it.[146]

The *San Francisco Call* said fans expected Johnson to outpoint Kaufman handily. "Kaufman was never built for a boxer and he never laid any claim to either speed or skill in the 24-foot ring. He is a big, strong, husky young fellow who can take a punch and deliver one. Generally he needs plenty of time in which to wear his man down."

The bout would at least furnish the locals with a line on how the championship version of Johnson would do when up against a big, strong, powerful, sturdy young heavyweight. "He is said to have improved wonderfully in every department of the game since he became champion. … The Johnson of old never set San Francisco on fire."

---

146 *San Francisco Evening Post, San Francisco Chronicle*, September 1, 1909.

On August 31, Johnson did his usual morning roadwork. Jack could outrun any of his training mates. In the afternoon, in front of a large crowd, on the open-air platform at his Emeryville training quarters, he boxed 6 speedy rounds (3 each) with Young Peter Jackson and Dave Mills.

Johnson stepped around his sparring partners at will and fired off all of the punches at his command. One observer said, "Johnson is a splendid gymnasium worker. ... He surely looks good and has improved much in appearance and speed during the week." Another said Johnson used his left jab and left hook, as well as uppercuts and short rights. "In none of these blows did Johnson appear to draw an arm back before delivery. He just struck out in a snappy way and stood flatfooted while doing so. For all the trouble either Jackson or Mills gave him, Johnson might have sat in a chair and sparred equally well." Mills was nearly as tall as Johnson, and received stiffer blows, particularly left hooks to the body. It appeared though that Johnson was holding back, for he did not want to inflict unnecessary injury upon them. Still, he far outclassed his sparring partners, who were "dusky boxers of no mean ability." Even after more than an hour of bag punching and sparring, he was breathing regularly and appeared unruffled by it all.

INTERESTING POSES OF HEAVYWEIGHT CHAMPION

Johnson believed that his sparring partner Young Peter Jackson still was a great fighter. Jack said he would wager on him. In 1906, Jackson had stopped Langford in the 5th round, though Jackson subsequently lost 1906 and 1907 15- and 20-round decisions to Langford, the latter fight being Jackson's last loss. Johnson had pounded on Jackson in a 1905 12-round no-decision, winning every round.

Speaking of Jeffries, Johnson said, "He will come back to this country with bands playing and he'll work the theatrical game for all it is worth. He may sign articles and appoint a date for the fight, but mark my words, when the time draws near there will be an accident or a doctor's certificate, setting forth that Jeffries' health will not allow him to fight."

Were they to fight, Johnson said he would not fight Jeffries in the South. "I will not fight at Oklahoma, or south of the Mason and Dixon line, or at any outside place. I am not crazy. I want to fight in or near a big city, where I will have all the protection the law affords and every chance to show that I am a better man than Jeffries."

That day at Millett's, Kaufman sparred 6 rounds (3 each) with Joe Willis and Jack Cordell. Kaufman's trainer Mark Shaughnessy encouraged Al to use his left jab. The Kaufman camp was concerned about Johnson's jab, and wanted Al to be able to send some jabs in return. The *Chronicle* said Al blocked and countered well, and was looking shifty and fast on his feet, to an extent never before shown. However, the *Call* said, "If anything Al looks bigger and more formidable than he ever did, but he is no faster and no more clever. … He still relies on his ruggedness and his punch."

Kaufman said, "That fellow Johnson isn't going to stop me, and maybe I will surprise him. I am not going to be as slow as he figures and I know he isn't the gamest man in the world when it comes to taking a punch." Al thought he had a good chance to win.[147]

On September 1, promoter Jim Coffroth visited Johnson. In the morning, Jack did 7-8 miles of road work. In the afternoon, he punched the bag and did his usual gym exercise, which included toying with pulley weights and shouldering a large dangling bag. Then he boxed 7 rounds – 2 with Frank Kaufman (of no relation to Al) and 4 with Dave Mills. Bob Armstrong's lips were in bad shape, so Johnson went easy with him for 1 round only, because Bob wanted no more than that. After his rubdown, Johnson weighed 213 pounds. However, when asked his weight, Jack humorously told spectators, "230 pounds."

Johnson told Coffroth, "If I don't knock out that big white man for you in nine rounds, you don't need to give me my training money."

Coffroth said, "Johnson looks spryer to me than he did two years ago. He is a little bit higher in flesh than he was in those days, perhaps, but he is certainly faster."

Johnson failed to appear in court for his speeding trial in Oakland, so his $25 bail was forfeited. His manager George Little announced that Jack was too busy getting into shape to allow ordinary Police Court business to interest him.

Little declared that Johnson would have taken on Kaufman for 100 rounds if he could, but the Kaufman side wanted a limited-rounds no-decision bout.

That same day, Kaufman boxed 3 rounds each with big Joe Willis and Jack Cordell.

Most writers and experts opined that Kaufman's only chance of defeating Johnson was to wade in, make it a slam-bang fight, and hope to

---

[147] *San Francisco Call, San Francisco Chronicle, San Francisco Examiner,* September 1, 1909; *San Francisco Bulletin,* September 8, 1909.

land a big bomb or wear down the champion. However, "if he believes he can box with the colored champion he is a subject for the funny house." Kaufman's forte was not speed, but strength and a good punch.

Kaufman said of Johnson, "Oh, he's a great fighter, all right. He can be hit, though, the same as anyone else. And if I can land on him just once I think I'll bring him down. I expect to get a bit of a mauling in the beginning, but from what I have seen of him with Flynn and others I don't think he can punch hard enough to make me stop fighting."

In response to Little's claim that Johnson would have fought a bout of any length, Morris Levy insisted that it was the Johnson people who wanted it to be 10 rounds.

The *Evening Post* did not think a knockout was likely. Johnson had never been a very aggressive fighter, and Kaufman was known for his toughness. Johnson likely would outpoint Kaufman. "The big negro knows how to fight. He is clever, a much better hitter than most persons imagine, and altogether a good ring man. Kaufman is the very best of a bad lot of white heavies."

Although Referee Eddie Smith of Oakland was prohibited from rendering an official decision, he was not barred from stating his opinion afterwards. Smith said he would tell the newsmen who he thought had won the bout. That opinion could serve to satisfy wagering on the outcome.

Essentially, he would render an official unofficial decision in the no-decision bout.

Referee Smith said he expected the men to fight every minute of the bout, and he would not allow stalling, or else he would rule it a no contest. Straight Marquis of Queensberry rules would govern.

The odds were 2 to 1 that Johnson would win the unofficial decision. However, Kaufman was favored at 10 to 6 to last the full 10 rounds. Most experts thought it would go the distance, but that Johnson would win.

23-year-old Al Kaufman was listed as standing 6'2" tall and weighing 202 pounds. He looked bigger and taller than that. Some said Al was closer to 216 pounds. Johnson was 31 years old, stood 6' ¼" tall, and weighed about 213 pounds.

Kaufman was taller and had 3 inches greater reach than Johnson. He also had a bigger chest measurement. However, Johnson had bigger arms and legs.

Ketchel manager Willus Britt said Johnson was correct to have a lot of respect for Kaufman. Britt was nervous about the bout, for he did not want it to derail the Johnson-Ketchel fight. "Al has the kick, and he has a chance to land it on anybody. It is our one fear now that Kaufman may beat us to the championship. ... Al can knock any man endwise that he hits, and he is just as liable as not to nick Jack on the chin and put him away." Britt said that despite Jack's comments after Ross-Kaufman (that they both were a joke to him), Johnson was not taking any chances. Jack knew that Kaufman inflicted terrible punishment on Ross towards the end of the fight. That explained why Jack was working hard to be in good shape.

Still, the biggest fight on sportswriters' minds was Jeffries-Johnson. "For the past year these big bruisers have taken up more space in the newspapers than anybody else in the country."

Although Johnson had been saying that Jeffries would not fight him, Sam Berger said Jeffries had put himself on record that he would fight Johnson, and Jeff was a man of his word. "During his entire career Jeffries has never once run out on a match." However, "Johnson, after promising to fight Langford for the National Sporting Club of London, fell down on that match and refused to fight the little Boston negro. ... Jeffries always

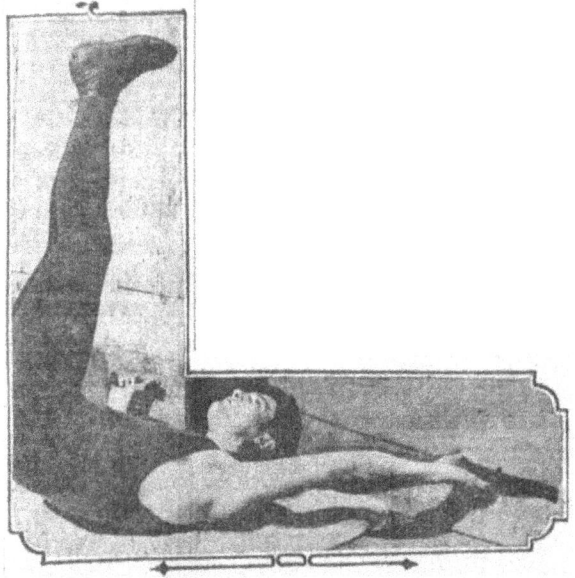

fought when he said he would fight. … But that much cannot be said for Johnson." Berger said Jeff was sore at Johnson and would give him the best walloping he ever got in his life, one that he would never forget.[148]

On September 2, Johnson did his usual roadwork. Spectators gathered at the open-air pavilion at the Cokrell resort in Emeryville to see him punch the bag for 15 minutes and then spar 4 rounds with Dave Mills.

Despite the fact that the mulatto Mills was no slouch, and "for speed has Kaufman looking like January molasses beside a spring flood," Johnson completely outboxed him. Jack waited for Mills and then countered his leads with his famous left hook and lightning right uppercut.

Although Johnson normally toyed with him as a cat does with a mouse, in the 2nd round, Mills landed a solid stinging straight left to the face. Johnson made him regret it. His smile disappeared, his eyes flared, he feinted, stepped in briskly, and tore in with a retaliation of uppercuts and a bewildering volley of blows to every part of the anatomy, until timekeeper Little warned him to cut out the rough stuff.

Actually, Little was concerned about Johnson's hands. He did not want him to hurt them so close to the fight. Jack always kept his hands well wrapped up. In general, Johnson was very touchy about his hands, one of the reasons why he "looks twice before he strikes a hard blow." However, if someone landed a good one, he liked to get payback.

Johnson's footwork was lively, and he drew away from swings in the nick of time. Sometimes he waited like a statue for the attack, and then disarranged his opponent's aim with left hooks that were delivered with wonderful quickness.

After the workout, Johnson tipped the scales at 213 ¼ pounds.

Although Kaufman was big, strong, tough, well-conditioned, and had a tremendous blow, after seeing Johnson in sparring, the *San Francisco Bulletin* writer opined that all of Kaufman's good traits would not matter.

> Kaufman hasn't one chance in a million of winning from Johnson on points; he hasn't one in a thousand of knocking the champion out. … From the manner in which the big dinge blocked, side stepped and evaded Mills…it would appear that Al will have but little chance to reach Johnson with a haymaker. …

> Jack Johnson is today in the greatest physical condition of his career – which means that he is bigger, stronger, faster and more scientific than he has ever been before, and able to make monkeys out of ninety-nine one hundredths of all the heavyweights in the world, with the possible exception of James J. Jeffries. The black champion is broader of beam, fleeter of foot and shiftier of arm and glove than he has been during his previous visits to the Coast.

---

[148] *San Francisco Call, San Francisco Evening Post, San Francisco Chronicle, San Francisco Examiner, Philadelphia Evening Bulletin,* September 2, 1909.

When Referee Ed Smith told Johnson that they would have to protect themselves at all times, including in clinches and on breakaways, Johnson said, "Let him come any time he wants to. I've got Aunt Betsy (indicating his left) and I guess that I can protect myself with that. I'm going to jab this fellow Kaufman into little pieces and he will not have much chance to clinch with me in that fight of ours." Referee Smith asked, "You understand that you can hit in the clinches?" Johnson replied, "Yessah, I understands that perfectly, and I'm going to hit all the time." Johnson also said, "They can't come too fast for me. The faster Kaufman comes the oftener I'll hit him, and I expect to muss his feathers some." Johnson was confident that he could blindfold himself and go 10 rounds with Kaufman.

That same day, Kaufman boxed 4 lively rounds with his new sparring partner, Lew Taylor.

Tickets were on sale for $1, $2, $3, and $5.[149]

On September 3, Kaufman did medicine-ball tossing, shadow boxing, and bag punching, and he also sparred 3 rounds with welterweight Jack Cordell and 4 rounds with 204-pound amateur heavyweight Lew Taylor.

Kaufman showed decided improvement. He had strength, a particularly potent right, and he could take a punch and come back strong and wear down his man. Al was in very good shape, and he would have to try to use his condition to wear out the champion. "Johnson is too clever a boxer and too wise a ring master to be outgeneraled by such a man as the blacksmith."

Johnson did his usual gym exercises, but did not spar. Although he was looking a trifle fat, his wind was good and his boxing a revelation. He appeared to be faster and cleverer than he was when last seen in San Francisco nearly two years ago against Jim Flynn.[150]

Scouting the bout, the *San Francisco Call* said,

> Johnson is one of the most clever big men who ever donned a glove. It stands to reason that he will experience little or no difficulty in walking around the ponderous blacksmith and jabbing him as hard and as often as he pleases. In the past Johnson demonstrated beyond the question of a doubt that no slow man could hit him, though it must be admitted that he never showed much disposition to do any hitting himself. … If Johnson figures that Kaufman is too tough and too rugged he will keep dancing around and sidestepping. After the fight he will offer the usual excuse that he did not want to take a chance of hurting his hands. … Johnson's past performances in this city were enough to turn all the fans against him, but he may have improved since the championship crown came his way.[151]

What many said about Johnson was, "The most dashing boxer in the gymnasium I have ever seen, but in the ring nothing more than a marvel of

[149] *San Francisco Call, Examiner, Chronicle, Bulletin, Evening Post*, September 3, 1909.

[150] *San Francisco Examiner, San Francisco Call*, September 4, 1909.

[151] *San Francisco Call*, September 5, 1909.

defense." That saying "fits him to a nicety when most of his fights are concerned." Johnson promised that he would fight and not stall. The champion was "quick, clever and strong."

Kaufman did not have the speed, but he had the punching power, and he knew it. Al said, "I know that he will punch me about some. I expect to be rough handled in the beginning. But just let me hit him once and he will know that something has happened to him. If I can land just one blow I'll be satisfied, for I am sure I will bring him down."

The bout would show whether Kaufman could whip Johnson in a longer fight, or if he would be so thoroughly outgeneraled that he would stand no chance. Johnson could show what he could do against an opponent bigger and taller than he, with a greater reach and a staunch heart.

Johnson took pride in his great arm and shoulder strength. He said that he was a specialist at handling strong men in clinches. Discussing his chances with Jeffries, Jack said that he was not at all concerned by Jeff's strength. He argued that in subduing strong men like Frank Childs and Sam McVey, he had proven to be the master of greater in-fighters than Jeffries had ever taken on. "Any one who will watch Johnson in his sparring bouts at Cockrell's camp can tell by the way he twists his partners in the clinches that his claim of wondrous arm power is not an idle boast."

However, Kaufman was a very strong man. Like Fitzsimmons, he had been a blacksmith by trade. Swinging a 20-pound sledge for three years had made his muscles as strong as steel. W. W. Naughton said, "Kaufman is a wonder at breaking the arm-locks that are common to breast-to-breast milling. I am wondering which of the men will have the upper hand if there is much rough work at close quarters."[152]

One expert believed that Kaufman would do better than many thought. He was the type of fighter who fought to the level of his competition. His best performances had come against his highest quality of opposition, while his worst outings had been against men who were considered his inferior. Regardless of performance, he usually found a way to win.[153]

W. W. Naughton said Kaufman's winning record possibly was as good as any heavyweight ever. However, sometimes when he won, he failed to impress, causing the comment, "He won, but that's about all." Many had once said that about Johnson. Still, most thought Kaufman was a harder puncher than Johnson, could stand rougher usage, and was more courageous. His pluck was a proven quantity, for he had withstood gruelings and still won. "This is not an imputation that Jack possesses the despised 'yellow streak.' He simply hasn't been pounded and pummeled like Kaufman." Al had proven his grit, whereas Johnson did not have to do so. "Johnson has simply established that he is an exceedingly clever ring man."

Jim Coffroth told a cute story about Johnson. One night while they were in New York, Jack was commenting on the fact that certain critics doubted his courage: "They say that, I suppose, because they haven't seen me punched to pieces?" Coffroth responded by asking, "But on the level, Jack, are you game?" Johnson pondered a moment and responded, "I don't know." After they both laughed, "Jack explained that he had contrived to avoid being bruised and beaten so far, and that until a man came along who was equal to the task of hammering him, he would have to remain in the dark in regard to his own stout heartedness."[154]

Just two days before the fight, on the morning of Tuesday September 7, Johnson ran 10 miles. He worked for an hour in the gym, boxing 4 rounds with Dave Mills. Jack claimed that he would enter the ring weighing 209 pounds.

Kaufman punched the bag, skipped rope, and wrestled with Mark Shaughnessy, his trainer. Then he boxed 3 rounds with Lew Taylor, engaging in considerable roughing.

The odds were 10 to 4 that Johnson would win on points, and 2 to 1 that Kaufman would last the limit.[155]

Kaufman said,

[152] *San Francisco Chronicle, San Francisco Examiner,* September 5, 1909.
[153] *San Francisco Bulletin,* September 6, 1909.
[154] *San Francisco Examiner,* September 7, 1909.
[155] *San Francisco Chronicle,* September 8, 1909.

They say that one good punch deserves another. Well, that doesn't go in pugilism. I know that I will be satisfied to trade one good punch for a half dozen of Johnson's. Yes, and I'll be satisfied too, for I believe that my blow, if it lands, will do more damage than any six of the jabs and uppercuts I may get from Johnson.[156]

The *Call* said that although Kaufman's best chance was to land a haymaker, Johnson "is an artful ringman and too careful to fall a victim of a wild swing." He was "one of the most careful ring tacticians in the business, and one who never takes the slightest chance of leaving himself open for a decisive punch." Typically, Johnson had been "content to lay back and wait for his opponent to open up the fire before he would battle. At this line of milling he is an adept, but it does not please the spectators. This usually brings a slow battle, unless one of the contestants is aggressive." His style was effective, but it was too defensive for the fans to enjoy or appreciate. "This has undoubtedly detracted from the colored man's popularity." The general opinion was that Johnson would box carefully and win on points.

Some speculated that Johnson would not try to stop Kaufman, and might even carry him so they could fight again and make more money. "The fans seem to think that Johnson will save Kaufman. The heavy weight field is rather shy of material and the champion may take it into his head to be careful with his tool and save him for another day."

The *San Francisco Evening Post* said the "lazy negro champion" was expected to give a tame exhibition of cleverness. Although many doubted Johnson's courage, his cleverness was undisputed. "The big negro knows every trick and artifice of the game." Kaufman was rugged and powerful enough to send anyone to sleep. However, he needed to land his punch, and the oscillating Johnson was masterful at making an opponent miss.

Eddie Smith said, "The best man will win, regardless of color or prejudice. Of course there will be no official ruling on this contest, but I will make a statement for the press in which I will fully cover all details of the match and this statement will do just as well as an official ruling."[157]

Facts About Heavyweights

COFFROTH'S ARENA.

Mission Street and Sickles Avenue, San Francisco.

2 P. M.

Tommy McCarthy vs. Roscoe Taylor, 130 pounds; 15 rounds. Tiv Kreling, referee. Men weigh in at Corbett's, 1517 Ellis street, 10 a. m.

3 P. M.

JACK JOHNSON, Heavyweight Champion of the World,

Versus

AL KAUFMAN of California.

Eddie Smith, Referee.

Take Cemeteries cars along Mission, San Mateo Suburban from Fifth and Market, Valencia along Market, Fillmore and Mission, and Polk, Larkin and Onondaga avenue. Cars all run through on day of fight. Also S. P. train from Third and Townsend streets, 11:30 a. m.

Bleacher doors open at 10 o'clock. Reserved sections, 12 noon. 4000 bleacher seats at $1. No scalping.

Downtown box office at 800 Market street open until 2 p. m. day of contest.

156 *San Francisco Examiner*, September 8, 1909.
157 *San Francisco Call, San Francisco Evening Post,* September 8, 1909.

Heavyweights Anxious
to Clash in the Ring

Kaufman planned to enter the ring at about 205 pounds. The *Call* said that although he could not outbox Johnson, with proven assimilative and recuperative powers, he could take all of Johnson's punches and patiently await his opportunity to land a terrific knockout wallop. "If he is successful in driving home a few of these wicked body blows – any one of which would set a yearling bull on his haunches – Johnson will indeed be a fortunate man to still retain the heavyweight crown." Al had "repeatedly shown that he can take a fearful lot of punishment and still be strong enough to deliver a sleep-producing smash. ... It is doubtful if any man in the ring today is better equipped for a grueling mill than this same Kaufman."

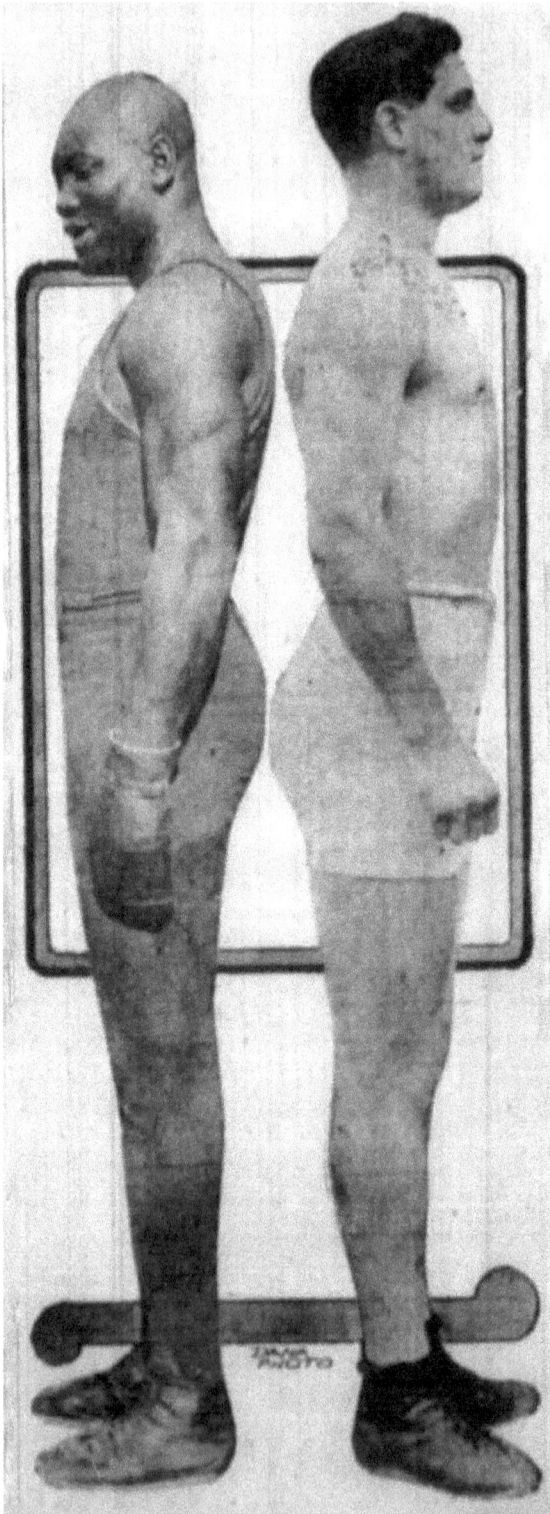

Kaufman was "about to go in against one of the cleverest big men who ever pulled on a glove." He would pit his heart, strength, and condition against Johnson's "cleverness, ring experience, and cunning." Most fans believed that Johnson would step around Kaufman and keep shooting his left into Al's face. The *Call* said Kaufman appeared to be in better shape. "Johnson, on the other hand, spent more of his time scorching in that big red automobile of his than performing in the gymnasium." Still, most experts opined that Jack had trained well and was ready.

Some local fans remembered Johnson's "miserable exhibitions" against McVey, Hart, and Ferguson, in which he was "hooted and hissed for his dogged tactics." However, he was a gate draw because he was the champion. "It is only Johnson's fame as heavyweight champion that has made him the great card he is today."[158]

The *Chronicle* agreed that in previous local matches,

> [Johnson] has never created a brilliant impression. Essentially a defensive fighter of the first caliber, the fight-going public has found fault with his lack of aggressiveness and the length of time that it has frequently taken him to dispose of his opponents. For all that, there is a tendency to underrate Johnson and his right to the championship title.

The point was that the mere fact that fans did not like or appreciate his style did not mean that Johnson was not very effective.

The *Chronicle* also agreed with the *Call's* analysis of the fight. If the comparatively slower but stronger and tougher Kaufman stood off and boxed, Johnson would "jab him into pieces." He needed to rush and keep a fast pace. "Fighters who have stayed the longest with Johnson have been men of the rushing type, as Jim Flynn, with no particular style, but an aggressiveness that was disconcerting."

The *Chronicle* said Kaufman's manager had demanded the no-decision clause. His logic was that if Johnson outpointed his fighter, he did not want to have it count too much against him. However, the referee would offer his opinion, and everyone would know who won anyhow.[159]

On Thursday September 9, 1909 at the Mission-street arena in Colma, California, the Jack Johnson vs. Al Kaufman 10-round no-decision bout took place. The doors opened at 10 a.m., and the preliminary would start at 2 p.m. The main event was set to start at around 3 p.m.[160]

The weather was ideal, though there were ominous banks of fog clinging to the hills surrounding the arena. Delegations of fans from Los Angeles,

---

[158] *San Francisco Call*, September 9, 1909.

[159] *San Francisco Chronicle*, September 9, 1909.

[160] The following account is an amalgamation of the local day-of and next-day reports from the *San Francisco Evening Post*, September 9, 10, 1909; *San Francisco Chronicle*, *San Francisco Examiner*, *San Francisco Call*, and *San Francisco Bulletin*, September 10, 1909.

Sacramento, Fresno, and Stockton were in attendance. A crowd of between 6,000 and 8,000 taxed the capacity of Coffroth's fight pavilion.

Johnson was the betting favorite at 10 to 4 odds. The line on whether Kaufman would or would not stay 10 rounds was the most popular proposition. Kaufman was the 2 to 1 favorite to last the distance.

Upon his entrance at 2:50 p.m., Kaufman was given a great reception. "There was a genuine ovation for the white man." He smiled and nodded to his friends. With him were manager Morris Levy, Jack Cordell, Mark Shaughnessy, and Lew Taylor.

In contrast with Kaufman's reception, a few minutes later, as Johnson slowly cantered down the aisle, stepped over the ropes and into the ring, the crowd hooted and booed him. The *Chronicle* said the fans were markedly unfair to Johnson. The hisses and groans that greeted his appearance represented a majority of those present, though some gave him a friendly greeting. His lack of popularity was well known, "but black or white, he was entitled to fair consideration. … As a fighter, Johnson has been uniformly fair in his actions in the ring. There are few men quicker to obey the referee or none who will fight a more fair battle than this same Johnson."

Regardless of the cold reception, Johnson smiled derisively and simply walked over to Kaufman and shook hands.

Accompanying the champion were George Little, Bob Armstrong, Barney Furey, Young Peter Jackson, and someone called "the Cocoanut Coon." Most likely Dave Mills was present as well, if the latter wasn't him.

Billy Jordan announced Kaufman as "the Native Son of the Golden West." The crowd again cheered him to the echo. Indeed Kaufman was the local San Francisco native, in part explaining his popularity.

Then Jordan said, "The heavyweight champion of the world, Jack Johnson." Again there were hoots, hisses, and boos. Jack obviously was extremely unpopular. Neither fighter seemed nervous.

Johnson again shook hands with Kaufman and examined the tape and bandages on his hands. Kaufman's seconds did the same to Johnson.

The gloves were selected, and while they were being fitted, Referee Eddie Smith entered the ring.

Jordan announced that tickets were being sold for a benefit fund to aid famous veteran California actor L. R. Stockwell, who recently was stricken with blindness. Johnson and Kaufman engaged in some good-natured bidding on tickets toward the fund, which made it seem more like a poker game. Jack opened by pledging $20. Al then said, "I'll take $30." Johnson grinned and said, "I'll raise you ten." Kaufman replied, "Make it fifty." Johnson countered, "Make it $100 then." Kaufman ended matters with, "I'll cover the hundred and call you." Each time that one man raised the other, Billy Jordan announced to the crowd what the boxer had said.

They stripped and posed for photographs. Both appeared to be in good condition, though some said Johnson looked a bit fat. Kaufman was taller and seemed to have the better of it in the reach.

Johnson wore blue fighting breeches. Kaufman wore white tights. Each man wore a red, white, and blue Stars and Stripes American flag belt.

Referee Ed Smith confirmed that they were going to fight using straight Queensberry rules. The boxers returned to their corners to await the clang of the bell.

The ring was cleared, and at 3:04 p.m., Uncle Billy Jordan made his familiar cry of "Let 'er go!" and the bell rang to start the fight.

1 - They fiddled and feinted until Johnson landed a well-placed left hook to the stomach. Johnson began beating a tattoo on Kaufman's head and body. They mixed it at close range, with Johnson landing short rights and lefts to the jaw. He landed a left to the face, and when coming out of a clinch, shot in his left twice more. Three, times, Jack jabbed the nose with his left. Jack smiled and shot right and left to the face. He landed at least a dozen stinging lefts to the head and body without a return.

By the middle of the round, Johnson had his famous right uppercut working, and Kaufman started bleeding from his nose and lip. Jack seemed to have his man measured properly, and spent his time jabbing his left and landing an occasional right uppercut in the clinches. It looked as if Johnson would tear him to pieces. Kaufman could not break through Johnson's guard. "It was an illustration of the mastery of the colored man." It was one-sided, and the crowd was silent.

Near the round's end, Kaufman landed a light left jab to the lip and the crowd applauded with joy. Roars of "Good boy, Al!" were heard, even though it did no damage and barely landed with any force. Johnson simply smiled. Still, "It was about the only clean blow that Al landed."

All of the local papers agreed that it was Johnson's round. "Johnson had much the better of the round." From the first landed punch until the end of the round, it was all Johnson, who clearly demonstrated his superiority. "Kaufman seemed very slow in comparison with the fast work of Johnson."

2 - Johnson landed his hard left jab to the face. They clinched and Johnson showed his strength by wrestling and pushing Kaufman against the ropes. A moment later, Jack drove a straight left to the face. He shifted the left to the body, and then fired it back up to the head. His left was like a piston rod, and Kaufman was powerless to avoid it. Three times in succession Jack's straight left sent Al's head back. Johnson landed a hard left to the ear, staggering him.

Kaufman appeared a bit at sea, for he had not yet been able to land anything. When Al did try a lead, Johnson simply stood away, held up his hands, and laughed at him. They closed in to a clinch and Johnson rocked Kaufman's head with short left and right swings to the face, bringing blood.

Some writers said Kaufman landed a few jabs to the head and rights to the body, but they had no effect. Each time, Johnson simply flashed his golden smile. He even cracked jokes at the spectators, who tried to encourage Kaufman.

Johnson was outlanding Kaufman by far, doing the same thing he did in the 1st round. He showed that he could outwrestle Kaufman in the clinches or hold him off almost at arm's length. When close, Jack used his blood-letting right uppercut. As the round ended, he jabbed Al into a neutral corner. Kaufman took it all manfully, showing his toughness.

The local writers unanimously agreed that Johnson had the better of the round. One said it was a relatively tame round. The *Examiner* said Al landed some, but the *Chronicle* said, "Again Kaufman had failed to land a blow."

3 - Johnson set a fast pace, repeatedly using lefts and rights to the body and head. Jack drove a wicked left to the jaw and followed with a hard clout to the stomach. He cut loose with more right uppercuts, one of which badly cut Kaufman's lip and broke his teeth, causing the blood to spurt and spray from his mouth in profuse torrents. Al held on to save himself. Johnson continued landing uppercuts. There was a continual great stream of blood coming from Kaufman's mouth.

The remainder of the round was a series of Johnson punches, the right uppercuts doing the most damage. Johnson planted a fearful right wallop to the bleeding face, which caused the blacksmith to stall. Johnson taunted Kaufman and landed two hard jolts to the jaw. A left to the stomach weakened Kaufman. Al was short with a left lead and Jack crossed him heavily with the right. The champion stood away and grinned triumphantly. As Kaufman came in, Johnson landed two lefts to the face. Al landed a right on the stomach, but Jack struck his chin with a right uppercut.

Near the end of the round, in a fierce rally, Johnson rushed and forced Kaufman into a corner and hammered him with heavy left and right hooks to the head and jaw that hurt him badly. Al looked helpless, and the crowd sensed the end of the uneven contest.

When the bell rang, Kaufman went to his corner in bad condition, for he was covered with blood and his eyes were glassy. He tumbled into his chair with blood flowing in a veritable stream from his mouth and nose.

The *Evening Post* said that thus far, Kaufman had not landed one effective blow. It was all Johnson. The *Call* said, "It was apparent that Johnson was clearly Kaufman's master and could finish him at such times as he was ready to cut loose."

4 - Kaufman landed to the ribs several times, but never in a way that told. Johnson used his left elbow to block some body smashes. Still, some of the body blows riled the champion, who in response badly battered Kaufman. Johnson put more sting into his blows and showed a dash of aggression. He landed several left jabs. He walked Kaufman around the ring.

In one rally, Johnson's fierce swings with both hands carried Kaufman to the ropes, and Al bent across the top rope until it looked as though he would topple over onto the ringsiders. The referee stepped in and separated them.

After that, Johnson stood off, and with open gloves, laughed at Kaufman. This gave the crowd the impression that Jack was playing with Al and merely trying to show him up. Johnson slowed down a bit, but still continued with his left leads, right uppercuts in the clinches, and an occasional swing to the jaw or body.

Kaufman's face was covered with blood, and there were even smears of his blood on Johnson's shoulders and back as the result of their coming together in clinches.

Kaufman sent a nice right to the ribs, and repeated it. Jack grinned and winked at his seconds. Al landed another right on the ribs and Jack dealt him a right uppercut which sent his head back. Al scored another right under the heart. Johnson landed a left to the head and then twice hooked his right to the head.

Both eased up, with Kaufman seldom leading. The *Chronicle* said that toward the close of the round it was evident that Johnson was playing with him. The *Call* said the round ended tamely and it looked as if Johnson deliberately slowed up. They were clinched at the bell. It was another clear Johnson round.

5 - Early on, Johnson forced Kaufman all over the ring. He hooked in many ugly rights and lefts to the body. He cut up Kaufman considerably about the face and punished him severely with lefts over the heart, blows which were tiring even for the big fellow. Johnson jabbed the mouth and then twice hooked his left into the stomach. He continued blocking most of Kaufman's blows.

Johnson slowed up, though at intervals he continued to work left jabs and right uppercuts. When Al came at him, Johnson showed a few more of his golden smiles and kept him at a safe distance. He seemed to know there was no danger. Johnson yelled at one of the photographers, "Keep quiet over there."

Kaufman worked him into a corner and landed a right to the body. They clinched. After Al broke away and stepped back, Johnson remained standing with his back to the corner and dared Kaufman to come in and return to the attack, in taunting fashion saying, "Come on Al! Walk right into them! Youah tough big man." Al accepted the invitation and went after him, swinging several blows, but Johnson parried, blocked with his arms and elbows, and grinned, for he was so clever that Kaufman could not land on any part of the scoring area. At the conclusion of the bombardment, Al received an uppercut.

The fans expressed their disapproval. "Why don't you fight, you big zobs?" "Oh, if Jeffries was only in that ring we'd see a fight." "Where do you think you are at; in some picnic grounds?" "We paid to see a fight, not a minstrel show." It had no effect on the champ. Johnson was out to give a boxing lesson, and Kaufman could not hit him.

Eventually, Johnson started his own rally. He followed Kaufman across the ring, sending in left and right hooks to the face. Al landed a couple rights to the ribs, but Johnson landed four snappy right uppercuts between the chin and nose, each one tilting and lifting Kaufman's head a foot in the air. Al tried hard to land to the body, but Jack blocked the blows. "Johnson was quickness and nimbleness personified." They were clinched at the bell. Once again, it was all Johnson.

6 - At first, Johnson sparred cautiously. He was in a loafing mood again. One spectator yelled, "Look out, here comes Jeff!" Jack laughed. He held out both gloves until he touched Kaufman's gloves, and then he brushed aside straight lefts and body rights.

Kaufman missed a swing and Johnson smashed him with a left across his bleeding face. In a clinch, Jack landed uppercuts.

Suddenly, Johnson broke loose and landed a fusillade of blows, including left hook to the body and right and left to the jaw, beating Kaufman backwards across the ring to the ropes. Johnson followed with some hard stomach blows that sent Kaufman halfway through the ropes and almost into the press stand.

The referee momentarily came to the rescue. When Al came out from between the ropes, Jack made another rush at him.

However, Johnson quickly slowed down again. He liked to vary defensive tactics with "spiteful spurts of fighting in which he cuffed Kaufman until the blood fell from Al's face like rain." Then he would return to playing defense again.

The crowd yelled, "Mix it, Al," and he did so. However, Johnson was waiting for him, and showed that he was master of the situation at any style of fighting. Kaufman landed two lefts and a right on the face, but they were light blows. Johnson landed left jabs and right hooks, and every punch told. After a clinch and break, Johnson blocked a right with his elbow and then hooked his left. Jack waved his hand at someone in the audience. At close quarters, Johnson uppercut him with his right and hooked with his left. Jack drew back from a left and clinched. He leaned his chin on Kaufman's shoulder and chuckled and laughed as they pushed around. Johnson was having everything his own way. It was another Johnson round.

7 – Although Al came up looking weak, he rushed and landed a left to the jaw, and bothered Johnson for a moment with a couple of solid body punches. He landed a particularly nice right to the body, his best punch of the fight. This set the crowd to cheering for him. For the first time in the fight, he was coming on, showing aggression and setting the pace. Johnson had slowed down and seemed content to allow Kaufman to do all the work.

However, it was only a flash of solid lands from Kaufman, and most of the time Johnson blocked cleverly. Jack momentarily brought his left hand into action. He landed a couple lefts to the stomach and used his short right uppercut in the clinch. He drew away from Al with ease and laughed.

Johnson went on the defensive again, just to show how he could block the blows. Holding Kaufman off with outstretched arms, Johnson grinned at Al's feeble efforts to break through his guard. At times, Jack liked to stand as still as a statue and catch the leads in the hollow of his open glove. He was content to play defense for a while. Jack backed and fiddled. Kaufman tried to be busy, but Johnson smothered every attempt like a skilled mechanic.

Suddenly Johnson loosened up his offense again and quickened the pace, hooking and uppercutting Kaufman clean across the platform, rocking his head with left and right. Jack then returned to firing in straight lefts. In the clinches, he pushed Al away and jolted him with both hands. As they broke from one clinch, Johnson sent Al across the ring with a succession of lefts and rights to the face.

Clearly, Johnson was alternately holding back and cutting loose. "It was apparent to all that Johnson was holding himself in reserve and only opened up when the fancy took him." The locals again agreed that it was Johnson's round.

8 - Johnson infused more ginger into his work. The round started with one of his usual straight lefts to the face, followed by two body punches with both hands. Johnson also swung right and left with considerable force to the jaw and mouth. He came after Kaufman and chased him around the ring. Kaufman backed away, seldom leading, despite his advisers' instructions to do so. Jack beat him back to the ropes with lefts and rights, and the blood again flowed from Al's mouth.

Johnson stood still and winked as Kaufman brushed his face with a left. As Al closed in, Johnson twice landed left uppercuts to the jaw, but Kaufman responded with a hard right to the ribs or stomach, about the best blow he had landed. In the clinches, Al smothered Jack's uppercuts. Johnson hooked a hard left into the stomach and hit the face with a left.

Kaufman landed his solid right to the jaw, and with a straight left tilted Johnson's head. This started the crowd cheering. It was his best sequence to that point, but the punches did no serious damage. Jack kept drawing Al's fire and stepped in with lefts and rights to the face.

Kaufman blocked some blows, but mainly suffered severe punishment. He scored more frequently than before, but his punches did not disturb the champion. The locals still agreed that Johnson won the round.

During the one-minute respite between rounds, Johnson kept up an incessant verbal exchange with the crowd.

9 - Johnson landed a left hook to the ear. Al removed the smile from Jack's face by clouting him in the stomach with a pile-driving right. For a fleeting moment Johnson fought back a bit wildly. He quickly regained his composure, though, and sent right and left with great force to the jaw. Johnson waited for a while, and blocked Al's lead. In the clinch that followed, Johnson landed his right uppercut five times in quick succession. Kaufman's nose started bleeding again. Jack's smile returned.

Kaufman hit the ribs with his right. During a clinching rally, Johnson kept his left hand free and clouted Al's mouth many times as they struggled across the mat.

After breaking, Kaufman did the forcing and tried to mix it, but Johnson was too clever and kept him away. Al received a left to the face and right to the body. He kept trying for the ribs with his right, but Jack either stepped away or blocked it. Johnson stopped his every lead and gave a wonderful exhibition of blocking.

In a half clinch, Johnson hooked his right to the head twice and also uppercut twice. He forced Kaufman back to his own corner in order to get away from a beating. Jack rocked his head with a high left hook. He then smashed the left into the stomach twice in succession.

However, Johnson then backed off again. Some hissed and hooted at the champion and complained that he was not working fast enough, but he made no reply. They felt that Johnson had not been doing his best to extend himself to the utmost to try to stop his opponent. It may have been that he was pacing himself and conserving his energy. He had his mouth open and was breathing heavily, as if he was tired. The round ended with the crowd jeering at Johnson. Some spectators started to leave the arena.

10 - They shook hands. Johnson crouched slightly and tore in, landing a left to the jaw, left on the body, and a right on the jaw. He seemed determined and serious. It looked as if he had saved up his vitality for one grand effort in the final round, for he was trying to land a finishing knockout blow. Johnson rushed Kaufman and fired away, landing left hooks to the

stomach, head, and mouth. He sprang at him like a tiger, sending heavy rights and lefts to the head. He forced Kaufman to the ropes and beat him about the face with short lefts and rights that had plenty of steam. They slugged, but Johnson did the greater execution, smashing Al on the body with both hands.

However, Kaufman took it all well, and then Johnson slowed down. One writer opined that either Johnson was not in condition to finish him or he was a very poor hitter for a big fellow. Perhaps Kaufman simply was that tough. After all, he had been stopped only once, early in his career, and even then it wasn't until the 17th round.

Johnson rested for a bit, played defense, and then shot in a jab. Kaufman came back with a left. He landed a solid right on the ribs, and in a clinch reached the ear with a right. The referee split them apart. Al landed another right on the ribs. They clinched again and Jack kept Al's head tossing with right uppercuts. Kaufman kept smashing at the ribs.

Overall, Johnson was still scoring three to one. Just before the close of the round, Johnson sent in another volley of body blows. They were mixing it up when the gong clanged. There was a scattered cheer for Kaufman because he had lasted the distance and still seemed strong.

All of the local reports unanimously agreed that Johnson had won easily, winning every round. Kaufman was no match. He left the arena with a bloody mouth and nose. Johnson was as unmarked when he left as when he entered the arena.

What observers were not sure about was whether Johnson had carried Kaufman or just was not able to knock him out. Various interpretations proliferated. Of those who thought he could not knock him out, some believed Kaufman was too tough to be stopped in a short period of time, while others thought Johnson simply did not have much of a knockout punch, or he was not a great finisher in a short fight owing to his cautious, methodical style. Of those who thought he had carried Kaufman, the reasons included: Johnson did not want to risk getting hit or fatigued by trying to stop him, for attacking too much or long involved greater risk of getting hit back, and if he gassed himself trying to finish but failed, he then would be vulnerable; Johnson's history was to open up only when stung or angered, but if not, he was content to win on points; Johnson was in a good mood and just chose to play around in a no-decision bout for which he would be paid regardless of result; Johnson either wanted to leave open the possibility of a rematch, to stimulate interest in other upcoming matches, or to encourage others to fight him.

The *San Francisco Evening Post* said Johnson easily won a tame and uninteresting bout. It was not a fight, but a boxing lesson administered to the awkward Kaufman. The way the clever Johnson loafed and joked with the newspaper men during nearly every round made it seem more like a minstrel show than a fight, which disgusted the fans. Jack appeared to be out of shape, but nevertheless, the fight was one-sided. He was not forced to fight hard. He knew that Kaufman had no chance to beat him, so he played with him. Johnson only tore after Kaufman in the final two rounds.

Despite his efforts, Kaufman could not land solidly on the "dancing, dangling black" any more than one could land a knockout blow on one's own shadow. "The big black man danced before Kaufman's glazed eyes like some giant shadow, which Al tried as vainly to capture as did the little boy who chased the rainbow." During the entire fight, Al landed only four or five good blows, which had no effect.

Bill Delaney seemed heart-broken as he saw the man into whom he had put so much time and effort be picked to pieces. Bill had wanted a longer bout, to be held at a later time. "But younger and less scrupulous men than Delaney induced Kaufman to take a chance with Johnson, cleverest of all heavyweights, in a ten-round exhibition." Delaney said Kaufman would have been the next world champion had he heeded his advice. "Kaufman should have taken his time making a match with Johnson. He is really the only white competitor that the negro has, and I think that if Al had waited for several months he would have won a world's championship for himself."

Johnson hit him where and when he pleased, content to coast. "Johnson simply toyed and played with Kaufman, and there was a general suspicion around the ringside that the giant negro was not trying very hard to put Kaufman away." "On more than one occasion Kaufman's eye took on the glassy stare of a man in deep distress, but on these occasions Johnson would step back and allow Al time for recuperation."

> It was simply an afternoon's play for Johnson. The big negro exchanged pleasantries with the newspaper men and spectators, and was as unconcerned about coming to grief at the hands of Kaufman as though Kaufman were in the next county.

During the bout, the crowd hooted, hissed, and taunted the grinning Johnson. Particularly when he rested, Johnson would talk with all comers. Once fan in the bleachers yelled, "You ain't game! You've got an awful yellow streak, Jack." Johnson retorted, "Mebbe, but they can't find it." Several laughed at the comeback. Jack added, "Nobody has found it yet." Another yelled, "You're a big dub." Johnson chuckled and cleverly responded with, "That may be so, but I'll help spend some of yoah money tonight." To another he said, "I got your $3." Yet another said, "Wait till you meet Jeffries." Jack replied, "Then I'll get some money." Jack was "as playful as a black kitten."

It was noted that Sam Berger had managed to deck Kaufman several times in the 3rd round of their bout (which Al came back to win by KO), yet Johnson could not drop Kaufman even once (although once or twice only the ropes saved Al from going down). He hit Al with open gloves as often as he did with clenched fists. The feeling was that he was a big clever defensive fighter "without much heart and with no very damaging punch." Nearly everyone at ringside said Johnson would be easy pickings for Jeffries.

The *San Francisco Chronicle* was much higher on the champion. Every round was overwhelmingly in Johnson's favor from any point of view. To Kaufman's admirers' disappointment, Johnson actually was the more powerful of the two, as well as being cleverer. Kaufman hardly laid a glove on Johnson, "a marvel of cleverness," who "proved himself the best piece of fighting machinery in the world the way he beat Al Kaufman." Kaufman lasted the distance and still seemed fresh at the end, but that was all that could be said for him.

> [T]here was no element of the game in which Johnson was not his master. He handled the Californian much as one would a child, jabbed at will with his left or sent in thundering lefts to the heart and right uppercut him with such ease that in the minds of many there was a feeling that at any time Johnson might have sent Al down for the count.

The reason why Johnson had not stopped Kaufman was because he waited too long to open up. After the 3rd round and up to the latter part of the 7th round, Johnson deliberately played with Kaufman. He even allowed himself to be backed into a corner, and with his hands stretched down at his sides, he laughingly dared Al to come and get him. When Johnson finally picked up the pace, got serious and tried to end the fight in spectacular fashion in the 8th through 10th rounds, he discovered that Kaufman had more strength left than he had reckoned. Plus, Kaufman was good at surviving. When Al held in close, Johnson said, "Break, Kaufman, break." But Al did not break, and with blood streaming all over his face from the wicked uppercuts, he managed to stay and recover.

In the final round, Johnson relentlessly followed Kaufman around the ring and cut loose forceful blows, looking for a knockout. A volley of lefts and rights sent Kaufman against the ropes and partially through them. But Al came back, and Jack slowed up. At the close, Kaufman fought the best he had in the contest, sending in body punches in the clinches, though they were not strong enough to bother Johnson.

In contrast with the *Evening Post*, the *Chronicle* said the fight pleased the crowd, and was worth watching. The champion's cleverness and coolness with which he blocked the blows, combined with the fact that he rarely missed his own punches was amazing and brought forth admiration. Whether in the clinches or out of them, he beat Kaufman as he pleased. At long range he jabbed the face and brought blood. In the clinches he showed the development of his right uppercut, which experts had claimed he could not use successfully against Kaufman. They were wrong. Johnson dealt many a blow that must have hurt.

Some said Kaufman hurt Johnson in the 7th with body shots. However, Jack did not show it in his appearance or by his actions. He only smiled the more as he held Kaufman off in the clinches and proceeded to trounce him with more lefts.

During the fight, Johnson waved his hand to various friends in the audience, or smiled at his wife, who was seated in a ringside box. She never failed to smile back. He also carried on a rapid-fire repartee with Kaufman's fans; sometimes during the round, and sometimes in the corner.

Johnson was cautious, as always, but not unduly so. Though he waited for Kaufman to come to him, Johnson always was ready to return the blows. He was quick as a flash, with the faculty of making one hand do double duty, starting a left for the body and then quickly transforming it into an uppercut. His confidence showed in his every action.

Kaufman could not hit Johnson, while Johnson could hit him. Kaufman appeared doubly slow when compared to a man of Johnson's great speed. Johnson anticipated his every move and smothered and picked off Al's leads at will, rendering them harmless. Conversely, Johnson landed whatever blow he wanted and wherever he fancied. Jack was very efficient with his efforts, rarely missing.

Some opined that Kaufman would have a chance in a much longer bout. Others said he had no chance at all, regardless of the distance. The *Chronicle* writer agreed with the latter opinion.

> Johnson showed plainly yesterday with what ease he could handle Kaufman. That he did not knock him out may have been due to his cautiousness or the fact that he started too late. However that may be, it is questionable whether Kaufman would have lasted much longer. Unable to hit Johnson, it was apparently only a case of how long his physique would bear him up.

Another *Chronicle* writer said Johnson toyed with Kaufman, making him look like a clumsy plaything, though he played too long to beat him down. At the end, Kaufman was "spilling great gushes of blood from his mouth and the white of his eyes showed ghastly and staring." "It was ape strength and ape cunning against blind stolid courage and endurance." Kaufman could scarcely place a glove on the "alert man-animal before him. The black landed on him at will, making the white man look like a big, befuddled thing, a lumbering automaton. Race prejudice, which is strong in the crowds that see fights, was much in evidence."

The crowd wanted to see Johnson back up, but he never did. "His gorilla arms coiled and recoiled and struck at the mealy white body before him with the speed of a rattlesnake striking."

Johnson, mocking and self-confident, treated Kaufman with contempt, his "wicked grin" never coming off, which upset Al's legion of white followers. The "pitifully helpless" Kaufman could not strike under or above Johnson's "squirming, twisting baboon arms." Al also was puzzled by the rain of blows that showered on him from all directions. Kaufman's chance to land one devastating smashing blow never came.

In the last round, Johnson sprang forward and pounded on Kaufman, who struck back blindly and clung to Johnson tenaciously to save himself from being stopped. "The fight showed that Johnson is wonderfully clever, that he has the strength and the cunning of an ape." Kaufman had strength and courage, but was too slow for Johnson. "In any kind of a contest the alert black man animal is his master."

The *San Francisco Examiner* said the fight "proved that the negro is a marvel at defensive work and that he is peculiarly effective with punches for which he might almost claim a patent." Johnson "assuredly gave an exhibition of avoidance that was a treat to witness." His best blow was his right uppercut, which was a damaging punch and almost impossible to avoid. He also had wonderful knowledge of timing and distance. The only criticism of Johnson was that he lacked a knockout punch. Still, "One thing that Johnson made clear is that he is stronger in the arm than Kaufman, the blacksmith. This was shown in one clinch after another, for Johnson bent and twisted Al whichever way he wished." Johnson was a lot stronger than folks realized.

Although a large number of spectators believed that Johnson purposely allowed Kaufman to last the distance, W. W. Naughton did not believe that. "The trouble with Johnson is he does everything so easily that it looks as though he could accomplish a great deal more." Although there was no doubt that he stalled in some rounds, either because he was pacing himself or because he was cautious about getting hit, he still administered punishment throughout. "It may have been that some of those raps in the ribs that Kaufman gave him warned Johnson to steady himself and think it over, and it may simply have been the promptings of the Johnson temperament." He wasted time in some of the rounds, but tried hard to stop Kaufman in the last two rounds, though by then he was a bit fatigued.

Kaufman was game. Even when beaten back to the ropes, he would go after Johnson again. Al landed a number of left jabs and connected with his right to the ribs. He was cheered whenever he scored cleanly, but there never was what one might call a thoroughly solid smash. "It might have been different if Johnson had not been such an adept at twitching his head or his body away at the critical moment."

The *San Francisco Call* said Johnson played with the giant California blacksmith and slowed up when it was time to finish him off. Johnson lived up to his past record as a nonaggressive performer who generally went the distance and won on points. Regardless, it was a one-man fight. "Repeat the name of Johnson for 10 rounds, with a little additional emphasis and force in the third, sixth and tenth, and you have the story of the battle." Kaufman was entitled to some credit for lasting the distance, "but none of us know whether or not the same Jack willed it this way." In general, Johnson's performance was lauded.

> The black man gave an exhibition of boxing and clean hitting that fairly opened the eyes of every spectator. No cat ever played more skillfully or more successfully with a tiny mouse than did he with

Kaufman. He never lost his famous golden smile. ... Apparently he never breathed heavily.

Throughout, Johnson landed his right uppercut, his best blow, with stinging effect. Al never could block it. Jack had a knack for pinning him down with his left and then bringing up his right. These jolty blows rocked Kaufman and robbed him of much of his fighting spirit.

Though Kaufman managed to weather the storm, "he failed in his effort to convince the fans that he was the tearing, dauntless, game fighter that the fans had long considered him." He was more dogged than game. Johnson made him more cautious than usual. Al stayed back, content to wait, seeming half frightened. The crowd called for him to wade in, but he kept his distance and took his medicine anyway. Perhaps he did not like those right uppercuts that Johnson landed when he did get close, or he was afraid of running into blows as he advanced. In the clinches, Johnson would hit him with the right uppercut, and then shove him away and swing right and left on the jaw. Kaufman scarcely ever returned the blows, and when he did, he rarely landed. From the outside, Kaufman could not block Johnson's left at all. "Kaufman had no more chance of blocking one of Johnson's lefts than a turtle has of running down a Bakersfield jack rabbit."

Johnson had proven his dominance over all other active heavyweights. "The fight goes to show that Jeffries is the only man who has any license to make a legitimate showing against Johnson." The only other possible exception was Sam Langford, but he was black, and the white population did not want to see the title go from one black man to another. "The San Francisco fans should raise the Jeffries cry louder than ever now, that is if they want to see a man in the ring who is capable of making the black champion extend himself."

The only criticism of Johnson was that he would "never make a great or a spectacular fighter, simply because he can not summon up enough courage or spirit to go in and finish his man when he has him on his way." He possibly could have put on the finishing touches as early as the 3rd round, but was content to just keep far ahead on points.

The *San Francisco Bulletin* said Johnson "so clearly demonstrated that he is Al's master at every point of the game of fisticuffs that it is doubtful if the men will ever again clash in the ring." It was hopeless for the obviously outclassed Kaufman, who would have to show marvelous improvement to justify a re-match. "It was child's play for the smoke and Kaufman can thank his lucky stars that Johnson was in a good humor and fought under wraps." A decision was not necessary. "No man with good common sense...would have conceded Kaufman a look-in at any stage of the game." Since last seen in the San Francisco area, Jack Johnson had "improved to a remarkable degree."

Kaufman did not land half a dozen clean punches. Those that he did land only had the effect of stirring Johnson to action, sending in a torrent of blows to the face and body that made Kaufman wince and cover. At the end, Kaufman was bleeding and sore from the terrific pummeling, while Johnson was unmarked and unhurt. "And at that the big dinge did not open up and show his true speed more than twice or thrice in the contest. Most of the time he stood half-crouching in the center of the ring, daring Kaufman to come to him, and laughing derisively at the latter's attempts to land a blow."

Occasionally Johnson approached Kaufman with outstretched arms, placing them on his shoulders, and then he would drive cruel right and left swings to the face and body. These blows, along with his famous right uppercut and short one-two to the mouth, were Jack's main stock in trade, developed to their highest efficiency.

From the start of the fight to the final gong, Johnson toyed with the ex-blacksmith, punished him when he wanted to, carried him when he chose, danced away from his lunges, wrestled him around at his pleasure, and jeered and leered whenever Kaufman landed a punch or missed one.

Johnson started with a bewildering volley of blows, blocked all of Al's leads, and responded by halting him with rebuking wallops to his face and body. Within two minutes, a torrential stream of blood flowed from Kaufman's mouth, which never stopped. Kaufman vainly hunted for an opening. Like a cat, Johnson watched him, brushed aside heavy rips aimed at his stomach, and countered hard with both hands.

Successive rounds were for the most part a repetition of the start. Johnson pounded and jabbed away at the mouth and body, punishing Kaufman severely and laughing at his attempts to retaliate.

Johnson was criticized for smiling and laughing at his foe. "This grinning and grimacing, by the way, will gain Johnson little save public opprobrium and is certainly an undignified exhibition for a champion. The sooner he cuts it out the better it will be for himself and the game."

Johnson also was censured for his waiting tactics, "which makes the contests in which he appears seem slow and uninteresting. The public does not pay to see a fighter stand in the center of the ring and look pretty." Of course, the *Bulletin* granted that Johnson should not be condemned for fighting according to his own ideas, which were effective. But it noted that he would have been more popular if he had been more aggressive and not inclined to smile at and taunt his opponents.

> Outside of these petty criticisms Johnson seemed to have everything. He beat Kaufman to every punch, blocked those which came near landing, ducked away from the few that passed his guard, and sent myriads of lightning-like punches into his adversary from every possible angle. Even then he did not seem to be half trying, and the writer firmly believes that he could have knocked Kaufman out if he had cared to. As it was, the latter was in a bad way at the conclusion of the bout, and whatever he received as his 'bit' could hardly repay him for the punishment he received.

The "gorilla" Johnson gave "the lion" Kaufman the drubbing of his life. Respect for Johnson's abilities had risen.

> To be sure, the white race still has another lion up its sleeve and is by no means ready to admit that the tawny one from Texas can whip him. But after yesterday's exhibition the consensus of opinion is that Jeffries, if he ever does decide to fight, will have one of the toughest arguments of his career before he puts Jack Johnson to the mat. In short, the pride of the fistic world will have to be in top-notch condition and use every ounce of strength and gray matter to subdue the black champion and it is freely predicted that the battle will be one of the milestones in the history of the American prize-ring. Johnson demonstrated, beyond all question of doubt, that he is the greatest heavyweight exponent of the fisticuffs now before the public, and that it will take a wonderful fighter to beat him down.

Regardless, the *Bulletin* opined that Kaufman still was a factor in the division and could beat a lot of top fighters. Just because Johnson beat him did not mean that Al wasn't a very good fighter. "Any man who thinks he has a chance with Al because of his showing against Johnson would do well to encase himself in armor-plate before entering the ring. Otherwise he may be carried out on a stretcher a few minutes later."

After the contest, Referee Eddie Smith told the newsmen that Johnson was the clear winner, for he had outboxed Kaufman in every round. That would be the accepted verdict throughout the sporting world. Smith said,

> Jack Johnson certainly demonstrated beyond any shadow of a doubt that he is one of the cleverest boxers we have seen in the ring during the last ten years. At all times he had the better of Kaufman and was robbed of a knockout only by the wonderful assimilating powers of the big blacksmith. Kaufman displayed great pluck and endurance, for he was punished more severely around the body than perhaps many thought.
>
> In the seventh and ninth rounds Kaufman showed best. In these rounds he obeyed the coaching of his seconds and tried to take the lead from the clever negro. Johnson was either tired, or he laid off in these rounds, for he contented himself with trying to block the punches hurled at him by the challenger and seldom tried to hit back. Kaufman in these rounds landed several times to the body with telling effect, but his punches to the head did little harm, owing to the fact that Johnson always moved his head with the punch just as a ball player catches a ball.
>
> In the sixth and tenth rounds Johnson tried hardest to finish his man. This can especially be said of the tenth, when during the first two minutes of the going he tried every punch at his command, but could not land solidly. Johnson tired the last minute and Kaufman

came at him and finished the round on the aggressive. Whether Johnson could have finished Kaufman had he been more aggressive, or whether Kaufman could have shown better in a long fight still remains to be seen, but Johnson had all the better of the ten rounds fought yesterday. Johnson's most effective punch was the right uppercut, with which he beat Tommy Burns. He time and again pulled Kaufman into it, and with it first started the blood coming from Kaufman's nose and mouth.

Smith declared that Kaufman had hurt Johnson a few times with his body blows, and also said that Kaufman was coming on strong at the end. The *Bulletin* opined that he was correct in his latter assertion, but was not sure about the first claim, feeling that if Johnson was hurt at all, it was slight. Either way, afterward, Johnson paid Kaufman a compliment, saying, "He was a better boy than I thought he was; but I fought better than I thought I would."

Johnson said,

Kaufman is a big, tough fellow and is a hard man for any one to beat, but I would like to fight him over a longer distance. I didn't do any too much training for this match, but he didn't bother me. I thought I had him a couple of times, but he always came back fresh. I found Kaufman a tougher chap than Tommy Burns and he can beat a whole lot of them in the heavyweight division. I was too clever for him, that's why he hardly laid a glove on me.

Johnson also was quoted as saying,

Kaufman is a big, strong fellow and can take a world of punishment. I hit him many hard blows, but he took them and showed that he is game. Why, he can whip nearly all those big fellows. Why, he can beat Tommy Burns any time. Kaufman is a tough fellow and it will take a great fighter to beat him. He is game and can hit hard. They said I would back up. Well, did any one see me back up? I forced the fighting throughout. If the fight was longer I think I could have finished him. I am willing to fight Kaufman 45 rounds, or any distance. I believe I could have knocked him out in a longer battle. I will go to San Jose tomorrow, where I have a theatrical engagement. Then I will go to Los Angeles, where I am matched to fight Barry. I expect to do my training for the Barry fight here.

Johnson said Kaufman was the toughest man he had ever met, much tougher than expected, and that no one could knock him out in 10 rounds.

Al Kaufman said the distance was too short, that he could not properly warm up and get started in a mere 10 rounds with such a clever big man as Johnson. One reporter responded that indeed, Al never did get started. Kaufman wanted to fight Johnson in a longer bout, one of at least 45 rounds, and felt sure that he would win by knockout. "I can't get started in ten rounds. That was my trouble. Johnson is certainly a clever boxer, but he hasn't got the punch. He didn't hurt me and he never can hurt me. I want to get at him over the long route, then I will show who is champion of the world."

Kaufman also was quoted as saying,

> I am now convinced that I made a mistake in taking Johnson on for 10 rounds. I did not get started until the eighth round, and I certainly need a long fight to show what I can do. Johnson is so clever, a man can not make an impression against him in a battle of short duration. He covers up so well and is so fast that a man can not begin to slow him down in 10 rounds. In the eighth round I was beginning to open up and was just going along well. Johnson hit me often but I was never in danger. His most effective blow was a right uppercut, which he delivered when we were clinched, or at close range. These blows did not stagger me; they merely cut my lip. I hope I can get another chance with Johnson in a 45 round contest, and I believe that I could defeat him in a long battle, as I would have a chance to slow him up.

The *Bulletin* claimed that contrary to reports that the show generated $11,000; allegedly only $7,209 was taken in, of which Johnson earned 40%, or $2,883, Kaufman 25%, or $1,803, and Coffroth 35%, or $2,623. The gallery was well-filled, but the reserved seats, especially those at $3 and $5, were not purchased as eagerly. There was little or no ticket scalping, Coffroth having arranged his sale of seats in a way that spectators were not able to purchase a considerable number of seats at once. However, the *Bulletin's* claims seem inconsistent with the reports of a big crowd. Someone was wrong in their accounting.

The *Chronicle* said the reported Kaufman fight receipts of $11,224 were correct, within several hundred dollars of the box office statement. If Johnson was to earn 40% of the gate as reported, then he made $4,489.60 for 10 rounds of work.[161]

Promoter Tom McCarey, who had scheduled a Johnson vs. Jim Barry bout for September 20 in Los Angeles, called it off. He said that Barry's health would not permit him to appear on that date. Jim had not passed the physical exam.

The news that the Jim Barry fight was off came within hours of Johnson's decisive victory over Kaufman. Many noted the interesting timing of the cancellation, which led sports to believe that the real truth was that McCarey had decided that Barry would be led to slaughter should he fight Johnson, and so he called it off. Some reported that before the Kaufman fight, McCarey had said to friends that if after seeing Johnson in action, he saw that Barry would have little chance to make a showing, he might cancel the bout.

The *Bulletin* comically opined that Barry and McCarey had developed a case of "tonsillitis Africanus."

---

[161] *San Francisco Chronicle*, September 11, 1909.

It is strange how general is this 'tonsillitis Africanus' in the fistic world. Johnson, Langford, Young Peter Jackson and a few other chocolate and coal-colored bruisers seem to be human generators of throat trouble. Let one of them get a match with a white slugger and immediately the latter feels a tickling in his throat. ... Sometimes this condition is even transmitted to the promoter.

McCarey believed that once Jeffries returned from Europe that he would sign to fight Johnson, and that either he or Coffroth would promote the bout in California. Tom considered Johnson "to be one of the greatest - if not the greatest – heavyweights that ever donned a glove." He further said,

Johnson is the ideal of a defensive boxer and I have yet to see him opposed to a man whom he could not beat under double wraps. He has lost one or two decisions on account of his lack of aggressiveness, but when he harnesses up with Jeffries and realizes that he has to go the limit to win, you can mark my words that there will be all kinds of fur and feathers flying.

McCarey said the Kaufman fight was a joke, matching herculean cleverness against brawn and stout-heartedness, but Kaufman was outclassed so clearly that it looked almost pitiful.

McCarey also said that if he could obtain Johnson's word of honor that he would extend himself against Ketchel, he would wager that Jack would knock out Stan within 5 rounds. However, Johnson rarely extended himself, and usually won however he saw fit.[162]

In an interview from New York, Stanley Ketchel said,

I do not expect to penetrate Johnson's wonderful defense in the first few rounds, but I propose to weaken him with attacks on the body until he is ready to lower his guard. ... There is no doubt that I will be the champion pugilist in a short time and that Jeffries will be spared the ignominy which he dreads so much in meeting a negro. ...

Yes, I have taken on a lot of weight. It's fighting weight. ... I can't make the middleweight limit without getting weak. I weigh from 182 to 185 pounds stripped now, and I need that weight to have my full strength. ...

I'd never quit. As long as I could get on my feet I'd get up and turn my face to the enemy if I knew the next blow was going to kill me.

Some said that Stan was exaggerating his weight, that he actually weighed closer to 170 pounds.

Regarding the heavyweight champion, Ketchel said,

Johnson is a big man. Before he was champion he always fought in the same style. Now he'll have to change. All he had to do in other

[162] *San Francisco Bulletin*, September 11, 1909.

fights was stand off and set himself on his big flat feet and catch you coming. He was mighty clever at that. I'll make him come to me, and when we meet I'll have at least an even chance. ...

Johnson is a good-natured sort of a big coon. I always liked him pretty well. You can't blame him for the things he has done. For years he was the under dog, and had to take the worst of everything. He fought his way up in spite of everybody, and now he's champion it would be strange if he didn't take his revenge. Of course, he does a lot of crazy things, but what should you expect? He's just a great big uneducated coon come into a lot of money and a sort of popularity, and he's lost his head a little.

Regarding Langford, Ketchel said,

He's slow. Langford is a dangerous man in the first round or two. Sam is a hard hitter, and like all negroes, he's a great man when he's winning. I'll take the heart out of him. ... I'll hit Langford whenever I want to. We'll try that out right from the start, and see who weathers the storm. I have as much endurance as he has – perhaps more. Langford has always fought men who were afraid of him. I'm not. That helps. ... I know I can drop any man I hit on the right spot, no matter how big he is. I figure Langford as being easy to hit.[163]

Experts agreed that Johnson was a "wonderfully improved fighter." Some said he had improved at least 50% since last seen in San Francisco. Although he remained cautious and still possessed the "hesitancy that has characterized his work and that comes after a flash of brilliancy against an opponent," he "has more confidence."

Most observers agreed that he would give Jeffries a hard tussle, and that Jeff would have his work cut out for him. "Many of those who saw the [Kaufman] fight are convinced that Jeffries in his best days would have had work with Johnson."

However, opinion was divided regarding whether Johnson extended himself against Kaufman, so far as his punch was concerned. "If the black used the best punch at his command against Al Kaufman, there is no question but that he needs to improve to beat down Jim Jeffries, but at the same time there are a number of close observers who believe that the negro was under wraps and did not give Kaufman the best he could."[164]

Neither O'Brien, nor Ross, nor Kaufman had impressed newspaper reporters or the public sufficiently to garner any momentum for lengthier title challenges.

---

[163] *San Francisco Bulletin*, September 11, 1909. Stan also said he hurt both of his hands in the Papke fight. After the Kaufman bout, many of Ketchel's friends feared that he would receive a severe beating, and wanted him to avoid the champ.

[164] *San Francisco Chronicle, Philadelphia Evening Bulletin*, September 11, 1909.

On September 10, Johnson and George Little went to San Jose to fulfill a three-night theatrical engagement there.

A few days after the fight, W. W. Naughton said that those who railed at Johnson because he did not fight like a whirlwind in every round had gotten over their ill humor and were "now freely admitting that the champion is the marvel of the age in the boxing line even if he does fool away much valuable time when he is in action." One had to take Johnson as he found him. He always was erratic, and it seemed hopeless to get him to change his style. "When he boxed George Gardner in this city he began to loaf just as soon as he had established a fairly strong lead. With Marvin Hart he dominated the white man for a few rounds and then loitered so long that he lost the decision." His local bouts with Ferguson and McVey were fairly dull as well. "He slows or quickens as the whim seizes him and he defends his tactics by saying that he usually brings the decision away with him."

Johnson explained and argued,

> I came out of the Kaufman go without a scratch or a bruise and I left the other man pretty badly punched up, didn't I? What more do they expect? I don't advertise to kill a man every time I enter the ring. I have lots of fights to look forward to and I have to keep my hands in good shape and protect the title I have gained in the face of greater difficulties than any man deserving of the championship ever encountered. Those who blamed me for using my cleverness to my own advantage would be the first to howl with joy if I blundered and was knocked over by some lumbering opponent. I win my fights and I intend to win them my own way. There is no complaint when a favorite in a horserace comes home eased up half a length ahead of the next best, is there? Those who handle him know there will be other races on other days and the nag isn't asked to burst a blood vessel when there is no occasion for it. And on top of all this I'll tell you something. Knocking Kaufman out isn't as easy as it may look.

Naughton said that as a rule, Johnson was not the best puncher. Ironically though, unlike most other clever men, Johnson actually was more offensive on the inside than on the outside. At long range, he mostly was cautious and defensive. When up close, Johnson would show his great arm and shoulder strength as he twisted his adversary about and disentangled his right for uppercutting. "And my! What a punishing soak it is. It may fall 40 per cent short in the force that generally accompanies a knockout blow, but in a long fight it would eventually subdue a behemoth like Jeffries, even."

Despite his faults of omission, "Johnson is now regarded by the sporting public as a real champion. It is felt that no one in the lists at present can conquer him, and our thoughts turn to Jeffries more than ever. The alfalfa baron is our only dependence." However, as a general rule, experience had shown that fighters on the comeback performed in a "desultory manner."

Sam Berger said that Jeffries would require another six months at least to be prepared properly for a Johnson fight.

Jeff's father did not want him to take the Johnson fight. The Reverend Alexis Jeffries said, "If my son should ever fight Jack Johnson, I would be tempted to disown him." Of course, Mr. Jeffries had never wanted his son to box in the first place, feeling that the sport was devilment. But implicit in his statement that he might disown his son if he fought Johnson was the abhorrence at the thought of his son engaging in a mixed-race championship fight.[165]

The black-owned *New York Age* said the Kaufman bout proved that Johnson was a great and wise ring general who could whip any man in the ring, including Jeffries. "One thing about him is that he has made up his mind to fight according to his own ideas and not in the manner ofttimes desired by the white writers and the public." Johnson had Kaufman at his mercy, and with other important matches on the horizon, took no chances of injuring his hands or exposing himself and getting caught with something big. It was not his job to win by knockout, but not to lose the title, for if he did lose his crown, he would not be given the chance to win it back.[166]

---

[165] *San Francisco Examiner*, September 12, 1909.
[166] *New York Age*, September 16, 1909.

CHAPTER 6

Stanley Ketchel

Jack Johnson's next scheduled championship bout was set to be held in mid-October 1909 against world middleweight champion Stanley Ketchel.

Known as the Michigan Assassin, the 23-year-old Ketchel originally was from Grand Rapids, Michigan. Of Polish descent, his birth name was Stanislaus Kiecal. A pro since 1903, he had nearly 50 career victories to his credit. His fights included: 1905 KO12 and KO11 Jerry McCarthy; 1906 KO7 Kid Fredericks; 1907 D20, KO32, and W20 Joe Thomas; 1908 KO1 Mike "Twin" Sullivan, KO20 Jack "Twin" Sullivan, W10 Billy Papke, KO3 Hugo Kelly, KO2 Joe Thomas, LKOby12 and KO11 Billy Papke; 1909 WND10 Jack O'Brien, WND6 Kid Hubert, KO4 Tony Caponi, KO3 Jack O'Brien, and W20 Billy Papke.

As of mid-September 1909, promoter Jim Coffroth said Ketchel had to come to San Francisco by September 21 or the fight would be called off. He needed the fighters to be present locally in their training camps for at least three weeks in order to promote the bout adequately and arouse local public interest.

Coffroth was upset at Ketchel's manager Willis Britt for making the interim Langford match. He thought such a fight should not have been made until after the Johnson fight. "Anyone with a grain of sense must admit that a September 17th date in New York and an October 12th date in San Francisco are things which tread on one another's heels."

Britt asked for a postponement of the Johnson fight from October 12 to October 23. Coffroth was willing, but Johnson refused, alleging that he had arranged to travel to New York shortly after October 12 for theatrical engagements there. All parties had signed a contract agreeing to October 12, and Britt had put up a $5,000 forfeit and side-bet guaranteeing Ketchel's performance on that date, so Johnson had the superior position.

Regardless, there was some doubt about whether Ketchel-Langford would happen. New York Governor Charles Hughes (who defeated newspaper magnate William Randolph Hearst in the 1906 election) did not look upon the battle with favorable eyes. "Already there is a strong suspicion that Mr. Hughes may step in and prevent the fight."[167]

With "lawyer-like volubility," Johnson went to Coffroth to convince him not to call off the fight. Johnson noted that when he had put up $5,000 to bind a match, the managers of Langford, Kaufman, and Ketchel all covered it. At Coffroth's request, Ketchel was chosen, which caused some to roast Johnson for selecting a small man. However, Coffroth thought the Ketchel

[167] *San Francisco Examiner, San Francisco Evening Post*, September 14, 1909.

bout would be the most lucrative financially, so Johnson agreed to fight him. Jack said,

> You know, Mr. Coffroth, I entered into a contract with you and Britt, representing Ketchel, in New York. October 12th was named as the date. ... I have kept the date in view, and have made all my arrangements to suit you and Ketchel. ... It is true you have no forfeit up to bind your side of the agreement, and the principal reason is that I considered your reputation for square dealing a sufficient bond.

Johnson wanted to make sure that Coffroth did not cancel the fight just because Ketchel had not arrived by a certain date. "I think, in fairness to me; and in consideration for the way I have trusted you, you should go ahead with the match." Coffroth agreed that Johnson had made a good case, and said that as far as he was concerned, the match was still on.

Johnson selected new training quarters at the Seal Rock Hotel, near Ocean Beach. Barney Furey/Fury would assist him as trainer.

In New York, acting on the district attorney's advice, the police commissioner declared that the Ketchel-Langford bout could not be held. Governor Hughes was the real reason the bout was stopped. He had wired the police commissioner, district attorney, and sheriff, informing them that it was their duty to see to it that the law was not violated. Clearly, he wanted the mixed-race bout canceled. The fight was off.

Britt said Ketchel was in the best shape of his career, and surely would have beaten Langford. Instead, they would leave for San Francisco to continue preparations for the Johnson bout.[168]

Ketchel was upset by the Langford match cancellation. He said, "I would have whipped Langford easily, and am sorely disappointed, because we had a hard time bringing Langford to terms. ... I wanted to give him a good beating before I whipped Johnson, so that with Johnson, I would have cleaned up the entire circuit of negro fighters."[169]

From Carlsbad, Jim Jeffries said that as soon as he returned to the U.S. he would sign to fight Johnson. "I am more confident than ever that I will be able to beat the big tar baby."[170]

Sam Berger said Jeffries would fight Johnson "more to uphold the precedence of the Caucasian, and wipe out some personal insults that the negro has heaped upon him, than for the money that will be in the fight." Continuing, Sam said,

> Jeff never wanted to lick anyone so badly in all his life as he wants to lick this big tallow smoke. You see, Jim has a personal grudge against Johnson, and he wants to clean up this score. The negro has taken

---

[168] *San Francisco Evening Post*, September 16, 1909; *San Francisco Examiner*, September 16, 17, 1909. Governor Hughes would later become a U.S. Supreme Court justice.
[169] *San Francisco Evening Post*, September 17, 1909.
[170] *San Francisco Evening Post*, September 14, 1909.

every occasion to belittle the big fellow, and this has made the alfalfa man as sore as a boiled owl on the negro. There is absolutely no doubt that Jeffries will fight. ... The big fellow doesn't know what the word 'insincerity' means. ... Jeffries was never a bull-con artist. He was not and is not like Tommy Burns and that sort, who squeeze every penny out of the game that they can get.

Berger said Jeff was a man of his word, not just a talker, and if Jeff said he was going to fight, then one could bank on it. Sam said Jeff was training hard and was perfect physically. "Training is a religion with Jeffries."

When Jeff goes into the ring with Johnson the public can rely on his condition. He will be just as good as he ever was in his entire career. He has taken off a lot of weight. ... So far as cleverness is concerned, I don't see where Johnson has anything on Jim. He is a very fast big fellow. Do you know that there are very few professional sprinters who can beat Jeffries in a hundred-yard dash? Well, that's a fact. He is not flat-footed like Johnson, and he is much speedier on his feet.

Berger said Jeff would beat Johnson because he was aggressive, big, strong, clever, and fast, and Johnson would not be able to withstand his fierce rushes. Johnson could not do with Jeffries what he had done to others. Jeff could manhandle Johnson in the clinches too. He could hit the ordinary fighter on the arms and paralyze him. Plus Jeff could take a punch, never having been down. "To compare Jeffries with Johnson on a mental, moral or physical basis is all rot. Jeff is his superior every way."[171]

After Australia's Hugh McIntosh offered $50,000 for a Johnson-Jeffries match, he told a London correspondent,

Johnson is willing and ready; he has been all along; he has never changed. Oh, yes, I think he is looking after himself all right; you see he cannot afford to lose his title. And Jeffries is going to meet him, but Jeff wants to postpone the day as long as he can. It is not a question of physical fear with him, for Jeffries is absolutely fearless. What he does fear is loss of prestige, and so he will not be soon in the ring until he is absolutely sure is really fit. And it will be a bitter contest. That between Burns and Johnson was bitter enough, but this will be more so. There is the color prejudice, and — and Johnson's talk.

Jeff's theatrical tour had been very successful. He had made $40,000 during a 20-week engagement, and was a huge fan favorite.

Americans will not hear of him being defeated. Listen to the list of things they call Johnson: Nervy Nubian, Big Chocolate, Giant Ethiopian, Scientific Senegambian, Ebony-Hued, Husky, Heaved, Lil

---

[171] *San Francisco Evening Post*, September 16, 1909.

Artha, Tantalizing Texan, Galveston Cyclone, Big Smoke, and Cloudy Clouter.[172]

Jeffries said he was rising every day at 6 a.m. and doing two hours of roadwork. He also did an hour and a half or two hours of gym work. He went to bed every night at 9 p.m.[173]

The *New York Age* noted that Johnson's training length and intensity depended upon how much of a threat he perceived his opponent to be. It advised him to take everyone seriously, for often it was the fighter who was held the cheapest that gave one the most disagreeable surprise party.[174]

Men in the know said Johnson evidently held Ketchel in high regard and had more respect for him than previous foes that year, because he was training hard and not riding around in his automobile as often as usual.

Comparing Ketchel with Johnson, W. W. Naughton said Johnson was bigger in every way, stronger, had a punishing uppercut, and was a talented, tricky boxer on top of it all. Ketchel was a whirlwind finisher and a big puncher. Most said of Stan, "If he ever lands…"[175]

Local San Francisco fans eagerly awaited the arrival of the cowboy pugilist. "With local boxing fans Ketchel is the biggest favorite in the ring today." They knew that he went in to fight hard and all the time, no matter who he was fighting.

According to those who were collecting donations to aid the blind actor Stockwell, Johnson had failed to come through with the $100 that he had promised before the start of the Kaufman fight. Attempts to get him to pay up had failed. They wanted it to be known that he was a welcher, counterfeit philanthropist, and a four-flusher.[176]

Stanley Ketchel and manager Willis Britt

Ketchel promised to give Johnson a trouncing. The *Bulletin* said, "If any one can develop the 'yellow streak' which Johnson is said to possess Ketchel is the man to do it, and he will never let up trying until the

---

[172] *San Francisco Evening Post*, September 18, 1909.

[173] *San Francisco Examiner*, September 20, 1909.

[174] *New York Age*, September 16, 1909.

[175] *San Francisco Examiner*, September 19, 1909.

[176] *San Francisco Evening Post*, September 20, 1909. On September 19, Johnson did his usual morning road work, and in the afternoon, he boxed 6 rounds at the Seal Rock house.

champion has knocked him cold. … If there is one thing in the world the sporting world wants him to do that one thing is to beat Johnson." Although few experts thought Ketchel had much chance to win, nevertheless almost every fight fan wanted to see him try.[177]

On September 20, as usual, Johnson ran 10 miles in the morning, and in the afternoon, he spent 20 minutes on the punching bag and 20 minutes at footwork before sparring 4 rounds with Dave Mills.

Johnson was confident, as always. "Johnson is nothing if not vain of his fighting talents and to hear him talk even Jeffries will give him a small amount of trouble." The champ said,

> I'll take care of this Ketchel man the same as I've taken care of everyone else. There was some talk that I wasn't trained for either O'Brien or Kaufman and that I seemed to be shy of a knockout punch. Well, I'm going to show the San Francisco sports a well-trained champion this trip and I think I'll treat them to a knockout, too.[178]

Latest Photograph of Stanley Ketchel, the Middleweight Champion of the World, Who Is Due to Arrive in San Francisco Some Time Today. The Fans Are Awaiting Ketchel's Arrival With Great Interest.

On September 23, Ketchel, known as the "lion," the "assassin," and the "sensation of the prize ring," arrived in San Francisco. Folks were eager to see Stan train, for he was a "spectacular worker and the longer he works in camp the greater the interest in a fight. Ketchel is the most ambidextrous fellow in the ring today and the most sensational of fighters."[179]

Stan's talkative manager Willis Britt said, "Ketchel weighs 172 pounds now and will give that big shine the fight of his career." Ketchel already was in splendid shape, for he had been training for the Langford fight. Britt discussed Stan's strategy:

---

[177] *San Francisco Bulletin*, September 20, 1909.
[178] *San Francisco Examiner*, September 21, 1909.
[179] *San Francisco Evening Post*, September 22, 24, 1909.

Ketchel will make things lively for Johnson, but he will not throw himself on the spears the way Jim Flynn did. He will fight Johnson the way Walcott fought Joe Choynski. He will crouch and draw Johnson's fire, and then he will just hurl himself at the big negro and smash away for dear life with both hands.

They figured that was the best way to fight him, after having seen Johnson against O'Brien. They saw Johnson struggle to stop O'Brien, but then two weeks later Ketchel easily did away with him. Britt continued, saying, "Ketchel figures that he is Johnson's master. ... I know that it was never in Johnson to knock out a man of Ketchel's caliber in twenty rounds. Tommy Burns was the best that Johnson met, and I, for one, am certain that Burns would be a mark for Ketchel."[180]

On the afternoon of September 24, in the presence of a large crowd, Johnson sparred 2 rounds with Dave Mills and 2 rounds with Joe Lanum.

Although Jim Coffroth was pleased with the attention that the bout was receiving, he wanted to postpone the fight from the 12th to the 23rd. "The Portola week date means at least $10,000 more in the box office." He believed that many folks from places like Los Angeles would attend the fight if the date was changed, so that they could enjoy both the bout and the Portola week celebration. Patrons were not as likely to travel up north twice for two different events, and he did not want to force folks to choose between the two. Coffroth and Britt reasoned that hosting the fight during the Portola week would mean a greater population would be in town, which would mean greater ticket sales. Johnson would benefit too, but continued to insist on the contractually agreed-upon October 12 date.[181]

Willis Britt was great at promoting the fight, making statements on a daily basis. With his usual big talk, he said,

> Why, that big dinge didn't even knock Al Kaufman down, and according to the reports I read of the fight, he hit Kaufman when and where he pleased. Can you imagine Ketchel hitting any one and failing to put them down if he lands properly? Why, if Ketchel lands on that big smoke they'll have to get a smoke consumer to dig up Johnson's remains from the debris. The Lion is going to roar loud in this fight, and I am certainly confident that he will beat Johnson and beat him so thoroughly that Jack will never be heard of again.

The *Evening Post* said Ketchel was the gamest, grittiest, most spectacular two-fisted fighting machine, confident and fearless. "He is a fighter, pure and simple." Ketchel was said to be a vastly more courageous fighter than Johnson, with a daring, slashing style, loving the bombardment of fists.

Johnson's style was much more cautious:

---

[180] *San Francisco Examiner*, September 24, 1909.
[181] *San Francisco Examiner*, September 25, 1909.

As well compare a wharf rat to a Bengal tiger in courage. Yet, what Johnson lacks in courage, he makes up in cunning. Like some ghoulish coyote, Johnson will hang to the flank of a harassed foe until he drops from sheer weariness and then will beat him.

There is nothing, barring finesse and finish, in the boxing of Johnson that can appeal to any one. There is more of the weasel than the lion in the negro.

However, the *Evening Post* also noted that Johnson was much bigger than Ketchel in height, reach, and weight, and the old ring adage was that a good small man rarely beats a good big man, "and even Johnson's worst enemies must admit that the Galveston tar baby is a very good big man."

Lacking heart, Johnson has all the other qualifications of a good fighter. He is without cavil or doubt the most scientific heavyweight now before the public. Johnson is a master of defense. The big dinge does not carry a leaden blow, but he is a ripping puncher, and when he finishes with his opponents he usually has them looking as though they had just completed a six-weeks' course with a sausage grinder.

Were Johnson a game, smashing fighter, he would be one of the best men at any weight that ever entered a ring, for the negro surely knows that little boxing business like some connoisseurs know painting.[182]

The *San Francisco Bulletin* said the "Galveston Shine" inherited ancestral traits which made it hard to fight him and even harder to make him fight. In ancient times, there were battles for supremacy between white nations and the darker ones, but the whites eventually won out. "Nevertheless, they gave us a strenuous tussle for a couple of thousand years, and did not give up until a few adventurous spirits, of the Ketchel and Jeffries order, rolled them over a barrel and packed them off to Africa, where they have resided in more or less quietude ever since." Jack Johnson was said to be an ancestor of the ancient warriors who gave the whites a tough time of it.

[He] has shown the ancestral trait of avoiding punishment. On the other hand, however, he has seemed somewhat loathe to administer it, and up to the present time it is safe to say that Jack has never extended himself, being content to stall along under wraps and take a decision where he might have had a knockout just as well.

[Even against Hart] the big Galveston smoke seemed to be holding something back which he either would not or could not let loose. Critics say he could have knocked out Tawmy Burns in ten rounds and Al Kaufman in five – if he had wanted to.

---

[182] *San Francisco Evening Post*, September 25, 1909.

On September 26 at the Seal Rock House, over 1,500 people paid 25 cents each to watch Johnson train, including Ketchel admirers who felt that Stan had a great chance against "the dinge." They saw Jack box with Joe Lanum, Bob Armstrong, and Dave Mills, showing all of his skill in a very pretty exhibition. Still, one observer who watched Johnson toy with his sparring partners said, "He stalls too much. … Ketchel will never allow him to get away with that waiting game. Stanley is going to tear right after him, and unless Johnson perfects his defense – both of head and body – he will be a gone goose before the tenth round is over."

The *Bulletin* agreed that "Johnson might have to call in some of his reserve forces before the Ketchel battle is over. The Michigan lad is pounding his big sparring partners all over Millett's gymnasium. … Willus Britt is having the hardest sort of a time keeping him supplied with human punching bags." Ketchel had shown improved form and power.

Johnson told the *Bulletin* that he intended to fulfill his promise to purchase $100 in tickets for actor Stockwell.

On the 26th at Millett's, fans who watched Ketchel train "expressed their astonishment at the wonderful condition of the middleweight champion." After his brisk morning run, in the afternoon he punched the ball, skipped rope, played handball, and toyed with the pulley weights. Then he sparred.

Ketchel looked heavier than ever, but was as pliable as rubber, catlike and graceful in action, and showed his usual fire and abundance of vim. He boxed 6 fast and furious rounds with three different men, taking on each one for 2 rounds. Gunboat Smith, the navy champion, was first to spar with him, and he showed a lively display of courage, weathering the rounds in good fashion and putting up an admirable exhibition. Ketchel dropped Al Kreiger in the 1st round with a deadly left shift. Thereafter, Stan eased up on him. Steve O'Connor was pelted for 2 rounds.[183]

On September 27, the crowd enjoyed watching the "lion" Ketchel welt several different sparring partners - Steve O'Connor, Dick Eilers, Oscar Gentry, Kid Wallen, and Charley Miller. Each attempted to box 2 rounds, but each one in turn either was knocked out cold or Ketchel had to back off and take it easy after decking or hurting them. Halfway through the 1st round, Ketchel dropped 230-pound Charley Miller with a left hook to the chin. Miller rose and complained of a sprained ankle. Assistants had to help him out of the ring.

Ketchel had been extremely rough on his sparring partners, which cut their supply short. Some thought that they were not good enough to give him any kind of a challenge. "What Ketchel needs is a sparring mate like Bob Armstrong, some big, clever fellow who boxes a little like Johnson."

That day, after his usual morning run, in the afternoon, before a packed pavilion at the beach, Johnson sparred 4 lively rounds with his principal sparring partner, Dave Mills, "a raw-boned mulatto."

---

[183] *San Francisco Bulletin, San Francisco Evening Post*, September 27, 1909.

Ketchel knocks out Steve O'Connor in sparring

W. W. Naughton said there was no more of a weight difference between Johnson and Ketchel than there was between Jeffries and Sharkey. History had proven that smaller men could give bigger men a tough go of it.[184]

Naughton said he had never seen Johnson work as steadfastly as he was at present. Despite the size difference, Johnson obviously had more respect for Ketchel than for the average opponent.

Johnson said,

> So Ketchel knows how I'll fight through watching the Johnson-Burns pictures and through seeing me in the East with Jack O'Brien. Well, it's a good thing, in a way, as what he thinks he has discovered will give him confidence, and this means that he will fight his best. I have only to repeat what I told them in the East after the fight with O'Brien. I knew that both Ketchel and Kaufman were at the ringside with their eyes bulging out taking in every move I made. I guess I showed Kaufman one or two things that he didn't see when I boxed O'Brien, and I guess Ketchel will say that I kept a few tricks in reserve for him, as well.

---

[184] *San Francisco Evening Post, San Francisco Examiner,* September 28, 1909. Also on September 27, Ketchel did road work in the morning. Before the afternoon sparring, Stan played handball, punched the bag, buffeted the sand-sack and did a lot of shadow boxing.

From Australia, Tommy Burns said he would like to fight Johnson again. He knew that the public would not think he had much of a chance, but he felt that he did not do himself justice in their fight. Tom said,

> If I had let Johnson do some of the leading, there would have been a different story to tell. … I, like a fool, played into his hands. I rushed and rushed, and his superior reach and strength told its tale. I know one thing. Johnson had to go to a hospital the day after the fight. He may not admit it, but two of his ribs were splintered.

Regarding a potential Johnson-Jeffries match, Burns said that if they did meet, "mark my words, Jeffries will be close enough to his old form to beat Johnson."[185]

Initially, Johnson said he would not bet anything on the particular number of rounds that the upcoming bout went. "I am no one or two round fighter. I am going to win and that's good enough for me. I don't want any of that round betting in mine."

Gallery seats sold for $2 each, while the reserved section seats sold for $3 and $5. Box seats sold for $10.

Anyone who had ever seen Ketchel in action knew that he would try all that he could to drop Johnson. Fans wanted to see if Stan could spring one of his surprises. He had the power to do it. They also knew that Ketchel had $5,000 wagered that he would win, showing his confidence.[186]

Jack Welch (or Welsh) was selected to referee the bout. He was Johnson's one and only choice. There was no dissenting voice to his selection, for he was considered capable and honest, and was very popular with fight followers.

On September 29, just before Johnson was about to start his sparring exhibition at the Seal Rock hotel, policemen appeared and informed him that until he had secured a license, which happened to cost $1,200, he could give no further boxing exhibitions when an admission fee was charged.

Johnson immediately

John Arthur Johnson, the Black Cyclops, Who Will Fight Stanley Ketchel at Coffroth's Arena on the Afternoon of Discovery Day, Tuesday, October 12.

---

[185] *San Francisco Examiner*, September 29, 1909.
[186] *San Francisco Evening Post*, September 29, 1909.

jumped into his automobile and drove to Chief Cook's office. Johnson told the police chief that he believed he was being discriminated against, for others had been allowed to take in money at the doors while training, including Ketchel. The chief informed Jack that he would have to secure a license to box if he charged admission. He asked Jack to file an application with the board of supervisors, and said that if he did so, he could continue his sparring bouts temporarily, pending action on the application by the board's police committee.

That day, the champ boxed a 4-round exhibition with Dave Mills, and "showed such undoubted marks of skill as a defensive boxer as to convince the most skeptical that he is a master of the art of boxing." Jack was content to play with "his fellow Senegambian." He caught and blocked every blow with utmost precision and merely laughed at Mills' best attempts to land.

Spider Kelly was impressed, and declared that he could not recall many fighters who could outdo Johnson in defensive skill.

Tom Corbett announced that Johnson was a heavy favorite at 10 to 4 odds. The betting odds that Ketchel would not last 12 full rounds were even. Regardless of the odds, Ketchel was such a terrific and sensational ringman that most everyone wanted to see the fight.[187]

Willis Britt, who loved to talk tough, said that he and Ketchel were firmly convinced that Johnson would be dragged out of the ring by the heels. They thought Johnson did not want to postpone the fight because he did not want to give Stan additional time to train, and was nervous.

On September 30, Ketchel sparred with Gunboat Smith, Kid Lafayette, and Steve O'Connor, and he handled them all neatly.

From Paris, Jim Jeffries said, "As soon as I get to America I want to sit down immediately and sign articles with Johnson. ... I want to get him in the ring with me, and when I do get him there I will give him the trouncing of his life." Jeff also said, "I am the champion of the world. I have everything to lose and nothing to gain. Therefore I won't want to fight for a purse of less than $150,000. ... I am quicker than I ever was and am confident that I can lick Johnson."[188]

Johnson said Jeffries was afraid, and had been for years. Jack would insist on a winner's and loser's end if they fought. He was not about to give Jeff the best of it financially unless Jeffries could defeat him.

> I think he fears me more than any man living. ... I have been chasing Jeffries for six years trying to get a fight with him, and I am still on his trail. ... When he was at his best he could have gotten as much money for fighting me as he can now. He was champion then and he

---

[187] *San Francisco Evening Post, San Francisco Examiner*, September 30, 1909.

[188] *San Francisco Evening Post, San Francisco Examiner*, October 1, 1909.
On October 1, in the morning Ketchel spent an hour on the road, and followed up with an hour in the gymnasium, after which he sparred Steve O'Connor 3 rounds and finished up with Kid Lafayette. Jack Johnson took a rest from training that day, saying the wet weather had prevented him from working. He and Dave Mills would be at it again the next day.

could have demanded 90 per cent of the purse, but I could never drag him inside of the ropes with me. ... He was afraid of me then, and he's more afraid of me now.

Johnson had heard about Jeff's statement that he didn't want Johnson to run out of the match and that he wanted to get Johnson in the ring so he could give him the trouncing of his life. In response, Jack said, "High-handed words, considering the fact that I have been chasing Jeff all around the country seeking the match and practically challenging him. .... I am not yet convinced that he wants a fight with me."

Johnson said the reason he did not want to delay the Ketchel match was because he believed that Britt was looking for a way out of the $5,000 side bet. He claimed that Britt offered his manager George Little (also spelled "Lyttle") $1,500 in gold coins if he would call off the bet.

The champ was confident, as always. "Ketchel is a pretty tough boy, but I feel sure that I will knock him out in less than fifteen rounds. I will weigh about 196 pounds when I enter the ring with Ketchel. ... I was never in better condition in all my life."

Britt countered Johnson's statement by saying that it was Little who remarked that it would be worth about $1,500 for someone to call off the bet. Britt had responded, "Yes, if one thought he was going to lose, but let me tell you that we have no idea of losing." The inflammatory Britt said,

> Ketchel will knock the golden smile from the countenance of that big hippopotamus. Say, on the level, if Johnson was in Africa right now, where he belongs, he would be in a cocoanut throwing competition for the championship of the world with the other baboons of the Jungle Athletic club. That smoke has got a tail a yard long sure, and Ketch will show it to the public. Johnson's got a streak of yellow in him richer and broader than the Chinese war flag.

Britt said Little was just Johnson's messenger and was not even drawing a messenger boy's pay. Britt wanted a postponement because it would mean more money in the house, which meant more money for everyone.

> And I do not understand why Johnson will not agree to a postponement, unless it is that his Simian brain cannot see where it would be to his advantage.

> Johnson's talk about theatrical engagements is all poppy skalum. That dinge couldn't get booked in a nickelodeon after Ketchel gets through with him.

> Stan is going to be in great shape for this match, and he's going to flatten Johnson sure. Why, there's not a chance in a million for Johnson beating Ketch inside of twenty rounds. It ain't in the dinge to do it.

Britt further said, "It's funny to me to hear this big dinge talking about what he is going to do with Ketchel. Steve and myself laughed ourselves sick over the interview in which Johnson declared he would win by a knockout. Why, who has he ever knocked out? … Johnson is scared."

Johnson responded,

> Personally, I don't want the fight during a big celebration. I tried that in Philadelphia and we didn't have the money there should have been in the house. When people come to the Portola festival they are not going to see a fight. … Coffroth and Britt set the date six months ago, and they knew when this Portola festival was scheduled. If they wanted a different date, that was the time to name it.

> I am not afraid of giving Ketchel any more time in which to train. That's child's talk, but it won't stop me. Ketchel and Britt are trying to wriggle out of this side bet, but I'll tell you right now that if there is any trouble over that $5,000 bet, there isn't going to be any fight. I'll pack up my things and go to Europe.[189]

The *Freeman* printed the opinion of ex-middleweight champion and former Jeffries trainer Tommy Ryan, who said Johnson would whip Jeffries:

> Don't think that just because Jeff and myself are on bad terms that I am taking the Johnson side. I honestly believe that the Negro will win. … Johnson is not only as clever as Corbett, but he is a punishing fighter, even if he is not a strictly knockout man. He has one punch that will land Jeff – that uppercut. This is the Negro's one best bet, and he will use it until he finally wears down the big fellow.

> This Johnson is a cool, crafty fighter. He never wastes a punch. He will enter the ring intent on wearing out Jeff, while, on the other hand, Jeff will tear in like a bull. Jeffries has seen his best days, and he will never go the route again. … I look to see Jeff fight himself out in ten rounds, and then go down.[190]

Some thought that Ryan was prejudiced as a result of his personal differences with Jeffries.

Tom Corbett said gamblers were willing to bet even money that Ketchel would last 15 rounds. However, the *San Francisco Chronicle* said betting on rounds in Johnson fights had never been a good proposition.

> He is too uncertain a quantity and too much inclined to take things easy when in the ring. Johnson may never let Ketchel land a decisive blow, but he is naturally timid and will prefer to take no chances that might result in a speedy conclusion of the affair. Ketchel is not to be gainsaid a chance with his remarkable punch and his fearlessness, but that is as far as one can go when the past performances of these two men are considered. Johnson, apparently, is too strong and far too

---

[189] *San Francisco Evening Post, Call, Chronicle, Bulletin*, October 2, 1909.
[190] *Freeman*, October 2, 1909.

clever for his smaller opponent. Be that as it may, it should be a fight worth watching.[191]

The *Call* agreed that although Ketchel was admired for his gameness, fearlessness, grit, and power, a victory for him would be a surprise. Johnson had all of the advantages – height, reach, weight, experience, and defense. Still, Stan "can hit like a trip hammer and he can take a punch if necessary."

Some noted that Ketchel had twice knocked out O'Brien, whereas Johnson had failed to do so, and O'Brien had held his own against the champ. "According to popular belief, Johnson is always afflicted with faintness of heart when under fire, and instead of fighting back he was wont to run for cover in the old days. According to these theories and deductions, it is up to Ketchel to bring out this so called yellow streak." However,

> Johnson's fight with Kaufman last month did more than any other feat he ever performed to convince the fans of this city that he is a great fighter. He certainly showed them practically everything that day. He was fast and clever and more aggressive than he used to be. His blows were so accurate that only two of them went shy of the mark during those 10 rounds. There was class in every move of Johnson's that day.[192]

Johnson drew criticism for his penchant for automobiling, but several noted that his training did not suffer. He was a bear at covering many miles of road work. "Johnson is not a man who replies to criticism in the ordinary manner. He is inclined to be sullen, and makes no attempt to explain things." The champ said, "They think I'm not training. Well, if they notice I am not asking for a postponement. Just let them come and see me box Ketchel, and then they'll know whether I am trained or not."

Although Ketchel had attended several exhibitions of the Johnson-Burns moving pictures, and had seen Johnson box O'Brien live, conversely, Johnson said he had never seen Ketchel fight and did not care to do so. He disagreed with those who said that he could pick up ideas about how to handle Stan by watching him. Jack said,

> Ketchel has never fought a man who fights the way I fight, and that means that Ketchel will have to fight in an entirely different way when he meets me. How then could I have learned anything by seeing him box others? I had a chance to see him fight O'Brien, but I declined to go. … Now I know all this will seem strange because most fighters think it will be of benefit to them to see a man they are going to box in action. Ever since I have been in the ring I have had notions of my own, and I have lived up to them strictly. One of them is that I don't want to see the other fellow until we are face to face

[191] *San Francisco Chronicle*, October 3, 1909.
[192] *San Francisco Call*, October 3, 1909.

with the ropes all 'round us. I can learn more about an opponent in the first round of the fight than I could by seeing him in twenty fights with other men.

In fact, Willus Britt confirmed that Ketchel would fight differently against Johnson. "It is a mistake to think that Ketchel is going to hurl himself at Johnson. He will press Johnson continually, but not in an aimless slam bang way as Burns and Flynn did. Many of the men who have boxed Johnson say that it is next to impossible to get him to lead. Mark my words, Ketchel will make him lead."[193]

On October 3, Ketchel started the day with his usual 10-mile run along San Mateo County's muddy highways. In the afternoon at Millett's, he sparred Steve O'Connor, Kid Lafayette, and Young Sharkey, a new-comer, 3 rounds each. Ketch then pulled and tugged at the gym machinery for about an hour. "His wonderful strength and his ability to hit from most any old position seemed to make a great impression on the big crowd." After finishing up at Colma, Ketchel went over to the Chutes, sparred 6 more rounds, 3 each with Lafayette and O'Connor, and repeated the performance in the evening. The crowds cheered long and loud when they saw his hard blows. That day, in total, he had boxed 21 rounds.

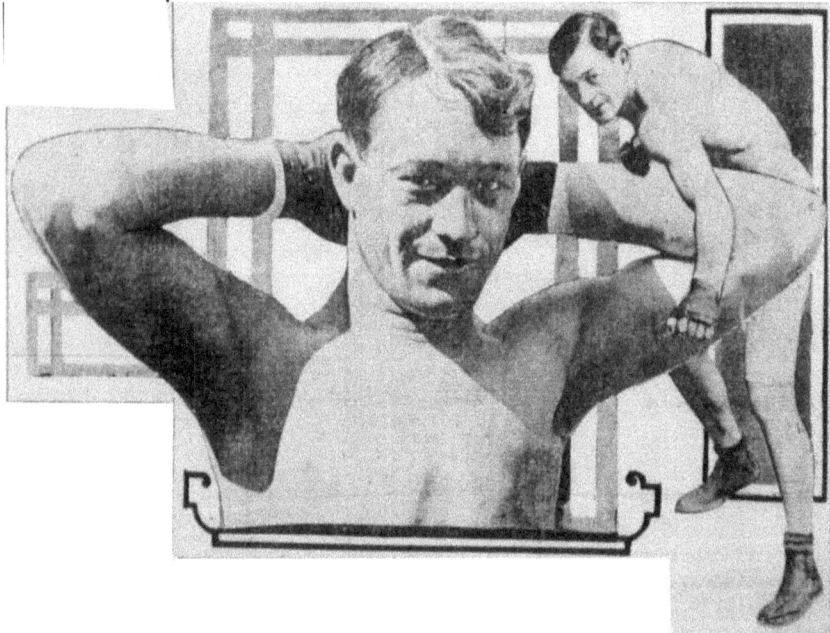

That same day, amateurs Tom O'Neil and Joe Lanum worked 3 rounds each with Johnson, and Dave Mills went 4 more rounds, for a total of 10 rounds. Johnson boxed in his usual classy, careful style. None of the sparring partners were able to lay a glove on the champ, who seemed able to do most anything he pleased with them.

---

[193] *San Francisco Examiner*, October 3, 1909.

George Little said,

> In reply to Britt's statement I will say that I might be a messenger boy for Jack Johnson and I might not be drawing a messenger boy's salary, but I will have the satisfaction of jingling part of that paltry $5,000 side bet.
>
> When a boy, my grandfather used to take me on his knees and talk like this: "George, when you grow up to be a man never buy any hair restorer from a bald headed barber, and never take a broken man's advice."
>
> As for Johnson being in Africa throwing cocoanuts for the championship of the world, when he gets in the ring on October 12 he will land a few on Ketchel's cocoanut that were never there before.

The *Evening Post* opined that Ketchel had no chance whatsoever against Johnson, who could beat him any time he wanted. It would be like betting on a one-legged man in a hundred-yard dash. Yet, fans wanted to see the fight. They knew that "the Lion will fight to the last ditch. He is game, and spectacular, and the fans always pull for this sort of scrapper, even though they give him little chance to win." The *Bulletin* agreed that although few believed Ketchel had a chance to win, most thought it would be a great battle and that the "Michigan Lion" would land some solid blows on the "Galveston Gorilla" before it was over. Johnson remained the 10 to 4 favorite, but there was plenty of money being wagered at even odds on the proposition that Ketch would last 15 rounds.[194]

On October 4, Johnson finally compromised and consented to postpone the fight date by four days, from the 12th to the 16th, the Saturday before the Portola festivities. However, he only agreed because all of the parties signed a contract that day which stated that every other clause in the original contract, including the $5,000 side bet, would otherwise remain the same. Willis Britt signed for Ketchel, Johnson signed for himself, and Coffroth for the club. The parties also decided to take moving pictures of the fight, and a contract was signed with the Miles Brothers to film it.[195]

That day, after Johnson did his morning road work, afternoon gymnasium stunts, and 4 rounds of speedy and clever boxing with Dave Mills, he hopped on the scales, which showed 199 ½ pounds. Johnson was solid muscle and bone, and in top shape. His eyes were clear and his movements catlike and spry. Jack said,

> I never try to hurt any of my sparring partners. I consider it unfair for a champion to take on sparring partners and cuff them about. …
> When I spar I always try to improve myself in some particular and I

---

[194] *San Francisco Call, San Francisco Evening Post,* October 4, 1909; *San Francisco Bulletin,* October 5, 1909.
[195] *San Francisco Chronicle,* October 5, 1909. The fight would take place at 3 p.m.

don't think a man can improve much when he goes whacking away as though he intended to cut down a lot of oak trees. I never let go wild punches, because one is always liable to injure his weapons in such foolish forays, and I don't care to enter into any fight with the handicap of injured mitts. … Tip O'Neill, who boxed with me last Sunday, is quite a boy. Young O'Neill showed me considerable cleverness, and he has a good punch.

James J. Corbett said that although he hoped Ketchel would win, he feared that Johnson was too big and clever for him.

Tommy Ryan said Johnson should not hold Ketchel too lightly, for men like Fitzsimmons and Sharkey had beaten much bigger opponents, and Ketchel had the power to do so as well.

Johnson did not mind Jeff's statement that he was his physical superior, but Jeff's claim that he had it on Johnson in terms of intellect had hurt the feelings of the "heavyweight from Zamboanga," for he took pride in his intelligence. The *Evening Post* quoted Johnson as responding,

> What? Jeffries mah superior in intellect? Dat ain't so. Ah'm a smart niggah, Ah am. Ah know litterchure. Ah know joggafy. Ah knows where New York and Chicago is, and Ah knows 'rithmatic, too. Ah can beat Jeffries in a spellin' match or any form of culture he cares to meet me in. Ah'm a smart niggah.

The *Evening Post* said that six months ago Jeffries was weighing 272 pounds. When he reached Europe his weight was down to 240 pounds, and as of September he was down to 232 pounds.[196]

Willis Britt said, "We are going to make that big smoke do just as much leading as we do. There is an impression that Stanley intends to wade into Johnson the way these other boobs did; well, I only hope the dinge thinks so, for then he will get the surprise of his life." Britt said Stan would land his pile-driving smashes into the body.

Johnson again reiterated his intention to make good on the $100 pledge to Stockwell, though he had not yet done so.[197]

On October 5 at Colma, in his 9 rounds of sparring, Ketchel fought in his usual wade-in, slam-bang, tear-away manner. He knocked out Lafayette in 1 round. He then boxed Steve O'Connor 4 rounds, and though Steve was a big fellow, Stan toyed with and roughed him, landing slashing blows that made O'Connor wobble. Britt had to cut two rounds short to prevent a knockout. The very large Charles Miller also boxed 4 rounds.

Ketchel appeared to weigh at least 175 pounds. "Camp information has it that Stanley weighs more than 180, but then camp information is seldom to be given full credence." Britt said Stan was big and strong enough to beat

---

[196] *San Francisco Evening Post*, October 5, 1909. Jeffries was traveling with his little German wife, who was a native of Frankfort-on-the-Main.
[197] *San Francisco Bulletin*, October 5, 1909.

any man alive. When Johnson got hit, he would go out. "We're going to win sure."

Johnson took a day off. He said he was in top condition already, and feared going stale. Instead, he went to take a look at U.S. President William Taft, who was in town giving speeches. Jack then strolled about town a bit.

However, another local source said Johnson sparred 3 rounds each with Dave Mills and Bob Armstrong.

Jeffries, who had arrived in London from Paris, said, "If Johnson is half as ready as I am for the fight it won't be long after my return to America before we are at it." Jeff also declared, "I am going back to clinch a match with that big flat-footed bluffer. I know that Johnson does not want any of my game, but I am convinced that public opinion will force him to fight."

Johnson replied, "Just what I want, and the sooner Jeff gets here and signs up the better he will please me and the public."

George Little added, "Jack has been trying to get Jeff in the ring for six years, and while the prospects now look fairly bright it is by no means certain that Jeff will not find some way to get out of the match."

Jim Coffroth said it was looking as if the arena would be packed on the 16th. He regretted not setting the seat prices even higher.

> However, what will be lost at the gate will be made on the moving pictures. I have practically closed with Hammerstein's in New York to display the films there the first week after the fight. All the large eastern cities are rapidly falling into line, and it looks as though the pictures will go like wildfire all over the United States.[198]

Johnson, Ketchel, and Coffroth agreed to pay outright the entire cost of filming the fight, which meant that they would reap all of the profits. Johnson secured the greatest share at 40%, while Ketchel and Coffroth each would earn 30%. "If Johnson should win in a round or two, the pictures will be worth little, but if it is a sensational match, or by any hook or crook Ketchel would be returned the winner, there would be barrels of money for the men concerned."

The film expenses were significant. The films cost 50 cents a foot. A round required 200 feet of film. Hence, about 4,000 feet or $2,000 would be needed if the fight went the 20-round limit. It also cost another 15 cents a foot to develop the positive, which meant $600 more. There would be another 1,000 feet of film used for the scenes depicted at the training camps and prior to the big fight in the arena (another $650). Hence, the total investment might be in excess of $3,000, and possibly a set of pictures that would not be valuable if folks were not interested in seeing the fight on film afterwards. Hence, the more interesting the bout, the more valuable the films would be to the investors, including Johnson, who stood to earn the most money.

Johnson appeared to be in better shape than when he fought Kaufman. He had taken off all of his excess poundage. He had been doing more road

---

[198] *San Francisco Chronicle, San Francisco Evening Post, San Francisco Call, San Francisco Bulletin,* October 6, 1909.

work than usual. On October 6, he ran 10 miles and boxed 4 rounds with Dave Mills, "the chocolate colored negro." Jack looked fast and catlike.

On the 6th, Ketchel boxed 3 rounds each with Steve O'Connor, Charlie Miller, and Johnny Loftus, for a total of 9 rounds. Stan showed his usual dash and vim and had all of them wobbling, save Loftus, who managed to stay away. Britt said Ketchel was getting heavier and stronger every day.

Unlike Ketchel, who was rough with his sparring partners, Johnson had been kind and gentle with them, not attempting to hurt them. "The big negro is very easy with his sparring mates. He does not slug them or batter them up like Ketchel does, and working with Johnson is soft work compared to boxing with the ordinary pugilist." Jack kept them coming at him and softened his blows, though he still easily outboxed them.

The *Call* said Johnson was forced to ease up on his sparring partners because he

Jack Johnson in a Favorite Fighting Pose and in His Automobile Outfit. Johnson Posed for These Pictures Especially for The Evening Post.

did not want to lose them, for he had so few already. Dave Mills was the only one who reported to the job on a daily basis. Bob Armstrong was being saved up for special occasions, for he was suffering from swollen lips and head injuries. Johnson's blows did more damage than some realized.

Eastern followers of the game thought Ketchel had a splendid chance "to cop Johnson." Odds there had tightened up from 10 to 4 to 10 to 6. Although Stan was a strong underdog, many were willing to wager that he would last the distance, or close to it.

Al Kaufman conceded Ketchel a chance to win. He said,

> Johnson cannot hit as hard as the public thinks he can. I guess I should know about that if anyone does, for if ever one man tried to knock out another Johnson tried it on me – but his efforts did not even bruise me up and had it not been for the cut in my lip, which made my face bloody, it would have been easy to see that Johnson was not hurting me in the slightest degree. If he cannot hit Ketchel any harder than he did me I think the latter has a good chance to win: that is, if he can get past the negro's guard, which is really the hardest thing he has to contend against.[199]

---

[199] *San Francisco Chronicle, San Francisco Evening Post, San Francisco Call, San Francisco Bulletin,* October 7, 1909.

On the 7th, Britt was smoking a cigar in promoter Jimmy Coffroth's office, telling his friends that Ketchel would be a sure winner. Johnson walked in, wearing his automobile uniform. Smiling, Jack said, "Evenin', Mistah Britt." Willis replied, "Well look who's here….if it isn't Jack Johnson himself. Well, Jack, I'm glad you dropped in. I was just telling Mitchel that Ketchel was going to give you a fine larruping, and telling him how Ketch is going to do it." Britt continued, "I hear you're going to box with Armstrong. Well I wish we had Armstrong at our camp. I guess the reason you haven't been working with him before is because he is too tough."

Johnson replied, "You come out and box with me just once, and you can have Armstrong at your camp. I'll tell you what I will do. If you will come out I'll let you have Armstrong and give you $100 to boot." Britt replied, "Nothing doing. You might crack my jaw and I want to be behind Ketchel when that fight starts. I want to tell him to wait and let you lead and caution him against going in too strong." Johnson retorted, smiling, "Nothing to that. Ketchel is coming in at me this way," and he whirled his arms in windmill fashion, "and I'll get him like this," and Jack fired his right uppercut in the air. Britt replied, "That's just where you are mistaken. Ketchel isn't going to fight you that way and you're going to be the most surprised man that ever stepped into a ring. I want to tell you something, Johnson. You will have to do some leading for this fellow. You will not be able to play your old game of wait and let the other fellow come in. That's too soft. You will have to do a little fighting on your own account."

Johnson then replied, "That's the only way Ketchel has a chance to beat me. If he doesn't come after me in pell-mell fashion he hasn't a chance in the world. If he tries any other way he is a gone duck. I ain't goin' to fool too much with Ketchel. I'm going to beat that boy up some." Britt told Johnson, "You are one who holds caution almost to the point of hysteria. You never fought an aggressive battle in your life. … But Ketchel is of a different mold. Lion or tiger like, he loves to fight, and there is not a bit of yellow in the Ketchel make-up. You know, Jack, that if yellow pigment ever became extinct all the artists would have to do would be to trepan you and they could get enough yellow to paint the North Pole."

Johnson responded, "Lawdy, how that man do talk." Britt told Johnson that he wasn't going up against Tommy Burns. Jack replied, "No, but I will have a softer one." Britt said Jack had been beating a lot of suckers who came at him just the way he wanted, so he could jab them. Jack said, "Well, let him come at me any way he wants. I am used to the tough fellows and the clever ones and the fast ones and the slow ones. I can get them all." Johnson said Ketchel was in for a beating before a holiday crowd. "I'm saving up for him."

The conversation drifted into the topic of their respective performances against O'Brien. When asked how he accounted for the fact that O'Brien went the distance with Johnson but Ketchel stopped him, Johnson replied, "I'm a different kind of fighter. I am more careful than Ketchel and take my time. Besides that I wasn't in any sort of shape. I weighed 222 pounds then, and 212 for Kaufman, but now I am weighing 198, and will be down to 197 for the Ketchel fight." He only had to box 6 rounds for O'Brien and 10 for Kaufman, but since this was a 20-round bout, Johnson had gotten himself into top condition and was going to "clean him up."

After Johnson left, Britt said he could not understand why so many thought Ketchel would be soft for Johnson, given that Johnson's record was not exactly replete with knockouts. "What is there in Johnson's past record to give him any license with this knockout talk? ... Whom has he knocked out in the ring that Ketchel couldn't dispose of in less time than Johnson did?" He noted that men who had lasted the distance with Johnson at some point included Pete Everett, Hank Griffin, George Gardner, Denver Ed Martin, Sam McVey, Sam Langford, Joe Jeannette, and Marvin Hart. (However, Ketchel had not fought any of those men, and Johnson had stopped Martin and McVey in subsequent matches, and decked Langford and Jeannette more than once.) Britt said that Johnson was not a "knocker out." "He hasn't enough of the bull terrier in him for a knocker out. He stalls along and beats his opponents by being more clever than they are." Britt said Johnson's best wins were against Flynn and Burns, but Langford had stopped Flynn in 1 round, while Burns had been unable to knock out fighters such as Jack Sullivan and Hugo Kelly, both of whom Ketchel had stopped. (However, Burns fought them as a middleweight, not heavyweight.) Continuing, Britt said,

> The trouble with Johnson is that he has never been opposed to a real, live, sure-enough top-notcher, and he's trying to cover up his fear of the experiment by a lot of big talk. ... Jack's record is about the saddest excuse for a championship title-holder anyone ever looked at. It's filled with Denver Ed Martins and Sam McVeys and Joe Jeannettes, Black ills and so forth – men who have nothing but bulk as an excuse for being in the prize-ring – but there aren't many like Corbett, Ruhlin, Sharkey and those fellows. ... Ketchel, on the contrary, has been meeting the best in his class all the time.

Britt said Stan was never better in his life, was hitting harder, and was bigger and stronger than ever. Willis Britt was the best talker in the game.

Of course, Britt overlooked the fact that Johnson usually won, had taken on some big and tough black fighters who were amongst the best in the business but avoided by white fighters, and that top white boxers, including Jeffries, had ducked him for years.[200]

On October 8, Ketchel did mountain climbing as part of his morning road work. He worked in the gym for 65 minutes, slamming the punching bag, playing handball, wrestling with the sand bag, and doing gymnastics on the floor, until he finally took on Miller and O'Connor for 2 rounds each.

---

[200] *San Francisco Chronicle, San Francisco Evening Post, San Francisco Call, San Francisco Bulletin,* October 8, 1909. On the 7th, Ketchel did no boxing, but rested. Johnson did his customary 4 rounds with Mills.

He took no rest between rounds, boxing one man right after the other. Stan said, "I was never afraid of anyone in my life, and least of all Johnson. I can't figure where he has a chance to knock me out, and when I land on him he is going to know it. He is so big that I can't help hitting him."

After the workout, Ketchel stripped, stepped on a scale for the reporters, and weighed 174 pounds. He stood 5'11". Hence, he was about the same size as elite fighters like Fitzsimmons, Choynski, and Sharkey. He looked firm, strong, and healthy, and did not have the drawn and haggard appearance that he had when he last fought at middleweight. Stan thought he would gain a few more pounds leading up to the fight and would enter the ring at about 180 pounds. The general belief was that Johnson would have about a 25-pound weight advantage.

In an interview with a *Bulletin* lady reporter who visited both camps that day, Willis Britt said of Ketchel, "Oh yes, he's heavy enough, 180 pounds, and a nigger is easy to beat, for a nigger is never as game as a white man."

That day, Johnson and Bob Armstrong sparred 2 very fast and clever rounds. "Armstrong in his day was one of the cleverest of the heavyweights and he is still a past-master with the gloves, so tricky, in fact, that Johnson can not make him step around and miss like he does with the ordinary ones." Johnson also sparred 4 rounds with Dave Mills.

George Little said, "Johnson is better now than he ever was. ... Johnson does not underrate Ketchel. He considers the Montana man a very formidable opponent, but for all that he expects to win inside of fifteen rounds."

The lady reporter noted that Jack Johnson used to be a sparring partner at a salary of $1.50 a week. However, winning the championship had brought him fame, money, and a newly acquired ego.

Since winning the championship, Johnson had gained a lot of weight. Little said Johnson loved to eat and always had an appetite. "He'll eat twenty-five or thirty pancakes at night and go to bed and sleep."

Regarding his age, Johnson said, "Thirty-two is my stage age. We still have stage ages. It wouldn't do for me to tell what my REAL age is." Jack was actually 31 years old.

The reporter said that current opinion was that Johnson periodically got himself arrested by the automobile police for advertising purposes. Little maintained that it was because the police liked to boast of arresting a champion. Johnson said, "It's a curious thing, I always get arrested when I'm going slow." The reporter asked him whether it was perhaps because of his reputation for speeding. Johnson exclaimed, "Ah! That is not right. The law reads that a man cannot be arrested without showing cause." The reporter asked, "But suppose when you're speeding, something should go wrong with the car; the danger from accidents is so much greater?" Johnson again replied,

> Ah! 'If' and 'suppose'! Two small words, but nobody has ever been able to explain them. ... I would just as soon go seventy-five miles an hour as five. One man falls out of bed and is killed. Another falls from a fifty-foot scaffold and lives. One man gets shot in the leg and is killed. Another gets a bullet in the brain and lives.

Johnson spoke of crashing his car into a tree in New Jersey on a slippery night, which cost him $1,800, but he was not hurt. "I always take a chance on my pleasures. We gets in this world what we're going to get." Johnson indeed had the courage (or foolishness) characteristic of a fighter.[201]

In England, Hugo Corri said Tommy Burns was a far better man than he received credit for being. Just because Johnson beat him did not mean that he was not a very good fighter. Because Johnson was taller and had a much longer reach, Burns had to go to him. However, that suited Johnson, "who is, perhaps, the greatest defensive fighter the world has ever seen."

Johnson relied on defense more than offense (though he had a wicked uppercut), having no problem with boxing many rounds and winning on points as opposed to a knockout, just as long as he was winning. "For instance, it took him 8 rounds to knock out Ben Taylor, while Iron Hague did the trick in just over one round. But who would dream of comparing

---

[201] *San Francisco Call, San Francisco Chronicle, San Francisco Evening Post, San Francisco Bulletin,* October 9, 1909.

Hague with Johnson?" The champ liked his opponents to come to him, and if they would not oblige him, he had ways of tricking them into doing it.

Some argued that Johnson would be easy for a much more powerful fighter like Jeffries. However, Corri disagreed, saying,

> I fancy that Johnson would win. He is three years younger…[and] is one of those negroes who have the trick of aging slowly, more slowly, that is, than the average white man. Then, again, Johnson has not quit the ring and Jeffries has. A very big item this. Johnson is still habituated to taking punishment, while Jeff has forgotten the feel of it.

Johnson would not carry the fight to Jeff, and "Jeffries' racial feeling may combine with circumstances and impel him to go after Johnson, a course which will just suit the black's marvelous powers of defence. Johnson is, I think, the greatest defensive fighter the world has ever seen."

Corri opined that Langford was too small to defeat Johnson, for a good big man always beats a good little man, "even when the little 'un is such a marvel as Langford. For Langford is a marvel, a wonderfully aggressive fighter with an almost impregnable defence." Sam also had a good chin. Hague had decked him, but Langford came back to knock out Hague.

Bob Fitzsimmons said Langford was too slow to be a champion, was vastly overrated, and never would be able to extend Johnson.

Fitz thought Johnson's career would be finished when he met Jeffries. "Jeff will beat Johnson to death. … Jeffries is in a class by himself. He is a mountain of a man. Johnson will never be able to hurt him enough to win, and the coon will never be able to stand big Jem's punches."

Bob said he had been too old to do anything with Johnson, plus Jack cross-buttocked him heavily in the 1st round, which affected him.

> Yes, I am pretty confident that Jeffries will beat the nigger if ever they come together. It all depends on Jeffries, of course. If he says that he will meet him, he will. He is a man of his word, is Jem Jeffries, one of the most thoroughly straightforward men who ever pulled on a boxing glove. … That coon Johnson is a great hand at kidding, both outside and inside the ring. But he won't kid Jeffries. It is said he succeeded in making Burns lose his temper, 'got his goat,' as they call it in the States. … Anyway, champion kidder as he is, he won't succeed in ruffling Jeffries' temper. Jeff is far too cool and collected for that.[202]

The *Call* wondered who would be Johnson's best foe if Jeffries did not face him next. "A careful survey of the field reveals only one man, Sam Langford. As Langford is of the same color as Johnson, a meeting between this pair would not stir up enough interest to warrant any promoter coming forth with the guarantee that these men undoubtedly would demand for a

---

[202] *Boxing*, October 9, 1909. A British magazine.

championship battle." Johnson was not going to take on a tough man unless he thought the fight would be a big gate draw or unless he was guaranteed a lot of money.[203]

The *San Francisco Bulletin* said "Beggar" Sam Langford was begging for matches, but top middleweights and light heavyweights side-stepped him. His victories were like defeats in that they caused many to avoid him. Some thought he allowed Sandy Ferguson to stay the limit in 12 uninteresting rounds so that he could obtain more matches.

"BEGGAR SAM" LANGFORD.
The Chocolate-Colored Bombardier, Who Has the Goat of All the Middle and Light Heavyweights in the Country.

The *Bulletin* felt that Langford's record, though somewhat formidable, was not so great that it should cause top men to avoid him. "He has succumbed to Danny Duane, Young Peter Jackson and Jack Johnson and several other men have fought him to a draw – Jackson twice, Joe Jeannette three times, Jack Blackburn four times, Dave Holly twice, Andy Watson three times, Joe Walcott and Billy Chisholm each once."[204]

The *San Francisco Chronicle* said the Johnson-Ketchel fight was looming up much more than it did at the start. Fans believed that Stan's dangerous punch would give him a chance to win throughout the 20 rounds; a likely distance given that Johnson usually was content to win a decision. "There are many who cannot get away from the belief that Johnson has a streak of yellow, and that if hard pressed and hit he will quit." Ketchel was a man who could press and hit hard.

Ketchel held a KO32 over Joe Thomas, and stopped Jack Sullivan in the 20th round, so he had stamina and carried a wallop late into fights.

Although it would be better for Johnson's reputation to win by a knockout, one never knew what Johnson would do. "The Johnson spirit, however, is peculiar and he might be satisfied with results that would spell victory even if not a knockout."

Responding to critics who compared the relative performances of Johnson and Ketchel against O'Brien, and to those who claimed that he was chicken-hearted and afraid to try to knock out a dangerous man, Johnson said,

[203] *San Francisco Chronicle, San Francisco Examiner, San Francisco Call,* October 10, 1909.
[204] *San Francisco Bulletin,* October 11, 1909.

I'm not a slugger, but a boxer and a scientific hitter. You all know what a great racehorse Sysonby was. Well, he never broke a record in his life, but he never ran second, either. That's me. I'm not for tearing in and knocking 'em out, just to get the name of being a hurricane. I would rather size my man up in the right way, beat him down carefully, if slowly, and then win without taking a chance of allowing him to put over any wild haymakers on me. This has always been my style and I am not going to change it now, simply because I am champion of the world.

The *Chronicle* summed up, "And there you have Johnson. Confessedly, he doesn't care for the spectacular as so many fighters, but is satisfied if he gets the verdict." As a result, many did not like Johnson's style.

W. W. Naughton noted that Ketchel often crouched against his opponents, but felt that such would be foolish against Johnson, who was a master of the uppercut. He also did not think Ketchel could force Johnson to lead, for Jack was the cleverer of the two. Although there had been more upsets and surprises in pugilism than in any other sport, he thought Ketchel had little chance to win. Still, "interest in this particular event is keener than it has been in any match that has taken place in this city during many years." Ketchel's confidence and wager on himself helped stimulate that interest.

Those who saw the Johnson-Burns moving pictures agreed that Burns, a former middleweight like Ketchel, simply fought right into Johnson's hands. He waded in and tried to penetrate Johnson's guard, but Jack's superior reach and his wonderful judgment of distance proved fatal. Ketchel claimed that he had seen the films and had a plan to defeat Johnson. "Many a fighter has told us how he was going to fight when he got into the ring, but then it was a very different story. Theory is all right, but execution is what brings home the money."

The fighters were to take 60% of the house, and they were to divide their end 65% to the winner and 35% to the loser. There also was the $5,000 side bet, which meant that if Ketchel lost, even with a filled arena, which would yield around $25,000, he would come away with no money, except what he earned in film rights and exhibitions, which still could be quite significant.

On October 10, Johnson took his auto out for a spin, but suffered a flat tire. Ketchel happened along as Johnson was repairing the tire, and offered to help him, but Jack declined. Nevertheless, Ketchel talked with the champ, good-naturedly. "Say, Jack, you ain't so big, are you? Why, from the way they talked about you I thought you were as big as one of the twin peaks. Why, you ain't got much on me, Jack, I'm nearly as big as you are." Johnson responded, "I may not be so big as they say, but I think I'll be big enough to beat you up some, Mr. Ketchel." "Well, that's where we differ, Jack. You know that little song, Jack. You know how the chorus runs, 'And he rambled till the butcher cut him down.' Well, Jack, I think I'm going to cut you down next Saturday. I like them big like you because you'll fall harder than a small fellow and it won't be so easy for them to pick you up, either." Then Ketchel left while Johnson smiled and continued fixing his flat.

TYPICAL FIGHTING FACES OF THE TWO CHAMPIONS AND CHARACTERISTIC POSES WHEN THEY ARE SET FOR ACTION

That day, before capacity crowds at the Chutes, Ketchel sparred both in the afternoon and evening, 4 rounds each time, dividing up the rounds between Charley Miller and Steve O'Connor, hammering them.

Ketchel said, "I feel as strong as an ox." Stan enjoyed hill climbing, feeling that it had improved his endurance. He also felt better bigger. "To tell you the truth, I realize now that I have been making a mistake for the last year in making the middleweight limit. ... I think I will enter the ring with Johnson weighing about 175 pounds. I won't say that I expect to beat Johnson easily, but I will say that I do expect to beat him."

What happened in a sparring session at the Seal Rock house that afternoon, October 10, 1909, has been the subject of some historical debate. The *San Francisco Evening Post* claimed that in the 4th round of his sparring exhibition with Jack Johnson, the able navy seaman Gunboat Smith, who had been a Ketchel sparring partner, knocked the heavyweight champion to the canvas.

> And it was no fluke knockdown. Coming out of a clinch near the end of the last round, 'Gunboat' swung a right overhand chop, which took Johnson flush on the chin. The negro went down as prettily as any fighter ever hit the mat in the ring, and when he got up he was dazed so much that George Lyttle, Johnson's manager and timekeeper, called time, cutting the round short fully a minute, and seeing to it that the naval scrapper did no more sparring with the champion during the rest of the afternoon.

> Smith had shown in the first three rounds that he boxed with Johnson that he could reach him with a right overhand chop, and he landed this blow on Johnson frequently. Smith and Johnson slammed each other around good and hard and the fans who visited the Seal Rock camp to see a sparring exhibition felt before the end of the second round of the Smith-Johnson bout was over that they were seeing the real thing.

Smith showed little fear of Johnson's punches and mixed it with him at every opportunity throughout the 4 rounds. In the 4th round, Johnson caught many of the blows with apparent ease, but after about 2 minutes, coming out of a clinch, quick as a flash Smith sent his right to the point of the jaw and dropped Jack flatly to the mat. The 500 fans present cheered vociferously. Jack did not smile.

The relatively inexperienced former amateur armed forces champion Smith had just turned professional, and did not even seem as big as Ketchel. Many said that if a game amateur could reach Johnson and drop him that Ketchel could do the same and more.

However, despite being dropped, Johnson still sparred two others, for Smith was just the first of three. Johnson rested up a bit and then sparred Arslinger, a Los Angeles lightweight, and Johnny O'Keefe, a middleweight, for 2 rounds each.

> Johnson did not care to discuss the punch much. He seemed inclined to take the incident lightly and pass the matter off as a slip rather than a knockdown, but there was not one fan who saw the trick turned who could be convinced that Smith's blow was any less hefty than a real knockdown punch.

However, not every local paper reported a knockdown. The *San Francisco Call* said several hundred fans paid 25 cents each to watch the champ train. Johnson had a new sparring mate in Gunboat Smith, the hard-hitting Oakland middleweight who had been flattening so many of them across the bay of late. "Johnson and Smith went four rounds and the exhibition proved a good one." Nothing about a knockdown was even hinted.

It said Bob Armstrong, who had recovered from his recent injury, then worked 2 rounds with Johnson. "This pair always puts up a clever exhibition, for Bob is nearly as clever as the champion himself." Joe Lanum and Dave Mills worked 2 rounds each with the champ as well.

The *San Francisco Examiner* also described Johnson's Sunday October 10 training. In the early morning, Johnson put in a couple hours of hiking. In the afternoon, before a crowded Seal Rock Pavilion, Johnson boxed 10 rounds. He went 4 rounds with Gunboat Smith, who had transferred his allegiance from the Ketchel camp to that of the enemy. Then Johnson took on Armstrong, Mills, and Lanum, 2 rounds apiece. This newspaper did not mention anything about a knockdown either.

The other local next-day newspapers did not even bother to print anything about the training that day.[205]

Some national newspapers via dispatches ran with the knockdown story, printing it on the 12th. The story's promotional value was that it could serve to stimulate even more interest in the upcoming championship fight, because it made Johnson seem vulnerable.

In subsequent days, some of the local newspapers discussed the knockdown claim. George Little was busy sending out telegrams contradicting the report that Smith had knocked down Johnson on Sunday the 10th. "I don't know that I ought to bother about making denials, at that. The thing is a cheap attempt to gain a reputation at Johnson's expense." The question was whether the *Evening Post* was engaging in yellow journalism, potentially being paid by Smith's backers to circulate the story.

The *San Francisco Call* reported, "There are a number of contradictory stories about the knockdown which Gunboat Smith is said to have scored on Johnson." Some said that Smith landed a looping punch on the jaw which "took the champion off his pins and landed him on his haunches." Johnson said it was no knockdown. Little said it was a slip, although it was a slip after Smith had landed a blow. Some who saw them box said it was the real thing, insisting that Johnson was dropped. Smith was a good fighter, for he had boxed with Ketchel some days ago and gave Stan a good time of it.

The *San Francisco Chronicle* said, "The story that Gunboat Smith knocked Johnson down in a sparring exhibition Sunday afternoon was a bit stretched. Johnson slipped on the canvas and the balance of the yarn was easy to concoct." Little said the canvas should have been sprinkled, but that was neglected, and "Johnson's foot slipped and he partially fell. That's all there was to the story."

The *San Francisco Evening Post*, which had generated the story about Johnson being decked, noted that Little was hard at work denying the story.

---

[205] *San Francisco Evening Post, San Francisco Call, San Francisco Examiner*, October 11, 1909. At the end of the training, Johnson stepped on the scale and weighed 198 pounds.

Lyttle denied the knockdown and tried to say that Johnson slipped, and some of the unwise swallowed Lyttle's statement complete. … There were quite a number of fans present when Smith knocked Johnson down, and Mr. Lyttle would have a day's work convincing any of them that Jack's discomfiture was a slip. You don't often see champions slip to the mat when they are boxing ring novices, do you? And Johnson's canvas dive was no slip, but the result of a well-timed whack on the chin.

On October 11, Ketchel did his usual road work, and showed excellent form in sparring 6 rounds total, rotating Miller and O'Conner in and out for 1 round at a time, 3 rounds each, while Stan took no rest between rounds.

Ketchel said he was sure that he would win, despite the fact that the public did not think so. He was fighting Johnson, not the public, and felt that he could hit harder than Johnson and would land too. "There never was a fighter in the world who could not be hit, and…I will hit Johnson, and hit him good and hard." He noted how Fitzsimmons eventually found a way to hit the unhittable Corbett.

Billy Papke opined that Ketchel had a great chance to win. "That Ketchel boy is no cinch for anyone. … Ketchel is a terrible hitter, and he is very liable to knock out anyone whom he hits, and I think that he will hit Johnson. … I feel sure that Ketchel will outgame Johnson."

Already there was a demand for the moving pictures. Orders had come in from New York, Chicago, Boston, Pittsburg, and Philadelphia. The day after the fight, Coffroth would head to New York with the films.

A man close to Johnson said Jack could knock out Ketchel any time he wanted to do so. However, it was acknowledged that the motion pictures might be worth more if the bout lasted several rounds.[206]

On the 12th, Ketchel boxed 3 rounds each with Miller and O'Connor. He also did his long morning run and an hour of afternoon gym exercise.

---

[206] *New York Times, San Francisco Examiner, San Francisco Call, San Francisco Chronicle, San Francisco Evening Post*, October 12, 1909. On the 11th, Johnson did not box, but just did road work. Little said Jack was tapering so that he would not go into the ring overtrained.

Stan said he had a system to avoid Johnson's punishing uppercut. "Flynn and Burns and a few more just threw themselves on that uppercut in a suicidal way. I think I will profit by their mistakes. … Whether Johnson comes after me or backs up, it isn't in him to knock me out in twenty rounds. He is not a knocker-out and never will be."

On October 12, Johnson boxed 11 rounds, besides his usual gymnasium routine. Gunboat Smith was very willing and went right after Johnson, swinging viciously for 4 rounds. However, Johnson blocked all of his efforts, and Smith could not land effectively. Still, Johnson was forced to cover and do a good deal of clinching, and the sailor kept him very busy.

Johnson then sparred 3 rounds with Johnny O'Keefe, 2 rounds with Los Angeles welterweight Charley Ashlinger (or Dave Anslinger), and 2 rounds with local heavyweight Joe Lanum.

When he called it a day, Johnson looked as fresh as a daisy. After a rubdown, he stepped on the scales and weighed 196 ½ pounds.

Scouting the bout, an *Evening Post* writer said,

> Coming right down to taw, and without any aspersions being cast and with all respect due the colored race, I tell you from personal knowledge that I never yet have seen a negro that didn't quit under fire. … Ever since the dawn of day the white man has been in the supremacy. It will carry in the present issue. … Now you might think from this talk that I'm prejudiced against the colored race. Never in a thousand years. I know some of the most brilliant fellows in the world who are colored men and I am proud of their company and associations.[207]

On the 13th, Johnson went downtown to talk business with Coffroth regarding the European rights for the moving pictures.[208]

George Little understood that Johnson had made some slow fights in California, but said this one would be different. "While he does not undervalue Ketchel's punch, Johnson thinks he can win about as he pleases." Little insisted that Johnson would put Ketchel away as fast as he could. "I know some persons think that on account of the pictures that Johnson will be inclined to let Ketchel tarry a while, but such is not the case." Little said Jack was never better, as strong as an ox, and had prepared properly. "I am certain that he will win inside of fifteen rounds and I am going to bet my money that way, and I intend to bet a good chunk, too."

Sam Fitzpatrick said Ketchel only had a remote chance to win.

---

[207] *San Francisco Chronicle, San Francisco Call, San Francisco Examiner, San Francisco Evening Post,* October 13, 1909.
[208] The parties were arguing over the distribution of the film rights in Europe. "The black thinks there is a world of money to be made with the pictures in Europe." Willis Britt disagreed. He said that although over $100,000 had been made on the Battling Nelson - Jimmy Britt films in the U.S.; only $7,000 - $8,000 was made in Europe.

Johnson cannot lose this fight, because he is too scientific. He knows how to block better than any big man I ever saw. He is quicker with his hands than with his feet and can pick blows out of the air in wonderful style. There is no doubt about his gameness, and when it comes to fighting it should be remembered that he never has been extended.

He further said that Ketchel was plucky and a great slugger, but lacked the generalship and skill that Johnson had, and therefore would be an easy mark. "I doubt whether he can land an effective blow. Burns is a better boxer than Ketchel, yet he never put a glove on Johnson."

Fitzpatrick thought Jeffries was the only one with a chance against Johnson, and "if they come together Jim will have the hardest fight of his life on his hands."

After his work on the 13th, Ketchel said, "I feel stronger now than I ever felt before." Making the middleweight limit had left him totally dried out and weakened. The added weight was good solid muscle, and he would have every ounce of his strength. Stan said,

> If Johnson beats me I will have no excuse to offer. ... I believe that my superior punching power will bring Johnson down to my size before we have gone very far. ... Nearly every man of the least bit of class that he has fought went twenty rounds with him, and I think I am a much better man than any one that the negro ever met.

Ketchel further said, "I do not intend to do all the fighting." He would not go after a bigger man the way he did with smaller men, and intended to make Johnson do some of the leading. Stan said he would make a studied, careful fight, and not give Johnson the opportunity to hit him with the uppercut, as he had done with others.

> I have made a careful study of the Johnson-Burns fight pictures and I have mapped out a plan of battle that I believe will be a bit disconcerting to the negro.

> He likes his opponent to come to him so that he can counter and use his right uppercut. I am not going to rush in to Johnson open and uncovered. I will fight him carefully and I think that Johnson will know that he has been in a fight before the mill has gone very far.

> Of course, if I get Johnson in trouble I will fight like a wildcat, but I am not going to offer myself up as a sacrifice to that famous right uppercut of the champion. ... Johnson moves faster and better when he is going backward. I am going to force him to come to me, and if he does I feel certain that I will be able to give him all he can stand and a little bit more.

The *San Francisco Evening Post's* title of its article was, "Lion Will Pursue Waiting Policy in Battle With Gorilla." However, Stan also said, "If I ever get Johnson going I will never let up on him."

Willis Britt said the loser's share would be a little more than $5,000, and given that there was a $5,000 side bet, if Ketchel lost, they would not make any money. He said they would not put themselves in such a position unless they were convinced of victory. "Ketchel will go into that ring carrying 180 pounds of solid muscle and sinew. ... A man weighing this much is just as formidable as one weighing 20 pounds more."

From London, Jeffries said Johnson ought to defeat Ketchel, although he would be rooting for Stan. He thought Ketchel was tough but not big enough to defeat the heavier and cleverer Johnson. "I only hope Ketchel leaves Johnson for me." "Johnson will be the easiest proposition I have ever tackled."

The *San Francisco Bulletin* opined that if Ketchel knocked out Johnson, the motion pictures would be worth half a million dollars at least. If the battle went 20 brisk rounds, the films would be worth $250,000, and "even if Ketchel should lose to the champion in twelve or fifteen rounds, but succeed in knocking him down or punishing him badly at any stage, they would easily be worth $150,000 to $200,000." That type of money could be incentive enough for Johnson to carry Ketchel for a while, and perhaps do more.[209]

---

[209] *San Francisco Call, San Francisco Chronicle, San Francisco Evening Post, San Francisco Bulletin,* October 14, 1909.

On Thursday October 14, two days before the fight, the Miles Brothers filmed the fighters at their respective training facilities. Coffroth asked Johnson to get in his auto and drive towards the picture machine. With his manager in the vehicle, Johnson dashed up at a whirlwind clip, "and if the camera caught anything at all it must have looked like a night picture of Haley's comet." They asked the champion to drive at a slower gait, which he did, and this time the operator said, "I've got him."

Johnson and Barney Furey were filmed doing roadwork. For the cameras, Jack also shadow boxed and did some fast sparring with Gunboat Smith, who managed to land a good left on the chin and make the bout highly exciting for the spectators. Johnson followed up with dumb-bell exercises and more shadow boxing.

Even after the cameraman was done, Johnson sparred some more, boxing with Gunboat Smith, Dave Mills, Johnny O'Keefe, and Joe Lanum. He also did some burlesque with Dave Aingslinger (or Charles Anslinger) in a comedy act. After his workout, he tipped the scales at 198 pounds.

The motion picture folks hoped that the fight went more than 10 rounds. That would make more patrons want to see it.

On the 14th at Millett's, for the motion picture camera, Ketchel did much the same activities as Johnson. He punched the bag; shadow boxed, and did various exercises. Then Stan sparred a few rounds with 236-pound Charlie Miller, and as usual, the big German took a severe pounding.

After the pictures were concluded, Ketchel spent another hour at handball, medicine ball, dumb-bells, and the like.

Willis Britt said,

> Ketchel will win this fight as sure as you are alive. ... I had a chance to duck out of that $5,000 side bet, and the fact that I didn't lift my hand is the best proof of how we feel in the matter. ... Johnson has only one thing over Ketchel. He has experience and boxing ability. Ketchel has gameness, strength, a wonderful punch and the speed. ... As I have said, Johnson must do some leading; but if Ketchel hurts the big fellow he will tear right in.

Johnson and Coffroth held a mysterious private conference. Some speculated that Johnson threatened not to fight if the side bet was called off. Others wondered if it had something to do with the films.

George Little said Johnson just wanted to have an understanding in regard to certain little matters so as not to consume time when they entered the ring. Motion picture films were very expensive, and he did not want a long delay debating issues before the bout started, which would cost them all money. It was decided that the managers would have a conference with Referee Welch to settle all matters that might arise and cause friction.

The *Bulletin* said their discussion pertained to the side bet. The stakeholder in New York said he consented to hold the money as a forfeit guaranteeing appearance, but could not pay it out as a wager for fear of violating the Otis-Walker betting bill. He wanted to be relieved of further responsibility. Johnson accused the Ketchel side of trying to put one over on him, seeking a way out of the bet. He said he would not fight without it. He called attention to the fact that the Ketchel side could have selected many topnotchers when it came to depositing the wager, but selected this particular one. The parties agreed to move the $10,000 into the hands of another reliable business man.

The *Evening Post* said that so far as moral support, Ketchel would be the overwhelming favorite. "The public is with Ketchel almost to a fan." If he happened to win, he would be "the greatest ring hero of modern times."

Johnson's cautious, defensive style was again criticized. "This writer does not accuse Johnson of cowardice, but he surely lacks the quality of aggressiveness that usually goes with a champion." The writer speculated that perhaps Johnson was lazy, and speaking figuratively, preferred to do sitting down what he could do standing up. The writer also opined that Johnson feared being hit hard. "The negro never was fond of taking a punch even from mediocre hitters." His gameness was questioned. "Johnson has seldom shown many very open signs of courage, and there is a public belief, well founded or not, that Johnson is not a game man. ... Johnson is the reincarnation of some coyote that, though strong and gifted of speed, cares not to mingle too closely with an enemy." On the other hand, Ketchel was a lion who would rather die fighting than take a backward step.

Another writer noted that unlike Ketchel, "Johnson…has boxed in a patchy manner in all his most prominent contests. He has slowed or quickened as the whim seized him, and when criticized later for 'fighting in spots' has offered the defense that he always boxes to win and that he does not advertise to kill a man every time he enters the ring."[210]

Ketchel said he had no fear of Johnson, though he appreciated his abilities. Stan had been able to eat what he wanted, and had built himself up. He would not be surprised if he entered the ring weighing more than 178 pounds. "He will never knock me out. … Johnson has never developed a knockout punch, except for a lot of dubs, and he is not going to start on me." Ketchel further said,

> I intend to battle carefully and at the same time force Johnson to lead. In his other fights the men have rushed him and have suffered accordingly. I don't mean to say that I will make a runaway fight. I will press the big fellow continually, and it will be hard luck if I do not create an opening in one of the rounds. If I hit Johnson and get him going, he will not have a chance to recover.

Willis Britt said Ketchel weighed a rock-solid 177 when he woke up on Friday morning, the day before the fight. He did no work on Friday, and therefore "ought to reach 180 pounds by the time the fight starts."

Britt said Ketchel had better sense than just to wade in on Johnson, but was going to draw him into a lead. "Johnson will have to open up some time, and when he does, this lion will be ready with that swing and with that shift. I tell you that Ketchel is going to win." He also said, "I consider Ketchel the most sensational fighter the world has known. He is game through and through and can hit from any angle. He is a much harder puncher than Johnson and has no fear of the negro."

The day before the fight, on the 15th, Johnson weighed 199 pounds. He said he would dry out overnight and come into the fight weighing 195 pounds. "When I fought Jack O'Brien I was fat as a Jap wrestler."

Johnson further said, "I am going to win, but I can't say how, nor how long it will take me. I always win, don't I?" He would take his time and figure out Ketchel. "I always study my man out carefully and I will study Ketchel out this time, too."

However, Johnson also said that he and Little were both betting at even odds that he would stop Ketchel within 15 rounds. That was how he was advising his friends to wager. When asked if it would be safe for his friends to bet that he would win inside of 10 rounds, Johnson replied, "No-o. But they can go as far as they like on the fifteen round proposition. Tell 'em to bet that I stop Ketch before the end of the fifteenth round. I say 'stop' instead of 'knockout' because the police may have to interfere in order to

---

[210] *San Francisco Chronicle, San Francisco Call, San Francisco Examiner, San Francisco Evening Post, San Francisco Bulletin*, October 15, 1909. Neither boxer did much work on the 15th. Ketchel took a short run, while Johnson engaged in a brisk walk.

save Ketchel from useless punishment." Hence, Johnson was prognosticating the bout's termination during rounds 11 through 15.

Latest Pictures of Stanley Ketchel, Middleweight Champion of the World, and Jack Johnson, Heavyweight Champion of the World. This Pair Will Hook Up at Coffroth's Arena in a Twenty-Round Battle for the Heavyweight Title Tomorrow.

George Little said, "In my opinion it is all over with the exception of paying over the money. ... Johnson was never better trained in all his career than he is now."

Little heard that Jeffries was on his way back to the U.S. Little was so confident in Johnson that he said he would bet Berger and Jeffries any amount up to $20,000. Johnson was happy about Jeff's return, but still pessimistic, saying, "I don't think he will ever take a chance with me. He knows I can beat him."

Bob Armstrong, who once had been a Ketchel sparring partner, warned Johnson not to overlook Ketchel. "Never mind Jeffries. Jeffries can wait, and you'd better get past this other fellow first. If this lad, Ketchel, lands on you he'll make you forget there is such a man as Jeffries on earth, and I know what I'm talking about."

Johnson said,

> I realize that Ketchel is a tough, hard-hitting scrapper, and for this reason I have trained faithfully for him. I expect to knock Ketchel out in less than fifteen rounds tomorrow. I am betting my money that way. ... I see that he says he will make me do the forcing. The chances are that I will do more forcing than Ketchel will care to handle when we hook up. ... Maybe he thinks I am not a very wicked puncher, but I think he will change his mind before I am through with him tomorrow afternoon. ... I wish it was Jeffries instead of Ketchel I had in the ring with me tomorrow. I know I would surely beat him.

The day of the fight, the *Chronicle* opined that Johnson ought to win. Ketchel was a hard puncher, but "Johnson is far too cautious and careful a fighter to rush matters where there is a danger of a punch being landed. He cares little for a knockout, so long as the decision goes his way. This characteristic of the black makes it hard to say how long the go will last." The *Call* agreed that Johnson would win.

The *Bulletin* said that "if the darky has a streak of yellow anywhere in his makeup the Michigander is the one who will bring it out. ... Besides, almost every lover of the boxing game who has seen Johnson in the ring wants to see him get a licking."

On the morning of the fight, Johnson weighed 196 pounds.[211]

San Francisco Chronicle, October 16, 1909

On Saturday October 16, 1909 at Jim Coffroth's arena, located at Mission and Sickles Avenue in Colma, California, in the San Francisco area, Jack Johnson defended his world heavyweight championship against Stanley Ketchel.[212]

As early as 11:30 a.m., Valencia Street was congested heavily with automobiles and street-cars. A line of spectators a half-mile long was pushing its way into the arena. The first preliminary wasn't scheduled to start until 1:30 p.m. Men of almost every nationality were in attendance. Even some women were there. Four operators guarded the moving picture machines on the high platform erected in front of the gallery.

At 1:35 p.m., Promoter Coffroth announced that every seat had been sold. "With the standing room customers that will be squeezed in within the next half hour I figure to have $40,000 when I count up tonight."

No bigger crowd could have been packed into the arena. It was a record crowd, with many thousands in attendance. Even the aisles were crowded. Thousands were turned away at the door, with absolutely no room to fit them. The bleacher seats had sold for $2, while standing room sold at $5 a head. "Many negroes were scattered through the crowd, but were outnumbered forty to one by the white followers."

---

[211] *San Francisco Chronicle, San Francisco Call, San Francisco Examiner, San Francisco Evening Post, San Francisco Bulletin*, October 16, 1909. Johnson said that Gunboat Smith was one of the best young heavyweights he had ever boxed.

[212] The following account is an amalgamation of the local next-day accounts from the *San Francisco Chronicle, Examiner*, and *Call*, October 17, 1909. The *Chronicle/Call* accounts were nearly identical and apparently written by the same author.

South of the arena, far up at the top of the green hill, dozens of onlookers assembled and used field glasses and telescopes to obtain a free view.

Police officers were stationed around the corners of the ring, and many special officers were distributed throughout the crowd, which was something new.

At 2:54 p.m., announcer Uncle Billy Jordan climbed between the ropes carrying new gloves. They were dark red, and had light-blue ribbon strings. A dozen photographers took up their positions in the ring, awaiting the participants. From ring center, a moving picture was taken of the crowd.

At 3 p.m., Johnson made his way down the center aisle to the ring, followed by manager George Little, Bob Armstrong, Dave Mills, Harry Foley, Jack Leahy, and Young Peter Jackson. Barney Furey probably was there as well. Jack wore a long dark gray bathrobe.

As he climbed between the ropes and into the ring, the spectators gave Johnson a poor reception, which included hoots, hisses, groans, and catcalls. Jack only smiled. A chorus from the bleachers called out, "Where is that $100 which you promised to give a blind man?" One taunted, "Wait till Jeffries gets at you. He will not be so easy to handle as the little boy you are meeting today." Another fan told Johnson that Ketchel was going to beat him, and the champ responded by saying that he was going to give Ketchel the beating of his life. Harry Foley, who was in Johnson's corner, offered to bet that same ringside patron that Johnson would win.

Within a minute, Ketchel followed, accompanied by manager Willis Britt, Johnny Frayne, Johnny Loftus, Kid Lafayette, Jimmy Leonard, Charlie Miller, and Steve O'Connor. Stan wore a gray sweater and black pants/trousers.

The popular Ketchel received a huge ovation; akin to a royal welcome. He seemed bashful. Ketchel smiled in appreciation of the applause, but as he went to and sat in his corner, it appeared that his eyes were filled with tears. He tried wiping them away. He either was consumed with nervous tension or touched by the warm reception. Stan told the newsmen that he had received a message from his mother wishing him success.

Johnson stood in the center of the ring and gazed about the audience.

The moving picture men were kept busy, taking views of the scene.

Johnson went over to Ketchel's corner. The men shook hands. Johnson examined Ketchel's hands. He also examined Stan's gloves, but when he tried to remain in Stan's corner so he could observe the gloves being put on, Britt got in the way, objected forcibly, and argued with him. Johnson insisted that he could stay there if he wanted to, but Britt stood his ground. Jack wanted to make sure no horseshoes were inserted. The crowd hooted and hissed. Britt shouldered Jack away, and the big crowd cheered. Britt said to Ketchel, "We've got his goat already, Steve." Johnson returned to his corner to stand amongst his own seconds.

As the gloves were tied to Johnson's wrists, he looked over the sea of hostile faces with a half-grin.

Billy Jordan led Ketchel to the ring center and introduced him as the middleweight and light heavyweight champion of the world. The ovation was such that Ketchel was overcome and he went to his corner with tears in his eyes. Johnson was introduced as the heavyweight champion of the world. His reception was modest in comparison with Ketchel. Referee Jack Welch was also introduced.

After the introductions, the men stripped to their fighting costumes and posed for the newspaper photographers. Johnson towered over Ketchel by several inches. Johnson wore knee-length blue trunks with a flag belt. Ketchel wore pinkish red trunks with no belt.

Ketchel's weight was given out as 174 pounds, and Johnson's as 196 pounds. As neither man took the scales, no one knew for sure what they weighed.

Referee Welch ordered the ring cleared. Billy Jordan announced the start of the fight by saying, "Let 'er go." The bell rang at exactly 3:09 p.m.

1 - To start matters, Johnson slammed in a hard left to the stomach and

they clinched. After breaking, Stan threw a right that landed on the shoulder. The spectators yelled to Ketchel, "Make him lead!"

Stan sparred for almost half a minute, trying to get Johnson to lead. At long range, Johnson twice shot his left to the face with lightning-like rapidity and Ketchel was forced back to the ropes, but wriggled away. In the clinches, Johnson easily handled Ketchel. His gold teeth glistened as he smiled.

Johnson landed a left to the face

and Stan swung a right on the ribs. A left struck Stan's forehead and they clinched. Both feinted a great deal. Johnson's left jabs were quick but light, and he was very wary. He put in two more jabs and blocked a left for the stomach. Jack scored with two more jabs. Stan backed him to the ropes and drove a left to the stomach. Jack landed another jab.

The *Chronicle/Call* accounts said the utterly tame round was all Johnson. Both fought with extreme caution. Ketchel looked nervous, while Johnson wore his golden smile. The *Examiner* said, "So far Ketchel was true to his promise to force Johnson to lead." It also said Jack was playing a clever boxing game, feeling out his man.

2 - Both feinted. Ketchel blocked a left jab and they ran into a clinch. Referee Welch pried them apart. On the break, Johnson landed a left jab to the nose, and soon thereafter did it again. Johnson was often whipping his left to the nose. In every clinch, Ketchel was working short-arm blows for the stomach, particularly his left hook. However, mostly Johnson held Stan powerless in the clinches, or was able to twist his body to avoid the blows.

In one clinch, Ketchel managed to land a hard left uppercut to the upper body or jaw, but Jack just smiled. In a fast mix, the champion landed a right uppercut and then straight right to the jaw, backing up Stan, and in the follow-up near the corner, as Ketchel tried to stop and fire a right; Johnson landed a shorter, faster clean right to the jaw that dropped Ketchel to the floor with considerable force.

Johnson walked to his corner. Ketchel grabbed the lower rope and rose from the knockdown at the count of six. Stan rushed in, but had great difficulty in getting under Johnson's long reach. Johnson clinched, and then sparred cautiously, not trying to follow-up his advantage. Jack jabbed three times in succession. Stan landed a left on the body and a left hook on the jaw. They clinched, and Johnson grinned. Johnson merely toyed with him, mostly cautiously jabbing and defending until the bell ended the round.

3 - For about 30 seconds, Johnson posed and waited for Ketchel, who pawed the air and did not lead. Jack feinted rapidly, trying to draw a lead. They closed in and swung left and right to the body and head at close range. Stan landed both hands to the body. Johnson landed left, right, and left on the jaw. Johnson also landed two right uppercuts. The referee separated them. They again rushed in close. Johnson landed several short-arm rights and lefts to the stomach. As they broke, Stan uppercut his left to the face.

Johnson held both hands extended and then suddenly shot in a straight left. Ketchel missed a right swing for the jaw. Johnson landed a left to the face, and Stan landed a left on the body. A long clinch followed. Johnson missed a left but landed the next one. They clinched. Johnson smothered Stan's blows while holding, and drove a stiff right to the stomach. Both feinted for a while. Stan was short with a left and Johnson rapped him hard on the jaw with a right. At the bell, Ketchel went to his corner dancing and looking fresh. During the minute's rest, Johnson kept up a running conversation with his seconds.

4 – For a while, Johnson stood still like a statue, and then began feinting. Stan's corner shouted, "Make him lead." They sparred, and Johnson landed right and left cleanly on the face without a return.

Johnson rushed in, forcing Ketchel to the ropes. After Stan clinched, Johnson literally lifted him up off his feet like a baby and carried him to ring center, five feet from the spot where the clinch started. Johnson's strength was obvious.

They sparred again. The fans and Britt called to Ketchel, "Make him lead." Stan barely missed a long-range right swing, though some fans thought it grazed the face, so they howled with glee. Johnson grinned and shook his head. Jack was short with a couple of lefts.

Johnson steadily backed away as they sparred for a lead, with Ketchel following. After a long spell of sparring, Johnson rammed home a hard left to the mouth. Ketchel kept trying to get Johnson to lead. Johnson landed a hard right to the jaw. Stan landed a light left on the mouth and they clinched.

The *Examiner* said both men were fighting very carefully. The *Call* said, "It was a tame round, characterized by a few bursts of speed." The *Call* also said it was another Johnson round.

5 - Johnson kept feinting and moving toward Ketchel. Stan opened with a left to the body, but the champ replied with a couple light lefts to the face. Johnson blocked a left and they clinched. Jack landed a left jab to the mouth. Stan's head went back from another hard jab to the nose. Johnson followed with another jab and blocked a left hook in a clinch.

At long range, Ketchel tried to get him to lead, but the champ would not respond. They sparred again. Johnson twice flung his left jab to the face. Johnson's long left visited Ketchel's red nose several times in this round, and he always got away without receiving a return.

Ketchel tried for the body with his left but was short. Johnson landed two left jabs to the face and a hard right to the body. Ketchel reeled. In the clinches, Johnson's system of defense was perfect. On the outside, he drove in two more quick left jabs without any drawing back of his elbow. There was blood on Ketchel's lips.

Few leads marked the round, but Johnson had all the best of it.

6 - Ketchel landed a left to the body and followed with another left to the jaw. Johnson countered with a left to the stomach. Jack landed two left jabs and Ketch landed a right to the body.

Johnson sent Ketchel reeling with a left on the jaw, and dropped him to his haunches with a straight left. Another version of the knockdown said Ketchel ran into a straight left on the chin and he went down to the floor. A third version said Ketch blocked a left on his guard but still went down.

Stan had been caught off his balance, and without waiting for the count, he rose with a half-hearted smile. Another left jab landed on Stan's mouth, and Ketch hooked Johnson in the ribs with his left. Johnson seemed to have his range with his left jab now, and repeatedly prodded Ketchel with it.

Johnson landed his right uppercut to the jaw. He also raked Stan's face with a succession of lefts to the jaw. Ketch continued forcing the pace, but was met with two lefts on the nose that started the blood flowing.

The crowd laughed as Johnson backed away. Ketchel followed him and swung a left on the body. Johnson came back with a left jab on the mouth. As Stan was going through the motion of a shift, Johnson nailed him with left and right on the face. He then followed with a left jab at the bell.

Johnson had a good lead in the round, though it looked as if he was holding back. In every clinch during the fight, Ketchel was bent backward by Johnson's superior weight and strength. Ketchel's nose bled during the round and while he sat in his corner.

7 - Johnson swooped in with two lefts on the nose. Stan countered with a hard left hook to the body. Johnson peppered the sore nose with his left, causing it to bleed freely. Jack used his left in a punishing way, reaching the face repeatedly. Ketch swung his left to the body.

In a clinch, Johnson began pumping in right uppercuts for the first time, reaching the face and body. Ketchel used Johnson's shoulder as a mat to wipe the blood flowing from his nostrils. In close, Johnson landed several times on the nose and face. He sent Ketchel reeling with a right. In a clinch which followed, Johnson worked his uppercut again, tilting Ketchel's head. Stan tried hard to land lefts on the body, but Jack baffled him and then made him pay, scoring hard to the stomach.

Suddenly, Ketchel swung his left with terrific force and it caught Johnson solidly on the jaw, raising a big lump there that immediately was perceptible to the spectators. It was by far Ketch's cleanest and best blow of the fight, and the immense crowd rose to its feet yelling gleefully. However, the *Examiner* disagreed with this version, saying that the left caught Johnson on the glove and made a noise. The crowd cheered, thinking Ketchel had landed, but Johnson laughed.

8 - Johnson immediately closed in, landing twice with his left jab on the face, sending Ketchel's head back. Stan's nose was pouring blood. They clinched and each punched the body with the left. Johnson then hit the ribs with his right and Stan again hit the body with his left. They roughed it in close, and Stan worked in a hard right uppercut on the jaw. The referee separated them, and Johnson landed a left and right on the face as they broke. Ketch got in another left on the body. He missed a right swing and almost went through the ropes from the force of his own effort. Jack stepped back and grinned.

Johnson forced him back gradually and landed a left to the jaw. Ketch swung a left on the body and Johnson twice scored with left jabs. Stan missed another right swing and the misdirected force spun him around like a top. At the bell, Stan ran to his corner smiling as the crowd cheered.

9 - Johnson planted his left to the face continuously without return. Jack had started to put more steam behind his blows. More than once, Ketchel winced under the steady punishment.

Johnson stood still for a moment, and then rammed home a straight head-tilting left. They clinched until the referee broke them. Another clinch followed. Johnson either held Stan's arms so that he could not score, or he smothered Ketchel's body blows. The champ landed four stinging left jabs to the face, but Stan did not break ground.

Ketchel landed a left on the ribs and Johnson countered with short left hooks to the jaw until they clinched. There were two or three clinches in which Ketchel landed lefts to the stomach.

As Stan ducked, Johnson caught him with a right hook to the mouth, which sent him into the ropes. Ketch missed another wild right swing. A couple of nasty Johnson left jabs, one of which sent Stan's head back, brought blood from the lips. The champ enjoyed the honors.

10 - After a clinch and break, Johnson landed two straight lefts to the stomach and quickly shifted the left to the jaw, where he twice connected. Ketchel started spitting blood. Johnson landed several lefts on the mouth and nose. He also landed a right uppercut. Ketchel seemed quite tired.

During a clinch, Johnson rammed in a series of body punches. As they scuffled and wrestled, Johnson landed some short left hooks to the ear and jaw, and Ketchel stumbled and almost went down to the floor, but Johnson held, lifted, and swung Stan up to a standing position again, preventing Ketchel from going down.

After breaking, back on the outside, Johnson stood statue-like and straightened out his left every few seconds, landing several jabs, bringing fresh blood from Stan's sore mouth and nose. Jack sent Ketch reeling with a left hook on the neck. Johnson again wrestled him almost off his balance.

Johnson drew back from a left swing and clinched. Stan against missed a left hook and Jack rushed Ketch to the ropes in a rally, putting in a punishing left on the stomach. Stan winced. At the bell, Jack patted him on the shoulder with his open hand.

The *Examiner* said Ketchel was badly whipped in this round. It also said, "Up to this point Johnson seemed to be under a wrap," meaning that the writer believed that Jack previously had been holding back and was carrying Ketchel. At two points in this fight, Johnson literally did carry Ketchel, lifting him up off the canvas.

11 - After some desultory sparring, Ketch whipped his left to the kidneys and missed two hard swings for the jaw. Johnson landed a straight left and used his right uppercut several times in a clinch, but did not seem to put much force into the punches. Johnson was not using or landing his right uppercut as often as he usually did. A left jab sent Ketch's head back.

Stan sent the crowd into convulsions by landing a terrific hard right on the face, almost on the jaw. Johnson immediately clinched and seemed content to rest. Ketchel forced the fighting, trying to follow his advantage, but could not penetrate Jack's clever defense any further.

Suddenly Johnson loosened up and was all over him, whipping in hard punches with both hands from every angle, driving Ketchel across the ring until Jack felt that he had avenged the blow. In the clinches, Johnson avoided Stan's left uppercut. Johnson launched his right uppercut, landing each time. Jack then swung his left into the body, scoring repeatedly.

At the bell, the crowd cheered Ketchel vigorously. However, his face was battered badly from the effects of the constant left jabs.

12 - Johnson stepped briskly from his corner and met Ketchel with a straight left as Stan advanced. They clinched and broke. Someone yelled, "Now then, Stanley," and Ketch let go a right swing. His glove seemed to curve around Johnson's neck, though it possibly came down on the jaw. It was too fast to be seen well. Johnson sank clumsily to the floor, his left glove catching himself. The champion was down! The crowd was shocked.

Johnson took his time to rise, flipping around, and ever so slightly shaking his head. The *Examiner* claimed there was a bit of a grin on Johnson's face, so evidently he was in possession of all his senses.

As soon as Jack rose, Ketchel rushed in to finish him, but Jack met the advance by lashing out with a series of five blazing-fast rights and lefts thrown in combination. The finishing blow appears to have been the first right that Johnson threw, which landed as Stan was throwing his own right.

Johnson threw his vicious combination with so much ferocity and abandon that he flung himself over the top of the prostrate Ketchel and went tumbling down to the canvas in his own corner. Ketchel fell on his back with his arms outstretched, as if he had been shot dead. Johnson turned around, rose, and then swiped some of Stan's teeth out of his glove.

Ketchel was completely out cold as referee Jack Welch counted off the ten seconds. He lay prone with blood streaming from his mouth.

After the count concluded, Stan started to rise, lifting his back off the canvas, but his seconds had to lift him up and assist him to his corner before taking him to his dressing room.

It was a wild and spectacular ending, given that the champion had been on the canvas, apparently dropped and hurt, and just seconds later it was Ketchel who was down and out.

Overall, the fight had been a dominant Johnson performance. He had administered a gradual beating, even though Ketchel had been true to his word in his attempt to try to force Johnson to lead. Johnson dropped Ketchel in the 2nd, 6th, and 12th rounds, and picked him up and prevented Stan from going down in the 10th round.

Debate about this fight has continued to this day. Most of it centers on two issues. The first was whether Johnson was carrying Ketchel and could have finished him at any time, or simply was administering his usual cautious gradual beating. The second issue was whether Johnson intentionally took a dive before finishing Ketchel in order to make the motion pictures more valuable, and/or to bait Ketchel into a trap. Another theory was that Johnson wanted to seem vulnerable, so as to induce Jeffries to fight him. Others thought Ketchel simply was a very hard puncher who caught Johnson well, and that Jack, though slightly stunned momentarily, struck out in an attempt to get payback, as he always did when hit hard. Fans, writers, and experts engaged in the same debate then as today.

Afterwards, Johnson said,

> Ketchel is a good tough boy, but I had things all my own way. The time he knocked me down was because I was coming in too fast. His punch hit me back of the ear, but the force of both of us coming together was what sent me to the floor. Of course it hurt me. Why shouldn't I admit it? … Jeffries can have his chance any time. I guess I showed the fans that I have a good punch.

Of course, as will be discussed, the films showed Johnson's version to be incorrect. He was not moving forward at the time.

Another paper quoted Johnson as saying,

> A lad game to the core with a terrible punch – that's Ketchel as I found him today. But with all his gameness and punch, he can thank his luck that he scored a knockdown on me. It was not alone the force of his right-hander clipping me behind the ear that felled me; it was the fact that I was coming in, as well. I was stunned, I can assure you.
>
> As for the fight I put up, I fought safe all the way and that's all I wanted. I will admit, though, that once or twice I allowed Ketchel to come too close, when I might just as well have held him off. This scar on my chin from one of his left hooks tells me that.

A third paper quoted Johnson as saying,

> Ketchel is a good, game man and put up a hard fight. He hit me on the jaw when I went down in the twelfth round and there is no good of saying that I was not dazed when I really was. ... It was a wild blow that caught me on the jaw. ... He came at me wildly and I waited for him with lefts and rights and beat him to the blow. The blow which knocked him out was a right to the jaw. I beat him to the punch.

Hence, in some versions Johnson said the punch hit him in the back of the ear, while in others he said he was hit on the jaw.

The films are old, not very crisp, do not have a sufficient number of frames for a good slow-motion view, and the angle is not perfect. Therefore, it is not entirely clear where Johnson was hit. Today we know that filming a fight from several different angles demonstrates that often one angle can be deceptive, and another can give a better view of where a punch actually landed. Often, a punch that appears to miss or land on the neck from one angle can be seen to land on the jaw from another. One can watch the existing films and draw one's own conclusions.

Ketchel said he landed a hard punch. He wanted a rematch.

> I was too careless, that was all. From the start I was laying back waiting for a chance to land a hard punch. ... I hit him a good stiff left when he dropped [actually it was a right]. But then I lost my head. How did he hit me? I don't know. I only realized that when I came to. ... I weighed 178 pounds and never felt in better condition for a fight.

Ketchel also was quoted as saying,

> I knocked Johnson down fairly and squarely with one of my swings and I came within an ace of winning the heavy weight championship. ... Just where I hit him I can not say. ... I must admit that I was too

careless. … Had I kept my head I might have knocked him out. … I was never afraid of Johnson and I carried the fight to him round after round. He never hurt me till he landed the punch that knocked me out. Here are three of my teeth which fell out after that last punch.

Referee Jack Welch said,

It was the same old story of the good little man against the good big man, and the good big man won. Ketchel fought the best fight that was in him, and he was game to the core. He hurt Johnson when he put the black down in the twelfth with a right swing behind the ear, but it only served to arouse Johnson's ire, and the negro came back and made short work of him. At no time did Ketchel have a chance against the wonderful defense of the negro. He showed remarkable courage, however. … Johnson is a wonderful fighter and took no chances throughout the contest. Both men fought cleanly.

Another paper quoted Welch as saying,

Ketchel fought the best he knew how, but he was hopelessly outclassed. It was simply a case of a very game man biting off more than he could chew.

I believe the flooring of Johnson by Ketchel in the twelfth, just before the fight ended, was a clean knockdown in every way. Ketchel made a vicious right swing as Johnson came in and caught him behind the ear, sending him down.

Ketchel wasn't set when Johnson rose to his feet, and so, when the big negro lashed out with a left and a right, catching him about the jaw, he went down like a log. Just look at the glove on Johnson's right hand and you will see where Ketchel caught that final right. His teeth tore holes in the leather of the glove big and ragged, as though it had been hacked with a saw.

Welch confirmed his belief that the knockdown of Johnson was genuine. "Johnson was inclined to fool around too much, and I think Ketchel sneaked one over on him." Welch also said that after knocking him down, Ketchel went after him wildly, without any defense, leaving himself open, and Johnson met his attack with the faster blows, which were terrific wallops that were so hard that Johnson also went to the floor from the force of his own punches. "Up to this time Johnson fairly outclassed the white man. He was too big and too clever for him. Johnson fairly smothered Ketchel with his cleverness and was beating him down systematically. Ketchel showed wonderful gameness, as he forced the fighting, although he was badly stung at times."

The *San Francisco Chronicle* said Ketchel never had a chance to win, but the bout had one of the most spectacular finishes ever. "It was a sensational wind-up to what had been a thoroughly one-sided bout in favor of the black." In the middle of the 12th round, Ketchel swung a hard right.

To the writer and to 90 per cent of those who were in a position to follow closely what was happening, the punch seemed to glance around the back of Johnson's head. Apparently, also, it had little force, and there was genuine surprise when Johnson dropped down, spun around on his knees with a smile on his face and took advantage of the count that the rules of the prize ring permitted him.

This writer noted that it was significant and telling that as soon as Johnson rose he was not so dazed as to be prevented from immediately rushing Ketchel more viciously than he had at any previous stage of the match, and had so much force behind his right and left swung in rapid succession that the right glove showed where Ketchel's teeth pierced through the leather. Ketchel's front teeth had been knocked out. The timing of Johnson's sudden increase of speed and power seemed interesting, particularly given that he had never thrown like that at any earlier point in the fight. The suggestion was that he had been carrying Ketchel. Still, even prior to that point, Stan was bleeding freely about the face, and bruised all over his body.

The *Chronicle* wondered whether it was a legitimate knockdown of Johnson. It conceded that it might have been a straight knockdown and that Johnson could not save himself from going down, but "the writer did not see a punch that would have such an effect, and it must also be remembered that such an ending would be of fast assistance to the handling of the moving pictures." The strong suspicion was that the punch was not that good, and Johnson intentionally went down to increase the market value of the films so he could make even more money. Noted was the fact that "Ketchel was apparently too weak to have landed a telling blow in the ninth, and the way he fairly collapsed when Johnson put his force behind two punches is the best indication of his condition."

Another *Chronicle* writer said that even while Johnson was down, it was obvious that he was planning his opponent's downfall, like a cat ready to spring, and a few seconds later he completed the job. "Whether Ketchel hurt Johnson when he half knocked and half shoved the champion to the floor in the final session will always be a disputed point, but the fact that a few seconds later the white man was in the land of dreams can never be questioned."

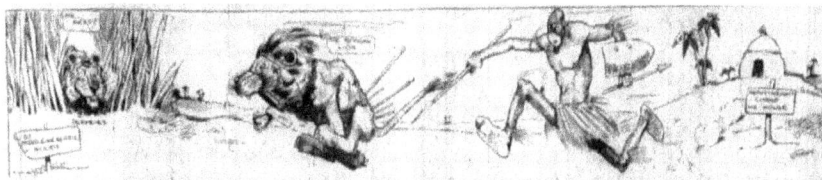

San Francisco Call, October 17, 1909

The *San Francisco Call* said Johnson won after reeling from a "mysterious punch" that fans failed to see. The champ quickly recovered and immediately finished Ketchel with a right and left that landed flush on the jaw. A few seconds before Johnson was down, Stan had started a wild right swing for the head.

> It landed some place – nobody knows where – but as the blow was delivered Johnson staggered and reeled to his knees. He floundered around for a few seconds, and then came like a panther at bay and delivered the two wallops which brought the uneven contest to an end. Now the question is: Was the battle on the square, or did Johnson take his ungraceful stumble for the purpose of swelling the gate receipts of the moving picture shows that are to follow, or had he stalled up to this point to help the wise betters on the 15 round end of it?

The end came so suddenly and was executed so deftly that it electrified and mystified nearly everyone. Veterans shook their heads and said, "It was a good show, but the last act was rotten. They should have had a stage manager to give them a few practical rehearsals." The crowd, for the most part, thought Johnson fell to help the moving picture revenues.

Referee Welsh said Ketchel hit Johnson on the back of his ear. Johnson said it landed on his jaw and severely stung him. He was caught off guard when he least expected it. Many were unsure. "But even the champion himself can not explain how he came back with the speed and fury with which he responded." As soon as he was down, Johnson smiled as he steadied himself, rose, rushed in, and knocked out Ketchel. Fans found it mysterious for Johnson to be dropped, but within a few seconds thereafter, be able to pulverize his opponent into total unconsciousness. "Nobody ever saw anything quite like it before. It was a new one in ring tricks."

No one doubted that Ketchel was legitimately knocked out cold. "Johnson apparently hit Ketchel so hard that he fairly sprawled on top of his small opponent and fell over him in his own corner." He quickly rose, while Stan remained out.

The *Examiner's* W. W. Naughton said the closing round was both sensational and peculiar. After Johnson went down from a punch that curved around his neck, he rose and met Stan's rush. Ketchel fairly impaled himself on Johnson's fast-flying fists and fell.

Naughton noted, "Johnson has the habit of infusing buffoonery into his fights at times, especially when he has matters well in hand." Naughton suspected that this was just such a moment. After the bout, he asked Johnson why he went down grinning from what was at best a glancing blow. Jack replied, "Oh, he hurt me, sure enough. He caught me on the bone behind the ear." A medical student said Johnson was struck on the mastoid process. Naughton said Johnson fell like a clown, which in part caused many at ringside to say it was bogus. Naughton thought that if he was hit harder, it might have looked more genuine. When Ketchel went down, it was like a soldier whose heart had been cleft by a sword-thrust.

Naughton agreed that the knockdowns in the last round would add to the value of the pictures. Thousands had paid to watch the Gans-Nelson films to see if Nelson indeed had fouled. In a like manner, they would go to see whether Johnson had sprawled in earnest.

Another *Examiner* writer said that a few seconds into the 12th round, a right to the back of the head, just behind the ear, dropped Jack to the floor. Every one of the 10,000 or more spectators screamed, bellowed, shouted, and cheered. Slowly Johnson turned over and then slowly raised himself. Once he regained his feet, a wonderful transformation occurred. Like a tiger upon a fawn he went at Ketchel, fighting and lashing out with all of his wonderful strength behind his punches, "fighting for the first time during the afternoon." Two short punches landed to the face with enough force to leave the imprint of teeth upon the glove. Ketchel dropped flat onto his back like a dead man, his arms and legs spread far apart. Carried by the violence of his own assault, Johnson staggered into the falling body and tripped to the floor, sprawling on his hands and knees. Nothing so sensational had ever been seen.

After the battle, the newsmen swarmed into the ring. Johnson admitted that he had been hurt badly. However, it was "hard to believe that the battered Ketchel had a damaging blow left in him by the time the twelfth round had been reached." The only thing that this writer was sure about was that Jeffries was the only man in the world who could force Johnson to extend himself.

The *Chronicle* believed that Johnson had carried Ketchel during the bout. It was apparent to those at ringside that Johnson could have finished the fight much sooner than he did, proven by the fact that "he was merely saving Ketchel even to the extent of holding him up in the earlier rounds, when the white man was almost falling."

Even before the fight started it was rumored amongst the press that Johnson would fight for the moving pictures for 12 rounds and then cut loose. George Little was credited with having told several friends that Johnson would win in the 12th round. In the 10th round, when several people remarked that Ketchel might last the limit, Little offered to bet any amount of money that Johnson would knock him out before 15 rounds had passed. Little even said to those in and around the corner, "What round do you want Johnson to knock him out? He can do it now. Just say the word." No one thought Ketchel was in on it, but "there is reasonable suspicion that Johnson, for the sake of the pictures preferred to allow his opponent to last a reasonable length of time." Even prior to the fight, Johnson had told friends not to bet that the fight would end before the 10th round, but to bet that it would end before the 15th, meaning that Jack felt confident it would end between rounds 10 and 15.

An *Examiner* writer also said Johnson so far outclassed Ketchel that he could have knocked him out in any round he wanted, including the 1st round, had he cared to extend himself. The finish was so spectacular that a suspicious mind might believe that it had been planned for the benefit of the moving picture man.

Summarizing the fight, the *Chronicle* said that for the most part, the rounds were much the same. Johnson had the better of matters at any style, though he was wary of the Ketchel swings and never left an opening. In the early rounds, Johnson's favorite punch was the left jab to the face, which rarely missed.

Johnson also had the advantage at infighting. At times he welcomed the clinches so that he could land on the body, and so easily handled Ketchel that the latter was tied up in a knot with no chance of punching back. Johnson's blows traveled a short distance.

Once Johnson saw that Ketchel was tottering and could not land, the champ changed his tactics. Instead of leading to the head, he fired his lefts into the body, and many a left rip to the stomach must have hurt.

Johnson was "a marvel of boxing skill." He feinted, led with lefts for the stomach or head, closed in with a right uppercut, and all the while rendered Ketchel ineffective. Stan's rushes and shifts were futile. Johnson could move back out of danger and grin.

Ketchel tried to stick with Britt's game plan. True, much of the time he forced Johnson around the ring, but he also tried to force him to lead. Johnson was willing to do so when the opportunity offered and he saw that he would receive little in return. Some criticized that Ketchel could have done better had he adopted his usual rushing tactics, but the *Chronicle* disagreed, feeling that if he had done so that Johnson would have stopped him even sooner.

As early as the 2nd round, Johnson showed a flash of his strength when he right uppercut Ketchel and sent him to the mat for a six-count. In that round, Stan's left eye showed signs of being cut.

In the 3rd and 4th rounds, Ketchel was bleeding profusely. "He seemed utterly unable to cope with the more massive Johnson, or to land any punches on his own account."

In the 6th round, Johnson sent him spinning across the ring from the force of a short-arm punch, and finally dropped him with a left. Ketchel immediately rose, but finished the round with his face covered in blood and his legs tottering.

Ketchel had his best showing in the 7th, when he landed two hard punches, one of which was a left swing flush on the point of the jaw. Johnson just shook his head and laughed. However, when the fight was over, he had a badly swollen jaw, and in one spot the skin had been taken off. That showed that Stan had real power. The other punch was a corking good left to the body, but once again the blow did not stop Johnson. "If anything, he carried the fight more aggressively than ever, and at the finish of the round was leading by a wide margin, as he led in every round of the battle."

Ketchel was puffing much more than one would expect from someone who had trained so well. Once he discovered that he was powerless, a discouraged look came over his face, and several times between rounds he shook his head sadly at his friends at ringside. On the other hand, Johnson's seconds were elated at how easily he was handling Ketchel.

Willis Britt said Ketchel lost the fight through his own carelessness, just when he had the fight almost won. The *Chronicle* disagreed. "Ketchel was as easy for Johnson as have been any of the men he has met in recent months." Ketchel showed his courage and gameness, but "at all times in the bout Johnson handled his man much as he would a child, swinging Ketchel clear off his feet in some of the clinches and outboxing him so that Ketchel's vaunted shift missed by a foot on the many times that he tried to connect." He was no more formidable than Kaufman, and his efforts were impotent.

Another *Chronicle* writer said Ketchel was the crowd's idol, but an easy mark for the whirlwind black who outclassed him at every stage of the bout. This writer said that had he been anyone other than Ketchel, or been of a different color, the fans would have jeered and hooted him. Instead, they heartily cheered his every puny effort. Ketchel was cheered at the slightest excuse. Even when he swung and missed, he was cheered for his courage. If he waited and made Johnson carry the fight to him, he was applauded for his wisdom, and if he landed even a light blow, the crowd burst into a howl of delight.

On only two occasions did Ketchel land telling blows. One was a powerful left swing early on that raised a welt on the champ's jaw. The second was the knockdown. Each time, the crowd went into a frenzy. Stan was cheered even as he left the ring. However, "It was Johnson all the way, even during the spasm of renewed hope which brought the crowd to its feet in the twelfth round."

Johnson towered over the "assassin," made him look foolish, and "often during the bout spared him, displaying rare good-nature until the moment when it suited his purpose to end the fight."

Ketchel was the idol not only because of his skin color, but because of his courage in standing up and taking punishment. He absorbed left jabs, right uppercuts, and heavy left jolts to the body, "which would have discouraged and sickened any fighter of his weight but himself." Johnson was his superior in skill, and was a giant of marvelous quickness and science, as well as relative size. "Added to the natural support of a white man by the white race, was the added hatred of Johnson for his offensive ways, which have made him the most unpopular fighter in the ring."

Unlike Ketchel, Johnson was jeered and booed. The champ simply grinned and showed his gold teeth, further increasing the fans' dislike for him and strengthening their hope that he would be defeated. Johnson's white wife was in the stands, smiling confidently.

Johnson received no applause, not even when he generously picked up Ketchel from the different corners of the ring and whirled him around to a safe space in the center, after which Jack stepped back momentarily and allowed Ketchel to get his bearings. The crowd simply hated him.

> The crowd groaned and exchanged estimates as to how close Ketchel had been the heavy-weight crown, but in the opinion of the writer, and I would have been pleased to see him win, the middle-weight champion had no more chance than the much talked of rabbit.

Angered by the result, the crowd began discussing how Jeffries would make pulp out of Johnson.

The *Call* said it was one of the most uneven and discouraging bouts ever seen, and just a bad matchup. "Ketchel never figured for a single second. He was too small, too clumsy and too inexperienced. If he ever did happen to hit Johnson once, Johnson would respond with at least 10 punches, just to even up the score and show the crowd that he was still in the game." The fight was lopsided and uneven throughout. It "resembled a setto between a hawk and a sparrow."

Ketchel was game and sincere, but Johnson easily hustled and bustled him around the ring. "Johnson never seemed to be in earnest. He spent as much of his time watching the crowd as he did watching Ketchel. He would answer his critics and then come on and cuff Ketchel with a right or a left, whichever suited his purpose." Ketchel was outclassed in every aspect of the trade, with the possible exception of gameness, "but what is the use of gameness for a man like Johnson, who seldom, if ever, is compelled to show this quality? There was no necessity for his taking any punches."

Johnson was not overly aggressive. He stalled and smiled and took his time. When he threw, his punches generally landed. When Stan missed, Jack smiled and winked at the crowd. Time and again he informed everyone at the ringside that the battle would end before the 15th round.

The *Call* said there was little to tell of the battle, round-by-round. Johnson started off by using his piston-rod left to the face. He brought the blood running from the nose in the 1st round and blackened Stan's eyes. Stan looked dangerous, but that was all. "The black man did the fighting and everybody saw it." In the 3rd, Johnson's left landed quite often. Ketch was bleeding, and even his breathing seemed to be labored. They clinched and exchanged a few body punches, but Stan's efforts were feeble. It was the same in the 4th, though Johnson started to bring his right uppercut into play. From the 6th round on, Ketchel seemed to tire, while Johnson improved. Ketch bled profusely from the nose and mouth. He tried to land his famous right and left shifts, but missed by many feet each time.

Johnson kept jabbing him and smiling to the crowd. He seemed to land wherever and whenever he pleased. Stan would bore in and try for the body, but invariably got the worst of the mix-ups. Johnson seemed to have a perfect sense of distance and range, and was able to vary his blows from the head to the body without being harmed. He always remained safe, whether at a distance or up close in the clinches. Ketchel was game, but it did not appear as though Johnson was hitting him as hard as he might have had he felt so disposed.

The crowd was with the white man. Johnson had several hundred black admirers, but they were afraid to cut loose vocally. "If Johnson did any damage the crowd would hold its breath, but if Ketchel landed one everybody seemed to jump to his feet at once and tear loose with a volley of cheers."

Johnson did not seem to mind the fans' jeering at all. He worked his smile all the time, and the further the fight went, the broader his smile became. He was heard to remark many times that he intended to give Ketchel the worst beating of his life, and he did.

The *Examiner*'s W. W. Naughton said Johnson outclassed and toyed with his smaller opponent for 11 rounds before putting him out with a fierce volley of smashes. Summarizing, "Jack Johnson is a wonderful fighter. Stanley Ketchel is a game one."

Naughton said Ketchel was a wonder when equally matched, but had as much chance with Johnson as a rabbit with a greyhound. Johnson's final blows were so vicious that the skin of Johnson's glove was torn through contact with Stan's teeth. Ketchel fell heavily; spread-eagle on the floor on his back, with his arms thrown out, lifeless as a log. After the count, Johnson seemed concerned, and heaved a big sigh of relief when Ketchel slowly came back from his slumber.

Naughton said it was a lamentably one-sided fight. Before the 2nd round was over it was obvious that Ketchel's one hope lie in landing a big blow. Occasionally, Ketchel managed to force Johnson to lead, but when Johnson led he landed. Throughout the fight, Johnson stood like a statue, and suddenly would snap left jabs to Ketchel's face, tilting his head back and drawing blood from his lips. For about 6 rounds the champ mainly relied on left jabs, and Stan's bleeding lips and blood-smeared face bore out Johnson's accuracy. Stan mostly tried to land his left swing to the ribs. He succeeded a few times, but he mostly missed.

Ketchel faced the music doggedly, though without his usual dash. Instead of fighting like a tiger, he boxed in a rather subdued manner. He seldom took a punch without trying a return, but all he could do was try. He was not successful in landing. Not much in the bout could encourage him. His body hooks were brushed aside. His left leads to the face fell short. When he swung his right Johnson drew his head out of range. Stan missed his shifts and big swings, and his blows lacked their usual snap. Johnson was able to dance out of harm's way and Stan would swing himself off balance. When Johnson held out his two hands, Stan went for the body, but fell short. "When Johnson holds a man at bay in this manner the champion's arms seem to be as long as oars."

Johnson kept his dangerous right uppercut in reserve until the 7th round. That blow was strong enough to tear through a man's guard and loosen his teeth. However, he did not use it as often as usual. In fact, he hardly used it at all. Some speculated that he wanted to carry Ketchel, while others thought he felt that he did not need it.

When Johnson masterfully feinted, Ketchel would begin throwing, as if punches were coming. Hence, Johnson could get him to lead. At these times, Stan was confused greatly. It appeared as though Johnson allowed numerous openings to pass unnoticed.

Johnson was very clever in the clinches as well. He showed that he knew more in one round than the average fighter had learned in a career. He did not grab, but rather placed his gloves against the biceps or shoulders and used pressure to render Stan as helpless as if he was tied up with ropes. Ketchel usually was way above average at clinch fighting, but he was powerless against Johnson. He couldn't free himself, and Johnson looked down at him and chuckled. Even when Ketch did escape and land, it almost seemed as if Johnson allowed him to do so. Regardless, Johnson twisted and turned so that his hip acted as a bunker, and he gave Ketchel a stiff dig with the right in the stomach to show him that he could work inside too.

The clinches showed Johnson's immense strength. Several times he lifted Stan off his feet in a playful manner and swung him half around. Once when Stan's legs became entangled, Johnson picked him up with one arm and placed him on squarely on his feet. "Johnson has always assured his friends that Jeffries' strength has no terrors for him. After watching the champion closely in his recent fights, it seems to me that even big-framed Jeffries will not be able to take any liberties with ebon-hued Johnson when they lock arms and begin to pull and haul."

Johnson was very careful, watching his man as a cat does with a mouse. He did little execution early on, which made Ketchel followers glad. However, in the 5th round, Johnson doubled up on his straight lefts and added power to them. Stan began to take on the look of one up against it. He bled freely, while Johnson showed how easy it all was. He stood motionless, poked out his hands straight in front, blocked the blows, and jabbed the bleeding mouth.

In the 6th round, Ketchel was sent reeling from a solid right, and a moment later he was dropped by a straight left. He rose and stalked, and the crowd laughed derisively as Johnson backed away, along the ropes. Whenever they laughed, Jack grinned. "Whatever else may be said about him, he is a cool-headed customer and ringside reviling does not rattle him for an instant." While the crowd was guffawing, Johnson moved in, and Stan began to set up his shift, but before he could, that left jab fired out like a piston-rod and sent blood from Ketchel's nose.

In the 7th round, Johnson used his uppercut for the first time, while holding in the clinches. After using it a few times, he stopped using it again, only employing it on rare occasions. In that round, Stan got a loud cheer when he landed a hard left hook. Many thought it landed on the chin, but Naughton said it did not. "It landed on his raised glove."

The 8th round saw Ketchel working his right swing, trying it several times, almost throwing himself off his feet when he missed, which was on every occasion.

In the 9th, a Ketchel blow sent Johnson against the ropes, and there was a ripple of excitement amongst the crowd. However, the throng sobered when Johnson spurted and prodded Ketchel with left hooks.

By the 10th round, Stan appeared tired. The question most asked was whether he could last 15 rounds. Some thought he could, given how carefully Johnson was fighting.

Johnson loosened up a bit in the 11th round, but took a couple of fairly hard blows in return for the ones he landed. As Johnson went to his corner, there was a slight smear of blood on his right cheek. It looked as though Stan had nicked the skin with a high left hook.

In the 12th round, Stanley took the aggressive, as if he had been given instructions to abandon his attempts to make Johnson lead. He hurled himself right into the thick of things. However, 34 seconds into the round, he was stretched out unconscious on the mat.

Another *Examiner* writer also said it was a one-sided, totally unequal bout. Johnson was unharmed, and never took a long breath during the fight. "It was a crime to send Ketchel in against Johnson. At long range boxing the negro punished the white boy at will, and during the clinches Ketchel was as helpless as an eel held in a vise."

Afterwards, Jim Coffroth estimated the receipts at $32,300, though before the fight began, Coffroth said he expected the gate to yield about $40,000. The fighters received 60%, from which Johnson's winner's share was 65%, or about $12,597. Plus he won an alleged $5,000 side bet. He also would earn a great deal more from the film revenues, of which he had a 40% interest. Hence, it was a very nice payday for him. Ketchel earned 35% of the 60% fighters' share, or about $6,783. However, if he lost an alleged $5,000 side bet, then he only earned $1,783. The parties claimed the side-bet was paid, but no one knew for sure. Either way, Ketchel would have a share of the lucrative motion picture receipts.

One newspaper reported that there were 8,401 paid admissions at the fight, the second largest crowd that ever attended a fistic contest there. 8,704 had attended Corbett-Jeffries II. Another report said the 8,400 paid admissions were just 600 less than the Jeffries-Corbett bout. Every ticket was sold and several hundred stood up in the aisles and in the gallery.

In subsequent days, the newspapers and fight-goers continued talking about the 12th round knockdown that Ketchel scored on Johnson, wondering whether Ketchel actually knocked Johnson down. The referee said yes. Some fans doubted it. It was a much debated question. Many asserted that Ketchel did not land hard enough to budge a lightweight, and that Johnson took a dive to enhance the value of the moving pictures.

San Francisco Evening Post, October 18, 1909

The *Evening Post* believed the knockdown was legitimate. "The blow was one of those sudden and spectacular ones for which Ketchel has been noted." It felt that Referee Welsh was in the best position to opine regarding the blow, and he said it was legitimate, though it only momentarily jarred Johnson. The *Post* noted that after being knocked down, for the first time Johnson showed fire in his eyes, indicating that he had been hit hard and wanted revenge. "His face took on a demoniac look, half human, half the expression of some wild thing goaded to desperation. Johnson's…gorilla-like arms began to beat a very hailstorm of blows on Ketchel." Before that, he wore a "dreamy, languid expression." The sudden and ferocious attack took Ketchel by surprise.

The *Chronicle* said the 8,500 spectators were still talking about the peculiar incidents. Some thought it was a fake, but there was no doubt that Ketchel was trying and had been hurt badly. The day after the fight, Ketchel's face was bruised, nose swollen, and there was a gap in his mouth where Johnson had knocked out several teeth. This writer felt that there was no foundation for the assumption that the two were working together.

However, there was "plenty of reason for argument that Johnson delayed the knockout until the twelfth in order to give the moving pictures a chance. The suspicion also continues that Johnson did the spectacular in falling to the floor of the ring when he was hit, if hit at all, by a glancing blow," which did not have the force of the punch that Stan landed in the 7th round, when "Ketchel failed to stagger the black." It seemed suspicious that an even harder blow which landed solidly on Johnson's jaw had not budged him, yet this blow took him off his feet. Several parties were advised against betting that Stan would last 15 rounds.

The *Call* said that not in years had any fight caused the tongues to wag the way they were about the Johnson-Ketchel fight. The result had sports guessing. Nine out of ten were sure that there was some sort of a job framed up, but none were sure exactly what it was. Everyone was talking about the mysterious punch with which Ketchel allegedly floored Johnson.

The two fighters and the referee all said it landed. "If the punch was landed it certainly was the fastest and most deceptive in history."

The *Examiner* agreed that the main subject of argument was whether or not Ketchel had knocked Johnson down. The general opinion among those at ringside was that the champion had done the tumbling act for the benefit of the pictures. Those who saw his golden smile as he went to the mat found it hard to reconcile the smile with a knockdown.

Johnson's wonderful cleverness was acknowledged. He was so decisively superior such that no one wanted to see a rematch. The only blot on his performance was his "flop to the floor, which was voted amateurish."

Another writer said Johnson handled Ketchel as if Stan was an amateur. He boxed 10 rounds for the benefit of the moving pictures, and then, having fulfilled the obligation, whipped Ketchel in less than two rounds of actual fighting. Nine out of ten failed to see Ketchel's knockdown blow land.

The *Bulletin* agreed that the big crowd reviled the black man for faking his own knockdown to give the film men what they wanted. Over 8,000 watched Johnson play with his pygmy opponent for 11 rounds, until finally becoming serious about knocking him out.

The spectators paid an average of $4 a seat in the hope of seeing Johnson get a trouncing, but they only saw a repetition of Johnson-Burns, with a few spectacular sidelights thrown in for the cinematograph men. The few who claimed to have seen the knockdown punch land said it hit the base of the brain, not the jaw as Johnson claimed. However, Jack could not hold back his grin once he went down. "If Johnson can recuperate from a swat like that in three seconds and then come back strong enough to knock his opponent cold a second later he is supernatural and must be ranked in the same class as…the Wizard of Oz."

The *Bulletin* called Johnson's flip-flop "grotesque." Many believed that he was a "manipulator of the worst type," whose actions would hurt the game more than Jack O'Brien's confession several years ago.

This writer condemned Johnson for carrying Ketchel. Noted was the fact that when Johnson's friends asked him if it was advisable to bet on him to win in less than 10 rounds, he cautioned them not to do so, but said they could bet that he would win within 15 rounds. "How does it sound to you, gentle reader? At that, he had a hard time to keep faith with his friends. … In the second round, and again in the tenth, Johnson almost knocked his opponent out, only saving the day by holding the latter in his arms until he had recovered his senses." Ketchel usually missed his punches badly. "In most instances Johnson simply grinned and allowed the Michigan Lion to recover his equilibrium – probably fearing he would finish the battle if he followed Ketchel up."

Despite its racially denigrating language, the *Evening Post* said the boos and catcalls that accompanied Johnson into the ring were uncalled for.

Black or white or brown or red, when a man enters the ring he deserves fair treatment, and this was more than the local fight fans accorded Johnson. No matter what may be said against Johnson's antics out of the ring, once he finds himself between the ropes with an opponent in front of him, he is the fairest and cleanest of fighters, and a good sportsman. He never takes unfair advantages.

Memphis, Tennessee reported that the fight reports had tied up traffic on the Mississippi river. There was a shortage of labor, for black deckhands wanted to remain ashore in order to hear returns from the fight as it was taking place. Even after the victory by one of their race, they remained ashore to celebrate, which caused the big steamboats to remain docked. It was called a "Big Negro Jubilee."

Eastern followers were surprised that Johnson displayed such remarkable skill, strength, and agility. Although Ketchel's defeat was no surprise, the way Johnson handled him with such ease was surprising.

> Sporting authorities now agree that Johnson has been underrated, rather than that Ketchel was overestimated, and that Jeffries has a much more difficult problem with which to contend than was known before the Ketchel fight. The consensus of opinion here is that Jeffries' vulnerable point will be his wind, which, it is feared, has not improved through five years of idleness.

Willis Britt wanted a rematch for Ketchel, but the press said the public would not demand it, having seen the easy way in which Johnson had handled him. Britt had a couple of Stan's teeth, but still believed Ketchel almost beat Johnson, but was careless and got caught. He said Ketchel would fight Langford any time there were sufficient inducements.

The *Examiner* noted that Ketchel sobbed like a child before the fight. It was not known whether it was the result of sheer nervousness, if he was overcome by the immense crowd's demonstration in his favor, or whether it was the thought that sure defeat awaited him.

In Australia, Tommy Burns said he wanted a rematch with Johnson. However, the consensus was that the only opponent left for Johnson was Jeffries. No promoter would care to handle a second meeting between Johnson and Burns, given the dominant lacing Jack handed Tommy the first time, as well as the similarly-sized Ketchel.

Given how easily Johnson had handled light-heavyweight-sized fighters like Burns and Ketchel, there wasn't going to be huge interest in a Sam Langford fight either. Johnson simply was too big and clever for smaller foes. Plus, Johnson already had defeated Langford clearly once before.

Langford wanted to fight Johnson, and he and his manager Joe Woodman said they would immediately post any size forfeit Johnson named to go as a side bet. The *Call* said, "It does not appear that there will be much of a chance to make this match, however, for the reason that two colored fighters would not draw much money."

The *Examiner* opined that Jeffries was the only opponent for Johnson.

> The sooner the big boy arrives home the better it will be for the peace of mind of the fight followers of this country. ... Outside of Jeffries there isn't a man in the game today who could even make a respectable showing against this wonderful negro. Johnson is a big man in a big puddle, and what's more, he knows it.

The public wanted Jeffries for Johnson. There was some talk of a Burns-Langford match. It was said that Burns would have a chance against anyone but Johnson.

Everywhere he went, the champ was the center of attraction, and his victory brought money and joy to all those of his color who had bet on him.

The day after the fight, Johnson was seen in his racing auto, as usual. He said his jaw was still sore from the effect of Stan's mysterious punch, but otherwise he had no marks.

Jack said he was in the business to make money, and fighting made him money. A Jeffries fight could make him the most money. He wanted Jeffries, but would not chase after him. "I'm not going to run after him. I am the champion and Jeffries can come after me."

Johnson was not interested in a Ketchel rematch. "Let him fight some one else. I knocked him out, all right, and that ought to be enough for the time." However, Johnson also said he would fight anyone if there was enough money in it.

Johnson, who had fought both, thought Ketchel could beat Langford. "They are pretty evenly matched, except that Ketchel has a better punch than Sam."

When asked if he had received the money from the side bet, Johnson replied, "Yes sir, I have the money, and what is more I am just counting it."

From overseas, Jeffries said that upon his arrival in New York from Europe, he would instruct Sam Berger to make the Johnson match. Jeff said that he was in fine health, and if Johnson ever entered the ring with him, the championship would be returned to the white race. "Johnson is not much of a fighter and he never met a good man. His fight with Burns was no test. Burns is a newspaper fighter. I can only hope that Johnson will cover my money. I would not fight him if I did not think I could beat him." Jeff said he was weighing about 230-235 pounds.

Jim Corbett said Jeffries surely would meet and defeat Johnson:

> Johnson's defeat of Ketchel should not be given too much significance. It is merely a case of a little man going down before a big fellow and was to be expected. While Johnson isn't a dub, he is by no means a great fighter. ... He has appeared at a time when there has been a remarkably poor lot of heavyweights.

Corbett said Jeffries had delayed fighting Johnson simply because he wanted to see whether or not he could get into condition again. He currently was in the best condition that he had been in years.

The American public may take my tip. He will easily wrest the heavyweight championship from the Texan brunette. As a matter of fact, Jeffries in my opinion does not need to be in first-class condition to whip Johnson, because Johnson is not and never was in the same class with Jeffries. Johnson is only able to fight defensively. His only blow is a counter. Burns, Ketchel and others have always fought Johnson's fights for him.

Jeffries won't do anything of the kind and Johnson will find his uppercut unavailing against the Californian, while if Jeffries ever lands on Johnson, which he will, it will be good-by Mister Colored Champion.

The *Bulletin* said the Ketchel bout only intensified the sporting world's desire to see Jeffries come back and "give the black champion a drubbing that will drive him from the prize-ring forever." Johnson had prolonged Ketchel's agony 10 rounds longer than necessary, had made a plaything of him, leering and laughing when Stan tried to hit him, calling out to the crowd to watch his antics, "and generally behaving like the denizens of the forests from which his ancestors came. Even the fight-followers who are hardened to the sight of a negro opposing a white man in the ring do not relish the idea of a sneering, grinning gorilla slowly annihilating one of their own race." They were praying for Jeffries to lick the "Galveston coon."

Coffroth was wise to place two uniformed policemen and a dozen plain-clothes officers in Johnson's corner. Coffroth said, "I don't want him to come to any harm at the hands of the crowd."

Although some said Ketchel did better than Kaufman, this writer strongly disagreed. Johnson was never close to stopping Al, and Kaufman did better late in the bout. Conversely, Johnson could have stopped Ketchel any time he wanted to do so. Stan simply was too small. He would have a good chance against similarly-sized men such as Langford and Burns.

The Miles Brothers said the moving pictures were the finest ever taken of a fight, even better than Britt-Nelson. The negatives had been developed already and would be taken to New York to be exhibited.[213]

A fair amount of the Johnson-Ketchel fight films still exist. In the 1st round, Johnson mostly stepped in with jabs and then quickly would step back or to the side, capitalizing on his obvious height and reach advantages. When close, Johnson easily suppressed Ketchel's attack by placing his gloves on Stanley's gloves and arms. Throughout the bout, Johnson used a quick peppering left jab lead, slick circling footwork, feints, reach outs to block or smother, and clinching when close. His movement was quick but efficient, moving no more than necessary. Sometimes he would lean back away from blows as well.

---

[213] *San Francisco Evening Post, San Francisco Chronicle, San Francisco Call, San Francisco Examiner, San Francisco Bulletin,* October 18, 1909.

In the 2nd round, Johnson threw a flurry of solid punches, including a right uppercut and straight right that sent Ketchel back. Johnson continued the attack and dropped Ketchel with a short right. Johnson did not try to finish him, but returned to his cautious defensive style, parrying, feinting, clinching, and carefully selecting his moments to punch.

Johnson demonstrated his typically methodical and cautious style, where he gradually broke his man down over time without taking needless risks against a known puncher. He fought similarly against Burns. It was not anomalous for a Johnson bout to go many rounds. Either he did so because he wanted the fight to last rounds so the motion pictures would be more valuable, certainly a strong possibility that many writers and fight observers believed at the time, or he was just being careful and taking his time, as often was the case with him.

In his autobiography, Johnson claimed that he took it easy on Ketchel and carried him in order to make an entertaining show. He thought he "must carry on the fight in a way that would make the pictures snappy and worth seeing."[214] This would help boost film revenues, of which Johnson was to receive a sizable percentage.

Some aspects of the fight bolster the argument that Johnson was carrying Ketchel. In the 9th round (or so the intertitles claim)(it appears to be the 10th based on the newspaper descriptions), Johnson was holding Ketchel's left arm with his right hand and hitting him with his left hook a few times. Ketchel started to sag to the canvas. Johnson actually lifted Ketchel up and did not allow him to fall, preventing a knockdown.

Another interpretation of Johnson's "assistance" could be that Jack was aware that he had fouled by holding and hitting and did not want to give the referee an excuse to disqualify him should Ketchel go down, so he kept him up. Disqualification losses were not all that uncommon at the time. Johnson realized such a potential, having suffered a disqualification loss previously in his career, to Joe Jeannette. That said, typically in straight Queensberry rules fights, most referees allowed subtle holding and hitting.

Johnson either was carrying Ketchel, toying with him, torturing him, or methodically and carefully breaking him, depending on how you want to interpret it. It was never easy to peg entirely what Johnson was doing. Whatever he did, he did because he wanted to, and it worked for him.

Ketchel's nose and mouth were bloody, and Johnson was administering his usual gradual beating, in the same way he did with Burns, though with more outside work than in the Burns fight.

Later in the 10th round, Johnson again knocked Ketchel off balance with a right uppercut followed by a swinging left hook. So even if Johnson was carrying him, he still was beating him up, though without finishing him.

Regardless, Ketchel threw some dangerous punches throughout, particularly with the right hand, and appeared to be giving it his all. Johnson

---

[214] Johnson, *In the Ring and Out*, at 194-196.

was content to stick jabs, maintain his range, feint, tie up, and only occasionally launch combinations. When Ketchel threw his right, Johnson would attempt a quick right hand counter, usually the uppercut. He utilized many tactics similar to the Burns fight: either quickly attacking and then grabbing, then occasionally sneaking in short uppercuts or hooks, or he would wait for Ketchel to attack so he could counter and suppress Ketchel's arms. Both fighters were cautious, and the pace was relatively slow, neither moving very much, each carefully selecting their moments of attack. When waiting on the outside, Jack occasionally pumped in a jab.

In the 12th round, Ketchel threw a lead looping overhand right and Johnson went down. It looked as if Johnson was attempting to duck the overhand right, putting his head down, and he actually lifted his left leg off the ground, bent his knee and moved his left foot towards his right foot, either just before and/or as the blow landed, leaving him less than stable. The blow came over the top to land, apparently in the neck or behind the ear region, or possibly on the jaw, the force sending the off-balance Johnson down. Jack put his outstretched left arm out to the ground to catch himself after his left knee and rear end hit the ground. He pushed his body up off of the canvas and then flipped around while on the ground, moving to a face-down position. His right knee momentarily touched the ground, but then he pushed up so only his hands and feet were on the ground. Throughout, it seemed as if he wanted as little of his body to touch the canvas as possible, or for as short a time as possible, other than his hands and feet. He ever so slightly shook his head momentarily, as if a bit dazed and clearing his head. Johnson rose slowly. Whether he was slightly hurt or was just acting in order to fool Ketchel and the public is the real mystery.

What is odd about this sequence is that there is no logical reason for a fighter to lift his left leg off the ground, bend his knee, and move his leg to the left as a blow is on its way, because that obliterates all semblance of balance. Accidental or intentional, such an act would make it easy for any kind of blow to drop him. Hence, it certainly is possible that Johnson was in the process of throwing himself down intentionally. However, it is possible that the blow landing is what momentarily took out Johnson's leg. Poor footage and camera position can be deceptive.

In his 1920s autobiography, contradicting what he said that the time of the fight, Johnson claimed to have gone down intentionally, saying,

> I was hoping for something of a sensational nature and tried to devise a plan to that end. On the day of the fight...I was busily thinking how I could make the fight picturesque, and a plan occurred to me. This plan I did not divulge to any of my party though I told Bob Armstrong...that if he should see me down in a certain round he need not get excited. ... [Ketchel] sent over a punch which landed on my jaw. It did not hurt nor disconcert me. My brain had been working rapidly – so rapidly that I recognized this to be a clean cut blow with apparently much force back of it. I said to myself, 'Now's

your time! Now's your time! Here's your chance,' and so I hit the canvas. ... I pretended to be groggy, but in reality I was ready to deliver the knockout.[215]

After Johnson rose, Ketchel moved in to finish, advancing with a lead right, but just as Ketchel's body turned towards the left from the force of his own right hand punch, Johnson immediately landed his own perfectly timed powerful right to the jaw. Ketchel literally had flung himself directly into the path of Johnson's punch, doubling its force. Johnson continued to swing wildly and viciously in combination with both hands to the head, left-right-left-right as Ketchel went to the canvas, a mere few seconds after Jack had been down. It is unclear whether the follow-up blows landed, because they were delivered so quickly and the film footage is not of the best quality, but most appear to miss or are grazing. Johnson's punches are blazing fast and ferocious at this point. Johnson swung so hard; he actually lost his balance from the force of his own blows, which threw him to the canvas momentarily. It was a stunning turn of events.

After rising, Johnson can be seen wiping some of Ketchel's teeth out of his gloves. Mouthpieces were not worn at that time, and were not used until about 1915, when Ted "Kid" Lewis fought Jack Britton. The combination of small 5-ounce gloves and no mouthpieces led to a lot of knocked out teeth. Ketchel was counted out.

It is possible that Johnson reacted late to the surprise punch, and in ducking, lost his balance, and then was hit hard and sent down. After all, Ketchel was known as a true puncher. A slightly stunned Johnson was upset, and used the opportunity to catch Ketchel coming in recklessly. He possibly later claimed to have faked the knockdown to save face, not wanting to admit that he had been decked.

Typically, throughout his career, Johnson would coast along and outpoint his foes, but if they landed something significant, he would turn tiger and get payback. He had done so on a few occasions earlier in the Ketchel fight. So, if Johnson was stunned and angered, he might have wanted immediate payback, and Stan obliged by running right into the blow, thinking Johnson was more hurt than he was.

However, reporters made a good point that Johnson threw with more ferocity and power at that moment than at any other time in the fight, opining that he could have done so at any time, and had held back until then. Those were some brutal fast blows, too.

Some later made the claim that Johnson was angry with Ketchel, the man he had been carrying pursuant a gentleman's agreement, for having double-crossed him and nailing him with a good one. However, this claim is not supported by the evidence. Both men had struck each other with hard blows on occasion throughout the contest.

---

[215] Johnson, *In the Ring and Out*, 194-196.

At the time, Johnson claimed he was stunned. Certainly, Ketchel was known as a tremendous hitter. Still, most suspected that Jack was fibbing. However, one does have to consider that believing the worst sold more newspapers and cast the most doubt about Johnson's integrity.

We will never know for sure, but the fact that Johnson made no attempt to finish after decking Ketchel early on, and literally held him up on occasion, combined with the odd look of the knockdown, and Johnson's instant recovery, certainly led to a strong belief that Johnson was playing a game, which he later claimed and admitted.

Another thing to consider is whether Johnson's going down against middleweight Gunboat Smith in sparring from an overhand right, the same punch that Ketchel dropped Johnson with, actually was somewhat of a rehearsal, to see whether he could pull it off and fool folks, and was another ruse to generate interest and ticket sales, of which Johnson would earn a percentage. There was debate about the legitimacy of that knockdown as well. Or perhaps Jack's apparently impregnable defense simply was vulnerable to the overhand right.

A couple years after his autobiography was published, Johnson claimed that he was a good business man, and stood to make a lot of money from the moving pictures. He knew that if he stopped Ketchel quickly, there wouldn't be much demand for the films. The motion picture houses would not want to purchase a film of a black man easily and quickly defeating a white man. Jack claimed that he carried Stan, and then, after enough rounds had elapsed, intentionally went down, feigning grogginess. He saw that Ketchel was determined to finish him, so he set himself and readied to counter with a right that had everything on it. The punch knocked Stan unconscious and ripped out all of his front teeth. Johnson said his only regret was hitting him so hard. "But that last round made those motion pictures sell like hot cakes. I made a small fortune out of them." Of course, another way to view the confession is that Johnson really was decked and momentarily stunned, but preferred to tell a fanciful story rather than admit that he was dropped. Such stories also sold more books.[216]

A few days after the fight, the *San Francisco Bulletin* said the popular impression was that Johnson deliberately allowed his much lighter opponent to stay on his feet long enough to make a good moving-picture film, and then intentionally took a dive before finishing him, thus assuring himself many extra thousands of dollars.

The *Bulletin* said this theory was strengthened by the statements of several of Johnson's seconds and camp members, who claimed that the champion told them not to worry if he were to fall or be knocked down. Also, Johnson had wagered several hundred dollars that Ketchel would not last 13 rounds, and was very confident about it, but advised friends not to wager on a knockout before the 10th round.

[216] *Saskatoon Star-Phoenix*, Apr 26, 1929.

The *Bulletin* said the pictures would show how unconcerned Jack's cornermen all were when Johnson dropped to the mat. "He practiced it daily in his training quarters." This lends credence to the theory that when he went down with Gunboat Smith that Johnson was seeing if he could fool the public. The unnamed Johnson camp sources claimed that Ketchel actually missed his right swing.

The *Bulletin* opined that Johnson could have beaten Ketchel in 2 rounds if he had tried. He almost stopped him in the 2nd, causing one of the men on the moving picture platform to call out, "Not so fast, Jack!" He again almost had Ketchel out in 10th round, but allowed and helped him to stay.

The *Examiner* said the majority thought the knockdown was bogus. Ketchel supporters said it was legitimate and that saying otherwise was to rob him of a little credit "where his credits were lamentably few."

W. W. Naughton opined that Johnson's fall was unreal and stagey. At first he thought that Johnson, who had gone down clumsily with a grin on his face, was throwing the fight and was going to stay down and take the count. Most gamblers did not care what Johnson did in the way of asides, as long as he protected their money and won.

It looked as though the debate over the knockdown indeed would prove the best possible advertisement for the pictures. Everyone would want to see them so that they could opine for themselves, or confirm what they thought they saw.

A local civil engineer wrote a letter condemning the *Bulletin* for race prejudice, saying that "it is contemptible the way you and other sporting writers abuse and revile Jack Johnson because he is black!" The *Bulletin* replied,

> In the first place, neither the writer nor any other reputable sport critic would think for a moment of condemning Johnson because of his color or race. Sam Langford, Young Peter Jackson, Joe Gans, and even Johnson himself have always received fair play at the hands of American sporting writers until they did something for which they deserved opprobrium. Then, and then only, they got what was coming to them. In the second place, the public or San Francisco goes to see two men doing their best, not one great hulking piece of fighting machinery playing for twelve rounds with a smaller – though gamer – opponent for the benefit of the cinematograph. And, in the third place, Johnson has made such evident attempts to belittle every one of his white opponents that he has made himself universally unpopular throughout the entire country.

Of course, this perspective overlooked the fact that writers, fans, managers, and opponents often used racially derogatory terms towards Johnson, verbally abused and belittled him as a fighter, and had drawn the color line on him and others for years. It also overlooked the fact that men like Corbett had laughed at and taunted his opponents, had hippodromed, and had a cautious style, and yet the press had treated him well.

The *Bulletin* also reported that those in Johnson's camp claimed that the side-bet was called off the night before the fight. Ketchel would not appear in the ring if Johnson insisted on the wager. San Mateo officials supported Stan, declaring that they would stop the contest and arrest the principals if the bet was allowed to go forward.

The *Call* said it had been many a day since any big fight had attracted more unfavorable comment or aroused the fans' ire more than this one. Coffroth insisted that Johnson made $21,000 total, more money than Jack ever saw in his life before. However, no one believed that Johnson ever received such an amount. The general belief was that Coffroth got Johnson to call off the side bet two nights before the fight. "It will take many a long day and many a strenuous effort to convince all the fans that there was nothing wrong."

Although it was claimed that Ketchel had lost all his money in the side bet, noted was the fact that he had just purchased a $6,000 racing automobile. If the side bet was legitimate, he only had about $1,600 coming to him. "Does this look as though the defeated middleweight champion went broke last Saturday afternoon? The signal is not all convincing."

Although Ketchel's weight was given out as 176 pounds or more, in New York, they thought that misleading statements were made about his weight so as to make the fight appear to be less of a mismatch. Some said he actually weighed 168 pounds. Others said Johnson weighed more than 205 pounds. By claiming Ketchel was larger and Johnson smaller, the match did not seem so uneven. There was no proof of this, but speculation was rampant.

Sam Langford wanted to meet Ketchel for a $5,000 side-bet at catch-weights or at 158 pounds. Langford wanted to whip Ketchel in order to justify a match with Johnson. However, insisting on catch-weights against Ketchel was not exactly the way to convince folks that he was a true heavyweight.

Johnson told Tom McCarey that he would fight in Los Angeles against whatever opponent he selected. However, "The almost hopeless condition of the heavyweight division was brought straight home to McCarey when he tried to figure on a possible opponent for Johnson."

The disapproval of the Ketchel bout and Johnson's ways only served to intensify the desire to see Jeffries fight and beat him. "Johnson started upon a career of local unpopularity when he sneered and laughed at Al Kaufman. … He rounded it out when he pitilessly and unnecessarily punished Stanley Ketchel." The sport-loving population of San Francisco, which perhaps was larger than that of any other metropolis, would go en-masse to see Jeffries against Johnson, no matter what the ticket prices.

Naughton most wanted a Jeffries fight. "The negro so far outclasses all the other heavyweights…that it must be hard work for him to hold himself back sufficiently to make the exhibitions interesting. Such being the case, it is little use expecting satisfactory results from any bouts that Johnson may engage in before he stands toe to toe with big Jeffries." Jack Johnson had come full circle, having gone from being criticized for not being good enough, to being too good for his own good.

Sam Berger, who had not seen the fight, called the bout a burlesque. He had thought Johnson would be under a pull. He confirmed that Jeffries would fight the "so-called champion."

Given that Johnson-Ketchel had generated large box office receipts, and the fact that Jeffries-Johnson was a "100 per cent better card than Ketchel and Johnson," it was understandable why some promoters would be offering a $50,000 purse (or more) for Jeffries-Johnson.[217]

When Johnson was in Oakland, he heard someone mention something about a fake. Johnson replied, "Who said dat?" A "dusky admirer of the champion" pointed to an "unoffending citizen" who was accompanied by two women and said, "Dat's the fellow ova' there." Johnson walked over in wrath and swung at him and they got into a fight. The women with the man scratched at Johnson. "This sort of thing adds nothing to the popularity of the heavyweight title holder." The fight-goers were "disgusted" with him and his tactics. "He has taken on airs that are insufferable." The hope was that Jeffries would "everlastingly wallop the pretensions out of this black fighting man."[218]

George Little said Johnson had been chasing Jeffries for six years without success. "What he wants most is to get Jeffries in a ring with him so that he can show him

Jack Johnson, the Heavyweight Champion of the World, and George Little, His Manager, Who Continue to Claim That Jim Jeffries Is Afraid to Meet Johnson in the Ring.

how much superior he is." The public demanded that Jeff fight him.[219]

It was looking almost positive that Jeffries would re-enter the ring "in the hope of regaining the heavyweight championship of the world for the white race." He had gone too far in his public statements to back out.

---

[217] *San Francisco Evening Post, San Francisco Examiner, San Francisco Bulletin*, October 19, 1909; *San Francisco Call, San Francisco Examiner*, October 20, 1909.

On October 18, 1909, Mike Schreck easily outpointed Tony Ross in their 10-round bout, but the referee declared it a draw. Schreck had the best of it throughout and almost knocked out Ross in the final round.

[218] *San Francisco Bulletin*, October 20, 1909.

[219] *San Francisco Evening Post*, October 21, 1909.

Johnson's recent easy victories, from Burns on, made it apparent that no man of ordinary caliber or size had any chance with him. A fighter needed skill, ability, and size to defeat him. Johnson would have the advantage of never having been out of shape, and fighting and winning all the time during the years that Jeff had been idle, giving him great confidence. Hence, he was apt to give Jeff a long, hard struggle. He would be a dangerous proposition for any man.

Some noted that although Johnson had objected to a date delay of the Ketchel match owing to his alleged engagements back East, Jack had remained in the local area following the bout and had not yet left.[220]

The black-owned *New York Age* said that by defeating Ketchel, Johnson had not only strengthened his hold on the title, besides boosting his stock several points higher in the realm of pugilism, but he also had established a record for nerve. It was easy to do one's best when the crowd supported and cheered for you. "What a difference when you find yourself confronted by a crowd of 10,000 excited spectators who clearly make known to you that you are not their favorite contender by hoots and groans and loudly cheer the other fellow." Jack's nerve under such circumstances further served to dispel racial stereotypes and myths.

> Colored fighters have been charged with possessing a yellow streak, which after all means an exhibition showing lack of nerve at a critical period. Possibly there have been such cases, the fighters having been discouraged by the hoots and groans of the crowd; but not so with Champion Jack Johnson. He is evidently one of those who at all times considers the source, and instead of becoming awed or nervous at the unfriendliness of the big crowd, showed that he was master of the situation by looking around cynically and then handing out one of his famous golden smiles.

Not many could face a huge audience that was against them and still keep their nerve. The *Age* saw Johnson's smile as a way to combat the ill-feeling against him. Still, the *Age* understood the racial sympathies.

> The writer does not bewail the fact that Ketchel, a white man, was the more popular. It was natural that such a situation should exist. How many colored men could you find in the United States who were pulling for Ketchel? A white man was arrayed against a colored man, and consequently there was a crossing of racial sympathies, generally speaking.

Still, the *Age* noted the bias of white newsmen.

> Speaking of some of the white writers, the class that has not yet become reconciled to the fact that the champion heavyweight of the world is a Negro, they have been made monkeys of by Johnson for

---

[220] *San Francisco Bulletin*, October 21, 1909.

some time. A few of them reside in New York City, and they are certainly a bunch of sore-heads. Johnson has made them welch, dispute themselves and appear ridiculous in the eyes of their readers. One of them told in bold face type Saturday just how Ketchel was going to put Johnson, a fourflusher [bluffer], out. Sunday morning he begged that he be awarded the first prize in the guessing contest, declaring that he had predicted before the fight that the champion would knock out Ketchel. …

This article said Johnson was master of the match from the 1st round on and carried Ketchel so he could make more money with the moving pictures. Jack showed that he was a general on defense, and pulled off a foxy trick in order to make a dramatic ending, playing possum and acting dazed so as to draw the deceived Ketchel in for the finishing blows.

The *Age* opined that Johnson had not yet shown what he really was made of, for he had not yet been made to do his best.

> Now, about Jim Jeffries, to whom the prejudiced writers again turn to lead them out of the wilderness of embarrassment and humiliation. If Johnson and Jeffries ever fight it will be a big surprise to the sporting editor of THE AGE who does not believe Jeffries will ever re-enter the ring. And if he does, he has so lost his fistic prowess of former days that he would not be able to battle successfully with Johnson.

> From the way things look, the disgruntled had better resign themselves to the inevitable and find solace in the thought that an American, one who was born in this country, is fittingly wearing the championship honors. … It looks very gloomy for the Caucasian; for all the fighters who are to be taken seriously as contenders for the heavyweight title are of ebony hue – truly a most unique state of affairs.[221]

The *Freeman* said the fight settled the "question of the physical prowess of the Negro." The bout was a sad spectacle. Yet, "it requires so much to convince the white man that the Negro is his physical equal." Johnson had something that the white man wanted.

> Prize-fighting has always been a conspicuous factor in the world's sensations, but never before has a championship title been worth so much to the white man as now. And the humane societies should prevent the many inhuman sacrifices that the white man will undergo in his frantic desire to wrest the title from the giant Negro. And whatever may be said of Johnson, good, bad or indifferent, you are cheating yourself if you say he is not a fighter, even though his fight with Ketchel had many shady appearances. And the writer takes the liberty here to say that if this Johnson-Ketchel fight wasn't a

---

[221] *New York Age*, October 21, 1909.

prearranged affair, there was some awful clear catering to the moving picture machine.

This writer opined that not in a thousand years could Ketchel legitimately drop Johnson. "Ketchel was out in the second round with an unintentional punch." But Johnson made no attempt to finish then, because that was not the plan.

However, even some blacks were susceptible to prejudiced views about black fighters. A couple years later, Johnson trainer Professor Watson Burns, a black man, said it wasn't yellow that made colored fighters quit, but the fact that they could not take the beating that white men could. They had less assimilative powers. However, they were not quitters. It was a physical fault more than a moral one.

Burns also said Johnson had feared Ketchel, and held Stan's punching powers in holy dread, which is why he trained hard for the fight. Johnson used to say, "Boy, that man jes' like lightnin'. If he ever hits you then you are daid, jes' th' same is if a bolt of lightnin' smashed into you."[222]

Although Johnson was known for speeding, wearing nice clothes, and taunting opponents while inside the ring, the *Freeman* said that when in the presence of white men outside the ring, he conducted himself in an unassuming gentlemanly manner, such that no one might take exception.[223]

[222] *Freeman*, September 23, 1911.
[223] *Freeman*, November 27, 1909.

CHAPTER 7

Making the Jeffries Fight

On October 22, 1909, James J. Jeffries returned from his trip to Carlsbad, Bohemia, arriving in New York on the steamer *Lusitania*. He was greeted by hundreds of fans "eager for a glimpse of the man who is expected to regain individual physical supremacy for the white race."

Jeffries looked solid, without superfluous flesh. He said he weighed around 228 pounds the last time he checked. In Europe, he had done 10 miles of road work every morning. In the afternoon, he worked in the gymnasium.

Jeff said he was ready to fight Johnson as soon as possible. "The sooner the articles are signed the better." He denied saying that he wanted a $150,000 purse. He said the promoter with the highest bid would get the contest. When asked about Johnson, Jeff said, "I care not about Johnson. That negro has made more noise and done less than any man I know."[224]

The day before, on October 21 in San Francisco, Jack Johnson was arrested for speeding again, this time on Market street. At the City Prison, where he was booked, when asked his occupation, Johnson replied, "Lawyer." When the bond and warrant clerk commented on the number of times Johnson had been arrested for his speed mania, Johnson replied, "If I want to speed on Market street I intend to do so. There is a good road there, the best in the city. I never killed any one. If it suits me to speed that is my business." The *Examiner* noted the humorous irony that although Johnson kept himself in reserve when in the ring, he liked to extend his auto to the last notch when driving. It cost him $100 bail to be released.

Despite encouraging reports about Jeff's condition, many doubted whether he could regain his old form. "It is one of the tenets of sportdom that a horse or a man that has been out of competition for a few years can never be brought back into the game again and made to perform as

---

[224] *San Francisco Evening Post*, October 22, 1909; *New York Times*, October 23, 1909. Mrs. Jeffries had accompanied Jim on the trip and had spent some time at her home in Saxe-Meiningen. Jeff had not done any boxing while abroad, but was working on his physical fitness.

brilliantly as before." However, Jeff had taken his time to work back into shape gradually. Jeff's confidence that he could fight well again gave many doubters confidence.[225]

Boxing, a weekly magazine based out of England, said Jeffries was the great white hero "whom we can look to wrest the title for the dominant race." It claimed that it was not just a matter of racial pride, but one of existence, which caused the urgent desire to see Jeff triumph. It said the colored races outnumbered whites, but hitherto had been kept in subjection by recognition on their part of physical and mental inferiority. Great changes had taken place of late. The Russo-Japanese War proved that a colored nation could defeat a white nation. Ever since then, there had been signs of unrest amongst the dark nations.

There was powerful symbolism in the fact that the dominant race was compelled to recognize that a black descendant of a slave was the sport's master. Johnson's success had political, racial, and sociological implications. Such success inspired colored peoples with hope. A Jeffries victory was needed to help quell that hope. "While, if after all, Johnson should smash Jeffries – But the thought is too awful to contemplate." The white race's entire hope was pinned on Jeffries.

Jeffries said Johnson had never been fond of meeting a man with a dangerous punch. "He would never have lost to Marvin Hart if he had only gone after him, but he wouldn't risk doing so. … So he was content to lose on points rather than run the risk of getting badly hurt by a man he could have cut to ribbons if he had only gone after him."

Jeff also said Johnson was not very popular even amongst his own people. "He hasn't had any too good a time in the States as it is; even the niggers are getting tired of him. They support him, of course, because he is their colour, but they are a bit sick of him, all the same."

The writer noted that Jeff was undefeated and had never even been knocked down. "Fitzsimmons surely hit him harder than Johnson will ever be able to hit him, and Jeff took Bob's blows, and still came on unruffled." As masterful a boxer as Johnson was, "he cannot be said to be quick on his feet, while Jeffries is as quick as ever." Plus he was heavier than Johnson, which would tell its tale. "We can't see Jeffries losing, and that's a fact. Even if they made it a fight to a finish, Jeff ought to outlast the negro."[226]

---

[225] *San Francisco Examiner*, October 22, 1909. Some said the reports about Jeff's training overseas were exaggerated, that he had done more relaxing than hard work. However, he was looking good, and he was a man who easily took on weight when not working.
[226] *Boxing*, October 23, 1909.

On October 22, Johnson left San Francisco via railroad for Chicago. He forfeited the $100 bail on the speeding charge. "For a few months, at least, the last has been seen of Jack Johnson and his gilded giggle."[227]

The *Chronicle* said the Ketchel bout had served to boost Johnson in discussions of a potential Jeffries match. Many boxing followers were now saying, "That chap Jeffries wants to be in the best possible shape when he meets the black man." No longer was Johnson being underestimated. "There seems to have been an awakening that Jack Johnson is a fighter to be reckoned with. He has been underrated." His recent matches had opened the eyes of many who previously dismissed him. "They are willing to concede now that Johnson has never shown them his best form and that he has never been compelled to extend himself. They realize that he is possessed of unusual strength, particularly in the arms; that he is crafty and experienced in the ring, and is acquainted with the tricks of boxing as are few heavyweights."[228]

The most likely places for the fight were San Francisco, Los Angeles, or Nevada. Johnson did not want to fight in Australia. While there, he felt that promoter McIntosh was in partnership with Burns, and that they did everything in their power to stir up public sentiment against him.[229]

Sid Hester, the Mission fight club matchmaker, wired an offer of a $75,000 purse for Jeffries-Johnson. Hence, Coffroth would have to do better than what he had offered. It marked the beginning of a campaign by various promoters to obtain the bout, never before rivaled in history. England's National Club also made offers, but neither man wanted to fight anywhere but America. A promoter would have to be cautious about offering too much, for although the bout undoubtedly would be the richest in history, it still took a lot of ticket sales at high prices to generate that type of money, plus cover expenses and still make a profit.[230]

Jeffries and Berger planned to watch the Johnson-Ketchel films every afternoon in a New York theater in order to get a line on Johnson. They did not attend the first showing on October 25, owing to the large crowds.[231]

---

[227] *San Francisco Examiner*, October 23, 1909.

[228] *San Francisco Chronicle*, October 24, 1909. The *Chronicle* also noted that a vast of amount of space had been devoted to commentary about the Ketchel fight. The majority felt that Johnson stalled round after round when he might have finished matters, and the knockdown of Johnson was accomplished by a glancing swing that could not have done any damage.

[229] *San Francisco Evening Post, San Francisco Bulletin*, October 23, 1909. Berger said Jeffries and Johnson both preferred California.

[230] *San Francisco Bulletin*, October 25, 1909.

[231] *San Francisco Evening Post, San Francisco Bulletin*, October 26, 1909.

Johnson arrived in Chicago. Aside from a lump on the side of his jaw, he looked to be in perfect shape. Jack said, "That knockdown was on the square in our fight, but the blow landed on the left side of my neck or the ear or somewhere, I don't exactly recall now. It was a peachy punch, too, that I misjudged, slipping in on it just in time to get the full force of it."[232]

On October 26, a doctor burned out the right nostril of Jeff's nose and removed a fleshy obstruction. Jeff said he was able to breathe well again. He said Fitz had pounded his nose so hard in their first fight that he had not breathed properly ever since. That afternoon, he worked out in the gymnasium. The following day, he would have the other nostril burned out.

After watching the Ketchel films, Tom Sharkey said he thought Jeff would not have such an easy time with Johnson. Tom said that unless Jeff was absolutely fit; he would be beaten.[233]

The *Examiner* printed photos of Jeff which showed that he had lost the paunch he previously had, and was 50 pounds lighter, proving that the stories of his systematic training were true. It said that Jeff, like other fighters, always was inclined to prevaricate when discussing his weight. However, he looked relatively trim.

[232] *San Francisco Examiner*, October 26, 1909.

[233] *San Francisco Examiner, San Francisco Evening Post, San Francisco Bulletin*, October 27, 1909.

The doctor told Jeff his nose was not broken, but there was a fleshy growth in the nostrils. The doctor wanted Jeff to take opiates for the procedure, but he refused. The doctor finally got him to consent to allowing him to rub a little cocaine on the inside of the nose. Jeff did not flinch at the procedure.

Yank Kenny filed a civil suit in Chicago against Johnson for $2,000. He alleged that Johnson had hired him on April 25, agreeing to pay him $60 a week for one year to act as a trainer, but Jack had deserted him at Cedar Lake, Indiana last August, having paid him only $220.

Some wondered whether so much weight reduction could be accomplished without losing one's vitality. They recalled when both Sullivan and Mitchel lost a lot of weight to fight Corbett, but also lost all of their speed, force, and energy. Both were around age 33 at the time, and both had been out of the game for quite a while before fighting again. Jeff was 34 ½ at present and likely would be 35 years old when the fight took place, and he had been out of the game longer than either Sullivan or Mitchell were before they fought Corbett. However, unlike the others, Jeff had lost the weight gradually and properly, rather than overtraining in a short period of time.

Fight fans were given quite a jar when John L. Sullivan said Johnson would whip Jeffries. Sullivan said,

> The negro is not being credited for what he has done. Neither is he given credit for being as good a fighter as he is. I think that when he meets Jeff – if Jeff ever consents to a meeting – that the black boy will beat him to a frazzle. I am a great admirer of Jeff and would be one of the first to bewail the fact that a negro claims the championship, but I fear that Jeff is not the man he was five years ago and that he will be unable to cope with this wily Zulu. I don't like negroes any better than I did twenty years ago, but in this case I think credit must be given to the better man, and I look upon Johnson as being the fighter of the day.

On the 27th, Johnson left Chicago for New York. He said, "I know that many of my own race say that I will have no chance in a battle with the Californian, but I have confidence enough in my own ability to think that I can beat him." For years it had been his ambition to get Jeff into the ring. Jeffries had accused Johnson of using his name to further his own interests, but Jack said that if Jeff did not sign to fight, it would prove that the opposite was true, and the public would become disgusted with Jeffries.[234]

Proving his confidence, Johnson was willing to fight Jeffries winner take all, or whatever division of the purse Jeff wanted, as long as the winner received a larger share. "If Jeffries thinks he can lick me I don't see where he can have any complaint on the proposition." He thought Jeff would stall and call him names, but ultimately would crawl out of the match in fear.

On October 28 at 9:30 a.m., Johnson arrived in New York. A big crowd of about 5,000 members of his race were on hand to greet him at the train station. Jack grinned from ear to ear. He said he was weighing about 205 pounds and wanted to meet Jeff as soon as possible. Jack also said,

> We will now see who is the 'four-flusher,' the black or the white man. If Jeffries signs up and behaves himself properly I will doff my hat to him and at the same time promise him the greatest thrashing of his life. ... There must be both a winner's and loser's end in the division

[234] *San Francisco Examiner*, October 28, 1909.

of the purse. To show that I am a good sport I will allow Jeffries to name the percentage which the winner and loser shall receive.

This is the opportunity of my life and I propose to show the world that I am the best man that ever donned a mitt if I succeed in getting Jeff into the ring with me. It has always been the ambition of my life to get this man in the ring. ...

It frequently has been said that somewhere in my anatomy runs a yellow streak. Does it not strike you funny that no one has ever been able to find it? And just take it from me, Mr. Jeffries will not be able to locate it, presuming that I have one somewhere.

Upon my word, I can't see how the dopesters can give Jeff a chance with me. It is certain that he is not nearly as clever as I, and I have been fighting right along and am in the pink of condition, while James J. has been in retirement for five years. ... Let me give you this little tip: When Jeff and I get in the ring, don't let anybody's prejudice against the negro prevent you from getting a good-sized bet down on the black man. Of course, if you can afford to lose, why, bet on Jeffries.

George Little said the $5,000 he had put up to bind the Jeffries fight could be used as a side bet, and he also was willing to wager up to $20,000 more at prevailing ringside odds that Jeff would be defeated. Little further said, "I understand that Jeffries spoke contemptuously of the pictures of the Johnson-Ketchel fight and that he said it was a bout between a washerwoman and a boxer. If Jeffries thinks Ketchel fights like a washerwoman, let him fight him. Ketchel has a terrible right hand."[235]

When Johnson arrived at his hotel on the corner of 35th street and 8th avenue, a hotel reserved for blacks, he was the hero of an admiring throng of "his own people," who blocked the streets on both sides of the hotel and for more than a block in every direction. Jack smiled and shook the hands of hundreds of admirers. He said of Jeffries, "All I want is to get him in the ring good and fit, so there will be no excuses."

Jeffries was working hard at Cooper's gymnasium on West 42nd street, where he had been doing daily work since he arrived in town. Jeff said, "I'll kill that fellow. It will be a short fight. In less than fifteen minutes the big negro will get all that's coming to him. I saw the pictures of his fight with Ketchel last night. He's a good defensive fighter, that's all. He couldn't hurt me with an ax. But wait till I hit him. Good night."[236]

In the evening, Johnson went to Hammerstein's and was introduced to the audience before the showing of the Ketchel fight pictures. Jack thought the films had been doctored a bit, for he remembered knocking Stan down in the 8th round, but it wasn't there.

---

[235] *San Francisco Bulletin, San Francisco Evening Post*, October 28, 1909.
[236] *San Francisco Chronicle*, October 29, 1909. Jeff walloped the 150-pound sandbag.

Johnson noted that Jeffries had objected to experts saying that Johnson was as clever as James J. Corbett.

What does Jim want me to do in order to be classed with James J.? Hop around like Jim Corbett did? Says I'm flat footed. All right, I'll be flat-footed. That's better head work than jumping around like a clown and wearing yourself out. Joe Gans didn't hop around, did he? Guess he was considered passingly clever.

I will beat Jeffries as sure as you're born. Go bet on it. I could have gone a million rounds with Ketchel, I felt so good and strong. He was a game little fellow, though. It was a shame that the last punch spoiled his teeth. It shows you what a crack I hit him. I went down, too, don't forget to tell 'em that. I'd look fine taking a chance going down there with so many fellows who liked Ketchel and who would have jumped in and cheated me out of my title in a flash. Besides, I'm not stuck on getting floored. Ketchel was game. … He took a fearful beating. …

I think Ketchel will have a great chance to beat Burns if they ever meet, although people seem to think Burns can't hit. You bet your life he can hit. He's got a good punch.[237]

The *San Francisco Bulletin* said the result of the Jeffries-Johnson fistic argument would bear "almost as much weight upon the Anglo-African question as did the Civil War."[238]

On October 29, 1909 at New York's Hotel Albany, James J. Jeffries and Jack Johnson signed articles of agreement to fight 45 rounds or more, the fight to be held no later than July 5, 1910, before the club that offered the largest financial inducements within the next 30 days, or December 1, that club being required to post a $5,000 guarantee. The winner would take a side bet of $10,000 and 75% of the purse, and the loser 25%. Jeffries, Berger, Johnson, and Little had all met and agreed.

Johnson wanted his name listed first, and to be called the present champion. Jeffries assented. They did not decide on a referee at that time.

Jeffries said the public would insist on a finish fight, so he wanted no less than 45 rounds. He wanted no debate about a potential decision. When Johnson said he thought San Francisco only allowed 20-round bouts, Jeff said, "Then San Francisco won't get the fight. Make it 45 rounds or more." Johnson agreed.

Jeff wanted a $20,000 side bet, but Johnson wanted $5,000. They compromised on $10,000. Jeff said, "All right, but I wanted that $20,000."

Jeff was willing to do the fight winner take all, and Johnson was agreeable, but Little objected, saying that if something went wrong, he was not prepared to come away with nothing. So they agreed to a purse split

[237] *San Francisco Examiner*, October 29, 1909.
[238] *San Francisco Bulletin*, October 29, 1909.

that gave the winner a hefty 75%. The terms, both financial and otherwise, showed both fighters' confidence.

They agreed the bout would have to be held outdoors in order to accommodate the huge crowd that would want to see it. Hence, winter would not work for the bout's date. Plus, Berger urged the necessity for ample training time. The most likely dates for the big fight would be either May 30 or July 4, both big holiday dates. Most likely the bout would be held in California or Nevada. They would fight straight Queensberry rules with 5-ounce gloves. All parties signed the contract, including James J. Jeffries and John Arthur Johnson. They posed for photographers, and champagne was served.[239]

The *Chronicle* said that as a spectacle, nothing could surpass the Johnson-Jeffries bout, "combining as it does the world's title with the supremacy of the white over the black race."

On October 30, 1909, after a week-long illness, Stanley Ketchel's manager Willis Britt died from a hemorrhage flowing from a lung disease. Some said he had died of a broken heart.[240]

---

[239] *San Francisco Call, Chronicle, Evening Post, Examiner, Bulletin*, October 30, 1909.

Sam Langford issued a challenge to Johnson, saying he wanted Jack to fight him before Jeffries. He was offering to bet $5,000 a side, with the winner to take the entire purse or 75%. However, this challenge would fall upon deaf ears, given the pending vastly more lucrative Jeffries fight. The *Afro American Ledger* noted that Langford would be a dangerous man for Johnson to meet, for Sam had a punch with the force of a mule's kick, and also had remarkable cleverness. Other than Jeffries, Langford was the only man with any chance against Johnson. *Afro American Ledger*, October 30, 1909.

[240] *San Francisco Chronicle*, October 31, 1909.

Some thought that Jeffries, with his ferocious-looking, imposing frame, might intimidate Johnson. "If he is the Jeffries of old, he will not be buffaloed or kidded by Johnson." Many thought Jeff had the footwork advantage in the bout. For a big man he was the fastest fighter in the world on his feet, showing marvelous speed. Johnson was a relatively flat-footed fighter, generally waiting for his man to come to him and then picking him off. "Nobody was ever able to stop Jeffries in this way, but they all admit that Johnson has a far better chance on account of his quickness and his natural strength." San Franciscans had seen steady improvement in Johnson over the past six years.

Race would factor in the betting. "There is no question but that the national prejudice against the black race will install Jeffries a 10 to 7 or 10 to 8 favorite over Johnson. ... Hundreds of thousands of dollars will change hands" on the fight's result.[241]

Johnson had been sending money monthly to his mother in Galveston. He was in the process of investing $10,000 in a home for his mother and two sisters so they could come live in Chicago. Jack said he would never live in Texas again. Mrs. Tiny Johnson said,

> My boy has always been good to me and his sisters. He promised to build me a fine home, and I am going to Chicago to be near him. He wrote three weeks before the Ketchel match that it would not last 15 rounds, and told me I could mortgage the old home and bet the money he would win. He sends me money regularly, about $200 a month.[242]

Eventually, Johnson paid $11,000 for a 12-room home and real estate on Wabash Avenue in Chicago.[243]

On November 2, 1909 in Boston, Sam Langford knocked out Klondike Haines in the 2nd round.

Langford had challenged Johnson and offered to bet him $5,000. Johnson said he would not fight Langford unless he put up $10,000 as a side bet.

> When he planks down that amount for a side bet I will cover it, and then we will fight. I have licked him before and I can do it again. The reason I won't fight Langford for any share of the receipts is that I don't believe two blacks would draw well, either in this country or over in England. I want to know what I am going to get if I win, and it will have to be $10,000 or there will be no battle.[244]

George Little said Johnson would defeat Jeffries because he was the fastest fighter the ring ever saw. He would be able to elude Jeff's blows,

[241] *San Francisco Call*, October 31, 1909.
[242] *San Francisco Call*, November 2, 1909.
[243] *Freeman*, November 20, 1909.
[244] *San Francisco Call*, November 3, 1909.

while Jeff would not be able to elude Jack's blows. "I think that the Johnson of today could have whipped the Jeffries of seven years ago."[245]

The English magazine *Boxing* said Americans were opposed to Johnson not only because of his "personal failings" but because of his color.

> It is repulsive to the American nature that a black man should hold a world's fighting title over a white man. If there was another Caucasian in sight of his prowess 'we' could look to as having a chance to wrest the championship from Johnson, he would be as much favoured and lauded as Jeffries is. The simple truth is that, with the present stock of 'heavies'…there is not one who would have the remotest chance with Johnson. He simply outclasses all existing heavyweights.[246]

Picking Johnson to defeat Jeffries, Marvin Hart said Jeff could not come back after such a lengthy period of idleness and easy living.

Johnson was full of confidence. He said, "If I thought I could not beat Jeff, I'd never have signed articles." Jack noted that Jeff did not speak directly to him at all when they met, and he did not expect him to do so.

> If what has been said about his feelings is true, then he surely is sore, and as I didn't go into that meeting to make friends with him, I am just as well satisfied. It will serve my purpose just as well to have him good and mad when he enters the ring. He will get a worse licking than ordinarily if that is the case. A man enraged can not show good judgment at any time.

Apparently the contract that he and Jeff signed did not preclude either from taking an intervening match. However, "If Jeff should happen to take anybody on and be beaten, the big fight will be off as far as I'm concerned. But I'll take on the man who licks him instead." When asked how Jeff looked, Johnson said he looked tired, and perhaps was stale. "I will be as confident as the night I fought Stanley Ketchel. Jeff will never beat me. If he needs a few fights under his belt to help him, I hope he gets 'em. Then he will have no excuse to offer if I beat him."[247]

Boxing trainer Tim McGrath did not like the way Jeffries had been doing his "so-called training on the vaudeville stage." He opined that Jeff should be engaging in hard, rough training in the mountains, with good sparring, rather than theatrical engagements. It appeared that Jeff and Berger were trying to earn as much money as possible in light exhibitions,

---

[245] *Seattle Star*, November 5, 1909.

[246] *Boxing*, November 6, 1909. On November 10, 1909, Gunboat Smith won a 10-round decision over Young Peter Jackson.

[247] *Freeman*, November 13, 1909. Within a month, Johnson would begin a theatrical tour. Speaking of Langford, Johnson said, "I see my colored brother, Sam Langford, is getting up on his high horse and yelling for a match. He can have one, you bet, but as I have said before, he must post a forfeit of $10,000 to show me that he is not using my name to advertise himself, and that he will go through with any contract that we may sign."

rather than getting down to serious work. "If anything does more to beat Jeffries it will be lack of condition or shortness of wind," which was not going to be improved by short vaudeville performances.

McGrath said Jeffries seemed to be suffering from what many other analysts had suffered from – underestimation of Johnson. Many were starting to realize just how good Jack really was. "Jeff needn't think that he can blow this negro over. He's got to have the good old punch, that keen eye and that old speed. Johnson isn't afraid of him, so get that out of your head. The colored man is the best front runner in the world."

The fear was that if Jeff was not in top shape, which he would need to be for up to 45 three-minute rounds, then he would beat himself just as Sullivan did with Corbett. "Johnson is just as clever as Corbett and he's a much better fighter. Take it from me that Jeff will have his hands full when the battle begins."

His advisors had been telling Jeffries that he was as good as ever and that he "can beat that coon in a few rounds," such that he might be underestimating Johnson and failing to prepare as well as he should. Even though Jeff was one man in millions, five years of idleness and no hard boxing had to have its effect on his constitution. No fighter ever stayed out of the game as long and then came back with the form he used to display. It simply was not human nature, "and the sooner Jeff wakes up and takes this for granted the better it will be for himself."

Johnson, though not much younger than Jeff, had been fighting steadily all along. "He is coming, while Jeff looks to be going. Here lies the difference. Johnson has been improving with every fight." Johnson was hard to hit, and if Jeff could not hit and hurt him early, then as the rounds progressed, stamina would become a factor, and the present Jeffries did not appear to have stamina like he once did. And Johnson was a very relaxed fighter who knew how to pace himself and go rounds without getting hurt. "Without wind Jeffries will never beat that negro."

Lacking top conditioning, Jeffries would beat himself. "Three or four rounds will tell whether the big fellow's breathing apparatus is all right or not. A man of his bulk will show this weakness, if he isn't fit, in jig time. If he lacks the proper stamina it will be good night to the white race and the heavyweight title." Johnson would not have to punch him into submission, but rather could content himself with picking off Jeff's blows and allow him to wear himself out. "What an agonizing spectacle it would be to sit at that ringside and watch this great undefeated champion of all the champions fade away before that negro simply because his wind fails him." McGrath also opined that it might do Jeff a lot of good to engage in one or more tune-up fights first in order to sharpen up.

McGrath believed that Johnson never would fight Langford, for he feared the latter. However, Johnson was in a position to ignore him, owing to the Jeffries fight, the fact that he had defeated him already, Sam was a black challenger and the public wanted to see a white man regain the championship, and because Langford was no bigger than men like Ketchel and Burns, whom Johnson had dominated.[248]

Jeffries made it clear that he did not want to fight anyone other than Johnson. Bill Brady had challenged Jeff to fight Al Kaufman, but Jeff was not interested. He was coming back for only one fight.

On November 23, 1909 in Pittsburg, after Sam Langford twice decked Mike Schreck in the 1st round, the referee stopped the bout in Sam's favor.

The *San Francisco Call* said talk of a Johnson-Langford match was not taken seriously.

> Why should Johnson take a chance at Langford for a comparatively small sum with the Jeffries match but six months away? It would be foolish for him. He can make just as much money on the road, without running the slightest risk. Johnson and Langford would not draw a large house. No two negro fighters ever did, and no two will. It is not at all probable that any promoter would be willing to give up as much money as Johnson and Langford will surely demand.[249]

Little said Langford was bluffing and would not come up with the side wager, or would insist on odds. He said Johnson would defeat Langford as easily as Ketchel.

However, Langford's manager Joe Woodman indeed posted the money. It was opined that Johnson never thought he could get that sum, but now that he had, it was believed that Jack would sidestep the match anyhow. It simply did not make financial sense, given the upcoming Jeffries fight.[250]

When Johnson was appearing at a New York vaudeville house, from the stage he made a speech saying that he was willing to fight Langford or anyone else. The police arrested Jack and charged him with attempting to violate the prize-fighting statute. At his arraignment, the local magistrate discharged him. "There is no violation here, and the police were wrong."[251]

On December 1, 1909 in New York, bidders for the Jeffries-Johnson fight included Tom McCarey, Ed Graney, John Gleason, Tex Rickard, and others. The bids were astronomical and unprecedented. Graney offered 80% of the gross receipts with a $75,000 guarantee, with the management having sole ownership of the motion pictures. Another offer was 80% plus $70,000 guaranteed, and $20,000 for 1/3 of the pictures. Another was 90% of the gross with no guarantee. Gleason and Coffroth jointly offered $125,000, but they keep full picture rights. Another offer was $75,000 plus 66 2/3% of the pictures, or 80% of the gross plus 66 2/3% of the pictures. McCarey offered the entire gate receipts plus 50% of the moving pictures, or $110,000 cash plus 50% of the moving pictures. Hugh McIntosh offered £7,500 ($37,500) for a fight to be held in America, £8,000 ($40,000) if the

[248] *San Francisco Call*, November 14, 1909; *New York Sun*, December 5, 1909.
[249] *San Francisco Call*, November 28, 1909.
[250] *New York Sun*, November 28, 29, 1909; *Freeman*, December 4, 1909.
[251] *Los Angeles Herald*, December 1, 1909.

fight was held in England or France, and £10,000 ($50,000) if the bout was held in Australia, or the fighters could have the whole gate less $10,000, with a minimum $25,000 guarantee to each fighter, or without deduction if in Australia, with a guaranteed minimum of $37,500 to each man, with McIntosh keeping the motion picture rights, or a $50,000 purse plus 1/3 of the films.

G. L. "Tex" Rickard of Ely, Nevada, who had promoted Gans-Nelson, believing that an immediate show of money talked loudest, offered $15,000 cash, which he had with him right there at the meeting, and a check for $5,000 ($20,000 up front) as a guarantee for a total cash purse of $101,000, plus the fighters would receive 66 2/3% of the motion picture rights, for a July 4 fight. If his bid was accepted, he agreed to deposit $30,000 within 60 days of the fight, and the remaining $51,000 within 48 hours of the fight. It was believed that the pictures would be worth a fortune, for the Britt-Nelson fight pictures earned around a quarter of a million dollars. It was anticipated that the films for this fight would generate a half million.

When Johnson saw all of that cash, his eyes glittered. Berger was at the meeting representing Jeffries, while Little and Johnson were both present.

Rickard announced that John J. Gleason was in with him on the offer, forming a strong alliance to bankroll the fight. Determined to co-promote the fight, Gleason had partnerships in offers with both Coffroth and Rickard.

Soon thereafter, Rickard claimed that he and Gleason had won the bid, though no official announcement would be made for a day, owing to New York's anti-prize-fight laws.

Also on December 1, at New York's Madison Square Garden, before 4,000 spectators, both Jeffries and Johnson gave exhibitions. Johnson appeared first and sparred with white opponents in a mild manner. After some interim wrestling matches, Jeff appeared and skipped rope, shadow boxed, and sparred 3 short one-minute rounds with Sam Berger.[252]

On December 3, 1909 in Hoboken, New Jersey, articles of agreement signed by Jeffries, Berger, Johnson, Little, Rickard, and Gleason stipulated that Jeffries and Johnson would meet in a 45-round fight using straight Queensberry rules, wearing 5-ounce gloves, that they would start training no later than 90 days before July 4, 1910, the date of the contest, and would not engage in any other fight until the championship bout. Each party had to deposit $10,000 to guarantee performance. The $101,000 purse would be split 75% to the winner ($75,750) and 25% to the loser ($25,250). The fighters would each have a 1/3 share of the film profits (2/3 total). The promoters would deposit $20,000 right away, another $30,000 60 days before the bout, and the remainder within 48 hours of the fight. There was no reference to a side bet.[253]

---

[252] *New York Sun, San Francisco Call, Los Angeles Herald*, December 2, 3, 1909. Jeff's breathing was somewhat impaired, showing that he still had a lot of work to do.
[253] *New York Tribune*, December 3, 1909; *New York Sun*, December 4, 1909.

On December 11, 1909 in Paris, France, Joe Jeannette and Sam McVey fought to a 30-round draw in a rematch of their epic battle.

Jeffries assured the public that he would not stall, and would try to knock out Johnson as soon as he could. He wrote,

> When I presented Marvin Hart with the world's championship title, a little over four years ago, I had fully made up my mind to retire from the ring, because the public did not think there was any one in my class who could give me an argument.

> I came out of retirement because the public demanded it, and because, under the circumstances, I felt it my duty to regain the title.
> …

> No one seems to doubt my ability to beat Johnson if I was in the form which made it possible for me to win the championship and beat all the heavyweights, but there does seem to be some question as to whether I will ever be able to come back. I don't believe there is any one in a better position to judge my condition than I am myself, and it was only after I had convinced myself that I could come back that I announced my intention to fight Johnson. I am absolutely confident that when I enter the ring, on July 4, I will be in as good condition as I ever was in my life. I will beat Johnson, and do it in much less time than any of the followers of the ring expect me to. You can rest assured that when the sun sets on July 4, 1910, a white man will be the champion pugilist of the world.[254]

The *Freeman* said that fans should anticipate a long fight. Jeff's prediction of a fast knockout was more of a dream than anything. First of all, Johnson was too cautious and defensive to be stopped quickly. Second, Johnson liked to take his time in breaking down his foes, rarely taking a chance by wading in and slugging away, or doing so on a consistent basis. Even if Johnson could stop Jeff quickly, he would not risk robbing himself of the film profits that he would lose by terminating the fight too quickly. Jeffries himself usually gradually broke down his foes, dealing out bone-crushing blows when he did punch, but took his time about it unless he saw that his opponent was not much to worry about or he felt forced to pick up the pace. This writer also believed that the fighters would split the proceeds 50/50 rather than what the public was told. There was no reason for either man to risk only earning the short end of the purse.

The *Freeman* said the black race could take pride in its sporting achievements. "We should feel proud of our race from a sporting standpoint, because we have reached the top round in every line of sport that we have been permitted to take part in." This writer predicted that Johnson would defeat Jeffries in a hard fight. "This should be a happy Christmas day for us, recollecting that we have been so much deeper down

---

[254] *Richmond Planet*, December 18, 1909.

in the mire than other races on the globe, and now we are on the top round in the world of sport." Such successes were symbolically important to the oppressed.[255]

JACK JOHNSON.

Jack Johnson had not seen his mother, Mrs. Tiny Johnson, for seven years, but they spent Christmas together in Chicago, for he had purchased her a home at 3344 Wabash avenue. Present were Johnson, his wife Hattie, his mother, sister and her children, his son, brother, manager, manager's friends, and a few distant relatives. Jack kissed his six-year-old son (who actually might have been his nephew), who was playing with a toy automobile. He presented his wife with a set of diamond earrings. He and his manager discussed his $1,500 a week theatrical engagement, which would continue until mid-April. Jack intended to start training for Jeffries around May 1 at Ocean View, near San Francisco, sparring with Gunboat Smith, "who knocked me down," Jack Heinen, and Monte Cutler.

Speaking of the upcoming Jeffries bout, Jack's mother said, "Win that fight? Why, he'll knock that white man's head off." Jack planned to win within 15 rounds. "I intend to adopt a style of fighting that will make Jeff come to me. There will be plenty of infighting. When I get him coming I intend to use my uppercut. I think that will fix him."

The local colored aristocracy paid their respects to the champion, coming and going all day. "And those who don't believe that it is a fine thing to be a world's champion heavyweight ought to see the way that Jack Johnson is idolized by the colored population."[256]

Christmas was not a happy time for everyone. According to the *Chicago Defender*, in 1909, 325 black men and women had been lynched, shot, and burned at the stake for fun. 28,000 colored females had been victimized by mobs or rapists. Southern state governments had failed to protect black folk.[257]

---

[255] *Freeman*, December 25, 1909.

[256] *Freeman*, January 8, 1910.

On Dec 27, 1909 in Sydney, Australia, Bill Lang scored a KO12 over 46-year-old Bob Fitzsimmons to retain the Australian heavyweight title. Since his 1908 LKOby6 loss to Tommy Burns, Lang was on a three-fight win streak, including 1908 KO5 Jim Griffin and 1909 KO17 and KO20 Bill Squires. Johnson had stopped Lang in 9 rounds in 1907.

[257] *Chicago Defender*, January 1, 1910.

THE NEW YEAR DINNER

meone Overlooked—As Usual

Chicago Defender, January 1, 1910

THE DAWN OF THE NEW YEAR

Brings Fear Upon Those Without Hope.

Freeman, January 1, 1910

"TAKE OFF THAT UNIFORM!"

The Governor of Georgia has decreed that no "Negro in that state shall wear a uniform." Will he be stripped of civilian cloth next in their effort to make him an animal?

Chicago Defender, January 22, 1910

Jim Jeffries continually expressed confidence that he would defeat Johnson. "If I didn't feel sure I wouldn't fight. I've never stood up in a ring yet without feeling sure, and I am certainly not coming back after four years of farm work to be beaten by a nigger, even if that nigger did beat Burns. You can bet your life on that."[258]

Joe Gans opined that Johnson would conquer Jeffries:

> It will be a case of science against brute strength, and in this affair the science of Johnson will come out on top. I want to say that I am not favoring Johnson because we are of the same color. If I thought that Jeff could whip Johnson I would be one of the first to express my convictions. … It's simply a case of which man I consider the superior, and my choice is Johnson. … In his prime Jeffries was a bunch of muscle and bones that no man could hurt. He has had years of rest, and at present the retired champion is simply a mass of soft flesh that is in such a condition that it will be impossible for him to get back to the old days. … When he faces Johnson he will be far from the Jeffries of old.

> Jeffries may manage to get rid of a lot of overweight and may appear as fine as a fiddle when he sits in his corner, but take it from me, that old vitality which is absolutely necessary for any kind of a battle will be missing, and then what can you expect?

---

[258] *Albany Advertiser*, January 8, 1910.

It is almost a positive fact that all the folks who refuse to give Johnson a chance with Jeffries simply figure through prejudice against the colored fighter. He can't hit, he always backs up, he hasn't got the punch and he is always stalling, are a few things that they charge to Johnson. Now, in my estimation, and you know that I have seen them all, I think that Johnson is one of the greatest fighters of the past twenty years. ...

When they start you can go broke that Jack will use all his cleverness to prevent Jeffries landing in the early rounds. ... That means that Johnson will keep on the defensive until he thinks Jeffries has lost a lot of his strength and is having trouble with his wind.

When Jack is satisfied that he holds the upper hand, then he will change his tactics and try to beat Jeffries down with those sharp uppercuts and stinging jabs that will take the big fellow's energy away and leave him a mark for his colored rival.[259]

Famous trainer and manager of champions Billy Madden said Johnson would win, and it would be easy, for no man could come back. He also said that Johnson was better at present than Jeffries ever was. If Jeff used his crouch on Johnson, the current champ would whip in his terrible right uppercut. However, most whites disagreed with him.[260]

De Witt Van Court said the consensus of opinion was that if Jeffries could come back that he would defeat Johnson easily. "In my opinion, Jeff will win inside of six rounds." Van Court believed that with proper training, Jeff could be as good as ever. He made this statement to counter the argument of folks like Billy Madden, who said that Jeff was as good as beaten before he even entered the ring.

Van Court noted that as a result of public demand, Jeff was returning to regain the title for the Caucasian race, and after a year of light training and good living, Jeffries had proven to his own satisfaction that he could do it. He was not a man who would take a chance of ruining his unbeaten record if he thought otherwise.

Van Court believed that Johnson's speed and cleverness would mean nothing when up against Jeff's great strength, terrific slugging, fast footwork, and excellent generalship. Jeff had retired at the top of his game, not on the down swing, and had not endured any punishment over the last several years. He was only three years older than Johnson, was heavier than him, and had fought a higher class of opponent, usually with superior results to Johnson. Johnson had scored a much lower percentage of knockouts. Van Court noted that a man like Griffin had twice fought Johnson to a draw. Jeff had knocked out Griffin. Jeffries had proven that he could take punishment, whereas Johnson had not. "If there is anything that

[259] *Freeman*, January 15, 1910.
[260] *Spokane Press*, January 15, 1910; *Freeman*, February 26, 1910.

Johnson has done at any time in the ring that would give him a chance to whip Jeffries when the big fellow is in half shape I am unable to find it. If he classes with those men of the ring whom Jeffries has beaten insensible to the mat I am no judge of fighting class." For the past year, Jeff had not touched liquor or cigarettes, whereas Johnson was known to eat and drink and enjoy life between fights. Plus, as of mid-January 1910, Jeffries still had another five and a half months to train.[261]

Jim Corbett picked Jeffries to win, and said he would assist him. Corbett was training so that he could be fit enough to be a Jeffries sparring partner.

On January 20, 1910 in New York, Jack Johnson was arrested on a charge of assaulting a fellow black man named Norman Pinder. The event took place between 1 and 3 a.m. at Barron Wilkins' saloon at 253 West 35th street. Allegedly, Pinder offered him a drink, and Johnson said he wanted wine. Pinder said he could buy him one, but could not afford more. Johnson said he never drank anything else. Pinder came back by saying there was a time when Johnson was not so particular. "You used to drink beer. I've seen you drink it – and out of a bucket too, with your face in the bucket like a horse." Johnson then struck him several times. When asked at police headquarters why he had done it, Johnson said, "Honest to God, Cap'n, I'm sorry I didn't hit him harder. He has been casting aspersions and insults on me for a long time and I just had to hit him." Apparently there was history between the two.

Johnson called his manager George Little, who obtained a bail bondsman. The champ said his real name was John Jackson, age 31, and that he was a boxing instructor by occupation.[262]

Boxing noted that Jeffries' supporters liked to claim that Johnson had a yellow streak. Tommy Burns had claimed the same. "The man who could face with a calm, broad smile such hostile receptions as those which greeted him when he entered the ring to meet Burns and Ketchel, to say nothing of others, cannot be much of a coward."

Battling Nelson picked Johnson to defeat Jeffries. "Fighters never come back. … I won't believe that the Negro is not game till I see him lie down. … Jeffries has fought four rounds in six years, and he hasn't led a Sunday school teacher's life. I don't see how he will last."

A Harvard doctor declared that Johnson had a remarkable reach - 78.8 inches.[263]

There were rumors that if Jeff was on the verge of being beaten that his adherents either would throw in the sponge or do something to get him

---

[261] *Los Angeles Herald*, January 16, 1910. Johnson had also fought a draw with Mexican Pete Everett, whom Jeffries had stopped.
[262] *New York Sun, Washington Herald*, January 21, 1910.
 On January 19, 1910 in Philadelphia, Al Kaufman won a 6-round no-decision bout against Philadelphia Jack O'Brien.
[263] *Boxing, Freeman, Chicago Defender*, January 22, 1910.

disqualified, rather than allow Johnson to score a clean knockout. An angry Jeff disputed this rumor, and said it was a lie to say he was not fit to fight. Johnson would have to knock him out cold to win.

> But that nigger never can win from me. I'll give him the worst pounding that a man ever received. In my previous fights I always held back some steam, because I was afraid of maiming my opponent. With Johnson, however, I am not going to hold back anything. He will receive the limit, and just one punch will lay him so low he won't get up for an hour.

Bill Brady said Jeffries would win if he made Johnson lead. He noted how Jim Corbett had been inactive but trained for a year and then showed his old-time form against Jeffries when they fought 23 rounds. Brady felt that Jeff was a better fighter than Corbett, so he could do the same.

Still, Brady admitted that Johnson was the best fighter that Jeff had ever faced.

> I have seen Johnson fight, and take it from me that he's there with everything. He has the best left hand of any big fellow the ring ever produced. Don't let them gull you with the stuff about the negro having climbed to the front at the expense of little men. The little men he beat are pretty shifty fighters. Johnson is a better man than Peter Jackson ever was. … I think the big fellows of today are cleverer, faster and can hit just as hard as the big 'uns that Jeff flattened out.[264]

Joe Woodman said that Sam Langford could defeat Johnson and any other heavyweight in the world except Jeffries. He said Jeff would defeat Johnson, and did not even need to be half as good as he once was to win.

> Langford occupies the unique position of being a popular colored fighter. The prejudice that usually attaches to negro fighters does not apply to Langford in the same degree that it attaches to Johnson and other black gladiators. Sam always attends to his own business and does not go about the country bragging about his prowess and issuing challenges to every fighter in his class.[265]

Jeffries said he would start formal training about February 15. He did not care where the fight took place. "I know that I can defeat Jack Johnson at sea level or on top of Pikes Peak." Jeff said he would tear into Johnson from the start and never let up until Jack hit the canvas. "I will demonstrate again the superiority of the white race."[266]

---

[264] *Los Angeles Herald,* January 23, 1910.

[265] *Los Angeles Herald,* January 25, 1910.

[266] *Los Angeles Herald,* January 29, 1910; *Seattle Star,* February 1, 1910. In light of Utah Governor Spry's expressed opposition to the fight, Jeff thought the fight most likely would take place in San Francisco.

SAM LANGFORD.

The *Freeman* opined that with the exception of Jeffries, Langford was the only logical opponent for the champion. However, "the physical advantages of the champion over Langford are so great that the public would hardly concede the latter a chance." This writer believed that only father time would defeat Johnson, whom it called the age's marvel and the greatest ring general ever.[267]

Jeffries denied published statements that he would win quickly, and encouraged fans to ignore wild bull stories. He would keep his intentions and strategies to himself. He reminded the public that it was he, not Johnson, who insisted upon a 45-round battle. He would be in top shape, ready to knock out Johnson no matter how long it took. He never felt better in all his life, and would not deceive his supporters by telling them that he was in great shape if he was not.

World champion wrestler Frank Gotch said he had wrestled with Jeff over the past couple of months and was certain he would win, and win easily. Jeff was in top condition and very strong.[268]

An impressed observer who saw Jeffries exhibit with Sam Berger in Spokane on February 3 said,

James J. Jeffries is going to give back the heavyweight championship to the white race. I am as confident of this, barring accidents of an unforeseen nature, as I am that the sun will rise tomorrow morning. I must confess that I am slightly prejudiced, racially, but with that in mind, I can see no one but Jeffries in the coming struggle for the pugilistic supremacy of the world.[269]

Jim Corbett said Johnson was flat-footed, but he slid along, always backing away, making the other fellow lead and fall short. He thought that if right, Jeff was too fast with his feet for Johnson to beat him flat-footed. "I know that Jeff came after me so fast that I couldn't get out of the way, and I was going like a race horse on my toes."

In response, Jack Johnson said that lots of great fighters fought flat-footed, including ones that had beaten Corbett, so Jim should hardly criticize. "Flat-foot boxers made him call for the police."

---

[267] *Freeman*, January 29, 1910. A writer for the *Freeman* saw Jeffries give a New Year's Eve exhibition in Chicago. Jeff tired perceptibly at the finish, and the consensus of unbiased opinion was that the Jeffries of the present was anything but the Jeffries of yore.

[268] *Seattle Star*, February 1, 1910.

[269] *Spokane Press*, February 4, 1910. This writer had seen Jeff a year ago, and he was then fat and out of condition. However, Jeff's exhibition on February 3 had convinced this observer that he had rid himself of superfluous fat, and was now fast and vigorous and his wind good.

HE WILL HAVE THEM ALL TO BEAT.

The Future Welfare of His People Forms a Part of the Stake.

Chicago Defender, **February 5, 1910**

John L. Sullivan knew how hard it was to come back after several years, which is why he picked Johnson to win. He did not think old man Corbett would make the best sparring partner either.

> Take it from me that Jeffries can't come back. I know it, and nobody knows it better than Jeffries himself. I don't care what Corbett says, his talk to me has the same weight as the ashes on a cigar. He couldn't punch a hole in a pound of butter. With Corbett as his trainer, it would be all off with Jeffries. Corbett, of course, is boosting the game, but that fight, if it ever comes off, will demonstrate what I have said. Jeffries can't come back. If he intended to, he ought to get some husky youngsters, who would punch him around a little.[270]

Sullivan also was quoted as saying, "Will Jeffries lick Johnson? No. Not unless Johnson lays down for him. ... None of the rest of us was able to quit the ring and come back strong ... Jeffries won't have the endurance."[271]

---

[270] *Richmond Planet,* February 5, 1910.
[271] *Freeman,* February 12, 1910.

Some speculated that the fight would be fixed for the white man to win, because if he did, the pictures would be worth a million dollars. If the black man won, whites might refuse to see the films. Hence, the feeling was that Johnson would be bribed to take a dive. Of course, this was sheer speculation. Jeff had never been involved in a fixed fight. Johnson at worst only carried some of his foes, but never intentionally allowed them to win. Plus, Johnson had told all of his friends and family to bet on him.[272]

The French were backing Jeffries to win. The English thought Johnson was the best bet. Americans liked Jeff.[273]

On February 8, 1910 in Los Angeles, Jim Flynn unofficially won a 10-round no-decision bout against Sam Langford. The *Los Angeles Herald* said Flynn won decisively, having won nearly every round, carrying the fight to Langford throughout. Referee Charles Eyton said Flynn had the best of it from start to finish. This put a damper on Langford's challenges to fight Johnson, for Johnson had handled Flynn and knocked him out.[274]

Johnson and then-girlfriend Etta Duryea. Jack called her his wife.

In a letter to the editor of the *Freeman*, one man criticized Sam Langford for challenging Johnson and talking about his ability to beat him, even though the middleweight-sized Langford knew he had no chance to do so. "Every time one Negro gets a little prominence, along comes another, and instead of emulating his example, tries to assist the white man in tearing him down. ... Sam knows there is neither money nor glory in a fight between him and Johnson, whichever wins. Let him build up in his own field."

The *Freeman* warned Johnson that if he did not slow down and be more careful about comporting himself with the law, that he would wind up in prison. Jack also failed to realize his political

[272] *Richmond Planet*, February 5, 1910, quoting the *New York Journal*.
[273] *Salt Lake Herald-Republican*, February 6, 1910.
[274] *Los Angeles Herald, San Francisco Call*, February 9, 1910.

importance, which could have an adverse impact on the black race, as well as himself. No one ever heard of Peter Jackson creating any scenes in a barroom. He lived decently and was a gentleman. Yet, when he fell off the map, "the white man silently rejoiced." Ten years ago, no one would have imagined there was even a possible chance for a black man to be heavyweight champion.

> Johnson is undoubtedly the recognized heavyweight champion of the world, and for that one reason the colored people have something to be proud of; aside from this, there's nothing to stand on your head about.

> The heavyweight championship of the world carries with it a great deal more than the mere title, especially if you take into consideration the amount of good or bad that can be done the race to which such a fighter belongs. The world generally knows every 'hook or crook' made by a champion, and for that reason the colored race is up against two great obstacles; First, the adverse feeling such a condition will naturally arouse; and second, the inability to control to any sensible degree the conduct and general deportment of such a 'crazy' champion. The white man has no real love for Mr. Johnson. ... Then why not stick with and try and be an honor and a credit to his own race. As a matter of fact, Johnson has shown no particular liking for the colored race since he has been heavyweight champion of the world, and this is shown conclusively in his recent mix-up with Norman Pinder, a little consumptive colored man of about ninety pounds, who had about as much chance in a battle with Johnson as a bedbug would have trying to kiss him during his favorite dream. ... The cold hand of the law is reaching out for Mr. Johnson in no uncertain terms, and it looks to take the leading role in his future conduct. Why shouldn't it, when the lives, liberty and happiness of over nine million Negroes are being antagonized and jeopardized by his folly? If you don't believe it, holler 'hurray for Jack Johnson' in the hearing of any group of white men, and see how much trouble you will have. Then when you get close enough to say 'howdy-do' to Mr. Johnson, let me know if he answers. ... That Jackson Johnson is a big, strong, burly, rough darkey, I'll admit, and being champion of the world he may feel that he has a perfect right to run over, beat up, ignore and otherwise make life miserable for others, but he should not forget the fact that Samson ruled the world with his strength, but his love for a woman got him killed. ... So, when you look back into Mr. Johnson's police record, you will agree with me that unless he puts a quietus to his wild methods, the strong hand of the law is apt to chain him down.

This writer listed several legal issues which Johnson had become entangled with since his arrival back to America as champion:

On landing in New York City from Australia, after he had defeated Tommy Burns for the heavyweight championship of the world, he was arrested and charged with committing rape on a colored girl; was fined $250.

May 21, 1909—Johnson's automobile seized by sheriff in Philadelphia on a writ of attachment in suit for board bill.

May 22, 1909—Forced to settle a bill of $406 for nursing his brother.

May 30, 1909—Arrested, charged with violating speed laws of Boston; was fined.

June 2, 1909—Johnson pleaded guilty to violating speed regulations; was fined $5.

June 9, 1909—Arrested in Boston in suit to collect old debt of $41; later smashed his auto in wild ride through city.

July 16, 1909—While at Crown Point, Ind., had road race with auto; machine skidded; opponent's axle was broken; young white woman seriously hurt.

August 5, 1909—Arrested in London, Ont., on telegram from chief of police of Woodstock, charged with exceeding speed limit; in wild ride ran down another auto and smashed it; was fined.

October 21, 1909—In a parade in San Francisco, drove auto recklessly through the streets; arrested. On leaving San Francisco after his fight with Ketchel, his auto was attached for a debt of $180. The Overland Limited was held twenty minutes while Johnson was sought for debts he owed; refusing to pay, his auto was held.

January 2, 1910—Jumped contract with Terre Haute theater; manager attached trunks; was arrested by police.

January 4, 1910—Held up by constables and made to pay costs for jumping contract to show at Duquesne Garden, Pittsburg.

January 14, 1910—Arrested in Boston, charged with assaulting taxi driver and breaking window in cab.

January 20, 1910—Arrested in New York, charged with assault on another Negro (Norman Pinder), in Barron Wilkin's Cafe; held in $1,000 bail for grand jury.

Freeman, February 12, 1910

Johnson's assault case was before a New York grand jury.

That Mr. Johnson looks upon these conditions as a very huge joke is demonstrative of another phase of his ignorance. The grand jury is in duty bound to indict him, then he is up against a No. 1 district attorney, with twelve white men in the jury box. If found guilty, the least he will get is six months, unless the judge suspends his sentence, and what judge can you find who will do this after seeing Johnson's police record. … It's a 'pipe' that a colored man won't have any more chance of getting on that jury than Johnson will have beating it. And with twelve white men on a jury trying Johnson, all betting that Jeffries will lick him, while down deep within their hearts they are praying that Jeffries will kill him. Can you beat it?[275]

---

[275] *Freeman*, February 12, 1910.

The grand jury indicted Johnson with a charge of second degree assault on Norman Pinder. His bail was set at $2,500. Conviction carried a maximum sentence of 5 years, or a fine, or both.

JOHNSON SUPPRESSES HIS LAWYER.

When Jack Johnson was arrested the other week in New York by order of Judge Mulqueen of the Court of General Sessions by reason of an indictment charging him with assault in the second degree for having belabored Norman Pinder with a chair, a very funny incident happened.

When the Judge suggested that Johnson had offered $3,000 cash bail earlier in the day, that it might be accepted. Johnson looked uneasy. Lawyer Nugent started to address the court in Johnson's behalf when suddenly the mighty Jack clapped his hand over the lawyer's mouth,

forcing him back to his chair. "Your honor," said the fighter, "when I came to court this morning I had that $3,000 with me. I didn't tell you a lie. Now I have only $2500—the rest went for legal expenses." Then everybody laughed as they looked as his lawyer drawed up in a chair.

Freeman, **April 9, 1910**

Several newspapers observed that Johnson was breaking police records. In less than one year, he had been arrested thirteen times. The twelfth was a charge of assault on Norman Pinder, a "consumptive negro who claims Johnson floored him for offering to buy beer instead of champagne." Johnson alleged self-defense and was awaiting trial in New York. The thirteenth arrest came in Detroit, when Johnson's bull pup chewed the coat off a pedestrian and Jack was hailed into court. One newspaper said he had been sued for $20,000 in damages and had paid $800 in fines.[276]

Supposedly, after Sam Langford had beaten Mike Schreck in late November 1909, Johnson and Langford were in the same Negro club. Within earshot of Langford, speaking to Bob Armstrong, Johnson teased Bob about the company he kept, that being Langford. Sam became angry and threatened to whip Johnson then and there. Johnson's hand moved towards his hip pocket. A black detective grabbed and took something away from him, and was heard to say, "It's good that gun is empty or I'd run you in."[277]

---

[276] *Salt Lake Tribune,* February 20, 1910; *Salt Lake Herald-Republican,* March 5, 1910.
[277] *Freeman,* February 19, 1910.

Amongst some gamblers, Jeffries opened as a 10 to 7 betting favorite.[278]

C. E. Van Loan said Johnson was making as much money as he could while the sun still shone on him. Like Jeffries, he was traveling from town to town giving theatrical exhibitions. He was a great spender and it took a world of money to keep him going. Jack was making up for all of the long, lean, hungry years. "Johnson never used a manager for anything, except to draw money from hm."

One writer said Johnson played it safe in his battles, preferring to win by a shade without endangering his face. His supposed cowardice was based on the fact that he fought cautiously against men he might have knocked out had he taken more risks. His answer to his critics had always been, "I won, didn't I?" The only time that answer was wrong was against Hart, and even then, many thought Johnson indeed had won the bout on points. [279]

The English publication, *Boxing,* discussed the uneasy feeling about the Jeffries fight, which disturbed the "complacent American mind." They feared the consequences if Jeffries lost.

> Well, then, as every American realized, things would be in a very parlous condition indeed. It was bad enough to have a negro strutting about as cock of the walk as it was, although he was only enabled to strut by virtue of his triumph over a little fellow – a game and clever fighter, but nevertheless a smallish man – in Tommy Burns.

> But a victory over Jeffries, the chosen champion of the white race, has become a contingency almost too awful to contemplate. Should Johnson win, not only he, but all the coloured inhabitants of the United States would commence strutting at once. And this would be a serious state of affairs from every point of view.

Boxing admitted that from a racial viewpoint, it wanted to see the white man win. If Johnson lost, it accurately prophesized what would happen thereafter – the color line would be drawn more firmly than ever.

> Of one thing, however, we may rest assured. Should Johnson lose his title…the black man will have enjoyed his last tenure of the world's championship. He will never be given another chance.

> The first step which any future white holder will take will be to draw a most portentous and well-defined colour line. In fact, it would not be a very wild prophecy that this will be insisted upon by fight promoters, press, and white public alike.

> It may not show commendable pluck on the part of the white race, but there are numerous reasons for their adopting such a course.[280]

[278] *Call,* February 13, 1910.
[279] *Freeman,* February 19, 1910.
[280] *Boxing,* February 19, 1910.

Billy Madden said that any claims of a new school vs. old school of boxing were all bunk.

> Fighters are only human. Go way back into history and you will discover that everything now used in the fighting game is exactly the same as years ago. ... It's a remarkable thing that every new crop of fighters swell up and pronounce themselves far superior to the former stars. I have been hearing this since I was seventeen years old, and now I am fifty-seven. Men don't improve in the prize ring. The game has been the same and can never change.

Fighters always did and would need speed, strength, gameness, endurance, and skill, and would use or combine them in varying ways, depending on the individual.[281]

In late February, the *Los Angeles Herald* said Jeffries had been proving that he would be the same old gladiator. His appearance and condition of late had been removing doubt about him.[282]

The *Freeman* said that either Jeffries' left to the body or Johnson's right uppercut would win the fight between them. They could punch well with both hands, but Jeff was better known for his left, while Johnson was more noted for his right.[283]

On March 9, 1910 in Oakland, California, Jim Barry scored a KO9 over Gunboat Smith. Smith would have to wait awhile before he could claim to be a legitimate heavyweight contender. Jim Barry was the man whom promoters were afraid to match with Johnson, fearing for Jim's health.

From a Minneapolis pulpit on March 11, speaking to the congregation of the St. James African Methodist Episcopal Church, Johnson said there was nothing one couldn't accomplish if he listened to his mother. "When I first broached the prize fighter idea to her she didn't like it, but when I showed her that it was a business proposition, she said, 'Go ahead and win,' and following that suggestion I have done my best."[284]

A *Freeman* writer said it was foolish to expect Johnson to be a Booker T. Washington or a paragon of culture and refinement. Regardless, it felt that Johnson's actions were overblown by the press. "While he is in the limelight, his every act is noticed, purposely misconstrued and exaggerated. Jack is a really good fellow, never a bully, and his errors of deportment are more the caprices of an overgrown schoolboy than a hardened sinner."[285]

On March 17, 1910 in the Los Angeles area, Sam Langford avenged his loss to Jim Flynn, dominating the bout and knocking him out in the 8th round with a right uppercut.[286]

---

[281] *Freeman*, February 26, 1910.
[282] *Los Angeles Herald*, February, 27, 1910.
[283] *Freeman*, March 5, 1910.
[284] *Freeman*, March 19, 1910.
[285] *Freeman*, March 12, 1910.
[286] *Los Angeles Herald*, March 18, 1910.

On March 18, Johnson was in yet another auto accident, a single car collision. Many wondered how long he could continue driving the way he did without being injured or killed.

Former Jeffries trainer Tommy Ryan announced that he would assist Johnson with his training. He would give Jack tips about Jeff.

Jeff's theatrical manager said he had been watching him closely for several months, and was convinced that Jeffries would defeat Johnson.[287]

A *Freeman* writer said that analyzing the upcoming fight from an unprejudiced point of view, Johnson would win. Although in his prime Jeffries was the greatest fighter ever, six years of idleness would prevent a comeback against a man who had been improving all the time, working with different men, and fighting consistently. Johnson had shown generalship, coolness, great endurance, and was the better defensive fighter of the two.

> Watch and see if Jeff doesn't go down in eighteen rounds and that will be the limit. I do not believe that Jack will lay down, for he knows that it is something for him to do that no other man has done. … This alone will make that giant from Texas fight the battle of his life.

> We are with you, Jack, old boy. … He has proven to the race that he is worthy of their race pride. … The white race says that Jeff must win and that the whites must be supreme. But we say that the black man must win.[288]

A writer for the *Salt Lake-Republican* said he would rank Johnson, Langford, Kaufman, and Jeannette ahead of the present version of Jeffries.

> Take all the reports of the strenuous training of Jeffries with a grain of salt. … Jeffries is making the mistake so often fatal to the unbeaten – that of underestimating his opponent. I believe that the giant boilermaker has such a contempt for the abilities of Johnson that he is deceiving himself into the belief that he can beat him in a punch.

This writer said Jeff had been smoking 20 cigarettes a day for the past six years. Mix that with all the drinks he had over that time and "you will find that Jeffries has consumed enough booze to make a good sized pond, and enough cigarettes to stretch from Chicago to New York."

The writer also said Langford hit harder than Johnson and was just as fast and clever, but Johnson was too rangy for a man of Langford's build.

Al Kaufman had a good punch and could assimilate punishment. "He would wear Jeffries out in a long fight."[289]

On March 23, 1910, Johnson was in New York to stand trial for his assault charge upon Norman Pinder. None of the witnesses showed up, but

[287] *Salt Lake Herald-Republican*, March 19, 1910.
[288] *Freeman*, March 19, 1910.
[289] *Salt Lake Herald-Republican*, March 20, 1910.

nevertheless, showing his bias, the judge increased Johnson's bail to $5,000, which he could not pay, so he had to spend time in jail for half a day, locked up while bail money could be secured. The judge continued the case to the next day, with warrants for the arrest of the witnesses. However, it appeared that the charge would have to be dropped, which eventually it was.[290]

Los Angeles Herald, **March 26, 1910**

No fan of the black man, the *Los Angeles Herald* said the champ was disgracing himself. "Johnson seems to disregard all common decency by almost insisting upon open defiance of law and order everywhere he goes, and he constantly is getting into trouble with officers of the law." He loved to joy ride at high speeds. Right after being released from jail on the assault charge, he was served with a breach of contract suit in Chicago. He was losing supporters even amongst his own race.[291]

During March, Jeffries was on a hunting trip in the Tehachapi mountains in California.

On March 31, 1910, Jack Johnson celebrated his 32nd birthday.

On April 3 in Chicago, Johnson sparred 6 rounds with Kid Cotton. Jack said, "I was surprised at my own condition. I expected to be winded and

[290] *Salt Lake Herald-Republican,* March 24, 1910.
[291] *Los Angeles Herald,* March 26, 1910.

tired after six fast rounds, and the fact that I was not shows that I'm in pretty good shape already."

Ministers in the Oakland, California area said they would attempt to stop the big fight, which they denounced as a brutal and bloody exhibition. They would seek an injunction and make an appeal to California Governor James Gillett.[292]

A SOUTHERN EASTER CELEBRATION.

Good Friday Was Celebrated Thus in Arkansas—An American Citizen Void of Protection by Our Great Government.

Chicago Defender, **April 2, 1910**

[292] *Los Angeles Herald,* April 5, 1910.

CHAPTER 8

A National Obsession

The public and press were so intrigued by the Jeffries-Johnson championship fight, dubbed "the fight of the century," such that for the next three months, from April to July 1910, the press issued daily reports on the two fighters' activities and training, and the thoughts, predictions, analysis, and expert opinions of those associated with the fight and those involved in the sport of boxing. The public eagerly read it all. The constant attention helped gamblers assess the two men. No fight or sporting event ever had received such a huge amount of daily coverage, or for so many months ahead of the event. It further built an already hugely significant fight to epic proportions.

On April 5, 1910, Jim Jeffries arrived at his training camp at Rowardennan, Ben Lomond, California, in the Santa Cruz mountains north of Santa Cruz. He would train there for the next three months. Jeffries said, "I have practically been in training for this fight a year." He did not plan to take off much more weight.

Jeffries received a letter from a Brooklyn man who "deeply deplores the fact that the colored youths of the Church City have corralled the goats of all the white boys there. Mr. Harmon implores Mr. Jeffries to give Mr. Johnson a proper beating, in order that the youngsters of his neighborhood may enjoy peace and, incidentally, get the upper hand in the future." Jeff received daily letters of that nature from folks across the country, urging him to restore the championship to the white race.

Tommy Ryan backed out of his agreement to train Johnson, fearing that it would make him very unpopular.

In Boston, Jack Johnson won his breach of contract suit with Alec McLean on a technicality. The court held that the contract made four years ago was illegal, for a fight agreement was a felony and could not be enforced.

Johnson had demanded a jury trial on his latest speeding charge in Chicago, and the jury acquitted him.

Former Johnson manager Sam Fitzpatrick said Jeffries would win the upcoming fight. Johnson called Sam sour grapes.[293]

In the early days of training camp, Jeff primarily focused on general conditioning. On a daily basis, he did things like play baseball and handball,

[293] *San Francisco Call, Spokane Press,* April 6, 1910; *Richmond Planet,* April 9, 1910. With Jeffries were his wife, wife's two nephews Tod Boyer and Russell Kissler, manager/trainer Sam Berger, wrestler Farmer Burns, and friend Dick Adams. Bob Armstrong arrived that evening. Eugene Van Court said that except for less hair, Jeff looked the same as he did a number of years ago.

row on the San Lorenzo river, run 10 miles through the mountain trails, skip rope, and punch the bag. He also liked to spend time fishing.[294]

The Emeryville race track in Emeryville, just outside of Oakland, California, had been selected as the fight site.

Proving that the fight was of universal interest, Rickard and Gleason had received ticket orders from as far off as Australia and Great Britain. All nations were interested in the outcome. The *Freeman* wrote,

> There is not a patriotic Negro in America today, no matter what his views may be in regard to the prize ring and its principals, who is not proud of the fact from the depths of his heart that one of his race reigns supreme in his vocation. … Supremacy in one vocation begets supremacy in another. … The constant dropping of water will wear away a stone, and Jeffries is no exception to the rule. We hope that when the smoke of battle clears away, so to speak, that the question of supremacy between Caucasia and Ethiopia will have been settled from a gladiatorial standpoint on its merits, and the victory achieved on Ethiopia's side.[295]

Johnson told a *Boxing* correspondent, "We all know that he has been a great fighter, but he is not the Jeffries that once fought so well. … I am sincere when I declare that I do not believe he ever can get in fit condition to put up a hard battle."[296]

Johnson was exhibiting and doing some preliminary training in Chicago.

The *Call* said Jeff's face looked old and haggard, like a 45-year old, but he worked like a youngster.

On April 9, Jeff ran 10 miles with Farmer Burns and Bob Armstrong. He hit the punching bag for a few rounds and skipped rope. He also played three games of handball, worked with the dumbbells, and sparred a few rounds with Armstrong. Some feared that Jeff might go stale by working too much so far from the fight.

On a rainy April 10, one-hundred sporting men saw Jeff engage in rope skipping, wrestling, and shadow boxing, totaling 16 rounds. Jeff said he felt just fine, was not tired, and was going easy. He was not concerned about overtraining.[297]

On April 11, 1910 in Chicago, Jack Johnson boxed Kid Cotton for over an hour. Jack said he was just feeling himself out. He still was on an exhibition tour, with stops planned in Omaha, Denver, Salt Lake City, and Los Angeles. He intended to start real work in May at Seal Rock, California.[298]

---

[294] *Reno Evening Gazette*, April 7, 9, 1910.
[295] *Freeman*, April 9, 1910.
[296] *Boxing*, April 9, 1910.
[297] *San Francisco Call*, April 10, 1910; *Reno Evening Gazette*, April 11, 1910.
[298] *Salt Lake Herald-Republican*, April 12, 1910.
  Also on April 11, 1910, in Sydney, Australia, before a crowd of 17,000, in his first fight in over a year since losing the title, Tommy Burns won a 20-round decision over Bill Lang, the

On April 12, in his sparring, Jeffries doubled up Sam Berger in the 2nd round with a body wallop. The 3rd round only lasted a minute and a half, as Berger called it off early. Jeff then shadow boxed for 10 minutes, punched the bag for 6 rounds, and wrestled with both Farmer Burns and Bob Armstrong. Jeff ran 10 miles that day as well. The day's work encouraged everyone. Jeff was looking well, showing speed, snap, and accuracy, and his breathing was good. Jeff said, "I never felt better in my life."[299]

On April 15, Jeffries celebrated his 35th birthday, but put in a full course of hard training and sparring nevertheless.[300]

That day, in Chicago, Johnson ran about 10 miles. He boxed with Marty Cutler and Kid Cotton and did about an hour of gym work.[301]

Jim Corbett said Jeff would knock out Johnson, and just one good punch would do the trick. He believed the fight would not last longer than 6 rounds. Jim said the only way Jeff would lose was if he beat himself by working too hard chasing Johnson around. He did not think Johnson could put Jeff out with a punch. "I don't believe he could knock Jeff down, even if he had a horseshoe in his mitt, because I've been there myself, and I know, take it from me." Although Jeffries was left handed, "he can hit as hard with either hand as Johnson can with both. Besides being the hardest hitter that ever donned the gloves, Jeffries is a sure and crafty fighter. He's there on both the aggressive and defensive tactics. Johnson's defensive work is good, but his aggressive work is very bad."

Corbett cast the usual aspersions on Johnson, saying he was flatfooted and had a yellow streak. He also said Johnson was just the colored champ, not the world champion. "Jeff is the champ, and he will be until he dies."

Corbett expected to join Jeff's camp sometime in mid-May. He said he wasn't getting paid, except for expenses. He was doing it out of friendship and because "I don't want to hear the people say, 'We have a colored champion.'" Jim said Ketchel and Burns were too small, and Kaufman too slow, but Jeff had it all.[302]

---

man whom he had stopped in 6 rounds in 1908 when he was champion. Burns weighed 181 pounds to Lang's 188. Burns held the lead early, but tired and clinched often in the last 8 rounds, while Lang fought cautiously as well. Hugh McIntosh refereed. *Reno Evening Gazette*, April 12, 1910.

[299] *Reno Evening Gazette*, April 13, 1910.

On April 14, 1910 in the Los Angeles area, in a vicious battle that featured terrific slugging and roughing, 166-pound Sam Langford scored a KO16 over 196-pound Jim Barry. *Chicago Defender*, April 16, 1910.

[300] *Reno Evening Gazette*, April 17, 1910. That day, in the morning Jeff ran 10 miles and rowed on the river. In the afternoon, he sparred, skipped rope, shadow boxed, hit the bag, tugged the pulley weights for a half hour, and played a game of handball. In the 2nd round of sparring with Bob Armstrong, who was under instructions to punch as hard as he could, Jeff caught one on the chin that put a cramp in his neck, which required massage before he continued for a 3rd round.

[301] *Chicago Defender*, April 16, 1910.

[302] *Los Angeles Herald*, April 17, 1910.

On April 20, Jeffries sparred 3 rounds with Bob Armstrong. Jeff landed some telling blows, and Bob was eager to quit after the 3rd round.[303]

On April 21, 8,000 people gathered at the train station to see Johnson leave Chicago, heading west to give exhibitions in various cities. The *Chicago Defender's* entire staff was on hand to bid farewell to their hero.[304]

On April 22 in Omaha, both whites and blacks gave Johnson a nice reception. The champ said, "I like Omaha. It's a dandy city, and I am glad to be here. They are certainly treating me fine here today. I didn't expect such a warm reception." That evening, Johnson attended a big dance given in his honor. A line had to be formed to permit all those who desired to get a handshake with the champ. At a local café, Johnson performed upon the bass violin for half an hour.[305]

While in Omaha, Johnson said,

> Of my fight with Burns I can truthfully say that I never before entered the ring with a heart so full of malice. Mr. Burns had said many unkind things about me, and in the ring that day I remembered them all. Every time I forced him to his corner I would ask him if he remembered when he had made some certain statement and I followed it up with one of my best blows.

Jack said Jeff had said many harsh things too, and on the day of their battle, he would remember them all and make Jeff atone as well.[306]

In Sydney, Australia, Johnson was the betting favorite over Jeffries at 6 to 4 odds.

On April 22, in addition to his other usual training, Jeffries sparred 3 rounds with Armstrong and 2 rounds with Berger. Sam worked on his right uppercut, coaching Jeff to block it, knowing that was one of Johnson's favorite blows.[307]

Johnson told *Boxing*, "I've wanted this so much that now I've got it, it seems hardly true." He had long wanted to fight Jeffries.

> I expect to knock Jim Jeffries out in 18 rounds, though perhaps we may go to 20. But the last is the outside number. …

---

[303] *Reno Evening Gazette*, April 21, 1910.

[304] *Chicago Defender*, April 23, 1910. Johnson was with his wife, George Little and wife, Sig Hart and wife, Marty Cutler (a.k.a. "Monte"), George Cotton, Barney Furey, and Tom Little.
Also on April 21, 1910 in Pittsburgh, Al Kaufman won a 6-round no decision bout against Philadelphia Jack O'Brien.

[305] *Freeman*, May 7, 1910.

[306] *Los Angeles Herald*, April 24, 1910.

[307] *Reno Evening Gazette*, April 23, 1910. Jeff's measurements allegedly were: height 6'1 ½", chest 45 inches, 50 inches expanded, waist 36 inches, thigh 26 inches, calf 17 inches, biceps 16 inches, forearm 13 inches, and weight 228 pounds.
Joe Choynski had arrived, and was quite surprised at Jeff's physical improvement. Still, he believed Jeff needed some good, stiff boxing bouts to put him into his old fighting trim. That day, Jeff also ran about 12 miles, participated in two sessions of handball with Berger and Billy Papke, and punched the bag.

The man doesn't live who can yank me around just as he wants to. Jim Jeffries may be strong, but when he bumps against me he will bump up against one quite as strong, and who knows how to use his strength quite as well. Some silly dopesters get the hunch that I am a chicken beside him. Well, when it comes to mauling round at close quarters he'll find I'm not an easy guy.

You can have it from me right here now that I have never yet mixed it with a man that has extended me to my last link nor anything like it.[308]

As of late April, Johnson said he would not begin hard training for another couple of weeks. He did not want to overtrain and go stale. He had never trained more than 2 months for a fight.

On April 25, Johnson exhibited in Salt Lake, sparring 4 rounds, 2 each with George Cotton and Marty Cutler (a.k.a. Monte). He was weighing 224 - 226 pounds, but planned to fight at 210. Jack said, "In late years no one has ever hurt me, nor hit me to speak of." When asked if he was going to even up things on July 4 for what Jeff had said about him, Johnson replied, "I know that Sam Berger has said more than Mr. Jeffries, but Mr. Jeffries has said enough, and I will make him account for them when we meet."[309]

On April 27, 1910 in Philadelphia, Sam Langford and Stanley Ketchel fought to a 6-round no-decision. A poll of newsmen on scene had it 7 for Langford, 4 for Ketchel, and 2 votes for a draw. Even those who said Langford won said he only had a slight advantage and that a draw would have been a fair decision as well. Many thought Langford was under a pull, not trying his best. Others said Ketchel's hard-punching non-stop aggressiveness gave Langford all he could handle, though Sam was the better boxer.[310]

When Johnson arrived at the Los Angeles train station on April 28, 500 cheering blacks greeted him.[311]

On April 29, 1910 in San Francisco, Owen Moran knocked out Tommy McCarthy in the 16th round. McCarthy never woke up, and died from the injuries he suffered. Moran faced a manslaughter charge. The ministerial community and religious folk used the death as ammunition to appeal to California Governor James Gillett to prevent the Jeffries-Johnson fight.[312]

On April 30 in San Francisco, Johnson boxed Marty Cutler and Kid Cotton 3 rounds each and appeared to be in fine shape. Jack believed that

---

[308] *Boxing*, April 23, 1910.

[309] *Salt Lake Herald-Republican*, April 26, 1910. Pursuant to Choynski's orders, Jeffries rested on the 25th. On the 26th, Jeff ran 10 miles with Bob Armstrong, Farmer Burns, and Joe Choynski. In the afternoon, he worked the chest weights, medicine ball, and skipped rope. *Los Angeles Herald, Reno Evening Gazette*, April 26, 27, 1910.

[310] *Reno Evening Gazette*, April 28, 1910; *Washington Times*, April 28, 1910. On the 27th, Jeffries walked 5 miles and then ran 5 miles. He also did rope skipping and helped repair a dam.

[311] *Spokane Press*, April 28, 1910.

[312] *San Francisco Call*, May 1, 1910.

his sparring partners were superior to the ones Jeffries had. He said, "[I]n Jeffries' camp will be a number of men who will be unable to stand the beating which Jeffries will give them and consequently Jeff will not derive the proper kind of benefits."[313]

Johnson had a point. Choynski was 41, Armstrong was 36, and neither one had fought since 1904, though Armstrong had made a living as a sparring partner. Corbett was 43 and had not fought since 1903. Berger was the only young one at age 25, but even he was inactive, not having fought since 1906. However, the thinking was that each one only had to go a few rounds with Jeff, and each had enough size, strength, skill, and experience to give Jeff plenty of good work combined. Iowa's Frank Gotch was the best wrestler in the world, so he would give Jeff good wrestling practice.

As of May 1, Johnson had set up his training quarters at the Seal Rock house on the beach. He seemed larger and stronger than ever before.[314]

On May 3, Tex Rickard made his second required installment deposit, at 11 a.m. stacking 1,500 $20 gold pieces totaling $30,000 on the table of Rickard and Gleason's offices in the Flannery Building. The Metropolis Bank would hold the money until the July 4 fight. Johnson commented, "Look at that nice new money, Mr. Berger. You all better take a good look, for that's as near as you'll ever come to it. Ain't it pretty?"

Putting up the money for the big fight. Reading from left to right: Tex Rickard, Jack Johnson, Sam Berger, Vice President Meyerstein of the Metropolis bank, George Little and Jack Gleason.

On May 3, Jeffries sparred 4 rounds with Bob Armstrong, keeping Bob on the run most of the time.[315]

---

[313] *Freeman*, May 7, 1910.
[314] *Reno Evening Gazette*, May 2, 1910.

The parties were wrangling over the choice of a referee, and on May 4 they held a meeting to discuss the issue. Johnson wanted either Jack Welch/Welsh or Eddie Graney. Berger wanted either Eddie Smith of Oakland, Phil Wand, Charley Eyton, Billy Roche, or Johnny Herget. Johnson said, "I object to Smith because he gave me the worst of it when I boxed Hank Griffin in Oakland several years ago. I thought I won that fight, but Smith called it a draw." Johnson saw Phil Wand give Joe Walcott the worst of it one night in a bout with Kid Carter. He did not want Charlie Eyton, owing to the fact that he resided in Los Angeles, which was Jeff's hometown. Johnson did not want Herget, because he was close to Fitzpatrick, his former manager.

Sig Hart, Jack Johnson, George Little, Sam Berger, Tex Rickard, Jack Gleason

Johnson said he had to protect himself because of his color. Berger accused Johnson of using his race as a stall tactic to get the best of it. Berger did not want Johnson's selections of Welsh or Graney, though few could understand why. Both had good reputations, were white, and were known for honesty and integrity. Berger simply said Johnson and Welsh were too friendly. He said nothing about Graney.

Johnson said he could name fifty men who would be suitable to himself. Berger said perhaps one of them would suit him. Jack replied: "I know that none of them will suit you." Berger: "Well, why not?" Johnson: "Because they are all smokes."

Gleason noted that the opposing parties were supposed to choose a referee by May 4 or the club could make the selection. Johnson replied that

315 *San Francisco Call*, May 4, 1910; *San Francisco Evening Post*, May 3, 1910.

if the club named Berger's man there would be no fight. Deadlocked on the referee question, they agreed to postpone the issue until May 16.[316]

Throughout his training, each day, in the morning Jeff did his roadwork. In the afternoon, either before or after sparring, Jeffries played handball, rope-skipped, punched the bag, and shadow boxed. He varied the amount of sparring.

On May 5, Jeffries sparred Billy Papke. In the 2nd round, Jeff landed a right over the eye which shook up Billy and raised a lump. After that, Jeff just used his left.

Next, Jeff sparred Choynski for the first time, going 3 rounds. Despite his advanced age, Joe had enough cleverness and experience (over 75 fights) to give Jeff some work for a few rounds, showing his agility and prowess. Still, Jeff easily handled him and was gentle. Afterwards, Choynski said Jeffries would win the fight in about 7 rounds.[317]

On May 7, Jeff sparred 6 rounds with Papke and 3 with Choynski.[318]

On May 9, Jeff sparred 3 rounds with Choynski and 4 rounds with Armstrong. He was not as effective as he was in prior sparring sessions.

Joe Choynski, Sam Berger, James Jeffries, Farmer Burns

On May 9, Johnson ran 12 miles at a good pace with George Cotton, Barney Furey, and Marty Cutler.[319]

---

[316] *San Francisco Call*, *Reno Evening Gazette*, May 5, 1910.

[317] *Reno Evening Gazette*, May 7, 1910. *San Francisco Evening Post*, May 6, 1910.

[318] *San Francisco Call*, May 8, 1910.

[319] *Reno Evening Gazette*, May 10, 1910; *San Francisco Evening Post*, May 10, 1910. Cutler dropped out long before they had gone half the distance. Jack admitted that it might have been too many miles so soon.

On May 10, Jeff roughed it for 6 rounds with Choynski and Armstrong. His eye was still blackened from a blow he received the previous day. Jeff seemed faster on this day, and his sparring partners were glad when it was over. Jeff said he had taken off 25 pounds since beginning his training, and was weighing 225 pounds.[320]

On the 11th, Jeff sparred with Choynski and Armstrong and showed vast improvement. In addition to his usual training work, he also did a challenging abdominal exercise. He sat on a backless chair, with his feet on the rungs of another, leaned back until his head touched the floor, and rapidly rose to a sitting posture. He said he did this exercise for ten minutes before sparring a couple days ago, which accounted for his poor showing.

On May 12 in Washington D.C., an Iowa Congressional representative proposed a bill that would make it unlawful to send by mail or any other manner to any other state any picture or description of any prize-fight, with a penalty of up to one year of imprisonment or a $1,000 fine.

That same day, Jeffries gave both Armstrong and Choynski a grilling, showing his speed. Armstrong's face was bruised and he had a half-inch square of skin peeled off near the eye. Choynski was bleeding from his mouth and his right eye was discolored.[321]

A *Freeman* writer, cognizant of the powerful symbolic racial importance of the fight, wrote, "Jack, please show this haughty world that color don't make the man."[322]

Boxing reported rumors that Jeffries did not like training and had grown tired of hard work. Annoyed by such stories, Jeff said he was working harder than ever before in his life.

Boxing did not believe rumors that the fight might be fixed. Both men obviously were determined to win and were training hard. Even if the fight was fixed, neither one could trust the other. Plus, "the negro's vanity would compel him to knock the white man's head off at the first opening which presented itself." Jeff entertained powerful sentiments, and Johnson was fully aware that Jeff wanted to hurt him as much as he could. Johnson had wanted to beat Jeff for so long, and for so many years had endured taunts that Jeff would beat him, such that there was no way he would throw it. It was the fight he always wanted to win, and it meant too much to him. Plus there was the race angle. "There is far too much at stake and there are far too many prejudices concerned for any 'frame-up' to come within the bounds of possibility."

Some pointed to the opening odds being strongly in Jeff's favor as evidence that Johnson was going to throw the fight. However, there were some explanations for it, though the reasoning might have been in error:

---

[320] *San Francisco Evening Post*, May 11, 1910. Jeff also did three miles of short sprints.
[321] *San Francisco Evening Post, Reno Evening Gazette*, May 12, 1910.
[322] *Freeman*, May 14, 1910.

People are remembering all Jeff's doughty deeds, and are also remembering that Johnson put up a comparatively poor show against a decided second-rater in Marvin Hart, to whom, it was asserted, he quit as soon as he got hurt. Jack, we were reminded, had all the best of that encounter until Hart got home some heavy body blows which hurt, and that after these visitations he confined himself to hanging on, clinching, and avoiding Hart's attacks to the best of his ability.

It was this fight which revealed, according to his opponents, the existence of a broad "yellow streak" in Johnson's make-up.

But there have been a whole host of rebutting statements that the Hart affair was one of the biggest "frame-ups" in the whole history of the boxing ring.

How one viewed the Hart fight influenced the analysis of Johnson. Some thought Jack showed yellow in that fight. Others thought Johnson clearly won and had been robbed, that the fight was fixed for Hart to win if there was a decision, so that a Hart-Jeffries fight could be set up, knowing that Jeff refused fight Johnson while he was champion.[323]

Other reasons for Jeffries being the betting favorite were the fact that he had never lost, had never even been down, typically hurt or dropped his opponents even in fights that went the distance, both early and late, and had superior results against common opponents: Jeff/Johnson vs. Choynski (D20 vs. LKOby3), Pete Everett (KO3 vs. D20), Hank Griffin (KO14 vs. L20, D15, D20), Joe Kennedy (KO2 vs. KO4) Jack Munroe (KO2 vs. WND6), and Bob Fitzsimmons (KO11, KO8 vs. KO2). Plus, there was race prejudice – whites simply could not believe that the vaunted representative of their superiority could be defeated by a black man.

No one knew for sure just how much the Jeffries of the present compared with the one of old until they could see him in an actual fight. Opinions varied. Some said he was just as fast and strong as ever, while others said he was an old man and only a shadow of himself.

With Johnson, it was different. "Anybody who knows the first thing about the game can see that the black champion has improved 200 per cent in every possible department of the game. He is more clever, hits harder and is a better ring general than he ever was." He also had a champion's confidence.[324]

On May 15, Jeffries ran 5 miles under a broiling hot sun. In the afternoon, he skipped rope 20 minutes, shadow boxed, sparred 3 or 4 fast rounds with Bob Armstrong, and struck the punching bag 15 minutes. In all, he did 60 minutes of gym work. Amongst the visitors to the camp that day were the San Francisco mayor, the sheriff, and local supervisors. Charlie Eyton expressed himself as astonished at Jeff's splendid condition.

---

[323] *Boxing*, May 14, 1910.
[324] *San Francisco Call*, May 15, 1910.

That same day, Johnson did his first real gymnasium training at the Seal Rock house. Before a crowd of about 2,000 which jammed their way into the big dance-hall pavilion, Johnson did his usual routine exercises and boxed 8 rounds.

Johnson's first 3 rounds were with George Cotton, a colored boxer from Chicago who weighed about 185 pounds (though some later said he was over 200). Cotton was strong and willing, and they really went at it. On the inside, Johnson handled him like a sack of wheat. Jack drew blood in the 2nd round with a sick uppercut. Cotton kept the pace fast in each round.

Marty Cutler, also of Chicago, was smaller than Cotton, but ably boxed 3 rounds as well. Cutler fought a bit like Ketchel, but Johnson mostly kept him at arm's length, smiling. When close, Jack would tie him up and uppercut him. The champ could get inside of Cutler's swings or sidestep his rushes with an artist's class. Jack's defense was beautiful. Johnson almost dropped Cutler in the 2nd round, but took it easy on him in the 3rd.

Denver Jack Geyer, a Los Angeles heavyweight, worked 2 more rounds with Johnson. Geyer showed dash and vim, but Johnson easily handled and punished him.

Johnson appeared bigger and stronger than ever, and there was no question as to his ability as an all-around clever boxer and systematic puncher from any angle with either hand. He was wonder in every department of the game, though primarily he played defense. The crowd marveled at his form. His sparring partners were playthings, for he did with them as he pleased. This was no easy task either, for each was strong, young, rugged, and always coming. But the faster they came, the more marked was the champion's great blocking and golden smile. Johnson did not cut the rounds short either. "Jack boxed them cleverly, mixed it with them, swapped and countered with them and then held them helpless before him." He knew every move and trick of the game. In the clinches, he pinned their hands and held them while he laughed. At other times, he waded right in and forced them to the ropes. But he was careful not to do any real damage. At the end, he was not even drawing a long breath. Jack remarked that he was better than he imagined.[325]

The referee discussion was ongoing, and the parties met again on May 16 to address the issue. Although Johnson had accepted Eddie Smith for the Kaufman contest, he said he had done so because it was a no-decision bout. Jack did not trust Smith's judgment, owing to the Griffin decision. Johnson named Ed Graney, Jack Welsh, and Tex Rickard as suitable referees. Welsh had refereed his last contest and did a good job. Graney had refereed many of Jeff's bouts, so Johnson thought that he should be acceptable to Jeff. "If Graney was not square then why did Jeff take Graney to referee...?" Graney and Welsh had reputations for competence, fairness, and integrity, and that is all Johnson wanted – a fair man. Jack said, "There

---

[325] *San Francisco Call, San Francisco Evening Post, Reno Evening Gazette*, May 16, 1910.

is not a man that lives that would dare to give Jeff the worst end of the contest. The white people would hang him to a tree. It would be very easy for any one to give me the worst end of this contest on account of my color."

During the debate, Johnson's black trainer Barney Furey thought he heard Sam Berger use a derogatory term about Johnson. Furey said, "I hear you and I told him." Johnson rose and said, "If you care about doing any fighting, I'm ready for you." Berger also rose. Johnson said, "You are an educated dog." Jack Gleason interfered, played peacemaker, and got them to address the issue at hand.

Johnson blamed the Hart loss on the referee and added that this was the principal reason why he was taking such pains to see to it that the proper man refereed. Eventually, Berger asked Tex Rickard if he would referee. Rickard said, "Yes." Berger said that suited him. Johnson said, "All right," and the debate was over.

Tex Rickard

Promoter Tex Rickard had never refereed before. However, the parties could not agree upon anyone else. Rickard said he would accept the position pro tem, but if they agreed to someone else, he would step down.[326]

On May 18, Johnson ran 12 miles. "As everybody knows, Johnson is a bear on the road. He's one of the greatest runners and walkers of the whole crowd and when he does road work he does it with all his heart and all his mind."

In the afternoon, Johnson mauled three sparring partners for 9 rounds – 3 rounds each. A good percentage of observers were women, including white women. Kid Cotton was first, and though he tore after Johnson, he failed to make an impression. At the end of the 3rd round, the Kid was bleeding from his nose and mouth.

Marty Cutler tore in like Ketchel. In order to avoid the white boxer's rushes, Jack stepped around quickly and landed many a hard uppercut and straight left to the face, and rocked him on several occasions with rights to the jaw. Cutler took all that Johnson could give and came back for more.

Dave Mills, the other colored conditioner (other than Cotton), was not as aggressive, but he was fast and shifty. Johnson displayed improved footwork. "Of course he is still a flat footed boxer and he always will be, but when he wants to he can move around at a clip that surprises many of them."

While he was in Chicago, California Governor James Gillett said he did not foresee any reason why the big fight could not be held in California.

[326] *San Francisco Evening Post*, May 16, 1910; *San Francisco Call*, May 17, 1910.

"The law authorizes the contest to take place and there is nobody to prevent it. I haven't the slightest doubt the club can get a permit in San Francisco without any trouble." He also said,

> The fight seems to be of the biggest national interest, and I do not believe there is any desire to prevent it. … It will bring hundreds of persons to the coast and leave thousands of dollars in San Francisco. … To the people of the United States, at least, it is a bigger thing than the passage or defeat of important legislation, Roosevelt's triumphal tour, or even the approach of the comet.[327]

After a discussion with local San Francisco politicians, Tex Rickard confirmed that the fight would be held in the San Francisco area. The local supervisors and police commission had stamped their approval upon the bout.

However, the religious community was trying to apply political pressure to stop the fight. A delegation of local San Francisco church confederations, accompanied by their attorney, called upon the district attorney and demanded that he take action to stop the bout.

Jack Johnson and Tex Rickard

On May 19, Johnson again boxed 9 rounds.[328]

Jack Johnson's status as champion had symbolic value and served to uplift black folks' spirits. A *Freeman* poet wrote, "Dear people, take it from me: I'm no fighter and don't want to be; if both were white I wouldn't care

---

[327] *San Francisco Call*, May 19, 1910.
[328] *Reno Evening Gazette*, May 19, 20, 1910.

a minute. But since our race is represented, we all would like very much to shout: 'Hooray! Jack has knocked Jeffries out!'" The *Chicago Defender* said, "While pugilism does not compare favorably with the intellectual forces of mankind, yet, the same pluck, patience, perseverance and stick-to-itiveness characterized by the colored champion is essential to success in all vocations in life." Hence, "we do hope as a loyal race" that Johnson would win.

The *Defender* said that never before in pugilism's history had the public been aroused to such a pitch of excitement. When the big fight was signed, the question was whether Jeff could return to his former condition. Now that Jeffries was rounding into form, there seemed to be no doubt left in the minds of the public as to his ability to regain his former condition.[329]

Although Corbett had not yet joined Jeff's training camp, Choynski wrote him a letter saying that Jeff was in fine shape already and was alternating work with periods of rest so he would not get stale. In general, Jeffries was following the hard-easy principle, sparring and working hard one day, and then going easier the next.

However, the *Call* said there were many conflicting reports from the Jeffries training camp. Scarcely any two of the supposed knowing ones who visited brought back the same impression. Half said he was in grand form, while the other half said he was only a shadow of the great fighter he once was. "One thing is certain, if Jeffries feels as old as he looks he is far from being anywhere near the class of the heavyweight champion who retired from the ring six years ago." However, looks could be deceiving.[330]

Many observers of Johnson's training said he was lazy. They felt that he was not training hard or often enough. Some said Jack had been working in the gym only twice a week. Johnson said he did not want to overdo his training so far from the fight. "I am going to train just as suits myself and not the public. ... I have always attended to my own training and am too old to let the public disturb me. ... With as much time ahead of me I would be a fool to knuckle down to boxing. I would be sure to go into the ring stale, and I want to be right for Jeffries."[331]

In general, on a daily basis, Johnson ran 12 miles in the morning, and in the afternoon, he tossed the medicine ball, shadow boxed, punched the bag, and worked with weights before doing any sparring.

On May 22, Johnson mauled sparring mates Kid Cotton and Marty Cutler for 8 terrific rounds. His wind seemed perfect. He was a "wizard in the clinches." In close, he snuck in his snappy uppercut, while at long range; he fired his piston-rod jab. He rarely missed. Jack also showed his ability to side-step. In the 4th round, a punch to the stomach made Cutler feel sick. By the end, Cutler's mouth was bleeding. Impressed with Johnson's work, the crowd, about one-third of which were women, applauded him.

[329] *Freeman, Chicago Defender*, May 21, 1910.
[330] *San Francisco Call*, May 22, 1910.
[331] *Los Angeles Herald*, May 22, 1910.

After his training concluded, Jack stepped on the scales and registered 218 ¾ pounds. He expected to weigh 208 for the fight.

That same day, Jim Jeffries sparred 9 fast rounds with Jack Jeffries, Joe Choynski, and Bob Armstrong, and showed that he too was fit. All those who observed the sparring believed that Jeff was in excellent condition.[332]

Johnson said he might go see Jeffries box in San Francisco at his public exhibition on Friday. "Jeffries would certainly be surprised. But why shouldn't I go and see him box? Of course I have seen him in action before, but then I might like to know what condition he is in."[333]

Billy Delaney, who had trained both Corbett and Jeffries, agreed to join the Johnson camp. The two had come to terms. Delaney was wise, experienced, and knew Jeffries well. Johnson also intended to get former opponent Al Kaufman to box with him, because he was big and strong like Jeffries. Kaufman had defeated Jack O'Brien twice in 6-round no decision bouts in Philadelphia in January and April 1910. Jack said his sparring partners, Cotton, Mills, and Cutler, were superior to Jeff's sparring mates.

On May 24, Jeffries boxed 11 rounds. Armstrong went 3, using his clever defense, which would help Jeff prepare for Johnson. In rip and tear fashion, Jeff also sparred with his brother Jack Jeffries, Sam Berger, and Joe Choynski. Joe emerged with a broken tooth and damaged ear and nose.[334]

On Friday May 27 at the Dreamland rink, "the hope of the white race" exhibited in front of a crowd of 4,000 - 5,000. Billy Jordan introduced him: "A Native Son, the California Wonder; the cleverest man who ever stepped into a ring; the great and only undefeated champion of the world, James Jeffries." The house roared with delight, stood up, and tossed their hats in the air. He was popular in part because Johnson's claim to the title was "savagely resented by the Caucasians who follow the fighting game." The fans were also pleased, impressed, and encouraged by the fact that he looked like the big and strong Jeffries that stopped Corbett years ago. The fans were certain that he would slaughter Johnson.

Jeffries sparred 3 rounds with Joe Choynski and another 3 rounds with brother Jack Jeffries. One reporter said, "It was a great showing for the former champion – positively the best that he has made since he started to 'come back.'" Both sparring partners were playthings in his hands. He danced around like a baby lion and crouched and sprang forward like the Jeffries of old. The only question was how much stamina he had, which could not be answered in a mere 6 rounds. Still, he had several more weeks of training time. He appeared to weigh about 230 pounds.

[332] *San Francisco Call, Reno Evening Gazette*, May 23, 1910. After sparring, Jeff shadow boxed, skipped rope, and played two games of handball. That morning, Jeff had run 5 miles on the road and rowed on the river for an hour.

[333] *Reno Evening Gazette*, May 24, 1910. Ultimately, Johnson decided not to go watch Jeff spar.

[334] *San Francisco Call, San Francisco Evening Post*, May 25, 1910. After sparring, Jeff skipped rope and played handball. In the afternoon, he put in another hour in the gym.

Another reporter was more guarded with his praise. He said Jeffries was accurate with his left and showed speed, but his judgment of distance was somewhat faulty and he left his face unguarded. "Jeffries cannot hold his face out for Jack Johnson to peck at as he did with his sparring partners last night. There is power in those massive black arms." Still, Jeff had shown wonderful improvement from four or five weeks ago.[335]

The *Call* said that although his true stamina was not yet known, if he fought as well as he boxed in sparring exhibitions; Jeffries would spring a surprise on the world. Still, although Jeff had removed all of his excess fat, some pointed to the wrinkles in his stomach and wondered if he had taken off too much weight and never could be as rock solid as he once was.[336]

The *Chicago Defender* found all of the white Christian clergy and religious organizations' fight-opposition to be amusing and hypocritical. It said the Sunday school convention and white Presbyterian Ministerial Association had set a new Christ-like mark in their color line, for they were working

---

[335] *San Francisco Call, San Francisco Evening Post*, May 28, 1910. Present but not sparring were Sam Berger and Jim Corbett. Corbett and Choynski buried the hatchet and shook hands.
[336] *San Francisco Call*, May 29, 1910.

overtime in an endeavor to prohibit the match. These religious folks were taking up the matter even with the U.S. President. The real "national disgrace," as these organizations liked to call the fight, was the fact that "supposed Christians faint at the sight of prize fights, but laud the raping of colored girls and lynchings. ... If this is Christ, excuse me."

> Why, sure these gentlemen object to the national disgrace of a white and black man struggling for physical supremacy as man to man, etc. I wonder if these same men have stopped to consider how hypocritical their present efforts seem to the fair-minded public, who cannot help but wonder if these gentlemen are really sincere from a Christian standpoint ... [W]ith all of the lynchings and mob violence that is prevalent in this land of supposed freedom, you have never heard or read of a Christian body of white ministers even raising their voices in their annual conferences, much less appealing to the authorities to put a stop to it. But possibly they reason this way: That lynchings are perpetrated by a mob against one man, and as the motto of our beloved country is 'In Union There is Strength,' it is no national disgrace. But in the case of Messrs. Johnson-Jeffries, it is man against man, and as a Negro has an equal chance, that in itself, in their opinion, is enough to constitute a national disgrace. Now I may be wrong, but it seems to me that if this same 'Christian' body would direct their combined efforts to abolish Jim Crow cars and advocate the enforcement of the fourteenth and fifteenth amendments, along with the abolishment of mob violence, they would be following a course more in keeping with the Christian consistency that we all expect to see in one who wears the cloth. But for them to ignore these vital questions that affect the moral and Christian welfare of seventy-five millions of people, and concentrate their influence upon an incident that only affects a few, is, in my opinion, the very zenith of that most despicable of curses known as hypocrisy. Wake up, my white brethren, and show to us that your hearts are right. ... [A]s this is the first time that a black man and a white man have met as the pick of their respective races in a contest of this kind, on behalf of the Negroes of this and other countries may Jack succeed in knocking Jim's block off, just to make it a good national disgrace.[337]

On the morning of May 28, Johnson ran 12 miles, part of it over hills, finishing the last 100 yards in a little better than 12 seconds. In the afternoon, Johnson sparred 9 rounds: 4 with Kid Cotton, 3 with Walter Monahan, and 2 with Marty Cutler. A short right uppercut to Cutler's jaw knocked him out. Johnson took some hard blows that day without flinching, and showed his brute strength. He weighed 217 pounds.[338]

---

[337] *Chicago Defender*, May 28, 1910.
[338] *San Francisco Call*, May 29, 1910.

Jim Coffroth saw Jeff train on May 29 and was surprised at how good he looked. "I did not think that Jeffries would ever get down to so fine condition as when training for Munroe in Harbin Springs. I have never seen Jeffries look quite as husky and healthy and I have watched him closely in many a fight. I am of the opinion that he is a better man today than he was ten years ago."

However, John L. Sullivan criticized Jeffries' choice of sparring partners. "Jeffries doesn't need old fellows like Corbett and Choynski. ... What he needs is young fellows with a lot more speed than he has."

True to the traditions of his race: Jack Johnson holding a prize chicken about to be transformed into pie for the champion's dinner

San Francisco Call, May 31, 1910

About 100 spectators watched Johnson train on the 29th, and all agreed that he was in top condition. Jack punched the bag, tossed the medicine ball, did body exercises on the mat, handled weights, and shadow boxed. An impatient observer shouted, "Oh, put on the gloves. Quit your kidding." Johnson grinned and won the house when he replied by inviting him to come up and do a little boxing. There was no further disturbance.

Jack sparred 8 rounds: 5 with George Cotton and 3 with Marty Cutler. Cotton retired with a bleeding mouth. Cutler was cautious, for he had been knocked out the previous day. The champ did not seem winded even after boxing hard and fast.

Johnson noted the conflicting reports about Jeffries. Many said he was demonstrating his old-time form, while some said he was just old. "Now, how can I get a line on him when I hear such reports as these? ... Well, I just hope that Jeffries is as good as they say he is. I want to beat him at his best." Johnson wanted Jeff to be in good shape so there would be no excuses and he could receive full credit for victory. "But now that the San Francisco public has seen Jeffries and given him the stamp of their approval, I want credit should I beat him." Johnson said that he would have Jeff down on the canvas for the first time in his career within 15 rounds, and would stop him within 20 rounds.[339]

[339] *Reno Evening Gazette, San Francisco Call, San Francisco Evening Post*, May 30, 1910.

On May 30, Johnson sparred 3 rounds each with Cutler, Cotton, and Mills.[340]

Jim Corbett's comment that Johnson had a "yellow streak" roused Johnson's ire. Johnson said no one had been able to find it, if he had one. Jack also noted that in Jim's first contest with Tom Sharkey, Corbett hollered to the police many times to help him. When they fought again, after a few rounds of taking a good licking, his second jumped into the ring "by a prearranged plan to again save this coward, Corbett." Johnson asked whether those bouts showed that Corbett had a yellow streak.[341]

After laying off of sparring for several days, on June 1, Jeffries sparred again, telling his partners to let go and hit hard. He worked 8 fast rounds. Up first, Armstrong set a lively pace for 3 rounds. Just before

San Francisco Chronicle, June 1, 1910

time was called, Jeff drove his glove into Bob's midsection and he doubled up with a grunt. Choynski next worked 3 rounds and displayed more skill than usual. Berger was last, and for 2 rounds they went at it in slam-bang fashion, roughing it around the ring. Berger hit hard and Jeff replied in kind, much to Sam's discomfort at the close. Jeff was bloody from the nose and mouth, while Berger's nose was also bleeding.

That same day, on June 1, Johnson ran 12 miles in the morning, taking 1 hour and 40 minutes to do it (approximately 8 minutes, 20 seconds per mile pace). Then he had a rubdown and took his automobile out for a ride for a couple hours. In the afternoon, Johnson did his usual gym work – pulleys, medicine ball, shadow boxing, and speed bag, but no sparring. The *Call* said the "big smoke" was "lazy" and lacked ginger in his work.[342]

While in Chicago, California Governor James Gillett shockingly said the Jeffries-Johnson fight was a "frame-up" and that Jeffries would win. He further said, "All fights are fakes" to fool fools, and this fight was just a scheme to make a lot of money.

> Anybody with the least bit of sense knows that the whites are not going to allow Johnson or any other negro to win the world's championship. … Johnson is no fool. He knows he would have to

---

[340] *San Francisco Call*, May 31, 1910. Johnson was down to 215 pounds.
[341] *San Francisco Call*, June 1, 1910.
[342] *Call, Chronicle, Bulletin*, June 2, 1910. Afterwards, Johnson weighed 215 ½ pounds.

whip every white man at the ringside in order to win. He would no more think of trying to knock out Jeffries than he would think of trying to stop a lightning bolt.

There was no chance to get Jeffries back into the ring until he had been assured that he would win. He does not need the money. He had too much to lose and not enough to gain. Johnson has little to lose and the prospect of getting a lot of money.

Suppose the affair is not a frame-up, what chance would Johnson have? None. He would knock himself out if necessary to avoid winning. ... Undoubtedly it will be a fine sparring match, as that is necessary for the moving pictures.

I would like to interfere if I could, but the only thing that would justify my interference is a riot. I do not think that will occur.

When Jeffries wins, every white man in the country will be told that a white man has demonstrated his physical superiority over a negro and everyone who has no sense will rejoice in the victory.

Gillett also said that he would stop the fight if he could, but "all sorts of frauds are allowed that nobody has the power to stop."[343]

Gillett's interview caused a storm of comment and increased suspicions about the fight's genuineness.

The day after making his statements about the bout, some reported that Governor Gillett denied making such statements.

Others reported that Gillett admitted making the statements, but said he merely was expressing his own private personal views, and did not intend his words to be used for publication and dissemination.

Most commentators believed the fight would be fought on its merits, for Jeff had a reputation for being the ring's squarest man, and Johnson had too much pride to take a dive. They thought the governor did not know what he was talking about and either was seeking publicity or "talking through his hat." His comments were given little weight, particularly since just a month or so prior he had said that he knew nothing about the fight game.

Jeffries denied that the fight was fixed, and said he never had been involved in a fake in his entire career. He had too much integrity to be involved in a fix. Jeff felt insulted by what Governor Gillett had said.

Jim Corbett, who had yet to spar with Jeffries, believed that Jeff would overtrain if he kept up his present grind. Corbett wanted Jeff to lay off the sparring for a while. Jim said, "This big fellow does not need so much boxing as the majority of the people believe. He has done a pile of work already – more than any man that I know could have got away with. A little light boxing, a little more work and some gym exercise is sufficient. Jeff is in grand shape right now." Later, Corbett would change his tune.

[343] *San Francisco Bulletin*, June 2, 1910.

On June 2 and 3, Jeff heeded Corbett's advice and only ran and walked (either 9 or 12 miles), played handball, and worked with pulley weights for a half hour.[344]

Corbett said there was no question that Johnson would make a careful fight. Jeff knew it too, which is why he was getting into superb condition to be prepared for a Marathon match. "Nobody can tell him anything about slugging or making a rough house. … What a chance Johnson would have if he stood up and tried to mix with this big fellow. Why, the fight would not last a round."

Jeffries, Corbett, and pals swim at Santa Cruz

On June 3, Johnson exhibited at the Dreamland rink. The crowd was not nearly as large as the one that assembled at the same place a week ago to watch Jeffries, nor was the reception as warm. Upon Jack's appearance, there was scattered applause, but also hisses.

Johnson squares off with George Cotton; with George Little at center

Johnson sparred 4 rounds with 200-pound George Cotton and 2 rounds with Marty Cutler. Despite their best efforts, his sparring mates were unable to land. Although the champ did nothing particularly exciting, and though he wore big mitts, the power behind his short blows was noticeable. In the 2nd round, Johnson dug in a few hard blows which shook up Cotton. At the

344 San Francisco Bulletin, San Francisco Call, June 3, 1910.

finish, Cotton was bleeding from the mouth and nose. Jack just played defense with Cutler, and his "defensive tactics are nearly perfect."

Half the gallery was friendly, and half hostile. During the exhibition, some interrupted with verbal misuse of the champion. Between rounds, while the crowd was deriding him, Johnson walked over to the local news writer, smiling, and said, "I got their money, anyhow, so let 'em holler."

After the sparring, in a speech, Johnson said that when the crowd congregated at the fight, he hoped that "they will see," and then someone in the gallery immediately hollered "a nigger funeral," and then laughter followed, "two well trained men, both in the very best physical condition, and that the battle will be between man and man and may the best man win." The champion was applauded loudly.

The *Evening Post* said that no matter what private thoughts one had about Johnson, it was unsportsmanlike and reflected ill-breeding to treat him unfairly and indecently with jeers, hisses, and interruptions.

During Johnson's boxing, there had been loud calls for Sam Langford, who was in the audience. When Johnson left the arena, Langford took the stage and Billy Jordan introduced him. "The reception given to the Boston tar baby was, in fact, better than the greeting accorded the champion." Although called "Beggar Sam" because he was begging for matches, at that time he had a bout scheduled against Al Kaufman.

Joe Woodman denied that Langford had carried Ketchel in their 6-round no-decision bout, saying that Stan was very tough and a lot better than some thought. Langford tried all the way, but needed more rounds to be able to stop him. The *Bulletin* said, "If that was the best Langford could do against Ketchel he is a vastly overrated fighter."

From Kansas City, Billy Papke, who had sparred with Jeff, said Jeffries was in excellent shape. "I like his chances in his fight with Johnson."

New Yorkers who wanted to see Jeff win offered his old trainer Bill Delaney $10,000 to train Jeffries instead of Johnson. Delaney replied that under no circumstances would he work with Jeff. "I quit Jeffries for welching on a gambling debt and running out on the Squires match. Jeffries has selected a good training staff and can get along without me. From a white man's standpoint I admire the stand you take – but I could not conscientiously have any more dealings with James J. Jeffries."[345]

Al Kaufman accepted the invitation to spar with Johnson, feeling that it would be a good learning experience. Some thought Delaney wanted to see Johnson defeat Jeffries, so he told Kaufman to help Johnson. The other belief was that ever since Kaufman knocked out Sam Berger, Jeff's current

[345] *San Francisco Call, Reno Evening Gazette, Chronicle, San Francisco Bulletin, San Francisco Evening Post*, June 4, 1910. Jeffries had failed to pay a gambling debt accrued in Reno when he was there to referee the Hart-Root fight in 1905. Delaney claimed that Jeff had agreed to fight Squires back in 1907, but Jeff said he never agreed to terms, for the financial inducements were insufficient. Jeffries had wanted $25,000 guaranteed, but they only offered $20,000.

manager, the two were at odds, and Al had heard that Sam made unkind remarks about him, so he wanted to see Berger's fighter beaten.[346]

The *Call* said the retired champion certainly was a wonder. Watching him work provided ample evidence that Jeff still was a great fighter.

The *Chronicle* believed that both fighters were holding the other too cheaply. Johnson and his followers argued that the "hope of the white race" had been out of the ring too long. Jeff's camp said Johnson hadn't whipped anyone, had done nothing to show that he was a good man, and would quit as a result of Jeff's rushes. Both arguments were unfair. Jeff appeared far from broken down. Johnson was underrated long before he obtained the championship, and still was.[347]

On the afternoon of June 5, before 500 spectators at his Ben Lomond training camp, Jeffries skipped rope for about 20 minutes and then boxed 3 speedy rounds with Choynski. Jeff's storm of blows in the 2nd round nearly had Joe out, and Jeffries had to check himself to save Joe from being stopped. Jeff showed much speed, strength, and power, and the crowd gasped at his tremendous abilities. He tossed Choynski about as if he were a novice and not one of the fastest and most scientific fighters ever. "At one stage of the bout Choynski all but went down for the count." As usual, Jeff also punched the bag, shadow boxed, spent some time

Choynski, Jeffries, Corbett

with the chest weights, and put on an elastic chest exerciser.

Corbett said Jeff was like a brand new youngster. "I can't look at him without feeling sorry for that poor fellow Johnson. He thought he was picking a fight with a has been; and here is Jeffries looking for all the world like the same old Jeff. ... Jack will get the surprise of his life, mark my words." Jim said Jeff had speed and judgment, and actually had to hold back or else he'd blow through his sparring partners. Jeff was smiling and in good humor.

---

[346] *Freeman,* June 4, 1910. Tom Flanagan was Johnson's conditioning trainer. Joe Rogers, the nearly 300-pound wrestler, was also helping Johnson train. Johnson decided not to attend a Jeffries exhibition because he did not want to stir up trouble or cause Jeff to think he was trying to aggravate him.

[347] *San Francisco Call, San Francisco Chronicle,* June 5, 1910. Johnson did not do much work on the 4th, and did no sparring.

Despite the fact that the religious and ministerial community had been sending him petitions to stop the bout, Governor Gillett declared that he would not interfere with the fight. "You may say that I will not interfere no matter how many petitions are sent to me, unless I am satisfied that a condition has arisen demanding the interference of the Governor of California." He said the remark he had made the other day was a casual one, not meant to be taken seriously, and unfair advantage was taken of it.

On June 5, Johnson sparred 4 rounds with Cotton, 5 rounds with Cutler, "pounding the white boy well," and also worked a bit with Dave Mills.

News out of the Johnson camp was that Jack had fired George Little as his manager and would turn over his affairs to Billy Nolan. However, Little said he had a contract to earn 25% of the champ's profits, which he intended to enforce. He also said he helped pay Johnson's bills.[348]

Johnson was not able to finalize an agreement with Nolan, so initially he decided to be his own manager, but then the next day, Johnson announced that he had appointed Tom Flanagan to manage him.

First Action Picture of Jeffries and Corbett in Training—They Were Snapped During an Exciting Handball Game.

Corbett estimated Jeff's weight to be about 218-220 pounds. However, Jeffries would not step on the scales, feeling that his weight was not relevant. He said, "I don't care if I weigh 250 pounds. It is not the weight, it's the way a man feels. I'm feeling like my real self now and could step into the ring next week if necessary."[349]

As of June 7, Jeffries and Corbett still had not sparred. Instead, the two ex-champions played a game of handball.

---

[348] *San Francisco Bulletin, San Francisco Examiner, San Francisco Call,* June 6, 1910. On June 5, Jeffries did no morning road work, but instead rowed for 45-minutes on the river.

That morning, Corbett and Choynski engaged in 3 gentle rounds of sparring, the first time they had been in the ring together since 1889, but they put aside their bitter feud and "came together to aid Jeffries in his attempt to return the pugilistic honors to the white race."

On the 5th, Johnson also did his usual morning road work and engaged in shadow-boxing, weight-pulling, muscle-grinding, and bag punching.

[349] *San Francisco Call, San Francisco Bulletin,* June 7, 1910. On June 6, Johnson did road and gym work, including shadow boxing, bag punching, and throwing the medicine ball.

Jeffries rested on the 6th. Corbett noted that rest was needed as much as work. Jeff had been working for over a year.

In Chicago, a $10,000 bet was made on Jeffries, with Jeff the odds favorite at 6 to 10. This gambler had faith in the "hope of the white race."[350]

On June 8, Johnson sparred 5 rounds with Kid Cotton and 4 rounds with local semi-pro heavyweight Walter Monahan, punishing both severely.

That same day, in his 3 rounds of boxing with Armstrong, Jeffries showed wonderful speed. Jeff worked his left hand in piston-rod fashion, despite the fact that "the colored man is a faultless blocker." The ex-champ smothered and blocked every blow and drew blood from Bob's mouth with a right. Jeffries hit Armstrong with a right uppercut and Bob was about to topple over when Jeff caught him. Jeff also demonstrated the fast footwork of a lightweight. It was even said that Jeff's ability to shift and move around quickly was better than that of the champion.

Critics opined that Jeff had improved his condition by 50% in the past two weeks. Some skeptics refused to believe that he would be as good as he was when he fought Munroe, but still they argued that he would prove formidable enough to defeat Johnson. Others said he was as fast as or even faster than when he was champion. "On the surface he looks as good as ever, but that asset, stamina, which is not apparent to the naked eye and can only be determined by a real test in the ring, is the only point that keeps admirers in doubt."[351]

The majority of New York sports were picking Jeffries to win. Tom O'Rourke said, "If Jeff is half way right he ought to beat the nigger good and proper." George Considine said, "Put all you got on Jeffries. Where does the negro shine, anyway?" Bat Masterson and Kid McCoy said if Jeff could get anywhere near back into shape, he would win easily and Johnson would regret taking the fight.[352]

The *New York Age* said members of the black race in the East had raised $17,000, all wanting to bet on Johnson. They formed a pool and forwarded the money to Johnson for him to bet on their behalf. Jack had told them that the odds in California were better, so he would place the wager for them. Betting was very brisk. Jack said, "Am in tip top shape and will win sure." This was taken as evidence that the fight was not fixed. If Johnson was intending to lie down, he would not wager black friends' money on himself. Hence, The *Age* said:

> There is going to be thousands of dollars placed on the Johnson-Jeffries fight on purely sentimental grounds, and the money will not be bet and lost by Negroes, either. Really, when you look at the

---

[350] *San Francisco Call*, June 8, 1910. On June 7, Johnson ran about 12 miles in the morning, but he took the afternoon off. *Reno Evening Gazette*, June 8, 1910.

[351] *San Francisco Call*, June 9, 1910. That day, Jeff hiked to the summit of Mount Lomond and back, a total distance of about 8 miles. Farmer Burns was giving Jeff wrestling tips.

On the 8th, Al Kaufman arrived at Johnson's training quarters. Al was scheduled to fight the 165-pound Langford on June 18.

[352] *San Francisco Chronicle*, June 9, 1910.

pugilistic situation void of racial prejudice and only from a true sportsman's standpoint, it looks as if Jack Johnson is the one best bet.

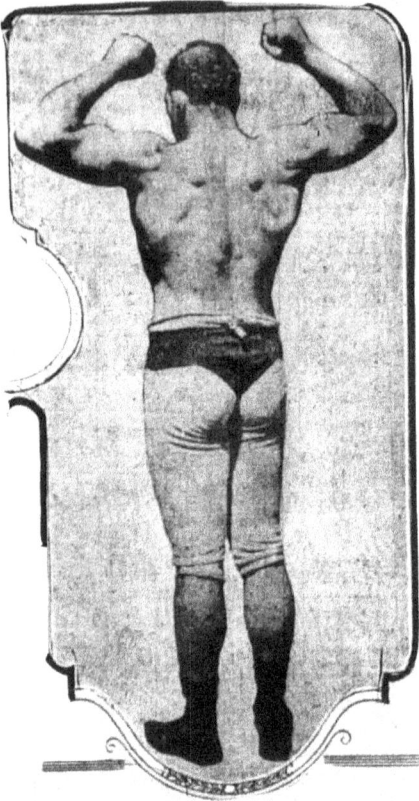

However, whites were not only betting on Jeffries, they were so confident in him that they were giving odds, making him the betting favorite. Hence, blacks could make a lot of money by betting on Johnson, the underdog, if he won.[353]

Jeffries would work hard one day, and rest the next. The rest day allowed him to recover, not go stale, take on some weight, and reserve his force, so that the next day he would be full of vim.

On June 9, Jeff went on a fishing trip. Corbett said Jeff was training the way he thought best, and was taking the bout very seriously, despite some concerns by those who wanted to see him working every day. Corbett said folks could put their minds at ease:

The call of the white race has brought Jeffries out of retirement and believe me, if the white population of the United States knows what a game, determined effort this man Jeffries has made to get back into condition to make good and what a terrific grind he has put himself through to attain his present splendid shape, he'd be a popular hero on the strength of that alone.[354]

On June 9, Johnson sparred 4 rounds with Al Kaufman. At 212 pounds or more, the 24-year-old Al was big, strong, and young, so he was a perfect sparring partner. Johnson landed several stiff ones to the jaw and body, but Al took them all with his usual good-natured smile and always was willing to come back for another rally. He kept boring in all the time, and managed to land a couple of telling body blows. Johnson was happy to have the work, and his boxing was even faster than it had been against his other sparring partners. Jack said he would back Kaufman to defeat Langford.[355]

---

[353] *New York Age*, June 9, 1910.

[354] *San Francisco Bulletin*, June 10, 1910.

[355] *San Francisco Call*, June 10, 1910. That morning, Johnson and Kaufman were out on the road for a 12-mile run, and both finished like sprinters doing the 100-yard dash. Al was in good shape, having been training at Harbin Springs for his upcoming fight with Langford.

On June 10, Jeffries worked the pulley weight machines, skipped rope for 15 minutes, and then went back to the pulleys. He went from one machine or exercise to the other without taking any rest. "A few minutes with the weight machine will make the ordinary man blow like a grampus. Jeff put in fifteen minutes at top speed and skipped the rope the other fifteen, and at the end of the half hour he was as fresh as at the beginning." He also hit the punching bag for a half hour.

After all of that work, for the first time in training camp, Jeffries and Corbett sparred 3 rounds. It had been nearly 7 years since they last fought. Corbett imitated Johnson's style, based on his observations of the moving pictures of the Burns and Ketchel bouts. He tried right uppercuts, but Jeff was able to elude them. Jeff was careful not to unload with any big power, though he cuffed Jim a few hard ones in the 3rd round, which was the fastest of the three. Jeffries was as fast and clever as Corbett. "As soon as Jeffries had tested Corbett and found himself the absolute master he almost played with him."

Next, Jeff went 3 more rounds with Choynski, handling Joe rather severely, landing several hard blows. Jeff also showed good defense, feinting, ducking and turning from blows all while maintaining pressure and staying on top of Joe, who only landed once.

Jeffries worked for 1 hour and 25 minutes, but appeared fresh at the end. Afterwards, Corbett walked over to Jeff's wife and said, "You do not need to lie awake any at night, Mrs. Jeffries, worrying about how this fight is coming out. The big fellow has got the old punch and everything else. Honestly, he is a marvel."

Some book-makers who had wagers on Johnson were surprised at Jeff's performance and condition, and likely would hedge their bets. They had thought that he could not return to his old form, but now thought they were mistaken. "The hope of the white race worked impressively today, and there was not a spectator in the audience who did not think he was fit."

Jeff said he knew how to condition himself, having trained for many fights. He never felt better. "When I was hunting in the Tehachapi mountains there wasn't a day that I didn't walk thirty miles over rough country, and that took the weight off me without my knowing that I was doing it. I'll be ten pounds lighter in the ring than I am now. The drying out process will do that."

Regarding the fight, Jeff said, "It will be a short one. I do not think it will last ten rounds. I'm not underestimating the other fellow. I have never done that in my life." Another quoted Jeff as saying that the black fellow would jump with fright when he met him. "That fight is not going to last any longer than I can help. The minute I get one good chance at that fellow I am going to pop him and he will go down for the count." However, Jeff also said he was in shape to go 100 rounds if necessary, though the fight was only scheduled for 45.

Corbett said he tried to open up on Jeff, but Jeffries covered up so skillfully that he could not get at him. Jim said that punches had no effect on Jeff, while conversely, being hit by him was like running into the bathroom door in the dark. Jeff's judgment of distance was excellent. Wrestling with him in the clinches was like being tossed by a bull.

Some writers said Jeff's condition was marvelous, but neither Corbett nor Choynski could give him the quality work that he needed, for they were too easy for him, and Jeff had to hold back too much. Regardless, Jeff showed none of the labored breathing he had when he first started his comeback. Jeff's left thumb had been slightly sprained for the past week, which perhaps also explained why he held back, and why he had not been sparring as much.

The *Examiner's* C. E. Van Loan said Jeff had no superfluous flesh, was remarkably light-footed, had accurate judgment of distance, and was able to work for nearly two hours without drawing a labored breath. "Jim Jeffries is right when he says that he is ready to fight to-morrow." The verdict was unanimous amongst all of the expert spectators present that Jeff was in top form.

Some wondered whether Jeff would look so good in an actual fight against a fit and prime champion who could make him miss and land a few good ones himself. A Johnson admirer said, "After he misses half of his blows and the other half are blocked by Johnson, Jeff will suddenly realize that he is not all there. There is nothing so disastrous to an old timer as the sudden realization that he is not there any more. He feels like a drowning man with the life saving station 20 miles away."

The *Evening Post* said that both Jeffries and Johnson were defensive fighters, and neither was a quick finisher. Hence the bout likely would be cautious and methodical. Their strength difference was not great. Jack did not care to trade blows with anyone, even those who were his inferior. He preferred to defend, counter, and sharp-shoot. He had power, but did not always show it. However, when he grabbed an opponent, they were helpless to do anything. Johnson likely would have the better condition.

Another writer used a racial analysis, saying that blacks were followers more than leaders, and whites had better brains. Others questioned Jack's courage, saying that as soon as he found himself in trouble he would run.

On the 10th, Johnson ran 12 miles but did no sparring. He preferred to race his car. Some questioned his training methods, but Jack said, "I have trained for enough fights to know what is good for me. I am not worried over my trouble with Little nor am I bothered by what the critics say about my carelessness in training." This writer agreed that Johnson was in very good shape, and within a few pounds of his fighting weight.

George Little wanted 25% of Johnson's share of the purse, and a like share out of the moving picture profits. He had a contract that did not expire until May 1911. He declared that Johnson owed him $18,000.

The *Freeman* reported that the San Francisco authorities had issued a permit for a 45-round contest.

Tex Rickard said that neither man would be favored by him when he refereed the contest, and the moving pictures would show that.

Tom O'Rourke said Jeff would win if he was in top condition. However, he acknowledged that Johnson was very clever and a hard man to knock out, for he lacked aggressiveness, which for him was not a fault. Hence, Jeff would need to be in great shape to get to Johnson.[356]

Jeffries had convinced most of those who had seen him in action at his training camp that he had come back. He remained the 10 to 7 odds favorite. After all, he had never been beaten, had never been hurt or dropped, and he had beaten the best men of his day, men who in general were considered to be superior to the men that Johnson had fought, although it seems that many writers overlooked the top black opposition that Johnson had met; only seeing white.

Johnson's record, particularly early in his career, was not as clean, but he had been a bread-winner for the bettors, consistently winning once he had come into his own. He had speed, cleverness, gracefulness, and all-round ring generalship, which convinced even casual observers that he could beat anyone if he could beat Jeff. He also was a hard and accurate hitter. As a holder in clinches, he had no equal. Whether or not he could get away with clinching against a man of great bulk and strength like Jeffries was another question.

---

[356] *San Francisco Call, Examiner, Bulletin, Evening Post, Freeman*, June 11, 1910. Both Johnson and Little had hired attorneys.

On June 11, Johnson boxed 10 rounds total with three sparring partners: 4 with Al Kaufman, 4 with Kid Cotton, and 2 with Dave Mills. Jack was the master of the situation at all times. Kaufman was bigger than Johnson, tough, rugged, always ready to tear in, and he kept Jack busy blocking, but Johnson had the superior skill and science. Johnson generally cut loose on each of them in the last round, and except for Kaufman, the two others were used up at the finish. "The big black is a wonder at mixing, for he can keep well out of range and step in and out at will. At the conclusion of work, Johnson stepped on the scales at 214 pounds."

Afterwards, Kaufman said, "Johnson is a wonderful fighter. He is improved over the day I fought him. ... I know that he can hit harder. I look to see him beat Jeffries, and I don't think that the retired champion will be able to lay a glove on the negro."

Eddie Graney said he never saw Johnson work as hard. He was punching harder and was more aggressive. "Don't let anybody talk you into thinking that he is loafing on the job." Johnson was running from 8 to 12 miles a day.

Some were startled by news that Jack ate from 8 to 12 chickens a day. Chicken was his favorite food, and he had a poultry yard with over 100 chickens. He was doing enough work that he needed to eat well.

The *Call* said Jeffries had spent over a year trying to recover his old form, and from all appearances, he had succeeded. He was surrounded by experienced and expert trainers, despite the fact that some called them "dead ones." They were skilled, clever, and fast enough to give him good work, particularly since each was working only for a few rounds, while Jeff remained in the ring. Comparing the two staffs, this writer opined that Jeff could cripple Marty Cutler easily. Cotton could not stand Jeff's left rips to the body. Jeff had injured his own brother Jack with a left to the ribs when sparring a few weeks ago, and Jeff wasn't even trying to hit hard. Brother Jack's ribs had been hurting ever since. Big Bob Armstrong and hefty Sam Berger could give Jeff comparable work to Kaufman.

Some thought that Jeffries should be boxing more rounds. However, Jeff was confident that he was training properly for a long bout, for he had never shown fatigue late in fights.[357]

On June 12, nearly 1,000 people gathered outside under the broiling hot sun to watch Jeffries train. He skipped rope for 15 minutes without a break, worked the pulley weights and wrist machine, sparred with Corbett and Choynski, and wrestled with Farmer Burns.

In the 1st round, Jeff neatly blocked Corbett's blows. In the 2nd, Corbett tried to land uppercuts, but mostly missed. Jim showed bewildering speed, but Jeff was able to elude the punches. The ones that did land made no

---

[357] *San Francisco Call, Chronicle, Examiner,* June 12, 1910. Jeffries rested from sparring on the 11th and went fishing. He walked 3.5 miles and then ran back the same distance in 23 minutes, showing what great shape he was in.
Also on June 11, Corbett and Choynski sparred each other at a benefit.

impression. In the 3rd round, Jeff opened up more, and by the end, Corbett was not clamoring for another round.

Although he was up second, Choynski fared worse than Corbett in his 3 rounds, blocking several fast ones with his face. A wicked left on the forehead almost dropped him.

Jeff then tussled and wrestled for 2 rounds with Farmer Burns. Jeffries was convincing more and more of the skeptical that he was himself again.

Corbett said he was amazed by Jeff's speed. Furthermore, Jeffries was impervious to punches. Jim said he sprained his thumb when landing. Corbett observed Jeff's sparring with Choynski, and said that although Joe was getting on in years, he still was mighty clever, shifty, and had a punch, but scarcely landed on the alert and clever Jeffries.

That same day at Ocean Beach, 1,000 spectators saw that the 212-pound Johnson was in superb condition. He worked the medicine ball, and then sparred 4 rounds with Kaufman, 4 with Cotton, and 2 with Dave Mills, for a total of 10 rounds. Both Cotton and Kaufman weighed over 200 pounds. Against big Al, Johnson demonstrated his ability to box, side-step, and hold a stronger man. Johnson showed no signs whatsoever of being affected by the few hard blows that did land. Jack was able to land his right uppercut on Kaufman. He slugged more with Cotton. Mills was told to go for the body in the 1st round, which he did, but when Johnson chased after him in the 2nd, there was no escape.

The crowd was surprised at Johnson's nimbleness and cleverness. The *Call* said Johnson showed more class, cleverness, aggressiveness, and strength with each workout. Those who saw him opined that Jeff would have to go some to lick him. Jack was in good spirits, always smiling.

From Chicago, Stanley Ketchel said that Johnson was one of the greatest, if not the greatest fighters the world had ever seen. He said that even if Jeff was able to come back, he still could not beat Johnson.[358]

---

[358] *Reno Evening Gazette, San Francisco Call, Bulletin, Evening Post,* June 13, 1910.

Attorneys for the church federation were continuing to pressure the governor to stop the big fight.

On the evening of the 12th, both Berger and Corbett told Jeffries that although he had done great work on the road and in the gymnasium, they believed that he needed more sparring, because he needed his muscles and wind to be ready for actual combat. Jeff agreed to do more sparring.

On the morning of June 13, Jeff boxed 9 total rounds with Armstrong, Berger, and Choynski. First, Armstrong and Jeff went at it hammer and tongs for 3 rounds. Bob tried to land a right uppercut, but Jeff blocked and countered with short thudding wallops to the body. Bob covered well and proved his reputation as a great gym fighter, although in the 3rd round he tired and ran a bit to save himself. Bob grinned, Jeff stepped in and nailed him with a wicked right to the pit of the stomach, and Bob's eyes rolled. After the round concluded, Armstrong sat down and said, "That's plenty." Jeff took a brief rest.

Next, 6 rounds were boxed without any rest for Jeff, while Choynski and Berger alternated back and forth 1 round each until each man had gone 3 rounds with Jeff. Jeffries did not even take the minute break between rounds, while his opponents got 3 minutes of rest after each round.

Jeff opened up more on his sparring partners than before, tearing into them fast and fierce, pounding them hard. "Berger and Choynski at times took punishment that would have flattened many fighters." As big and burly as Berger was, Jeff tossed him about as if he were a lightweight. It was a good thing that they only went one round at a time. Still, at the end, both sparring partners were winded. It was opined that Jeff could not do this every time with them or else he would be in need of a new staff.

Afterwards, Berger said, "It is the most discouraging thing in the world to box with Jeffries. He is always on top of you, and when you hit him you cannot hurt him. ... Hitting Jeffries is too much like driving your fist against the trunk of an oak tree."

Armstrong said a man who can hit like that can knock out a foe with either a body or head shot. If those raps did not drop Johnson they would take the fight out of him until Jeff landed on the vital point.

Joe Choynski still thought Jeffries would win the fight within 7 rounds.

Corbett said Jeff had plenty of speed and tremendous physical strength combined, punches had no effect on him, and he came on all the time, so even if he was outboxed for a while in the early rounds, eventually he would outstay, out-game, and knock out Johnson. "No boxer has a chance against a strong, fast fighter like Jeffries." "You simply can't hurt this fellow."

Jim thought a couple weeks of boxing would make Jeffries just right. Jeff thought that "drying out in the last three or four days will make his wind perfect." Of course, today we know the opposite is true. Johnson also practiced drying out.

There was no taking of weight at Jeff's camp, so everyone had to estimate. Corbett thought Jeff was about 222; Choynski estimated 230,

Armstrong 225, Farmer Burns 220, while Cornell thought Jeff was about 218 pounds. Jeff said he thought Cornell was about right.

Many gamblers were banking on Johnson showing the yellow streak after he realized that Jeff was too strong, powerful, determined, and impervious to being hurt. Sam Berger placed a $1,000 wager on Jeff, who remained the favorite at 10 to 7 odds.[359]

As the camera shows Jeffries in his present condition.

Jeffries was elated by his condition. He said he was ready to fight, and if defeated, would have no excuses to offer; and furthermore, he would be satisfied that Johnson could have beaten him at any time during his career. Those who saw him train said he was as good as ever.

William T. Rock, president of the Vitagraph company, and representative for several other film companies, offered $150,000 total to Johnson, Jeffries, Rickard, and Gleason to purchase the moving picture rights. Johnson sold his rights for $50,000. Jack received his money and was satisfied, saying, "Some of my friends tell me that I can make more by taking a chance, but I am satisfied to get this money outright. Then there will be no chance to mix me up in any suits. The ready cash looks good."

Johnson said it did not matter whether the fight lasted 1 round or 45, because the picture men were taking all the chances. "They can't say now that I am fighting for the films, because I have sold my interest in them."

Rock said the films would be exhibited in big cities just one week after the fight. Up to 8,000 theatres would show them in the U.S., Canada, and Europe.

On June 14, 400 spectators watched Johnson spar Al Kaufman only 4 rounds. "The big black champion was a bit lazy and did not move around so rapidly as the fans hoped he would." He almost entirely played defense, showing his wonderful blocking ability.

Afterwards, Johnson said, "Why should I box hard? I am in condition and practically down to weight. I am only weighing 212 pounds and as I will be boxing every day I don't want too much exercising just now."[360]

---

[359] *San Francisco Call, Chronicle, Examiner, Bulletin*, June 14, 1910. After the sparring, Jeff shadow boxed for 15 minutes. He also worked the pulley weights and wrist machine, and did stomach exercises.

[360] *San Francisco Call, Reno Evening Gazette*, June 15, 1910. Also on the 14th, Johnson ran 12 miles in the morning, and in the afternoon, before sparring, he tossed the medicine ball and punched the bag. Marty Cutler had left the camp, for he had not been in good humor ever since Jack had knocked him out.

On the 14th, Jeffries did 7.5 miles of road work, punched the bag for 15 minutes, played 3 games of handball (which lasted 1 hour), worked with pulley weights for 6 minutes, did 7 minutes of shadow boxing, used the wrist machines, and engaged in strength exercises.

Despite previously having said that he would not stop the fight, in mid-June, California Governor James N. Gillett buckled under to the religious community's anti-fight political pressure. He sent a letter to the attorney general instructing him to take steps to prevent the contest. In a total about-face, his new position was that boxing was illegal in California.

Upon hearing about the governor's letter, Jeffries responded, "I can't believe it. I did not think that the governor would do that after he has repeatedly said he would not interfere." A politician failing to be a man of his word? Never heard of such a thing.

Tex Rickard was quite upset by the unexpected turn of events, and criticized the governor's "11th hour" pronouncement.

> I am sick and tired of all this fooling, and I am willing to throw up the sponge so far as bringing off this contest in the state of California. I have already expended $25,000. … Why Governor Gillett should wait until this late day in declaring that he would stop the fight, particularly in view of his accredited statements in the past that under no circumstances would he interfere, is inconceivable. … I do not know what caused the governor's sudden change of mind, but presume the pressure brought upon him by the many church federations has had its effect.

BIG FIGHT PAVILION WELL UNDER WAY
WORK THROWN AWAY IF FIGHT IS STOPPED

Rickard had spent a great deal of money in reliance upon the governor's prior representations, having constructed a special arena for the fight. San Francisco businessmen, particularly hotel owners, were not happy about the governor's new position either. Big fights boosted the local economy.

As a result, Reno, Nevada was hoping to obtain the fight. It was only a one night run east of San Francisco, and a bit closer to all the eastern enthusiasts who wanted to come see the fight. A local Reno businessman offered to pay the $1,000 state license fee and to build a suitable arena if Rickard would move the fight to Reno.[361]

Further explaining his actions, Gillett said that boxing was illegal, corrupted morals, was offensive to the citizenry, and should be abated as a nuisance.

Governor Gillett also said that what he said in regards to the Johnson-Jeffries fight applied equally to the upcoming Langford-Kaufman fight,

361 *Reno Evening Gazette*, June 15, 1910.

which was scheduled to be held in just a few days. The governor said they would be arrested if they fought. Therefore, a potentially great fight between Kaufman and Langford was called off.

Cynics might say that it was no surprise that the governor was preventing two high-profile mixed-race bouts. Another way of looking at it was that politicians historically had given in to anti-prizefight pressure that often arose in conjunction with high-profile fights. This was nothing new.

San Francisco's mayor criticized Gillett for his timing, saying that if he had informed everyone a couple months ago that he would prevent the fight, they would have avoided a great expenditure of money.

The *Freeman* said the fight had been advertised so notoriously that the authorities could no longer sit back. Big publicity fights often brought out the politicians, for they were responsive to their powerful anti-boxing church and religious constituencies.

On June 15, Johnson boxed Kaufman and Cotton 4 rounds each. Both sparring partners bled from their mouths. "The Johnson of today is a better man than he ever was in his life." Afterwards, Jack stepped on the scales at 213 pounds. He said he never felt better in his life.

Reno, Carson City, and Goldfield, Nevada, as well as Juarez, Mexico all wanted the bout. Rickard was considering his options.

Johnson said he did not care where the fight took place. It made no difference to him.

Jeffries also said he would fight wherever Rickard and Gleason wanted. He said Nevada's altitude would not bother him, given that he had been doing a lot of work in mountains that took him to an elevation of 2,000 feet above sea level. However, Reno was at an altitude of over 4,000 feet. In general, Ben Lomond was only a few hundred feet above sea level. That said, Johnson had done no altitude training for this fight whatsoever.[362]

The black-owned *New York Age* noted that many newspapers were promoting the race aspect of the bout. "An unsportsmanlike attempt of some writers to inject racial prejudice in the coming championship contest…has been severely criticized by a number of fighters who well know that the question of color should not figure in the big fight." Some

---

[362] *San Francisco Call, Chronicle, Reno Evening Gazette,* June 16, 17, 1910; *Freeman,* June 25, 1910. Also on June 15, as usual, in the morning, Johnson ran 12 miles. In the afternoon, prior to sparring, Johnson punched the speed bag for 15 minutes, shadow boxed, and tossed the medicine ball. Johnson said he intended to cut down on the long runs.

On June 16, Johnson took a brisk 8-mile walk, took a dip in the surf, and played a game of ball. Gym training reports differed. One said that he did his gym work, but did not box. Another said Johnson sparred 4 rounds with Cotton, and slaughtered him unmercifully. Bill Delaney had arrived to assist Johnson.

Jeffries did not box on the 16th. He played 3 games of handball, punched he bag for 14 minutes, jumped rope for 14 minutes, and then used the pulleys for 12 minutes. Corbett thought he should be boxing more often. Earlier, some had said Jeff was overtraining, but now some were saying he was undertraining.

newspapers were critical of this aspect of the reporting. The *Cincinnati Commercial Tribune* wrote,

> A number of the daily newspapers both in the North and the South are working themselves into a terrible state of excitement over the possible consequences of the defeat of Jeffries by Johnson.... They refer to it as a struggle between the champions of the Negro and Caucasian races.

> Now this is in no wise a struggle for supremacy between representative champions of the two races. It is utterly foolish to attempt to surround the fight with any sentimental halo of race supremacy. ...

> The only danger of any racial difficulty arising from this battle comes from the ill advised and unthinking people and papers who try to make a struggle between two bruisers...assume the guise of a battle for race supremacy. Such characterization of the fight will make the ignorant members of both races have an exaggerated idea of the importance of its result.

Likewise, the *New York American* said many folks were concerned by the pervasive racial overtones and hype surrounding the fight, and feared violence.

> In many quarters there has been an evident desire to stir up a racial prejudice in the coming battle. ... Some have even gone so far as to claim that the Negroes throughout the country would become unbearable in the event of Johnson winning and race riots would surely result. ...

This writer did not believe such was the case, for several black men had won championships and defeated white fighters, and no race riots had resulted. "The big affair is a contest between men, not race of men." However, not everyone agreed. For many, this fight was about race.[363]

The governor ordered two companies of the California state militia to go to San Francisco to ensure that the Langford-Kaufman fight did not take place. He said that California had been disgraced long enough and the intolerable outrage would not be allowed. Any man who attempted to stage a boxing bout would have to fight the State of California first. So the governor was willing to use violence to prevent a violent sport.[364]

Conversations on the streets heard folks saying things like: "Boxed nine rounds yesterday." "Faster than ever." "Can't get the Black to work hard enough." "Had his auto out." "Not training." "Corbett'll do it for him." "Too old." "Good as ever." "Bet you."[365]

---

[363] *New York Age*, June 16, 1910.
[364] *San Francisco Bulletin*, June 17, 1910.
[365] *Boxing*, June 18, 1910.

Johnson heard that Jeff was as strong as a lion. "If he can shove Bob Armstrong and those boys around he must be right. I had Armstrong with me in the Ketchel go, you know." Jack knew how strong Armstrong was and what he could stand, which was a great deal. If Jeff could shove him around, then the ex-champion had to be strong. "If Jeffries wasn't there he would not be throwing Bob around. I don't want to get into that ring under 200. Jeffries will weigh near 230 and if he has thirty pounds on me it's going to hurt in the clinches." Hence, Jack did not want to lose any more weight.

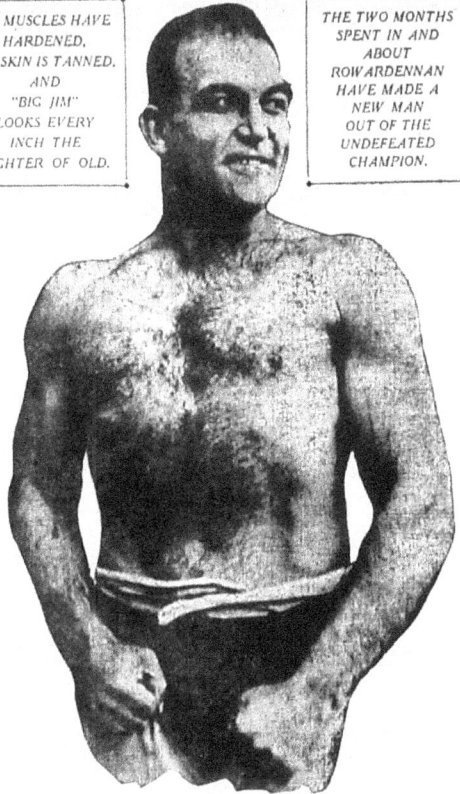

Jeff After a Year of Strenous Stunts

HIS MUSCLES HAVE HARDENED, HIS SKIN IS TANNED, AND "BIG JIM" LOOKS EVERY INCH THE FIGHTER OF OLD.

THE TWO MONTHS SPENT IN AND ABOUT ROW ARDENNAN HAVE MADE A NEW MAN OUT OF THE UNDEFEATED CHAMPION.

The *Freeman* opined that black folk would wager around 1 million dollars on Johnson. White gamblers were very confident in Jeffries. One man who bet $10,000 on Jeffries, giving 10 to 6 odds on the underdog Johnson, said Jeff did not have to be as good as he ever was to win, for Johnson was not in the same class with him, and Jeffries would win in short order.

The *Freeman* said, "It will be noted that the object is to have the white man win if there's any way to do it. It is squarely a case of Negro versus white man in the matter of brawn and nothing will be undone to make for the supremacy of the white man." It believed that the odds were designed to boost Jeffries and reduce Johnson's courage and his friends' faith.[366]

Jeffries believed dirty politics were mixed up in the governor's actions. "I really don't think the governor has acted fairly in this matter." Jeff felt badly for Rickard, who had invested so much time and money into hosting the bout in the San Francisco area. If the governor was going to prevent the bout, he should have notified the parties much sooner. Instead, they acted in reliance upon the permit issued and his statement that the bout would not be stopped.

---

[366] *Freeman,* June 18, 1910.

Reno appeared to be the alternate location. Jeff said he would transfer his training camp there on the 19th or 20th. "That high altitude will not affect me as much as it will the other fellow. You know I have been dwelling around these mountains for a long time and am right at home in them."[367]

Many friends said Jeff's long absence from the ring should cause him to do more sparring to make sure his judgment of distance was at its best. However, Jeffries declared that he never did a great deal of sparring when training for his fights, so he was not worried.

Sam Berger reserved living and training quarters at Moana Springs, about three miles south of Reno.

Johnson engaged Laughton's Springs to be his Nevada quarters.[368]

On June 19, Jeffries boxed at the Casino at Santa Cruz. With Corbett, he only worked 2 rounds of 1.5 minutes each. Choynski then sparred Jeff 3 interesting rounds. Jeffries also skipped rope for a few minutes and did a like amount of shadow boxing.

On the 19th, a large crowd came to watch Johnson's afternoon training. He punched the bag for several minutes and then boxed 5 rounds with Cotton and 3 with Mills, slaughtering them. Several times, Johnson put his hands on Mills' shoulders and invited him to hammer his body as hard as he could, and Mills complied. Jack just grinned and seemed to feel no effects from the blows. Throughout the 3rd round, the champ dodged punches and then jumped in and rapped Mills. Johnson's two days off had been good for him, for he went at his work with vigor.

After the sparring, Jack hit the punching bag again for one round and then did a little shadow boxing. Johnson imitated well-known pugilists and their styles, and was clever enough at it to rouse the merriment of the men watching. He concluded with the medicine ball. After the day's work was over, Johnson took the scales and weighed 212 pounds. Bill Delaney, who recently had arrived, was present, but only watched.[369]

---

[367] *San Francisco Call, Reno Evening Gazette,* June 18, 1910. On the 17th, Jeff only did road work. However, Johnson wasn't doing much training at that point either.

[368] *San Francisco Call,* June 19, 1910. On June 18, Jeff punched the bag for 20 minutes, shadow boxed for 15 minutes, worked with the wrist machine for 10 minutes, and then the pulleys. Next, he wrestled with Farmer Burns and Jack Jeffries.

On the 18th, Johnson ran about 8 miles. That was all he did that day.

[369] *Call, Examiner,* June 20, 1910. In the morning, Johnson ran 12 miles.

On June 21, Tex Rickard confirmed with Jeffries and Johnson that the fight indeed would be held in Reno, Nevada. They would take trains to Reno.

To obtain the fight, the city of Reno had promised to construct a special arena, furnish the site, and pay the $1,000 state license fee. Nevada was a sparsely settled region in need of money for development, and the fight would be good for the economy.

Upon hearing the news of its acquisition of the fight, Reno went wild with excitement, and a brass band played in celebration.

The Reno sheriff said no intoxicating liquors would be sold or allowed in the arena. He planned to have extra deputies on hand to ensure order, including plain-clothes men.

Billy Delaney (to the Left), Who Took Charge of Johnson's Training Camp Yesterday Afternoon, and Tom Flanagan, the Champion's Manager.

Rickard said Goldfield, Nevada had made a very tempting offer of a guaranteed $200,000 gate. However, Reno was the better location in terms of its accessibility. Folks from San Francisco could see the fight in Reno on Monday July 4, leave that night, and be back to their businesses on Tuesday morning. That would cause a couple thousand more to show up.

Letters addressed to Nevada Governor Denver S. Dickerson arrived, asking him to prevent the fight. However, legal experts said there was nothing in the law that would empower the governor to interfere. Boxing was perfectly legal in Nevada.

John L. Sullivan said he could not predict the fight's exact result, but thought it would end in about 15 rounds. He gave the impression that he thought Johnson would win, for he believed that Jeff was sparring with too many "has beens" rather than young men [370]

However, another paper quoted Sullivan as saying, "Being a white man, I naturally want Jeffries to put Johnson to sleep. I have been quoted as saying otherwise, but I want to deny that. I am looking for Jeffries to win."

Johnson ran up against the color line even in Reno. The owner of the Laughton Springs resort said he would not allow Johnson to train there. "The color line has always been drawn tight in Reno. Old-timers relate that a black face was never seen here in the early days and up to four years ago a

---

[370] *Reno Evening Gazette, Nevada State Journal,* June 21, 1910. Sullivan said Jeff should get seven or eight young men, fight 3-minute rounds, and let a fresh youngster come up every round. "If at the end of nine or ten rounds Jeffries finds that he can stand for the punishment then he will be fit for the battle of his life."

colored hotel porter was the only negro in the city." Jack would have to locate alternate living and training quarters.[371]

It was around this time that Jeffries' autobiography, *The Life and Battles of James J. Jeffries*, was published. Newspapers contained advertisements for it. Naturally, a biography would help market the upcoming fight, for it was about the "man who today is the most talked of man in the world."[372]

The fight would take place in a rock-strewn field in East Reno, about 1.5 miles from the heart of the city. It was familiar as the scene of the Hart-Root bout for Jeff's vacated title, which took place exactly five years ago from the date of the upcoming contest, on July 4, 1905. The area was flanked by the Southern Pacific railroad tracks and a trolley line known as the Reno-Sparks interurban railway.

Tom Flanagan had to struggle to find a place that would accept Johnson. He finally secured a roadhouse three or four miles southwest of Reno, known as Rick's resort. "Certain persons interested in it were against letting it out to a colored man."

Apparently, Johnson and George Little held a conference and came to a financial settlement.

On June 21, Johnson ran 9 or 12 miles (depending on the source), did his usual gym stunts, and also sparred 8 fast and entertaining rounds, 4 each with Kaufman and Cotton. Afterwards, Jack weighed 213 pounds.

Johnson figured that Jeff would try to wrestle and grapple and use his size and strength to try to tire him out. Jeff was working with wrestlers Farmer Burns and world champion Frank Gotch.

> I'm no wrestler, but if he thinks that he's going to push and haul me around like a baby I'll fool him. … [I]t isn't fighting, no; but it's part of the game. It's the easiest way in the world to tire a fellow out. … Kaufman is a 200-pounder and if they can find anyone stronger than Cotton I'll make a little bet. Those two have been working that stuff with me and I'm well backed with a good pair of thighs for any roughing.

Johnson was not concerned by Reno's altitude. "I don't mind that altitude thing at all. I've been all over Colorado, where it's high, and never felt it. … I trained Sharkey in Colorado and had a few fights there myself. I know all about it."

That day, John L. Sullivan sat beside Bill Delaney while Johnson worked. Sullivan said he still was uncertain about his choice in the fight. However, he was impressed with Johnson. "This is the first time I have ever seen the big black, and to say that he has impressed me favorably would hardly be expressing my meaning. He is a big, husky piece of humanity… [with a] well

---

[371] *Bulletin*, June 20, 1910; *Call*, June 21, 1910. On June 20, once again Jeffries did not spar. He had not done much work during the last four days. He just ran 7 miles. He did no gym work. Johnson did not do much either. He only ran 12 miles.

[372] *Bulletin*, June 21, 1910.

developed body." John L. was not surprised that Jeff was training so long and hard for him. "The retired champion evidently does not underrate this fellow, because, as a matter of fact, Jeffries has laid out and gone through a better and more thorough course of training than any man ever did before preparing for an affair of this sort." Continuing, Sullivan said Johnson "went at his work with an alacrity that was really surprising, in view of the twelve-mile plug on the road earlier in the day."

> What surprised me more than anything else in Johnson's work in the ring was his stealthy method of action. He seemed a good bit like Fitzsimmons in this respect. Apparently he does not move around on his feet and he gives the impression unless you watch him closely that he is not judging distance at all; but when his opponent gets within the proper range, a short straddle gives slight advance forward as the glove goes out and then you can see that he has judged his distance to a nicety.

Sullivan also said that the way Johnson dropped his elbows and held his upper arms loose to his body gave the impression that he had given some thought to a plan of body defense. Still, the ex-champ did not see anything of startling nature that was an improvement over old methods. "I should feel complimented, because these latter-day young fellows have thought sufficiently well of our old methods to adopt a good many of them."

John L. Sullivan greeting Jack Johnson at the latter's training camp; Billy Delaney, as master of ceremonies, is seen between the two famous fighters.

Sullivan wanted to correct some misinformation which was so common at the time.

> There have been a great many reports published in the papers throughout the country that I said that I thought Johnson would beat Jeffries and that Jeffries' training methods were all wrong and there was this and that wrong with the method itself. I do not know who circulated these stories, no more than I knew who circulated the stories that have been told about me and my opponents when I was in the game for fair.
>
> All I can say is that I never made these absurd statements, either about Jeffries or Johnson.[373]

On the 21st, Jeffries worked for 65 minutes without showing the slightest sign of fatigue. He was unusually light on his feet and moved about like a lightweight. Jeff said his wind was great. Those who saw him work were convinced that he was as good as ever. He and his crew then left his camp at Rowardennan, Ben Lomond to travel to Reno.

Thought to be of potential impact on the fight, even more so than the altitude, was the intense heat. The Hart-Root fight at the same location on July 4 was extremely hot. Even audience members were prostrated. The 4th was forecasted to be boiling hot. James Jeffries hated the heat. He was so upset by the hot conditions of his championship bout with Sharkey as a result of the hot lights required to film the indoor fight that he refused to allow his bouts to be filmed for quite some time thereafter, until the technology improved, forgoing thousands of dollars in revenue as a result.

Joe Gans picked Johnson to win. He figured that Jeff had been away from the ring for too long to come back, no matter how good he looked in training. "If Jeff were in his prime he would be a 10 to 1 favorite over Johnson. But six or seven years without battle makes more difference than the average man can conceive." He said Jeff may look good on the outside, but years of inactivity were bound to put his inner workings to the bad.[374]

Johnson heard that Jeff was working on defending the uppercut with great success. However, Jack laughed, saying that the men with whom Jeff was sparring did not know how to throw it properly, and showed the punch in advance, including Corbett. He also said that Armstrong "is about as fast as a horse car, anyway, and if Jeff couldn't get away from it he'd have to have malaria or something." Johnson could not tell if or when he would use the uppercut on Jeff. He had no set plan of attack, but would take whatever openings were there, and react to the style his foe used.

Battling Nelson wanted to see Jeffries win, but said the fight would be no cinch for Jeff, who would have to fight a harder and faster battle than

---

[373] *San Francisco Examiner*, June 22, 1910.
[374] *San Francisco Call, Chronicle, Bulletin*, June 22, 1910. Jeff's work on the 21st included bag punching, rope skipping, wrist machine, pulleys, and a chair exercise.

any other in his career. "Jeffries, at his best, would have the time of his life to defeat the negro."

> Sentiment should be cast aside in this battle, because a fighter is a fighter when he enters the ring, no matter what his color may be. Perhaps a lot of people don't like Johnson, and perhaps I don't, but that isn't blinding my judgment. I know him to be a fighter through and through, and Jeffries would have had his own trouble with him at any time. Jeffries never did care much about boxing him at any time, and I doubt if it was altogether because of his color.

Terry McGovern said Jeffries would defeat Johnson decisively. "Jeffries has an awful wallop. If he lands it in true style he'll cave in Jack's ribs. ... [T]here is no question in my mind as to who will be the winner. The negro is a good man; but it's a case of him meeting a better one."[375]

UNCLE TOM'S CABIN — AS IT WILL HAVE TO BE PLAYED IF JOHNSON WINS.

UNCLE TOM (to Simon Legree).—DID AH HEAH YO' SAY, WHITE MAN, DAT YO' DONE OWN MY BODY AN' SOUL? HUH?

Puck, June 22, 1910

---

[375] *San Francisco Examiner,* June 23, 1910.

Bill Delaney said Johnson surely would defeat Jeffries.

> I know Jeffries well and know that he is now and always has been afraid of Johnson. The mention of Johnson's name sends cold shivers up and down Mr. Jeffries' spine. He never wanted any of Johnson's game. When I was with Jeffries merely mentioning the black man's name was like casting a pail of cold water in Jeffries' face. … Jeffries very likely looks good today, but he can hardly be as good as he was six years ago, and I believe honestly that Johnson, as good as he is today, could lick Jeffries the best day he ever saw. Make no mistake about it, this Johnson is one great fighter. He is one of the cleverest big men the ring has ever seen.[376]

PHOTOGRAPH OF IMMENSE CROWD THAT GREETED JEFFRIES AT RENO STATION, TAKEN BY EXAMINER STAFF PHOTOGRAPHER—ARROW INDICATES JEFFRIES AND TEX RICKARD

On June 22, twelve days before the fight, Jeffries and his crew arrived in Reno. The city's entire population came to greet him at the train station, giving him the greatest welcome ever afforded to any celebrity who ever visited, including U.S. presidents. Jeffries was the "wonder of the age, the most important man who had ever found his way into the Sagebrush state." Not caring for attention, Jeff tried to avoid the huge crowd of thousands of men by nonchalantly exiting from the last train car, but he was seen and cornered. So he bowed his head and smiled.

... JAMES J. JEFFRIES AND TEX RICKARD ...

Tex Rickard and the mayor greeted Jeffries. Eventually Jeff was taken to a home in Moana Springs via automobile, a few miles south. There, Jeff and his team would reside.

That day, the contractor started work on the large arena, which would be built close to the site where Hart-Root took place. Rickard wanted it to be able to fit 20,000 people, for already he was swamped with ticket orders.

<hr />

[376] *New York Age*, June 23, 1910.

JEFFS HOME AT MOANA SPRINGS

Jeffries' training facility

WHERE THEY WILL BOX

Corbett advised Jeffries not to take any more long runs. Jeff agreed, saying he mostly would engage in shorter runs and 200- or 300-yard sprints. Corbett said,

> Jeff has been a constant surprise to me. If he is not in better shape right now than he has ever been two weeks before any of his former fights, then I am a very poor judge of fighters. ... I am convinced beyond the shadow of a doubt in my own mind he will be as good, and likely better, than the Jeffries I fought several years ago.

Special trains between San Francisco and Reno were being arranged with the Southern Pacific railroad, in addition to the Pullman company.

On June 22 in San Francisco, Jack Johnson once again was arrested for speeding. The officer claimed that he saw Johnson speeding at about 45-miles per hour and allegedly ordered him to stop, but he did not. He went

to Jack's hotel and attempted to place him under arrest. Initially, Johnson refused to be arrested, saying, "Take your hands off me, or I'll kill you." The officer then went and got a couple other officers. Jack went to his room and locked the door. When they returned, the police broke the door in and seized Johnson, who resisted their efforts until Delaney advised him to allow the law to take its course. Jack unsuccessfully attempted to convince them to let him go, given that he was leaving town the next day. When the police chief greeted him, he said, "Arrested again?" Johnson replied, "Yep, but it took three of them."

Johnson paid $10 bail and returned to his training quarters. "Being arrested has become such a common thing with Johnson that his admirers are not alarmed when they hear that their idol has been taken before a magistrate. He seems to thrive on this kind of recreation."

Some thought that Johnson would really like Reno, given that there were no speed laws in Nevada.

That morning, the champ had run 8 miles. In the afternoon, after punching the bag for 15 minutes and throwing the medicine ball, Johnson boxed 3 or 4 rounds with Kaufman and 5 with Cotton. Kaufman showed improved speed and gave Johnson plenty of work, for Al was strong and not afraid of getting hit. They swapped some stiff blows. After his work was completed, Johnson stepped on the scales at just a trifle over 211 pounds.

Johnson said,

> Many sports seem to think that I can not take a punch. They say I am not game. They got this impression from my style of fighting, because I have never been in a hurry to finish my man. I am glad I am meeting a big, strong man like Jeffries, because it will give me a chance to show the public what I can do. Nobody can say that I can not take a punch because I have never allowed my opponents to get close enough to hit me. I pick off the blows before they get started. I have had everybody guessing for years and am glad to get the opportunity of showing the public that I am a real fighter and not a staller.

Johnson said he had settled with George Little for $16,000 so that he would not have to run back and forth to court. Little said he still had money wagered on Johnson, and intended to bet even more.

The *Call* said Johnson was a 10 to 6 underdog in part because of the "common feeling that the powers in control – human and otherwise – will not allow the black man to win over the pride of the white race."

In Reno, nearly everyone faithfully supported Jeffries. "It's Jim all the time. This goes for them all. They would fire Governor Dickerson tomorrow and give the job to Jim if he only put it up to them." Most of the big gamblers were betting on Jeff.

Nevada Governor Denver Dickerson assured everyone that he would not stop the bout, for boxing was legal, the laws had been complied with, and he was convinced that the fight would be on the level. He would follow the law, no matter how many anti-fight petitions he received.[377]

June 23 was Jeff's first day of training at the Moana Baths. In his morning roadwork, he showed plenty of speed, and was not puffing hard, either. He sprinted the last 200 yards in what seemed to be world record time. Jeff then played baseball for 2 hours.

"BIG JIM" AND HIS FAITHFUL TRIO OF TRAINERS, JIM CORBETT, JOE CHOYNSKI AND FARMER BURNS. THE BUNCH HAS JUST RETURNED FROM A RUN AND IS IN A HAPPY MOOD. FROM NOW ON ROAD WORK AND BOXING WILL BE A PART OF THE DAILY PROGRAM AT MOANA.

In the afternoon, in the presence of 400 spectators, Jeff hit the speed bag for 15 minutes, worked with the pulley weights, skipped rope, shadow boxed 10 minutes, engaged in 3 rounds of wrestling with Farmer Burns and Jack Jeffries, and finished with abdominal exercises. One said the gym work took 1 hour and 10 minutes, while another said it lasted 2 hours. Jeffries looked great. "They were all unanimous in their belief that the white man's only hope will bring back the championship."

Jeff believed he would become fully acclimated to the air at altitude in a few days, but said it hardly bothered him at all.

Jeffries also said he would start the drying out process. He would not drink much, feeling that it was time for him to tighten up his skin. Back then, many believed that water was a detriment, unlike today; for we now know that fluid helps the body. We also know that dehydration is even more likely to occur at altitude.

---

[377] *San Francisco Call, Chronicle, Nevada State Journal, San Francisco Examiner,* June 23, 1910. Rickard was seeking to prevent a rival promoter from hosting a potential Langford-Ketchel bout on the same date as Jeffries-Johnson.

JEFF AND CORBETT TALKING IN RENO RING—JEFF PUNCHING THE BAG BEFORE BIG CROWD

When John L. Sullivan showed up at Jeff's training camp, Jim Corbett barred him and had the gate closed. Sullivan asked "Why?" Corbett replied, "Because you have knocked the big fight and called it a fake. Jeff wants me to say that he will not shake hands with you." Sullivan responded, "That's a mistake. I've been misquoted." Jim replied, "I don't believe you were misquoted." Corbett accused John L. of being jealous because Corbett had beaten him, and said he had held a grudge ever since. "I licked you, and you have never forgiven me." Eventually, Sullivan left.

CORBETT TELLING SULLIVAN TO LEAVE JEFF'S CAMP

Tex Rickard would attempt to effect reconciliation, saying that John L. would be treated with the same courtesy as any other newspaper correspondent.

On June 23 at Seal Rock, Jack Johnson ran 8 miles, but did no gym work. He did not want to lose any more weight, and wanted to take on some more, particularly given the Nevada heat.

Johnson said the high altitude would not bother him any more than it would Jeffries. Since they would be breathing the same air, everything would be even.

That day, Johnson left camp to take a train to Reno. With him were his "wife" Etta Duryea, Sig Hart and wife, Rawhide Kelly, Doc Furey, George "Kid" Cotton, Frank Sutton, Dave Mills, Al Kaufman, Johnny Loftus, Walter Monahan, R. J. Comiskey, local police Sergeant Magee, and Professor Burns. Bill Delaney would come later.

Sig Hart, Jack Johnson, and Jack's "wife"

Johnson and others about to leave the Seal Rock House to head to Rick's Resort, near Reno. L to R: Professor Burns, Barney Furey, Sig Hart, Sandy Griswold, Jack Johnson, Billy Delaney, Al Kaufman, Frank Sutton, George Cotton, Dave Mills. Behind the champion is Jack Welsh.

Promoter Sid Hester said he and Tom O'Day had purchased Johnson's fight picture interests, not the eastern syndicate, and they had deposited $50,000 into Johnson's bank account. They were negotiating with Jeffries for his portion of the film rights.

When Johnson did not show up in court to answer the recent speeding charge, the judge declared his $10 bail forfeited and asked the policeman if he wanted a bench warrant to be issued for Johnson's arrest. The officer replied, "No, I do not think that will be necessary. I think that will be enough." The judge agreed and dismissed the case.

Hosting the fight in Reno had the desired effect. Already, the local hotels were packed. Gambling joints and restaurants were thriving.[378]

---

[378] *San Francisco Call, Nevada State Journal*, June 24, 1910.

Johnson told *Boxing* why he would win the fight.

> I know pretty certainly just how good I am, and I can guess pretty accurately just how good Mr. Jeffries can possibly be.

> You can reckon, too, that I have been doing quite a lot of thinking about this fight. I could see it away off as soon as I had beaten Tommy Burns out in Sydney, just because I left dead certain that you white men wouldn't like to see me riding around as champion; and there wasn't any other man you could possibly pick but Jeffries with anything like a chance of knocking me out of the championship. ...

> I shall have to be mighty spry in the early rounds. ... Jeffries is going to be mighty dangerous during the first few rounds, and the only thing I can't quite make up my mind about is just how long he is going to stay dangerous.

> Sooner or later, though, he is going to get tired and weak. I don't need to be a prophet to tell you that. A man can't live as he lived and take off all the weight he has taken off and then come into the ring as fit as he ever was in his life. Then, too, he may reckon on doing a bit of stalling on his own account. He may play at being tired, just to get me to come at him; but well, if he catches me doing that, he is sure entitled to do so. ....

> Jeffries hasn't had a young fellow out with him. ... Boxing with them can't help but slow him down ... [I]t really looks to me as though Jeffries is going to be a lot slower than he is said to be. ...

> He has got to get home on me to make his weight felt, and he has got to land for his punch to be effective. Well, what do you think I shall be doing? ... I'll admit that he can take plenty of punches. He could always do that, and I don't reckon for a moment that he has gone back at that. But then, I am not figuring on beating him with a punch – or with a dozen punches, for that matter.[379]

Johnson told the *Afro American Ledger*,

> I expect to knock out Jim Jeffries within eighteen rounds. ... It may take a trifle longer than I look for, but not a minute over twenty, and that goes. ...

> Now...fighting is a simple matter of business with me. I'm in the game for what I can make out of it, and personal likes and dislikes don't cut any ice with me any more than they do with any other business man who lays his plans to clean up a bunch of money. Of course I'm proud of being the first Negro that has held the world's heavyweight championship. It's only human nature that I should be. ...

---

[379] *Boxing*, June 25, 1910.

The man doesn't live on this earth who can throw me around just as he wants to. Jim Jeffries is a strong fellow all right, but when he bumps into me he'll be buckling up with a man that's every bit as strong as he is. Where do some of these dopesters get the hunch from that I'm a chicken compared to him? I know I don't look the part, and you can ask any one I've boxed with if I'm an easy guy to man around at close quarters… . I'll set him the fastest pace he was ever up against in his life, and believe me, he won't be able to stand it.[380]

Joe Jeannette picked Jeffries to win within 10 rounds. He said, "Jeffries has speed and the wallop to whip Johnson. I think that Jack is a wonderful boxer and that he will make Jeff look awkward for a couple of rounds. Then Jeff will sail in and beat him to a frazzle. Johnson cannot stand the gaff. Give him a couple of blows on the stomach and he wilts."[381]

In Reno, Jeff was the favorite at 10 to 6 odds. One writer said Johnson's prowess was up against the courage and sentiment of the whole white race.

The arena construction was underway on East 4th street. Six carloads of lumber had arrived, and more were coming, to make a total of nineteen train cars of lumber. Telephone, telegraph, and electric lights were installed on the site. The arena would measure 300' x 300'.

SCENE AT THE DEPOT WHEN CHAMPION JACK JOHNSON REACHED RENO.

Rickard and Jeffries sold their motion picture rights to William Rock for $100,000 total. Jeff would receive 2/3 ($66,666.66) and Rickard 1/3 ($33,333.33).

On June 24, about 5,000 people greeted Jack Johnson's train when it arrived in Reno.

Johnson was assured that the color line would not be drawn on him in Reno. Jack smiled and rode off by auto. He and his crew would reside in a nice large house.

In the afternoon, at Rick's roadhouse, Johnson did a little light training.

[380] *Afro American Ledger*, June 25, 1910.
[381] *San Francisco Bulletin*, June 25, 1910.

During his leisure time, Jack liked to play bass violin.

On the morning of the 24th at Moana Springs, Jeffries boxed 5 rounds - 3 with Bob Armstrong and 2 with Jack Jeffries. James was so rough with his brother that the last round had to be cut short to save Jack. Jeff punched, clinched, pulled, mauled, and tugged, wearing out his brother, while the punches that Jack landed had no effect at all. After the sparring, Jeff skipped rope and shadow boxed. He did his road work in the afternoon. It was said that the drying-out process agreed with Jeff. Also, the high altitude did not bother him. "This altitude is not going to hurt me a bit."

Jeff said he was not talking about the fight. "I never was one of those who liked to tell how they are going to knock the other man's head off. It is foolish to talk that way." All he could say was that he would do his best.[382]

DeWitt Van Court, Well-Known Boxing Instructor, and Life-Long Friend, Poses With Jeff in Camp.

---

[382] *San Francisco Call, Examiner, Bulletin, Nevada State Journal,* June 25, 1910.

One observer of both Jeffries and Johnson's training said,

> Jeff is tremendous. ... The white race have got the best man they could get to represent them in the battle. As for Johnson, he is the finest specimen of his race I ever saw. ... The colored race has in this man a real representative, a man that will be very hard to lick, for he knows if he can win this fight he will do more to make the white man respect his color than a thousand Booker Washingtons.

William Muldoon, the wrestler who had trained Sullivan for the 1889 Kilrain bout, said he was agreeably surprised at Jeff's condition. Jeff's constant training for the past year had worked.

> No man ever stepped into a prize ring with greater responsibilities, in the fact that he will represent the white against the black race. He

fully appreciates the importance of his undertaking, as he is attempting to do what no other man in the world today can do. … He knows the entire world has their eyes upon him, expecting him as the white man, to make good. It is an awful responsibility for any one man.

Jack London said Johnson and Jeffries were vastly different types. Johnson was "happy-go-lucky in temperament, as light and carefree as a child. He is easily amused. He lives more in the moment, and joy and sorrow are swift passing moods with him." Jeffries was "more primitive, more ferocious, more terror inspiring." He was like a warrior from thousands of years ago; a perfect type of physical manhood.

London opined that the fight did not mean to Johnson what it meant to Jeffries.

> If Johnson loses the fight, he won't be worried much. If Jeff loses, it will almost break his heart. Under that dark and rather somber seriousness that characterizes him, there is a race pride of which he is intensely self-conscious. Then, too, there is the pride in himself as a man and as a subduer of men. … Of one thing I am certain the loss of any half dozen of his other fights would be less of a blow to Jeff than the loss of this coming fight with Johnson.[383]

On June 25, the Sullivan-Corbett feud came to an end. At Jeff's request, Sullivan visited the camp again, and when John L. met Corbett, they shook hands and engaged in cordial conversation.

Upon meeting him, Jeff said, "Hello John." Sullivan responded, "How are you, young man?" Jeff told

SULLIVAN AND CORBETT BECOME FRIENDS AFTER LONG BITTER ENMITY

CORBETT AND SULLIVAN SHAKING HANDS; WILLIAM MULDOON, PEACEMAKER, ACTING AS MASTER OF CEREMONIES, AT RIGHT, RECORD-UNION

Sullivan that he was willing to take his word for it that John had not knocked him off the bout. Rickard's and Muldoon's peacemaking efforts had been successful.

---

[383] *Reno Evening Gazette, San Francisco Evening Post, San Francisco Chronicle,* June 25, 1910.

That day, Jeff rose early and ran 5 miles. An hour and a half later, at 10 a.m., he rope-skipped, shadow boxed, punched the bag for 20 minutes, and sparred with Bob Armstrong, Jack Jeffries, and Joe Choynski. He worked for a couple of hours. He planned to go fishing in the afternoon.

Jeffries was cheerful and showed a good temper. He was wonderfully well-built. His legs were like mighty columns, and he was symmetrically proportioned.

Jeff said, "I know that this altitude is not going to affect me." He quickly had gotten used to it. He also said the heat was not bothering him either. "I believe that I am going to win quickly."[384]

On the 25th, in the morning, Johnson ran about 8 miles. In the afternoon at Rick's resort, Johnson punched the bag for five minutes and threw the medicine ball for several minutes. For his 9 rounds of sparring, first he boxed Kaufman 4 rounds, demonstrating his marvelous blocking, guarding, and dodging, and amused the crowd with his frequent grins. Jack also showed his offense, drawing blood from Al's nose.

Next, Johnson boxed Cotton for 3 rounds, maintaining his grin. Jack said, "Come on, kid, put it over." Soon Cotton was dripping claret.

---

[384] *San Francisco Chronicle, Call, Nevada State Journal,* June 26, 1910.

Both Kaufman and Cotton were glad when their sparring was concluded, for they had been pummeled and were bleeding profusely from their mouths and noses. Jack London said, "I should not like to be a sparring partner in Johnson's camp."

Johnson also sparred Dave Mills for 2 rounds, allowing him to pound on his stomach. Jack said, "What's the matter, Mills? Can't you see I'm all in? Come on, come on."

Afterwards, Jack said, "This altitude business is a joke. Why, I feel fine, even better than I did at the beach." Johnson was confident and relaxed.

Trainer Tim McGrath said Johnson never showed a yellow streak for as long as he knew him, and the style Johnson used accounted for the erroneous opinion of many.[385]

After watching both men train that day, Jack London opined that barring a lucky punch, which was extremely unlikely, the fight certainly was not going to be short. "Johnson is so clever on the defensive that it would take a long time for Jeff to get him, while, on the other hand, Jeff is no slouch at defense himself, and he is such a behemoth that it would not be in two punches, nor forty, that Johnson could get him. Whoever gets it will have to work for it and work hard."

[385] *Nevada State Journal*, June 26, 1910.

London said Johnson looked stronger and better than he did in Sydney against Burns. He had his entire bag of familiar tricks –

> [His] cleverness of defense; the old letting his opponent hit him repeatedly on his unguarded stomach; the old dreaming and sudden awakening to fierce onslaught for three or four seconds; the old placing of his hand on his opponent's biceps to stop a blow; the old smiling into the camera while in a clinch and the old rubbering trance-like at the audience or passing of facetious remarks while at the same time cuffing his opponent or blocking and withstanding a violent assault.

There was no evidence of exertion, even at altitude. Kaufman devoted himself to stomach blows, something they expected from Jeff. However, Johnson was not bothered.[386]

The *Call* said the majority of sports were picking Jeffries to win. The current San Francisco Olympic Club instructor, as well as Billy Gallagher, gave Jeff the nod. One man predicting a Jeffries victory said, "I'll be there to assist at the autopsy." A real estate man who rented to blacks said, "If Johnson wins I will have to raise my rents to get even." Most Jeffries supporters thought he would win quickly and easily by knockout. Alec Greggains said, "It's a cinch for Jeff. I saw enough of Johnson in his fight with Marvin Hart to let me know what he is like." The confident Tom

---

[386] *Call, Chronicle*, June 26, 1910.

Corbett said, "Jeffries will win. ... I look for him to bring the heavy weight championship back to the white race. I am going to bet everything I have on him." Eddie Hanlon said Jeff had the strength, heart, and punch. Tiv Kreling said Jeff would rush and corner Johnson and nail him. Johnny Loftus said Jeff would win, but insisted that it would take a while. "None of them, I don't care who he is, can crowd Johnson to the ropes and knock him out in a few rounds. He's too clever a boxer and too great a ring general." Another man said, "I can see nothing to it, only a badly frightened negro, fighting on the defensive, trying to withstand the rushes of the greatest heavyweight punisher that ever climbed into a ring. I can not see anything to it but a white celebration."

Sam Langford said, "I think that I can beat Johnson and I know that I can't beat Jeffries, so that's my answer. Johnson is not there with the heart to trim that great, big white man." Joe Woodman said Jeff would win without a doubt. He was too big, strong, and game, and could not be hurt.

James J. Corbett said, "I look to see a big, clever, defensive coon trying to keep out of the way of the greatest fighting machine that ever stepped into a 24 foot ring." Joe Choynski said, "I have been up against both and know a little about their fighting qualifications. I honestly think Jeff is better than ever and will win this fight sure." Bob Armstrong said Jeff was a cinch to win.

Most of those who had been skeptical about Jeffries' ability to come back had been convinced otherwise since seeing his physique and form in training. They thought he indeed was back. Others said he did not need to come all the way back to lick Johnson, he was so good.

Johnson had his supporters, though. One color-line advocate said, "Any white man who fights a negro ought to lose." Many said Jeff simply could not come back after such a long retirement and defeat a man of Johnson's class. The feeling was that Johnson would box on the defensive and wear Jeff out, for after so many years of not fighting, regardless of how Jeff looked externally or in training; the stamina would not be there in a long hard fight. Tom Flanagan said that even if he was not managing Johnson he would bet on him. "Jeffries is the remains of a once great fighter, but his day has passed. He's only the shell of a man who beat them all a few years ago. He can't come back." In picking Johnson, Stan Ketchel said, "Johnson is the hardest hitter who ever lived." Some gamblers were quite happy that Johnson was the underdog, because it meant all the more money for them. Harry Foley said Johnson was the "greatest big man of them all and I am not barring anybody. I do not see how Jeff can come back after being out of the game for six years." Despite the fact that he was no longer Johnson's manager, George Little said he was betting on Johnson to flatten Jeff. He called Johnson the greatest big fighter ever.

There were those who were on the fence. Jim Coffroth said he originally thought Johnson would win, but after seeing Jeff come around and show great form, he was not so sure. "Both are terrific hitters and one never can tell what may happen." Jack Welsh said it was a tossup. Ed Graney said it was too hard to say.[387]

On June 26 at 4 p.m., after preliminary exercises, wearing his blue trunks with the American flag knotted about his waist, Johnson sparred first with Al Kaufman. "Johnson's defense was a revelation of speed and accuracy." Despite boring in hard, Al could make no impression, while Johnson smiled and made Al's head bob back from blows, drawing some blood. The

spectators wondered whether Kaufman was not able to land any punches because Johnson's defense was too speedy and wonderful or because Al was too slow. After the 4th round, Kaufman was breathing heavily, while Johnson showed no signs of his wind being affected.

Next, Walter Monahan, San Francisco's 4-round champion, went 4 rounds. Johnson split his lip and made his nose bleed. A mass of red spread over his entire face and made him look as if he had taken a bath in a slaughterhouse.

Some who saw Johnson train that day said he looked inert, sluggish, tired, and lacking vim and ginger. They said he was a careless worker.

Others said that Johnson picked off the blows with such ease that he appeared to be loafing, and he fought the same way. He boxed without any apparent effort, for the game came naturally to him. Jack smiled and joked with his sparring partners, but also knocked their heads back. He had them breathing hard at the end, while he seemed to be taking things easy, toying with them. He was far superior.

---

[387] *Call*, June 26, 1910.

Some said Jeffries rested on the 26th, preferring to go fishing. However, two Reno papers said he did train. He woke up early, took a walk, punched the bag for 10 minutes, shadow boxed, did pulley work, and wrestled with Farmer Burns and Bob Armstrong.[388]

[388] *Reno Evening Gazette*, *Nevada State Journal*, *San Francisco Call*, *San Francisco Examiner*, June 27, 1910. Johnson's morning road work on the 26th consisted of alternating fast walking with an occasional sprint (for either 6, 8, or 10 miles - depending on the source), which is what he did the day before. In the afternoon, prior to sparring, Johnson punched the speed bag for a couple minutes, creating a pretty rat-a-tat tune. He then threw the medicine ball with Kaufman, Mills, and Denver Jack Geyer. Cotton did not spar, owing to his swollen lip, the result of Jack's smashes from the day before.

Battling Nelson said it was difficult to say who would win. The overall impression from his comments, though, was that he favored Johnson. He opined that it would be a tough fight for Jeffries. Nelson said the general public did not give Johnson due credit for his fighting ability. They liked to say he was a big black faker, quitter, no good, not game, and would lie down. Nelson said Johnson had never quit or thrown a fight, and it appeared to him that the fight was on the level. It was true that Jack had pulled and stalled in several fights, but he had never once quit or laid down.

A number of scribes lay particular stress on the Johnson-Hart battle held in San Francisco, at which I was a ringside spectator and on which I had $40 bet on Hart against $100 on Johnson. The only reason I bet on Hart was that I was figuring that the promoters were laying plans for a championship battle between Hart and Jeffries, and that if there was anything crooked the white man would win, which he did through the referee, and only through the referee.

After the twentieth round was about one minute old I offered to sell my bet, which would amount to $140 if I won, all for a five-dollar note, to Billy Benner, with whom I had made the bet. He said: "No. If you want $5 I will give it to you, but I wouldn't buy the bet." The next thing we knew the referee held Hart's hand aloft, signifying he was the winner. If that's what they call quitting or laying down on Johnson's part I am willing to string with the quitters all the time.

Nelson believed Johnson obviously defeated Hart.

Nelson said the claims about colored fighters - that they lacked gameness, would not take punishment and fight back, would run away and quit - were false. He said just as many white fighters were quitters as black fighters. The public and so-called experts had claimed incorrectly that Johnson would quit against Burns. He believed that both Jeffries and Johnson were game.

He further opined that Jeff would have the job of his life on his hands even if he was at his best. Smaller men like Sharkey and Corbett had given Jeff close fights. He also noted that champions don't come back with success even after a couple of years, let alone six. Johnson was a serious proposition. Hence, it likely would be the hardest fight of Jeff's career.

Nearly every white American hoped that Jeff would win, given that he was a white man. "The general public at large seems to think that we should not have any negro champions in their respective classes because this is a white man's country – and I agree with them." However, that was not clouding Nelson's judgment when scouting the bout.

Nelson did not think it made sense for Jeffries to take the fight. Even if he won, he would retire again and Johnson would remain the best fighter before the public. If Jeff lost, "a white man would stand a fat chance of walking down Market street, or any other one, without being humiliated, or otherwise roughly treated, if he passed by any of Johnson's race."

Ultimately, Nelson said,

> As for the winner, it is awfully hard to pick. One thing certain is that I consider Johnson one of the best men Jeffries has ever been called on to meet. He is very nearly of equal poundage, almost as tall, a little cleverer, younger and right in the active part of his fighting career and unquestionably he ought to be in better shape. Jeffries has the harder punch, is tougher and possibly the gamest of the two, but has been out of activity too long. I think he must win inside of fifteen rounds, if at all.

Nelson also said that if one knew nothing about the two fighters, but just looked at photographs of their bodies and was asked to pick a winner, race prejudice aside, most likely one would pick Johnson.

T. P. Magilligan said that although Jeff was the odds favorite, and folks were saying that he looked as good as ever, it remained to be seen how he would perform in actual combat against the champion.

The more this writer saw of Johnson, the more impressed he became. "Johnson has the peculiar faculty of growing on one. The more one sees of the big black the stronger one is impressed with his fighting prowess." Some thought Jack was not serious, but his apparent carelessness and indifference actually was studied defense. He was very elusive. He was a ring paradox. He appeared easy to hit, but then opponents found him unhittable. "His simplicity is more complex than the most complex system."[389]

Reno police planned to have plenty of law enforcement present, both plain clothes and uniformed, to maintain order. Local police captain Cox declared that the first fellow to shout "Kill the Nigger" would be hurled out of the arena. No alcohol would be allowed. Quite frankly, the tickets prices were high enough such that the rough element would be minimized.[390]

The *San Francisco Bulletin* questioned Governor Gillett's motives in preventing the fight. Obviously, it was done for political reasons. He had not prevented boxing for three and a half years of his administration. "He wanted the approval of the many good citizens who in their indignation against prize-fighting might forget that far worse evils were demanding their attention." Gillett would allow pugilists to maul each other every day of the year if he thought there were enough votes in it. He had gained the support of clergymen who showed more concern over a boxing match than they did about overworked children. Boxing lovers were upset at Gillett.[391]

One week before the fight, on June 27, Jeffries worked the punching bag for 20 minutes, and then the pulley weights. For sparring, Jeffries started out with 3 rounds with Armstrong, tearing into Bob and forcing him to do all he could to prevent Jeff from stopping him. For the next 5 rounds, Jeff alternated rounds back and forth with Choynski and Berger, with Joe doing 3 total rounds and Sam 2. In the 2nd round with Berger, Jeff landed a right to the stomach that decked Sam. Jim Corbett then worked 2 rounds, and Berger sparred 1 more. Jeff worked his right very well, planning to surprise Johnson with it, for Jack had said he only feared Jeff's left. At the conclusion of the sparring, red blotches were all over Berger's body.

Finally, Jeffries pulled, tugged, and wrestled with Farmer Burns for 2 rounds. He had worked for 13 total rounds – 11 boxing and 2 wrestling. "Jeffries' wind and condition stood the test of hard boxing, and were all that could be expected."

Jeff liked Reno. He was playful, in good humor, and feeling well. He said he felt stronger and his wind even better. "I feel better in fact than when I was in Rowardennan. I think that the air is clearer here. I don't breathe a bit faster than I did down there and as for weakness, why I can throw Burns around easier right now than I could do two weeks ago." He also said, "I

[389] *San Francisco Evening Post*, June 27, 1910.
[390] *San Francisco Call*, June 27, 1910.
[391] *San Francisco Bulletin*, June 27, 1910.

feel like I could fight all day now. … I was feeling so good that I was afraid to cut loose on the boys. … I was in shape a month ago."[392]

[392] *Chronicle, Examiner, Nevada State Journal,* June 28, 1910; *Reno Evening Gazette,* June 27, 1910.

321

Oakland referee Eddie Smith said, "I have watched Jeffries train for thirteen years, and I can honestly say that he boxed better today than at any time before. … His eye was good in gauging distance and he was aggressive at all times. His footwork was good and firm."

It was a hot day, too. John L. Sullivan said the thermometer registered 87 degrees when he looked, though he was told that some thermometers showed 96.

That day, Jack Johnson took a 10-mile morning run.

In the afternoon, under the broiling sun, Johnson tossed the medicine ball for 10 minutes, and then hit the punching bag. He boxed 4 fast rounds with Kaufman and 4 more with Walter Monahan. Walter bled from his mouth and nose. When Monahan wiped his face on Johnson's shirt and arms, Jack said, "Don't blood me all up. You are an awful looking fighter." Finally, Dave Mills worked 2 rounds. In total, Jack had sparred 10 rounds.

John L. Sullivan said Johnson showed a little more activity than the day before. Mrs. Johnson was there and was an interested spectator.

Like Jeffries, Johnson also said the altitude did not affect his wind at all. He was weighing 211 pounds and expected to weigh about 208 at ringside. "In the two days previous to the start of the contest I'll dry out three pounds and that will bring me to my fighting notch."

Johnson was confident that the spectators would give him a square deal, regardless of his color, and just would see them as two boxers.

Jack Root had arrived in town and watched Johnson train that day. Several years ago, while Root was training to fight George Gardner, Johnson had been his sparring partner.

> At that time I was considered pretty fast and pretty good, I believe – yet Jack made me step around pretty lively every time I donned the gloves with him. What I have seen today…convinces me that Johnson is a hundred per cent stronger and better than he was when he acted as my sparring partner – and I think Jeffries will only win after the hardest sort of a battle if he wins at all. Another thing – if Jeff can win (and, being a white man, I naturally hope he can) it will be the first example of a man coming back that I have ever known. … Why, every fighter knows what an awful task it is to get into shape after even a year's idleness and as for five –well, he will be a wonder if he can do it.

Root noted that most of the time, Jack was on the defensive, save for the occasional counter when his sparring partners became overconfident.

> He did it easily, apparently with about as much effort as when he is sawing the bow across the cello strings. That is the way he works. Sometimes his work is so slow that it looks slovenly. Sometimes the big fighter appears to be loafing, but he works so easily that it is hard to comprehend how much effort there is behind his careless motions. It is always noticeable, however, that no matter how little he appears

to be working his sparring partners are steaming and puffing and are doing their best to land on the big fellow without having the least effect.

Johnson was described as being a "big, good-natured darkey out for a frolic." He always wore a smile, and had a light-hearted demeanor. As a fighter, "Johnson's work is deceptive."

After training, Johnson played cello and piano.

In general, most fighters favored Johnson. Sporting experts and newspaper men were about equally divided.

Jeffries did not train as good-naturedly as did Johnson. However, this was only a matter of temperament. Sullivan said, "I was a good bit like Jeffries. I hated the confounded work. It was all work and no fun. I used to look at my trainers as personal enemies." However, later he could see that everything his trainers did was for his own good.[393]

William Muldoon was amazed by Johnson's work, and said that Jeff was facing his greatest battle. Muldoon called Johnson an enlarged edition of Fitzsimmons. He had very long legs, with his lower leg being particularly long. That gave his legs the appearance of slenderness and lack of development, but the appearance was deceiving. "His legs are well developed; it is only their extreme length from the knee to the ankle which makes them appear slender." As for his upper body, "I have never seen more powerfully developed arms, shoulders and back muscles than I found on Johnson." Jack carried no superfluous flesh.

Muldoon called Johnson's boxing careless to a certain degree. He looked like a sparring instructor teaching beginners, and seemed somewhat disinterested. "He spent too much time watching the crowd and in looking at the men at the ringside over the shoulders of his sparring partners." He worked lightly, though obviously he was in good shape.

Ultimately, Muldoon thought Jeff would have his work cut out for him.

> If there is any man in the world who can beat Johnson, that man is Jeffries, but if Jeffries fails we must accept Johnson as the world's heavyweight champion for some time to come. Outside of Jeffries we have no man who would stand a chance with the negro, and I believe that Jeffries will have on his hands the most serious contract of his life on next Monday afternoon.

In terms of his personality, Muldoon said Johnson liked to have people of his own color around him. He was courteous, respectful, and very polite.

Like Johnson, Jeffries was drying out, eschewing liquids, which he believed would increase his speed and improve his endurance, so that he would enter the ring weighing 217 pounds. Jeff claimed he was close to 220, but most thought he looked about 230.

Jeffries was a silent, serious, introverted, iron man who avoided attention and found his huge popularity and adulation annoying. He preferred private training as opposed to performing in front of the big crowds and reporters that were determined to watch him train. He trained how and when he liked, rarely letting anyone know when he would work, and at times he would vary his schedule based on how he felt. This upset some fans and reporters who wanted to know when he would train so they could be there to watch. Reporters wanted scoops and needed to write daily training reports, for which readers hungered. Jeff said he was training for a fight, not running a three-ring circus. He wasn't doing anything for show, and wanted to be left alone. He had a brusque way of speaking.

Some took it as nervousness about the fight, but that was just Jeff's normal personality. "He is merely himself, with the strength of character to be himself." He felt no impulse to be pals with everyone he met, "and he is

---

[393] *Call, Chronicle, Examiner, Bulletin, Nevada State Journal,* June 28, 1910.

honest enough not to simulate a feeling he does not possess. All the same, it is darned hard on the public." Despite his distaste for large crowds, Jeff had never shown stage fright in any of his fights, most of which were before huge crowds.

With Johnson it was just the opposite. He was care-free, happy, personable, and reveled in and craved attention. He was jealous of the fact that the fans and reporters were more interested in seeing Jeff than him, and was upset when they did not come out to his camp. He enjoyed talking with and entertaining reporters, and liked performing for them. This actually caused many reporters to take a liking to him, for Jack was affable, congenial, and accommodating.

> Nobody was ever more gregarious than he, ever happier to greet old friends and make new ones. He likes crowds, thrives upon them, and in turn does his best to give them a good time. Let him decide on a certain day that he is not going to spar, and then inform him that 200 persons have journeyed all the way out to his camp to see him work, depend upon it, Johnson simply couldn't let them go away disappointed.

Johnson would spar and give the fans something to talk about. Conversely, if Jeff had decided not to spar or work, then he would not do so even if a massive crowd was on hand to see him.[394]

C. E. Van Loan said that three points should be watched closely when the fight began, for they could show how the fight might go – the first right uppercut that Johnson landed, the first clinch, and first body punch that Jeff landed. "The short right uppercut which Johnson lifts into an opponent who comes at him is surely his most deadly punch, and he shoots it like a flash, seldom missing, for he reserves his fire until he sees a sure opening." Johnson would land, but the question was whether he could hurt Jeff. "It is foolishness to say that Johnson cannot hit Jeff fairly on the point with his right uppercut. Johnson can hit any man in the world if he tries, and this time he will be trying as never before." Jeff had a proven jaw, for even Fitzsimmons, who was considered the hardest puncher in boxing, could not budge him. "Jeffries has always been able to take a terrific punch without showing its effect." It remained to be seen whether Johnson could handle Jeff's strength in the clinches or his very powerful body blows.

Famous authors and boxers from all over the country and world had flocked into Reno, which was seeing a celebrity a minute. Never before in boxing's history had such a galaxy of boxing stars and famous men been congregated for a fistic show. Everywhere one turned there was a group of celebrated men. Over 150 writers from all over the country were in town. A majority had been in Reno for a week or more, watching the fighters work.

---

[394] *San Francisco Chronicle*, June 30, 1910.

Members of the Australian party which arrived on the steamship *Wilhelmina*, l to r: Bill Lang, W. F. Corbett of the *Sydney Referee*, Hugh McIntosh, and Tommy Burns.

Bob Fitzsimmons had arrived from Australia. He picked Jeff to win in over 20 rounds, for he had endurance, persistence, aggressiveness, and power. Johnson was clever, particularly defensively, but lacked the punch.

Frank Slavin, former top Australian heavyweight, picked Johnson. He cited his elasticity and strength.

Lou Houseman of Chicago said he was willing to wager $10,000 that Johnson would not last 7 rounds.

Jack London said men wanted to see and hear about the fight so badly that it hurt. "When the pages of all the newspapers are daily filled with it, the only conclusion is that a very large portion of the people of the country are interested in it." It was estimated that between 15,000 and 20,000 people would pay from $10 up to $50 for tickets to the fight.

London said boxing was developed by and belonged to whites, and was inherently part of the white race, suggesting that was why Jeffries should be the favorite in the fight.

> This contest of men with padded gloves on their hands is a sport that belongs uniquely to the English speaking race and that has taken centuries for the race to develop. It is no superficial thing, a fad of a moment or a generation. No genius or philosopher devised it and persuaded the race to adopt it as their racial sport of sports. It is as deep as our consciousness and is woven into the fibers of our being. … We like fighting. It is our nature.[395]

On June 28, Johnson trained in front of a large crowd that included Nevada Governor Denver Dickerson, Tex Rickard, and Superintendent of State Police Cox. After some gymnastic exercises, skipping around the ring lightly and actively while shadow boxing, bag punching, and work with the medicine ball, with his same care-free expression, Jack boxed 12 rounds – 4 with Kaufman, 4 with Cotton, 2 with Monahan, and 2 with Mills.

---

[395] *San Francisco Bulletin, San Francisco Chronicle*, June 29, 1910.

Against Kaufman, Johnson didn't just play defense, but did some leading and jabbing.

Cotton was the heaviest and most willing of the sparring partners, but this led him to being the most battered. After Cotton drew some blood from the champ's lip, Johnson nailed him with a left hook to the jaw and dropped him to the mat, knocking him out. A little cold water soon brought him around.

Johnson treated Monahan easily, though a few jabs opened up Walter's lips and started the blood. Jack was as fast on his feet as the lighter man.

Although Mills was fresh and the fastest of the sparring partners, he had nothing on Jack.

Johnson had drawn blood from each sparring partner. "Old-timers who were out there say that they didn't believe the negro had so much life and go in him. They had imagined him a trifle sluggish, but not now."

The 209-pound Johnson said he never felt better or fitter in his life. Regarding the dropping of Cotton with a left hook, Jack said, "I had no intention of knocking him down, and, in fact, I didn't think I could hurt him very much with the big twelve-ounce mitts. I will show some of these people who think I have no punch that there is some steam behind my blows, even if they are left-handed ones."

Johnson was upset by stories that said he was slow and lazy. By tearing into his trainers, he proved such tales to be untrue.

Nevada Governor Denver Dickerson said Johnson was wonderfully clever and the embodiment of strength, agility, aggressiveness, and good nature. His sparring partners were playthings in his hands. Governor Dickerson was amused by the fact that Johnson liked to kid around with his sparring partners and the spectators.[396]

---

[396] *San Francisco Chronicle, San Francisco Examiner, Nevada State Journal,* June 29, 1910; *Reno Evening Gazette,* June 28, 29, 1910. Johnson did not do any roadwork that morning.

Hugh McIntosh picked Johnson to win. He said he did not care how great Jeff once was, he never saw an athlete come back and amount to anything. Jeff might have looked great on the outside, but he wouldn't be on the inside. He had a $500 wager with Tommy Burns, who bet on Jeff.

Burns said Johnson was no match for Jeffries and did not have a chance. He said Jeff was too good for anyone, including himself. He also said Johnson was afraid to fight him again.

Bill Lang, who had once fought and lost to Johnson, and served as a Johnson sparring partner before the Johnson-Burns fight, said Johnson was a big, strong, clever fellow and would give any man a long hard fight.

On the 28th, Jeffries ran 7 miles. However, he did not box, saying that he had a stomach ache after eating that day. Hence, he disappointed Governor Dickerson, who had come to see him work. Jeff suffered from some dysentery that day, though it soon abated. Still, that was not good for someone who was limiting his intake of liquids, because dysentery tends to cause the loss of more fluids from the body, leading to dehydration.[397]

The *San Francisco Chronicle* said the consensus of opinion was that Jeffries would be the best conditioned man.:

John Foster, *New York Telegram* – "I consider Jeffries to be in much better condition than Johnson." .

Edwin Park, *Boston Globe* – "I consider Jeffries to be a better conditioned man than his colored opponent. I am greatly impressed with the grand improvement shown by the white man."

E. B. Moss, *New York Sun* – "I should say that Jeffries has a shade over Johnson on the score of condition. … Jeffries was not winded after his fast work-out extending over two hours. It may be that Johnson did not require as much exercise as Jeffries."

Tad Dorgan, *New York Journal* – "I should say that Jeffries looks to be in the best condition, but I am not prepared to say that he will live up to his looks."

Sandy Griswold, *Omaha World-Herald* – "I have thirty years' experience, and I flatter myself that I am a good judge of condition. I consider both men in fine form. There is no doubt that Jeffries is in superb condition."

Hugh Keough, *Chicago Tribune* – "Jack Johnson should be in the better condition, taking everything into consideration."

Frank O'Connell, *New York Herald* – "My opinion is that both men are good."

B. W. Ritchie, *New York Sun* – "I should say that both men are in good condition. I am not altogether too certain about Johnson. … Johnson has a lazy style in his boxing. He appears to accomplish a good deal with a minimum effort. Jeffries works under a nervous strain, and is always keyed up to a high pitch. I think it will take Jeffries some time to break through the colored man's defense. I look for Jeffries to win in something over fifteen rounds."

John Seys, *Chicago News* – "Jeffries is in the best condition. I look for him to be too strong for Johnson. He should wear down the colored man."

E. G. Brown, *New York World* – "Externally Jeffries probably looks in the best condition, but I am not prepared to say whether he has taken the best method to reduce to his present weight."

---

[397] *Call*, June 29, 1910; *Examiner*, June 30, 1910; *Nevada State Journal*, June 28, 1910.

Eddie Smith, *Oakland Tribune* and *Chicago American* – "Both men look fit to me." "Prior to the workout of Jack Johnson today, I had feared that he had overtrained. This belief being strongly impressed on me by the rather indifferent manner in which he worked the first two days after arriving at Reno. Johnson's work of today, however, forbids any such thought, and it is my belief now that he is the best conditioned athlete I have ever seen. His boxing is superb and at the end of twelve hard rounds today he was breathing normally. Johnson is faster and stronger than I have ever seen him. Jeffries is the surprise of the athletic world. … His boxing and gymnasium work are all that they ever were, and if it were not for the fact that we know Jeffries has been out of the game so long, everyone would agree that he is in the best condition of his life."[398]

On June 29, Johnson ran 9 miles in the heat. He boxed 10 rounds - 4 with Kaufman, mostly playing defense, 4 with Monahan, in which some blood showed on the champ's lip, and then 2 rounds with Mills.

That same day, Jeffries met Governor Dickerson and shook his hand. In the presence of more than 1,000 spectators, Jeffries trained in front of the motion picture machine. Jeff skipped rope, punched the bag, shadow boxed, and did gym exercises. He boxed 6 rounds - 2 rounds each with Joe Choynski, brother Jack Jeffries, and Sam Berger.

Having seen both men in training, Governor Dickerson said Johnson was faster than Jeffries and would land more often, though Jeff had more power and was sturdier. Johnson was the cleverer of the two and his defense harder to penetrate. "It is safe to say, I think, that Johnson will hit Jeff more times than Jeff hits him, but his blows will not have the same telling effect."

---

[398] *San Francisco Chronicle*, June 29, 1910.

Footage from this day still exists. Fans may be familiar with a segment that shows Corbett and Sullivan shadow sparring, feinting, and then shaking hands.

Pistols were banned from the arena. Anyone who tried to bring one in would be barred from taking their seat.

Taking no chances on his security, Johnson had hired an army of gun fighters to ensure that no one tried to make trouble for him. Both he and his intimate friends kept guns with them.

An influx of wagers on Johnson caused the odds to move from 10 to 6 ½ to 10 to 7 ½, with Jeff still the favorite.

However, in Chicago, a scare had been thrown into the black population. They were not as willing to bet on Johnson, in part because Eastern sporting men were so confident and eager to wager large sums of money on Jeffries, and even were offering 2 to 1 odds to Johnson backers.

Johnson sent a telegram to his mother saying, "Don't believe what you see in the newspapers. I am in condition. Will win sure."

Jack Root believed that Jeff's crouch combined with his great body blows would earn him the victory.[399]

The fighters agreed to box in a 22-foot ring. Some thought that Johnson would demand a larger ring, but he did not.

Some wondered whether Jeff could stand the effects of the sun's rays. It had been very hot and dry recently, which might make the fight a contest of stamina. However, Jeff liked the outdoors and had been training outside.

Frank Herman said Johnson's training showed that he was planning to win through defensive tactics, hoping to sap Jeff's strength gradually by causing Jeffries to waste his energy missing blows, which would also dishearten the ex-champ. Jack was clever, efficient, and wasted no energy. Johnson likely would cut up and puff up Jeff's face. Regardless, Jeff was game and always had come through with victory. The questions about

---

[399] *Reno Evening Gazette*, June 29, 1910; *Nevada State Journal, San Francisco Call, San Francisco Bulletin*, June 30, 1910. At that time, Root was a theatrical impresario in Burlington and Ottumwa, Iowa.

Johnson's gameness made him the underdog, although Johnson's cleverness ensured that he never had to take a severe grueling. Ultimately, this writer thought Johnson had the edge.[400]

The *New York Age* said the coming contest, dubbed the Battle of the Century, had aroused more widespread interest than any other match in prize-ring history. It was the all-absorbing topic of discussion everywhere. A massive number of articles were being written on a daily basis. Most thought it would be a long time before boxing saw another fight of this magnitude.

The *Age* predicted a Johnson victory, and emphasized that Johnson's race did not factor into its analysis. For years, Johnson had chased the white fighters, Jeffries included, making futile efforts to obtain top matches.

> After trying unsuccessfully to get the colored man's 'goat' in the opening rounds, Jeffries will find what he is up against. Johnson will evidently try to tire his white opponent, and then 'cut loose' as he has never done before. As he has been waiting for years for big game, also big money, he will have no hesitancy in showing all his fighting wares.[401]

On June 30, the motion picture machine filmed Johnson bag punching, medicine-ball throwing, and shadow boxing. Then he sparred 4 rounds each with Kaufman and Cotton. Against Al, he demonstrated his neat blocking skills and almost instinctive ability to find the smallest opening, whipping in some nasty blows. Johnson cut Cotton's mouth, after which he asked, "Wasn't that a beaut?" In the clinches, Jack winked over Cotton's shoulder.

The consensus of opinion was that Johnson's blocking tactics and guard were beyond criticism. He generally held back against his sparring partners, causing some to question his power, although occasionally he whipped in some sudden short vicious blows, even against seemingly invincible guards, before going back to playing defense again. On occasion Johnson demonstrated his footwork, though he hardly moved at all in his workouts.

Johnson's lip still showed a little cut that Cotton had caused two days prior, and it bled a little. The big fight was four days away.

Before Johnson had sparred, John L. Sullivan tried his hand at the punching bag, which the camera filmed. Some of that footage still exists.

Joe Woodman, Langford's manager, had shown up there that day, and upon seeing him, Johnson said, "Mr. Woodman, there have been differences between us and I must request you to vacate these grounds." Woodman felt he had a right to be there because he had a partial interest in the films, but Johnson insisted there would be no films if he remained. Eventually, Woodman complied with the demand and left.

---

[400] *San Francisco Evening Post*, June 30, 1910; *San Francisco Examiner*, July 1, 1910.
[401] *New York Age*, June 30, 1910.

Jack Johnson Drawing His Entire Training Crew and Manager Flanagan in an Automobile That Doesn't Break the Speed Laws

Johnson said he was through with hard work. He only would do some limbering-up exercise. He was down to 209 pounds. "I am well satisfied with my condition. I am stronger and bigger than I ever was before and I know that my speed has not diminished. There is no chance of my becoming worn out during the fight through lack of condition. I feel as if I could fight a hundred rounds."

Johnson said he would end the battle in short order should the opportunity present itself, but would not fight recklessly and risk getting nailed and taken out.

> No one can ever convince me that it is good judgment to stake everything on the chance of one blow. Rushing at an opponent and trying to tear his head off may be just the thing to give him the chance to do a little tearing on his own account, and in all my fights I have studied to win without giving any thought to the number of rounds. When the proper time comes I am always ready to complete my job, and I have been fairly successful so far.

Jack was glad to hear that Jeff was in fine condition, for it meant that when he won it would earn him more credit.

Responding to Tommy Burns, Johnson noted that Burns had sought a fight with Jeff when Tom was champion, so obviously Tommy did not think Jeffries was as invincible as he was claiming.

Johnson said he had to chase "fourflusher" Burns all over the world for years demanding a fight, but the frightened Burns was more interested in two fake fights with O'Brien. Jack had to take a relatively paltry amount of money to get Burns into the ring, while Tommy received a huge guarantee.

He also didn't think Burns really wanted a rematch, despite his claims in order to save face. "Burns's statement after I beat him was like the statement of a lot of people who after the storm has blown over, assert, 'well it can never happen again.'" Jack said Burns could come to his camp to spar, and if Tommy could last 10 rounds, he'd give him $10,000. "He knows in his heart that I am his master."[402]

Jim Corbett said Jeff was impervious to punches. Both Corbett and Fitz had landed perfect punches on his jaw and Jeff did not budge. When Johnson hit him and Jeff kept coming in, Jack's heart would evaporate.

Corbett also said it was a contest between men not only of entirely different races, but of different traditions.

> Jeffries is the embodiment of all that is powerful and brutish in the white man. He has always lived close to nature. ... Had Jeff lived thousands of years ago, when strength and courage made kings, he would have reigned supreme among his fellow men. It must have been the same with Johnson, say you, and you are right. But don't you remember reading the tales of how the blacks bowed down to, worshipped, and feared – there's the word – feared the white man.

> Psychologists say that in times of great stress, in great moments, we go back to original principles, the inborn characteristics that, while they may be buried deep by disuse, invariably spring to the surface when a great crisis arrives...Will Johnson be able to check and master the overwhelming fear of the powerful white man...? I doubt it.

> No one realizes better than I do the fact that I am prejudiced in favor of Jim Jeffries. I am. ... I know that Jeffries is the pugilistic marvel of the age. Why, then, shouldn't I be prejudiced in his favor? Undoubtedly there is a racial prejudice there, too. In sizing up this fight I have made allowance for that prejudice and have not allowed it to influence my judgment. I have carefully weighed Jeffries' fighting abilities and compared them one by one with Johnson's. And Johnson has suffered by the comparison.[403]

---

[402] *San Francisco Call, San Francisco Examiner, San Francisco Chronicle, Nevada State Journal*, July 1, 1910; *Reno Evening Gazette*, June 30, 1910; July 1, 1910.
[403] *San Francisco Bulletin*, July 1, 1910.

On the 30th, Jeffries said, "I am ready to go into the ring to win the championship back for the white race." His said his training was finished and he would do little work for the next few days.

Jeffries said he had not overworked, but had trained just right. He gave himself sufficient work, but also sufficient rest. He did not risk leaving his fight in the training camp. He had enough experience training for big fights to know what he was doing. "I have more to lose than anyone else. That's why I must take my own judgment for certain things," including not giving sparring exhibitions whenever the press or public wanted him to do so. Jeff said the way he was feeling at present; he did not think any man in the world could beat him. He would keep in mind all those who had bet on him. He had worked for more than a year preparing for the fight. "It has been a long, hard pull, but I believe I have brought myself into the greatest physical condition of my life." Jeff also said, "I'll win because Johnson hasn't got a blow hard enough to floor me, and because I am going to tear after him with every ounce of fight and strength I have in me, and not stop until he lies on the flat of his back in the ring."[404]

Jeffries' confidence made believers out of many. After all, he always had been right before. He had never lost a fight. His resume included: 1893-95 KO14 Hank Griffin; 1898 KO3 Joe Goddard, KO3 Peter Jackson, KO3 Mexican Pete Everett, W20 Tom Sharkey, and W10 Bob Armstrong; 1899 KO11 Bob Fitzsimmons and W25 Tom Sharkey; 1900 KO1 Jack Finnegan and KO23 James J. Corbett; 1901 KO2 Joe Kennedy and KO5 Gus Ruhlin; 1902 KO8 Fitzsimmons, 1903 KO10 Corbett; and 1904 KO2 Jack Munroe.

Jeff's weight was still a mystery, for he refused to step on the scales. His trainers thought he was about 218, though others estimated anywhere from 220 to 230. Jeff had taken off weight early on in his training, and then maintained it, while Johnson had reduced his weight gradually.

William Muldoon, who had trained Sullivan for Kilrain, said Jeffries appeared to be in great physical condition, and showed more spirit and enthusiasm in his sparring than Johnson. His movement was quick and springy, and he had dash. All of the offensive and defensive moves and punches were there. He still had power too.

---

404 *San Francisco Call, Chronicle, Examiner, Nevada State Journal,* July 1, 1910.

Johnson seemed to be toying with his sparring partners, holding back more, but he was in great shape. Muldoon believed that Jack could stop any of his sparring partners whenever he wanted.

Regardless of his positive statements about Jeff, Muldoon believed that Jeffries should have sparred more often, every day from 10 to 20 rounds. He felt that Jeff's judgment of distance and timing were not good, owing to the fact that it had been such a long time since he last fought. Furthermore, "He leaves many openings which lead one to believe, after studying the two men and their methods, that Jeffries is due to receive a great deal of punishment."

Battling Nelson modified his earlier comments and said that although Jeff was a great man, Johnson was greater. "Jeff rushes in and half the time he doesn't know just where he is going to land and that is meat for this big colored boy. I am afraid that Jeff is like the old pitcher that went to the well too often."

Jeffries wanted to test the ring floor boards to make sure they were solid. He said the boards were too loose and springy when he fought Fitzsimmons in San Francisco, and when he started after Bob; he sunk, whereas the lighter Fitz was able to move easily.[405]

The *Chronicle* said nine out of ten men in Reno were picking Jeffries to win. Regardless of who won, it opined that no fighter alive would have the right to challenge the winner, for he would have no rival.

Stanley Ketchel said that despite the fact that he would root for the white man, he was picking Johnson to win, not for personal reasons, but because that was his honest opinion.

> I consider Johnson one of the greatest fighters of the present time, and I ought to know what I am talking about, because I fought him. He is more than a wonderful defensive fighter as the critics have remarked. He has a punch that few people, and I am one of them, appreciate. He will win surely, and I am going to have a good bet down on him. ... Johnson is an underrated man and he will surprise the people. ... Johnson is a wonderful blocker, the best in the world. I don't believe that Jeff will be able to land a hard punch on him. I consider that I am a faster man than Jeffries and I know that it was practically impossible for me to land. In our fight at Colma Johnson landed at will and there was nothing that I could do to stop him. ... Don't believe those people who try to tell you that Johnson can't land a hard blow. He can hit and I know it. He knocked some of my teeth out for me in California, and I was so stunned by the force of the punch that it was some little time before I could begin to understand things. Now, I am a middleweight, but, all the same, I can stand a punch as well as the next man.

---

[405] *San Francisco Examiner,* July 1, 1910.

TOMMY BURNS (AT LEFT) GREETING STANLEY KETCHEL AT RENO.

Ketchel also said, "Jeffries will be disappointed and sad at heart when he finds that he cannot land. I think, too, that his long absence from the ring will operate against him." Stan figured the fight would last a long time, owing to the fact that Johnson was a cautious fighter. "Big, game man that he is, Jeffries will stand as long as he is able to stand, and when he does collapse it will be simply because he can't stand up any longer under the strain."[406]

Jack London also thought it would be a long fight. Both men liked to wear out their opponents gradually and rely on the cumulative effect of their blows. Jeff was more of a puncher, but often took some rounds to warm up and get going. Since it essentially was a fight to the finish, neither was likely to take great chances of being reckless or wearing himself out too soon. So they would feel each other out for a while. He opined that Jeff would suffer early punishment, for "the man never lived who could prevent Johnson landing on him." Jeff was willing to take three to land one, believing he had the superior ability to assimilate punishment and administer telling blows. Jeff always was fast, but might not seem quite as fast owing to the fact that Johnson was phenomenally quick and clever. However, Jeff's own cleverness would be a surprise to those who had never before seen him in action. Nevertheless, it was likely that Johnson would nail him with his sneaky right uppercut. Johnson also would better measure time and distance. London wondered who would loaf in the clinches. Johnson often did. Jeff might try to use his superior weight to wear him out, but if he crouched, Johnson might lean on him. The other question was whether Jeff could hit him, as powerful as he was. Johnson was noted for eluding, moving away, blocking, and entangling a man's arms. It was unclear whether such tactics would work against a man who was bigger and thought to be stronger.

Some said that Jeff seemed grouchy, just as he was in the old days right before a fight.

---

[406] *San Francisco Chronicle*, July 2, 1910.

De Witt Van Court, who had known Jeff from the start of his career, said Jeffries was better than ever. He did not expect Jeff to have a great deal of trouble with Johnson. He thought Corbett was three times as clever as Johnson, though not as strong. He classed Johnson with Ruhlin, and said Jeff would humble the black man the same way. "Those stomach punches of the big fellow will fix Johnson."[407]

Sam Langford said, "I hope Jeff breaks Johnson's jaw in the first punch. I think Jeff will win the fight inside of 15 rounds if he is in shape. ... Johnson is pretty clever but can't hit hard enough to knock Jeff out." Another newspaper quoted Langford, speaking about Jeffries, as saying,

> Goodness Lordy! Ah never believed dat any man could look so powerful strong. He looks big enough to eat up de whole black race. Ah'll fight Johnson any morning before breakfast, but Ah'd rather step in de 'lectric chair than stand up before dis terrible being. All Ah can say is dat Johnson had better look very carefully over his insurance policy befo' he gets into do ring on Monday afternoon.

Burns said Johnson was a good boxer but not much of a fighter. It would take more than boxing to defeat Jeff. He admitted that Jack had a hard right, but said the left was not as useful. "I know Johnson's limit. He is certainly a clever fighter, but I don't think he has the heart to withstand the tremendous force of Jeff's blows."

Corbett said Jeff was better than ever, and one blow from the giant would do more harm than all of Johnson's punches. This time, Johnson was not going up against a smaller and weaker man, but just the opposite. Jim anticipated a hard fight, but said Jeff would win hands down.

Corbett said that Johnson's supporters, friends, and backers did not have the confidence in Johnson that they professed. They would not place wagers at even money, instead demanding odds before they would bet on Johnson. The odds still had Jeff as the strong 10 to 7 favorite, meaning that not enough folks were wagering sufficiently on Johnson to shift the odds in any meaningful way. Most of those who had seen Jeff in training thought he would win. Johnson remained the underdog.

From Louisville, Marvin Hart said he hoped Jeffries would win, but in his heart, he thought Johnson would have it on him. "Jeffries has loafed too much." He might look good on the outside, but on the inside he was no longer the same. He thought the fight would last 15 to 20 rounds.

The *Call* said the fight had been sized up from every angle, working up the fans' interest to a fever pitch, and still many remained undecided regarding what the bout's outcome would be.

Abe Attell was utterly surprised by how good Jeff looked. He originally thought Johnson should be a heavy favorite, but, "Now I think there is nothing to it but Jeff."

---

[407] *San Francisco Chronicle*, July 1, 1910.

Hugh McIntosh was surprised by Jeff's shape, but still liked Johnson to win. "He would prefer to see it rest with the white race, but he can not forget the way in which Johnson won the championship from Tommy Burns a year and a half ago." Jack had youth and cleverness combined. "I am putting my money in the dark column."

The highly respected Young Peter Jackson, who had fought Johnson, said Jack would wear Jeffries down before landing a knockout blow.

> I believe that Jack Johnson is the cleverest fighter that ever donned the gloves. I fully expect to see him beat Jeffries and make a good job of it. Jack is a remarkable boxer. I have yet to see the man that can compare with him in that line. Jeff is going to have a hard time hitting Jack, and it's safe to say that Jack is going to cut him up some. ... I think it is highly possible that the fight will not be aggressive on either side. It's a cinch that Johnson will make his end of it defensive.

He thought the battle would be lengthy, lasting 25 to 30 rounds.

Famous sportswriter Robert Edgren picked Jeffries. He had seen Jeff work for the past month and simply could not picture him on the floor. Jeff had great strength, which was even greater than his size, and he had proven toughness, never having lost or even been down in a boxing match.

Jeff told Edgren that his critics were fools who didn't know a damn thing about training. He had given up a year of his life to prepare for the bout. "I'll make fools of them all. I must win this fight; I shall win it." Jeffries also said, "I may take a devil of a licking, but I will get him."

On July 1, Johnson ran 6 or 8 miles (depending on the source), sprinting the last 200 yards. He stepped on the scale at 209 pounds. Jack laughed at predictions that said he would be lucky to last 6 rounds. "That's what they all say." The champ felt great. He was through with work and would rest.

> Many a time when I was training for my early fights I didn't have any attention at all, and sometimes I didn't have any too much to eat, but I pulled through. Later I was matched with so many fighters who were so far inferior to me that I didn't have to train, and I have gone into the ring weighing as high as 220 pounds and won.

Because Jeffries had been a champion, and was the bigger and heavier man, Johnson had taken him seriously.[408]

The *Freeman* said the big bear Jeff was gruff and grum. His camp was quiet and solemn, like a funeral. "Jeffries has the white man's burden. ... Will it help Jeffries, this terrible responsibility?" Another *Freeman* writer noted the immense pressure upon the ex-champ. "Jeffries knows that he is the Atlas of the white race in fistic matters. The white man's terrible responsibility is on him and he is leaving nothing undone to give a satisfactory report of himself."

---

[408] *Reno Evening Gazette*, July 1, 1910; *San Francisco Call, Nevada State Journal, San Francisco Examiner*, July 2, 1910. On the 1st, Jeff ran 5 miles.

Johnson's camp was more like a picnic. Jack had no ill humor, talking and kidding with his sparring partners, despite the fact that some said he looked slow and sloth-like. However, Johnson showed his speed when he felt like it. For recreation, he would shoot craps and play roulette.

The Governor assured Johnson that if he was good enough to whip Jeffries that no race prejudice or outside influence would be permitted to wrest the decision from him. Johnson said, "I'll go to sleep on that, Mr. Governor. I'll trust to the square men of Nevada and the others around the ring to see that I won't get none of the worst of it from anybody but the man I'm fighting, and I'll attend to that part of it myself."

Jack Johnson at the roulette table. Jack has been playing them pretty high up in the sagebrush State, and has been having about an even break with Dame Fortune.

The *Freeman* noted that John L. Sullivan had gotten himself in bad with certain folks when he gave out a very favorable report about Johnson. Honesty didn't always pay.

The *Freeman* said the nation's birthday would see the two best specimens of mankind contend for the biggest prize in sport. Its writer thought Johnson would not rush the fight, but would box on the defensive, outgeneral Jeff, take his wind, and eventually Jeffries would "collapse like a punctured dirigible." Jeffries had the pile-driving blows, and if he could land, he would put Johnson to sleep in a hurry. However, if he was not able to land, "he would be but an elephant versus a tiger."

Ultimately the *Freeman* opined that given that youth and endurance were in Johnson's favor owing to the laws of nature and Johnson's uninterrupted activity, Jeffries needed to try to blast Johnson out quickly or he probably would not be able to do it at all.

Yet another *Freeman* writer said the entire civilized world was interested in the outcome, owing to the fact that was promoted as a race supremacy battle and the last big contest the generation would ever see. Fearing harm to blacks, it cautioned,

> This is by no means a race supremacy battle. It is a battle for thousands of dollars. The race question was raised by sporting editors throughout the world on Jeffries as the bull fighters would raise the red flag to enrage the bull. And it had its effect on Jeffries. It is well that the colored man does not take this race question too seriously. … This race question will get many a man in trouble on the Fourth of July if he carries it too far.

This writer gave Choynski indirect credit for Johnson having become champion. By sending him into dreamland for a minute, when Johnson came to his senses he realized that he needed not only to hit the other fellow, but above all things, not to get hit.

No living man had gone through what Johnson had gone through to get to the highest point. "He has been accused of everything – yellow streak, quitter, four-flusher, trickster and all kinds of denouncements." He had to whip all of the top colored fighters before the whites would face him. Even after doing so, many still drew the color line on him, or he had to suffer a raw decision against Hart. "All this went to make him what he is today. His record will show that he has defeated more men than any heavyweight champion has ever defeated; traveled the world over to do it."

Johnson's method was compared with "Isaac Murphy, the race horse rider, who made all of his finishes close. The same with Jack Johnson, no matter what class of fighter he fought he would slow along with his man. He has never been classed a slugger; for if he had been so classed he would not have got the chance he has today."

Johnson was meeting the greatest man he had ever faced, who could hit twice as hard as any and could stand double the punishment. Jeff was a whale. However, this writer predicted a reproduction of Corbett-Sullivan.

> Sullivan was kind enough to tell the world what caused his defeat. Too old and too long between fights; the game had gone back on him. Had Jim Jeffries read John L. Sullivan's ring record carefully, he would never have returned to the ring to fight a man like Johnson. …
> Jeffries will last as long against Johnson as his vitality will allow him.

Johnson would study Jeff for a while, and the fight would be rough for 5 or 6 rounds, and the crowd would encourage Jeff, but they could not fight for him. "Johnson won't care how much noise they make; he is used to that – in fact, all colored fighters are. After this grand rally of Jeffries, Johnson will set about slowly putting things to an end. … All this talk about Jeffries putting Johnson away with one punch is silly talk and bad noise."

Before Johnson had left Oakland, he told a crowd of 500 blacks, "I want to advise every one of you to bet on me, but not to bet on the duration of the fight. Don't bother about the number of rounds, just get your money down that I will bring home the bacon and then sit back and wait until the time comes to cash in."

Veteran trainer Mike Murphy had seen Jeffries. He came as a skeptic, but had been convinced that Jeff was perfect.

> If Johnson had seen some of the bull rushes Jeffries made while shadow boxing he might not be so confident that he will stop the hope of the white race within seventeen rounds. They were simply terrifying and the speed and power with which he hurled himself across the ring like a 13-inch shell caused the women spectators to shriek with fright.

Upon seeing the fight grounds, Jeff said, "It was on this very spot that I gave away my title exactly five years ago, and now I have come to get it back."[409]

The *Chicago Defender* wrote, "Think, in 1776 the colored man fought the British to give the American his freedom and today (1910), which should be a nation's fight, the colored man is forced to fight Jim Crow delegations, race prejudice and American public insane sentiment. If he wins in the face of all this, he is truly entitled to a Carnegie Hero Medal." For security purposes, 500 detectives would be in the arena and around the ring. This writer opined that $2.5 million dollars had been wagered on the fight.

The *Defender* believed that Johnson had been able to fight for the championship by carrying fighters and not knocking them out. Peter Jackson had been too brilliant, and by showing his true form he had robbed himself of the opportunity to be champion. Champions did not want to fight tough propositions. Johnson never was forced to extend himself, and showed rare business tact by not giving it his all.

> Had he shown his true form the laurels of champion would never have rested on his sable brow. … Knowing that his color would be a barrier to him in reaching the coveted goal of his ambition, if he performed too brilliantly, hence he fought his battles systematically.
>
> Johnson, being a past master of feints and guards, his exceptional cleverness, great speed and almost impenetrable defense, enabled him to wage battle the full limit of scheduled rounds, winning by a narrow margin, whereas a quick victory over his opponents would have put his future interests in jeopardy. Hence the public was misled as to his real form.

His long quest for the championship showed unparalleled pluck, patience, and perseverance, for no one had to work harder or longer to obtain a title shot.

Johnson was a real champion, and would show his true form against Jeffries in the biggest fight of his life. "When the smoke of the battle clears away, so to speak, and when the din of mingled cheers and groans have died away in the atmosphere, there will be deep mourning throughout the domains of Uncle Sam over Jeffries' inability to return the pugilistic scepter to the Caucasian race."[410]

Responding to those critics who said he did not spar enough, Jeffries told the *Examiner* that he never sparred all that much for his fights. He didn't box for a week before he fought Corbett the last time, but still won in brilliant fashion. "I believe I am in condition to make good. … I feel in my

---

[409] *Freeman*, July 2, 1910.
[410] *Chicago Defender*, July 2, 1910. Johnson had a brother named Henry Johnson. He also had a foster brother named Charles Hurley, who was an orphan boy that Mrs. Johnson raised from one and a half years old. They soon would live together in Chicago at the Johnson home on 3344 Wabash avenue.

heart that I am as good as I ever was in my life." Jeff was resting and preserving his vitality at this point, given that the fight was close, and he did not want to overwork so close to the fight. That way, he would not leave his fight in the gym. He was not going to train or spar just to satisfy those who wanted to see him work. He had been training for nearly a year and a half, and knew what he could do. He always had trained faithfully and well for his fights, and successfully. "I would like to say that I am in as good condition as ever in my life, and I judge this by my own feelings." Jeff felt that he had arrived at the nearest point of physical perfection possible. "As I sit here this minute I feel in my heart that I am as good as I ever was in my life. ... I know now that I am going to be able to deliver the goods; that I am going to be able to show the public that its faith in me has not been misplaced."

Jeff said he still had not decided on his plan of battle. He might rush, and he might not. He could do either, depending on what he saw from Johnson. If Johnson was careful, it might be foolish to be wild.

W. W. Naughton said Jeff had a jolly demeanor, and was playing practical jokes on his training camp mates. Fears that worry had marked the big fellow were unwarranted. Jeff was laughing, joking, and in good humor. He planned to wear some tape and bandages on his hands, owing to the fact that he had injured his hand early on in his training.

Allegedly, John L. Sullivan again said Jeff should have sparred more. Although John L. never placed a great deal of stress on sparring, this was "probably because boxing came more naturally to me than it does to Jeff."

Another *Examiner* writer, scouting the bout, said, "Johnson is big; Jeffries massive. I should say that Johnson is the quicker, Jeffries the stronger of the two. When I watched Johnson box, I couldn't see how any man could hit him. When I watched Jeffries box, I couldn't see how any man who stood in front of him could keep from being hit." Jeff probably was about 225 pounds. He was not a fast rusher like Sullivan, but more deliberate in his methods.

The betting odds varied, depending on the locale. Throughout the U.S., the odds were 10 to 7, with Jeffries the favorite. In London, England, the fight was at even money. However, one said Johnson was the slight favorite amongst British bettors. In Australia, Johnson was a slight favorite.

Famous sportswriter Tad Dorgan said the Jeffries men outnumbered the Johnson men three to one, but both sides had strong arguments. Johnson would be up against the roar of the crowd, the hardest hitter he ever met, a bigger man than he had been fighting, and a man who was in much better condition than Johnson realized. Jeff's supporters said he was one in a million. One noted that after Hank Griffin hit Johnson on the jaw, Jack played it safe. Jeff stopped Griffin in his first pro fight and dropped him several times in their 4-round exhibition.

Johnson supporters said no man could come back after six years. Some thought that losing all that weight, about 75 pounds, would sap Jeff's strength. Others said Jeff made his reputation on older fighters. Of course, he beat young men too. However, Johnson was the best boxer Jeff had ever met, was just as strong, and about as tall. He did not weigh much less. Jeff essentially was forced into the match, and never really wanted it.[411]

A *Chronicle* writer agreed that Jeff should have boxed longer and more often than he did, particularly in light of the fact that he had not fought in years. Except for Fitzsimmons, who was a rare exception and thought to be a freak of nature, long layoffs in one's 30s never helped. This writer also believed that a man who had not fought in years could not take punishment the same way that a boxer who had been active and regularly fighting could. Given that Johnson was much cleverer than Jeffries, likely Jeff would have to absorb punishment in order to land his big blows.

Another *Chronicle* writer who had observed Johnson said his muscles were as flexible as rubber and his movements quick and wonderfully lithe. His breathing was good. He was smiling, relaxed, and confident.

There was a rumor that Langford might box Jeff on July 2, but given what Jeff had said about being done with his training, it sounded false.

Famous writer Jack London said that the equals of Johnson and Jeffries would not meet again in a generation. Viewed from every possible angle, there never had been anything like this fight in the history of the ring, nor was there likely to be anything like it for the duration of the lives of those alive to see it. It truly was the fight of the century.

No comparable giants had ever met. "Johnson is a dusky wonder. For his size there has never been so clever a defensive boxer. Nor has there ever been a cooler-headed boxer. … So cool is he that his fighting at times seems lackadaisical." Johnson had sudden fierce moments, but he was not a killer by nature. Jack had great instincts. He could be looking away and talking to someone at ringside and still block, roll his head, or pull back just enough to make punches miss, all the while continuing his conversation. "A wonderful fighter, indeed, is Johnson, utterly unlike any other fighter, a type by himself."

Jeffries also was remarkable, huge, rugged, symmetrical, a man from the days when the world was young and humans were monstrously strong, but also with the skill and science of modern man. Johnson was a fighting boxer, Jeffries the boxing fighter. Both were cool and experienced. "It is the fight of fights, the crowning fight of the whole ring, and perhaps the last great fight that will ever be held."

Ten miles of film would be taken just of the preliminary incidents, which would cost around $25,000. The moving pictures likely would generate more money than the purse or the house. Vitagraph Company President William T. Rock was in charge. Ten cameras would be at ringside. At least three machines would be running at one time. Each camera would take an average of 200 feet per round. As soon as the fight was over, the negatives would be rushed to Chicago and New York for development and the first

---

[411] *San Francisco Examiner*, July 2, 1910.

show would be held a week later. About 400 - 500 sets of films would be scattered around the U.S., the greatest fight film distribution ever.[412]

The *Bulletin's* writer opined that Jeff appeared to have the better chance of winning, likely after about 12 to 14 rounds. He would struggle and have to take punishment to land the knockout blow, but eventually he would do it. That said, this writer also believed that they were so evenly matched that no result would be surprising, except a quick victory for Johnson.

Another *Bulletin* writer said, "Jeffries should win this fight." He was stronger. He had the better punch, "and as for courage, he lays over the darkey like wool over a sheep. These little advantages, combined with race psychic reasons, give him an edge that makes the 10 to 6 price figure about right." This writer also believed Jeff's defense was a lot better than folks realized, for he had good head-movement. "Personally, I believe that Jeff, with all his natural speed and agility, will make a positive fool out of Johnson."

Fitzsimmons, Choynski, and Munroe, who had fought both, favored Jeffries. Bob thought Jeff would win quickly. Choynski said, "I met both men early in their career at a time when I could hold my own with any of the heavies. Jeff was by far the better man." Munroe said Jeff's punching power would prove too much for Johnson.[413]

Bill Delaney never thought Jeffries would fight Johnson.

> When Jeffries was fighting and at his best Johnson used to follow him about the country and hurl challenges at him. Jeffries refused to meet him on the ground that he was black. The fact that he had already fought colored men like Bob Armstrong, Peter Jackson and Hank Griffin cut no ice: Jeffries turned Johnson down cold. Why? Because he was afraid of him.

Of course, Jeff argued that he did not want to give a black man a chance to win the championship. Back then, Delaney was as insistent or more so that Jeff would not cross the color line as champ; that he would not allow it.

Delaney said of Johnson and the upcoming fight,

> [T]he sporting world does not know how good a fighter he really is. In my mind he has been fighting under wraps. The public has not really seen him extended in recent years. Fighters of the type of Ketchel, Burns and Flynn could not push him hard enough to get up a sweat. ... Of recent times he has done all that has been asked of him, and no competent judge of a pugilist will deny that he is not a vastly improved mechanic. While I am singing Johnson's praises I will be fair and give Jeffries the credit of being the greatest heavyweight of his time. ... After the gong rang and the seconds left the ring and the gloves were raised to parry and punch he feared no man born of

---

[412] *San Francisco Chronicle*, July 2, 1910.
[413] *San Francisco Bulletin*, July 2, 1910.

woman. Before the gong no fighter suffered more from stage fright; but I am talking about Jeffries as I knew him six years ago. ...

Six years is a long time to be out of the ring. Jeffries likes the good things life affords, and he has indulged himself to some degree. ... Johnson has kept his eye clear, his foot quick and his muscles pliant by frequent appearances in the ring, and for six years Jeffries was rusting. It stands to reason that he has slowed up in consequence of his inactivity. ... I understand that Jeffries has trained conscientiously and arduously for this affair. Friends who have visited him were surprised at his condition, which shows that he has worked hard. ... There is no pleasure in beating a man who is out of shape. You get no credit for winning. Hence it pleases me to know that Jeffries can have no excuses when he is defeated, which he will be. ...

Gymnasium work never reveals how much a fighter has left. I have seen fighters set a gymnasium on fire in training and blow up in a couple of rounds in a fight. Fighters themselves don't know how good they are until they have boxed a few rounds in the ring. And this is why we are not going to make any plans until we have gone a few rounds with Mr. Jeffries and seen how much he has left in him.

It has been stated in the press, and I have heard experts who have seen Johnson perform, say that Johnson was a coward. In reply to this attack upon his courage, please name me a fighter, white or black, that he has ever refused to fight. As I have already mentioned, when Jeffries was in his prime Johnson was dogging his footsteps with challenges. Cowards never taunted Jeffries. Johnson loves to fight, and he was never known to go hunting for easy game. Ten times more fighters ran away from Johnson then he ever sidestepped. Furthermore, Johnson is an improved fighter, if ever there was one. He will face Jeffries weighing about 208 pounds – probably the largest good man Jeffries ever met. ... Another point they attempt to make against Johnson is that he can't punch – can't deliver a knockout. They said that about Corbett, who was a greatly underrated fighter. Jim Corbett could hit, and Jim Jeffries will find that Jack Johnson can hit before he is through with him. ... Jack is the sort of fighter who can travel a long distance before tiring. Fighting he makes easy. He wastes fewer punches than Corbett would if he were fighting. In my long connection with the ring I have seen few fighters who knew more about fighting than Johnson. He has lots of brains. Should Jeffries crowd him – have him in distress – Johnson will beat a retreat, as any fighter should, until he can recover. It is only the brainless kind that rush in after being stunned.

The betting odds do not startle me. I looked for Jeffries to be the favorite. There are four or five reasons for it. Johnson's undeserved reputation of being a coward, also his reputation of being a weak hitter, and Jeffries a hard one, his color and the suspicion that if there is anything doing in the crooked way Jack would be the one to lay down, all these have contributed to make Jeffries a red-hot favorite. But that does not fease me. Sullivan was a 4 to 1 favorite when Corbett beat him; Corbett was a 2 to 1 favorite when Fitzsimmons downed him. ... In regard to the fight being 'shady,' there is no reason to have any fear. If I even suspected a crooked angle I would never have consented to go behind Johnson.[414]

Johnson said the talk of his having a yellow streak made him laugh. He said it was Jeffries who could not stand the gaff.

I don't think Jeffries can come back; and, even if he is in the same condition that he was when he defeated Fitzsimmons, Corbett, Sharkey and the rest of the heavyweights, I feel in my own heart that I am his master. I'm just as strong as he is, am faster, cleverer and can hit just as hard as he can. ...

I am glad that all of the critics pronounce him to be in the best shape of his entire career, for then I'll get the full credit for licking him. ....

With my superior science, I can't see how Jeff can stand up under the punishment. That talk of 'yellow streak' in my make-up is a joke. Nobody ever saw me show it, did they? Well, I'm just as game as he is and I'll hit him fifty times where he will hit me once. It's only a question of how long Jeff can stand the gaff. It may be a few rounds, and it may be forty, but I'll be on my feet at the wind-up. I am trained to the hour and could fight all afternoon, if necessary.

Jeffries too was sure of victory:

I never was in better shape and I never was more confident of winning a battle. I can't tell how long it will take me to defeat Johnson, as he is a clever, shifty boxer, but in my present condition I know that I shall get him before the limit. ...

While I have been criticized a great deal for not boxing more, I couldn't have got into any better shape than I am if I had boxed a hundred rounds every day. I never did much boxing in the training quarters for any of my battles ...

The American public can rest assured that I realize the responsibility that rests on my shoulders in this battle, and I shall fight just as hard to win the championship as I did to get in perfect trim for the encounter.

T. P. Magilligan said Johnson was good-natured and enjoyed joking and kidding his opponents. He loved to be flashy and relished the limelight. He relied on skill more than mixing it up. No one doubted that he could now

---

[414] *San Francisco Bulletin*, July 2, 1910.

decisively defeat all those who once had beaten him – Choynski, Klondike (avenged), Jeannette (on a dq which was avenged), and Hart. He used to say, "Jeffries can't touch me." Most writers believed that Johnson held back in his fights. His defense was almost impregnable, as hard to crack as a burglar trying to crack a safe with a bologna sausage. Although some criticized his power, he managed to badly puff up and cut up most of his opponents, and he knocked out Ketchel's teeth. Most were hurt and decked along the way to decision losses. His style was unique in that he would stall along seemingly unconcerned, and then all of a sudden there was life and animation as he landed wounding blows.

This writer felt that Johnson never was given full credit for his ability, because in many fights he had his hands tied by stipulation. "No one knows exactly how good Johnson is. He has never been extended anywhere near the limit of his capacity. He beat all his men of late years with such apparent ease that even the veriest novice might see he was holding back." This time Johnson would not hold back. Rumors of a fix were false, for over 100 reporters were on the scene and not one of them could produce any evidence of such.[415]

William Slattery said many picked against Johnson because of race and personal prejudice. "He is not a popular fighter, even with those of his own blood. Many of them bet against him because of their hatred for him." However, when picking a fight, one had to use cool, calculating judgment and overlook "caste hatred." Also, when making a selection, neither a fighter's own words, nor his trainers', were convincing, because they had their pride and loyalty and were not going to be objective.

Many Southern white citizens had dire apprehensions, intensely fearing the social result of a Johnson victory. Many black folk believed that the bout would settle the status of the races.

The negro population of the south is intensely interested in the outcome of the great battle, believing that the fight will determine the social position of the black man in the society of the nation.

It is the contention in the south that if Johnson wins at Reno white ladies will be crowded off the sidewalks and insulted generally.

---

[415] *San Francisco Evening Post*, July 2, 4, 1910.

Southern congressmen...see many dire evils in the defeat of the white man by the black.

"Dangerous exultation" is the term used by those who deplore the effect of the fight.

Negro government clerks are said to be nervous and excited as they expect their race to be greatly exalted in a social way by the fight.[416]

Black churches would be praying for a Johnson victory. About a thousand "dusky sports" were expected to be on hand at the fight, and most of them were betting their money on Johnson.

Public interest in the fight was so tremendous, one writer called it ravenous. Newspapers throughout the nation were devoting an enormous amount of space to the fight on a daily basis, having sent their best men to cover the training preparations and the fight.[417]

One writer who gave Johnson the edge said Jeff's stamina and ability to wear down opponents would not be the same as when he was young.

Of Johnson, it can be said that he is an underrated fighter as far as the outside world goes. Prejudice against the colored race has had much to do with this, while the undue caution exhibited by the champion in all of his matches is another thing that has told heavily against him. The fight fan likes an aggressive, rushing fighter, and therefore is inclined to belittle the Texan.

Denver Ed Smith, a black fighter, picked Jeffries as a sure winner. The sporting editor for the *New York World* picked Jeff. W. F. Corbett, editor of the *Referee*, picked Johnson. He said Johnson was fit, had a hard punch, and was a clever boxer, while Jeff appeared to be overtrained and a little stale. Tiv Kreling picked Jeff. Joe Woodman said Johnson was a dog and Jeff would bring it out within 15 rounds. Tad of the *New York Journal* said he thought Johnson would win. Former Johnson foe Denver Ed Martin said, "There will be one 'white' colored man in the ring next Monday afternoon." He liked Jeff. Bob Edgren of the *New York World* also picked Jeff.

Johnson would face a hostile audience. It was safe to predict that fully 90% of the spectators would be rooting for a Jeffries victory, regardless of whom they had wagered upon. However, Johnson was used to facing a hostile audience. "If the truth must be told, Johnson is the least popular of colored champions in the last quarter of a century." Men like Joe Gans, Peter Jackson, and George Dixon were all very popular with fans, "but for some reason Johnson has never been a favorite."

Jack Johnson said,

I feel satisfied that I am in better condition now than I ever was in my life before. I pride myself upon being an expert on condition, and

[416] *Nevada State Journal*, July 3, 1910.
[417] *San Francisco Chronicle*, July 3, 1910.

I have with me one of the greatest trainers who ever lived – Tom Flanagan. ... So far as Mr. Jeffries is concerned, I have nothing to say, only that I believe that I am his master.

Another quoted him as saying,

I have everything in my favor. I have never been out of training for long, I have taken care of myself, and I have the advantage of being the better boxer. ... I have been panned to a certain extent for not being aggressive. But I use my head, and I have never taken unnecessary chances. I believe this to be the best part of ring generalship. I know that I can land a knockout, and you will be surprised when you see it.

He further explained his style:

They talk about my being slack in the ring. They have long yarns about Jack Johnson not being aggressive. Well, young feller, I want to say any time I feel like it was time to loosen up I loosen so quick it makes their heads swim. I am glad to have a chance to state for publication that what they call my lack of aggressiveness is not due to any desire to prolong the agony; it is simply that I know when I have my man going and it would be absurd to take chances of a lucky swing that might put me down.

Johnson had been looking forward to this fight for over six years. Jeff had said that Jack was the softest mark he ever heard of, yet Jack noted that Jeff had been training harder for him than ever before for anyone else.

Jack said the only thing wrong with him was that he still had a cut lip from a head butt from Cotton. "Oh, yes, I'm strong as a bull. Jeffries won't rough me much. I know that he will have some weight on me, but if he can push me around that ring he's going to surprise me a lot."

When Sullivan asked Johnson how he felt, the champ responded, "Captain John, I never felt better in my life. If I felt any better I would be afraid of myself." When asked if he was just a bit anxious, Johnson said he actually was more nervous before the Burns fight.

On July 2, Johnson said he was just loafing around his camp until the fight. One report said he ran about 8 miles. Other than that, Jack mainly was just shooting dice, playing craps, and horsing around. He said he would not drink any liquids on the 3rd and would allow his weight to drop to 208 pounds by the drying-out process. He was happy with his weight, for it did no good to put on a bunch of meaningless pounds. He was all hard muscle.

Johnson was not bothered by the odds, which had him as the underdog.

I am not at all surprised at the big odds which are being bet on Mr. Jeffries. I expected that he would be favorite when the public had been led to believe that he is as good as he was when he retired from the ring. They think so now, and as most of the folks who will attend the battle and wager their money on the result are white, it is only natural that they should select Jeffries to carry their money. It makes it nice for my friends because they are getting good odds for their money. … How the man who makes the odds figures I don't know and I don't care. It is a funny price to lay against a man who has defeated everybody who stood between him and the championship of the world, and especially when he is going against a fighter who has been out of the ring for five years, and who may or may not have 'come back,' as they call it.

One writer noted Johnson's supreme confidence. Jack was not concerned by all the stories that Jeff looked great in training. Johnson had once told the writer, "I could take any rattle-trap of an automobile and with some paint, grease and varnish make it look like new. If I tried to start on a journey with it, though, it would fall to pieces." This idea seemed to be deeply embedded in Johnson's mind.

All of Johnson's camp mates said he would win. Jack Geyer said Johnson was the finest boxer ever. George Cotton said he was the hardest hitter he ever ran up against, as well as the hardest to hit. Jack had the heart and the confidence. Dave Mills said Johnson was fast on his feet, clever with his hands, and had a knockout punch in either mitt. "I think the fifteenth round will see the finish." Walter Monahan said he was lighter and faster on his feet than Johnson, but could not begin to get away from him. Johnson would hit Jeff at will and elude counters. He said Johnson would end the fight between the 10th and 20th rounds. Sig Hart said, "Of course Johnson is going to win. I do not make a habit of going behind losers. … Johnson has the punch, he has the stamina, and he has the cleverness."

Al Kaufman said Johnson was cleverer than ever and had a kick in either hand. Johnson was in perfect condition, and it was nearly impossible to land on him. Jack was very strong in the clinches, and could grasp an opponent and swing or throw him about as he pleased. Kaufman was a big strong man, but admitted to getting the worst of the short-arm work. Johnson's way of throwing a man around on the inside was wearing, and Johnson could keep it up for a long time. If Jeffries tired he was in for trouble. Despite the size difference, Jeff would find Johnson to be abnormally strong. Folks did not realize how strong and powerful Johnson was because he was not aggressive, and liked to play a waiting game and take no chances. "But Johnson has a punch and aggressiveness when he likes to let them go." Al said Johnson's short jolts were no love taps, and even when he appeared to be loafing, he actually was just relaxed, thinking, playing defense, and setting up his opponents for a good blow.

Johnson trainer/manager Tom Flanagan opined that Johnson would win within 20 rounds. Jack was in perfect condition. "I have no fear of Jeffries sending a thrill of terror through the black man, as so many people imagine. I know that he is as game as a pebble and that he will put forth his greatest ring effort against the conqueror of Corbett, Sharkey and the balance of the old time champions."

Hugh McIntosh said Johnson was in even better condition than he was in Australia, and he had never seen a man more physically fit. Jack had the punch and the stamina.

Jack McAuliffe said the quicker thinker would win the fight, and he felt that was Johnson.

On July 2, Jeff said he was doing nothing and did not intend to do anything until the fight. He said the fight might be easy or hard, long or short, but he was prepared for anything. "I am going to keep faith with the public that has kept faith with me." Jeff was happy with his training staff, valuing their veteran skill and advice. He also said that shaking four- or five-hundred hands a day was a tough game. "I guess that Johnson and myself can claim the record of bringing together more celebrities of the sporting world than any two boxers ever drew before."

> I am fit and ready and in the best condition for any fight I have had on the Pacific Coast. I knew I was right a month ago and have been gradually working on edge until I feel better today than I ever have in my life. I don't care whether the fight goes four or forty-five rounds. I am in shape to go the route and I am confident of winning. I have worked long and hard for the chance to come to show that I can lick Johnson and I am going to take full advantage of it Monday. If I lose I will not have an excuse to offer.

Jeffries further said,

> I never would have signed for this match unless I felt absolutely certain that I could get back into condition. It took me a long time to make up my mind, because I was feeling myself out. Once I believed that I was fit, I consented to fight. Now I am ready. I feel that my condition is perfect and it has been perfect for the last month. ... I know that I can go 100 rounds under the blazing sun, so the longer the fight progresses the better it will be for me. I know that Johnson is a big, clever, wonderful, defensive fighter, but I know that I can and will beat him.

Jeff claimed that he once told Johnson that they could both go down into a cellar together and the man that came back up would be champion. Johnson said, "I ain't no cellar fighter." He wanted to fight in a ring before the public. Jeff took it as a sign of fear.

Speaking of why he had come back, Jeff said the whole world was begging and pleading with him to defend the white race's supremacy, feeling that he was the only man on earth who could beat Johnson. Bill Delaney had told him that no champion could remain out of the ring for more than two years and ever come back at his best. Jeff had gained weight and lost the champion's ambition. However, "the pressure became too great." He started working out to see if he felt that he could come back. In time, he felt good again and decided that he could regain his old form. Hence he signed for the fight. He felt that he had reserve strength that he had never needed to use in a fight, but he knew it would be there if he needed it.

All of Jeff's camp-mates picked him to win. Joe Choynski said Johnson would "find himself pitted against a man much faster, cleverer, and stronger than himself and he'll surprise me if he lasts longer than seven rounds." Joe said Jeff had marvelous strength. He was in the best possible shape and had trained properly and well, leaving no stone unturned. Jeff's judgment of distance and timing was right, and he would have no excuse if he lost. "I know I for one will be right on hand to wish the negro well if he accomplishes the unexpected by defeating our man."

Sam Berger called attention to the fact that Jeff had been working steadily for sixteen months. It would be a long, hard battle, with Jeff the aggressor throughout, crowding slowly and surely.

> I know absolutely that Jeffries is in condition. He is just as good as he ever was and unless he knew this he would never have made the match. The honor of being the retired, undefeated heavyweight champion of the world means more to Jeffries than millions of dollars. He has plenty of money and he does not have to fight unless he wants to. These arguments go to show that the great white fighter is on the level and on the square. He wants to bring the championship back to the white race and he is going to do it beyond the question of the slightest doubt.

Jack Jeffries said Jeff would make Johnson jump over the ropes before the fight had gone long. "Jim has had at least a half-dozen fights harder than this one, and he went into the ring nowhere near the condition he is now. Jeff will only have to hit the negro once and it will be all over."

Jim Corbett said both he and Jeffries were very confident. Jeff was "just as formidable a fighter today" as he was back when they fought. "He has the heart, the strength and the punch to beat Johnson." Jeff could land his terrible punch early or late, it did not matter. "Johnson is a big, clever fellow and one of the greatest defensive fighters who ever stepped into a ring, but he lacks the heart and the courage and Jeffries will surely beat him down."

Bob Armstrong, who had fought Jeff and sparred with Johnson, said if Johnson fought he would be finished quickly, and if he ran away it would be a slow death for Jack. As soon as Jeff hit Johnson the fight would be over in short order. However, it did not matter in what round that punch came. Bob was going to bet on Jeff. He believed Johnson would be scared.

Tommy Burns did not believe Jeff was as good as he was a few years ago, but did not think he had to be. He said Johnson was not a hard hitter, and Jeff had never been hurt, so he just did not see how Johnson could stop him. Burns said he was a pigmy next to Jeff. Johnson would not have the size advantage against Jeff that he had against him. "Take it from me, Jeff will rush that big 'coon' off his feet. Why, every time they go to a clinch he'll take some sap out of Jack and it will not be many rounds before the spectators will see Johnson wilt before Jeff's furious onslaughts."

Burns said Johnson did not like to take a beating. Tom claimed that his body punches had cracked Johnson's ribs and caved them in, that Jack had spent time in the hospital after their fight. "He cannot stand up to Jeffries' punches. Jeffries will drive right through him." He said if Jeff's left hook hit the body, Johnson would be down squirming on the mat.

Sam Langford said, "I know that the champion has no punch and that he does not like to take a beating. Jeffries is too big a man and he will simply win as he likes."

Burns and Langford met, and they appeared to be about the same height and weight. Each was surprised by the other's small stature.

Jack Root said Jeff looked great. "Remember Jeffries beat the best at a time when there were more good heavyweight fighters than there are right now."

Bill Lang said Jeff was a bigger and stronger man than Johnson.

Tom Sharkey said Jeffries would win. "Johnson trained me for a couple of fights. He is a classy boxer, but he hasn't the steam."

Jack London believed that Jeff had come back. "A trifle of prophecy, if the fight goes any decent distance, bent and dented ribs for Johnson, if not broken ones."

Fight announcer Billy Jordan, famous for his call of "Let 'er go," anticipated that Jeffries would win in about 15 rounds. "He is going out to bring the championship back to the white race, where it belongs." Still, he realized that Jeff had his work cut out for him to beat the "speedy negro."

Odds were at 10 to 6 ½, with Jeff holding as the strong favorite. It was even money that the fight would go 20 rounds.

Some thought Jeff would tear right in, while others said he would take his time and methodically break him down. Jeffries was noncommittal regarding his tactics.

Sportswriter C. E. Van Loan said Jeff had the best of it on form. Johnson had never whipped anyone of true championship class, and Jeffries would be an entirely new experience for him. Jeff had the superior record. However, Johnson supporters said he always was under a pull, but would not hold back against Jeff.

Stakeholder Tim Sullivan was holding the $101,000. It was reported that George Little would earn $30,100 from the fight.

On the evening of July 2, some folks were being loud outside the Jeffries camp, disturbing his sleep. When it happened a second time that night, they believed it might have been done intentionally by those wagering on Johnson. So it was decided that a guard would be posted outside to ensure that Jeff's sleep was not disturbed.

Jeff had sent for water from Germany to be used for the fight. His wife was watching over it.

A *Call* writer said the 10 to 6 odds were ridiculous in light of Johnson's remarkable showings in his recent battles, "and they have been made ridiculous because of the prejudice against Johnson on account of his color. He is not a popular fighter, even with those of his own blood." This writer thought Jeff should only be a slight favorite, or perhaps it was an even-money fight. For whatever reason, the public was overwhelmingly betting on Jeff, and few offsetting wagers were being placed on Johnson.

Picking a winner was very difficult. The two were total opposites. Jeff was serious and more focused on offense, not minding a punch here and there. Johnson was playful and took it all lightly, but focused more on defense and landing the occasional punch. "The fact is, they don't know how good Johnson really is and they don't know either whether Jeffries has even started to come back." This writer said Johnson was a far better fighter than his fights showed.

Burns and Johnson met. Tom said he wanted a rematch. Jack said he could have one if he obtained sufficient financial backing.

Burns said Johnson took the scales for him on July 2 and weighed 206 pounds.

Johnson said Burns could beat Langford, and if the match was made, Jack would bet on Tom. Since he had fought both, Jack was in a position to judge.

Johnson didn't mind that Burns was picking Jeff or rooting for him. He said he was glad so many folks thought Jeff would defeat him, for it increased interest in the match and generated more money.

CHAMPION JACK JOHNSON INSPECTING THE NEWLY CONSTRUCTED RING IN THE ARENA AT RENO.

After inspecting the ring, at Johnson's request, the platform outside the ropes was extended out a couple more feet to four feet. Jack did not want to get pushed through the ropes and off the platform.

The *Call* reported that the $101,000 purse actually was going to be divided evenly, 50/50, and not based on winner and loser. Such was decided in a secret meeting in Hoboken. It said the real truth had leaked out. Jeff had sold his motion picture rights for about $67,000, while Johnson sold his for $50,000. Others said the $101,000 purse would be divided 75% to the winner and 25% to the loser, plus a $20,000 bonus to each fighter.[418]

[418] *San Francisco Chronicle*, July 3, 1910; *San Francisco Examiner, San Francisco Call*, July 3, 1910; *Los Angeles Times*, July 4, 1910.

Reno was jammed to its limit. The ticket office opened on July 3, and $60,000 in tickets were sold that day. Scalpers were selling $10 seats for

$15. The $15 seats were quickly sold out.

Perhaps hoping to rattle the ex-champion and former protégé, Bill Delaney said fear was why Jeff would lose, for Jeffries dreaded Johnson.

> For years Jeffries has been afraid of Johnson, and he has never gotten over that feeling. Some seven years ago Johnson was dogging the footsteps of Jeffries for a fight, but he never got the chance. I had to take all the blame and act as the bumper. Jeffries told me that he didn't want to fight Johnson, and while he did not admit it in so many words, I knew that he was afraid. After Johnson beat Jeffries' brother, Jack, he came to me and pleaded for a fight. I told him that Jeffries didn't want to fight him, and he said to go and tell Jeffries that he (Johnson) had licked Jack, and that he could lick Jim.

Delaney said Jeff did not want the fight, regardless of financial inducements.

A *Chronicle* writer opined that for Jeff to win he had to do so quickly, or else age and long absence from the ring would catch up with him.

U.S. President William Taft said he would receive reports of the fight through a local newspaper wire. His son Charley was betting all his money on "the pride of the white race."[419]

Jack London believed the fight would be on the square. They had trained too hard and long for it not to be.

In response to boxing's critics, London said there were many things a lot worse than prize-fighting, a sport which had rigid rules that gave its participants more fair play than the outside world offered. In the real world, food was adulterated, legislators were bribed, children worked in factories, and merchants compelled women to labor long hours on a semi-starvation wage. By comparison, boxing seemed lucrative, safe, and fair. "If some of the fairness of the prize-ring were carried into business life it would be a much more beneficial world in which to live."

A southerner told Jeff that the South was with him, and emphasized the fight's larger implications. "For God's sake, Jeff, beat the negro. We are all with you; do your best. It is more than the fight to us."

On July 3, Jeff continued resting, while Johnson ran 5 or 7 miles. Both fighters were drying out. Jeff again confirmed that he never felt better.

Jeff stood 6'1 ¼" to Johnson's 6' ¼". Jeff had not taken the scales for reporters, while Johnson was about 209 pounds.

---

[419] *San Francisco Chronicle*, July 4, 1910.

Mrs. Jeffries did not want to see the fight. She did not think women should attend fights. However, Mrs. Johnson would have a good seat. Jack wanted her to see him win.

Jim Corbett said he was certain that Jeff would win, for he had trained faithfully and was in magnificent condition. He could not picture that giant of a man on the canvas. Although Corbett wanted to see more actual boxing from Jeff, he did not think that would interfere with the result.[420]

The arena doors would open at 12 noon on the 4th. Billy Jordan would start making introductions at 1:30 p.m., and the fight would start at 2 p.m. Tex Rickard would referee. Charlie White was the substitute referee, if needed. The official timekeeper was George Harting (also called Harding). Jeff's timekeeper was Billy Gallagher. Johnson's timekeeper was Stanley Ketchel.

Writer Rex Beach opined that Jeff would win, in part because "he possesses a mentality lacking in his antagonist, and mind after all is stronger than matter. In his training he has had the counsel and stimulus of better minds than has the negro. ... The man of education will outlast the man of ignorance in any test of endurance be they evenly matched in strength."[421]

Battling Nelson, who was picking Johnson, said, "Racial prejudice seems to influence almost everyone here." Folks asked who Johnson had beaten, but Nelson asked them the same thing about Jeffries.

A *Call* writer said the battle would "decide whether the white or black race shall rule supreme over the pugilistic world." The giants stood in stark contrast. One white, one black. One mean and surly, taking it as serious business, the other light-hearted, happy, and childlike, treating the fight as a mere everyday ordinary effort. Both were meeting their most formidable opponents. "It will be a question of strength, endurance and lion heartedness with the white man, and a question of speed, skill and ring science with the black monster."

---

[420] *San Francisco Chronicle,,* July 4, 1910.
[421] *Reno Evening Gazette,* July 4, 1910.

Another *Call* writer said those who insisted that Johnson was a dog with a yellow streak had no basis for such claims. True, he had loafed a good deal during his career, but he had never quit cold. "And they say Johnson must be a dog because he's colored." However, other colored champions like Dixon and Gans had never dogged it. "No man should be branded with the failings of his race until he has exhibited these failings himself. There is no trait that is absolutely universal in any one race."

Both fighters were highly motivated. Jeff wanted to restore pugilistic supremacy to the white race. For Johnson, this fight had been his one great ambition. It was the cap to his career that he had always sought.

When Stanley Ketchel came to visit Jeff at his training camp on the 3rd, he was ousted. Obviously, Jeff was upset that Stan had picked Johnson and would act as his timekeeper.[422]

On July 3, the day before the fight, Jeff wrote that he was glad the fight was the next day, for he was hungry and anxious for it to come, like a boy waiting for Christmas day. He was confident that he was going to bring home the honors, for he was in perfect condition and ready to fight. He was not going to say how he was going to fight, lest he might tip off his opponent. Anyone who wrote otherwise was just guessing.

> When the gloves are knotted on my hands tomorrow afternoon and I stand ready to defend what is really my title, it will be at the request of the public, who forced me out of retirement. I realize full well just what depends on me, and I am not going to disappoint the public. ... That portion of the white race that has been looking to me to defend its athletic supremacy may feel assured that I am fit to do my very best. ... If I had so much as a slight pain, a sore finger, or the most trivial thing imaginable that might annoy me, I would immediately insist on a postponement. Fortunately I am as sound as a dollar. I think I will surely beat Johnson. I would not have signed to fight at all unless I was reasonably certain of victory.

Jeff also said that some had discussed what harm might come to Johnson should he win. "They have pictured the negro as being shot, hanged or mobbed in case he won." Showing his true sportsmanship and humanity, Jeffries said,

> I would consider any move to intimidate Johnson as cowardly and a disgrace to the American spirit of fair play. It is my honest belief that should Johnson be fortunate enough to win from me that the negro would not only be allowed to walk unmolested from the ring, but that he would be accorded all the honors due to the victor. I want it understood that I want no friend of mine to make a hostile movement towards Johnson. . ... If Johnson should by any chance win...he must not be harmed. I demand this.

---

[422] *San Francisco Call*, July 4, 1910.

Jack Johnson considered Jeffries to be a dangerous opponent, but nevertheless was confident that he would win. "A man of his bulk and strength is a hard man to handle at any time, and I know that Jeffries is a good boxer and a hard hitter, but I feel confident that I can show as much and more in all of these lines." He also said, "I honestly believe that in pugilism I am Jeffries's master, and it is my purpose to demonstrate this in the most decisive way possible." Johnson disagreed with the argument that Jeff would be able to wear him out. Jack had not yet met anyone who was superior to himself in boxing, and he hit hard enough to stop anyone.

W. W. Naughton wondered whether the odds still having Jeff as the 10 to 6 favorite and the greater wagering on Jeff had more to do with the fact that there was a conflict between judgment and sentiment. A very strong man like Al Kaufman, one of the biggest and strongest top contenders in boxing, was saying that he could not budge Johnson when they sparred. Al said, "I have exerted myself against him day after day and I haven't been able to force him or back or budge him an inch. Johnson is the strongest man I ever went against." Yet the gamblers still believed in Jeffries. Some said Jeffries didn't do much boxing because he feared being exposed or injured. There was a great deal of speculation.

Another *Examiner* writer said that to all outward appearances, Jeffries was as good as or better than he was when he quit the ring.

It was estimated that Jeff weighed around 220 pounds and Johnson 206, though no one knew for sure.

Despite some of his previously expressed reservations, William Muldoon picked Jeffries to win. Sullivan said he was not selecting either, though most believed that he actually favored Johnson. Abe Attell, Frank Gotch, and Jake Kilrain all picked Jeff.

Respected sportswriter Tad Dorgan said Jeff's fighting days were over, Johnson was too clever, and would win easily. Johnson took a long time to mature, but now was at the top of his game. Johnson was cunning, catlike, cautious, fast, and tantalizing. He liked to play with his foes like a cat does with a mouse. "He won't try to kill him with a punch, but will nose him out round after round until the big fellow either falls from exhaustion or is beaten so badly that his seconds will come to his rescue." Johnson had the right sparring partners, young men who roughed it with him and tried to knock his head off. Jeffries surrounded himself mostly with old men. "Sam Langford probably would clean every one in Jeff's camp in ten rounds."

An *Examiner* writer said that Johnson had toiled for years, fighting anyone who would fight him, battling against the color line. He had heard the hisses of race feeling in the shouts and yells at countless ringsides. Despite his best efforts, the color line had prevented a Jeffries fight. He knew that if one day he held the championship, public clamor would force Jeff out of retirement. Jeffries had never intended to return to the ring, but eventually had yielded to the public pressure. "And had the championship remained in the keeping of a white man, he never would have fought again. So, after all, it is Johnson's black skin that has won him his chance to fight

Jeffries." The irony was that his skin had kept him from a fight with Jeff, but now that he was champion, his black skin is what got him the fight.[423]

On the morning of the fight, Jim Corbett said they were fighting "for glory, money, title, and to prove the physical superiority of the white race." Jeff was prepared to wear down Johnson gradually, systematically, and persistently, keeping after him all the time. Johnson was prepared to do the same. "It is peculiar that both men will go into the ring with the same premeditated plan of action, that of exhausting the other man." Jeff was prepared for a long hard battle. "Jeff will get Johnson eventually." He was a lion who would attack the wolf. "Johnson is of the wolf kind that fights only when cornered." Jim expected a long battle because he did not believe Jeff had done enough boxing in his training to win quickly. "However, as I have so often said before, I do not believe this lack of boxing on the part of Jeffries will affect the ultimate result of the battle today." Jim cited Jeff's prodigious strength, wonderful hitting power, and gameness under punishment as "the things that will bring the pugilistic supremacy to the white man." Regardless, Jim gave Johnson credit for having really "great ability. Outside of Jeffries he is the greatest man in the ring in the whole world today." Corbett insisted that Jeff was not a shell, but was as good inside as out. His stamina was there. "It is true that Jeffries has taken off an astonishing amount of weight and flesh in the last year. But he has done it gradually and by natural means."[424]

Ashleigh Simpson said that if the colored man were white, the odds would be considerably different from what they were.

Many suggested several potential negative effects if Johnson won. "If Johnson wins there will be a riot in the south. If Johnson wins the game of pugilism will suffer."[425]

Johnson too was cognizant of his own importance, and the fight's importance. He recently had been heard to say that he thought he was a greater deliverer of his own race than Frederick Douglass or Booker T. Washington.[426]

Thousands of pages of newspapers had been devoted to the fight, analyzing and discussing it exhaustively, more than any single upcoming sporting event in history. The wait was almost over.

[423] *San Francisco Examiner,* July 4, 1910; *New York Times,* July 4, 1910.
[424] *San Francisco Bulletin,* July 4, 1910.
[425] *Nevada State Journal,* July 4, 1910.
[426] *San Francisco Evening Post,* July 4, 1910.

CHAPTER 9

Battle of the Races

On Independence Day, July 4, 1910 in Reno, Nevada, Jack Johnson fought perhaps the most racially charged fight of all time when he took on undefeated retired ex-champion James J. Jeffries. For whites, it was supposed to be white Independence Day, for Jeffries was supposed to liberate whites from a black champion who never was supposed to be in such a position, and to put blacks in their place. The fight was hyped as a battle for racial supremacy.

Jeffries was 19-0-2 with 16 KOs. He had become champion in June 1899 and fought until August 1904, before retiring in 1905. Since early 1909, immediately after Johnson had won the title, Jeffries had been in training to come back and reclaim his crown for the white race.[427]

Reno was packed with people. There were so many celebrities that no one even took notice of them. The town had been so overflowing with humanity that the restaurants ran out of food.

The night before the bout, Johnson sat with his friends and said that he was thinking of the hard road that he had traveled since he left home when he was 12 years old. "I ran away as a kid and stowed away on a cotton steamer and landed in New York. I didn't have a nickel." Since then, he had traveled most of the world, had his ups and downs, but his ambition had been realized. He had taken his mother out of the Galveston shanty where he was raised, and put her in a big house in Chicago. "She's got everything she wants, and I'm happy."

The morning of the fight, Jeffries was the 10 to 6 betting odds favorite. Los Angelinos were willing to place their money on the Southern Californian at practically any odds. Johnson money started to come in heavily from the East, though.

At 8 a.m., as required by law, two doctors examined the fighters and declared them to be fit and in perfect physical condition.

Jeff's personal physician said Jeffries was a slow starter, but once he warmed up, Johnson would not be able to tire him.

Jeff seemed cool and collected, joshing and joking with his friends.

Most elaborate preparations were made for Jeff's corner. In addition to the regular paraphernalia, his corner would be equipped with a sunshade, an electric fan, "and drugs enough to start an apothecary shop." All of the

---

[427] The following account and discussion of the fight is from an amalgamation of sources which had reporters on the scene, including: *Nevada State Journal, San Francisco Chronicle, San Francisco Call, San Francisco Evening Post, San Francisco Bulletin, San Francisco Examiner, New York Times,* July 5, 1910; *Reno Evening Gazette,* July 4, 5, 1910; *Freeman,* July 9, 1910.

material nearly filled an automobile, which trainer Van Court took to the arena.

The day before the fight, Berger thought the ring canvas was too loose, the ropes too slack, and the padding too soft. The first cloth was white, covered with rosin and dirt. Berger wanted to use the floor padding and canvas which had been used to cover the platform in Jeff's training camp.

At 8:25 a.m., Jack Gleason arrived on scene to decide a quarrel between Corbett and Berger on one side and Sig Hart on the other regarding which canvas should be used – the one from Jeff's camp or the one from Johnson's. Gleason decided in favor of the Jeffries canvas because it was painted a dull red or pink and was much easier and restful on the eye than the glistening white canvas from Rick's, which caused a sharp glare of light.

After the doctors' examinations, Johnson took a drive downtown. Upon his return, he ate breakfast, consisting of four lamb chops, three soft-boiled eggs, tea, and bread.

Jeffries took a short stroll and had breakfast at 9 a.m. A barber gave him a shave and a haircut. He was not irritated and did not seem nervous at all. Mrs. Jeffries was the most worried, having tears in her eyes continually.

Doctor William Porter visited Jeff and administered some medicine to him for the prevention of nose bleed.

At 10:45 a.m., Johnson was in the yard posing for news photographers. He was laughing and joking as though he had not a care in the world. The last hour before going to the arena, he rested quietly.

Rex Beach was one of those who harped on the bout's racial significance. "Out from the jungle shadows of Ethiopia had stalked an Afric-giant to measure his strength against the white man's champion. It was again a battle of the races." As a result, people paid enormous amounts to watch. Tickets were sold for $10, $15, $20, $25, $30, $40, and $50. It was like the Roman Coliseum. Even women were there.

In the days leading up to the fight, demand for seats had been so great that $10 seats were being purchased for $12.50 and $15.

The day of the fight, ticket prices had advanced even more, not only for the cheaper seats but for those at ringside. Ticket scalpers had more than doubled their investment. The cheapest seats had been marked up to $25, and there were more takers than offers. Crowds eagerly attempted to purchase tickets. Rickard admitted that his friends had been correct in advising him to ensure that a large arena was built.

It was a very hot clear day, with dry air, and not a cloud in sight. Despite the intense heat, it was faintly tempered by a slight cool breeze, which folks hoped would continue.

Shortly before 11 a.m. at Moana Springs, Jeff began playing cards with his training buddies. He played cards for a couple hours, as well as craps.

At 11 a.m., the betting was 2 to 1 on Jeffries to win, with plenty of money in sight on the white man. Even odds were given on the over-under, which was 20 rounds, meaning one could bet on whether the fight would or would not go 20 rounds.

The ringside telegraph instruments had begun to hum. A force of 100 expert telegraph operators had gathered in the town. Offices of both the Western Union and Postal Telegraph companies said at least 750,000 words of press matter at an average cost of two cents a word were sent out over the wires before the day was done.

Thousands were thronged around the four arena entrances. Above each of the entrances was an American flag, dropped on its staff.

At 12 p.m., the arena gates were opened. The crowd was orderly.

Many tried to enter illegally. Some presented business cards and asked the door-keepers to have them sent in to someone in authority. Each entrance was policed heavily by deputy sheriffs, and all such proposals were coldly spurned.

Before entering, men were frisked. So as to prevent rowdiness or violence, alcohol and weapons were forbidden. Only the police were armed. At each entrance, several bottles of alcohol were confiscated. Joe Murphy tried to bring in wine bottles, but they were seized. There was no drunkenness. Hence, the police did not have to do much.

Inside, the arena's bare pine boards generated a terrific amount of heat from the scorching sun, which beat down fiercely.

Boxes built for women were at the top of the enclosure's outer walls. These boxes soon were filled with women who wore striking gowns and gaudy hats.

Nine motion picture machines were present.

At 12:37 p.m., more than a thousand holders of $20 and cheaper seats made a demonstration, for they were located directly behind the motion picture shed, which was obstructing their view. Rickard pacified them by ordering the obnoxious shed removed.

The Reno military band entered the 22-foot ring and played various American airs to celebrate the nation's birthday. At 12:50 p.m., they played "The Red, White, and Blue." An enthusiastic fan jumped into the ring, waving a silk American flag, and the vast crowd cheered. The band next played "Dixie" to another tremendous cheer.

At 1 p.m., the arena was nearly filled. The heat was intense, as the midday sun poured its rays into the crater-like structure. Green visors were sold by the hundreds for eye shields against the glaring sun. They cast reflections across the ring.

Timekeeper George Harting entered with the gloves in a big green box. There were two pairs for each fighter, in case one burst.

When the band played "America," the crowd made a feeble attempt to sing, but soon they went back to their fans and handkerchiefs. The brass band also played "Just Before the Battle, Mother," "Star Spangled Banner," and other tunes appropriate on the nation's birthday.

Contrary to popular belief, it merely was rumored that the brass band would play "All Coons Look Alike to Me," but it did not do so, for racial feeling was too high. The authorities had barred anything that might cause a disturbance.

There was an undertone of fairness and good fellowship amongst it all. There was little bad language, and no disputes or disturbances in the crowd. Lemonade was the only beverage served.

At 1:10 p.m., word was passed that every seat in the arena was sold. Several thousand persons were still in line at the booths.

Never before had so many women attended a fight. Every section was dotted with them, from the cheapest seats to the $50 ringside section, in addition to the 75 - 100 women in the long booth on the crater's rim.

Barbed wire had been stretched in front of the outer rows of $10 seats.

At 1:30 p.m., Jeffries got ready to depart for the arena. Corbett said he delayed their leaving as long as possible so as to avoid the anxious wait at the arena which had unnerved so many boxers.

At 1:32 p.m., Jack Johnson arrived at the arena.

Tex Rickard announced that they were fighting for $121,000. The purse was $101,000, which Rickard said the fighters were splitting 60% to the winner and 40% to the loser. However, Rickard also awarded a $10,000 bonus to each fighter, regardless of result.

It was reported that the purse division was brought about by Johnson's refusal to enter the ring unless it was agreed that there would be a larger winner's share and smaller loser's share. However, some later reported that vice-versa was the case, that it was Jeff who wanted such a division.

Ringside betting favored Jeffries at 10 to 6 odds, and remained so.

Estimates of the crowd size varied. Some said there was a paid attendance of 15,769, with another 760 complimentary tickets given out. Many unpaid viewers also slipped in at various places around the arena, breaking in through holes or climbing up to the rim, estimated to be about 1,500. Jack Gleason thought 2,000 to 3,000 people got over the fence and saw the fight without paying admission.

Some said the structure seated about 17,000, but another 4,000 to 5,000 were jammed in like sardines in the standing-room sections and on the circle at the extremes. Every seat was occupied. A six-foot platform that extended around the upper edge was covered with a human fringe of standing spectators. Some newspapers estimated that at least 18,500 were in attendance.

The promoters' staff placed the attendance at between 18,000 and 20,000. Rickard said the seating capacity was a little over 19,000, but 20,000 people were in the arena. Others estimated that 20,000 or 21,000 were crowded into the bowl-shaped yellow pine arena. Either way, it was the biggest crowd that ever saw a prize fight, and the receipts were so far ahead of any similar event that the record was shattered.

Reports regarding the gate receipts also varied. The most specific numbers offered were $270,775 and $277,775. Some said the gate was as good as $380,000.

Rickard estimated that the San Francisco losses, including the cost of the unused arena, cost him about $30,000.

After deducting both major and incidental expenses, Rickard estimated that they would make a profit of about $120,000 to $125,000, which he and Gleason would split. If true, the gate had to yield at least $271,000. Plus, the promoters would profit from their interests in the motion picture proceeds. Rickard sold his 1/6 interest for $33,333, but Gleason still held a 1/6 interest.

Jack Gleason said that even after all of the expenses were paid, he and Rickard would split evenly about $150,000 total between them, excluding their share of the motion picture receipts. It certainly was the battle of the century from a financial perspective; by far the most lucrative fight ever up to that point.

One reporter claimed that someone brought a thermometer to ringside and it registered 102 degrees in the sun. The *Nevada State Journal* later said the temperature got up to a high of 86 degrees. Either way, it was hot.

It was a wonderful crowd in that it was most orderly and well behaved, even under the broiling sun. Perhaps the sun had something to do with it. It was so hot, no one wanted to perspire any more than they had to. Also, the deputy sheriffs helped ensure that the crowd would be respectable.

Jack Johnson's wife entered the arena and was seated near the ring.

At 1:45 p.m., Billy Jordan, the veteran announcer, entered the ring. At 1:55, he cleared the ring of photographers and hangers on. The preliminary introductions took up a great deal of time.

William Muldoon entered the ring and gave a speech, saying,

> I want to say something of the only broadminded state in the union, the one free state. I therefore suggest a token of our respect and esteem to one citizen, a man who has the courage to stand by the laws without being influenced and say that those people who enjoy this sport shall be protected. I ask all here as a token of esteem and respect to this gentleman, Governor Dickerson of Nevada, the man who has carried out the laws as they are in the statutes and allowed the people to enjoy their sport, to stand up with heart and soul and give three rousing cheers for Governor Dickerson of Nevada.

The entire vast assemblage rose and gave three rousing salvos for Nevada Governor Denver Dickerson, who was in attendance, sitting in the north section with a friend.

At 2 p.m., Jeffries arrived at the arena and went to his quarters.

At 2:05, Billy Jordan reviewed Tex Rickard's connection with the fight game and introduced Rickard as the "gamest sport of the world. All the credit you can give belongs to this great sport, Tex Rickard. I call for three cheers for Our Tex." The crowd responded with a will.

Tim Sullivan, the stakeholder, was presented as "the famous stakeholder, the Honorable Tim Sullivan of New York." Rickard and Sullivan then stood at ring center and were photographed.

A mob of folks tried to tear away a hole to sneak into the arena, but Gleason called out a platoon of police who were listening to Jordan's speeches. They rescued the fence and saved it from further destruction.

Never in history were so many pugilistic celebrities at a fight. All of the old-timers were there. Billy Jordan continually introduced the vast throng of celebrities. John L. Sullivan climbed through the ropes, which set the spectators wild. Jordan said, "I introduce to you the great and only champion, big hearted John L. Sullivan." Responding to repeated calls, Bob Fitzsimmons jumped into the ring. He was introduced as "the greatest warrior of them all." Tom Sharkey also entered. Frank Gotch, world's champion wrestler, was introduced next. "Gentlemen, the great Roman gladiator, Frank Gotch." Others introduced included Hugh McIntosh, Jack Gleason, timekeeper George Harting, Tommy Burns, Stanley Ketchel, Jack O'Brien, Los Angeles promoter Tom McCarey, and moving picture man William Rock. The crowd finally started to show some impatience, growing tired of all the introductions. However, further introductions included Bill Lang, Jimmy Coffroth, New York promoter Charley Harvey, Joe Choynski, Abe Attell, Battling Nelson, Jack McAuliffe, and Sam Langford. Langford announced that he would challenge Johnson for $10,000, win or lose. The crowd began yelling for the big fellows to appear. Jake Kilrain was the only great former fighter not introduced to the throng. The entire group of notable fighters and promoters stood together and were photographed.

McIntosh, Burns, Sullivan, Coffroth, Gotch, Jordan, McCarey, Lang, Fitzsimmons, Sharkey, Harting, Ketchel

At 2:28 p.m., Johnson came down the aisle and entered the ring from the northeast corner. Some said he was given a chilly reception. Others said that a friendly cheer greeted Johnson's appearance. Another reported that although his reception was not marked, he did receive a few scattering cheers, and the jeers were not very noticeable, though a few did stand up and hiss him.

Johnson was preceded by his manager Tom Flanagan, and followed by his other trainers and seconds: Bill Delaney, Al Kaufman, Professor Walter "Doc" Burns, George Cotton, Doc Furey, Dave Mills, Harry Foley, Sig

Hart, and Jack Leahy. Johnson's timekeeper was Stanley Ketchel. Kaufman and Delaney were in his corner.

Johnson wore a mocha or black and gray striped silk dressing gown/bathrobe with thin white and black stripes running through it vertically. Jack smiled, waved his hand, and bowed to the crowd, which included a small sprinkling of folks of his own race. He greeted friends and acquaintances. He was not nervous, but seemed happy, calm, and only semi-serious.

Ed Cahill said Johnson entered wearing an elaborate gorgeous robe. "Don't get away with the idea that his high sense of his own importance is offensive. Not at all; he is just the simple-minded, elemental savage, basking in the sunlight of popular admiration. There is no pose. He can not help it."

Johnson's girlfriend Etta was sitting on the west side of the ring in a $40 seat under the moving picture stand. Jack waved to her and she responded in kind.

A few minutes later, at 2:31 p.m., Jeff's approach was like the coming of an emperor. With Jim Corbett leading the way, Jeff's entry was the signal for a tremendous outburst of enthusiasm. The cheer was far more powerful than the one which greeted Johnson. "The crowd was there to yell, and to yell for the white man." Jeff was given a great ovation.

Jeffries entered the ring from the southeast. His seconds were Jim Corbett, Jack Jeffries, Abe Attell, Joe Choynski, Bob Armstrong, Eugene and De Witt Van Court, Farmer Burns, Roger Cornell, and Sam Berger. His timekeeper was Billy Gallagher.

Bob Armstrong acted as a palm-bearer, holding a great fan or sunshade which could be used to cool the fighter between rounds and shelter Jeff from the sun.

Jeff was attired in an ordinary old street suit - plain shirt, coat, and trousers, and he also wore a cap. He was not the glass of fashion that Johnson was. As had been his custom in prior fights, he was chewing a big chunk of gum nonchalantly. One said he looked primordial as ever, with an expressionless face. Another said he was dark, somber, ominous, grim, serious, and savage. Most thought he seemed calm. One observer said Jeff chewed gum in a way that did not indicate that he was suffering from any attack of nervousness. However, one Reno writer said Jeff seemed nervous.

Corbett requested a toss for corners, but Delaney said Johnson would allow Jeffries to take either corner. As he sat in his chair, Jeff said, "I don't care what corner you put me in, it's all the same to me." There was no change in position. Jeffries took the corner with his back to the sun.

At 2:35 p.m. Johnson was led to ring center and presented by Billy Jordan: "Gentlemen, the heavyweight champion of the world, Jack Johnson." Some said he was given a fair reception, while others said a very weak reception was tendered to the champion. Richard Barry said, "When Johnson was introduced he got about nine handclaps and there were upwards of twenty thousand people within sight." While being introduced, Jack smiled and waved his hand at his white wife. His hands were bandaged with black adhesive tape.

Johnson was stripped and ready, wearing blue trunks with a silk American flag as a belt, entwined around his waist.

Abe Attell wound cotton or white muslin bandages around Jeff's hands. At 2:37 p.m., he still was winding the surgical bandages around his wrists. Some tape was also applied.

At 2:38 p.m., Jeff stripped. He wore purple trunks (slightly of a blue hue) and the American flag for a belt. The multitude stared at him in awe. He looked good, like a gnarly rugged oak, huge, stolid, stoical, and well-tanned.

Jeff came to ring center and was introduced: "The great and only undefeated heavyweight champion of the world, James J. Jeffries." The adoring crowd roundly cheered, howled, clapped, tossed hats in the air, and punched each other with joy. Johnson smiled and clapped along with the rest of the crowd. Coffroth thought Jack was pretending to applaud. Jeff folded his arms behind him and gazed over the vast assemblage which cheered again and again. Both looked fit to fight any number of rounds.

At 2:40 p.m., the men donned their gloves and Jordan cleared the ring. Johnson's golden smile was much in evidence as he sat in his corner.

Referee Tex Rickard and alternate referee Charley White were introduced.

Tom Sharkey interrupted by re-entering the ring and challenging the winner. The mob jeered, booed, and cat-called the sailor.

Johnson was willing to shake hands, but Jeffries refused, saying there would be no handshake, so Johnson assented with one of his many smiles.

Billy Jordan said, "Gentlemen, this will be a forty-five round contest, honest and on the square. They will break by the order of the referee. May the best man win. Let 'er go!"

George Harting rang the bell to start the fight at 2:46:30 p.m.

1 - Johnson smiled and Jeff calmly chewed gum. They engaged in a long session of cautious sparring. Corbett said both were grinning. For about ten seconds, Jeff circled and then feinted his left. Johnson grinned and stepped back. Both feinted lefts. Johnson worked him around until the sun was in Jeff's face.

Johnson led first and landed the first blow, shooting a light stabbing left to the nose or mouth. They clinched. Jack pushed Jeff's arm backwards and showed much strength. After pushing him back, Jack swung his left to the jaw. In the clinch that followed, Jeff roughed it at close quarters, crowding Jack around and slightly bearing his weight upon him. They kept close and seemed unwilling to break. Both worked their lefts to the body. The crowd cheered whenever it appeared that Jeff had landed. Jeff ducked a left and clinched.

Corbett said, "Wonder how long that black man is going to do the brother act? Will he never let go? Break 'em, Tex." However, John L. Sullivan said it was Jeffries who was doing all of the clinching. Both men seemed willing to rough it at close quarters.

As they sparred again, Jeff tried to land his left, but Johnson threw his head aside. Another clinch and they slowly walked around hugging each other. On the break, Jeff landed two short-arm lefts to the face and the crowd yelled. Corbett shouted, "Why don't you laugh?" Johnson winked and smiled back. They continued in a locked embrace, slowly pushing each other around. Jeff was chewing gum calmly. After the break, they sparred.

Johnson landed a clean left to the chin. They clinched and jostled again. Jack pushed out of the clinch and landed another left. Neither landed much, and what they did land was not landing very hard or with much effect. Jeff landed a left to the body. Corbett said, "That's it, Jeff, right there, that's where it hurts."

In the clinch, Johnson pushed Jeff's left forearm back so that he could not use it. Jack stopped a left with his shoulder and landed a left on Jeff's cheek.

They were still clinching at the gong. After the bell rang, Johnson grinned and playfully tapped Jeffries on the back of the shoulder. Jeff returned to his corner smiling as well, and winked.

Summarizing, observers said it was a tame, uneventful round with considerable hugging and clinching. Some said Johnson was doing the clinching, while others said Jeff was doing all of the clinching. It might have been that they both were clinching, taking turns doing so.

It was a feel-out round, and both were exceedingly cautious and careful. They were experimenting, getting their range, and testing one another's strength in the clinches. Both held well. Jeff showed momentary flashes of his cat-like quickness, but the hitting on both sides was light. No telling blows landed, although Jeff received cheers for anything he did. Jim Corbett said, "Looks to me as if Jeff were stalling." Most said the round was about even. Tension was high. The *Call's* William Slattery believed that Johnson was a bit nervous at first, trying to hide it with smiles and by talking to his opponent.

Between rounds, Jeffries told his seconds to leave him alone; that he would fight his own battle. Each fighter was given cold water.

Throughout the bout, between rounds, Corbett stood in the ring opposite Johnson's corner and taunted Jack with cutting remarks. Clearly, Jim was trying to rattle him. At first, Jack was surprised, but he soon became accustomed to it and had a ready and witty answer every time that Corbett flung a remark his way. Corbett yelled to Johnson, "Why don't you smile?" Jack replied by winking and smiling.

2 – Johnson came up chatting and smiling, while Jeff advanced with his famous crouch and smiled in return. Jeff stood with his left well forward. Jack blocked Jeff's left for the face and they both laughed. Jack feinted and jumped away. Johnson then landed a stinging straight left on the mouth and they clinched, with their arms entwined.

Jack London said a repetition of what happened in Australia when Burns fought Johnson took place. Each time someone said something harsh to Johnson in the hope of making him lose his temper, Jack responded by giving the white man a lacing. Jeff did not talk as Burns did, but Corbett spoke, and each time Jim cried out, Johnson promptly landed a blow. Corbett yelled, "He wants to fight a little bit, Jim." Jack retorted, "You bet I do, Mistah Corbett," and as Jeff held on, the champ landed a stinging right uppercut to the jaw which tilted Jeff's head. Another quoted Corbett as crying out to Johnson, speaking about Jeffries, "He's going to fight a little bit now." Jack replied, "All right, Mistah Corbett, I feel like fightin' a little bit myself."

As they separated from a clinch, Jeff swung his right to the ribs and Johnson retaliated with two ripping left uppercuts to the jaw. Johnson blocked a left swing. However, Jeff landed a left on the ear.

They closed together and clinched, with Jeffries leaning his weight against the champ. Jeff tried to crowd and put his weight on Johnson in the clinches. With his golden smile, Johnson said, "Don't love me so much, Jim, don't love me so." Jack followed his comment with a short right uppercut to the jaw. For the most part, Jeff ignored the kidding and maintained his solemn expression.

They tried short-arm jolts without effect. Jeff reached the body a bit with his left. Both were tensely careful. Jack feinted a left and Jeff ducked.

After another clinch, both were careful in breaking away. Jeff feinted, and as he came in with his usual crouch, Johnson landed a right on his eye which caused it to flush.

Johnson attempted to break out of clinches and punch. Corbett hollered, "That left hand hook is a joke. Jim, he can't reach you with it. It's a little slow yet." However, Jack landed some short left hooks.

Van Loan said that two or three times, Jeffries tore into a clinch head first, and toward the end of the round, blood showed on Johnson's lips as a result of the head clashes. Naughton said Jeff drew first blood with a left on the mouth. Another said Jeff opened the lip with a chopping right. The cut on the lip that Cotton caused in training several days earlier had been re-opened. The crowd drew inspiration from the blood.

In the clinch, Jack tilted Jeff's head with a right uppercut again. Using his right, Johnson pushed Jeff's left arm back as if in a hammerlock. Jeff ducked a left uppercut and clinched. They swung around. Jack landed a light left uppercut. They parted from a clinch just before the bell. Johnson was as jovial as ever and laughing gleefully.

Summarizing, the *Bulletin* said Jeff's punches missed most of the time. Johnson's aim was by far the more accurate. Every blow he landed meant business, especially a left hook that hit the right eye. The *Evening Post* said the round was similar to the 1st, except Johnson put a little more steam into his left jabs, which disconcerted Jeff. The *Nevada State Journal* said they kidded and talked to each other continually. The *Reno Evening Gazette* said, "It was a case of strength against cleverness, with the Nubian having the better of it." The *Chronicle* and Jack London said the fighting was very tame. Both exhibited extreme cautiousness. Jeff was not making the whirlwind fight generally forecasted. Richard Barry said that in the middle of the round, they scrapped for the first time in earnest. Everyone said, "Now wait till the coon feels that bear strength." However, Johnson lifted Jeffries and set him aside a foot, easily and gracefully, without effort. That stunned everyone and they groaned. Robert Edgren then said, "It's all over." Tom Sharkey said, "My God, it's no contest."

Between rounds, each fighter took some cold water. Johnson and Corbett kidded each other incessantly during the minute rest.

3 – Both came up slowly. Jack either was careless or very confident, for he smiled and talked to Jeff, deriding him as he made feints for his head. "Come in Jim." Jeff half-crouched, feinted, and advanced, but Jack stepped back and landed a hard left hook to the stomach. They clinched and fought at close range, wrestling. Back on the outside, Jack twice jabbed the nose, and as they closed in, he whipped a left uppercut to the jaw and neatly blocked Jeff's blows. Johnson swung his left on the neck.

During the action, Corbett yelled, "You've got a fat chance of hurting him, Jack. Everybody is laughing at you. He's making you look like a fool. How do you like that stinger to the stomach, eh? It hurts, don't it? Wait till that yellow streak begins to show. Go on, Jim, you'll knock his block off."

As they circled around the ring, Johnson kept up a constant cross-fire of conversation with Jeffries. It appeared that they were smiling and kidding one another. Johnson twice jabbed the face and also whipped in a short right to the face. A long clinch followed. Johnson took Jeff's left forearm in his right hand and deliberately pushed it back, holding it as long as he wished. Jeff could not move. No one ever before had done that to him.

Johnson landed a right uppercut in the clinch and Jeff rapped him on the jaw with a right. They hung together for quite a while. Jeff swung a hard right on the body and they clinched again. Corbett said, "Dat's funny; I know that feeling myself." Johnson winked over Jeff's shoulder at Corbett and said, "Come in and help him." Corbett then became very vulgar, and everyone around Jeff's corner was susceptible to his remarks. However, some of the crowd did not appreciate Corbett's mouth and fired back at him.

Jeff ducked a short left hook. They clinched and broke. Jeff blocked a left but Johnson landed another one clean on the mouth. They clinched on the ropes and Johnson landed a sharp right uppercut. Jeff rushed and landed a left on the body. Jack tried another uppercut but missed.

Both clinched and hung on a good deal. Jeff attacked but Johnson blocked well. He often took blows on his arms, shoulders, and gloves. The *Chronicle* said, "The white man finds it hard to break through the clever defense of Johnson." Jeff rushed in but Johnson neatly blocked a vicious right swing and clinched. When the round ended, Jack again patted his antagonist on the shoulder. Johnson waved his hands to friends in the audience and chuckled as he went to his corner.

John L. Sullivan said Johnson had the better judgment of distance, and had done all the hitting thus far, though his punches were not damaging. It seemed that Johnson was starting to think the big fellow did not have anything to show. His big smile showed his confidence. Still, although Jeff was receiving blows, he did not seem worried. His face was flushed, but he looked on sarcastically as Johnson struggled around with him.

The *Evening Post* said Johnson was blocking blows cleverly, and Jeff only landed a few harmless punches. The *Reno Evening Gazette* said, "Johnson, on points, has a good advantage, but there was not much power behind his stings." Jack London said it was the same story as before. Richard Barry said that in the clinches, Johnson was able to seize Jeff's left, his best arm, and prevent its use, which was like a death blow. Conversely, Jeff's defense was no use. He took the punches - right uppercuts, chopping lefts, and short snappy jabs. The *Freeman* said Johnson's wide grin was apparent to all.

However, the *Call* said it was Jeff's round. Jim Coffroth and W. W. Naughton called it an even round. C. E. Van Loan said Johnson was fighting cautiously, taking no chances.

4 – Johnson seemed more confident. He swung for the head but missed. Jeff feinted with his left but Johnson guarded with his right arm. Jack landed a left hook above the ear. They clinched. Jack landed a right

uppercut, but did no damage. Jeff missed a left swing. Johnson swung a left and Jeffries laughed at him. Johnson rushed in with a nasty left stab to the face and Jeff clinched. Johnson was all smiles. Jeff hit the body with his left, but Johnson landed two stiff left uppercuts and smiled some more. Jeff also smiled to show that he could stand the gaff.

Johnson kept joshing and taunting Jeff all the time. Rickard admonished him that it was a fight and not a talkfest. Jack London said Jeff showed up better, rushing and crowding and striking with more vim that before. This appeared to have been caused by a Johnson sally, and Jeff went at him in an angry sort of way. In response to Jeff's rush, Johnson said, "Don't rush me, Jim. You hear what I'm telling you?" Jack backed his statement with a right uppercut to Jeff's jaw. Despite attacking more frequently, Jeffries found it difficult to land often, owing to the clever blocking. As Jeff rushed in, Johnson landed a left.

After Jeffries landed a couple lefts to the body, one of which landed well in the pit of the stomach, cries of glee came from Jeff's corner. Corbett hollered, "You've got him winded, Jim." While Johnson was talking, Jeff landed a good hard right to the mouth, which started the blood flowing from Johnson's lips again. The blood was more noticeable this time. Some in the crowd cried, "First blood for Jeff." As Johnson brought his two hands around Jeff's neck, the ex-champ repeated his right to the body.

Some said that for half a minute, Johnson quit smiling and kidding, was more serious and cautious, and boxed in real earnest, strictly tending to business. They rushed into a clinch and fought while holding.

Others said Jack's golden smile had not faded from his face. Johnson shot a hard left to the mouth and almost wrestled Jeff against the ropes.

Another said Jeff forced Jack against the ropes and landed half a dozen short body shots in rapid succession. He also landed a left on the mouth.

They held for quite a while, and the crowd yelled for them to fight. After breaking, Johnson shot in a straight left to the mouth and Jeff closed in and dug three lefts into Johnson's stomach. However, Johnson landed three uppercuts in succession, lifting Jeff's chin in the air each time.

Jeff landed a low blow and Jack called attention to it. Corbett was trying to disconcert Johnson, but as Jeffries advanced and ducked into a clinch, Jack timed him on the way in and landed a short right on the jaw.

After breaking, Johnson landed another good hard left jab to the head. In the clinch that followed, Johnson dared Jeff to bring forth those demon punches for which he was famous. However, it was Johnson who landed a hard left on the jaw.

The *Reno Gazette* and *San Francisco Evening Post* agreed that it was Jeff's round, and the best one so far. The *Call*, which had given him the 3rd round, said, "Jeffries did the better work in this round also, though Johnson was just beginning to start." Jack London said it was anybody's round, and more Jeff's than any preceding one. W. W. Naughton said the round was even. Jim Coffroth said Johnson showed his superb skill in blocking. Jeff led but was baffled, while Jack occasionally countered. The round was even or

Jeffries. The *Bulletin* said it was evident that Jeff's body punches were lacking in steam. He had planted a few choice raps on the body, but Johnson only smiled. The *Chronicle* said Jeff rushed at him but could not land with any effect. Fighting at close range, Jeff jolted Johnson in the stomach with several blows, but they lacked force. Johnson's mouth was bleeding. However, "Fight uneventful up to this period."

In the corner between rounds, Johnson looked down at Sullivan at ringside and told him that Jeffries could not hit hard.

5 – As usual, Johnson came up with a volley of verbiage. He chuckled, "I am all open if you can find the place and land it." Jeff paid no attention but rushed in close with his low crouch and they wrestled for a spell. The question of strength between them remained unsettled, for there was not much to choose between them in the wrestling. Corbett said, "Johnson is trying to goad Jeffries into losing his head, but it doesn't work. He might as well talk to a stone wall." Corbett called out, "Why don't you go in and mix it, Jack?"

Johnson was fighting with open hands. They clinched several times, each taking turns rushing in. Jeff stepped away from a left jab. They feinted into a clinch. Jeff said, "Break free," and then leaned his weight on Johnson.

They fought at close range. Johnson landed above the hip with a left and they clinched. Jeff hit the body with his left and Johnson twice left hooked him in the face. Johnson met Jeff with a left jab and Jeffries drove in a solid right to the body. They hung together. After breaking, Jack poked a left into the face, repeated it with more force, and then danced around. A short

Jeffries left to the face brought more blood. Although there was a slight smear of blood on Johnson's lips, Jack smiled nevertheless.

Johnson feinted as Jeffries stepped away, crouching. Johnson kidded and said, "I will straighten him up in a minute." Someone in the crowd heard him and said, "He will straighten you up, nigger." Johnson led and landed his left on the stomach. In the clinch, Jack looked over Jeff's shoulders and grinned. Jeff smiled and remarked, "Gee, I love you, Jack."

Jeffries shot two rights to the body, but Jack responded with a left uppercut that cut Jeff's lips a bit. Sullivan said it was a short right that cut the upper lip. Corbett said, "Johnson gets over a right and a fleck of blood shows on Jeff's upper lip. He got that from that last left stab." Eventually, Jeff's lip bled more profusely than Johnson's.

More clinching followed. Jack drove his right to the jaw and followed with two left uppercuts to the same spot. He jarred Jeff with a straight left to the mouth and they clinched. Both bled from the mouth. Some noticed that Jeff's nose was bleeding as well. Jack London said the right nostril was bleeding.

Jeffries led but fell short. Johnson met and caught him with a straight left and right on the forehead. In close, Johnson brought his right hand up to the mouth. Johnson caught Jeff's left lead and Jeff seemed bothered, because he could not find an opening.

Suddenly, from the down-low crouching position, Jeffries sprung up to his toes with a straight left to the mouth that sent Johnson's head back a foot. It was a clean punch and the crowd cheered. Sullivan said it was the first straight blow to his credit during the fight, a straight left on the forehead. Corbett's version said, "Jeff jolts his left to Johnson's head and the coon's head wabbles back. Don't cry, Johnson, the worst is yet to come." However, Johnson was not jarred, for he clinched and laughed loudly. Still, Corbett was trying to get his goat. It was so quiet at ringside that his comments could be heard from far away. Corbett said, "My, oh my! That's an awful bad left! Worst left I ever saw! Jim, I thought this fellow could box. He can't box a lick on earth." Johnson looked over and grinned.

When the bell rang with the two men in another clinch, they patted each other on the back. Johnson's customary round-ending back pats were more noticeable than Jeff's. Jeffries went to his corner with a split upper lip.

The *Reno Gazette* said Johnson looked a bit serious as he took his seat, though no real damage was done on either side. The *Chronicle* said very little fighting was done in this round, and it had been a repetition of the preceding four to a great extent. Jim Coffroth said feints and clinches marked the round, though Jeff landed some good ones. Naughton said the round was even.

Jack London said that from this round until the end of the fight, Jeff's face was never free from blood, a steady stream starting to flow from his lip and right nostril. Corbett's running fire of words served to make Johnson smile even more merrily and to wink at him over Jeff's shoulder in the clinches. To this point, Johnson had shown no yellow streak, but Jeffries had neither bored in and ripped awfully nor put it over on Johnson in the clinches. Jeff was not as fast as once he had been.

The *Bulletin* said Johnson had started an assault on Jeff's features, landing as often as he liked, splitting the lip with a left, and starting Jeff's nose bleeding. Jeffries could not land effectively. With ease, Jack blocked everything and never missed an opportunity to send a few through Jeff's defense.

The *Call* said Johnson had started to fight in earnest, lading several body shots, his famous uppercut, and a left across the mouth that caused Jeff's lip to bleed. Johnson was better in this round than in any of the others.

The *Evening Post* said Jeffries seemed encouraged by his success in the previous round and looked more confident. However, Jack was not flustered in the least, talking to Jeff in a manner that exuded confidence and relaxation. The round was a tame one, though Jack kept ripping in rights and lefts that had a wearing effect. Jeff landed a few lefts through the guard, but the force was spent before they reached the face. Generally, Johnson was able to wriggle out of harm's way.

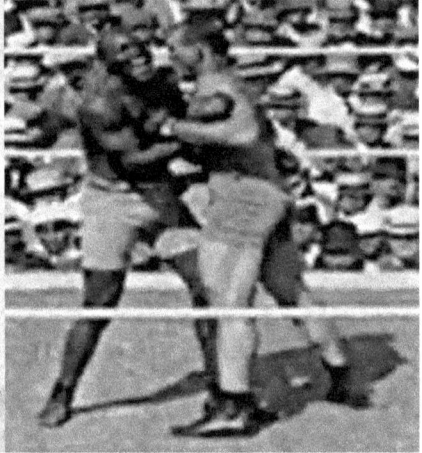

6 – Before the round began, Jeff remarked to his seconds, "I'm going to mix with him now." He continued chewing gum. At first, they sparred cautiously. Jeff crouched, and then he straightened up and attacked, but did not land to any effect. Corbett yelled, "Go it, Jeff, slam 'em in. Make him back up." Jeff ducked a left and shot a right to the body. A fan asked Johnson if he would like a drink. Jack responded, "Too much on hand now." He then said, "Now we'll mix it a bit."

Johnson showed his class in a flash of real fighting. With startling quickness, Johnson fired a hard left to the body and three stinging left hooks on the sore mouth and face, driving Jeffries to the ropes. They were the most effective blows of the fight thus far, and Jack's first real fierce aggressive rush. It only took a second or two, but at its conclusion, Jeffries clinched, and it could be seen that blood was seeping from a slight cut high on his left cheek bone, and his right eye was closing. The blood oozed continually from the re-opening of an old cut. Jack laughed, "Ha ha."

In Corbett's ringside report, he said, "Yes, I guess Johnson did have the better of that. I'd like to see Jeff cut loose a little. Gee, he's got Jim's right eye on the blink. Be careful, Jim, take it easy, you'll get him." Corbett didn't speak much during this round.

Jeffries kept trying to rush and get in but was awkward and his blows lacked accuracy. Johnson's left went around Jeff's neck and they clinched. Jeff blocked a left and right and drove his right against the ribs. Johnson quickly ripped in three speedy left uppercuts to the jaw. Jeff hit the body with good force and they clinched again. In a hot rally, Johnson landed a double lead on the eye.

Johnson shot his left to the stomach. They broke and sparred. Jack feinted and Jeff stepped back out of the way. Richard Barry said Jeffries began backing away, which was surprising. Sullivan said Jack was showing all the cleverness, but Jeff did not seem disturbed. He constantly chewed his gum.

As Jeffries rushed in, Johnson caught him with a hard straight left to the jaw, probably his hardest blow thus far. They engaged in fierce fighting, but Johnson fired the quicker blows, and more of them. They hugged persistently in the clinch that followed. On the inside, Johnson worked his short-arm blows and landed.

A hard left caught Jeff's eye. Sullivan said Johnson's blows were harder than they seemed.

Jeff waded in, but on the inside, Johnson freed his arm and met Jeff with a nasty left uppercut that further puffed up and closed his right eye. Johnson also landed his right uppercut. After the bell rang, as he went to his corner, Jeffries rubbed his swollen eye.

All of the ringside reporters agreed that it was Johnson's round by far, and it was his round throughout. Jeffries was bleeding from his nose, lip, and cheek, and his right eye was closing and getting blacker. His face was all marked up. Jeff had been aggressive in the round but was all at sea. Johnson was fighting and smiling strong. C. E. Van Loan said that during this round, Jeff rushed and landed on the body, but Johnson jerked himself loose from clinches and fought back savagely with both hands. The *Call* said Johnson peppered and hooked Jeffries, who seemed bewildered by the attack. Jeff tried but could not reach Johnson. Jim Coffroth said Johnson started a sudden rally and rained blow after blow with the left on Jeff's head. Jeff tried to duck but Johnson landed nevertheless.

The *Bulletin* said Jeff's right eye had been wounded in the 2nd round, and a blow in this round closed it. Richard Barry said the closed eye had begun swelling in the 4th round, was puffed in the 5th, and several lefts in this round left him blind at the end. The *Nevada State Journal* said the right eye had been hit in the 1st round, and by the end of the 6th round it had swollen nearly closed.

During the intermission, his seconds worked hard on Jeff's damaged optics, but it seemed to irritate him more than it did him good. He motioned for them to leave him alone.

7 – Jeff came up with a ferocious frown. They closed in, but Johnson was first to lead again, stepping in with left hooks. Jeff blocked two of them, and as they clinched, Johnson said, "Come on you, Jeff." Johnson was showing more aggression than he did in the opening rounds. Jeff crouched low but found it difficult to land.

Johnson began feinting rapidly and Jeff circled around. They fiddled around for twenty seconds without a blow being struck. Jeff was being more careful. Johnson was grinning while looking for an opening.

Although Jeff's eye was badly bruised, he never lost his poise. He rushed to a clinch and received a right jolt to the jaw. When Jeff tried a right at close quarters, Johnson laughed sarcastically. Jeff rammed his left into the body. He landed a left to the face and Johnson laughed. Johnson was fighting cleverly and stopping leads, or at least smothering them.

Locked in an embrace, Johnson freed his left, jolted Jeff three times over the damaged right eye, and followed with a right uppercut to the jaw. Jeff landed a straight right to the jaw, but Jack countered with left and right to the sore face. Johnson landed a left on the nose, bringing blood from one of Jeff's nostrils.

At this stage, Jeffries certainly was getting the worst of it. He still was rushing, but not displaying the same judgment that he did earlier. As Jeff came forward, Jack stepped back. Finally Jeff got in, but his left lead went around Johnson's neck. Rickard told them to break from another clinch. Tex was doing very little, as both were fighting very fairly. Jeff's nose kept bleeding. He sent in a high left that landed on the chin. In the clinches, Jack kept freeing his left and jolting Jeff's head. Johnson landed a mighty powerful left on the chin, his most effective blow, followed by a right.

Most observers and newsmen (*Reno Gazette*, *Chronicle*, *Bulletin*, Naughton, Sullivan, Barry, and Van Loan) said Johnson clearly won the round and had taken a decided lead in the fight. Jeffries was showing the effects of the punishment. His right eye was swollen, his upper lip puffed, nose bloody, and cheek bone cut with gore dripping from it. The eye seemed to bother him. He showed signs of weariness as well. The hot sun beat down on the fighters and they perspired freely. Even Corbett noted that Johnson landed several good left swings to the jaw and hammered Jim with the right on the chin. The *Bulletin* said it had become apparent that Jeff had little or no chance, for his blows were missing. Already he had taken enough of a beating to make a regular human quit. Richard Barry said that at one point, Jack forced Jeff to a corner.

Conversely, Jack London said this was a mild round. Jeffries was grim and silent, Johnson was leading and forcing, but both were careful, and little happened except for a few exchanges of blows. Thus far, Jeff's roughing, crowding, and bearing on of weight had amounted to nothing. Also, he was doing less and less of it. The *Call* also said the round was slow, with honors even. Jeff began to show signs of distress, while Johnson seemed content to lay off a bit and study his man. Jim Coffroth said both were cautious. The round was enlivened only by the persiflage between Corbett and Delaney in opposite corners.

Between rounds, Johnson kidded Corbett, who was watching what was being done in his corner. Jack said, "Too late now to do anything, Jim; your man's all in."

8 – As Jeffries quickly rushed in to close quarters, Johnson drove a left to the mouth. Jack clinched, but used his free left on the face. Shortly after breaking, Johnson landed two left jabs to the face and jaw with considerable force. Johnson said to Corbett, "Hello, Jimmy. Did you see that one?" Jack began jeering Corbett, asking him how he liked the looks of things. Corbett replied, "He who laughs last laughs best."

Sullivan said Johnson kept after Jeffries all the time. As Jeff led, Jack stopped him with a left on the chest. Jeff led again but caught a right on his ear and hard left on his face. In the next lead, Johnson landed a terrific straight punch on the nose. Jeff grunted and bored in with a show of anger, but Johnson clinched. Through his blood-bespattered face, Jeff shouted, "Break away, Johnson." But the champ did not break for a while. Jack drew back away from a vicious left swing, making it miss, and then laughed.

During the fight, Bill Naughton was dictating blow-by-blow to a telegraph operator. He said, "Jeff took a left hook to the jaw." Johnson heard him and replied, "Is that all he takes, Mr. Naughton?" Jack then landed twice with fast, short jolting hooks that brought blood.

Jeffries landed rights to the body, but they had no effect on Johnson. During a long clinch, Jack poked a left to the body, and also used his right to the back. When they broke, he landed a left to the face.

In another clinch, Johnson grinned over Jeff's shoulder, and, winking to the newspaper men, kept his left hand busy, generally landing.

To encourage Jeffries, Corbett said, "It only takes one or two, Jim." Then Johnson, as if to answer, landed a stinging left uppercut to the battered eye and said, "That's all it takes, Mister Jeffries." After a pause, Jack landed another, and said, "See that?"

Jeffries attempted to land a left to the head but missed as Johnson stepped away. Johnson then stepped in again and landed a left on the chin. They hugged around the ring and took their time to break. As they sparred,

Jeff led and landed lightly on the jaw. In the clinch, Johnson whipped his right across and grazed the chin.

Jeff swung another hard left for the face but missed. They clinched. Jeff pushed his man about the ring and the bell rang with the fighters clinched. As they separated, there was the usual back patting.

Naughton and Sullivan both said it was Johnson's round, and from the perspective of both points and effectiveness, the fight was going all Johnson's way. A Reno writer said that even ardent Jeffries admirers practically were admitting defeat. Jack London said Jeffries showed perceptible signs of tiring and slowing down, rushing and crowding less often. He had not received much punishment, but his condition appeared poor. It was obvious that he had not come back. Conversely, Johnson was maintaining or increasing the pace, and was as quick as a flash.

Jim Coffroth said Jeff tried to rush in close, for he was being cut to pieces and worn down from a distance. The *Chronicle* said Jeff tore in but was not landing much, for Johnson blocked well, and the ones that did land were not well directed and had no effect at all. Both men clinched quite often, particularly during the last part of the round, which was very slow. Richard Barry and Jim Corbett both noted that Johnson was good at pulling his left arm out of the clinches and hitting. Corbett said Jeff also was a sucker for Jack's right, and could not get away from it. "Johnson is showing up better, just as I said he would."

The *Evening Post* said Johnson was making his final calculations. He kept measuring Jeffries with his rangy left, and varied it with a right uppercut. Johnson was confident, but still careful to avoid any chance blow that might snatch away his victory.

Conversely, the *Reno Gazette* said the round was a "rather featureless session." The *Call* said this round practically was a repetition of the previous one, which it had called even. The *Chronicle* said Johnson gamblers now were willing to wager on their man at even odds, for apparently he was making a winning fight. However, many still believed that Jeff eventually would land a big one and turn things around, as he always had done.

Between rounds, Johnson's corner was calm, with not much happening. Jeffries' handlers were as busy as bees. Abe Attell gave most of the advice.

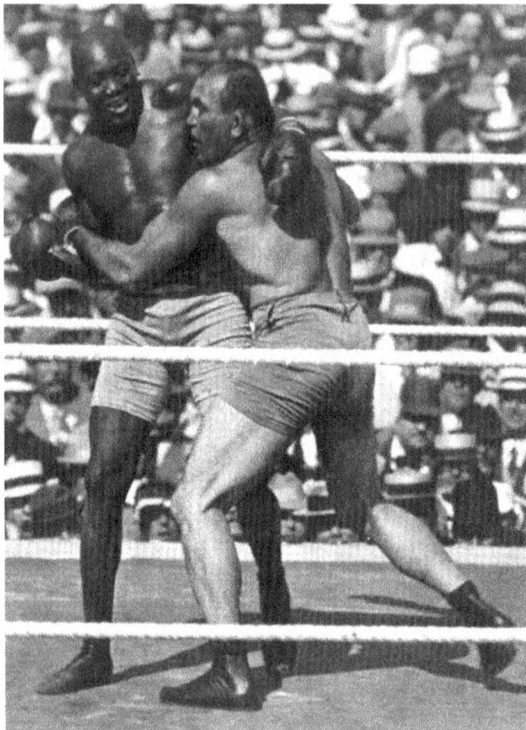

9 – In his corner, before the bell rang, Johnson kept up a constant conversation. When the round began, Corbett said to Jeffries, "Go in and make that big stiff fight, Jim." Johnson replied, "That's right; that's what they all say." Jeff grinned and said, "Come along." Johnson replied, "Come on, I'll mix with you." Jeff led and landed a left on the body. Corbett hollered, "That's it, put that left in there again."

Johnson hooked his left to the jaw with great force. While they were clinched, he continued to hurl terse statements at Corbett. Jack hooked another powerful left hook to the jaw. Jeff's right uppercut was blocked. As they broke, Johnson landed a left on the chin and a right on the jaw.

After Jeff butted with his head, Johnson flung his left to the stomach or midribs and they clinched. Jeff crouched lower than ever and Jack drove in another wicked left to the stomach. Corbett noted, "Johnson rams the left to the body. That was a pretty punch." Jeff clinched. After breaking, Jack sent in two left jabs to the mouth and eye, but Jeff paid little attention to them. Jack again jabbed away at Jeff, stopping his forward progress. Corbett said, "Look out, look out. Keep away from those lefts, put up your guard. Don't let him keep putting them over." After another clinch and break, Johnson stepped in quickly and drove his left into the stomach.

Between clinches, Jeff shot in a couple of rights to the ribs and stomach. Corbett said, "Stick it into his stomach there, he can't take them." While breaking, Johnson landed a left on the face. Jeff landed a left on the ribs and they clinched.

In one clinch, Jeff leaned his chin on Johnson's right shoulder, where he was safe from the uppercuts. Johnson was smiling, and seemed brighter and happier than when he entered the ring.

However, Jeff stepped in, ducked a left, met Johnson coming and drove a solid right into the pit of the stomach that sounded like the beat of a bass drum. Johnson grunted and lost his smile for a few seconds as he backed up for a moment. Jeff's men said, "That's the stuff. A few more like that, and he'll stop!" However, Johnson again smiled and invited Jeff to punch his body as hard and as often as he pleased. After the gong, as they passed each other going to their corners, Johnson again kidded the boilermaker.

The *Reno Gazette* said it was Johnson's round. Newsmen agreed that Jeffries was looking very bad, for his face was bleeding from several places; his right eye was almost closed, and was blue underneath.

The *Bulletin* said that in this round, Johnson opened a gash on Jeff's forehead and staggered him with successive left uppercuts. Jeffries planted an occasional body punch, but his efforts were weak and only brought smiles from the confident Johnson. Jack London said Johnson clearly demonstrated that he could drive in the left in a way that was surprising. Many, like Burns, had denied that he had a left. Jack proved otherwise. He landed a blow near the heart that must have been discouraging. W. W. Naughton said it began to look a little dismal for Jeffries.

The *Chronicle* said that overall, there was little fighting. Both showed extreme caution, and every round was a lot like the preceding rounds. Jim Coffroth said the rounds from the 9th onwards were monotonous. Jack landed an assortment of blows, while Jeff could not land with any considerable force.

Conversely, C. E. Van Loan said this round gave the Jeffries men their only chance to cheer. Richard Barry said, "This was the only round that could be given to Jeffries." Jeff had landed some solid body blows.

10 – They slowly came to ring center, fiddling and feinting. Johnson shot two lefts to the head and followed with a short right to the ear. A long clinch mixed with wrestling followed, and Jeff swung his right around the body. After breaking, Jeffries bore in but Jack held his arms. They leaned into one another while clinched, and neither seemed stronger. On the outside, Jack landed a straight left on the face and they clinched again.

After breaking, Jeffries feinted his left and followed Johnson around. Jack poked a couple lefts on the mouth. He tried a third and Jeff swung a left on the jaw.

Sullivan said Jeffries had not landed a real clean blow. He missed a right counter and they clinched. Outside again, Jeff threw a half-hearted lead but it just led to a clinch. Another break and Johnson shot over a clean straight right to the face, landing just as Jeff was coming in. Jack then landed a hard left to the stomach. Jeff landed both hands on the ribs. Corbett said, "Ha ha, he's getting tired now, Jim."

In the clinch, Johnson did effective work with short lefts and rights to the face. Corbett said, "Look out for that right swing. I guess that one must have stung." Jeff led and they clinched. Johnson used the left on the cheek. Jeff landed a left on the face. Jack came back with a left and Jeff drove a good left on the belt line. A spectator said, "Why don't you smile Jack." Over Jeff's shoulder, Johnson grinned at the crowd.

Jeffries blocked and eluded some blows. Corbett said, "That's it, Jim, block 'em; show him up. You've got it on him. He can't hurt you." Farmer Burns tried to encourage him as well, saying, "Jeff, you're getting better."

However, Johnson always was on the alert to land or block. He whipped in two lefts and a right uppercut to the jaw that made Jeff yell, "Oh." Jeff's head kept bobbing up with the blows. Corbett lamented, "Jeff always lets them uppercuts go through." Jeffries hung on for a bit, but after breaking, he made a rush which brought a cheer. They were clinched at the gong.

Sullivan said Jeffries appeared tired as he went to his corner, and his handlers looked worried. Johnson was cool, and no one in his corner was the least bit flustered. Mrs. Johnson, from about the sixth row, shouted to her husband, "Keep it up, Jack."

The majority of writers and experts said Johnson clearly won the round. The fighters confined themselves mostly to infighting and short streaks of wrestling. Jack peppered, pecked, and jolted Jeff's sore face with his left, drawing more blood. He was making a careful battle, and was content to jab Jeffries at intervals. Jeff's badly puffed and bleeding upper lip, the blackened, slowly closing right eye, and the gore trickling from the cut on his left cheek all distorted his face, making him a sorry spectacle. Overall though, the round was tame.

The *Call* and Jack London said it was plain to all that unless Jeff could land a lucky blow that could turn the tide, his chances for victory were fading quickly. Jeffries was growing slower and more tired. His few rushes had been futile. Johnson was fresh, aggressive, and smiling with confidence, for the fight was all in his favor to that point. He seemed to realize that he had Jeff in a hole, and being less afraid of consequences, kept up a steady rain of lefts to the jaw, varying occasionally with a right uppercut or left to the body. Johnson practically did all the work in this round. His blocking was marvelous.

London said Johnson had shown no yellow, but rather condition and speed. He had not used his right uppercut that much, but had used a savage unexpectedly-quick left. He held his own in the clinches, had gotten the better of both the infighting and outfighting, and had been unhurt and smiling all the way.

Conversely, unlike the others, W. W. Naughton said the 10th round was even. That's boxing for you. Take or believe what you like.

11 – They fiddled for an opening and then wrestled. Corbett said, "Short, snappy one, Jim." Johnson replied, "Huh. Easy to say, but hard to do." Johnson feinted his left and landed the right sharply across the jaw as they clinched. Jeff shook his head as though stung. They wrestled for a while. Several times Johnson landed his left hook to the face. Jeff laughed. As Jeff broke away, Jack was right on top of him with left and right. Jack landed a right uppercut, and as they clinched, Jeff hit the body with a hard right.

Jeffries was getting all the worst of it, but kept trying to fight back like a tiger. However, he didn't seem to worry Johnson one bit. Jeff's judgment of distance was poor. He often missed in the air. He was spitting quantities of blood and breathing laboriously. Jeff held on a lot too.

As a master of clinch fighting, Johnson was very good at yanking or working his arms free from the clinches and smashing in his famous short punches like piston rods. He was working his close blows to perfection, and in every clinch he managed to land a right or left uppercut. Corbett said, "There's that right to the jaw. That coon certainly is outboxing Jim. Go on, I've handed him the same thing, Jack, and he just eats 'em up. He don't even feel 'em."

Jeffries appeared both angered and quizzical, astonished by Johnson's ability. Jeff kept trying to hit Jack's body with both hands. What punches he did land had no effect. However, Corbett said to Johnson, "You're getting tired, ain't you? That's it; now Jim, bore in. That's what he should have done at the start and he'd have taken the heart out of that coon."

Johnson smashed Jeffries time and again with left and right to the jaw. Jeff fought back wildly. Jack swung a couple terrific clean right uppercuts to the jaw and Jeff appeared almost to weaken. Johnson followed with more left and right uppercuts to the jaw, varied with left and right swings to the jaw. The blood spouted freely from Jeff's mouth and nose in a stream.

As they broke, Johnson turned Jeff's head around with a left on the jaw. Jeffries was doing all the clinching. He didn't seem to have the punch, and Johnson was landing almost as he pleased. A straight right on the chin caught Jeff and he wobbled.

Although Jeffries was a bad-looking sight, suddenly he electrified the crowd by making a rally, landing his right to the jaw and hard left to the body. This brought the crowd to its feet. However, Johnson banged him a left on the bloody mouth just as the round closed.

Most said it was another Johnson round by a large margin. No one was betting against Johnson anymore. Jeffries freshened up for the first minute and did some good work, but then he started laying against Johnson for support. His stamina was gone. Each round was slower than the one before. Jeff worked his left rips to the body, but none had the slightest effect. Jack was smiling and confident all the time, toying with him. Eventually, Johnson opened up on the "hope of the white race" with a flash of fast fighting.

The *Chronicle* said they continued the same kind of fight. Jeffries kept rushing and boring in, fighting like a cyclone, but he could not land effectively very often. Instead, he was receiving a bombardment of terrific punishment from both rights and lefts, and was unsteady on his legs. He kept rushing in, but was very tired. They were fighting furiously at the gong, with Johnson doing nearly all of the landing.

However, there were some differing viewpoints. Jack London said this round looked better for Jeff. After being stung by a Corbett remark, Johnson rushed and provoked one grand rally from Jeffries. It was faster fighting, and more continuous than at any time previous. It culminated in a fierce rally in which Jeff landed hard. W. W. Naughton called this an even round, though that seemed typical for him.

12 – At the start, Johnson looked at Corbett and laughed, saying, "I thought you said you were going to have me wild." Some of the crowd laughed at Corbett, who did not respond. Johnson missed a hard left and they clinched for a while. Jack cleverly blocked body blows and landed a straight right to the mouth, starting the blood afresh. Jeff was worried, for try as he did, he could not land. Whenever he came in he caught a left or right somewhere where it hurt. As Jeff rushed in, Johnson met him with a left jab and a right uppercut to the jaw. Jeff landed a left to the body. In close, Johnson landed hard left hooks to the body and face.

On the outside, Johnson boxed neatly, blocking effectively. Whenever he saw a friend at ringside, he smiled, nodded, or winked. He'd say, "Howdy, Joe." Then he sent a left to the eye. "Hello, Tom." Then he followed with a right uppercut. Corbett noted, "Look at that coon nodding and bowing to the crowd. He's grinning now, but will he keep it up?" Jack landed a left lead on the face.

A Johnson straight left sent Jeff's head back a foot. In the clinches, Johnson punched Jeff's face repeatedly with the left. Jeffries was slowing perceptibly and weakening in the clinches. He tried to fire his left, but Jack put out his right, touched him on the biceps and stopped the blow before it was started. Johnson blocked leads in clever style and jolted Jeff's jaw with an uppercut. In the clinches, Johnson kept ripping away with his right.

Jeffries clung to him. He was very tired and weakening. His face was covered with blood, showing the punishment very plainly. He rarely tried to hit Johnson, but instead was hugging all the time.

Johnson was landing hard lefts and rights on the nose, mouth, and jaw. Jack caught him with another hard right and straight left and Jeff clinched again. As they broke, Johnson landed another left in the face and right on the jaw. Jeff's swelled right eye became bigger and bigger from the effects of the jolty blows. Blood ran from his mouth and nose.

Corbett said,

> I'd like to see Jeffries do something. He looks too slow to me. Why the deuce didn't he take my advice and do a little more boxing? Johnson is making a sucker out of him. Look at those lefts and rights. He's hitting Jim whenever he pleases. And Jim's taking it. I wish I was up there. I can hardly restrain myself. Jim will get one of those lefts over yet, and then it'll be good night. Johnson is landing left and right almost at will. Jim's bleeding pretty freely from the mouth.

At the bell, Johnson went to his corner smiling. In his corner, Jeffries was very tired and spitting blood. Jeff's seconds were ominously quiet. Conversely, Johnson's corner hummed with life and bustle.

The local Reno papers said Jeffries was slow, missing leads, and in a pitiable condition. The *Call* said Jeffries was gone, fast losing what little speed he had when he started. He tried to punch and rush now and then, but Johnson smiled and made sarcastic, cutting comments. Jack London said Johnson was quicker and more aggressive than ever. As usual, every Corbett remark brought more punishment to Jeff. By the end of the round it was clear that Jeffries had not come back. Richard Barry said it was obvious that the battle would end with a Johnson victory. Still, the spectators hoped that Jeff had one big rally left. "If the white race must go down, we wanted it to go down in a blaze of glory." However, it appeared that the last big punch was not there, for it had been sapped by the vicious grinding mauling that Johnson had administered. Jack landed as he pleased.

Conversely, as usual, W. W. Naughton, who seemed intent on spinning things in as favorable a way as possible for Jeffries, said the round was only slightly in Johnson's favor.

13 – The round opened with Johnson saying to Corbett, "Hello, Jimmie; isn't that wonderful." Jeff's legs seemed sturdy, but his bruised face gave him a discouraged look. Regardless, Jeff was not nearly as spry on his feet as Johnson, though he kept chewing gum. They fought without damage into a clinch, and wrestled about the center of the ring. Over Jeff's shoulder, Johnson called to a friend in the crowd, "Hello Tom." Jeff's efforts to mix matters were futile.

Johnson broke the clinch with a volley of rights and lefts to the face and mouth. He was landing most all of his blows, several times with both hands. Jeff clinched, but Johnson freed his left and landed three times. They had been clinched for nearly a full minute, while all the time Johnson was yanking his arms loose and mercilessly landing uppercuts. Jeff could not elude the hurtful short blows at close quarters. Johnson was landing pretty much as he pleased.

Jeffries was a sight; his face cut and covered in blood, though he still was going after Johnson. Jack cleverly evaded Jeff's attempts. The blows that did land were so weak that Jack just laughed. Corbett saw Jeffries land a left to the body and thought it might have hurt Johnson. "No, there Johnson comes back with the left to the jaw. That's a terrific punch. Can Jim take those things yet? He's a marvel. That punch would have killed an ox." Others noted that in the clinches, when Jeff threw his lefts to the stomach, Johnson looked over his shoulder, smiled, and did not attempt to resist the punches. A Johnson right uppercut almost lifted Jeff from the floor. Jack was dealing out severe punishment with every punch, for Jeff's defense was failing him. The champ yanked his arms loose from clinches and rapped Jeffries again and again. Jeff's arms seemed like lead and he could scarcely raise them, let alone hit Johnson. As the round progressed, Corbett was noticeably silent.

Near the round's end, Johnson drove Jeff back against the ropes and, all inside of a second, smashed him full in the face with a right, left, and another right. Jeff tumbled forward into a clinch, the blood pouring from his nose and mouth.

Jeffries pushed Jack back to a corner and nailed him twice to the face, but the blows had no power or effect. Johnson watched him closely in the clinch. When they broke, three times Johnson threw and landed his right to the jaw. The round ended with Corbett advising Jeff to cover up and stay away.

At the bell, Jeff stared rather blankly into the middle of the ring. He appeared very tired and slowly returned to his corner bleeding profusely. His face was all cut up, bloody, and swollen.

Sullivan said Jeffries seemed to be broken up, and his seconds could not encourage him. Johnson was jovial at all times. It looked like the beginning of the end.

Corbett, who had been standing over where he could look into Johnson's corner between rounds, came back and leaned over Jeff, who sat huddled over his chair with his chin on his breast, his head hanging low as he sat in his corner. Jeff nodded as Jim spoke to him.

All of the writers agreed that it was Johnson's round and that things looked very dim for Jeffries. The tiring Jeffries was fading, and his efforts were futile, for he could not land, while Johnson could hit him at will with either hand. Even the hardiest Jeffries admirers were abandoning hope, for it appeared to be only a matter of time. Johnson had chaffed Jeff's corner-men, defeated Corbett in the mouth fighting, and battered Jeffries in every way, inside and out. Even Naughton said it looked bad for Jeff. Like a fighting mechanism, Johnson flashed from defense to attack and back again.

14 – Johnson wasted no time, for he immediately planted his left in his foe's face, and Jeffries hugged. After breaking, Johnson feinted rapidly and landed two more jabs, one landing as Jeff advanced, followed by a right uppercut before they clinched. Jeff swung a left on the cheek, but Jack just bowed to the audience and smiled. In the clinch, Jeff only lightly landed his right to the jaw. His punches never bothered Johnson. Jeff's leads were ineffectual because Johnson got too close. Jack kidded all of his attempts.

Jeffries tried a right swing but Johnson beat him to it with a left lead to the face. Jeff straightened, and the crowd yelled. Jeffries landed a left jab but it made no impression except to bring a laugh from Johnson.

They drew close and Johnson said, "Ain't that a nice belly Jim, why don't you hit it?" Jeff did not do so. Corbett warned his man to beware of the dangerous uppercut. Jeff's right eye was almost totally closed.

Johnson again dared Jeffries to hit him just to see how hard he could do it. Jeff put all his weight into a body blow. Johnson pushed him away and landed a left on the jaw. Jack sent some rapid-fire left jabs to the mouth, and Jeffries shook his head. There was a long clinch, with Johnson consistently ramming away at the face with both hands, bringing the blood. After Johnson struck him with a left hook, Jeff said, "Oh." Corbett said, "Gee, but Jim's right cheek is battered up. That coon must be hitting hard. There goes that left again. It doesn't help Jim's face any. He tells me that he can't see out of the right eye."

Members of the audience called out, "Talk to him, Corbett." Corbett had said little from the 7th round on. He was relatively silent, for he had seen the end coming.

Yet, Johnson took one of his characteristic loafing spells, laying back and playing with the big man. He was as cool as a cucumber, smiling broadly as ever, confident that he was master of the situation, yet also careful as ever. He was taking no chances, for he had matters well in hand, pacing himself very well, gradually punishing and breaking down his foe.

Jeffries landed a high left on the mouth, and in the clinch that followed, Johnson jolted him back in the mouth with his left. As usual, Jeff was unable to protect himself from this blow. Corbett said, "Jeff lands a left high on the head. I wish Jim would lead oftener. He seems satisfied to just wade in and take them."

Jeffries lowered his head while clinching and shoved his left against the body three times. Johnson was not distressed, but just laughed. In the clinch, Jack said to Jeff, "My belly's gone to pieces – eh?" After breaking, Jack came back with a left jab on the face and hook on the chin before they clinched. Corbett observed, "Johnson rests and then suddenly shoots over those punches and Jeffries looks as if he expects them, but he doesn't block 'em."

Johnson grinned and said to Jeffries, "Right on the hip; hit me heah, hit me heah." Jeff managed to land a left on the hip. Johnson said, "They say my belly is awful weak, Jeff. Awful weak." Taking body shots with a smile was Johnson's response to all those, including Jeffries, who claimed that Johnson and other black fighters could not take it and would show yellow as soon as they absorbed body punishment. Corbett then said to Johnson, "Why don't you do something? You're doing a lot of talking, why not fight?" Johnson replied, "Too clever, too clever, like you." The crowd laughed.

The *Reno Gazette* said the round ended tamely, but Johnson had all of the honors. Jeff's seconds looked blue. The *Call* said Jeff was just about done, for he barely was able to stand, while Johnson was fresher and faster than ever. Richard Barry said Johnson was still cautious, fighting the same fight. He gave no openings, and slipped in an uppercut when he saw the chance. The *Chronicle* and *Nevada State Journal* both said Jeffries kept coming forward and springing in with blows, but the clever Johnson was able to block leads with the greatest ease, while frequently landing his own blows.

Between rounds, only water was used in Jack's corner, while in Jeff's corner they were using everything that they had.

15 - There were no bright faces in Jeff's corner, for it looked as if he was fading away. Jeffries came out with his guard held high. Naughton said he blocked a straight left and they clinched. Sullivan said Johnson sent his left

on the eye before they clinched for a while. After breaking, Johnson shot a left jab from the hip straight into the face, and then followed it up with another. They clinched near the ropes.

Johnson freed his right arm from the clinch and fired a vicious right uppercut to the point of the chin that jolted Jeffries' head back. Then Johnson fired three consecutive left hooks to the jaw, each one knocking Jeffries backwards towards the ropes, where he turned around and went down, grabbing the lower rope with his right hand. It was the first knockdown of his career.

Showing his inexperience, Tex Rickard failed to count. Johnson hovered close to Jeffries, a few feet away. Corbett hollered, "Get up, Jim. For God's sake get up. Throw some water there, you fellows, are you turned to stone?" Of course, he was suggesting illegal assistance.

Jeffries got to a position with one foot and knee on the floor, looking at timekeeper Harting, who was calling out the count. When Jeff started to rise, Johnson began moving closer, eager to pounce and land a finishing blow as soon as Jeff rose. The ex-champ saw this and wisely momentarily checked himself and kept his knee down. Rickard stepped in and slightly pushed Johnson back with one arm so that Jeff could have some space to rise. Jeffries rose in about nine seconds; though some said it had been more.

As soon as Jeffries rose, from one pace away, Johnson quickly took one step in and nailed him with a powerful left hook to the jaw, and Jeff tumbled backwards through the ropes in nearly the same place. His rear end and right arm were on the canvas outside the ropes, but his legs were draped over the ropes, hanging there, with his left hand grabbing the lower rope. Essentially, Jeff was in a sitting posture outside the ring with his legs caught on the ropes. Hundreds of his friends and admirers yelled, "Don't let the old man get knocked out; stop it." Other spectators cried and repeated several times, "Don't let the negro knock him out."

Once again, Rickard failed to count. In violation of the rules, Jeff's cornermen mounted the apron. One walked on the apron over to Jeffries, outside the ropes. Two others entered the ring, one of whom looks like Corbett. Berger remained in the corner, standing on the apron. Another person who was not a second, whom Sullivan said was a newspaper man, mounted the ring from the other side of the ring and ran to Jeff, and he, along with one of Jeff's cornermen, lifted and picked up Jeffries from the canvas and helped him get back inside the ring again. A photographer had also entered the ring and moved over to the far side. Appearances were that they had stopped the fight and were acknowledging defeat. The fight seemed to be over. Johnson coolly watched.

Yet the fight was not over. Once Jeffries was back up and in the ring again, Johnson quickly advanced and attacked. The cornermen exited the ring as the fight resumed. Johnson fired a left hook, and then momentarily paused with his left outstretched in stiff arm fashion and his right help up high, as if he was uncertain. Jeff moved backwards and then across the side of the ring as Johnson gave chase, firing two more left hooks, a right, and another left hook as Jeff staggered on the retreat and slightly turned away and went down again on his hands and knees, on the opposite side of the ring from where the first two knockdowns had taken place. The crowd rose to its feet, some yelling and some cheering. Some in the crowd yelled, "Save him from a knock out; throw the sponge into the ring."

Once again, Rickard seemed confused, failing to count, while Johnson hovered about, calmly walking around his foe. Timekeeper Harting was counting the seconds. Tex put his arm out so as to prevent Johnson from pouncing too quickly. Once again, several of Jeff's cornermen entered the ring. The huge Sam Berger seemed intent upon stopping the fight, and approached Johnson, apparently hollering something and raising and pointing out his arm as he spoke, acknowledging defeat. In the meantime, Jeff had risen, unassisted. Johnson pointed towards Berger and stepped away, to the side. Billy Delaney demanded the fight for his man. Tex said he already had awarded the fight to Johnson. Berger led Jeff back to his corner as Johnson's cornermen entered the ring and started celebrating Jack's victory, surrounding him on his side of the ring, while Jeff's seconds surrounded him over on his side of the ring. Others who were sitting at ringside entered the ring as well. The fight was over. John L. Sullivan congratulated Johnson.

Sig Hart allegedly said to the champ, "Go over and shake hands with the poor fellow, Jack." Johnson replied, "No, I don't owe him anything now." Sullivan said Johnson started to walk over to shake hands but the crowd inside the ring was too much for him and his seconds dragged him away. Later, he went over to Jeff's corner to shake, but Corbett and Jack O'Brien waved him away. Richard Barry said that Jack went to shake, but Jeff waived him aside. "He has never shaken Johnson's hand. He probably never will." Conversely, the *Bulletin* said Johnson showed sincere sportsmanship by going over and shaking Jeff's hand, assuring him of his appreciation of his gameness and expressing the hope that there should be no hard feelings.

Jeff remained on his chair in his corner for several minutes, bleeding profusely from the mouth, with his seconds trying to bring him to some kind of respectable shape before he left the ring. He was in a stupor, with his head bowed down.

In his corner, Johnson was besieged by a mob of excited fans. The crowd inside the ring was so dense that the police had to keep people back. Jack seemed a bit concerned about potential violence to his person. His trainers and seconds formed somewhat of a circle around him. Johnson told Delaney, "No, I don't want to go through that crowd. They might mob me." Delaney replied, "Oh, come on, they are all your friends." Eventually, Johnson walked out, but he had his seconds around him as bodyguards.

Spectators tore the ring to pieces as souvenirs. In five minutes, the ropes, canvas, and other material had vanished, as if swept away by a hurricane.

Overall Analysis

The press, fighters, trainers, and managers all virtually were unanimous in their analysis of the fight. They agreed that Jeffries was not even a shadow of his former self, while at the same time granted that Johnson was a magnificent boxer who could not be beaten.

They agreed that Jeffries gradually faded as Johnson methodically broke him down. Jeff could not land effectively against Johnson's magnificent defense. Jeffries was not strong on the attack, and his quickness quickly evaporated. He was dead game, smiling through the blood, always trying, but always failing. Conversely, Jack could land almost at will, chopping away, particularly on the inside, slowly beating Jeffries down.

The *Reno Evening Gazette* described the bout as a courageous struggle of a well-meaning, big, strong, and clever white man against a gigantic greyhound with phenomenal speed, brute force, gameness, and stamina. Johnson had met the giant of a century, a bull in the form of a man, and had shattered the idol and made him a pitiful sight. It was a case of skill, an alert eye, an active brain, and clever actions against the brawn of a tired giant with a sluggish brain and worked-out muscles.

Pauline Jacobson said the fight was all Johnson. "To a novice it was palpable that Jeffries was getting beaten to a pulp, that he was getting groggier and groggier." Jeff's thick swollen lip drooped. His eyes were swollen. Blood spattered over his cheeks and over the ropes.

Johnson outclassed and played with Jeffries, and was not extended or hurt at all. Throughout, he was smiling, light-hearted, and nothing but good nature. Even when the battle was at its thickest, his golden smile was the most prominent feature in the ring.

The only damage Johnson suffered was a cut upper lip, which he received in training from Cotton, and simply was reopened. Some said a punch reopened the cut, while others said it was from a head butt as Jeff rushed in to close quarters.

Most said it was not a great fight, except in terms of its significance. Jack London said it was a slow fight, even for a heavyweight bout. Tommy Burns put up a faster, quicker, livelier battle than Jeffries did. "Faster, better fights may be seen every day of the year in any of the small clubs in the land." The *Chronicle* said the contest was a disappointment in that it was one-sided, and not the anticipated fast and spectacular fight. Jeff was less aggressive and vicious in his work than expected, and failed to make the necessary hurricane battle. Johnson, liking to size up his foes, as he always had done, held back and fought as he wished. John L. Sullivan said, "I don't think it was such a great fight. It was simply a case where nature asserted herself and Jeffries' vitals were gone. The wheels of motion refused to work." It was one-sided from start to finish, and Jeff never was in the fight. His vaunted preparation and condition availed him nothing. He was but a helpless shell of his former self. It was the sorriest sight Sullivan had ever seen. Battling Nelson said it was the greatest event in history but not the greatest fight. "The fight was the poorest exhibition of fighting for a championship I ever saw. Johnson was master of the situation." Johnson was not aggressive enough to please the bloodthirsty fans, but he was effective. The *Chronicle's* Ben Benjamin said there was a sameness to every round. Jeff could not land, for Johnson blocked him with ease and gradually beat him down with a succession of uppercuts. Writer Jack Densham said the fight was less exciting than Johnson's sparring sessions with George Cotton. Conversely, Helen Dare called the fight a wonderful contest of skill, strength, courage, and finesse.

Chances as the Fight Progressed

Early on, Johnson showed that he was the better boxer. The *Reno Evening Gazette* said it was Johnson's fight from the start, and "even a novice at the art could see that." After the first few rounds, it was evident that Jeff was fighting a losing battle. However, no one dared express such a belief amongst the thousands of Jeffries admirers, who greeted every blow Jeff landed, and even ones he attempted, with cheers. He remained the favorite with the vast throng of people, who cheered whenever he happened to land on some portion of Johnson's anatomy, regardless of whether the blow carried any force or was of any damaging effect. "The mere fact that Jeffries had reached the negro with a blow was considered sufficient for loud applause." Seldom was there a word for the dark man, who was slamming away at Jeff's face, bringing the red blood flowing. A *Chronicle* writer said that from the 3rd round on it was altogether Johnson's fight. During the bout, Pauline Jacobson said of Johnson, "Oh, he is giving it to him; he is giving it to him!" A spectator told her, "Oh, shut up! We've got to hope for the best. All the more credit to Jeffries if he wins." However, in the next breath, that same spectator then said, "Oh, where are his famous stomach punches?" Later, Jeff's adherents admitted their favorite's defeat long before the actual end came.

The *Nevada State Journal* said Jeff's right eye was damaged in the 1st round and closed in the 6th. Between each round, Choynski swabbed out the cut left optic and injected a healing lotion into it. As the fight progressed, the congested blood turned the skin under the eye a deep blue.

John L. Sullivan said Johnson won easily, never showing the slightest concern. From the 4th round on, Johnson's confidence was the most glaring thing he ever saw.

T. P. Magillian said that except for the 4th round, "the writer could not see any round where Jeffries so much as held this black man even." It was all Johnson, for he toyed with Jeffries.

Jack London said that after the fiddling of the first few rounds, the issue never was in doubt. Honors were with Johnson from the start, and strongly so after the 7th or 8th rounds. In the closing rounds it was all Johnson.

A woman who witnessed the battle said Johnson was calm, smiling, and confident. Every point was in his favor during the first 4 rounds, but it wasn't until the 5th that she fully started to appreciate the skill that Johnson was using to play a game at which his knowledge was complete.

The *Chronicle, Nevada State Journal, Bulletin*'s William Jacobs, Waldemar Young, and W. W. Naughton agreed that after the 6th round, it was all Johnson, and it was obvious that he was going to win. Some said that Jack's closing of Jeff's eye in the 6th was the beginning of the end, and it was obvious that he was a beaten man. Most agreed that it was one-sided from the start, that Jeff never really had a "look-in," but from the 6th on the "tragedy" headed towards the only conclusion possible. The *Nevada State Journal* said Jeffries had a chance up to the 2nd round, but agreed that after the 6th round it was plain that Jeff was weakening and outclassed. Jeff landed a few body blows, but he was being chopped to pieces gradually.

Sam Fitzpatrick, who wanted to see Jeff win, left the fight toward the end of the 7th round. When asked where he was going, he said, "I am going out. I don't want to see the finish." He saw that Jeff was slow and slowing.

The *Reno Evening Gazette* said that in about the 8th round it started to become evident what the result was to be. Ben Benjamin said Jeff's defeat generally was prognosticated after the 8th round. T. P. Magillian agreed.

John L. Sullivan said Jeffries clinched often, but when Johnson threw him away from him in one clinch in the 8th or 9th round, Sully was further convinced that Johnson would win.

Frank Herman said that in the 9th round, someone remarked that Jeff's only chance was a lucky wallop.

The *Nevada State Journal* said that Jeff's lower lip, driven against his teeth by a swinging right to the jaw, bled freely after the 10th round. His mouth puffed out to a grotesque smile, and his swollen eye gave him the pitiful appearance of winking weirdly. The *Bulletin* said that from the 10th round on, it was little short of a slaughter. The end obviously was approaching. Nothing but courage carried Jeffries through the last 4 rounds. Ben Benjamin said Jeff was almost in a state of collapse at the end of 10 rounds.

Jack Densham believed that Johnson decided to finish things in the 11th round, for he rocked Jeff's head. Helen Dare said that in about the 11th round, Johnson's face took on a stronger, bolder confidence, a laughing but ever watchful impudence. Jeff's fierce aggressiveness wavered from his eyes and a sort of angry wonder came into them. Corbett's face suddenly looked grave. The *Nevada State Journal* said that after the 11th it was hopeless for Jeffries. Frank Herman said that in the 11th round, when Jeff was hammered all over, someone remarked that he would be lucky to last 15 rounds. Jeff's look of determination left him, while Johnson winked at the crowd.

In the 12th round, another driving uppercut caught Jeff under the nose and tore the skin around the nostrils. Blood trickled continually from the wound. The constant hammer of blows on his right jaw had puffed the side of his face out of proportion. Pauline Jacobson said that by the 12th round, it was obvious that Johnson had him: "He's got him now; he's got him now; why don't they call it off and give it to the negro now? There's one thing, by God, they can't say now this was a frame-up. Johnson got him outclassed in every way; he's got him outboxed." A spectator responded, "Ah, cheer up. Jeffries is liable to get Johnson yet when Johnson is looking at the grandstand. He's too fond of that." But Jeff continued growing groggier. Jack smiled, placing his blows wherever he wanted on the defenseless man, beating him to a pulp. Between rounds, Choynski put his lips to Jeff's cheek and sucked the blood; all while the other seconds were splashing water and waving towels frantically. Johnson's corner was serene. "God, it is awful."

The *Bulletin* said Johnson had Jeffries in bad shape in the 13th round, and it looked like curtains. Lou Houseman left the arena, saying, "I've had enough. I can't stand any more of this." Jeff was surprised, bewildered, and helpless under the volley of blows that were landing at will. His guard was of no use to stop the trip-hammer blows. The drubbing he had received was telling on him, and he had no strength to fight back.

Some said Jeff's showing in the 14th round gave some of his supporters hope. However, Jack Densham said both men slowed in the 14th, making it seem nearly even, but Jeff was gone. After the round, Jeffries told his cornermen, "It's no use."

Naughton said that as of the 15th round, Jeffries had been cuffed for at least the last eight rounds. By the end of the first minute of the 15th round, Jeff was down for the first time in his career.

C. E. Van Loan said the end came with suddenness, but it was not a surprise, for it had been in plain sight since the 5th round. Even the most rabid Jeffries fans could not deceive themselves. Johnson had been manhandling him in the clinches, systematically and methodically whipping in blows, and easily blocking Jeff's punches, such that there was nothing to do but wait until the fight's end. Frank Herman said that although Jeff had been fading away since the 9th, in the 15th he still looked strong enough to last a couple more rounds. Hence the end was somewhat sudden and surprising. The *Chronicle* said that when it was over, a hushed silence fell over the audience, like a funeral. The end was no surprise, for most saw it coming.

Round by Round Fight Summary

Frank Hall said he sat alongside John L. Sullivan, and was only three feet from Johnson's corner. He could see and hear everything. The coolness that Johnson displayed "was the most remarkable exhibition of nerve I have ever had the good fortune to witness." When Johnson entered the ring and shook hands with Hall and Sullivan, Hall asked him how he was feeling. Jack said, "Very, very fine."

After Delaney gave him his water, the gong sounded and the men faced each other to start the fight. Johnson said, "Now, come on, Jeff; do your best." Jeff made no reply but kept chewing his gum. In the latter part of the 1st round, Johnson said to Jeffries, "Be very careful, for you have got one too many eyes to look out of." Jeff just swung his left, landing on the hip. Then, for the first time, Johnson used his uppercut, and Jeff's head went back. It made Hall think back to when Jeff once said, "How is this fellow going to knock me down when I have never had my head knocked back. There is no man living in the world who can knock my head back much less put me out." Hall had once told Johnson what Jeff said, and Jack replied that not only would he knock Jeff's head back but he'd knock him down.

The *Chronicle* said not much took place in the 1st round other than a wonderful exhibition of defense by Johnson. Jack landed the first punch, a left to the face, but Jeffries brought first blood with a light left to the underlip, a slight cut that later bled profusely.

Naughton said that from the start, Johnson kept a strong look-out for Jeff's powerful left, pressing against Jeff's left forearm with the palm of his own right glove.

Hall said Corbett tried to coach Jeff in the corner with all of his skill and knowledge, and kept up a streak of fire at Johnson, telling him that he was yellow and it would appear shortly. Jack responded by smiling, showing his golden teeth.

The *Chronicle* said Johnson started the 2nd round with two left hooks to the face. Corbett said, "He wants to fight, Jim. Let him." Hall said Johnson was superior in the 2nd and 3rd rounds. After receiving a blow in the stomach, he stood up tall and said, "Try it again, Jeff; once again, Jeff," and then drew Jeffries nearer to him, putting his arm around his neck and uppercutting him with his right. That started the blood flowing from the ex-champion.

Naughton believed that Johnson was not confident at the start, but his confidence grew after a few rounds. Regardless, contrary to the belief of those who thought he would run away, Johnson never did. From the start, he was content to hold his ground and fight in the clinches.

As the bout progressed, Hall recalled John L. Sullivan's prophetic words; that after Jeffries had been fighting for 3 or 4 rounds he would feel as if he had a dumb-bell in each hand. Such was plainly visible in the 4th and 5th rounds.

T. P. Magillian said Jeff tried hard in the 4th, managed to land a hard left to the stomach, and made Johnson grunt. However, Hall said up to that point, Jeffries had learned that one good blow simply made Johnson laugh. Conversely, Johnson's blows were effective. Johnson said to Corbett, "They all say I can't hit – here is one of them," and he fired a blow which knocked Jeff's head as far back as it could go.

Jeffries was very game, took the punishment round after round, and swallowed the blood.

The *Chronicle* said the 4th and 5th rounds were much the same. Jeff tried to land but could not do so effectively. Johnson contented himself with landing body punches that had a weakening effect, even if they did not appear to be spectacular. However, Jeff's nose and lips became bloody in the 5th round.

The tide truly turned in the 6th round. Determined to mix, Jeff valiantly rushed several times, but could not land. Conversely, Johnson left-hooked him repeatedly, and also landed left uppercuts. Naughton said Johnson suddenly freed his left from a clinch and landed well enough to close Jeff's right eye. A few seconds later, Jack freed his right and uppercut Jeff on the mouth, and the blood flowed. A cut opened under Jeff's left eye as well. From then on, throughout the bout, Jack continued to free himself from clinches and land short shots.

T. P. Magillian said Johnson was his master at infighting as well as at long range. Johnson's famous right uppercut jarred Jeff's head back. Jack grabbed Jeff around the shoulders and said, "That's right, Jim, do just as your seconds tell you." Jeff seemed surprised that Jack had no fear of him and was totally unconcerned.

Naughton said Johnson became flippant. At one stage, he said to Jeff, "Well, old man, it's all over but the shouting." He frequently talked to Corbett in a sneering manner. With every round, Johnson became "more overbearing." He laughed in Jeff's face, and when the mood seized him, he pulled himself free from clinches and fired in short shots. Jeff could not cope, and rarely rushed. He managed to duck some long range shots, but after he ducked and they ended up in a clinch, Johnson hooked and jolted him from the inside.

The *Chronicle* said Jeffries' eye bothered him considerably in the 7th round. He could not land and he was having trouble seeing. When he went to his corner, someone remarked, "He's a beaten man."

T. P. Magillian said a right uppercut in the 8th round lifted and hurt Jeff, who cried out, "Oh." Johnson took his time, though, going about things in a cool, workmanlike fashion. He hit the body and face with an assortment of jarring blows that were punishing. Jeff was game, and though he fought carefully, he showed no trace of cowardice. Few big men would have taken the pummeling as stoically as he did. The men were good-natured, jesting with each other throughout. At the conclusion of several of the rounds, Johnson gave Jeff an encouraging and patronizing slap on the shoulder.

Naughton said that by the 9th round, things looked worse still for Jeffries. He tried to land body blows, but in the main, Johnson's forearms intercepted the efforts. When going into a clinch, Jeff landed one forceful right to the pit of the stomach which caused a roar of delight. Jack just grinned, and then laughed some more when Jeff landed a left on the ribs.

Naughton said the 10th round was a bit slower. Battling Nelson said that at the end of the 10th round, Jeff received a good hard left hook on the liver that put a sickening expression on his face. He reeled like a drunken sailor, but the bell came to his rescue.

According to Naughton, in the 11th, Johnson was confidence personified, laughing and nodding to various folks while in the clinches. He also amused himself with chaffing Corbett. Jack feinted rapidly and then sent a snappy right to the jaw. Jeff shook his head as though stung and clinched. Johnson suddenly yanked his left clear and jolted the face rapidly. Blood dripped from Jeff's nose and lips and his right eye was more swollen than ever. Yet, Jeff laughed good-naturedly. It seemed that Jeffries was hell-bent on landing one good smash in the body. However, he rarely landed solidly, for Johnson blocked well. Whenever the crowd voiced its approval of what appeared to be a well-placed body shot, Johnson giggled and then peppered Jeff's face with several left hooks in the clinches.

Battling Nelson said the 11th round was tame, for Johnson was willing to wait to land the knockout.

One *Chronicle* writer said the only round that Jeff truly gave his supporters something to cheer about was the 11th. Johnson had subjected him to terrific right and left blows that were some of the hardest of the fight. Jeff was in bad shape in the early part of the round, but he recuperated and landed a right to the face that appeared to stagger Jack, who stalled a bit. It was a fast round, and it had the crowd on its toes.

However, from the 12th to the 15th, it was all Johnson. He fought as he pleased, systematically chopping Jeff to pieces. He even left openings, because he knew that Jeff was a whipped man and had nothing left. The ex-champion had lost his execution, strength, speed, and defense.

Naughton noted that in between rounds, Corbett liked to stalk along the edge of the ring to the other corner, across from Johnson, perhaps trying to observe Johnson's condition, or perhaps to annoy him. However, Jack was cheery and buoyant. After the 13th round, Corbett ventured forth no more.

By the 14th round, it seemed uncanny how easy it was for Johnson to free his left and land it. Jeff was bloody from ear to ear, and his right eye was a mere slit. He had a "woe-begone" expression. He still tried to hit the body, but Johnson did not cringe or budge.

Hall said the first knockdown in the 15th round took place on the side of the ring near Jeff's corner. For the second knockdown, blood from Jeff's throat spattered all over the timekeeper and himself.

When it was all over after the third knockdown, after he returned to his corner, Johnson said to Hall,

> Frank, I could have fought him for two hours longer easily. Wire to my mother at once. I was only having some fun when the finish came. Not one blow hurt me. It is Jeffries that can't hit. He will never forget two punches I landed on him, and he will never order John L. out of his camp again for giving his opinion of a fighter. He won't be so grouchy now. … Don't you think I boxed well. I fought this fight different than I ever did before and I fought a better one.

When Hall asked for Johnson's gloves, in declining, Jack replied, "I will give one to Corbett and one to Jeff." "Where is my lucky bathrobe? I don't want to miss that."

The End

By the 15th round, Jeff's right eye was closed to a slit, his left eye was swollen and cut underneath, his nose was split, and blood trickled from his lips. The smile of victory was upon Johnson's face. According to the *Chronicle*, when the 15th round began, the men engaged in a long clinch. Corbett shrieked advice. Johnson chuckled, "Do as they told you, Jim," and then landed a left to Jeff's stomach that hurt. Johnson landed a right uppercut and then shot in three wicked lefts to the face and Jeff sank to the floor. Sam Berger yelled to Jeff's brother, "For God's sakes, Jack, throw in the towel and stop this fight."

The *Chronicle* felt that Jeffries should have been counted out the first time he went down. It said Harting counted twelve seconds, but Rickard did not hear the count and allowed Jeff to rise. "Timekeeper George Harting tolled the count with uplifted finger, but Tex Rickard, unaccustomed to his position, and excited at the tenseness in the air, lost track of affairs." Of the first knockdown, Jim Corbett said, "He was on the floor many seconds more than ten, but it seemed a year to me."

Conversely, the *Examiner's* Alfred Lewis, William Slattery, and the *Reno Evening Gazette* said Jeff rose nearly at ten, but beat the count. He was a bloody, tired, beefy human being.

The *Bulletin* provided another perspective regarding Rickard's demonstration of inexperience and lack of knowledge when Jeff was down. "The rules call for a man to retire to his own corner when he floors an opponent. Johnson stood directly over the prostrate Jeffries." Rickard only pushed Jack back one pace. Hence, from this perspective, the count should have been suspended until Johnson moved back further.

As soon as Jeffries rose from the floor, like a flash, Johnson immediately hit him with another left hook and Jeff went down again, his huge body sprawling backwards outside the ropes, his legs dangling over them. C. E. Van Loan heard some folks yell, "Stop it, Tex! Stop it!" Corbett asked, "Why don't the bell ring?!"

Rickard's voice was not strong enough and no one heard a count. Jeff laid there until Jack Jeffries and a newspaper man picked him up and tossed him back into the ring.

Van Loan, Naughton, and Slattery said Jeff was up just before or at the count of ten. He spat a mouthful of blood. Some thought the fight was over. Slattery said, "It is a question as to whether Jeff ever would have risen but for the assistance of his brother, but, anyhow, [his brother] Jack committed a rash foul, and had Refcree Tex Rickard acted in accordance to the rules, he should have disqualified Jeffries then and there and awarded the battle to Johnson."

Richard Barry said that after the second knockdown, Farmer Burns and Roger Cornell helped Jeff up. "Technically, the fight should have been stopped right there, but Tex Rickard, the referee, who had not said a word nor lifted a hand until that moment, paid no attention to the irregularities." Jim Coffroth said no towel came into the ring; only a handful of seconds.

The *Bulletin* said the illegal act of lifting Jeff up and back into the ring "brought a roar from the Johnson supporters," but Johnson did not complain or appeal to the referee. He knew that he had his man safe, and wanted no technical victory, but to end it cleanly. There were enough of Jeff's advisers in the ring to have disqualified Jeff had the referee so chosen.

The *San Francisco Evening Post* said that in the clamor that followed the second knockdown, Johnson did not realize he was the victor, and while Jeff retreated, Jack followed and knocked him down again. Berger entered the ring to stop the fight and prevent further punishment. Upon the third knockdown, Corbett said, "There he goes. I don't want to look at it. Jim, Jim!" Coffroth said, "He would have gone down for a fourth time had not Berger made himself understood to Rickard that defeat was acknowledged by the Jeffries corner."

The *Bulletin* said that as soon as Jeffries was lifted to his feet illegally after the 2nd knockdown, Johnson attacked, slugged, and mauled the "tottering hope of the white race" across the ring with hooks, rights, and a left uppercut and Jeff went down for the third time. He placed one hand on the lower rope.

Jeffries was not counted out. "Whether or not, it probably will be counted as a knockout." Jeff actually rose at eight. However, as the timekeeper was tolling the seconds, Berger humanely stepped through the ropes and entered the ring to stop the fight. Robert Edgren said that when Rickard saw Berger, he told Johnson, "Stop. Don't hit him." Wanting to prevent further slaughter and cruel and unnecessary punishment, Berger said, "We lose, Tex." Jeff was like a man in a trance. Delaney, Johnson's chief second, hollered his claim for the fight based on Jeff's handlers' breach of the rules. At least eight men then entered from both sides. There was a moment of confusion. No one heard any formal decision, but obviously it was over. Some noted that Rickard raised Johnson's glove as a signal that he had won. Others said Rickard could not make himself heard, but had announced that Johnson had won.

Johnson stood at ring center and received congratulations from Delaney and his other seconds. His breathing was normal, not as if he had been engaged in an athletic endeavor.

The Formal Decision

The *Call's* William Slattery said Tex Rickard did not initially give a formal technical decision as to how the bout ended. All folks knew was that Jeff went down three times and obviously had enough, Berger entered the ring to ensure that the fight was stopped, and Rickard declared Johnson the winner. The question was whether Jeffries was disqualified or knocked out.

Jack London said the end was pitiful. "Never mind the technical decision. Jeff was knocked out. That is all there is to it." London noted that Jeff was knocked through the ropes by a left, too, the punch that no one believed Johnson possessed.

W. W. Naughton opined, "Johnson will receive the credit of a knockout. It is the law of the ring that if anyone intervenes when a knockout is imminent, a knockout is recorded."

Another wrote, "Rickard finds it difficult to make an official ruling on the technical points involved, but is disposed to rule that the interference of

Jeffries' seconds in helping him to get up after the second knockdown constitutes a disqualification."

Rickard said,

> Jeffries was not counted out, although I am satisfied he could never have got up within the ten seconds when he went down the second time if his seconds had not put their hands on him and pushed him up. This assistance disqualified Jeffries and I was trying to get between the fighters to stop the fight on that account when Johnson sent him down for the third time with a left and right on the jaw. The pictures will show that I got between them when this third knockdown came and gave the fight to Johnson before the timekeeper could count ten. Therefore I believe it should stand as a disqualification, although as I have said, Jeffries would have been counted out had the disqualification not occurred.[428]

Rickard also was quoted by several reporters as saying,

> I awarded the fight to Johnson after Jeffries went down the second time because he was lifted to his feet and pushed back to the middle of the ring by Berger, Attell, and I think, Choynski. But before I could get between them they were fighting again, and Jeff went down the third time.

> The fight was won and lost when Jeffries went through the ropes... This is official. ... It was this way: Jeffries was brought to his knees, and, as he arose, dazed, Johnson hit him with a succession of lefts that sent him through the ropes. As he lay there several of his seconds caught hold of him and helped him to his feet. Under the rules of the game, which I have read thoroughly, while certain people were saying that I couldn't referee a fight, this disqualified Jeffries and Johnson was the winner. I thought the seconds were going to carry Jeff to his corner, Instead, they shoved him into the ring again to be beaten further, while I was doing all I could during the confusion to stop the fight.

Yet, another quoted Rickard as saying, "I stopped the fight only when I saw that Jeff could not keep on his feet. It would have been brutal to have let Johnson hit him again."

Regardless of what he said, Rickard's statements were not at all consistent with Rickard's actions in the ring, and do not match what the films show. Even though he could have disqualified Jeff for the assistance given to him in rising after the second knockdown, in truth that is not what he did. He allowed the bout to continue after Jeff was assisted up, and does not appear to make any attempts to stop the bout at that point. He also

---

[428] *San Francisco Bulletin*, July 6, 1910.

appeared willing to allow it to continue even after Jeff went down a third time, until Berger entered and made it clear that he wanted it stopped.

Some writers said the general custom was that if a second entered the ring to stop the fight and signify that he was throwing up the sponge because his man had enough, that it was the equivalent of a retirement and technical knockout rather than disqualification. It appeared that Rickard was making his disqualification ruling ex post facto, or after the fact. They all knew that the real reason it was over was because Jeff had enough.

Official timekeeper George Harting (or Harding) said time was called to start the fight at 2:45 p.m. The bout was terminated at 2 minutes and 27 seconds of the 15th round. It ended at 3:41 p.m. Harting did not count out Jeffries. Jeff was down for nine seconds, then eight or nine seconds when he was assisted to his feet, which was against the rules which require a fighter to rise unassisted. Harting said he did not think Jeff could have risen unaided from the second knockdown. For the last knockdown, Jeff's cornermen rushed in for the second time, which "earned for him his second disqualification." Regardless of their entry, "There is no doubt that, independent of this action; Jeffries would have been counted out." Of course, it would have taken at least another knockdown, for Jeff rose at eight after the third knockdown; but clearly he was near the end. Harting noted that Rickard awarded Johnson the fight after the third knockdown, after Jeff's seconds "sprang into the ring when they saw that their idol was helpless."

Harting had told Rickard before the fight that if a man was dropped that he had to keep the other boxer from standing directly over the fallen fighter, and to watch him for the count. He complimented Rickard's work. However, Rickard had not exactly prevented Johnson from standing over Jeffries.

The contest's result could be considered a technical knockout, retirement, or a disqualification, depending upon how you want to view matters. Regardless, Johnson had won, for Jeffries was in no condition to continue without ultimately being beaten into total unconsciousness.

"Long absence from the ring tells the story." - Ben Benjamin

All of the writers agreed that as the fight progressed, Jeff showed a lack of stamina, strength, and steam. He never showed a flash of his old-time ability at any stage, but was just an empty shell of a once great fighter. The march of time had killed his vital spark. It proved that no man can defy the laws of nature and come back after a long absence from the ring.

Naughton said the fight was reminiscent of the Corbett-Sullivan and Corbett-Mitchell fights, which Corbett won against men who had been inactive for years. Years of inactivity and poor habits had cost Sullivan all of his speed. It also was like Jeffries-Jackson. Against Jeffries, Peter Jackson had been a shadow of his former self. Now it was Jeff's turn, "poetic retribution" in a way. It reaffirmed the adage, "youth will be served."

The *Chronicle* said, "Jeffries put up a sorry fight." "It was pitiful in a way, this vanquishing of the hope of the white race, the effort of a man to drag himself back into athletic condition in order to wrest back to his own race the title that he had relinquished." However, Jeff did show gameness by absorbing a beating and rising from the knockdowns.

Rex Beach said it was no fight at all, but a pitiful tragedy. Although not much happened in the first three rounds, Johnson gradually awoke to the fact that the march of time cannot be disputed, and so too did Jeffries.

T. P. Magillian said Jeff's efforts were feeble, half-hearted, and ill directed. He missed his blows and was countered. He clinched to avoid punishment, but received frequent uppercuts on the chin. He was game but slow, fighting a losing uphill battle all the way. "Men compared his ineffectual blows and his incessant clinches with the slashing fights of his earlier years. They forgot that it needs but the loss of a fraction of a man's speed to convert him from a champion into a has-been."

<u>Further Analysis and Plaudits for Johnson</u>

Despite the criticisms of and explanations about Jeff's performance, nevertheless, Jack Johnson was given a great deal of credit. Newsmen agreed that there was nothing that Johnson could not do. He was a marvel of accuracy, a whirlwind for speed, and a giant for strength. He shoved the giant Jeffries about the ring. He was a masterful boxer and game fighter, with superb cleverness and ring generalship. The *Nevada State Journal* said Johnson was like a panther, beautiful in alertness and defensive tactics. The *Chronicle* called Johnson the "most wonderful big man that the prize-ring has ever seen." He fought a remarkable battle, showing great ring generalship, boxing in his own way. Johnson's defense was everything that proponents claimed. He boxed in superb style, blocking the blows and landing effective uppercuts. Ben Benjamin said Johnson was confident all the way and scored an easy victory owing to superior cleverness. C. E. Van Loan said Johnson was clean, fair, masterful, and unquestionably superior. The *San Francisco Evening Post* said the game, courageous Jeffries was outclassed by a crafty, clever man with strength and skill.

The *Reno Evening Gazette* said Johnson was in his prime, presented an "almost impregnable defense," and was a "cracking good hitter."

> [P]ossibly never in the prize ring's history has there been a man possessing more varied powers than this dark hued giant, whose muscles are trained to a combination of strength and quickness and accuracy such as has never been excelled, and whose guiding brain works in perfect harmony with his muscles. …
>
> Johnson rightfully deserves the glory that should be his. All names of the fighters of today dwindle when his is called. How long his reign will be one may tell. But that he has earned the right to wear the crown, no one who believes in fair play will deny.

Another Reno writer opined that Jeff's strategy was all wrong. He threw caution to the wind and rushed into clinches, playing the infighting game with Johnson, but it was he who was being hit, rocked, bloodied, cut to pieces, and sapped of vitality from volleys of uppercuts and hooks. Even before the 5th round, his face looked bad. The faces of the Jeffries bettors took on a drooping expression.

The *San Francisco Chronicle* said Johnson handled Jeffries as he pleased in an unequal contest, landing at will and blocking nearly every punch, which prepared the crowd for the end that was bound to follow the awful beating. Many of his fans retained hope that Jeff could land one big one to turn the tide, but that hope never was realized. The end was quick and dramatic.

The *Chronicle* opined that Johnson's short jolting body blows did more to wear down Jeffries than anything. Jeff was bothered when his eye was closed, but the body shots made him breathe heavier and his legs weaker.

Jeffries was "just as far from being the Jeffries of the days gone by as Johnson was different from that black man who fought Marvin Hart in San Francisco once upon a time and who was roundly hissed and hooted for his indifferent work." Jeff had retrograded and Johnson had wonderfully improved in both defense and aggressiveness, "a style that is born only of confidence." "The best man did win. No one of us can gainsay that, black man though he is."

Most said Jeffries was beaten terribly, while Jack London and C. E. Van Loan said he was stopped but not so badly punished. A Reno writer said Jeff's face was "cut to ribbons and his bloody visage" presented a "pitiful sight." Homer Mooney said it was like a baseball game with a 23-0 score. The *Chronicle's* Ben Benjamin said Jeffries was a badly beaten man.

W. W. Naughton said Jeffries was mastered, whipped, and cut to pieces by a grinning, jeering negro's merciless attacks. Johnson was stronger, and whipped Jeff primarily with left hooks and left uppercuts while clinching. "It was a one-sided fight. Johnson overpowered Jeff in the clinches, which was thought to be Jeff's long suit. Johnson proved more clever than many expected. Where formerly he had been using to great purpose his right, in this fight he resorted to his left."

Naughton said the odds saw Jeffries sliding after the 6th round. He had been a 10 to 6 favorite, but was even by the 7th. A round or two later Jeff was the 10 to 6 underdog. By the 12th round, no one would bet on Jeff, no matter what the odds.

Another *San Francisco Examiner* writer, Alfred Lewis, said Johnson was quicker, cleverer, hit harder and more often. His defense was perfect – he could step back, duck, dodge, or block. Jeffries frequently sought the clinches, and yet he got the worst of it there. Johnson hooked him repeatedly and badly beat his face to a pulp, although Jeff calmly chewed gum continually. Johnson's mouth bled a little in the first two rounds, but he smiled throughout and was smooth in his work. The bout seemed like a joke to him. When he wasn't making flippant remarks to Jeff he was tossing one to Corbett or members of the audience.

The *Bulletin's* William Jacobs said, "Johnson must get full credit for his victory. Even though Jeff was lacking in the 'dash of youth,' he was still probably the most formidable man in the heavyweight ranks." Jeff was in good condition, but Johnson was his master at every stage and aspect of the game.

> It is safe to say that Johnson landed five blows to Jeffries' one throughout the fight. Jeff, perhaps, led as many times as the colored man, but, whereas his blows left his shoulder like a slow-moving piston rod and were promptly blocked by the black, Johnson's blows started like a torpedo and usually landed right where they were meant to land. Johnson had speed, direction and strength in abundance. Jeffries had nothing.

This writer approximated that Johnson had landed 14 clean uppercuts to the chin, 60 straight left jabs, 40 or more right and left hooks to the face and body, and "heaven only knows how many solid jolts with both hands secured in the infighting."

Jack Densham said, "But it was interesting to see how Johnson followed the lines he had laid down for himself, his cool and careful calculation at all times and the almost reflex action with which he defended himself." The scientific Johnson never took a chance, but he never missed an opportunity. He did no showy boxing. There was no unnecessary movement. He guarded against every attack and sent in his own blows with uncanny rapidity. Jeff landed few blows, and what he did land had little effect, and usually Johnson smiled. When Johnson clinched, it looked like he was using no energy, yet Jeff could not do anything. It was so easy for Johnson it almost appeared lazy. Jack took body blows with nonchalance, to the surprise of those who expected him to be hurt. He even intentionally allowed Jeff to land some body blows, causing wonder to sweep throughout the crowd. "Perfect temper, perfect fitness, wonderful skill and uncanny accuracy all combined to assist Jack Johnson in winning the smoothest and most easily won battle that was ever fought for a championship."

Ed Hamilton said Jeff was beaten down by the jolts, hooks, and uppercuts of infighting. An Australian said it was worse than the Burns fight. Many thought that Jeff was stalling, holding back, taking his time, and trying to wear down Johnson, and eventually would loosen up and show something, but he did not and could not. That was all he had.

Douglas Erskine said Johnson proved himself to be a marvel in boxing skill, strength, speed, and condition, growing stronger in each round. However, most said that Mother Nature had beaten Jeffries, who was relatively weaker by the 7th round.

The *Call's* William Slattery said that except for the first few rounds, Jeffries was slow and unable to block punches. He was exhausted, outfought, outgeneraled, and outgamed from start to finish. There might have been a few rounds which may have been even, but they were very few, and were even only because Johnson did not attempt to extend himself. He laid off, rested up, and studied his foe's every move. "Johnson had proved to the world that he is the greatest heavyweight fighter of them all."

Ed Cahill said it simply was a case of too much Johnson, a great man. "Johnson is the perfect fighter, compact, of whipcord, and steel." Jack sat on the sunny side of the ring, and unlike Jeffries, required no sunshade protection, for his black skin protected him. "No naked lizard on a rock was more immune from heat stroke than he. Is the Caucasian fighting man played out?"

Throughout, Johnson landed wicked uppercuts. Jeff kept boring for the body, and landed many times, but Johnson just grinned, and on occasion patted Jeff on the back in a patronizing way. Jeff simply could not affect Jack's good nature. Cahill called Johnson a "grinning savage."

San Francisco Mayor P. H. McCarthy said Johnson was the ring's greatest fighter. He must have had steam behind his blows to whip Jeffries.

Frank Herman opined that when Jeffries saw how easily Johnson blocked his rushes and checked ripping lefts in a nonchalant, almost indifferent manner, he lost heart. He never landed a blow that had the least effect. Conversely, Johnson had no trouble landing all over, with any punch. "He used a left cross to good advantage and this punch, together with his right uppercut, gradually sapped Jeff's strength. The stomach blows that the shifty coon planted every time he had the grizzly bear off his guard, trying to protect his sore mouth, also were distressing."

The *Nevada State Journal* and *Chronicle* believed that Johnson could have finished off Jeffries earlier had he wished. Some thought he fought for the moving pictures, wanting to give them a longer reel, even though he already sold his interests. Others said he fought for his friends who had wagered on him to win over a certain number of rounds or under a certain number of rounds. Some said that pounding on Jeff over a period of time would serve to show conclusively that he was his master. Or it could be that he wanted to punish Jeffries for the things he had said, and for drawing the color line on him for years. And still others might say he employed his usual cautious methodical style to wear down his man gradually and only finish him when he was certain that he would not risk being caught. He took his time, for there was no need to rush and get reckless.

Jim Coffroth said Jeff's accuracy and judgment of distance was so poor that early on it drew comments of derision from Johnson. As early as the 7th, Jeff shook his head, showing his discouragement. Coffroth said Johnson won every round.

Tom Flynn said not much had changed in the art of boxing from the old days. Johnson used the time-honored tactics of Jem Mace and Peter Jackson, using the left until the opening for the right came.

Boxing said of Johnson, "He clinched, wrestled, and roughed it with Jeffries until he had the white man worn down and weakened, and then, and not until then, he cut loose, and went in to finish the worn-out athlete."[429]

The *Afro-American Ledger* said Johnson manifested his superiority in every department of the game. However, "To many Johnson is still a mystery, for he has hidden behind that gigantic muscular structure some latent powers yet unrevealed." Regardless, he was "today without fear of contradiction the undisputed champion heavyweight of the world."[430]

The *Freeman* said that after the 3rd round, Johnson treated Jeffries almost as a joke. He fearlessly and playfully smiled and blocked, warding off rushes with a marvelous science, tucking blows under his arm or plucking them out of the air as a man stops a baseball. Johnson proved himself to be Jeff's master so absolutely that experts such as Australian sporting writer W. F. Corbett said that Burns had put up a better fight against Johnson. Except for a few rounds, the fight was tame. Jeff had lost his powers of defense, and did not have the punching power to hurt. After receiving blow after blow on the jaw, his power ebbed.

Johnson was "as cool as an iceberg." Although as the white man's hope, Jeffries plainly felt the greater responsibility, Johnson had longed for this fight for over six years. He wanted Jeff to have everything in the way of terms so that there could be no excuses afterwards. When Berger asked him to toss for corners, Johnson said, "Help yourself. Take that one over there so that Jim can have his back to the sun. I'll sit in the other corner. I don't mind a bit." Jeffries would not shake hands or pose together with Johnson for photos before the fight, a clear indication that he thought Johnson was beneath him. After it was over, the spectators looked like they were returning from a funeral. "Johnson is invincible and will remain so for years." "Long live Johnson!"[431]

Alleged Yellow Streak Disproved

Nearly every reporter and expert unanimously agreed that the fight had disproved the theory that Johnson had a yellow streak, "the thing that has been written and talked about ever since he came into ring prominence." Johnson did not show a trace of yellow. London said he went up against a bigger man with a huge reputation, but was not intimidated or scared at all. "And he played and fought a white man, in a white man's country, before a white man's crowd."

Pauline Jacobson said everything was against Johnson, because the audience was white and the referee was white. She asked how Jeff would feel if he was fighting in front of a colored audience with a colored referee. Before the fight, upon entering the ring, Johnson told Rickard, "I don't want any of the worst of it and I don't want any of the best of it."

---

[429] *Boxing*, July 9, 1910.
[430] *Afro American Ledger*, July 9, 1910.
[431] *Freeman*, July 9, 1910.

The *Bulletin* said Johnson was the coolest and most unconcerned man in the arena. His golden smile never deserted him. He won through his marvelous defense and infighting ability, "but more credit is due him for his gameness in facing unruffled a man whom experts had pronounced invincible."

> Nor can credit be denied Johnson for winning under conditions absolutely unfavorable. There are many States in the Union where black men enjoy a greater vogue than in the sagebrush commonwealth. The talk of possibly gun play in event of the negro's winning, taken in connection with the fact that practically every cent of Nevada money was bet on Jeff, was not idle twaddle. In the arena not one person in twenty was an admirer or backer of the negro, and not one person in forty was of his own blood. But the champion never worried and never laid aside his good-natured grin, not even when jeers and even insults were hurled at him by those about the arena.

Another *Bulletin* writer said Johnson "proved to the satisfaction of the writer, at least, that the 'yellow streak' so commonly reported to be one of natural inheritance of the negro was 'left at home' in his case, and that he could take, as well as administer, a glove punching at the hands of the foeman of equal girth and measurement." Of course it was also true that Jeff scarcely landed one solid blow to a vulnerable spot, so some still wondered what would happen if Johnson had to take a beating.

The *Nevada State Journal* said Johnson betrayed no nervousness, let alone fear. After the first two rounds, Jeff was willing to hug Johnson often.

Even Tommy Burns said, "Let no man now say Johnson has a yellow streak. He demonstrated beyond any manner of doubt that he is game to the core." Jack was cool and remained in fighting range at all times. He never missed a chance to score, even when Jeff hugged him.

Jim Coffroth said,

> Let us now call Jack Johnson the champion of the world and not tell about all his poor fights and the little men he has whipped. He was asked today to meet in the ring the greatest fighting animal we have known. He met him in an arena where but few of his race were about him. ... He was fighting on a soil that has been referred to by the effete east as the 'wild and wooly west,' where gun plays are thought to be as common as the click of the ball on the roulette table. ... We will no longer hear of the 'yellow streak.' That's good.

War of Words

Throughout the fight, there was a running comedy of witty sallies which brought amusement to the spectators. With his golden smile much in evidence, Johnson kept up a running conversation with Corbett, Jeffries, ringside spectators, and newsmen. Edgren said Jack smiled and joked with exaggerated good humor. Slattery characterized Johnson's grin as one of hatred, malice, and revenge.

The ongoing war of words and wits between Corbett and Johnson always resulted in a Johnson victory, and Corbett was made the butt of laughter. Corbett usually referred in some way to Johnson's alleged yellow streak, calling on Jeff to "show the yellow streak in the nigger." However, Jack always sent back keen verbal and physical shots. In the 6th round, Johnson warned Jeff that he would mix it, and he carried the fighting to him. He did the same in the 9th. Several times when Jack whispered to Jeff to break or he would uppercut, he did exactly as he threatened. After the 6th round, Jack laughed and joked with the crowd, winked at Corbett, "who had been boisterously noisy during the opening stages," and time and again told Jeff to try to land a body punch. One writer said that after the 8th round, Johnson so completely was the master of the situation that Corbett's remarks were checked. Another said that after the 10th round, all hope vanished, and Corbett's taunting remarks almost completely subsided. C. E. Van Loan said that up until the 10th round, Corbett had been laughing and making fun of Johnson. However, he realized the tide was not going to turn, and therefore his face turned grey and sullen, and he was silenced. The *Reno Evening Gazette* said the "white man with a grouch has been defeated by a colored man with a continual smile, one that won't wipe off, and the battle of all battles has been finished."

Fighters' Opinions

Tom Sharkey said Jeff had no punch and was stalling from the start. "It was the worst fight I ever saw. Jeff never had a chance from the first sound of the gong till the end. It was one big, disgusting joke. I could knock Jeff cold in three rounds." He also said, "If Jeff caught me like that I'd lick him fifteen times. He didn't fight that way when he met me." Tom said he could defeat Johnson and would not stall like Jeff did.

Jake Kilrain said that although once a wonderful fighter, Jeffries was not there at all, not for a minute, for there was no life or snap in his work. Jake knew by the 3rd round that Jeff had not come back and was just a shadow. Still, he gave Johnson credit:

> Johnson is without question a great fighter. I believe that he would have been a great fighter at any period of the pugilistic game. Of course, it is hard to compare him with the famous old-timers, but I think he probably could have fought them an even fight. He is fast and clever. I don't believe Jim Corbett at his best was any better as a boxer. It will be a long time before we find a man to beat this black fellow.

Stanley Ketchel said the fight was no contest. Although Jeff was a weakling compared with the Jeffries of old, he still had a hard punch. "Therefore, you have to give credit to the black."

Johnson could have knocked his man out in any round after the first, but he was holding back, perhaps for the sake of the moving pictures and perhaps because he had told his friends that the fight would go a little distance.

Jeffries displayed absolutely no aggressiveness, and when Johnson began to punish him with uppercuts the yellow showed in the Californian. He was looking for a gate to get out of his trouble, and I am surprised that he lasted as long as he did. ...

Jack Johnson deserves a lot of credit for his showing today. He proved himself to be a strong, clean fighter and a man with a powerful punch. I don't think I have ever seen a man so clever as he is, and I ought to know something about him. He proved to the world that he can be an aggressive as well as a defensive fighter. If he wants to be aggressive, he can be terribly aggressive.

John L. Sullivan said:

I was in such a peculiar position. I all along refused to announce my choice as to the winner. I refused on Jeff's account, because he was sensitive, and I wanted to be with him some time during his training. I refused on Johnson's account, because of my well-known antipathy to his race, and I didn't want him to think that I was favoring him from any other motive than a purely sporting one. He might have got this impression, although since I know him better in these few weeks I am rather inclined to believe that he has not many of the petty meannesses of human character.

You will deduce from the foregoing that I really had picked Johnson as the winner. My personal friends all knew it, and even Jeffries accused me of it one day, but I denied it in this way. I said, "Jeffries, I have picked a winner, but haven't done it publicly."

Sullivan had based his prediction upon the same theory that got him, which is that you cannot come back after long inactivity and obesity.

Tommy Burns said Johnson's showing was a big surprise. He hardly could believe his eyes when he saw Jeffries at Johnson's mercy. It was a one-sided fight from start to finish. Jeff did nothing effective. Johnson never felt the force of his body blows, as he checked some and blocked others. "I heard hundreds of people applauding Jeffries for scoring body blows when from my seat I could plainly see that they had been cleverly blocked by the other fellow."

Bob Fitzsimmons said there never was even a flash of Jeff's old-time self. He looked great, but left his vitality on the road. He overtrained and lacked vim, dash, vigor, strength, force, and power. The fight had not gone 4 rounds before Fitz was convinced of this. "He wasn't even a quarter of the man he was when he met me."

Fitzsimmons gave his thoughts on the rounds. "In the first round I thought Jeffries had a shade the better of it, but he did not display the aggressiveness that I had expected of him." The second and third rounds were about the same. Bob kept waiting to see Jeff display his old irresistible tactics. After the 4th round, Bob realized that Jeff no longer was what he once was. After the 11th round, it was all Johnson. In the 13th, Bob expected to see Johnson put him out. The 15th round was the sorriest sight he ever saw. Jeff had nothing left.

Conversely, Fitzsimmons said Johnson was one of the ring's most dangerous fighters ever. The way Johnson patted Jeff on the shoulder after the rounds was as if to say, "Poor old fellow, I am sorry for you, but I have to do it." It was such a pitiful sight that Bob had tears in his eyes. Fitz said of Johnson:

> He is a big, strong, clean fighter, and has a powerful punch. He is one of the cleverest fighters we ever had. I used to think that he was only a defensive fighter. He showed today that he is an offensive fighter as well. When he wants to he can be terribly aggressive. I believe that if he had forced the fighting in the first round it would not have gone four rounds. But Johnson worked along his own previously made plans. He fought a clever, cool and masterly battle from the start. He made me change my opinion of him as a fighter.

> I don't think there is a man in the ring today who would have a chance against Johnson. Notwithstanding that, he met a weakling compared with the Jeffries of old. He showed by his work that he is a terrific hitter, a most clever blocker and one of the most dangerous aggressive fighters the ring has ever seen.

Sam Langford said he was as willing to fight Johnson as ever:

> This fight don't make him any bigger fighter than he was before. Any one that saw this fight knows that it was no fight at all. Jeff had no business in that ring, that's sure enough. Why, he had no fighting strength and he had no punch, and he had no aim, and he couldn't hit anything, even if he had the strength to land a knockout punch. He did not get any hard body punching at that. Any good middleweight could have taken all the blows he got. Why, say, there were not half a dozen good wallops in the whole fight. I hope that big black man gives me a chance to fight him. I'll promise there will be something doing in the ring that day, boss, yes, sir.

Bill Lang said it was a very slow bout with too much clinching and not enough exchanges. Jeff did not go after Johnson as expected, and after 6 or 7 rounds, Lang concluded that Jeff was outclassed and it would take a fluke for him to win. "It proves that an athlete cannot give up a sport and fatten up and then take off the fat and get back this former muscular strength."

Battling Nelson said Johnson was stronger, cleverer, faster, in better condition, and a better judge of distance. "He scarcely got a sweat. It wasn't

Johnson's hard punching that won as much as it was his untiring, tantalizing, wicked jabs, hooks and uppercuts, along with Jeff's poor condition." Jeff had gameness, determination, and heart, but lacked condition and showed nothing of the great fighting ability that made him famous.

Abe Attell said Jeff was the greatest fighter ever in the heavyweight division, but had passed his prime and could not come back. He lacked his former fire. He could not get at Johnson and his blows were weak.

Jack Root said Jeffries was beaten down round by round in the same spot where Jeff had given away his title to Marvin Hart (after Marvin beat Root). When he visited Jeff's training camp, Root saw that Jeff's judgment was bad; for he was missing blows all the time. So he bet on Johnson. "I found Johnson more clever than ever. I won $3,700."

Ed Smith said, "Jeff's vitals were gone. ... Jeff didn't box enough. There was too much fishing in his training."

William Muldoon said Jeff was nervous and forgot all he ever knew about boxing, though he had strength and condition. Except for the 9th round, Jeff was outclassed, both outside and inside.

Jack O'Brien admitted that he was wrong in his estimation of Johnson. "Although I boxed him and a majority of the papers had given me the decision as far as cleverness was concerned, I feel that he would defeat me in a long contest."

In a later interview, Jack McAuliffe said that after Johnson grabbed Jeff's arms, pinned them behind him, and laughed in his face, Jeffries had an amazed and concerned look on his face.[432]

Opinion of Officials Involved

Various reporters quoted referee and promoter Tex Rickard as saying,

> After Johnson colored Jeffries' eye with that left hook in the second round I knew it was the negro's fight. No other man in the world but Jim Jeffries could have stood up under that blow.

> I saw after Jeff got that jolt that closed his eye that Johnson had it on him in every way. He didn't have the steam. There was no snap and his footwork was slow.

> Jim put in some nice work in one or two of the later rounds, but Johnson hit harder and cleaner as the fight progressed.

> Jack Johnson is the most wonderful fighter that ever pulled on a glove. He won as he pleased from Jeffries, and was never in danger. I could not help feeling sorry for the big white man, as he fell beneath the champion's blows. It was the most pitiable sight I ever saw. As a matter of fact I thought, way down in my heart, that Jeffries would be the winner of the fight.

---

[432] *Boxing,* January 14, 1911.

Jeffries couldn't hit Johnson, and Johnson could hit Jeffries whenever he pleased. Jeff was not so good as the last time he fought.

Jeffries wasn't there. That tells the whole story. He was mistaken in thinking he could come back. Johnson had the best of the fight all the way. Jeffries landed few blows, and none of them hurt Johnson.

It was Johnson's mallet left which wore Jeffries down. The white man fought a game fight, but he was not the Jim Jeffries of old. Early in the fight Jeff showed signs of weakness and seemed to be much hurt by Johnson's blows.

Rickard further said, "Jack Johnson was a perfect wizard at defensive work, while his terrific punches worried Jeffries from the very start." "Johnson worked his left uppercut with telling effect and Jeff seemed unable to block the blows. Jeff lacked speed. He lacked endurance and showed less of his old skill than ever before."

During the fight, Johnson continually joshed Jeff, saying, "Hit me again. You haven't found that weak spot in my stomach. Now, hit me in the belly, won't you?"

Rickard said it was a clean bout, with little fouling. Twice Johnson did not break when told, and held on when he had no right to do so. Jeff pushed Jack's head back, and unintentionally butted. Tex cautioned them and the slight breaches were not repeated.

Concluding, Rickard said, "It was the same old story. No two men can whip Johnson today. He fooled the whole world. All his previous fights have apparently been phony. He had Jeffries whipped in the third round when he closed his eye."

Jack Gleason said Jeff was not the man of old, for he lacked speed and force in his blows.

Timekeeper George Harting said Jeff never had a chance.

Johnson put it all over him in every department of the game. He merely toyed and fooled with the white man. It is hard to imagine any fighter going back as far as Jeff has gone back. ... Johnson proved to the world that he is not yellow. On the contrary, he is game and aggressive.

The end almost came in the 12th round, when Johnson landed a terrific right on the jaw and dazed Jeffries badly. Only the call of time saved him.

Johnson was cool throughout, and showed that he was a wonderful judge of distance, an accurate hitter, and "his defensive work and blocking was simply marvelous." Jeff only landed twice, and even those blows were partially blocked. Harting said Johnson had won every round, and would have deserved victory had the bout been stopped at any time.

Johnson's Camp

Afterwards, in his dressing room, Johnson spoke with all of the reporters, who quoted him. The following is an amalgamation of those quotes.

Of the fight, and his confidence that he would win, various reporters quoted Johnson as saying, "It was no easier than I expected." "I defeated Jim Jeffries in much easier style than I expected." "I whipped him with greater ease than I anticipated." "It was one of the easiest victories I ever achieved." "I never had any doubts about licking him, as I had seen him fight Corbett, Sharkey, Munroe, Ruhlin, and several other men and knew that I was his master." "Before I entered the ring I was certain I would be the victor. I never changed my mind at any time."

> I knew that I had the big fellow from the very start. I was not hurt at any time. It is true my lips bled, but I had a slight cold sore and they were almost bleeding when I entered the ring.

> When I set him aside in the second round I knew for sure I had him. That's when I got his goat. I wasn't so sure the first round, but when he found he couldn't budge me by shoving his eyes widened and the smile left his face.

> I knew that I had his goat in the second round when I blocked his most effective punches and turned his arm sideways when I stuck out my hand to stop the blow. He thought he had it on me in strength and tried to rough it early in the fight but I just toyed with him so much that he even quit that sort of tactics.

> I knew that I was Jeffries' master the minute we sparred off. I could feel all through the battle that I had him, and that it was only a question of a short time before I would knock him out.

Johnson said he wished that the fight was twice as long, for he was having some fun. Jeff had not hit him a single blow. Conversely, Jeffries would not soon forget some of the stinging uppercuts that struck him. "He was only half the trouble that Tommy Burns was. And what is more, he will never order John L. out of any fight camp just because he gave an honest opinion."

Telling how he won, Jack said, "I won from Jeffries because I outclassed him in every department of the fighting game."

> I had heard so much about his wonderful strength and his awful left hooks that I thought he might be able to hit me once or twice during a round. Instead of that he never got past my guard except when I was jollying him, and none of his blows hurt me. In fact, I can't tell when or where he hit me, his punches were so light.

> I haven't got a mark on me and I'm not at all fatigued. I could have boxed all afternoon.

It was a game and courageous man whom I defeated. I never met a better. He simply could not hit me. I had him at all points of the game. The blows that did the damage were the left crosses to the jaw – not left hooks. It is a different blow from a hook, for it passes outside of the other man's defense. I also landed on his stomach and I think I hurt him there, but it was the constant cutting of his jaw that really did the work. ...

Jeffries never could hit me. He couldn't penetrate my defense. I have always known this and he just found it out. When he crouched I made him straighten up and then I pecked him to pieces. I used everything that there is in pugilism on Jeffries, and he couldn't stand the strain.

The first few rounds I looked him over, after which I settled down to hard work. I cut him down with straight lefts in the face. In the sixth I closed his eye.

I won just the way I thought I would – by keeping my left going into Jeff's face and body to worry him and my right always ready for the heavy work. I knew Jeff could not stand the pace and that I would gradually wear him down. At that he made a great fight, considering the handicap he was under, and I was forced to be cautious all the time. Otherwise I should have finished him before I did.

Jeffries did not hurt me once. ... I gave Jeffries a beating he will never forget. As I thought, I was too fast for him. Jeffries did not put two hard punches on my body in the fifteen rounds. I might have won sooner, but why take chances when so much was at stake.

I outboxed him at every point. I was stronger than he was and was in better condition.

He landed several hard body blows on me during the fight, but they did not bother me at all. I don't feel the least bit damaged in any way.

I didn't expect to win in such a short time, but when I saw that my blows were taking effect I knew that I need not fear for the title. It may have looked easy, but Jeffries was certainly a tough one to put away.

Jeffries fought a game fight and had more in him than I thought. ...

I took my time and played a waiting game, as I knew that it was only a question of how long he could weather the storm of blows. From the thirteenth round on the big fellow began to wobble, and in the fifteenth when I saw his arms down and his knees shaking I stepped in quickly and slipped over a left cross that had just enough power behind it to bring home the bacon that will entitle me to wear the championship crown without any 'ifs' or 'buts' to it.

Johnson believed the fight debunked several myths about him. Regarding his ability to absorb stomach punishment, Jack said,

> Jeffries blows had no steam behind them. ... I heard people at the ringside remark about body blows being inflicted upon me. I do not recall a single punch in the body that caused me any discomfort

> Not once when he reached me with his glove did the blow jar me, and I want to tell you that many times when the crowd cheered thinking I had been hit in the stomach, my glove was between Jeffries' blow and my body.

> Those clinch blows to my stomach did not bother me in the least. I have been saying it for years, and I say it again, although nobody seems to want to believe me, my stomach is the least vulnerable part of me. I am not bothered by blows there. I can stand up and let Jeffries do what he did to me in the clinches all day long and never bat an eyelid.

> It's a funny thing that every pugilist who fights me thinks he can hurt me by playing for my stomach. I can stand a lot of beating there, and it's a wonder some of these wise figurers did not come out to my camp and see Dave Mills beat me as hard as he could on the body without me making any attempt to guard it. Those who did notice did not see me writhing in pain after Dave got through.

Amused by those who liked to claim that he had a yellow streak, Johnson asked, "Did I back up? Did I run away? Who did the most of the leading? Who made the first lead?" He said he was afraid of no man.

> One of the many things that are said by the people who cannot bring themselves to acknowledge that I am any good as a fighter is that I have no punch. Well, I think today's exhibition of punching should send that story to the waste basket along with the 'yellow streak' fable.

> As for running away from Jeffries and winning by tiring him out, I never for a moment thought of doing any such thing. I am the champion and I would make a fine spectacle running away from anybody. Anyhow, what would I run for when I was sure that I could beat Jeffries at any kind of game he wanted to start?

> I made the first lead in the fight; I landed it; too. I kept on leading and landing, and I must have led ten times to Jeffries' once, and I landed a greater proportion of blows than that.

> I think I showed the people that I didn't have any yellow streak, and that I am entitled to the championship.

Johnson said it was a clean and fair fight.

I was much gratified today with the fact that there was nothing to make it unpleasant.

Jeffries did not try any mean tricks, but boxed as fair and square as any man could, and you could see that there was no attempt on either side to take an unfair advantage.

I must say that Jeffries is a game fighter and that he is an awfully clean fighter. He didn't try to foul me when I had him whipped. I was afraid that he would try to lose on a foul if he saw that he was licked.

One thing I must give Jeffries credit for is the game battle he made. He came back at me with the heart of a true fighter. No man can say that he did not do his best.

Regarding his interactions and talk with Jeffries inside the ring:

Jeffries was quite good-natured in the ring. The only words we spoke to each other were joshes. There was no bitter feeling on my part, and I do not think there was any on the part of the big fellow. There was no personal satisfaction in knocking Jeff out, only the mechanical pleasure of winning a big fight.

Jeffries and I talked to each other several times, but there was nothing of a bitter nature in the remarks. It was just a little exchange of words relating to what we were doing, and once or twice we joshed a little, but not much.

He joked me and I joked him. I told him I knew he was a bear, but I was a gorilla and would defeat him.

Regarding Corbett:

I had a lot of fun with Jim Corbett while today's fight was going on. Corbett is one of the men who thinks he can outbox me, and also that I am lacking in courage. He shouted to Jeffries this afternoon, "He will show the yellow soon." I answered over Jeffries' shoulder, "Well, he made you show, and if he makes me quit I'll come out and get you. That will make us even."

Corbett was a failure as a second. He tried to rattle me by his talk, but what a chance! At no time did I feel like a loser.

Johnson also said of his verbal jousts with Jeffries and Corbett,

I had great sport in kidding Jeff and Jim Corbett.

They thought I would get rattled when 'Gentleman Jim' joshed me, but I'm just as good a jollier as I am a boxer and after the sixth round the vaudeville star didn't work off any of his stage jokes on me.

During the entire fight I kept asking Jeffries to hit me in the stomach and find that yellow streak he said I possessed. He made a game effort to do so, but he was too slow and I had no difficulty in reaching him with a left cross and right uppercut whenever I saw an opening.

Johnson complimented Rickard's refereeing:

> Rickard only had to say 'break' once or twice, and the fear that his position would be one of turmoil and strife was wrong. I do not remember any fight between either large or small men in which there was so little for the referee to do. Rickard did not put his hands on us once, yet there was no hanging or holding that could interfere with the progress of the fight that would give the spectators reason to call it a 'hugging match' or a 'wrestling match.'

Of the treatment accorded him by the spectators and Reno public, Johnson said:

> Another thing that I want to boost is the crowd. It was the most orderly bunch of fight fans I ever saw. I wasn't insulted once and nobody had a word to say against me. There was no hooting and when I walked out of the ring and winded my way through the crowd, instead of getting shot or hit on the head with pop bottles as some of the people expected if I won the sports all congratulated me and gave me credit for winning. I have a warm spot in my heart for Reno and the thousands of spectators that were in the arena.
>
> I want to thank the spectators for the consideration shown me during and after the contest. ...

Later in the day, when he saw that the people did not intend to molest him, Johnson went into town and was surrounded in front of the Golden Hotel. He gave a short speech thanking the people of Reno and Nevada for their courteous treatment, which would be one of his "most pleasant memories." Bill Delaney said if Johnson were white, he'd be Vice-President of the United States in a few years, given how affable and bright he was.

Johnson again said,

> Before I leave Reno I want to thank the people of the State of Nevada and the many visitors from other parts of the country for the excellent treatment which has been accorded me. I could not have been more pleasantly received or more hospitably treated while I was training and I am glad that the people at the ringside today upheld me in my published statement that I had no fear that any advantage would be given my opponent. I could not ask for a more fair-minded gathering than the one that saw me win today and applauded me when I had proved that I was still the best of the world's fighters.
>
> I want to say that the treatment I received in the ring from both public and promoters was everything to be desired. I was treated like a gentleman, and it will always be my endeavor to act as one.

> I want to thank the people of Reno again for the cordial reception they have given me. It is one of the things I shall always remember.

Johnson also complimented and thanked all of his cornermen, trainers, and sparring partners for helping to prepare him and handling him well.

Speaking of his career, Johnson said, "It was not my fights themselves, but my fight to get those fights that proved the hardest part of the struggle." He had believed all along that Jeff could not touch him, and for years had wanted to fight him.

> It was my color. They told me to get a 'rep,' but how was I to get a 'rep' without meeting fighters of class? But I made them fight me. I just kept plugging along, snapping up what chances to fight I could grab, until by and by the topnotchers saw that sooner or later they'd have to take me on. As soon as I had shown what I could do, the fight public – most of the fans, anyway – took sides with me, and that helped a whole lot.

It was the general belief that Johnson held back in his fights, lest he make potential opponents too afraid to fight him. He preferred to toy with his foes. He had a good temperament, was never rattled, and usually smiled during his fights, even in the face of "coarse and insulting jibes that frequently greet him from fight spectators." He never lost his poise.

Johnson celebrated briefly at his training quarters, but planned to leave that evening on a train for Chicago, where he had investments. He would stay in Chicago for a short time before going to New York to appear at Hammerstein's for a couple of weeks, where in a vaudeville show opening on July 11 he would deliver a monologue describing the fight. He would then rest at Atlantic City and take on other engagements.

Johnson displayed a check for $60,600 for his share.

Regarding potential future fights, Johnson said, "I don't care who I fight next. Anybody who can draw a gate will be acceptable to me, but now that I have been in a battle in which $101,000 was the purse I'm liable to become an expensive luxury for the promoters, and it isn't likely that I would be attracted by anything but a big purse." If they wanted Johnson, they would have to pay him very well. He knew his value.

> As for Sam Langford, he can have me any time he makes a noise like a live one. I wonder how he feels now. I shall have great satisfaction in doing the same thing to him some time, since he has taken occasion to abuse me.

Tom Flanagan, Johnson's acting manager, said, "It was all Johnson from the beginning. ... Jeffries...wasn't a match for Johnson."

George Johnson said, "I came out from Chicago to see my brother Jack win, and I felt all the way out that there was no chance for him to lose."

Chief trainer Professor Watson Burns, who had been with Johnson for many years, said,

I am very glad that Jack won. All of us worked hard to condition him, and I believe that my method of training Jack and of keeping away all worrying matters so far as possible is the best for a man of his temperament. I was quite certain about the result before the first round was over. I could see where Jack had it on the other fellow and that he could not be hit.

Professor Burns also said, "Johnson is one great fighter and in spite of the fact that he is thirty-three years old, he is not likely to go back for a long time yet." Jack was in magnificent condition.

Sig Hart said, "I won a nice little bet at good odds that Jack would win before the 15th round was over."

George Cotton said he knew Johnson would win decisively, for Jack could hit, had heart and confidence, and it was nearly impossible to hit him. He thought Johnson was the greatest boxer ever.

Trainer Barney Furey said,

I have been with Jack for seven years now and I have always thought that he was the hardest hitter in the business. He showed today that he has a punch that hurts. … Jack was unruffled throughout the fight. … He can lick anybody that is before the public now, and it will be some time before he gets to the stage where he will have to extend himself to the utmost to win.

Al Kaufman knew that Johnson was strong enough, clever enough, and had enough endurance to beat Jeff easily. "He didn't take a real punishing blow in the whole fight. Jeff was game to the core, but he was not there with his old-time form. He was not the Jeff of old. That is all there is to it."

Johnson's "wife" Etta said,

I had a good seat, facing Jack, and at the end of every round, I waved my hand at him and smiled my encouragement. I always knew that he could whip Jeffries. …

I hope the public will give Jack due credit for what he has done. He is the best fighter that ever stepped into a ring. . …. It was a grand sight to see him batter down that big fellow, and the way he shoved him around and handled him with the ease that he would an Indian club in the gymnasium proved that he is the strongest boxer in the business.

I certainly like to be at the ringside and watch Jack win. I never get nervous, because I always have great confidence in Jack's ability to win. He is too clever to get hurt. I hope that they will hold another big fight here, as the people of Nevada certainly treated Jack good. He got a square deal and he didn't have to stand any insults at the camp or in the ring.

Johnson sent a wire to his mother in Chicago, telling her of his victory. His mom was upset and insulted by the fact that Jeff had declined to shake

Jack's hand before the bout. She said her son promised her that he would win, and he always kept his promises.

Jeffries' Camp

After the fight, Jeffries had tears in his eyes. In the ring, Corbett said, "Jim, sit down. You lose, we lose and thousands lose, but we are your friends still. You are done with fighting. What care you for any more of this." Jeff dropped down onto his chair with his head drooping.

As he sat in his chair, Jeff said, "If it was only four or five years ago. I felt I was gone after the third round. It's no use; my stomach went back on me. Oh, this is awful." Jeff's seconds tried to console him. Frank Gotch said, "That's all right, old man. We are going fishing and forget all of this."

Once in his dressing room, Jeff sobbed, broken-hearted from the poor fight he had made. "Just think, he knocked me out; yes, knocked me out. Oh, this is awful."

Corbett, ever the spin artist, told him that the bell rang right at the end and he was not knocked out, which was not true – the bell had not rung.

> You are not 50 per cent the man you were. You are done with this game forever. Had you been yourself at all you could have beaten him in two rounds. I thought the same as you did, but I found nature beat me, too. It gets everybody, Jim. You thought you were there, and I did too, but it is the same old story; you have gone back.

Jeff said, "I tried hard to get going, but I couldn't. God how I felt in that ring. If I only could have had my old-time steam."

The doctor told him that everyone has to lose some time. He had beat men and now he was beaten. Gotch told him he was not knocked out.

Jeff said, "I thought I might get going. In the first I thought I would warm up, but I couldn't."

Jeff's wife said the loss would break his heart. He had worried and worked so hard for such a long time.

One of Jeff's friends said his steam and punch were gone. "He was forced into the match, and now I guess the people who lost on him will roast him. This is the saddest day I have ever known."

Later, various newspapers quoted Jeffries as saying:

Reno Evening Gazette: "The colored fellow beat me fair and square, but I thought I would get to him before he got me. In this I found I was mistaken."

San Francisco Chronicle:

> I am done. I was not there at any time. My old steam was lacking woefully. Gee, I wish it was five or six years ago. My stomach went back on me. It hurt me and I knew I was done. I thought I was there. I trained well, and felt better than I ever did in my life. It is no use, though. I am done with the fighting game forever. Johnson is cleverer than a great many people give him credit for. He did not hurt me

with his punches. I was simply not there. I knew what to do, but I could not dance around like I did at other times and dash into my man. This hurts me worse than anything I have ever experienced in my life. I do not hold anything against the negro. He fought fairly, and beat me fairly, and I am not going to make excuses. He knocked me out, too. I was too tired to get up. I knew what was happening all the time, but my old steam was lacking and I could not follow the dictates of my will. I have beaten many men and now I know what it feels like to hit the floor. I am not hurt, my face is cut up a little, but I feel all right now. I did my best, that is all I can say. I trained hard and thought I was there and my friends lost, that's what gets me. It's all over now. I am glad of it and am going to keep out of the ring. I fought my last battle, and fought my best, but it was not good enough. I guess it is Old Jeffries now, and people will knock.

San Francisco Examiner:

I tried. That's all I ask credit for doing. I was beaten fairly and squarely. I have no excuses of any kind to make. Let full credit be given Jack Johnson for his victory. He is truly a great fighter.

I would have remained the retired and undefeated heavyweight champion of the world but for the fact that the American public demanded of me that I try to take away the championship from a black man.

I don't regret the fact of my defeat so much as I do that it was a negro who beat me, thereby establishing himself as the best man in the world. I would rather have been beaten three times over by a man of my own race than to have been the means of placing a negro in this position. It was to tear Johnson away from this honor that I consented to fight. I shot at the mark but missed it. There is nothing left to do but congratulate the winner. The color line should be drawn outside the ring. It cannot be done inside the ropes. When two men face each other for battle one of them must not be discriminated against because his skin is black. Keep him down entirely or give him fair place. …

I went down trying with every ounce of energy in my body to bring back the world's heavyweight championship to the white race. … That I will never fight again goes without saying. I did everything that mortal man could do to bring myself back into fighting form. I actually believed that I had accomplished this. I felt that I was myself again … I was mistaken. … Had I met Johnson when I was in my prime the result would have been different. I would have beaten him. As it was I wore myself down and was beaten as much by the effects of my own exertions as I was by Johnson's blows.

The good judges of fighting say that I had no chance to win after the fifth round, yet if you will read over the details of the first five rounds you will not find that I was punished to any extent.

We merely felt each other out in the first round. I was testing the negro's stock in trade – he was testing mine. We both joked through the slow second round. We were starting out over the long 45-round route, a fact that we both were thinking of at this time. There wasn't a real hard punch exchanged in the third round, not one. I figured that I had a good round in the fourth. I got through with a couple of wallops to my man's body and I reached his face. Johnson's mouth was bleeding when the bell rang at the end.

The fifth was a fairly hard round. My lip was cut along about this point. They say that the pictures will show that I was looking worried at the finish of this round. If so what was I worried at – surely not over the slight amount of punishment that I had taken. This worried look, if it was there must have been the first sign I was showing of my loss of strength. If Johnson was outboxing me in the sixth I gave no heed to it. I know that at this time I felt that I could win by getting in my best punch to the right spot.

Johnson's seconds shouted wildly in the seventh when my nose began to show blood. This meant nothing to me. I have had bloody noses and black eyes before and yet I always conquered the men who gave the unpleasant badges to me.

I knew as well as anybody that I was tiring in the eighth, but I guess the picture films will show that I was still fighting. From this point until the fifteenth round I was trying, always trying to send in some sort of a punch that would weaken the negro.

As I said in the beginning I only ask credit for trying. I slaved to obey the will of the public. Had I neglected one single item in my long battle for condition I would feel that any criticism directed toward me was deserved. As it is I believe that I deserve consideration from my people; what is more, I feel that I will get it.

San Francisco Bulletin:

I'm too old. I could not come back. … I did the very best I knew how. Whatever excuses I might have to offer for my defeat I'm going to keep to myself. Maybe I haven't any at all. He licked me, and that settles it. There isn't anyone to blame but myself. … I'm glad of the chance to get back to private life again. I think I was game enough, but Johnson was the better fighter.

Jeff later said that Johnson's left hook affected his vision, and he saw double.

San Francisco Call:

My stomach went back on me. I entered the ring in the best shape I could have possibly put myself in. I felt confident and trained as faithfully as any man could. The people demanded that I return to the ring after my long retirement to face Johnson and I went through a long siege of work before I announced that I would fight. I thought I could regain my old form and I worked hard in an effort to get into the best possible shape. Johnson is a great fighter and the people cannot imagine how clever he is. I have nothing to say against Johnson. He fought fairly and won the battle strictly on its merits. As early as the third round I found my stomach troubling me and I did not have the speed and strength I thought I had. I was not knocked out completely, but I was all in and it did not matter whether the fight ended in that round or the next as I was exhausted.

Freeman:

I did not have the snap of youth I used to have. I believed in my own heart that all of the old-time dash was there, but when I started to execute the speed and youthful stamina were lacking. …

I suppose most of my trainers and helpers will say that I did not box often enough. It would not have made any difference. … I simply was not there, and that's all there is to it.

I guess it's all my own fault. I was getting along nicely and living peacefully on my alfalfa farm, but when they started calling for me and mentioning me as the white man's hope, I guess my pride got the better of my good judgment. At that, I worked long and hard to condition myself and I was fit, so far as strength goes, but the old necessary snap and dash, the willingness to tear and crush, were not with me.

Six years ago the result would have been different, but now – well, I guess the public will let me alone after this.

That evening, Jeffries was quoted as saying, "What will mother say when she hears that I have ben licked by a nigger!" His mother was a Southern woman.

I felt that I couldn't win that fight after the first round. My arms were heavy and lifeless. I was all right in the first, but in the second round my arms felt as though they were paralyzed. It wasn't long before I found out that I wasn't the Jeff of old. Old nature had me beaten. I thought I had come back, but I hadn't. I am mighty sorry for my friends who bet on me.

Jeff's trainers all rendered their opinions of matters. Several reporters quoted Jim Corbett, who had given up a theatrical tour to help Jeff train:

I knew Jeffries was beaten after the fourth round. He did not have anything at all. I have passed through the same experience, and know how it is. You feel you have the old steam, and the old punch, but when you hear the call of the first gong you know you have done your last work. ... Jeffries seemed in marvelous condition, but he would not box, and that was where the rub came. It is no use to howl now. Jeffries and all of us realize that he has gone back over 50 per cent; otherwise he would have licked Johnson in a round or two.

It was simply the old story of the pitcher and the well – once too often. It has happened to a whole lot of us, and that it must happen to Jeff some day was just as sure as fate. Jeff did not box often enough to give us a line on him. We all knew him to be in great shape as far as ability to run miles and miles on the road was concerned, but he did not spar enough for any of us to guess just how he would show up on the ring line. As soon as he had boxed two rounds today, I knew that he had nothing. He was all right enough in spots where he did not need to be good, but the muscles used mostly in actual fighting, because of lack of practice during the training, failed to respond when called upon. ... It was only his courage and his condition that kept him there as long as he stayed.

Corbett said it was not the Jeffries who beat him and Fitzsimmons twice. Jeff lacked his usual vitality, power, and endurance. He thought his condition was right, for Jeff looked good and worked well in training, but when it came down to the real test he was not there.

We all foolishly thought and believed that Jeffries was immortal. ... We hailed Jeffries as the hope of the white race. Now we must hail him as the 'goat of the white race,' for it was the clamor and the howl of the white people who dragged Jim Jeffries out of retirement, who hounded him and fired him, by this hounding, to go into the ring against his will, and this was the result. The blame is upon our shoulders.

Corbett thought that Jeff could have performed better had he sparred more often, though he probably would have lost anyhow. He also thought that once it became apparent that Johnson was outboxing him and obviously had more endurance, Jeff should have torn into him as hard as he could, gone for broke to obtain a knockout, or get beaten fast. That at least would have given him a chance to win. "As it was, Jeff fought carefully until he was worn down by Johnson's punches."

The fact that Jeff was beaten by a black man is what hurt Corbett the most. "If it had been a white man that beat him I would not feel it so keenly. But it gets to me pretty hard to think that Jeff was never knocked down in his life and after fighting half of the greatest fighters the world has produced, until he lifted the color line and fought a black man."

I am ready to concede that Johnson is a great fighter and put up a marvelous exhibition of defensive work and fought a great fight. He never backed up and took many chances. However, I am convinced that Jeffries was far from the man he was. ... Jeff simply got exhausted. ... I wanted him to box a little more during his training. ... If I had had any say I would have had him have one or two real tests before he entered the ring. However, it is too late now and there is no use of depriving the winner of any of his honors.

When Corbett and others tried to cheer up the ex-champion, Jeffries responded, "Now don't give me that sort of talk. I worked hard to get into shape and thought I was back to my best form. I went into the ring confident, but found out that I wasn't there. I got a good licking and that's all there is to it: so don't worry over it."

Sam Berger said, "Jeff believed himself to be fit and so did the rest of us, but the vim of youth was entirely lacking." After the 3rd round, Berger was convinced that Jeff was not himself. His ginger was missing and he did not seem to have anything. His judgment of distance was off and he lacked his strength. He said the Jeff of old would have torn Johnson to pieces.

Choynski agreed that Jeff was not himself after the 3rd round. "When Johnson pushed Jeff's left arm back I could see that he did not possess the strength which he possessed during his palmy days." "He did not have the steam. If he was the Jeffries of six years ago he could have beaten Johnson easily. Johnson is not much different from when I fought him. To beat him you have to take a punch to land one." Joe said perhaps Jeff did not do enough sparring. Regardless, Jeff simply had gone back. "Jeffries isn't a shadow of his former self. He showed it in the first two rounds."

Farmer Burns said Jeff made a game stand, but nature was against him, which was something that was not brought out until the actual fight. You never can know how a man really is inside from training alone. He felt certain that Jeff would go the route, and was greatly surprised when he weakened.

Jack Jeffries said,

> I did not like to throw in the sponge when the end came, because I have seen my brother in far worse shape on at least a dozen other occasions, but that was when he was himself. Six years ago he could have taken the beating which Johnson gave him today and would have smiled for more. But that was six years ago. He has lost his steam and punch and we might as well make the best of it. ... He thought he was right and he looked right to all of us, but perfect condition is evidently judged only by the test that follows in the ring.

Roger Cornell said the blinded right eye was the main cause of defeat. It swelled up in the 2nd round. Jeff saw double and could not see blows coming from his right side. "Johnson hammered him with the left almost at will, and Jeff could not block them. He did not see them."

Frank Gotch said Jeff's head and heart were right, but he lacked the speed of hand and foot, as well as shape, of his younger days. Early on he noticed Jeff fail in some of the stunts he used to perform so well.

Deception About Jeffries and His Ability to Come Back

A *Reno Evening Gazette* writer said that leading up to the contest, people believed that Jeffries had come back, or made themselves believe it. When it came, reality was pathetic and grim. After a few rounds, everyone knew that the magic and flame of Jeffries was gone, "although we fought against admitting it." "Poor Jeffries!"

Frank Hall said it was axiomatic that no athlete can come back after a long layoff. "As I have claimed all along no man ever did and Jeffries could not come back." The public had fooled itself into thinking that Jeff could do so. "We fool ourselves every day more than other people fool us."

Edward Hamilton said fans clung to their idolatry for Jeff almost to the end, expecting the great white fighter to come back at any moment. "The race feeling was strong within even the men who had taken the benefit of the odds."

The chairman of the Board of Police Commissioners said, "Most people thought the negro would win, but they didn't like to say they thought the black would whip a white man."

San Francisco's mayor, P. H. McCarthy, said California's governor had claimed that the fight was fixed for Jeffries to win. The result spoke for itself, and showed how little he knew.

The *Nevada State Journal* said Jeffries allegedly had trained and conditioned himself faithfully and carefully for over a year, working longer and harder than anyone ever had before to get back into top shape. He claimed he was better than ever. Yet he went down to defeat with ease.

Sam Davis said,

> The odds in favor of the white man were purely fictitious and arose from the ridiculous touting of his condition and endurance from the pens of the so-called sporting writers of the San Francisco papers. These men have little judgment in such matters, but are influenced almost solely by their sentiments.

Writers had offered descriptions of Jeff's wonderful speed and strength. He showed neither in the fight. Jeff was no longer able to judge distance and his face was an easy mark. He did not have his vaunted punch. "This fight demonstrates that you cannot add an ounce to a fighter's blows or endurance by newspaper touting and the backing of the betting ring. Johnson could have licked Jeffries and all his training camp in the same ring this afternoon."

The *Bulletin* also said the glowing tributes of his trainers, Corbett, Berger, and Choynski, and newspaper scribes who were all more than friendly towards Jeff, deceived the general public and installed Jeff as a betting favorite at a false price. "It is all too plain now why much of Jeff's work was done in secret." Excuses given for Jeff's laying off were that he was getting too light in weight or feared going stale. Also affecting the odds were the constant qualifying phrases used in conjunction with Johnson's chances: "If he did not show his yellow streak." "If his disposition did not make him weak." "If he had not been bought off." Such statements fooled the public into the belief that Johnson was just bluffing in his training and was going into the ring to lose. It caused many to bet on Jeffries. "The popularity of Jeff with the fight-loving public of the world caused them to be easily swayed to bet on him against their better judgment."

Jack O'Brien said the majority of reports from the training camps were that Jeff had regained all of his old-time speed and cleverness, but he absolutely failed to support the truth of such reports. Jeff had lost his snap, judgment of distance, and his ability to receive and assimilate punishment. "He may have done his best but it was a poor best." O'Brien knew Johnson was very clever, and had favored him in a general way, but thought if the reports from Jeff's camp were true that Johnson would be defeated.

Frank Brady, a Montreal promoter, said the betting public had been tricked by reports of Jeff's training, which had to be false. "If he believed he was in condition he was either ignorant of the game or hasn't much gray matter in the top of his head. So far as the exhibition was concerned, we might as well have had some one from an old ladies' home."

Tommy Burns agreed that Jeff's training reports were too glowing, and caused many to bet on Jeff. Nearly every day for weeks, many newsmen, experts, and friends told Johnson that he was a lamb being led to slaughter, that Jeff would kill him. The Jeffries that Burns had read so much about was not there, nor anything like him.

Bob Fitzsimmons admitted that he had allowed his sentiments to carry him away and blind him to the fact that Jeff had aged and lost his vitality. Deep down he thought Johnson might win, but he pushed that thought from his mind and could only think of Jeff's former greatness.

Gamblers on Jeffries lost a great deal of money. It was estimated that over $250,000 was won and lost on wagers in Reno alone. The estimated amount bet on the fight in the U.S. was over $3 million. One of those who had lost, Adolph Sprekels, said,

> I was misled by the reports of Jeffries' condition. The truth is, he is but a hollow frame of what was once a grand, big athlete. The old theory that boxers cannot come back to form after years of absence from the ring was simply verified today. It was a shame to put Jeffries in the ring again.

The *Evening Post* said the hope of the white race cost at least 1 million dollars to gamblers who wagered on him in the "wrestling contest." The Johnson bet proved to be the greatest short-end wager ever. Jim Coffroth was said to have won $8,000 wagering on Johnson. Matt Larkin won $27,000. They believed that no one can come back after a long retirement.

In another interesting twist, the *Evening Post* took a jab at the *Bulletin*, which prematurely claimed that Jeffries had won. The *Bulletin's* effort to be first, to have an inside scoop before anyone else, led to the early release of an incorrect special edition. A member of the *Evening Post* secured a copy of the first fight extra, which it teasingly called the *Bulletin*'s only scoop in the past two years. When one man saw the paper announcing Jeffries' victory posted in the *Post's* window, done to embarrass the *Bulletin*, he growled, "Get out! The coon won all the way. I saw it. What does this mean?" Someone explained the meaning to him and he laughed. Such was the integrity of some newspapers. Even today, some news agencies will rush to publish before having all of the facts.

Whether Result Would Have Differed In Years Past

Naturally, everyone liked to speculate about what the result of a fight between Jeffries and Johnson would have been had they fought years ago, with some opining that Jeff would have won, while others said the ultimate result would have been the same. All of Jeff's trainers said the Jeffries of six years ago would have defeated Johnson with ease. Jack London said, "Jeff was not the old Jeff at all. Even so, it is to be doubted if the old Jeff could have put away this amazing negro from Texas, this black man with the unfailing smile, this king of fighters and monologists."

The *Nevada State Journal* said,

> Regardless of his long absence from the ring, Jeffries would have been beaten by Johnson when he was at his prime in the opinion of the men who saw yesterday's battle. Impregnable and invincible to all the other heavyweights, Jeffries would have been as easy prey to the colored champion seven years ago as he was yesterday.

> Superb in his exposition of ring generalship and boxing, Jack Johnson excited the admiration of even the staunchest Jeffries' fans.

W. W. Naughton said it was futile to argue whether Peter Jackson could have beaten Jeffries in his best days, or whether Jeffries could have beaten Jack Johnson years earlier. It simply could not be answered. All we know is that at one point in their careers, these men were better than their peers. It was Johnson's time.

Frank Herman said Johnson was too fast, too clever, and too crafty, and won with ridiculous ease.

> In my opinion Jack Johnson is the most wonderful heavyweight that ever donned a glove. If his color was white instead of black he would be the most popular boxer in the world. His cleverness, combined with his coolness and great hitting powers, as well as his good-nature, would make him as big an idol as John L. Sullivan was in his prime.
>
> I believe Johnson would have defeated Jeff when Jeff was in his prime. I think that the coon-hued swatologist is the most marvelous piece of fighting machinery that the prize ring has ever known. He has every requisite that goes to make a champion.
>
> His enemies have always pointed to his past battles as flukes, and they have never failed to refer to the 'yellow streak' that he has never shown in any of his contests. Yesterday he proved that he was game when he refused to run away and back up against a man who was supposed to be the strongest and most powerful heavyweight in the country. ...
>
> Of course, many will try to console themselves by saying that Jeff wasn't in condition and that he would have wiped up the earth with Johnson when he was in his prime. However, the most expert trainers in the country pronounced the big giant to be in perfect trim, and they backed up their opinions with real money.

Stanley Ketchel harshly said, "Jeffries never could fight." Stan claimed that he was not saying that because he was sore for being kicked out of Jeff's camp. "He has been all along the most overrated fighter that ever lived, and I don't believe, as he stands today, that he could lick anybody." Ketchel said he would fight Jeff winner take all and place a $10,000 wager at 10 to 7 odds. "I never said a harsh word about Jeffries in my life; yet he ordered me out of his training quarters just because I picked Johnson to win this battle."

William Muldoon said, "I believe he would have whipped Jeffries at any time during his professional career."

Bob Fitzsimmons said, "If Johnson had met the Jeffries I met there would have been a different story to tell. ... But there's no use in speaking as to what might have happened now, for it is all over."

Bill Delaney said he always knew Johnson would win.

> I do not believe there is a man in the world who can defeat him. I have always claimed that no man living today could bring the yellow

streak out on Johnson. Whether there is one or not, he is a wonderful fighting machine. When fighting his hardest Johnson is resting easy. He is the coolest thing I ever saw.

I knew that Jeffries was afraid of him, and I knew that would cause his defeat.

Delaney said that he had told Johnson long ago that he had nothing to fear from Jeffries.

No man can beat another man if he is afraid of him and I know that Jeffries never cared for the idea of fighting Johnson, even when he was champion and Johnson was not so good as he is now. When I matched Jeffries with Bill Squires and he went back on the arrangement and let Tommy Burns get in and win from the Australian in a punch, Jeffries was opening the way for his defeat of today. Johnson probably never would have been champion had Jeffries come out then, before he had gone back too far. Johnson did not need any seconds today. He could have won without me or any of the others.

Delaney further said,

Fear lost the heavyweight championship of the world for Jeffries yesterday at Reno. He was afraid of Johnson.

Form had nothing to do with it. Jeffries made a desperate, game fight, and did all any man could do to regain his laurels, but it wasn't in the cards for him, or any other man, to beat the Jack Johnson who fought him yesterday. Jeffries was fighting the cleverest heavyweight that ever stepped into the ring, not barring Jim Corbett. Jeffries was always afraid of Johnson. When I was with him he repeatedly refused to sign with Jack. When I found that he was afraid to fight the negro I left him.

Jeffries promised me faithfully he would fight Squires. I made a match at his request and he ran out on it. Had he met Squires, as he promised to do, he would have defeated Squires and Burns, the man who lost the championship to Johnson. Johnson would never have become champion, and, therefore, Jeffries is directly responsible for Johnson being champion of the world today.

Ed Hamilton said there would be debates for years to come regarding whether Johnson could beat the Jeff of old. He certainly was Jeff's master at all points on this day. "The gorilla is greater than the bear."

The *San Francisco Evening Post* said some still thought that Jeff at his best was the greatest ever, but as he was at present, he was no match for Johnson.

Tommy Burns thought the present Johnson might have beaten Jeff even at his best. Johnson was "unquestionably a stiffer proposition than he has been given credit for being. ... I had no idea that Johnson was so skillful, game and enduring a boxer." This was coming from a man who had fought him.

Georg Harting said,

> I may be mistaken, but I think that the Johnson of today could beat Jeff the best day he ever saw. ... It was too one sided. Jeffries could not do anything, even rough work in the clinches, for which he used to be so famous.

However, Harting granted that Jeffries had lost his speed and hitting power, as well as judgment of distance, strength, stamina, and ability to absorb punishment.

C. E. Van Loan said that whether the Jeff of years ago could have won was a matter of conjecture. Regardless, Van Loan opined that in Jeff's present form, or lack of it, several men at that time could beat him. However, "Not one of them could have beaten him as cleverly or as decisively as Johnson."

The black-owned *New York Age* said Johnson landed 77 telling blows to Jeffries' 24. The clever Johnson was his master at every stage, for he toyed and played with him as he saw fit. After the fight, Johnson said the match was not as fast as some of his sparring bouts.

> Jack Johnson has proven to all that he is the cleverest heavyweight fighter that ever stepped into the prize ring. His defense is impregnable, and he left the ring without a scratch, while Jeffries' face brought to one's mind a hamburger steak – it was so cut up. And that left uppercut of the Galvestonian's! ... It certainly was a mean, cruel punch. ...

> Nature, after all, reigns supreme, and in the case of Jeffries it was a case of while the mind was willing, the flesh was weak. Yet, even in noonday of Jeffries' existence I do not think he could have defeated Jack Johnson. Of course, had the contest taken place a number of years ago the colored champion would have had a more strenuous a time of it, but the result would have been just the same.[433]

Crowd Response and Reaction

Helen Dare said the crowd was kindly, considerate, orderly, and good-natured. It was a good-looking crowd, well-dressed and groomed. "I could name if I could get the time and space, hundreds of the best known men in the country." Women were scattered from ringside to the topmost row, not just confined to the special boxes at the top that had been prepared for women. "I have shared with zest and felt the thrill of what has always been regarded as exclusively a man's game, a man's holiday. Shocking? Is it?"

---

[433] *New York Age*, July 7, 1910.

C. E. Van Loan said it was the most remarkable assemblage of sporting men ever gathered in the history of the game.

The *Bulletin* said the crowd was more sportsmanlike than expected.

> Some of us had been led to believe that an anti-negro demonstration would take place in case Johnson won. On the contrary the crowd seemed almost evenly divided between Johnson and Jeffries. Notwithstanding the fact that every white man wanted to see Jeffries win, as a matter of principle, Johnson received a generous ovation when he entered the ring and another when he left it. This is perhaps due to the fact that Johnson had been friendly with the people, while Jeffries and some of his trainers – notably Farmer Burns – had been exactly the opposite. At any rate, there was no time during the contest that any protection was needed for Johnson, and he was actually cheered when he left the ring.

Another *Bulletin* writer said the enormous gathering had but a sprinkling of colored folk as spectators. Everything was against Johnson, yet he was unperturbed. His clean fighting won him many friends. He did not transgress the rules, and he never even appealed to the referee when Jeff butted him with his head or put his forearm across his throat. Still, his victory was not popular. He was given less applause upon leaving the ring than his vanquished opponent received.

One *Chronicle* writer said the crowd response was muted. "It was like the passing of a funeral. Hardly a white man cheered, and few blacks." The end was taken with solemn silence. Helen Dare said Johnson's victory was unpopular, unanticipated, and undesired.

Another *Chronicle* writer said,

> Jeffries was carried to his corner by his seconds and intimate friends, Johnson waiting the while to give the final handshake that ring custom demands. Then the crowd, ever fickle, ever inclined to turn to the winner, showered its attention upon the negro and shouted his name as he turned his grinning face toward them to acknowledge the reception.

The crowd appeared to treat it like a regular fight. "Race feeling? There was none manifested this afternoon," for "there was no thought given to the fact that he had been defeated by a colored man." Afterwards, local crowds that saw Johnson gave him a cheer.

Sullivan said the fans pitied Jeffries. Although no friendship was exhibited towards Johnson, and little cheering, he was treated fairly. "The negro had few friends, but there was no real demonstration against him. They could not help but admire Johnson because he is the type of prize fighter that is regarded highly by sportsmen." He fought fairly and only demanded fairness in return.

Richard Barry said practically there were no cheers for Johnson.

Ed Cahill said the crowd scarcely said a word about race, and when someone did say something offensive, there was a strong outcry of crowd disapproval; "Cut that out!"

Fred Bechdolt said the crowd was strangely quiet throughout the bout. They broke into spasmodic applause, but then quickly fell back into silence. When Johnson won, the crowd mostly was silent. The cheer that was heard was when Jeff rose from his corner well after the fight was over.

Battling Nelson said the applause Johnson received for annexing the undisputed title was anything but flattering.

Bill Delaney noted that whites were upset with him for working with Johnson. "I received all sorts of threatening and insulting letters."

Tom Flanagan said it was the best crowd he ever saw, the largest and easiest to please. "The people were fair and I admire them for it."

Tom Flynn noted the advances in racial tolerance.

> Thirty or forty years ago if Johnson had commenced to whip his white antagonist, the ropes would have been cut, the ring invaded by ruffians and he might have been lucky to escape with his life. He got few cheers today at Reno, but nevertheless, his treatment as compared with that of the old fighters was courteous.

W. W. Naughton said the crowd reaction at the end differed from most fights. There was one yelp when Jeff went down the first time. "Then those who yelled seemed to suddenly remember that a negro was beating down a white man. In the other knockdowns Jeffries fell in silence." After Berger entered, there was not the acclaim that usually was in evidence when a fighter had won. There was more silence as the big throng filed out.

Former San Francisco Mayor E. E. Schmitz said, "I'm sorry to see a white man go down that way." He "spoke what was in everybody's mind."

THE SAN FRANCISCO EXAMINER — SPORTS—EDITED BY W. W. NAUGHTON—SPORTS — TUESDAY, JULY 5, 1910

EXAMINER FIRST TO FLASH "KNOCKOUT" TO WAITING THOUSANDS

PHOTOGRAPH OF THE DENSE MASS OF HUMANITY THAT PACKED MARKET STREET AT THIRD TO SEE AND HEAR "EXAMINER'S" RETURNS

15,000 FANS SEE FIGHT REPLICA AT AUDITORIUM
Remarkable Living Representation of Battle in Reno Given by "Examiner" at Rounds Progress.

80,000 SEE 'EXAMINER' STREET RING THIS PAPER FIRST TO FLASH FINISH

DENSE THRONG FOLLOWS BATTLE AT VALENCIA
"Examiner" Bulletins Come Quick and Fast, With Graphic Description of Great Battle.

Throughout the country, huge crowds stood in front of newspaper bulletin boards reading news dispatches flashed from the ringside. Some newspapers hired look-a-like boxers to demonstrate the punches from inside a makeshift ring. When the fight ended, there was no applause.

Further Meaning and Significance of the Victory

Helen Dare said that for over a year the entire civilized world had been interested in this fight to a most extraordinary degree, and for the past two months had talked about little else. More than a million dollars had been spent, and even more wagered. An arena had been built for one day. Men from all over the world had made special journeys. An army of writers had been engaged. Advisers, trainers, and attendants had been busy for months. Governors of two states and opposing and supportive moral factions had been mightily exercised. Jeffries had been training for more than a year. Yet the actual event which meant so much to so many only lasted sixty minutes.

Rex Beach said the victory would help the black race.

> It is doubtful if even in his best days Jeffries could have won, for the African through all the combat showed a marvelous speed and aggressiveness that only occasional moments in his previous fights had hinted at. He demonstrated further that his race has acquired full stature as men; whether they will ever breed brains to match his muscles is yet to be proved. But his heart, his yellow streak of which so much had been said, it was not there. He fought carefully, fearlessly, intelligently. He outpointed, he outfought, he outlasted his opponent. There remains no living man to dispute his title as the world's champion.

Clearly the fight could serve to dispel many racial myths about the inferiority of blacks, which could uplift the spirits of black folks.

One man said,

> I'm ruined. Think of it! A big black man beating Jeffries. Why, I would have bet old Bearcatcher against a truck horse that Jeffries could whip all the black men fighting at the same time in the same ring. ... This is a big blow to a man from down where we think a white man can whip a whole passel of men of Johnson's color. I can hardly believe it. It is a shadow on the white race. It's awful. I tell you I hate to look my friends in the face.

A captain of detectives said,

> Johnson did the trick, but he had to do it to convince the people that he was made out of championship material. He is a great fighter no doubt. ... There was more interest taken in the fight than in any similar contest, and the fact that a negro won it is not a fact that the average white man takes to kindly. Race prejudice should not interfere with judgment in boxing contests, and in this case the stronger, cleverer man won the fight.

It was noted that there was little betting by blacks, which helped keep the odds in Jeff's favor. They thought Johnson was better, but incorrectly believed that Jeffries would not take the fight unless it was fixed.

Frank Hall said,

> It seems a terrible thing for a white man to go down to defeat at the hands of a black. There was too much sentiment in this battle. People seemed to forget that it was a question of which was the best fighter, and there is no question of a doubt in my mind that that was the cause of the odds.

A *Bulletin* writer said it was doubtful if there ever was a less popular champion than Johnson. "There are several reasons contributing to this, but probably no one factor was more potent than the sight of the beautiful and apparently educated and refined white woman whom Johnson calls wife standing up in the arena between rounds and throwing kisses and waving salutes to the black man."

The *Call* called Johnson, the son of a former slave, the "new champion." The fact that some did not give Johnson recognition as the true champion until he defeated Jeffries explains why the bout was so important to Johnson, aside from economics. He needed the victory to obtain full universal status as champion.

John L. Sullivan noted that even though Johnson technically was champion with his victory over Burns, the rank and file of sporting people never gave him the full measure of his title. Jeffries always had been the bugaboo of his championship, so it meant a great deal to Jack to defeat him.

The *Nevada State Journal*'s H. G. Wales, Jr. said the world in general and the sporting element in particular had refused to recognize Johnson as the true champion, and claimed that the previously undefeated Jeffries was the man. Now that Johnson had defeated Jeffries, they had to give Johnson his just due recognition.

Jack London lamented, "Once again has Johnson sent down to defeat the chosen representative of the white race, and this time the greatest of them all. And, as of old, it was play for Johnson."

A local Reno writer called it the greatest tragedy in ring history. As the "pride of the white race," Jeffries had been the idol of countless thousands throughout the world.

Pauline Jacobson said some had wondered whether blacks throughout the country would become demoralized and refuse to work if the white man won. Instead, the opposite had occurred.

Afterwards, when a black woman who was boarding a train took off her hat, someone asked why she removed the hat, and she said, "Cause ah wants everybody to know that ah's a niggah, das why, an' ah'm prahd of it."

James J. Jeffries no longer was the idol he once had been. His world tour was cancelled. His ability to draw had taken a big hit. The only salve to a broken reputation was the big money he had earned.

Years later, Johnson said that he wanted to punish Jeffries, as he had done with Burns, for all the rumors that Jeffries had spread that were intended to attack his courage. Jeff had spread the story that he had offered Johnson the opportunity to fight him in a cellar, alone, but that Johnson had said, "I ain't no cellar fighter. I want to fight in public, with a referee." Jeff replied, "Oh, you aren't even a four-flush. You're a three-flush." Johnson said he wanted to prove that he wasn't the man he had been made out to be, for it was Jeff who was afraid to fight him. Jeffries had "indulged in many hateful and venomous remarks" towards him. Even James J. Corbett, who was in Jeffries' corner, called Johnson names in an effort to upset him. In retaliation, during the fight, Johnson laughed at and taunted Jeffries and spoke to Corbett and ringsiders to reflect his confident control over matters. He wanted revenge, and he got it.[434]

The Money

Tex Rickard said Johnson made $70,600 from the fight purse. Jeff got $50,400. Johnson sold his motion picture interests for $50,000, Jeff sold his for $66,666, while Rickard got $33,333 for his end. Gleason refused to sell his share. Johnson earned a total of $122,600. Jeff earned about $117,066. "Yet some people say fighting is a bad business." Jim Coffroth asked, "How would you like to be a 'white hope'?"

Others noted that Jeff also had made another $75,000 in theatrical engagements, which is what Johnson could now make.

A few weeks later, Rickard said the receipts were $270,778.50. After the purse was paid, and $21,000 in expenses, he would have $128,000 left to split with Gleason.

What the Films Show

Some portions of the fight films still exist. Keep in mind that it was a 45-round fight at altitude under the hot Nevada desert sun at 3 p.m. in July, not an easy task for anyone in any era. With such a potentially great number of rounds to fight, essentially it was a fight to the finish. Under such circumstances, it is understandable that the fighters would want to be efficient and methodical. They did not care about points. It was all about landing effective blows that eventually would lead to a knockout, and preventing one's foe from doing the same.

The films show that for most of the bout, the 32-year-old Johnson smothered the 35-year-old Jeffries' offensive attempts, slowly wearing him down with single shots on the inside and then going back to the clinches. Johnson is clever and cautious. He does not allow Jeffries to get off very often, nor does he allow him to land cleanly anything meaningful. His defense is very efficient. He raises his hands to block, suppress, or clinch. He also moves, rolls, or leans away at just the right moment and at just the right distance, doing so with no more energy than necessary. When Jeffries

---

[434] *My Life and Battles* at 90-91. Johnson, *In the Ring and Out*, at 171.

advances, Johnson knows how to step or slide just out of range, or quickly move in to suppress or fire something before either man clinches.

Rickard did not get involved much. Back then, referees did not inject themselves too much, properly preferring to allow the fighters to fight in the clinches or to work their way out, something which more referees today should emulate.

Johnson was able to suppress, punch, then suppress again, not allowing Jeffries to get off with much of anything, controlling the inside, where the fight mostly seems to have been fought. From the outside, Johnson could step in quickly with a straight punch and then tie up. Or Jack would wait for Jeff to attack, and then block with his arms and tie up.

Johnson does not waste his energy on combinations, rarely throwing more than one or two at a time, and he quickly defends, clinches, or suppresses any counters. When Johnson fires, it is as fast as lightning and sneaky too. Sometimes you barely can see the punches. One can tell the footage is projected at the proper speed, because the referee's movements are slow and deliberate. Jack occasionally yet consistently lands crisp shots, round after round, until his foe wilts. Johnson lands some nice straight rights, short hooks that are hard to see coming, and his stinging uppercuts are short, blazing fast and snappy, and even harder to see coming. Jack's reactions are quite fast, but he is also so calm, relaxed, and minimalist that you may not realize just how blazing-fast his speed and reactions are. He rocks the head of a very large and strong man.

Johnson's brand of ring generalship is something which many do not understand until their favorite aggressive power puncher has been in there with a boxer who can do these things, and then, after they are defeated, they come to appreciate it. It was a deceptively effective methodical neutralizing and dismantling of a bigger man, even though it might not have been done in the most entertaining style.

San Francisco Examiner, July 5, 1910

CHAPTER 10

The Aftermath:
Riots, Repression, and
Repercussions

There was much more on the line in the Jeffries-Johnson fight, psychologically, than a mere battle between two men. The fight was promoted in the press as a battle of racial superiority between the white and black races. During this era, many scientists and social theorists believed that blacks were inferior to whites in every way, physically, mentally, and socially. They believed that whites were in superior power positions as the result of the natural order. Because world heavyweight champions had been viewed as symbols of national and racial superiority, Jack Johnson's victories challenged such theories.

Racial myths led the public to believe that Johnson lacked the physical and mental abilities needed to beat Jeffries – that the best black never could beat the best white. For example, relaxation and pacing in the ring, something actually beneficial to a fighter's speed and condition, something which Johnson exhibited, was considered black laziness, lack of focus, and lack of training. The public and press had so built up Jeffries as invincible and so believed racial myths of black inferiority that it helped make Johnson the betting underdog.

The fight's racial contrast hyped it, making it financially successful, but caused its symbolism to have serious consequences. Not only was race pride at stake, but also there was fear that a black victory could be used to upset the social caste that placed blacks at the bottom. Whites feared that a Johnson victory might mean that blacks would demand more rights.

Johnson too realized that the magnitude of the event went beyond boxing. "It wasn't just the championship that was at stake - it was my own honor, and in a degree the honor of my race." These strong racial feelings led to serious repercussions that resonated not only in the immediate future, but for many years to come.[435]

Although the spectators inside the arena and in Reno had been civil and well-behaved, it is an understatement to say that such was not the case elsewhere. Despite the attempts of some to minimize the racial aspects of the fight, the reality was, for a great many, the fight indeed was about race. The fight's result set off an immediate wave of racial violence and riots

---

[435] Johnson, *In the Ring and Out*, at 183.

across the nation, "between whites, angry and sore because James J. Jeffries had lost the fight at Reno, and negroes jubilant that Johnson had won."

When the fight bulletins came in on July 4, 1910 announcing Johnson as the victor, many whites did not appreciate blacks celebrating their de facto representative's victory over the whites' representative in the battle for supremacy. The psychological impact and toll was tremendous, and it brought out the worst in many whites who did not want the fight's result to threaten the status quo or for blacks to think it was an argument for equal opportunity. Therefore, they felt the need to lash out at blacks, particularly those who celebrated the victory. It was sheer anger meeting unmitigated joy; which in the racial climate of the time, proved to be a powder keg that ignited into violence throughout the nation. However, the violence was not simply limited to white on black; it included black on white, black on black, and white on white.

Thousands were injured in the national riots, and there were several deaths. Not until the assassination of Martin Luther King, Jr. in the late 1960s would one event cause such widespread national rioting. Incidents in various cities included, but were not limited to:

Atlanta, GA – Whites chased many blacks, one of whom the police saved from being killed.

Baltimore, MD – As a result of arguments regarding the fight, several blacks were stabbed and injured in a race riot. One was cut badly, and two others assaulted by whites were injured severely. 70 blacks were arrested for disorderly celebrations.

Charleston, MO – Unrelated to the fight result, two blacks were lynched for allegedly committing a murder. A third lynching was threatened when a crowd captured a black man who used rough language when addressing a white woman, but eventually he was set free. The sheriff and his deputies claimed to be powerless against the crowd which attacked the county jail. An exodus of the black population was reported to be in progress.

Chicago, IL – Until daylight the next day, the streets were filled with blacks celebrating Johnson's victory. Whites were made the butts of boisterous wit. Scores of blacks were arrested for disorderly conduct and for blocking traffic. Women were as wild as men in the excitement, and children accompanied them. The next morning, 36 men were arraigned.

Many fights and riots were reported in the negro section, called the "black belt." Scores were injured. A negress was shot by a negro. One black man was stabbed and dying.

Cincinnati, OH – Intermittent rioting followed the announcement of the fight result. Whites took blacks from their homes and beat then. A mob of hundreds of whites chased a black man who allegedly made offensive remarks.

Clarksburg, W. VA – Angered by black celebrations of Johnson's victory, a posse of 1,000 white men drove blacks off the streets. One black man was being led with a rope around his neck when the police interfered.

Covington, KY – Several whites stabbed a black man, who barely was saved from lynching.

Enoka, LA – Three blacks were killed in the riots. Wild with enthusiasm, blacks paraded the streets cheering for the champion and taunting whites. A man and his father were beaten and shot to death. Infuriated whites also followed and shot to death a negress who shouted for Johnson.

Fort Worth, TX –There were many fights and race disturbances between whites and blacks. Two negresses badly beat a white woman with beer bottles.

Houston, TX – When a negro on a street car vociferously announced the fight's outcome, a white man slashed his throat from ear to ear, and he later died. Another version of this incident said a white man, who was stabbed by a negro, killed his negro assailant.

White men attacked and badly beat three blacks. Reports of a few persons shot. Police were called to quell several minor disturbances.

Hutchinson, KS – More than a thousand blacks that had gathered specifically for the purpose of praying for Johnson's victory were jubilant upon hearing of his victory. No riots.

Kansas City, MO – Street rioting.

Keystone, W. VA – In most instances, whites could not stand the blacks cheering for their hero, so they attacked. Blacks fought back and eventually took possession of the town. A negress stabbed a negro to death.

Lake Providence, LA – A white man killed two negroes, and a negress was struck by a stray bullet.

Little Rock, AR – Several fights on trains. White men killed two blacks. A white conductor was killed.

Los Angeles, CA – Several clashes between whites and blacks occurred throughout the night. The *Call* wrote, "Flushed with small cash winnings, several negroes sallied forth, filled themselves with liquor and looked for trouble." Four whites and five blacks were injured in interracial fights, and were treated at hospitals. A dozen were arrested on charges of drunkenness. When a white man spoke disparagingly about the champion, a black man severely cut him with a razor. Another white received two rib fractures from a fight with a black man who declared that he could lick any white man in California. Another white man suffered a broken rib and battered face after a fight with a black man. Yet another white took a beating when he disagreed with an "arrogant negro" on Spring Street.

The next morning, the courthouse was packed with more than 200 cases of disorderly conduct and battery charges from the riots the previous day. Blood-stained bandages covered wounds made by clubs and knives. Fines of $5 to $10 were the rule. One white man, defending his actions in fighting, said a colored gentleman was using some awful language in the presence of women and children, including that white people did not have any business on the street.

Louisville, KY – Crowds of blacks attack white newsboys selling extras telling of race riots and the fight.

Macon, GA – Authorities doubled the police force to prevent a race clash. Blacks were boisterous in celebrating the victory. Several were beaten. "The negroes have angered the whites by insolent remarks about Jeffries."

Mounds, IL – Four blacks killed a black constable who was attempting to arrest them for shooting up the town in celebration of Johnson's victory. One white man was killed and another mortally wounded.

New Orleans, LA – There was rioting near newspaper bulletin boards issuing fight result reports. Two whites shot and seriously wounded two blacks. The whites approached and said, "Johnson won, but we will get even with all negroes." Then they started shooting. One was hit in the head and the other in the arm and side. A negro who shouted, "Hurrah for Johnson!" was seized and beaten severely until the police rescued him. Several other relatively minor outbreaks of violence occurred as well.

Newport, RI – Between the announcement of the fight result and 1 a.m., there were 24 conflicts between blacks and whites.

New York, NY – Race rioting between whites and blacks broke out in the seven different points of the city, affecting all of the boroughs. "The irritation caused by the defeat of Jeffries at the hands of the negro caused scores of street fights, negro hunts through the streets and outbreaks all through the night." There was rioting from the time the result was announced until long after midnight.

A negro waiter was killed in an altercation with a white man over the question of what Jeff in his prime could have done to Johnson. The white man ended the argument by striking the black man over the head with a blunt instrument. He later died in the hospital. His assailant escaped.

Whites pulled blacks from street cars and beat them. Some were found in the streets unconscious. One negro was dragged from a street-car and badly beaten before being rescued. Some white men were beaten in negro sections of the city.

One black man was almost lynched for yelling to a crowd of white men in the San Juan section, "We blacks put one over on you whites and we're going to do more to you." After his revolver missed fire, the crowd was upon him. He was being hauled to a lamppost when the police rescued him.

A gang of white men set fire to a negro tenement on the West Side, but it quickly was put out.

One report said that sailors from the various battleships in the port were the leaders in nearly all of the attacks on blacks.

About 50 badly injured blacks were in hospitals recovering from injuries.

Police reserves were out in all negro sections. Time and again, reserves were called upon to quell mobs.

The police were still keeping patrol the next day in the "black belt" to try to check any further race trouble engendered by the bout's outcome.

Norfolk, VA – Fifty blacks and several whites were taken to hospitals for injuries received in riots. They had broken faces and stab wounds. Many blacks were in severe condition. There were riots in all parts of the city. Much of the trouble was caused by enlisted men from the various battleships who attacked blacks wherever they met them. Nearly a score of white U.S. sailors were fined from $5 to $20 for their assaults on blacks.

Omaha, NE – One negro killed and several injured.

Philadelphia, PA – Fights with fists, bricks, and missiles broke out nearly everywhere in the city where the two races intermingled. Police freely used clubs to quell the disturbances. Over 100 whites and blacks were arrested.

The next day, the arrested rioters, some with heads bandaged, went before a police magistrate. Most received a fine, but those more seriously involved were held with bail or sent to country prison for short terms.

Phoenix, AZ – A mob seriously injured a negro.

Pittsburg, PA – In the negro district, street cars were held up and insulting epithets were hurled at white passengers until police used their clubs to beat back the crowds to permit the passage of cars.

Scores hurt in race riots in which a thousand blacks attacked white men. 100 rioters were arrested.

Pueblo, CO – Two white men were stabbed and 25 hurt in a white-black race riot in Besemer City Park.

Roanoke, VA - There were street scuffles all over. Mostly, there were broken heads and black eyes. However, some knives were used and a few scattering shots were fired. Six blacks were beaten and dying from broken heads. One was fatally wounded. Six white men were locked up.

One negro, upon hearing the fight result, said, "Now I guess the white folks will let the negroes alone." A white man replied, "No," and they clashed. The police jailed the negro, but allowed the white to go free. However, another black man shot that white man in the head. The bullet went through his skull.

St. Joseph, MO – A mob of whites attacked a white man who came to the defense and aid of a black man who was being struck by another white man. A policeman finally rescued him.

St. Louis, MO – Blacks blocked traffic and made threats. Initially, the police were powerless to cope with them, but eventually, a score of police came and the blacks were clubbed into submission and dispersed.

Blacks had planned a celebration to be held the day after the fight, but the authorities interfered and forced the plans to be canceled. Blacks were cautioned against assembling in the streets.

Shreveport, LA – Three blacks killed, one white fatally injured, and scores of both races hurt in the post-fight riot.

Uvalda, GA – Riots led to the deaths of three blacks; and many injured.

Washington, D.C. – With the black population numbering over 100,000, the largest black population in the U.S., they were in a frenzy of delight over Johnson's victory. The police were ready for trouble and quickly stopped many fights. The *Call* said, "The negro saloons were crowded with coons filled with gin." Hundreds of drunken blacks proceeded through the streets.

Blacks were wild with enthusiasm, and their boisterousness increased as the evening progressed. Police tried to quiet them but there was invariable conflict, and several persons were injured seriously.

7,000 blacks and whites rioted throughout the night.

Three white men chased a negro who had been shouting, "Hurrah for Johnson, champion of the world!" Fight after fight followed in quick succession. Police arrested whites and blacks for rioting.

Some blacks attacked whites. Three negresses dragged white women into the streets and beat them and tore their clothing away. An enlisted U.S. marine had his throat cut and was at a hospital in serious condition. Another white man was found unconscious after a free-for-all fight on Pennsylvania avenue. He was taken to a hospital, where it was determined that he had a concussion. A negro stabbed a white man, which required hospitalization.

Every policeman was on duty. There was a question as to whether federal troops should be ordered into the national capital to restore order. The fighting was continuous along Pennsylvania avenue between the Capitol and the White House. Rioting continued all night.

At least 200 blacks were arrested and more than 30 whites. Others said there were 246 arrests.

Two hospitals were crowded with injured whites and blacks.

Heavy police detachments patrolled negro settlements. Daylight brought little cessation to the celebration.

One or two shooting affairs occurred during the evening. Many were severely injured, but none fatally.

Washington, PA – Blacks shot two persons in cold blood.

Wilmington, DE – Whites attempt wholesale lynchings. Scores of persons were injured in the resultant riots. Police clubbed whites and blacks who were fighting. Police threatened to shoot into a crowd of 5,000 whites that were throwing stones at an arrested negro.

There were race riots in nearly every sizable city in the U.S. Thousands of blacks were beaten and several were dead or dying. The mob spirit seemed to rise up wherever a negro cheered for Johnson or permitted his exultation over the victory to grow to an extent that made it offensive to whites. Blacks were chased through the streets.

The *Bulletin* said scores of cities saw fighting that raged all night. Most victims were black. Up to noon on the 5th of July, 19 blacks and 5 whites had been killed, hundreds of both races were injured, many fatally, and hundreds were in jails and prisons. Hospitals were filled as well.

The *Chronicle* reported that at least 12 men had been killed and more than 100 seriously injured as a result of riots in the wake of reports of the fight's result. Most of the trouble was in the South, but large cities in the North were not immune.

Ironically, there were almost no troubles in Reno, where the fight had taken place. The week of the fight, at least 300 known crooks were arrested. Over half were drunks. A large percentage was taken into custody on suspicion of theft. The police were on guard to arrest anyone who even hinted at making trouble.

Some blamed whites for the riots, some blamed blacks, and some said it was a mixed bag, varying from situation and locale. The *Call* said the blacks celebrating Johnson's victory precipitated trouble with whites. The *Evening Post* said the irritation caused by the defeat of Jeffries at the hands of a negro caused scores of fights and negro hunts.

Mrs. Tiny Johnson, the champion's mother, deplored the riots, and said it was all due to white unwillingness to allow blacks to express themselves. "The white ones do not like for a black man to be on top, but Jack's there, and his victory will help the entire negro race."

She said her son planned to retire from the ring. Arthur told her that he would whip Jeffries, remove all possibility of the slightest dispute as to his right to the title, and then quit fighting.[436]

Blacks rejoiced at the victory in the greatest celebration since the issuing of the Emancipation Proclamation. To them, it proved what they could do if allowed to compete on an equal footing. The fight provided a huge psychological uplift. Furthermore, Johnson and his victory was the symbolic representation of black revenge upon white indignities.

The powers-that-be were aghast. The fight result and the riots had a ripple effect. Some wanted to ban boxing; some wanted to ban the fight films; while others attempted to disavow the very racial meaning that much of the press and public had conferred on the bout before it had occurred.

In Los Angeles, it was said that the city council would pass a law to prohibit all boxing exhibitions.

---

[436] *Nevada State Journal, Reno Evening Gazette,* July 6, 1910; *San Francisco Evening Post, San Francisco Call,* July 5, 1910.

The *Los Angeles Times* was concerned that as a result of Johnson's victory, blacks might become too uppity, confident, and demanding of more rights. It sought to disabuse blacks of such notions, and to diminish the fight's significance. It told whites that the fight meant nothing, and to take the loss in a more honorable fashion.

> It was a fight between a white man and a black man, but it is well at the outset not to pin too much racial importance on the fact. The conflict was a personal one, not race with race. ... Even if it were a matter of great racial import, the whites can afford the reflection that it is at best only a triumph of brawn over brain, not of brain over brawn. ...
>
> Pugilism and civilization bear no direct connection, but are in inverse ratio. ...
>
> The white man's mental supremacy is fully established, and for the present cannot be taken from him. ... His superiority does not rest on any huge bulk of muscle, but on brain development. ...
>
> The members of the white race who are not a disgrace to it will bear no resentment toward the black race because of this single victory in the prize ring. That would be to manifest lamentable weakness, not strength; stupid foolishness, not wisdom; a cowardly disposition, not manliness.
>
> Let the white man who is worthy of the great inheritance won from him by his race and handed down to him by his ancestors "take his medicine" like a man. If he put his hope and the hope of his race in the white man who went into the ring, let him recognize his foolishness, and in his disappointed hope let him take up this new "white man's burden" and bear it like a man, not collapse under it like a weakling.
>
> And now a Word to the Black Man.
>
> Do not point your nose too high. Do not swell your chest too much. Do not boast too loudly. Do not be puffed up. ... Remember you have done nothing at all. You are just the same member of society today you were last week. Your place in the world is just what it was. You are on no higher plane, deserve no new consideration, and will get none. ... No man will think a bit higher of you because your complexion is the same as that of the victor at Reno.

The *Times* further said that the fight did not mean that the black man was on top. "You are no nearer that mark than you were before the fight took place." It said brains mattered more than muscle. But it also said,

"White men who are men worthy of the name will not join in any fresh crusade against your race, already too long and too cruelly persecuted."[437]

The fact that whites spent so much time trying to diffuse the Johnson victory was an implicit acknowledgment of what a powerful occurrence it really was. Whites also were trying to quell further violence.

Ministers throughout the country started a movement to get the fight films banned. Christian societies like the Christian Endeavor Society believed the films were as bad as the fight itself. They lobbied politicians, saying that the film exhibitions would be demoralizing, the cause of more violence, and harmful to the morals of women and children. Most police chiefs supported the ban, fearing that public exhibitions would encourage race riots and crime.

Given the national violence which had occurred merely in the wake of verbal and written fight reports, many politicians throughout the country feared that the film exhibitions might cause further violence. As a result, many cities and states banned the exhibition of the Jeffries-Johnson fight films.

Some cities said they would allow the films, some banned them outright, while other cities said the films would be permitted provided that no disturbances were created, taking a wait-and-see approach. Usually the films were barred by order of the mayor, or sometimes by emergency legislative action. Sometimes the police simply banned them on their own.

The following are examples of how several locales, city and state, throughout the nation, dealt with the Jeffries-Johnson fight films issue:

Alabama – The governor said he would recommend prohibition of the fight pictures.

Alameda, CA – Films of the fight were barred.

Arkansas – The governor said he gladly would cooperate in the movement to bar the pictures.

Atlanta, GA – A bill prohibiting the display of moving pictures of any prize-fight was introduced in the general assembly. The mayor expected the films to be banned. "The pictures would inflame the anti-negro sentiment and the result would be disastrous." Fearing bloodshed, he did not want race clashes to be renewed.

Baltimore, MD – Pursuant to the police commissioners' request, the mayor said he would prohibit the exhibition of the moving pictures. The local marshal said, "We have a large colored population here and the exhibition of the pictures might cause racial troubles." A local Cardinal said children had to be protected from the films. The showing of the pictures would have a bad effect upon the community, and would "tend to induce attacks upon

[437] *Los Angeles Times*, July 6, 1910.

the blacks," as well as cause riots. "The black people could not profit by seeing the pictures and I am sure the whites would not."

Bellingham, WA – The films would be welcomed. No race trouble had resulted, for there were few black persons there.

Berkeley, CA – The police chief said the fight film exhibitions would not be allowed.

Boston, MA – The mayor said Boston would bar pictures of all boxing contests.

Buffalo, NY – The police superintendent said the city ordinance prohibiting prize-fight moving-picture exhibitions would be enforced strictly.

Cairo, IL – The mayor said he probably would prohibit exhibitions, because he believed they may arouse race prejudice.

California – Confident that local mayors would prohibit the films, the governor said he would take no formal action. "The interest in the fight was exaggerated into hysteria. Now comes the natural reaction, following the collapse of that hysteria." The *Bulletin* noted, "The Governor intimated that the prejudice against the pictures might not have been so general and so pronounced had the white man defeated the negro."

Chicago, IL – The Women's Christian Temperance Union started a movement to prevent the exhibitions. However, the police chief said he did not think the pictures would injure the city's morals. Ultimately, the city decided to allow the pictures to be displayed, but would take action if anything happened. (This position later changed, as will be discussed.)

Cincinnati, OH – The mayor said the pictures would not be permitted to be exhibited publicly, for he thought they would promote race hatred.

Colorado - The governor said he would attempt to bar the pictures.

Connecticut – Supported the ban of the films.

Covington, KY – Would not bar the films.

Denver, CO – Would not ban the films. On July 7, the Denver Fire and Police Board denied the petition of the juvenile Court and Citizens' Union representatives to forbid the fight film exhibitions.

Des Moines, IA – A state law already prohibited the exhibition of such pictures, and the law would be enforced.

Detroit, MI – The mayor said if the police and he decided that the fight pictures would cause race hatred, they would be excluded from the city.

East Liverpool, OH – The mayor said he would not prohibit the pictures, for there was no more harm in showing them than in presenting Wild West shows. "This agitation over the country is simply advertising the pictures. If people remained quiet the public soon would forget the fight."

Fort Worth, TX – In response to the mayor's request, the city commission passed an ordinance prohibiting the exhibition of the Johnson-Jeffries fight pictures.

Frankfurt, KY – Won't bar the films.

Fresno, CA – The mayor instructed the chief of police to prevent the fight pictures from being shown.

Geneva, NY – Barred.

Harrisburg, PA – The mayor issued an order prohibiting the showing of the pictures.

Helena, MT – Barred.

Houston, TX – Barred.

Illinois – The governor said he would join the governors of other states in the movement to suppress the fight pictures.

Indiana – The governor was opposed to the exhibition of the films and would prevent exhibitions if possible. "If there is any law to prevent the exhibition it will be enforced."

Indianapolis, IN – Initially, the mayor said he would permit showings, and was anxious to see the pictures. Later, after the mayor held a conference with city officials, they decided the films would not be shown.

Jefferson, MO – Films allowed.

Johnstown, PA – Barred.

Kansas City, MO – Initially the mayor said he would take action to prohibit the pictures. A subsequent report said the pictures would be allowed unless they provoked race rioting.

Lexington, KY – The local police judge declared that the moving pictures of the fight could not be exhibited there. The black population was about as large as the white, but no troubles had yet been experienced.

Lincoln, NE – The police chief said he would enforce the ordinance prohibiting the showing of prize-fight pictures.

Little Rock, AR – The mayor issued a proclamation prohibiting the films.

Los Angeles, CA – Given that boxing was illegal, the mayor likely would ban the films. Furthermore, the city prosecutor said he would enforce the city ordinance prohibiting the exhibition of motion pictures that were subversive of morals or harmful to the young.

Louisville, KY – The mayor said the pictures would be prohibited.

Lynchburg, VA – Pictures barred.

Maine – The governor said that in the interest of peace and morals, he gladly would assist in the prohibition of the pictures.

Maryland – The governor said he would not permit the showing of the Johnson-Jeffries fight pictures.

Michigan – The laws did not prohibit pictures, but the films could be suppressed by mayors, the police, and city ordinances. The governor said he would use his influence to bar the pictures throughout the state.

Milwaukee, WI – The mayor sent word to all theater managers advising them against entering into contracts for the presentation of the fight films, for such exhibitions were detrimental to public morals.

Minneapolis, MN – Barred by mayor.

Missouri – The governor said that if the fight pictures started race riots or produced public disturbances in the state, he would prevent their display as a public nuisance.

Mobile, AL – The mayor informed all moving picture show operators that they would not be permitted to show pictures of the fight.

Montana – The governor said the laws did not prevent the exhibitions.

Natchez, MS – Barred.

Nebraska - The state attorney general said there was no state law, so each community would have to take action regarding the matter if they chose.

New Brunswick, NJ – Barred.

New Orleans, LA – Initially, the mayor issued an order to the chief of police to arrest the proprietor of any theatre attempting to show the moving pictures. Later, New Orleans decided to allow them to be shown, but only when blacks and whites saw the films at different times. Segregated exhibitions would reduce the possibility for violence.

New York, NY – The International Association of Police Chiefs said boxing film exhibitions were illegal because prize-fighting was illegal in New York, and therefore exhibitions would be the reproduction of an illegal act.

However, New York City mayor William Gaynor had a tolerant attitude towards the films. He said, "New York hasn't a large negro population, and I am sure the pictures will not engender any race feeling here." The mayor said the pictures could be shown without interference. He had no more right to stop the films than to stop publication of the stories of the fight. He would not use arbitrary power to suppress the exhibitions. In a letter to a reverend who represented an international reform bureau, the mayor said,

> Ours is a government of laws and not of men. ... I shall not take the law into my own hands. You say that you are glad to see that the mayors of many cities have 'ordered' that these pictures shall not be exhibited. Indeed? Who set them up as autocrats? ... The growing exercise of arbitrary power in this country by those put in office would be far more dangerous and is far more to be dreaded than certain other vices which we all wish to minimize.

Norfolk, VA – The mayor would not permit the films to be exhibited.

North Dakota – Films barred by executive order.

Oakland, CA – The mayor said he would exercise his police power to stop the films, feeling that prize-fighting was brutal and degrading.

Philadelphia, PA – The mayor refused to prevent the picture exhibitions. He did not anticipate further rioting.

Phoenix, AZ – The mayor announced that an ordinance would be introduced prohibiting the exhibition of the fight films.

Pittsburg, PA – The police said the pictures would be allowed unless when shown they proved to be the cause of race trouble.

Portland, ME – Barred.

Portland, OR – The police chief said that most likely the picture exhibitions would not be prevented. However, another report said the fight picture exhibitions were prevented by a law passed in 1897 which said, "Whoever publicly exhibits any photographic or other reproduction of a prize fight shall be punished by a fine not exceeding $500." Another report said the mayor would allow the films to be exhibited. He said, "I cannot see that the displaying of the pictures is any worse than the printing of the minute details of the fight in the newspapers."

Portsmouth, VA – Barred.

Providence, RI – Laws enacted three years ago against the exhibition of moving pictures of fight films would be enforced rigidly.

Richmond, VA – Barred.

Riverside, CA – Barred.

Rhode Island - The governor said he would leave it up to individual towns and cities.

Roswell, NM – Barred by mayor.

Sacramento, CA – Won't bar the films.

St. Joseph, MO – The mayor said he would not interfere with the films. "I want to see them, and I want my boys to see them." However the Federation of Churches would petition the city council to pass an ordinance against the pictures.

St. Louis, MO – The president of the police board of commissioners said they would not permit the exhibition of the fight films. "The police officials believe that negroes in St. Louis eager to show their admiration for Johnson and the belief that the black can whip any white man living will become riotous after viewing the pictures." They thought the films would arouse bitter race feeling and bloodshed.

San Bernardino, CA – The majority of councilmen said they would not oppose the showing of the moving pictures.

San Diego, CA – The superintendent of police said no steps had been taken to prevent the exhibition. He knew of no reason why they should not be shown, as others had been in the past.

San Francisco, CA – The local Church Federation argued that the films were the reproduction of an illegal act. The mayor said that if the board of supervisors found the films to be subversive to general public morals, the censors would bar the pictures. Ultimately, San Francisco's Board of Motion Picture Censorship banned the films, making their exhibition unlawful. One member of the board of censors said pictures of prize-fights had a demoralizing effect on the young. Another said suppression was necessary to prevent race war.

San Jose, CA – The mayor refused to be swayed by the ministerial hysteria, and allowed the showing of the films.

> I do not see any reason why the Jeffries-Johnson pictures should not be shown in San Jose. Under the English common law every idiot, insane person and incompetent, as well as every minor, was provided with a guardian to care for him, but anyone else might do as he pleased. So it is here and it seems to me that the proper way to deal with the situation is to prohibit those from seeing the exhibition who are incompetent. There is nothing about the pictures of the fight which can be very injurious to persons of sound mind and faculties.

Savannah, GA – The mayor would not permit the fight pictures to be shown.

Seattle, WA – The mayor said there would be no interference with the fight pictures. He was confident that the police could do their duty and handle any problems. "Whenever I am convinced that the city is unable to handle any riot that may result from the exhibition of fight pictures in Seattle, I will immediately tender my resignation."

South Carolina – The governor would recommend prohibition.

South Dakota – In the interest in preserving law and order, the governor said he would approve a prohibition of the pictures.

Springfield, IL – Barred by city council.

Springfield, MA – Barred.

Texas – The governor said he would submit legislation to prohibit the moving pictures of the Jeffries-Johnson fight. He feared such exhibitions would stir up racial feelings and result in bloodshed.

Topeka, KS – The mayor said he would never allow the fight pictures to be shown. "I will see that the police department stops the show and arrests the managers."

Utah – The governor said prohibition of the pictures was impracticable.

Van Buren, AR – The fight pictures were prohibited.

Virginia – The governor said he would request officials of every city and town to prohibit the showing of the fight pictures.

Washington, D.C. – Washington D.C. was first to issue an order preventing the public exhibition of the Jeffries-Johnson fight films. Fearing more riots, at the request of the police chief, the commissioners of the District of Columbia ordered the films barred.

Even foreign cities and countries considered whether or not to allow exhibitions of the Jeffries-Johnson fight films. Most who banned them feared the incitement of racial animosity. One must keep in mind the political and racial context. Much of the world contained nations whose dark majorities had been conquered and colonized by white minorities. From the conquerors' perspective, the films potentially could send a dangerous message to those who were oppressed – that their lot in life was not inevitable. Such a message could foment agitation, demand for more civil rights, and ultimately rebellion. The films' potentially powerful symbolic message led to their banishment by many towns and countries throughout the world:

British Columbia, Canada – Films barred by executive order.

Calcutta, India – The demand to prohibit the pictures was spreading. The newspapers there suggested that the American authorities destroy the films and compensate the owners.

Cape Town, South Africa – There was widespread demand to prohibit the films, "owing to their effect on the natives. Signs already are evident among them of excitement on account of the victory of the negro." South Africans were refusing to order the films, fearing racial unrest.

Havana, Cuba – The government prohibited exhibition of the fight pictures.

Johannesburg, South Africa – All of the newspapers demanded the suppression of the moving pictures. It was believed that the town council intended to forbid the exhibition as detrimental to the public peace.

London, England – A movement in favor of government action to suppress the fight pictures was extending to a considerable section of the House of Commons. Both parties supported the movement. Some morning papers advocated for a general suppression. Sir Howell Davies said he would ask the Home Secretary in the House of Commons to prohibit the fight films in the interest of public decency. The London City Council voted to deprecate the showing of the films. Although there was no law preventing the halls from showing them, it was thought that theaters would be hesitant to do so, given that the Council granted discretionary licenses every year and the halls would not want to incur their ire.

Manila, Philippines – Fearing the effect that the bout might have on the Filipinos, the municipal board of Manila resolved to prohibit the picture exhibitions.

Melbourne, Australia – The clergy sent a petition to the premier of Australia asking him to prevent the pictures. A similar movement was afoot in New Zealand.

Mexico City, Mexico – The pictures would be welcomed. The Governor of the district said, "Happily, we have no negroes here."

Ontario, Canada – Barred by executive order.

Pretoria, South Africa – The government sent instructions to the police to prohibit film exhibitions of the fight.

Victoria, British Columbia, Canada – A resolution to forbid the exhibition of the pictures failed to pass at the city council meeting. The government would not interfere with the motion picture exhibitions.

The majority held that the fight films were injurious to the morals of the young and provocative of race war. The feeling was very strong in the South, where the black population equaled or exceeded the white population. Many reverends said the pictures would have a demoralizing effect, that children would be influenced by them, and that the films "would inspire them with false ideals," whatever those were.

Those of us today who understand our 1st amendment constitutional rights to be something time-honored and sacrosanct might be asking how they could censor and ban fight films. Well, the U.S. Supreme Court did not hold that the 1st amendment was applicable to the states until 1925, in *Gitlow v. New York*, 268 U.S. 652 (1925). Hence, until then, the 1st amendment only applied to the federal government. At that time, cities and states could do what they wanted when it came to censorship.

Various noted clubwomen joined the hysterical war on the fight pictures. They demanded the protection of children from the degrading spectacle. The District President of the San Francisco Federation of Women's Clubs said, "Any sort of prizefight is debasing, but the one at Reno was particularly degrading. It aroused primitive passions. The white race is not depending for supremacy on brute force, and no man of the caliber of a prizefighter fosters the ideals of our civilization." The lady Vice-President of the California Club wrote,

> The fact that this man Johnson is the champion fighter of this country deludes the colored race into believing that they have made great progress. It gives them a false security, sets up a degrading ideal for them, and immeasurably retards their growth in real intelligence.

> One reads about these race riots everywhere. The pictures prolong the degrading event that happened in Reno on the Fourth by emphasizing it in the minds of children and of persons of immature

intelligence. The negroes are to some extent a child-like race, needing guidance, schooling and encouragement. We deny them this by encouraging them to believe that they have gained anything by having one of their race as champion fighter. Race riots are inevitable when we, a superior people, allow these people to be deluded and degraded by such false ideals.

Let alone the injury that will be done our children by allowing them access to such a spectacle as these fight pictures, we also owe something to these negroes. As a superior people we are under responsibility show them a better way than this.

Naturally all of this was a big concern for the companies and men who had invested a great deal of money into the films, such as the American Vitagraph Company. Financial interests were at stake.

The motion picture syndicate said they would not show the pictures in any city where adverse legislation existed. They did not intend to buck the law. "We do not think these pictures are any different from those which have been displayed of the Johnson-Burns and Johnson-Ketchel fights, but if we find that popular sentiment is against them we will lay them on the shelf and not show them at all." However, they reputedly had invested $200,000, so they were going to need to show the films in the locations that would allow them, or via underground private exhibitions.

Subsequently, the picture-men released a statement to the effect that the films would not be displayed in public places, at least not by the Vitagraph Company of America. They said the reels only would be made available to private clubs and at stag parties, in order to ensure that the younger generation would not be allowed to see them.

Apparently, the motion picture men made this announcement because they felt that putting up a fight to show the films would have resulted in the passage of additional laws making the exhibition of fight pictures a crime. By gracefully withdrawing, without opposition to public clamor, the pictures still would have the option of making money via private displays, which could give them a chance to earn some money, although not as much as would have been the case with public exhibitions. Plus, perhaps when the hysteria died down, the films could be displayed publicly.

The motion pictures, including the fight, scenes at the training camps, and the preliminary program at ringside occupied two hours.

Black folks wanted to see the films. Unlike most white ministers, the Negro Ministers Conference, composed of pastors of the African Methodist Church of Pennsylvania, New Jersey, Delaware, and New York, refused to endorse a resolution favoring the suppression of the fight films. One bishop admitted that he had prayed that Johnson might win. "[He] wanted to see the black man win, especially as the whites had made a race issue of the encounter. He urged that no appeals be made by colored men to suppress the pictures and declared that men advocating such suppression were doing so only because the black man had won."[438]

THE FIRST MESSAGE FROM MARS---By WESTOVER

San Francisco Evening Post, July 8, 1910

And Not a Friendly Port in Sight

San Francisco Examiner, July 9, 1910

[438] *San Francisco Chronicle*, July 5-7, 1910; *Reno Evening Gazette*, July 5-7, 12, 13, 1910; *San Francisco Bulletin*, July 6-8, 1910; *San Francisco Call*, July 5-8, 12, 1910; *Nevada State Journal*, July 6, 8, 1910; *San Francisco Evening Post*, July 6, 11, 12, 1910; *San Francisco Examiner*, July 9, 10, 1910.

Sympathizing with American whites, many newspapers in London, England were excusing the white violence that followed in the wake of the fight result, feeling that it was understandable, and perhaps even necessary. A *Freeman* correspondent said the queer thing about the reaction in London, England, was that the English, who usually took delight in anything that reflected adversely upon Americans, suddenly reverted to support for black suppression. Race appeared to trump nationality. "The *London Afternoon Star* is practically the only afternoon paper that has criticized the outbreak of anti-Negro violence." The London *Globe*, which usually was anti-American, was not so in this instance. It said,

> Our sympathy runs more to the man with the rope than to the blatant blacks. It is against human nature to expect white men to accept the negroes' insolent assertion that Johnson's victory established the superiority of the black without instant protest. The Reno contest was the most injudicious one ever permitted and the racial effects will continue for years.

> The Americans are the trustees of the predominance of whites over blacks and we believe they will prove true to their trust.

The London *Daily Telegraph* wrote in support of white-upon-black violence,

> It is useless to hold up the hand of reprobation here. These things are brutal and vile, but behind them lies the absolute necessity to keep the negro race a little in check, for if it once gets out of hand there will be worse scenes under the stars and stripes than have yet been witnessed there.

The *London Times* said the fight proved nothing, for a thousand American whites probably would beat a thousand negroes in any conflict or form of physical endurance. It commented on the fact that Americans disliked seeing a white man beaten by a Negro, and remarked,

> The American feeling must frankly be recognized. The feeling, we think, is not confined to America. It is very easy for us in England, where we have no color problem, to talk with indignation and abhorrence of the lynchings and the outrages which occur so frequently in the Southern States of America. We have yet to see how the English would act if confronted with entirely similar conditions. There is much reason to fear that our attitude would be no more tolerant.

The *San Francisco Evening Post* wrote, "The *Times* thinks that the pivot of the whole question is the world-wide instinctive feeling against color intermarriages."

Many newspapers deplored the fact that a white man had consented to meet a black, and some reiterated condemnation of former champion Tommy Burns for ever having consented to fight Johnson just so he could earn money. They blamed Burns for having given a black man a chance at the title, which ultimately forced Jeffries out of retirement.[439]

Several writers said pugilism's death seemed imminent. John L. Sullivan said that talk of boxing's future being gloomy was ridiculous. He said the future would take care of itself and the game would be just fine. "It's been the same old story all the time." They said the same things after his big fights, but such was not the case. "Now this Jeffries-Johnson fight marks the end of the sport. BOSH. When they change human nature, and put a mollycoddle's heart in every good, red blooded American citizen then the game might die," but until then, there was scant danger of pugilism ceasing.[440]

Thomas Bannerman, president of the San Francisco Board of Education, said the fight's result was a "proper rebuke to the Caucasian race." He was glad that the black man won.[441]

The *Bulletin* said the fight game was dying by inches, for politicians used the sport to serve their own personal ends. It looked as if California officials had their minds set upon boxing's complete abolition.

Tex Rickard said the country was being run by crooked politicians. He called the anti-fight-film movement hypocritical. He noted how San Francisco Mayor McCarthy had been a friend, had brought the fight there, fully supported it, and a permit was paid for and granted, but now the mayor was joining in on the bandwagon saying that the showing of the pictures was against the law and corrupted morals. "I suppose it is a case of politics." The *Bulletin* also called the mayor a hypocrite.

Rickard argued that if the fight really was such a brutal affair, the best way to convince people for all time that such was the case would be to let them go and see the pictures in question and judge for themselves.

> Every day in the week all over the country the youth of the big and small cities are shown on the canvas the commission of murder, robbery and trickery of all kinds, and these shows go on without censure. Why this sudden disposition against the pictures on moral grounds is hard to understand.

He said there was more brutality in amateur bouts with raw and inexperienced youngsters than in a pro bout with trained and experienced fighters.

Tex said the attempts to ban the pictures would make the investors more money in the end, for it was the best advertising in the world. And the film folks needed the motion pictures to be exhibited, for they, backed by Lubin, had invested a great deal of money purchasing the rights. Special lenses and film stock had been purchased. They paid for the operation of twelve machines at ringside. Development of the films also cost a great deal.

---

[439] *Reno Evening Gazette, San Francisco Evening Post,* July 7, 1910; *Freeman,* August 6, 1910.
[440] *San Francisco Bulletin,* July 11, 1910.
[441] *San Francisco Examiner,* July 5, 6, 1910.

Rickard said it was impossible to promote fights unless one first got himself "right" with the politicians, "and I guess you all know what that means." He said Governor Gillett misled him willfully, told him in person that he would not interfere with the fight, but then when the time was right, turned on him by panning the fight and getting it barred, making a play of political pyrotechnics. "I don't know what politics is behind this, but you can gamble it's crooked politics." It showed that the whole game of government was "rotten to the core." "If Gillett had told me that he would not allow the fight to be pulled off in this state I would never have thought of coming here. But Gillett lied and lied repeatedly." Tex said stopping a fight or the fight game never was done to serve any alleged high moral purpose, but to secure further political power.

Rickard said Governor Gillett had been drinking a few too many highballs on the day he gave the purported interview in Chicago alleging that the then-upcoming fight was fixed for Jeffries.

Tex said the fight game would go on. In a year or two there would be even more of it. Some states would legislate against it, while others would be more liberal. He would stage any bout he thought would draw a crowd and make money. To him, it was just like mining or oil-drilling. If he saw a chance to make money, he would take it.

Rickard further said that in order to get the fight, he had to offer $10,000 bonuses to each fighter two days before the opening of bids.[442]

The next day, Rickard said his alleged interview printed in the *Bulletin* the night before, criticizing the mayor, was a fake. He denied having said anything. Regardless, the point was made.[443]

Professor W. L. Hamilton of the University of California, in a lecture before a sociology class, declared that the Jeffries-Johnson fight proved that the negro no longer belonged to an inferior race. Johnson's success demonstrated the improvement of the entire race, and was an instance of the black race's remarkable rapid advances in the last century in all areas. "He is rapidly approaching equality with the white so far as civilization is concerned and I should not be surprised, were I alive to watch his progress, 300 years hence to see the negro and the white intermarry and meet everywhere on common ground."

A black reverend in Washington, D.C., preaching the lessons of the fight, said,

> I believe that because Johnson won, prize fighting will be stopped forever. The white people are unjust to Johnson, but this does not change the principle that fighting is wrong. The newspapers are most to blame for the interest in prize fighting. If negroes attach undue importance to this fight, the whites are no more rational.

---

[442] *San Francisco Bulletin*, July 7, 8, 1910; *San Francisco Call*, July 8, 1910.
[443] *San Francisco Evening Post*, July 8, 9, 1910.

Johnson should be allowed to appear on the stage just as Sullivan and other pugilists have done.[444]

The *New York Age* said even presidential elections had never aroused the interest manifested by millions of Americans of all races in the fight. Blacks were joyous, while whites were somber. It estimated that the country's blacks were richer by nearly half a million dollars by betting on Johnson.

> And the result of the fight has had a peculiar effect on the populace. … Seldom was a white brother seen to smile and appear as if pleased. The only people whose faces were bright and who went about in a light-hearted manner were the colored citizens. …

> For the Negro citizens to enthuse over Johnson's victory and try to buy up all the newspapers is perfectly natural. I have never seen so many colored people reading newspapers as since the fight. I saw one enthusiastic citizen of color with every New York daily paper of July 5, including a German and a Hebrew paper. He told me that he wanted to cut the pictures of the fighters out of two papers he could not read. Then, again, never have I seen such few white people read the papers as within the past two days. …

> That the Negro race should feel highly elated over the fact that a member of their race is champion of champions is to be expected. There would be something wrong with us if we felt otherwise. All other races feel proud of their members who achieve name and fame; then why not we?

> There is one regrettable feature about the Johnson-Jeffries fight that I deem it opportune to comment upon at this time and that is the attempts of many white writers and Caucasians to provoke a race issue. The fight between Johnson and Jeffries was not to decide whether the colored race was the superior of the white race as fighters. It was to settle the question of who was the superior…Jeffries, who happened to be a white man, or John Arthur Johnson, a Negro.

The *Age* noted that many writers unnecessarily attacked Johnson simply because he was a colored man. Whites liked to contend that a black fighter would always show the yellow streak when he faced a white man, and that black fighters lacked heart. Even Jack London, who admitted that Johnson did not show a yellow streak in the fight, despite so many predictions that he would, still did not grant that the question was settled for all time. "How nonsensical! How can some of the 'doubting Thomasas' be convinced that Negro fighters do not possess yellow streaks?"

---

[444] *San Francisco Bulletin*, July 7, 1910.; *Afro American Ledger*, July 23, 1910.

Some black folk had not wanted the fight to happen, feeling that the contest would do more harm to colored citizens than good. However, this writer disagreed.

> I have always wanted to see Jeffries and Johnson meet, in the first place believing that Johnson would win, and secondly, feeling that the victory of the Negro over the white man would cause the white brother to hold us in higher esteem.
>
> Despite the fact that we are acquiring education as well as wealth, we are not only as a race, but as individuals considered the inferior of the Caucasian. Almost any white man, no matter how ignorant or illiterate, thinks he is the superior of every black man, and while any Negro would be foolish for a moment to compare his race with that of the dominant race, yet we are willing to make comparisons as to superiority when it comes to individuals.
>
> The case of Jack Johnson shows the superiority of individuals, irrespective of color, and by defeating Jeffries we are bound to be more highly respected. From now on the white man will not generally underestimate us as he has been guilty of doing heretofore.
>
> Some of the yellow journals are endeavoring to work up race riots throughout the country, now that Johnson has won.[445]

Lithographs of Johnson appeared in the windows of practically every black apartment in New York. Most blacks lived in the negro districts of San Juan Hill and Harlem.

The Irish district of "Hell's Kitchen," which was next door to San Juan Hill, was agitated, and a number of bitter clashes between whites and blacks took place on July 7. "Serious trouble seems inevitable and the 'cockeyness' of the colored population seems to have increased a hundredfold since July 4."

The police reported that shops had sold more revolvers in the four days since the fight than at any similar time in recent years. Most of the purchasers were white.[446]

Baltimore's *Afro-American Ledger* noted that amongst the crowd that stood by the news office where the fight returns were being megaphoned out to the multitude, a white man said, "I hope Jeffries will kill the damn nigger." The writer replied to him, "Johnson is right there in the ring with him." The white man said, "If Jeffries can get at him he will knock his damn head off." The writer again replied, saying, "There is nobody in between Johnson and Jeffries and Jeffries has every chance in the world to get him."

The *Afro American Ledger* criticized white newsmen and others for hyping

---

[445] *New York Age*, July 7, 1910.
[446] *San Francisco Bulletin*, July 8, 1910.

the racial aspects of the fight, which in part caused the riots and all the trouble regarding the fight films.

> [The] world stood spellbound, with eager anxiousness never occasioned before by any event in the sporting world. The prime reason for this anxiety was the unwise accentuation of the racial features of the fight. The world was made to feel that it was the white man against the black man, and that in order to show the superiority of the Saxon brain and brawn over the Negro brain and brawn, Jeffries must win. He was published up as the hope of the white race, and as their representative must show his superiority over the Negro. … This emphasizing of the racial element in the contest, prepared the way for the trouble which has arisen throughout the country, as we had expected and the newspapers, these public educators, are responsible for it.[447]

Providing another black perspective, the black-owned *Broad Ax*, published in Chicago, Illinois and Salt Lake City, Utah, said the whole civilized world stood against the cool, steady nerve and boldness of Johnson, whose well-directed, scientific, sledge-hammer blows could defeat any heavyweight on the face of the earth.

Many erroneously believed the rank speculation of Governor Gillett, who said the fight was a frame up, that Johnson had a weak back and like any common Negro would lie down or would be bought off. His wild talk, combined with racial prejudice and stereotypes, caused many white sporting men to be guided by false sentiment, and therefore they went bust by placing their money on their white idol. On the other hand, colored folks raked in lots of money by betting on Johnson at long odds.

To the great astonishment of those who knew nothing about Johnson's fighting qualities, he did not display the yellow streak so much talked about by the California governor, the fans, the white newspaper writers, and the public in general, aside from black folk, for the former falsely labored under the impression that Jeff would lay Johnson out cold with one or two body blows, and that "no Negro could look him or any other white man in the eye and live thereafter." The entire civilized world was aghast.

The fans and Jeff's cornermen were so hell-bent upon making sure Jeffries was not knocked out by a black man that they urged the fight to be stopped, and the cornermen rushed into the ring to save him.

Still, the fans who attended the bout "displayed more tolerance than the preachers and so-called Christians who hated to see the black Samson win, and who think it is a burning shame and an everlasting disgrace for a Negro prize fighter to knock out a white prize fighter."

Throughout the country, there was great rejoicing by the colored population. Because of this, some "pinheaded" city and state officials would not permit the moving pictures to be exhibited. "Many members of the so-

---

[447] *Afro American Ledger*, July 9, 1910.

called superior race have vented their spite and bitterness against the Colored people because they were on the losing side." The fight's outcome settled none of the serious problems which confronted the American people.

This writer opined that it was wonderful that a black man held first place in at least one thing in the world. It proved that if given the chance, blacks were capable of producing folks who were tops in other fields as well.[448]

George Knox, publisher of the *Freeman*, also commented on the racial hype, analysis, and impact of the fight.

> It has been well said that the white people are responsible for the turn of affairs in pugilism, especially as it concerns the Johnson-Jeffries fight, and which, by the way, will have much influence in the future in affairs of the kind. The impression was made that the aim of the fight was to win back the laurels from the Negro, a contention never denied at any time up until the day of the fight. The championship, according to men, means that the one who wears the title of champion is the best man physically in his particular class.

Being a champion of the human race was an honor and a symbol of great manhood. However,

> [Johnson] is a Negro, and the Anglo-Saxons are not quite prepared to see Negroes shattering their traditions. … The many expressions in the newspapers at all times and in Jeffries' favor always were inflammatory to a race like the colored people, who feel to be getting the nasty end of things always. …

> The result of the fight will be far reaching in its consequences; the end is not promised. But whatever the end, the white people should think as to who knocked the chip off of the shoulder. Already conditions are assuming an ugly shape. The fight pictures are being prohibited in localities and mostly because of who Johnson was. The colored people did many silly things; to be honest, they aggravated the white people, but simply through a spirit of victory, and one must confess of race rather than of individual. It should have been the other way; it would be far now for the general peace if the fight had been considered merely a contest for the supremacy of man, physical man, rather than a contest for race superiority which counts nothing for more than the moment, excepting prejudice.

The *Freeman* recognized that the fight "meant nothing by the way of securing supremacy for the race." It saw the fight as a contest between two individuals and not a matter of race. Johnson himself had avoided talking about the fight in racial terms. And yet, "The *Freeman* feels as though the

[448] *Chicago Broad Ax*, July 9, 1910.

race should be grateful and thankful for having an opportunity to display its athletic ability, which has been denied by Sullivan, Corbett and others."[449]

Fight fans dreamt that Johnson had a yellow streak that Jeff would bring out, but it was only a dream, and they were just awakening to reality.

Race analysts believed that the white man's weak spot was his chin, while the Negro's body was his vulnerable part. "And that you may beat him over the head all you care to and that he will not even be dazed. This is carrying a joke too far." The fact was that fighters of both races had been knocked out with punches to either the body or head.[450]

A New York theater on Broadway claimed to be showing the Reno fight films, but when the spectators realized that the films were fakes and the theater owners were swindlers, they rioted and tore up the theater.

A writer for the black-owned *New York Age* said the question in the wake of the fight was whether its result would intensify race feeling. Being an optimist, this writer felt that more good would result than bad.

> Those of the white race who have heretofore held the Negro cheap at all times will commence to regard the race to which Champion Johnson belongs in its proper light – a child race, while true, but having members who are capable of competing with other races in most every walk of life, providing an opportunity is given. There is no doubt that the Negro will be accorded more respectful consideration.

True, the fight caused several disturbances in which white toughs attacked blacks, and several people died.

> Yet, if one does not size up the post-fight situation in the role of an alarmist he will find that at a general election more murders are committed and more brawls take place between whites of opposite political parties than occurred between the two races after July 4.

> Of course, the sensational newspapers will seek to attribute every clash between whites and blacks for the next year to Johnson's victory over Jeffries, but the people of this country are beginning to learn that the yellow journals incite more race antipathy than do the most radical elements of both races.

> All Negroes and all well-thinking white citizens regret that a number of colored persons were killed because Jack Johnson won the fight. But had Jeffries come out winner I venture to make the statement that the list of Negroes killed by white toughs would be three times as large as it is today. Irrespective of the termination of the fight, conflicts between the races would have been inevitable, but in view of the far-reaching effect the fight at Reno is bound to have on this body politic I think the casualty list has been small. There is one thing

[449] *Freeman*, July 9, 1910.
[450] *Freeman*, July 9, 1910; *New York Times*, July 5, 1910.

the Negro must learn, and that is that races, as with individuals, must sacrifice in order to succeed. Many races have lost thousands of people to gain a point.

There was an issue involved in the fight on July 4, one which the Negro did not make but which was brought on by many of the white newspapers and Caucasians. A week or so before the fight even a colored minister, clothed in his ecclesiastical garb, could not talk for long before he was called Jack Johnson in derision. No one can deny that by reason of color the Negro has been greatly underestimated. To be other than white usually means inferiority to the majority of white citizens, and when Johnson whipped Burns it was then that Jeffries was called upon to regain the championship title and relieve the white race of what was considered an embarrassing situation.

So, before the fight at Reno when the betting should have been even money the odds strongly favored Jeffries to win, and not because conditions should have been rightfully such, but because one fighter was white and the other colored, and the white bettors could not for the world see why in such a great contest for physical supremacy a Negro should come out first best.

Therefore, the blindness, due to color prejudice, cost many a white man a neat sum of money, and any time you touch a white American's pocketbook it is then he sits up and takes notice. In an endeavor to correctly size up the Johnson-Jeffries contest the white bettors will very likely conclude that after all color is no bar to success and does not necessarily mean inferiority.

But the movement against the exhibition of the fight pictures is about the most childish and idiotic crusade that has been inaugurated for some time. Had Jeffries won there would have been no opposition to showing the pictures, but as Johnson came out victorious the cry "Don't show the fight pictures" was set up which now extends as far as India. In fact, even abroad various authorities do not favor the pictures being shown to the darker races in which a black man is pictured as soundly thrashing a white man. The attitude of the anti-fight picture clan reminds one of the hesitancy of some mothers to put long trousers on their overgrown sons- fearing that the young men will become too fresh and mannish.

What is particularly pleasing is that both races are taking the result of the fight in a becoming and praise-worthy manner. True, a number of white toughs have seen fit to vent their spleen by attacking Negroes, but they are the dregs of society, and their actions must be attributed to ignorance. And the colored brother has exhibited unusual reserve during these moments of unbounded enthusiasm for him and has not been arrogant or insulting as many whites presumed he would be. So, despite the fact that a Negro is the undisputed champion of the world, the sun continues to rise and set and there are no evidences that the affairs of this great country are to be chaotic and unsettled because Johnson won.[451]

Some blamed white newspapers and Jeffries himself for causing the riots, for they made too much of the race issue. The *Washington Times* noted that Jeff was advertised as the "champion of the white race," and announced that his only purpose in re-entering the ring was to re-establish Caucasian supremacy. He forced the race issue, which resulted in riots, largely precipitated by white men and boys who attacked blacks. He stirred up needless animosity, and was aided and abetted by the news writers who incessantly demanded that he leave his farm and "uphold the supremacy of the white race."

The *New York Sun* said some thought Jeff would win because of his race, some simply wanted the white man to win, so they picked him, and others thought Jeffries would win because business interests would make it worth Johnson's while to lie down, because they could make more money long-term if the more popular man won. Johnson's victory saved boxing by showing that it was not always or necessarily the most popular man that won. "As for the talk about the bad effect of Johnson's victory, it seems to be largely nonsense. If a white man is willing to go into the ring with a Negro, he and his friends ought to be willing to take the consequences."

The *Indianapolis News* said, "Fairness to the Negroes compels the statement that all the talk about the fight Monday as a struggle for race supremacy came from the white man. As far as we know no colored man made this silly assertion. Johnson himself said that it was simply a battle between two men, which, of course, is all it was." The race issue was "nonsense," but Jeff and many newspapers supported and fostered the idea. "What wonder is it that some of them [black people] came to accept the white view, and to celebrate the triumph of Johnson as victory for their race?" The whites were to blame for the black exuberance, for whites were the ones who advanced the "idiotic theory" that there was a race question at issue. It opined that Jeff did not fight for race, but for a big purse and a share of the motion picture proceeds. Of course, one might argue that white newspapers were trying to diminish or minimize the race aspect only now that Johnson won.

Psychologically, some whites overcame their disappointment in the race aspect of the fight by viewing Johnson's victory as a victory for the South. The *Richmond Times-Dispatch* noted that Jack was Southern born and raised, which made him fit for a fight with a Northern Yankee.

This newspaper further noted that most post-fight racial disturbances had taken place in the North, such as "Pittsburg, which Andy Carnegie has blessed with his benefactions and where he has preached his homilies on the race question, and in New York, where the sainted members of race

451 *New York Age*, July 14, 1910.

equality live," or in cities of the new South, like Atlanta. "In the old South, of which Richmond is the soul, there has been no trouble."[452]

A white minister in Cleveland said that the attitude and movement against the fight films was unworthy of the white race.

> While I deprecate the prize fight, and the display of the brutal in these moving pictures, I believe there is in this matter an issue more serious than the fight itself. It is the race prejudice that it reveals.
>
> The prize fight has always tended to arouse the brute in man, but why should the matter be treated differently when a Negro participates? Race prejudice is a contemptible passion, and is only aggravated by the present discussion.
>
> Reports show that white men have been the great offenders in the post-fight disturbances – men who are not sportsmanlike enough to wish to see the better boxer win. If the white man had won, the white man would have exulted, the Negro would have borne defeat, and the pictures would have been shown. The disgrace is to the white man whose mean intolerance belies his boasted superiority....
>
> It is a pity to degenerate into lovers of the prize fight; but it is a greater pity to become self-confessed slaves of an intolerance that is bigoted and fanatical. Let every white man prove his worth by bearing defeat as a 'white' man should.[453]

The black-owned *Chicago Broad Ax* said religious organizations, preachers, and the press throughout the country were crying out against the fight pictures because a black prize fighter put to sleep a white fighter.

Their hypocrisy was duly noted. Neither religious organizations, preachers, nor the press ever attempted to suppress the *Clansman*, which depicted a black man raping a white woman. On the contrary, they "glorified it from their pulpits as the noblest work of their hand made God." Nor did they cry out against bloodthirsty anarchists such as Benjamin Tillman, James Vardaman, Reverend Thomas Dixon, Jr., and their brood of rank enemies to society, law and order, whose sole object was to stir up race hatred and prejudice and to uphold mob and lynch law so that the "highly civilized Christians" could to their hearts content murder innocent and law-abiding colored men, women, and children in cold blood, upon some pretext or other.

The newspapers were bitterly opposed to the moving pictures, even though those same newspapers for months had extensive daily coverage of the training and the fight, including photos, which had entered into millions of homes where children resided. Those same papers crying out against the pictures had set forth gleefully all of the details of thousands of fights, as

---

[452] *New York Age*, July 14, 1910, quoting the *Washington Times, New York Sun,* and the *New York World* in quoting the *Richmond Times-Dispatch.*
[453] *New York Age*, July 14, 1910, quoting *Cleveland Plain Dealer.*

well as the most revolting crimes committed by mankind, in particular when it came to illustrating black crimes. Newsmen were hypocrites as well.

The *Broad Ax* opined that those who were fearful that Jeffries might not defeat Johnson, mainly the "so called Christians," were the ones who cried out against permitting the fight. They were afraid of the message that a potential Jeffries loss would send. Other Christians felt that Jeffries' likely victory over Johnson could be used to instruct the colored folks never in the future to attempt to fight anyone with a white face. Millions of Christians sent up prayers to the heavens calling on their white God to ensure a Jeffries victory. Others protested because the fight would not put any money into their pockets. Ultimately, they all were upset that a black had defeated a white.[454]

The *Afro American Ledger*, based in Baltimore, printed the views of the black press about the fight:

Lodge Journal and Guide, out of Norfolk, Virginia:

> Prize fighting is becoming a menace to the peace and happiness of the races and ought to be abolished. In a great fight like that between Johnson and Jeffries race feeling will creep out and race pride will be injured. … For the sake of peace let us have no more prize ring comparisons of the physical prowess of the Negro and the white man.

West Virginia's *Advocate*: "Racial superiority is not decided by tests of physical endurance."

Atlanta Independent: "It is quite natural that the blacks should sympathize with Jack Johnson and the whites with Jim Jeffries."

Nashville Globe:

> If the daily papers would stop publishing the groundless rumors about riots and near-riots the matter would soon be forgotten.
>
> The latest agitation about the moving pictures is another mistake the daily press is making. It is a case of making mountains of mole hills. … The whole affair shows inconsistency of the rankest nature. When the "Clansman" was staged a few years ago the doors of every theatre in the country were thrown open. Billboards were covered with pictures that were of a nature, of a truth, to create a hatred toward a helpless people, but no city forbad the show being exhibited, but when a Negro prize fighter defeats a white prize fighter, a great howl is set up about race riots, race domination and the like. If the perpetuity of this government is now threatened by one Negro prize

---

[454] *Chicago Broad Ax*, July 16, 1910. James K. Vardaman was Mississippi's Democrat governor from 1904-1908, and later served in the U.S. Senate from 1913-1919. Known as "The Great White Chief," he advocated for slavery's return. He further said, "If it is necessary, every Negro in the state will be lynched; it will be done to maintain white supremacy."

fighter the predictions of the statesmen of the old world that our form of government would not stand the test of time has virtually come true.

Philadelphia Tribune:

> The white Philistines throughout the country bet on their Goliath and when he was done up they got sore in the head as they were in the pocket and began to maltreat black people. He is a poor sport who howls like a dog when he is whipped and tried to take revenge of those of him who whipped him. ... There may be no more legalized prize fighting in this country. In that case the championship of physical prowess will remain with the black Samson and his people. Very good.

A black reverend of Philadelphia's Mount Olive African Methodist church said that Johnson's decisive victory would have a tendency to increase the spirit of independence in the Negro race.

A writer for the *Afro American Ledger* said the effect of Johnson's victory upon the country had been phenomenal, disastrous, and far-reaching. Regrettably, it had rekindled race prejudice in people and sections where it barely existed or was dormant.

The blame was laid at the door of those who were dissatisfied with the result and gave vent to their feelings by mercilessly attacking the innocent.

> The rough element of both Negroes and whites has brought disgrace upon themselves and the community by their thoughtless acts of violence. As to the legal suppression of the moving pictures...it is absurd and looks more like child's play than the work of grownups in a civilized country like this, the boasted land of the free and home of the brave.

Allowing whites to brutalize blacks in mob violence fostered general lawlessness, which would have a greater social impact.

> There is a class of persons to be found in almost every community which seems to have lost all respect for the law. The reason for such misguided judgment may be traceable to the fact that the law winks at crime and disorder when it ought to apply its legal authority. However, we are thankful that greater civil war did not follow Jack Johnson's victory.[455]

Even the white-owned *Brooklyn Daily Eagle* said:

> The effect of the Negro's victory on the ruffians or animals of his race and on the animals and ruffians of the white race has been what was expected. ... A strain has been put on law and on the police as the enforcers of law. Had the result been reversed there would still

---

[455] *Afro American Ledger*, July 16, 1910.

have been a strain, but it would have been less, and law and civilization would not have been so severely wrenched.[456]

The black-owned *Washington Bee* also quoted what the Negro Press throughout the nation said about the fight's implications:

Dallas Express:

> The fight, however, is not without its helpful lesson to us all. We have had placed before us a striking example of the fact that excellence along no line of human endeavor lies in race or color. Superior training is the thing. Preparation is what counts. … Johnson has taught his own race a lesson from which they should take courage – not courage to fight, perhaps, but courage to try.

Afro American Ledger:

> It was a race question from the start to the finish, for which the negro was not and is not responsible. The results, riots, deaths, and injuries lie at the door of the white man and his prejudices, and the negro is not and should not be held responsible.

Kentucky Reporter: "What Johnson has done in his line of work is only a demonstration of what the negro can do in any chosen profession, if given a fair chance."

Muskogee Cimeter, based in Oklahoma:

> If the Ministers' Alliance and other organizations which are fighting the exhibitions of the Johnson-Jeffries fight pictures would put forth as much energy in suppressing such plays as *The Clansman* and suppressing the lynching and burning of negroes, then the general public could well commend their efforts.

Advocate Verdict, based out of Harrisburg, Pennsylvania:

> "To win back the championship for the white race" was the keynote of the entire affair. The race issue was raised by the white men alone. Besides, some of them were so sure that Jeffries would win back the championship that they bet large sums of money on him. Naturally, a man would feel a little sore after losing a big sum, or his last dollar, but he would be a better sport if he shouldn't try to take his revenge on an innocent person.

Atlanta Independent: "Our white neighbors ought to be liberal enough to allow the blacks to exult a little enthusiasm over the victory of Johnson, and the negroes ought to have sense enough not to tantalize our white neighbors over the defeat of Jeffries."

---

[456] *Afro American Ledger*, quoting *Brooklyn Daily Eagle*, July 16, 1910.

Amsterdam News, based in New York: "The negro race rejoices over the victory, and why not? The white people would have done the same if the results had been the opposite. We needed a Booker T. Washington, a Kelly Miller, a Paul Lawrence Dunbar, and certainly a Jack Johnson."

Chicago Defender: "This fight has taught the white man that boasting has caused him to lose heart as well as his money, and that the other fellow, though black, can fight like hell."[457]

The *Freeman* said the general belief was that there would have been no trouble had Jeffries won. In the opinion of clearer-thinking people, whites should have been better sports and taken their medicine like men instead of being poor losers and getting ugly over their champion's defeat. Jeffries and his backers were criticized for forcing the race issue into the equation.

Some tried to minimize the fight by saying Johnson only proved that he was the biggest brute. Notwithstanding this, most sporting experts could not help but give Johnson credit for being the most scientific boxer the world had ever seen, one whose brains helped quite as much as his muscles.

White preachers and newspapers deplored the disorder and vociferated loud and long about prize-fighting's brutality. Colored ministers, while not sanctioning prize fighting as such, could not conceal the satisfaction they felt over the victory that had come to a member of the black race, and the practical demonstration Johnson had given to the world that blacks were not inherently inferior to whites.

The *Freeman* said that most thinking people recognized that the opposition to boxing and the films was all due to race prejudice. There would have been no hue and cry raised had Jeffries won.

The only reason whites put forth for barring the films was that they might infuriate the mob. However, this writer asked why society should concede so much latitude to the mob such that the course of events must be disturbed to appease its angry passions. The correct position that officers of the law should take is that people should be able to enjoy their natural rights, and if mobs do not approve of obedience to the constitution and insist upon getting ugly, the right thing to do is for the police to suppress the mob, not the films. "The Negroes of Washington [D.C.] are particularly sensitive on this score, for the policy of yielding to every objection of the mob to the civil equality of the races here on federal soil, has gradually forced us out of every place of public enjoyment, of intellectual profit and of ordinary public accommodation."

There was no more reason to suppress the films than there was to keep the pictures and articles out of the daily papers, which reached everyone. Newspapers had done more to stir up the excitement than any other agency. "Why cry down the pictures, which reach a limited number, and allow the newspaper undisputed sway?"

---

457 *Washington Bee*, July 16, 1910.

Another *Freeman* writer said that if the pictures were opposed merely on the score of brutality and immorality, then all should join in. However, that hardly was the case. The truth was that such arguments were a front for the real reason - that there was a "darkey in the woodpile." The omitted argument was well understood by everyone. The opposition was an example of hypocrisy and a growth of the race feeling.

One poet wrote,

> They called big Jack a smoke, out at Reno;
> Said his boxing was a joke, out at Reno;
> But despite his yellow streak,
> And his heart so very weak,
> He put big Jeff to sleep, out at Reno.[458]

England's *Boxing* said the big fight was over, "and now we are being told that the racial war is going to commence. Was there ever a more lamentable confession of panic?" The "prophets of evil" were inciting "the more truculent white men in America to ensure that bloodshed shall follow the defeat of Jeffries."

> That some bloodshed was bound to follow, everybody who knew anything about the racial trouble in the States was aware. The black man is, and will be for many generations, very like a child. ... But the negroes could no more help strutting round and gloating over their champion's triumph than they could help breathing. Their boastings may not have been in the best possible taste perhaps, but one might have expected that the whites would have been sufficiently strong-minded to recognize that the blacks were only children showing off in somewhat noisy fashion. If the white men hadn't been so sore about the matter!
>
> Because there is no use in disguising the fact that the whole white race is feeling a bit sore over this Reno battle.
>
> Everybody has been telling everybody all about the yellow streak which every Negro conceals in his make-up, and which Johnson was certain to reveal in the ring. Well, every negro may conceal a yellow streak somewhere, as quite a number of white men do (although we never acknowledge the fact); but its existence has still to be discovered in Jack Johnson's composition.
>
> Had Jeffries emerged victorious from the struggle should we not have heard of bonfires, feastings, and general jubilation? Here and there a negro would probably have been killed, but these murders would only have been isolated cases, for the simple reason that the negroes would have accepted their hero's defeat with more equanimity than the whites have done; while, on the other hand, the white men's

---

[458] *Freeman*, July 16, 1910.

jubilation would have been more restrained and less personally offensive. The white's superiority to all the races, which is his cardinal faith, would merely have been confirmed, and he would consequently have been far less excited.

As matters turned out, however, the black's growing hopes of equality, as well as his peculiar vanity, the vanity of a subject race, were all appealed to, and no power on earth could have prevented him manifesting his joy over the event.

The attacks on boxing as a sport, and its meaning, were related to race. A year prior, generally boxing was recognized as the finest form of physical exercise and hailed as the "Noble Art." Now, everything had changed. It was "brutal," "degrading," "a relic of the barbaric ages," and "a blot on our civilization."

And all this just because a white man – who was coaxed, badgered, and bullied out of a well-earned retirement – found it impossible to recover his old prowess...and consequently went down to defeat before a despised negro.

The Americans built the fight to a racial conflict of the highest order.

They lifted, of their own free will, this championship contest out of the realms of pugilism and converted it into a racial trial of strength. The negroes would probably have still regarded it as such, without any assistance from the white men; but it was because the white men insisted that Jeffries "would show the nigger what a contemptible thing he was when he came up against a real good white man" that the coloured people were so dead-set on the issue. ...

It was the whites, and the whites mainly who converted the Reno contest into a test of racial superiority. They insisted on this fact from every standpoint. Brain, brawn, speed, agility, stamina, wit, and courage were the points to be tested. ... Can it be wondered at that the black men were jubilant?

The fight was not just about boxing superiority alone, as it might have been, "but moral, mental, and physical superiority, as one race insisted and the other accepted, with the under dog's champion coming out on top."

So now the white men wanted to stop the fight pictures.

Why? He may say that they are indecent. Some of the influential whites are built that way, but they have only just discovered that boxing pictures are indecent; they never found it out before.

Then they say that their exhibition will conduce to race riots. Well, the rioting so far has been mainly on the white side, though we will readily admit that the blacks probably went about asking to be ill-treated. What do the mayors, town councilors, and other guardians of law and order say of the pictures?

That the blacks will ask for more ill-treatment and will be accommodated, or is it that they are anxious to avoid all reference to their champion's downfall.

Really it looks as though the latter were the sole reason which appeals to them. We can rest assured that, had Johnson been beaten, there would have been a tremendous run on these pictures. Everybody knew this beforehand, and it was openly asserted that such would be the case.

Governor Gillett's claim that the fight was a fake, and American pressmen's insinuations that it was only because he feared that Johnson intended to bring off a double cross that he refused to allow the contest to take place in San Francisco, was "an absurd story, which subsequent events proved to be absolutely baseless. ... Yet we have heard nothing save those rumours which sprout so readily from the brain of the American pressman."

Jeffries was credited with the crowd being sportsmanlike, for he had issued a statement prior to the fight demanding such, and they acceded to his appeal.[459]

Some said the present wave of agitation against boxing would pass over and the game would resume its normal condition. Others thought the recent happenings had injured it rather seriously.

The *San Francisco Bulletin* blamed many in the press for instigating riots by continually harping on the racial aspects of the bout. Those who were amenable to the powers of suggestion eagerly devoured such talk. It opined that in truth, Johnson beating Jeffries was not such a big deal. Johnson was not the first black man to beat a white man. Other blacks, like Gans and Walcott, beat whites, and no racial difficulty took place. However, for Jeffries-Johnson, the press and some participants "went Hades bent on telling open-mouthed fools that it was to be an ethnological test, a test of the physical superiority of the races. Merest balderdash, but it was bad seed and grew a bitter harvest." This writer said no sensible white man would believe that racial superiority depended on a Jeffries victory any more than would any black man believe that Johnson's victory meant the superiority of his race. The hysteria had hurt pugilism, potentially beyond recovery.

Also noted was the fact that Johnson's victory did not lead to one scrap at ringside. The paying boxing fans behaved themselves. It was the general public that did not.

Georgia passed a bill barring the exhibition of any fight pictures of fights between whites and blacks, although films of whites against whites or blacks against blacks could be exhibited. The majority of the legislators felt that black-white fight pictures would be degrading and lead to riots.[460]

---

[459] *Boxing*, July 16, 1910.
[460] *San Francisco Chronicle*, July 19, 1910.

Some white writers opined that Johnson's victory over Jeffries had been a serious set-back to black boxers in all classes. "There will be quite a number of cities, not only in the South, but in the North as well, that will bar the black fellows." City officials in Memphis had told promoters not to match any colored men.[461]

Mayor Brand Whitlock of Toledo, Ohio noted that the press, after discussing the details of the anticipated brutality for months, was now against the fight pictures, and even against boxing. The hypocrisy was "simply sickening." He also scored his fellow politicians.

> For months newspapers, periodicals and magazines have been filled with intimate personal accounts of both fighters, giving as if it were of the last importance to humanity, the thoughts and opinions of defeated former pugilists. ... And now, after reveling for two months as a nation in all this, we experience a recrudescence of Anglo-Saxon morality and suddenly wake up to the fact that all this is brutal and likely to corrupt somebody. This is declared in resolutions, and interviews and hundreds are greedily seizing the opportunity to obtain a reputation for morality by opposing prize fighting. Meanwhile in the tenements and slums of New York, yearly, children are dying; half of all the children in these districts die before they reach the age of six years. Furthermore, last year by the industrial machines of the country, half a million men were killed or maimed. Most of these lives might have been saved by the improvement of working conditions, by the enactment and observance of safety appliance acts. They or their families might have been recompensed in a measure by the passage of employers' liability acts or by the repeal of many ancient provisions of the law such as the fellow servant rule. No resolutions now, no appeals, or threats. Why? Because to oppose this kind of brutality is dangerous – economically dangerous.

> Because to oppose this kind of brutality involves an economic risk – it might hurt business, it might cost men their soft positions.

> Since the fight ended it has suddenly been discovered that some questions of race superiority was involved in it.

> That question is not involved and it can't be settled that way anyway. For instance, I have no doubt that Jeffries, even in his battered and bruised condition, could whip Booker T. Washington, or that Johnson could whip Tolstoy whenever he wanted. Perhaps he could whip Colonel Roosevelt and many other of the leading representatives of our race. But even if he could and did, nobody

---

[461] *San Francisco Evening Post*, July 21, 1910.

would say that demonstrated the superiority of one race over the other.[462]

A writer for the *Chicago Broad Ax* said the U.S. constitution would be violated if the fight-film exhibitions were stopped. Article V of the Constitution required that the government not take private property for public use without just compensation. He argued that the films were of no value if they could not be exhibited, and therefore were as worthless as if destroyed. A great deal of money had been invested in the enterprise. The public could not ex post facto pass a law against what was legal at the time of the fight, which was to film it and exhibit the pictures.

This author noted that subsequent to the fight, white writers had been encouraging the idea that not too much importance should be placed on the fact that Johnson won, that all it proved was that one black man whipped one white man. "All that froth talk before the fight about the white man being so superior to the black man has quit. It was confidently said that the presence of Jeffries in the ring would scare Johnson out of it." The sudden change in discourse, now that Johnson had won, was noted. However, the writer agreed that blacks could not improve their race's standing just by hurrahing for their prize fighters. Much more would be necessary.[463]

The *Freeman* further quoted expressions from the black press throughout the nation:

"Yet Jeffries was the most perfect specimen of the white man's superior physical manhood." - *Exchange.*

"Both Johnson's 'yellow streak' and Jeffries' 'superior stamina' received some severe jolts." – *Detroit Informer.*

"The *Atlanta Constitution* published for the first time in its history a Negro on the first page when it placed Jack Johnson on there. Great Scot!" – *Chicago Defender.*

"Why suppress moving pictures of the Jeffries-Johnson fight and allow Dixon's lying, vulgar book to be sold and theaters to play the disgusting dramatization, 'The Clansman'?" - *East Tennessee News*, Knoxville.

"Well, the white press and white sports, and as for that matter the whites generally, made the Johnson-Jeffries fight a race issue. Then why get mad? If the whites had been victorious they would have been yelling yet. Let us have a little fun out of the victory." – *Georgia Broad-Axe.*

"We knew that the white man is drunk with power and pride, but we contended that since he had so many monuments to his achievements to point to that he could stand a 'little thing' like a Negro whipping a white man in an exhibition of brute force without any display of feeling." - *World*, Indianapolis.

---

[462] *New York Age*, July 21, 1910.
[463] *Chicago Broad Ax*, July 23, 1910.

"Pride of race made the white man's friends beg the black champion to desist, that the 'hope of the white race' be saved the humiliation of a knockout at the hands of the greatest fighter the world has ever known – a Negro." - *New Century*, Norfolk, Virginia.

"We fear the victory of the brutal encounter of Jack Johnson and Jim Jeffries and the success that came to the Afro-American, if extra precautions are not exercised, will stir up racial strife." – *Philadelphia Courant*.

"If the Negroes are boasting and rejoicing elsewhere in the United States as they are in and around Muskogee over the victory of Johnson over Jeffries, their actions are going to damage the race in many sections." – *Baptist Informer*, Muskogee, Oklahoma.

"Johnson is undoubtedly the most skilled fighter that ever donned a glove. Thus we plainly see that when individual members of our race are given half a chance in America they prove the equal of the best of the Anglo-Saxon and often their superior." - *Iowa State Register*.

"It was a clear case of science and endurance triumphing over bigotry and egotism." - *Columbian*, Louisville, Kentucky.

"In this hour of Johnson's victory the Negroes of the country should exercise considerable self-control, good judgment and discretion and should refrain from indulging in demonstrations." - *Southern Reporter*, Charleston, South Carolina.

"The success of Jack Johnson on the Fourth of July should be an inspiration to the Negro of this country. He has shown in unmistakable manner what can be done by thorough preparation for anything he undertakes." - *Star*, Newport News, Virginia.

"Jeff was not doped; that was sure; he was examined by the best experts in the business." - *Seattle Searchlight*.

"The Johnson-Jeffries fight may have injured us in some sections and increased race prejudice in some others but on the whole it has proved a God-sent blessing in showing that certain traits and characteristics are inherent in us and when fairly and fully developed make us one of the most powerful races of people on the face of the globe." – *Richmond Planet*, Virginia.

"The exhibition of race and color hatred was the most marked feature of the whole affair. There was enough of it before the fight, but the amount since the battle clearly shows how far away we are from the sentiment which has made the Star-Spangled Banner one of our famous National airs." - *Dallas Express*.

"That which the daily press tried for months to make a racial contest for supremacy passed off as a mere contest of gladiators, in which the better man won fairly. Now that same daily press is trying to recede from the position it has been holding and is offering such editorials as sane, fearless organs should have offered long ago." - *New Age*, Los Angeles.

"Before the battle was waged the public press, with all energies that it was capable of, declared that this would prove the assertion that the darker-skinned race could not achieve the physical condition; could not undergo the stamina that the Caucasian race, with its thousands of years of development behind it, has achieved. They claimed it absolutely impossible; the developments of this fight have emphatically refuted this argument and have proven that such is not the case." – *Advocate*, Portland, Oregon.

"The most intense race prejudice was the occasion of the Johnson-Jeffries prize fight. This city was a scene of the most bitter race feeling. The police could not handle the mob. Hundreds of fights were allowed to go on, and dozens of colored citizens were assaulted almost under the eyes of the police without being molested. Of course, the defeat of Jeffries was a bitter pill for a prejudiced class to swallow." - *Bee*, Washington, D.C.[464]

Commenting on race analysis in boxing, the *San Francisco Bulletin* said,

> As for the superexcellence of the white race, it is almost doubtful if negroes have not been their equals in the ring game at all stages of the sport's history. ... At the present time negroes rule the prize ring with Johnson, Langford and Jeannette at the helm.

> Boxing is undoubtedly a good sport, but the writers always maintained that certain "authors" placed too much stress on the racial aspect of the Reno battle. ... The head, not the fists, make for a superior race. ... Barring the difference in the color of their skins, Johnson was a far more civilized and better mannered man than Jim Jeffries, with a better intelligence, a keener sympathy for the amenities of life, and as he has subsequently proven, possessed of a better fighting brain, better fighting hands and a better fighting heart.[465]

The Illinois Attorney General wrote a legal opinion arguing that the fight pictures should be barred as immoral.[466]

The *Chicago Broad Ax* noted that the Chicago mayor and chief of police, while originally not objecting to the fight films, did an about-face and said they would not permit the exhibitions of the Johnson-Jeffries fight. This paper opined that there would have been no storm of protest against the films had Jeffries won the championship, but it was "galling to many so-called Christians to think that a Negro carried off that honor."

Initially, the mayor had said that in the past, white fighters had been knocked out by colored ones, there was nothing to get excited about unless acts of lawlessness were committed during the exhibitions, that there was

---

[464] *Freeman*, July 23, 1910.
[465] *San Francisco Bulletin*, July 27, 1910.
[466] *San Francisco Evening Post*, July 28, 1910.

not as much race prejudice in Chicago as in the South, and no harm would come from the exhibitions, for pictures of the fight already had been scattered to all parts of the world through the daily papers.

However, the mayor had changed his mind. The *Broad Ax* opined,

[I]f Jeffries would have won in his contest with Johnson; he would have been hailed by the so-called Christians throughout this country as divine evidence of the superiority in every respect of the white race over the black race.

But as it turned out the other way, it is very galling indeed to hypocritical Christians, who roll up their eyes Heavenward in holy horror at the very idea of permitting the exhibition of the moving pictures. But if a lynching bee was on tap, of a Negro, charged with raping some low white woman, who wanted to be raped, thousands and thousands of this same class of Christians who are bellowing out against the moving pictures, would attend the lynching bee with their sweet innocent little children to witness the Negro being burned at the stake and gladly pay out their money for slices of his quivering flesh, and the preachers would have exclaimed from their pulpits that such demoralizing scenes have been productive of much wholesome and moral influence.

And yet they are bitterly opposed to one class of moving pictures, the Johnson and Jeffries, and we are again reminded that there is more hypocrisy to the square inch among the Christians in America than any other country in the world.[467]

In Chicago, a black man who came to collect from another black man on a one dollar bet on the big fight stabbed to death his debtor, who apparently would not pay up.[468]

William Pickens, a Talladega College professor, gave his analysis of the fight and the race issues it revealed. He noted that Johnson had said before the fight that if he whipped the white man, Jeff would never forget it, but if the white man whipped him, he would forget it in fifteen minutes.

These words pretty accurately express the difference in the feelings of the two races. The average Negro wished to look at the fight as only a pugilistic contest between individuals, while certain clamorous newspapers of the white race, north and south, insisted and kept insisting that it was to be "a great race battle." ...

If Jeffries had won the fight, it would have aroused no resentment in the Negro race against the white race.

However, blacks knew that if Jeff won, whites and their newspapers were ready to preach lies about black inferiority. Many editors already had

467 *Chicago Broad Ax*, July 30, 1910.
468 *Chicago Broad Ax*, July 30, 1910.

composed such editorials before the fight. Therefore, blacks could not conceal their satisfaction at Johnson's big fist figuratively knocking such homilies and editorials into the waste basket. "In this he did missionary work."

Contrary to what they said before the fight, whites ex post facto tried to spin the fight as just being about brute force, but really it was about more.

> We are not sorry that Johnson showed other points of superiority besides mere physical superiority. Most of us had already conceded the latter. But during all the months of preparation and clear through the battle he has carried the sunshine and good-nature of his race. His good-nature was impregnable against insult and unshaken by the battle itself. ...

> Even the insulting words of Corbett, the "bully," could not shake him. The jeers of the audience fell on him like rain upon the testudinate back of a turtle. ... The black man was merry all through the game. ...

> And not only in physical and temperamental qualities, but in magnanimity the black man was superior. His race has noted with pride that he has never tried to bully his enemies or to detract from the worth of his opponent. ... [H]e gave them choice of corners without "tossing." ...

> White editors who so nobly fought Jeffries' battles before the fight, have found one consoling reflection since the fight, viz; that the victory of the black man "will do the Negro race harm." How, I ask, in the name of heaven can it harm a race to show itself excellent? ... These results have simply impressed the Negro with an undue sense of its importance. It was poor tact again on the part of white people.

> But, sincerely now, it was a good deal better for Johnson to win and a few Negroes be killed in body for it, than for Johnson to have lost and all Negroes to have been killed in spirit by the preachments of inferiority from the combined white press. It is better for us to succeed, though some die, than for us to fall, though all live. The fact of this fight will outdo a mountain peak of theory about the Negro as a physical man – and as a man of self-control and courage. ...

> It will do Johnson's race good and no one knows this better than the white men who are responsible for the overestimation of the event – before the event. After the event, however, it is called a pure contest of brutality, and Johnson is represented as simply the "best brute."[469]

A black author wrote a poem about the fight for the *Freeman*:

> The Fourth will be remembered, as long as we are a race;

---

[469] *Chicago Defender*, July 30, 1910.

For a noble black man, who wore our flag about his waist.
Jeff, he was a good man, as ever struck a brace.
But when he walked up to Jack, Jack struck him in the face.
Hurrah for the champion of the world! For he is of our race;
Hurrah for Jack Johnson! Sound it in every place.
The flag has floated from the mast, it has floated from every place.
Henceforth it will always be worn, around the Negro's waist.
I hope he long may live, and bear his distinction with grace.
Jealously maintaining your honor, for you are one of the race.

The *Freeman* said Johnson's victory revealed a great deal about society.

Johnson, by defeating Jeffries, has brought about the true color of the average American white man. … This fight has drawn them out from Governor on down. Their actions after Johnson had won proves beyond the slightest doubt the brain and blood of this fair country, which is advertised the world over "the land of the free and liberty." Ministers laid down their Bibles, lawmakers set aside their duties to meddle with the much-called low, degraded pastime of prize-fighting. All these choice picked public servants, whom the public has selected from among the thousands of men to help lead the nation to peace and prosperity, turned and advocated race riots on the whole-sale order. …

Their reason for objecting to the pictures being shown is that it would ruin the morals of the young American. Because Jack Johnson, black-born American, defeated James J. Jeffries, white-born American, the child must not see this horror; yet they have seen "The Clansman," heard the great Tillman lecture, read for years what Vardaman had to say and know the art of burning Negroes at the stake by heart. All this they claim as pastime, but a picture that would show them what a Negro can do if he is given a fair chance would ruin their little pure hearts. … If Jeffries had won…these same persons would have advocated that these pictures be shown in the public schools every Friday in order to show the little tender buds of morals the superiority of the white man over the black man. … They would claim that the pictures and books would give them courage. …

[A]ny Representative from the South can shoot a defenseless Negro while lying helpless on the ground and should be awarded a Carnegie brave medal. Yet it is a state's prison offense to show a picture where a Negro defeated a white fair and square.

The hypocritical daily papers showed photos of the fight and provided descriptions of the bout in order to sell newspapers, while at the same time knocking the pictures, of which they had no financial interest. Hence, if prize-fighting was a disgrace, then so too were the newspapers that described it in every detail. This writer accused the newspapers of creating and promoting race hatred and riots.

The battle was a white man's own affair. Had it been left to the colored race to finance and promote the fight Mr. Johnson and Mr. Jeffries would have received about a two-thousand-dollar guarantee and it would have been a hard matter to collect…if they had depended on the Negro for their support.

In truth, the fight was not about race supremacy. Blacks had been winning championship battles for the past 15 years. Jeff's fall was the same as his predecessors. They all eventually lose if they keep at it long enough.

The past champions in their day were as good as the men of the present day. Champions must fall or the game will die out. They have fallen and will fall. There will be prize fighting as long as the world stands. It is a lot of folly to hear the comment that the last heavyweight fight has been fought in this world. There will be another fight here in this country just as soon as a man shows up who can beat Johnson. The same crowd that has been doing all the hollering will demand it. Don't be worried – Johnson will never retire. The sporting writer will not allow him to. As money is a factor, he has his price, the same as James J. Jeffries, who returned to the ring to get that pile of money regardless of whom he was to fight. [470]

Some wondered if the protests about the big fight would cause the sport's obliteration, or whether it would survive the jolts being handed to it. Many states already either outlawed boxing or had restrictive laws.[471]

On July 29, 1910 in Slocum, near Palestine, Texas, white racial hatred ignited again. White mobs took up rifles and shotguns and hunted down and slaughtered an estimated 18 to 25 blacks. Most of the known victims were unarmed and shot in the back. Investigation of the "race war" revealed that it was a "'nigger killin' pure and simple. Hundreds of white men, armed to the teeth, forayed through the district and shot the scurrying blacks wherever they overtook them."[472]

An English observer reporting on the race riots said, "I see that white hoodlums in various American cities have been manifesting their sportsmanship by shooting down the Negroes for no other offense than that they made merry over the victory of their black champion."

A black correspondent to the *Freeman* in Glasgow, Scotland, gave a Scottish view of how the fight result was received. The result there created great excitement among all classes and races.

They are true sportsmen here. The American whites are now showing up their ignorance, unjustness and brutality to the world in a way that will make them less popular than ever in sporting circles at any rate.

---

[470] *Freeman*, July 30, 1910.
[471] *San Francisco Chronicle*, July 31, 1910.
[472] *Reno Evening Gazette*, August 2, 1910; *Washington Post*, July 31, 1910; *New York Times*, July 31, August 1, 1910; *Fort Worth Star-Telegram*, February 27, 2011.

There is no doubt but that the whole population of the white world would rather have seen "the white man's hope" at the top of the pole. ... The true sporting spirit then admires the hero who did get there – "our Jack." If the civilized world knew more of what the American Negroes were doing, it would go a great way in obtaining world-wide respect for the race and more denunciation of the treatment dealt out to them by the unjust white Americans, who wish so much to be at the top of the pole in all things.

Johnson had "established world-wide fame for himself and the downtrodden race." His victory, one of brain and muscle, judgment and tact, was a threat to whites, for it had symbolic value.

This Scottish correspondent believed there undoubtedly would be a world-wide move to prevent the picture exhibitions.

> Why? Because the black man was the victor. Our victories must not be kept before the youth of a white man's country; it's too humiliating. Here in religious Glasgow the town council has been petitioned not to allow them to be shown. ... Had Jeffries won would this be so? No, they would have been used to cower these poor, simple, good-hearted natives, to make them fear the power of the white man and make them feel their own insignificance before him. The world must know only of the white man's superiority and only of the inferiority of the Negro and all dark races, robed in its shadiest garb. ...

> The press, as you all know, is the greatest educator today. ... Bear in mind that there are many here, and elsewhere, as bitter toward the black man as can be found in America. Why drink in all the poison of the one-sided press against the colored man, who is stigmatized as being possessed of all the vices America contains and not a single virtue. ... My eyes are open to all that is going on through the press, commercially, socially and otherwise. One thing is certain: The black man must make his own way; no white man will do it for him, nor yet help him to do it. Why not? Because the united white press, the united white Christian civilization, and the united white state rulers are at one in all things where a Negro's interest is at stake. In America they are bold with it – out and out – in other countries they are sneaking.

> They would rather not offend the American cousin. He is generally wealthy. Why should he not be rich, I often ask, after obtaining for nearly 250 years the unpaid labor of from three to ten millions of slaves. ... Jack, the slayer of the white man's hope, which I hope may be forever, has opened many new avenues for the Negro if he will take the opportunity to work upon them. Take new courage now. Three cheers for Jack the Giant Killer and the same for the colored journalists and the Afro-American press, the black man's hope.

The *Freeman* noted that the *Chicago Tribune* had "received and printed a number of communications calling attention to the ludicrous inconsistency of the newspaper protests against the display of the Johnson-Jeffries fight pictures." The correspondents were "appalled by the journalistic hypocrisy which can devote a year to giving publicity to the preparations for the fight, surrender pages to a detailed account of it, supplement this by printing photographs of its most agonizing moments, and then complacently demand the suppression of the moving pictures."[473]

Some saw the Johnson-Jeffries fight films. The motion pictures ran 2 ¼ hours long, including both pre- and post-fight scenes, and the entire 15 rounds. They were the clearest and best fight films ever taken.

One reporter who saw the films said Johnson slowly but surely mowed down Jeffries. It was a slow affair, and Jeffries made no sensational rallies. He simply received blows. The effect of Johnson's ripping uppercuts could be seen plainly as Jeff's big frame quivered and rose every time a right shot upward to his jaw.[474]

An editorial in the *Evening Times* of Glasgow, Scotland noted that there was fair play in the fight, despite the strong racism in the U.S.

> Emphasizing still further the point regarding fair play is the fact that into the contest entered the very strong racial feeling of black and white. It is difficult for the citizens of this country to thoroughly appreciate the depth and the vehemence of these feelings in America. The animosity which unfortunately exists between the white man of the Southern States especially and the Negroes can not be exaggerated. It explains the vast difficulty surrounding that bugbear of the American statesman, the color problem. Yesterday's exhibition of a white man getting publicly pummelled into partial unconsciousness by a representative of the hated and despised Negro race, must inevitably tend to fan the flame of racial hatred. Perhaps the best feature about the business is the fact that despite the existence of these feelings, Johnson was permitted to defeat Jeffries. That is at least a further evidence of fair play.

The fight pictures were big in Ireland. Despite denunciations by Archbishop Walsh, threats by the police, and protests, the pictures were drawing tremendous houses in places like Dublin. At the end of the day, the "Celt is a dead game sport," and folks wanted to see the fight.[475]

The *Chicago Defender* reported that in order to justify, explain, and minimize the racial impact of Johnson's victory, a desperate Kentucky colonel named Jack Collins was telling his black workers that Johnson actually was white. Collins said,

---

[473] *Freeman*, August 13, 1910.
[474] *Boxing*, August 6, 1910; *San Francisco Evening Post*, August 15, 1910.
[475] *Freeman*, September 3, 1910. The fight pictures were being shown in Denver as well. The pictures showed that "Jeff had no business in the ring with Jack Johnson."

The negroes, seh, have shown signs of becomin' unendurable. It was a matter for diplomacy, seh. We did not like to use force upon the negroes, foh they are mere children, seh. Also, we need 'em to work the crops. So I delivered 'em a lecture.

"This heah Jack Johnson," I says to them, "is the finest example of a Numidian athlete that ever lived. The Numidians are a white race, but owing to their having lived in a southern latitude for many generations, they looked somewhat dark on the outside. But they most fiercely resent being called negroes." ...

"Col. Collins," says my old Jack darky, "we folks always been told this heah Misteh Johnson is a cullud man." "Don't you believe it, Jack," says I. "Johnson is a Numidian. No coon could ever lick a white prizefighter." .... "All right, cunnel," says mah old Jack, "But them Numidians mus' be mighty dahk w'ite folks, cunnel."[476]

Hugh McIntosh said this was not the first time that issues related to Johnson fight films had arisen. He discussed the impact of the Johnson-Burns films, as well as the effect of Johnson's victories on non-whites.

The coloured superiority in the sport of boxing – the greatest of all athletic sports, wherein the actual domination and complete mastery of an opponent is the strongest and, we might say, the most striking feature – is exciting the minds of thinkers as to the possible influence for evil this will have upon the coloured races.

McIntosh said the earth's colored people took a keen and eager interest in Johnson's personality, life, and career. The Burns-Johnson film exhibitions caused thousands of Kaffirs in South Africa to surround a poster of Johnson. They were so excited that the police asked the management to refrain from exhibiting posters, photos, or "from publishing in their advertisements anything that might excite the Kaffir mind. Each exhibition of the pictures was attended by Kaffirs, who were highly delighted each time their coloured champion landed a decisive blow."

So concerned about Johnson's impact were they, that the South African Parliament discussed whether to bar the Johnson-Burns fight film exhibitions. McIntosh did not want to annoy the white race's feelings. Hence, he terminated the film tour there, and decided that no pictures would be shown in South Africa in which there was a colored contestant.

In India there was a similar state of affairs. The "Hindoos" and "Cingalese" on the island of Ceylon flocked to see the Johnson-Burns pictures. There was fear and concern that the films would inspire the natives to rebel, emboldened by seeing a member of a darker race beating up a white man. There was unrest and discontent prevailing amongst a section of the natives, given that they had been colonized by the British.

476 *Chicago Defender*, September 3, 1910.

Hence, there was clear recognition of the fact that the films and the fight had potential political, racial, and social influence. That concern was intensified when it came to the Jeffries-Johnson fight films.[477]

ONE PLACE WHERE FIGHT PICTURES WILL BE POPULAR

San Francisco Bulletin, July 16, 1910

THE STRONG ARM OF THE AMERICAN LAW

Chicago Defender, July 30, 1910

---

[477] *Boxing*, September 24, 1910. The Burns-Johnson films were shown and reaped large profits in places like Siam, Portugal, Rangoon, Japan, Manila, West Indies, India, Egypt, and Mexico. Fijian natives paid as much as six shillings each for the privilege of witnessing the exhibition.

CHAPTER 11

Revisionism

In the wake of James J. Jeffries' loss to Jack Johnson, excuses and explanations proliferated. Some thought Jeff was in top form, but lost confidence at the last moment. Others thought it was a swindle all along, that the public was deceived, and that Jeff and his trainers all knew that he had no chance, but wanted to make as much money as possible, so they sold the fight. Still others thought Jeff was confident and felt good, and was as good as he could be after such a long layoff, but Johnson simply was too good for him, although folks were trying to spin his defeat and come up with excuses after the fact. Another theory later put forth was that Jeff was doped or ill with dysentery.

A *San Francisco Evening Post* writer said that for picking Johnson before the fight, some accused him of having some grudge against Jeffries. It seemed as if folks felt it was the press' duty to boost Jeff and show race loyalty, rather than write what they honestly felt. "The public was led badly astray by the mass of conflicting tales that poured in from Jeffries' camp." Most authors praised Jeff's condition and other qualities.

Now that Jeff lost, many were attempting to take cuts at him and say he quit, which was false. He was game and courageous under adverse circumstances. This writer felt that Johnson would have been a tall order for Jeff even at his best, and hence had written that the odds were far astray. Yet, Jeff's admirers were saying that if he was half as good as he once was that he'd make Johnson jump over the ropes. They were hysterical in their belief in him and in their denigration of Johnson, whom they treated with contempt, saying he was yellow and a quitter. The fight showed that Jeffries was overrated and Johnson underrated.

San Francisco Examiner, July 7, 1910

Jeff's training was criticized. He worked with wrestlers and men who were well past their primes. Even then, he did not spar much, and Corbett still hit him plenty. Jeff's flatterers were his worst enemies all along. They filled his head with his invincibility and told him that Johnson was not trained, that he was yellow, and could not fight. Anyone who fairly criticized Jeff's training or picked Johnson to win was banned from the training camp.

Jeff worked more to take off the weight and make his body look good than he concerned himself with preparing for a fight.

Although on the day of the fight Jeffries said that in years past the result would have been different, the day after the fight, allegedly Jeffries said in very humble fashion, "I never could have hit that fellow in my prime. He is the devil. I never could have reached him in a thousand years." When asked whether age or race had something to do with the loss, Jeff responded, "I don't know what it was, only that I never could have whipped him at my best."[478]

Jeffries refused to answer the assertions of Muldoon and others that he was all-in before he entered the ring. They said he seemed to be a nervous wreck before entering his dressing room before the fight. Jeff just said, "My steam was gone. I knew it in the fourth round. I tried to fight, but I could not." Regarding the reasons which led to his "peculiar condition," he had nothing to say. Mrs. Jeffries replied, "It is what we might have expected."[479]

Jeffries had lost his friends in a degree never before experienced by a former champion. Typically, an ex-champion still found sympathy, praise, and applause. Not with Jeffries. The public was fickle. Jeff was goaded into a fight by a public which convinced him he had to do it, and that Johnson would be easy prey. "He suspected all along that Johnson was his master, but the flatterers led him into molasses, and when big Jim began to sink they deserted him."

Many said Jeff was overcome with fear, which shattered his nervous system. "But the public remembers that these 'wise ones' did not stir the air with any warning note of Jeff's disinclination, his unfitness to fight, that they dropped no ink to warn them of such conditions."[480]

Some said that seeing Bill Delaney in Johnson's corner also served to unnerve Jeffries. Jeff had failed to pay a gambling debt in Nevada, despite Delaney's urgings to do so (he eventually did before coming to Reno), and had failed to keep his promise to Delaney to fight Squires. That caused their estrangement, and for Delaney to help Johnson. "Thus, one by one, Jeff's chickens all came home to roost."[481]

Famed referee Jack Welch had feared a fake, for there had been some talk that Johnson would lay down. However, Johnson told him that there was nothing to such rumors, for they were rank speculation. Johnson told him that he would win. "I am sure that Johnson could have beaten Jeffries when the white champion was in his prime. If Johnson fought the battle he did at Reno, Jeffries could never have beaten that black man, never in the days of his prime."

Many admired Johnson for his sportsmanship and ability. "Casting aside race prejudice and sentiment, Johnson showed himself the champion. He is

---

[478] *San Francisco Evening Post*, July 6, 1910.
[479] *San Francisco Bulletin*, July 6, 1910.
[480] *San Francisco Evening Post*, July 7, 1910.
[481] *San Francisco Bulletin*, July 8, 1910.

a wonderfully powerful fighter. His short blows - ones in which his fist traveled less than a foot – had punishing powers almost unbelievable."

Many were angry with Jeffries, accusing him of hiding the facts from them. They felt that he had to have known that his speed and punch were gone. Frank Brady said Jeff had no right to allow it to be given out that he was in superb condition. Some blamed Corbett and the other trainers for constantly boosting him in the press; accusing them of deliberately misrepresenting Jeff's true condition.

Some thought lack of condition was why Jeff was reluctant to box before the fans very often, or to let folks know exactly when he would be sparring. Gamblers said his failure to box more, or with younger men, cost them dearly. If he had boxed more often, longer, and with better men, his lack of condition would have come to the surface and they would have realized he was not so good. He took the weight off and looked good, and the majority took him at his word when he said he was as good as ever.

Tim Sullivan believed that Jeff realized at least a week prior to the fight that he could not win. He was sullen and uncourteous, in part because he knew that his friends were being misled by the false reports of his condition. He said Jeff merely went through the motions of training.[482]

However, others said that Jeffries usually was grouchy before a fight, even in his prime years.

Jeff drew little sympathy from the *Bulletin* and other reporters, owing to the fact that during training, he was morose and uncivil, "and nowhere nearly as highly civilized a person as the black boxer who opposed him." Jeff had welched on his gaming losses after the Hart-Root fight as well, which reflected poorly upon him.

Unlike Jeffries, who was surly and gruff towards the reporters who had helped make him a fortune, Johnson made friends and was a gentleman to the reporters. He proved that "he is a likeable negro." He was always smiling, and his quick wit gained him "as many friends as any black man could expect to gain." Jack was pleasant and very obliging. He had open training and gave the press full access, unlike Jeffries, who trained when and how he pleased. If the crowd wanted to see Johnson box, he boxed. If the photographers wanted pictures, he posed. If correspondents wanted inside information, he gave it to them. True or not, he gave them good copy. He shook hands with the people and gave speeches. He was everything that Jeffries was not. "It is little wonder, therefore, that we of the fourth estate have kindly feelings toward him for his unfailing courtesy." The only excuse made for Jeffries was that it was his nature, and he had been just as discourteous to others, including the governor, as he was to the newsmen.

---

[482] *Nevada State Journal, San Francisco Bulletin,* July 6, 1910.

Johnson's abilities were also lauded. "No expressions as to Johnson's ability as a fighter can be too strong." Jack was big, fast, powerful, and a clever ring general in every way.[483]

The *Examiner* asked whether Jeff was doped with some opiate preceding the fight. A story to that effect had been circulated. The story was "generally discredited. Most people here believe Jeffries was nervous to the point of panic." Corbett said the suspicion that Jeff had been doped was ridiculous. Rickard did not believe it either, but felt that Jeff appeared to be very nervous. Jack Root thought Jeff was scared. "Don't fall for any story that Jeff was doped, because all the trouble with Jeffries was that he was badly scared."

A *Chronicle* reporter said a nervous collapse paralyzed Jeffries, who shook like a leaf at noon the day of the fight and entered the ring in a daze. His nerves went to pieces. Trainer Roger Cornell said, "Jeff suffered a mental and nervous breakdown in the rubroom shortly after noon of the day of the fight." Others thought he was in a daze because he was doped, but that was just a rumor without substantiation.

Jim Corbett gave several reasons for Jeff's defeat, including nervousness over his responsibility to the big bettors and his friends who had all of their money on him, his grief over Delaney's desertion and fact that he'd be aiding Johnson, and worry about the battle having been driven out of California and Gillett's criticism about the bout. Corbett said, "Physically, he was all right until three days before the fight. Then a change came over him and he seemed to be like a man dazed. All this talk about his being the hope of the white race had got on his nerves." Corbett said Jeff was worried to death, for the magnitude of the affair staggered him.

Corbett said that before the fight started he went to Johnson's corner and looked at his hands, but his real purpose was to see if he was nervous. Jim believed that he was. When he came back to Jeffries, he said, "Jeff, you have got that nigger scared to death. If you wade into him you can lick him in one round." However, "Jeffries acted like a man who didn't hear what was being said to him. … [H]e acted as if he was in a stupor. … Jeff didn't have a punch that would break an egg."

Corbett also said that Mrs. Jeffries told him the day after the fight that Jeff walked the floor the entire night before the battle. He worried a great deal because so much was expected of him, and so much depended on his showing. "At the eleventh hour, Jeff lost his confidence." He said trainer Roger Cornell realized that Jeff was all-in before the fight, in the dressing room, and broke into tears.

Boxing quoted Corbett as saying that in the dressing room before the fight, Jeff was like a man in a trance. When he tied his shoe laces, he had tears running down. It was as if he knew what was coming and he was in a state of nervous collapse.

---

[483] *San Francisco Bulletin, San Francisco Examiner,* July 5, 6, 1910.

Corbett said that when he kidded and taunted Johnson, "I really didn't mean any of the things I said." Jim's plan was to talk to Johnson and take Jack's mind off the business at hand, and then Jeff could follow up on any slip of concentration on Johnson's part and land the winning punch. However, "I was there with the gab, but Jeff wasn't there with the wallop."

In the 1st round, when Corbett started to yell at Johnson, some fan bawled out, "Aaw, shut up, Corbett!" Jim replied, "Shut up? Why, man alive, this is only the first round, and I'm going to be yelling in the forty-fifth and just as loud!" The critic remained quiet after that.

Corbett admitted that he had to admire Johnson's ready wit. It made him harder to whip, for Jack combined humor with hitting and footwork and never got flustered, which simply threw his opponents into a frenzy. He was self-control personified in the ring.

Corbett yelled to Jeff to hit him one good punch and the yellow streak would come out. Johnson clinched, smiled, and said, "That's what they ALL say, Mistah Co'butt." Once, Corbett said, "Why don't you fight, Johnson?" He replied, "I can't; I'm clever, like you, Jim." Corbett admitted that he had to hold his face straight then, for he wanted to laugh.

The fact that Delaney was in Johnson's corner also broke Jeff's heart. He could not get over the fact that Bill was planning a battle against him. At one point, Delaney looked over at Corbett and said, "Why don't you smile, Corbett?" Jim was stumped for an answer, for "I had shot my bolt, so I blurted out: 'Bill, he who laughs last laughs best.'"

Corbett called Jack Jeffries over and said, "Jack, your brother's whipped. What are we going to do?" Brother Jack said, "For God's sake, do something, Jim. Let's do something – we can't let that black fellow knock my brother out. Make Jim lose the fight on a foul."

Joe Choynski said Jeffries lacked courage, not condition. Just three days before the fight, Jeff was the invincible giant of six years ago. But then his courage faltered, and he suffered a mental collapse. On Sunday, he began to get nervous and fret. He must have thought about his long life of ease over six years, the public demand that he come back, and the long strain of training, "with its thousand and one worries that no one but his trainers will ever know. I tell you he had his mind loaded to overflowing." This was despite the fact that on the surface he smiled and impressed some that he was carefree and eager for the battle. For weeks on end Jeff received hundreds of letters daily from admirers imploring him to whip Johnson, telling him that he was the hope of the white race. "That preyed upon his mind" and "unnerved him." Joe was still convinced that Jeffries could whip Johnson, and wanted to see a rematch. .

Choynski said that after the 1st round, Jeffries complained about a right to the back of his ear that did not look very hard, but Jeff said dazed him. In the 2nd round, a blow landed on his right eye, and that also hurt him. In the corner, Jeff said he saw double. Joe sucked the blood from his nose for five rounds and kept his eye from closing entirely. "I knew he would lose, but I was awaiting the inevitable. Jeff was not hurt any; he simply collapsed." Joe said Jeff simply could not take the punishment that he once could, and his courage was gone, for he was afraid to mix it.

Ben Benjamin said many thought the fight was fixed for Jeff, which created false odds.

> Since Jeff's inglorious defeat there are many unkind enough to say that the colored man could lick Jeff the best day he ever saw. But that can never be proved and will always be a matter of opinion. It is a certainty that Johnson made Jeffries look like 10 cents on the 4th of July. The way Johnson stopped Jeffries' swings was a revelation and took all the heart out of the previously undefeated champion.[484]

Benjamin opined that it was the same old story of when a once-great man starts downhill everyone who was not great who envied his prior success gave him a kick. They now were doing it to Jeffries, just because he couldn't do what no one could - come back from years of idleness to beat a champion. Men had glorified him and made capital out of his reputation and friendship, but now were doing all they could to blacken his character, saying they knew he had no chance and that he did not prepare properly. Such was contrary to what they had said before the fight, including his own trainers. Regardless, if Jeff had been a bit friendlier and more obliging to the press and public, he would have received more sympathy.

Tex Rickard revealed that he had gotten both fighters to sign for the fight with him two days before all of the bids came in. Rickard offered Johnson a $10,000 bonus and told his wife that he would buy her a sealskin coat if her husband signed. He also loaned Jack $2,500.

Rickard said Berger, Jeff's manager, told him that he couldn't get the fight without Gleason, so that was why Tex took Gleason into the combine. He did not know whether Berger was in on it with Gleason as a partner, so as to get a better cut for himself. He also gave Jeff a $10,000 bonus.

Tex said the fighters initially agreed to cut the purse 75/25 based on winner-loser, but three days before the fight, Johnson suggested that the purse be cut 50/50, showing that he had some doubts about his ability to win. That made Rickard think that Johnson believed he had a tough fight on his hands. However, Jeffries refused to split it 50/50, which showed just how confident Jeffries actually was, despite reports to the contrary. They finally agreed to split the purse 60/40.

Regarding the fight, Rickard said, "Jeff was game, and don't let anybody tell you that he showed the yellow streak. It was a case of nervous prostration. He could do nothing. … I was as much surprised as any one at the result."[485]

---

[484] *San Francisco Chronicle, Bulletin,* July 7, 8, 1910; *San Francisco Evening Post, Nevada State Journal, Reno Evening Gazette, San Francisco Bulletin,* July 12, 1910; *San Francisco Call,* July 12, 13, 1910; *San Francisco Evening Post, Bulletin,* July 19, 1910; *Freeman,* August 20, 1910; *Boxing,* August 13, 1910.
[485] *San Francisco Bulletin,* July 7, 1910; *San Francisco Chronicle, San Francisco Call,* July 8, 1910.

Rickard was very high on Johnson. He said that during the fight, Johnson allowed Jeff to punch him in the stomach.

> He just pulled his right hand away, leaving Jeff's left free, and then told him to punch him in the stomach. Jeff did and then Johnson offered him a chance to punch him there again. Well, Jeff pulled his hand back to send in the other one, but like a flash Johnson uppercut him on the jaw. The next round I heard Johnson tell Jeff that he was welcome to punch him in the stomach again if he wanted to, and pulled his hand away, leaving the opening, but Jeff didn't bite.[486]

Rickard was contemplating suing Governor Gillett for damages incurred.

Jeff's friend and business partner, A. F. Jack Kipper said the idea that Jeff was doped was ridiculous. "This dope stuff is all rot." Jeff did not even know about the rumors because he had not read the papers yet. However, Kipper said Jeff was not himself mentally when he entered the ring. Worry ruined his chances. He received hundreds of telegrams from men who pleaded with him to win, saying he had to win, that they had bet all their money on him. That sort of thing preyed on his mind.[487]

The *Bulletin's* W. J. Jacobs said Jeffries was being maligned by the same men who egged him on to come out of retirement and return the title to the white race. His failure to win the fight was looked upon as "such a grievous and unpardonable sin that his honor has been assailed, his courage doubted, even his disposition held up as a horrible example. And all this because he lost a fight." Every fighter tasted defeat at some point, and yet Jeff was being made a "fall guy" because his turn came.

Some criticized that he fought a miserable fight. Yet, Jacobs asked, "What fighter hasn't? Take, for instance, Jack Johnson's fight right here with Marvelous Marvin Hart." Most fighters had a bad performance or two in their careers. Jeff was guilty of the same crime a thousand others had committed – the crime of losing, which was unpardonable for some.

Jeff also was roasted because he had been less than genial. However, he never had been a social mixer. He always had kept close within his own small circle of friends and avoided "glad-handing every Tom, Dick and Harry." His unwillingness to mingle made him enemies, but he was just being himself. There was no hot air or bull-con stuff in his make-up. "In an ordinary human being, open-facedness of this sort would be a trait to be generally admired, but because it happens to be in the loser of a championship battle it's downright surliness."

The public had enticed him to fight, and it had been to his and their detriment. Jeff had trained long, hard, and faithfully, and was in great shape. Many a condition expert looked him over and all agreed that he was

---

[486] *Bulletin*, July 20, 1910.
[487] *Reno Evening Gazette, Call*, July 9, 1910.

physically perfect. "He might have fooled one or two, but he could never have gotten by the keen eyes of all those who watched him. ... Surely, with the country's acknowledged best judges on the job and enthusiastic over his physical fix, he cannot be roasted on that score." It seemed that the critics were kicking a man when he was down.[488]

Some had thought the story of a frame-up was plausible, which caused them to wager on Jeffries, or be hesitant to bet on Johnson. Fans recalled with disgust Ketchel's "knockdown" of Johnson. "That Ketchel fight always had a queer look, and that supposed knockdown of the champion in the last round was declared by 80 per cent of the crowd who witnessed it at Coffroth's Coloma arena to be of the 'phony' order. Nobody saw the mysterious blow which knocked Johnson down." Most were willing to bet that Stan never landed and that Johnson intentionally flopped to make the motion pictures more pleasing and marketable to the audience. "It mattered little so far as Johnson was concerned whether he won in a round or in 20, for he probably could have stowed the middle weight champion away at any time he wished, as he outclassed Ketch from every angle."

Folks did not think Johnson tried his hardest against Kaufman either, for he was going to be paid well either way, and had no fear of losing his title because it was a no-decision bout. Hence, he was merciful and did not deal out as much punishment as he could have done had he so desired.

Regardless, George Little's claim that the fights were fixed was given little credence, for "his standing generally does not call for much. He is vindictive and is trying to even up old scores with Johnson." No one doubted that Ketchel and Kaufman were trying their hardest, and everyone knew Stan had been badly knocked out.[489]

One paper noted that a year prior to the fight, Delaney on behalf of Kaufman had challenged Jeffries. When then asked why he had done so, Delaney said, "Why, Jeffries is all in. He can never regain the old form. His wind is gone and no matter how hard he may train he will blow up because of weak bellows if he fights again. He has been out of the ring too long and is not in the best of health. Kaufman can beat him and so can Johnson. If he fights again he will be taking desperate chances with his reputation." Bill proved himself to be a shrewd judge. Two weeks before the fight, Delaney had said, "Johnson is the greatest fighter in the world. Jeffries will not be able to go 15 rounds. Johnson will outbox and outstay him as sure as the sun rises and sets." Others who predicted a Johnson victory included Ketchel, Battling Nelson, Kaufman, Tim McGrath, and Jim Coffroth.

Some thought that Corbett's post-fight declaration about Jeffries was characteristic of Corbett, who was trying to save face. He made himself a laughing-stock because he had told everyone that Jeff was in magnificent condition. He needed an excuse for the performance, for now everyone

[488] *San Francisco Bulletin*, July 9, 1910.
[489] *San Francisco Call*, July 12, 1910.

thought he had been falsely boosting Jeff, so he was claiming that Jeff did not box enough and was nervous.

Jeffries probably should have taken tune-ups with guys like Kaufman, Barry, and Ross to better prepare himself, or to discover how much he had left. Of course, if he lost, then he'd be out of a massive payday. Still, even with winning tune-ups and sharpening up further, most believed it was doubtful if Jeff could have escaped the beating that Johnson handed out.[490]

Some were saying that Jeffries took the fight for the money. However, although a huge purse was a big incentive, the truth was that the public had hounded him, and he felt it was his obligation as a white man. He risked his prized reputation, and had to undergo a lengthy and difficult training regimen.

Boxing wondered whether the quotes attributed to Jeffries were even genuine at all, or fabricated by news reporters, press agents, trainers, or managers on Jeff's behalf. Jeff was not a talker. He was not a bragger, nor was he the kind to say that he could not whip Johnson at his best. Most likely, he would not say anything at all.[491]

Some wanted to see a return match, while others thought it would be pointless.

Tex Rickard opined that Jeffries was suffering from dysentery the afternoon of the fight, which is what Jeff meant when he said his stomach went back on him. One can wonder what effect drinking imported German water might have had on him, as opposed to fresh water. Indeed, Jeffries had suffered from some dysentery earlier that week. That, combined with cutting down on water intake as the fight approached, in a hot climate could have left him dehydrated and weakened. Of course, it is also possible that Tex was trying to get a sense for what type of interest there would be in a rematch. Excuses were needed to justify one, to convince the public that the result could be different the next time. Jeff thought about it, but ultimately decided to remain retired.[492]

Since the fight, Jeff's café, which usually had been jammed packed, was as silent as a cave.

Bill Delaney was given credit for helping Johnson defeat Jeffries. Delaney knew all of Jeff's strengths and weaknesses. He had Jack hold his right in reserve and use his left. He cautioned Johnson when to expect a rush. Jack was able to forestall Jeff's rushes almost before they began. This caused the impression that Jeff was not trying. The fact was that he was trying, but Johnson always stopped him. Even Bill got in on the act of taunting Jeff. At the end of the 5th round, he said to Johnson, "You are bringing out a bit of the yellow he showed when fighting Fitzsimmons. Keep at him."

---

[490] *Reno Evening Gazette*, quoting the *New York Sun*, July 13, 1910.
[491] *Boxing*, July 16, 1910.
[492] *San Francisco Evening Post*, from a Los Angeles dispatch. July 15, 1910.

A couple years later, when asked about Bill Delaney's benefit to him in the Jeffries fight, Johnson said,

> I felt, of course, that it did not do Jeffries any good to see his old standby behind the other man. But Delaney did not dictate to me; he just asked me to be guided by him in one thing. He wanted me to fight very carefully, and I did so. I believe I could have whipped Jeffries in eight rounds, but to please Delaney I went at the job cautiously and took longer.

A *Freeman* writer opined that it would be six years before Johnson was old enough to be beaten, or to "get in shape for a licking."

Although it was given out that Jeff said that he could not have whipped Johnson in his best days, even the *Freeman* wondered whether it was a genuine quote. "It does not sound quite reasonable that he made the statement because it is not like men to admit so much."[493]

Bulletin writer T. P. Magilligan said that for giving his honest opinion before the fight that Johnson would win, he was scored severely. Folks told him that he was wrong, that Jeff would tear Johnson in half.

This writer still questioned Johnson's toughness, and still wondered whether he had a yellow streak in him. He thought that Johnson showed fear in the first few rounds. In the 4th round, Jeff landed a pile-driving left into Johnson's stomach, which turned Jack nearly white. Those who watched saw that Jack cared little for the gaff. He had been taunting Jeff, but all of a sudden he gained respect even for the shadow of Jeffries. "It was this punch that convinced the writer that Johnson is far from being an unbeatable pugilist." Jack got careful, and Jeff failed to follow up his opportunity. The writer felt that Johnson was a grand boxer with an enormous wallop, but did not like a grueling, and if a man could be found who would tear into him regardless of consequences, he would have more than an even chance. Jeffries never really tore into him.[494]

England's *Boxing*, in answering why Johnson was pre-eminent, noted that Johnson himself declared that he was always learning and improving on the job. He took lessons from his opponents, refraining from the use of his own heavy punching powers until he had picked up all the wrinkles he could gather from them.

Boxing thought that ironically, prejudice actually had benefitted Johnson's career. "Had he been a white man it is certain that he would have been snapped up by some enterprising manager quite early in his career, billed as coming world-beater," and then thrown into fights with the elite prematurely, before he had acquired sufficient ring experience or knowledge.

For a long time, early in his career, Johnson often went hungry and rarely had enough money. He lived from contest to contest. When in jail

---

[493] *Freeman*, July 16, 1910; *San Francisco Examiner*, July 1, 2, 1912.
[494] *San Francisco Bulletin*, July 22, 1910.

with Choynski for several weeks, they were given gloves, and Choynski sparred with Johnson and gave him invaluable lessons.[495]

Charlie White, who had been the back-up referee for the championship fight, said,

> Johnson is a great fighter – in fact, one of the best we have ever had. He has the best defense of any man in the business. He is a hard hitter with either hand, especially with his left, which hooks and shoots as straight as an arrow. He stands up straight – never crouches – thus gaining the advantage of height and reach. If he keeps in his present form he will be champion for five years at least, and don't forget this: If he were a white man the public would accord to him the title of the greatest heavyweight that ever donned a boxing glove.

Jeffries had known that he was going to be in a tough fight. When he started training after his trip abroad, he told one writer, "This - - nigger is going to give me the toughest fight I ever had. He won't lead and I will have to carry the fight to him, and do all the breaking away in the clinches."[496]

In late July, James J. Jeffries joined the claims that he was doped. He said, "There was something the matter with me. They sure did something to me and it will all come out in time." He did not specifically use the word "drugs," but essentially he was alluding to it.

Bill Delaney discredited the "dope" story, the start of which Jeffries had nothing to do with, and which Jeff initially discredited when excuses were first put forward for his defeat. Bill said, "No, Jeffries could not have been quoted correctly… If he is looking for a chance to show that he was not himself that day…he can win a good bet for himself by beating Al Kaufman." The best way to prove he was doped was to have another fight and perform well. However, Jeff did not enter the ring again.[497]

Boxing said the talk about Jeff being doped was "silly." "He wanted no doping; he was already doped with the dope of age, and the yet more killing dope of three years' saloon-keeping. That's dope enough to stay the powers of the best man that ever drew breath. The dope of the cocktail."[498]

Still, Jack Jeffries later said he would carry to the grave with him the belief that Jeff was drugged before he fought Johnson. "Anyone can see by the pictures that all Jim's old-time rushing tactics were missing and that he wasn't there. Nothing could have slowed him up like that unless it was dope."[499]

Although few believed the dope claim (Fitzsimmons claimed the same after his loss to Jeffries), before the fight, Jeffries was administered a drug to

---

[495] *Boxing,* July 23, 1910.
[496] *San Francisco Evening Post*, July 27, 1910.
[497] *San Francisco Bulletin*, July 25, 1910; *San Francisco Evening Post*, July 27, August 2, 1910, citing the *New York Telegraph*.
[498] *Boxing,* August 13, 1910.
[499] *Freeman*, September 24, October 1, 1910.

prevent nose bleed, which one could speculate might potentially have affected him. If one really wants to engage in speculation, one might also ask whether Abe Attell might have slipped him something. Attell worked Jeff's corner. Years later, Attell was involved in the fixing of the 1919 World Series, possibly in conjunction with Arnold Rothstein. There was a lot of money to be made on a wager on the underdog Johnson.

Jack Gleason criticized Tex Rickard's refereeing. He said Rickard showed his inexperience by allowing Corbett to use the raised platform between rounds and stand in the neutral corner to look in on and taunt Johnson, and by failing to stop the fight and award Johnson the decision as soon as Jeff's seconds boosted him back into the ring, which was a flagrant violation of the rules.

Gleason attributed Jeff's poor performance to his failure to box more frequently. He said Jeff spent too much time fishing and not enough boxing, and "he knew it, I believe when it was too late."[500]

Australian promoter Hugh McIntosh, who had promoted Johnson-Burns, said the story was rife in America that the bout originally was a frame up, that Johnson had agreed to lay down to Jeffries, but then in Reno, when Jack saw Jeff train, he had an idea that he was Jeff's master. He then decided not to throw it. McIntosh clearly bought the story.

> There can be no denial of the fact that from the moment Jeff reached Reno he was in the throes of a grouch that would not impress a disinterested, unprejudiced spectator that he was confident of the outcome.
>
> The eve before the fight he walked his room all through the night. He must have learned then that Johnson had no intentions of giving him the battle and meant to double-cross him. ...
>
> When Jeff entered the ring he was plainly very nervous. When he stood up to be introduced his knees shook ... The reason was plain: Jeff knew that he had not come back. ... Johnson told me he could beat Jeffries in the latter's best day; now I believe it.

McIntosh said Jeffries looked like a man who was not trying. Johnson was the game man, and Jeff the one who had the fright. Only once in the fight did Jeff let himself go. He landed a left to the body that clearly hurt Johnson, but instead of following it up, Jeff returned to his previous tactics of trying to avoid the inevitable. "Towards the conclusion of the very much one-sided contest, Jeffries showed palpable signs of a desire to chuck it."

In his training camp, Johnson was lively and cheerful, playing craps games and the cello to the accompaniment of rag-time music. He seemed not to have a care on his mind.

McIntosh claimed that one of Jeff's admirers insisted on the band playing "All Coons Look Alike to Me," which was received with great

---

[500] *San Francisco Evening Post*, August 8, 1910.

enthusiasm. This claim contradicted the news reports that this tune was not played, having been barred by the authorities.

McIntosh said Johnson dominated the fight from start to finish. "The white champion was outclassed in speed, strength, and hitting ability and the hopes of his admirers were speedily dashed when they observed that in the clinches the negro was the stronger."

As for the future, "The search for a white man to wrest the championship from the black holder has commenced, and the white sporting public of the world will not be content until they have proved the white superiority in the sport of boxing."[501]

The Future

At this point, most writers and experts believed that Jack Johnson was invincible, no heavyweight had a chance with him, and only Father Time would defeat him. Jack London concluded, "Johnson is a wonder. No one understands him, this man who smiles. … And where now is the champion who will make Johnson extend himself, who will glaze those bright eyes, remove that smile and silence that golden repartee?" *Boxing* said the white heavyweights of the day were not as good as the leading colored exponents: Johnson, Langford, McVey, or Jeannette.

PRETTY EASY FOR JOHNSON FOR AWHILE—By WESTOVER

San Francisco Evening Post, July 7, 1910

[501] *Boxing,* August 13, 1910.

The *Reno Evening Gazette* said Johnson reigned supreme and was without true challengers, for he had proved himself to be "invincible." "Ring followers agree that no man now in the game measures up to the job. Very little attention is paid to Sam Langford's challenge and the black champion himself regards it as a joke."

Alfred Lewis said no one showed the slightest promise of being able to defeat Johnson.

Ed Hamilton believed that Langford was the only man in sight who even remotely could compete with Johnson. Some said the bone-crushing demon Langford and Johnson would draw a big crowd. However, Hamilton believed it would be a long time before any fight could draw anywhere near the type of gate that the Jeffries fight did.

H. M. Walker did not think any fighter had a remote chance to beat Johnson.

> Nowhere in the world of pugilism is there a man who has one chance in a thousand of wresting the title from the shambling, smiling, good-natured black. He whipped the grizzled Jeffries in each and every one of the fifteen rounds, and what is more, Jack accomplished this feat with such ridiculous ease that his continual tantalizing smiles and nods wore a deep canker into the souls of the friends and supporters of the white champion.

Johnson's defensive skill alone was so superb that it would bring discouragement to any opponent, big or small. They simply could not hit him. "His cleverness is marvelous. He punishes in a cruel, rasping, deliberate manner that suggests the snake prolonging the torture of a helpless victim. His sting is poisonous." No man could compete with, much less extend or conquer him. "Jack Johnson's skin is black, but he is a real heavyweight champion of the world."

Ketchel said of Johnson, "There is no man in the world who has a chance with him." Stan included Langford, with whom he had been in the ring with as well.

George Harting believed that Johnson was without peer. "I do not know of anybody in the heavyweight class who can give Johnson a semblance of a fight, and believe that he will hold the championship for years to come."

Bill Delaney said father time eventually would get Johnson, but it would take a while to find a white man to do it. Kaufman was the only man with a chance, but he needed at least another year and a half of work and improvement, combined with Johnson's aging. Langford would be no match for Johnson. He was too small and would not be able to land.

Jim Coffroth said promoters would have to find another white hope. "An opponent for the champion will be difficult to find. No one appears on the pugilistic map at this writing. Still, one never knows what a year will develop."

The *San Francisco Bulletin* said for the first time a negro was the undisputed heavyweight champion, and there did not appear to be any white man in sight who could change that. It opined that he had no capable challenger, and it would take many years to develop any man good enough to beat Johnson. Some talked of a match with Langford, but "the Boston middleweight is too small a man" to be given a serious chance against such a grand champion.

Most felt there was not enough championship stuff in Al Kaufman to beat the champion. Not enough folks would be willing to travel to Nevada to see that fight. And at that time, Nevada was the only place where such a fight could be held.

Johnson essentially was without a big fight on the horizon, and therefore probably would not fight for a long while. "Here he is loaded down with money, a fine theatrical engagement, and nobody to fight. Nothing to do but pose, show those gold teeth, and strut about the world. It's a safe bet that Johnson will be the heavyweight champion for at least six years."[502]

> Probably the best [challenger] is Sam Langford, but the latter is also a negro, and a fight between two colored men is not especially attractive from a box-office standpoint, and it is not believed that they will ever meet. …

> The man who is to dethrone Johnson will have to be developed. It may mean a wait of one or two years, but somebody will get Artha if the latter sticks to the game long enough.

> The colored man is master of his class today, but just the same he will go the way of the Sullivans, Corbetts, and Fitzsimmonses.[503]

Naughton opined that Langford at least would make Johnson hustle, even if he did not defeat him.

Tex Rickard did not support a Langford-Johnson bout, saying, "Langford could not make a showing against Johnson. He's too small. Then, two black men fighting would not draw a crowd. Johnson told me he would be willing to meet Langford, but he knew that a fight between blacks would not make any money. The champion tells me he does not intend to fight again for a year." The paying public was white, and they wanted to see a white man regain the title. "I don't think there is a man in the world who classes with Johnson and the only man who will ever beat him is himself. If he takes care of his health he will retire a champion." Rickard said the next best match would be Burns-Langford, for he did not think Ketchel was as good as either.[504]

Bulletin writer E. D. Burrows said he would bet on Langford if he and Johnson met. "At any rate, we would almost surely see a better battle than the one recently staged in Reno – for 'Beggar Sam' is neither a has-been nor is he liable to be intimidated, in the least degree." Next to Kaufman, Sam

---

[502] *San Francisco Bulletin*, July 5, 6, 1910.
[503] *San Francisco Bulletin*, July 16, 1910.
[504] *San Francisco Bulletin*, July 7, 20, 1910.

had the best chance to beat Johnson. Though short, he had speed, science, and a wallop that instilled fear. Sam was game to the core and undoubtedly one of the toughest nuts in the business.[505]

The *Call* said that only father time would defeat Johnson, for he was the greatest fighter of all. It said the most interesting potential future bouts were Johnson-Kaufman, Johnson-Langford, or Kaufman-Langford.

In the meantime, Johnson was enjoying his fame and fortune, and did not need to fight to earn good money. He reveled in wine, women, and song. He delighted in being in the limelight. "If Johnson cares to he can act just like the other champions. He can lay off for the next year and reap the golden harvest which the theatrical field offers. Notwithstanding his color he is a great attraction before the public."[506]

New York fight promoter William Gibson said he would help raise the $20,000 that Johnson demanded Langford put up for a fight. However, he did not believe the fight would happen. "I don't believe you could pay Johnson enough money to fight Langford." He claimed to have offered Jack $5,000 to box the "Boston Bone Crusher" Langford 6 rounds a year ago, but said Jack turned it down.[507]

A Los Angeles sportswriter said, "Of course Langford really couldn't beat Johnson in a fight. Too much class. He is the kind of fighter, however, that a man like Johnson hates to meet. ... He hates concentrated, continued fighting. He dreads a man who keeps boring in without regard to punishment." The feeling was that Johnson would win, but it would be a tough fight that would require him to work hard. Supposedly, Langford had gone broke betting on Jeffries.[508]

The *Freeman* opined that in the meantime, Sam Langford would make the most out of issuing challenges that he knew were perfectly safe, given that there was not a great likelihood of them fighting. Johnson had said of Sam's challenge, "That nigger better hunt some one in his class." Langford had been sure that Jeff would "kill that nigger Johnsing." Johnson had given Langford a licking several years prior (1906 W15, decking Sam twice), but Sam had gained weight since then, and was walking around at about 180 pounds. Of course, Johnson had gained a lot of weight as well.[509]

Langford manager Joe Woodman said he was prepared to post a side bet of $10,000 for Langford to fight Johnson. "I'll admit that Johnson is a great pugilist, but Langford, though forty pounds lighter, can beat him. If Johnson goes to England, France or Australia, I will follow him with Langford to force him to fight."

Another *Bulletin* writer said that although Langford was much smaller, he was the only one with even a glimmer of a chance against Johnson. He had

---

505 *San Francisco Bulletin*, July 8, 1910.
506 *San Francisco Call*, July 10, 1910.
507 *San Francisco Bulletin, Evening Post, Chronicle*, July 14, 1910.
508 *San Francisco Evening Post*, from a Los Angeles dispatch. July 15, 1910.
509 *Freeman*, July 16, 1910.

confidence, heart, and the punch. "This is the one reason that Johnson is putting financial barriers between himself and Langford. If Johnson was certain he could beat Langford half as easily as he beat Jeffries there would be no talk of $20,000 side bets." Still, Johnson would have all of the physical advantages.

In late July, the *Bulletin* said much of the Langford-Johnson talk had "died out a bit," but "Langford seems to be the best equipped of all Johnson's challengers, and Johnson, though he won't admit it, has more respect for the fighting ability of his brother of color than he has for the rest of those who are seeking a match with him." Some were talking about a potential Langford-Ketchel re-match in a longer bout.

The *Evening Post* said, "While a match between the pair might not be the best drawing card, it should furnish an interesting fight, as Langford is a very classy scrapper."[510]

The *Chronicle* opined that Johnson was due for an extended rest before he defended the title. There was no formidable opponent on the horizon. Plus, there were few places where a big fight could be held.

Langford was talked of, but the *Chronicle* opined that he still would be a 2 to 1 underdog, so there would not be sufficient public demand for the bout to be financially lucrative. Despite how good he was, Langford appeared to be too small a man to humble the giant and clever Johnson, and therefore, "he is not given much consideration." No promoter would be willing to put up a purse the size of which Johnson would demand, for not enough white fans were going to be willing to pay big money for tickets and to take trains to Nevada to see two black men fight. In general, they wanted to see a white man attempt to take the title.

Al Kaufman would be a 3 to 1 underdog, and no big crowd was going to turn out to see a white man battle against a black man with the odds so much against him.

This writer opined that the top contenders should fight it out amongst themselves, to garner sufficient public clamor to make a fight with Johnson lucrative, such that promoters would want to make the fight and Johnson could earn enough money to make it worth his while to train and enter the ring again. That could take a while.[511]

Eugene Corri said England had a man who could whip Johnson, named Bombardier Billy Wells. He was 21 years old, stood 6'3" and had many knockout victories.[512]

Some thought Jeffries would do better in a return match, for he would not be carrying the same weight of responsibility, he'd be the underdog, no one would be telling him that he was the white race's hope, and Jeff would spar more often and surround himself with better trainers. Still, others thought a rematch simply would not sell after Jeff's poor performance.

[510] *San Francisco Bulletin*, July 18, 20, 22, 27, 1910. *San Francisco Evening Post*, July 20, 1910.
[511] *San Francisco Chronicle*, July 24, 1910.
[512] *San Francisco Evening Post*, July 16, 1910.

A *Bulletin* writer said the lack of class that Jeffries showed in their fight would make it doubtful if in a rematch they would draw 1/3 of the house that they drew.

Jeffries was the latest pugilist to discover that Johnson had a very telling punch. Writers and fans previously had contended that Jack's punching powers were only mediocre. However, during the fight, Jeff said in his corner, "Gee, but that coon can hit some. I feel as though my jaw was cracked." Stan Ketchel had told everyone that Johnson could punch. "Say, when they tell you that Johnson can't hit, you just tell them that I say he is the hardest hitter in the world. Look here, if a fellow couldn't hit, how could he dislodge three teeth?" What deceived some folks into thinking Johnson could not punch was his cautious, defensive, methodical style. He generally did not like taking big risks to finish a man. He was content to take his time about matters. But he could hurt his foes when he wanted.

Despite the fact that Australians had wagered on Johnson, his victory was unpopular, for they had rooted for the white man. They thought a great deal of Jack's fighting ability and admired his skill, but they did not care too much for him on his two visits, for his flashiness made him unpopular.

Rumors that Burns would rematch Johnson were regarded as a joke. The average man in Australia said, "Why Johnson will kill him next time." Still, many thought that Burns would put up a better fight than Jeffries did. Burns had worried himself until he was positively ill before the Johnson fight. It seemed that all those who talked confidently before the fight showed their true fear when they entered the ring with Jack Johnson.[513]

San Francisco Evening Post, July 13, 1910

---

[513] *Chronicle,* July 27, 1910.

CHAPTER 12

Life After the Big Fight

When Jack Johnson's train from Reno arrived in Ogden, Utah, heading to Chicago, Johnson said, "Well, people I turned the trick and I'm going back to Chicago to my old mammy. I went there determined to turn the trick, and I had no trouble in doing it. … I'm just the same old fellow that I was before I had the pleasure of Mr. Jeffries' company for a short time." Jack said Jeff stung him only once, jarring him a little with a left hook. "He made a mistake to fight me, but the people forced him to do it. Therefore he should not be roasted too strong. If you will believe me he did the best he could all the way through."

Johnson also said, "We were kidding each other continually. … When I landed on him he usually asked me if I did not think he had a hard old head, and I would retort by asking him if he did not think I was a pretty clever fellow."

Between rounds, Corbett came over to his corner and glared at Johnson. "That only amused me. I don't think he had a right to step over that way as it is a time-honored custom for the seconds to keep their own corners. But I did not mind in the least. I kept talking to him and kidding him all the time and don't consider that I had the worst of the verbal exchanges."

George Cotton said, "When Jeffries and Johnson clinched in the eighth round, Jack said to Jeffries, 'I've got your measure, Mistah Jeffries, and I am going to put you out any time I want to.'"

Before Johnson left Utah, three burly young toughs walked up to the open window and used a vile epithet to Johnson in the presence of his wife and dared him to come to the platform. Jack's companions stopped him from doing so. However, one of Johnson's trainers exited, spat a mouthful of tobacco juice onto one of the young toughs, and then kicked him. Officers rushed up and forced the crowd back.

As a result of the incident, railroad officials placed two detectives on the train to accompany the champion.[514]

On July 6, from Grand Island, Nebraska, Johnson said he would not consider Sam Langford's challenge, for he was not going to fight again for a year. "Just say for me that Langford has not got a chance. I'm not going to fight again for one year. … I have put up five fights in rapid succession. I believe I am entitled to take some time before going into the ring again. I am going to Europe to fill some of the numerous contracts I am receiving and that I have here now."[515]

---

[514] *Call*, July 5, 1910; *Nevada State Journal*, July 6, 1910; *Examiner*, July 6, 1910.
[515] *Reno Evening Gazette*, July 7, 1910.

When Johnson arrived in Chicago on July 7 at 2 p.m., he was accorded a welcome such as no other black man of modern times ever received. About 5,000 blacks and a big sprinkling of whites were at the railway station to greet him. The crowd yelled, "Jack, Jack, Jack." Miles of sidewalks were lined with a living wall of humanity seeking to catch a glimpse of him. Men, women, and children cheered and waved banners. Some pinned the extra papers with Johnson's picture across their breasts. No one entering the city ever received a warmer welcome than the "black king of the fistic ring."

It was estimated that blacks in Chicago had won at least $600,000 wagering on Johnson.

Some were saying that he was so popular that if Johnson ran for alderman in Chicago's Third Ward that he would win in a walkover.

In a new car, Johnson drove to his home at 3344 Wabash Avenue, where his mother Tiny Johnson and members of his family awaited. A huge crowd was outside their home as well. Amidst roars and drums, Jack made his way into the house and embraced his mom.

Mrs. Johnson said Jack always kept his word to her, and he had promised to win the fight. She served him chicken and watermelon.

Jack's mother said that as a little boy, her son was a regular cry baby. His sister Janey often would beat up the bullies for him. However, one day his mom told him that he should be ashamed for allowing his sister to fight for him, and if he did not fight back for himself, she would give him a worse whipping. Thereafter, Jack always fought back, and did well for himself.

When asked about a potential fight with Langford, Johnson replied, "Sam Langford? You make me laugh. I am not running around now looking for fights. Let Langford put up his $20,000 first, then he can talk. Just now, I'm going to rest. I am going to New York Sunday afternoon to begin a thirty weeks' vaudeville tour. ... If it looks like a good thing I may accept offers to go to Europe." Johnson was quite wealthy, could make even more easy money on the stage, and did not need to fight any time soon. Joking, he said, "I have enough money to last me till next week."[516]

Johnson said Jeffries fought a game battle to the end. Those who said otherwise were just sore about losing their bets. Gameness was all Jeff had left in the last few rounds. "I am sure sorry I had to put him out."

Jack recalled the early-round kidding they engaged in. Jeff said, "This is a tough old head to crack." Johnson responded, "I'm a sure enough nut cracker." When Jeff asked if Jack had hurt his hand when hitting him, Jack replied in the negative and hit him again. Once when Jack missed and his blow slid off Jeff's hairy chest, Jack said, "Jeff, you've got cocoanut oil on yeh." Jeff replied, "You ain't got no cold if you can smell that good."

---

[516] *Nevada State Journal, San Francisco Call,* July 8, 1910. *Freeman,* July 9, 1910; *San Francisco Evening Post,* July 7, 1910.

In about the 6th round, Johnson said, "Come right on, Jeff, let's mix it." Jeff replied "All right." Johnson opined, "At the end of that round I knew I had Jeffries' number."

> It amused me the way that fellow, Corbett, tried to get my goat. And believe me, kiddo, I certainly put a rope around his angora before I was through. When we got to the end of the fatal fifteenth Jim Corbett looked nearly as bad as poor Jeff and twice as disappointed. Jeffries never mixed things so hot for me that I couldn't answer back to Corbett.
>
> I was in a clinch, plugging away at Jeff's ribs when Corbett, in his A No. 1 sneer, cried: "Jim will make you show your yellow streak after awhile." "Then we'll be in the same class, Corbett," says I, still plugging in the clinch. "He certainly made you show plenty of yellow once."
>
> As the mill went on I kept laughing at Jeffries. It was a good-natured laugh, but it bothered Corbett. "That's the old bull," he cried to Jeff. "It's a strong bull," was what I passed him. "Go on, Jeffries, he's only stalling," cried Corbett. "Great stall it is, too," says I.
>
> That ended the most elaborate attempt that was ever made to kid a man out of the championship. Believe me, boy, I'm some kidder myself. …
>
> After the thirteenth round I didn't kid him any more. I knew he was all in and I didn't want people to think that I was a braggart. I ended it as gently as I could and made sure. You see, Jeff had to be done up brown. To the last knockout there was always a chance that he would come through with a wallop and this colored fellow was taking no chances.
>
> I only really felt two of Jeffries' blows. He busted open a cut in my lip early in the game. I got the cut from that bear Cotton, and it's the only mark I'm bringing home. The other blow was in the eleventh when he got to my body with a punch that had real steam behind it.[517]

Johnson told his feelings about the fight to a *Boxing* correspondent. In that interview, he complimented Jeff's power. "He could hit, too. … [H]e landed several punches that let me know that I had been hit." Johnson figured that he would have to size up Jeffries and get him tired before risking cutting loose on him, and that is just what he did.

Jack noticed that Jeff had wrestlers Farmer Burns and Frank Gotch with him in training camp, so he expected that Jeff would try to maul him in that

---

[517] *San Francisco Evening Post*, July 13, 1910.

way. Therefore, he had all his sparring partners, who were young, strong, husky fellows, haul him about as much as they could. He was prepared.

Summarizing the fight round by round, Johnson said,

> I never do rash things in a fight. There is no sense to it. I just planned to fight my usual fight, to be as sure and careful as I could, and never take a chance with my hands once.
>
> I figured that it would take me about three rounds to size up the situation and lay my plans, and then I would know just the way to beat Jeffries. ...
>
> Mr. Jeffries feinted a bit, and then tried the clinching game. I was ready, and we did a lot of pulling about, landing only a few punches in the first round.
>
> Jeffries crouched and let out at long range in the second, but I dodged him, and got home left and right, and we had another clinch. We wrestled a bit, and I was feeling very comfortable. Mr. Jeffries was pushing me about, but I was feeling quite fresh and going easily, able to hit him when I wanted to, while, though he was looking happy and easy, I could tell that he wasn't going to beat me for strength. ...
>
> We wrestled a lot more in the third. I could tell that things were going my way. Jeffries seemed happy and easy in his mind, but I could see that Corbett was beginning to get anxious. He had been talking at me all the time ...
>
> Jeffries started out to cut me down in the fourth, which was about the only round he did real well in. But he didn't do me any much harm, except when he opened that old cut in my mouth. He got home some hard ones to my body as well, and I went back into the ropes at times, but I was going back as he struck, so the blows didn't tell as the crowd thought they did.
>
> He started out confidently next time. ... I blocked his left and let him have it from both hands, cutting his mouth and bringing him into another clinch. I upper-cut him as well, and this made him shove me about. I went quite easily, but the work and the heat tired Jeff more than it did me, and the game was suiting me fine.
>
> He crouched again for the sixth, and we had a little spell of long distance work. That was when I showed them that I had the left punch they all said I hadn't got, and cut his right cheek open. He rushed at me, and we went into more clinches. I talked to him a lot, but I don't think that he was worried any. He kept cool, though he missed all the hard ones he sent at my face, and I could feel that he was getting weaker.

I knew then that I had the fight safe, but I didn't want to throw it away by being careless, so I just met him with my left when he tried rushing. We had a clinch or two, but I was getting home easily, and could tell, too, how weak he was getting. I don't know how he was feeling himself, because he kept very cool, but his punches weren't anything like so hard as they had been, and he was missing me more than he had been doing.

It was clear that he felt that he couldn't box with me, because he kept rushing at me in the eighth, hoping to beat me down, perhaps, with body blows at close range. I was dead sure that he couldn't do that, but though I didn't mind him clinching, I felt that I would jab him some as he came in. ... He did some more pushing about, and landed a few blows, but he was feeling pretty sore as he went to his corner, I can tell you.

Corbett was getting rattled, and tried some more talk. ... [Jeffries] came at me like a bull in the ninth, and got home some heavy blows to the stomach. He did a lot of pushing as well, and felt much stronger to me. I bashed him in the face and body, but he didn't appear to mind, though he was badly cut about.

Mr. Jeffries is a good, game fellow. He must have known by now that he was in for a beating, but he laughed and joked when I landed on his jaw and ear. He again got home on my mouth, and though I had his eye nearly shut he was as cheerful as at the start. But his wind was going fast, and the end wasn't very far off. It was only a question of how long he could last.

He came at me for all he was worth next time, and fought as hard as he could. He got right home on me several times. ... But I didn't mind mixing it at this stage. I was beating him in every department of the game, and open fighting would only mean punishment for him. The crowd cheered him, but he wasn't feeling good himself, and he was getting weak and wild before the gong came. We had wrestled a bit, too, and this sort of thing wasn't doing Jeff any good. His arms were getting weak, and he couldn't put them up to block or stop my blows. ...

The only thing left to be decided was how much Jeffries could take. Some people say that I might have finished things quicker, and perhaps I might. But it wasn't safe to take chances with a man like Mr. Jeffries. He had pulled round once or twice, and had come at me so fiercely that I couldn't be certain he wouldn't be able to do it again, and it was surer to get him well beaten before I went in to finish him. But he took a lot of finishing. Don't let there be any mistake about that. Mr. Jeffries fought a square fight and a game battle. No one can say he didn't do his best. I went all out for him from the eleventh round, but though he was weak and badly beaten, he was still so strong that I didn't judge it wise to take any chances. He was almost blind, and badly cut about, but though I landed all sorts of upper-cuts, and hit him hard, he wouldn't drop till the fifteenth round. I nearly had him down twice in the fourteenth, but he still staggered at me in the next, and struggled up to his feet twice after going down. ...

Yes, I was a bit sore when they introduced Mr. Jeffries as the champion of the world, because you see I fancied that that title belonged to me all right. Well, it does now, you know, so I am not kicking about it at all any more.

No, I don't guess that I shall fight again for a year, at least. ... I've got some good Vaudeville engagements, and I don't mind easy money at all.[518]

Johnson alleged that former manager George Little attempted to get him to throw the Jeffries fight, which explained why he broke away from Little. George asked him how much it would take to get him to throw it. "I asked him what he meant by asking me to throw away the title which I had worked hard for eight years to win." Little said someone was offering big money for him to lie down. "Now if I ever called a man in my life I certainly told Little a few things then and wound up by telling him I was through with him."

Little told Jack that he could not dismiss him because he owed him a lot of money, and also threatened that he would let the world know a few things about Johnson. "By this he meant that I was not training, that I was not leading a decent life, and a lot of other things which he knew were not true." Johnson called upon the authorities for protection, and after they had heard his story, Little was compelled to keep away from his camp. Little then circulated stories that Johnson was not training, was sick, and in no condition. Johnson wanted the public to know, "I am an honest fighter."

I could have dragged down $350,000...had I agreed to throw the fight, but no amount of coin is ever going to induce me to figure in a shady deal as long as I am in the ring. I intend to retire and nobody will ever accuse me of pulling off a crooked fight. ... I might have cleaned up more than $350,000 had I agreed to figure in a crooked act. I felt, however, that I was the better man and wanted to win, for I knew I had thousands of friends in various parts of the country all banking on me to beat Jeffries. Besides, I had given my promise to my old mammy in Chicago.

Johnson said Al Kaufman was the next best man in the world. Kaufman would be dangerous in a long fight with anyone, for he had the punch and

[518] *Boxing*, July 16, 1910.

stamina combined. "Naturally, I think I can beat him, but I'd rather go against Jeffries any day in the week."

Jack was winning numerous admirers by "carefully avoiding the 'racial' issue."

Johnson was also praised for remembering those from his past. He sent gifts ranging from $250 up to $750 to eight men in Galveston who had helped him early on in his career. Ed Harrison, an old-timer in Galveston, had taught Johnson how to fight when he was a young boy on the docks. He had promised Harrison that when he became wealthy he would fit him in fancy clothes. Jack sent him $750. Receiving a gift of $500 was Cafferty Williams, who once had saved him from drowning in the bay at the docks, when Jack was sucked under a vessel.

Jack financially supported his brother and his mother. He also had three sisters living, all of whom were married.

On July 8 in Chicago, a St. Louis machinist was arrested after he attempted to force his way into Johnson's home. He was armed with a rifle. Neighbors thought he intended to kill Johnson, so they called the police. The man admitted that he had lost $25 on the fight, but denied that he intended to harm Johnson. Why then was he attempting to break into his home with a rifle in hand?[519]

Jilted manager George Little alleged that Johnson had promised the film folks to allow the Jeffries fight to last 7 rounds and the Ketchel fight to last 12 rounds. He claimed that Johnson and Ketchel rehearsed the double knockdown. He further alleged that the Kaufman fight was fixed, for both fighters agreed that there would be no knockout or else they would forfeit their share of the purse plus have to pay a $2,500 penalty, which had been put up as an alleged side bet.

Johnson said all of Little's charges were false. He said he had never faked a fight in his life and would sue Little for libel. Certainly, at the very least, the fact that Johnson knocked Ketchel's teeth out and knocked him out cold disproved that that knockdown was a fake.[520]

Johnson said Langford and his manager Joe Woodman were looking for free advertising at his expense. Some felt that Johnson was not overanxious to fight the "bone crusher." However, "Very few of the fans who saw the monster black man beat Jeffries up think that Sam would have any great chance to beat Jack, but at that it must be admitted that Langford is Johnson's most formidable opponent right now."

However, Johnson was so rich at that point that he wasn't going to fight anyone any time soon. If he was going to take a tough fight, it would have to be because there was enough public demand for it such that it would be worth his while financially. And at that time, most considered Johnson unbeatable. There was no reason to take a tough fight when he was making

[519] *Reno Evening Gazette, Call,* July 9, 1910; *San Francisco Chronicle,* July 10, 1910.
[520] *San Francisco Chronicle,* July 11, 1910.

a great deal of money without having to train or risk his title. Being champion and just being seen on stage had great monetary value to Johnson. He was not going to risk the status for which he had struggled and worked so long to obtain unless he was paid very well.

In an effort to build momentum for a rematch, on various occasions, Langford and Woodman claimed that in their 1906 fight, Sam knocked Johnson down twice. However, Johnson offered to bet them $5,000 that such was not the case, and was willing to leave it to the next-day local Boston newspapers to decide the issue. Neither Langford nor Woodman evinced any desire to make the wager, obviously because in fact, the next-day papers said Johnson dropped Langford twice, not the other way around. Johnson claimed that he knocked Langford down for 22 seconds, but the referee would not allow him the knockout.

Ultimately, the *Evening Post* opined that Langford was far too small for Johnson, in both height and weight. It would be a matter of the old ring adage that a good small man cannot beat a good big one, as proven by Johnson's bouts with Ketchel and Burns. "Sam is too small for Johnson. He may be the best man of his poundage that ever climbed through the ropes, but Johnson would have all the natural advantages over Langford, and these advantages in the favor of a fighter of Jack's class would be too large a handicap for even so clever a battler as Langford to overcome."[521]

On July 11, 16,000 citizens of the San Juan Hill area of New York, also known as the "Black Belt," swarmed the train depot to see Johnson arrive from Chicago. They were there even though the train was several hours late. The police, fearing trouble, refused to permit a parade.

Baron Wilkins, reputed to be the city's wealthiest black man and the champion's close friend, was to have made a welcome speech from his saloon's balcony. However, fearing that hundreds of idle whites might start a riot, the police told him not to give the speech, and he complied.

Jack would make his first appearance that night at Hammerstein's roof garden, and would collect $3,000 per week.[522]

Johnson said, "Jeffries was forced to fight me. He did not want to, but the newspapers and magazines haunted and hounded him until there was no other course left him but to come out of retirement and take up the white man's burden."

Johnson said he had been fighting for 15 years and always tried to conduct himself honorably, including when he married Daisy Champlain. "I have proved that a Negro can be honest. ... I want my colored friends to do everything they can to be an honor and a credit to the race." He liked all of the accolades, but hoped black folk would not be like the French were with Napoleon. The people were with Napoleon when he was winning, but turned against him when he lost. Jack said he never would be broke.[523]

---

[521] *San Francisco Evening Post*, July 11, 1910.
[522] *San Francisco Evening Post, Chronicle*, July 11, 1910.
[523] *Freeman*, July 16, 1910.

That evening, Johnson made his first New York vaudeville stage appearance before a crowded theater. There were no riots.

Johnson had sold his rights to the fight pictures in part because generally he believed that a bird in the hand was better than two in the bush. He liked money up front. He figured that if he had not sold, he would have to pay folks to look after his interests, and after the various parties got through cheating one another, there would not be much money left for him. He was content with what he had received. "I hope they make a million out of it."

On July 13 at the Vitascope film company's plant in Flatbush, New York, Johnson and his wife saw the fight films at a special private exhibition. Whenever her husband landed a punch, his wife chuckled and patted Jack on the back or shoulder. When asked to point out the blow that closed Jeff's right eye, Jack said to watch close, that it was when they broke from a clinch. As they separated, Jack's arm shot out and landed on the eye. Mrs. Johnson remarked, "It was a dandy." Jack only occasionally spoke after that, saying things like, "He didn't hurt me much that time," or "I felt that." In the 10th, he said, "Here is where he starts to go away. It is almost over now." Afterwards, he said, "Those are the best pictures I ever saw."[524]

Some gamblers had made money simply by betting the odds variations in different locations. The French had Johnson the favorite at 3 to 1. In England, Jeff was the favorite. So some bet on the underdog Jeffries in France and then bet Johnson in England. This way, they were going to make money no matter who won.[525]

Regarding George Little's claims, one paper wrote, "Little isn't a very high grade man and little credence can be placed upon his accusations, although they may be true." Johnson won his fights, and no one could ever say he laid down. If Little was so honorable and if something really was wrong, he should have protected the public before the fights, not had a hand in them and then throw "mud on the coon" after Johnson had jilted him. "If he wanted to gain the confidence of the public he should have become conscience-stricken long ago."[526]

Johnson said Little offered him $50,000 to lay down to Jeff inside of 8 rounds. Little reasoned, "Don't you see, Jack, the pictures will be worth $1,000,000 more if Jeffries wins? Get wise." Johnson laughed. The second time Little approached him, Jack said, "See here, George Little, there isn't enough money in the world to make me throw this fight. I think I can whip this man the best day he ever saw, and besides, I have too many friends who believe in me and will bet their money on me to lay down."[527]

---

[524] *San Francisco Bulletin*, July 14, 1910; *Evening Post*, *Chronicle*, July 14, 1910. Johnson said the left clout he landed on Jeff's right eye in the 2nd round sent Jeff towards defeat. Jeff rubbed his glove over it many times, indicating that it gave him trouble. Before the fight, Bill Delaney had told the *Bulletin* writer that Johnson planned to close one or both of Jeff's eyes as soon as possible.

[525] *San Francisco Evening Post*, July 15, 1910.

[526] *San Francisco Evening Post*, July 16, 1910.

[527] *Freeman*, July 16, 1910.

Johnson wanted to engage in automobile races on the track. He loved to speed, and wanted to prove himself a champion race-car driver as well.

In New York, Johnson was arrested for reckless driving. Jack was mad. He said the police were dogging him and trying to get him however and whenever they could. He was arrested at 47th Street and 8th Avenue, after he followed the instructions of a police inspector who told him after leaving the theater to get away as quickly as he could from the admiring crowds. Johnson told the judge that it was a matter of necessity. "I had to drive hard to dodge the hoodlums, who call me names and throw stones at me. The officers told me to go fast and get away as soon as I could. I have never run down or injured anyone, but I don't want to be struck by stones." The judge told Jack that he would wind up running down someone yet, and noted that he had been arrested in almost every city that he had visited. Johnson said the arrests were made for advertising purposes. He pled guilty and paid a $15 fine.[528]

The *Bulletin* said, "There is very little disposition on the part of promoters to match whites and negroes since the Johnson-Jeffries affair."

However, Sam Langford was scheduled to box Al Kaufman 6 rounds in Philadelphia in August. Johnson had said that Kaufman could lick Langford. Hence, if Sam could defeat Al, it would garner much greater momentum for a Johnson-Langford match, given that Johnson had said Kaufman was the best heavy other than himself.

The *Evening Post* opined that although a Johnson-Langford bout would attract a good-sized crowd, there would not be as much interest in such a contest as would be the case when a white boxer was challenging for the crown, because "two negroes never make an ideal card."[529]

The *Freeman* said, "The effort to get up a go between Johnson and Langford is amusing." In order to compel a fight, writers claimed that Johnson was afraid of Langford. No one could blame Langford or his backers, for he had all to gain. Nagging sometimes paid.[530]

Hattie McLay, who lived in Philadelphia, claimed that Johnson was her husband, and she was about to sue him for divorce and $50,000 in damages. However, she could not produce her marriage certificate. She claimed the champ had carried it off. McLay said she first met Johnson in August 1907 in Marshall's café, and went with him to Atlantic City, and then to Boston, where she was married to him on September 28, 1907 by a magistrate. She had lived with Johnson until December 30, 1909. She had witnessed his fights during that time, including the one with Burns. She said Johnson had deserted her, and for the last six months George Little had supported her.

Johnson denied that she was his wife and accused Little of influencing her to make trouble for him.

---

[528] *Bulletin*, July 20, 1910; *Chronicle*, July 21, 1910.
[529] *San Francisco Bulletin, San Francisco Evening Post*, July 21, 1910.
[530] *Freeman*, July 23, 1910.

The *Broad Ax* could not opine as to the merits of McLay's claim, but was amused that a white lady was willing to acknowledge to the world that "she has been seeking social equality with Colored people; and that she is willing to call Johnson her black darling in order to grab on to some of his money."[531]

George Little said Johnson's charges that he tried to get him to lie down were ridiculous, for he had nothing to gain by having the fight thrown when he already had wagered on Johnson.

Governor Gillett explained that he had heard that the Jeffries fight was a frame-up and would go 15 rounds to help the pictures. He said dishonesty was rampant in boxing, and nearly all of the matches were fixed. Owen Moran admitted that he had agreed to let Tommy McCarthy to stay 15 rounds, though McCarthy died as a result of the fight. The governor said frame-ups included Papke-Thomas, Johnson-Kaufman, and Johnson-Ketchel. "It makes me laugh when I read that Johnson has demonstrated that a Negro can be honest. He's a fine example of an honest Negro. He'd double-cross his best friend."[532]

On July 25 in New York, Jack Johnson was arrested, not for speeding, but for traveling too slowly and standing still. He was accused of obstructing traffic by stopping his car seven feet from the curb. He was also charged with having a wrong number on his car. He gave $100 cash bail for his court appearance.

The next day, Johnson was found not guilty of obstructing a highway. Jack said, "Most generally, they get me for speeding and always fine me, too. This time I was caught for standing still, but they let me off."[533]

Paul West composed a poem about the police harassment that Johnson endured:

> Jack Johnson on a summer's day
> Motored up Broadway, blithe and gay!
> He wanted to get from Thirty-fourth
> Maybe a dozen blocks up north.
> But the moment he showed his visage bright
> A million policemen hove in sight,
> And each individual copper grim
> Fell on the Smoke and arrested him.
> They hailed him to court without a word,
> And these were the charges that Johnson heard:
> Disturbing the cop upon his beat,
> Casting a shadow across the street,
> Tooting his horn till it lost its breath,

[531] *Chicago Broad Ax*, July 23, 1910.
[532] *Freeman*, July 23, 1910. Gillett claimed that three or four times at Willus Britt's, Johnson and Ketchel rehearsed the knockdowns. Gillett also claimed Johnson and Kaufman agreed not to try to knock each other out. Gillett essentially was repeating Little's allegations.
[533] *Bulletin*, July 26, 1910; *Chronicle*, July 27, 1910.

Making men cheer themselves to death,
Wearing the pavement asphalt down,
Making a Jeffries bettor frown,
Waking a copper from his rest,
Scaring a sparrow from its nest,
Stopping the trade in five saloons,
Distracting attention from three balloons,
Scattering fourteen swarms of flies,
Straining a hundred thousand eyes,
Crossing a street without a permit,
Stretching the neck of a Harlem hermit,
Neglecting to check his hat and coat,
Getting Jim Corbett's peevish goat,
Doing as other people do,
And smiling without a license, too,
Battery, arson, theft and treason,
Blinking his eye with no good reason,
Mayhem, piracy, breach of trust,
Beating the customs, spreading dust –
Every crime and felony,
From truancy up to bigamy –
And he paid his fines and he went away,
To travel again that great Broadway,
And to be arrested from time to time
And charged with every heinous crime
Because – the reason is easily found;
He knocked out Jeff in the fifteenth round! [534]

The Indianapolis Motor Speedway turned down Johnson's request and refused to allow him to race there at the upcoming September automobile races. Blacks resented the Speedway's refusal to allow Johnson to participate. Indianapolis had a large black population. However, leading white citizens commended the decision.

Johnson instead asked to be allowed to engage in an exhibition race, but the directors also refused that request. "Johnson has been opposed on account of his color, barred from entering certain automobile races, including one in Indianapolis."[535]

The alleged Mrs. Jack Johnson was in town with fire in her eyes. "He can't run out on me. I've got the deeds to his house in Chicago in a safe deposit vault and I've got the key to the vault." She also had love letters from Johnson. One letter said, "With a million kisses I am now going to the ring to slip a sleeper over on that stiff, Philadelphia Jack O'Brien." Johnson

[534] *Freeman*, August 27, 1910.
[535] *Bulletin*, July 27, 1910; *Evening Post*, July 28, 1910; *Freeman*, August 20, 1910.

had left Hattie McLay in late 1909 and had been with Etta Duryea ever since.[536]

Johnson was making $3,500 per week in a 40-week theatrical tour, which would include Europe.

Johnson's brother, Charley Johnson, said Jack would not fight Langford unless and until he had beaten the top men whom Jack had defeated, including Burns, Ketchel, and Kaufman.[537]

JACK JOHNSON

Champion of the World

*His Statute 18 in. high fin-
ished in bronze*

An Ornament for every Negro
home as he is the first Negro admitted to be the best man in the
world, sent upon receipt of price
$2.50. Agents wanted in every
locality. Send $2.50 for outfit and
liberal terms.

The Champion Statuary Co

1535-41 Melrose St.. Chicago, Ill.

Freeman, July 30, 1910

Johnson turned down Hugh McIntosh's offer of $75,000 for a one-year tour which included three fights - with Sam Langford, Tommy Burns, and Bill Lang as his opponents. Johnson believed he could make more. He was making nearly that amount in vaudeville, without having to train or risk his title. Given how much money he had made and would be making, he wasn't desperate to fight, and could be patient about what offers he accepted.[538]

Reports were that the white woman whom Johnson currently called wife (Etta Duryea) never was married to him. His real wife was driven away from his Chicago home to make room for the present woman. The *New York Telegraph* thought Johnson should stop motoring around the streets with the new white woman, declaring that such an exhibition was subversive to the city's morals, conducive to race hatred, and should be the matter of police regulation. It said his real wife, though very light, had a trace of negro blood. This newspaper asked whether the moving pictures of the Jeffries fight were more vitiating than the spectacle of Johnson in real life parading with his white paramour through the streets in an automobile.[539]

As of August 1, race-car driver Barney Oldfield said he would accept Johnson's challenge to race him on the Brighton Beach track.

When asked if he would fight Langford, Johnson said, "I will if he puts up $20,000 as a side bet and some club will offer a large enough purse." Responding to Langford and/or his manager's claims that Sam knocked him down in their fight, Johnson said, "As for being knocked down, the only man who has ever knocked me down was Joe Choynski." Interestingly,

---

[536] *Bulletin,* July 28, 1910. Norman Pinder, the man who refused to buy wine for Johnson at Baron Wilkins' resort the previous spring and got a licking, also had Johnson served with a lawsuit he filed.

[537] *San Francisco Evening Post, Bulletin,* July 29, 1910; *Chicago Defender,* July 30, 1910.

[538] *Freeman,* July 30, 1910.

[539] *San Francisco Evening Post,* August 2, 1910, citing the *New York Telegraph.*

he left out Ketchel, unless of course Johnson threw himself down in that one.[540]

The *Evening Post* said Langford could help his case to fight Johnson by defeating Kaufman decisively. Regardless,

> Just whether two colored boxers would be able to attract a large enough crowd at Sydney to warrant McIntosh guaranteeing the fighters a big purse is doubtful. In this country, no matter how evenly matched or how clever the scrappers may be, the promoters have found it to be a risky undertaking to bring two colored boxers together.

However, Johnson would have to take Langford's challenge seriously if he beat Kaufman, given that Johnson had been singing Kaufman's praises.[541]

Langford took a big hit in the press when he pulled out of his scheduled bout with Al Kaufman. Just before the fight was to be held, he refused to fight unless the Philadelphia promoters guaranteed him $7,500 for the 6-round bout, regardless of result. Langford also refused to box Kaufman if the bout was delayed for one day. This "poor excuse" lost him many friends. Some said it was an act of cowardice. "Did Jack Johnson's repeated statements to the effect that Kaufman would surely whip Langford get Sammy's angora? It looks very much like it. The run-out will now give Johnson a chance to roast his colored nemesis." Sam's stock took a tumble.[542]

The *Post* said Langford would have been the real noise had he whipped Kaufman. His failure to fight Kaufman merely because the promoter refused to accede to his "exorbitant demands" caused some to call him "Hold-Up Sam" instead of "Beggar Sam." It seemed that Joe Woodman had played right into Johnson's hands. Still, Woodman thought a Johnson-Langford fight would be lucrative, and said that Johnson was resorting to subterfuge when he claimed there was no money in an all-colored fight.[543]

Johnson said Langford would not draw, and he did not think Sam could beat Kaufman or Ketchel anyhow, "and everybody knows neither of these men have a chance with me."

The *Freeman* said Langford had no business whatsoever in the ring with Johnson. "Jack outclasses him in every way in the world." Sam was too short and light and his punch would in no way affect Johnson, assuming he could land one. Johnson had 40 pounds of weight, several inches of height and reach, and was one of the most scientific as well as most powerful men in the world. "Langford can never become the man that Johnson is today,

---

540 *Boston Guardian, Freeman,* August 6, 1910.

541 *San Francisco Evening Post,* August 8, 1910.

On August 7, 1910 at Neuilly, France, Sam McVey and Battling Jim Johnson fought to a 15-round draw.

On August 10, 1910, Joe Gans, the old master, passed away as a result of tuberculosis.

542 *Evening Post,* August 11, 12, 1910.

543 *San Francisco Evening Post,* August 15, 16, 1910.

for the reason that Johnson has acquired a knowledge of ring generalship that few men have ever possessed." It also said, "It is now a settled fact that Sam Langford is in no way the real qualified opponent of Jack Johnson. Sporting men of the East will tell you in a hurry that Sam is too small, and he certainly is. ... Few men of the powers in science and strength combined that Jack Johnson now possesses are born in a generation."

The *Freeman* also opined that if Johnson took care of himself, it would be a long time before any man would be able to take the crown from his head. He was so much better than everyone else that the white race's only hope lay in the development of some unknown.

Johnson noted that legislators were attempting to kill boxing. "I have practically given up all hope of defending my title in this country. ... I don't care where they hold them as long as they offer purses which are worth training and fighting for. I still am firm in my assertion that I won't fight a long battle again for a year."[544]

Boxing said Johnson had been a first-class show-business headliner at Hammerstein's, attracting large crowds. Many thought no whites would pay to see a black man, but they did. "This proves for sure one of two things, either that the real American values the satisfaction of his curiosity above his race prejudice, or that he deems the successful man the god in the car to be run after, whether he be black or white in colour."[545]

Apparently, Hugh McIntosh had signed a Langford-Burns bout to take place in London for $25,000.[546]

Johnson told a *Boxing* writer,

I need not tell you that in America the racial question is very rampant just now. Our country taken from us is ruled by whites, and any sign of superiority on our part is regarded as a crime. They regard people of my colour as little better than dogs. Education does not count, and neither does refinement nor high breeding. Colour with them is everything. ... Here am I, a cultured man, fit to converse on any subject – from astronomy right down to ancient classics – tabooed by white individuals whom I regard, both as regards race and education, as my inferiors.

These people – these Christians – attend church, pray regularly, and yet pick out of the New and Old Testaments only those things which are agreeable to themselves. Worse than this, the very clergymen recognize that unless they pander to the popular taste they might as

[544] *Freeman*, August 13, 20, 1910. Johnson had returned to Chicago briefly for some business. He had decided not to go to England until April 1911.
[545] *Boxing*, August 13, 1910. Johnson left Chicago on August 14 for Cleveland, where he would give a boxing stunt.
[546] *Evening Post*, August 24, 1910.

well shut up shop. My blood boils as I think of these things, and only deep and solemn prayer calms me.[547]

On September 5, 1910 in Philadelphia, Al Kaufman unofficially won a 6-round no-decision bout against Bill Lang.

On September 6, 1910 in Boston, 170-pound Sam Langford won a clear 15-round decision over 190-200-pound Joe Jeannette in a fierce contest. Some said that defeating a respected heavier and taller fighter like Jeannette justified Langford's challenge to fight Johnson.

At her brother's home, Lucy Johnson, the champion's sister, got married to Otto Bowlden of Oklahoma City, a professional ball player for the Oklahoma City club. As a gift, Johnson gave his sister a check for $3,000.

The English kept talking about Bombardier Billy Wells, who they thought had a chance to defeat Johnson. The 6'3" 21-year-old had many fights in India while in the army and was impressive. Eugene Corri said, "I am quite confident that he is the coming man – the man to whom we can look to wrest the championship from Johnson."

In September 1910 in Boston, when Jack Johnson and Sam Langford met, Langford asked Johnson to put up his $20,000. Johnson replied, "Oh no, you put up and I am ready to cover it. I am the champion and not supposed to put up first." Langford: "Yes, you are the champion, but you said last night you would do so." Johnson: "To save any further argument on that, I will acknowledge I did say so last night, but I was a bit hasty. I had a good sleep since and I think differently now." The two went back and forth for a bit. Johnson said, "You know that a bout between two colored men would not be a drawing card…and for that reason I want the side bet."

Johnson had the superior negotiating power, because he was the champion and had something Langford wanted. Langford opined that Johnson was afraid to meet him. Johnson replied, "I met you once, Langford, and defeated you." Langford: "Yes you did, but I was only a child then." The truth was that Langford could not post the money.

Stanley Ketchel, who had boxed both, said Johnson would beat Langford easily. Speaking of Langford, Ketchel said, "I believe he is overrated. He hasn't got a ghost of a show with Johnson. I believe I could whip the Boston fighter easier than I could Burns." Stan said Burns would be the toughest fight for him.

A Paris promoter offered Johnson $20,000 to fight Joe Jeannette to a finish in Paris. Johnson did not think the offer was large enough for such a fight. "My theatrical contracts run for 30 weeks more, and in April I am going to Europe to fill more engagements."[548]

---

[547] *Boxing*, September 3, 1910.

[548] *Freeman*, September 17, 24, October 1, 1910.

On September 26, 1910 in Baltimore, Al Kaufman won a 6-round decision over Al Kubiak. On October 8, 1910 in Philadelphia, Al Kaufman won a 6-round no decision against Tony Ross.

On October 15, 1910 in Conway, Missouri, Stanley Ketchel was murdered by Walter A. Dipley, who shot him in the back, took Stan's money, and then fled with his girlfriend/wife Goldie Smith. Both Dipley and Smith were captured, tried, and convicted of murder in the 1st degree. Smith's conviction was overturned after she spent 17 months in prison. Dipley's life sentence was confirmed.

On October 25, 1910 at the Brighton Beach track in New York, Barney Oldfield defeated Jack Johnson in two consecutive 5-mile heats of auto racing in a best two out of three competition. Afterwards, Oldfield said,

> I raced Jack Johnson for neither money nor glory, but to eliminate from my profession an intruder who would have had to be reckoned with sooner or later. If Jeffries had fought Johnson five years ago, the white man would have won. ... I am glad if my victory over Johnson today will have any effect on the 'white man's hope' situation.[549]

The American Automobile Association later blacklisted Oldfield for racing Johnson without obtaining a sanction.[550]

Jack Johnson's impact was still being felt. A *Freeman* writer said, "From the racial standpoint, the victory of Johnson over Jeffries furnishes food for a wide range of thought. It helps the Negro to tell the world that opportunity is its greatest need in any avenue of life." Johnson was a racial asset and a powerful symbol in the sense that he showed what a black person could do if given the opportunity.[551]

On November 2 in Chicago, Johnson unintentionally got caught up in a labor dispute. Thousands of taxicab workers were striking. Johnson got into a non-union taxicab that drove past a crowd of striking union drivers, one of whom threw a brick through the window. It hit Johnson in the forehead, cutting him badly and stunning him for a few minutes.[552]

Hugh McIntosh reported that Tommy Burns had to postpone his December bout with Langford, owing to a twisted knee he suffered while playing in a lacrosse game.[553]

On November 10, 1910 in Joplin, Missouri, Sam Langford scored a KO2 over black Jeff Clark.

Abe Attell claimed that in order to get Jeffries to fight him, Johnson had agreed to throw the fight, but gave Jeff the double cross. Allegedly, John L. Sullivan also asserted that the fight was to have been crooked, but Johnson experienced a change of heart during the last 24 hours.

Jeffries branded these stories as lies. "Never from the moment that I signed articles in New York until I came into the ring at Reno was there any

---

[549] *Salt Lake Herald-Republican*, October 26, 1910; *Freeman*, November 5, 1910. Oldfield won either a $5,000 or $10,000 wager with Johnson.

[550] *Freeman*, December 24, 1910.

[551] *Freeman*, October 29, 1910.

[552] *San Francisco Call*, November 3, 1910.

[553] *El Paso Herald*, November 5, 1910; *Chicago Defender*, November 26, 1910.

understanding between Johnson and myself other than that the fight was to be decided strictly on its merits. Any man who speaks to the contrary tells a lie." He challenged those who claimed otherwise to prove it. Basically, the feeling was that they were engaging in rank speculation, and feeding off of rumor, as boxing folks often did and still do.

Jeffries did claim that he had been doped. "You may say for me that I am positive that I was doped some time during the last three days that I spent at Moana Springs. ... Whoever he or they were, their tracks were covered up so thoroughly that it is next to impossible to prove anything."

The *Freeman* opined that the only thing that ever would make fight fans believe Jeff's dope story would be for the guilty person to confess, if such a person existed. No one believed Fitzsimmons either when he claimed, after he lost the first time to Jeffries, that he was doped.[554]

In November 1910, while in Lawrence, Massachusetts, Jack Johnson was suffering from memory loss and depression. He told his wife to take his revolver, for something told him that he might do harm with it. On November 17, a Lowell doctor told Jack to stop stage work for a while and rest, for he was suffering from nervous prostration. Jack said, "I attribute my condition to overwork. I haven't had a rest since my fight with Jeffries. ... I'm going to take a long rest. I'm going to give up my world tour until I recover."

It might have been that the champ was suffering from a bad concussion, given that recently he was hit in the head with a brick. In his vaudeville performances, he was sparring 3 rounds with Walter Monahan, so perhaps he was not allowing his brain to heal.[555]

From New York, the National Negro Committee, speaking about the black race's condition in the U.S., said,

> Our people were emancipated in a whirl of passion, and then left naked to the mercies of their enraged and impoverished ex-masters. As our sole means of defense we were given the ballot. ... No sooner, however, had we rid ourselves of nearly two-thirds of our illiteracy...than this ballot...was taken from us by force and fraud. ...
>
> This attempt to put the personal and property rights of the best of the Blacks at the absolute political mercy of the worst of the Whites is spreading each day.
>
> Along with this has gone a systematic attempt to curtail the education of the Black race. Under a widely advertised system of 'universal' education, not one Black boy in three today has in the United States a chance to learn to read and write. The proportion of school funds due to Black children are often spent on Whites ...

---

[554] *Freeman*, November 19, 1910, January 28, 1911.
[555] *Chicago Broad Ax*, *New York Times*, November 19, 1910.

In every walk of life we meet discrimination, based solely on race and color…

We are, for instance, usually forced to live in the worst quarters. … When we seek to buy property in better quarters we are sometimes in danger of mob violence, or, as now in Baltimore, of actual legislation to prevent.

We are forced to take lower wages for equal work, and our standard of living is then criticized. Fully half the labor unions refuse us. …

A persistent caste proscription seeks to force us and confine us to menial occupations where the conditions of work are worst. …

A widespread system of deliberate public insult is customary, which makes it difficult, if not impossible, to secure decent accommodation in hotels, railway trains, restaurants and theaters, and even in the Christian church we are in most cases given to understand that we are unwelcome unless segregated.

Worse than all this is the willful miscarriage of justice in the courts. Not only have 3,500 Black men been lynched publicly by mobs in the last twenty-five years, without semblance or pretense of trial, but regularly every day throughout the South the machinery of the courts is used, not to prevent crime and correct the wayward among Negroes, but to wreak public dislike and vengeance and to raise public funds. This dealing in crime as a means of public revenue is a system well-nigh universal in the South.[556]

On November 19, 1910 in Paris, France, Sam McVey scored a KO21 over Battling Jim Johnson to become European champion. The two previously had fought to a 15-round draw in August.

Countering Jeannette manager Dan McKetrick's offer of $20,000 for a finish fight, Johnson's manager said the champion would accept a Jeannette fight if it was 20 rounds and Johnson was guaranteed $25,000.[557]

Despite some claims that he had offered more (or would), Hugh McIntosh actually had offered Johnson only $15,000 plus expenses to fight Langford, and he wanted Johnson to post that same amount as a performance guarantee. Langford manager Joe Woodman, who had a letter from McIntosh, confirmed the information.[558]

On November 25, 1910 in New York, Jack Johnson was arrested for assault and disorderly conduct. Allegedly, the previous month, on October 24 or 25, he had made an indecent proposition to Annette Cooper, a show girl, and then grabbed her wrists when she repulsed him. However, when

---

[556] *Chicago Broad Ax*, November 19, 1910.

[557] *Freeman*, November 26, 1910.

[558] *El Paso Herald*, November 5, 1910; *Chicago Defender*, November 26, 1910; quoting a letter from Hugh McIntosh published in Boston by Joe Woodman on November 25.

Cooper failed to appear in court the next day, on November 26, claiming she was ill and requesting that the case be continued for two weeks, the magistrate refused to hold the case over, and discharged Johnson.[559]

In the wake of Stanley Ketchel's death, the heir to the middleweight championship throne was in question. Joe Woodman said Langford was willing to meet any man in the world at 158 pounds and would bet $2,500. "In order to make certain that he can weigh in at 158 pounds, Langford stepped on the scales with his clothing on and weighed 174 pounds. ... Langford says it will be no trouble for him to make 158 pounds."[560]

Jack Johnson was investing in Chicago real estate. He had a cash balance in a local savings bank of nearly $165,000. Johnson said, "I will show you one prize fighter who never will end up broke."[561]

In early December, Tommy Burns pulled out of the Sam Langford fight, citing the injured knee he twisted some time ago playing lacrosse. Tom said he was retiring for good, for his knee no longer could stand hard training.[562]

The highest offer Johnson received from either French, British, or Australian promoters to fight either Langford or Jeannette was $20,000. "Johnson has repeatedly sneered at challenges from Jeannette and Langford and has been practically safe in so doing, as no American promoter has shown a desire to secure either match, but with real money hung up in Paris and London, Johnson, it appears, will be compelled to place himself finally on record one way or another." However, Johnson believed he was worth more, for he had just earned three to six times that amount from one fight.

Johnson came home to Chicago for a brief respite; for the continual monotony of one-night vaudeville stands all over the East Coast had worn him out. However, he said he would continue out West in January. He also had received several tempting offers from theatrical agencies in Europe. Jack said his pulse was between 82 and 84 beats per minute, not bad for being out of training.[563]

The *Freeman* said there was no good reason for thinking that McVey, Jeannette, or Langford could beat Johnson. However, in time, every champion eventually had to lose.

John L. Sullivan said the fight game was not dead, but was in critical condition. The one chance for its recovery was to find a young talent who could beat Johnson.

> This colored fellow isn't invincible, you know. He's a great fighter and I predicted two years ago he would beat Jeffries. ... But you know when a fellow gets to the top of his profession he falls into many temptations. He finds many who are willing to buy him a drink,

[559] *Salt Lake Herald-Republican*, November 27, 1910.
[560] *Freeman*, November 26, 1910.
[561] *Chicago Broad Ax*, December 3, 1910, quoting *Chicago Tribune*, December 3, 1910.
[562] *Spokane Press*, December 5, 1910.
[563] *Freeman*, December 10, 1910.
On December 6, 1910 in Boston, Sam Langford stopped Morris Harris in the 2nd round.

and he goes along for a year or two and thinks all the time he's as good as ever. Some day he'll put on the gloves and get into the ring against some clear-headed strong and well trained fellow with young blood running through his veins, and then he'll suddenly awake to the fact that his old activity and spirit have gone and he's bound to be beaten down.

Sullivan was speaking from experience.

The Jeffries-Johnson motion pictures had been displayed in various parts of the U.S., Canada, England, and Australia, but the profits were minimized by limited distribution, due to all of the political and legal opposition to them. The fact that Jeffries lost also dampened the interest in seeing the films. It turned out that Jeffries and Johnson had been wise to sell their motion picture interests before the fight.[564]

After seeing the Jeffries-Johnson fight films, a *Boxing* writer said he was surprised, feeling that the written reports had exaggerated how badly Jeff had been defeated. Jeffries rose from the final knockdown fairly quickly, and nonchalantly wiped the blood from his face. Jeff's boxing was more forceful and good than reported, and his ducking and footwork brisk. "In short, I saw none of the old-man movements attributed to Jeff." He was just beaten by the better man. Johnson boxed carefully, with the intention of wearing his man down. His strategy worked. "It certainly is not a pretty fight, but one continual clinch."[565]

Carl Morris of Oklahoma was an emerging white hope. He was a huge 6'4", 235-245-pound heavyweight. On December 20, 1910 in Sapulpa, Oklahoma, Morris stopped former champion Marvin Hart in 3 rounds.

Johnson said he would not fight Al Kaufman again for anything less than $25,000.[566]

On December 21, 1910 in a Pittsburg bar, Brooks Buffington, a white Southerner, shot and killed Robert Mitchell, a black man, after the two engaged in a racial debate over the fact that earlier that evening, Jack Johnson had seconded a white boxer, while the black opponent had a white cornerman. One report said Buffington actually had sought to kill Johnson, but the intoxicated man was not allowed to enter the arena where Johnson was, so, perhaps frustrated, he killed a Johnson admirer instead.[567]

At year-end 1910, the *Chicago Defender's* editor lamented,

> When in the last days of departing year we look backward and see the bodies of 200 heroes lynched and 5,000 innocent girls rushed into motherhood by our Southern white friends, we mourn and hide our faces in shame at a government, the greatest the world has ever seen, which would permit such crimes to be instituted in her domain. We

---

[564] *Freeman*, December 17, 1910.
[565] *Boxing*, December 17, 1910.
[566] *San Francisco Call*, December 23, 1910.
[567] *Washington Times*, December 21, 1910; *New York Times*, December 22, 1910.

look with shame upon our churches for not raising a dissenting voice; and we look with shame on American priests who at no time during a lynching have they tried to stop the mob or offer a prayer for the lynched. While others of the race rejoice and gloat over their success, we humbly beg God's mercy on the American government and its citizens.[568]

On January 1, 1911, Jack Johnson left his mother's home in Chicago. Allegedly, he had a disagreement with his mother over his white girlfriend Etta Duryea, whom for the past year Johnson had been calling wife. Earlier in 1910, Duryea had been divorced from her white husband Charles Duryea. Mrs. Tiny Johnson allegedly barred Etta from entering the home again. Johnson's devotion to Etta caused him to leave his mother and sisters, or so the story was told.

On January 10, 1911 in Boston, Sam Langford won a 12-round decision over Joe Jeannette. Sam dropped Joe in the 1st round with a left uppercut to the jaw, and thereafter, Langford gave him the beating of his life, punching him at will, winning every round.

On January 11, 1911 in London, Gunner Moir knocked out Bombardier Billy Wells in the 3rd round.

On or about January 18, 1911 in Pittsburg, Jack Johnson formally married Etta Duryea, whom he had been calling wife for some time.

Jack Gleason allegedly offered $50,000 for a Johnson-Kaufman fight. Johnson said, "I only hope it's true, for I don't know any easier way to make a pile of money." Still, Johnson looked upon Kaufman as the best heavyweight except himself. He said Kaufman could defeat Jeannette, McVey, and Langford.[569]

Johnson alleged that Carl Morris was developing his reputation on fake fights. He said a representative of an Oklahoma club recently visited and asked him to permit Walter Monahan, Johnson's white sparring partner, to lay down to Morris. Johnson also said that Mike Schreck told him in Pittsburg a few days ago that the reason his fight with Morris was postponed was because he refused to lie down.

Although colored folk wanted Johnson to keep the crown forever, some thought he should fight and not maintain the crown by default. However, "Johnson is not going to do the worrying, and he's not to be blamed a bit. His incontested victory is a splendid asset, and to take a chance jeopardizes it. While it is fairly true that he can whip anything standing on shoe leather, yet he takes a chance of being defeated every time he steps in the ring." The bottom line was that Johnson had worked long and hard to get where he was, and he was not going to risk what he had toiled to obtain unless he was paid very well.[570]

---

[568] *Chicago Defender*, December 31, 1910.
[569] *Freeman*, January 14, 21, 1911.
[570] *Freeman*, February 4, 1911.

During the first week of February 1911, Johnson appeared in Indianapolis at the Empire Theater. In the twice-daily performances of "The Rector Girls" Company, when Johnson appeared, the band played "Hail to the King." Jack then sparred 3 rounds with Walter Monahan and gave an exhibition of shadow boxing and bag punching.

After his stay in Indianapolis, Johnson headed to California with Monahan and Bob Moha, the Milwaukee welterweight.

Hugh McIntosh and Jimmy Britt allegedly offered Johnson $25,000 to fight the winner of Langford-Lang in London.[571]

W. W. Naughton said the overwhelming desire to locate a "paleface" capable of defeating Johnson caused some to overlook the fact that some of the best fighters in the world were black, including Langford, Jeannette, and McVey. "Comparison between the white and black will make it apparent that dusky-skinned heavyweights at present before the public are not inferior to the whites."[572]

Despite the fact that some international promoters wanted to see Johnson fight top black fighters, few American promoters wanted to see him defend against another black fighter. They and the fans wanted to see a white man recover the crown for the white race. If Johnson lost to a black fighter, it made no difference to whites, for the crown still would remain in black hands, a situation they wanted to correct.

On February 21, 1911 in London, England, Sam Langford defeated Bill Lang via 6th round disqualification. Despite having a big weight advantage, Lang was outclassed. Langford dropped him in the 2nd, 3rd, and 5th (twice) rounds. However, in the 6th round, when Lang was almost out, in a fast rally, either Lang decked Langford or Sam slipped down. While Sam was on the ground, Lang struck him heavily, leading to his disqualification.

At that point, Johnson said he was willing to fight Langford, but insisted on a $30,000 guarantee. He would not fight for a $30,000 purse to be split 60/40, which Hugh McIntosh had offered. Jack said,

> I do not understand McIntosh. He gave Tommy Burns £6,000, or $30,000 to box me in Australia, and I, who won the fight, received $5,000. I informed McIntosh some time ago that I would require as much as Burns received if I was wanted to defend my championship. Surely if he could afford to give Burns $30,000 in Sydney he can offer me an equal amount to box in a city like Paris or London.

---

[571] *Freeman,* January 28, February 11, 1911.

Against Monahan, Johnson mostly played defense, though he let out just a bit in the 3rd round to show what he could do if he wished.

On January 23, 1911 in London, Battling Jim Johnson, the colored heavyweight of Galveston, defeated Jewey Smith of South Africa in the 11th round when Smith retired owing to a twisted arm. Tommy Burns had stopped Smith in 5 rounds in 1908.

[572] *Freeman,* February 18, 1911, quoting W. W. Naughton in the *Cincinnati Enquirer.*

Regardless of economics, Johnson's opinion of Langford had not changed. "I still believe I can beat him easily."[573]

Following an exhibition of the Jeffries-Johnson fight films, an Indianapolis theater proprietor was arrested. However, a judge held that exhibition of the pictures was not unlawful under the city ordinance. It was no more unlawful to exhibit the pictures than it was for newspapers to publish the scenes which had transpired. The case was dismissed. The reels started going on March 6 and were in full blast thereafter.

On March 8, 1911 in London, Bombardier Billy Wells won a 20-round decision over Porky Dan Flynn. This proved to be significant, because on March 24, Flynn would win via 4th round disqualification over Gunner Moir, who had defeated Wells. Flynn had dominated Moir, who was disqualified for throwing Flynn down.

John L. Sullivan said Sam Langford had no chance to defeat Johnson. "Sam Langford is too small to ever expect to cope successfully with a man of Jack Johnson's size and skill. No little man is ever going to whip Johnson." Sullivan said Langford was wonderfully strong, but it would take a big man, at least as big as Johnson, and a clever one, with a terrific punch in either hand, to whip Johnson. "I don't think he is in sight just now."

When asked when he would fight again, Johnson said, "Any time that a suitable purse is hung up, and with any man." There had been talk of a Kaufman fight, but nothing definite had come of it. He was willing to fight whomever the promoters wanted, as long as he was well compensated.[574]

Johnson said McIntosh knew his price. "Now, if Langford thinks he can win the battle from me, let him do as I did, take the small bundle of coin and all the glory. I am not in need of money, and am not fussy about fighting, anyway, so if I fight it will be on my own terms." As champion, he was well aware of the fact that he had strong negotiating power. "I am wise to McIntosh. He is in partnership with Langford's manager, and they are going to promote fights in Paris. They can't ring me in. I'll have my own way or I won't fight."

Other than Kaufman, emerging white hopes included Carl Morris and Jack Lester. Morris was big, fast, and powerful, standing 6'4" and 240 pounds. Lester stood over 6 feet and weighed 210 pounds. The second tier included men like Jim Stewart, who weighed 220, but was beaten badly by Jim Barry and also stopped by Jack Sullivan. Barry held victories over Gunboat Smith and Sandy Ferguson, but had been beaten by Kaufman and Langford. Bombardier Wells had been stopped by Gunner Moir, whom Burns had defeated. Gunboat Smith had been stopped by Jim Barry and Joe Willis.

On March 16, 1911 in New York, Joe Jeannette had all the best of a 10-round no-decision bout against Jim Barry.

---

[573] *Freeman*, March 4, 1911.
[574] *Freeman*, March 11, 18, 25, 1911.

On March 25, 1911 in San Francisco, Jack Johnson pled guilty to speeding and was sentenced to 25 days in jail. Johnson admitted that he had been traveling at 62 miles per hour. An auto dealer, who was trying to sell a car to a white man, was about to be passed by Johnson. The dealer's prospective client said, "I'm a southerner, and if you let that fellow pass you, I'll not buy your car." So the dealer raced Johnson. That got them both pinched.

Justifying the lengthy jail sentence, the judge cited Johnson's lengthy record of speeding infractions. Jack started his jail term on March 28. Subsequently, the judge agreed to reduce his sentence slightly and release him on Easter morning, Sunday April 16, but then, for whatever reason, the judge had a change of heart and made Johnson spend the full 25 days in jail. This was the second time that Johnson had spent nearly a month of his life in jail; the first being when he was arrested for fighting Joe Choynski.[575]

The black-owned *Chicago Broad Ax* opined that the jail term might do Johnson good, "to learn that he must have at least some respect for the laws of this country and not to feel just because he has plenty of money that he can just for the pleasure of the thing run his automobile at full speed at all times."[576]

However, others said the sentence was excessive in the extreme, for Johnson had victimized no one, the sentence was disproportionate to the crime, and was just a way the white man was trying to attack and punish Johnson for beating Jeffries, and to weaken him by feeding him jail food.[577]

Johnson said the judge had treated him unfairly.

> I think I was stung just because Judge Tredwell wanted to get a little notoriety out of me. They have never put any one else in jail for speeding. ... [Judge Treadwell] told me that if I would plead guilty he would fine me. ... He promised to release me on Easter Sunday. When Saturday came, although I had a parole paper signed by the district attorney and the sheriff, the judge refused to sign it.

When leaving San Francisco, heading home to Chicago, Johnson was asked, "Are you going to be good now, Jack?" Johnson replied, "I think I will drive as fast as ever. I have never hurt any one." However, Jack was not interested in returning to California, for boxing or for any other reason.

On March 28, 1911 in Sapulpa, Oklahoma, Carl Morris knocked out Mike Schreck in the 6th round.

On April 1, 1911 in Paris, France, for a $10,000 purse, Sam Langford and Sam McVey battled to a 20-round draw. Many thought Langford deserved the verdict. Still, Johnson had dominated McVey three times.[578]

---

[575] *Freeman,* April 1, 8, 1911.
[576] *Chicago Broad Ax,* April 1, 1911.
[577] *San Francisco Call,* April 23, 1911, quoting the *Wisconsin Weekly Defender,* a black newspaper.
[578] *Freeman,* April 8, May 6, 1911.

Hugh McIntosh offered Johnson $25,000, win, lose, or draw, if he would fight Kaufman or Langford, but Johnson responded that he must have $30,000, the same amount McIntosh had paid Burns. McIntosh was waiting to see how Langford-McVey had come out financially before making a counter proposition.[579]

Speaking about Johnson, Joe Choynski said,

> Jack has one physical gift that makes him hard to beat in the ring. The darkey carries his weight high and rides a foe all around the ring, using his weight on him, thus tiring out his rival. Until there is developed a man as big, as powerful as John, who can play the same game there is a slim chance of the sable hued hitter being dethroned from his high perch. Johnson is also most skillful at the art of blocking and shoving off. Has marvelous strength in his fore arms.[580]

Staunch slavery advocate Senator Ben Tillman was suffering from brain trouble, and his mind was decaying. "Tillman was the monster who once incited mobs which caused maddened, sweating men to abuse the golden rule as imps do in the lowest depths of hell with all its iniquity." Yet, the *Chicago Defender* granted, "After all his rage and after all his vilification of the race and all that, great credit is given him for being a man to fight out in the open and not like the Northern assassin."[581]

On April 24, 1911 in London, Bombardier Billy Wells knocked out Iron Hague in the 6th round to win the National Sporting Club's British heavyweight title.

On May 5, 1911 in Kansas City, Missouri, Jim Flynn knocked out Al Kaufman in the 10th round. This was a huge upset victory for Flynn, for many, including Johnson, had considered Kaufman the best of the white hopes. This victory once again put Flynn on the map as a contender.

On May 15, 1911 in New York, Jack Johnson was cited for driving his auto too slowly, at 5 miles per hour, and for having Chicago plates. Johnson noted that they pinched him for going too fast and for going too slow. "Next thing somebody'll arrest me fur bein' a brunette in a blonde town. Ef I goes fast they arrests me, and now it seems like ef I go slow they does the same. White men, whut's the trouble now?" However, the magistrate dismissed the charges.[582]

Speaking of the Jeffries fight and Jeff's claims of being doped, Johnson said,

> All his talk about him being doped is a flimsy excuse to set himself right with the public. ... He was in the pink of condition, and all those who knew him intimately said so before the fight.

[579] *Boxing*, April 8, 1911.
[580] *Pittsburgh Press*, April 14, 1911.
[581] *Chicago Defender*, April 22, 1911.
[582] *New York Evening World*, May 15, 17, 1911; *New York Times*, May 16, 1911.

The kind of dope he was full of was FEAR! He was scared to death. I always knew he wasn't game, because he spent so much time telling others what a yellow streak I had, and the man who does that is always a quitter. ...

As soon as Jeff saw that he had a hard fight on he began to stall; in the clinches he held on. ... It turned out to be the softest fight I ever had. I was only surprised at the ease with which I won.[583]

Set to exhibit in England, Johnson said he would fight Bombardier Billy Wells if guaranteed $30,000. He wanted the same amount for Langford or Jeannette. He hoped that when he returned to America that a white hope would have been discovered who could give him a good fight.[584]

Fighting Face That Scared Jeffries Into Defeat

Freeman, February 11, 1911

---

[583] *Boxing*, May 29, 1911.
[584] *Evening World*, June 5, 1911.

CHAPTER 13

Bombardier Billy Wells and the British Empire's Color Line

On June 6, 1911, Jack Johnson, accompanied by his white wife Etta Duryea Johnson, his black chauffeur, white trainer, and one white and one black sparring partner, sailed from New York for England on the German steamer *Kronprinz Wilhelm*. The trip's main objective was to make money in theatrical engagements at English music halls. However, Johnson said if he was offered $30,000, he would fight a bear. When asked, "Will you fight Langford?" Johnson replied, "He ain't no bear. He's a wild cat."[585]

Johnson landed at Plymouth, England on June 12, 1911.

When he arrived in London at Paddington station, the cheering crowd was so large, dense, and frantic to get a chance to shake his hand; it required the police to assist Johnson and his wife through.

Johnson was booked to see King George's coronation. He said, "I'm going to see King George try on his new hat."

Johnson's jovial good nature and his flow of stories quickly made a decided hit with all those whom he met. Jenkins, the theatrical manager in charge of Jack's tour of the music halls, was delighted.[586]

---

[585] *Evening World,* June 6, 1911; *Freeman,* June 17, 1911. While en route, in the ship's gymnasium, Johnson gave a boxing exhibition with his sparring partners. The passengers greatly enjoyed it, and showed no race prejudice.
[586] *Manchester Guardian,* June 13, 1911; *Freeman,* July 1, 1911.

The *Defender* said, "Perhaps the reason why Theodore Roosevelt condemned prize fighting in America is best described from the lionization of Mr. J. Arthur Johnson in England. ... When the black world laughs the white world cries. ... But sport has done its holy work; it has demonstrated that black is the hard chalk and white is the soft cheese."

The Jeffries-Johnson moving pictures were running at full blast in London.[587]

On June 22, 1911, Jack Johnson attended the coronation of King George V and Queen Mary.[588]

The English magazine, *Boxing*, said Johnson was totally unlike the average man's idea of a pugilist or a black man.

> He is a man well worth meeting – and studying, too, at that, for the simple reason that even a brief acquaintance with him at once disabuses your mind of numerous prejudices which you first imbibed with your mother's milk, and have since sedulously cultivated by the study of much expert opinion from ethnological and education authorities so called.

> In the first place, Johnson belongs to a race which is frequently asserted to be only partially developed from our animal ancestors. All the apologists for the ill-treatment of coloured men and women by white lords of creation have always insisted that the black man was, and is, a brute, and must be treated as such.

> In the second, Johnson is a man of comparatively humble origin, who went through a long series of hardships in his youth, and who at many times during his career has known what hunger, thirst, and the lack of a roof to cover him mean in reality. ...

> For Jack Johnson in the flesh is really a merry, unaffected, shrewd, and likeable man. He will deliver himself of his views on life in a carefully-reasoned, philosophic fashion which affords instant proof that there is not only plenty of brain inside that shaven skull of his, but that brain has also undergone careful cultivation.

> He is a consummately cool man, indifferent to danger, and yet in many ways as simple almost as a child; kind-hearted to a degree, sentimental of course – like most coloured folk – wonderfully humorous, especially in a dry vein, and positively a really charming host.

> Musical taste is almost universally allowed to be convincing evidence of a refined disposition, and Johnson is not only a great lover of

[587] *Chicago Defender*, June 17, 1911.
On June 16, 1911 in Winnipeg, Canada, Sam Langford won a 10-round no-decision against Tony Caponi.
[588] *Manchester Guardian*, June 23, 1911.

classical music, but also a really good executant himself on his favourite instrument, the bass viol. He might even earn a decent living as a musician were he not able to collect a much better one with the gloves.

Jack preferred talking about most anything but fighting, but would talk about boxing if pressed. He delighted in motor-driving, horse-racing, swimming, athletics, and books. Johnson's wife was an excellent pianist.[589]

The champ said if a challenger sufficiently proved himself worthy, there would be great demand for a fight, which meant that a promoter would be able to offer Johnson what he wanted. It was up to the challengers to garner sufficient public demand.

Johnson said he once put up a $5,000 side-wager to bind a match with Langford, Kaufman, or Ketchel, but the only one who had the nerve to cover it and fight was Ketchel.

> Now to settle this tiresome controversy, let me say that if any responsible promoter in America, England or France hangs up a suitable bunch of coin and there is no interference I will fight Langford under any conditions Woodman may name. ... But I'd rather box with a white man because that's where the interest is, and also the money.

Johnson mentioned possibly fighting the winner of Jim Flynn vs. Carl Morris. Although Johnson had stopped Flynn back in 1907, "they tell me he has improved a lot. He must have shown better form to have stopped Kaufman the way he did. If Morris can put Flynn away in a hurry he'll look like the only real white heavyweight in the world, and just say that I'll give him a match just as soon as he is ready."[590]

The *Freeman* noted the irony of the fact that Jeffries had begun his career by stopping a black man, but ended it by being stopped by one. Regardless of the impact the latter fight had on his legacy, the fact was that he got paid mighty well for the beating he received. Similarly, no one could fault Johnson for wanting to get paid handsomely for taking risks as well.

In July, it was announced that Johnson had signed to fight a boxer named Patrick Curran in early August in Dublin, Ireland, for $25,000, plus 45% of the gate after the purse and expenses had been paid going to the winner, with the remaining 55% to be divided equally between Johnson and his manager, Tom Flanagan. This offer made no sense unless Johnson and his manager were self-promoting the bout, or the promoter was looking to make money with the film rights, or the terms were reported incorrectly.[591]

Also in July, it was announced that Johnson was going to fight England's champion Bombardier Billy Wells in England for a guaranteed

---

[589] *Boxing,* June 24, 1911.
[590] *Freeman,* July 1, 1911.
[591] *Freeman,* July 15, 1911. Johnson was said to be weighing 245 pounds.

purse of $30,000, win, lose, or draw. Johnson's demands were met, so he took the fight. Wells weighed about 190 pounds.

Other potential matches being discussed for Johnson were Sam McVey in Paris in November or December, Bill Lang in Sydney on Easter 1912, and possibly Bill Squires or Jack Lester.[592]

Johnson was going to fight whoever made him the most money. If two men generated the same purse offers, then logically, Johnson was going to fight the one who presented the least risk to his title. If someone wanted to win the title badly enough, they had to make it worth Johnson's while, and perhaps take less in order to obtain the title shot, just as Johnson did with Burns. Or they would have to put up a sufficiently large side bet.

Johnson had a lot of money, so he was not desperate to fight. Plus, he was making easy money with vaudeville appearances. The reason he made that money was because he was champion. Hence, there was little incentive to risk the title without a very large guarantee. He was following in the footsteps of the champions who came before him, all of whom made easy money between fights. It would not be easy to convince him to fight again for less than a very tempting offer, particularly when he had just earned over $100,000 from his last fight. Once a man has fought for big money, it can be hard to convince him to fight for a much smaller amount.

Johnson was training on the outskirts of London for his August 5 fight in Dublin with Petty Officer Curran, the Irish champion. However, for whatever reason, the Curran fight was called off. Still, Johnson was supposed to fight Wells in September.[593]

In late July or early August, for a short period of time, Johnson gave nightly exhibitions inside a large dance hall at Magic City amusement park in Paris, just east of the Eiffel Tower. He even sparred with then welterweight Georges Carpentier.

On August 1, 1911 in New York, which on July 26 had legalized boxing with the passage and signing of the Frawley Act, 190-pound Joe Jeannette fought 200-pound Tony Ross to an unofficial 10-round newspaper draw.[594]

Johnson said the English people treated him very well. "Johnson seems to be very popular in England – much more so than in the United States." Jack said he even would consider making England his home. He did not like how he was treated in America on account of his race. "What has America done for me? Has it ever given me a square deal? Did it give me a shout when I won? Not on your life." He was even quoted as saying that he would never take up a musket for the United States.

The question was whether Johnson was just playing to his hosts, or genuinely meant what he said. Another question was whether the good

---

[592] *San Francisco Call,* July 16, 1911; *Freeman,* July 29, 1911. Johnson was demanding a minimum guaranteed purse of $25,000 for everyone but Langford, for whom he said he needed to be guaranteed $30,000, and Sam would have to put up a $10,000 side bet.
[593] *Freeman,* August 5, 1911.
[594] *New York Sun,* August 2, 1911.

treatment he was receiving was just the honeymoon phase for a famous athlete who was just visiting. The *Freeman* cautioned that the race struggle knew no national boundaries; something Johnson soon would learn.

Americans were upset with Johnson for making what they called unpatriotic remarks. Perhaps to garner favor and distinguish himself, Sam Langford responded by saying that he was a loyal U.S. citizen.

Subsequently, Tom Flanagan, Johnson's manager, denied the reported interview in which Johnson was "alleged to have declared against America and for England."

BOMBARDIER WELLS, BRITAIN'S "WHITE HOPE."

The Jack Johnson vs. Bombardier Billy Wells fight was set to be held in England in late September. "Wells is by far the best boxer and the most promising fighter that the country has produced for many years." However, "It is regarded as tantamount to professional suicide for him to meet Johnson at this stage of his development." Wells had been out of the army for only 18 months, and although he had improved a great deal, was clever for a big man, had a good punch in either hand, and was game, he still was relatively inexperienced. However, Johnson was guaranteed $30,000, so he agreed, and Wells wanted to fight Johnson.

On August 15, 1911 in New York, before a crowd of 5,000 spectators, 170-pound Sam Langford stopped Philadelphia Jack O'Brien in the 5th round.[595]

Sizing up a Johnson vs. Langford matchup, Bob Fitzsimmons said Johnson had better defense, though Langford could hit just as hard, and it was a toss-up regarding ring knowledge. He seemed to think that Johnson's greater height, reach, and weight might prove too much, though it was uncertain whether Jack could stand up under Sam's body blows.[596]

On August 24, 1911 in New York, Sam Langford stopped Tony Ross in the 6th round. Ross had a weight advantage of almost 35 pounds, but still received a severe beating.[597]

Demonstrating that race relations were not improving in the U.S., Georgia Governor Hoke Smith, who was President Grover Cleveland's

---

[595] *Freeman*, August 5, 12, September 2, 1911. Johnson would train at the Norfolk Arms.

[596] *Pittsburg Press*, August 19, 1911.

[597] *Freeman*, September 2, 1911. Langford dropped Ross in the 4th round. Tony came back strong in the 5th, but then in the 6th round, a right uppercut to the chin staggered Ross, and then a left to the jaw sent him down and out.

former Secretary of the Interior and also Georgia's future U.S. Senator, and the former publisher of the *Atlanta Journal*, whose fostering of racial animosity had led to riots, spouted off inflammatory racial rhetoric and encouraged and signed into law bills designed to disfranchise and deny blacks the vote so as to give the white man the ability to control government under all circumstances. He did not believe that blacks were citizens, but rather simply a "debauching influence" that reaches "the man who uses the ballot." Governor Smith said, "The true policy in the United States should be the development of the white race, with no mixture in matters of government by the yellow, the brown or the black races." He believed white men must rule even where blacks outnumbered them, as was the case in Georgia. "[W]e made it lawful to keep 200,000 Negroes from registering and voting, and only permitted 10,000 to register. ... The Negro has been permanently eliminated from politics in Georgia."

The *Chicago Defender* lamented the fact that blacks had to pay taxes to support white men who spent the money to benefit only white men. The spirit of white rule had sunken so deep into the hearts of white Southern citizens such that "some of them count it a privilege to insult a Negro anywhere and in any place." It opined, "The blood of the soldiers that was spilt in the Civil War ought not to be spilt in vain. The Negro cannot protect himself unless he is given a fair chance. He must have the ballot."[598]

In late August in London, Jack Johnson gave a sparring exhibition at Earl's Court in London, and thousands watched him train. He then returned to Paris to exhibit there again.

Although odds on Wells started at 20 to 1, the odds had dropped down to 5 to 1. Lance Corporal Wells' supreme confidence was infectious to some gamblers.

Johnson was receiving 20% of the gate receipts for his exhibitions, with all expenses paid, so he continued exhibiting as long as possible before buckling down to intense training for the Wells fight. He expected to train for five weeks for Wells.

Apparently, in August, Johnson had signed a one-year contract with Hugh McIntosh to begin October 31, for a guaranteed $125,000, which would include fights in Australia against whomever McIntosh selected, including Sam McVea, Sam Langford, Bill Lang, or Jack Lester. Supposedly, Johnson was next going to fight in Australia on December 25.[599]

There were reports that Johnson's white wife was being treated for nervous prostration in Paris.[600]

---

[598] *Chicago Defender*, September 2, 1911.

[599] *Freeman*, September 2, 1911, *Rock Island Argus*, August 16, 1911; *Hawaiian Star*, August 25, 1911. Since his last loss, a 1909 LKOby49 to Jeannette, McVea had been undefeated in 19 bouts, with 16 wins (including victories over Jim Barry, Fred Drummond, Al Kubiak, Jim Stewart, Battling Jim Johnson, and George Rodel) and 3 draws (D30 Jeannette, D15 Battling Jim Johnson, and D20 Sam Langford).

[600] *Freeman*, September 9, 1911. Some estimated Johnson was weighing 245-250 pounds.

Before his upcoming bout with Joe Jeannette, Sam Langford said, "Jeannette ain't human. I'd rather Johnson 20 rounds than Jeannette 10."[601]

On September 5, 1911 in New York, before nearly 8,000 spectators, Sam Langford unofficially won the 10-round newspaper decision against Joe Jeannette. Still, Joe put up a game and clever fight, giving Langford all he could handle. Some said the fight was a draw, for on scientific points, Jeannette won, landing three to one, but Langford landed the harder blows, hurting and dropping Jeannette on several occasions. However, Jeannette was one tough cookie, not easily subdued by anyone, and fought back well all the time, landing a lot of good clean blows of his own. As a result, some said the fight dropped Sam's stock and did not strengthen his claim for a fight with Johnson. One writer said Langford would be no match for Johnson.[602]

In early September, less than a month away from the Wells fight, Johnson was training at the Pelican Club in Paris. Also, twice a week, on Wednesdays and Sundays at 4:30 p.m. at Magic City, Johnson was giving 3-round exhibitions with Bob Armstrong, amongst others. Jack did not appear to be in very good shape. He was slower, less supple, and very much overweight, carrying a "superabundance of tallow."[603]

Every night at 10:30 p.m., Johnson sparred with Bob Armstrong and Monte Cutler, and conducted other miscellaneous training activities.

On September 9 at Magic City, a crowd of at least 250 people watched Johnson train. "Kid Cotton could not stand more than 4 rounds before Johnson's mighty punches."

That evening, welterweight Georges Carpentier also sparred with the champ.

There was something strangely prophetic in the picture that Johnson and Carpentier afforded in the ring together – a world's champion in the being, and an embryo laurel-wearer; the present and future generation; what is and what may be.

---

[601] *Pittsburg Press*, September 2, 1911.

[602] *Freeman*, September 16, 30, 1911. A reporter who called the fight a draw said Jeannette outpointed Langford by a large margin in the last 4 rounds and had the better of the 3rd round as well. Langford won the 1st, 4th, 5th, and 6th, with the 2nd being even. Jeannette was the better man at long range. However, Joe was dropped in the 1st, 4th, and 10th rounds, more due to slips than to the glancing blows. Sam gave his weight as 169 pounds, while Jeannette said he was 180 pounds. Both appeared heavier than they admitted.

Another account said in the 1st round, Langford dropped Jeannette for an instant. Joe withstood terrible body blows and jabbed away at the face with his left. He landed several rights squarely on Sam's jaw. In the 2nd, Jeannette landed a right and Langford went to the floor. In the 4th, Joe staggered Sam with a right uppercut, but Langford landed a left to the body and right to the jaw and Jeannette dropped. Several times thereafter, Sam had Joe in a bad way, but Jeannette was fast on his feet, clever with his hands, and outboxed Langford constantly, sending Sam's head back continually with jabs. Both were bleeding, cut, and bruised. Joe beat up Sam in the 8th. Langford's left eye was closed and his mouth was cut badly. He kept running into hard left jabs.

[603] *Boxing*, September 9, 1911.

Although 6 stone lighter than his partner, Carpentier showed that in science he was well up to academic form, and but for the difference in avoirdupois might stand more than a passing chance with the burly title-holder. Carpentier has a long way to travel before getting to the highest rung of the fistic ladder.

Boxing said Johnson had been fortunate to meet many of his foes past their primes or before their primes, or they weren't very good, or they were much smaller. Johnson got Fitz when he was a goner, although ironically "it turned on the first rays of popularity around Johnson." "Johnson is a fortunate being. Such a man as Tom Sharkey in his prime might have put the extinguisher on the present world champion's career before it had even had time to flicker its first ray." Of course, Sharkey drew the color line.[604]

For the upcoming title fight, Johnson would earn $30,000 and Wells $10,000, regardless of the fight's result. The picture rights had been sold to the Barker Motion Picture Company for $100,000. Heavyweight championship boxing films were big business.

The motion picture contract contained interesting incentives. If Johnson won, he would not receive any royalties. However, if he lost the fight, he would earn a 33 1/3% royalty. This caused some to speculate that Johnson might throw the fight to make more money. However, the point of the term was that if he lost, it would cost him valuable contracts that he could earn only as champion, so this would compensate him in the event of a loss.

The *Freeman* did not think Johnson would throw a fight. "The Negro knows what honor is; he loves it, and if he has sufficient means to sustain himself he will never be guilty of selling out. Johnson is very proud, and for his life would do nothing wrong along the line suggested. He has money. He only needs honor and respect."

Johnson was a diplomat. While in England, he praised everything English, and while in Paris, he praised everything French. He told the Parisians that after he disposed of Wells, McVey, and Langford, he would retire and live in France.

> There is no present prospect of any one licking me. ... Bombadier Billy hasn't got a ghost of a chance with me. Then I am going with Hugh McIntosh to Australia where I will lick McVey and Langford. I expect little trouble from either one of the pair. ...
>
> After defeating the last of these three men my theatrical engagements will keep me busy for some time. Finishing with the stage, I am coming back here to Paris, announce my retirement from the ring and open a big gymnasium.

After returning to London, Johnson saw moving pictures of Wells. Jack said, "Wells might not be so easy after all. He seems pretty husky and exceedingly fast, and it looks as though I will have to fight hard to win."

---

[604] *Boxing,* September 16, 1911.

However, many reporters disagreed, feeling that Johnson had far too much class and experience for Wells.[605]

The *London Times* said that while in England, Johnson had avoided the ridiculous braggadocio so often heard from many transatlantic boxers. He also never made the mistake of belittling his opponents. "He is popular, and has so far deserved his popularity."

The *Times* opined that with the possible exception of Gunner Moir, Johnson was the strongest living pugilist. Even Jeffries could not outwrestle him in the clinches. "He has a trick of knuckling-down the upper arm-muscles of an opponent, which is worthy of the cleverest exponent of ju-jitsu." He annoyed opponents with such clutches, and also adroitly used his tongue with bitter-sweet taunts, uttered in a purring voice with an infantile smile that caused foes to lose their temper.

The characteristic feature of Johnson's style was subtlety, speed without haste, and unerring judgment of distance, which made him an artist. Some could not appreciate his tactics because they were so subtle that they were veiled in obscurity. Yet he was very effective. They said he did not have a punch, but that was because they did not see how the shifting of his weight from one foot to the other supplied all the force required for the leisurely lightning hooks and jabs. His subtle blows to useful spots did more to break down an opponent's resisting powers than a more spectacular punch. For the most part, he was defensive, allowing opponents to do the bulk of the leading, preferring to counter, usually landing. His favorite counter was a right uppercut that came from nowhere, with jarring effectiveness. He protected his body well with the use of his arms and elbows.

Johnson was a fast man, who could run 100 yards in 10.8 seconds or less, and might have been a sprinter.

Billy Wells was quick with his feet and hands, had a long reach, and accurate and powerful blows which came out easily, with good timing. He had a nice long left jab.

The *Times* regretted that Wells was fighting Johnson before he had come to his full strength and experience. However, it also said that Wells was the speediest and most skillful of the many "white man's hopes."

The fight had been moved to October 2, to be held in the Empress Hall, Earl's Court, London. The match was attracting a lively amount of interest, including from professed critics of the sport.[606]

Despite claims that race prejudice was not as great in England as in the U.S.; a *Freeman* writer feared that such was not true entirely. "If Johnson wins, I am very much afraid that prejudice will come up a bit in England. Even that fairly fair country does not care to have a black-a-moor putting it over Englishmen, the very lords of the fighting business in all respects. I

[605] *Freeman*, September 16, 1911.
[606] *London Times*, September 12, 1911.

may be mistaken in this, but we shall see what we shall see. Kindly watch the prediction." It turned out that this writer was onto something.[607]

With the Johnson vs. Wells fight looming large, race, religion, and politics coalesced and garnered momentum to prevent the bout. During September, the Regent's Park Chapel's Reverend F. B. Meyer, a Baptist secretary of the National Free Church Council, a coalition of churches in England, in the name of religion began a crusade against the scheduled October 2 Johnson-Wells contest, as well as its reproduction and exhibition via cinematograph films, saying it would be bloody and degrading. Specifically referenced was the fact that it was a white vs. black fight. Meyer urged Winston Churchill, the Home Secretary, to prevent the fight.

On September 13, London City Council chairman Edward White sent a letter to W. H. Bond, the Earl's Court Exhibition, Ltd.'s licensee, strongly urging that the Johnson-Wells contest scheduled to be held there had to be prevented, and threatening that if the show was not stopped that the location's license might be endangered when it came up for renewal. Noted was the fact that the council had received a resolution passed unanimously at the meeting of the Wesleyan Methodist Church's Second London District's Synod, emphatically protesting against the fight. The City Council already was on record with its opinion that public exhibitions of the Jeffries-Johnson motion pictures were undesirable. "Bearing in mind the very widespread feeling of disgust which the Johnson and Jeffries contest in America caused in this country, I feel bound to add my personal view that if the proposed contest takes place at the Earl's Court Exhibition it may very seriously imperil the renewal of the licence by the Council in November next."

The Earl's Court directors responded that they had nothing to do with the contest other than leasing the Empress Hall to the promoters. Legally, it was impossible for them to take steps to stop the contest, for if they did, the promoters then would be within their rights to enter suit against the Earl's Court, Limited, for damages.

James White, one of the promoters, said, "Boxing contests take place in London every week during the winter, and no efforts are made to stop them, so why should this one stop? The law will not be infringed in the slightest degree, and absolute order will be maintained throughout the building. The police authorities will be invited to be present."[608]

In America, the *Freeman* reported that Reverend Meyer had "protested that prize fighting was demoralizing and brutal and also that it would embitter the feeling of the white people against the Negroes in America, South Africa and India." Home Secretary Winston Churchill was looking into the fight's legality. The promoters said they would not be deterred by ignorance, prejudice, and misconception.[609]

---

[607] *Freeman*, September 16, 1911.
[608] *London Times, London Daily Mail*, September 14, 15, 1911.
[609] *Freeman*, October 7, 1911.

Reverend Meyer and the National Free Church Council said they were not attacking the art of self-defense generally, but argued that this particular fight would be a brutal match and not self-defense. Meyer claimed that the Reno fight had attracted a horde of profligate people, there was much gambling, and the pictures were banned.

The Earl's Court Press Manager questioned the London City Council's jurisdiction over the matter, saying,

> The only distinction between the Johnson-Wells contest and others was that this one might conceivably be complicated by the colour question. It might be urged that Imperial considerations rendered it undesirable that such a contest should take place at all. If that were so, the matter was for the Home Secretary and not the London City Council.[610]

The National Free Church Council was urging ministers in England to speak out against the fight from their pulpits and arouse the national conscience against the spectacle. The Johnson-Wells fight was denounced in countless sermons in London.[611]

The London weekly *Observer* supported the bout's prohibition, saying, "We think that there are objections which may be legitimately taken to the exhibition, and its subsequent display at the music halls, and should not be sorry to see it prohibited." Its objection had nothing to do with boxing's purported brutality, for it did not believe boxing was brutal. Quite the contrary, it believed boxing was a fine physical and moral exercise. "We do, however, think that the great publicity given to the heroes of these events has a tendency to cause the youth of the realm to follow after false gods. Estimable a darkey as Mr. Jack Johnson may be – and, we believe, is – we do not want him as a popular hero." The fact was that even the English were uncomfortable with the thought of a black man defeating their white champion, for such an occurrence had symbolic value beyond boxing.[612]

Members of Parliament, metropolitan mayors, members of city and county councils, and the clergy overwhelmingly opposed the fight. Alderman A. Shirley Benn, a member of parliament and the London County Council, said,

> I am strongly in favour of the London County Council doing everything in its power to prevent boxing contests between white men and negroes. My objection is based not on any dislike to boxing pure and simple, but on the effect on the minds of negroes of contests such as the one to which you refer.

[610] *London Times*, September 16, 1911.
[611] *London Daily Mail*, September 16, 1911. *Freeman*, October 7, 1911.
[612] *Observer*, September 17, 1911.

The Southwark mayor said, "I think boxing is good sport, but such contests as suggested between Johnson and Wells do not meet with my approval."

Reverend Meyer said, "At this time we ought to bring the races of the world together rather than increase the bitterness of the antagonism between white and black."

One reverend who opposed the opposition said, "Why all this fuss? There are so many real evils to be got rid of that it seems a pity to waste energy on matters of this sort." A Lord who supported the bout said those who did not approve of the fight were under no obligation to witness it.

James White, the contest's promoter, said of Reverend Meyer,

> I make him the following sporting offer: If he can prove there will be more brutality in this contest than in any of the contests being staged nightly at all the boxing halls throughout London and the provinces, including England's premier club, I will cancel this contest, though it would mean serious financial loss to me.

He also said that he would stop the bout if Meyer would agree to indemnify him from loss.[613]

White said the contest would take place, so far as he was concerned. All of the seats in the Empress Hall had been booked. At least 10,000 would witness the contest. White "ridiculed the idea of a match between Johnson and Wells being calculated to create racial prejudice, as had been put forward in argument by certain persons, including a member of the London County Council."[614]

The *London Daily Mail* called it a "Black & White Fight." Many focused on the brutality of boxing in general. However, they could not overcome the argument that they opposed this specific bout but not others. Lord Harris said, "I think it inconsistent to oppose one and not others." One London Council member admitted why there was a difference. "I am most emphatically against the proposed contest between a white man and a negro, as it is bound to create racial antagonism in certain quarters, whatever the result may be."

A London Council member who was not opposed to the fight said, "My own personal view is that the colour or racial question is not of very serious importance in this country." Hence he did not see any reason for an objection, as long as they complied with the Queensberry rules. The Fulham mayor said if people wanted to spend their money to witness the contest, there was no valid reason why they should not be able to do so.

Jack Johnson said he could not understand the objections to the fight, for black men already had fought white men in London without trouble. He said his championship title gave him the right to defend against England's

---

[613] *London Daily Mail*, September 18, 1911.
[614] *London Times*, September 18, 1911. Wells was giving exhibitions before large crowds at Princes Hall, sparring with three opponents.

best man. "I see that they are trying to raise a storm of protest against the match. I don't see why, as it will not be different in any way from scores of others which take place nightly in London."[615]

There was some degree of hypocrisy to the opposition. However, the difference was that this fight had greater symbolic value, because it was a black world heavyweight champion going up against the white British heavyweight champion, so it was not just an ordinary contest. Really, the opposition was not about boxing but the potential symbolic political message that the world would receive, particularly British colonial subjects, should a black champion pummel a white British champion.

Several public school headmasters went on record against the match. Even the Archbishop of Canterbury wrote a letter to the Home Secretary opposing the fight. They feared the contest's influence on British youth.

A sportsman who was not opposed to the fight, Sir C. Champion-De-Crespigny, said, "I most certainly do not agree with the London County Council in trying to stop the contest. My only objection is that if the 'nigger' is fit and fine it will prove a burlesque and probably not last a full round."

Some argued that Reverend Meyer was not in a position to criticize the Johnson-Jeffries fight, for Meyer admitted that he had not even seen the fight films. Regardless, Reverend Meyer thought the Home Secretary would support his viewpoint.

The *South African News* was leading an agitation against the fight as well. It appealed to the Union Government to prohibit the importation of the bioscope films into South Africa should the contest take place. "The paper further expresses fears as to the effects which the fight may have upon the South African natives, and protests that the country cannot afford to invite any expansion of the black peril."[616]

Despite promoter James White's efforts to work with and appease Reverend Meyer, the reverend refused to relent in his crusade against the fight. Meyer said,

> The eyes of millions of the black and subject peoples are watching the issue of the contest (so widely advertised by the fact of it being held in the heart of London) as being in their judgment a decisive test in the matter of racial superiority, and, however you may guard it, you cannot alter its essential effect.

---

[615] *London Daily Mail*, September 19, 1911; *Boxing*, September 23, 1911. Johnson was training hard in Paris. Each morning, he left his villa at Neuilly at 9 a.m. and took long walks and runs, sometimes as much as 10 or 12 miles, through the Bois de Boulogne. In the afternoon, he went to the Pelican Boxing Club and worked for an hour and a half.

When he arrived in Paris three weeks prior, Johnson was 17 stone (238 pounds). On September 18, he was weighing 15 stone, 13 pounds (223 pounds).

Johnson said he expected to defeat Wells, but only after a hard and stiff battle. Wells was known for being smart, fast on his feet, and having a good kick in each hand.

[616] *London Daily Mail, London Times*, September 20, 1911.

Whatever safeguard you may adopt in the matter of referees, you must admit that the present contest is not wholly one of skill, because on the one side is added the instinctive passion of the negro race, which is so differently constituted to our own, and in the present instance will be aroused to do the utmost that immense animal development can do to retain the Championship, together with all the great financial gain that would follow.

In South Africa, the Cape Town correspondent said many prominent men, including the Moderator of the Dutch Reformed Church, warmly approved of a suggested prohibition in that country of any illustrations or newspaper descriptions of the Johnson-Wells fight.[617]

The *Freeman* reported, "There is no doubt that the feeling against the match is of the strongest sort and that it is growing stronger."

[T]he color question has been introduced, and never before has the color question been so discussed in England. It is not based upon conditions in England, but upon conditions in parts of the British Empire where the question looms large.

The *Outlook* asks the pertinent question: "If we were convinced that Wells could outclass the victorious black should we be so serious to deny him the triumph?"[618]

Wells was listed at 6'2 ½" and 13 stone, 10 pounds (192 pounds). He was slightly taller and had a longer reach than the champion, but Johnson was superior in every other way, including skill. That led to the objections about the bout, for the feeling was that the black world champion would crush their white champion.[619]

A large number of prominent people, including the Archbishop of Canterbury, the Bishop of London, and even Lord Lonsdale, who was a lover of boxing, supported Reverend Meyer. Several London newspapers supported him as well, including the *Times* and the *Daily Telegraph*. Major General Sir Alfred Turner said, "The Home Office should prevent the exhibition, which my lead to lamentable racial disturbances."

The *Times* and the *Daily Telegraph* argued that race relations in Africa were such that Great Britain could not afford an encounter likely to cause the racial ill-will that was provoked in the U.S. after the Reno affair.

Lord Lonsdale objected to the fight because he thought Johnson was too superior to Wells. "Johnson, to my mind, is one of the most scientific boxers I have ever seen. Wells is exceedingly good, but in my humble opinion he is lacking in experience." Still, he did not think the fight was more likely to cause a breach of the peace than any other contest.

[617] *London Times*, September 22, 1911.
[618] *Freeman*, October 7, 1911.
[619] *London Daily Mail*, September 22, 1911.

The *Freeman* noted and predicted, "Never in the history of public sport has so much government influence been directed against the holding of a glove contest; and there will be no fight."

From Paris, Johnson said, "It's just this, you don't want me to win, and that's the truth, but I am going to win. ... Lonsdale is sore at me because I would not fight for $5,000. Why should I fight for $5,000 when I can get $15,000? I am over here for the money. If the fight is stopped in London we can fight here in Paris and get a larger crowd."[620]

Petitions to the Home Secretary said the fight should be stopped in the interests of public order and national well-being. A South African man said,

> I state unhesitatingly, and I write with inner knowledge, when I say that such a contest, with all its concomitants, must necessarily have a most harmful effect throughout South Africa, where white and black are seeking amid great difficulties to establish permanent and equitable relationships based on justice to both.
>
> We have hitherto in South Africa attempted, with success or with partial success, to maintain the supremacy of the ruling caste – viz., the European element. ... Surrounded, as we are, by natives in all stages of civilization, from the sea to the Zambesi, we seek to establish our supremacy ...
>
> How can we look them in the face when such a fight is permitted to take place in the heart of the Empire? It will have a bad effect on the native races within the Empire and it will inflame race feeling throughout South Africa. ...
>
> Why pit black against white at all, and why do so with all the odds in favour of the black man? ... The baneful effects will be felt far beyond the spectators who witness the fight. It will make the position of the white man more difficult still in distant parts of the Empire.[621]

Hence, the truth was that when push came to shove, the British Empire had a vested interest in maintaining white supremacy and suppressing anything which symbolically threatened it.

South Africans argued that in English dominions, there was race danger incidental to mixed-race championship contests. South Africa had prohibited the exhibition of the Jeffries-Johnson fight films, and would do the same with the upcoming fight. Blacks could not be allowed to see a black man beating up the best Englishman either.

A writer named Stanhope said that even a few weeks after Johnson beat Burns, when the writer arrived at Suva, in the Fiji Islands, a policeman told him that he had more trouble with the colored people since that fight than at any other time previously. A colored man said to him, "White man he no

---

620 *Freeman*, October 7, 14, 1911; *London Daily Mail*, September 23, 1911.
621 *London Daily Mail*, September 23, 1911.

use; black man he knock him down every time." The policeman promptly proved to him that not every colored man was a Johnson. "The fact remains, however, that physical force had to be used, and once that is the case the safety of a white population, many times outnumbered by a coloured, becomes seriously menaced." Press reports of the contest were sufficient to cause trouble. This man believed that boxing in general produced more good than harm, but once the color question became injected, the analysis changed entirely. Blacks were taught that it was a heinous offence to attack a white. A mixed-race bout shattered that doctrine. Therefore, a mixed-race championship fight would have "effects which both we and those who live under the British flag in distant lands may live bitterly to regret."[622]

South Africa's Bishop of Grahamstown said, "I am Bishop of a colonial and missionary diocese where there are nearly as many Kaffir adherents of our Church as there are Europeans, and I believe a fight between a black and a white man cannot fail to do infinite harm and cause bitter racial feelings."

A Nigerian correspondent argued that the Johnson-Wells fight would weaken the British Administration's supreme authority.

> There can be no doubt that in this part of British West Africa, and in such places as Sierra Leone and Cape Coast, the news flashed over the wires that a physical struggle between a white man and a black man, attended by thousands of spectators, has been waged in the capital of the Empire, would have a thoroughly mischievous effect – especially if the black man won.

Because Johnson was so well respected, it was presumed that he would win, even if the talented Wells gave him a tough time of it. This writer said that "one can imagine few things more calculated to do us (and them) harm…than the…astounding incident of masses of Englishmen assisting at the public thrashing – if it so turned out – of an Englishman by a negro."[623]

The *Freeman* was not surprised that Johnson's Dublin fight had been canceled, and believed that the Wells bout would be canceled as well.

> Not one word has been uttered as to why Jack Johnson didn't fight at Dublin. He should have had the feeling that white men are white the globe around and that black men are black men in the meanwhile. They can't doff their feelings like they can their shoes, and furthermore they don't want to.

In the *Freeman's* opinion, no big fight would take place for Johnson in Europe. They were not going to pay him the big money he wanted, and racism and political fears would do the rest. White men of whatever nationality did not care to see Johnson beat up on a white man in a

[622] *London Times*, September 23, 1911.
[623] *London Times*, September 26, 1911.

heavyweight championship fight. It was a time in which conquered darker races were trying to assert themselves, and whites were resisting, in all ways. South Africa, England's Cape colony, was a reflex of the United States. In fact, the British Empire's racial conditions in many ways were even more problematic than in the U.S., given that fewer whites ruled over a far greater number of darker people.

> Other countries yet in South Africa are beginning to take notice, and England hopes to avoid a peril from its black belt stretched around the globe. So it does the very wise thing – from its viewpoint – self-preservation, keeping down all unnecessary possible causes of race comparison and friction. ... Great Britain has a race problem of her own. Such a notable defeat of a white British champion by a Negro would have its effect, it is thought, upon British South Africa, where there are one million whites dominating five million blacks, and in India, where only 150,000 whites are ruling over 300,000,000 nonwhites. And so in Jamaica and other parts of the empire.

> The Briton who has been spending his time analyzing our colored problem and writing gloomy predictions suddenly awakens to the realization that our colored question is nothing compared with his, for in the British Empire there are only sixty million whites, as compared with almost 350,000,000 nonwhites.

The Brits feared the fight's psychological effect. The Russo-Japanese war had shown the effect of the defeat of a white country by a nonwhite one. It was the germ of unrest in India. Time after time in the white-ruled world, "it has been shown that it is unwise to let the nonwhite races physically humiliate one of the 'ruling race.'"[624]

A Johannesburg correspondent lamented the fact that South Africa's white population was not keeping pace with the colored population, and feared the implications. At such a pace, eventually the darker peoples would outnumber the whites even more than they did already. "And what will become of the system of self-government under such conditions? Bearing in mind the progress of the backward races, is it certain that half a century hence twelve millions of coloured men will be content to be ruled without representation in the Legislature chosen by a few hundred thousand white men?" Black and brown races already constituted over 78 percent of the Union of South Africa's population, but they had no say in the government.[625]

Ultimately, regardless of the fact that boxing bouts took place all the time in Great Britain, Home Secretary Winston Churchill, on behalf of the Home Office, concluded that the Johnson-Wells bout would be illegal, and issued an edict that unless the promoters abandoned the contest voluntarily,

---

[624] *Freeman*, October 7, 1911.
[625] *London Daily Mail*, October 9, 1911.

steps would be taken to prevent it by issuing a summons against promoter James White in the Police Court for a prospective breach of the peace.

However, James White did not want to give up on the promotion. He said the bout's rules would be no different than others held in England. If there was no breach of the peace for all of those bouts, there should not be one this time either. White felt that he had the right to be treated the same as any other boxing promoter. "It had been alleged that the publication of a report of the contest would be very harmful. There were those who would take great care that no report should be published by any newspaper."

Reverend Meyer was pleased. He believed the fight would be demoralizing, degrading, undo the results of education and social reform, and threaten racial disturbances in all parts of the Empire. Meyer had received several letters from reverends and bishops in Durham, Uganda, Kent, Australia, and New Zealand, all saying that a fight between a black and a white man would be harmful and cause bitter racial feelings.[626]

Reverend Meyer said a conference about boxing should be held to discuss three points: 1. The abolition of the knockout-blow, 2. The prohibition of black vs. white contests, and 3. The elimination of all money stakes or prizes. Reverend Meyer further said,

> So far as battles between coloured men and whites are concerned, I am absolutely opposed to them. … When white opposes black it is not a game of skill, for the black nature has more fire in the blood than the white, and has more passion. The reason men like to see blacks fighting whites is because the black men fight so passionately; it introduces the element of animalism which you do not see in the case of two white boxers. …

> As I have lived in one country – South Africa – where the racial problem enters into these matters, I emphatically endorse the 'Stop-the-Fight' campaign now being engineered in that country, where it is believed by many that the contest will have a grave and harmful influence on the natives, who place altogether exaggerated importance upon the fact of a black successfully pommelling a white man.

Meyer admitted that he had never seen a professional boxing contest in his life. In response to this admission, *Boxing* said, "Comment is needless."[627]

On September 26, a local magistrate issued summonses to John A. Johnson (who was back in England), Billy Wells, James White, and others to answer for the contemplation of a breach of the peace.

Johnson was served at his new training quarters at the Royal Forest Hotel, Chingford (having moved from Whetstone). He had just finished sparring 7 rounds with two of his sparring partners.

---

[626] *London Times, Manchester Guardian*, September 26, 1911.
[627] *Boxing*, September 30, 1911.

Johnson told the detective who served him that he intended to represent himself, rather than hire a solicitor. Jack said, "If they stop this fight it means that every other boxing contest, no matter where held, must be stopped too. If they stop this fight, England can never claim again that she is a nation that allows fair play." Johnson said he had spent more money in England than he had earned from it. He also said if the fight was stopped, it might take place in Paris.[628]

Supporters of boxing said that what was taking place was an absolute farce. People who knew nothing whatsoever about boxing were dictating what was or was not brutal. There had been many black vs. white fights without problem. Boxing fans feared that the upcoming legal proceeding could deal a death-blow to the sport.[629]

The Metropolitan District Railway Company, the owner of the property where the bout was to take place, filed a suit to obtain an injunction against the fight being held on its premises. The company feared that if the fight was allowed, its license to operate would not be renewed. Specifically cited was the letter from the London Council threatening such.

The Defendants cited fights such as Slavin-Jackson, Johnson-Burns, and Langford-Lang, all of which were black and white fights that had taken place without incident.

The judge, Justice Lush, granted a temporary injunction against the fight, given that the bout had a strong probability of endangering the owners' license. The justice passed no judgment on the contest, but simply agreed that because there was a reasonable likelihood that the license was imperiled, the injunction could be granted.

On September 27 at the courthouse on Bow-Street, there was a separate case and hearing brought by the Crown at the instance of the Home Office, regarding the alleged contemplated breach of the peace. As Johnson predicted, the place was packed. Well-known sporting men were present, showing support for the fight. Reverend F. B. Meyer had a seat upon a back bench. Outside the courthouse, a crowd of about 2,000 people was dense enough to hold up traffic. Wells, who had been training at Leigh-on-Sea, arrived in a taxicab. Great cheers greeted him. The police had to help him get through the crowd.

John A. Johnson entered the courtroom with his shining golden smile. Even Magistrate Marsham was amused. When the Solicitor-General said, "Mr. Johnson will defend himself," Johnson replied, "Absolutely." His voice's emphatic strength left no doubt about his confidence in his ability to plead his own case. Jack stood beside Wells, as well as their respective managers, James Maloney and R. C. Jenkins, promoter James White, and the lawyers. The hearing began shortly after 2 p.m.

---

[628] *London Daily Mail*, September 27, 1911.
[629] *London Times*, September 26, 1911.

When permission was given for the men to be seated, Johnson chose to remain standing. During the Solicitor-General's opening statement, Johnson leaned easily against the rails, looking about and smiling. When Johnson had occasion to speak, his words were clear, and his sentences as straight to the point as one of his left leads. He addressed the Magistrate as "His Worship," and referred to opposing counsel as "the honorable solicitors."

The government argued that the fight would constitute a breach of the peace and was illegal, as opposed to a legal sparring match. The Solicitor-General said that the last time a championship contest was decided, it took place at Reno, and the title was maintained successfully by "Jackson." Johnson interrupted, "Johnson, if you please." The Solicitor-General bowed his head in acknowledgement of the correction. Continuing, counsel argued that a sparring match was legal, but intent to injure or do harm was illegal.[630]

The Solicitor-General said that Johnson had taken part in three championship contests. Johnson interrupted, with a broad smile, "A few more than that, if you look into the records." The Solicitor-General replied, "Well, three or more." Burns, Ketchel, and Jeffries all had been stopped before the contest had gone 20 rounds. He argued that was proof of intent to injure.

Police Superintendent McIntyre was called as a witness. Subsequent to defense lawyers' objections, legal argument ensued regarding whether he could be questioned about published records of the results of previous championship contests and newspaper descriptions of them contained in the *London Sporting Life*.

The magistrate asked Johnson whether he had objections he wanted raised. Johnson said,

> Yes, I object, for the witness is refreshing his memory of something he probably knows nothing about. I object because these papers printed in England are no authority upon contests in America. In these records which the honorable solicitor holds it is said, Jack Johnson fought Jim Scanlan 14 rounds. The contest only lasted 8 rounds; the records are wrong. From these records the witness is simply refreshing his mind. Reading a paper refreshes his memory of things he has perhaps never known.

Nevertheless, the magistrate overruled the objections, admitted the newspaper into evidence, and the fight descriptions contained therein were read into the record. When asked whether, after hearing the descriptions,

---

[630] In Johnson's agreement for the Wells fight, entered into evidence, he sold the picture rights to White, agreed to give exhibitions while training, and agreed not to divulge any matters to the press in connection with the contest except with White's permission. He agreed to write exclusive articles for the newspapers during training, to write his impressions of the contest, and a magazine article which was to be White's exclusive property. On the signing of the agreement, Johnson was to receive 1,500 pounds, another 1,500 one month before the contest, and 3,000 paid an hour before the contest took place ($30,000 U.S. total). Wells was to receive 2,000 pounds ($10,000 U.S.). They agreed to use 5-ounce gloves.

the witness apprehended that the upcoming contest would lead to a breach of the peace, the Superintendent replied, "I do."

The lawyers reserved cross-examination for a later time, but Johnson wanted to cross-examine him at that point. "I want to cross-examine him now." The magistrate suggested that it might be better for him to leave it until the legal gentlemen had undertaken theirs. Johnson persisted, however. "Are you familiar with the Queensberry rules?" "No, I am not." "Why did you say I knocked Tommy Burns out in the fourteenth round?" The superintendent started to look at the records. Johnson: "Don't look at the book. I object to you looking at that book every time I ask you a question. You are simply refreshing your memory." The superintendent said he meant the contest ended in 14 rounds. "I said at first that you knocked him out, but I find that the police interfered." Magistrate: "He admits he made a mistake." Johnson said, "The witness does not know what he is talking about. If he only goes by the book his evidence is very thin." Continuing, Johnson asked: "Why do you say that when Jack Johnson and Mr. Wells box on October 2 there will be a breach of the peace?" "I said I feared there might be." "Did Sam Langford and Bill Lang cause a breach of the peace?" "I do not know." "Did you see that fight?" "No." "Have you ever seen a boxing contest?" "No." "Then you have no idea of what they are like?" "No." With a scornful wave of his arm, Johnson turned to the magistrate and said, "The witness may go now. I am through."

Johnson's cross examination of the police officer was a "very sharp, swift attack, very skillful for one not experienced in courts." Of course, what they did not realize was that Johnson had been in court many times in the U.S. The case was adjourned until the following day.

As they left the court, huge crowds loudly cheered and hailed the Defendants. It took a while for Johnson's taxicab to drive away, for it had to move slowly, given that a crowd of men clung to it as it went down Bow-street. Wells literally ran down the street to escape the cheering crowd.[631]

The next day, on September 28, 1911, matters came to a sudden and unexpected conclusion. The bout was declared off "voluntarily." Pursuant to the agreement of the parties, the Justice of the Police Court granted an injunction against the fight. It appeared that promoter White had agreed to abandon the bout, fearing the potential repercussions of an adverse decision against boxing in general. Such would hurt potential future contests as well. So instead of risking a decision that might implicate boxing's legality in general, they agreed to abandon the contest. Another reason given was that in light of the injunction issued by Judge Lush, it was impossible to hold the contest at Earl's Court, and as no other premises were available in London, it would be impossible for it to take place as advertised.

Unfortunately, the Johnson-Wells fight could not be held anywhere in the British Isles, where it would be the most attractive and financially

---

[631] *London Times, London Daily Mail,* September 28, 1911.

lucrative, given that Wells was the British champion. However, the injunction would not affect Johnson's friendly sparring exhibitions at music halls, which continued.

The *London Times* was happy that the fight had been called off. It said the pressure of public opinion had achieved the desired result.

> We have assumed throughout the Empire great and unparalleled responsibilities, and it is impossible to ignore the widespread effect which this contest must undoubtedly have had in those countries where "colour feeling" unhappily exists. We have opposed the fight in the belief that it was contrary to the best interests of the Empire for this country to allow it to be held. The fine and manly English sport of boxing has been neither assailed nor displaced by its prevention, nor has the opposition been based upon any personal feelings towards either Johnson or Wells. Indeed, it is only fair to recognize that both men have adopted an attitude of most commendable restraint ever since public opinion began to range itself against their meeting. In his cross-examination of Superintendent McIntyre in the proceedings at Bow-street on Wednesday, moreover, Johnson showed a power of advocacy which proves he is possessed of an acute brain as well as formidable fists. Neither the men nor boxing as a sport have been arraigned and the justification for the opposition to the holding of the contest at Earl's Court is founded, as we have declared from the first, upon the public interest of the Empire.[632]

The *Freeman* noted that the Earl's Court lease had been secured for 21 years, but the London County Council had full powers over the granting or revoking of licenses, and without its consent, it was impossible to run the place. Hence, long-term economic concerns forced the promoter to acquiesce to those who sought to stop the fight.[633]

Johnson returned to the Royal Forest Hotel at Chingford, where he had been staying for the past week, and announced his retirement.

> I am now through with boxing. I will finish my contracts in England, but I will never put on the gloves again in public after those contracts are through. I shall retire as the heavyweight champion of the world. … I may say that I am not retiring on account of the contest which was arranged between myself and Wells. I had decided that even if the contest had come off I should retire.

He also was quoted as saying,

> I have fifteen weeks to do on the music-halls in England, and after that I go to America to appear at a few music-halls there. But when

---

[632] *London Times*, September 29, 1911.
[633] *Freeman*, September 30, 1911.

my contracts are finished no one will ever see me fight in the ring again unless it be boxing at some benefit for a charity. This is a genuine retirement.

I am going to do what no other heavyweight champion of the world has done – retire and not come back to defend my title. The title of heavy-weight champion will have to remain vacant for a year or so, but after that time I mean to get the five best men available to fight it out and name the best among them as champion. It is not because of the result of the court proceedings to-day that I have come to this decision. I have been thinking about it for some time past, and Mrs. Johnson has persuaded me a great deal.

I had only one other fight fixed up, and that was in Australia. But as Australia is governed by England, I do not want to run the risk of making that journey and then find the fight declared illegal. So that fight is off.

Clearly, Johnson had grown tired of the fight game, particularly with all of its legal impediments, and at that point was content just to lead an easy life.

The *Freeman* quoted Johnson as saying,

I have fought and defeated the best heavyweights in the world and have made enough money in the ring and on the stage to last me for some time, the remainder of my life, in fact, I hope. I can still earn quite a little on the American stage, and am satisfied to retire on my laurels. I had hoped to fight Bombadier Wells here, but as the English public has seen fit to prevent that, I will return to the states as soon as my theatrical contract expires here and retire from the game.

Some thought the fight might be moved to Paris, but Johnson's statement made that prospect seem slim. Wells remained interested in fighting, particularly after training so hard. Even if Johnson was willing to move forward, the question was whether Parisians would pay the same amount of money to watch a British champion fight Johnson, who was not going to fight unless a French promoter offered the same money. Another question was whether France, which also had vast colonial holdings, would allow the fight or object to it on the same racial grounds.

That evening, Johnson said,

I had originally intended to fight three more fights, but as Australia is governed by British law, and they don't seem to want me any more in this country, I don't want to force myself on the public. I have made enough money to retire on, and the last chance the British public will have of seeing me with the gloves on will be at exhibitions which I am about to give in the music-halls through the British Isles.[634]

---

[634] *Manchester Guardian, London Daily Mail, London Times,* September 29, 1911; *Freeman,* October 7, 1911. Johnson continued giving sparring exhibitions at the London Palladium.

Johnson had a contract with McIntosh which began October 31, but the fulfillment of that contract appeared to be in doubt.

Some hoped that a 10-round Johnson-Langford bout could be arranged in New York. The Langford-Jeannette bout drew in $16,350, so it was believed that a Johnson-Langford bout would draw at least double that.

However, in New York, the club that had been using Madison-square Garden for boxing contests had its license revoked. The local powers-that-be once again were coming down on boxing.

New York Governor John Dix, who recently had championed boxing, had changed his mind and was discussing with Senator Frawley the advisability of repealing the enacted law that legalized the sport. "The English opposition to the Johnson-Wells match commands much sympathy here, even in sporting circles."[635]

A month after the bout was prevented, in the House of Commons, Mr. Thorne commented, "Does the right honorable gentleman think that if there was any possible chance of Wells beating Johnson we should have heard anything about it?" Laughter followed, and no answer was given. The point was that if they thought Wells had a chance to beat Johnson, most likely those whites in power would have allowed the bout. No white member of the British Empire wanted to see a black champion beat up a white challenger, owing to the message it sent to the darker races who were the Empire's subjects.[636]

In the end, Great Britain and the British Empire was no better than the U.S. in its racial attitudes about white/black competition on a championship level, despite what it often professed about itself. Ultimately, in a world where whites sought to dominate the darker races, concerns about racial conflict came to the forefront, and a Johnson-Wells fight was viewed from a racial and political perspective. The English had colonies throughout the globe, dominating darker folk. Fear about the bout's symbolic effect, particularly if Johnson won, are what derailed the bout. Johnson was a symbol of subversion to the racial status quo. These concerns were particularly sharp in South Africa, where in the Second Boer War (1899-1902), the Brits had sustained massive casualties in obtaining Afrikaner lands. Nationalist movements threatened British rule in places like India and Egypt as well. In all of these places, non-white subjects outnumbered the whites. A black man defeating a white British champion sent a message the Empire did not want and did not think it could afford.

It was important for Great Britain not to have an international boxing contest take place, be filmed, and then have news about the fight and those films be disseminated to its subjects showing or describing a black man dominating its white champion.. That could foster ideas it did not want

---

On October 4, he even sparred with comedian George Robey. *Manchester Guardian*, October 5, 1911. In mid-November 1911, Johnson sparred at the Palace in Manchester.

[635] *Freeman*, September 30, 1911; *London Times*, September 29, 1911.

[636] *Manchester Guardian*, November 2, 1911.

encouraged. European countries that held colonial empires over darker nations throughout the world could not afford to be any more tolerant than Americans.

In the meantime, while Johnson was overseas, on September 15, 1911 in New York, "Fireman" Jim Flynn won a 10-round no-decision bout over Carl Morris, the emerging 6'4" 230+-pound heavyweight who had earned knockout victories over Marvin Hart and Mike Schreck. Despite being five or six inches shorter and weighing about 50 pounds less (180 vs. 230), Flynn badly beat Morris, showing that he could handle much larger men, as he had proven in his 10th round knockout over Al Kaufman earlier that year. Flynn broke Morris's nose, closed both of his eyes, and had his lips badly puffed. The right side of his head was battered and swollen. The Kaufman and Morris victories made Flynn a top white contender.

The *New York Age* opined that the world's top four heavyweights were black (Johnson, Langford, McVey, and Jeannette), and no white man in sight was a serious contender. It noted that the *New York Morning Telegraph* lamented this situation, feeling that no white man really had any chance of beating Johnson, including Flynn, whom Johnson already had knocked out. It asked, "Where is the white man who will take the conceit out of the big Negro, Jack Johnson? It seems as if this gross dark throwback stood invincible in the prize ring and defied the world to find a white man who can whip him." However, no white man appeared to have a chance with him. The *Age* agreed, saying, "Never before in the history of the ring has the superiority of the black fighter over the white fighter been more pronounced than at this time."

Since the recent Langford-Jeannette contest, there had been less talk about Langford putting up a great fight with Johnson.

> As Jeannette, who is not nearly as clever as Johnson, gave Langford all he could do…it must be acknowledged that it is not highly probable that Langford would prove the champion's master were they to ever fight. A combat between the two would simply be the case of a good little man meeting a good big man, and unless Johnson has gone back since he defeated Jeffries, he should have no difficulty in winning out in such a contest.

Hence, in asking where the man was who could defeat Johnson, the *Age* answered, "Nowhere, so far as we can see."[637]

The *Ogdensburg News* agreed with the *Age*, saying that Johnson had a 5 ¾" height advantage, the longer reach, and was much heavier in weight than Langford. Plus he was very skillful and had underrated strength. Although Langford recently had won the popular verdict against Jeannette, the fight showed that "any man with a good left jolt can worry Langford."

---

[637] *New York Age*, September 21, 1911.

Now, if Jeannette with a light stab could slow up Langford what would a man like Johnson, who has a terrible jab, do to the Tar Baby? Then another thing – Langford is an easy man to reach with an uppercut. How could he keep away from Johnson's left and right hand head rockers? … The Johnson who met and defeated Jeffries would stow away Sammy Langford with his terrible left jab and heavy uppercuts.

This paper opined that no man could hope to defeat Johnson if he was anything like as good as he was when he fought Burns or Jeffries.[638]

On September 30, 1911 in Sydney, Sam McVey (a.k.a. McVea) won a 20-round decision over Australian heavyweight champion Jack Lester, who recently had won the Australian championship with a W20 over Bill Lang.

McVey said Johnson had never suffered much punishment, for he blocked or eluded all of the punishing blows. McVey said Langford was a dangerous hard hitter who could take punishment, but was handicapped by being small, and was not the cleverest. "At the same time, if he was as big as Johnson or myself, neither of us would have a chance against him."[639]

Bombardier Billy Wells still wanted to fight Johnson, in Paris, and was disappointed to hear that Johnson was retiring. Billy did not think Johnson's decision made any sense, for as a retired champion, his value as a music-hall draw would decline. Wells was certain that Johnson would fight again, and argued that since they both had trained for a fight, they might as well fight in Paris. Johnson had expressed sympathy for Mr. White, and could help him recoup his losses. However, it was unclear whether White could make Johnson the same large guarantee for a fight in France.

Wells thought that either Johnson feared him or his heart was no longer in it and he only wanted easy marks. It is doubtful that Johnson feared a man who was knocked out by Moir, whom Burns stopped. Most experts believed that Johnson would beat Wells with ease. That was their fear. Still, Johnson was carrying too much flesh when he started training, and found training to be a real burden.

> [Training] becomes in time a veritable torture to boxers once they have passed their thirtieth year and have gone in for self-indulgence to any extent. And when a man has gathered as much wealth as Johnson he cannot help taking things easy between matches, especially at his age, any more than he can help asking himself every day why he submits to the grind and deprivation of training.[640]

There was no guarantee that a white-black heavyweight championship fight could take place in France, given that France had its own colonial empire, ruling over several darker nations in Africa, Asia, and the Americas.

---

[638] *Ogdensburg News*, September 30, 1911.
[639] *New York Age*, October 26, 911. On October 6, 1911 in New York, Sam Langford knocked out Tony Caponi in the 3rd round.
[640] *Boxing*, October 7, 1911.

It easily could have the same concerns as Great Britain. Plus, allowing Johnson-Wells to take place on its soil would aggravate political relations with its neighbor. Clearly, Johnson no longer was interested in training for a fight that might not be allowed to take place, or one in which he would not be guaranteed to be paid very well, and so he drew down his $1,000 forfeit. "That ends it."

While at the Grand Hotel in Paris, Johnson reiterated that he was retiring. He said, "There's nobody going to risk enough money to make it worth my while to put in a lot of hard training."

It was reported that Johnson had many quarrels with his white wife, the last occurring in a Paris café, where she declared that Jack did not pay enough attention to her, and he allegedly slapped her face.

In his October exhibitions at the English music halls, in places such as Newcastle-upon-Tyne and Leeds, Johnson sparred with Fred Drummond. There were some rumors that Johnson was low on cash and had to pawn his car. Allegedly, his sparring partner Monte Cutler said so. Tex Rickard allegedly claimed that Johnson had spent $120,000 since fighting Jeffries. Others countered that Johnson had over $150,000 in various forms of securities, and had plenty of money.

From Chingford, England, on October 20, Johnson denied the rumors that he was broke. "I possess more than $100,000 cash, four automobiles, three here and one in America, and all fine ones, a bag full of diamonds and a lot of other property." He recently had a car made according to his own ideas and specifications, which cost more than $7,500. His wife wore jewelry worth between $60,000 and $70,000. Johnson said that when he finished his work in Europe, he would return to America to fulfill vaudeville engagements. "My trip to Australia has been indefinitely postponed. I have more business than I know what to do with. Tell them that Jack Johnson is still a long way from the bread line."

Johnson blamed the ministers for the fight game's decline. "It is all the preacher's fault. ... This is supposed to be a free country, and it would be but for the preachers. They look sharply after everybody's morals except their own. ... I am a sober man. I am told the great majority of preachers in England are boozers." "Great fighting is dead from an overdose of sanctimoniousness." He said he was going to Paris, which was the warmest town on earth.[641]

On October 28, 1911 in Sydney, before a crowd of over 6,000, Sam McVey scored a KO2 over Bill Lang.

A *Freeman* writer said Johnson's declaration of retirement was met with little comment, owing to the fact that ever since defeating Jeffries, "the

---

[641] *Freeman*, October 7, 14, 21, 28, 1911.

On October 23 at King's Hall, London, welterweight Georges Carpentier defeated Young Joseph, England's welterweight champion, when Joseph's seconds retired him after the 10th round. *London Daily Mail*, October 24, 1911.

Galveston black has made himself obnoxious to both the members of the white and black races as a result of the way he has conducted himself."

Unlike Johnson, the 173-pound Langford was quiet and unassuming. Still, he was a black man, and white folk wanted a white champion, not a black one.

At that time, Jim Flynn was the best white heavyweight. However, he had not the "ghost of a chance against either Langford or Jeannette."

Johnson was in somewhat of a Catch-22 position. White patrons wanted to see a white man recapture the crown. They did not care as much to see another black man challenge for the title, because at the end of the day the title would remain in black hands. Hence such a fight would not be as lucrative. However, whites did not want to see or even allow a fight in which the white fighter had little chance to win. That sent the wrong message too. They only wanted a fight in which the white fighter had a good chance to defeat Johnson.

The *Freeman* again noted that the reason why Johnson was not allowed to fight was owing to the potential "bad influence on the darker races, so many of whom are of the English possessions." The potential Wells fight had "quickened the public conscience."

In Newcastle, England, Johnson was fined $100 for speeding his auto.

W. W. Naughton said Johnson's pompous ways and the flashiness he displayed with his white wife had caused a reversal of feeling against him in England. He put himself on too high of a pedestal to suit even mild-tempered Britons. "In spite of the strong feeling against Negroes in many quarters, Johnson would never have been as unpopular in America as he is now if it were not for his actions outside of the ring since he won the championship." Naughton was arguing that it was more than mere race prejudice which explained why folks did not like Johnson.

However, the *Cleveland Gazette* said the truth was out at last.

> The plain fact was, in the case of England, that the spectacle of a Negro whipping a white man would give too much encouragement to the blacks of the English provinces, in several of which that country was and is having more or less trouble to keep them subjugated. The same thing is true in the case of the whites and our people of the South.

The *Freeman* agreed. "The truth plainly presents itself, if we conclude that racial relations are similar around the globe, a fact patent for years." In fact, many English newspapers had agreed that Johnson was likeable.[642]

Dr. T. Rhoudda, a Brighton, England Congregationalist preacher, called attention to religious leaders' hypocrisy by asking, "Will the forces that came together to stop the fight remain together to stop the terrible treatment which the white man is dealing out to the black?"

---

[642] *Freeman*, November 4, 11, 18, 1911, quoting *Cleveland Gazette*.

The *Freeman* noted that Johnson had brought attention to the worldwide color line and race politics, regardless of country. In the end, race mattered throughout the world, not just in the U.S. It opined, "Poor, innocent Jack Johnson and his Reno have brought forth this world discussion, and perhaps for the better. What has been brought out had a latent existence, and which would out at some period, sooner or later." Johnson made it obvious that the world's whites did not want racial fairness.[643]

On December 6, 1911 in Clifton, Tennessee, a black farmer and his two daughters were lynched by a group of "white caps," or white farmers who sought to eliminate competition from black farmers by using violence and intimidation. They shot the father, hung his daughters, and then burned them.

The Home Edition · The Chicago Defender. · If you see It in The Defender It Is so

VOLUME VI. NUMBER 49. CHICAGO, ILL., SATURDAY, DECEMBER 9, 1911. PRICE 5 CENTS

United States Government Responsible For 1,000 Colored Men, Women and Children Murdered

In America during 1911; Educated Men and Women, both North and South, Decry these Conditions. The Christian Church Is Called Upon to Ask God's Mercy. Jews in Russia Have No Trouble Compared to That of the American Negro. The Cry of 12,000,000 Black People who Fought on Both Sides of the Conflicting Armies of the 60's Beg You for a Man's Chance and Equality Before the Law

On December 11, 1911 in Brisbane, Australia, Sam McVey knocked out Jack Lester in the 8th round.

In England, Johnson was called to court to pay an IOU for $2,500 given to promoter James White. Also, a jewelry firm was seeking the return of diamonds or payment for them. Johnson was "facing more lawsuits and complications than any man who has ever worn the world's championship title." He constantly was being sued by folks who claimed he owed them money for various breaches of contract.

Johnson also had failed to return the money that Hugh McIntosh had advanced him. He was supposed to fight McVey in Australia on December 26. However, owing to his retirement, and given his frustration with the British Empire, of which Australia was a part, he was not going to honor the McIntosh contract. Instead, McVey would take on Langford there.[644]

---

[643] *Freeman,* November 25, 1911.
[644] *Freeman,* December 9, 16, 1911.

CHAPTER 14

Fireman Jim Flynn

In late December 1911, just before Christmas, Jack Johnson returned to the U.S. to spend the holidays with his mother. When he exited the Twentieth Century Limited train, Johnson sighed, "Well, I am glad to be in Chicago." He had brought back from England his valet, as well as 13 trunks of clothes.[645]

The *Freeman* believed that black success in sports served to defy arguments that denied black ability to shine. Blacks found success in boxing more than any other sport. However, the black race came up against the demand for white supremacy in all areas of life. "There seemed to lurk a fear that the Negro all over the land would feel his ability to meet the white man on an equal footing." Sports had symbolic political value which threatened the race caste. Yet, men such as Johnson, Langford, Jeannette, and McVey had no peer.

As a result of black success, "The press has taken an unusually active part in trying to push the Negro out of the limelight. … For two years the papers have been devoting column after column to Jack Johnson and magnifying whatever little thing the champion may do into some act against the public safety." Some policemen never saw their names in print until they grasped the opportunity to secure a medal by arresting the champion. "If he is to be made the scapegoat of every little cheap newspaper reporter it is because he is black and a member of a race which most people of other races take a delight in looking down upon." The *Freeman* hoped that a white hope in whom white men had confidence would be produced, so that Johnson once again could prove that he was the most marvelous heavyweight ever.

Scouting potential bouts between Johnson and Langford and Johnson and Jeannette, a *Freeman* writer said,

> I fail to notice where any fair-minded, good judge has offered an opinion that Langford and Johnson would be a real contest. It has been said that Langford would give him a hard fight – that would be about all – if Johnson was in any kind of condition. … Langford is without a slight doubt the best little man that ever donned a pair of gloves. … As far as Langford is concerned, he could never whip Johnson.

Joe Jeannette has been named by some few writers as a possibility. Jeannette has never shown championship form and never will. ... At the present time there's no one to fight.

This writer opined that when a good man finally showed up, Johnson would be too old to get into proper condition. Aging fighters who grew fat and stale never were the same again, and that was proven time and again with men like Sullivan, Jackson, and Jeffries. "The above three men were all as good in their day as Jack Johnson in his." Yet, when they finally fell, they fell easily. To be a top fighter, one had to be used to hardship. Johnson was living the good life, and did not have to train or work hard to earn. Over time, that would make him soft.

In a few years, when a good white fighter eventually came along, one whom the best judges said could lick a past-it Johnson,

> [T]he fight would be pulled off in Washington, D.C., in front of the Capitol. ... It would be a greater feat than the coronation of King George. The moving pictures of the event would be shown in every church, Sunday-school and day school on the globe, to the savages in Africa, to show how much greater the white man's powers were than the black man's. ... These same level-headed kickers would readily welcome the contest that would surely show Johnson beaten helpless on their front lawn.[646]

On December 26, 1911 in Sydney, Australia, before 18,000 spectators, Sam McVey won a 20-round decision over Sam Langford.

Langford hotly disputed the decision. Many hooted the verdict. They thought Langford at least had earned a draw. Tommy Burns said the decision was a very bad one, that McVey only won 3 rounds.

Others said McVey landed the greater number of blows and outboxed Langford. McVey was both aggressive and clever. He scored the only knockdown, in the 3rd round, bloodied Langford's mouth, and swelled up and discolored Sam's right eye with constant lefts. Some said that those who supported Langford were amongst a vocal minority. Earlier that year in Paris, the two had fought to a 20-round draw. This victory boomed McVey's stock. Plus, it was the largest crowd to attend a fight there since Burns-Johnson.[647]

---

646 *Freeman*, December 23, 1911.

647 *Hawaiian Star*, January 31, 1912; *Freeman*, December 30, 1911; *New York Age*, December 28, 1911, February 15, 1912. One report said McVey put up a very aggressive battle and landed the greater number of blows, although few of them had any telling effect on Langford, who was trying to land a decisive punch. McVey showed remarkable cleverness in avoiding punishment, for his defense had Langford puzzled.

Another report said both men fought hard until they tired. The 1st and 2nd rounds were fairly even, both showing caution, but landing hard blows. In the 3rd, Langford landed a heavy right to the jaw, but McVey came back with a hook that dropped Langford to the floor, though he rose immediately. McVey won the 5th, landing his left to the jaw. Langford's mouth and tongue were bleeding, and he seemed dazed. By the 9th round, McVey had piled

Bill Lang, who had been defeated by Johnson, Langford, and McVey, said McVey was the stiffest of the lot. However, Johnson had defeated McVey thrice: (1903 W20 and W20 (scoring three knockdowns), and 1904 KO20 (scoring 2-3 knockdowns).

On December 27, 1911 in Salt Lake City, Utah, Jim Flynn knocked out Tony Caponi in the 3rd round.

Back in Chicago, Jack Johnson vigorously denied the "rumor" that he had retired, and said that he had no intention of retiring. "With me it is purely a question of money whether I will fight again, but I have not retired and do not intend to do so for some time yet. I was sorry I did not get to fight Bombadier Wells in England. …. [A]ll those stories about me running around and drinking a lot of champagne are lies." Either he had changed his mind about retiring, or the initial reports of his retirement were false.

The champ said promoters only had to meet his $30,000 price, the same as what Burns got for fighting him, and he would fight anyone.

Rumors were that Johnson was nearly 300 pounds and his wife was seriously ill. Jack said he was weighing 233 pounds.

> If I am supposed to be down and out, why don't some of these promoters take advantage of staging a fight between me and one of these 'hopes,' whom so many persons think have a chance of beating me in a contest?
>
> Since my return from Europe I have heard a great deal about Jim Flynn. It is true he beat Al Kaufman and Carl Morris, but he has been doing so much talking since those fights that I will meet him, winner take all, if there is enough money in the house. I have beaten Flynn before, and I'll stop him with a punch if necessary. Don't think for a minute Jack Johnson is all in. … I am tired of hearing these stories about my retirement.[648]

New York promoters were offering Johnson only $15,000 for a 10-round bout with Joe Jeannette. Joe would earn $5,000. Jack said he would fight Jeannette if a $30,000 guaranteed purse was posted, and Joe also had to bet him $10,000 on the side to show that he had true confidence.[649]

Hugh McIntosh offered $30,000 for a Johnson fight with McVey, who

---

up many points. Both showed signs of punishment. Langford had a marked discoloration and swelling over his right eye. McVey's mouth and nose were bleeding. It was give-and-take in the 10th round, but the 11th and 12th were Langford's. McVey's left, which had done considerable execution up to that time, began to lack steam. For the next 5 rounds, the men sparred, and few heavy blows were exchanged. Langford was aggressive, but McVey outboxed him. Langford's eye was closed tight, for McVey frequently landed there. Both were tired and cautious in the 19th, and in the 20th round they were too weary to do anything but clinch.

Also on December 26, 1911, in Buffalo, New York, Joe Jeannette won a 10-round no-decision bout against Jack "Twin" Sullivan.

[648] *New York Age*, December 28, 1911. *Freeman*, December 30, 1911; January 6, 1912.
[649] *Call*, January 4, 1912.

was coming off his victory over Langford. Johnson said he would accept as long as the money was deposited in a reliable bank before he left Chicago.[650]

On December 30, it was reported that Johnson had agreed to fight Sam McVey in Sydney on or about Easter Monday, April 8, for a $30,000 guaranteed purse plus $5,000 in training expenses. McVey's victory over Langford made it a lucrative bout. Johnson said, "McVey is made to order for me." Jack also said, "Furthermore, I will meet Jim Flynn, Al Kaufman, Carl Morris, or Al Palzer before I leave for any distance if the promoters will give me $30,000 for my end."[651]

Unfortunately, Sydney's clergy immediately began agitating for the prohibition of the scheduled McVey-Johnson fight. Fearing a repeat of what had taken place in England, businessmen interested in the fight engaged legal counsel to test the contest's legality; to ensure that they would not be investing money in a venture that could not proceed. Once again, it appeared that another potential Johnson bout might be derailed by opposition.

Promoter Jack Curley offered Johnson a flat fee of $30,000 to fight Jim Flynn in July 1912, as long as Curley retained all of the motion picture proceeds, or $20,000 plus training expenses and a 33% interest in the films. Negotiations were ongoing.[652]

As a result of all of the opposition to the fight being held in Sydney, Johnson received notice that the McVey match would have to be moved to France, to be held on June 23 instead of April. Of course, that was very close to a potential Flynn bout date. Johnson would not be able to do both matches around the same time. Between the two, a Flynn fight made more business sense because it seemed to involve less risk for the same money.[653]

White hopes were the craze of the nation. Every promoter was trying to develop a white heavyweight who could defeat Johnson.

Chicago's *Day Book* said, "Flynn looks like the best 'white hope' in sight at present. He is a rough and ready, tearing, clashing fighter, who does not know the meaning of fear."[654]

Promoter Jim Coffroth also said that he would give Johnson his $30,000 price to fight Flynn. He said, "Flynn is fighting in remarkable form. His showing against Kaufman entitled him to a chance at the championship."

On January 6, 1912, Jack Johnson and Jim Flynn signed articles of agreement to fight in July 1912 (with the exact date to be set by May 1) in a fight to the finish. Johnson would be paid a guaranteed $30,000, $1,100 for expenses, and 1/3 of the moving picture rights. Five-ounce gloves would be

---

[650] *Freeman*, January 6, 1912.
[651] *San Francisco Call*, December 30, 1911. *Observer*, December 31, 1911.
    On December 28, 1911 in Brooklyn, New York, Al Palzer knocked out Al Kaufman in the 5th round.
[652] *Manchester Guardian*, January 3, 1912; *Salt Lake Tribune*, January 4, 1912.
[653] *Call*, January 4, 1912.
[654] *Day Book*, January 6, 1912.

used, soft bandages allowed, with straight Queensberry rules to govern. The referee was to be mutually agreed upon. Johnson and Flynn agreed not to engage in any bouts after May 1. Flynn's undisclosed share would be paid by his manager, Jack Curley, who represented the promoters, whose identity was a secret. Curley would post $10,000 as a guarantee, while the fighters each would post $5,000 for their performance guarantees. If one party failed to perform, his guarantee money would be forfeited and divided evenly between the remaining two parties. Tim Sullivan of New York was the forfeit stakeholder, and the money had to be in his hands by February 16, 1912. The bout location would be named at a later date. Originally, it was thought the fight would take place in Nevada, though that later changed.

Jim Flynn had a record that began in the late 1890s, and included 1904 D10 George Gardner; 1906 D15 Jack "Twin" Sullivan and LKOby15 Tommy Burns; 1907 W20 and D20 Jack "Twin" Sullivan, KO18 George Gardner, KO7 Dave Barry, WDQ13 Tony Ross, LKOby11 Jack Johnson, and KO6 Bill Squires; 1908 DND10 Jack "Twin" Sullivan, D10 Jim Barry, LKOby9 Al Kaufman, LND10 Jim Barry, and LKOby1 Sam Langford; 1909 WND10 Billy Papke and LND6 Philadelphia Jack O'Brien; 1910 WND10 Sam Langford and LKOby8 Langford; 1911 KO9 Tony Caponi, KO10 Al Kaufman, WND10 Carl Morris, and KO3 Tony Caponi.

Flynn held a 1910 10-round no-decision victory over Langford, although sandwiched around that victory, Langford had stopped Flynn in 1 and 8 rounds respectively. However, since losing to Langford in March 1910, Flynn would go on a ten-fight win streak with nine knockouts, including victories over highly touted big men in Kaufman and Morris. Many thought the 184-pound Flynn had the experience, toughness, strength, power, and aggressive, fast-paced, spirited style to give Jack Johnson a stiff challenge.

Johnson said he would ask McIntosh to postpone the McVey bout until the fall. Jim Corbett said Johnson took the Flynn fight in order to stall off potential tougher matches with colored challengers.[655]

---

[655] *New York Times, Washington Herald,* January 7, 1912; *El Paso Herald,* January 6, 1912; *Freeman,* July 20, 1912; Boxrec.com. Copy of the signed articles of agreement.

H. C. B. Fry, publisher of the new *Fry's Magazine* in London, England, opined that the Negro was constitutionally a better scrapper than the Caucasian, for he was quicker and had superior ability to absorb punishment. Fry claimed that England did not have anti-color feeling, yet admitted that "we do not much like not having a man who is either champion of the world or thereabouts, one of our own blood, I mean – a white man."[656]

There had been talk of Johnson boxing in a 10-round bout in New York, to be held prior to the Flynn fight, most likely against Joe Jeannette.

However, on January 11, 1912, New York Boxing Commissioner Frank O'Neill said he would not allow Johnson to box in the state against anyone. "I have come to the conclusion it is against public policy and expediency to have Johnson box here. This is final."

That same day in Chicago at O'Connell's gymnasium, Johnson sparred 3 rounds each (for a total of 9 rounds) with Walter Monahan, Marty Cutler, and 120-pound featherweight Jack Hirsch. Against the featherweight Hirsch, the champion twice went down and took a count. Of course, he just was clowning around for fun, and the fans enjoyed it.

Putting to rest the rumors that he weighed close to 260 pounds, Johnson took the scales and tipped the beam at 229 pounds. Jack said he had plenty of time to get into shape for Flynn, only needing four months of training for a finish fight.

Afterwards, when Jack read that the New York boxing commissioner was barring him from fighting there, Johnson responded that the commissioner could not ban him without reason.

> Do you know why they try to bar me in New York and London? Well, it is because they know no white man alive can whip me. They believe in their hearts that Jack Johnson is the greatest fighter that ever lived and just because he is colored they don't want to give him a chance.
>
> Why, if they had a big white fellow in New York that they thought could trim me, there wouldn't be the slightest objection in the world to the match. They would let me fight Jeannette, too, because he also is colored. But just because I have it on the white fellows, they say, 'Let's bar him.' That's not justice and I will leave it to any fair-minded person if it is.

---

[656] *New York Age*, January 11, 1912.

Talking about Corbett, Johnson said,

> Corbett says he could have whipped me ten years ago. Say, I could have beaten Jim Corbett every afternoon just for fun when he was at his very best. He never knocked out a good man. John L. Sullivan and Charlie Mitchell were fat dead ones when he fought them.

Dan McKetrick, Joe Jeannette's manager, had been offering Johnson $15,000 to fight Joe in a 10-round bout. Johnson wanted $30,000, preferably for a longer fight. After all, he would earn that for fighting Flynn.

> This McKetrick makes me tired. At first he said Jeannette was a Marathon fighter, that he could beat me over a route, but would have no chance in ten rounds. Now he wants to make it ten rounds and bunk the public, because he knows I can make Joe look foolish. However, if he comes across with a $30,000 bid he can have a ten-round whirl before I box Flynn.[657]

On January 17, 1912 in Toronto, Jim Flynn knocked out 200-pound Al Williams in the 2nd round. Williams claimed to be the Canadian champion.

On January 29 in Cincinnati, the Methodist Ministers Association adopted a resolution protesting against the Johnson-Flynn fight, and sent its protest to the U.S. Congress.

Black newspapers often liked to call attention to the clergy's hypocrisy, for religious folk condemned boxing while engaging in total blindness regarding lynchings and the barbarism of mob rule. The *Chicago Defender* noted that white members of the cloth rarely concerned themselves with prize-fighting until Jack Johnson was champion. Hence, it said Christianity was a "peculiar kind of religion. Can these worthy (?) men of God explain?"

> It is a peculiar coincidence that the barbarism of prize fighting is never uppermost in the minds of the more sanctimonious (?) of the white race until the name of Johnson is mentioned. ... Can these worthy (?) men of God explain why the battles between the white exponents of the art fail to arouse their antagonism? Truly the ugly sprit of prejudice is a most opposing force and Christianity is powerless to obliterate it. For the protestation against prize fighting is no more than another exhibition of the white man's pet hobby – prejudice, and only a true insight into a Christian life and a casting of the sham religion will uncover the eyes of the divines to the things that warrant protesting against. Daily, yes, hourly are members of the other race scheming to degrade and perpetrating the crime of lynching on their fellow-man and if the religion of the white man was a thing of the heart and not of the head their bills to Congress would

---

[657] *Salt Lake Tribune*, January 12, 1912; *Tacoma Times*, January 11, 1912.

be filled with prayers and entreaties of the suppression of such diabolical crimes against humanity.[658]

In February, Las Vegas, New Mexico was chosen as the Johnson-Flynn fight site because New Mexico had just been admitted to the Union as a state on January 6, 1912 and had no laws against prizefighting. Local businessmen welcomed the publicity and revenue which would flow from a big fight.

However, as soon as the site was announced, the usual anti-boxing folks came out in force and protested the bout. New Mexico Governor William McDonald said he would stop it if he could, for he did not want to permit a white-black fight. He appealed to the legislature to pass a law against prize fighting. As usual, church groups supported this position and called the bout a detrimental disgrace.[659]

In early February in Chicago, Johnson was appearing on stage at the Haymarket theatre, two shows a night, singing and playing the bass violin in a show called "Down in Melody Lane."[660]

On February 24, 1912 in Milwaukee, Jim Flynn knocked out Leopold McLaglan in the 3rd round.

On March 8, 1912 in Indianapolis, Jack Johnson exhibited 4 rounds with Frank Hoe.

During March, Johnson was in Louisville, visiting the owner of the finest colored café there. He created so much excitement that the mayor had to call for more officers.[661]

The U.S. government was pursuing Johnson, intending to prosecute him for smuggling, alleging that he failed to declare and pay taxes on a $6,000 diamond necklace when he returned from abroad. The government claimed he owed $9,600 in duty taxes on the necklace, including the penalties. Despite Johnson and his wife's vigorous protests, secret service men raided his home in Chicago and departed with the necklace.[662]

On April 8, 1912 in Sydney, Sam Langford avenged his defeat by winning a 20-round decision over Sam McVey.

On April 15, 1912, in its maiden voyage, the largest passenger ship ever built to that point, the RMS *Titanic*, struck an iceberg and sunk. As a result of the ship having an insufficient number of lifeboats, 1,502 people died. There were no safety regulations requiring more lifeboats. In an ironic twist of fate, owing to the color line, there were no black Americans allowed on board, although there was one Haitian family.

---

[658] *Chicago Defender*, February 3, 1912.

[659] *New York Times*, February 9, 1912.

[660] *Chicago Defender*, February 10, 1912.

On February 12, 1912 in Sydney, Australia, Sam Langford won a 20-round decision over Jim Barry.

[661] *Chicago Defender*, March 23, 1912.

On March 16, 1912 in Sydney, Sam McVey won a 20-round decision over Jim Barry.

[662] *Chicago Defender*, April 6, 1912.

Jack Johnson was earning money performing in a burlesque tour.

On April 24, 1912 in Pittsburgh, Jack Johnson and his brother Henry Johnson were passengers in the back seat of the champ's car, which was driven by valet Randall Wright. When the car came to a stop, a heavy truck rear-ended it, crushing the car like an egg-shell. The impact strained the tendons and muscles in the champ's back and spine. Johnson had been set to start active training for the scheduled July 4 Flynn fight, but on the doctor's advice, he would rest for a while instead.[663]

On May 3, 1912 in Springfield, Missouri, young promising white heavyweight Luther McCarty knocked out Carl Morris in the 6th round.

On May 23, 1912 in Albuquerque, New Mexico, Jim Flynn sparred 3 exhibition rounds with his regular sparring partner, Al Williams, a former opponent.

After promoter Jack Curley introduced him to the crowd, Flynn gave a short speech, saying he would bring back the championship to the white race, "where it belongs." He was cheered loudly.

One month after being injured as a passenger in an auto accident, on May 25, Johnson left Chicago, heading to Las Vegas, New Mexico, the fight site. With him were his wife and four sparring partners - Marty Cutler, John Perkins, William Brown, and Professor Burns.[664]

On the evening of May 26, en route to Las Vegas, a mob of people met Johnson at the Santa Fe train station. Jack said,

> I can't see anything but victory for me. All this talk about Jeffries being down and out when I fought him is good boosting for Flynn. … I could beat Jeffries the best day he ever saw. I'm the best boxer in the world and I don't say it to brag either. Flynn simply can't whip me, that's all. … He has kidded himself along for months now and he actually believes he can beat me.

Johnson said the fight would not go over 10 rounds.

Tommy Ryan, who agreed to train him, said Flynn had a chance, for Johnson never had beaten a great fighter. Ryan discounted the Jeffries victory, saying Jeff was not fit to fight. He also said that no one knew how far Johnson had gone back as a result of two years of inactivity.[665]

Johnson's initial training camp was at Forsythe's ranch, six to eight miles northeast of Las Vegas, New Mexico. Jack planned to do road work for a while before starting gym work.

---

[663] *Chicago Defender*, April 27, 1912. *New York Times*, April 25, 1912. As a result of his injuries, Johnson canceled his engagements to appear at the local Academy Theater.

From 1891 to 1911, the official spelling of the city's name was changed temporarily to "Pittsburg," but from July 19, 1911 on it was known by the original spelling, "Pittsburgh."

[664] *Albuquerque Evening Herald*, May 24, 25, 1912.

On May 13, 1912 in Melbourne, Australia, Sam Langford stopped Jim Barry in the 11th round. On May 24, 1912 in Plymouth, England, Joe Jeannette scored a KO11 over George Rodel.

[665] *Albuquerque Evening Herald*, May 27, 1912.

At that time, Flynn was weighing about 215 pounds, but intended to train down to 195. Johnson said he was weighing 232 pounds.

Jack Curley said he would construct an arena in an exclusive residential section of Las Vegas, on a vacant lot at the corner of Sixth Street and Friedman Avenue. It was only a short distance from the center of the city, and one could walk to it within 15 minutes.

The Forsythe Ranch training camp did not last long, for Johnson did not like it. He said it was lonesome, the coyotes kept him awake all night howling their heads off, there were no trees, the roads were dusty, and water was scarce. He decided to train in town, in Las Vegas, where the people could see him. "Then there will be no stories told of me fooling away my time." He found a place to his liking in West Las Vegas.[666]

On the morning of May 28, Johnson ran 10 miles in 2 hours. He repeated the stunt in the afternoon. Jack said the altitude did not bother him in the least.[667]

At that point, the bout was scheduled for 45 rounds.

Flynn was training in Montezuma, 5.5 miles northwest of Las Vegas, working in the hotel ballroom. Tommy Ryan said Flynn was bigger than he thought, big enough to become champion. He believed that Flynn's strong build, ferocious style, and powerful explosive blows were well-adapted for Johnson. Flynn loved hard work, was a good listener, and was known as the toughest man in the business. He did not drink or smoke. Ryan thought Jim would weigh just under 200 pounds for the fight.

Flynn was 32 years old and had been fighting for almost 12 years. His experience would serve him well, as it had against Kaufman and Morris.

---

[666] *Albuquerque Morning Journal,* May 27, 28, 1912. Chief Johnson trainer Tom Flanagan would arrive in about a week. Jack's sparring partners included Marty Cutler, John Perkins, Jack Debray (also called George DeBray), and Bob Barnes.

On May 27, 1912 in Melbourne, Sam Langford stopped Porky Dan Flynn in the 14th round.

[667] *Albuquerque Morning Journal,* May 29, 1912.

Jack Curley said Flynn would win with superior fighting and unexcelled gameness.

Although New Mexico Governor William C. McDonald had asked the legislature to pass a law prohibiting prize fighting, it did not appear that it was going to do so. Further, his appeal made it evident that he believed that he was powerless to stop the fight without a law being in effect.[668]

Johnson appeared to be taking Flynn seriously. He was running two hours in the morning and taking a long hike in the afternoon. He had a 30' x 30' platform in the back-yard of his dwelling in Old Town, or Las Vegas proper. He sparred with Marty Cutler and George DeBray, his two massive white sparring partners, both of whom said they could not hit Johnson more than once a week. Cutler said that in order to win, Flynn had to hit Johnson, and he did not think he could do it.

Johnson said, "Mistah Flynn will touch me but twice in our coming battle. The first time will be when he shakes hands at the beginning of the fight, and the other will be when he tries to hold on to keep from being knocked out, when I put over the anaesthetic punch."

On June 1, using 10-ounce gloves, Flynn sparred with Al Williams and Tommy Ryan. Flynn was fast with his short-arm blows to the stomach and jaw. "He can put a world of strength in a mighty short punch."

On June 2, while Flynn was doing roadwork, a farmer mistook him for an escapee from the local mental hospital/asylum, which was about four miles from Flynn's camp. The farmer told the superintendent, "One of your patients has got away and is running for the hills as fast as he can go." They caught up with the Pueblo fireman at his training camp, but soon realized he was not a patient. Flynn explained, "I am not crazy on any subject, but one. ... I have it so strongly implanted in my bean that I am going to win, that Jack Johnson will have to give me some tough pounding to beat it out of me. I am just crazy enough or just wise enough to believe that he can't do it and that I will be champion about the fourth of next month."

Jack Curley said there was no chance of the fight being stopped. The legislature would adjourn on June 8, and most of them favored the fight.

Curley said Flynn was looking good and would win for sure. "Johnson looks to be aging to me and is not so fast as he was. Flynn is a different man. He weighs 210 pounds and is a great big fellow."[669]

On June 2, Johnson boxed 9 rounds.

Philadelphia Jack O'Brien, who had boxed both Johnson and Flynn in 6-round bouts in 1909, said Flynn would be hard to whip and would give the champ a great battle. If the odds were right, O'Brien would wager on Flynn.

> I think [Flynn] has a great chance, although Johnson is one of the greatest exponents of boxing that ever lived. ... Johnson at all times is a dangerous proposition and liable to pass one over when least

[668] *Albuquerque Evening Herald, Albuquerque Morning Journal,* May 30, 1912.
[669] *Albuquerque Morning Journal,* May 31 - June 3, 1912.

expected. I hardly think he is any better, if as good, as he was some years ago, but, nevertheless, he is too good to be fooled with.

Jack Curley wanted to bet on the Fighting Fireman at 5 to 2 odds. "There's no limit in what I'll bet on Flynn."

On June 3 in the heart of Las Vegas, a great crowd saw Johnson train. Jack sparred 3 rounds each with Marty Cutler (white) and Rastus Respress (black) (a.k.a. Calvin Respress). One observer said, "The big smoke was at his best, so far as his feinting and footwork was concerned, though he refrained from beating up his two boys." Another said, "Johnson looks slow, compared with his former speed. However, to one who has never seen him before, he appears as fast as a streak of very quick, but very black lightning." Jack also went through his full course of gym work on his spacious outdoor platform, finishing with a dazzling exhibition of bag punching. Johnson said he had lost five pounds since coming to camp, and weighed 227 pounds.

Despite the fact that Flynn's Montezuma Springs resort was several miles from town, there was a splendid crowd on hand. The 204-pound Flynn was so harsh with his sparring partners that he stopped both Ray Marshall and Al Williams in the 2nd round. Howard Morrow was happy to be done when the 3rd round of their sparring was completed.[670]

Flynn's work was the exact opposite of Johnson's. Enjoying give-and-take fighting, Flynn was a game, rugged, willing, hard-hitting fighter who daily lambasted his sparring partners. "It was a case of slug, slug, slug and butt, butt, butt from the time each setto starts until it ends." He roughed it so viciously that his three sparring partners were crippled, badly used up, and ready to quit. Al Williams' ribs were injured, and Howard Morrow had an ugly cut below his right eye. Flynn's proven reputation for being the roughest, toughest scrapper in the business was fully justified. He said, "I'll only win by fighting the big smoke. He would make me look like a huge sucker if I tried to box with him."

Flynn loved to train hard, and tabooed smoking and beer. All of his sparring partners said Flynn was as strong as any man in the game and dealt the hardest blow of them all. Flynn could be relied upon to rough it every inch of the way. There was no chance of him collapsing like Jeffries. Flynn had been active throughout his 50-fight career, and had gone 10-0 with 9 KOs over the course of 1911 and 1912 alone.

Conversely, Johnson was coming off a two-year layoff, during which time he had engaged in a great deal of high living, so many thought he would not be as good as he once was. Plus, he was 34 years old.

Flynn was very confident.

> I'll knock the big smoke stiff. … I'll win and win sure. Why shouldn't I win? Doesn't every good white person around the country want me to trim Johnson? Then, won't the best people at the contest in Las

---

[670] *Albuquerque Morning Journal, Albuquerque Evening Herald,* June 4, 1912.

Vegas July 4th be white people? I know I won't disappoint, and inside of a month's time the whole world will know what I know now.

Flynn sparring partners Howard Morrow and Ray Fairchild went to the Johnson camp to watch him work. On June 5, they saw Jack spar Marty Cutler, Rastus Respress, and Kid Skelly. They believed that Johnson had gone back. They said his blows lacked steam and he was not nearly as fast as he once was. Of course, Johnson might have been kidding them and holding back.

Every morning, Johnson was engaging in a brisk two-hour run over the hills. He was boxing with four sparring partners – Marty Cutler, George DeBray, Kid Skelly (all white), and Rufus Rastus Respress (black). He was sparring from 6 to 10 rounds in his daily public workouts on the platform he had built. Some said Johnson was puffing badly during his sparring.

One writer said Cutler and DeBray were painfully slow, and Skelly and Respress undersized. To date, Johnson had boxed about 24 rounds. However, he had yet to rough it at all. Jack was content to allow his sparring partners to do the work, satisfied to duck out of harm's way and act as if he was going to start a punch, only to pull it back. Still, his defense was there. Kid Skelly, who made Flynn's teeth rattle in an exhibition a few days ago, was not able to touch Johnson.

Regardless of any criticism, Johnson was pleased with his progress and was sure of victory. "While I figure Jim Flynn a tough ringster, the best of the white crop, I am confident I will defeat him July 4th inside 15 rounds." He said there was no doubt about it. Still, showing his respect for Jim, Johnson said he would back Flynn to beat any man in the world except himself. "I have a month before me, and I am confident I will be in the pink of trim July 4. Those experts who said I had gone the pace that kills and would never be able to come back will be proven a foolish lot next month. I sure do feel sorry for Mr. Flynn."

When asked what he would do after the fight, Johnson said, "I'll fight a man a week up to and including Labor day. Then it will be curtains with Lil' Artha for all times."

Johnson said he would fight Sam Langford if Sam and his manager Joe Woodman posted a large enough side bet to make it worth his while, and if they could find a promoter willing to put up his required guarantee. "Yes, my sweeping defy includes Sam Langford if he and Joe Woodman, his manager, can scrape up enough money to give me the right sort of a side bet." Jack had his reasons. "Johnson always refused to meet [Langford], alleging that two black men would not draw a large enough crowd to pay expenses, let alone accrue enough mazuma to buy gasoline for Johnson's big racing automobile."[671]

Curley said the advance ticket sales had exceeded his expectations. Of course, no one knew if that was true or if he was just puffing.

---

[671] *Albuquerque Evening Herald, Albuquerque Morning Journal*, June 5-6, 1912.

Tommy Ryan expected that Flynn would weigh between 185 and 188 pounds for the fight. At the close of his workout on June 6, he weighed 195 pounds, having come down from 215. Ryan did not like excess weight on a fighter, and thought Flynn would be at his best a bit lower. "If he weighed more his speed would be slowed just that much and his blows would not be any the harder."

Johnson said his weight was coming off rapidly, having removed about 10 pounds. He weighed 222 to 223 ½ pounds. His camp expected him to weigh about 219 for the fight. However, many who had seen him "declare he is fabricating concerning his weight and that he weighs a good ten pounds more than he is willing to plead guilty to."

Johnson allowed his sparring partners to come at him as fiercely as they wanted, while he merely side-stepped their wicked yet unavailing leads, holding back his offense and not being rough with them.

Harry Smith said two years of idleness could not have done Johnson any good, though he doubted that Jack had dissipated as much as some alleged. Johnson was too shrewd to allow that. He did no less than 12 miles of daily roadwork and had not missed a day of work since he started training.[672]

On the evening of June 6 at the Santa Fe Elks' theatre, Johnson exhibited for the New Mexico Athletic Club, boxing with George De Bray, Marty Cutler, and Kid Calvin Respress. The locals said Johnson did not appear to have an ounce of superfluous flesh, wearing his weight well. "His fighting attitude is a natural erect posture with one foot advanced. Lightning-like rapidity in action is combined with a grace of movement that is unusual in one of almost monstrous proportions." The three sparring partners were fine physical specimens, but seemed like pygmies beside the titanic champion who punched them about at will. His boxing set to rest the rumors that the "Big Smoke" was not in the best of condition. The locals were impressed, feeling that Flynn had his work cut out for him.

When called upon for a speech, Johnson said,

> I wish to show the people of Santa Fe that a boxer can be a gentleman. It is the first time that I have been in your new state and the impression that I leave with you I desire to be favorable both to myself and the sport of which I am an exponent.

---

[672] *Albuquerque Morning Journal, Albuquerque Evening Herald*, June 7, 1912.

In regard to the battle which is coming I wish to say that I shall do all I can to defeat Jim Flynn, and I will use every fair means to that end. But above all may the best man win.

Jack said he never felt better, and smiled, showing the gold in his teeth.[673]

Johnson's sparring partners resented some newsmen's statements that they were too slow to bring out the fine points of Johnson's boxing. Cutler said it was a crime to call him slow, for he had more speed and class than any sparring partner that Flynn had at Montezuma.

As of June 7, Tommy Ryan, who had been in the Flynn camp for eleven days, said Flynn had the strength, gameness, and willingness, but would need to work on his defense, for Johnson would be tough to defeat.

That day, before a crowd of 150 spectators, Flynn sparred 3 rounds each with Howard Morrow, 220-pound Al Williams, and Ray Marshall. Although he landed some damaging body blows, Flynn was not as rough as usual, working on his defense and showing a level of skill at blocking that surprised even his closest friends. His gym work lasted 1 hour and 15 minutes, and his condition was said to be phenomenal. The impressed crowd gave Flynn a pleasing round of applause.

On the evening of June 7, Johnson again boxed in Santa Fe.

W. W. Naughton said Johnson was earning the lion's share of the money. Flynn's incentive was that if he won, he'd earn a king's ransom, particularly from the motion pictures.[674]

Johnson had planned to exhibit in nearby Albuquerque the following week, but declined to do so as a result of the fact that no assurance could be given to him that he would be permitted to stay at a first-class hotel. He was told that there were a "lack of accommodations," but the truth was that the color line was at work. Johnson said, "I don't want to be humiliated by being refused first class hotel accommodations." Johnson put his principals ahead of money.[675]

On June 12, Ryan and Flynn sparred 3 rounds, their fourth sparring session together. Afterwards, Ryan said that when the match was first made, he considered it a joke. "I had another laugh when Curley offered me a big bunch of money to handle Flynn. The offer was too big to be turned down." However, Flynn's condition, ruggedness, strength, and confidence had impressed Ryan, and Jim was improving every time they worked together. Ryan said Flynn had a legitimate chance with Johnson.

I honestly believe that if the contest goes ten rounds Flynn stands a better chance than Johnson to be the victor. Jim's condition is bound

---

[673] *Santa Fe New Mexican*, June 7, 1912. Professor W. Burns, also black, was Johnson's trainer.

[674] *Albuquerque Morning Journal, Albuquerque Evening Herald*, June 8, 1912. *Kansas City Star*, June 7, 1912. The *Star* had a reporter on scene.

Flynn was highly motivated, having given up a theatrical contract that was bringing him $750 a week, in order to go to Las Vegas and train.

[675] *Albuquerque Morning Journal, Albuquerque Evening Herald*, June 11, 1912. Johnson had been paid $600 for exhibiting in Santa Fe the previous week.

to be better than Lil' Artha's. Then Jim will take better to the high altitude than the black. Don't say that I am claiming that the title is going to be returned to the keeping of the white race, but if Johnson doesn't cop Flynn while he is fresh I think my entry will just about score.

Flynn told Ed Smith, the Chicago sporting writer who had been mentioned as a strong candidate to referee the bout, "Ed, I want to die if I lose to Johnson. I'll give any man in the country full permission to shoot if I don't win."[676]

On June 14, Johnson was given a list of fifteen names as potential referees, but he objected to eleven of them as unfit as a result of pronounced antipathy against his race. The *Chicago Defender,* which had a special correspondent with the Johnson party, wrote, "They tried to fake him, but he wouldn't stand for it. ... At least a half dozen of those crossed off were men known as Negro haters. One of them openly declared that 'the Negro had no business at the head of anything.'" Jack favored either Ed W. Smith of Chicago, Jack Welch/Welsh of San Francisco, Mark Levy, who was the director of the New Mexico Athletic Club of Albuquerque, or Edward Cochrane of Kansas City.

Ed W. Smith, the *Chicago Examiner*'s sporting editor, was chosen to referee, for he got along with both Johnson and Curley, and was acceptable to both. He had witnessed every championship battle since Sullivan-Corbett. His selection met with the sporting world's approval.[677]

On June 15, Flynn boxed only 5 rounds, because Ryan and the others were on the disabled list. Ray Marshall had to retire after 1 round. Al Williams and Howard Morrow each were able to work only for 2 rounds.

Dr. Shaw examined Flynn and declared him to be in perfect condition, saying, "I regard Jim Flynn as one of the most remarkable specimens of physical development I have ever examined." According to Dr. Shaw's measurements, Flynn weighed 196 pounds and stood 5'10 ½". Johnson was listed at 219 pounds and 6' ¼" tall. Flynn's reach was 70 inches, while Johnson's was 75 inches.[678]

On June 17, Tommy Ryan abruptly quit and left the Flynn camp. Ryan wrote, "Am disgusted with Flynn. He is hog fat and has no chance whatever with Johnson. I refuse to have my name used any further in connection with this affair. Please notify Associated Press."

---

[676] *Kansas City Star,* June 13, 1912.

[677] *Chicago Defender,* June 15, 1912; *Albuquerque Morning Journal,* June 16, 1912. Edward W. Cochrane and Abe Pollock, both writers, were the second and third referee choices.

[678] *Kansas City Star,* June 16, 1912; *Albuquerque Morning Journal,* June 17, 1912. Flynn took a dip in the hot waters, and Abdul the Turk rubbed him down.

On the 15th, Johnson limited his boxing to work with Marty Cutler, and he also tossed the medicine ball for 10 minutes, shadow boxed 5 minutes, and punched the bag for 5 minutes. In the morning, he covered 12 miles. Flynn's hike was the same.

On June 15, 1912 in New York, Joe Jeannette won a 6th round disqualification over Black Bill.

Although Ryan intimated that he did not like the way that Flynn was training, most believed the real reason he left was financial, for he wanted a more definite understanding from Curley regarding what remuneration would be forthcoming for his services, and got the wrong answer.

Others reported that Flynn practiced foul tactics on his sparring partners, so much so that a disgusted Ryan quit and left the camp. He predicted that Flynn would lose on a foul.[679]

Responding to Ryan's allegations that Flynn was fat and had no chance, Promoter Jack Curley said both Flynn and Johnson were training hard in public daily, so folks could see for themselves that both men were rounding into prime form. Flynn was training as no man ever trained before. He weighed 198 pounds, and "not one of the hundreds that watch him work every day will hint that he is hog fat or untrained. And his quarters are open to the public at all times. There is no excuse for anyone to miss seeing and hearing for himself." Curley said Ryan was just sour grapes and had left several other fighters after some discord.

Much to Curley's chagrin, thus far Governor McDonald had declined to put himself on the record regarding whether he would attempt to stop the fight. Curley feared that might cause lower attendance, for folks would not want to spend money and travel to a fight which might be prevented. Las Vegas men of prominence who were interested in the venture's success allegedly had spent from $65,000 to $75,000 on the enterprise.

Curley declared that any report that the governor was determined to stop the fight was false, generated by persons who had been denied complimentary tickets and wished to injure the bout's prospects.

Curley insisted that the fight would happen. There was no law to prevent it in New Mexico. The bout likely would be better than the Jeffries fight, for Flynn was younger, more consistently active, and in great shape.

On June 18, Flynn worked at top speed for 50 minutes, including 3 rounds of tugging and hauling with Ray Marshall and 3 rounds of boxing with Al Williams. When the training concluded, Flynn was barely puffing. Those who watched "the hope of the white race go through his training are almost a unit in the belief that he stands more than an even chance to carry off the heavyweight title."

All expressed surprise at his size and strength, and agreed that Flynn was in excellent shape. "Tommy Ryan, Flynn's discarded trainer, who quarreled with the firm of Flynn & Curley over money matters, has made himself a laughing stock here by declaring that the white boy was 'hog fat.' Flynn is nothing like that, as anybody who goes to his camp can see." Dr. Shaw said he doubted if Jim was carrying over four pounds of superfluous flesh.

Abdul the Turk Malgan, who had become the chief trainer, said Flynn was working harder than any other fighter with whom he ever had been

---

[679] *Albuquerque Evening Herald, San Francisco Examiner, Call,* June 18, 1912; *New York Times,* June 22, 1912.

associated. "Flynn deserves to bring the heavyweight title back to the white race. ... He is a bear for work, is behaving finely, and if confidence counts for anything, the July 4 battle already is in."

Referee Ed Smith said Tommy Ryan's statement that Flynn was fat was not true. He obviously was in great shape. Smith said Ryan admitted it to him. Ryan told Smith that he was upset with Flynn because he wouldn't pay attention and wanted to do things his own way.

Unlike Flynn, who charged no admission fee, Johnson charged the public 15 cents apiece to see him work a matinee. He punched the bag for 15 minutes, threw the medicine ball for 10 minutes, and then boxed 5 rounds with Marty Cutler and 6 rounds with Calvin Respress. Afterwards, he stepped on the scales and weighed 220 ½ pounds.[680]

An army of workmen were constructing the great arena that would accommodate 17,000 people. The most distant seat would be only 80 - 90 feet from ring center, with the highest seat five feet above the ground.

The arena was located on 6th street, within a five-minute walk from the Santa Fe train station. The street-car line passed within 200 feet of the structure and was a short walk from the business district.

Although Queensberry rules required a 24-foot ring, or as near to that size as practical, Johnson said he would fight Flynn in any kind of ring, including a 17-foot one.

On June 20, Flynn ran 10 miles in 65 minutes. As usual, he hit a huge 300-pound bag of oats and hay. He engaged in 3 rounds of pulling and hauling with Ray Marshall, and then 3 more with Al Williams. A short left hook wobbled Williams badly. Flynn also skipped rope, something Johnson did not do.[681]

On June 21, 1912, federal officials indicted Johnson and his wife for smuggling, alleging that

---

[680] *Albuquerque Evening Herald, Kansas City Star*, June 19, 1912.
[681] *Albuquerque Evening Herald*, June 20, 21, 1912. Flynn occasionally was boxing with Abdul the Turk as well. The outdoor ring at Johnson's Old Town training quarters was flooded with rain.

they had failed to report and pay import duties on a $6,000 diamond necklace that Jack had purchased for his wife in England.[682]

Tommy Ryan said Curley was trying to use him to boost a man who was not a fit opponent for Johnson. "The match is one that never should have been made."

Claude Johnson, the *Kansas City Star*'s sporting editor, who was on scene, allegedly said,

> Flynn looks good to me. Tommy Ryan was kidding himself and trying to kid the papers when he stated that the fireman was hog fat. That is absolutely absurd. ... The Jim Flynn in training here for Jack Johnson is a hundred per cent better Jim Flynn than the one that did up Al Kaufman in Kansas City last May.

> Jack Johnson also looks good to me. I doubt if he was any better at Reno. ... He is confident of the result of the big match, and at this stage of the game, is my pick. As I see the Las Vegas encounter on the Fourth two splendidly trained fighters, the best white man and the best black in the world, will go to the post and the fistic enthusiasts should see a spirited encounter.

However, Claude Johnson's *Kansas City Star* report differed slightly, saying that the reason Jack Johnson wasn't training all that hard was because he was figuring on winning relatively quickly, with one punch. "Johnson looks good and healthy – looks like he could step in the ring right now and put up a fast battle for a short distance – but, really, he doesn't look as if he had trained for an endurance contest."

This reporter also said that the Mexicans, who outnumbered the American citizens in that area four to one, were strong for Johnson.

> Every afternoon at the ink's camp the insurrectos congregate and applaud his efforts. John Arthur can spell a fair line of Spanish, while a smattering of English and profane is Jim Flynn's line. The negro appeals to the 'Mex' because he is good natured and looks lazy. They don't like anything here in the animated line.[683]

Tom Flanagan had joined the champ's camp and got his first glimpse of Johnson on June 22, the first time in nearly two years. After Johnson hit the punching bag, tossed the medicine ball, and boxed 3 rounds with Marty Cutler and 3 with George DeBray, Flanagan said, "He hasn't aged a day. He looks every bit as good to me as he ever did in his life." He thought Flynn had almost no chance to win, for Johnson was fit to fight for a month.

Professor Watson Burns, trainer-in-chief, said, "Jack is every bit as good today as he ever was in his life. ... We are not underrating Flynn, but

[682] *New York Times*, June 22, 1912.
[683] *Albuquerque Morning Journal, Albuquerque Evening Herald, Kansas City Star*, June 22, 1912.

honestly I don't think that he has better than an extreme outside chance of defeating Johnson."

John Perkins, Marty Cutler, George DeBray, Jack Johnson, Professor Watson Burns, Calvin Rastus Respress, Kid Skelly, William Brown

The consensus of opinion of those who saw him in action was that the Pueblo Fireman Flynn would give Johnson the fight of his life. Jim would carry the fight to Johnson every minute and not tire. He could not be stalled or kept off, and therefore it would be a toe-to-toe bout. "One and all scoff at Tommy Ryan's statement that the Puebloan is 'hog fat' and stands no chance with Johnson. If the best conditioned man is going to win the battle July 4 it will be Flynn's championship."

However, Johnson was known as the hardest man in the business to hit cleanly. Despite a lengthy career, he had no bruises, no cauliflower ear, no flattened nose, and no marked-up face. The feeling was that his defense and ring generalship were so tremendous that he never really had a hard fight.

On the 22nd, Flynn did his full course of gym stunts, hugged and tugged for 10 minutes with Ray Marshall, and boxed 4 rounds with Abdul the Turk, 3 rounds with Al Williams, and 2 rounds with Chic Coleman.

The betting odds were 10 to 4, with Johnson the favorite.[684]

On June 23, 2,000 people paid 15 cents each to watch Johnson spar 10 rounds. The "inky champion" was down to 215 pounds after his workout.

Some told Flynn that Johnson considered the fight a joke and was not training. On one hand, Flynn was happy in that he would be the better prepared, which gave him a better chance to win. On the other hand, he was mad because he felt that people would not come to see the fight if they did not think Johnson was taking the bout seriously owing to his feeling that it was a mismatch. That did not help to promote it.[685]

In his autobiography, Johnson claimed that during training camp for this fight, a 23-year-old Harry Wills sought a place as a sparring partner, but

[684] *Albuquerque Evening Herald*, June 24, 1912.
[685] *Kansas City Star*, June 24, 1912.

only remained a few days. "He proved wholly unable to stand the grind and was compelled to acknowledge that the ordeal was too much for him."[686]

Ten days before the fight, on June 24, New Mexico Governor William C. McDonald said that as long as the law was obeyed, the fight would not be prohibited. He wanted county and city officials to enforce the state laws strictly, his main concern relating to the suppression of public gambling.

Governor McDonald explained that as early as February 9, he expressed himself as opposed to the fight, but the attorney general advised him that the bout could not be prohibited legally. All he could do was enforce existing laws, and the legislature had passed no law against boxing. As of March 11, two laws were introduced in the legislature, one prohibiting and one allowing boxing. The one legalizing it passed the house, but both bills were smothered in the senate committee. On May 28, the governor requested that the legislature take action. However, neither house did anything, so he could not prevent something that was not illegal.

Las Vegas met with jubilation the news that the governor would not intervene. A big fight of this kind could be a big boost to the local economy. The city's leading businessmen had invested a lot of money in the promotion. The news caused a healthy stimulus in the sale of seats. Seats were selling for $10, $20, and $25. Seating capacity was 17,150.

Mayor Robert Taupert said the city would be kept clean and gambling suppressed. "I gladly vouch that no city ordinance or state law will be violated and that aside from saving the local business men their money invested in the coming venture, we will all combine and assert our local pride so that every visitor will leave these parts with the opinion that we are a law-abiding country."

Tommy Ryan said Flynn would not last long.

> If Johnson does any kind of fighting at all, he will put Flynn out of the game in eight rounds…ten at the outside. … Take that report that Flynn is five feet ten and one-half inches tall. It's all bunk. He is five feet nine inches and not a hair taller. … I could have made good money by staying, but I quit because I saw that Flynn never had a chance and never will have with Johnson. … And the reports of what I said when I got to the camp were about all faked. I watched Flynn work out and I thought less of him every time I saw him. Yes, he did what I told him for awhile, but he soon got to knowing it all. … Flynn has no defense. He has a crouch that Johnson will soon take out of him and that is rotten as a defense. His foot work is pretty good, but taking it all around Flynn is no fighter. Ten rounds is the very most I would give him in the fight.[687]

---

[686] Jack Johnson, *In the Ring and Out* at 66. At that point, Harry Wills only had about eight pro bouts of experience.

[687] *Albuquerque Evening Herald, Albuquerque Morning Journal,* June 25, 1912.

Hugh McIntosh allegedly was offering Johnson $30,000 to come to Australia to fight. Most presumed the opponent would be Sam Langford. Johnson would require assurances that the British Empire/Australian authorities would allow him to fight there before he would travel such a long way and spend time and money training, forgoing other opportunities.

Tom Flanagan noted that the champ was criticized regardless of whether or not he fought.

> They roast and they pan and they pan and they scold and never get through talking about a champion who doesn't fight. Yet, when the champion gets his price and starts to prepare for a battle they begin to pan him and scold for taking on easy marks.

> Now, the average man thinks a champion ought to battle every time some young fellow bobs up with a challenge. ... If Flynn isn't the best of the white men, then why isn't he? Hasn't he done everything that has been asked of him in the last two years or so?

> And then the average man doesn't consider what it costs to train for a real battle, both in a financial and a physical way; doesn't consider at all how infrequent are offers of the kind that come from Jack Curley for this Las Vegas battle and doesn't consider a hundred and one other things that stand in the way of big affairs of the kind.[688]

The confident Johnson did not see how he could be dethroned. His trainer Professor Watson Burns and his sparring partners all declared that Lil' Artha was absolutely invincible.

In Flynn's camp, trainer/sparring partner Abdul the Turk said Johnson had to be every bit as good as he was in his battle with Jeffries to win. "If Johnson has gone back at all and is unable to go at top speed over twelve or fifteen rounds, he will be carried out of the ring."

On June 25, although it rained from noon until after 3 p.m., both men were in action at their respective camps. That morning, Flynn ran 12 miles. Flynn's boxing workout lasted 55 minutes, and he sparred 10 rounds: Al Williams went 4, while Ray Marshall, Chic Coleman, and Abdul the Turk each did 2 rounds. Flynn was weighing around 190 pounds.

The now 215-pound Johnson punched the bag about 15 minutes, tossed the medicine ball for about the same length of time, and then sparred 8 rounds with Marty Cutler, working in particularly fine fashion. Tom Flanagan said Johnson was as fit and good as ever, and Flynn doomed to defeat. "Father Time, no one else, is going to dethrone the champion."

Intrigued by the contest, W. W. Naughton arrived in East Las Vegas. He noted that Flynn had been the underdog against Kaufman and Morris, but won in emphatic fashion against both, annihilating and beating up two very

---

[688] *Albuquerque Evening Herald*, June 25, 1912; *New York Times*, June 26, 1912.

big, strong men. He beat Morris so badly that he wasn't the same since. Thus, Flynn had proven himself to be the best of the white hopes.[689]

There were the typical rumors and speculation that Johnson might throw the fight. The rumor was that Flynn was scheduled to win between the 10th and 15th rounds. Harry Smith responded, "Johnson thinks too much of his title and the glamour with which it surrounds him to give it up for what Flynn and his backers could afford to hand over." Although the motion pictures would be much more valuable if Flynn won, Curley probably was promoting the bout on the chance of Johnson not being in the best of shape owing to his long inactivity, not because of a fix. "Naturally such gossip is to be expected."

Both Flynn and Johnson were confident and appeared well prepared. "[Flynn] boxes in his roughest style, with head down and fists before his face as he crouches." "This talk of high life and wine dinners for Johnson seems to be a joke." Jack said he would win soon after the 10th round. "Johnson should still be the greatest heavy-weight of them all and even if not, Flynn should be easy for him."

Johnson was guaranteed $30,000 for the fight, win, lose, or draw. And if they didn't pay him up front, "You can rest assured the colored man will stay out of the ring."[690]

It had rained considerably for the past month, but as of the 26th, there was not a cloud in the sky.

Johnson's sparring partners were in bad shape. The ailing Marty Cutler had been taking the blows for three weeks and needed a rest. George DeBray, the Chicago heavyweight, allegedly sprained his knee in Sunday's workout. Another reporter said DeBray had boxed only three times owing to a bad foot which rendered him unable to get out of the way fast enough.

On June 27, Johnson did 12 miles of roadwork and sparred 8 rounds with his black sparring partners, Calvin Respress and Bob Watkins, the Denver heavyweight. He also hit the bag for 15 minutes and threw the medicine ball for the same amount of time. Following his rubdown, he weighed 214 ¾ pounds.

The *Star* reported that the 5'6" Calvin Respress, who was built like Joe Walcott, was the only man left who was able to assimilate Johnson's jolts. "Johnson appears to take keen delight in slaughtering this gorilla-like ink spot. … [Respress]] was so cute [that Johnson] brought him along with the other animals."

Jack Dugan of Kansas City, Kansas said the "smoke" looked as if he was ready to put up a real fight.

It was anticipated that the Rocky Mountain Athletic special would bring upwards of 1,100 Colorado blacks to the fight.

---

[689] *Albuquerque Evening Herald,* June 26, 1912.
[690] *Albuquerque Morning Journal,* June 27, 1912.

One betting proposition was that the Fireman would be on his feet at the end of the 15th round, but even those who sought to make that bet were asking for 10 to 8 odds.

Captain Fred Fornoff of the state mounted police arrived and voted Las Vegas the state's cleanest city.

Although Johnson was willing to fight in a ring of any size, his handlers, Tom Flanagan and Professor Watson Burns, objected to the 17 ½-foot ring. They said that they would not permit the champ to enter a ring of less than 20 feet. Apparently, the ring's dimensions could be increased only up to 19'10", and they accepted that.

On the 27th, Flynn ran 12 miles and trained before another great crowd. Jim said, "How do I feel? Bully." After going through his full course of gym stunts, he boxed 4 rounds, 2 each with Ray Marshall and Al Williams. After his hour of fast work, he said, "I wish the fight was tomorrow. ... I feel sorry for Johnson. I'll beat him and beat him sure."

George Morrison, a Denver sporting authority, said Flynn was as hard as a brick and trained to take a beating. "All this talk about Flynn being fat isn't true." Still, he predicted that Johnson would win sometime after the 14th round. However, if the bout lasted 20 rounds, Flynn's chances might increase, for he was in great shape and could take punishment. "If Flynn is knocked out he will be senseless when Eddie Smith does the count."

Seeking more sparring partners, Johnson announced that he would give $200 to anyone who could last 2 rounds with him. His sparring partners were too badly battered and injured to continue. Instead, Johnson was doing long stretches of road work.[691]

On June 28, 1912 in New York, 228 ¼-pound Al Palzer knocked out 188 ½-pound Bombardier Billy Wells in the 3rd round. Although Wells had decked Palzer in the opening round, Palzer came back and dropped Wells once in the 2nd and twice in the 3rd round. Both stood 6'2 ½".[692]

The *Chicago Defender* opined that Johnson would not sell out and throw the fight, for he had too much at stake. "Such report seems absurd when one views the obstacles that the champion had to overcome to reach the coveted goal of his ambition. ... The champion would struggle to stem the tide of defeat as long as an ounce of strength would respond to his dominating spirit."

Flynn was the pugilistic "Titanic of the Caucasian race." However, Johnson outclassed him in strength, speed, and cleverness. His defense was almost impenetrable, which would enable him to wage battle for many rounds without defeat, even if the high altitude affected his breathing. The *Defender* opined that the title would not be transferred "to the brow of the Anglo-Saxon."[693]

---

[691] *Kansas City Star,* June 27, 1912; *Albuquerque Evening Herald,* June 28, 1912.

[692] *Albuquerque Morning Journal,* June 29, 1912.

[693] *Chicago Defender,* June 29, 1912.

The *Freeman* noted that every effort was being made to boom the match as much as possible, yet the interest was nowhere near as great as had been the case for Johnson's last match. It found it ironic that just two years ago the eyes of the entire world were focused on the Jeffries fight. For months, every move they made on a daily basis was covered and wired to the four corners of the globe. Johnson was doing the same training at present.

> But there are no feverish cries for news from headquarters. No descriptive writers are painting word pictures of the wild country in which the battle is to be fought.

> No blue-blooded sporting men are risking their futures on the outcome. No tired business men are arranging their vacations to stretch over a period covering the fight. ...

> And the funny part of it all is this: The Johnson-Flynn fight, which no one cares to see, will undoubtedly be a better fight than was the Johnson-Jeffries affair, which drew the biggest house in ring history. It cannot be any worse as a battle.

> We are not trying to make this situation fit any law of logic.

The same holds true today. The press and public often overlook a much better and more entertaining matchup and promote and get excited about one that likely will not be as good, but is between two "big name" fighters in a long-desired match.

Jim Corbett said no man ever accomplished anything worthwhile unless he had pluck, and "it fairly oozes out of the Pueblo man. He will not admit the possibility of defeat." Corbett said stories of a frame-up always were circulated before big fights, but he did not believe them.

Tommy Ryan said Flynn was too small and knew nothing about fighting but to slug. In somewhat contradictory fashion, he also said he thought Flynn should not weigh more than 175, but was weighing much more. "He has a very short reach and a bad disposition. I could not tell him anything let alone teach him. ... I can't understand how any sane man can make himself believe that Flynn can beat Johnson, if the contest is on its merits, which I think it is. Of course, as a white man, I wish to see Flynn win."

Ryan said he had accepted the offer to train Flynn for a certain amount of money. However, Curley later told him that "we were all to take a chance on the gate. Of course, as Curley has tied up so much money for expenses here, I could not see my way clear on what the fight would draw, and so I quit." Hence, the real reason for his departure was economic.

Flynn was a courageous battler who fought like a tiger, and it was anticipated that win or lose, his performance would command the spectators' respect. In his first fight with Johnson back in 1907, "Flynn tried to fight close from the first smash of the gong, and that even when tossed back by the force of Johnson's uppercuts he returned to the charge again and again." However, in doing so, he fought right into Johnson's hands, hurling himself onto the spears and taking a fearful whaling until the end.

However, Jack Thompson of New York said Flynn had improved 50%, while Johnson had declined 50%. Hence, he thought Flynn had a chance.[694]

Top row: Jack Johnson, Ed Smith, Jack Curley, Tom Flanagan. Second row: Jim Flynn, Otto Floto, W. W. Naughton. Bottom: Paul Armstrong.

Field correspondents on hand in Las Vegas included Omaha's Sandy Griswold, Denver's Otto Floto, Kansas City's Claude Johnson, Milwaukee's Tom Andrews, and San Francisco's W. W. Naughton, amongst others.

A straw ballot of 24 votes saw 17 favoring Flynn as the victor.

In the final days of training, Johnson had almost no sparring, working only with Respress, who was too small and light. However, he was no slouch. Years later, Respress would last 15 rounds with hard-punching 220-pound Luis Firpo.

Although the champ's condition was looked upon with some suspicion, many who saw him train were satisfied. They noted that he had come down in weight from 234 pounds at the start of camp to 214 ¾ pounds.

Flynn continued to weigh just a bit over 190 pounds, which is what he weighed after his workout. He too was not doing much sparring, for his glove-mates were in bad shape as well, and he had to take it easy on them.[695]

The critics assembled in Las Vegas believed that it would be a worthwhile fight and one of the hardest-fought battles ever seen. Sports-writers from all parts of the U.S. were in town. Most anticipated that the bout would last at least 15 rounds. The methodical Johnson was not one to win quickly, and his defense was too good for Flynn to beat in a hurry. Flynn would have to wear down the "Big Smoke." Flynn's confidence and faithful manner of training had made a big hit with the local fight crowd.

Tom Flanagan thought the bout would last at least 17 rounds. Johnson thought he would win in 10 rounds, and was willing to bet $2,500 that

---

[694] *Freeman*, June 29, 1912.
[695] *Kansas City Star*, June 29, 1912.

Flynn would not survive the 15th round. Conversely, Abdul the Turk said, "Flynn will win, and win sure."

Although it was raining on June 29, 433 people paid 15 cents each (generating $65) to watch Johnson spar 3 rounds each with DeBray and Respress. Some said Johnson lacked dash and seemed weary even at the start. Others might say he was just taking it easy.

That day, Flynn boxed 6 rounds as well, and weighed 191 afterwards.

New York's Garden City Athletic Club wired Johnson an offer to fight Al Palzer in that city on Labor Day. "How Johnson is to fight in New York unless the boxing commission relents hasn't been explained. Six months ago the commission announced that the champion ink was barred."[696]

Johnson was perturbed by reports of his going back. The champ asked, "What is all this foolish talk about Jack Johnson having become old and crippled just because it is two years since he had a championship fight?" He said Flynn's backers had better not believe that their man was going to win owing to Jack's inferior condition.

Johnson kept a private clipping bureau and remained thoroughly informed regarding what the sporting critics were writing about him all over the country. "Woe betide the fight correspondent who has said things about Johnson, and who comes to the Johnson camp looking for news. He will find the Johnson scrapbook a bar to progress. It has come to a point where Johnson has the sport writers graded." If they were not on the preferred list, they might be barred from his training quarters or from receiving interviews. Johnson said,

> People don't stop to think and I think newspaper men above all should look at things from every angle before putting their ideas in the paper. ... [T]his thing of giving out to the public that Johnson has done nothing for two years but take life easy is entirely wrong and very misleading. If that is the one thing Flynn's friends are building on to bring him home a winner over me, goodness help them and goodness help Flynn.
>
> I have done more boxing during the past two years than Flynn has done. Every one seems to forget that I put in a full course of training for a fight with Bombadier Wells in England. The fight did not come off, but I had the benefit of the preparation. And for one year and eight months of the two years that have elapsed since I defeated Jeffries I have sparred constantly on the theatrical circuits all over the world. I have been meeting all comers in my stage bouts and I have been in constant training and constant practice. ... Flynn will find me an opponent who has been working union hours right along and has had mighty few holidays. ... Why, I am better than ever. ... I am faster and I hit much harder.

[696] *Kansas City Star*, June 30, 1912.

Flynn supporters wanted 2 ½ to 1 odds, but the Johnsonites were offering only 2 to 1.

On Sunday June 30, as a result of the pleadings from the local baseball club, which said that if he gave a free show, the baseball game set for the same day might just as well be called off, for the first time, Flynn charged admission to watch him train, and fully one thousand paid 15 cents each.

Flynn's final hard workout impressed all of the experts present. After his usual gym stunts, he boxed 7 rounds: Ray Marshall went 2, Abdul the Turk the next 2, and then Al Williams boxed the last 3 rounds.

Flynn gave a speech to the crowd, saying he was ready for the big smoke and would bring the championship back to the white race. He would devote no further time to boxing until the fight.

On the 30th, Johnson mercilessly and soundly battered DeBray and Respress, drawing the ruby fluid from each. However, with Marty Cutler, who just recovered from poison oak, Johnson mostly played defense.

W. W. Naughton was impressed. The talk had been that Johnson had shown a falling away in the hitting department, that he could not hurt his sparring partners no matter how hard he tried, and that he missed 40 per cent of his blows. However, that day, he slaughtered them, snapping their heads backward with vicious clean slashes, sending them to the floor. Johnson gave abundant evidence that even if he was not as forceful as he was before the Jeffries fight, he still was a marvel at finding the range and sending in a hurtful smash. "Johnson was as fast as chain lightning and never an effort was wasted that I could see."

Ultimately though, Naughton opined that "Johnson, no matter what he says, has gone back some, but even if he is the Johnson of old, he is not a knocker-out of the Fitzsimmons type." Naughton noted that it took Johnson 11 rounds to defeat Flynn even when Jim was much lighter and less experienced and knowledgeable. Flynn now was smarter, craftier, more experienced, bigger, stronger, and more confident. Some believed Flynn would do better at altitude owing to the fact that he was from Colorado and was more used to it. "I don't think it's possible for Johnson to knock out the Jim Flynn of today." Even if Flynn lost, he was so splendidly trained, hard as nails, and chock full of fighting spirit that the bout was sure to be enjoyable.

Johnson said he was weighing 213 pounds. Flynn was 192.

Johnson told his detractors,

> Stick to your opinion, but don't back it with your money. Then when it's all over you'll know better and you won't be poorer in pocket. ... One of the wagers I would like to make is a few hundreds at even money that Flynn will not hit me ten clean blows during the fight. And even those he does hit me will not hurt, for Flynn cannot punch. And here's a hunch for you. The last man I licked was named Jim. I

have been beating Jims all my life and I don't think Flynn ever got the better of a man named Jack.[697]

Tommy Ryan made an interesting and insightful prediction. He said Flynn might lose the fight on a foul.

I would not be surprised to hear of Flynn losing the fight by a foul. When he sees that he can not hit Johnson he will do anything he can… [A]ll he can do is what he has done in all his fights, put down his head and start slugging and I do not think that kind of fighting will do to whip Johnson. Flynn is just a fair good little man against a very good big man. … [N]owadays the butthead fighter is a thing of the past.

Ryan also said Flynn's measurements were false, that Jim was 5'9" and no taller, and about 200 pounds, not less.[698]

The *Albuquerque Evening Herald*'s W. H. Lanigan opined, "So far as condition goes the Puebloan will be the superior starter of the two."

[Flynn's] present form is marvelous. He will go into the ring a three to one better man physically than Johnson. He can go a route; Johnson can't. Flynn never puffs after his hour's work in the gym and the Fireman's work is WORK compared to what Johnson pulls. Johnson always puffs, to an extent, after completing his toll. A colored man does not belong in this high altitude. It's in the swamps where they thrive. Johnson is one sterling, high-class, likeable, appreciative fellow. The ring would have owned its most popular champion were he a white man. He is confident. … But give me a ticket on Flynn Thursday. Jim will win sure, and I think he will cop inside of 11 rounds.

John Day, the *Chicago Inter-Ocean*'s sporting editor, said, "When Tommy Ryan sent out word to the pugilistic world that Jim Flynn was hog-fat he lied." He said Ryan made the statement out of personal spite. Day noted that while Johnson had been idle for two years, Flynn was fighting all the time, so he was sharp and at his best.

Despite the hype, Johnson remained a 2 to 1 betting favorite.[699]

On July 1, Jack took things comparatively easy. Neither man sparred.

If Johnson won, it was "highly probable" that his next fight would be in Australia. McIntosh had offered him $30,000 to fight either Langford or McVea, promising to place a $10,000 guarantee in the hands of a reputable sporting man before Jack sailed. Johnson said, "That looks good to me. I will cable McIntosh today, asking for further particulars. If everything is satisfactory I will sail for Australia in September."[700]

---

[697] *San Francisco Examiner*, July 1, 2, 1912.
[698] *Albuquerque Morning Journal*, July 1, 1912.
[699] *Albuquerque Evening Herald*, July 1, 1912.
[700] *San Francisco Examiner*, July 2, 1912.

W. H. Lanigan said if Johnson was to win, he had to do so within 15 rounds or Flynn's stamina would prevail. "The Pueblo boy has made a big hit with all the big critics and fistic experts in Las Vegas. There is nothing to it but that he is a wonderful specimen of humanity."[701]

Meanwhile, in Washington D.C., in the U.S. Congress, a Senate bill had been proposed which would prohibit the interstate shipment of moving picture films of prize fights. Representative Thetus Sims of Tennessee, a Democrat, proposed the bill and sought to pass the measure immediately, explaining that the Johnson-Flynn fight was scheduled for July 4, and he hoped the picture films might be barred from leaving New Mexico. However, a quorum was not present in the house, so the bill was blocked temporarily, despite Mr. Sims' vehement protests. Still, the bill was pending.

Johnson jolts Marty Cutler's head back with a right uppercut

Jack Curley was paying San Francisco's Miles Brothers to take the motion pictures.

The moving picture machines were at the camps on July 2, but the wind was severe enough that further photographing was delayed at Flynn's camp until the 3rd. Johnson was filmed only for a short while, because as soon as he started sparring, the rain came in torrents. However, the champ kept right on toying with his sparring partners.

According to his manager, Johnson weighed 214 pounds. "He appeared to be in splendid form, and as full of energy as a boy."

Fearing hand injury, Johnson planned to do only light road work on the 3rd, as well as toss the medicine ball.

Johnson said that in all probability, he would accept Hugh McIntosh's offer for a match with Langford. "It looks likely. I think I will go to Australia in October, perhaps sooner." There also was talk of a potential match against Al Palzer on Labor Day.[702]

W. W. Naughton predicted a small attendance and financial failure. Folks were not tumbling into town in overwhelming numbers. Naughton said he would be surprised if one-quarter of the 17,000-person stadium was filled. If so, Johnson would be the only one to make money, for his $30,000

[701] *Albuquerque Evening Herald,* July 2, 1912.
[702] *Albuquerque Morning Journal,* July 2-3, 1912.

purse was guaranteed, and he would insist on receiving it before the fight began. What this analysis overlooked was that Curley and Flynn still could make money with the moving pictures. They also were gambling on the riches that would be earned if Flynn won the fight.

Curley believed Flynn would win. Johnson had been leading an easy life, visiting the "high places of the big cities," and had not fought for the past two years, while the younger Flynn had been living a monastic life and fighting regularly. His wife died 18 months ago, and Jim was broken up over it. He stopped drinking and gave up cigarettes. He gained good solid fighting weight, increased his speed, and as an underdog defeated both Al Kaufman and Carl Morris. "Johnson may or may not have gone back. Some people think they notice a difference in him, while others think he hasn't changed. Anyhow, there is a doubt about it and a strong suspicion that when the test comes he will show a falling away. In Flynn's case there are palpable incidents of improvement."

Johnson, Curley, Flynn

Johnson men were laying 5 to 2 against Flynn.

Referee Ed Smith met with the fighters on the 2nd to discuss the rules. The combatants agreed to fight according to straight Queensberry rules, which meant they would protect themselves at all times, including in clinches and on breaks. They could use the free arm as long as they were not holding with the other. Hitting as they stepped out of a clinch was permissible. They agreed to break at the referee's command. Smith impressed upon them that they must follow fair play at close quarters. It was thought that the two might forget ring manners. Flynn was particularly fierce and impetuous when infighting.

Referee Smith was happy about the agreed-upon rules, saying he would not work a fight that used rules other than straight Queensberry, for with modified rules, one or the other was bound to forget himself, and whenever that happened, as usually was the case at some point, those who bet on the contest jumped up and yelled "Foul!" That was annoying to the referee, principals, and the spectators. It gave an excuse for needless discussions.[703]

Writing for the *Denver Post*, Referee Smith said both men were quite confident. Flynn said, "More confident than ever. ... You're in for the surprise of your lives, that's all I'll tell you now." Flynn was not willing to bet, but that was because he did not have the money. The only way he could make any money on the bout was to win. If he did, there were mountains of gold in sight. Johnson wired Zeke Abrams, asking him to wager $5,000 at the best odds obtainable.

Smith did not anticipate a short contest. "Johnson is not a quick finisher. His whole record breathes of his having taken his time with every job that he ever undertook, excepting...unimportant matches. ... The champion may have to take more than the ordinary amount of time in disposing of Flynn." Smith anticipated that the longer the battle went the better it would be for Flynn. However,

> I am not one of those who so freely express the opinion that Johnson has gone back too far. ... I have been looking at him almost daily for a month and I believe that he is in grand shape. ... As for the fireman, he never was in such shape as he is at the present time. ... One thing is sure: The fireman will be forced to set the pace, for in all of Johnson's contests he has made every single one of his opponents come to him.

Professor Watson Burns said he trained Johnson exactly as he had for Jeffries, so the champ was in great shape, strong, and physically perfect. He weighed 214 pounds on the evening of the 2nd. "I look for him to win between the twelfth and fifteenth rounds. ... I look for him to make his own pace and win as he pleases. ... Johnson is greater today than he ever was."[704]

On July 3, the day before the fight, Johnson donned the gloves for a few moments, just to remain sharp. He said, "No excuses if I lose."

That day, Flynn said, "I am going to be champion tomorrow. ... Johnson can't best me. He knows it. A lot of so-called authorities, who panned me at first, are now beginning to realize that I have a bigger chance and a better chance than they ever conceded to me. ... I am going to win. Get down on that."

Flynn intended to tear in with his head down and arms crossed to intercept uppercuts, and to land some of his overhand swings. Johnson

---

[703] *New York American, San Francisco Examiner, Denver Post*, July 3, 1912.
[704] *Denver Post*, July 3, 1912.

expected Jim to do the rushing, and evidently it was his purpose to stand his ground and receive the charge.[705]

Flynn also said,

> I know how to protect myself better and those who expect to see Johnson nail me with those uppercuts whenever he wants are going to have their eyes opened. I only wish I could make the public feel the way I do about this thing. But my reward will come later. The crowds that are following Johnson now, will be trailing after me when I get back from that arena tomorrow afternoon.[706]

The day before the fight, special trains from Denver, Pueblo, Kansas City, El Paso, Trinidad, and other places arrived. As a result, prospects for at least a modest crowd were much brighter. Some folks arrived on horseback, some in automobiles, and others via train. The genial Johnson met all of the trains and gave folks an opportunity to meet him.

Some suspected that Johnson, who was extremely vain, was viewing the struggle more seriously than he wanted the world to believe. Still, Johnson said, "I could have finished Flynn in any round last time if I had wanted to. I saw that he was bent upon rushing me, though, so I took things coolly and made him lick himself, practically." Someone recalled that Flynn showered verbal abuse on Johnson during the contest. Johnson agreed: "He surely did, but you bet he suffered for it. He called me vile names in the sixth round and after that I gave him the punching of his life."

Flynn once had obtained a popular newspaper decision over Sam Langford. For the return bout, he was brimming over with confidence, just as he was at present. The result was that he got knocked out. Naughton remembered that, so he was not overly swayed by Flynn's confidence.

Naughton said there always were rumors of fixes, and there was a rumor that Johnson had agreed to transfer the championship for a monetary consideration. However, crooked fights always were paid for out of money cleaned up on the betting market. In the present case, there practically was no wagering of note. Hence, he did not believe there was a fix.

The day before the fight, Johnson had another talk with referee Ed W. Smith. In view of Flynn's reputation for hotheadedness, he urged Smith to keep a sharp watch on him. Jack said, "So much has been said about this match that I wouldn't like to see it end through a foul. I will promise you that I will be strictly on my good behavior and a timely warning from you if Flynn becomes unruly will have a good effect. I want nothing but a square deal." Smith said he would insist upon both men adhering to the rules.

If he won, Jim Flynn did not intend to defend the title against any black fighter, and would draw the color line. "It is his idea that the white and

---

[705] *New York American*, July 4, 1912.

[706] *Albuquerque Evening Herald*, July 3, 1912; *San Francisco Examiner*, July 4, 1912. The *Albuquerque Evening Herald* advertised that folks were invited to its offices on the afternoon of July 4 to hear the returns of the fight from direct wire.

black races should have separate champions and he argues that there would be less prejudice against boxing if the promoters of the future would set their faces against 'magpie matches.'" He would refuse to give Johnson the same opportunity that Johnson gave him. Hence, one can understand why it was so important for Johnson not to take too many risks inside the ring, for if he lost, he knew he would not be given another chance at the title.[707]

On the evening of July 3, Johnson told Otto Floto,

> If I am beaten there will be no excuses offered. I won't send out a story the day after that I was doped. ... I will win, and win with something to spare. I have placed my own money in the poolrooms at odds of 2 to 1. If I were not confident of success you don't think I would do anything like that. When I stepped on the scales this morning I weighed exactly 214 pounds.

Johnson said he would dry out overnight to about 212 pounds. "I don't care what corner I take." If he was in a corner that Flynn wanted, he gladly would give it up to him. "We'll have no argument on that point." Jack said he would win within 15 rounds.

Flynn was equally confident. "Tomorrow at this time I'll be the champion of the world." He would not receive any pay until Johnson received his $31,000 and the other expenses were deducted. Then Curley and Flynn would divide the remainder.

> It may be a bloomer and I may get a beating, but I have risked all that in an attempt to restore the title to the pale-faced race. If I win I wouldn't care if the receipts were only three dollars, for I feel that I will get mine after that. But if I lose I may have my beating as my reward in attempting to down the black. ... But take it from me; I am not going to lose; I am going to win in the ninth round.

Jim said he was in perfect condition, and if defeated, he would have no complaint. He said men like Hart, Russell, and McVea were able to back Johnson around the ring, and if he backed him up, he had the kick in his wallop to force Johnson to make a stand and fight.

The night before the fight, Johnson attended and watched the Unholz-Yoakum fight in the same arena that he would meet Flynn.

That night, Flynn also paid a visit to Las Vegas, his first in several days. A mob of fight fans followed him.

The *Omaha World Herald*'s Sandy Griswold, who was in Las Vegas, said there had been very little gambling of any note. Flynn supporters were not wagering, demanding 3 to 1 odds, which they could not obtain.

Flynn was as uproariously confident as ever, while Johnson was cool and indifferent. Griswold recalled that when Flynn fought Johnson the first time, he was just as confident and declared himself to be just as fit. "Johnson did not receive a mark, while Flynn was battered out of all

---

[707] *San Francisco Examiner*, July 4, 1912.

semblance to a human being." Jim tore into Jack just as he would the next day, but nevertheless, Johnson tore his head off with uppercuts. Jim's eye looked like a ripe gourd. Flynn called him names and admitted he was too clever. Johnson invited him to rush in so the farce could be ended. Flynn obliged and Jack made good.

On Thursday July 4, 1912 in Las Vegas, New Mexico, Jack Johnson defended his world heavyweight championship crown against Fireman Jim Flynn.[708]

The morning of the fight, the odds remained at 2 to 1, with the champ the favorite. Johnson offered to bet $10,000 on himself. He also telegraphed $5,000 to San Francisco to be wagered that he would win within 15 rounds. Johnson bet $40 to $100 that he would drop Flynn in the 1st round, and $30 to $100 that Flynn wouldn't hit him with a clean punch in the first two rounds.

As usual, the men's exact weights were not recorded officially, but it was estimated that Johnson would be around 212-214 pounds. Some said Johnson was closer to 219. The morning of the fight, Flynn weighed 192 pounds at his quarters. Johnson was 34 years old to Flynn's 32 years of age.

That day, Johnson said, "I am as good as ever. … [T]he fight will not go over fifteen rounds. May the best man win."

Flynn said, "I know a lot of people think I am crazy, but I firmly believe that I will be the champion of the world before the sun sets tonight. Johnson has gone back. That's a certainty. I have improved 100 per cent since he whipped me. I look for a long fight."

Tom Flanagan said, "Johnson is fit for the fray. He will win, but I expect Flynn to make a desperate struggle before he succumbs. Johnson is good enough to hold the title at least two years more."

Jack Curley said Flynn would win and startle the pugilistic world, just as Corbett did with Sullivan. "The gate will not be as big as I expected, but a Flynn victory will bring in the money afterwards."[709]

The weather was nice and warm, but not too hot.

The arena walls were built of pine lumber and canvas. Outside of the seating space was a barbed-wire fence running around the arena. Between the barbed wire and the outer wall, the state mounted police were on duty.

Sandy Griswold said the fight attracted all kinds of people. Rich ranchers, stockmen, miners, men of the commercial world, summerishly-gowned women, Americans, Mexicans, Indians, Negroes, and Chinese were all in a jumbled mass.

---

[708] The following account is an amalgamation of the same-day and next-day July 4 and 5, 1912 reports from the *Las Vegas Optic*, *Albuquerque Evening Herald*, *Albuquerque Morning Journal*, *Santa Fe New Mexican*, *Denver Post*, Claude Johnson of the *Kansas City Star*, W. W. Naughton of the *New York American* and *San Francisco Examiner*, and Sandy Griswold of the *Omaha World Herald*, all of whom were at the fight or had reporters present at the fight.
[709] *Freeman*, July 20, 1912.

Unfortunately, the crowd was small, far less than expected. Only about 3,000 men and 500 women paid admission. About 4,000 total were present.

Promoter Curley wore a sorrowful face that could be cured only by a Flynn victory. Curley said the total gate receipts did not amount to over $29,000 and were below Johnson's $30,000 guarantee. Some said Governor McDonald's action in delaying his statement that he would not interfere with the fight cut down on the attendance. Whenever there was some uncertainty about whether a bout would be allowed to take place, patrons held back. Still, Curley could earn good money with the films.

The affair was carried out in orderly fashion. The streets were filled with visitors, and the restaurants and hotels filled as well, but there were no serious troubles.

Shortly before noon that day, Jack Curley handed the champ a certified check for $31,100, which represented his purse and expense guarantee. For Flynn, who was an equal partner with Curley in the venture, it would be a fight for glory and potential future earnings.

The betting picked up at noon, and considerable money was wagered. There was little sentiment in the wagering. Men who were hoping for a Flynn victory still bet on Johnson. The prevailing odds in Chicago were 3 to 1, with the champ the favorite. It was even money that Johnson would win within 13 rounds. The champ was telling his friends to accept that wager.

Dr. Benjamin Franklin Roller was selected as Flynn's official doctor. He examined Jim at noon and said he had reached the acme of physical perfection. He said if the fight went 15 rounds, Flynn would win.

Tom Flanagan said it might go 25 rounds, but predicted Johnson's ultimate victory without great exertion.

There were few notables at ringside. Miss Fannie Vetter, Flynn's fiancée, was amongst the early arrivals. She took a seat in a box on the west side of the ring. She did not look happy.

Mrs. Etta Johnson drifted in, holding $30,000 in rocks, including a $7,000 necklace. She looked happy, as if the battle was over already. Mrs. Johnson and the wives of the champ's trainers occupied a box near the ring.

About 200 of Flynn's hometown Pueblo fans, distinguished by white rooter hats, were on hand to cheer for him. They sat together.

Fans could buy most anything in the arena. Soda pop was retailing for 15 cents a bottle. Soft cushions were selling for 25 cents. Souvenirs included everything from Mexican gold-work to official programs containing maps to the locations of Las Vegas's most prominent citizens.

The fight probably would start late, as Curley was waiting for a train from Salt Lake, hoping it would bring more money. Another purported cause for delay was that the moving picture films had not yet arrived.

The arena, inside and out, was patrolled by 75 armed members of the state police, under the leadership of Captain Fred Fornoff. "They look like moving picture bandits and carry more artillery than a first class cruiser. That they maintain the peace at all hazards, the betting is 1 to 10."

One man offered to wager $10,000 to $8,000 that Flynn did not survive the 15th round. A local man accepted the bet.

At 1:50 p.m., ten minutes before the scheduled start, there was no sign of either fighter. The Las Vegas silver cornet band started playing.

At 2 p.m., the original start time, the fighters still were not at the arena. They dressed at their own quarters and came to the arena in autos.

Seconds after 2 p.m., Flynn was the first to arrive. He was given a tremendous ovation. The Mexican band greeted him with "All Coons Look Alike To Me." Jim was smiling confidently, and said he would be champion before the sun set. "I am going to win." He went to his dressing room.

At 2:03 p.m., Johnson arrived in his motor car. Jack said he would win in 15 rounds. He too retired to his dressing boudoir.

At 2:04 p.m., announcer Tommy Cannon of Oklahoma City entered the ring and called attention to the "several hundred ladies who have graced this occasion by their attendance." He asked the spectators to remember the ladies' presence when it came to shouting comments.

Cannon then announced a 4-round preliminary between two small boys.

For the main event, Otto Floto of Denver kept time for the club, Flynn had Al Tearney of Chicago, and Johnson had Tom Flanagan. The timekeeper had forgotten the gong, and they were sending for it.

There was plenty of Johnson money in sight, with few takers.

The moving picture men were all set and waiting.

Flynn's brother Lou Flynn entered the ring, followed by Jack Curley with Flynn's gloves.

As Johnson approached the ring, there were calls of "There he comes!" At 2:27 p.m., Johnson entered the ring. The champ wore the same striped bathrobe that he had used in Reno. He took the east corner. He was seconded by Professor Burns, George DeBray, Kid Skelly, and Bob Watkins.

Eleven minutes later, at 2:38 p.m., Flynn received tremendous applause as he approached and entered the ring. He took the west corner. Flynn's seconds included Abdul the Turk, Chick Coleman, Ray Marshall, Louie Haines, Dr. Roller, Lou Flynn, Al Williams, and Jack Curley. Jim was in exceptionally good humor, and spent much of the time sauntering about the ring greeting friends. Upon seeing Mrs. Johnson, Flynn shouted, "Ain't you pulling for me, Mrs. Johnson?" The champ's wife smiled but said nothing.

At Johnson's request, Mrs. Johnson was transferred to another box in order to be nearer to his corner.

The McMahon Brothers of New York telegrammed an offer to be read at ringside. They offered $20,000 for a Johnson-Jeannette bout to be held in New York. Another telegram from Joe Jeannette himself was read, challenging the winner, guaranteeing Johnson $20,000 for his share. Victor Breyer of Paris offered Johnson $30,000 for a 30-round contest there with Jeannette. Al Palzer wired a challenge to the winner, saying he had posted a $5,000 forfeit. Luther McCarty wired Flynn a challenge.

The announcer introduced Sam McVey manager Billy McLain/McLean, Kansas City Judge Casimir Welch, and promoter Jack Curley.

At 2:40 p.m., Referee Ed W. Smith of Chicago entered the ring and ordered it cleared as soon as possible.

Abe Pollock of Denver and Eddie Cochrane of Kansas City were presented as alternate referees, if needed.

The fighters donned their gloves. Johnson withdrew his objection to the gloves the ring officials provided, and wore them. He had ordered a special set for his own use.

Flynn was introduced as the "Fighting Fireman of Pueblo." His earlier warm reception of cheers was duplicated. Johnson was then announced as the champion heavyweight of the world. His reception was lukewarm.

Sandy Griswold described Johnson as supple, smooth, and sinuous, like polished ebony or a graceful snake. He was indifferent to the July sun. The white challenger looked rough and rugged, like a chunk of granite.

At 2:45 p.m., the men were at ring center, taking instructions from the referee. They briefly discussed the rules.

At 2:48 p.m., the ring was cleared again. Announcer Tom Cannon made his final remarks, referring to the rules governing the contest.

At 2:49 p.m., time was called to start the fight.

1 - Flynn asked, "Will you shake hands, Jack?" and then proceeded to rush into a clinch. Jack then replied, "Gee." Flynn fired a left to the stomach. Johnson held and smiled. Flynn came in with his head down and rushed Johnson to the ropes, but Jack smothered the punches and clinched. As they broke, Johnson scored with a right uppercut. Flynn kept in close but Johnson easily avoided his attempts. Johnson was too clever for Flynn and shoved him off. The champ hooked his stiff left to the ear before they clinched. They broke and again clinched. Johnson smiled constantly and fought with great care, sending in light jabs. They clinched and Johnson sent a sharp left to the head and hooked his right to the ear.

As he rushed in, Flynn butted Jack in the chest and Referee Smith cried, "Look out." Johnson laughed as he held Flynn and tilted his head with a right uppercut. Flynn tried for the stomach but was stopped with a right to the head. Jim covered up and rushed. Johnson landed a left tap to the jaw.

Flynn backed him to the ropes and the champ replied with a right uppercut that cut a deep gash under his left eye. The blood showed on Jim's cheek. Johnson again backed to the ropes, laughing, and landed another uppercut. As Flynn struck him in the stomach with hard lefts, Johnson laughed again. Jack pressed his body forward as if inviting punches, or to smother them. Flynn tried to infight, but Johnson easily baffled him. Jack cuffed him on the jaw with a couple rights. Jim tried to get in again, but Johnson held him off. They were in a fierce rally at the gong. Johnson went to his corner smiling.

The local press agreed that it was all Johnson's round.

About 23 minutes of the films still exist, including portions of each round. Since they are incomplete, they cannot be the final word on what took place, but certainly they assist our understanding.

What the films show is that throughout the bout, in nonstop fashion, Flynn bulled his way in with his head lowered and leaning forward or slightly crouched to the side, with his hands up or arms crossed in front of him.

From the start of the 1st round, Flynn immediately advanced to the inside, and Johnson immediately clinched. Throughout the round, from the inside, while clinched, Flynn tried to work short overhand left hooks to the head, as well as body shots. Johnson often smiled and looked into the crowd as he played defense.

Johnson was very good at either holding around the arms or just placing his hands on Flynn's arms, shoulders, or elbows, applying some force to smother and suppress so that Flynn either could not punch or had the force of his blows greatly diminished. Sometimes Jack would push Flynn off to move him back to the outside. Occasionally Johnson would hit him with a jab or give him a stiff arm, or try to time him on the way in with a hook or uppercut. The champ tried to keep him off a bit, and would slide back or step around to the side. Jack moved just a bit, not wasting energy moving too much, for Flynn was relentless, quickly moving in to the inside, where Johnson clinched immediately. Up close, Jack would play defense for a while and allow Jim to work. The champ also would let go, fire in a short inside blow, and then suppress Flynn's arms again. This would be the fight's pattern.

2 - Johnson landed several left jabs to the face and sent a right to the body. Flynn kept trying to get inside, bulling forward all the time. Jack landed an uppercut and jabbed Jim another five times. As Flynn rushed, Johnson simply grasped him about the shoulders and held him at bay, all the while "grinning like an ape." The champ pecked at the face with light lefts, toying with Flynn. As they clinched, Jack twice more shot heavy right uppercuts to the jaw, one of which sent Flynn's head bobbing. In the clinch, Flynn hammered the body and Johnson laughed.

The champ was coolness personified. Time and again he exchanged his usual repartee with the spectators.

Flynn landed an overhand left to the mouth and rammed his right into the stomach. Johnson landed a right uppercut and left hook, and Flynn replied with a right hook. Flynn stopped Johnson's uppercuts with his crossed arms and used both hands on the body. Johnson scored with a right uppercut before the bell. Johnson laughed and winked to a friend as he took his seat. Flynn's mouth was bleeding as he went to his corner.

The press agreed that it was Johnson's round, for he very much bested Flynn.

The existing films show that Johnson was again clinching, suppressing, and smiling. Flynn kept working at a good rate. Jack hit him with several blows from the outside, especially the jab, and then clinched as Flynn advanced quickly. He would push Flynn off, and then strike him from the outside again. Jack landed most of what he threw. Flynn was very aggressive, on the inside trying to launch ferocious overhand hooking blows to the head and ripping body shots, though Johnson was good at either smothering and diminishing the force, or blocking, or eluding with a slight movement of the head. Jack calmly smiled as Jim worked diligently and incessantly. Here and there, in the clinches, Johnson jolted Flynn's head back with a sneaky short right uppercut.

3 - Flynn immediately rushed in to close quarters and butted Johnson's chin with his head, but the champ just held and winked at the referee. Jim pounded the stomach. On the break, Johnson shot in a left jab to the nose and repeated it with good effect. They clinched again. Several times Flynn tried for the stomach but either was blocked or held. Jim landed a right to ribs and an overhand left to the head.

Flynn cut short a witty Johnson remark by twice hooking his right to the jaw. This nettled the champ and he cut loose with several short right uppercuts to the jaw, tilting Flynn's head. Jack drove in a hard right to the chest. Jim landed a left uppercut to jaw. They clinched and Jim pounded the stomach.

Flynn landed a left to Johnson's mouth, which started bleeding slightly. Jack held him by the shoulders as Jim drove both hands to the body and attempted a left hook to the head. Johnson rocked Flynn's

head with several fierce lifting right uppercuts. Flynn covered and hung on.

Flynn's face was badly damaged. He spat blood in a stream, for the champ had cut his mouth, eye, and nose with the volley of rights and lefts. Johnson twice rocked Flynn's head with stiff uppercuts and Jim clinched at the bell.

Johnson went to his corner with his usual golden smile. Flynn was bleeding profusely from the nose and mouth, which covered his face with blood. It was another Johnson round.

On the films, once again Flynn advanced and Johnson clinched. Flynn tried to dislodge himself, but found it difficult. Jack smiled. Jim quickly advanced with his low crouch, moving in and firing upward his overhand hook. Throughout the round, Jack clinched, and as he was holding, he looked off into the crowd and smiled. The smile did not leave his face even as Flynn jolted hooks over. Jack seemed to take them, but rolled enough with the blows such that they did not land solidly.

From the clinch, Johnson landed several short uppercuts with both hands, each time smothering Flynn's attempts to counter. The vicious Flynn was very eager and active, but found it quite challenging to penetrate Johnson's brand of defense, and even when he did, despite his ferocity, he could not land very solidly or with much force, owing to Jack's tactics. Johnson timed Flynn with a nice right uppercut as Jim advanced. Even when Jack landed, usually he would clinch immediately after. After more clinching, Flynn attempted a right uppercut and hook, both of which were grazing, and Johnson retaliated with several right uppercuts before clinching again and smothering Flynn's attempts.

4 - Johnson shot in straight rights and lefts as Flynn advanced. Flynn rushed in close but was met with the customary rain of right and left uppercuts to the face. Still, it seemed as if Johnson was holding himself in check. The champ pressed his palms against Flynn's arms, which kept him from fighting back too well. Johnson hardly attempted to protect his body from Flynn's body attacks. Instead, Jack constantly invited Jim to blaze away at his stomach.

Johnson kept cutting up Flynn's face with short uppercuts. Flynn kept trying for the stomach. They broke from close quarters and Jack used his left jab to the nose, starting the blood afresh. Jim missed an uppercut, and Jack laughed out loud. Flynn elicited a great cheer when he rushed Johnson to the ropes and planted a solid left to the jaw. Johnson landed a right hook to the jaw three times in succession. The round ended with Flynn's face covered with blood.

The observers again agreed that it was Johnson's round.

The film version shows that Jack jabbed and then grabbed. Flynn tried to hook him. Jack snuck in a right uppercut and then grabbed again. Flynn kept trying to work his hands free from the pressure of Johnson's mitts on his arms, so he could fire short body jolts. A usual, Jack landed an occasional uppercut and clinched, or pushed him away, as his mood suited him. The champ fired a right on the head of the advancing Flynn and then grabbed again, followed by the inevitable uppercut. Flynn continually tried to free his arms enough to let go some body shots, a right uppercut, and a hook, but he mostly missed or landed with little effect. Johnson landed several jabs in a row before Jim covered his face and got inside. After breaking, Jack hit him with several metronome jabs again. Flynn leapt in with some hooks until Johnson grabbed hold again and smiled. Soon thereafter, Jack snuck in one of his short right uppercuts.

5 - Johnson started the round nonchalantly, turning his head towards the spectators and hardly noticing Flynn, who at close quarters banged away at his stomach with half a dozen blows. Johnson only smiled and made no apparent attempt to protect his midsection. Mrs. Johnson waved at Jack. On the outside, Johnson shot six lefts to the nose in quick succession. Flynn rushed into a clinch and tried to drive in body shots. Johnson rocked his head with a left uppercut to the jaw. Flynn again pounded the stomach four or five times. He was bleeding profusely.

Johnson aroused the crowd to merriment by releasing his hold on Flynn and clapping his own gloves together "like a happy school girl." In another clinch, Johnson patted Flynn on the back of the head and rebuked him for butting. Flynn loudly protested to the referee, "Make him let go. I can't fight while he's holding me."

The round ended with the two in a clinch, while Johnson was carrying on a running conversation with his wife and seconds. Flynn's face was a mass of blood. Conversely, Johnson apparently was as fresh as ever. However, for the first time, Flynn smiled as he went back to his corner. It still was Johnson's round.

On the films, from the start of the round, Flynn leapt in and Jack immediately clinched. Soon thereafter, Jack snuck in a jolting right uppercut that sent Jim's head back. Jack smiled, and then slowly pushed Jim off. Flynn stepped back in and punched ferociously, but found the clutches of Jack's arms. Jack pushed off and jabbed.

Several times Flynn stepped in and tried to fire away, but again Johnson eluded or smothered the blows. Jim mostly landed some short body shots that did not seem to bother Jack very much. Johnson pushed him out, and then landed several jabs before grabbing and smiling. Flynn kept digging at the body, forcing his punches through Jack's clutches, while Jack snuck in a right uppercut. Amidst Flynn's body shots, occasionally he tried the overhand right or left hook to the head, but either Johnson rolled away and eluded, blocked, or grabbed.

At one point, Johnson indeed smiled, let go and clapped his hands together behind Jim's head as Flynn was leaning forward. Then Jack applied pressure onto Jim's arms with his hands and smiled again. Gradually pushing off to the outside again, as he did when he felt like it, Jack landed some jabs before Flynn got in again. Some wrestling followed, and Flynn tried his overhand hook and right but could not land cleanly. When the mood suited him, Johnson worked his right and left uppercuts.

6 – Flynn drove five or six vicious blows to the stomach. Johnson caught him in his arms and held. Flynn complained as Jack held him, hollering to the referee to call him off. Then Flynn flagrantly butted with his head three times. Jim hit the wind as the referee warned him for butting. Flynn complained that Johnson's holding made his actions justifiable. Jack's seconds were in an uproar. The referee severely reprimanded Flynn for deliberately butting. Several newsmen opined that it looked as if Flynn was seeking a loophole to stem the beating being administered to him.

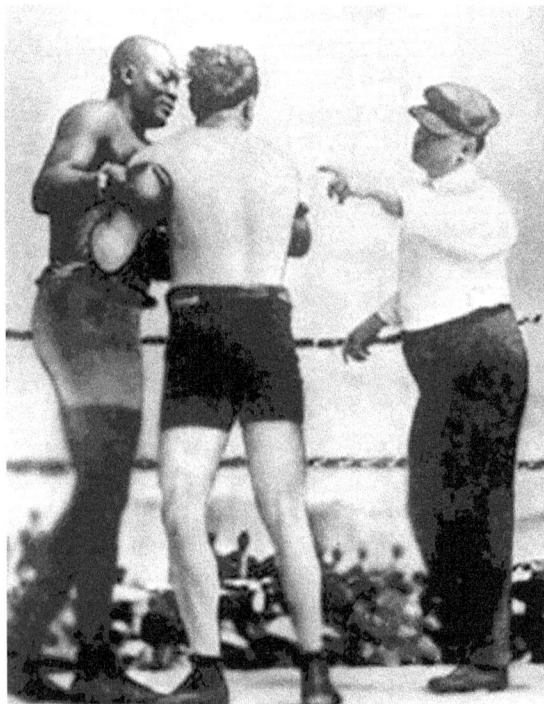

The bout continued. "Show me," said Flynn. Johnson dazzled him with his speed, landing left and right to the face. As he was being held, Flynn pummeled the stomach and again butted. Referee Smith again warned Flynn for butting. This time, Johnson objected strongly. Flynn's excuse was, "He's holding me."

Maddened, Johnson, landed a volley of straight lefts and rights to the face, fairly bewildering Flynn. Then Johnson stopped, either to pace himself or to prolong the bout. Flynn again intentionally butted and again was warned. He offered Johnson his hand to shake or touch gloves, and Jack slightly extended his right but did not shake, perhaps fearing a sneak blow. Flynn kept charging in and firing body blows. Johnson pummeled his head.

Johnson complained that Flynn was butting and using foul blows. The referee parted them and chided Flynn for butting, which was about his fifth warning. Jim said that Jack kept holding him, and such was the case. At the end of the round, Johnson was pounding Flynn's face.

Flynn's work in this round had been very rough. Sandy Griswold said it was Johnson's round on clean fighting. Conversely, the *Denver Post* said Flynn was administering vicious punishment and won the round. Spider Kelly went over to Flynn's corner. Between rounds, Flynn's seconds warned him to stop butting.

The film version shows that Flynn got inside and hooked to the head and body, but was being grabbed as usual. This time Flynn allowed his frustrations to get the better of him. While being held, Flynn slightly jumped up into Johnson's face with his head. Johnson kept holding, and slapped Flynn's ear with a right. Jim tried a left hook that was blocked, and then jumped up with his head into Jack's face again. It obviously was an intentional head butt. While the fighters were still in a clinch, Referee Smith pointed at Jim, cautioning him, as the boxers looked towards the referee.

They resumed and Flynn attacked the body with both hands, while Johnson grabbed both of his arms to make him less effective. Leaning forward on the inside, Flynn jumped up with his head into Jack's face again. This drew another stern warning from the referee.

Johnson pushed him off and then jabbed him several times before Flynn got in and tried to break free from Jack's grasp. Flynn pushed him into a corner, working short body shots. Johnson pushed him off a couple times and landed some jabs. Back on the inside, Flynn kept trying to land, but Jack grabbed or pushed off with his hands on Jim's arms or shoulders. Jack used more jabs, stiff arms, a right, and a little footwork to maintain some range. He then landed a right uppercut before grabbing the advancing Flynn.

Flynn flagrantly and brutally launched himself into the air and landed the top of his head into Johnson's face. The referee broke them and again administered a warning. Flynn reached out with his right to touch gloves, and Jack reached back, but they did not touch, as Flynn pulled his hand back just as Jack's glove came close.

Johnson jabbed and Flynn immediately stepped into the inside. Jim worked short body shots as Jack simply placed his palms on Flynn's arms to diminish the force of the blows. Johnson then grabbed again, and Flynn leapt up into the air with his head, striking Jack's face. The referee broke them to administer yet another warning, and this time Flynn complained.

After resuming, Johnson got into action, firing off a combination of several short blows to the head, mostly jabs and right uppercuts before grabbing again. Flynn gave him a more subtle butt and Jack turned and looked at the referee. Flynn stood up straight, looked at the referee, and appeared to say something, likely complaining about the holding. The referee said something and they broke.

Flynn advanced and swung an overhand right that missed as Jack turned away from it. Johnson walked about, jabbing away until the bell.

Flynn had head butted intentionally about six times in the round.

7 - Spider Kelly was in Flynn's corner and was advising him. Johnson landed a dozen rapid-fire jabs to the face without return, playing with Flynn like a kitten with a mouse. Johnson worked on Flynn's sore bloody nose at will, beating a tattoo there with left and right, but did not appear to be trying for a knockout, for his punches were rather light. Jack's left was going fast and Flynn could not get to close quarters.

Finally, Flynn carried Johnson into a corner and landed a hard stomach blow. When they broke, Johnson twice drove his right uppercut to the stomach. Flynn sent half a dozen jolts to the stomach with both hands. Jim blocked two uppercuts but a left hook caused his face great damage. His nose was bleeding badly, and his face dripped blood. Johnson right uppercut the face, sent a left to the nose, and followed with right and left to the head, all damaging punches. Flynn landed an overhand right to the face. Johnson's uppercuts with both hands kept Flynn from working close.

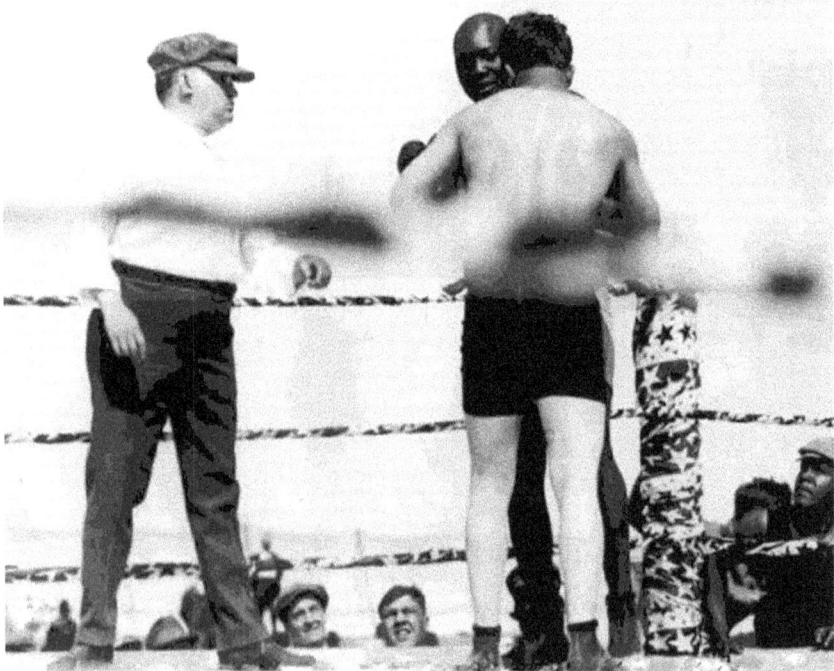

A spectator called out to Johnson, urging him to end it, but Jack replied, "Wait a minute." Flynn's nose was mashed flat, and he complained to the referee that he was being held. Referee Smith replied, "Fight. I'm referee of this battle." Jim attempted to land several wild swings to the head, but missed by a yard. He could not penetrate the impregnable defense. His face flowed blood. They were again clinched at the bell, and the crowd yelled to Johnson, "What you holding for?" Jack replied, "Because I'm strong."

It was all Johnson's round. W. W. Naughton said it was a bad round for Flynn.

On the films, as usual, Flynn was really good at getting inside, but Johnson was good at grabbing or suppressing his arms, then gradually pushing him to the outside again. From the outside, Jack jabbed him multiple times in rapid succession and then pivoted away back to ring center. Jack kept jabbing and walking away, trying to maintain his range as Flynn crouched and advanced while taking most of the blows.

Once Flynn got to the inside, Johnson placed his palms on Jim's arms to suppress them, and then looked into the crowd and smiled. Flynn fired a fast hook to the head and Jack rolled away from it. The champ used a jab and stiff arm and moved away until Jim got in and worked the body as Jack again pressed his hands on his arms, eventually pushing him out. Johnson stepped in and held as Flynn, as usual, tried to work to the body and head.

Flynn landed several to the body as Johnson smiled. Flynn followed and landed a right uppercut that jolted Jack's head. This caused Johnson to get into action more, landing a right uppercut and then a left uppercut. Flynn advanced and Jack landed a right uppercut and followed with some jabs and stiff arms to keep him at range.

Johnson again grabbed as Flynn fired some hooks and looping rights to the head while being held. Johnson kept sneaking in the occasional uppercut to the head with both hands, even as he was grabbing. Even when held, Flynn kept trying to work the body and follow with a looping shot over the top. When Johnson got some room, he jabbed and used his left stiff arm to set up a right uppercut, after which he held again.

8 - Johnson landed a left to the jaw and they clinched. Jack kept him at arm's length with his left and shot a right to the nose. Flynn rushed in and Johnson sent a left uppercut to the badly battered nose, starting the blood afresh. Jack lifted Jim's head with a right uppercut, and then sent two lefts to the head. He also hooked him and shot a right to the nose.

Johnson would punch, clinch, punch, and clinch. Sometimes he would push Flynn off and then hit him with jabs as Jim forced his way inside.

While being held by Johnson, Flynn intentionally butted. Johnson called the referee's attention to the butting, and Referee Smith warned Jim.

Johnson drove a right to the jaw and straight left to the mouth. They clinched. After the break, Flynn tore in, driving in two hard body blows. Johnson scored heavily with his right to the nose.

After yet another clinch, Flynn deliberately butted Johnson three times. Referee Smith gave Flynn a stern warning.

Flynn tore in, forcing Johnson to the ropes. Flynn sent three rights to the body and was trying desperately, but Johnson was his master at all stages, uppercutting him whenever he liked. As they parted, Johnson scored a telling right uppercut, and twice lifted Flynn's head with left hooks.

Johnson held, and Flynn twice jumped up and twice butted Johnson on the chin. The referee lectured Jim and threatened to stop the fight, saying, "Once more and I'll disqualify you." Flynn said the champ was holding him. Some erroneously thought he had disqualified Flynn, but they were ordered to resume just as the bell rang. At the bell, Flynn was covered with blood.

Summarizing the round, Naughton said Johnson kept holding and Flynn kept butting. It was an unfair round on the part of both men. Griswold said it was Johnson's round. Several local observers said Flynn was warned for butting at least three times in the round. The round was like its predecessors, with Johnson uppercutting and Flynn butting viciously, at the same time losing a world of blood. Flynn was helpless, and for the tenth time in the fight, warned about butting.

The films show that as usual, while being held, Flynn was working short body shots and looping hooks and overhand rights to the head. Johnson snuck in the occasional uppercut. Jack used a stiff-arm with his left, placing his open palm into Flynn's face, and then followed with light rights to the head. After more clinching, Johnson used his left stiff arm again and followed with a big right uppercut to the jaw before the usual clinch.

While in the clinch, Jack jolted in a couple left uppercuts, the second of which really lifted Flynn's head upwards. As the referee stepped in close to break them, Flynn flagrantly jumped up, butting Johnson in the face. Jack then strongly grabbed both arms and spun around. Flynn followed with two more leaping head butts in a row. The referee broke them, spoke to Flynn, and then waved them on to continue.

As Flynn advanced, Johnson hooked him and stepped around. Jack again pressed his hands on Jim's upper arms and held while Flynn hit the body. Flynn stood up, looked at Johnson, and leaned in with his head again. The referee broke them and talked to Flynn, who was looking directly at the referee. They resumed and it was more of the same – Flynn getting in and trying to punch while being held. Jack would jab from the outside and uppercut on the inside, though he mostly held and smothered.

9 - Johnson landed a left uppercut and then held. They wrestled. After a break, Flynn immediately got to the inside again and was held. He worked the body. Johnson pushed him off and kept the fireman at arm's length in an attempt to safeguard himself against the constant butting. As Jim advanced, Jack hit him with a right uppercut and held again. Jack pushed him off, hit him with another uppercut as Jim advanced, and then pushed him off again. Flynn got inside and was held, and he butted again. The referee broke them. At ringside, Jack Curley was talking to the sheriff.

Flynn got to the inside, jumped a foot in the air and landed with the top of his head against Johnson's jaw, intentionally butting yet again, and then hit the body as Johnson held. The referee broke them and again sternly warned Flynn, who complained about Johnson's holding. The referee waved them on to continue.

Captain of the Mounted Police, Fred Fornoff, realizing that the referee seemed loath to terminate the fight on a foul, entered the ring and declared, "The fight is over." He had his men with him, and they carried revolvers.

Referee Ed W. Smith awarded the fight to Johnson. The champion was given a terrific cheer, while the crowd vented its wrath on Flynn with jeers and boos. They had wanted to see the fight come to its natural conclusion, but were sore at Flynn for his intentional fouls which forced the stoppage.

The film version shows that Johnson pushed Flynn off and then timed him on the way in with a right uppercut. He pushed off again and then struck with a left hook and held again.

Flynn threw a hook to the body and then leapt up with his head, butting. The referee simply broke them.

Johnson landed an upward jab and then grabbed. The leaning-in Flynn launched himself up into Jack's face, butting again. Flynn followed with some body shots as the referee broke them and issued another warning.

Flynn put his hands on his sides and appeared to be arguing with the referee, motioning with his hand as if upset. Flynn then grabbed the referee as if to demonstrate Johnson's holding. The referee pushed him back and waved them on to continue.

However, at that point, law enforcement entered the ring and ordered a termination of the proceedings. Flynn briefly protested, grabbing hold of the policeman, but was gently pushed back. Johnson's cornermen entered the ring, followed by many more folks. The fight obviously was over.

After Flynn is warned for intentionally butting yet again, state Police Captain Fred Fornoff enters the ring to stop the fight.

The sportswriters put forth two extreme views about this fight. Some argued that Johnson was dominating every round, toying with Flynn, could have put him out at any time, and was breaking him down gradually. A frustrated and bloody Flynn foresaw a bad ending for himself, so he fouled to get himself disqualified.

Another view was that although Johnson was outpointing him, he was tiring from Flynn's relentless attack, throwing less punches, and holding more as the fight progressed. Had the bout continued and Flynn not lost his head, he had a chance to wear down Johnson eventually, for Jack was not in his best condition, while Flynn was strong and active throughout and in excellent, superior shape.

The truth probably lies between the press' two extremes. Johnson used the style he typically used, and he used it from the start. He clinched early and often, played defense, allowed Flynn to work, and carefully chose when to punch, usually landing. He was not punching very hard or often, and though he might have been marking-up Flynn, Jim never once was hurt.

Flynn was an absolutely relentless ferocious ball of energy, firing away on a consistent basis, moving in quickly, and constantly trying to work his hands free to punch. He obviously was very frustrated by Johnson's defensive tactics and holding, feeling that he could not land effective blows. He totally lost his composure and fouled flagrantly and often. It appeared that both men could have continued fighting in the same manner for many more rounds. At the time the bout was stopped, it was not clear how the 45-round bout would have ended had it been allowed to continue.

The local *Las Vegas Optic* reported that the scheduled 45-round bout was brought to a close in the 9th round when Captain Fred Fornoff of the state police, Governor William McDonald's personal representative, declared that it no longer was a boxing match, but a brutal exhibition, and that Flynn's foul tactics made its continuance impossible. He jumped into the ring with his deputies and drove the fighters and officials to their corners. Referee Ed W. Smith then announced that Johnson had won and the fight was over.

> Flynn displayed no ability throughout the fight. He was cut about the face until blood ran down his breast in a stream. He was utterly helpless from the first round on and by the sixth was deliberately trying to butt the champion's chin with his head. Time after time, as Johnson held him powerless in the clinches, Flynn lifted his head upward. Smith warned him repeatedly but it did no good. In the seventh he began leaping upward every time he could work his head under Johnson's chin. Flynn's feet were both off the floor time and again with the energy he put into his bounds. Sometimes he seemed to jump two feet into the air in frantic lunges at the elusive black jaw above him.

> Referee Smith forced Flynn back toward his corner a half dozen times. "Stop that butting," he would say, shaking his finger in Flynn's face. "Stop it or I will disqualify you." "The – nigger's holding me," Flynn roared back. "He's holding me all the time. He's holding me like this," and he offered to illustrate on the referee. Smith evaded the blood-smeared arms held toward him and waved the men together again.

In the eighth round, in a clinch, Flynn flung himself up again. Smith jumped between them and warned him again. "Next time you do it I'll disqualify you," he shouted. However, Flynn did it again and again in that round without being disqualified. He again did it repeatedly in the 9th round, before the police stopped it.

Through it all, the champion was smiling. He evaded Flynn's attack with the utmost ease. The *Optic* said ringside opinion was unanimous that he could have put Flynn out at any time he happened to fancy it. The champ opened up only once, early in the fight, when Flynn landed his only good blows, right and left hooks to the jaw in a clinch. Johnson appeared nettled and smashed a right uppercut through the guard, which rocked Flynn on his feet. Then the champ smiled again and went back to his monotonous chopping uppercuts in the clinches, which reduced Flynn's face to a bloody mass.

It appeared that Johnson was not attempting to hit hard. He was content with a slow, coldly scientific chopping, every blow finding its way through the barricade of gloves and elbows behind which Flynn crouched. Johnson gave a perfect exhibition of guarding and hitting in the clinches. Not a blow Flynn started reached him with any steam behind it. They were smothered or tossed aside unless Johnson chose to allow his opponent to batter away at his stomach, smiling all the while over Flynn's shoulder.

When it was over, there was not a mark on Johnson's body, other than a cut inside his lower lip, which bled slightly for a few minutes.

The fight lacked interest, for it was a like a training bout at Johnson's camp. There were no cheers. The crowd accepted the police's action with apparent relief. "Long before the end did come, ringside opinion seemed to favor the view that Flynn was eager to be disqualified. He was helpless as a child and certainly made no effort to disguise his attempt to do with his skull what his gloves could not accomplish."

Although the consensus of opinion was that Johnson could have won at any time by knockout had he so desired, Flynn was not hurt. Cuts and bruises on his face were the only damage done. "He had nothing to say in defense of the showing he made."

Both the decision to stop the bout and Referee Smith's decision in Johnson's favor were popular ones. The crowd was confident that Johnson would have won by knockout. Flynn was roasted roundly for his unsportsmanlike tactics. Undoubtedly Smith could have disqualified Flynn and stopped the bout much earlier, but he hated to deprive the fans of their amusement after their long journey and the money paid.

Some questioned the propriety of Fornoff's action, for it was discourteous to the local sheriff's office to jump in. Many thought it should have been the sheriff who stopped the fight, if interferences were made, according to precedent.

Some thought it a strange coincidence that a police finish occurred. At a conference held a few days before the fight, both Flynn and Johnson anticipated and dealt with the potential issue of police interference. Both agreed that a decision should be given if the police stopped the contest.

The *Optic* opined that the police interference saved Flynn from the humiliation of a knockout loss. Captain Fornoff stopped it on account of the many fouls. The champion landed at will and showed that he still was the master of the game. Flynn was getting much the worst of it when the bout came to a conclusion. Hence the decision went in favor of the "inky boxer," a decision which received approval from the vast majority of the crowd, which included many Southerners. The challenger showed less class than had been expected. The crowd size was a bitter disappointment.

The *Albuquerque Evening Herald* had a same-day report. It said Flynn was slaughtered and beaten unmercifully, outgeneraled and outfought at every stage in every round, so therefore he resorted to persistent butting tactics. Flynn's face was chopped and cut frightfully, and he was on the verge of being disqualified when Chief Coles of the Las Vegas police ended the unequal contest in the 9th round, declaring it a brutal exhibition.

For three rounds, Flynn realized his inability to defend himself, and frantically tried to butt his way to victory. At times he leapt a foot from the ground, endeavoring to crash his skull against the champ's jaw. Time after time, Referee Smith warned him to stop it. Flynn would respond, "He's holding me; he's holding me," and then he would butt again.

Johnson made no serious effort to hurt Flynn at any time. Apparently he held himself in check even when Flynn's butting tactics were at their worst. Johnson bore not a single mark beyond a slight cut inside his lower lip.

Claude Johnson of the *Kansas City Star*, who was on scene and published a same-day report, said Johnson was too strong and skillful for the gritty Pueblo fireman. It was a bloody fight. From the 1st round, the white hope's fight was hopeless. Johnson was as fast as ever, his wind held out, and he had all of his cleverness and punch. Flynn threw many punches, but Johnson seemed to thrive on them. The crowd was small, but the relatively cool weather kept the spectators happy.

This writer noted that he had predicted that if Flynn lost, it probably would be through disqualification. "Flynn told the writer this morning that he would never take the full count and if the going got too rough he was liable to bite or kick rather than suffer humiliation at the hands of a negro."

Flynn, incensed by the scarcity of funds, was keyed up to the point where he would do almost anything. He had been training heroically for eleven weeks, climbing hills and pummeling his sparring partners. He firmly believed his share of the tickets would be equal to Johnson's. Now he knew the truth, and rather than go down to defeat without pay for his trouble, he would do anything to prevent a knockout loss.

Johnson was worried about Flynn's fouling propensities, and told the writer that morning that he expected Flynn to use unfair tactics. He again asked the referee to watch the fireman closely. "I don't want to win on a foul nor do I want to be bitten. An even break is all I want, and ten rounds will end the battle."

The next day, the *Star* reported that the crowd was disgusted. Flynn was battered and beaten at all stages, so he plainly attempted to force the referee to give Johnson the contest on a foul. Repeatedly warned, he still repeatedly offended by butting into Johnson until Captain Fornoff stopped it. No longer was it a boxing match, but a slaughter and brutal exhibition.

Flynn's nose was broken, eyes black, cheek cut open, and his lips and both ears were puffed. Johnson only had slightly puffed lips from the deliberate butts to the mouth.

The *Santa Fe New Mexican's* same-day report said the fight ended in a fizzle when Flynn, bleeding profusely from the mouth, and his face beaten to a pulp, repeatedly fouled until the city marshal, Jim Coles, sprang into the ring and stopped it. The fireman never had a chance. Johnson played with him like a cat with a mouse.

The *Denver Post* said fight fans were disgusted. John Bramer said Flynn seemed to know that he had no chance to win, but that he had to make as good a showing as he could, and took his chances with fouling. Dan Arnold, an enthusiastic fan, said Johnson could have put Flynn out whenever he wanted. He merely was playing with him and seemed to have the situation under perfect control from start to finish. The crowd's general opinion was that Flynn had nowhere near Johnson's fighting abilities.

W. W. Naughton had a completely different perspective than the locals. He agreed that Flynn's incessant butting caused the police to stop the bout. However, he said Johnson broke the rules as well and was used up badly at the end. Flynn's fast pace quickly told on Johnson. Hence, Jack looked to the referee to give him the battle on a foul. Flynn had squandered his chance at victory, for if only he had kept his temper in check, he possibly could have worn Johnson down and won.

Captain Fred Fornoff of the state police entered the ring. Referee Ed W. Smith, after thinking about it for a few seconds, gave Johnson the decision.

Referee Smith said the fight was not won on a foul, but via a points decision. Johnson had held on to Flynn's arms and shoulders, and, frustrated at his inability to use his arms and fists, Flynn used his head. Johnson said he held in order to prevent Flynn from butting him. Smith said,

> They both transgressed the rules, Johnson by holding and Flynn by butting, but Flynn was the greater offender. The decision was given to Johnson because he had the better of the fighting up to that time. They agreed fully a week ago that if there was any interference of any kind the man in the lead at the time the bout was stopped was to be declared the winner.

That Johnson had scored the most punches and had brought the most gore could not be denied. So, although the bout was stopped as a result of Flynn's flagrant fouling, the referee technically awarded a points decision to Johnson based on the work done up to the police stoppage. Technically, it was not a disqualification, although in reality it was Flynn's flagrant fouling that led to the bout's termination.

Naughton questioned whether Johnson looked like an eventual winner when the bout was stopped. "It was the opinion of the majority of the spectators that if Flynn could have kept his temper and fought cleanly he could have worn Johnson down." Naughton felt that Johnson lacked stamina. Flynn was the better trained. He was full of fight and ginger at all times, while Johnson, grinning, stalled for fully half of the round in each round.

By the 6th round, Johnson was somewhat bedraggled. The constant punches to his stomach had affected his stamina, and he no longer maintained the "idiotic grin" he wore in preceding rounds. Flynn rushed ferociously from his corner to start the 6th, as if he sensed that Johnson was weakening. He tore at him like a bull and had him on the ropes. Johnson clasped his forearms and leaned his elbows in the hollow of Flynn's arms in such a way that Flynn was as powerless as a man handcuffed.

Flynn lurched and twisted violently in his effort to free himself, and finding that he could not do so, used his head as a battering ram. Johnson still held on and glanced appealingly at the referee. Professor Watson Burns jumped upon the ring ledge and shouted at Smith, "Can't you see that Flynn is butting?" Johnson chimed in as well, looking concerned. Smith pulled them apart and shook a warning finger at Flynn. Jim's blood was up and he said, "He's holding me! He's holding! Why don't you make him quit and fight as a champion should?" Smith turned to Johnson and told him that the charge against him was true, and that while he was not as culpable in the manner of unfair fighting as his opponent, he certainly was departing from the agreement that had been entered into as a fair stand-up boxing match.

They resumed fighting, and once again Johnson clasped Flynn's arms and pinioned him. Try as he might, he could not free a glove. He was mad and immediately resorted to butting again, while Johnson shouted for help. Professor Burns waved his arms and cried about the unfairness of things.

Four times did Smith have to break them and shake a warning forefinger at Flynn. Johnson stood there noticeably limp. Flynn said, "What am I to do? What am I to do? I am licking the big stiff and he is holding me like grim death all the time."

In the 7th round, Johnson bent forward with his arms well out and met the rush with a straight left that snapped Jim's head back. Flynn rushed and rushed all the time, but got the left pumped between his eyes. Johnson struck him about a dozen times, keeping him at bay. However, Johnson slowed down and held, and Flynn broke both gloves free and pounded away at the short ribs and stomach and even landed an overhand punch that knocked the champ's head aside. Johnson then pushed Flynn away and tilted his head with two uppercuts, "and altogether it was a bad round for Flynn." The round was devoid of butting.

The 8th was another foul round. Flynn had been warned by his seconds, and Johnson had slowed up perceptibly toward the close of the previous round. This round, instead of meeting Flynn with the jab or uppercut, Johnson threw out his arms and clasped him often, strengthening the suspicion that the pace, altitude, and rough work combined were having their effect on the champ's strength. Several spectators commented, "If Flynn will only keep his head he will lick the negro, for Johnson is giving out." However, Johnson knew how to hold Flynn safely, and was strong enough to do so.

Flynn tried to tug away in an effort to free himself from the embrace, but baffled, he jumped from his feet and pounded with his forehead into Johnson's chin and throat. Professor Burns flashed up to the platform side again and drew attention to the unfair fighting. Johnson kept holding on and appealed to the referee. Smith promptly split them apart. This time Smith warned both men; Flynn for using his head and Johnson for holding instead of breaking and fighting back.

For the remainder of the round, Johnson was clinging and Flynn ramming him with his forehead. During it all, there was tumult amongst the spectators and confusion in the ring. Two or three times it looked as if the referee was about to stop the fight and render a decision, but probably he balanced Johnson's holding against Flynn's butting and allowed it to go on. "It seemed reasonably clear that Johnson, at this time, would have liked nothing better than to have been declared the winner on a foul." He dropped heavily into his chair at the close of the 8th round and beckoned to the referee, "I thought you told me you were going to be fair." Smith replied, "I am trying to be fair, and to tell the truth, I can't make up my mind which of you is the worst offender."

Between rounds, Flynn's seconds implored him to keep his temper, telling him, "Johnson is all in and you will surely whip him if you keep your temper." Flynn replied, "I know it, but it makes me sore clean through when he grabs me and holds on instead of trading punches with me."

In the 9th round, Flynn again rushed and Johnson again held. The pinioned Flynn threw discretion to the winds and butted the chin again and again, and made his usual excuse speech when Smith broke them. After another spasm of holding and butting, during which Johnson seemed quite perturbed, police Captain Fornoff and one of his men climbed into the ring and said, "We will have no more fighting of this kind." Referee Smith pondered a few moments and then announced his decision for Johnson.

Naughton said Flynn was punished, but not to the extent that was expected, and nowhere near the extent that he suffered in their first bout. He received a number of uppercuts, there was a slight cut on his cheek, and the claret trickled from his nose, but there was no real damage done.

> No matter what Johnson thinks, or what any of his trainers or admirers think, he is not the man he was two years ago. His condition failed quickly today, and he did not punch with the old-time force. He did not even show the strength he did in the clinches with Jeffries, although he was powerful enough to blanket little Flynn when the latter decided to take a fighting chance and give blow for blow. ...

> When he was himself he never allowed any one to take liberties with him. An extra hard punch either in a practice bout or in a real fight brought retaliation from the champion in the shape of a volley of hooks and uppercuts. But here today he allowed a man lighter and several inches shorter than him to take liberties with him. If he had

followed his usual custom he would have shook himself free and batted Flynn's head from side to side with hurtful punches. But instead he clung to the undersized Fireman like a creeper to a fence, and wanted to be declared winner on a foul.

The *Denver Post's* Otto Floto, who was present at the fight, wrote, "Flynn lost the chance of his life. He had Johnson worried to death." Spider Kelly agreed, saying, "Good God! What a chance Flynn had, and tossed it off!" Kelly said Flynn had the fight won. Floto thought that Captain Fornoff was too hasty in stopping the bout when neither man was hurt. "Flynn's foul tactics and overofficiousness on the part of Captain Fornoff spoiled what probably would have given the white man an excellent opportunity to wear the crown of supremacy in the realm of fistiana." Johnson also violated the rules, for he held continually, and held and hit, but Flynn did so to the greater and more flagrant extent, for the way he butted left no doubt about his intentions. Smith's repeated warnings were to no avail. Still, Floto thought disqualification of either would have been unjust.

Floto opined that neither fighter had been punished to any great extent, and both could have continued for many more rounds. The cut on Flynn's nose bled profusely, but outside of external damage, he was uninjured.

Floto was not saying that Flynn would have won, but his chances to win were taken away by what he thought was law enforcement's hasty action. At the time of the stoppage, the fight was up in the air and in doubt. Regardless, "Johnson is still a great champion. He is cunning and shrewd and manages to cover up his transgressions of the rules in a manner that is surprising. But he is not the Jack Johnson of two years ago."

In the past, when an opponent would foul him, Johnson would laugh and say he did not mind. "Not so yesterday. One time when Smith walked to his corner the big black said, 'I thought you were going to be fair to me.' The referee looked at him and replied: 'That's just what I am, Jack, for you are committing a breach of the rules when you hold and hit. It's just as much your fault as his butting. I think I am treating you both fairly in this matter.'"

Floto believed that father time eventually would defeat the gradually slipping Johnson. Eventually, some young, strong fellow with a wallop would come along and "there will no longer be an argument as to whether the white race or the black race owns the title." Regardless, at this point, Johnson still reigned as champ, and still was very clever.

> Even when tiring fast toward the close of the battle, he covered it up with the golden smile and little by-play such as clapping his hands behind Flynn's back. Then he would wink to friends and laugh at his handlers in the corner. Yet the experienced eyes of the critics discovered his weakening, and the manner in which his bellows were asked to do duty.

Flynn fought like an enraged bull with his head down, boring in. A clinch usually followed, and then uppercuts were sent into his face.

Johnson used his left to great extent. He would jab five or six times without return, and then use short uppercuts. However, invariably, clinch after clinch was featured. In the close work, Flynn had no advantage whatsoever. "Rather he fared badly." "Johnson is cunning, as I said, and for that reason I believe he will retire before facing defeat."

Floto opined that Johnson would seek to confine his game to 10-round bouts in New York. "Ten rounds is the distance he can safely undertake without much harm coming to him as yet."

Some opined that Johnson was allowing Flynn to stay to make the pictures profitable. Others thought such speculation was absurd. Johnson had bet money that he would deck Flynn in the 1st round, which he did not come close to doing.

Regardless of the criticism, on a personal level, Johnson was fairly well liked. "No matter how we may criticize his fighting ability, we are forced to concede the fact that Johnson is a shrewd, clever diplomat who knows how to handle himself in all kinds of going. He is well behaved and impresses all he meets with his bearing."

One writer said the public, and especially the gamblers, had been handed a trimming. Referee Smith explained that ten days ago it was decided that if the police stopped the fight the decision would go to the man who was leading at the time. "That was a lovely arrangement, but the people who framed it forgot to take the public into their confidence and many a man lost good money who would not have bet counterfeit stuff if he had known of the arrangement. You can fool all of the people all of the time."

Another said the decision was "strangely suspicious." This writer thought that if a decision was given to Johnson, the referee should also have declared all bets off. Speculating, he wrote, "It looks as though Flynn was giving Johnson the beating of his life, and as the money was all on Johnson, especially the local money, the police interfered to save Johnson and the money bet on him. That's the honest conclusion, otherwise the fight should have been no contest and all bets off."

The *Omaha World Herald*'s Sandy Griswold, who saw the fight, said that although Johnson was a great fighter, he was luckier than he was great. He had been battered fiercely and mercilessly, but won anyhow. Flynn, enraged by Johnson's persistent illegal holding, at various times jumped upwards while clinched. Flynn's offense was the most palpable and damaging. As of the 9th round, Jim had been shaded in a majority of the rounds, and he shed most of the red fluid. Hence, the decision went against him.

Griswold thought the intervention was lucky for Johnson, whom he thought eventually would be beaten. Although Flynn had a split and fractured nose, his face a mask of smeary gore, and his torso and upper limbs swathed in a scarlet sweater, his eyes were wild, fierce, and terrible, with the ravages of hatred, vindictiveness, and victory. Griswold thought

Referee Smith was mistaken, but the greater mistake was Flynn's. Jim had "absolute victory" in his grasp, but his hatred and passion threw it away. "There was no call for his repeated butting the negro under the chin, he was winning with most astounding rapidity as it was." Griswold opined that if Flynn had been more patient, cool, and collected, and the mill had been prolonged, he would have had worn Johnson down and had him out.

Johnson had speed and skill, but Flynn had indomitable ferocity, courage, strength, and the full resolution of a wild beast, the unsubduable, uncheckable raging of a fiend. Johnson could only hold him off for so long. Jack was landing at will, but then Flynn would get inside and Johnson was forced to hold. Jim worked the stomach and landed overhand chops.

Griswold admitted that Flynn was in a bad way in the 8th round. Johnson was fighting, and though weakening, he gave Flynn's "bruised and busted visage an awful thumping, bringing the blood in torrents from gashes and rents in cheek and from mouth and nose and ears."

In the 9th round, Flynn attacked the "rapidly weakening and complaining black." When clinched, Flynn jumped clear from his feet time and time again, with the top of his cast-iron head under the black man's chin.

Griswold admired Johnson's tantalizing coolness and dazzling skill and science, which were the wonders of all, and he also admired Flynn's marvelous strength and ferocity. He summarized the diversity of opinion:

> [O]pinion seems to be pretty equally divided as to who really had the better of the fight, and was winning, and would have won, had it been permitted to go to a finish. There are many who think that Johnson, after all, was the wrongly judged party, that he was fighting clean against a ruffian who had made up his mind to win by fair means or foul, but if he saw there was no chance either way, he himself would give it up by fouling. They think Johnson was giving Flynn a proper trimming and that the only damage he sustained was by reason of the disgraceful tactics of Flynn and this all may be true. But the other side, they contend that while the champion made the fireman look like a helpless infant in the earlier rounds of the battle, and that all his sangfroid and humorous sallies were but the foil of a real fear that soon possessed him after Flynn's unquenchable efforts had enabled him to get in much deadly work, and that to save his crumbling fame and fortunes, he had to resort to the role of an innocent, to save himself with, that he soon had the bravo taken out of him via the stomach route and realized that desperate situations required desperate remedies and holding Flynn in his strong arms was the one that could save him. They claim that all that has been said about the champion's retrogression is true, that he is a mere apology for the big invincible that made Jim Jeffries look like a sucker, and that he now knows it himself, and that he will never fight again.

> So far as I am concerned, I am with the latter, although I realize that there is little preference between the two men. I do not think

Johnson is at all a great pugilist today, and that Jim Flynn is a dangerous rival for the best of them. I also think that Johnson has picked a fitting time to get out of the game. Such luck as was vouchsafed him today don't come to one man twice in a lifetime.

Tom Flanagan declared that Flynn should have been disqualified as early as the 6th round.

There was nothing to the battle but Johnson. In my mind at all times he had it well in hand and the danger line never appeared on the horizon so far as I was concerned.

I think that Flynn's foul tactics should have called for disqualification in the sixth round, when it became apparent that he intended to fight with his head instead of his hands. ...

I heard a lot about the way in which Johnson tired towards the close of the battle, but I am confident that it's a mistake. Johnson was in superb condition and could have gone the whole forty-five rounds without flying the distress signal, as some stated. ...But today in my humble opinion he is the same peerless champion he always was. ...

I do not agree with many present at yesterday's battle that Johnson hit while holding. It may have seemed so to others, but to me it looked like his natural way of boxing – the same manner in which he boxed his training companions while preparing for this battle.

Afterwards, Johnson addressed the crowd in his big room before he left. He was the picture of good humor and his golden smile in evidence. He insisted that he did not have to exert himself at any stage of the fight.

You know I have always fought on the level. I have been accused of having a yellow streak in numerous fights, but I have never been guilty. I have many times overlooked foul tactics of other fighters, but I cannot understand why this fellow Flynn was allowed to go on so long as he did without being disqualified. I complained to the referee several times, but there was nothing doing except warnings until the police took the matter into their own hands.

Johnson said that but for Flynn's foul tactics; he would not have a mark.

While Referee Smith decided in my favor, I hardly think I was given proper treatment during the fight.

Any one could see that I was taking all the fight out of Flynn with my straight lefts and uppercuts, and he was not hurting me a bit. I was handling him carefully, just as I did when I fought him before, and just as I did when I boxed Jeffries at Reno.

Flynn is a foul fighter, but he had the sympathy of the crowd with him just as an underdog always has when opposed to a champion. I am sure I could have knocked Flynn out in a few rounds more if he had continued to fight fairly instead of acting like a billy goat. However, I have retained the championship and will always be ready to box any man who is considered a suitable opponent.

Johnson said he wanted nothing further to do with Flynn, for he could not fight fair. The only time Jack was hurt was from head butts.

I was whipping him properly and thoroughly, and would have had him out in at least one or two more rounds. ... His aim was to lose on a foul. He was taking punishment the spectators neither saw nor understood, and while he did daze and hurt me a bit in the sixth and ninth rounds, not a single blow from his fists even made me wince.

Jack then drove his auto to the betting commissioner to collect his wagers on himself.

Before he left on the 9:15 p.m. train to Chicago, Johnson said,

Flynn is a joke. No matter what the wise fellows may say about me being tired, I could have gone twenty rounds more at the fastest pace. I was taking things easy and allowing him to fret himself. I did not want the fight stopped. I wanted to show the crowd that Flynn was a dirty fighter. Then I wanted to whip him.

They are saying that I did not train properly. I train to suit myself and produce the best results. I was perfectly trained and was well satisfied with my condition.

Now there is a prospect of my being matched with Al Palzer for ten rounds in New York. To show that I believe I am as good as ever, I will bet $10,000 of my own money that I will stop Palzer inside of ten rounds.

The *Star* said that although Flynn claimed he was robbed when the police captain entered the ring and told Smith to stop the fight; few paid any attention to his claim. Flynn said,

There was nothing to it. I had the big negro going, and he violated every rule of Queensberry fighting by holding me around the arms and shoulders and keeping me from punching him. He was able to do so because he is so much taller and stronger than I am.

I lost my head, and it seemed to me I was justified in doing what I did when he broke the rules by holding. I am sorry now that I did not keep myself cool, as the championship was mine beyond any doubt.

In other fights men have been disqualified for constant holding, and any fair man will say that Johnson should have been disqualified today.

Certainly my foul fighting was brought on by his.

I doubt whether Johnson will meet me again. I know by the look on his face he was fading away today, and he was a lucky champion that things turned out as they did.

Flynn said it was Johnson who started the dirty work.

All was well for three rounds, and while Johnson was landing mighty regularly his punches did not hurt. I knew in advance that he no longer had much steam behind his blows. … Yes, I guess Johnson poked me pretty nearly whenever he wanted to. But I was never hurt and was never in any trouble. I knew in advance that I had to take a licking in order to win and I think I was taking it in a manly way. … Furthermore, I am quite sure that I had started hurting him along about the sixth round. … I was just as strong at the end of the eighth round as I was at the end of the first, while I was confident all along. … I could feel Johnson's punches, never hard ones at any stage, getting weaker and weaker. Then, he was beginning to puff like a porpoise. … Johnson started the dirty work and never let up. He wouldn't fight and I had to do all the fighting…. I'll admit [Johnson's punches] came in fairly warm at the start, [but] I scarcely felt them from the sixth round on. … I would have worn Johnson down yesterday and fairly eaten him up if Referee Smith had paid as much attention to Jack's foul work as he did to mine, and if the police captain who stopped the fight had not been a simpleton and mistaken a blood-bespattered fighter for a well licked one. … I was in to keep going and break Johnson's heart and bring out the yellow streak that I know is in him. … I'll admit that Jack's start was an even better one than I figured.

Flynn said the cut nose was not bothering him at all during the bout. Conversely, "[Johnson] was beginning to tire badly and was the happiest man in the arena when the police interfered. He didn't care to go any further. He was as much to blame as I. He held me throughout and the only way I could force him to release me and at the same time even up for his violation of the rules was to butt him."

Flynn did not blame the referee for giving the contest to Johnson. He acknowledged that he was behind on points. "I am not a bit sore excepting at myself for having lost my head the way I did. But he started the foul work first and I think I was justified in doing what I did. Johnson should have been disqualified before the sixth round, for he wouldn't permit me to fight at all."

Most felt that Flynn only had himself to blame. Though he was being punished in every round, he was never even staggered and could have continued for some time had he fought fairly.

Promoter Jack Curley said Flynn was beaten fair and square, though he also said Flynn was still strong at the end despite the flow of blood from the cuts. Although Flynn failed to win, he convinced many leading critics that

Johnson was beatable. "I predict right now that if Palzer meets Johnson within a year he will rule favorite in the betting."

Still, Curley also said that boring in, willingness to mix, and a slam-bang style "will never beat Jack Johnson in his present shape." Johnson tired, but Flynn ran right into his punches, while Johnson did not have to move.

Flynn grew tired of being held. "There is no denying the fact that Jack held on repeatedly." Most felt that Flynn should have taken it easy during the clinches and rested along with Johnson. After all, he had 45 rounds to wear down Johnson gradually. Regardless, Flynn clearly was there to fight, for he was full of vigor and over-anxious to display his prowess. Early in the 6th round, tired of being held, he was forced to use rough tactics to break loose, and resorted to fouling.

In Referee Smith's eyes, Johnson had the better of it. "Flynn willingly admits that such was the case. But insists that he was in no danger of being knocked out and would have surely worn the big fellow down and won before the forty-fifth round." However, Johnson won, and "under the conditions was entitled to the verdict." Flynn received a very small sum.

Referee Ed Smith was very critical of Flynn. He said Flynn disgraced everyone and fought a foul battle when he saw that he was outclassed. He fought as foul as a man could, bringing down the police's wrath. Flynn deliberately tried to lose the contest on a foul when it was plain to him, as it was to the spectators, that he was a beaten man. "There is much more praise for a man who will take a punch on the jaw and die the death of a real gladiator on the floor than there is for the man who, seeing himself in for a trimming, will seek the subterfuge of a foul, the cowardly refuge of the man who is not game."

Smith admitted that Johnson was not fighting entirely fairly. Johnson was guilty of the trick of placing his glove around and behind Flynn's arm or shoulder, yanking Flynn forward into him and slashing at him at the same time with the other hand. All around the ring there were cries that Johnson was holding.

> Johnson was not holding as much as he was smoothing Flynn at all stages. He placed his thumbs in Flynn's elbows and simply held the fireman's arms helpless, completely blocked. ... It was not a foul move, because Flynn's arms were free in a way and he was able to tap Johnson's stomach and short ribs with both hands, but in a way that did not seem to do much damage.

Ultimately, "Maddened by the fact that he was being checkmated and outguessed at every stage of the contest, Flynn resorted to the most barefaced system of fouling." Smith said he was about to disqualify Flynn when the police entered the ring. He had waited to do so because he did not think the fouling had jeopardized the champ's chances to win.

Smith said Johnson was superior from start to finish:

It was the champion's battle from the first tap of the gong. He ripped Flynn with a straight left and murdered him with his old right uppercut.

It was not a good battle to look at.

Johnson did not put up an impressive battle, albeit he won by a mile and had all the better of it.

There did not seem to be the old cutting force to his drives, despite the fact that he opened a gash on Flynn's left cheek in the first round and started the blood to flowing from his nose in the second round.

Later on he opened a triangular shaped cut on the bridge of the fireman's nose, and this, too, poured blood in a stream.

The Pueblo man was so bespattered at the close that every punch the champion landed sent a shower of gore in all directions.

Johnson was unmarked, although in the third round the blood showed in the mouth, the 'golden smile' being colored by the gore that trickled out of a lip cut, evidently on the underside.

Johnson was never hurt at any time, even when Flynn deliberately jumped up into his chin. Still, the champ was smart enough to get his head out of the way most of the time.

Johnson is immeasurably superior to the Flynn class as a boxer. So far does he overreach the Flynn standard there is no comparison at all. Johnson stabbed out with his left and always found the mark. In one round he shot nine straight lefts to the face in almost as many seconds, pumping them in with the precision of a machine gun. And that right uppercut seldom failed to find a resting spot on the swollen face of the man from Colorado. ...

Johnson seemed to tire a lot in the sixth and the eighth rounds, but I doubt if it was a serious thing at all and certainly not because of any punishment that was meted out to him. Flynn got many a glancing punch at his body and landed a few overhand wallops on the face, but in the main the force of these was exhausted before he found the target.

Hundreds in Chicago's "Black Belt" celebrated the news that their man was still champion. The returns had been received in nearly every café, saloon, and theater in the black belt. A riot call was sent to the police, and the blacks, who had begun a parade through the streets, were routed by a small army of bluecoats. One black man who fired a revolver several times in the street was arrested.

Johnson returned to Chicago. He "gave the impression he likely would accept the offers he has had to go to Australia and fight Sam Langford."

Flynn was at his Montezuma camp nursing his mashed nose.

Sportsmen were divided on the question of whether the contest should have been stopped. Some said Referee Smith should have disqualified the white man. Others believed that as long as Johnson was willing to continue, the bout should have continued with warnings. They criticized Captain Fornoff and the state police for interfering, feeling that ultimately it should have been left up to the referee. The fight overall was very tame. Few blows landed. Flynn was bleeding from the nose but he was not hurt. "That Flynn had no business in the ring with Johnson is generally conceded." However, some felt that he should have been allowed to stay until he was knocked out. Many felt that the local sheriff or the city marshal were the proper persons to act, if someone did, and the state police should have remained in the background.

A couple days after the fight, the *Omaha World Herald* said Flynn was battered and beaten at all stages, and evidently attempted to force the referee to give Johnson the contest on a foul. Although Flynn declared that he had been robbed, "there were few who attended the fiasco who paid any attention to his claim."

The consensus of opinion was that it would be many years before a heavyweight was developed capable of wresting the title from Johnson. Flynn made a foul and hopeless fight. "As early as the third round it was evident he had no chance."

Johnson refused to take the fight seriously; good-naturedly joshing and joking with the crowd and Flynn. "Johnson displayed a cleverness and ease in blocking and getting away that made Flynn look like the veriest Tyro."

Johnson overlooked the dirty work, but Flynn insisted on butting continually. In the 8th round, Johnson could stand the fouling no longer, and appealed to the referee. In the 9th, Johnson seemed serious, and split open Jim's nose with a vicious left jab. Flynn, angered by the blow, deliberately ran at Johnson and butted him three times, until the bout was stopped.[710]

The *New York American* repeated the view that Flynn was bested and on his way out, but for Johnson's carrying him.

> Ringside opinion was that Flynn would have been neatly cleaned in a short time. On three occasions during the fight Johnson landed from five to seven straight punches on Flynn's flattened nose in as many seconds. … Flynn was groggy and Johnson could have used his famous punch to the jaw with either hand and put Flynn to sleep. Still Flynn declares he was not whipped, and asserts the police robbed him of a victory.[711]

Back in Chicago, Johnson said he cleared $31,000 from Curley, and won $5,000 betting on himself. "Flynn was easy." He said he had planned to knock out Flynn in the 10th round. Johnson also said, "Well, it was not

---

[710] *Omaha World Herald*, July 6, 1912.
[711] *New York American*, July 6, 1912.

much of a fight at that. I had him whipped from start to finish and would have finished him in a round or two more. Those experts who said I was tired and worried at the finish did not know what they were talking about."

Johnson said he had no desire to fight ever again. He never wanted to see another pair of gloves, and intended to retire after Labor Day. He said he would fight Al Palzer as long as the bout took place no later than Labor Day, for after that he intended to retire forever. "If Al Palzer wants to fight me he will have to do it not later than Labor day, for on the day following I will retire from the ring forever. That's final – I quit then for good."[712]

Many praised Johnson for maintaining his poise and composure even when Flynn was acting in a rank manner.

Although it had been the largest crowd ever gathered in the city's history, it still was far smaller than expected. Jack Curley said about 3,000 men and about 500 women paid admission to "witness the failure of Jim Flynn to restore the pugilistic championship to the white race." Several hundred who did not pay admission helped swell the crowd.

Curley said the gate receipts were not sufficient to pay the expenses. Some quoted him as saying the receipts did not exceed $29,000, while others quoted Curley as saying the gate receipts were about $35,000.

Allegedly, Curley stood to lose about $15,000 out of his own pocket, while the local Las Vegas businessmen who joined the venture stood to lose $10,000. Some said Flynn would receive nothing. Curley said he gave Johnson $31,000. He believed that he would lose money even with the moving picture receipts. "It is safe to predict that Las Vegas will never again be the scene of a heavyweight championship contest."

Some subsequently said that Johnson actually received only $21,000, that when ticket sales were looking bad, a couple days before the contest he agreed to take less - $12,000 in cash and $8000 in notes.

Later, it was reported that Curley and his partners had put up about $65,000 for the promotion. The city of Las Vegas posted a $10,000 bonus for it to be named as the battleground. The receipts barely totaled $28,000, so it was a case of the promoter and Flynn working for Johnson, who earned a $30,000 purse plus $1,100 for training expenses.

Within a month, Curley said he lost about $12,000 on the venture. "I knew I stood to lose when Governor McDonald threatened to stop the fight and didn't give out a statement to the contrary until ten days before the Fourth."

Curley said he paid Johnson $31,000, not $21,000 as some claimed. He gave Johnson an IOU for $8,000, which was honored and made good only one week after the fight.

Curley gave Flynn his automobile, which he had promised him if he won, but despite the loss, he gave it to him anyway. It was all Flynn earned

[712] *Albuquerque Morning Journal, Albuquerque Evening Herald*, July 6, 1912; *San Francisco Examiner*, July 7, 1912.

from the fight. Although Curley also gave Flynn $5,000 cash, Curley denied paying Flynn that money for the fight, but said that amount was paid in settlement of their theatrical business. Of course, without the fight being scheduled, Flynn would not have been a theatrical attraction.

Curley said he would never again promote a bout in Las Vegas, New Mexico. However, he also said he would continue promoting boxing, and was willing to put Johnson in the ring with any white man who seemed to have a chance with him, "but I will never promote a match between Johnson and any other colored man for the title, because I am quite sure it is not what the public wants and would fail as an attraction."[713]

Regarding the fight, several days later, Curley said,

> Flynn wasn't hurt, and I believe he had a chance to whip Johnson. … He was bloody from his bleeding nose, but you can't hurt Flynn by hitting him on the nose. The police rushed in to stop the fight as soon as they had an excuse. If it had gone on, there might have been a different story to tell. … As for Flynn, he expected to take a terrible beating during the first fifteen rounds. He was still in good shape when the fight was stopped. It was pretty rough, but fighting is a rough game.[714]

Governor William C. McDonald said the fight was peaceable and well handled, and would help the town of Las Vegas. Certainly, the bout had garnered much publicity for the town.

JACK JOHNSON FAIRLY PLAYED WITH JIM FLYNN

DAR'S SOM'PIN MIGHTY FUNNY 'BOUT DESE WHITE-FOLK'S LAWS. DEY ARRESTS A GUY AN' PUTS 'IM IN JAIL FO' FAST DRIVIN' IN A AUTO' AN' DEY ARREST 'IM AN' RAISE A AWFUL ROW WHEN HE BUYS DI'MONS IN LONDON AN' FERGITS TO PAY DE DOOTY— BUT, LAN'S SAKES! DEY FRAMES UP A SCHEME FO' DAT SAME GUY TO BEAT UP A PO'-LIL' WHITE MAN' LIKE MISTO FLYNN FO' A BIG POT OF MONEY, WHICH IS SHOLY LIKE STEALIN' CANDY FROM A BABY, AN' DEY AINT NO LAW 'BOUT DAT NOHOW — SEEMS MIGHTY FUNNY, DA'S ALL!

Chicago Day Book, July 5, 1912

[713] *Freeman,* August 17, 1912.
[714] *Albuquerque Evening Herald,* July 9, 1912.

The *Chicago Defender* reported that Flynn was a battered and hopeless white hope. He was bathed in blood from head to toe, with a knockout his inevitable finish, until the police interfered at 1 minute and 45 seconds in the 9th round. Captain Fred Fornoff of the mounted police stopped it, packing a .44 that spoke louder than words. He said the bout had ceased to be a contest of boxing skill. Both fighters had resorted to foul tactics, though Flynn was the first and worst offender, repeatedly disregarding the referee's warnings. Eight times the referee warned and threatened to disqualify him. Five times Smith called the champ for holding and locking Flynn's arms. "Flynn early awakened to the fact that his chances were slender, grasped the only alternative, that of roughing it." Flynn's nose was broken from a terrific right uppercut in the 4th round, and a long slit in his left cheek let blood spurt out upon the resin-bedecked canvas. However, Flynn was far from through. He was outweighed by 22 pounds, but never slackened the pace.[715]

The *Freeman* said "Caucasia" had "long been humiliated by Ethiopia. ... I have begun to feel ashamed for the white people at the poor prospect for their fighters. Will they abandon the field, feeling it unworthy of them...?" The point was if whites could not beat the black champion, they might simply quit trying, and instead denigrate and attack the sport itself as barbaric and try to taboo it.

> But regardless of the rhetoric; the white fighters are cutting a sorry figure. And yet as long as the game is in vogue it's right from the viewpoint of race pride to keep up the attack. ... From our viewpoint: We, the Negroes, have so little by way of triumphs to make merry over that we religiously cling to our one pugilistic hero. ... [T]he victories of old Jack Johnson are glory added unto us. Where but little is expected a little will do very well. ... Jack Johnson won over Jim Jeffries two years ago. The victory stood for an idea. Oppression lifted a bit. Negro stock did a little bulling on the racial market.

This writer wondered whether Johnson actually would retire as advertised, or "do the well known farewell stunt usual with retiring prima donnas." It said even Jeffries could not resist the temptation to come back, have his name in circulation, and hear the applause. Jack liked being somebody.[716]

Although W. W. Naughton believed that Flynn's rough-house tactics were not warranted, he realized that Johnson's persistent holding irritated Flynn and caused him to resort to foul methods. Naughton insisted that Johnson was not the powerful man he once was. He was not the same man who lifted Ketchel from the floor by the pressure of palms against arms and swung him around and placed him on his feet again. Nor was it the Johnson who took hold of Jeffries' thick left arm and twisted it hammerlock fashion

---

[715] *Chicago Defender*, July 6, 1912.
[716] *Freeman*, July 6, 1912.

behind his back. "If it had been the Johnson of old Flynn would have suffered for the liberties he took." The old Johnson would have lashed out and punished Flynn.

Naughton noted how tricky Johnson was. "Johnson is so artistic in everything he does in the ring that it requires great watchfulness to detect when he is not fighting according to Hoyle." He grasped Flynn by the shoulder and leaned his forearm into the hollows of his arms in such a way that Flynn was as powerless as a man bound to a stake. He also had a trick of holding and hitting, which was not according to the rules of fair play. He would yank Flynn towards him and then deliver an uppercut with the other hand, which gave the blow double force.

However, from the 6th round on, Johnson did more holding than hitting. In the early rounds he waited for the rush and met it with either a hook or uppercut. Later he simply threw out his arms and blanketed the Pueblo man as he rushed in. "Johnson's laurels will be in jeopardy the first time he meets a man who is as big as himself and younger and more rugged."[717]

On July 9 in San Francisco at the Miles Brothers' establishment on Mission Street, W. W. Naughton watched the films of the fight. Spectators were limited to newspapermen and friends of Jim Coffroth, who had secured the western film rights. The films were 2,000 feet long and ran for 40 minutes.

Naughton said it was perfectly plain before the 3rd round that Johnson had lost his punch. There was not a staggering blow, let alone a knockdown, in the whole fight. Despite being subjected to occasional spells of hooks and uppercuts from Johnson, Flynn tore in to close quarters, and under his persistent boring, Johnson gradually grew tired and less inclined to trade punches. Johnson held and blanketed Flynn for about two minutes of every round, time that should have been devoted to fair stand-up boxing.

Just before the end, Flynn tried to persuade Referee Smith that butting was his only recourse when being held. When the police entered, Flynn pled with the captain to be allowed to continue, but the official shook his head and waved his arm to signify that the affair had gone far enough.

Spider Kelly opined that Johnson put up a wretched fight and was in danger of being worn down if the police had not stopped it. He said, "When Johnson boxes again, no matter where it is, I will be at the ringside to bet against him. He has had his day and will surely be defeated if his next opponent is a rugged fellow with plenty of pluck."[718]

A *Freeman* writer, T. S. Andrews, said Flynn put up a surprisingly poor fight. Flynn made his best showing in the 3rd and 6th rounds. However, up to the end it was Johnson's battle on points clearly, for he gave the fireman a terrific beating, punishing him badly with right uppercuts and left jabs to the face. Johnson fought in the same careful manner as he did against

---

[717] *San Francisco Examiner*, July 9, 1912.
[718] *San Francisco Examiner*, July 10, 1912.

Jeffries. He was accurate in his hitting and seldom missed. He was a past master at blocking. Flynn threw away his chance by butting so palpably that it could not be overlooked. If law enforcement had not interfered the chances were that Referee Smith would have disqualified Flynn.

Some said Johnson seemed determined to drag out the rounds, "maybe in order to give the picture people a chance. Flynn was at his mercy all along."

The *Freeman's* Billy Lewis said Johnson was more secure in his title than ever, for his victory served as a set-back for white hopes. Flynn fought like a boy in the hands of his school-master. Lewis opined that Johnson was the best champion who ever lived.

Lewis noted that in a great series of fights in Australia, Sam McVey was victorious in all of his bouts with white men, leading to the Australians making racial conclusions.

[The Australian papers] attempted an analysis of the races physically, concluding that white men were not meant to cope physically with black men; insisting that black men more nearly approached the brute creation. … Whatever it may be, it can be set down, that, with equal conditions, weight, age, preparedness to fight, a white man will not whip a black man. … The Negro boy will concede a white boy long on intellect…he will see something almost superhuman at his case in doing intellectual things….

However, in athletic endeavors, the tables were turned. "Now the pale faces hover alongside, struck with amazement at the ease with which Negro boys do physical things. … No Negro boy thinks a white boy of equal age and size has any business monkeying around him."[719]

Lester Walton of the black-owned *New York Age* said the fight was responsible for exploding the ancient and decrepit opinion that the Negro was the possessor of butting proclivities. Flynn with malice aforethought sought to use his head in billy-goat fashion, contrary to all the rules, compelling the police (not the referee) to stop the farce. Those who argued that the Negro skull was thick and that butting was "as much of a racial trait with him as it was with the goat tribe, are now reluctantly confessing that the black man has no corner on the butting game. The admission is also made that in recent years the prize ring has shown the Caucasian to be more addicted to using his head as a human battering ram than his dusky brother." Therefore, the "American idea that the Negro is instinctively a butter has been dissipated." Johnson used good judgment and showed a cool head in not butting back.

Unfortunately, the arena was only one-third filled. The *Age* said that promoters needed to remember that large crowds only assembled when it looked as if the Caucasian had a good chance to win. However, the only

---

[719] *Freeman,* July 13, 1912; *Omaha World Herald,* July 5, 1912.

fighters with any real chance were black – Langford, McVea, and Jeannette.[720]

The *Freeman* also noted the importance of the fight outside of the boxing world. "The very Negro nature cries out for the great splendid things as the desert yearns for the rain; and Johnson stands for the idea at its best. He has wrested the key from the hand of adversity."[721]

Some felt that Johnson held Flynn so cheaply that he did not train as hard as he might have if he had respected him more. Johnson had such a high opinion of himself that he might have underestimated his adversary. One New York expert said, "Now, I do not agree with those who think that Johnson was in serious danger of petering out when he began to hold Flynn so tightly in the sixth round. That he was tired, I admit, but he was simply taking a means of resting himself and if Flynn had not retaliated by butting – thus causing the fight to be stopped – I think Johnson would have cut loose in spots and eventually scored a knockout punch." Opinion was that next time; Johnson would train more faithfully, not drink as much beer, and go to bed early the night before the battle instead of attending a fight.

As for Flynn, he had disgusted his well-wishers by his infernally bad ring manners. Those who had wagered on him were particularly wrathful; for they felt that he had lost the battle though criminally foul tactics, throwing away his and their chances to win. His seconds implored him to keep his temper, but it was like talking to a crazy person.[722]

W. W. Naughton again said he believed that the current Johnson tired more readily and was a less formidable puncher than he used to be. Naughton believed he was in a good position to judge, owing to the fact that he had seen Johnson in action in most contests of note for the past decade. However, one could not always tell with Johnson, who often liked to hold back and fool around.

> Incidentally Johnson is one of the hardest men in the fighting world to get a line on. He is such a consummate ring general and everything he does within the ropes is done so artistically that it is anything but easy to tell when he is in trouble.
>
> In the affair with Flynn he held on and stalled around with a grin on his face and with no particular appearance of being flurried, but he was an exceedingly tired champion of the world just the same. If he had been the Johnson of other fights, instead of looking hungry-eyed at Referee Smith when Flynn began butting, he would have broken his hold and punched Flynn clear across the ropes.

Still, Naughton acknowledged that there were many different viewpoints regarding Johnson.[723]

---

[720] *New York Age*, July 18, 1912.
[721] *Freeman*, July 20, 1912.
[722] *San Francisco Examiner*, July 14, 1912.
[723] *Freeman*, July 20, 1912. *San Francisco Examiner*, July 21, 1912.

T. S. Andrews said that some accounts of the Johnson-Flynn fight varied from the real facts.

> How any one who witnessed the battle could figure where Jim Flynn had an even show, or for that matter, any kind of show against the colored master, is hard to understand. What slim chance Flynn did have he forfeited by his unfair tactics. Flynn made the claim that Johnson was holding him, but even if the colored man did hold, it was not cause enough to make Flynn fight foul by butting with his head. ... Jim started out rough, for he butted Johnson in the stomach in the first round and offered no apology for his action. One thing must be said in favor of the colored man – he fought fair throughout and never took advantage of the white man. ...
>
> Smith was in a peculiar predicament, for had he given the fight to Johnson on a foul in the sixth or seventh round when Jim began his butting tactics, the crowd would have howled and there might have been cries of fake, etc. So, as long as Johnson was not seriously hurt, he determined to let the men go along in hopes that Flynn would stop his foul work. However, it became so flagrant in the eighth and ninth that there was nothing left but to disqualify Flynn for fouling and that is what the referee was about to do when the captain of police stepped into the ring and stopped further proceedings.
>
> The two fighters had agreed beforehand that in case of interference the referee should give a decision to the one having the best of it at that time, or if there was no advantage to either one, to declare it a draw. The referee could not do otherwise than give the verdict to Johnson, for the colored man had it on points by about 100 to 1. There was no chance for argument as to the verdict, and those around the ring, no matter how much they would have liked to see Flynn win, could not have rendered a different decision.
>
> How much better it would have been for Jim Flynn to have made a grand battle of it, even if he went down to defeat, than to have lost the way he did. His friends would have been stronger for him than ever before. ...
>
> Flynn did not have the colored man in distress at any time, if appearances count for anything. When Jim was pounding away at Jack's body, it was because Lil' Artha let him. He deliberately pushed his stomach out toward Jim and said: "Go ahead, Flynn. Hit it hard. Go ahead, man." Then, when he wanted to, he simply drew his stomach back and shot a couple of nasty uppercuts to Jim's chin that lifted him off his feet. ... Jack had wagered $3,500 that the fight would not go into the eleventh round. ...
>
> Had Flynn fought on the defensive he might have put up a creditable battle, for he is surely bigger and stronger than ever, and today can

whip practically all the 'white hopes' in the country, barring Al Palzer. It will take a big man to whip Johnson, one who can stand a grueling and be able to hit as well.

Johnson should be able to clean up Langford, McVey and Jeannette.[724]

Sportsmen as a rule were fair, and Flynn lost their sympathy when he resorted to foul tactics. Conversely, there was an increased respect for Johnson, for he fought in a refined and scholarly manner and did not retaliate. "Johnson is one of the fairest and most decent men ever known in the prize ring, and his complexion is all that prevents him from being the most popular pugilist of his time. He has many charms and fine graces of manner, he is tirelessly good natured, he appreciates favors, he is generous and he is loyal to his friends."

When Flynn was training, he talked a great deal, and referred to Johnson "in contemptuous terms and called him by insulting names." When Johnson heard about it, he simply smiled and said, "I certainly do feel sorry for Mr. Flynn." Although he was the most promising of the white hopes, Flynn was helpless in Johnson's hands. The only decent white fighters remaining were Al Palzer, Carl Morris, Luther McCarty, Jim Stewart, and Tom Kennedy. A lot of top white hopes were big, strong, and good-looking, until they faced a real test, and then they no longer were hopes.[725]

---

[724] *Freeman*, August 3, 1912.
[725] *Freeman*, August 10, 1912.

CHAPTER 15

Impediments and Tragedies

Following Jack Johnson's Independence Day July 4, 1912 victory over Jim Flynn, the press discussed who might be his next challenger. The *Freeman* wrote, "Sam Langford is next in line. Personally I hoped it would have been McVea since he is in Johnson's class physically. Langford is not of so good a physical build as Flynn." However, Langford had defeated McVea as well as Jeannette in their most recent bouts.

Johnson said he would fight Al Palzer if he got his price, and would bet $20,000 on himself. Palzer held victories over Kaufman and Wells.

Victor Breyer of Paris allegedly offered $30,000 (150,000 francs) for a 30-round Johnson-Jeannette fight to be held in France in the fall. Breyer offered to post the full amount in advance, but required that Johnson post a $10,000 forfeit to guarantee his performance. Some suspected that Johnson would refuse to meet Jeannette in a long fight, for Joe had the reputation of growing stronger as a fight progressed. [726]

> Johnson has never seemed to relish the meeting with Jeanette for any long contest. The New York Negro, who is well known to followers of boxing, has a persistent way about him that is very discouraging to an opponent. Joe is strong and game, and, while he is not as clever a boxer as Johnson or Langford, he is as game as either one of them, and he cannot be discouraged by one punch or a hundred, but he keeps coming back for more till the other man tires of the job of fighting him off.[727]

In Chicago, Johnson said he wanted to fight thrice more – against the Iowa lad Al Palzer, Sam Langford, and Sam McVea.

> I want to hurry up and convince everybody that there is none who can beat me. Then I will be willing to retire and let the rest of them fight it out for the championship. I would like to get Palzer next, say in New York, but I hope it is soon. The Langford and McVea battles, if they come off, I suppose will be staged in Australia. McIntosh is after them, but I want $30,000 for each fight and plenty of transportation and expense money.[728]

A frustrated Jeannette manager Dan McKetrick said he had pestered Johnson, but received no reply. "If Johnson is afraid to face Jeanette, why doesn't he say so and we'll claim the title. Jeanette will fight Johnson under

---

[726] *San Francisco Examiner, Washington Post,* July 12, 1912.
[727] *Freeman,* July 6, 1912.
[728] *San Francisco Examiner,* July 7, 1912.

any conditions. All he wants is to get him in the ring." Johnson had boxed Jeannette seven times: 1905 WND3 (scoring 2-4 knockdowns), LDQby2 (accidental low blow), and WND6 (scoring 4 knockdowns); and 1906 WND3, W15, WND6, and W/DN10 (scoring 1 knockdown).

Billy Gibson of New York's Garden Athletic Club said he would try to make a Johnson-Jeannette fight. He believed the State Athletic Commission's barring of Johnson only applied to a mixed-race bout.

A New York writer opined that Jeannette was the only one able to give Johnson a convincing argument. "The only man now in the game who would make Lil Artha hustle is Joe Jeanette. Johnson knows it; that's the reason he declines to answer Joseph's wave of the mitt." Unfortunately, the New York boxing commissioners had put themselves on record that they would not allow Johnson to box there.[729]

Hugh McIntosh was offering $20,000 per fight, plus $5,000 expense money ($45,000 total), for Johnson to fight both McVey and Langford in Australia, but that was well short of Johnson's $30,000 per fight demand.[730]

On July 10, 1912 in Chicago, at 41 West 31st street, Jack Johnson opened the Café de Champion. It was the most beautiful and elaborately furnished establishment of its kind. A crowd packed the streets waiting to get in. Tiny Johnson accompanied her son. There was an elaborate program of song and music played by an orchestra. It was not often that the mere opening of a café on a side street of the main line could attract crowds of such size.

On July 11, 1912 in Chicago, Johnson and his wife Etta appeared in federal court for their arraignments on the diamond necklace smuggling charges. They were released on $5,000 bail each. The maximum penalty they were facing was two years in prison and a $5,000 fine.

On July 12 in Chicago, Johnson was arrested and charged with striking and intimidating Charles Brown, a black chauffeur who was one of the government's principal witnesses in the smuggling case. Johnson formerly employed Brown. When Brown entered Johnson's café, Jack asked him what he told the Grand Jury. Brown declined to tell him, and Johnson allegedly struck him in the face.

Johnson was arraigned and furnished a $5,000 bond. He denied having assaulted Brown, and explained that when Brown came into his place he ordered him out. When Brown refused to leave, one of Johnson's friends pushed him out. Johnson denied touching Brown.[731]

New York promoters were negotiating with Johnson for a potential match with either Palzer or Jeannette. They believed that one of the boxing commissioners violently opposed to Johnson's presence there might withdraw his objection. Some thought Jeannette was better entitled to face

[729] *New York American*, July 8-10, 1912.
[730] *San Francisco Examiner, Washington Post*, July 12, 1912.
[731] *San Francisco Examiner, Washington Post*, July 12, 1912; *Chicago Defender, New York American*, July 13, 1912.

Johnson, while others thought the white-hope Palzer would be the more popular choice with the paying fight fans.

Any New York bout would be limited to 10 rounds, as required by law. The feeling was that Johnson would cut loose more in a short bout. He had to pace himself in Las Vegas, owing to the fight's potential 45-round length, and therefore was ultra-cautious. It did not necessarily follow that he would be as defensive in a short bout. Also, New York rules called for clean breaks, which would enable Johnson to fight at long range. Hence, "the prospect is none too rosy for Johnson's New York opponent, no matter who it may be."

A *San Francisco Examiner* writer opined, "Langford, McVea or Jeanette could whip Palzer and I think Jeanette is the best man of them all."[732]

On July 19, 1912 in Philadelphia, black boxer Battling Jim Johnson defeated Joe Jeannette in a 6-round no-decision bout. In the 3rd round, Jeannette tried some wrestling, and Johnson showed that he was a good wrestler too, tossing Joe to the floor. In the 5th round, Johnson dropped Jeannette with a hard punch to the jaw. Joe was shaken, but fought back hard. Both were tired in the 6th round. Joe used stomach blows, but Johnson was as hard as nails and Jeannette was forced to hold in order to avoid punishment.[733]

Billy McLean/McClain was the first and only black promoter of any note in the world. He wanted to engage Johnson to fight his man McVey in either Paris or Australia.

In late July, in front of his South-Side saloon, Johnson knocked out Homer Kerchfield, a black chauffeur, with a single blow. Jack said he caught him attempting to steal an extra tire from his auto, and when he ordered him away, Kerchfield struck him several blows in the face, and therefore he was obliged to strike back in self-defense. Johnson had Kerchfield arrested.

Negotiations for a Johnson–Jeannette bout were progressing. New York Garden A. C. promoter Billy Gibson offered $25,000 to Johnson for a 10-round match. However, the tough negotiator Johnson held firm in his demand of a $30,000 guarantee plus three round-trip train tickets on the 18-hour train. Johnson said it was his same old price, win, lose, or draw. "I don't care who you name to fight me, the price will be the same for my services or I won't appear."

Johnson preferred Palzer to Jeannette, but Gibson told Jack that there was no way he would be allowed to fight a white man in New York.[734]

Johnson explained why he was firm on his financial demands.

New York does not like me and I don't like New York. That is the reason why I will not lower my price to box there. They won't let me

[732] *San Francisco Examiner*, July 14, 1912.
[733] *Freeman*, July 20, 1912, August 3, 1912. Jeannette would later avenge the no-decision loss.
[734] *San Francisco Examiner*, July 26, 1912.

fight a white man in that town, but expect me to box only negroes. I don't care about that, of course, as long as I get the money. The reason they won't let me on with a white man is because they know I can beat Palzer and all the rest of them in one ring on the same night. However, this fellow Jeanette will be just as easy. I can punch holes in Joe for ten rounds and don't be surprised if I stop him. I'll be tickled to death to show New York just how easy Jeanette is if I get my $30,000.[735]

Little attention was paid to Johnson's claim that he would retire as of September 1. He was just about played-out as a theatrical attraction, and would have to fight to earn.

If Johnson does not succeed in his attempt to have the bars taken down for him in New York there only remains a trip to Australia or to Paris if he is to fight again. New Mexico, the only state in which a long distance fight could be staged, is now closed to the black champion. The captain of the state police at New Mexico, who stopped the bout with Flynn, was so disgusted with the affair that he has announced that under no circumstances will he allow another fight of the kind to take place in that state.

Johnson does not care for the long trip to Australia and will only accept one of Promoter McIntosh's alluring offers as a last result. The Australian wants Johnson to meet Sam Langford and Sam McVey. In Paris they want him to fight Jeannette. ... For some reason Johnson will have nothing to do with the Hoboken Negro.

The *Freeman* opined that although McCarty and Palzer might be able to take Johnson's measure at a later date, at present his most dangerous foes were members of Johnson's own race – Langford, Jeannette, McVey, and Jim Johnson, all of whom could box better than any of the big white hopes.

Jim Johnson was the only one yet to have boxed the champ. Although Jack Johnson had defeated all of his top black rivals, the fights took place back when he was a better man than it appeared he was at present. Langford and Jeannette believed they could whip him in a long fight. Johnson would have great advantages in height, reach, and weight over Langford. "Johnson has a good left hand and Langford is a mark for a straight left. With the big fellow in good shape, the odds would be big that he would win over Sam." Jeannette and McVey were closer in size to Johnson, were tall, big, and strong, could hit hard, and could stand a grueling. Johnson knew Jeannette would be a tough proposition, which explained why he was not overly eager to fight him.[736]

W. W. Naughton opined that if Johnson was allowed to break into the 10-round game in New York, he likely would retire undefeated as

---

735 *San Francisco Examiner*, July 27, 1912.
736 *Freeman*, July 27, 1912.

champion, for no one could beat him over a short distance. Given that New York had a very big population base, generating larger gates, Johnson could earn a lot of money without having to train for a long fight, and he would not have to suffer the potential punishment that a lengthy bout could bring.

A fight with Al Palzer would "excite more interest than any the champion could be a party to." Palzer was then considered to be the best of the white heavies, given his victories over Kaufman and Wells. Of course, Luther McCarty was on the rise as well.

However, matches with white heavies could not be made in New York because it was clear that in no event would the authorities allow Johnson to box a white man there.[737]

On July 28, from Chicago, Johnson said, "Unless Billy Gibson comes to my terms by tomorrow at midnight I am done with the boxing game for all time." That statement was the result of an all-day conference between the champion, Gibson (who managed Madison Square Garden), and Dan McKetrick, Jeannette's manager. Gibson offered only $20,000 for a 10-round bout with Jeannette. Johnson said,

> You can make the story of my retirement as strong as you like. I have a paying business here, and I am going to stick to it. There are no 'white hopes' worthy of attention. I have beaten Jeanette so many times that I have lost track of the number. Langford does not want to fight me, despite his repeated challenges. His challenges are merely to attract attention to his own person.
>
> I want at least a month in which to train, for I do not propose to go into the ring unless I am in good shape. I would have to train at least four weeks, and that would mean an outlay of $2,000. My business is in its infancy, and if I would leave it for a month I might feel the loss later on. I have $30,000 invested here, and it looks like a good living to me for the rest of my days.
>
> I traveled around the world to get a chance at the championship and took $5,000 for my part in fighting Burns. He received five or six times as much. I will not go to the expense of training and the consequent loss to my business unless I get at least as much as Burns did when he gave me a chance at the title.
>
> And this is no Patti or Bernhardt farewell, either. If they don't meet my terms before midnight tomorrow, I'm through forever. I won't be any Jim Jeffries. I have money enough for the rest of my life, and there isn't enough in the world to start me training again after a layoff for a year or so.
>
> Jeanette and myself would draw at least $60,000 in Madison Square Garden. I'm certainly worth 50 per cent of that amount. Jeanette

---

[737] *San Francisco Examiner*, July 28, 1912.

could not draw $10,000 with anybody else. There is no other match in the world that would draw as much in New York city. Jeanette ought to be satisfied with getting as much out of the match as I received when I fought for the title. That would leave the club a handsome profit for its trouble. Why should I take one-third of the gate, which is what $20,000 represents? All champions nowadays, when they fight with their title at stake, demand and are paid at least 50 per cent. I'm asking the guarantee because I do not want to be bothered with the thousand and one details that come up when a man is fighting on percentage.

Remember, at midnight tomorrow, if the word don't come that I've signed up the newspapers can print the story of my retirement, because that's the last hour for the battle.[738]

The next day, Johnson, disgusted with his treatment by the New York commissioners, who were barring a bout with Al Palzer, said he was through with boxing. "They won't let me fight a white man in New York, and there's too much red tape connected with the shorter bouts. I've got all that I can get out of the game now. Let the others go fight it out among themselves. No, there's no chance for me to come back. I'm through."[739]

The black-owned *New York Age* said, "It is about time that Johnson agrees to meet either Jeannette, Langford or McVea in the ring."[740]

On July 31, 1912, the United States Congress passed and President William Taft signed into law the Sims Act, which banned the transportation of prizefight films in interstate commerce, making it a criminal offense punishable by a year in prison and/or a $1,000 fine. For the next 28 years, until 1940 when President Franklin Roosevelt signed a repeal of the law, fight films only could be shown in the state where they were taken. This seriously limited the economic value of fight films, and limited fans' ability to see fights. However, widespread bootlegging allowed some folks to see fight films in private exhibitions. Boxing had taken a bit hit.

The motivation of Tennessee Congressional Representative Thetus Sims' bill against the interstate transportation of fight films was to prevent folks from seeing Jack Johnson beat a white man, to prevent race riots, and to limit the earning potential of those involved with boxing.

On August 3, 1912 in Sydney, Australia, Sam Langford clearly won a 20-round decision over Sam McVey.

The *Freeman* noted that Jack Johnson's fortune had come from the stage more than the ring. He and Jeffries had traveled the country making $1,500 a week before their fight. To make big money, a top notch fighter "has to

---

[738] *San Francisco Call*, July 29, 1912.
[739] *San Francisco Examiner*, July 30, 1912.
[740] *New York Age*, August 1, 1912.
On July 29, 1912 in New York, Jess Willard won a 10-round no-decision bout against Arthur Pelkey.

be more of an actor than a mitt artist." Top boxers knew that acting was easier than fighting, and more money was procurable from the stage than the ring.[741]

Dan McKetrick, Jeannette's manager, frustrated by Johnson's refusal to box Jeannette for anything less than $30,000, said he felt justified in claiming the championship for his man.

230-pound Al Palzer, who was being trained by Bob Armstrong, was willing to fight anyone for the right price, including Johnson. "If Johnson is willing to fight me on Labor Day I'll sign articles at once. I believe I am big and strong enough to beat him."

Luther McCarty, who had stopped Carl Morris, wanted to fight Palzer, and accused him of cowardice.

The *Freeman* opined that Johnson was so superior to all others that he could hold his championship for quite a while. Billy Lewis said, "It's a bad period for white hopes." The black contenders were better than the white ones, but Johnson had defeated all of the top blacks. Plus, "Johnson says contests of blacks versus whites get more money at the gate than a contest between two colored men. The all-black stars situation is unfortunate from that viewpoint." More whites were complimenting Johnson's cordial temperament and conceding him to be the finest physical specimen.

In Chicago, Johnson appeared in court to testify against a black youth who stole a tire from his car. Johnson said, "Your honor, I know this boy is guilty, but sending him to jail won't get me my tire back, and it may do him harm. If you are willing, I am satisfied to have the charge changed to one of disorderly conduct and a small fine imposed." The judge honored Johnson's request, and asked the champ what he thought the fine should be. Johnson said, "One dollar would suit me as well as anything else," and the judge made that the fine. Johnson showed that he could be merciful as well.[742]

On August 13, the government dismissed the charge against Johnson of intimidating a witness for the prosecution in the smuggling case.

Two weeks after his brief "retirement," on August 14, 1912, Jack Johnson signed an agreement to fight Joe Jeannette in a 10-round no-decision bout at the St. Nicholas club in New York City on September 25. Brothers Jesse and Eddie McMahon, New York promoters, made the fight. They got Johnson to sign by guaranteeing him $25,000 regardless of the gate receipts, but if the receipts totaled $60,000, Johnson would receive $30,000 plus an additional 25% (some said 35%) of any amounts exceeding $60,000. Johnson also would receive a one-half interest in the fight films, which could be shown in New York and overseas.

---

[741] *Freeman*, August 3, 1912.

[742] *Freeman*, August 17, 1912.

On August 8, 1912 in Saskatoon, Canada, Tommy Burns stopped Bill Rickard in the 6th round. It was Burns' first fight in over 2 years.

Johnson liked the contract because he expected to make more than $30,000 with that deal. He knew New Yorkers did not like him, but figured that fans would flock to see the fight, hoping to see the local man whip him.

Jack said he was weighing 242 pounds, but only needed to lose 12 pounds and get down to 230 for a 10-round bout.

Johnson was fully confident of beating Jeannette, saying,

> I whipped that fellow three times and can do it every day just for fun. The only time he ever did make a showing with me, I was under wraps a bit…. You know I had a hard time getting matches in those days.
>
> But believe me when I say I'll convince the public that I'm still a great fighter by whipping the life out of that fellow. … I expect to make more than $30,000 out of it, too.

The *Salt Lake Tribune* said that Johnson's assertion that he was under wraps when he met Jeannette was the truth. "Under wraps" meant that he had to agree to carry his foe in order to get the opponent to fight.[743]

Jess McMahon noted that although Johnson was given a one-half interest in the fight films, Jack also wanted to buy the other half of the film rights for $10,000. Johnson said, "They'll go big in Europe, for that fellow Jeanetty (the way Johnson pronounces Joe's name) is well liked over on the other side."

McMahon said the best white hopes were Palzer, Stewart, McCarty, and Gunboat Smith. Johnson offered to fight them all in a battle royal, insisting that none of them could hit him.

McMahon said Johnson lived like a king in Chicago, and was equally popular with whites and blacks. "His home on Michigan avenue is furnished magnificently and has a young army of servants. He has four automobiles and he uses every one of them daily."

Johnson was hurt by his lack of popularity in New York. Jack said to McMahon, "Why, I'm not a bad fellow, am I? Why do they always knock me in that big town. Here everybody is my friend."[744]

In negotiations with McMahon, Johnson had insisted, "I must have my price or otherwise I will accept the offer of Mr. McIntosh for three fights in Australia. I would not waste time stopping here for a smaller amount, and then you have picked out a tough man for me."

Generally, it was understood that boxing commissioner Frank O'Neill was opposed to a white man fighting Johnson, fearing it would put the game in a "bad light." Most believed that the commission would allow a black vs. black fight.

The *New York Age* theorized that some whites wanted to see Johnson fight a black man; because the feeling was that no white could defeat

---

[743] *Salt Lake Tribune*, August 15, 1912.
[744] *New York World*, August 17, 1912.

Johnson, but if he was defeated by a fellow black, then that fighter might be more vulnerable to a white fighter. Some black fighters, such as Langford and his manager, used that argument as a sales pitch to white promoters.

The *Age's* Lester Walton noted Johnson's symbolic value to the race, and was glad that he was dark enough such that no one could dispute that he was a black man. "That Johnson is a Negro without any question of a doubt has always been a source of gratification to me; for had he been even of a dark brown in hue, long ago some white writers would have sought to prove that he was other than of African extraction."[745]

Scouting Johnson-Jeannette, the *Freeman* said,

> Little chance is conceded Jeannette in a short bout with the champion, even though Johnson is not quite as fast as he was when the men fought their other engagements. In a long distance bout Jeannette's wonderful endurance and ability to assimilate hard punishment would give him a chance, but as ten rounds would be the limit here in New York many close students of the game give Jeannette little chance of copping first money.[746]

On August 19, 1912 in New York, 203-pound Luther McCarty and 224-pound Jess Willard fought a 10-round no-decision bout. There was a split of opinion regarding who won. Some picked McCarty, others Willard, while others said it was a draw.

That same evening on the same card, 195-pound Joe Jeannette scored a KO2 over 210-pound Jeff Madden.

Some suspected that the New York State Athletic Commission would not allow Johnson-Jeannette, even though it was not a mixed-race bout. The edict barring Johnson against boxing in the state mentioned nothing about who he boxed. The *Salt Lake Tribune* opined that his banishment was in part due "to Johnson's annoying way of seeking publicity in New York," and in part because "Governor Dix has noted the fact that practically every time Johnson had appeared in the ring there was trouble of some kind after the affair."[747]

On August 20, 1912 in Newark, New Jersey, the day after beating Jeff Madden, Joe Jeannette fought two black men, knocking out 195-pound Bill Tate and 201-pound Battling Brooks, both in the 2nd round.[748]

Johnson said that when the Jeannette match was made, the promoters told him that they had everything fixed with the commission, but according to recent reports, that did not appear to be the case.

> I honestly don't believe I ever will be allowed to fight in this country again. Whenever my name is mentioned in connection with a fight in any part of the country the ministers and reformers immediately get

---

[745] *New York Age*, August 22, 1912.
[746] *Freeman*, August 24, 1912.
[747] *Salt Lake Tribune*, August 19, 1912.
[748] *New York Evening World*, August 21, 1912.

busy with the governor, with the result that there will be nothing doing for Jack Johnson. Take it from me, I will not start training until I am shown my fight with Jeannette can take place as scheduled.[749]

Johnson had placed his $5,000 forfeit money in Al Tearney's hands, and demanded that the McMahon's $5,000 forfeit be given to him if they could not bring off the Jeannette match.

Unfortunately, on August 22, after holding a long conference behind closed doors with the state athletic commission, the McMahon brothers called off the Johnson-Jeannette match. New York boxing commissioners O'Neill and Dixon refused to allow Johnson to box anyone in New York, and threatened to revoke the license of any club which held a bout with him involved. "Johnson had been booted out of nearly every State in the Union, and it was believed that his appearance here would bring odium to the boxing game." It was said that Senator James Frawley, who had framed the bill legalizing boxing in New York, was opposed to Johnson's boxing there, and had urged the commissioners to stop it. The commission thought it best for the game of boxing to keep Johnson from appearing in New York, although they insisted that they had nothing personal against Johnson, nor was he barred on account of his color. They wanted to keep the boxing situation "healthy." Hence, their decision was spun as being for the betterment of the sport. Edward McMahon said, "The commissioners don't want Jack Johnson to appear in a match in New York City."[750]

Commissioner O'Neill said, "The commission decided long ago that Johnson would not be permitted to fight here. We believe now, as we did then, that the presence of Johnson in a ring contest in this state would be inimical to the best interests of boxing, the status of which has greatly improved under the Frawley law."[751]

That same day in Chicago, Johnson attempted to spar 3 rounds at a ball park to make a charitable donation to a local hospital. However, a policeman carrying orders from the chief of police said, "No boxing." Johnson replied, "Dis am foh charity, boss." The reply: "No sparring."

The *New York World's* Robert Edgren congratulated the commission for its decision, and said keeping Johnson out would greatly benefit the sport of boxing. "The trouble is that whenever Johnson appears race rancor develops. It's better to keep Jack Johnson out in Chicago, where they seem to love him, than to have more San Juan Hill troubles here."[752]

The *New York Age's* Lester Walton criticized the commission's decision:

They were not clear as to how the leading exponent of the manly art of self defense would cause boxing to deteriorate, and it is hardly probable that they could explain if given an opportunity to do so. Of

---

[749] *The Milwaukee Journal*, August 20, 1912.
[750] *New York Age, New York Daily Times, New York World*, August 22, 1912.
[751] *Freeman*, August 31, 1912.
[752] *San Francisco Call, New York World*, August 23, 1912.

course the action taken by the Boxing Commission was not due to Johnson's color. Such a charge most likely would be deemed unjust by them. But if the heavyweight champion was a white man how different things would have been.

If the word 'inconsistency' was not in the English language there would be times when the question of color prejudice would not be raised by the dusky citizens of this country. But so often do we observe instances in which the color of one's skin (not circumstances) alters cases that we have grown to regard with suspicion this 'Malice toward none, good will and equality of opportunity for all' spirit which is supposed to pervade every nook and corner of the United States.

It is difficult for colored citizens to understand why the leading fighter of the world is refused the privilege to exhibit his fistic prowess in New York when big, burly white fighters appear before the local clubs in boxing matches which are brutal in every respect and are oftimes so sickening that the police have to stop the gory and badly-battered contestants. Such contests, it will be presumed, are regarded with high favor by the Boxing Commission. In a match between Johnson and Jeannette, although both are big men, the absence of brutality would have been a pleasing feature, as they are boxers of great skill.

New York World, **August 23, 1912**

Bat Masterson, who wrote for the New York *Morning Telegraph*, did not think race had as much to do with the bout's prevention as some believed. He thought it was a question of political connections and pull. He believed that had the bout been secured at Madison Square Garden, it would have been allowed to go forward. Others said the commissioners simply were holding to their previous position that Johnson would not be allowed to box in New York. Masterson thought the McMahon Brothers were lucky that they were forced to call off the bout, for he opined that the show would have been a financial disaster. Regardless, even Masterson said the claim that it was for the good of the sport was all bunk.

Ultimately, Lester Walton said it appeared that the "door of hope" was closed against the champion, for he was barred from appearing in bouts in the majority of cities in the U.S., as well as England. France and Australia currently were friendly and disposed to have him appear there, "but if the color prejudice germ, which is so perniciously active in this country, is transplanted to such cities as Paris and Sydney, there will not be a place where Johnson can defend the championship title, unless it be at the North or South poles."[753]

Government authorities had prevented yet another Johnson fight.

Some white writers argued that Johnson was to blame for his banishment, not race.

> Johnson's personality alone is responsible for his being barred from the State of New York. It is a great pity that the big Texan has not had a more decent regard for the proprieties. He is the most unpopular Negro boxer who has ever been in the ring. ... There has been more scandal connected with Jack Johnson since he became prominent in pugilism than there was with the names of all the other Negro boxers put together.

Meanwhile, Johnson said McIntosh's offer of $50,000 (which included expenses) for two bouts in Australia did not look good enough to him. Plus, McIntosh had yet to post a forfeit.

Victor Breyer, a promoter of fights in France and Europe, said he was prepared to offer Johnson $30,000 to meet Jeannette in a 30-round bout in Paris or Monte Carlo.[754]

On September 2, 1912 in Pittsburgh, 163 ½-pound black Jeff Clark clearly won the unofficial 6-round newspaper decision in his bout with 197 ½-pound Joe Jeannette.

That same day in Daly City, in the San Francisco area, Jim Flynn won his bout against 218-pound Charlie Miller, when Miller refused to come up for the 16th round.

Johnson had a habit of retiring one day and coming back the next. He said he was so disgusted with the fight game that he would never fight again. However, he also said that he had heard nothing from Paris regarding any recent alleged offer to fight Jeannette, but would accept if the conditions were favorable.[755]

---

[753] *New York Age*, August 29, 1912.

[754] *Freeman*, September 7, 1912.

[755] *Freeman*, September 14, 1912.
   On September 9, 1912 in New York, 195-pound Joe Jeannette won via 7th round disqualification against 207 ½-pound Tony Ross. Ross was outclassed and outfought, and therefore deliberately fouled.

On September 5, 1912, a white woman in Forsyth County, Georgia claimed that an unknown black man had attempted to rape her, but fled when her family member opened the bedroom door. When a black preacher remarked that the woman was caught in bed with a black man and just claimed it was rape to save face, a group of white men whipped him with horse buggy whips on the street in front of the courthouse. Close to death, the sheriff took him into the courthouse and then locked the preacher in the vault after a crowd of 100-200 demanded he be lynched. Governor Joseph Brown had to send the National Guard to restore order to the town.

Several days later, on September 9, 1912 in the same county, a young black man raped and killed a young white girl. He freely confessed to several people.

The incidents led to the town's blacks being harassed, intimidated, threatened, and forcibly driven out of the town, fearing for their lives. Within four months, 98% of the county's over 1,000 blacks were gone, and from the surrounding counties, 50% to 100% were forced to leave as well, the largest mass exodus of black folk based on race in U.S. history. To this day, the county remains virtually all-white.

On or about the early morning hours of September 12, 1912 in Chicago, Etta Johnson, a.k.a. Etta Terry Duryea, a.k.a. Mrs. Jack Johnson, telephoned her sister-in-law, Mrs. Jennie Rhodes of 3344 Wabash avenue, and asked her to come over. Etta was in her room above her husband's new business, the Café de Champion, at 41 West 31st street.

Etta then called her two black maids to her, saying, "I want you to pray for me." They got on their knees and Mrs. Johnson joined them in prayer. She then asked them to leave her for a few minutes. As the maids were leaving, they heard her say, "God have pity on a lonely woman."

Shortly thereafter, at about 2 a.m., Etta Johnson took a revolver from a dresser and shot herself in the right temple. The bullet passed completely through her head, leaving a hole in both sides. Mrs. Johnson was lying on the floor, the blood oozing from her temple. She was not yet dead, but was unconscious.

Henry Johnson, the champion's brother, was running the café, and was told of the incident first. His sister, Jennie Rhodes, had arrived and was present as well. Henry ordered the orchestra to play loud music, and he rushed to his sister-in-law's room.

When the champ arrived, he was told that his wife had shot herself. He began wiping his eyes with a big handkerchief and cried, or as they then called it, "made audible manifestations of grief."

Etta was taken to the hospital, but there was nothing the doctors could do. At the hospital, by her bedside, Johnson said, "My little pal, you ain't going to take the count, are you?" At 3:25 a.m., Etta was declared dead.

Jack Johnson's wife Etta was 31 years old. She had been Miss Etta Terry of Brooklyn before marrying Clarence Duryea, a wealthy millionaire New

York and Long Island clubman and horseman. While married to Mr. Duryea for six years, Etta associated with an exclusive upper-class society.

In the spring of 1910, Etta sued for a divorce, which she soon obtained. She and the champion had been seen everywhere together well before that.

On January 18, 1911 in Pittsburg, at Frank Sutton's hotel on Wylie avenue, Etta and Jack Johnson were married. At the time, Johnson was appearing in a local theater. George Cole, a city detective, was Johnson's best man. The records showed Johnson's age as 32 and Etta's age as 29.

Immediately after her suicide, speculation abounded regarding why she had killed herself. Many believed that remorse for having left her place in exclusive high class white society and associating with those of Johnson's race ultimately led to her suicide. She was ostracized for marrying a black man. For more than a year, she had suffered from severe nervous prostration; brought on by the realization that she was forever barred from the world she voluntarily left.

On her recent trip to Las Vegas before the Flynn fight, Mrs. Johnson was said to have remarked to friends that everyone shunned her because she had married a Negro, and she was unhappy about it. She had been in ill health and despondent for a year.

Some said she was a depressive, and had been battling depression and suicidal thoughts for quite some time, even before she met Johnson. Her nervous ailment often caused her to become hysterical.

Johnson explained to the police that for the last two years, Etta had suffered from nervous attacks, and that several months prior, while suffering an attack, she had tried to throw herself through a train window.

Two maids were employed to watch her continually. She often spoke of dying, and said she never expected to recover from the nervous prostration from which she suffered.

Mr. Johnson had planned a trip for Etta to New Mexico, hoping that the air out there would do her good. She was to have gone to Las Vegas with Mrs. Ed Smith, wife of the *American* sporting editor who had refereed the Flynn bout. However, at the last moment, Etta decided not to go. Instead, she ended her life.

Others later said the champ was unfaithful, and some even suggested that he was violent towards his wife. Johnson was disgusted by the daily newspapers' efforts to make domestic friction the cause for the deed. "The champion was very much annoyed by several sensational stories in the daily newspapers harping on domestic troubles. He emphatically denies this."

Johnson wept as he denied that he ever was brutal to his wife. He also said he was through with the fight game.

> If it had not been for Etta I would have killed myself by leaping from a window of a hotel in Portland, Maine, a year ago. ... There is no telling what I shall do now. I may kill myself. There never was a better wife. I never expect to marry a woman like Etta. All talk of

family trouble is false. A few days ago I bought her a diamond ring and a sealskin coat.

Johnson said that his wife's efforts to keep him from committing suicide broke down her own health. He said the nature and extent of his suffering after the Jeffries fight had been kept secret by his wife and himself.

I am still suffering from the effects of that fight to some extent. ... I believe that I incurred brain fever or some similar derangement from the exertions of the Jeffries fight and the heat that prevailed at the time. I was not myself for a year, but the secret was closely kept between me and Mrs. Johnson. She saved me twice when I tried to choke myself to death. She seized me and struggled with me, and prevented the act.

She had an awful time taking care of me for over a year. ...

During the last two years she often told me she was tired of living. She tried twice before to kill herself. Once she attempted to jump out of a window in a London hotel, and before that she tried to take her life by leaping from a train out West.

I did everything I could to make her happy and spent money on her lavishly, but most of the time she seemed despondent. Her father died four months ago, and since then she seemed more nervous and despondent than before.

I employed two maids to watch her after she attempted to end her life the first time. ... The stories that there was much domestic trouble between my wife and my mother and sister are untrue. They both were very fond of her.

After Johnson declared that the Jeffries battle had done him harm, the *Freeman* asked, "Can it be possible that Jeff hurt the big Negro more than was apparent to those at the ringside?"

Etta's mother said, "My daughter was insane. She was insane when she married Johnson. She was insane when she ended her life. We did our best to prevent her marrying Johnson. But Johnson had money and we were poor, and she would listen to no one." However, if money was Etta's only concern, she could have remained married to Clarence Duryea.

Funeral services were set to be held at 11 a.m. on September 14 at Johnson's 3344 Wabash Avenue mansion. Fight promoter Jack Curley was in charge of the funeral arrangements.

Without Johnson's consent, the Pekin Theater arranged to take and exhibit films of Mrs. Johnson's funeral. The champ went before a Superior Court judge and obtained a temporary injunction against the theater's owners, restraining the management of the black theater from exhibiting motion pictures of the funeral. Johnson said, "The exhibition is an injustice to me and may cause the impression that I am profiting financially from the pictures." The chief of police said he would prevent any such exhibition.

Police estimated the outside crowds surrounding the funeral at 20,000.

Many used the suicide as an example of the adverse results of interracial marriage. The *Freeman* said of Johnson's wife,

> In view of racial relations, past and present, she ran a great risk of her personal happiness when marrying Jack Johnson. It is not urged that she was weighted down with unpleasantness owing to her marital relations, yet the marriage was ever considered unfortunate.

Some said the bitter fruits of the interracial marriage came when her friends and family in the East socially ostracized her. Johnson built a palatial Chicago home. However, the area's blacks regarded her as an outcast from the white race and thought she was after the money. They continually called her Johnson's "white wife." She was caught in the fire of two races, and both turned her down. "Like so many of the well-to-do of the white race, she had no way of knowing of the living death, socially, just across the line. … She possibly knew of some racial disadvantages… She did not know of the terrible sacrifice that would be hers to make."[756]

Hugh McIntosh was trying to put together a deal for Johnson to fight in Australia again. Via his representative, W. C. J. Kelly, he sent Johnson his assurances that he need not fear police interference. At that time, McIntosh was offering Johnson $25,000 per fight for two fights, for a total of $50,000, the first being with Sam Langford on Boxing Day, December 26 in Australia.

Johnson believed that he could and would negotiate for more money, but that once the details were ironed out, he expected to sign the articles.[757]

On October 9, 1912 at Perth, Australia, Sam Langford stopped Sam McVey in the 11th round. McVey's claim of a foul was not recognized.

On October 12, 1912, Jack Johnson announced that he had agreed with Hugh McIntosh to fight Langford and McVea in Australia for $55,000 for the two fights, plus $5,000 for training expenses ($60,000 total), plus five round-trip tickets to Australia for the members of his party. Forfeits of $10,000 to bind the matches were to be posted with Al Tearney.[758]

Also on October 12, 1912 in San Francisco, Luther McCarty knocked out Al Kaufman in the 2nd round.

On October 14, 1912 at a political rally in Milwaukee, Wisconsin, former President Theodore Roosevelt was shot, but not killed.

On the afternoon of October 18, 1912, just over one month after his wife passed away, Jack Johnson was arrested on a charge of abduction. He was released almost immediately on $800 bail. He was accused of abducting

---

[756] *Freeman*, September 7, 14, 21, 28, October 5, 1912; *Salt Lake Tribune*, *El Paso Herald*, September 12, 1912; *Manchester Guardian*, *Chicago Day Book*, September 13, 1912; *Chicago Defender*, September 14, 21, 1912.

[757] *Chicago Defender*, September 21, 1912; *Freeman*, October 5, 1912.

[758] *Freeman*, October 19, 1912; *Missoulian*, October 13, 1912. Johnson also said he would fight Flynn for a third time, in Paris, as soon as he was through with the Australian bouts.

Lucille Cameron, an allegedly 19-year-old white woman who was the daughter of Mrs. Cameron-Falconet of Minneapolis, a divorced woman.

Initially, Lucille Cameron had come to Chicago with her mother's consent. She met Johnson before his wife committed suicide. Rumors were that Mrs. Johnson killed herself after discovering her husband with his arms around the Cameron girl.

When a newsman told Mrs. Cameron-Falconet about her daughter's infatuation with the black pugilist, she immediately came to Chicago. She pleaded with her daughter to come home with her and leave Johnson, but Lucille refused, saying, "I cannot go back and I don't want to go back to Minneapolis. I expect to become the wife of Mr. Johnson shortly, though he has not proposed marriage to me. I love him and want to stay in Chicago." Her mother alleged that Lucille told her that she had "gone too far to go back." Mrs. Cameron-Falconet further said, "I was convinced at that time that the Negro had a hypnotic influence over her."

Mrs. Cameron-Falconet claimed that she called Johnson by telephone. He then came to see her in his auto. When she entered his car, she drew down the shades so as not to be seen. This nettled him. She alleged that Jack said, "Oh, some of the best white women in Chicago ride in this car." Mrs. Falconet also claimed that Jack laughed in her face and said, "Why I can get any white woman in Chicago."

She begged him to give up her daughter. "He said he would not and leered in my face." Johnson allegedly told her that "he would give every dollar he has to hold her."

Therefore, Mrs. Cameron-Falconet had her own daughter arrested on a disorderly conduct charge and Johnson arrested on an abduction charge. She also swore out a warrant charging that her daughter Lucille was insane, for she had to be insane to be with Johnson. Judge Owens in the County Court issued a commitment order for Lucille's detention at the Detention Hospital pending investigation as to her mental condition.

It was obvious that Mrs. Cameron-Falconet had her daughter and Johnson arrested in order to facilitate the breaking up of the relationship. It had nothing to do with abduction, for it was clear that Lucille Cameron was a willing participant in the relationship. But her mother was hell-bent on trying to break them up and was willing to use whatever means she could to make it happen. Law enforcement and the courts were willing to help her, even though it involved an abuse and misuse of power and the law.

Rumors were flying about that 90 of Johnson's white neighbors had met and formed a vigilance committee, sworn to drive Johnson out of the city by any means.[759]

The next morning, Johnson was arraigned in the Chicago municipal court. When attorney Charles Erbstein, representing Mrs. F. Cameron-Falconet, demanded that Johnson's bond be increased, Johnson replied to the court, "I don't think it is necessary to increase the bond. I am a responsible citizen. I have a business worth $60,000." Erbstein fired back, "It may be worth that to you, but it's illegal and you ought to be put out of business." Johnson replied with a laugh, "All right, 'Mr. Mayor.'" Erbstein retorted, "If I were mayor of Chicago you wouldn't be in business three days." Judge Hopkins then set the bond at $1,500, the usual amount in abduction cases. A professional bondsman posted a cash bond for the champ. The case was continued to October 29.

Two agents from the U.S. Department of Justice were present at the arraignment. Apparently, a few hours after Johnson's arrest, James Wilkerson, the U.S. Attorney for the Northern District of Illinois, ordered a thorough investigation, with the intention of pursuing prosecutions under the Mann Act, which prohibited aiding or assisting with the transportation of women from one state to another for the purposes of prostitution, debauchery, or immoral practices. "The government is determined to go the limit in investigating Johnson's alleged relations with the Cameron girl and others. Information has come to the department of justice that the negro prize fighter has associated frequently with young white girls."

On Wilkerson's application, U.S. Commissioner Foote granted an order detaining Lucille Cameron, holding her in custody under $25,000 bonds as a witness in a federal grand jury investigation against Johnson. Department of Justice agents questioned her for two hours, but she refused to discuss her relations with Johnson.

Johnson and his attorney attempted to visit Cameron, but were denied permission.

When they heard that Johnson planned to bail her out, at the request of federal officers, Commissioner Foote authorized Lucille Cameron's removal to the county jail at Rockford, Illinois. Wilkerson then ordered her taken to the federal building, where she would be held under special guard until she appeared before the federal grand jury. She told the police that she loved Johnson and expected to become his wife.

When Johnson was leaving a downtown bank, an unidentified man dropped a large ink-well from a 10th floor window and it narrowly missed the pugilist's head.[760]

---

[759] *Chicago Day Book*, October 18, 1912. *Freeman*, October 26, 1912. Johnson had planned to leave for Australia for the Langford fight and to take Cameron with him.
[760] *Ogden Evening Standard*, October 19, 1912; *Bennington Evening Banner*, October 21, 1912; *Freeman*, October 26, 1912.

Upon Johnson's arrest for abducting a white woman, even some black newspapers started to come down on him. The *New York Age's* Lester Walton said that since Johnson had become champion he had been the central figure in numerous escapades which tended to make him less and less popular with both black and white citizens. Walton called Johnson a mental weakling. Though he was shrewd and nervy, he also was so "deeply impressed with his own importance that he sincerely believes that he is a privileged character." He ignored those who implored him to avoid potentially hurtful notoriety.

There were some white writers who sought to prove that the death of Mrs. Johnson was the inevitable result of a marriage in which a black man and white woman were contracting parties. Of course, such talk was absurd. What the shooting of Mrs. Johnson really taught was the folly of two people becoming joined in wedlock with nothing in common intellectually or from a standpoint of culture. Mrs. Johnson was connected with a prominent New York family, and her environment with Johnson must have been vastly different from what she had been used to while living with her first husband.

Many blacks viewed Johnson's involvement with white women - from the death of his first wife and now a pending abduction charge - as a potential cause of prejudice and violence by whites upon blacks. Hence, he would be blamed, rather than the white perpetrators of the violence.

Johnson had mixed value as a symbol. When he defeated Jeffries, "the Negroes of this country were truly happy." It taught white citizens "a good lesson – that the color of a person's skin is not the determining factor to success. The race looked upon Johnson as a hero – one who would play an important part in breaking down prejudice."

However, Johnson also had proven to be a disappointment in some respects. "Instead of lessening prejudice he has increased it."

It is unfortunate in this country that the entire race is subjected to criticism when one member does something discreditable. It is not so with the white race, however. It is not pleasant to contemplate just what would happen if an insane Negro attempted to kill a high Government official [as a white man recently had done in an assassination attempt on Roosevelt]. In Chicago we learn that race riots are imminent. If there are any disturbances growing out of the Johnson-Cameron incident, investigation will show that the trouble all started over enraged whites attacking innocent Negroes who are in no way connected with the affair. The Negroes throughout the United States do not think so much of Johnson that they are willing to become victims of race prejudice unnecessarily occasioned by him. In the first place we have never relished any more than the white brother the unusual attention the fighter pays to white women...

True, he has a right to admire whatever type he sees fit, but the Negro has every type imaginable – the race really has a varied assortment.

There have been other colored fighters who have had white wives, for instance George Dixon. Yet Dixon was one of the most popular fighters that ever stepped into the ring. He did not crave for notoriety and was discreet. … But Jack Johnson, due to his woeful lack of judgment and his exaggerated ego, has become a menace.[761]

Black leader Booker T. Washington denounced Johnson, saying,

It is unfortunate that a man with money should use it in a way to injure his own people in the eyes of those who are seeking to uplift his race and improve its conditions…. In misrepresenting the colored people of the country this man is harming himself the least. I wish to say emphatically that his actions do not meet my personal approval, and I am sure that they do not meet with the approval of the colored race.[762]

The *Freeman* said Johnson was in bad as a result of the Cameron case, and was being condemned by his own race. "Never before in the history of Chicago has one man had as much newspaper matter printed about him in so short a time as Jack Johnson. … The daily newspapers have worked up an awful case on the champion." Even prominent blacks were calling meetings for the purpose of "taking action against" the champ, whatever that meant. Letters were being sent out to Johnson, even by members of his own race, informing him that he was a menace to humanity and the black race in particular.

As a result of all the legal trouble, Hugh McIntosh called off Johnson's fights with Langford and McVey. McIntosh cabled that Australian sporting people were disgusted by Johnson's relations with the Cameron girl. The allegations had so angered the Australian sporting public as to make Johnson a doubtful attraction, even though he was the world champion. Hence, the matches were no longer desirable.

Several *Freeman* writers commented on why everyone was so mad at Johnson. Given his white wife's recent suicide, many thought Johnson to be "obtuse" and "foolish" to be with another white woman, given the pain his previous wife had to endure. True, the woman was of age, a legal adult, and could make her own choices. "Granted. But Mr. Johnson should bear in mind that sentiment and custom are often stronger than written laws. For instance, most of the states have laws that permit Negroes to do what other men do, but when it comes to doing those things then it is something else." Hence, Johnson might have been in the right legally, but he had violated unwritten social rules.

---

[761] *New York Age*, October 24, 1912. Joe Jeannette had a white wife as well.
[762] *Afro American Ledger*, October 26, 1912.

Some blacks were insulted that Johnson only sought white women, for there were plenty of different types of black women from which he could choose. "Jack Johnson evidently thinks his own folks are not good enough for Jack Johnson." One said, "Let Mr. Jack Johnson kindly cut the female white people out of his operations and he will have plain sailing." Another said, "Some colored folks got together at Washington, D.C., and voted to repudiate Johnson as a member of the race. That's going a bit too far. ... All of us hope that Johnson will avoid doing things that stir up race feeling."

Another wrote that Johnson had shown a weakness for white women. His past relations had been somewhat overlooked. Most thought his marriage to a white woman was a "mere chance affair and not a thing studied out by the champion in the sense of a demand" which also implied the inferiority of his own race of women.

However, "The experiences of his wife should have cured him of all desire to take on another one, who, in the nature of things, would have to undergo the same experiences. The woman needs protection against the fate that awaits her should she step foot across the racial line." After what happened with his first wife, white and black folk alike thought it cruel and inconsiderate of Johnson to associate with white women. Blacks also feared a white backlash against their race.

We have been kindly disposed to Mr. Johnson, criticizing him some, but praising him more. We can not side with him in this matter in view of what we know. It is a humane question as well as a race question. The young woman, perhaps, thinks herself strong; thinks the strong support of affection and regard can buoy her up all her days. She is mistaken. When she finds that she must run a gauntlet of turned-up noses daily with only an occasional look of sympathy, she will find herself finally crushed between the milled edges of racial societies. ...

We should only be interested in knowing that the persistent pursuing of his course will cause a wide-spread feeling of opposition to Negroes. He has no moral right to anything that promises so much mischief. He's free, and all that, as he says, but there are 'invisible' laws to which he must subscribe – the agreements of society – if he would enjoy a large measure of that freedom of which he boasts.

Johnson needed to remember that as the king of boxing, unlike other boxers, he had no private affairs. "It's a mean condition all right, but it's the penalty of greatness and exacted by a punctilious public, most rigorously." Other black boxers could have white wives and go unnoticed, but the heavyweight champion had powerful symbolic meaning.

Despite the abuse of the law and courts, this *Freeman* writer opined, "I hope the mother and the courts will succeed in vetoing their 'hearts legislation.' More than the two are involved, since the race is held as one. I am satisfied the white people have no sympathy in the matter. I am satisfied that the Negroes have no sympathy in the matter."[763]

On October 21, federal authorities raided Johnson's café. Attorney Charles Eberstein (or Erbstein), Mrs. Cameron-Falconet's attorney, was with the officers. Johnson, who was eating dinner, called the attorney "the fighting name," and ordered him out. Jack said that unless he left, he would break him in two.[764]

Johnson emphatically denied the charges against him. He met with 100 representative black citizens at the Appomattox Club. He said he never made the remark attributed to him by Mrs. F. Cameron-Falconet.

> I want to say that I never made that statement, attributed to me, to the effect that I could get any white woman I wanted. I lay my hand upon the Bible, and swear that I never made such a statement.

> I want to say that I never said anything of the sort about any woman of any color. But I do want to say that I am not a slave and that I have the right to choose who my mate shall be without the dictation of any man. ... So long as I do not interfere with any other man's wife I shall claim the right to select the woman of my own choice. Nobody else can do that for me. That is where the whole trouble lies.

His lawyers declared that there were no legal grounds for his prosecution.

The Conference of Representative Chicago Colored Citizens issued a statement dated October 23, 1912. The black committee adopted strong resolutions asking the daily newspapers to be fair and not to condemn the entire race for the alleged misconduct of one person.

> That the tone of the daily newspaper expressions regarding this episode manifestly does the negro race an injustice by impliedly condemning the entire negro race for the alleged misconduct of one of its members.

> That we, as law abiding citizens in common with all good citizens of whatever race, condemn any immoral conduct or violation of the law...

> That we disavow any and all implied publications that the negro race as a race approve the alleged utterances of Jack Johnson or any alleged act or acts which either violate the laws of the land or are repugnant to decent society. ...

> That Jack Johnson at the invitation of this conference of representative negro citizens appeared in person and unqualifiedly denied that he made the statement, "He could get any white woman he wanted," or any statement reflecting upon the womanhood of any race, and being corroborated in such denial by Joseph Levy, a white

---

[763] *Freeman*, October 26, 1912.
[764] *Chicago Day Book*, October 22, 1912.

man who was present at the time the statement was alleged to have been made.

We therefore appeal to the sense of fairness of the public and press alike to discontinue the unfailing disposition to indict the entire negro race for any infraction of the law by an individual member of the race.

The *Chicago Broad Ax* said the minions of the law, like a pack of wolves, were hunting Johnson day and night. It also concluded that the statements attributed to Johnson were a pack of lies created by newspapers for the purpose of stirring up race prejudice.

The *Broad Ax* said white men were ready to shoot dead any Negro who even winked at a white woman. That was the white man's idea of fairness and justice in America. Lucille Cameron for several months had resided at an expensive hotel, and, being unemployed, it was obvious that a man was taking good care of her. She also demonstrated an inclination to associate with the "sporty element." She was no angel, and needed no protection. Her relationship with Johnson was consensual. Conversely, when black women were raped, they could obtain no justice whatsoever.

This writer alleged that newspapers were not interested in Cameron's welfare, but in selling newspapers. An incident such as this was exactly what they were seeking. They could not only "hurl their fiery and race prejudice darts" at Johnson, but at the entire colored race.

The *Chicago Defender* said the daily newspapers were engaging in malicious and vicious attacks upon a man who was not guilty. They were trying to incite riot. One newspaper suggested that if Johnson were living in the South he would be lynched, for they lynched folks for offenses much less severe than the one for which he was accused.

The Chicago City Council was attempting to close Johnson's café. On October 23, they adopted a resolution instructing the mayor to make an investigation of the café's conduct, and if any infractions could be found, to revoke his license promptly. They condemned his alleged boasts and said he was a disgrace to his race. Initially, Mayor Carter Harrison resisted, saying, "The council will pass resolutions on most anything so long as it is popular."

Cameron's mother was said to be hysterical, upon the verge of insanity, and under the care of physicians over the whole ordeal.

One man wrote the *Defender*, saying of Johnson, "His manner of living as regards his conduct and habits are to me revolting in the extreme. However, he is an American citizen and as such is clothed with all the rights and privileges of any other citizen of this city. If however, he has violated the laws…I am frank to say he should receive the full penalty of the law."

A black reverend said,

> Every man, colored or white, who acts in a way or conducts his business in a manner as to injure public morals, and who persists in

doing so after having been warned to desist, should be tried by the courts, and, if found guilty, punished; and whether he is convicted or not, he should be ostracized by all who believe in common decency and good morals.

Another local black citizen criticized the criticism of Johnson, saying,

The Johnson-Falconet case from the beginning, was plainly shown to be an out-burst of race prejudice. Hence, Mrs. Falconet's statement: "I would rather see my daughter spend the rest of her life in an insane asylum than see her the plaything of a nigger." Other statements show that it is merely Johnson's race and color that Mrs. Falconet objects to.

Now, any act or statement by anyone of his, Johnson's race, tending to favor the Falconet side of the case is treason, and this particular one is a traitor to his race. There is only one way to oppose race prejudice and that is by exercising race loyalty. ...

The charge of abduction, under which Mr. Johnson is held, and the many statements of Miss Falconet (who has passed the age limit of womanhood), of her determination, volition and love for Mr. Johnson, reveals the weakness of the law in this strange case of the color of skin. Our white brethren, whose minds are enslaved by prejudice, and whose daily papers, with their brimstone and blood-thirsty articles of condensed suggestions, seem to be laboring very energetically to provoke violence against this Negro whom the world has failed to conquer by fair play. The Negro as a man, as a race, and as a unit, should stand as a solid phalanx against and encroachment of his rights (no matter how insignificant), or any attempt that tends to limit the rights of a deserving and liberty-loving people.

Unrelated to the Johnson case, but insightful regarding the general perspective of the South regarding black rights, at that time, Hoke Smith, the U.S. Senator from Georgia, said,

The uneducated Negro is a good Negro; he is contented to occupy the natural status of his race, the position of inferiority. The educated and intelligent Negro, who wants to vote, is a disturbing and threatening influence. We don't want him down here; let him go North. I favor, and if elected will urge with all my power, the elimination of the Negro from politics.[765]

There were some allegations that Johnson recently had been shot in the leg by a married black woman, Mrs. Ada Banks-Davis, who may or may not have been his lover. The allegation was that she had shot him in a jealous rage over his attentions to the Cameron gal. Banks-Davis, who was a singer

---

[765] *Chicago Broad Ax*, *Chicago Defender*, October 26, 1912. *Freeman*, November 2, 1912. *Mahoning Dispatch*, October 25, 1912.

in Johnson's café, was called to testify before the grand jury, which was seeking something tangible against Johnson to substantiate the many horrible stories published in the daily newspapers. Banks-Davis said, "I never shot Jack Johnson. This story is ridiculous. I never handled a revolver in my life. ... I have tried to get the reporters to publish the facts, but you know that they are only looking for a new sensation." She said that while she was employed by Johnson, he was a considerate employer.

However, Banks-Davis' husband had filed a lawsuit against Johnson for $25,000, accusing him of alienating his wife's affections.[766]

U.S. government officials insisted that the singer had shot Johnson in his café. Some said that Johnson had been walking with a limp. Others said that he was seen at the bank the next day and seemed fine. Johnson strenuously denied that he had been attacked.

The grand jury also wanted to ask Banks about Johnson's alleged connection with the importation of Cameron into the city from Minneapolis, so as to obtain facts to substantiate a Mann Act charge.

Lucille Cameron was confined to the Oxford, Illinois jail. Johnson tried to get her released on a writ of habeas corpus.

A subpoena was issued for a West Side manufacturer, who federal officers said had introduced Cameron to Johnson.

Johnson deeded his property at 3344 South Wabash avenue to his mother, Mrs. Tiny Johnson.

The champ briefly went into seclusion, fearing for his life. A mob had besieged him in the First National Bank and forced him to flee through a side entrance. He received many warnings of assassination by letter, telephone, and personal messengers. Authorities declared and warned that widespread race war would follow if the threatened assassination took place.

> It is an unconcealed fact that plans are being discussed in various quarters as to some method whereby he can be killed, and his friends are urging him to forfeit his $1,500 bond to the government and get out of the country.

> It is realized by the authorities that his assassination or attempted assassination would precipitate an ugly race war, not alone in this city, but in other localities. Whites and Negroes in many cities would choose the occasion to even up old scores, dating back to the Reno battle.

Doing an about-face, Mayor Harrison said he was seeking some legal excuse whereby he could close up Johnson's café and drive him from the city. "The feeling against him and other Negroes is growing in intensity all the time, and trouble is being expected on the street cars and other places where the races meet. The killing of Johnson would start something that the authorities might have difficulty in handling."

---

[766] *Chicago Defender*, November 2, 1912. *Democratic Banner*, October 25, 1912.

During all of the tumult, Johnson had his brother Charles Johnson arrested for stealing some of his money.

Figuring correctly that Charles Johnson would not be happy with his brother for having him arrested for theft/embezzlement, the government subpoenaed him to testify before the grand jury, which he did for nearly two hours, giving them a fair amount of information about Johnson's trips from state to state with white women. He furnished names and addresses. Charles said Jack expected trouble, and as a result, deeded about $200,000 to their mother.

Joseph Levy, who was the champ's white secretary, Herbert Dan, a black chauffeur, and several others also were called to testify.

On October 30, 1912 in New York, Joe Jeannette won a 10-round no decision bout against 221-pound Battling Jim Johnson.

On October 31, the City Collector refused to renew Johnson's saloon license. Another reported that the license under which he was operating was owned by a brewery. His contract to use it expired on November 1, and it would not be renewed. Hence, Johnson was set to retire from the saloon business.[767]

Explaining why so many were against Johnson, the *Freeman* wrote,

Johnson bucked the unwritten laws of this country. These forbade racial amalgamation as it concerns Negroes and white people. Others may do so, may marry as they choose. ... With us poor sons of Ham, who live mainly by sufferance, this program of diversity is denied. And I may say right here that the Negroes have no desire, no general desire to change sentiment. ... He was aware of the sentiment against interracial marriages, and which is almost as strongly opposed by our own race as by the white people.[768]

West Liberty, Kentucky's *Licking Valley Courier* said that if the case had been south of the Ohio river, Johnson would have been "put over," for "The Southerner knows how to handle such cases." It said Johnson had "tried the stunt that every nigger who is given the opportunity tries – to equalize himself with white people." Johnson's money and the "glad hand" of "white negrophiles of the north" made him as good as white people, such that he married a white woman. "But the horrors of the situation was such that even she could not endure it and did the sanest act of her life in committing suicide." When he seduced another white woman, Chicago finally became shocked by his conduct, for Cameron's humiliated mother "managed to stir up enough of the dormant manhood in that Sodom."

---

[767] *New York World*, October 23, 1912; *Freeman*, November 2, 1912. *San Francisco Call*, November 1, 1912. There was an alleged offer out of Moscow, Russia for Johnson to fight McVey there for $30,000. Of course, some wondered if it was genuine, given that no big fight ever had taken place there. *Chicago Defender*, November 2, 1912.
[768] *Freeman*, November 2, 1912.

The Southerners know the nigger; know his nature, his capabilities, his limitations; hence know how to handle the problem that is becoming a grave national menace. But the Northerner's chickens are coming home to roost. The nigger himself is demonstrating to them the pitiful fallacy of their clamor to educate their black 'brother' and make a good citizen of him. The white man of the South long ago realized that Omnipotent Omniscience had made that impossible. The leopard can not change its spots. Neither can 'education and culture' make a good citizen out of the nigger. There's no moral foundation in his nature to build upon.[769]

On November 7, 1912, Jack Johnson was arrested on four indictments returned by the grand jury for violations of the Mann Act. His bond was fixed at a whopping $30,000, and Judge Kenesaw Mountain Landis refused to reduce it.

The Mann Act, a federal law officially known as the "White-slave traffic Act," was drafted by Republican U.S. Congressman James Mann of Illinois. The Act made unlawful the aiding or assisting the transportation of women (specifically including the aiding or assisting in the procurement of any tickets or form of transportation) across state lines for the purposes of prostitution, debauchery, or other immorality. Although intended to eliminate forced prostitution, the language of the act was so vague and overbroad that prosecutors could persecute even sexual encounters between unmarried consenting adults that didn't involve prostitution. It was a morality crime. Hence, anyone providing finances to a woman not his wife who traveled across state lines, if the intent was for them to have sexual relations, could technically be found guilty of a federal criminal felony. The law was approved by the U.S. Congress on June 25, 1910, signed by U.S. President William Taft, and went into effect on July 1, 1910.

Contrary to popular belief, Jack Johnson was not the first person prosecuted under this Act. In fact, in the Northern District of Illinois alone, there were forty Mann Act prosecutions brought before the Johnson case.

Initially, the U.S. Department of Justice alleged that on August 10, 1910, Jack Johnson had brought then 24-year-old Belle Schreiber of Pittsburg, a white woman, to Chicago for an unlawful purpose. Johnson had set her up in business as a part owner of a resort (another way of saying brothel) on the south side. A government lawyer said the case against him would not be open to dispute. "There could not be a plainer case of white slavery in violation of the Mann act."

Although briefly released, when there were issues surrounding the validity of the bond posted on his behalf by a friend, on November 8, Johnson was again taken into custody. At 9 p.m., when he was taken to a cell, handcuffed to a U.S. deputy marshal who was accompanied by two others as guard, Johnson struck a newspaper photographer with a cane that

---

[769] *Licking Valley Courier*, November 7, 1912.

he was carrying in his free hand. Jack did not appreciate the man's attempt to photograph him.

Johnson was forced to remove all of his clothing and wear prison garb. He was assigned to a cell in an upper tier. He asked for a dozen candles, a box of cigars, and a case of champagne. He was told that he could not have those items. Johnson replied, "You're not as accommodating as they were in San Francisco. I got everything I wanted there." Johnson requested a bottle of milk, and that was given to him.

Responding to the allegations, Johnson said, "I was in New York playing at Hammerstein's on August 10, 1910, the day they say I brought this Schreiber girl into this state. After that I played in Brooklyn for a week. I never transported her anywhere."

District Attorney Wilkerson opposed the acceptance of Johnson's cash bond. He said he understood that Johnson intended to leave the country on November 30 if he obtained his release. The offense with which Johnson was charged was not subject to extradition. Wilkerson wanted two men of good character with unencumbered real estate to post the bond. Judge Kenesaw M. Landis of the U.S. District Court agreed, and refused to accept cash. Johnson, who had been represented by Edward Morris, added another attorney, Benjamin Bachrach, to his team.

Belle Schreiber was the daughter of a Milwaukee policeman. She had preceded Etta Duryea in Johnson's affections. The start of their relationship pre-dated the passage of the Mann Act. The champ continued to associate with her after his marriage to Duryea, for she was his vaudeville combination after the Reno fight. She finally was abandoned by him, and at that time threatened to get even with him. She was a willing witness, and government detectives kept her in seclusion.[770]

Meanwhile, Lucille Cameron had been held in jail on a $15,000 bond, but when a bondsman offered to pay it, Judge Landis refused to accept it.[771]

The black-owned *Seattle Republican* opined,

> If Jack Johnson has broken the law he deserves the punishment of the law and we hope he gets it, but it looks to us as if all this publicity is given to it because Jack is a Negro and the women are Caucasians. Had Johnson mistreated girls of his own race in a similar manner the federal authorities would have considered it beneath their dignity to give it a moment's consideration. ...

> He was evidently untrue to the white woman he called his wife, which drove her to commit suicide, and he had no sooner returned from her tomb than he began to lionize a bunch of others, and became defiant

---

[770] *Freeman*, November 23, 1912. *New York Tribune*, November 9, 1912.
[771] *Daily Ardmoreite, El Paso Herald, Chicago Day Book*, November 8, 1912.

when the parents of one of the girls protested. In good plain English, he was a damphool and deserves no mercy.[772]

Many colored editors of various newspapers across the country were opposed to Johnson's affinity towards white women, for they considered it a slap at his own race, and believed it engendered further race prejudice:

St. Louis Advance, quoting Major John Lynch: "Some of his race have been proud of him as a prizefighter, but never as anything else."

Star of Zion, Charlotte, North Carolina: "This time he is arrested from trafficking in white slaves. A great injury is done the race when any of its members are exploited whose lives cannot be emulated by the youth of the race. We do not subscribe to the doctrine that the champion pugilist is a racial asset."

The Star, Newport News, Virginia: "No Negro, who has any spark of manhood and who prayed and hoped that Jack Johnson would win his battle with Jim Jeffries...now feels that he did himself the slightest tinge of honor. What a pity it is that Johnson ever was successful in obtaining the great amount of money which came to him if it is to be put to no better use than being spent in a desire to parade a white woman as his wife."

Exchange, Birmingham, Alabama: "As to the physiological ability of Jack Johnson, we believe we voice the sentiment of every intelligent Negro, when we say that we glory in him. ... [but] we say that we most indefatigably denounce his debase allegiance with the other race's woman, and only express our feelings mildly when we say that we hope that he will get everything that is coming to him as far as the law is concerned."

Detroit Informer: "The camel's back is broken with too much Johnson. That he is a menace to the race is conceded by all. Johnson should not nor does he deserve the touch of pity or defense from any source."

Pittsburgh Courier: "Negroes have had quite enough of Jack Johnson and his 'high life.' ... We think Jack Johnson a failure as a representative of the race; and experience no hesitancy in saying that we have had too much Johnson."

Illinois Idea: "Mr. Johnson may be the most scientific boxer in the world, but he is not the best diplomat...and he or no other man has ever suppressed public sentiment or public morals, and the moment that he attempts to do it he will be destroyed of his popularity and business opportunity as have all other men who defied public sentiment."

New York Amsterdam News: "It has been too often the case...that colored men who have achieved prominence have apparently sought to forsake their race by taking as the companion of their bosom either a cast-off or mediocre woman from the Caucasian race....an evidence of the black man's lack of race pride."

---

[772] *Seattle Republican*, November 8, 1912.

Texas Freeman: "Jack Johnson's temporary prosperity, his dense ignorance and misuse of power is doing more to crystalize sentiment against our race."[773]

However, Johnson had his defenders, too. The editor of the *X-Rays Democrat* of Topeka, Kansas said,

> Jack Johnson, the Colored champion pugilist of the world, is in the lime light once more. They claim he has disgraced Chicago. What a pity to disgrace so pure a city. Better see to the thousands of poor white girls who are living in the underworld of Chicago and give Jack Johnson and the 19 year old White gal a rest as she may not be worth the space she is receiving in the press.

The *Chicago Broad Ax* agreed. It said that the people of Chicago and the rest of the country were deceitful and hypocritical, and would hang their heads in shame when it fully dawned upon their race-prejudice-befuddled minds that they permitted themselves to go crazy not on behalf of a pure and innocent young lady, but an experienced prostitute who took money from both races. Cameron had been in his employment for a year.

The *Broad Ax* criticized that the law and law enforcement only sought to protect white women, but never black women.[774]

Lester Walton of the *New York Age* wrote,

> There is a difference between prosecution and persecution. If John has violated the White Slave Act then let the Chicago officials give him a fair trial and not seek to keep him in jail before he has been adjudged guilty. The actions of the Chicago authorities are more disgraceful than the notorious conduct of the champion.
>
> Evidently with a view to playing to the gallery and winning popular favor, the authorities are determined to make as much political capital out of the Johnson incident as possible. They are demanding all kinds of bonds and Tuesday refused a $40,000 cash bond, preferring to keep the fighter in jail. Investigation might show that the white women mixed up in the case are too low in morals to warrant the fixing of Johnson's bond even at $100.
>
> Johnson has been severely criticized in these columns for his lack of judgment, but we are unalterably opposed to seeing him railroaded to jail because of his color.[775]

The *Freeman* agreed that "it seems to us that they are pushing Jack Johnson too hard in the matter of his bond." A $40,000 bond was extremely high, and the court would not accept cash, but wanted it secured by property, which was an odd request. It seemed as if they wanted to keep

---

[773] *Freeman*, November 9, 1912.
[774] *Chicago Broad Ax*, November 9, 1912.
[775] *New York Age*, November 14, 1912.

him in jail. They were "pursuing the champion in a way not warranted by the custom of the courts." Although it did not support his relations with white women, the *Freeman* also opposed unfair treatment by the courts.

> We can not see that it is up to the law or court to see that Jack Johnson does not get Lucile Cameron, as much as we are opposed to it. We oppose it not as a thing of right and wrong, but as a matter of sentiment, knowing the general opposition to mixed relations and the possible bad effect on society as it is now constituted.

It was concerned that the court was being "too readily influenced by sentiment growing out of racial feelings," for it was looking as if judges were becoming prosecutors and persecutors, rather than neutral arbiters.

The *Freeman* noted that Johnson had assaulted the unwritten law of non-amalgamation. Although the country was filled with mixed marriages, including other fighters, they were "not advertised by men in high places." Johnson was the champion, the man on top. Hence, his marriages had greater symbolic value and were advertised in greater fashion. "Johnson laid on the last straw when he took on the Cameron girl. He broke the camel's back. Rage that had smothered and smoldered long – the old fires that had died down…revived, and are now fanned by the gust of passions that promise to cease when he has drained his cup of bitterness."

They were coming at Jack hard. He could furnish a sufficient bond, which already was huge, and yet they still sought to keep him in jail.

> Johnson's case is getting dangerously near to persecution if it is not there already. … Johnson is being maltreated right in the courts. … If the court means to punish him under the white slave law act, it acts extraordinary when it scours heaven and earth to find evidence, going into ancient history, so to speak. … The courts are to protect those whom others would devour, they are not to go into the devouring business themselves.[776]

The *Chicago Defender* lamented that it appeared to be the U.S. Government's policy of "All white people up, all black people down." The fundamental principle of the land of the free and home of the brave was justice to all. However, that principal seemed to have been trampled in the mud in the Johnson case. The world wanted to know why he was held in custody with three times the amount of bail required in his case as in any other, and the amount was guaranteed but still not accepted, which was unfair. "Has colorphobia such a stronghold in Chicago?" Johnson was being "persecuted beyond endurance."

Johnson's unsuccessful attempts to be released on bail had caused some of the public sentiment to switch in his favor, particularly his own race.

Johnson's lawyers, Morris and Bachrach, went to Washington D.C. to argue the case before the U.S. Supreme Court. The case was heard on

---

[776] *Freeman*, November 16, 1912.

November 11, 1912. They argued that the bail was excessive, that cash should have been accepted, and that the Mann Act was unconstitutional. "The Mann Act is particularly to prevent the traffic in women and is aimed at their debauchery. It cannot however interfere with the personal liberties of citizens and be constitutional." Johnson's attorneys argued that the regulation of morality was a matter for the states, not the federal government. They further argued that Congress lacked constitutional authority to make something not commercial a matter of interstate commerce. The case was continued so the government could respond.[777]

The federal grand jury returned four more Mann Act indictments against Johnson. Eventually, it would indict him on eleven counts. The penalty for each offense was maximum imprisonment of up to 5 years, or a fine of up to $5,000, or both.[778]

From jail, the champ declared his innocence. Hundreds daily visited him, white and black, including his mother, brother, and sisters. Johnson had both white and black lawyers working on the case.

Solicitor General Bulitt filed a brief with the U.S. Supreme Court, opposing the motion to admit the pugilist to more reasonable bail terms, arguing that Johnson might escape prosecution by fleeing the country.

U.S. federal Judge George A. Carpenter refused $40,000 cash bail on Johnson's behalf, and refused a bail reduction.

On November 15, 1912, after a week of incarceration in the Cook county jail, Jack Johnson was liberated. Friends and family furnished the $30,000 bond, guaranteed by $70,000 in property, including that of Mrs. Tiny Johnson and Matthew Baldwin, a real estate dealer. Johnson's mother put up the property at 3344 Wabash avenue, valued at $32,000. Baldwin also assured the Court that Johnson would be trailed by a private detective at Johnson's expense until the trial, which satisfied the judge.

Johnson walked out of court in company with his black attorneys Anderson and Wright, and his mother and sister, and three cheers went up for him.[779]

As Johnson was leaving the federal building, two Chicago avenue station detectives re-arrested him on a warrant sworn out by a newspaper photographer charging assault and battery, alleging that Johnson struck the photographer with a cane at the county jail entrance on November 8. The pugilist was taken to a police station, and a cash bond of $400 was accepted. The photographer also filed a civil suit asking for $10,000 in damages.

The *Freeman* said it appeared that Johnson's primary offense was "failing to get himself born white." "The spectacle of two great American cities lashing themselves into the fury of a Georgia lynching mob" over the allegations against Johnson was "contemptible beyond expression, and as much worse than Johnson's alleged offense as the Armenian massacres or

---

[777] *Chicago Day Book*, November 11, 1912; *Daily Missoulian*, December 13, 1912.
[778] *Washington Herald*, November 12, 1912.
[779] *Washington Times*, November 13, 1912; *Chicago Defender*, November 16, 23, 1912.

Russian atrocities surpass in degree a barroom row down in Bath House John's bailiwick."[780]

A black attorney wrote the *Freeman*, saying the Chicago press was exploiting the Johnson situation in a mischievous manner, which was a disgrace to the profession of journalism, and a sin against the peace of the community. "It has the effect to inflame the feeling of the masses of the white race against the Negro, who is having a hard enough time as it is."

This writer also criticized the black press and black religious community:

> Many colored papers, preachers and other Negroes continue to harp on one line, that Johnson owes the Negro race something. I disagree utterly with that assumption. The Negro race has done nothing for Johnson, has given him nothing, aided him in no way to attain any prominence and is entitled to nothing, considered as a race. When Jack Johnson needed money to go to Australia to fight Burns, did the Negro race come forward with help...? This idea Negroes have of criticizing is too common; just as soon as a Negro, great or small falls afoul of the white man's one-sided law all the Negroes like rats deserting a sinking ship begin to outdo the white in denouncing him. Cowardly conduct I call it. ... The fact that he likes white women is no reflection on the race; you make too much of that point. Most men like fair women, if you don't believe it just go into the best Negro homes...and you will find a yellow or almost white woman occupying the leading place of wife. ... If he gets in 'bad with the law' let him take his medicine, if he can't get out of it like other people have to do, but this eternal question of mixing up the race with everything he does is foolish and playing right into the white man's hands. Exactly what he wants us to do is to acknowledge that we are not good enough to marry his old bold, brazen women, while he takes great delight in running every black girl he can get his dirty paws upon. ... Don't let white folks bluff us all the time on this old mixed marriage question. ... and never admit for an instant that black men and black women are not good enough to mate with white men and women, for that is the whole thing in a nutshell and you know it. As long as we admit inferiority we are inferior.[781]

A white writer for the *Cincinnati Enquirer* said that Johnson was the greatest fighter who ever lived, and a lot of ill feeling against him, both personal and professional, had been caused by the fact that he was colored. This writer lamented the unfair way that Johnson was being attacked outside the ring in order to regain the championship for the white race.

---

[780] *Freeman*, November 23, 30, 1912; *New York Tribune*, November 9, 1912. *Evening Standard*, November 15, 1912.

On November 15, 1912 in Philadelphia, highly touted white hope Al Palzer unofficially lost a 6-round newspaper decision to Tony Ross.

[781] *Freeman*, November 23, 1912.

It is an unfair way to try to get the championship away from the Negro. I want it back to the white man and I want it bad, but I want him to win it like he lost it. … Now, to all men who want to be fair, let's give the Negro a fair deal and win back on the level.

If we could kill or put the ban on all men who get mixed up with the opposite race we should have about one-half of our own people out of business. I want to see the championship won as it was lost – in the ring. … I want to say if the championship is won back let it come through the ring, not the courts.[782]

On November 19, 1912, the abduction charge against Jack Johnson was dismissed quietly. Municipal Judge Jacob Hopkins dismissed it; owing to the fact that the prosecution was unable to prove that Johnson had abducted Cameron. The sensational story started by the daily newspapers and Cameron's mother had no basis in fact whatsoever. Of course, everyone had known this all along, yet they had put Johnson through the ringer anyhow, because they did not like his decisions. But using the prevarication was an abuse of the justice system, and it was unethical for the prosecution to pursue a case that had no factual or legal basis.[783]

Johnson compared himself to Napoleon. "Napoleon conquered countries. I had a lot of men to conquer. All great men have been persecuted."[784]

On November 21, Johnson pled not guilty to the charge of smuggling a diamond necklace into the country.

Jack dropped the case against his brother Charles, whom he had alleged stole $150 in furs.[785]

On November 22, at his arraignment, Johnson pled not guilty to the charges of having transported Belle Schreiber from Pittsburgh to Chicago, Milwaukee, and Detroit for immoral purposes.

Ida B. Wells-Barnett, a former slave, suffragist, journalist, and civil rights leader who documented how lynchings often were used as a way to control or punish blacks who competed with whites, often under the guise of false rape charges (when in fact most liaisons were consensual), called a meeting of 2,000 citizens. They passed a resolution declaring that the sensational exploitation of charges against Jack Johnson had done great injury to the civic, industrial, and business relations between colored and white citizens. They appealed to the public for the presumption of innocence to which every man was due, to the press for respite from harmful sensationalism, and to government officials to subordinate prejudice to principle.

The *Chicago Defender* said the Cameron case was a lesson for all races. Her mother had resorted to the hysterics of the stage in her spectacular

[782] *Freeman*, November 23, 1912.
[783] *Harlowton News*, November 22, 1912; *Chicago Broad* Ax, November 23, 1912.
[784] *Mathews Journal*, November 21, 1912.
[785] *Chicago Day Book*, November 21, 1912.

newspaper attempt to reclaim her adult child. In fact, "Cameron knew the turns and twists of State street before she knew the outs and ins of Café de Champion." Regardless, the entire black race was nailed to the cross. The lesson was that black folk should "move carefully in the future when they are called on to condemn one of their own upon the testimony of harlotry."

Tom Flanagan, writing for the *Evening Telegraph*, said that Johnson had never been forgiven for defeating Jeffries. On that day, Jack made thousands of enemies. He could have laid down and retired rich, but he did not because he was a better sportsman than the white gamesters who had hoped to clean up on the trusting public. Johnson was on the square, and could be depended upon to do his best in training and fight to win.

Flanagan said Johnson may have sinned against morality, but those who were hounding him probably were not any cleaner. "Jack Johnson is black and they are white. There seems to be a separate code of morality for whites and blacks in the United States and Johnson is the goat." Jack was no saint. He simply gave in to temptation. "Some people may be surprised to know that the famous pugilist has actually been hounded by women in nearly every city he has visited – white women, supposedly respectable."

Flanagan always found Johnson to be fair and honest. "He is black, and naturally can never hope for much justice across the line."[786]

The black-owned *New Amsterdam News* said there was no doubt about the attempt to put it over on Johnson. The government was run by white men, and they were only human, and were affected by race shame the same as anyone else. They did not like Johnson at the top of the ladder. The Cameron case was utterly groundless. Lucille was willing to testify all along that she was seeing Johnson of her own volition. "It is openly reported in Chicago that white men not related to the Cameron girl were behind the prosecution." Had the case come to trial and Johnson been given a fair hearing, the entire fabric of race persecution would have been exposed.

Noted was the inconsistency of Mann Act prosecutions, which were based solely on race. White men lusted after colored women in every city, in both the North and South.

> Yet in all this the government has never yet invoked the white slave law. The stench of the unjust and unholy race persecution in which the entire country is joining hands in railroading Jack Johnson cries to heaven for redress. ... The persecution of Johnson will not hurt only Johnson, but disturb for a long time to come the peaceful relations of the white and colored people of the nation.

It was obvious to this writer that the government was prosecuting Johnson because he was black, he slept with white women, and he was the world heavyweight champion, plain and simple.[787]

---

[786] *Chicago Defender*, November 23, 30, 1912.
[787] *Freeman*, November 30, 1912.

On December 3, 1912, Jack Johnson married Lucille Cameron at the family home at 3344 South Wabash avenue. Johnson placed a $2,500 diamond ring on her finger. Cameron was 18 years of age, as revealed by the marriage certificate, for her birthdate was February 22, 1894.[788]

The new Mrs. Johnson said,

I am a free woman and have a perfect right to marry whom I please. Why don't the United States government stop southern and northern white men as well from living and raising children by colored women out of wedlock; look in the south and see the advantage taken of the colored people. Look at that case where the white men in Georgia fought and killed each other for the love of a colored woman. There are no gleaming headlines in the nice big papers. Well, let them holler who will; all I have to say is I am happy and I did not go south either. I want my fellow citizens to know that I am still living in the 'land of the free and the home of the brave.'[789]

A motion picture concern offered Johnson $5,000 for pictures of the wedding, which he accepted. However, in most places, the films of Johnson's wedding were barred from being exhibited. Delegates to the convention of the Indiana Motion Picture Exhibitors' League decided to deny patrons the privilege of witnessing the mixed-race wedding.

JACK JOHNSON BRIDAL PARTY

Rev. John Balay, Mr. Donaldson and wife, Lucille, Jack, Mrs. Tiny Johnson

---

[788] *Chicago Day Book*, December 4, 1912; *Tacoma Times*, December 3, 1912; *Chicago Defender*, *Chicago Broad Ax*, December 7, 1912.
[789] *Chicago Defender*, December 14, 1912.

Picture show owners in Paducah, Kentucky placed a ban on any films showing the Johnson-Cameron marriage. They passed a resolution that the pictures were greatly deplored by all respectable people and were an insult to common decency, and would not be allowed to be displayed. Of the four local theaters, colored patrons were admitted to only one.

Not every black writer took Johnson's side. One wrote, "Another blot has been given the Negroes by Jack Johnson's craze for white women, which he exhibited in marrying Lucille Cameron, the nineteen-year-old girl."

It is said the citizens of Texarkana telegraphed Mayor Carter Harrison of Chicago saying that if Chicago wanted to get rid of Johnson to just send him to Texarkana for three minutes. It now begins to appear that Jack Johnson is determined to commit suicide.[790]

At that time, at a governors' conference, South Carolina Governor Coleman Blease said that those who lynched black men accused of assailing white women would not be punished.

I will never order out the militia to shoot down its neighbors and protect a brute who commits the nameless crime against a white woman. Therefore, in South Carolina, let it be understood that when a Negro assaults a white woman all that is needed is that they get the right man, and they who get him will neither need nor receive a trial.

Never mind due process, the right to counsel, the presumption of innocence until guilt is proven beyond a reasonable doubt in a court of law, or a unanimous verdict by an impartial jury. According to the state's own governor, mob justice was perfectly acceptable.[791]

The *Freeman* said black folk had become "more reconciled to Jack, since they saw plainly that they were trying to put something over him. At first they took the extreme attitude that white people took, insisting that the champion had committed an unpardonable sin." Noted was the difference in treatment based on race. John L. Sullivan was a drunk, who swaggered, bluffed, swore, and got into extracurricular activity not in his favor, yet he was treated as a "national pet."

After the Cameron case dismissal, Johnson said, "As soon as we can get away we will go to Paris." The *Freeman* wrote, "Not a bad idea, owing to the very much perturbed racial relations in this country. Of course, Johnson can stay in this country if he chooses, but he would not get very much pleasure out of the staying." However, the government was determined not to allow him to leave the country until it had its way with him.

The *Freeman* reported that a New York newspaper (which it did not name) had decided to draw the color line in pugilistic matters. Black fighters' names were barred from its columns. "Never again will the besmirched 'Jack Johnson' be set up on its linotype machines as part of a

---

[790] *Freeman*, December 21, 1912, January 4, 1913.
[791] *Freeman*, December 7, 1912.

boxing story, and the only way it can creep into the general news pages of the paper is as an essential integer in tales of justice meted out for criminal acts." That New York newspaper suggested that other papers should follow suit. "It meant further that Johnson is to be 'bludgeoned' out of his title in the one way that it seems possible to do it."[792]

On December 7, officials of the French boxing federation declared that they would take steps to prevent Johnson's boxing there. They said the police would forbid any fight involving Johnson on the ground that it might cause trouble.[793]

On December 10, 1912 in Vernon, California, in the Los Angeles area, 205-pound Luther McCarty of Missouri administered a beating to and stopped 190-pound Fireman Jim Flynn in the 16th round. Some called it an elimination bout for the "white championship."[794]

On December 11, both of Johnson's black attorneys, Anderson and White (or Wright), withdrew from him, saying that their disapproval of his recent marriage was so strong that they no longer desired to be associated with him.[795]

Also on December 11, U.S. Congressional Representative Seaborn Roddenberry, a Georgia Democrat, from the House floor demanded a constitutional amendment prohibiting the marriage of whites and blacks. He said, "We have heard much of slavery in the South, but in all the years of Southern slavery there never was such brutality, such infamy as the marriage license authorizing that black African brute, Jack Johnson, to wed a white woman and to bind her in the wedlock of black slavery." Roddenberry declared that in the South, blacks "respected the superiority of their former masters and would commit self-destruction before entertaining a thought of matrimony with a Caucasian girl." He prophesied that legal sanction of mixed marriages could bring the country to a bloody conflict.[796]

Keep in mind, at that time, 29 state laws prohibited whites and blacks from marrying one another, including Alabama, Arizona, Arkansas, California, Colorado, Delaware, Florida, Georgia, Idaho, Indiana, Kentucky, Louisiana, Maryland, Mississippi, Missouri, Montana (as of 1909), Nebraska, Nevada, North Carolina, North Dakota (as of 1909), Oklahoma, Oregon, South Carolina, South Dakota (as of 1909), Tennessee, Texas, Utah, Virginia, and West Virginia. Eventually Wyoming passed its own anti-interracial marriage law in 1913. In 1883, the U.S. Supreme Court had upheld such laws as constitutional in *Pace v. Alabama*, 106 U.S. 583 (1883).

---

[792] *Freeman*, December 14, 21, 1912, January 4, 1913.

[793] *San Francisco Call*, December 8, 1912; *Daily Capital Journal*, December 7, 1912.

[794] *Freeman*, December 21, 1912. Against McCarty, Flynn had been down three times in the 9th round and decked twice in the 16th round. Referee Charles Eyton, seeing that he was helpless, stopped it. The crowd supported his decision.

[795] *Omaha Daily Bee*, December 12, 1912.

[796] *Chicago Day Book*, December 12, 1912. The *Herald and News*, December 13, 1912; *Chicago Broad Ax*, December 14, 1912. Ultimately, no amendment passed and it remained up to individual states to pass their own laws regarding the interracial marriage issue.

On December 12, Johnson was fined $50 on the charge of assaulting a newspaper photographer with a cane.

Hugh McIntosh said Johnson was forever an exile from the Australian ring. "The whole current of popular feeling is so strong against him that no promoter would dare to bring him here." Several days later, McIntosh was quoted as saying,

As far as I am concerned, Johnson will never come to Australia again. He dare not show his face in London; he is barred in New York, and now that he will have difficulty in doing anything here, the only place that is left for him, as far as I can see, is France, and I doubt if they will stand for him even there.[797]

At that time, a claim was made that about a week before the Jeffries fight in Reno, Sam Langford knocked out Jeffries in the 4th round of a private sparring session, and that was responsible for Jeff's nervous breakdown. Joe Woodman claimed that Langford dropped Jeff twice in the 3rd round, and out in the 4th round. Few believed him.[798]

On December 26, 1912 in Sydney, Sam Langford knocked out Sam McVey in the 13th round. Langford dropped him in the 4th with an uppercut to the chin, and from then on McVey fought on the defensive. At the end, Langford landed a series of punches to the face, causing McVey to fall, completely beaten. A *Freeman* writer said, "It strikes me that Langford is the logical candidate for Jack Johnson's shoes."

On December 27, 1912 in San Francisco, Gunboat Smith won a 20-round decision over Frank Moran.

Jack Johnson intended to move his wife Lucille into a mansion in the Lake Geneva area in Chicago. However, many folks in the area were saying that they would try to keep him out, even if physical measures had to be taken.[799]

On January 1, 1913 in New York, Joe Jeannette won a 10-round no-decision against Battling Jim Johnson.

That same day, in Vernon, California, Luther McCarty stopped Al Palzer in the 18th round to win the White World Heavyweight Championship.

McCarty said he was drawing the color line, and considered himself the world champion. All fair-minded sportsmen knew the only way Johnson would lose the title was by being defeated in the ring. Hence, McCarty simply was the white champion, and one unwilling to fight Johnson.

Some said that blacks were suffering on account of Johnson, losing their places and jobs as a result of his actions. Whites were taking out their wrath over Johnson upon other blacks. Others said that the Johnson situation simply illuminated blacks' status in the country, and gave whites an excuse to do to blacks what they had been doing already. The *Freeman* said,

[797] *Honolulu Star-Bulletin*, December 16, 1912. *San Francisco Call*, December 21, 1912.
[798] *Evening Standard*, December 16, 1912.
[799] *Freeman*, January 4, 1913.

More than Jack Johnson is at stake. The Negro is on trial before the world. What is his status in America? The champion is simply a means to an end. He, if you will notice, has abused every canon of good taste from a racial viewpoint, socially considered, yet he has done no violence to the laws. He is an object lesson on the Negro's status in this country, whether by design or accident, and from a sociological viewpoint, worth the while.

When Johnson and his wife went to the dance of the Eighth regiment, a Negro regiment of the Illinois militia, he and Lucille appeared on the dance floor, but then the blacks present hissed them and backed away. The music ceased, and Johnson and his white wife stood alone in the center of the dance floor. All eyes were upon them, and the hissing increased until the entire place joined in. An upset Johnson said, "Come, Lucille, let's leave this place."[800]

Little known is the fact that Johnson made an attempt to leave the U.S. before his trial. On January 14, 1913, at the request of Charles DeWoody, superintendent of the Department of Justice in Chicago, local police in Battle Creek, Michigan stopped a Grand Trunk train and removed Jack Johnson and his wife from it. Federal officers received a tip that Johnson had left Chicago the previous night bound for Toronto, Ontario, Canada. They feared he intended to jump bond on the white slave charge, for it was not an extraditable offense.

Johnson said he only intended to remain in Toronto a couple of days, for he was on his way to see his old manager, Tom Flanagan, regarding an offer he had received from Tom O'Rourke for a fight in Paris against Al Palzer. A telegram from O'Rourke showed that Jack had been offered $25,000 or 60% of the house. The message to Johnson said, "Palzer was ill in McCarty fight. The latter refuses to box."

Superintendent DeWoody learned that the train was due to arrive in Battle Creek at 2:48 a.m. DeWoody called the local chief of police and asked him to stop the train, for Johnson was on it. At 4 a.m., DeWoody was awakened by a long distance call from Johnson, who pleaded, "You know I wouldn't leave my old mother and my country. I'd rather go to jail. I told my attorneys I was just going to Toronto to see my old trainer Tom Flanagan, and they said it was all right." DeWoody asked, "Did you have a round-trip ticket?" "No, I told them to get me one but they got it only one way. But I was going to get one." He begged to be kept out of jail.

DeWoody was not buying it, for Johnson, his wife, and valet all had one-way tickets. Another thing indicating that Johnson did not intend to return was the fact that he shipped his automobiles to Canada as well. DeWoody tersely declared to reporters, "A great chance he was coming back!"

That morning, at Johnson's home, two hours after Jack had been arrested at Battle Creek, without having been made aware of his arrest,

800 *Freeman*, January 11, 1913.

Johnson's mother said, "Jack is upstairs sleeping, but I can't wake him now. ... His wife is here with him. My boy would never run away." Johnson was taken back to Illinois and spent the night in the Chicago county jail to await U.S. District Court Judge George Carpenter's decision as to whether Jack's $30,000 bond should be forfeited.

On January 15, Johnson went before Judge Carpenter. Jack told the court that he had no intention of evading trial, but went to Toronto on business matters. The judge asked, "But you shipped two automobiles, didn't you?" Johnson said that was true, but he merely had intended to enjoy a few days' vacation before shipping them back to Chicago. His bond was allowed to stand, and he was given time to secure a $5,000 bond on the pending jewelry smuggling charge.[801]

Commenting on Johnson's potential attempt to flee the U.S., the *Freeman* said,

> It would not be much of a trick to slip out of the country incognito, had Johnson cared to have done so. I hope he had no such intentions in mind, for if so, under the circumstances, the history of human kind would scarcely contain a parallel of infamy – his mother is on his bond; he is obligated to friends.

The *Freeman* meant that he would cost his mother and others a great deal of money if he fled. Of course, what his mother had, he had given to her.

The *Freeman* opined, "What is happening to him is happening to every member of the race. Jack Johnson has violated public sentiment, not the laws, as far as it is known." It believed that a coterie of defeated, slanderous white reporters wanted to mob Johnson out of his title.

When Johnson went to O'Connell's gymnasium in Chicago, he was ousted. Jack had boxed 6 rounds there the previous day, but the next day, O'Connell told him he was barred. O'Connell told reporters, "Johnson's presence was hurting my business. Several of my pupils said they would quit if he came here again." It was believed that the same action likely would be taken against Johnson by all of the city's other big gyms.

Johnson hoped to travel abroad to fight Al Palzer in Paris on June 24 or 25 for a $30,000 guarantee. "Johnson realizes that he cannot get any bouts in the United States." Of course, he would have to win or successfully settle his legal battles first. Even if he could leave the country, it was not clear whether any locale would allow him to fight.[802]

On January 17, 1913 in New York, Joe Jeannette won a 10-round no-decision bout against Jeff Clark, avenging an earlier no-decision loss.

On January 21, 1913, in Providence, Rhode Island, Joe Jeannette won via 15th round disqualification against Battling Jim Johnson.

On February 3, 1913, the 16th Amendment to the U.S. Constitution was ratified, enabling the U.S. to levy an income tax.

---

[801] *Freeman,* January 18, February 1, 1913.
[802] *Freeman,* January 18, 25, 1913, February 1, 1913.

690

Also on February 3, 1913, the U.S. Supreme Court denied Johnson's habeas corpus appeal, holding that the issue was moot, since Johnson had posted bond and had been released. It also held that Johnson could not attack the Mann Act's constitutionality with an appellate court before trial, but rather he first had to exhaust all of his remedies, starting with the district court.[803]

However, on February 24, 1913, the U.S. Supreme Court decided *Hoke v. United States*, 227 U.S. 308 (1913), holding that although Congress could not regulate prostitution per se, as that was strictly the province of the states, Congress could regulate interstate travel for purposes of prostitution or "immoral purposes," finding the Mann Act to be a constitutional exercise of Congressional power.

That same day, the Supreme Court also decided *Athanasaw v. United States*, 227 U.S. 326 (1913), finding that the Mann Act was not limited strictly to prostitution, but to "debauchery" as well.

The ongoing race issues in the U.S. were not merely limited to the South. Legislatures in New York, New Jersey, Ohio, Michigan, and Minnesota were considering the interracial marriage question. The *New York Age* noted that the Jim Crow laws and the 'separate but equal' doctrine protected whites at every point, but left the darker races without legal protection. Whites were free to insult, order about, and even strike and murder blacks, and be justified by a judge and jury of their white peers. "The thing now happens at some place in the country every day, and is growing worse instead of better. Separate marriage laws and the discussion of them are adding fuel to the flames."

Matters had reached the point where a black man could not even look in the direction of a white woman without arousing a policeman's suspicions, which could lead to the black man's arrest on a disorderly conduct charge, which was the thin excuse the police used to arrest someone. Even today, alleged "disorderly conduct," or violation of noise ordinances, or interference charges seem to be the overbroad catchall way for police to arrest anyone for doing or saying anything they don't like. The *Age* urged,

> The Negro must fight for his rights, the least and greatest, whenever they are assailed, or he will have none in the end. The Separate Marriage law scheme should be fought to the bitter end. At the bottom of the whole scheme to isolate the Negro citizens in all of the public and private relations of life…in segregating them, separating them to themselves in living districts…and in branding them by law as so far inferior that they may not marry…as other races of the citizenship are free to do; in eating and drinking in places of licensed accommodation and amusement, and in accommodations in travel, by land and sea, as others are free to do – at the bottom of the whole scheme is to be found the slave-holders' doctrine, as formulated into

---

[803] *John A. Johnson v. Luman T. Hoy, U.S. Marshal*, 227 U.S. 245 (1913).

the law of precedent by Chief Justice Robert B. Taney of the Federal Supreme Court in 1856, that "it has been so far held to be good law and precedent that a black man has no rights that a white man is bound to respect."

Blacks could not vote, which destroyed their political rights. True, technically they could vote, but their rights had been destroyed by the violence of organizations like the Ku Klux Klan, the Knights of the White Camilia, and the Red Shirts, and by legislative enactments that the Supreme Court upheld, which functionally served to disfranchise most blacks. Only registered voters could serve on juries, so all-white juries passed judgment on blacks accused of crimes, and upon whites accused of crimes against blacks. Without political representation or protection in the courts, whites could pass whatever laws they wanted and practically do whatever they wanted.[804]

Jack Johnson was famous the world over. Even in West Africa, the Nigerian-based *Lagos Standard* reported that Johnson was a practical prisoner in his own hotel, where he was guarded by about a dozen of Chicago's biggest roughs. He was afraid of being mobbed if he appeared on the streets.

Although initially he drew the color line, Luther McCarty changed his mind and said he would fight only one black man – Johnson, if a club would guarantee him $30,000 or give him 30% of the gate. His manager Billy McCarney said he had given up the idea of drawing the color line for the next two years, as previously stated. "Johnson is the recognized champion, and we are after the real championship, and some money with it. Those dark skinned babies are real tough propositions, and I don't propose to give Langford a chance to earn all that Luther has worked so hard for, at least not right away." McCarty held victories over Carl Morris, Jim Barry, Al Kaufman, Jim Flynn, and Al Palzer.[805]

On February 16, Johnson became very ill and was confined to bed-rest. Dr. Carter diagnosed him with a severe case of typhoid-pneumonia. The pneumonia was so severe that it caused the postponement of his trial, which had been set to start on Tuesday February 25.[806]

Although there was discussion of Johnson fighting Palzer in France, the *Freeman* noted, "The bout is planned for June, but there is little interest, as Negro pugilists just now are under the ban in France."

The *Freeman* observed how the white press gave top white boxer Luther McCarty different treatment than Johnson. No one gave McCarty grief for

---

[804] *New York Age*, February 6, 1913.

[805] *Freeman*, February 8, 15, 22, 1913. The *Freeman* reported that in his close no-decision draw with Jess Willard, McCarty's work was so crude that some wondered how he managed to defeat Morris. New York was holding firm that it would not allow black fighters to box against white fighters. In Nashville, Tennessee, Johnson's prominence was blamed as being most responsible for the proposed bill to repeal the law allowing prize fighting.

[806] *Chicago Defender*, February 22, 1913.

asking for a guaranteed $30,000. When Johnson asked for that much money to box Langford, he was called a hog. "Yet Johnson is a world's champion. McCarty is hardly out of the preliminary class."

The Canadian government declared that owing to moral turpitude, Johnson had been designated as an undesirable and barred from admission into its country. The *Freeman*'s perspective was that Johnson was hounded by the government and branded as an undesirable because he was a black man who had won a white woman's heart. "Ten thousand pulpits refuse to thunder the Christ spirit as we understand it in this matter, seeing man as man."[807]

On March 24, 1913 in Brisbane, Australia, Sam Langford and Sam McVey fought to a 20-round draw. In June, after Langford also fought a 15-round draw with Colin Bell, the *Freeman* noted that although some argued that Langford had a chance to beat Johnson, "nobody much believes it."[808]

On March 31, Jack Johnson turned 35 years old. He celebrated at his residence at 3344 Wabash avenue.

On April 2, 1913 in Calgary, Canada, Tommy Burns fought Arthur Pelkey to a 6-round no-decision draw. Pelkey was down in the 2nd and 5th rounds, while Burns was down in the 4th.[809]

On April 16, 1913 in Philadelphia, Luther McCarty won a 6-round no-decision bout against Jim Flynn.

On April 22, 1913, Jack Johnson cut a plea deal in the jewelry smuggling case. Johnson's attorney Ben Bachrach had conferred with Judge Carpenter, and then asked to file the no contest (nolo contendere) plea. Johnson was fined $1,000 and compelled to forfeit the $2,000 diamond necklace. Judge Carpenter said there was no evidence to show that Johnson had smuggled the necklace personally. He merely attempted to conceal the fact of the purchase after his arrival in Chicago. Johnson initially had lied and said the necklace had been brought to Chicago by a friend three weeks after he and his wife returned home. The judge also referred to the white slavery charges, for which Johnson was set to face trial on May 5.[810]

On April 30, 1913 in New York, Luther McCarty won a 10-round no-decision bout against Frank Moran.

[807] *Freeman*, March 15, 22, 1913.
On March 14, 1913 in New York, Gunboat Smith knocked out Bombardier Billy Wells in the 2nd round.
[808] *Freeman*, June 28, 1913.
[809] When later they were in a contract dispute, Pelkey claimed that his bout with his manager Burns was faked. He said he was penniless, Burns induced him to frame up the match, and they rehearsed their battle beforehand. The two later reconciled. *Freeman*, September 20, 1913.
[810] *Chicago Defender*, April 5, 12, 26, 1913.

CHAPTER 16

The United States vs. John Arthur Johnson

On May 5, 1913 in Chicago, in the United States District Court for the Northern District of Illinois, Eastern Division, in federal Judge George A. Carpenter's court, Jack Johnson's "White-slave traffic Act" trial began. Formally, it was entitled, "The United States vs. John Arthur Johnson, otherwise known as Jack Johnson." The trial would last nine days.[811]

The White-slave traffic Act, otherwise known as the Mann Act, approved on June 25, 1910 and effective as of July 1, 1910, said in part,

> That any person who shall knowingly transport or cause to be transported, or aid or assist in obtaining transportation for, or in transporting, in interstate or foreign commerce...any woman or girl for the purpose of prostitution or debauchery, or for any other immoral purpose, or with the intent and purpose to induce, entice, or compel such woman or girl to become a prostitute or giver herself up to debauchery, or to engage in any other immoral practice; or who shall knowingly procure or obtain, or cause to be procured or obtained, or aid or assist in procuring or obtaining, any ticket or tickets, or any form of transportation or evidence of the right thereto, to be used by any woman or girl in interstate or foreign commerce...in going to any place for the purpose of prostitution or debauchery, or for any other immoral purpose, or with the intent or purpose on the part of such person to induce, entice, or compel her to give herself up to the practice of prostitution, or to give herself up to debauchery, or any other immoral practice, whereby any such woman or girl shall be transported in interstate or foreign commerce...shall be deemed guilty of a felony, and upon conviction thereof shall be punished by a fine not exceeding five thousand dollars, or by imprisonment of not more than five years, or by both such fine and imprisonment, in the discretion of the court.

The *Freeman* opined that Johnson was on trial for daring to brave public sentiment and continuing relations with white women. The charge against him, of white slaving, was an afterthought. Men were eager to see Johnson in prison owing to his known relations with white women, and because he

---

[811] Johnson was charged with violating 36 Stat. 825 (1910), 18 U.S.C. § 2421, by its own terms officially called the "White-slave traffic Act." (61st Congress, Sess. II, chapter 395, section 8). The bulk of the following description of the trial comes directly from the official court transcript and record.

was the "physical Zeus." The *Freeman* urged that under the circumstances, colored people, many of whom were hoping the worst for Johnson, should pray for his deliverance. If he was imprisoned, it would be the biggest calamity to the race since the days of freedom.

The *Chicago Defender* opined, "Public sentiment is largely in favor of the champion, many persons believing that he has not received a square deal." His friends claimed that the white newspapers had treated him unjustly.

Johnson complained that James J. Jeffries' admirers had hounded him since the Reno battle, and that this case was a direct outcome of his victory over Jeffries. Jack said, "All I want is a fair show." Johnson's attorney said, "If Jack goes free he will leave the United States at once."

The judge allowed in the courtroom only the champion's immediate friends and duly accredited newsmen. Comparatively few of those in the big courtroom crowd were black.

Pursuant to Johnson attorney Benjamin Bachrach's advice, Johnson's wife Lucille did not attend the trial, for fear of inflaming the jury's passions. Bachrach said, "I am afraid it would prejudice the jury against Johnson. The jurors might think he was flaunting her in their faces."

The early part of the week was consumed with jury selection. Attorney Bachrach asked each prospective juror whether he was a Jeffries admirer, if he was prejudiced against prizefighters, if he ever had been connected with a reform organization or a vice crusade, if he was opposed to intermarriage between a black and a white, or if he had any prejudice against colored men. Bachrach intended to exclude from the jury all persons of Southern birth. He preferred Republicans to Democrats. One prospective juror who was challenged and excused admitted that the circumstances surrounding Etta Duryea's suicide might influence his voice in the jury room. An all-white all-male jury was seated. Women could not serve as jurors, and blacks rarely were included in jury pools owing to restrictive laws.

The eleven-count indictment, obtained by U.S. Attorney James Wilkerson, charged that on October 15, 1910, Johnson caused, paid for, aided and assisted the transportation of Belle Schreiber, "otherwise known as Mrs. J. Johnson," from Pittsburg to Chicago by railway for various illegal purposes, depending on the counts, which included prostitution, debauchery, unlawful immoral sexual intercourse (sex outside of marriage), and for committing the crime against nature with and upon her (anal and oral sex), all against the peace and dignity of the United States.[812]

In his opening statement, U.S. government attorney Harry A. Parkin said that when traveling across the country, Johnson liked to have the company of women. Johnson had brought Belle Schreiber with him on a theatrical and fight tour for immoral purposes starting in 1909, taking her to

---

[812] At various times, "debauchery" has been defined as the leading of a chaste woman into unchastity, or to corrupt in morals, or to lead a lifestyle of habitual, excessive, unrestrained, or uninhibited indulgence, typically involving alcohol or drugs, which leads to sexually immoral activities.

New York, Boston, Pittsburg, Indianapolis, Toronto, Montreal, and then Oakland at the time he had the Kaufman and Ketchel fights. Subsequently, he took her to places like Atlantic City, Boston, Pittsburg, and Chicago. During this time, he "posed and passed her as his wife."

Parkin alleged that at one point, in one city, Johnson had three different white women, Hattie [Watson, a.k.a. McClay], Etta [Duryea], and Belle Schreiber, having sexual intercourse with each of them. From 1909 to 1910, he took the three with him to various cities at the same time, sometimes in the same train. He continued relations with these and other women even while married to Duryea, sometimes under the same roof where he lived with his wife, and said relations continued after her death.

The specific legally relevant allegations were that on or about October 15, 1910, Johnson paid Belle Schreiber's fare for a train ride to come from Pittsburgh to Chicago for immoral purposes. Johnson had a sexual relationship with her, both before and after her arrival in Chicago. Once in Chicago, Johnson provided funds for Schreiber to use to set up a house of prostitution, and he purchased her furniture. Johnson further engaged in debauchery. Finally, "Another immoral purpose is one which is too obscene to mention, almost, to the jury trying the case, the purpose being for the defendant to compel these women to commit the crime against nature upon his body."

Parkin also said,

> Now, it will appear, of course, that the defendant is a prize fighter; and in that connection it will be interesting, as the evidence develops, to see upon what victims he practiced the manly art of self defense. It will appear that these women who he carried about the country with him were, very, very many times, when he either had a fit of anger, or when the girls refused to do some of the obscene things which he demanded of them, - that he practiced the manly art of self defense upon them, blacking their eyes and sending them to hospitals, where he took care of them and paid their expenses until they recovered from the wounds which he had inflicted upon the faces and bodies of these women. Something may appear with respect to the prize fighting career of the defendant. We expect to put some evidence upon the stand which will develop the character of champion which the defendant professes to be; and also the real facts with respect to his championship, prior to the Jeffries fight.

Parkin further said that sometimes when Johnson had the three women with him, because of their differences and for other reasons, he would drop one off and put her into a "sporting house" (a polite way of saying house of prostitution) temporarily in order to relieve himself of the necessity of spending money carrying her about the country while he had the others.

In his opening statement on Johnson's behalf, defense attorney Benjamin C. Bachrach said that when Johnson came into prominence, "as is customary with a certain class of women, sporting women, they are attracted by an exhibition of physical prowess, and throw themselves in the way of a pugilist." Belle Schreiber was a member of the Everleigh Club, a sporting house (brothel) in Chicago, when Johnson became acquainted with her. Johnson did not put her there. She was an ordinary prostitute well before she met Johnson. She worked in sporting houses across the country. Bachrach said Schreiber consorted with several negro men, not just Johnson.

Bachrach said the law applicable to the case began on July 1, 1910, and hence anything done prior to that was irrelevant. The evidence would show that Johnson did not take Schreiber anywhere after the law went into effect, and did not send her a telegram asking her to meet him in Chicago or aid her in doing so, but that Schreiber came of her own accord, and then, once in Chicago, asked Johnson for money for her residence, because she wanted her mother and pregnant sister to come live with her. Jack then paid for her furniture. This was in November 1910, before he married Etta Duryea (in January 1911). If Schreiber subsequently changed the residence into a house of prostitution, Johnson had nothing to do with it.

Mervin Jacobowski (otherwise known as M. Mervin) was the government's first witness. In 1909 at Cedar Lake, Indiana, while employed by Roy Jones, a saloon-keeper who was Johnson's friend, Mervin saw Schreiber, who then was known as "Jack Allen," with Johnson at a party, along with George Little and his wife, Barney Furey, and Yank Kenny. It was sometime before the Ketchel fight.

About a year later, on August 14, 1910 (after the Jeffries fight), Mervin came to Chicago and started working for Johnson as his chauffeur. That month, Mervin left Chicago for Cleveland with Johnson and then girlfriend Etta, Sig Hart and his wife, Barney Furey, Walter Monahan, and Charlie Conners. While in Cleveland, Johnson sent Mervin to the Hollenden Hotel to go pick up a woman (who turned out to be "Allen") and bring her back to the Star theater, where Johnson was part of a twice-daily burlesque performance. Mervin did as requested. An hour later, Mervin took Allen/Schreiber back to the hotel.

Mervin again saw Schreiber in Detroit while the same Johnson party was there, again picking her up at Johnson's direction, and bringing her to the theater. An hour later, Mervin took her back to her hotel. He saw her again in Detroit that week. She was on the stage.

He also saw Schreiber in Toronto, while Johnson and Etta were there. This was all before Jack formally married Etta Duryea in Pittsburg in January 1911. Belle also was in Buffalo, Montreal, and Boston while Johnson was in those towns. During Christmas 1910, in Milwaukee, Mervin saw Schreiber in a hotel with Johnson. No other woman was there. Johnson was ill at the time.

Mervin said the only time he saw a woman named Hattie with Johnson was back in 1908 or 1909, in Chicago, and they were with George Little and his wife.

The government next called Lillian Paynter, who testified that in 1910 she ran a sporting house in Pittsburg. Belle Schreiber came to her house in March 1910 and stayed with her for about eight months. Julia Allen, a colored woman, also stayed there. Paynter was sick and hospitalized in late September or early October, and when she returned home in October, Belle was gone. "My sister put her out of the house because she heard that Belle was mixed up with a colored man." Paynter said she had never seen Johnson there. "I don't know if Mr. Jack Johnson was the colored man, the name wasn't mentioned to me." She did not know where Belle went.

Estelle Paynter, Lillian's sister, testified next. She ran the sporting house in 1910 with her sister. "Jack Allen," now known as Belle Schreiber, lived there for eight months, starting in March 1910. Belle briefly went to Atlantic City before returning. While her sister was in the hospital, after a man came to the house and spoke with Belle, Estelle ordered Belle out of the house, and she left the next day, somewhere around mid-October 1910. "I sent her away; I asked her to leave."

The next witness was John T. Lewis. He managed and rented apartment houses in Chicago. In 1910 he handled the Ridgewood at 28th and Wabash Avenue in Chicago. The building contained seventy apartments, from three to seven rooms each. He knew "Jack Allen." She rented a seven-room apartment, with first rent due on November 1, 1910, though she might have moved in sooner. She occupied that apartment for four months, until February 1911. She paid the rent. He did not know anything about her occupation. He stayed in apartment 425, while she was in apartment 424. Each apartment on the 4th floor was quite large, for there were only four on that floor, each one containing several rooms. He could not say how many flats of prostitution were in the building at that time, or whether there were any.

Bertha Morrison testified that during 1910 she ran a sporting business in the Ridgewood Apartment building at 28th and Wabash Avenue in Chicago. In November 1910, she was in apartment 757. She saw Belle there from November to January. The entrance to apartment 425 is near the elevator, so that as Morrison passed up and down in the elevator, she could look right at the door. "I know that was a sporting flat. All flats in the Ridgewood Building were sporting flats, all of them to my knowledge." She had seen Johnson in the building in the elevator, and saw him entering Apartment 425 two or three times from November 1910 on.

On cross examination, Morrison admitted that she had been inside only five of the seventy flats. She had never seen inside the Schreiber flat. She only knew they were sporting flats through hearsay.

Chicago police officer John O'Halloran specialized in booking women into houses of prostitution for two years, and had booked women into houses of prostitution in the Ridgewood. (Yes, you read that right – a police officer was a booker of prostitutes.) He said about 20 apartments were out and out houses of prostitution. The rest of the residents were "call girls" who went out on call to meet men at another location. However, he could not say for certain that every one of the residents was a prostitute. It just was the building's general reputation.

John T. Lewis was recalled, and again said he had no opinion or knowledge regarding the character of the apartments in his building.

Leopold Moss sold mattresses and furniture at Marshall Ventilated Mattress Co. at 908 Michigan Avenue in Chicago. During late October 1910, Johnson and Schreiber visited his business together. The government admitted into evidence a November 1, 1910 bill of sale, showing that the purchased goods were to be delivered to "Miss Jacque Allen" at 2730 Wabash Ave., Apartment 424, and included pillows, tables, beds, mattresses, springs, a three-piece suit, a rocker, chairs, dressers, commodes, rugs, carpet, table cloths, doilies, blankets, lace curtains, portierres, pillow cases, sheets, bed spreads, comforters, a table pad, sweeper, cuspidors, a kitchen set, socket poles, curtain poles, curtain rods, silverware, dishes, and pictures. Moss testified that Johnson paid $700 cash on a $1,196.53 bill, and signed a 30-day note for $500, which note was paid by Miss Schreiber sometime afterwards. The note was entered into evidence. After Schreiber telephoned to complain that some of the articles were badly scratched in delivery, Moss went to the apartment one afternoon to see about it, and he saw Schreiber, her mother, sister, and Johnson there, as well as the furniture.

During the trial, Johnson had not been wearing the flashy clothes that hitherto characterized his dress. He wore a blue suit, black bowtie, and black shoes. There was an absence of his normal flash of diamonds, stickpin, or diamond rings, and the golden smile was not so apparent.

On Thursday May 8, Belle Schreiber took the stand at 11 a.m. and remained until 4 p.m. She testified that she was born in 1886 in Milwaukee and was 26 years of age. She first saw Johnson in April 1909 (when she was 22) at the Everleigh Club, a Chicago sporting house where she was an "inmate." The Court overruled Bachrach's objections that information prior to the passage of the Mann Act was irrelevant. Bachrach said the defense was admitting that the relations between Johnson and Schreiber were "intimate carnal relations."

Belle Schreiber

Schreiber said she next met Johnson in New York City in May 1909. She received theatre tickets and several notes from him, and money via his manager. "I met him frequently in New York, and had sexual intercourse with him." Johnson paid her expenses. She then went to Boston with Johnson by motor car. A photo of Johnson and Schreiber seated in his automobile, surrounded by other persons, was admitted into evidence. Schreiber testified, "In my travels with the defendant I went under the name of Mrs. Jack Johnson, and registered at hotels under that name when

I lived with him." They next went to Providence, then New York again, and then to Chicago via train. For a while, she stayed with his manager, Mr. Little, at 22nd and State Street. "I met the defendant frequently; I lived with him as his wife." She next went to Cedar Lake with Johnson and lived with him there for a few weeks. Jack started training for the Kaufman fight.

Johnson then went to San Francisco, and took with him a woman named Hattie. Throughout the trial, Bachrach's objections to evidence regarding Hattie as being irrelevant and prejudicial were overruled. Johnson told Schreiber that he would send for her once he got located, which he did. "I received a telegram telling me to come to the ticket office, and to get a ticket and expense money and come out to San Francisco." She went to the ticket office and got the ticket and money that was waiting there for her. She arrived in nearby Oakland in about September 1909 and stayed there. At that time, she went by the name of "Mrs. Belle Leslie." Johnson met her there. At that time, Johnson was living with Hattie. However, "My intimate relations with the defendant continued during this time in Oakland."

After the September 9, 1909 Kaufman fight, Johnson took Schreiber to the Seal Rock Hotel in San Francisco. Johnson paid for her expenses. He kept introducing her as "Mrs. Jack Johnson." She lived with Jack at the Seal Rock hotel until after the Ketchel fight in mid-October 1909. Next, they traveled to Chicago, along with Hattie, George Little and his wife, and trainers. She said she saw Hattie with Johnson in New York as well.

When they arrived in Chicago, Schreiber lived on Indiana Avenue with a family. Johnson lived on Dearborn Street between 22nd and 23rd with Hattie. Nevertheless, Belle still saw Johnson frequently.

After Johnson went to Indianapolis in November 1909, he sent Schreiber money to follow him there. She used the name "Mrs. J. A. Gilbert." Little and Johnson both paid for her room, splitting the cost. She continued the same relations with Johnson there as at other places.

They went to Pittsburg for Thanksgiving. While there, she went by the name "Mrs. Jack Johnson." Then they traveled to New York.

Jack next went to Philadelphia, bringing Hattie with him, and subsequently sent Schreiber the money to purchase a ticket to Philadelphia. The same relations were maintained there. However, "This girl Hattie was living with him as his wife, and a girl by the name of Duryea, Etta Duryea." She claimed that Johnson introduced her to Duryea while all three were on the telephone line. Belle next left for Chicago and then home to Milwaukee.

Schreiber remained in Milwaukee until late January or early February 1910. However, at one point while she was there, she took a day trip to Chicago with her sister and saw Johnson, who told her to stay at home until he sent for her. When Parkin asked whether Johnson told her why he wanted her to stay home, Schreiber answered, "I was pregnant at the time." She told Johnson, who wanted her to have the baby. "He asked me to have this child and not to do anything to get rid of it."

Sometime during February 1910, Schreiber went to Cleveland, then Pittsburg, and then Detroit, where she saw Johnson. He bought her a ticket and sent her to Chicago, telling her to wait for him until he arrived. She went to Chicago with her sister. While Jack was in Milwaukee, he sent her money to come up there. Jack gave her money to pay the hotel bills.

Schreiber then returned to Chicago for a few weeks, before going to Pittsburg and residing at the Paynter home, which was a sporting house. She was an inmate there for several months.

A month after the Jeffries fight, in early August 1910, she received a letter from Johnson, along with money, asking her to come to Atlantic City. She went and stayed with him there for two days at Young's Hotel. While there, she used the name Mrs. J. A. Gilbert. Her relations with Johnson were similar to those described at other places.

Before leaving Atlantic City, Schreiber alleged that Johnson told her to come to Chicago and look for an apartment; for "he said if I was sporting I might as well make the money for myself as to make it for others. He gave me the money to come to Chicago. I came." Johnson paid for her ticket from Atlantic City to Chicago. She was not able to find an apartment at that time. Johnson subsequently joined her in Chicago, and they maintained relations, just as they had at other locations.

Then Belle went to Cleveland, where she saw Johnson again. Mervin, the chauffeur, came and got her and took her to the theatre. She stayed there for a week. Again they had relations.

Johnson took her to the train station, gave her money and told her to purchase a train ticket and go to Detroit and meet him there, which she did. He arrived the next day. They were not living together at that point, but they maintained relations.

The next trip was to Buffalo. He went first, but gave her the expense money to follow him, telling her to meet him there. They had relations there every day. At Cleveland, Detroit, and Buffalo, his immediate party included Sig Hart and Hart's wife. She did not see Etta at those places.

In early September 1910, again Johnson "gave me my money, and told me to get a ticket and meet him in Toronto." She did. Etta Duryea was with him at that time. Still, the same relations were maintained with Johnson in Toronto. Next stop was Montreal, and again he gave her money for the train ticket, and again they maintained relations. Etta was still with him. Johnson gave Belle money for a ticket to Boston, the next stop, which was still during September 1910. She said their same relations were maintained there. During her testimony, Schreiber often would use hotel bills provided to her to refresh her recollection of the dates. She had kept the bills.

Johnson gave Schreiber money to go to Pittsburg. That time, he purchased the ticket and gave it to her. She returned to the Paynter sisters' house. "Defendant knew where I was going, and what I was going to do when I got there. The Paynter house is the same house of prostitution that was testified to yesterday. I stayed there about two weeks. I was asked to leave the house." A man had come to the house and talked with Miss Paynter, and thereafter she was told to leave.

Belle went to the home of her maid, Julia Allen, and stayed nearly a week. "While there I received a telegram – I received several; I received money while I was there, $75. After I received the $75 I purchased my ticket and came on to Chicago."

At this point, Ben Bachrach made several objections, and outside the presence of the jury, argued in part that the White Slave Traffic Act was unconstitutional, for the power to regulate vice and immorality was within the exclusive power of the state, and hence the act violated the 10th amendment of the U.S. Constitution, and that under the commerce clause, Congress could regulate interstate commerce, yet the acts forbidden by the Act were personal and not commercial, and that transporting a woman from one state to another for the purpose of having sexual intercourse with her was not within the spirit of the Act. He also made jurisdictional challenges. Judge Carpenter overruled all of the objections.

Parkin resumed his direct examination. Schreiber said, "I received the $75 from the Postal Telegraph Company in Pittsburgh, on the 17th of October, 1910, while I was still staying with Julia Allen. I left that same day for Chicago. I got my ticket with that money that I got." When she arrived in Chicago, as per Johnson's directions, she went to a private family's rooming-house on Indiana Avenue. After arriving, Johnson telephoned her there and asked her to meet him at the Vendome Hotel, which she did. "I went to a room with him." Johnson asked her, "Did you receive the $75 I sent you?" She responded, "Yes."

Johnson spoke to her about looking for an apartment. He had to go away in a few days to New York. He said he would help her obtain furniture. "He said to me, to get my furniture and open a flat, and I might as well make the money as to give up half of what I was making to some one else, and for me to keep a couple of girls…and make money in that way." The next day, she met Jack again, and he gave her between $100 and $150 and told her that it was to pay her rent and expenses. She went out and got a flat at the Ridgewood apartment building. She then went to purchase furniture, but did not recall whether Johnson was with her. She paid for it with Johnson's check. After one month, Johnson gave her more money to pay the remainder owed for the furniture. Schreiber got a sporting girl to live with her.

Johnson came to the flat some time after she opened up. Belle remained in the sporting house from October 1910 through February 1911. "Defendant called upon me there from time to time, between the first of November and the first of March. My relations with him were the same as I have detailed in other cities."

Schreiber also claimed that she went from Chicago to Milwaukee with Johnson for Christmas in December 1910, arriving via auto, and returning with him, traveling back and forth every day via train.

After his marriage to Etta Duryea in early 1911, Johnson told Schreiber that he would send for her.

When Parkin asked whether she ever gave Johnson any money, Schreiber replied, "I gave the defendant some money that I made once, $20, - that was in Chicago."

Admitted into evidence was a photograph of Johnson with writing at the bottom in Johnson's handwriting saying, "To My Little Sweetheart, Bell, from Papa Jack, with best wishes." This concluded the direct examination.

Ben Bachrach cross-examined Schreiber. Belle said she lived in Milwaukee until she was 20 years old, and while there was a stenographer and typewriter. She then came to Chicago and became a regular sporting woman at the Everleigh Club, from December 1907 to April 1909. She first met Johnson while she was an inmate there. George Little was with him. She met up with Johnson a few days afterwards. "I received gifts from him in the way of theatre tickets and money." She saw him next in New York City, though Johnson had nothing to do with her going there on that occasion. "I practiced the profession of prostitution there." She and Johnson met up while there and became quite friendly.

Bachrach asked Belle about the photograph introduced into evidence, reading the inscription.

Q. Were you his little sweetheart? A. I suppose I was. Q. Were you in love with him? A. I don't know. Q. What? A. I don't know. Q. Don't you know now – did you think you were then? A. I don't know what love is. Q. The favors that you extended to him, were they extended simply for money? A. I don't know. Q. What? A. I don't know. Q. You cannot say now whether you were in love with the defendant, or not? A. No. Q. At this time? A. I don't believe I ever was in love. The Court: No. the question is, did you give yourself up to the defendant out of affection or for compensation. A. Compensation mostly.

Schreiber said Johnson gave her clothes, jewelry, and diamonds, and paid for her expenses during the many trips. Each time they went to a new city, he gave her some money. "I always received money from him when I asked him for it." It paid for all of her expenses, and "gave me a little over to have in my pocket." She had no explanation for why she had saved all of the hotel bills, and denied that her intent was to get out of him all the money she could. She usually showed Johnson the bill so he could see what expenses she incurred, and to ensure that he would believe her.

Belle went to Pittsburg in March 1910, to the Paynter's house of prostitution. She had not seen Johnson since January, owing to the fact that "the defendant and I were not on good terms between January and February at that time." Hence, going to the Paynter's home was her own decision and not influenced by Johnson. She went there to make money.

In early August 1910, Schreiber went to Atlantic City, and about the 15th of that month, Johnson's chauffeur Mervin came and got her. She had telephoned the theatre where Johnson was performing, informed them that she was in town, and gave the name of the hotel.

When she had been in a sporting house in Detroit in 1909, Mr. Little saw her there, and reported to Johnson, who came and got her out. Her treatment there had not been bad; it was just as good there as at any other location. However, Johnson gave her money to leave and come to Chicago. She had stayed at several houses of prostitution in several different cities, some for a short while, some longer.

After the July 1910 Jeffries fight, she sent Johnson a telegram congratulating him. She did not hear from him until she was in Atlantic City in August 1910 and had reached out to him. It had been six or seven months since she and Johnson had been in contact.

Schreiber said she occasionally contacted Johnson and requested money when she either was put out or refused admission into a house of prostitution, or was out of funds. She was put out of the Paynter house in Pittsburg in mid-October 1910. She attempted to contact Johnson in New York. She spoke with his chauffeur. "I told him that I was put out of this place; that I did not know where to go and that I needed some money, and he said he would talk to the defendant and wire me the next day, which he did. ... I got a telegram the next day, asking me what my expenses would be." She later testified that the wire was signed, "Jack." She did not recall the exact amount she gave in her reply. "I received a wire saying that he was sending me $75, for me to go to Chicago and stay at Graham's and wait for him until he came back. I have not got that telegram now."

She had kept all of Johnson's telegrams until January 1912, when she destroyed them. So, despite the fact that she had kept all of the hotel bills, she had not kept Johnson's alleged telegram at issue in the case. When Bachrach asked whether she had destroyed the telegrams at an earlier point in time, right after she heard that Jack had married Etta, Belle denied doing so then. Bachrach was trying to show that she was jealous. Belle said,

> I don't know when he was married to her, whether in January 1911, or not. I heard of it; Johnson avoided talking to me about it. He never talked to me about it. I heard it from his mother; she told me around Christmas time of 1910, -- either that he was going to be or was married, - I don't remember.

Continuing her testimony, Schreiber said,

> The place at Graham's is that of a private family on Indiana Avenue. I had been there before. ... When I was put out of that place in Pittsburgh, I asked the defendant for money to help me get away because I didn't have any more friends. I lost all my friends, and he was the only one I could turn to. I suppose I regarded him as my friend, too. I thought it was due for him to see me through my trouble. Q. And did you love him then? A. I told you I did not know what love was.

Schreiber rated all of the hotels where she had stayed in various cities. Some were better than others, and some were the best in the city, but she was perfectly satisfied with the accommodations at all of them. She was never forced to go anywhere. She was asked, and she willingly accepted.

Again discussing the telegram sent to her while she was in Pittsburg, Schreiber claimed that it said, "I am sending you $75; go to Chicago at Graham's, and wait until I get there," signed "Jack." She picked up the money from the Postal Telegraph Company, took a train to Chicago, and went to Graham's, arriving on October 18. Three or four days later, Jack called her on the telephone, and then she saw him at the Vendome Hotel.

Belle denied having asked Johnson to fit up her apartment so that she could have a home for her mother and sister. Her mother always had a home in Milwaukee. However, she admitted that she mentioned to Johnson that her sister was in the family way and had to be taken care of, and wanted her sister to come live with her. She claimed that she told that to Johnson after he told her that he wanted to get an apartment for her. Her mother came to visit, but did not live there. Her sister lived there while Belle was practicing prostitution there.

Schreiber testified that she had been in sporting houses in Chicago, New York, Pittsburg, Washington, and Detroit.

The first time she spoke with a government agent about Johnson was in Washington, in November 1912, at the time of the grand jury investigation. "I spoke to Mr. Horne, Chief of the Bureau of Investigation at the Department of Justice at that building in Washington." Since then, she had been earning money doing stenography work for a new reform association in connection with the Department of Justice in Baltimore. The Department of Justice was in charge of it. She was paid $15 a week, and the government paid her board at a rooming house, which was $5 a week. Government agents were watching and accompanying her everywhere.

She did not recall telling Horne about her claim that Johnson told her that she should get an apartment and he would fit it up, that as long as she was in the sporting business, she could make money for herself. "Q. Isn't it a fact that you did not tell it before the Grand Jury? A. I don't know." (The suggestion was that she had never before made such a claim.)

The only ones with whom she had discussed her testimony were DeWoody and Parkin. She had gone over her testimony two or three times with them. DeWoody told her to refer to Johnson as the defendant.

After Etta Duryea died on September 14, 1912, Schreiber sent Johnson a telegram saying, "Dear Jack, - Bernice King and I sympathize with you in your recent bereavement. Sincerely, Belle Allen."

On re-direct, Schreiber testified that the jewelry and diamonds which Johnson gave her were taken away from her by him, and then the next girl, Etta Duryea, was wearing them. She testified that Hattie had the same jewelry before she did. So the jewels were passed from one woman to another and then to another. She said the money Johnson gave her was enough to pay expenses, but no more.

Schreiber claimed that she practiced prostitution in Chicago from the time she got the Ridgewood apartment.

On re-cross, Schreiber stated that at the time she started the Chicago flat, Johnson gave her money besides paying for the furniture, about $100 or $150. When she left with unpaid bills, Johnson later told her that he had paid them for her. She gave some furniture to her mother, sold the rest, and kept the money.

Some newspapers said that it appeared that Schreiber was Johnson's girlfriend or common-law wife more than anything, and that he took care of her, starting well before the Mann Act's passage into law, but continuing thereafter as well.

Not reported in the official record, one newspaper claimed that Parkin asked her, "Did you have any discussion about coming here?" Schreiber responded, "No discussion. He beat me up so bad that..." An objection was interposed and the Court adjourned.

At that time, Judge Carpenter refused to allow the government to try to prove that Johnson beat Schreiber or other women, for such facts were irrelevant to the charge, even assuming they were true.

The next day, Julia Allen, colored, from Pittsburgh, testified that she had known Belle Schreiber since Thanksgiving 1909. Belle was known then as Mrs. Jack Johnson. That was how she was introduced. People called her Johnson's wife. Belle was in Pittsburg with the champ. In August 1910, Belle received money via telegram and then left for Atlantic City.

In October 1910, Belle was living with Allen at Allen's house. Allen had been Belle's maid. After a telegram came, they went down to the Postal Telegraph and Belle received $75. Allen went with Belle to Frank Sutton's hotel and had supper, and then Belle bought a ticket for Chicago and left.

Hattie Watson testified next. She first met Johnson in New York City in August 1907, after he had fought Fitzsimmons. At the time she met him, she was living in a "Call House," going out on sporting calls. The Court sustained Ben Bachrach's objections to further testimony from the witness, feeling that in light of the relations between Schreiber and Johnson and the admissions made already, it was not necessary to go into a state of affairs involving another woman. Regardless, the point was made. The woman named Hattie, whom Johnson for several years had been calling his wife, was a prostitute, like Schreiber. Both women had several aliases.

James Stillwell, attorney for the Pennsylvania Railroad company, testified that the rail company had routes between Pittsburg and Chicago during October 1910.

The government rested its case. At that point, Bachrach moved for a judgment of acquittal as a matter of law. He particularly asked that the counts for which no evidence at all was introduced be dismissed. At that point, the government agreed in part and asked for a withdrawal of counts 6 and 11, which charged that the purpose of Johnson's transportation of Schreiber was to commit the crime against nature. The Court granted the motion as to these counts. Bachrach again attacked the Act's constitutionality, as he had done before.

Regarding the lack of evidence in the case, Bachrach noted that no evidence had been introduced substantiating Schreiber's claim that Johnson had sent or asked someone to send on his behalf the purported telegram to Schreiber telling her to come to Chicago, or that the telegram said what she claimed it did. Furthermore, even assuming he had sent such a telegram, there was no evidence showing that his purpose at the time was for prostitution, debauchery, or some other immoral purpose. Further, even assuming that once she arrived in Chicago, he told her to make money in the business of prostitution, that was consistent with the theory that such thought and purpose occurred to Johnson *after* she arrived, not at the time the money was sent to her, which was required by the statute to show that such was his purpose when he assisted her in making interstate travels. The evidence was purely circumstantial, and the rule was that the circumstances proven must exclude the theory of innocence and not simply be consistent with guilt. The Court overruled the motions.

The defense called witnesses on its behalf. First up was Charles Lumpkin, whom Johnson had employed in 1910 as a chauffeur. On Christmas day, 1910, he drove Johnson, Barney Furey, and Miss Schreiber to Milwaukee. Johnson drank a little brandy, became sick and urinated some blood. Owing to his illness, he did not box at the theatre that day. Schreiber was not around when Johnson was taken to the train station.

Barney Furey testified that he had been Johnson's trainer for eight or nine years. Furey lived at 3344 Wabash Avenue, in Jack's mother Tina Johnson's house. The family lived there – Johnson, his wife, mother, sister, niece, nephew, Joe Levy, the maid, and himself.

In August 1910, Furey was with Johnson on all of his trips East. They left Chicago on August 15 heading for Cleveland, and traveled all over the East. Furey said he had seen Schreiber in Cleveland on the stage with Johnson. He did not recall seeing Belle in Detroit. The woman who traveled with Johnson was Etta Johnson, as he called her, though technically she was not yet his wife. He did see Belle on the stage in Buffalo, speaking to one of the show girls, but that was the only time he saw her there. He either saw her in Toronto or Montreal, on the same stage where Johnson was working. He did not see Belle in Boston. Belle was not in the traveling party; Mrs. Etta Johnson was.

The Johnson party was in Scranton on October 15, 1910, and left for New York on the 16th. They were in seventeen different cities over the next month or so, some for one or two days, some for a week or more, before returning to Chicago.

Back in Chicago, at the Ridgewood, Furey had seen Schreiber, her mother, and sister, and a girl named Lillian.

Furey was in the car with Johnson and "Jack Allen" when they went to Milwaukee in December 1910. On the train ride back, Schreiber was not there.

Mervin Jacobowski testified that Schreiber was not with their party in Milwaukee in December 1910, nor was she on the train ride back.

Charles Bud Redd said Schreiber came to Milwaukee during Christmas 1910 in an auto driven by Lumpkin, and was at his house that week.

Testifying next was Frank Sutton, a Pittsburgh hotel proprietor. In September or October 1910, Belle Schreiber came to his hotel seeking information regarding where Johnson was. "I says I don't know where he is at, he is somewhere with his show, and I says if you telephone to Barrett Wilkins on 35th Street, New York City, probably he can let you know just where the show is at." Schreiber got the telephone number. She called but they did not know where he was. She came back the next day and telephoned again. "I heard her say something about money and she said she was in trouble and she needed a favor of him."

A few days later, she came back and had a check in the name of Jack Allen. She couldn't get it cashed under that name, so he cashed it for her. It was $70 or $75. A colored lady by the name of Allen was with her, as well as Belle's sister and her sister's husband.

They had dinner, and after Belle finished eating, "she bid me good-bye, and she said her sister and her husband were going to Chicago and she was going to Washington City."

James Morrison, a theatrical man, said that during October 1910 he was in New York, and on October 17, he saw Johnson, who was there for several days.

Peter M. Doyle, an actor, said that on October 17, 1910, he was with Morrison in New York.

John A. Johnson, also known as Jack Johnson, decided to waive his 5th amendment rights and testified on his own behalf. He was 35 years old. He said that between October 1 and October 20, 1910, he was not in Chicago. "I did not receive any communication from any person about Belle Schreiber in October. The last part of September I received a telegram from her." He spoke with her via long distance telephone either on the 2nd or 3rd of October. "She asked me if I would send her $75, that she was sick and needed it, and I told her I would." He said that a couple days later, he sent her money via telegram, but not a written message.

> Only a money order. Q. Only an order for money? A. That is all. Q. Did you in the month of October or September…send a telegram to Belle Schreiber in Pittsburgh instructing her to go to Chicago at Graham's and wait for you there? A. I don't think I did. The Court: What is the answer? A. I don't think I did. Q. Well, do you know? A. I am not positive. Q. Have you any doubt about it? A. Well, I might have sent her one. Q. You might have what? A. I might have sent her one telling her that, but I don't remember doing so, and my reasons for that are that other fellows attended to all my business. … Q. What do you mean by that, you personally did not send one but somebody else might have? A. Yes, sir, that is it. Q. I am asking you, did you send one yourself? A. No, I did not. Q. Did you give any one authority to send it? A. I did not. Q. Did you instruct any person to

send a telegram of that kind? A. I did not. The Court: Do you know of any one at that time sending a telegram to that effect? A. I do not, sir. ... Q. When was the first time you ever heard of such a telegram being sent, if there was one sent? A. When I was sitting in the chair. Q. And when Belle Schreiber said it on the witness stand? A. Yes, sir.

Johnson said he was in Atlantic City in August 1910, but,

I did not, while in Atlantic City, tell Belle Schreiber that, inasmuch as she was engaged in the sporting business, it would be better for her to go into the business for herself, and that she should take an apartment and that I would furnish it for her in order that she might be in the sporting business, or words to that effect. At the time I sent that $75 to Belle Schreiber I sent it from New York, and at the time I sent that $75 I did not intend that Belle Schreiber should go from Pittsburgh to Chicago in order to engage in the business of prostitution. At the time I sent that $75 I did not intend that Belle Schreiber should come to Chicago for the purpose of leading a life of debauchery. At the time I sent that $75 I did not intend that Belle Schreiber should go from Pittsburgh to Chicago in order that I might have sexual intercourse with her. At the time I sent that $75 I had no intention at all as to where Belle Schreiber should go from Pittsburgh, or if she should leave Pittsburgh at all. She didn't say where she was going; she said she was sick. I had no intention on the subject. I did not directly or indirectly, -- by word of mouth or otherwise, give her any direction at the time I sent that money, or shortly before that time, to the effect that she should go to Chicago.

Johnson said the Barney Oldfield race took place about October 25, 1910, and a few days before that race he went to Chicago after Mr. Beerly telephoned him and asked him to come there, because they had a lawsuit pending with George Little regarding a diamond ring.

I did not go there to see Belle Schreiber. After I got to Chicago I met Belle Schreiber at the Vendome, she called me up at my mother's home. When I met her at the Hotel Vendome she told me that her sister was going to be sick, that she was pregnant, and that she wanted a place for her mother and her sister, and she asked me would I furnish a flat for her. I said certainly, I will do anything to make you happy; and she says, 'All right,' and she asked me where to go and I gave her a card of introduction to a furniture man, --- and she went there and got what she wanted, and I gave her the money to pay for it. ... Besides the furniture at that time I gave her $500 to start with, to start a home and keep her mother until she got a position, -- she told me she was going to work at stenography. She had done stenography work for me, lots of it.

Johnson denied several of Schreiber's claims, including her allegation that when they met at the Vendome in Chicago that he told her that since

709

she was sporting she might as well make money for herself with her own flat and that he would furnish it. "I never spoke any such words to her, or any one else. I never gave her any diamonds. I never loaned her any. I never permitted her to wear any. She bought some in Buffalo, but I did not pay for them."

Johnson said he paid some unpaid bills at the Ridgewood for Schreiber before he sailed to Europe on May 6, 1911. "I have not thought over the exact amount of money that I have given to Belle Schreiber since I have known her. As near as I can guess, it would be between nine and ten thousand; that includes all that I spent on her, everything – expenses and everything. She did not give me $20 at any time."

Regarding Christmas 1910, Jack said they made a trip by auto to Milwaukee. He, Lumpkin, Furey, and Belle were in the car. Jack was ill at the time. Schreiber did not return with him. She was not on the train. He later spoke with her. "In explanation, she said she was a little angry because I was coming to Chicago every day and was not paying the proper attention to her." He told her that preparations were being made for his marriage to Etta, which explained his lack of attentiveness to Belle.

Regarding Belle's claims that she was with Johnson on many trips in a drawing-room of a train car, Johnson said, "I never rode with her on a car any time in my life but once on a train, that was in 1909. Q. And since then you have never ridden with her? A. Never in my life." Johnson said he had nothing to do with her selection of the Ridgewood apartment. He went there when she complained that the furniture had been scratched, and saw the furniture dealer there, as well as her mother and sister. "I don't know that I was there at any other time. I think I was there once." He sent the $75 to her from either New York or Pennsylvania, but was not in Chicago at the time.

Of his testimony, a newspaper said that at first, Johnson spoke in a slow voice, and at times hesitatingly. Sweat stood out on his forehead and trickled down his face. After 15 minutes on the stand, his voice grew more distinct and he seemed more at ease. The direct examination lasted a little less than 30 minutes.

Parkin cross-examined Johnson. Jack said he told Belle in Milwaukee that he had become engaged and could not pay any more attention to her because of his approaching marriage. Etta was in the Chicago hospital at the time. Outside the presence of the jury, Parkin suggested that the reason Etta was in the hospital was because Johnson put her there, and he wanted to ask Johnson about it. Over Bachrach's objections, the Court allowed it.

Q. What was the occasion of her being in the hospital? A. She was sick, that is all I know. Q. That is all you know about it? A. That is all I know. Q. What was the cause of her sickness? A. I don't know. Q. As a matter of fact that was a sickness caused by blows from your hands, wasn't it? ... A. No. ... Q. Well, was it caused by blow or blows from your hand? A. No, no. Q. Was it not caused by blows received by Etta Duryea in Pekin Theater here in Chicago at your hands? A. No. Q. Did you not carry her out or have her carried out and put in the automobile and taken to the Washington Park hospital after you had beaten her up? A. No, no, and I will take an oath on it, no.

Johnson said he did not know Schreiber had been running a sporting house at the Ridgewood. He again denied ever taking money from her. He essentially pointed out that such a claim was ridiculous, given that he was making $2,500 a week. He said he did not see Schreiber in Chicago until a couple of weeks after he had sent her the money. He arrived in New York on the 16th. He did not recall exactly when or where he was when he sent the money or spoke with Belle. He again said he did not recall whether or not he sent her a telegram telling her to go to Graham's. He could not say he did not, nor could he say that he did. "I don't remember."

Jack denied having Belle come to Atlantic City, and said he did nothing with her while there. He did not give her any money on that trip either, or pay for her bills. He denied having sexual relations with her while there.

Jack denied knowing the character of the Ridgewood as a sporting house. "Q. And you did not know it was full of fast women? A. I didn't know anything about the fast women. I was not keeping up with them. Q. You were not keeping any of them. You kept Hattie, didn't you?" Objections were sustained.

Several times Johnson denied having as many as three women at a time in his travels. He denied having Hattie, Etta, and Belle with him at the same time. He did not have them traveling with him. Bachrach's objections to this line of questioning were overruled.

Johnson denied ever calling up Belle and introducing her to Etta over the telephone.

Jack said the woman who testified using the name of Hattie Watson was known by him as McClay. "She had three or four names. I called her by the name Mac – McClay. I called her Mac. Her first name is Anna, or something. I knew her by the name of Anna – Anna McClay. I never called her Hattie, never in my life that I know of." (One even has to wonder whether her alias was a comedic sexual stage pun – Mc "Lay.")

Johnson denied seeing Belle in Philadelphia.

Parkin attacked Johnson's relationship with Etta Duryea. "How long prior to the time she got her divorce were you living with her and going around the country with her? A. I don't know, I don't remember." The Court overruled Bachrach's relevancy objections, saying, "This is not a question of the cross-examination of an ordinary witness. The Government is entitled to go into the history of any defendant." Jack said he first met Etta in New York City in 1909. He was not certain of dates or who he was with when. "I have told you I never kept tab of those things. I am here today and gone tomorrow. I never kept any tabs. I was too busy; I had too much to think of."

Johnson said he did not have Belle and Anna "Mac" in San Francisco with him. He did not pay Anna's way out there. Lots of people came to see him. He denied having sexual intercourse with Anna "Mac" on the day of the Kaufman fight. "I did not. After a man has a fight, he is not feeling like it." The Court continued to overrule Bachrach's objections that such questions were totally irrelevant to the issues at hand regarding whether he violated the Mann Act, particularly since the questions pertained to acts prior to its passage.

Johnson denied having Hattie and Belle with him while training for the Ketchel fight in 1909. They may have been in the city, but they were not with him.

Parkin asked about the Ketchel fight:

Q. Did you win the Ketchel fight? A. Did I win it? Q. Yes? A. It is in the book, doesn't the book say so? Q. Just answer my question. Did you win the fight? A. I suppose I did. Somebody might say I did not. Q. You knew you were going to win it before you went into it, didn't you? A. I did. The Court: Now you are going into the question of a man's self confidence. Parkin: No, no, not at all. Bachrach: No, he wants to show that the fight was crooked or something like that. Johnson: They are all crooked.

Eventually, after some debate between Parkin and Bachrach, the Court sustained objections to this line of questioning.

Johnson did admit to bringing Belle and Mac back with him from San Francisco to Chicago. Part of the way, they were in the same drawing-room on the train. At times, they occupied the same state room as well. Of course, that was in 1909, before the Mann Act was passed.

Parkin again asked suggestive questions to Johnson about violence towards the women, and Bachrach's objections were overruled.

Q. Hattie was in the hospital while you were there, was she? A. Not that I know of. Q. Did you have any difficulty with her about putting her in a hospital? A. No. Q. Did you have any similar difficulty with Belle, -- fisticuff difficulty? A. I don't understand the definition of the word. Q. You had had with Belle, hadn't you? A. What is that? Q. You had struck Belle on various occasions? A. Never in my life. Q. Do you remember using an automobile tool on her? A. Never in my life. Q. You never did that? A. Never. Q. You say you did not? A. I say no; emphatically no. Q. And bruised her side until it was black and blue?

The Court finally put an end to this line of questioning, although prior to that point the judge had overruled all of Bachrach's objections.

Jack said Belle did not return from Milwaukee with him on the train in late December 1910. "She never made a trip with me but once in her life on the train." Belle left him in Milwaukee because she said he had not paid her enough attention. He told her that he was going to get married. He did not go to see her after that, but she came to see him.

Q. And you and she were living there together during that time? A. During what? What she? Q. You and Belle? A. What she are you talking about? You have got three shes mixed up. Which one? Q. Were there so many you couldn't tell? A. No sir. But there were three you just named. I want to know which one. Q. I am talking about the Milwaukee trip, did you have any more than one up there? A. I did not. … Q. I say subsequent to the time that you told Belle, and subsequent to the time that you made up your mind to marry Etta, you and Belle were living together at Milwaukee? A. Some of the time. Q. Yes. A. Yes, sure.

Jack said he married Etta Duryea on January 18, 1911 in Pittsburg.

Parkin asked him whether he had other women with him that he traveled with besides Hattie, Belle, and Etta since July 1910. "No." Parkin kept pressing the issue, suggesting there was a girl from New Jersey who was on the train with him in Philadelphia, upon whose finger he placed a diamond ring, took to Pittsburg, then sent back, and then gave the ring to Hattie, or "Anna Mac." Johnson denied the allegations contained in each question. Bachrach's objections to each question were overruled.

On re-direct, Johnson said that prior to being charged, he did not know there was such a thing as the White Slave Traffic Act. Bachrach again asked him whether he had sent a telegram to Schreiber telling her to come to Chicago and stay at Graham's. "I never sent such a telegram in my life. Not in my life. Never in my life. I never sent it. I never have known it was sent."

The Defense rested its case.

The government called rebuttal witnesses. First up was Roy Jones, who formerly had been in the saloon business. He had a conversation on Christmas Eve 1910 with Johnson about Etta Duryea. The Court overruled Bachrach's objections. Jones said, "Mr. Johnson asked me if I would not go out to the hospital with him to call upon his wife. … Well, he told me that his wife was sick, that she had been in a little trouble, and they had a fight or something." Jack told him the fight was at Bob Mott's café. "I guessed there was some misunderstanding between them, and he asked me – he told me that she had always – that she had always had a lot of confidence in me and had known me for quite a little while and he tried to get me to intercede and bring them together again." … "Q. I will ask you if he did not also state that he wanted to go there to see her so that any prosecution by her against him might be stopped? A. Yes, sir."

Jones saw Johnson in Milwaukee during Christmas 1910. He saw Johnson there with Schreiber.

On cross-examination, Jones admitted that he had his saloon license taken away a month ago, but recently had it restored. Bachrach implied that the government got him his license returned after agreeing to testify against Johnson.

The government rested its case.

Bachrach again made his motions for acquittal, which initially were denied, though subsequently, in addition to dismissing the charges of crimes against nature, the Court also dismissed the counts charging that Johnson's purpose in sending Schreiber the money was for travel for the purposes of debauchery.

A night session was held so the attorneys could make their closing arguments to the jury. Unfortunately, those arguments were not recorded by the court reporter. However, the press reported that in his closing argument, U.S. government attorney Harry Parkin said, "If you should find this defendant not guilty, knowing as you do the evidence in the case, I do not see how any of you can go home and look squarely into the faces of those you respect and admire."

Defense attorney Ben Bachrach maintained that the jury was not to consider Johnson's general record and behavior. "If he sent her the money to come to Chicago for immoral purposes he is guilty. That is the only thing to be considered by the jury." The argument was that Johnson sent money because Schreiber asked for it, because she was in need of help, not because he wanted her to come to Chicago for immoral purposes. Bachrach also argued that there was no proof that Johnson had aided or abetted in some way the transportation of one or more women from state to state for his commercial gain through their immorality.

Judge Carpenter then informed the jury that they were to determine whether, on or about October 15, 1910, Johnson caused Schreiber to be transported from Pittsburgh to Chicago for the purpose of prostitution, or for the purpose of having unlawful sexual intercourse with her. He also in part said,

> Gentlemen of the jury, you must realize, and I shall charge you, that a colored man in the courts of this country has equal rights with a white man. He is entitled to the same kind of a trial and the same laws protect him, and you must return the same kind of a verdict in this case as you would render to a man of your own color were he accused as is the defendant. ...
>
> When you get into your jury room and discuss the matter here you will look at these things from a great many different standpoints, but you are entitled to take into consideration that the prosecuting witness in this case is an abandoned woman, she is an unfortunate creature. You might, so far as the evidence in this case is concerned, call her the discarded mistress of the defendant. That you are entitled to take into consideration. You are also entitled to take into consideration the fact that the defendant himself testified. He did not have to testify. The law permits him, and when he does testify his evidence must be given, if you believe it, must be given the same weight that you would give the evidence of any other competent witness; but you not only have a right to take into consideration, but

you must take into consideration that the defendant himself is vitally interested in the outcome of this case, and so you must look at the evidence here from every conceivable standpoint. We have had prostitutes, we have had trainers, we have had hangers-on and we have had all kinds of unfortunate people here, but the mere fact that they are unfortunate does not bar them from testifying, it does not necessarily mean that they have not told the truth, but it is your duty, pleasant or unpleasant, to sift all this evidence through and through to see where the truth lies. ...

The law does not apply solely to innocent girls. It is quite as much an offense against the Mann Act to transport a hardened, lost prostitute as it would be to transport a young girl, a virgin. You are not concerned either with the location of the defendant when the money was sent or telegraphed, if you find from the evidence that he did send or telegraph the money. ... Now, he says that he sent it out of the goodness of his heart. She tells you an entirely different story. Now, it is for you to take all the evidence in this case and to satisfy yourselves beyond all reasonable doubt what the purpose of the defendant was in sending her the $75. The defendant himself admitted that he sent it. He claims that his purpose was good; the Government charges that his purpose was bad. Now, that purpose is one of the essential elements in this case and is something that you will have to settle to your own satisfaction beyond a reasonable doubt. ... You are not concerned with the defendant's morals save only as it may give you some light on his general character; it may give you some information as to what his intention was when he did the things, if he did the things that he is charged with here.

It is not necessary in order to constitute a violation of this law that it be charged that the defendant shall have received some profit out of the woman transported. I mean pecuniary profit. That is not an essential element at all.

But there is one thing that I neglected to state, gentlemen, that the Government has not introduced any evidence under counts 2, 4, 6, and 11 in this case, and I instruct you, therefore, when you take the indictment to your consultation room you are to disregard entirely those four counts, so that your deliberations will be based solely on counts 1, 3, 5, 7, 8, 9, and 10. ...

No evidence has been introduced on the debauchery counts, or on the counts charging the defendant with the crime against nature. The counts remaining are the counts which charge that the woman was transported from Pittsburgh to Chicago for the purpose of prostitution and the counts which charge that she was transported for the purpose of sexual intercourse.

Judge George Carpenter dismissed four of the counts as a matter of law, ruling that the government had presented no evidence of debauchery or crime against nature. Of course, the question is why then did the government put forth charges for which it knew it had no evidence, other than to try to prejudice the jury against Johnson by mere suggestions?

Summarizing the case, the *Freeman* opined that during the trial, Mr. Parkin, realizing his inability to make out a case, resorted to irrelevant matter wholly immaterial to the case at bar, in an attempt to prejudice the jury. Mr. Parkin unsuccessfully tried to show the jury that Johnson at times beat and slugged Schreiber and forced her to do things that otherwise she would not have done.

On May 13, 1913 at 10:45 p.m., the case was given to the jury to decide. After about one hour of deliberations (one said 98 minutes), the jury returned guilty verdicts on all seven counts of violating the federal White Slave Traffic Act, otherwise known as the Mann Act. When the clerk announced the word "guilty," Johnson's smile faded. The cherished hope of his enemies had been realized. A moment after the guilty verdict was read, a force of deputy marshals surrounded Johnson.

For each count, the maximum penalty was five years imprisonment or a $5,000 fine, or both. The *Chicago Defender* opined that it was improbable that he would get away with just a fine.

Johnson's attorney immediately made a motion for a new trial. Judge Carpenter scheduled a hearing for arguments on the motion for May 19.

Judge Carpenter overruled Parkin's motion that Johnson immediately be ordered confined in the county jail. Johnson would be allowed out on bond until he was sentenced.

Afterwards, Johnson said, "I have nothing to say. My attorney will speak for me." Bachrach said, "I can't account for the verdict. The case was a hard one but I was confident of an acquittal." Later, Johnson said, "I have fought a good fight but I lost." He also said, "I made a game fight and I lost but I am satisfied."[813]

Afterwards, gloating Assistant U.S. District Attorney Harry Parkin said,

> This verdict will go around the world. It is a forerunner of laws to be passed throughout the entire country forbidding miscegenation. Many persons believe the negro has been persecuted. Perhaps as an individual he was, but his misfortune will be a foremost example of the evil in permitting intermarriage between whites and blacks. He must bear the consequences.[814]

The *Freeman's* Billy Lewis said that Parkin's comments proved that Johnson had been struck below the belt. It was obvious that Johnson was

---

[813] *Chicago Defender*, May 10, 17, 1913; *Freeman*, May 10, 17, 24, June 7, 1913; *Daily Capital Journal*, May 8, 1913. *San Francisco Call*, May 9, 1913. *El Paso Herald*, May 9, 1913. *Day Book*, May 10-12, 1913.
[814] *East Oregonian*, May 14, 1913.

not being prosecuted for being good to Belle Schreiber, but persecuted for marrying his white wives.

Perhaps this is the first time in the history of the country where a federal court officer has given it out that a prosecution was not based on the charges preferred; that a race prejudice was the underlying motive of the prosecution; that it was in the interest of the race division. All of this is appalling in view of the source from which it came. Judge Carpenter completed this iron bed of Pisistratus, when he said that the "character of the prosecuting witness must not be considered." Says he further: "The fact that the prosecuting witness is a discarded mistress, an abandoned woman, does not affect the issue in this case."

And then this far fetched assertion: "We have had many unfortunate people here in this case – trainers, fighting camp hangerson and women of the underworld – but because of their status in life their evidence must not be disregarded."

Lewis said that he was sure that if other cases were cited, where men had been convicted and sentenced to prison,

I am quite sure not a single one will be anything similar to the Belle Schreiber affair. Here was a woman living with a man as her husband. She was carried about the country and introduced as Johnson's wife, at least. It was so understood. He sends her money, oodles of money, more money than most Negroes have ever seen, and she is worked within the meaning of the law. I am basing my judgment on Mr. Mann's sound sense, that his law was conceived to correct a well-known abuse, that of deceiving innocent, unsuspecting women into houses of disrepute, or decoying them to assignations of which they were not aware, and not to interrupt the movements of seasoned women of the world, when moving about with a full knowledge of what they are doing.

However, the judge also had said, "It is as much an offense under the Mann act to transport a hardened woman as an innocent girl. It is not necessary that a person accused of violating the act shall receive a profit through transportation of a woman."

Johnson's attorney rightfully contended that an individual's right to travel from place to place could not be denied. Johnson said that he did not invite Schreiber to Chicago, and especially did not state for the purpose named. If Johnson asked her to come to Chicago without stating a purpose, he clearly had that right. "He might send and invite the Queen of Sheba, and if she don't want to come, let her stay at home. Johnson beat the case to a frazzle, it is very evident to see. ... It is to be hoped that the government will not be put in the unenviable light of persecuting a race."[815]

On May 16 in Springfield, Illinois, the proposed Illinois state anti-interracial marriage bill was killed in committee.[816]

As of May 18, Johnson said he was broke and needed money, and wanted to fight Luther McCarty. He asked the court to defer his sentencing for 60 days, and for permission to leave the district so that he could fight. The Court denied his motion.[817]

On May 20, 1913 in Colma, California, Gunboat Smith won a 20-round decision over Jess Willard.

On May 24, 1913 at Tommy Burns' arena located just outside the city limits of Calgary, Alberta, Canada, after 2 minutes of fighting in the 1st round, 210-pound Arthur Pelkey knocked out 200-pound white heavyweight champion Luther McCarty with a clean left hook to the jaw. Referee Ed Smith counted him out. McCarty did not wake up, and was pronounced dead at the scene.

Some said it was a dislocated neck. A blood clot was found on McCarty's brain. His spinal cord was ruptured and there was a hemorrhage.

The next day, Tommy Burns' arena was burned down, likely by arson. The incident would end boxing in western Canada for a while. Burns had promoted bouts there for one year, successfully up to that point.

Luther McCarty was born March 17, 1892, and was only 21 years old. His father was an Indian "half breed" and his mother Irish. He stood a trifle over 6'3".

It was a shocker and major upset in every way, for McCarty was considered the world's best white heavyweight and boxing's hottest rising contender, with several quality victories under his belt. Now he was gone. Arthur Pelkey was a 6-footer with a record that contained no prior big-name victories, and a 1912 10-round no-decision loss to Jess Willard and an early 1913 LKOby2 to Jim Coffey. He had though, managed to deck Tommy Burns with a left hook in their 1913 6-round no-decision draw. Still, McCarty had defeated a much higher caliber of opponents, on a consistent basis, and never before had been stopped. Sometimes flukes happen in boxing. Some speculated that McCarty had died from a previous injury that was aggravated.

On June 1, 1913 in Belgium, Georges Carpentier, the French light heavyweight, won the European heavyweight championship by knocking out Bombardier Billy Wells in the 4th round as a result of powerful body blows. Georges had been decked twice by the hard-punching Wells and

[815] *Freeman*, May 24, 1913.
[816] *Freeman*, May 10, 1913; *Chicago Defender*, May 17, 1913. In the meantime, California was reconsidering the Brown anti-prize fight bill in the Senate.
[817] *Grey River Argus*, May 29, 1913.

took 9-counts in the 1st and 2nd rounds, but showed his resilience by coming back to win by knockout.[818]

On Wednesday June 4, 1913, after his motion for a new trial was denied, Jack Johnson was sentenced. When imposing sentence, Judge Carpenter said,

> It has been hard to determine what punishment should be meted out in this case. We have had many cases where violations of the Mann act have been punished with a fine only. We have had other cases where defendants have been sentenced to one or two years in the penitentiary. The circumstances in this case have been aggravating. The life of the defendant, by his own admissions, has not been at all a moral one. The defendant is one of the best known men of his race, and his example has been far reaching. The court is bound to take these facts into consideration in determining the sentence to be imposed. In this case the defendant shall be confined one year and one day in the Leavenworth penitentiary and that he shall pay a fine of $1,000.

Well known for his racial bigotry, U.S. Attorney General James C. McReynolds, whom U.S. President Woodrow Wilson had appointed earlier that year, had sent a telegram to James Wilkerson informing him that the Leavenworth penitentiary was designated as the place of confinement for Johnson. "This is special designation in this case only and does not affect generally existing designation Joliet institution for United States prisoners convicted [in] your district. Please have order court entered accordingly. McReynolds." Judge Carpenter had honored the request and ordered Johnson confined in Leavenworth instead of the usual Joliet penitentiary. The following year, McReynolds would be appointed to and confirmed as a U.S. Supreme Court Justice.

Ben Bachrach and Gustav Beerly were granted time to prepare a writ of error for an appeal. Johnson was allowed out on his liberty upon bond, pending his appeal's disposition.

Afterwards, Bachrach said he intended to base his writ of error upon several arguments: the unprecedented point that the jury had been prejudiced by the government's opening statement; the constitutional arguments made throughout the trial; the insufficiency of evidence; and the fact that the government had entered prejudicial and irrelevant evidence.

Many whites and those in the government thought the sentence was too light. Most blacks thought the sentence was way too harsh.[819]

The *Freeman* said the truth about the trial was that the evidence did not support the allegations. Billy Lewis said most colored folk could see nothing but color prejudice in the whole business, and with reason. The prosecuting attorney said as much, which sounded very bad coming from a government

---

[818] *Freeman*, June 7, 14, 1913.
[819] *Chicago Defender*, June 7, 1913. *San Francisco Call*, June 5, 1913.

official. "There are times when it does not pay to tell the truth. No; an individual can not doff his prejudices any more than a leopard can lose his spots, yet there is such a thing as sacrificing sentiment, prejudice in the interest of the general good."

Still, even the most liberal-minded blacks had thought all along that Johnson was a bit "too fresh" for his own good. No other champion had attracted so much attention to himself. Of course, some of that attention was owing to the fact that he was a *black* heavyweight champion.

Johnson's business had been taken away, he had been prohibited from boxing, thousands of dollars had been taken from him in bonds and defending court proceedings, and lost opportunities cost him many thousands more.

The *Freeman* felt that the iron had entered the judge's soul, for Johnson just should have been fined. Not only was the case not an aggravated one as the judge claimed, it was not a case at all. Furthermore, not a single case wherein a prison sentence was ordered paralleled Johnson's case at all. Schreiber was provided money to defray her expenses. Johnson lived with her. She was his girlfriend, and yet the argument was that he could not legally pay her expenses, which was ridiculous. The act was passed and conceived with the interest of protecting innocent people and to prohibit trafficking in immoral business. "Technically, the Schreiber woman falls under the classification because the inference is that she was transported for an immoral purpose. One can see how far reaching such an interpretation would be if it were generally applied." The case was a reach in terms of what the law was intended to prohibit. She was his common law wife, or a lover engaged, and as such had a right to receive money from her husband or boyfriend.

The judge viewed Johnson as a race leader, and as such treated him more harshly in order to send a message to blacks generally. The judge explicitly considered race in his sentencing, something which today would be illegal, improper, and grounds for reversal. Johnson might have been an immoral man, but again, Billy Lewis opined that such had no relevance to a proper legal sentencing consideration.[820]

On June 23, 1913, Benjamin C. Bachrach and Gustav Beerly, of 1320 Westminster Building, Chicago, filed Jack Johnson's appeal of the verdict. The appeal alleged that the verdict was not supported by the evidence; that District Attorney Harry A. Parkin made improper highly prejudicial remarks in his opening statement (including stating that Johnson beat women; that he kept three women at the same time, that when the three women he had with him had differences between them, he would drop one off and put her into a sporting house temporarily to relieve himself of the necessity of spending money carrying her about the country while he had the others; and alleging that Johnson committed crimes against nature even though the

---

[820] *Freeman*, June 14, 1913.

government had no evidence of such); that the court erred in admitting improper evidence, allowing irrelevant, immaterial questions not germane to the specific charges at hand regarding the transport of Belle Schreiber (including questions about Hattie McClay and Etta Duryea; questions about Johnson's violence towards women; and incidents that preceded the passage of the Mann Act), all designed to prejudice the jury; and that the Mann Act was unconstitutional because under the 10th Amendment, the power to regulate vice and immorality was a state function, not federal; and also that that Act was an unconstitutionally overbroad use of Congressional power under the Commerce Clause, for transportation of a woman for sexual purposes has nothing to do with commerce, because it isn't commercial; and that the court lacked jurisdiction because Johnson was not in Illinois when he sent Schreiber the money.

U.S. Attorney James H. Wilkerson and Special Assistant U.S. Attorney Harry A. Parkin represented the U.S. in the appellate process.

The *Defender* said there was a general difference of opinion as to Johnson's guilt or innocence. He was released on a $15,000 bond posted by Tiny Johnson and Matthew S. Baldwin, pending the hearing and disposition of his appeal (then set for November) by the U.S. Circuit Court of Appeals for the Seventh Circuit.[821]

---

[821] *Chicago Defender*, July 5, 1913.

CHAPTER 17

Escape and Exile

Twenty days after being sentenced, the day after his appeal was filed, on the evening of June 24, 1913; Jack Johnson left Chicago and escaped to Canada. He took a train to Canada disguised as a member of the Negro Giants baseball team. On Wednesday June 25, he and his wife Lucille reached Toronto via the Canadian Pacific railroad. They met Tom Flanagan, his manager, and then departed for Montreal. They intended to sail to Europe the following week.

Flanagan said, "Jack has forfeited his bond and is going to Paris. He has no intention of going back to Chicago, where he is positive he will have to serve out his sentence."

At Johnson's home, it was said he was on a fishing trip in Cedar Lake, Indiana. In fact, Johnson had been selling off his belongings, and even had shipped a couple of his automobiles so he would not have to come back.[822]

On June 26, Jack and Lucille arrived in Montreal. They already were booked to sail for Havre, France on the Alian steamer *Corinthian* the following week. Jack said, "I intend going direct to St. Petersburg, where I have a contract to fight Sam Langford and Gunboat Smith. These fights will be pulled off some time in September." He also said he did not intend to forfeit his bail bond, which called for his presence in the U.S. in November. Apparently, he was facing trial on additional Mann Act allegations.

Although Johnson said he intended to return to Chicago after fighting abroad, government agents believed he had left for good. Department of Justice Superintendent Charles F. DeWoody raised an outcry and urged the Canadian police to arrest and deport Johnson as an undesirable citizen, given his conviction. He said Johnson would serve his sentence at the federal penitentiary at Fort Leavenworth, Kansas. Still, the U.S. appellate court's decision on Johnson's case was not yet final. DeWoody said,

> There is a paragraph in the laws…which says the police have the right to turn back into this country any person whom they may deem objectionable. If that provision can be enforced and Johnson does not leave Montreal before we get the Canadian authorities to act he will be brought back and kept under surveillance until his appeal is disposed of.

However, Johnson's deportation was unlikely, for he showed that in Chicago he had purchased a through ticket to Havre, France via Montreal. Under such conditions, under the Dominion law, he could not be deported.

---

[822] *Rock Island Argus*, June 27, 1913.

By this strategy, Johnson tied the hands of the immigration authorities. They were powerless to act further than to see to it that he left the country on the ship upon which he was booked to sail.

Johnson's sudden maneuver was no surprise to his friends. He boasted for several days that he was about to slip one over on the government.

Tom Clark, a saloon proprietor, said both Johnson and his white valet Joe Levy had discussed their plans with a crowd of blacks for more than an hour before their departure. Johnson first went to a fishing resort in Wisconsin, and there donned some old clothes. He boarded a train containing members of the American Giants, a colored ball team going to Detroit, and he escaped notice. From Detroit he went to Toronto, and then Montreal; his wife and Joe Levy following. Once in Montreal, he telegraphed his friends in the U.S.

If Johnson remained abroad, the government would be enriched when it forfeited his bond. DeWoody said Johnson was in desperate straits financially. Bachrach said the bond could not be forfeited until after the court's decision on his appeal, probably the following April.

On June 29, 1913 at 3 a.m., Johnson and his wife left Canada for Havre on the Alian line steamer *Corinthian*. They boarded in the presence of Canadian immigration officers. Johnson reiterated that he had no intention of forfeiting his bond. He said he would be in Chicago when his appeal was argued in November. He took with him two automobiles, a limousine, and a high-powered touring car.[823]

The *Defender* opined that Johnson had been crucified and persecuted for being a Negro; one who whipped Jeffries. It did not believe it was anyone's business if he chose a woman of a different color for his companion, or if he married her. Johnson had done no different than any other big sport.

The *Defender* noted how governments had prevented the moving picture exhibitions of Johnson's victory over Jeffries. The federal government then prohibited interstate transportation of fight films altogether, in order to severely limit the exhibition of Johnson's victories, for such exhibitions "would make the white children grow up with certain fear or dread of the colored boy. It is the negro boy that would have to fear the white boy." They failed to beat him in the ring, so they had to discredit him, hide his victories, and prevent him from fighting.

To marry whom he pleased was a right guaranteed by the Illinois statutes and the laws of a number of Northern states. The country for centuries had mulattoes – black children with white fathers who did not recognize their own offspring, yet it was a crime against nature for a black man to marry a white woman by her own consent. Also, Jack lived in a mansion and had a $10,000 auto. "They don't like that, of course."

> How many congressmen, governors, judges and clergymen of the white race have consorted with colored women? From the present

---

[823] *Chicago Defender*, July 5, 1913; *Freeman*, July 5, 1913. *Chicago Day Book*, June 30, 1913.

day appearance of four millions of negroes in America, hosts of whom God alone can only tell whether they are white or colored, there must be left very little loyalty among white men, and less confidence among white women in them.

Johnson had invited the envy of his own race as well, and "pricked the ever-growing abscess of American prejudice by spending his money like he had a plenty." The spotlight was a fearful ordeal.

Likewise, the *Freeman* said that Johnson's own people sought to repudiate him because they believed that they were suffering prejudice which became more manifest owing to him. Consequently, he left a country nearly entirely turned against him.[824]

The *Mirror of Life and Boxing World*, based in England, said,

> No one should worry over Jack's departure, as the boxing game is better off without him. Negro boxers, like the black race riders, are a thing of the past. They have been eliminated from the sport to a great extent. ...
>
> [T]here has been a revolution of feeling against the black man in America, the true cause of which is hard to find, but which has been illustrated more clearly perhaps in connection with sport than in any other line. Legally the negro may be the equal of the white man in this country, but in sport there is little room for him any more. In professional baseball the negro never figured. He was never given a chance to figure.

In the meantime, on June 27, 1913 in New York, Gunboat Smith knocked out George Rodel in the 3rd round.

> Though Smith won because the Boer looked for a soft spot, the crowd wasn't convinced that the Gunner showed real championship material. Smith doesn't know what the left hand was made for. He has no defense. He does own a stout heart and a great wallop, but that lets him out.[825]

On July 1, 1913 in New Orleans, Louisiana, Joe Jeannette fought Harry Wills to a 10-round draw.

On July 4 in Chicago, Johnson's deceased wife Etta's necklace was sold at public auction for $2,160.

On July 10, 1913, Johnson, his wife Lucille, nephew Gus Rhodes, and Jewish secretary Joe Levy arrived at the French port of Le Havre.

Scheduled to return to the U.S. on October 1 to stand trial in federal court for another alleged Mann Act violation, Jack said, "I will return to

---

[824] *Chicago Defender*, July 5, 1913; *Freeman*, August 2, 9, 1913.

[825] *Mirror of Life and Boxing World*, July 19, August 2, 1913. Another observer said that although he was at the head of the white hope division, Smith needed to box more and not simply rely on his hitting power. The gate was $4,394.

Chicago in time for my trial. I have done no wrong, the whole world is with me and I am over here to make some money. … We return in time for my trial. I have never had any idea of running away. My attorneys have been fully advised." However, some reported that privately, Jack was saying that he would not return.

Harry Parkin, who prosecuted Johnson, said the judge had ruled that Johnson's appearance bonds could not be forfeited until Jack failed to appear at the time designated by the Court (which at that point was October 13).[826]

The *Freeman* said, "Everyone is free in the United States except the eight million Negroes. Prejudice on every hand is manifest against them." Ultimately, what brought Johnson down was that he "was indiscreet; he flew in the face of sentiment, but in doing so he stood for manhood rights."

Johnson said he would make Paris his headquarters, for that town did not take as much to the anti-Negro business. Paris loved McVea, and he had a white wife too; a beautiful French woman. However, there was some race prejudice in France, as was the case with the entire world. France had colonies of darker peoples as well.

Johnson had trouble finding a Paris hotel that would allow him to stay there. He was refused repeatedly at several good hotels before he finally found accommodation. The *Freeman* said, "It is just about the same prejudice which exists between races the world over. Whites and blacks will never be on rapport. They can get along, however, much better than they do in this country, just the same."[827]

On July 22, 1913 in New York, Joe Jeannette easily and soundly beat John Lester Johnson, another colored heavyweight, in a 10-round no-decision bout.[828]

It was reported that Johnson might fight either Al Palzer or Georges Carpentier.[829]

During July at the Lafayette in New York, Joe Jeannette was appearing in 3-round exhibitions with Frank Moran, who was regarded as one of the most hopeful of the white hopes. One evening, Joe landed a blow that cut

---

[826] There were two bonds, one of $15,000, which would be forfeited if the Court of Appeals decided his conviction was proper and he failed to appear to serve his sentence. The other bond was his personal bond for $30,000 cash on white slave indictments for which he had not yet been tried, which would be forfeited if Johnson failed to appear on October 13 to stand trial. The additional counts were that from December 26 through 31, 1910, Johnson transported Belle Schreiber from Chicago to Milwaukee over railway for the purpose of debauchery. *Chicago Defender,* July 12, August 9, 1913; *Freeman,* July 19, 1913.
  The *Chicago Defender* regularly covered Johnson while he was abroad. Johnson was a *Defender* reader and renewed his subscription.

[827] *Freeman,* July 19, 1913.

[828] *New York Age,* July 24, 1913

[829] *Chicago Defender,* July 26, 1913. The French idol Carpentier was clever, fast, and a hitter. Although he had losses to Papke and Klaus at the lower weight classes, he had performed better as a light heavyweight, for his strength had improved. He had stopped Wells despite the fact that the Bombardier outweighed him by 40 pounds.

Moran over the eye and caused the claret to gush from the gash. The *Age* opined that if Moran and Jeannette were matched in a real contest, Joe would beat him. "Maybe the Boxing Commission has been prompted to draw the color line from a humane standpoint."[830]

California was considering a bill to ban the 20-round bout. Jim Corbett opined that it would kill boxing, for true champions would be a thing of the past. "Some day I hope the reaction will set in and common sense will rule, but just now the fanatics seem to have the upper hand all along the line. As goes New York so goes the nation." Corbett also said that "Johnson was a disgrace to pugilism and his continued presence was a menace to the sport."

In order to make money, Johnson took to the stage in Paris, making his first appearance in *La Revue Chemise* at the Folies Bergeres music hall where Corbett appeared several years ago. There was some hissing, but there also was applause from a full house. Overall, Johnson was received favorably.

Each night, Johnson threw a medicine ball and boxed 4 exhibition rounds with various French heavyweights. After midnight, he danced the grizzly bear with Mrs. Johnson. He drew $1,200 a night for eleven nights.[831]

On August 8, 1913 in New York, before a crowd of 10,000, Gunboat Smith scored a 5th round knockout over Fireman Jim Flynn, who was floored five times in the round until Referee Johns stopped the fight. The Gunboat said he was ready and willing to meet Johnson, Langford, or anyone in the world in a finish-fight, winner-take-all.

Johnson was a spectator at a series of boxing bouts in Paris, and when the crowd discovered his presence, he was given an ovation.

Johnson visited Boulogne to purchase another automobile.

Jack planned to leave on a tour through Belgium's summer resorts, then to Bordeaux, Lyons, and Marseilles, leaving France on August 20 for a three-week Russian tour, as well as vaudeville tours through France, Germany, and Spain. He was making easy money.

Although there was some talk of matching Carpentier, the French champion, with Johnson, Chicago newsman Eugene Katz, who was in London, said, "[Carpentier] would last about three rounds with Johnson, even in Johnson's present condition. ... Langford, unless he has gone back greatly since I saw him two years ago, would lick [Carpentier] easily."

Joe Woodman, Langford's manager, reported that Langford and Johnson would fight in Paris in the fall for 20 rounds, with Johnson to receive a $30,000 guarantee, and Langford 20% of the gross receipts. However, it did not appear that a formal deal had been finalized yet.[832]

---

[830] *New York Age*, July 31, 1913. Jeannette was very expert and agile on his feet. For a big man he ducked quickly and gracefully.

[831] *Freeman*, August 2, 9, 1913. There was talk of Johnson possibly meeting Belgian wrestler Constant le Marin in a wrestling bout. Jack also had an engagement at St. Petersburg to put on exhibition bouts. *Mirror of Life and Boxing World*, August 9, 1913.

[832] *New York Age*, August 14, 1913; *Freeman*, August 16, 1913.

In New York, Sheriff Julius Harburger attended an August 13, 1913 bout between a white boxer named Paddy McCarthy and a Chinaman named Ah Chung, won by Chung via 6th round knockout. He and the New *York Morning Telegraph's* Bat Masterson called attention to the New York State Athletic Commission's hypocrisy, allowing this mixed-race bout but not those between blacks and whites.

Since the days when Abraham Lincoln issued his proclamation of freedom there was to be no distinction as to American citizenship, but how the Boxing Commission can come to the conclusion that a Chinese, who is a nonvoter and a non-citizen should have preference over a citizen is one of the mysteries that runs through the labyrinthian minds of commissioners.[833]

As a result of the black-white bout ban, local New York club managers were heard to say, "What sense would there be in matching a Negro and a white man and have the boxing commission revoke our license?" That in part explained why promoters refused to make such matches.

A writer for the *Evening Telegram*, James Crowell, looked at the commission's actions from a different angle. He said,

The boxing game has enough enemies already without trying to increase the number by opening the way for a hue and cry of much more extensive proportions than that which it already has to contend with. The racial prejudice that a bout between a white and a Negro boxer incurs is detrimental to the sport.[834]

On August 22, 1913 in Vernon, California, Jess Willard scored a KO11 over John William Young, a.k.a. Bill or Bull Young, a huge uppercut doing the trick. Young remained unconscious and died the next day after surgery to remove a cerebral hemorrhage. Willard and the promoters were arrested on a manslaughter charge.

Johnson was enjoying Paris and was being treated fairly well. Jack told a French sporting paper,

Since my return from France to America I must say that I have been the most persecuted man in the whole world. The Americans decidedly unable to stomach my victory over Jeffries...have tried to destroy and ruin me. There has not been a day on which I was not the victim of some plot, on some dubious charge, which ended only with great loss of money for me.

One day they accused me of violence to my chauffeur when in fact he menaced me and I was forced to give up heavy damages. At the same time I was in trouble for exceeding the speed limit when I had made

---

[833] *New York Age*, August 21, 1913. Recently, by a 2 to 1 vote, the New York State Athletic Commission had upheld the rule barring mixed matches between whites and blacks.
[834] *New York Age*, September 18, 1913.

10 miles an hour, and on the charge that my auto smoked, which was absolutely false, and the fines were always drained from me. They accused me of trading in white female slaves when I had simply traveled with my legitimate wife from one state to another.

I was arrested and was not released until I had deposited a bail of 50,000 francs. It was always my money that they were after... One day when I was punching the bag in public a cord holding the ball broke and the bag projected 10 meters, struck a woman spectator lightly, without hurting her in the least. The woman's lawyer hailed me into court and claimed enormous damages. Do you know what she demanded? Simply $2,500 ($125,000 francs). Notwithstanding the bad faith of the complaint, the court condemned me to pay $250 (12,500 francs) – a sum absolutely ridiculous under the circumstances.

In brief, with all these attacks and persecutions the American judges had already forced me to pay, in some months, more than 400,000 francs ($120,000) and as there was no reason why I would not be continually arrested until my last dollar was gone, I resolved to take to flight. But alas, that seemed impossible. They obtained an order of arrest, charging me with leaving Chicago. I resolved to use a ruse. I organized a baseball team composed of Negroes. I had chosen for it fifteen men as big and black as possible, all of whom resembled me marvelously. ... I sent a challenge in the name of the Negro team to one of the best teams in Canada. The challenge was accepted and a date quickly fixed. Disguised in baseball outfits, it was very hard to identify me. My secretary, wife, and domestic embarked for Canada by another route. I had bought in advance tickets direct to Harve by the steamer Corinthian. When I arrived at Montréal this precaution saved me. I had arranged with a big Negro who resembled me closely and when he said he was Jack Johnson the police would have taken him back triumphantly to my house in Chicago. I promised to pay him well. Fortunately all went well in Montréal. The local authorities, unfriendly, demanded how long I would stay in Canada, and if I had not had my ticket I might not have been so fortunate. As I was only going through their country, the Canadians could say nothing. Once on board the Corinthian I was safe. ... The officers and passengers of the Corinthian were truly charming to me. I count on settling permanently in [Paris] and never returning to the United States.

The *Freeman's* Billy Lewis said Johnson spoke the truth about his persecution. Johnson had traveled with a white woman who perhaps was a common-law wife. He sent for her to come to Chicago from Pittsburgh. On this point the government succeeded in making the case that Johnson was transporting a woman for immoral purposes. The government previously had the reputation of making out good, plain, unmistakable cases, but in this instance it fell to the small business of pettifogging (engaging in legal trickery or arguing about unimportant details), and the prosecution was glad to get rid of the pestiferous (annoying) Johnson at any cost. It was a flimsy case, one based on race prejudice and public demand rather than justice.

The *New York Age* also noted that the American spirit of fair play had not been in evidence since Johnson defeated Jeffries. Owing to the prevalence of "Negrophobia," law enforcement had harassed and inconvenienced him. Every police officer wanted publicity by arresting him for speeding. "We do not condone the champion's rank disregard for public opinion, for his indiscretions have done the members of his race much harm; but even had he not erred in judgment his color in this country would have operated against him."

The *Freeman* noted that despite black boxers' proven courage; there remained a certain class of boxing fans who claimed that every black boxer was "yellow." To the extent that some lacked self-confidence, it was because they suffered the effects of being subjected to the white man's will. Regardless, as a class, black boxers were every bit as game as the white boxers, as proven by men such as Dixon, Gans, Walcott, Jackson, Langford, and Johnson. Langford was so yellow that few whites in the world wanted to fight him. There were fifty white boxers for every black, and yet blacks had won many championships. Even the "unbiased critic will admit that the Negroes are natural-born fighters." Black soldiers also had been of great assistance to Uncle Sam, having fought well in the Civil War and the Spanish War, covering themselves with glory.[835]

In late August 1913, Johnson traveled to London, England. On August 25, Johnson appeared at a South London music hall called the Euston Palace, before a large and mixed crowd.

Two white American women comediennes told the audience that they refused to appear if Johnson did. One of the women, Beth Tate of California, said, "I do not object to Johnson on account of his color, but of what the man is alleged to have done." The gallery then replied, "What's he done?" The women were booed from the stage with whistles, cat calls, and hisses. There were only a few cheers. The average man on the street did not share the hostility towards Johnson. They regarded him as the victim of persecution due to color prejudice.

When Johnson appeared, the crowd roared with cheers for several minutes. Jack smiled and bowed. He appeared majestic to his supporters, and ignored with a wave of the hand those few who hissed and booed him. He made a speech, saying, "My only crime is that I beat Jeffries." Seeing that he was standing under the flag of the United States, he stopped talking, had it removed, and had the French flag hung in its place. Johnson thanked the crowd for its reception and remarked that he was glad that English people were so fair-minded.[836]

835 *Freeman*, August 23, 30, 1913; *New York Age*, September 4, 1913.
836 *Chicago Defender*, August 30, 1913. Jack's nephew Gus Rhodes was with him in London.

This is the first picture published by any newspaper of the champion since his exit from the United States. Facing the champion, with back ha'f turned towards you, can be seen **Mr. Joe Levi**, private secretary. Facing the champion with straw hat is Lord Pettiford, multi-millionaire and special friend, who has always admired the champion and is about to take his yacht to the lord's private summer home about thirty miles from London. Mrs. Johnson can be seen with her usual smile. Just outside the wharf are 10,000 or more people waiting to see the world's greatest champion, who has fought and won from Jeffries to Uncle Sam, making a clean breakaway, and has never fouled either. The champion says, owing to the ill health of his twenty-second cousin, he will not return to the United States on October 4.

Chicago Defender, September 27, 1913

On September 3, 1913 in New York, 194-pound underdog Frank Moran scored a surprise 7th round knockout over 6'3" 227-pound Al Palzer, avenging an earlier newspaper decision loss. England's *Mirror of Life and Boxing World* said, "Moran is now in the forefront of the white heavyweight division." Moran had won five fights in England, and they thought well of him.

Dan McKetrick, who managed both Moran and Jeannette, was trying to match either one with Johnson. Many felt that Jack was putting up the color bar against men of his own color, only seeming interested in white hopes. Regardless, "The champion cannot last forever, and the general feeling is that he may fall a victim to the first good husky fellow that comes along."[837]

---

[837] *Mirror of Life and Boxing World*, September 13, 1913. Moran had acted as a sparring partner to Bombardier Wells in 1911 when Billy was training for Storbeck. Since Frank returned to America, he had inconsistent results, losing to decisions/no decisions to Tom Kennedy, Al Kubiak, Tony Ross, and Gunboat Smith, though he defeated Sailor White, Tim Logan, Jim Cameron and others. In April 1913, Moran gave the late Luther McCarty a good fight, losing a 10-round no-decision. The Palzer victory was significant, given that Palzer had defeated Kaufman and Wells, and had lost to McCarty in the 18th round.

Johnson was a vaudeville attraction in England, appearing in the English music halls. The Variety Controlling Company booked a tour for him, and he received a $2,500 weekly salary, larger than any vaudevillian abroad.

Langford's manager Joe Woodman was claiming that Johnson would fight Langford 20 rounds in Paris on December 20. Johnson would receive a $20,000 guarantee and Langford a percentage of the gross. The bout would be promoted by Theodore Vienne at the Cirque de Paris.

Although France had colonial holdings in Africa, Asia, the Americas (including San Domingo and Haiti), and the Pacific Islands, apparently its racial concerns were not as great as the British Empire's. France seemed willing to allow Johnson to fight.

Sizing up the potential fight, "Most thinkers along the line of pugilism have it that Johnson can beat Langford; it looks that way, but it is by no means certain." Johnson had all of the physical advantages, as well as the defense and cleverness, although some said that he was in physical decay.

Regardless, the veracity of Woodman's claim was questionable, given that Johnson consistently had insisted that he would not do a Langford fight for less than $30,000.

Soon thereafter, an announcement was made that Johnson had agreed to fight Pittsburgh's Frank Moran, who recently had knocked out Al Palzer in 7 rounds. The fight likely would take place in December (later changed to January) at the Velodrome d'Hiver in Paris. Dan McKetrick, Moran's manager, arranged the bout. Leon See was representing Johnson in Paris.

On September 4 in London, Jack Johnson was injured when a taxicab collided with his motor car. Johnson sustained some tendon sprains, but nothing serious. A doctor was called to treat him. About $1,000 in damage was done to the auto. The taxicab driver was arrested. Johnson noted, "They would have me in the penitentiary by this time if this incident had occurred in the United States."

In an ironic twist, one of the federal grand jurors who indicted Johnson under the Mann Act, S. T. Vovee, was arrested for a violation of the same act in Los Angeles, after being trailed from Chicago by a woman who claimed to be his common-law wife. She had him arrested. Increasingly, women were using the act as a sword rather than as a shield, blackmailing their boyfriends from leaving them, sometimes demanding marriage or money, threatening them with prosecution under the Mann Act.[838]

Jim Corbett said that both Moran and Willard had lost hairline decisions to Gunboat Smith. A number of experts who witnessed both battles backed the fighters' claims that the verdicts were unfair. Still, the gutsy Smith was challenging Langford to a fight, the only white fighter to do so. Moran appeared to be a tough customer for anyone to put away. Johnson had

[838] *Chicago Defender, Freeman*, September 6, 13, 1913.

arrived at the stage of his career where money counted a great deal. Corbett opined that he might take a dive if there was enough money in it.[839]

On September 9, 1913 in New York, Sam Langford knocked out John Lester Johnson in 1 round.[840]

On September 12, by a unanimous vote, the New York State Athletic Commission refused to allow Sam Langford and Gunboat Smith to box in that state, again ruling that it was against the sport's best interests to allow blacks and whites to box each other. New York State Attorney General Thomas Carmody said New York was entitled legally to prevent mixed-race bouts if it believed they might prompt disorder or bitter racial feeling.[841]

The *Mirror of Life and Boxing World* opined that Johnson seemed to have drawn the color line. It believed that Johnson was following the example of white boxers in barring blacks, avoiding his toughest challengers. He showed no disposition to endanger his title in matches with either Langford or Jeannette. The suspicion was that Johnson realized that either they could beat him or at least had a much better chance than any white foe. It had been hinted that Johnson wanted to go down in history as the only colored man to become heavyweight champion, "but it might be a great deal nearer the truth to state that Johnson is in no way anxious to lose his crown, and that the possibility of defeat makes him pass up his tough coloured rivals and give preference to the more or less idolized white warriors." Johnson believed that although top whites were strong and could hit hard, they were not as adept at scientific boxing.[842]

Furthermore, Johnson could make as much or more money fighting whites. Few promoters were willing to put up big money for a black vs. black title fight. The general public wanted to see a white man win the title back, and far more whites than blacks paid to see fights.

Johnson earned money in the music halls of France and England, giving performances of sparring, dancing, singing, and bass violin. Some greeted him warmly, while others reviled him. Johnson could not escape global prejudice entirely.

In Paris, France, Johnson's home was the Grand Terminus Hotel. Jack had purchased property at Joiville le Pout, a Parisian suburb, and was building a bungalow there.

For two weeks, Johnson appeared at the Apollo theater in Vienna, Austria. Besides giving boxing exhibitions, he and Mrs. Johnson danced the tango, and the audiences went wild.

---

[839] *Freeman*, September 20, 1913.

[840] Langford earned $1,000. In 1916, John Lester Johnson would fight Jack Dempsey to a 10-round no-decision draw.

[841] *Freeman*, October 4, 11, 1913; *Thames Star*, September 16, 1913.

[842] *Mirror of Life and Boxing World*, September 27, 1913. Supposedly, Johnson was going to fight Moran and Pelkey.

While in Germany and surrounding countries, Jack and Lucille Johnson were received royally. He had a ten-week engagement at $5,000 per week.[843]

On October 3, 1913 in New York, 195-pound Joe Jeannette outpointed 199 ½-pound Sam Langford in a fast 10-round no-decision bout, winning 7 out of 10 rounds. There were no knockdowns, but each man was staggered. At the finish, the overweight Langford's right eye was damaged, his nose bruised, and his lips slightly puffed. Jeannette did not show a mark. Some thought Langford either had gone back or was out of shape. Joe controlled him with a long left jab.[844]

On October 9, 1913 in New York, Gunboat Smith defeated Carl Morris via 5th round disqualification, the result of low blows.

Thomas Dixon Jr.'s play, *The Leopard's Spots*, was having a successful tour. In North Carolina, in a speech given before the play, Dixon said that white civilization was being destroyed by educating the Negro.[845]

[843] *Chicago Defender*, October 4, 1913.
[844] *Freeman*, October 11, November 8, 1913; *New York Tribune, Chicago Day Book, Rock Island Argus*, October 4, 1913.
[845] *New York Age*, October 9, 1913.

CHAPTER 18

Battling Jim Johnson and the French

In late 1913, there was some suggestion that Parisians might be growing tired of Johnson. They thought he was funny, until he started talking about Napoleon. Jack said he possessed a library of works about Napoleon, and remarked to a reporter, "Napoleon was a great man, too." They believed that Johnson suffered from a badly swelled head.

The community of Asnieres, a Parisian suburb, was shocked at the thought that Johnson was going to live among them permanently. A movement was afoot to petition the authorities to bar him. They called him an undesirable creature. "To tell the truth, Parisians are heartily ashamed of themselves and the foolish enthusiasm with which they received this man."[846]

In October, the appeal of Johnson's criminal convictions was continued in the U.S. Circuit Court until the following April.[847]

As of October 29, Johnson, who was on a European tour, was in Budapest, Austria-Hungary, playing at the Royal Orpheum theater, which was packed nightly. He was a popular attraction wherever he went. "They wished to see the colossus of the nineteenth century." Johnson planned to leave in a few days for Bucharest and then Berlin.[848]

The world-famous Johnson had theatrical contracts to fill all over Europe, which would keep him busy for a year at $1,500 a week. Lucrative cozy contracts made it less likely that he would fight very often. This upset some French promoters, for it made it tougher to negotiate with him.

At a meeting of the French boxing commission, a letter was read from promoter Victor Breyer of the French Federation of Boxing Clubs in Paris. Breyer said Johnson should no longer be considered champion, and the winner of a fight between Langford and Jeannette should be declared the new champion.[849]

Bat Masterson, fight expert for the *Morning Telegraph*, wrote:

---

[846] *Freeman*, October 18, 1913.

[847] *Chicago Defender*, October 18, 1913. *Freeman*, October 25, 1913. Some reported that on October 13, when he failed to appear to stand trial on the seven remaining counts against him, Federal Judge Carpenter declared forfeit the $30,000 personal bond signed by Johnson. Whether this actually happened on this date remains unclear, for there are other indications that the bond was not forfeited until the following year.

On October 21, 1913 in Boston, Gunboat Smith knocked out Tony Ross in the 10th round.

[848] *Chicago Defender*, November 15, 22, 1913; *Freeman*, December 6, 1913.

[849] *New York Times*, October 29, 1913.

Word comes from Paris that the International Boxing Union, whatever that is, at a recent meeting there unanimously voted to bar Jack Johnson from boxing in France. Also, the union took it upon itself to declare vacant the heavyweight championship because Johnson had been sentenced to imprisonment in this country and for other reasons too numerous to mention.[850]

The *London Daily Mail*, which was published in London, Manchester, and Paris, said the International Boxing Union (IBU), in accordance with resolutions adopted at its November 5 meeting, consulted the federations of countries affiliated with it on the proposal that Johnson should no longer be considered champion. France was of the opinion that the title should be declared vacant, and named Joe Jeannette and Sam Langford as best qualified to compete for the championship. Of course, it was no coincidence that the French promoters who were members and voting accordingly were promoting an upcoming Langford-Jeannette bout, and that was good marketing for the fight. The United States still held that Johnson was champion. Belgium and Switzerland expressed no opinion. As a result of the lack of a majority vote, the IBU decided to summon an emergency meeting of its delegates, set for December 24 in Paris. So in truth, the IBU really had not declared the title vacant.[851]

However, some reported that the IBU declared the title vacant on the grounds of Johnson's conviction in the American courts and his refusal to fight. France's position had the approval of the English section of the union, which was not surprising given that the Brits had refused to allow Johnson to fight at all as far back as 1911. Regardless, Americans "will hardly take the verdict of the 'I.B.U.' seriously." Still, things did not look bright for Johnson. "Barred in this country by a jail sentence and popular sentiment as well, not wanted in England or Australia, and finally given the gate in France, the 'champion' is getting his bunches."

Some said Johnson was having financial difficulties and needed to fight in order to fatten his bank roll. He made money, but he also spent it. Yet, allegedly, Johnson said he wanted to put off any Langford match until February, so he could make as much easy money as possible.[852]

On November 7 in Spartanburg, South Carolina, Senator Benjamin Tillman declared that he favored lynching for all assailants of women. "He is the Senator who says 'to hell with the Constitution.' This is his stock in trade to get the vote of the 'red necks' in this section."[853]

Many black writers thought the U.S. Supreme Court would or should reverse Johnson's Mann Act convictions, for they believed that the trial and conviction were unfair. Had his conviction been obtained in a fair manner,

---

[850] *New York Times*, October 29, 1913.
[851] *London Daily Mail, London Times*, December 19, 1913.
[852] *Freeman*, November 15, 1913. *Chicago Day Book*, November 6, 1913. *El Paso Herald*, November 16, 1913.
[853] *Chicago Defender*, November 8, 1913.

no tears would be shed for him. However, "sending him to prison on the testimony of a notorious degenerate is quite another thing." Schreiber had testified that she made money in an immoral manner and gave the proceeds to Johnson. "But the woman's testimony was so glaringly false to all who heard it that even those who utterly detest the Negro refuse to believe it."

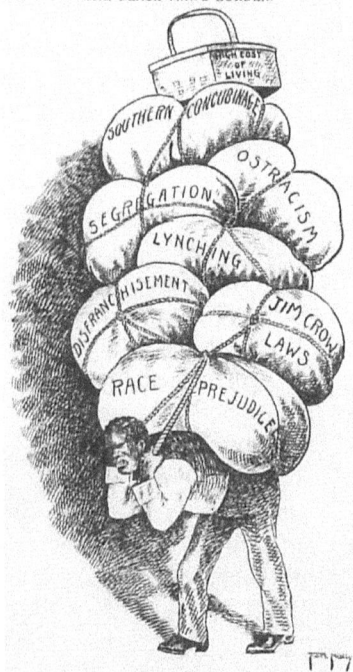

On the witness stand, Johnson did not deny that he had sent Schreiber money, but emphatically denied that he ever had compelled her to prostitute herself in order that he might financially benefit. He also swore, and his testimony was corroborated, that instead of forcing her to engage in immoral practices, he put her up in elegant apartments, and did the same for her mother and sister. All three women lived in luxury at his expense. "If such actions mean anything, they mean that Johnson was endeavoring in his own peculiar way to rescue the woman from a life of shame and degradation, which she had been following in Pittsburgh."[854]

On November 17, 1913 in Boston, 182-pound Gunboat Smith won a 12-round decision over Sam Langford, who appeared to weigh around 195 pounds.

Chicago Defender, **November 8, 1913**

Smith led in the early rounds, easily landing left jabs, clearly outboxing Langford by cautiously using his height and reach advantages. Langford did not concern himself with points, but threw powerful blows, which rarely landed. Smith tired near the end, and Sam landed more effectively, but Smith had accumulated enough of a lead to earn Referee Dick Fleming's decision. The victory was not a surprise to those who watched Langford get outpointed in 10 rounds by Jeannette a month and half ago. Sam did not appear to be in the best shape.[855]

On or about November 25 in Paris, Johnson engaged in a wrestling match against a German named Urbach. After Jack secured a couple falls and had won the bout, Urbach punched him on the jaw, but Jack did not retaliate. "A small riot followed and several arrests were made." Jack occasionally was engaging in wrestling bouts.[856]

To give one a better sense about the serious money that top boxers were earning, the New Jersey State Bureau of Statistics of Labor said the average

---

[854] *New York Age,* November 13, 1913; *Freeman,* December 13, 1913.
[855] *Freeman,* November 22, December 6, 13, 1913.
[856] *Chicago Day Book,* November 26, 1913.

wage of a person employed in factories there was $557 per year. The industries with the lowest average yearly earnings were the manufacture of shirt waists, with an average annual pay of $386.88, and women's and children's underwear, at $289.86 per year. Hence, one can understand why there were so many fighters.[857]

On December 3, 1913 in New York, Jess Willard won a 10-round no-decision over Carl Morris. Both fighters weighed about 235 pounds.

In early December, millionaire Matthew S. Baldwin, who had helped post a bond for Jack Johnson, was found dead.[858]

On December 6, it was announced that Jack Johnson would box fellow black Battling Jim Johnson 10 rounds in Paris on December 19, a mere 13 days away. Apparently, Johnson also had an upcoming bout with Frank Moran in January.[859]

On December 12, 1913 in Arran, France, Jack Johnson and his wife were injured when their auto collided with the safety gates at a railway crossing. Both were slightly cut about the head.[860]

The French Boxing Federation declared the world's heavyweight title vacant. Its director, Paris promoter Theodore Vienne, who also was the director of the Society for the Propagation of English Boxing in France, stated that Johnson was being stripped because of his criminal conviction in the U.S. and because he was refusing to box top contenders like Langford or Jeannette. Vienne said the upcoming Langford vs. Jeannette bout in Paris would be for the vacant heavyweight title. Vienne further said,

> The title held by Jack Johnson is declared vacant because it is not admissible in sport for a man to legitimately hold all his life, or at least as long as he pleases, a title which he obstinately refuses to defend against qualified aspirants. Nobody can contest that principle. Now, I have repeatedly offered Jack Johnson an opportunity of defending this title in Paris under the usual conditions of a participation in the receipts with a guarantee of $25,000 then $30,000. Jack Johnson has always refused.

> In an interview Jack Johnson had in Paris with Victor Breyer, then my associate, and later with Leon See, director of boxing and boxers, he made the same public declaration which remains still without denial, that "I will not box again even for a million."

> Since coming to Paris, Johnson made an engagement to meet me. He did not come himself, but his representative came, only to declare to me that Johnson did not wish to really box a capable adversary to maintain his title, but only adversaries of a second class. Under those conditions no one can be expected to submit to Johnson's fantastic

---

[857] *New York Journal*, December 19, 1913.
[858] *Chicago Day Book*, December 5, 1913.
[859] *Wanganui Chronicle*, *Northern Star*, December 8, 1913.
[860] *Freeman*, December 20, 1913.

demands. The sporting world has every right to rebel and to place open for public competition a title which the holder, because it is too much trouble, does not wish to have to defend.[861]

The French Federation's Victor Breyer and Paul Rousseau sent the New York State Athletic Commission cables stating, "French Federation proposes to International Boxing Union Jack Johnson no more world's champion. Please cable if in agreement with France."

However, the New York Commission responded that it recognized Johnson as the world champion until he retired or someone defeated him in the ring. This was somewhat ironic given that it refused to allow Johnson to box in New York.[862]

The *New York Age* opined that Johnson would be the world's champion regardless of what the IBU or the NYSAC decided. Any attempt to strip him via highway robbery methods would be to no avail.

Pugilists do not forfeit their titles because of acts of indiscretion in private life. If so, many white fighters would have been bated of their honors in the past. Rousseau stripped him because he refused to fight those fighters picked out for him to fight. On the theory advanced by Rosseau, the Philadelphia Athletics would be forced to forfeit its world's championship title for refusing to play the Lincoln Giants or some other strong colored baseball team.[863]

Arthur Pelkey said he would draw the color line when it came to Langford, Jeannette, McVey, and other blacks, but would step over the line if there was a chance to fight Jack Johnson for the title. Pelkey was in training to fight Gunboat Smith for the white championship.[864]

Jack Johnson wrote a letter to the *New York Herald's* European edition, saying,

I strongly protest against three or four so-called sportsmen who have pretended to form that which they called an international boxing union in the object of letting the public believe that I was no more the undisputed world champion.

But, as you have seen, some genuine sportsmen have taken up my defence and everyone knows now that I am still the real and only title holder.

Besides, I am willing to defense my title against any challenger, and those who will see me box my first opponent, 'Jim' Johnson, at Premierland, on Friday night will be convinced that I am still the man

---

[861] *Syracuse Journal*, December 14, 1913; *Omaha Daily Bee, Salt Lake Tribune*, December 15, 1913.
[862] *New York Herald, New York Journal*, December 17, 1913.
[863] *New York Age*, December 18, 1913.
[864] *New York American*, December 18, 1913.

who beat Jeffries, Tommy Burns, etc., and I really deserve the name of 'invincible,' which the Americans themselves gave me.[865]

On the evening of Friday December 19, 1913 inside the Premierland Francais, Elysee-Montmartre, 72 Boulevard Rochechouart, at Montmartre, a hill in the north of Paris, France, Jack Johnson fought Battling Jim Johnson. Some said Jim was from Memphis, others said Galveston, while later sources said he was born in Virginia but resided in New Jersey. Battling Jim was 26 years old to Jack's 35 years of age.

Battling Jim Johnson might not have been a big name, but he was no slouch. He was a big, strong, durable fighter, typically weighing around 225 pounds. He was very experienced, had fought a high caliber of opponents, including the big three – Jeannette, Langford, and McVey, and more than held his own. His record included: 1910 DND6 Tony Ross, LND6 Sam Langford, D15 Sam McVea, and LKOby21 McVea; 1911 KO4 Fred Drummond and KO11 Jewey Smith; 1912 L20 Fred Storbeck (despite dropping Fred three times and hurting him on several other occasions), WND6 Joe Jeannette (dropping Joe in the process), LND10 Jeannette, KO7 Black Bill, and KO2 Bill Tate; and 1913 LND10 and LDQby15 Jeannette, KO11 Con O'Kelly, KO8 Gustave Marthuin, KO10 Kid Jackson, and KO6 Bob Scanlon.

Battling Jim had at least 39 known bouts coming into the Johnson fight. The French thought of him as a good quality opponent, for they had seen Battling Jim box in France against McVea (D15), Jim Maher (KO3), and McVea again (LKOby21), all in 1910, and again in 1913 against Kid Jackson (KO10). He had fought and won several times in the United Kingdom as well, so Europeans were familiar with him. The *Freeman* had opined that Jim Johnson was amongst the top black fighters who were better than any white hope, for he was powerful, skillful, and could take a punch. Jim Johnson was the only top black fighter that the champ had yet to face and defeat.

En haut : JIM JOHNSON -- En bas : JACK JOHNSON
Ces deux boxeurs doivent disputer ce soir un match en dix rounds de trois minutes

---

865 *New York Herald*, December 19, 1913.

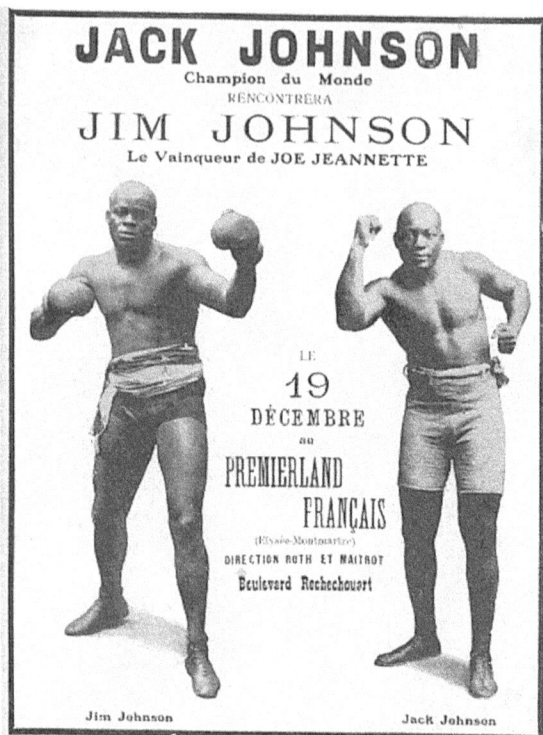

JACK JOHNSON
Champion du Monde
RENCONTRERA

JIM JOHNSON
Le Vainqueur de JOE JEANNETTE

LE
19
DÉCEMBRE
au

PREMIERLAND
FRANÇAIS
(Elysée-Montmartre)

DIRECTION ROTH ET MAITROT
Boulevard Rochechouart

Jim Johnson   Jack Johnson

The following is an amalgamation of reports written by several French, English, and American newsmen who were there.[866]

The *London Times* said Jim Johnson held a victory over Joe Jeannette, and many regarded him as likely to provide the champ with a serious fight. During the past year, in Brussels, Belgium, the gigantic Jim either had been mistaken for or passed himself off as the champion, fooling people into thinking he was Jack Johnson.

The *London Daily Mail* said that despite the fact that few regarded the battle as being of real importance, there was great interest in the contest due to the fact that it was Johnson's first defense in Europe. Plus, folks wanted to compare the champion with the other elite black fighters. So tickets were selling fast.

With the champ indeed about to fight, it would make it harder for the promoters of the Langford-Jeannette contest to declare that it was for a vacant title. Some believed that the reason why Johnson was fighting again was to forestall talk about his title being vacant. Jack's supporters seized the opportunity to motivate him to get back into the ring. Probably it was no coincidence that Johnson vs. Johnson was scheduled to be held the day before Langford vs. Jeannette. The champ likely also saw it as a tune-up in preparation for the lengthier upcoming Moran bout.

The day of the fight, *Le Matin* said,

Jack Johnson is really the champion of the world, all at the same time not being one. It's a big mess. Last November 5 the International Boxing Union said that because Jack Johnson didn't want to take on

---

[866] *London Times, London Daily Mail, New York Herald, Le Matin, Le Petit Parisien, L'Humanité, L'Intransigeant*, December 20, 1913; *La Presse, Le Temps*, December 20, 21, 2013; *Le Matin*, December 19, 20, 1913. The *London Times* presented its own correspondent's fight report. The *London Daily Mail* also had a special correspondent on scene in Paris. It provided one of the more detailed accounts. The *New York Herald* had a bureau at No. 49 Avenue De L'Opera, Paris and sent a special dispatch via its commercial cable company's system.

any other challenges he was going to be dethroned and the championship would be disputed between Langford and Jeanette. Said Jack Johnson, "What? I'm no longer the champion? We'll see about that." America is making trouble. The New York Athletic Commission still holds that Johnson is the champion.

Le Temps said the International Boxing Union, which included delegates from the U.S., France, Belgium, Switzerland, but not England, declared that the two men most qualified for disputing the title were Langford and Jeannette. However, truth be told, Belgium and Switzerland abstained in the vote, and the U.S. proposed that Johnson still was the champion. Hence, in actuality, only one member, France, voted that the title was vacant.

Some of the French press erroneously reported that Jack Johnson had not fought in two years, either overlooking or unaware of the Flynn fight. *Le Temps* said, "Jack Johnson, who calls himself the champion of the world, even though he hasn't accepted a fight for two years, will meet tonight Jim Johnson in a match of 10 rounds." *L'Humanite* agreed that since the fabulous feat of defeating Jeffries, the champ had done nothing other than evade the ring. Of course, this overlooked the fact that the Brits drew the color line on him in 1911, Johnson had fought Jim Flynn in 1912, most American cities would not allow him to fight, and even the Australians did not want him. Plus, there were the legal troubles.

L'Humanite called the bout a very rare and interesting event for Parisians. It said Jack Johnson was the most well-known person in the world, and the actual incontestable champion. In the face of the threat to take away his title, he was returning to the enchanted circle against Jim Johnson, a reputedly dangerous man.

Its writer further said that Jack had to flee his own country, but his real crime was not being pardoned by the Americans for defeating and crushing their idol, James Jeffries.

La Presse said the bout was the biggest pugilistic event of the year. "It's the return to the ring of the extraordinary pugilist, the best who ever existed." It anticipated an excellent and fascinating contest, for Jim Johnson was respected as "the strongest fighter in the world."

> Jim Johnson has shown himself to be the equal of Sam Langford in 1910, and he was only a novice. Since then he has made great progress, and is actually at his best form. Yes we said that Jim Johnson has shown himself to be the equal of Sam Langford. He has proven it in front of us with his draw match with Sam McVea, a performance that Langford could only faintly duplicate some weeks later. However, Jim Johnson has shown himself on two separate occasions to be the master of Joe Jeanette. Jim Johnson is thus one of the most qualified to meet the world champion. The combat tonight will be just as interesting as it is important.

Their measurements were listed as Jack Johnson – height 1 meter 85 centimeters, weight 97 kilograms (about 213 ½ pounds)(though he likely weighed much more), Jim Johnson – height 1 meter 79 centimeters, weight 101 kilograms (222 ½ pounds).

The fight was scheduled for 10 rounds (contrary to the erroneous belief of some that it was scheduled for longer). All of the local French press and on-scene correspondents from the *New York Herald*, *London Times*, and *London Daily Mail* confirmed and advertised the bout as being a scheduled 10 rounds of three minutes each.

The hall was well-filled with a huge crowd, and many women were present. Three contests preceded the main event. Hence, it was not until 11:35 p.m., more than an hour past the advertised time, that the two men faced each other in the ring. The contest started at 11:45 p.m.

1 - According to the *London Daily Mail*, after some preliminary sparring, Jack went straight in and jabbed his left home several times. Then he uppercut the right to the body and hooked a hard left on the other side. He shaped up well and got away from a left in exceedingly clever style. Both men were boxing well. It was evident that Jack was far from being the back number that some people reckoned him to be.

The *London Times* said the opening round showed both men in a good light. Jack appeared fit and in good form.

Le Matin said both men were playing a waiting game.

2 - The *Daily Mail* said they crouched cautiously. Jim tried a right uppercut but Jack slipped it and showed a mouthful of gold teeth in a broad smile. Jim stood up well and stopped some hard lefts to the jaw. The champ kept rushing, but could not land with effect. In a clinch, Jim showed his tongue in apparent derision.

Le Matin said Jack, who was getting closer and trying a couple of hard hits without results, was smiling and laughing, and the public was doing the same as well.

3 - In a clinch, Jack threw Jim off like a baby and tried to force the fighting. He put Jim's glove aside, but could not land even though the move caused laughter. Then Jim began to fight, and landed a clean straight right to the jaw, afterwards uppercutting Jack to the body. "The blows might have upset a weak white, but they only made Jack grin."

4 - Jack poked his right to the face, but Jim's long left and crouch were hard to get past. Jack landed a left hook to the jaw and a jab to the face. Jim's feet saved him, and he came back and landed a straight punch hard to the jaw. At the end of the round they were in Jim's corner with Jack trying hard to land. "The contest up to that point had proved not only that Jack Johnson was no back number, but that still another negro stood between the many white hopes and the world's championship." Jack Johnson still had it, but Jim Johnson was a good fighter as well.

5 - The *Daily Mail* said Jim fought hard, but Jack came back in dead earnest, and his fierce jabs would have finished most fighters. He kept hooking his left, and landed one hard to the body. Jack was the stronger fighter and better boxer in this round.

Le Matin said Jack was getting warmed up. He attacked, but the defensive Jim avoided most everything. From time to time, Jack hit the stomach, following with a blow of "Han!" like a lumber-jack hitting with an axe. However, it was clear that it was going to be a fight in which the skirmishes were monotonous, for there was a great deal of clinching and defense, and not a lot of punching.

6 - The *Daily Mail* said Jim started rushing from the gong, but got more than he could manage. Jack landed a right cross, and later a good jab to the face. Jim fought hard to the body, and twice landed well.

Le Matin said Jim socked it to the "café au lait wall" that was Jack Johnson.

7 - The *Daily Mail* said Jim was tired and fought poorly. A section of the crowd began to shout "fake." They were displeased with the little action that was taking place. The end of the round was greeted with hooting.

Le Matin said that in this round, Jack started to have labored breathing, and his blows were becoming weaker. With his force betraying him, his face became grave and almost tragic. Jim took the upper hand.

8 - The gong starting the round sounded with an uproar from the crowd. They wanted to see a fight, and let the fighters know it. Jim Johnson, in response to Frank Moran's shouted advice, stepped in and landed a straight right on the face. However, they again clinched, as usual.

The shouting broke out afresh, some calling out, "Give us our money back." The house had become very rowdy. They had expected a knockout, but the men's pace and style clearly was not going to give them that.

The *London Times* said Jim appeared to be fighting, but Jack seemed glad to rest in the clinches at every opportunity.

Conversely, the *London Daily Mail* said that despite the fans' discontent, the men seemed to be trying hard.

However, the "arrangement" idea had spread. The fans strongly believed the boxers were faking and working together, which caused spectators to shout their disapproval so loudly that it drowned out the sound of the gong.

9 - This was another monotonous round with a great deal of clinching and not much punching or landing on either side.

10 - *Le Matin* said that in the last round, the fat champion threw insults at his adversary. With derision, he presented the side of his face. Jack threw but missed, and got hit in the stomach.

The *London Daily Mail* said Jim fought cleverly and with effect. He landed two fine rights to the body, but in a rush slipped and fell. Both were hitting hard at the end.

The *London Times* said the last round was the same as before - dull. The spectators occasionally shouted, "Bravo, Jack," or "Fake." Jim landed several straight blows to the face. At the end, the malcontents were in the vast majority, and a terrific hubbub marked the conclusion of what it called a thoroughly unsatisfactory encounter.

Owing to the crowd noise, several minutes elapsed before the decision could be heard. The two judges, Frantz-Reichel and Georges Oudin, rendered their decisions. One gave it to Jim Johnson because he was breathing better, lasted to the end, and dominated the sparring in the last round. The other judge called it a draw. Referee M. Maitrot shared the opinion that the fight was a draw. Hence, because two out of the three officials called it a draw, the fight was ruled a draw. In today's parlance, it was a majority draw.

When the decision was announced, some spectators demanded their money back, while others cheered derisively. When the explanation was added that Jack Johnson had broken his left arm in an early round and had been unable to use it effectively, a shout of derisive laughter went up. The audience dispersed, continuing to express its disapproval of the proceedings.

Jack Johnson indeed complained of pain in his left arm, which was swelling. Two doctors examined him and issued a statement that his arm presented a fracture in the middle of the left forearm. He had a fracture of the third part of his left radius.

As of 1:45 a.m., a doctor confirmed that the radial bone in Jack's left forearm was fractured.

Jack said that his arm was broken when swinging on Jim's head in the 3rd round.

Le Matin said Johnson's broken arm explained to a certain degree the bad form that the champion showed.

Summarizing, the *London Times* said it was a draw after 10 inconclusive and most unsatisfactory rounds. After the first 3 rounds, the constant clinching brought forth outspoken criticism from the spectators, who shouted "Fake!" After the 7th round, the crowd's opinion about the fight found more definite expressing, all the way to the end.

The *New York Herald* said Champion Jack was spoiled by too much tango dancing and catch-as-can wrestling. He never showed a glimmer of his old form, and before half of the ten rounds had elapsed, was blowing like a bull. All of the bout's wrestling showed its effects on the champion, who was cheered derisively in a so-called battle. Both boxers seemed to treat the matter as a huge joke, and neither ever made a real effort to fight.

The *Herald* said the Paris press called it a huge fiasco. The *Matin* banteringly treated it more as a laughing contest than a boxing match. The *Excelsior* said it was grotesque, and felt that the referee should have declared it a no contest, for it was clear that neither man was trying.

Alluding to the recent dispute regarding whether Johnson should be stripped of the championship title, *Le Matin* said perhaps France was correct in the conflict which divided the two countries.

> In any case, what happened at Premierland between the two Johnsons was not to the advantage of the person who is trying to vindicate his championship claim, the famous Jack Johnson. Too much tango, too many special productions, too much catch as can, certainly drowned the form of Jack. Jack presented himself, as always, in admirable fashion, as always his café au lait skin color, smiling as always with gold teeth, but completely out of breath as soon as he started to try to force the opinionated resistance of Jim. Even though he was fat, he was as agile and flexible as a feline. Jack was hoping to have an easy victory. He was joking with his managers. Frank Moran challenged the winner.

Le Petit Parisien was not as harsh. It said the fans came in droves to see two famous colossal black fighters. However,

> To say that they returned satisfied doesn't exactly tell the truth, because a certain number expressed disappointment. Yet these two Negroes fought conscientiously. Jack placed many fabulous hooks to the jaw and not too shabby ones directly to the stomach. Already one counted on his victory, but when the fourth round was reached one remarked that he had stopped using his left arm. He continued nevertheless, and until the end of the fight he used only his right arm and resisted Jim. The referee declared that the match was a draw, and announced to justify this unintended result that Jack Johnson had his left radius broken.

L'Humanite said the fight represented the fall of an idol.

> The match last night did not give everything that was promised to the public, which came out in great numbers to watch the beginning of the Parisian world championship, and they vocally expressed their unhappiness. As soon as he appeared in the ring, the yellow Negro made a considerable impression. From the beginning there was the feeling that he would take down his adversary with ease.

> When I read the notes taken from the course of the match, I am astonished at the difference from the first rounds and the last ones.

> At the end of the 1st round, Jack had a huge advantage. He well defended with his left fist in front. He dominated against the large size of his adversary, who held himself in a low defensive position.

> For four rounds the champ was mastering the dance, hitting when and where he wanted. He was happy to show a golden smile when Jim would counter.

The following round, it was Jim's turn to do the forcing. Jack could hardly do much to stop him. This continued until the end of the match, when it was called a draw.

The public was informed that Jack broke his left arm in the course of the match.

Le Temps said that in front of a large audience, they boxed 10 monotonous rounds.

We have to recognize, and in accordance with the great majority of the public, that the impression Jack gave was rather to his disadvantage. He threw out a couple of lovely hits, but didn't show himself very combative except for a couple minutes during the 3rd round, and he obtained a draw against an adversary who dominated him during the last portion of the 10 rounds.

Poor Jack Johnson! Yesterday morning he wrote to the *New York Herald* a letter in which, having invited sportsmen to come and see him, he was going to affirm that he was still the man who beat Jeffries and Burns. He called himself invincible. "I am willing to defend my title against any challenger, and those who will see me box my first opponent, Jim Johnson, at the Premierland, Friday night will be convinced that I am still the man who beat Jeffries, Tommy Burns, etc., and I really deserve the name of invincible which the Americans themselves gave me."

What a pity! The invincible was able with all alacrity to secure a draw, even though he was meeting a man of the third order, who he dominated with his size and superior reach.

For those who are discussing who the actual champion is, Jack furnished an excellent argument against himself. It is clear that we did not find ourselves before a trained boxer carefully prepared. It will take 6 months to arrive at the same condition as that of Joe Jeannette or Sam Langford.

For the initiates of boxing, it was nevertheless interesting to see the slightly fat champion in the ring, because he is gifted with remarkable means. He possesses notably a left which he uses wonderfully to throw doubles with an astonishing virtuosity. But all of these qualities disappear after some rounds of a hard battle if one is not prepared for it.

The winner of tonight's battle [Langford-Jeannette] would seem to be more of a champion than the one who showed up yesterday. It is annoying to think that the invincible could consent to present himself before the eyes of the knowing public in such a state as he was in last night. This excellent athlete who is in retirement perhaps thought that we didn't know what boxing was in our country.

The *Los Angeles Daily Times*, *Omaha World Herald*, and *New York American*, via A.P. wire, had similar reports. One was entitled "Jack Johnson Hooted As Faker."

> The spectators loudly protested throughout that the men were not fighting, and demanded their money back. ... The organizers of the fight explained the fiasco by asserting that Jack Johnson's left arm was broken in the third round. ... During the first three rounds he was obviously playing with his opponent. After that it was observed that he was using only his right hand. ... When the fight was over he complained that his arm had been injured. Doctors who made an examination certified to a slight fracture of the radius of the left arm. The general opinion is that his arm was injured in a wrestling match early in the week, and that a blow tonight caused the fracture of the bone.[867]

The *New York Times* and *New York Journal* contained several A.P. wire versions. Some said that Jack Johnson was "battered" around the ring, barely saved from a knockout, and was "plainly groggy" when the bell ended the bout. The "three shades blacker" Jim Johnson crouched quite low and forced the action throughout, mostly attacking the body.

More in line with the local reports, also said was, "The bout, a ten-round affair, was a disappointment to the crowd in attendance, and Jack Johnson left the ring amid a storm of jeers and hisses from the angry assemblage." Disappointed by the lack of action, the crowd wanted its money back.

After being told that Johnson broke his left arm, the crowd responded, "When does he say he broke it?" The reply was, "In the 3rd round."

> This announcement was followed by more jeering and hissing, as the spectators had failed to notice any sign of an injured arm at that stage or later, Johnson feinted with his left continually, and showed much of his old-time skill in this part of his boxing. It was science alone that saved him from being knocked out within ten rounds. It was the general impression among the spectators that the injury had been sustained in the last minute of the fight, when Jim Johnson rushed Jack to the ropes and the two went to the floor with Jack's arms closed about Jim's waist. Both men jumped up quickly but Jack was plainly exhausted and he fell against the ropes as the gong sounded. Then he tottered to his corner, holding his left arm and declaring it was broken.

Jack appeared to be in good shape. He hardly could blame the poor showing on lack of condition. If he was overweight, it was only slightly so. He had been training for some time to condition himself for his bout with Frank Moran, set for January 19. He also had been promised a match with

---

867 *Los Angeles Daily Times*, *Omaha World Herald*, *New York American*, December 20, 1913.

the winner of the upcoming bout between Langford and Jeannette. He regarded Jim Johnson merely as a tryout or warm-up.

Johnson landed a couple of smashing body blows with his left in the 2nd round, but caused his foe no concern. He tried to use the same blow several times in the later rounds, but the efforts were all blocked. Jim Johnson, crouching in the style of Jeffries, but even lower, forced the fighting all the way, making his attack on the stomach. In the 7th round, he broke down the champ's guard three times, and each time he followed with terrific uppercuts which grazed the jaw. Only the champ's defensive cleverness saved him.

Jack showed plenty of confidence at the start, but his smile soon wore off when the going became rough. At one point he called over to Frank Moran, who was at ringside, and asked him if he wanted to get into the ring and hold Jim.

The fight was a big disappointment to the backers of the upcoming Moran-Johnson bout, for it was opined that the latter had lost most of his power as a drawing card. However, some noted that it was the general impression that if Moran had been in the ring that he would have won the championship. That made more folks intrigued by their upcoming fight.[868]

Overall, the general tone of the articles, particularly written by the local reporters, was that the crowd felt it had been denied a good fight, and that the broken arm was used to explain why Jack had done so little. Usually, crowds only demand their money back when they have been denied a good fight, not out of anger at a decision. If Johnson had been battered in the way that the *Times* article indicated, it would be unlikely that the crowd would have been dissatisfied and demanding a refund. It appears that the fight, for the most part, was a dull, cautious, defensive wrestling match.

As a result of Johnson's broken arm, his upcoming January 1914 bout with Frank Moran had to be postponed.

A couple days after the fight, the *New York American* offered another report from Paris:

> The poor battle which the champion made was the cause of much dissatisfaction here. Those who attended the bout believed that Johnson should have disposed of his lesser experienced opponent in short order.
>
> This dissatisfaction was appeased to some extent when it was stated after the fight that Johnson had fractured a bone in his left arm during the third round of the fray.
>
> He was to have met Moran here January 19.[869]

Jacques Mortane of *La Vie Au Grand Air* was not at the match, but described the fight based on what he heard about it from others. Many had

---

[868] *New York Times, New York Journal*, December 20, 1913.
[869] *New York American*, December 21, 1913.

believed that the bout would be a parody, but it was a sincere fight. Word was that Jack Johnson as a champion was only a vague memory, with merely photos and cinematograph films left to show what he once was. He thought his adversary would be easy, but his breath left him. He was himself for the first three rounds only. In the 5th he broke his left arm, the one he liked to use the most. The only good thing for Jack was a draw. It would not have been wrong to say that Jim Johnson had won. Jack Johnson's record forevermore would have the mark, "draw match with Jim Johnson." More than 2,000 spectators saw the bout.[870]

It was Johnson's first fight in over a year and a half, since the Flynn bout in July 1912. Prior to that, he had not fought since July 1910 against Jeffries. His inactivity was in part due to circumstances (including his race); as well as economics. Inactivity, lack of serious training, and the broken arm all contributed to the poor performance. And yet he still managed a draw against a solid, experienced, strong fighter. Given Johnson's propensity to play defense and neutralize his opponents, it can be understood why paying fight fans would not appreciate a Johnson fight; even without an injury hampering him. The fact that the fight was slow and dull did not mean that Johnson no longer had it. Regardless, many believed that at this point, Johnson was vulnerable and it was the beginning of the end of his career.

The very next day after Johnson vs. Johnson, on December 20, 1913 at the Wonderland Francais in Paris, in a match advertised as being for the world championship, in a hard contest, 185-pound (84 kilos) Sam Langford decisively won a 20-round decision over 187-pound (85 kilos) Joe Jeannette. In the 13th round, Jeannette was down 3 times for nine-counts. He was a pitiable figure at the finish. Many in France started calling Langford the world heavyweight champion.

Pour le championnat du monde de boxe

The French magazine *Le Plein Air* asked,

Is Jack Johnson still worthy of the title of boxing world champion? ... For us it is proven. ... [T]he black Langford, who brilliantly beat the other black fighter Joe Jeannette, is quite worthy of the title of world's boxing champion. ... Organizers should seek to establish in the shortest time possible, a Jack Johnson-Langford meeting, and this time definitely for the title. If Johnson avoids fighting such a competitor, Langford should be proclaimed the world's champion. Langford has undoubtedly defeated Joe Jeannette magnificently.

---

[870] *La Vie Au Grand Air,* December 27, 1913.

The magazine went on to voice its disgust with the Jack Johnson versus Jim Johnson match, calling the bout a big disappointment.[871]

After Langford's victory, the ex-middleweight champion of South Africa said, "I am convinced, after seeing the two Johnsons, Jeannette, and Langford in the ring, that Jack Johnson is master of them all, but that Langford has more chance than anyone else of defeating him."[872]

Gunboat Smith, who held a victory over Langford, was in training to fight Arthur Pelkey, who had upset Luther McCarty to win the white championship. Both fighters were amenable to fighting Johnson if they won, possibly in Mexico. Jim Coffroth said he had received word from Johnson asking for a match with the winner.[873]

On December 29, 1913 in New Haven, Connecticut, Jess Willard knocked out George Rodel in the 9th round with a single right uppercut. The *Freeman* reported that the fight fans believed that Willard could knock out any of the present heavyweights.

On January 1, 1914 at Jim Coffroth's arena in Daly City, California, in the San Francisco area, Gunboat Smith knocked out Arthur Pelkey in the 15th round with a right to the jaw, winning the white world heavyweight championship.

Johnson had discovered Smith and started him. Smith had been his sparring partner in 1909. The *Freeman* said,

> Then someone started the story that Smith knocked Johnson down while engaging in a little work-out bout. It was a good press agent yarn, and Johnson stood for it, as he was willing to get any publicity. He said a lot of nice things about Smith, and intimated that he could hit as hard as any man he had ever faced. It brought Smith to the notice of the promoters and he was given a start in the four-round game in Frisco. He was not much of a success in the short bouts, but Jim Buckley spotted him and via the long route has brought him to the top of the white hope class.

Smith had the Johnson stamp of approval, and that meant something. "The champ would not have stood for the advertisement that he was knocked down by a dead one."

Some said Johnson had forfeited his title by refusing to fight Langford. However, Johnson simply had said that he was not going to fight a top man for less than $30,000. Johnson had been promised $35,000 for his scheduled bout with Moran. He expected to get that much for a Langford fight.[874]

With his arm in splints, On January 8, 1914, Johnson said,

[871] *La Presse, New York Herald,* December 21, 1913; *Le Plein Air* December 25, 1913.
[872] *London Daily Mail,* December 22, 1913.
[873] *New York American,* December 21, 1913. Tommy Burns managed Pelkey, while Jim Buckley managed Smith.
[874] *Freeman,* January 10, 17, 1914, February 7, 1914.

I am ready to fight if the offer meets my terms, which are $30,000, but the fight must be subsequent to that which has been definitely fixed to take place in Paris during the first week of June against Frank Moran, the Pittsburgh heavyweight, for which William Astor Chanler…is guaranteeing me $35,000.

I expect toward the end of the same month to meet Sam Langford, provided the $30,000 I demand be forthcoming.

Johnson said his broken arm had been progressing well, and the splints were scheduled to be removed that Saturday.[875]

Jack Johnson and Frank Moran had signed to meet in a 20-round contest in Paris in June. Charles McCarthy, representing a group of three American millionaires who were supplying the money, handed Johnson a $35,000 check, while Moran was guaranteed $5,000. The checks were not payable until the day of the fight. The fighters agreed not to fight anyone else until the day of the fight. McCarthy intimated that the group he represented was motivated by the desire to see a white man re-take the championship, and, impressed by his annihilation of Palzer, they liked Moran's chances. Hence, they were willing to finance the fight.

Both parties signed the articles in the Pavillion Duphine in the Bois de Boulogne. After signing, Johnson and Moran drank to each other's health in goblets of champagne. Three moving picture machines filmed it all.

Billy Lewis said man's physical supremacy had been a theme of mankind. Therefore, the "best physical man is yet an object of distinction whether savage or civilized." Hence, the heavyweight championship, as the symbol of the world's top man, was important.

On January 13, 1914, a California jury acquitted Jess Willard of a charge of prize-fighting, which had resulted in John Young's death.

That same day, Jack Blackburn, future Joe Louis trainer, was paroled from the penitentiary after having served four and a half years of his murder sentence.

The New York State Athletic Commission's annual report showed that since the boxing law went into effect in August 1911, about $110,000 had been paid into the State Controller's office.[876]

---

[875] *New York Times*, January 9, 1914. William Astor Chanler was a former explorer, New York State Assemblyman, soldier and military leader (including the Spanish American War), Congressman (a Democrat), businessman (real estate and mining made him a millionaire), and hotel and race-horse owner. He later was known for anti-Semitic writings.

On January 26, 1914 in Taft, California, Tommy Burns scored a KO4 over Battling Brant.[877]

The *New York Age* noted that at first, white U.S. sporting writers were disposed to accuse Johnson of faking in his bout with Battling Jim Johnson.

> However, convincing evidence has been received by Tom Flanagan, a sporting writer on the *Toronto Evening Telegram*, that the champion actually met with a mishap.

> Flanagan has received two X-ray photographs of Johnson's injured arm, one showing it before it was set and the other after the cast had been removed. The first photograph showed the bone completely smashed, while the second showed that the arm had been set and was rapidly mending. ...

> Although in his fight with "Battling" Jim Johnson the champion broke his arm in the third round, he refused to quit and for seven rounds went through a most painful ordeal.

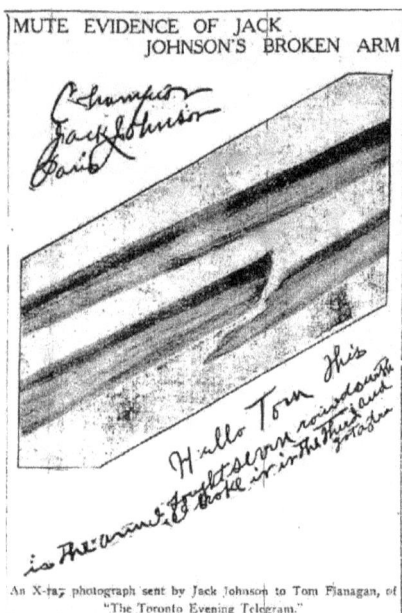

MUTE EVIDENCE OF JACK JOHNSON'S BROKEN ARM

An X-ray photograph sent by Jack Johnson to Tom Flanagan, of "The Toronto Evening Telegram."

Johnson was called nervy and courageous. There was no way to get his goat, although many tried. "Johnson first became unpopular with the white sporting writers of this country because of his refusal to do their bidding, many of them believing it was necessary for the champion to have white advisors."

The *Evening Mail*'s sporting editor opined that the reason why the New York Boxing Commission had drawn the color line was to protect white boxers from the humiliation of defeat by a black man. Of course that was manifestly unfair to black fighters, who had as much right to obtain the top rung in pugilism as in any other walk of life. "Fear is all that makes a boxer draw the color line. Either Jeannette, Langford or Johnson, if only half trained, could murder any white heavyweight now in the ring."[878]

---

[876] *Freeman*, January 10, 17, 24, 1914.

[877] *New York World*, January 27, 1914. Burns dazzled him with his speed and feinting. Brant was big and strong, but with inferior boxing knowledge. In the 4th round, Burns landed a hard left shift to the body that doubled up Brant. Then he landed three hard right uppercuts. Brant's arms dropped, and because he was helpless and practically out, Referee Blake stopped it.

[878] *New York Age*, January 29, 1914.

The *Freeman* opined that black supremacy in boxing was about over, for top blacks were starting to decline. "The black heavyweight dynasty is almost at an end, and with a big field of fairly good white heavyweights coming along, it seems only a matter of a short time before the white race will furnish an undisputed heavyweight champion." Langford had beaten McVea, but lost to Gunboat Smith, which hurt his reputation. "Jeannette's showing against Langford at Paris just about ends Joe's claims."

Gunboat Smith and Jess Willard were matched on January 18 to fight 20 rounds in San Francisco on July 4. Willard's manager guaranteed Smith $7,500. They had met the previous May, when Smith won a decision.

Gunboat Smith said that although he would rather be matched to fight Johnson, he was pleased to secure a match with Willard.

> I beat him before in twenty rounds, and I am sure I can do it again. He is a big, tough fellow, but I am sure I am his master. His victories over the other white heavyweights entitle him to a match with me. ... Willard has only one punch, and that is a right uppercut. If he can land with this wallop it is curtains for his opponent. When I fought him he never came close to landing. ... I only hope I can secure a match with Johnson after I trim Willard.[879]

On January 23, the London Olympic Sporting Club offered Johnson a $30,000 purse, split ¾ to the winner and ¼ to the loser if he would box Langford. London's National Sporting Club offered a $15,000 purse for a Johnson-Langford match. Even assuming England would allow Johnson to box there, Johnson was matched to meet Moran in Paris in June for a $35,000 guarantee regardless of winner, more than what they were offering for a Langford fight. Johnson knew he could get more than what they were offering. He practically could dictate his own terms, because most sportsmen believed he was champion until defeated inside the ring.[880]

Some remained bitter over the fact that Johnson had been allowed to escape the United States. In January 1914, various stories and rumors circulated insinuating that large sums of money changed hands in bribes to federal officials who had aided Johnson in his flight from Chicago. Johnson allegedly admitted making such payments. U.S. District Attorney James Wilkerson instituted a grand jury investigation, though ultimately no one was charged. Regardless, the reports only increased the government's ill-will towards Johnson.

---

[879] *Freeman*, January 31, 1914. Gunboat Smith was on a tear of late, though back in 1910 and 1911, he had been stopped by Jim Barry, Joe Willis, and Jack Geyer, and in 1912 had lost decisions to Geyer and Jim Stewart. Smith's victories since then included: 1912 KO7 Jim Stewart and W20 Frank Moran; 1913 KO2 Billy Wells, WND10 George Rodel, W20 Jess Willard, KO3 Rodel, KO5 Jim Flynn, WDQ5 Carl Morris, KO10 Tony Ross, and W12 Sam Langford; and 1914 KO15 Arthur Pelkey.

[880] *Freeman*, January 31, 1914.

The *Chicago Defender* contended that the champion was more sinned against than he had sinned. One Chicago newspaper said the whole case was a plot to get Johnson.[881]

Jack Johnson was persona non grata in England. Johnson tried to give an exhibition at Hanley, in North Staffordshire, England, but the newspapers raised such a holler that the lease on the football field was canceled and all the halls were barred against him.

> More than once I have said England is beginning to feel what the Negro problem means. She has nearly total Africa for redemption. … She must deal with the raw recruit from the bush. … The leading sentiment moulder, the statesmen, the politicians, have given it out that a bad precedent is established when a black man whips a white man. They have in mind the turbulent state of Africa…where England controls.

Dan McKetrick, Moran's manager, who also managed Jeannette, made the French government an offer of $4,000 to use the arena of the Grand Palais in the Champs Elysees for the Johnson-Moran fight.

Parisians had been spoiled by so many good fights. "Ten years ago if Jack Johnson and Jim Johnson had pulled off their little brother act before a French fight crowd, the chances are the spectators would have become hysterical with delight over the make-believe swings and the futile uppercuts." Instead, they yelled, "Throw them out. Give us back our money." That fight had hurt Johnson's popularity in Paris.

The notion that Johnson was through and all-in as a fighter was widespread. Thus, there was growing suspicion that whoever paid Johnson to fight was going to reimburse himself by betting on the other man. The feeling was that Moran's backers paid Johnson big money to fight because they believed Moran would beat him, and they would be rich as a result of the wagers, film rights, and future value of the championship.

Johnson vs. Moran was set to take place on June 27, the day before the Grand Prix, for a purse of 200,000 francs, or 8,000 pounds.[882]

In a letter dated February 24, 1914, Johnson said he barred no one, but wanted $30,000 for every bout staged.

> The whole world wants to see a white man champion. I have signed to fight a white man and because I refused a ridiculously small price to meet Langford the proposed promoters and Langford's manager tried to create the impression that I would never fight again. Langford or his agent never would induce anyone with real money to back him against me. That's the reason for his soreness.
>
> I am the same John Arthur Johnson, undisputed champion of the world, and after Moran I will fight the white man who stands out, be

[881] *Chicago Defender*, January 31, February 7, 1914.
[882] *Freeman*, February, 14, 1914; *Mirror of Life and Boxing World*, February 21, 1914.

he Gunboat Smith, Battling Levinsky, Jess Willard or Georges Carpentier.

I bar no one when I get my price. Moran's backers met my terms, and all the others have the same chance as Moran. I understand that Gunboat Smith defeated Langford. Here's the gunner's chance to get a crack at my title.

The public wants a white man to be my successor. I am ready to fight 'em all, and bar no one, at $30,000 apiece.[883]

The *Chicago Defender* noted that despite suppressing films like Jeffries-Johnson, the Chicago Board of Censors failed to suppress moving pictures that bred race hatred, allowing the projection of a recent film called *Levinsky's Holiday*, which featured a frolic called "Hit the Nigger." It used to be "Hit the Jew" or "Down with the Irish," but alert members of those races watched with hawk-like eyes any attempt to belittle their people. Instead of protesting, most black patrons simply laughed or remained silent.

Eventually, Chicago's colored citizens won their fight to get a member of their race onto the Film Censor Board. A local church pastor was appointed to the board which put its approval on every picture shown in Chicago, and he could object to the many pictures ridiculing blacks.[884]

On March 21, 1914 in Paris, Joe Jeannette won a 15-round decision over Georges Carpentier, the French and European heavyweight champion. Carpentier's defeat was a great surprise to his followers, who were of the opinion that he was the ring's greatest fighter, particularly after his KO4 and KO1 knockout victories over Billy Wells.[885]

On March 27, 1914 in New York, Sam Langford won a 10-round no-decision against Battling Jim Johnson. Clearly, Battling Jim was a tough cookie and not easily taken out, even by a puncher like Langford.

Frank Moran said his upcoming bout with Johnson was looked forward to as a big society event. In Paris, almost as many women attended bouts as men. A bound book containing the two fighters' records and history was being created. It would sell for $5 or $6 and would earn the fighters a lot of money, for there was a big demand for advertising space in it.

Moran returned to New York from Paris. He looked remarkably well conditioned and stated emphatically, without a trace of boasting, that he was going to whip Lil Arthur. "I'm in the pink of condition, because all the time that I have been away I have been taking care of myself. That doesn't go with Johnson, however, and I am confident that I will be able to whip him on points, if not a knockout. … I'm going to be the winner."

Johnson had done much to popularize boxing, not because of love for him, but because white men wanted to see a white man on the throne.

---

[883] *Chicago Defender*, March 14, 1914.
[884] *Chicago Defender*, February 28, 1914. *New York Age*, March 26, 1914.
[885] *New York Age*, March 26, 1914.

Hence there was a wide advocacy of boxing bouts almost everywhere in order to develop the man who would bring back the crown to Caucasia. Conversely, the Negro ranks were not being reinforced.

Johnson was in Stockholm, Sweden, scheduled to engage in wrestling matches. However, he was forced to leave Sweden, owing to the hostile demonstration against him.[886]

A lot of blackmailers were using the Mann Act to their advantage. Many men were being trapped into violating the law and then being forced to pay large sums of money to the female schemers in order to avoid threatened prosecution. "Those who have contended that the Mann white slave law was revived to persecute Jack Johnson declare that the champion pugilist is vindicated in the present dissatisfaction with the law. The department of justice will probably recommend an amendment of law, as a result of the operations of blackmailers in all parts of the county." The proposed amendment would limit its application to commercial vice. Most prosecutions had been one-sided affairs, with the man suffering and the woman, even if she was willingly guilty, going free, which gave them the power to blackmail.[887]

The latest report was that Johnson's $30,000 purse would be paid to his white wife on the day of the fight. "I say white wife, the words used in the dispatches, to show that that thing rankles deep yet. When Johnson went to Paris nothing was thought there of his intermarriage. It may be now that his new countrymen have gone to thinking about it. … [S]ome go so far as to say the authorities think of sending Johnson out of the country as an undesirable citizen."

Moran was doing vaudeville, making a nice salary because he was the man who was next to meet the champion. Frank said if he could deliver the knockout it would be worth a million dollars to him, "and he is right, it will be worth more; it will bring him the plaudits of the white civilization."[888]

As of April 1914, Jack Johnson was continuing to give boxing exhibitions and theatrical performances.

On April 14, 1914, Johnson's appeal of his White-Slave Traffic Act criminal convictions found a partial but significant legal victory. Although the U.S. Court of Appeals for the Seventh Circuit in Chicago sustained Johnson's conviction on two counts regarding his payment for the transport of Belle Schreiber across state lines for the immoral purpose of having sexual relations with her, and upheld the law's constitutionality and Congress' broad grant of jurisdiction, the evidence on the counts charging him with inducing Schreiber to come to Chicago so that she might engage in prostitution was held to be insufficient, and his convictions on those counts were overturned.

---

[886] *Freeman*, March 28, 1914.
[887] *Chicago Defender*, March 28, 1914.
[888] *Freeman*, April 11, 1914.

The government petitioned for a rehearing, which was granted, but on June 9, the Court again reversed the conviction on the prostitution counts and upheld the conviction on the sexual intercourse charges.

The Court remanded and held that the government could retry Johnson if it had additional evidence sufficient to support the prostitution counts. If not, the counts would be dismissed.

The Court also held that in light of the fact that his sentence improperly took into account his erroneous conviction on the now overturned prostitution counts, Johnson should be re-sentenced.

In its ruling upholding the convictions on the sexual relations counts, the Court found that the government had proven that after Schreiber (whom it called "the girl") had told a Johnson employee of her plight; the next day she received a telegram saying, "I am sending you $75. Go to Chicago at Graham's and wait until I get there, Jack." She drew the money from the Postal Telegraph Company, purchased a ticket from Pittsburgh to Chicago, and traveled there on the Pennsylvania Railroad. Johnson testified that he would not say that he had or had not sent the telegrams, but the fact that upon his arrival in Chicago he called Schreiber by telephone at Graham's, combined with Schreiber's testimony that Johnson asked her, "Did you receive the $75 I sent you?" warranted the jury in finding that he authored the messages.

Proof that Johnson's intent was to have sexual relations was bolstered by the fact that even before aiding her, "defendant habitually indulged in promiscuous sexual intercourse, that this girl was a prostitute; that defendant first met her several years before in a brothel; that throughout the period of their acquaintance they maintained sexual relations; and that frequently defendant in his journeys about the country took the girl with him, or had her travel to meet him, and always for the purpose of sexual intercourse." Johnson and Schreiber had traveled to and from Pittsburgh, Atlantic City, Chicago, Cleveland, Detroit, Buffalo, Toronto, and Montreal, and the finances were provided by Johnson, and at each place sexual relations were maintained.

However, the Court held that there was insufficient evidence that at the time he provided her with money to travel that Johnson's intent was for her to cross state lines for the purpose of engaging in prostitution. The mere fact that he subsequently supplied her with money to enable her to open up and run a brothel was not enough, for it only raised suspicion regarding his intent at the time he provided the money for the train ride. There were no supplementary facts. There was no proof that Johnson had been connected with or interested in brothels or had ever aided anyone to engage in prostitution. In fact, the Court held that the prostitution evidence was "slight and dubious."

The Court criticized the government for its attempts to inflame the jury's passions, and for not dismissing counts it knew it could not prove:

In his opening statement the government's attorney said:

"Another immoral purpose is one too obscene to mention, the purpose being for defendant to compel these women to commit the crime against nature upon his body. ..."

We must assume that the government's attorney, when he made the statement, believed he could produce the evidence. But at some time before he closed he knew that the picture he had drawn of the negro pugilist could not be verified. Yet not until after defendant's attorney had made a motion to that effect after the close of the government's case were the crime against nature counts withdrawn from the consideration of the jury. A desire, if not a duty, to be fair should have led the government's attorney to withdraw that heinous charge the moment he knew it could not be substantiated.

The Court opined similarly with respect to the unsupported and unproven claim in the government's opening statement that Johnson from time to time had three women with him and would drop one off and put her into a sporting house to relieve himself of the necessity of spending money carrying her about the country while he had the others. There was no proof of such allegations.

Further, the Court noted that the government improperly attempted to inflame the jury with its questioning of Johnson on cross examination:

Q. As a matter of fact that sickness (of a woman called Etta) was caused by blows from your hands, wasn't it?
A. No.
Q. Well, it was caused by blow or blows from your hands?
A. No, no.
Q. Was it not caused by blows received by Etta in Pekin Theater here in Chicago at your hands?
A. No.
Q. Did you not carry her out or have her carried out and put in the automobile and taken to the Washington Park Hospital after you had beaten her up?
A. No, no.
Q. Hattie was in the hospital while you were there, was she?
A. Not that I know of.
Q. Did you have any difficulty with her about putting her in a hospital?
A. No.
Q. Did you have any similar difficulty with Belle— fisticuff difficulty?
A. What is that?
Q. You had struck Belle on various occasions?
A. Never in my life.
Q. Do you remember using an automobile tool on her?
A. Never in my life.
Q. You never did that?
A. Never.

Q. You say you did not?

A. I say no, emphatically no.

Q. And bruised her side until it was black and blue?

The government's lawyer persistently repeated insinuating questions "with the obvious object of having his innuendoes taken in preference to the sworn answer."

A witness for the government was asked about a conversation he had on Christmas Eve, 1910, with Johnson regarding Etta. "He asked me to go to the hospital with him to call upon her. He told me he had had a fight with her at Bob Mott's Café on State street." The Court noted that such testimony was duly objected to. "We find nothing in the record to justify the injection into the case of the collateral question whether defendant exercised his fighting abilities upon women."

All of these questions "show the atmosphere of prejudice that pervades the record." Hence, "When the situation thus improperly created is measured against the doubtfully sustainable prostitution counts, we are all convinced that defendant did not have a fair trial on that issue."

Yet, despite the government's improper inflammation of the jury's passions, the Court did not reverse the sexual relations counts on those grounds, for "the record demonstrates that, no matter how improperly the prejudices of jurors may have been aroused, no other verdict could properly have been reached." Some folks, then and now, might strongly disagree.[889]

A less than pleased U.S. District Attorney James Wilkerson noted that although the evidence was held to be sufficient to sustain two counts charging improper relations, "Apparently the court holds the evidence insufficient to sustain the other counts, notwithstanding the known character of the woman and the known facts that Johnson met her in a disorderly house and subsequently furnished her money to run her flat."

Ben Bachrach was happy. "It is a great victory for us. Jack will come back now, pay a small fine and that will end it."

The *Chicago Defender* said the High Court's decision and recent efforts to amend the Mann Act showed the champ's friends that their contention that he was persecuted and not prosecuted was nearly right.[890]

In 1917, in three concurrently decided and reported cases (*Caminetti v. United States*, 242 U.S. 470 (1917), *Diggs v. United States*, and *Hayes v. United States)*, the U.S. Supreme Court confirmed that consensual illicit fornication (sexual intercourse between unmarried persons), whether or not for the commercial purpose of prostitution, was an "immoral purpose" under the Mann Act. Caminetti and Diggs had taken their mistresses from Sacramento, California to Reno, Nevada. Their wives informed the police, and both men were arrested in Reno. They were convicted on September 5, 1913; four months after Jack Johnson had been convicted.

---

[889] Johnson v. U.S., 215 F. 679 (7th Cir. 1914).

[890] *Freeman, Chicago Defender*, April 18, 1914.

In 1922, U.S. President Warren G. Harding nominated and the U.S. Senate confirmed James H. Wilkerson as judge for the U.S. District Court for the Northern District of Illinois, the seat vacated by Kenesaw M. Landis. On November 24, 1931, Wilkerson was the judge who sentenced Al Capone to 11 years in prison for tax evasion.

Judge Kennesaw Mountain Landis, who had set Johnson's bail at $30,000 and would not accept cash, and had helped keep Lucille Cameron in police custody, eventually became baseball's first commissioner. He was known especially for banning eight Chicago White Sox players in the wake of the fixing of the 1919 World Series, causing the team to be known as the "Black Sox." Their involvement, or lack thereof, has been the subject of historical debate. The players had been acquitted in their criminal trials.

Writing for the *Chicago Defender*, Ernest Stevens visited Paris and found the champ to be the most prosperous man of color in the city. He maintained a beautiful residence in a fashionable suburb.

Regardless, Stevens said the black race had a slim chance abroad. Stevens had not seen many blacks, and there were very few avenues of employment open to them. Both the writer and Johnson advised friends to remain in the U.S. France was not so great for blacks after all.

> There is only one Afro-American in Paris who can say that he is happy and that is Jack Johnson. I went to his house in Ansieres, a fashionable suburb, about ten miles ride from the city. He looks as robust and healthy as ever. He occupies a fine residence, with a large playground and poultry yard. He maintains a garage which houses several first class cars. He is prosperous and is kept busy running from one country to another doing theatrical turns. He sends greetings and like the writer, advises his friends to remain in the United States. There were also very few blacks in Holland and Hamburg. What few there are were of the unfortunate type that give the dominant race a bad impression of the whole. I may add that the German people give the race a squarer deal than the English.[891]

On April 13, 1914 in Buffalo, New York, 237-pound Jess Willard knocked out 207-pound Dan Daly in the 9th round with a smashing right uppercut.

On April 28, 1914 in Atlanta, Georgia, Jess Willard stopped George Rodel, the Australian champ, in the 6th round.

On May 1, 1914 in New Orleans, Louisiana, more than 5,000 fans watched 28-year-old Sam Langford and 24-year-old Harry Wills fight to a 10-round no-decision draw.[892]

---

[891] *Chicago Defender*, April 25, 1914.

[892] *Freeman*, May 30, 1914. Some writers thought Langford won, some said Wills won, while others argued it was a draw. The *Freeman* said reports differed as to who earned the decision. The local *Times-Democrat* said the local fighter Wills won. According to historian Clay Moyle, Langford's birthdate was March 3, 1886.

CHAPTER 19

Frank Moran

On May 6, 1914, the French Boxing Federation, which previously refused to recognize him as champion, reversed course and said it now was accepting Jack Johnson's claim to the title. Lending some insight into why the French Federation had changed its mind, Theodore Vienne, a prominent member, had assumed the general management of the fight between Johnson and Moran. He signed a contract to stage the match on June 27 as scheduled, succeeding Emile Maitrot, who retired. The fight would be held at the Velodrome d'Hiver, which contained 26,000 seats and had standing room for 4,000 more.

Moran arrived in Paris on May 16 and went to Butry to train.[893]

White folks wanted Moran to win, but questioned whether he could. Black folks were rather indifferent, because they did not like the way Johnson conducted himself. However, they had sublime confidence that Jack could more than hold his own.

Joe Jeannette said if Johnson had not fallen apart like some said he had, he would defeat Moran. Jeannette and Moran had sparred on the stage under Dan McKetrick's management. Jeannette said Moran had whipped no one of consequence and stopped Al Palzer when he was tottering. Johnson was weighing around 240 pounds, but still appeared to be in fine form. "Well, I tell you it's just this way; If all the stories that are going the rounds about the way Johnson has gone to pieces through drink and other kinds of dissipation are true, it ought to be easy for Moran to whip him. But, on the other hand, if these stories aren't true, Frank Moran won't win."

On May 20, 1914 in Philadelphia, 186-pound Gunboat Smith won a fast 6-round no-decision bout against 158-pound Jack Blackburn. Jack was dropped in the 1st and 5th rounds, but showed enough defensive prowess and cleverness to last the distance.

For whatever reason, the Gunboat Smith vs. Jess Willard fight had been called off. Instead, Smith was scheduled to travel abroad to fight Georges Carpentier in July. Joe Jeannette said Carpentier had a good chance to win, for he was a good boxer with a good stiff punch. "Yes, he is game enough. In a match I had with him, Carpentier stoop up, although his face was swollen to an awful size, and he could hardly see, but he fought on. I think he has a good chance to defeat Smith."[894]

---

[893] *New York Times*, May 7, 1914. *Freeman*, May 16, 23, 1914.
[894] *Freeman*, May 30, 1914.

In Boston on May 20, 1914, Dan "Porky" Flynn was given the 12-round decision over Jim Johnson, the ex-Paris waiter who had fought the champ. Johnson dropped Flynn in the 7th round with a left hook, but in the other rounds, Flynn had the advantage.

On June 9, 1914 in New Orleans, Joe Jeannette and Harry Wills fought a 10-round no-decision draw, though some thought Wills won.

On June 13, 1914 in Melbourne, Australia, Sam McVey knocked out Arthur Pelkey in the 4th round.

Apparently, while in Paris, Johnson had punched Charles W. Galvin. Galvin had been a Johnson masseur, and he uttered something about salary in a fashion which Johnson thought was rude, and the Dutchman had a vague recollection of being lifted from the floor and thrown through the air, landing with a bump. Johnson settled out of court with him by paying Galvin 100 pounds.

Both Moran and Johnson claimed to be fit and ready for their June 27 scrap. The *Mirror of Life* noted that the majority of Americans were confident in Moran, and a lot of money was backing him. They felt that Johnson was past-it. "Perhaps they take their wishes for realities!" Johnson was negotiating a potential agreement to fight Langford in October.[895]

In Paris, Johnson was giving daily training exhibitions which he called "afternoon teas." He shadow boxed, sparred, punched the bag, tossed the medicine ball, and skipped rope, all to the enjoyment of the fashionable crowds that paid money to see him train. His American followers delighted in making the remark, "I knew him in Chicago." Whether or not they actually knew him, they willingly planked down a five spot, the price of admission.

Johnson had regained much of his speed and stamina and looked to be well-trained. Judges were surprised at his condition. His sparring showed little evidence of his long period of idleness. Experts agreed that he was all-there, not all-in.

On June 12, when "Daddy" Vienne, the promoter, called Johnson at 10 a.m., Jack told him that he had covered 10 miles already that morning.

Moran, too, was hard at work at his Butry camp, an ideal spot on the River Qise, where he was sparring with Tom Kennedy, the former amateur heavyweight champion (who held a 1912 10-round no-decision victory over Moran), Willie Lewis (who often worked with Joe Jeannette), and a man named Hatton.[896]

A veteran of 39 professional contests, Pittsburgh's 27-year-old Frank Moran was a big, strong, husky, tough, and durable fighter. His claim to fame was his last fight, the September 1913 KO7 over the then highly touted 227-pound Al Palzer, whom Moran previously had defeated in a 1911 10-round no-decision. Moran had lost 1912 10-round no decisions to Al Kubiak and Tom Kennedy, a 10-round decision to Tony Ross, 20-round decision to Gunboat Smith, and 1913 10-round no-decision to Luther McCarty. He had won all five of his fights in London, including 1911 KO3 Fred Drummond, KO6 Tom Cowler, KO2 Charlie Wilson, and 1912

[895] *Mirror of Life and Boxing World*, June 13, 1914.
[896] *Chicago Defender*, June 13, 1914.

WDQ7 and KO12 Fred Storbeck. He had fought once in Paris and won. Other notable fights on his record included: 1909 KO6 Black Fitzsimmons and D6 John Willie; 1910 WND6 Thunderbolt Ed Smith and LKOby1 George Kid Cotton; 1911 LTKOby7 Jim Savage; 1912 KO8 Dave Mills, L4 Jake Geyer, W10 Charlie Horn, and D4 Charley Miller; and 1913 WND6 Sailor White. Moran usually weighed around 200 pounds.

Despite his noted strength and condition, many felt that a Moran victory depended upon how far diminished Johnson was. There were many "Ifs." If Johnson had slowed up, if he had lost his punch, if dissipation had cut down his stamina, if he failed to train properly or underestimated his more youthful opponent, etc. Although Moran's defeats seemed to classify him as a member of the second class, he was most competitive against his toughest foes, and had improved.

Word was that Johnson was training hard at Luna Park and was not taking chances. Jack took long and steady jogs through the Bois de Boulogne, perspiring freely. Big crowds came to see him work daily. He had five sparring partners, each boxing 3 rounds with him. He was

Frank Moran

looking like the Johnson of old, although his weight was 225 pounds.

Johnson said, "I never did put more into my training for any fight, and the man who beats Moran will be the same Jack Johnson who went into the ring at Reno." Jack also liked driving his auto, which he said had a steadying effect on the nerves and was good for the eye and concentration.

Apparently, word was that Johnson had signed an agreement with Richard Klein to fight Langford in London in September or October.

At the start of training, Moran weighed 207 pounds, but had worked down to 196 pounds. Frank was walking, skipping, rowing, ball-punching, and sparring.

Moran said he was training seriously, and the fight would not be a fake.

> I've only taken on this fight because I know I can win. … I'm in splendid condition. Not only do I feel confident of winning this big fight, but all those who have seen me over here are also sure of my victory, and I want all my American friends to rest assured that when I enter the ring I'll do all in my power to win.

During sparring on June 16 with Kennedy, Moran slipped and collided with his partner's head, splitting his left eyebrow. The 2.5-inch wound healed rapidly, but in order to avoid any risk of it reopening, he stopped sparring for nearly a week. Today, such a cut would force a postponement, but these were different times.[897]

It was announced in England that the Home Office no longer would allow any boxing matches between whites and blacks, for such fights were undesirable. A leading English promoter, C. B. Cochran, had hoped to arrange a Sam Langford vs. Gunboat Smith bout, but, "I was advised by the Home Office that it met with their disapproval and that they would take steps to stop any further contest between black men and white."[898]

Johnson had been a 3 to 1 favorite. However, a bunch of money came in on Moran, causing the odds to shift to 2 to 1. One French gambler offered to bet $8,000 on Moran at 3 to 1 odds. William A. Brady had a large wager on Moran in London. Many believed the odds would tighten further.

The 6'1" Moran was weighing 203 pounds. His reach actually was a couple inches longer than Johnson's. Allegedly, Johnson was weighing about 215 pounds.

The rules under which they would fight stated that all clinches must terminate instantly at the word "break." Moran's manager Dan McKetrick declared that this rule would benefit the white fighter and hurt Johnson, who ordinarily did a lot of damage during infighting. However, infighting and hitting in the clinches was permissible until the call to break.[899]

Otto Floto said that 999 out of 1,000 fights were on the square, but that the rare fake made folks become suspicious of even genuine fights.

Floto said Johnson finally admitted that he had a narrow escape from defeat when he met Flynn, and attributed it to lack of condition. Jack told Floto, "Flynn nor no one else will ever know how near I met defeat that day. It taught me a lesson, and henceforth I am not going to enter the ring unless in the best of condition. I had a narrow escape that time and won't allow it to happen again."

William A. Brady said the championship bout was going to be a real fight, and offered reasons why he thought Johnson would lose. Moran had everything needed to win. "I know that the big black is 36 years old; I know he has been drinking hard, living the fastest kind of life; going the pace that kills for five years." Such a life was bound to catch up with him eventually, especially at what was an advanced age for a boxer.

> Everybody insists that the black is a great fighter. The majority think he is the greatest that ever put on a glove. I don't think so. Never at any time in his ring history has he advanced one foot in the ring. He

[897] *Freeman*, June 20, 1914.

[898] *New York Herald*, June 21, 1914. Boxing itself was not under fire, for it combined the body and mind, and required courage and coolness under trying circumstances, and regular living for one to be effective.

[899] *New York Journal, Denver Post*, June 23, 1914.

has always backed away and made the other fellow carry the fight to him. That policy was all right as long as he was clever enough and fast enough to maintain an impenetrable defense; but to repeat the deadliest fact, the smoke is not 36 years old, and if he had lived a blameless life since his Reno victory he would still have no chance against a young man. No heavyweight champion in the history of prizefighting ever successfully defended the title at that age or anything approaching it, and the black is not the man to prove the exception.

If Moran will carry the fight to the big smoke from the tap of the gong and never stop, the world will once more have a white man in the top division of the boxing game, and I have reason to believe that Moran will do just this.[900]

Johnson was predicting victory within 12 rounds.

When all is finished I'll still be champion of the world. I never felt better in my life than now and one thing is certain, should anything unforeseen occur, I will have no excuses to offer. I feel as strong today as I did four years ago. I weigh today 212 pounds, but expect to enter the ring at about 204 to 206. I can easily get rid of the difference by simply drying out. Up to date I have drunk all the water I wanted, but during the last two days before the fight I will drink practically nothing.

Moran argued that Johnson represented a passing generation. It was time for a younger man to win the crown. He noted that since 1908, Johnson had trained seriously only twice, for Ketchel and Jeffries, the only men he feared. Other than that, Johnson had undermined his stamina by a life of ease. On the other hand, Moran said he worked hard all the time. Hence, he predicted the "black swan's" demise after the first few rounds.[901]

Bill Brady left London for the scene of the battle in Paris. Brady did not believe a word of the stories heard in London that the fight was fixed for Johnson. He thought such rumors were the result of British jealousy over the fact that the fight was being held in Paris. Regardless, the bout could not be held in England, owing to the ban on mixed-race battles.

Brady believed that after about 2 rounds, Moran was going to discover that Johnson was not the colossus he had been led to believe, and would loosen up and fight to win.

Also noted was the fact that initially, the Paris commission had declared that Johnson no longer was the champion, but after the commission's most important member, Vienne, had purchased the right to one-third of the

---

[900] *Denver Post*, June 24, 1914.
[901] *New York Journal*, June 24, 1914. Given that we now know that dehydration is counterproductive, it makes it all the more remarkable that Johnson was able to dehydrate himself and still have the stamina for 20-round fights.

profits from the Moran-Johnson fight, the commission reversed itself. Hence, essentially it had been bought off, or had financial motivations for stripping Johnson all along. Lack of integrity is nothing new to the sport.

James J. Corbett, notorious picker of losers in his fight predictions, said Moran had no chance, which made many think he did have a chance.

> I would give my right arm to see him put the black out of business, but it's my honest opinion…that the cinder will stall around and smile his way through the twenty rounds entirely on his cleverness.
>
> Even if the stories of the negro's dissipation are true – and I believe they are to a certain extent – he would have had to hit it up at a terrific pace to deteriorate enough for Moran to be in his class.[902]

MORAN BACKERS ARE BETTING ON HUNCH

Tad Dorgan of the *New York Journal* listed Johnson as 220 pounds to Moran's 197. Johnson was 6'1 ¼" and Moran 6'. He called Moran "a very fair fighter." Moran claimed that he would kid Johnson, rush him off his feet and make him fight. However, Tad disagreed. Tad said no boxer alive could compare with Johnson in kidding. He was without doubt the greatest goat-getter the ring ever saw. Jack took his time, and no one could rush him.

> It's his style. He never yet has made a great impression in the ring, because he is not a showy fighter. He is just a big strong fellow with an eye like a hawk and a slam like a pile driver. He ignores the yelps of the mob or the abuse from rival corners, looks his man over well and then gets down to work. He has no fancy footwork. He doesn't need it. . ... He can pick off punches that 99 out of 100 other boxers would stop with their chins. His strength is equal to that of two men. He showed that in Reno when he tossed Jeffries around like a baby.
>
> Just how Moran expects to beat Johnson is a mystery here. He isn't as big, isn't as fast, isn't as hard a hitter, isn't so experienced and is not as confident. … Johnson will be in shape, as he usually is, when a title is at stake, and just as careful.

---

[902] *Denver Post*, June 25, 1914. Brady was writing for the *Denver Post*.

Tad said many were willing to wager that it was time for Johnson to lose, and were betting on the hunch rather than the merits of the men. William A. Brady, former Corbett and Jeffries manager, was an ardent Moran admirer, and on a daily basis was writing that Moran was a cinch to win. He said Johnson was too old to win. However, Tad said Moran was an ordinary man facing an extraordinary one.

The confident Moran was writing a series of articles for *Boxing*, a London weekly. Moran wrote,

> I'll be far better than ever before. Johnson has been at the top, and he knows that his best time has passed. … A champion worries when he goes into a fight, because he's had all the good things, and he's afraid he may lose them. …
>
> I surely feel as confident as I sound. There isn't a doubt but I'll come home champion of the world. I've made up my mind that nothing can stop me, and that I'm going to tear into Johnson until he cracks. He'll fight hard for seven or eight rounds. He can do that on form. Then he'll begin to weaken and lose his speed, and I'll be going harder every minute. Even if he should get to me at the start, I can protect myself for a moment and then come back as strong as ever.[903]

On June 24, Moran ran 5 miles, and in boxing bouts with Willie Lewis and Tom Kennedy, showed rare speed and much skill.

That day, Dr. Gaston Dupau examined Johnson. He said that except for a slight trace of pneumonia, which Jack had back in March 1913, his condition was perfect. The trace was detected by a whistling sound near the top of the right lung while the breath was expelled. He said there was nothing serious in those symptoms, which usually followed pneumonia and disappeared within two years. Before his exercise, Jack's pulse was 68 and respiration 15. Afterwards, it was 102 and 20, respectively. Jack weighed 214 pounds.[904]

Two days before the fight, on the 25th, Johnson put in his last full day of work at Luna Park, training in front of 400 male and female spectators who paid 50 cents each. Jack had a retinue of black attendants. Although he was sullen and no longer smiling as he once did, his bag punching was as spectacular as ever. He looked and acted as if he was in perfect condition.

However, William Brady declared that Johnson was fat, not in shape, and had impaired wind.

> Everybody remembers the roasting handed out to Sam Langford the morning after his contest with Gunboat Smith in Boston, as Langford was over weight. I saw the fight, but Langford was sylphlike and in perfect condition compared with the Jack Johnson I saw punching a bag in a dance hall this afternoon.

[903] *New York Journal*, June 25, 1914.
[904] *New York Journal*, June 25, 1914.

Johnson is hog fat, great folds of flesh hang over his blue trunks, and although he showed no paunch, the old washboard-ridged stomach has disappeared and his mid-section looks very soft and flabby.

Brady called Jack's training that day a farce, a bit harsh given that it was a couple days before the fight and therefore understandably he was tapering. Johnson did 15 minutes of bag punching, 5 minutes of tossing the medicine ball with two white French gymnasts, and 5 minutes of shadow boxing with one-pound dumbbells. Brady opined that Johnson was at least 10 pounds overweight, and it was all in the wrong place – his waistline.

Brady asked Johnson what he wanted to tell the readers of the Hearst newspapers. Johnson replied, "I am going to win sure. I will knock him out in the twelfth round." Brady suggested that amount of time was just long enough to make the moving pictures valuable. Johnson replied, "I need the money, Mr. Brady." When Brady told Johnson that no one of his age ever had been successful at defending a boxing title, Johnson said he knew that, but felt fine, not like an old man. Jack said he had $5,000 to wager on himself at prevailing odds, but could find no takers.

Brady said he had it on good authority that Johnson put up $3,800 to purchase a 1/3 interest in the gate.

Brady opined that there would be a new world champion, one whose skin was white. "Moran will make the negro the most surprised individual a championship contest has ever developed." Moran had a college education and an "abundance of native intelligence." Victory would mean half a million dollars to him, plus "the lasting gratitude of the white people of the world."

Brady believed that if Johnson was less than his best, he would get whipped within 15 rounds. If the young Moran's condition was as good as he had heard; Johnson would be beaten within 10 rounds. "The boulevardiers actually believe the negro has taken off forty-three pounds in weight." Johnson admitted having put on 51 pounds over his fighting weight in the period since the Flynn fight, but declared that he now was weighing 213 pounds. Brady said, "My friends tell me Johnson's training has been a joke, including bouts with feather, bantam, welter and middle weights, Tony Ross being his sole vis-à-vis in his own class."

Moran was at his training quarters at Meriel-Sur-Oise, a few miles outside Paris. On Thursday June 25, Moran rose early and took a long, brisk walk, varied by sprints on the banks of the Oise. In the afternoon, he boxed with several sparring partners, including Tom Kennedy and Willie Lewis, dropping the latter twice. Moran said, "You can say for me that I have never been in better fighting trim in my life, and am absolutely sure of my staying power and soundness of wind. Of course I'll win."

Dr. Joseph Goode of Chicago examined Moran after he had sparred. The doctor said, "His heart pulse is only slightly above normal and his breathing is quite regular. I have seen Johnson also and I believe Moran is physically a better man."

Moran's boxing lessons from Tom Kennedy and Willie Lewis had nearly cured him of his crouching style. He now stood nearly as straight as Johnson, and his head blows were direct, bringing his full 203 pounds of force into place. There was immense power in his blows. His breathing was admirable. During a whole hour of strenuous exercise, he never once opened his mouth. In short-arm mix-ups, he worked rapidly and very effectively. Moran's footwork was a good deal livelier than that of Johnson's. Frank's action in general was much more energetic.

Tom Kennedy said if Moran lasted longer than 10 rounds, Johnson would be whipped. Willie Lewis said Johnson would be through after 5 rounds. Kennedy said, "The improvement Moran has made didn't seem possible to me when he began training. He is stronger now than I have ever known him to be." Lewis said, "Moran is really the first good man Johnson has ever met. None of the others could hit as hard as Moran." Moran said, "I look for absolute victory, judging by my condition. I cannot say anything about my tactics. You will see what they are when I get into the ring."

En haut, FRANK MORAN
En bas, JACK JOHNSON

Moran complained that the newspapers generally scoffed at him, most without sending reporters to his camp to study his form. "The Hearst newspapers are the only ones that treated me fairly by watching my work and honestly telling about same."[905]

Nothing was talked about in Paris other than the big fight, from the gutter to the homes of the aristocracy. Many women would be at ringside. The great amphitheater had been decorated with bunting from floor to roof. Ice-water coolers had been spread about the house. Old chairs had been re-cushioned. Physicians and nurses would be present in case they were needed for the crowd or the fighters.

The fight was being held on the eve of the Grand Prix, the greatest turf event of the year in France. It also was the height of the tourist season. Hence, Paris was chockfull of travelers and potential patrons.

Georges Carpentier's manager, Francois Descamps, had been watching Moran's boxing. He said if Moran won, Georges would challenge him.

[905] New York American, June 25-27, 1914; New York Herald, June 26, 1914; New York Journal, June 27, 1914.

French champion Carpentier was selected to referee.

Johnson cabled his mother in Chicago, telling her that he would win and there was nothing for her to be fearful about. He thought the fight would be over in 12 rounds.

Jack looked good, despite weighing 220 pounds. He still was speed personified and graceful in his every movement. He had worked hard in training. He had to, for when he began, he certainly was a "very fat athlete."

In physical make-up, the 204-pound Moran seemed to have an edge. He was younger at age 27 versus Johnson's 36. Nine years of youth was significant. True, Johnson had learned a lot more about fighting, but he also had dissipated frightfully for years. Moran was a clean-living youngster, while Johnson was said to be the opposite. Johnson only had a 1 ¼" height advantage. Moran actually had the longer reach.[906]

Moran had been training with Kennedy and Lewis for eight weeks. Bill Brady was impressed. "In all my experience with prize fighters I have never seen a more magnificent specimen of perfect condition than Moran."

The day before the fight, Moran said,

> I challenged Johnson because I thought I could whip him. Today I know I not only can whip him, but I shall whip him. … The Johnson I meet tomorrow night isn't as fit as Al Palzer was when I fought him. I'm not going to play the game Johnson wants me to play. Johnson is not going to make me beat myself. I am going to be just as much on the defensive as he is for the first seven or eight rounds, and if he wants me to mix he has got to come to me.
>
> In the eighth round I am going to start to roughing and hope my condition against his lack of condition and age will enable me to put in finishing touches at the eighteenth or nineteenth round.

Moran also was quoted as saying, "I have never trained so thoroughly and conscientiously before and my physical condition was never finer. My strength, speed, and stamina are at the utmost point of efficiency and to my mind it is a foregone conclusion that I will be the world's champion tomorrow night."

James J. Corbett said Moran had a chance if he would cut loose.

> Of course everybody seems to think Johnson is all in. I don't know how far gone he is. …
>
> Now Johnson, if he gets tired, will try to kid and bull his way through the twenty rounds. Smiling, and with his knowledge of the ring, he might make Moran think he is as good as ever. I would give my right arm to see Moran win because it would help boxing a lot.
>
> However, on form, Johnson should win, but from what I hear Johnson won't be in the best of form.

---

[906] *New York Journal,* June 27, 1914.

If Moran will just cut loose and keep up a fast pace and make Johnson fight every second and have the referee break them away quickly that's Moran's only chance.

Tom Flanagan said that although he was sure Johnson would win, he believed the battle would go the full 20 rounds.

Dan McKetrick said if Moran did not knock out Johnson, Frank would obtain the verdict on points.

William Muldoon said Moran had at least an equal chance of victory. "Moran is a fine specimen of manhood, blessed with a magnificent, well-proportioned physique, intelligent, level-headed, good habits… He should win in this contest."

Muldoon felt that Moran should refrain from clinching, wrestling, and shoving about the ring, for that would tire out his arms and play into Johnson's hands.

> Johnson's greatest skill has been displayed in his ability to injure his opponent while in the clinches. …
>
> He manages to get a hold of his opponent's wrists or forearm while in the clinches and twists and pushes them around to his back, compelling his rival to use strength in forcing his arms, and while he is engaged in that effort and his attention is attracted in that direction Johnson slips his body just far enough from his opponent to allow room for his right arm shooting up between them and catching his opponent under the chin or on the jaw with terrific force, and before the victim has time to recover from that jolt he brings in a short left-handed hook.

Muldoon further assessed Johnson's strengths. "Johnson at his best undoubtedly had the best judgment of time and distance of any pugilist I ever saw, excepting, perhaps, Peter Jackson." However, Muldoon also said everyone knew that it was necessary to keep active at the game in order to retain that good judgment of time and distance. Those who were inactive lost it, and there was no reason to think Johnson was the exception. "He hasn't faced on his merits a clever or even moderately clever boxer in years. … If Johnson defeats Moran in this bout, it will be by far the most creditable performance of his entire pugilistic career."[907]

The *New York Herald* said each man was fit. Their training bore out their assertions that they were well prepared. Moran's improvement in offense and defense, hard hitting, and ability to take punishment was noted throughout his training.

Johnson had trained assiduously, if not quite so strenuously. He actually began his work two weeks earlier than Moran, but had been careful not to overdo it. He remained a 3 to 1 favorite.

[907] *New York American*, June 27, 1914.

JACK JOHNSON'S BEST PUNCH

The day before the fight, on June 26, Johnson did his usual morning roadwork near his Asnieres training camp. Afterward, he rode his new auto into Paris to cash a check. In the afternoon, before a large crowd at his gym, Johnson sparred. In order to test his form, he extended by several rounds his customary five-round training bout, taking on three boxers successively for several rounds each. He also did some of his regular indoor exercises.

A big crowd was scheduled to be on hand for the fight. It was estimated that the receipts would reach at least $100,000. Carpentier's selection to referee likely would help attract a large following, for he was an idol amongst Parisians.[908]

[908] New York Herald, Omaha World Herald, June 27, 1914.

Conversely, the *Denver Post*'s Otto Floto said the public had not taken kindly to the mill. Still, if the bout went at least 10 rounds, the moving pictures would bring the backers their reward, regardless of the attendance. He believed that the "Inky Kink" was going to mix with Moran.

Everything seemed to hinge on Johnson's condition. The "Cinder" was able to win against Flynn, barely. "Had Flynn realized how far the black man was gone there can be no doubt about his winning the fight. But Flynn failed to see what those about the ringside observed. It was a lucky occasion for the Ace."

Floto agreed that Moran had a chance to win if he could make the "Cinder" carry the fight to him. However, saying one would do something was one thing, and doing it was another. Johnson had a way of forcing fighters to come to him, and on the defensive, with the battle carried to him, "he is a wonder and liable to beat any man who attempts – in fact, has beaten all those who assumed such presumption. ... The Cinder has a tantalizing way of forcing an opponent to come to him in spite of himself." Still, Johnson's dissipation was proverbial, with wine, women, and song being his slogan.[909]

The *Freeman's* Billy Lewis reported that Moran made a most favorable impression in training, and his sparring partners were superior to the champion's. Although Johnson had done excellent work, there was strong suspicion that the Paris night life had sapped his strength. H. B. White, a former all-around amateur athlete, who had watched both Moran and Johnson train, was confident that Moran would win, for he had trained scientifically with quality sparring partners, and was the picture of health and strength.

The *Cincinnati Enquirer* said,

> The trouble with Johnson is that he has had a flock of enemies to contend with and is seldom given his just dues. ... [I]t is not fair to judge a man's fighting ability by what takes place in his private life. Throw aside the prejudice and Johnson stands out as the champion in all the word implies. He is a natural-born fighter and did not get to the top by any boosting from the press agent. His color was against him, and he had a hard row to hoe.

Recently, Cleveland middleweight Tommy Garrigan had been in Paris, and he said, "Moran is a different fellow in every way to the one we saw box Tony Ross here in Cleveland a few years ago. He is thirty pounds heavier, much faster and can hit 40 per cent harder. But best of all he has got oceans of confidence ... He has wonderful speed and strength."

Regarding Johnson, Garrigan said,

---

[909] *Denver Post,* June 27, 1914.

I saw Jack fight Jim Johnson in Paris, and no man can make me believe that he can ever get back into the condition of the great fighting machine he was when he beat Jeffries.

Jack has been going back for some time, and McKetrick was foxy enough to see it. That is why I give him so much credit; for matching Moran and getting this great chance to win the title. ...

One day in a certain café in Paris, McKetrick asked Johnson to give Joe Jeannette a bout and Jack replied: "No, I won't fight Jeannette just now, but I will take on that big white boob, Moran. After I put him away and close his trap, I may give Jeannette a chance, provided I can see the price." McKetrick jumped at the offer and the Moran-Johnson match is the result.

It was said that Johnson weighed 218 pounds. Sparring partner Calvin Respress, who also had been with him for the Flynn fight, declared that Johnson was in better shape than he was against Flynn. Sparring partner Tony Ross, who held a 1912 decision over Moran, shared that opinion.

Johnson had increased the speed of his daily runs on the Bois de Boulogne, covering nearly 12 miles every morning. He did tremendous work at the punching bag. He allowed a French lightweight to pound at his stomach. In addition to sparring Respress and Ross, Johnson's sparring partners included Badoux (a clever Swiss middleweight), a French welterweight, and Roc (a French heavy), all of whom did some fast boxing with the champ.[910]

"McAuliffe" said that Moran was too young and inexperienced to deal with the greatest heavyweight of all time. "Johnson is a wonderful mechanic, with the build and strength of a giant; has a cunning head and is the greatest defensive fighter that ever entered the ring." Even when not in the best condition, Johnson still had his defensive prowess, and his style would wear down anyone, for he always made the other man do the work, and then he outgeneraled his opponent.

Moran said,

I am in the finest possible trim. I am the first big man Johnson has ever faced except Jeffries – a shell. I can hit. Al Palzer knows my right hand punch. I'll make Johnson come to me and fight. He may have a lead for a few rounds but before the fifteenth I will get the right over and it will be worth one million dollars to me.

Joe Jeanette said, "To beat a man you have to hit him, don't you? Moran can't hit Johnson hard enough to hurt him. I know how Johnson fights and I say Moran won't do."

---

[910] *Freeman,* June 27, 1914.

John L. Sullivan said, "If Moran whales away at the Negro's midsection with the viciousness of which he is capable, he will win. If he attempts to box Johnson, he will be beaten."

Jack Johnson said, "I never felt better. I have my old punch and I haven't forgotten how to box. If Moran thinks he will hammer my stomach he'll get a surprise. Jack Johnson can still protect himself. The reliable old uppercut is still hooked onto my hands."[911]

The *Chicago Defender* reported that every seat in the big arena had been engaged, including by some members of royalty. Some of the ringside seats were going for $75, $100, and $125. Advance sales already had reached $20,000. Public sentiment was pretty evenly divided, though the odds slightly favored Johnson.

Those who had seen Johnson train thought that he had lost some of his former speed, and that he tired more quickly than he did a few years ago. However, he still was strong, a keen strategist, and a hard fighter, with experience and all the tricks of the game. Johnson said, "Tell my friends, I am not fool enough to risk my title in a bout where I am not prepared. I never felt better, and if I lose I will not claim poor condition."

Moran said, "I am betting my own money on myself. I am going to fight warily and Johnson will not get a chance to pull any of his tricks on me."[912]

The *New York American* said Moran was a college student, baseball player, football player, sailor, clerk, and pugilist. He was born on March 18, 1887. He had been boxing as a pro since 1908. The day Johnson beat Jeffries; Moran scored a KO8 over a big black man named Dave Willis at Juarez, Mexico. His real claim to fame was that he knocked out Al Palzer in 7 rounds, after Palzer had stopped Kaufman and Wells.

Moran and Johnson actually had met in the ring once before, having boxed in an exhibition bout. "Four years ago the big Pittsburgher boxed four exhibition rounds with the champion on a Pittsburgh stage."[913]

---

[911] *Freeman*, July 11, 1914.
[912] *Chicago Defender*, June 27, 1914.
[913] *New York American*, June 28, 1914.

The *New York American* listed Moran as 203 to Johnson's 215 pounds. *L'Humanite* said Johnson weighed about 99 kg (218 pounds). Moran was nine years younger and weighed 8 kg less (200 pounds). The *London Times* agreed Johnson was 18 pounds heavier. *L'Intransigeant* listed Johnson as 100 kg (220 pounds) and Moran 92 kg (202.5 pounds). *La Presse* listed Johnson as age 36, 100 Kilos 500 grams in weight, and 1 meter, 85 centimeters tall. Moran was 27 years old, 92 kilograms 80 grams in weight, and 1 meter 85 centimeters tall. It said the fight would be the biggest in France's history.

L'Humanite said that for the past four years, Johnson essentially had abandoned the ring for exhibitions, punch bowls, and fun, dancing the bear-step in music halls. He knew that this was a big bout and therefore had trained seriously.

Le Petit Parisien anticipated a very good match. Those who saw Moran in training were unanimous in believing that Johnson had before him a white man capable of putting him on the ground and defeating him.

L'Intransigeant said the two boxers had almost equal chances. Johnson was heavier but Moran was younger. Those who saw Johnson in training would attest to his weight loss. He had lost much of his fat, was supple, and no longer tired. Those who saw him had trouble believing that this amazing athlete could be beaten.

Le Matin said Johnson had to flee the United States essentially because the Americans were not happy with his color. The U.S. population would be very satisfied to learn about Johnson's defeat.[914]

On the evening of Saturday June 27, 1914 in Paris, France, Jack Johnson defended the world heavyweight championship against Frank Moran.[915]

The day of the fight, Johnson said, "I was never surer of winning than I am today." Moran said, "I am in the best condition I have ever been, and I don't expect to be the loser." He also said that win or lose, he expected to be battered, but was prepared for it.

William Brady claimed that the afternoon of the fight, Johnson entered Todd Sloan's saloon and announced that he had $10,000 to bet at even money that he would knock out Moran in 10 rounds. Brady replied that he was willing to take the bet. Then Jack said he didn't have the money with him, but would go and get it and come back. He did not return.

The *New York American* said the $30,000 check, made out in February, had been photographed and placed in the Credit Lyonnaise's vaults, to be handed to Mrs. Johnson at noon on the day of the fight. That was in addition to the $5,000 in training expenses already paid to Johnson.

No one knew for sure what Moran was making, but generally it was understood that he would receive $5,000.

---

[914] *La Presse*, June 27, 28, 1914; *L'Humanite* June 27, 1914 *Le Petit Parisien*, June 27 1914; *L'Intransigeant*, June 28 1914; *Le Matin*, June 27, 1914.

[915] The following account is an amalgamation of *Le Petit Parisien, New York Herald, New York American, London Times, Le Matin, Denver Post*, June 28, 1914; *La Presse*, June 29, 1914; *Mirror of Life and Boxing World*, July 4, 1914. *La Presse* article by Daniel Cousin.

The night before, Johnson slept eight hours. His pre-fight meal consisted of chicken and vegetables. He dined at about 5 p.m. His wife superintended the culinary arrangements.

The fight was held at the Velodrome d'Hiver, where they hosted bicycling races, near Champs de Mars. Automobiles arrived by crossing the Alma bridge. The French said it was the largest arena in the world for this type of event. The place was beautiful and represented a small fortune. There were both upper and lower galleries.[916]

Several French reports said there were about 30,000 or 35,000 spectators. They said every seat or nearly every seat in the arena was taken. However, one reporter said there was a crowd of 8,000 spectators. Others said there were over 20,000 people present.

Ticket prices anywhere near the ring ranged from $40 to $60. Every ticket's price had a 10% surcharge added, the money going to charitable organizations.

The *Mirror of Life and Boxing World* said the reported gate was 12,000 pounds ($60,000), but its author, Con Murphy, believed that 7,000 or 8,000 pounds ($35,000 to $40,000) was closer to the truth. The *Herald* said the gate receipts exceeded $40,000 U.S. dollars.

The *New York American* believed that the gate would approach $100,000, and that Johnson would earn nearly $50,000, greater than his guarantee, owing to the generally accepted theory that he owned an interest in the promotion.

Le Matin said the gate receipts were 150,000 - 160,000 francs.

The *American* said William Brady and Dan McKetrick abandoned their plan to purchase the promoters' share of the motion picture rights. Hence, such rights would remain with Johnson, Moran, and Promoter Vienne.

The audience was strangely mixed. All of Paris was present, including every element of society - the poor, sportsmen, intellectuals, artists, and people of high society. Counts and Countesses, princes and princesses, dukes and duchesses were present. Famous French statesmen, boulevardiers, jockeys, American millionaires, and theatrical people were mixed in with rag-tag folks from the French capital. Even the English were there. A bunch of rowdy Americans had crossed the Atlantic just for this match. Local writers noted that a bout between a man of color and a paleface brought out a lot of passion.

The several hundred Americans present included Herman Duryea, former Senator C. W. Watson of West Virginia, William Brady, Bob Vernon, Frank Tennehill, Harry Pollok, Frank O'Neill, Tom Flanagan, Frank Gould, Alfred and Reggie Vanderbilt, Anthony and John Drexel, Willie Ritchie, and many others.

---

[916] Years later, the velodrome would be where they kept Jews before they shipped them off to concentration camps.

Several hundred women were in the audience, wearing beautiful gowns and jewels, including Baroness Henry de Rothschild. They supported Moran.

Johnson's wife Lucille occupied a prominent position, handsomely gowned and wearing many diamonds. During the fight, she would cheer and clap every time her husband landed a good blow.

Spencer Eddy, former American minister to Argentina, sat near the ring, as did the Duke of Westminster, the Earl of Sefton, former French Premier Louis Barthou, Baron James de Rothschild, as well as dukes and marquis.

There were some dark faces as well. Present were blacks from Senegal, Dahomey, and the West Indies, two black members of the Guadeloupe Chamber of Deputies, Prince Dauleep/Duleep Singh of India, and Omar Sultan Pasha of Egypt. It was an amazingly international crowd.

The Americans put in place a special telegraph post which allowed them to send direct trans-Atlantic cables, all at the expense of a couple thousand francs. Round by round reports were sent to New York.

The 16-foot ring was roofed in with a panoply of purple silk, beneath which were rows of yard-long tubes of electric lamps, whose lights cast reflections of different colors on the spectators, making them and everything in the vicinity of the ring appear ghastly. Some had a greenish tint, while others appeared pink, etc.

The bright lights combined with the mass of humanity made the arena quite hot. People were slightly uncomfortable. Men quickly removed their coats. Women in evening dress perspired. The *London Times* said it was doubtful if even the opportunity to see Georges Carpentier would have brought out so many women had they known before-hand about the lighting arrangements. However, the lights were necessary for filming.

At 10 p.m., the preliminary matches had finished. The crowd anxiously awaited the main event in silence.

The betting was 3 to 1 in Johnson's favor.

Mrs. Henry Tappe of New York, with her husband, met Moran at his dressing room door before the contest. Moran said to her, "Kiss me, I will win." She planted a kiss on his lips.

The fight was scheduled to start at 10:30 p.m. in Paris, which was 5:30 p.m. in New York.

According to *Le Petit Parisien*, as scheduled, the two combatants entered the ring at 10:15 p.m.

Le Petit Parisien said Johnson came to the ring smiling, looking superb and confident. His body was slightly thickened, but gave the impression of a black Hercules. *La Presse* said Johnson arrived to applause. C. F. Bertelli, Paris correspondent for the *New York American*, said Johnson entered the ring and dropped his long, striped dressing gown to the floor. Shouts of admiration went up as his tall, lithe form with big, enormous muscles bulged out. The *Mirror of Life and Boxing World* said Johnson was first to enter the ring, receiving a fair reception, to which he bowed and nodded with a smile. With the champ were Bob Armstrong, Gus Rhodes, Henri

Woolf, Calvan, Badoud, Tom Flanagan, and a couple of others. Johnson had both black and white trainers. James Preatt was Johnson's timekeeper.

Frank Moran, the "hope of an entire race," entered second, and he received a boisterous greeting. One said the crowd went delirious. The crowd was pulling for the blonde. After all, he was a white man. But Johnson had numerous supporters as well. Frank appeared to be in splendid form. He had with him Dan McKetrick, Willie Lewis, Tom Kennedy, Young Ahearn, Gus Wilson, and George Considine.

Le Petit Parisien said Moran was big, with impressive pectoral muscles, lots of muscle in his arms, and perfect legs. He appeared more serious than Johnson, but confident, with a will to win. Bertelli said Moran looked good, but lacked Johnson's natural robustness. *La Presse* said Moran, the hope of the white race, seemed very confident. The *Mirror* said Frank showed no trace of nervousness. The *New York American* said Moran looked trained to fine physical condition.

A lot of time was taken up putting on gloves and bandages. *La Presse* said each fighter had at least 10 attendants. In spite of this, their preparations were unusually long. While putting on his gloves, Johnson talked to his seconds, with all of the electric rays of light ricocheting off of his constantly smiling golden teeth.

It was announced that Sam Langford had cabled a challenge to the winner.

Johnson was wearing blue trunks. Moran wore green trunks with the stars and stripes flag around his waist.

Several writers said Johnson looked fitter than most people had expected, though there still was fat around his stomach, sides, and hips. Even eight weeks of hard training could not get rid of all the useless flesh.

Referee Georges Carpentier entered the ring to acclamations. He appeared very different from what folks were used to seeing. He wore flannels - a white shirt, white pants, and white shoes. Carpentier appeared to be the most nervous person in the ring.

The crowd was completely silent.

Dick Burge gave Moran a few words of advice. Carpentier called them together at mid-ring for a pow-wow.

Johnson objected to the rule prohibiting hitting in clinches. French rules provided for a clean break. Johnson said he understood he was fighting under Marquis of Queensberry rules. Mr. Vienne later said the rules were those of the International Boxing Federation, which did not allow holding and were a slight modification of the Queensberry rules.

After the rules discussion, they retired to their corners.

Announcer Max Sergy used a long megaphone to make the introductions. William H. Rocap, a former fighter, was the bout's official timekeeper.

At 10:33 p.m., the bell rang to start the fight.

1 - The local French press (*La Presse, Le Petit Parisien*) agreed that this was a feel-out round. The boxers mostly studied one another. There were some body shots and various attempts at offense, but nothing that really landed solidly or did any damage.

American observers (*Herald, American*, Bill Brady) reported that Moran fought for an opening and landed first with lefts to the stomach and head. Johnson succeeded in landing on the jaw. They mixed it hard, with Johnson landing on the stomach. Moran forced the fighting, but Johnson landed some hard uppercuts to the jaw.

England's *Mirror of Life and Boxing World* said that before the bell rang to start the fight, Johnson stood in his corner, cool, confident, and determined, while Moran made the sign of the cross and then turned around to face his adversary. When the bell rang, Johnson took to the middle of the ring. Moran halted before circling around his foe.

Johnson started earnestly; Moran carefully. For half a minute, not a blow was struck. Moran swung his left for the jaw but was short. Johnson tried his right for the head. Moran responded with two lefts. Johnson's every action betrayed the most earnest effort. He made a determined attack, but Moran's extended left hand caused the champ to pull up. A mix-up followed, with Moran coming through with credit. Johnson was serious and displayed more aggression than usual. However, he only landed a short right to the head. The round ended with honors even. Considine called out, "He can't hurt you, Frank."

Only some highlight portions of various rounds of the films still exist. The footage that remains shows a fairly slow-paced bout with both fighters being very cautious and defensive. During the 1st round, Moran circled, while Johnson remained alert at ring center, sliding forward. They took turns advancing and retreating, each trying to set up a moment to punch. When Johnson advanced, he would land a fast punch, usually a jab or straight right, and Moran would clinch. Occasionally they had a fast back-

and-forth scuffle of punches up close until the inevitable clinch. There was a lot of feinting and sliding back and forth. Moran liked to keep his left arm out to measure Johnson. Between rounds, the cornermen waived towels to cool off the men.

2 - *La Presse* said the round featured a couple hard hits here and there. Johnson's left was brilliant. *Le Petit Parisien* said Moran fired direct rights but they either struck badly or weakly. Johnson returned with a hook and an uppercut. Up to this point, the match was even.

The American writers said Moran forced the fighting, but Johnson landed some hard uppercuts to the jaw. In return, Moran landed hard on the head. Johnson sent a light left hook to the cheek.

The *Mirror of Life and Boxing World* said Moran swung left and right for the jaw but was out of distance, and Johnson smiled. Jack landed three uppercuts, but after breaking away, Moran rushed the champion, scoring with three swings on the head. Considine yelled, "He's a fine champion! Poor old man!" Jack responded to the verbal thrusts by thrice smashing his left on Moran's nose and winning the round.

3 - The French writers said Johnson had warmed up and figured out Moran. The battle became more animated. Johnson avoided Moran's attacks superbly and put more power into his blows, even putting Moran onto the ropes, though Frank took the blows well. Johnson's round.

The Americans said Johnson landed several terrific uppercuts to the jaw, while Moran responded with several jolts to the stomach. Johnson landed a hard jolt on Moran's eye and followed with hard knocks on the body. Jack crowded Frank, who stumbled against the ropes at the bell.

The English said Moran missed his blows, showing faulty judgment of distance and timing. Johnson landed his uppercuts. Moran landed three short rights to the body, but missed a right for the head. Johnson got busy with his left to the head and body, but Moran stopped a right uppercut with his left arm. Johnson rushed him to the ropes, hooking the left to the head, but missed his right at the gong. Moran smiled as he ran to his corner, but Johnson had won the round. Jack had been collecting the points.

4 – The French said Johnson attacked and repeatedly landed short, precise, heavy hits. He hammered Moran's head and nose, and Frank started bleeding a lot. Johnson was dominating more and more.

The Americans said Johnson drew first blood with a right to the nose. The crimson flowed. Jack smiled confidently as he met Frank's attack. Both led at the same time, each landing on the other's head without any harm or damage done. Johnson landed on the face at the gong.

The *Mirror* said Johnson's lefts had Moran's nose looking bad, and this was giving him trouble. Johnson led and tumbled into a clinch, and Considine yelled, "Can't you judge your distance?" Jack shook his head and smiled over Moran's shoulder. He sent the left on the nose again, and

Moran worked in close. Johnson feinted his left and sent the right on the jaw, but not heavily. It was a tame round, favoring Johnson.

5 - *Le Petit Parisien* said the fighting became slow, and did not appear to be very serious either. The spectators complained a little bit, crying out and trying to encourage the boxers to pick up the action. Moran grew tired of hitting Johnson in the stomach in the clinches. The punches had no effect, for the champion kept smiling, big and bright. At the end of the round, Moran landed to the jaw.

La Presse said this round was more of the same.

The Americans said Johnson appeared fresher and confident as the round began. Moran landed hard on the jaw and the crowd cheered. Johnson retaliated with several body blows. Moran blocked several hard uppercuts and landed lightly on the solar plexus, which amused the crowd.

The *Mirror of Life and Boxing World* said Moran missed a right swing for the jaw, and, in falling into a clinch, cut Jack's lip with his head. Jack scored with a straight left on the nose but Moran stopped another attempt and countered lightly. Moran feinted a left swing and sent his right home hard on the ribs. Johnson smiled broadly as Moran hit his body at close range. Moran showed up well and won the round.

The existing films show that Moran attacked and Johnson stepped back, countered, and they clinched. They would advance, fire, and clinch. Johnson was more aggressive, and Frank would duck and clinch. Jack snuck in several right uppercuts on the inside. He easily slid back from and eluded Moran's attempts. In a clinch, Moran dug in several right uppercuts to the body, but Jack didn't seem bothered in the least. He just smiled and then kept ripping in his right uppercuts.

6 - *Le Petit Parisien* said the black man seemed to have a nonchalant attitude. The round featured a couple of not very pretty hits. Advantage to Johnson. Conversely, *La Presse* said Moran got in a couple of nice hits.

The Americans said Johnson continued landing terrific uppercuts to the jaw. He struck a hard left as well. Moran landed with both right and left to the face, which brought a cheer from the crowd.

The *Mirror* said Moran was watchful and waiting. Not pleased with Frank's tactics, Johnson said to him, "Come on, come on!" Considine called out to Johnson, "You don't know how to lead; never did." Johnson replied, "No." Then after a moment's reflection, Jack said, "All right, Jim Corbett," playfully referencing the failure of Corbett's kidding at Reno.

Johnson did good work at close range, but when Moran swung a good right on the head there was great cheering. Johnson countered. Moran responded with another right and then gripped Johnson and whirled him around into a neutral corner. Johnson lost his usual attitude of calm composure and boxed wildly to the bell. Even round. Moran was making a fine effort.

7 - *Le Petit Parisien* said Johnson landed his left into his adversary's flank, but Moran was taking the punches well. It seemed that even if the white man could not win, he at least could resist. Johnson seemed to think exactly the same thing. He picked up his game but Moran responded. *La Presse* said this round was more of the same.

The American writers said Moran led and landed several hard ones to the head, while Johnson landed hard to the stomach. Moran landed a straight left jab to the chin. Johnson then rushed Moran to the ropes, though he did no damage. Johnson opened wider the cut on Moran's nose.

The *Mirror of Life and Boxing World* said that as he was leaving his corner, Johnson told his seconds, "I'll get him this time." However, Moran convinced him that he had a hard task on his hands by sending two lefts and a right to the head, though not very heavily. Johnson's left swing went wide, and the crowd cheered. Jack backed away as Moran led. Frank kept his left almost fully extended as a sort of feeler, but Johnson sent a right through his defense. Jack was treating his rival with the greatest respect now. Moran made a good rally before the end and won the round.

8 - *Le Petit Parisien* said the 8th and 9th rounds featured a couple of back-and-forth exchanges that were not very interesting. Moran led with his right to the face, doubled to the body, and the black man laughed. So far it was an even match. *La Presse* said nothing new happened in the 7th or 8th rounds.

The American press said Johnson followed his old style of fighting

on the defensive. He succeeded in landing three uppercuts to the jaw. In a clinch, Moran pounded the stomach, landing five or six blows, and blocked more uppercuts. Johnson landed a hard right to the jaw. Both did fine work.

The *Mirror of Life and Boxing World* said that early in the round, Johnson sent his left to the nose, and then both scored with lefts. The champ tried infighting without effect, for Moran covered up well. Frank grew angry for a moment at some remark Johnson made, saying, "You know as much about fighting as my boot." Johnson again tried close-quarter work, without doing any damage. The round ended tamely in the champ's favor.

9 - *La Presse* said nothing happened in this round.

The *Herald* said Moran landed a left hook to the body, while Johnson landed several hard ones on the jaw and head. Jack rushed the fighting somewhat, with Frank receiving a left on the jaw.

The *Mirror* said Moran took a right on the top of his head, but missed with his own right swing. Johnson sent in three lefts on the face, but Frank fended off another and drew back from a right uppercut. Johnson's round.

10 - *Le Petit Parisien* said that at early in the round, referee Carpentier warned Johnson for hitting after the break was ordered. However, the referee seemed to lack authority. At the end of the round, Moran was bleeding abundantly. The black man had a true advantage.

La Presse said that just after a break, Moran received a really hard hit on the eye. Johnson was taking over at this point.

The American version said they mixed it immediately at the start. Johnson was successful with infighting. As the referee told them to break, Johnson sent one to Moran's nose. Frank's seconds claimed a foul. The blow cut the nose. The referee warned Johnson, while the crowd hooted the champ. Hard fighting resumed. It looked as though Moran was weakening. His mouth was bleeding as well. This was all Johnson's round.

The *Mirror* said Moran's nose was bothering him, and Johnson played on it. The men had agreed to break away clean upon being told to do so, but Johnson infringed, and shouts of "Foul!" went up, with Moran going to his corner in protest. Carpentier cautioned Johnson, but overruled the claim of foul, with the crowd hooting. The remainder of the round was all Johnson. Jack sarcastically said, "How are you feeling now, Frank?"

Between rounds, it was announced that the referee had cautioned Johnson for hitting after being told to break, which announcement was greeted with both hoots and cheers.

The film version of this round shows that Johnson stepped in with a jab that landed, and then, in the clinch that followed, he scored with a left uppercut to the chin. While clinched, they exchanged close-in rights. Jack dug a right into the body.

Jack held, and as Moran was pushing him off to break out, Johnson landed a right uppercut that jolted Moran's head back, and Moran stepped back to complain. He walked to a corner as Carpentier warned Johnson. They resumed.

Johnson would fire a jab and a clinch would follow. While clinched, Moran threw some rights to the back of the head. More clinches and breaks followed. Jack landed some short rights and uppercuts in close. After a break, he attacked and landed a couple straight rights in a row. Moran lowered his head and grabbed. Jack jabbed and was held again. Jack would fire one or two punches before Moran would hold. At this point in the fight, Johnson was doing all of the leading and landing.

11 - *Le Petit Parisien* said Johnson inflicted punishment upon his adversary. A tired Moran hid his face behind his gloves on many different occasions. Huge advantage for Johnson.

La Presse said Johnson struck Moran around his eyes with three really awful hits. However, Frank still resisted courageously.

Americans said Moran landed a left to the head. Johnson then rushed him and received another warning for holding. Moran sent three hard blows to the body, but Johnson retaliated viciously with blows to the jaw.

The *Mirror of Life and Boxing World* said Johnson was cautioned for holding. The champ looked awfully serious. He had considerably the better of the round, cutting Moran's eyebrow and scoring frequently on the jaw.

12 - *Le Petit Parisien* said the round was really bad. Johnson hit what he could, but it seemed as if his hits were weak and without effectiveness. Blood was still flowing from Moran, though only due to the re-opening of cuts inflicted earlier.

Conversely, *La Presse* said Johnson accelerated and dominated.

The *Herald* said Johnson succeeded in landing several uppercuts to the jaw, as well as straight lefts to the nose and over the eye. Moran was breathing hard, and some wondered if he could last much longer. He cleverly dodged a hard swing to the jaw.

The *Mirror of Life and Boxing World* said Johnson again carried the honors, making special targets of Moran's nose and left eyebrow. He slipped a straight right for his jaw, and then tried to corner Moran, but Frank ducked smartly out and was applauded. Jack worked his right uppercut with good effect, and won the round. Moran was bleeding badly as he went to his corner. His attendants were solemn-faced, like pall-bearers.

13 - Moran returned to the battle with a smile on his lips and landed one hell of a hook. The blow made a lot of noise. Johnson let out a huge laugh and applauded with both hands. *Le Petit Parisien*'s writer wondered if the white man was coming back. Even round.

La Presse said Moran finally hit his adversary in the face. Johnson smiled and applauded.

The *Herald* said Moran led but could not land effectively, while Johnson sent one to the jaw. Frank landed hard on the jaw, which drew a cheer from the crowd. Johnson stood back, smiling, and then sent a hard right to Moran's jaw.

The *Mirror* said Moran rallied gamely and drew cheers. He attacked with determination, though Johnson presented a very fine defense and worked his right uppercut at every possible opportunity. Moran tried a right, and, shifting with lightning quickness, swung a hard left to the neck. It was the best blow struck in the contest, but Johnson was quite undisturbed and joined in the volley of applause by clapping his gloves together and smiling. He blocked another attempt similar in nature, and then Moran jabbed him on the nose, backing away as Johnson advanced to attack. Moran's round.

The films show that Johnson rolled away from a right and made it miss. Clinching followed. Jack was looking to land short rights and right uppercuts on the inside.

Moran missed a lead right but landed a follow-up left hook, after which Johnson landed a grazing right uppercut, and then clapped after Moran stepped away. They both smiled as Frank extended his right arm as if to shake as Jack applauded.

Moran quickly stepped forward again but they clinched. Between the several clinches that followed, Jack tried to sneak in a jab and left uppercut. Moran circled and attacked with a lead right that fell short and Johnson countered with a right uppercut and they clinched again. Moran moved around until Jack jabbed and they clinched. From the outside, Jack leapt in with a lead hook and Frank clinched. Johnson jolted Moran's head back with a snappy, sneaky-fast left uppercut. Frank held again. On the outside, Johnson landed a left jab before the bell.

14 - *Le Petit Parisien* said they furiously threw themselves at one another. Moran used his very long arms but the punches did not arrive at their destination. Johnson was serious and took a marked advantage just before time was called.

La Presse said this round was nothing new. This writer believed that Moran's only idea was to last the distance. On the other hand, Johnson seemed to be amusing himself, having a good time.

The American version said Moran tried hard but unsuccessfully for the jaw. Several of his blows brought smiles from Johnson. Frank ran into a punch on the nose. Moran made a futile swing and ran into the ropes.

The *Mirror of Life and Boxing World* said it was Johnson's round.

15 - *Le Petit Parisien* said the fight continued at a distance. The men changed their tactics. At least four times, Moran circled around Johnson, who pivoted in place and watched as Moran moved about the ring. There was no point in doing anything else.

La Presse said nothing of note happened in this round.

The Herald said Moran avoided Johnson, who stood still, laughing. Moran landed hard to the face. Johnson rushed him to the ropes.

The *Mirror* said both were eager for the fray, and Moran opened by scoring with two lefts on the head. He swung his right but Jack easily ducked it. Frank missed his left and right but hooked his left to the body with plenty of sting. Jack countered to the ribs. He occupied mid-ring, with Moran going round and round him. The crowd booed, while Johnson put his hands on his hips and smiled as he watched Moran circle him. Considine said, "You're the champion; show something." Even round.

The films show that Johnson did most of the leading from the outside, firing quick jabs, and he did all of the effective work on the inside. He kept ripping in right uppercuts. When Moran attempted to lead, Jack would just step back and make the blows fall short, and sometimes counter with a jab. Moran missed a right over the top and fell into the ropes. Moran continually moved about on the outside until Jack stepped in with a quick shot, and then in the clinch, tried to work his rights.

16 - *Le Petit Parisien*'s author questioned whether the last four rounds should be described. The fight had become tedious, consisting of faraway hits with little power. It was a good fight between two friends. The still-smiling Johnson kept hitting him again and again, but the white man's face showed no emotion, and he did not seem to be affected by the hits. Finally, Moran landed a couple himself.

La Presse said Moran received a dozen blows around the ark of his left eyebrow, which was bleeding abundantly.

The *Herald* said Johnson forced the fighting. Moran landed on the stomach and Jack sent a left to the nose. He followed with five more in rapid succession to the same place. Moran landed two straight lefts to the chin.

The *Mirror of Life and Boxing World* said Johnson scored with the right; and Moran with the left to the body. A series of Johnson uppercuts had the blood spurting from Moran's left eyebrow. Jack sent his left to the face, and both twice landed with lefts. Johnson's round.

17 - *La Presse* said nothing interesting happened.

The *Herald* said Johnson sent a hard left to the jaw, while Moran made wild swings. Moran sent a left to the face, which seemed to make little impression. Moran sent another left to the face which brought a cheer.

The *Mirror of Life and Boxing World* said that after Johnson had scored with a left, a right swing by Moran just grazed the camp's chin. Jack queried,

"How now?" Frank replied, "Pretty good." Frank sent a left on the jaw, missed twice, and then dug into the body. He missed a left swing, but brought his glove back smartly on the jaw. Johnson was puffing as he retired to his corner. Moran had the better of this round.

18 - The French papers said little or nothing happened.

The *Herald* said Jack sent one to the stomach, two to the face, and a hard left to the body.

The *Mirror* said Jack did some missing, but also put in some good and effective hits, mostly with his left. The crowd started shouting, dissatisfied with the combat, or lack thereof.

19 - *La Presse* said they stood close and landed some body shots for a time, but neither landed anything significant.

The *Herald* said Moran went after Johnson, infighting and holding at the same time. His tactics caused adverse comment. However, he did no damage. Referee Georges Carpentier frequently separated them.

The *Mirror* said Moran rushed in close and pegged away at the body with both hands. The champion tried to wrestle him off. It appeared as if Johnson's left arm had gone back on him, for he didn't strike a decent blow with it. Moran had him on the run, sending in his right on the jaw and ribs, winning the round.

The films show that as Moran advanced, Johnson smoothly moved away and scored jabs before clinching as Moran drew near. Moran worked the body, but so too did Johnson.

20 - *Le Petit Parisien* said that even before the 20th round began, the tired and upset audience started toward the exits. After the round concluded, when the referee appointed Jack Johnson as the winner, everybody recognized it. Without any possible discussion, Johnson was the winner.

La Presse said Johnson seemed to be at the end of his force. However, Moran faded into emptiness.

The *Herald* said they shook hands. Each tried for a knockout. Johnson sent several hard rights to the face. He also landed a left to the head. Moran's head rested on Jack's chest. Moran swung wildly, while Johnson landed frequently and at will. Moran hung on and tried ineffectively for the body. The gong rang and Johnson was declared the winner.

The *Mirror of Life and Boxing World* said Moran was tired as he stepped out and shook hands at the start, but so was Johnson. Moran fought as hard as he could and scored with his right on the ribs, but he lacked finishing power. Johnson landed a right cross-counter on the jaw. The bout was a scramble now, and it finished amid a terrific din, with the spectators in the cheaper sections screaming like maniacs. Pandemonium prevailed.

After a short wait, the announcer held up a card on which was printed the name of Jack Johnson, proclaiming that he was still "champion du monde."

On the films of the 20th round, Johnson kept sticking jabs and holding Moran safe on the inside. Moran's attempts to land from the outside were futile as well, for Jack always moved just out of range of the blows.

Scenes throughout the Johnson-Moran fight

In his next-day article, Max Hogmanay, who attended the fight for *Le Petit Parisien*, said Jack Johnson easily beat Frank Moran on points. Although Hogmanay also concluded that Johnson no longer hit very hard, he granted that it was possible that the white hope simply could take it very well. Regardless, Johnson had the science necessary to retain his title. Still, this writer opined that Langford could defeat him with little effort.

Daniel Cousin, writing for *La Presse*, said Johnson beat Moran in an amicable fight. From the first couple of hits, the fight seemed a bit bizarre and weird. It was not a fight, but rather a bunch of smiles and grimaces. Neither man was effective. Johnson was not in shape and was a shadow of what he could have been. His hits lacked both precision and power.

However, Moran did nothing. He rarely attacked, doing so only two or three times. But above all, Moran simply tried to finish the 20 rounds. During one of the rounds, Moran ran around the ring ten times. Johnson, fed up from following his not-so-courageous adversary, stopped and waited for him.

This writer opined that referee Carpentier would make a plaything of Moran, and when Carpentier added 10 more kilograms of weight (about 22 pounds) he would be champion. The fight proved that there were only four really great boxers in the world - Langford, Jeannette, Carpentier, and maybe Johnson, if and when he got his form back. This author believed that Carpentier would beat Gunboat Smith in their upcoming fight.

L'Humanite said Johnson had a bad fight but kept his title. At the start, Johnson stood there with his chest open, waiting for the attack, which came quickly. Moran threw right hooks and tried to hit him in the stomach. Johnson was happy to parry and escape the looping gloves by moving away.

In the 2nd round, the champion started to really work.

As soon as the 3rd round came, one could see Johnson's superiority. He allowed his adversary to hammer his chest; at the same time smiling, showing his big golden teeth. The golden smile stopped and Jack landed a left uppercut underneath his combatant's guard to the point of the chin, lifting up the white man's head. Johnson then let Moran work, which Frank did without any science. He kept hustling, while the champion was happy just to await the attacks and counter.

The match lacked beauty. Moran did not have the same class as the black man, while at the same time; Johnson was not as brilliant as he once was. Of course, Jack had a good time with his adversary, and was trying to mock him.

In the 13th round, Moran landed a left hook. Johnson stopped and applauded. The white man, shocked by such a gesture, stopped fighting.

In the 19th round, Moran, having hammered away at Johnson's stomach, saw that it was impossible to hurt his opponent, and nearly impossible to hit him.

This author said Johnson certainly won on points, but the proof was there that Johnson was no longer Johnson. This observer believed that without a doubt, Langford, Smith, or Carpentier would beat him.[917]

L'Intransigeant said that a more courageous adversary than Moran would have won. The two men's reputations led to the hope that it would be a heck of a fight. However, from the first-round, Moran gave the impression of being hypnotized. No meeting had ever been so solemn, sad, colorless, dull, or drab. Johnson did not have one moment where he could really

---

[917] *L'Humanite* June 28, 1914.

apply himself, but it wasn't his fault. He was discouraged from following his fleeing adversary around the ring. At one point, Johnson stood there with his hands on his hips, waiting for his foe to come to him and get back to work.

This author said there was no reason to doubt that Johnson was in the best condition possible. The fact that he could not knock out Moran showed that he was no longer the strong fighter from Reno. However, his 36 years, combined with his years at the café, in the car, and concert halls had not destroyed his athletic qualities. He still was quite good enough to defeat Moran. That said, he no longer was what he once was. The general sentiment of those who saw the fight was that the title soon would be Langford's. Moran lost the chance of his life.[918]

Le Matin said the exhibition was ridiculous and comedic. The match was nothing for Johnson, but he pretended for an excellent laugh and some fun. He enjoyed moving to the side with a huge smile, eluding blows. While Moran hit him in the body, Johnson smiled. Moran's seconds overtly mocked the champ, who reserved his biggest smiles for them. When the public booed and whistled, Johnson simply laughed. Americans would call out in anger, "That's the champion?" This writer said "the public had to sit there and watch the joy of this child, the infantile joy of this black person. His impudence was unconscious."

Johnson was heavy, fat, and slow. This writer opined that Johnson no longer was the world's best, for his decline was very visible, and Langford would beat him.

Moran did not show any of the excellent confidence which he had before the fight. He must have prepared himself too well for the match on paper and in his own imagination.

Moran found himself in the situation of a general who prepared a battle plan which would be excellent, but the response of his enemy was better than what he thought it would be. Close-up, Johnson was big and muscular, and Moran started to re-think, and he thought a long time.

From the 1st round to the 5th round, Moran only landed seven effective hits to the stomach. From rounds 6 to 15, he landed six hits to the face. From the 16th to the 20th, Moran did not land anything.

The Americans who were sitting at ringside would call out to him, "Go on Frank, hit him." However, Moran seemed more interested in not getting hit. Both men appeared to be holding themselves back. They smiled at one another amiably. There was mutual gallantry. It seemed as if they were politely apologizing to one another if they landed.

In contradictory fashion, this writer also said that Moran was courageous. He was hit in the nose and cut over the left eye. Blood sometimes blinded him, yet he continued to try to get at the black man. But courage alone is not what makes a champion and nobody seemed to realize

---

[918] *L'Intransigeant*, June 29, 1914.

792

it better than Moran. This writer opined that Moran never would be the champion.[919]

The *New York Herald* had a reporter at ringside. This observer said Johnson had no trouble outpointing the white hope. Moran was aggressive and game, but unable to land many effective blows. It was a hard-fought battle, but Johnson easily won on points.

The game Moran was stubborn and stood up to the champ, did most of the leading, and made many friends. However, Johnson's superior skill and effective uppercuts wore down his opponent and won the match. Moran was not able to block the terrific uppercuts. They were sent on the jaw repeatedly when Frank least expected them, and several times with such force that Moran was sent wobbling. However, there were no knockdowns or finishing blows. At the close, Moran was cut on the nose and under and over the left eye. Johnson showed no marks.

Towards the middle of the contest, it appeared as if Frank would not last the distance, but he showed courage and kept driving. Although he landed many times, his blows lacked force and were comparatively ineffective. Now and then he tried to land hard, but in doing so swung in the air, with Johnson being several feet away.

Moran took his punishment well. During parts of rounds, Johnson toyed with him when he saw that he could do so without danger to himself.

Toward the end, Johnson had the Pittsburgher absolutely at his mercy. Moran apparently feared that he would be finished, and clung to Johnson for support, trying at the same time to land, but without success. His manner of fighting and holding in the latter part of the fight caused some unfavorable comment. Johnson's tactics also brought a caution from the referee at one point, as well as a storm of jeers from the crowd.

Johnson's wife cried out shrilly from time to time. "Hit him daddy!" "Come along, pop." "Now then, Jack, let him have another."

The crowd sweltered under the heat. Many French spectators seemingly did not understand the fine points of boxing, and they voiced their objection to the infighting, though they cheered any resounding but harmless whacks.

William Brady, who was at ringside, was particularly hard on both boxers. He called it a second-rate exhibition. Neither one landed damaging blows. The big Paris crowd cried out in disgust at the fiasco. Johnson was tired out at the end, so tired that he forgot defense, but Moran's own exhaustion saved the champ. "In my opinion the referee could have called the bout a draw without doing injustice to either."

Johnson was in as good a condition as a man of his age could hope to be, but 10 rounds was as far as he could go well. Moran's condition was as expected, but his skills were not on par. "As a boxer Moran was absolutely outclassed." For five or six rounds, the public showed patience at the

[919] *Le Matin,* June 28, 1914

spectacle's slowness, but after the 6th and until the end, there was constant jeering, while derisive epithets were hurled at the combatants. One said, "Why don't you kiss each other?"

Moran did not deliver more than a score of really effective blows during the entire fight, while Johnson landed possibly a dozen in each round. Johnson fought like he did in all of his fights.

The champ never inflicted enough punishment to make Moran the least bit discouraged. A straight left and the old time right uppercut in clinches were all that Johnson had to offer, and the result of the blows merely was an abrasion of the left eye and on the bridge of the nose.

In the 11th round, Carpentier warned Johnson against striking in the clinches after the word "break." It only occurred once, through inadvertence, and it was not in the least degree serious. Throughout the fight there was no disposition towards foul play.

In one of the amusing clinches, Moran beat a tattoo on Johnson's stomach. Jack simply laughed outright, as he used to do in training while his sparring partners pounded him there at his request. The crowd went wild with good-humored laughter. At every stage, the French sympathies were with Johnson.

Johnson finished better. "It is certain that Johnson was in better general condition than Moran in the last round." In that round, Moran either attempted blows without clearly seeing where they might land or fell every other second upon Johnson's shoulder, putting his hands to his breast in an effort to avoid the uppercuts.

Brady opined that a second rater could defeat either fighter. He said it took less out of a man to stand still and let the other man do the work than it did to fight, which is what Johnson liked to do. Even so, Brady believed that there were half a dozen whites and at least one black who could have put the "waiting champion" to the floor, out for the count. Of course, this was coming from the man who incorrectly predicted a Moran victory.

Brady did note that in successfully defending the crown, Johnson had accomplished a feat never before achieved by a man of his age in the history of the ring.

Brady's report also was printed in the *New York American*, with some variations. He said Johnson, the "colored heavyweight champion," outboxed the challenger, although not one effective blow was struck by either man. There was never the suspicion of a jar, much less a knockdown. In the last three rounds, Johnson presented the spectacle of a champion superior in weight, science, experience, and strength, clinging to a smaller antagonist and eager for the final bell.

Moran did his best in the 18th and 19th rounds to obtain at least a draw, but his very exertions left him so fatigued that he appeared pitiful in the 20th round. He was gone, staggering about like a drunken man, swinging blindly at the thin air. Johnson was in worse condition, with his sole efforts to lean on his man. Their mutual exhaustion saved one another from being stopped. Brady further said the pictures would prove it to be the most disgraceful contest for a world's championship ever held.

The report of William H. Rocap, former fighter and the bout's official timekeeper, said the victory was little to boast of. Moran carried the fight to the champ, who refused to lead. His aggressiveness actually cost Moran the fight. Frank was always over-anxious and could not be patient.

In the 1st round, Moran showed that he could punch, when he caught Johnson with a right lead. The blow landed on the cheek bone and raised a large lump. Johnson was wary of his right thereafter and took no chances. He boxed carefully and let Moran set the pace.

Johnson was content to block and catch Moran coming in with a left hook and right uppercut. He showed flashes of his old-time cleverness, blocking and jabbing, and landing left and right uppercuts. All were well-timed, but they lacked speed. He let Moran do the bulk of the leading, and his younger foe fell into the trap.

After the 10th round, Moran fought under a disadvantage. He was bleeding from cuts on the nose and under the left eye, and at times was blinded by his own gore. Johnson slammed his crushed nose repeatedly, but Moran shook his head and bore in again.

Moran lost a great opportunity in the 13th; when he caught Jack flush on the jaw with a left hook. Johnson stood in the center of the ring and clapped his gloved hands. Moran could have caught him again, but was too slow.

In the 15th round, Moran moved around the ring, inviting Johnson to lead, but the latter stood still at ring center, dropped his hands, and invited Moran to mix it. Moran did and caught him with a left and right before the bell rang.

The bout was spoiled in the last two rounds because Johnson was not trying. "Johnson affected being tired, and Moran, weak from his own exertions, was quite satisfied to stay the limit." The crowd hissed and hooted as they left the great Velodrome d'Hiver arena.

Johnson emerged practically unscathed. Moran got to his head and body in the infighting, but inevitably Johnson smiled and brushed off his punches with little concern and no damage done.

On points, Rocap said Johnson had twelve of the twenty rounds. Two rounds clearly were Moran's - the 6th and the 15th, while honors were even in the other six. Hence, Rocap scored it 12-2-6 in rounds for Johnson.

Rocap said the fight was on the level. The champion rushed in the closing stages, hoping to put over a knockout blow. However, there were neither knockdowns nor anything that looked like a finishing blow. Johnson indulged in plenty of hard hitting, but Moran absorbed all the punishment and came back for more.

Also writing for the *New York American* was C. F. Bertelli, that paper's Paris correspondent. He said that at no time during the bout did a Moran victory appear possible. In the latter half it looked as if Johnson could have punished him more severely than he did, if he had so desired. Bertelli thought Johnson was carrying him. As a boxer, Moran was outclassed absolutely.

Johnson's boxing was superb, and his left-hand work was all that could be expected. However, Jack hardly ever followed up his advantages with sufficient keenness. Although Moran had boasted that he was going to make Johnson do the leading, the reverse was the case. Johnson got in his best blows after Moran's almost continuous ineffective leads.

As the rounds progressed, many suspected that the promoters knew all along that Johnson was going to win easily, and the spectators believed that the whole thing was designed as a way to make money off of the ignorant.

At times, Moran relapsed into his Jeffries style of fighting. A hundred times or more he covered his face with his arms, in a bending crouching attitude, to ward off Johnson's blows.

It was Moran, too, who did nearly all of the clinching, and here Johnson's skill in placing his weight to the best advantage on the other man's shoulder's came into full play. Not one blow of the few Moran landed seemed to affect Johnson in the least, while Johnson often succeeded in giving Moran such fierce jolts to the head as to stagger him.

Johnson's superior ring tactics frequently got Moran against the ropes or in a corner, and there Frank would crouch and bend and wait for an opportunity to charge and run away. Johnson would pursue him and force Moran to lead or clinch.

Moran usually would fall short with his blows, and Johnson would counter heavily with a left or right, and often with each in succession. In clinches, with one arm free, it was Johnson who always got in most of the short-arm blows. Early on, Johnson started Moran's nose bleeding, and he kept jabbing that member steadily with his left.

A little later, Johnson opened Moran's old cut on the left eyebrow, and from that moment, that cut became a special object of blows. It bled so profusely that the blood covered Moran's face almost entirely.

It is certain that Johnson finished stronger as well, and was in better general condition than Moran in the last round. Before that, Moran had wobbled slightly and it was evident that his continuous circling around had fatigued his legs greatly. The circling game was to Johnson's liking, for he turned it into a broad farce when he suddenly stopped in the middle of the ring and stood with his hands on his hips and turned his body slowly while watching Moran with a contemptuous grin. It was one of the moments when the mingled howling and scornful laughter of the multitude became deafening.

In the last round, all pretense of boxing by Moran was thrown aside, and he either attempted a blow without seeing where it might land, or every other second fell upon Johnson's shoulder, putting his hands to his bosom in an effort to avoid the uppercuts.

After the fight, Johnson's left arm was in considerable pain, but apparently there was no fracture. The trouble probably was due to a recrudescence of the fracture of the left forearm sustained in the Jim Johnson fight.[920]

The *London Times'* special correspondent's report said Moran was beaten on points, but Johnson was in poor form. Apart from the vexing question of Black versus White, the principal interest of the match was to see whether Johnson had deteriorated seriously during four years of leisure. It was inevitable that he should lose some ground, for in boxing, as in every other form of sport which depends upon perfect muscle coordination, it is only by constant practice that the highly-trained athlete can prevent a certain amount of degeneration.

The event proved that Johnson was not the man he was four years ago. This writer said that Johnson's career as a great fighter was over. Jeffries would be avenged not by a white man, but by the passing years. Jack still was a fine defensive fighter, but his defense was not impenetrable. He had lost his footwork and his timing was not as accurate as it once was. Johnson's days as champion were about over, but he still was good enough to beat Moran.

As for skill, Moran was a crude novice compared with Johnson. He could not hit either straight or hard. He did have pluck and endurance, though.

Both men started cautiously. Johnson waited for his opponent to bring the fight to him, which Moran was quite willing to do.

Early in the 2nd round, Moran landed a light left to the jaw which removed Johnson's smile, but Johnson soon retaliated with a much heavier left swing to Moran's face. By the end of the round, Johnson was sweating.

It was apparent that there was no sting in Moran's punches. On more than one occasion Johnson allowed himself to be driven around the ring while his opponent pommelled his stomach, but it was evident that he was never hurt and there was far more danger in the vicious right uppercuts which Johnson used to stop Moran's advance every now and then.

At the start of the 7th round, Johnson said to his seconds, "I'll get him this time." When he took the aggressive, he seemed to be able to penetrate Moran's defense quite easily and soon had the latter's nose and left eyebrow bleeding. However, he was unable to finish him off.

By the end of nine rounds, not a single really heavy blow had reached its mark. People began to wonder where the power for which Moran had been credited was.

At the end of the 10th round, the announcement was made through the megaphone that the referee had cautioned Johnson for hitting Moran after he had been told to break away. With the exception of this one incident, the fight was cleanly fought.

---

[920] *New York American*, June 28, 1914.

There was none of the running-fire of taunts which had been heard in Johnson's fights with Burns and Jeffries. Perhaps it was because Moran had not mouthed off and insulted Johnson, or at least not to the same degree.

The fight continued, and it was not only disappointing, but soon became tedious. Moran continued to do most of the leading, but his onslaughts were mostly of the windmill variety, and his swings were wide of their mark always by several inches, and sometimes feet. Usually, he was measuring his man with an outstretched left and preparing for a right which never came.

Towards the end, both were very tired and the crowd grew impatient. The spectators suspected the fight was not genuine. "This was a quite excusable, if mistaken, suspicion, and at times it was ludicrous to see Johnson in the middle of the ring revolving on his own axis with Moran strolling round the ring trying unsuccessfully to draw him – indeed, Carpentier once told the men to fight."

Some suggested that Johnson purposely refrained from finishing him off in order to secure a second fight, but this author did not believe that for a moment. It appeared to this author that Johnson intended to beat his man at an earlier stage, but was unable to do so, and was very tired at the end.

After the winner was announced, men and women in the crowd struggled to reach and mount the raised platform, and they almost fought to shake Johnson's hand. Husbands helped their wives to scramble through the ropes.[921]

Con Murphy, writing the report for the British publication, *Mirror of Life and Boxing World*, said Johnson went all out to win but was all-in at the finish. Moran did better than any other previous title foe. However, there never was any prospect of a knockout.

Johnson tried hard to obtain a decisive win from the start, but Moran was more of a match physically than others, and not decrepit and old. He did not waver or weaken.

In the 6th round, Moran startled and angered Johnson by putting his left around the champ's neck and then whipping him around and shoving him into a corner. It gave Jack an appreciation for Frank's raw strength, and he had a wholesome respect for him afterward.

In the 7th round, George Considine, who acted as Moran's timekeeper, yelled at the champ, "Moran's the first good man you ever fought." Johnson simply smiled back. Moran was standing up under the hardest blows that Johnson could connect with, and was giving very nearly as good as he received.

Johnson made free use of his jolting right uppercut at close quarters, but never hurt Moran much. The white man covered up well. Jack landed his straight left quite effectively; for Moran was open for it. However, Frank stopped the left swings. The jabs had Moran bleeding from the nose, and it appeared as if his nasal organ was broken. Blood flowed freely from the

---

[921] *London Times*, June 29, 1914.

nasty gash over the left eye, interfering somewhat with Moran's sight. Frank stood it all with gameness.

Georges Carpentier refereed capably. He clapped his hands when he wanted them to separate, or tapped a holding arm if one was at fault. His English was confined mostly to "Break away!" and "Don't hold!"

Parisians were dissatisfied with the contest, especially near the finish. Denied a knockout, they yelled, screamed, and hooted with peculiar shrillness. Cries of "Fake" went up, along with those who wanted their money back.

This writer opined that there never was a question of fake to capable judges who watched from ringside, though some spectators thought there was an arrangement between the men. The truth was that Johnson was unable to do any damage, though he tried. Johnson was in earnest, showing more aggression than was his custom, willing to do his share of the forcing, but Moran was cautious, though without showing fear. Moran was wanting in execution. His own futile exertions combined with the punishment he took left him fatigued, and he could not harm the champ.

Some time ago, Johnson was heard to say that he might allow Moran to stay a dozen rounds or so. "I'll string the big boob along for a while unless he stings me like Ketchel did." But it was one thing to prophesy, and another to perform. The strong Moran was not easily taken out.

Acting on instructions, Moran showed no desire to lead, making use of the ring instead, trying to counter the champion. He did not want to make the same mistakes that others had. These tactics didn't suit Johnson, who was at his best on the defensive. Johnson tried to goad him, saying, "Come on, come on!" Still, the slow pace actually helped an aging Johnson.

Johnson no longer stood out as invincible. The golden smile was fading. He was not as fast as he once was, his staying powers were diminished, and his punch had lost some of its sting. Age was slowly but surely getting him. He possessed all the boxing ability with which he had been credited. His fine defense had not lost anything. It still was sound. But the man who put many others onto the mat could not do so once with Moran, who never was in the slightest danger of being stopped. Johnson could not even daze him.

The champion was, however, always the classy boxer and sound ring general. This writer opined that Moran would have won if he had the boxing ability to match his height, strength, and stamina. Moran's work was badly wanting in finish. He never seriously troubled the champion, and though Johnson could do little but stall and play around in the last two rounds, the willing Moran could not put his good intentions into execution. He had gone through a grueling battle and had suffered in the process, as his cut faced testified, and was anything but fresh, as might have been expected after such a lengthy bout. There was no last desperate effort.

Regardless of the effects of age, inactivity, and an easy lifestyle creeping up on him, Johnson still clearly won. This author scored it 11 rounds Johnson, 5 rounds Moran, and 4 even. Johnson won rounds 2, 3, 4, 8, 9, 10,

11, 12, 14, 16, and 18. Moran won rounds 5, 7, 13, 17, and 19. Even rounds were 1, 6, 15, and 20.

Moran was entitled to credit for being the first challenger to extend Johnson. He was the first boxer to go 20 rounds with Johnson since Hart in 1905. That said, this writer opined that it might be possible that the champ's next performance might prove that it was nothing remarkable to last rounds with him, for any husky in-shape big man might do so with the champion in his present form.

Afterwards, Moran had a very nasty gash over his left eye, and his nose bothered him. But otherwise he was all right.

This writer opined that Johnson was nearing the end of his reign, but the question was who was best suited to dethrone him. Langford had a chance, but he was slowing up, and was greatly handicapped in height and reach. He would have to fight up and carry the battle to Johnson, and many feared it would be the Burns fight all over again, or a repeat of their 1906 Chelsea contest. Carpentier and Gunboat Smith might give him trouble, but it was unclear whether they could *beat* him. Either one would be forty pounds lighter than the champ, perhaps more, and not as strong.

This writer believed that a boxer with a snappy left would give Johnson trouble, were he to possess Moran's physical attributes as well. The contest was the "writing on the wall," so to speak, for Johnson. "He is about finished as an attraction in Paris, and while they would go to see him box Carpentier, in the hope of a victory for the French boy, there would be a very small gate for him against anybody else."

Referee Georges Carpentier said it was one of the best fights he had ever seen. When asked if he would like to fight Johnson, Carpentier responded, "Johnson is a little bit too heavy for me at present." Seven years later, Carpentier would fight for the heavyweight crown, giving him the distinction of having both refereed and fought in a heavyweight title bout.

In interviews, Johnson called attention to the fact that no champion of his age ever defended the title successfully. The *Herald* quoted him as saying,

> They thought I couldn't last 20 rounds. Well, didn't I? I am satisfied. I have done nothing for two years except ride fast. In another six weeks I will be ready to box anybody. Moran? He has a real hard punch with either hand. I know, because I have been there. If they always landed there is not anybody who could stand up against him. He is a good boy, all right, and I enjoyed the fight. Carpentier was a fine referee.

Brady and Bertelli quoted Johnson as saying, "Did I not box all right? I am as strong as ever and I never turned a hair. I'll fight any man in the world, within the next six weeks, too, if he comes along."

The *New York American* quoted Johnson:

> Did I not fight all right? Am I not as strong as ever? Wasn't the battle on the level? I am glad to win; most of all so that all these questions

about which there seems to have been some doubt, are now answered. I am ready for the next comer and will meet any man in the world within six weeks. Moran took a lot of punishment. His gameness held him on to the end.

William Rocap said Johnson excused his showing in the last rounds by saying that he could not get his left working. "I thought I had him in the earlier rounds, but I missed many chances. I am his master at any stage of the game."

According to the *Mirror*, Johnson was more inclined to make excuses for himself than anything else. "Moran is a big, strong fellow, you know, and I do not know any man in the world able to stop him quickly. I could have done with more training, and I would beat him sure if we were to fight again in six weeks' time."

According to the *Herald*, in the dressing room, Moran said,

> At the worst it should have been a draw. I was the aggressor throughout the whole twenty rounds and I was not hurt. The cut over my eye is only an old one reopened. It was received in training. I believe I had the best of practically every round. The blow that really hurt was one on my nose, and for this Johnson was warned. That stopped my breathing. That was the only real hurt Johnson gave me.

Brady and Bertelli quoted Moran, when answering why he lost, as saying something to the effect of:

> Well, the flow of blood from the re-opening of an old cut over my left eye in an early round prevented my seeing very clearly. You can also say that I admit Jack Johnson is a better boxer than I am, also that he got back into splendid form, finer than anyone would have expected of him. I am still sure, however, that in a fight to a finish I could best him. I was fresh and strong when the last round closed, and I only wish the fight could have gone on.

The *New York American* quoted Moran as saying,

> Jack Johnson is a better boxer than I am. The way he got into condition was remarkable and a big surprise to me. Although I got a cut over the eye I was still fresh when the fight ended, and am confident I can beat him in a battle to a finish. I have no apologies to make. I put up the best fight I could, but the negro's ring experience was too much to overcome.

William Rocap quoted Moran as saying, "I gave Johnson the best fight of his career. I am satisfied with my showing."

The *Mirror* quoted Moran as well:

> I am only sorry I did not beat him. He is a clever boxer and a great tactician, but I had him beaten at the finish, and would whip him for a certainty should we meet again. My nose and eye bothered me, but I

guess I am not going to make any excuses. I tried as hard as I could, but would do better in another attempt.

A couple days later, the *New York Herald* said Moran had a bruised nose from a punch he received in the 10th round, and a cut over his eyebrow. Moran said,

I don't look like a man who has been killed. I figured I could whip Johnson in view of his age, but I now believe him to be as strong as he ever was. I hope to secure a match with Sam Langford, as I want to meet the toughest man I can get. I believe I could have won from Johnson except for the foul blow on the nose in the tenth round, which sent the blood down my throat and sickened me.[922]

Arthur F. Bettinson, England's National Sporting Club's manager, called the contest "Rotten."
Dick Burge, the famous lightweight, said,

It wasn't such a bad fight for big fellows; I have seen much worse. I thought Moran had a good chance, and I told him before the fight to lead with Johnson every time and counter him as hard as he could, but he hasn't the finish, and was wide open for Johnson's blows. It was the first time I had seen the negro box, and I was not impressed. He is beaten now. Either Bob Fitzsimmons or John L. Sullivan at their best would have had Johnson on the floor, and that in jig-time.

The *New York Journal's* Tad Dorgan said that many observers simply did not understand or appreciate Johnson, and got their analysis of him and his performance against Moran wrong. Johnson's style of boxing never varied. Johnson-Moran was not a spectacular fight, but was of the same sort that Johnson had fought for the past ten years. Hence, it was no surprise that it was a somewhat slow bout. Tad said the "champ is not of the spectacular sort and never was. He fights the same cool, cautious battle every time." Everyone who followed his career knew that he fought his own way and no other, and that the fight would be slow and tiresome. No fighter had been able to make Johnson chase him, Moran included. Johnson was a master at imposing his tactics on everyone. He enjoyed playing defense and kidding his foes. He outclassed Moran without exerting himself. Tad said Moran was a second rater, as shown in his fight with Gunboat Smith.

Tad opined that the only two white men with any chance against Johnson were European heavyweight champion Georges Carpentier and Gunboat Smith. "Johnson cannot last forever. We all admit that." Most fighters of his age were done for and had lost their titles already, so it was just a matter of time before age was going to catch up with Johnson. He would be age 37 the following March. That said, Tad opined that Johnson still would be the betting favorite against either Carpentier or Smith.

---

[922] *New York Herald,* June 29, 1914.

Some were figuring that Johnson would lay down to Moran. However, he had never done it in his career, and there was no reason why he should do it with Moran when he could have done it with Jeffries and made a million. "Our dope here is that when Lil' Artha Johnson lays down it will be on the level. It may not be soon, but it will come."[923]

In the U.S., there was plenty of action surrounding the fight, and, as sometimes was the case with a Johnson fight, that action included racial violence. The *Herald* said that during the bout, vast throngs of men, women, and children stood outside newspaper buildings receiving fight bulletins. At least 1,800 swelled Broadway into 36th street in New York's Herald square to receive the *New York Herald's* bulletins.

Any time that the white hope made a particularly good showing, there was loud cheering. Many thought Moran's showing was so good up to the 15th round that they made wagers at even money.

Those of Johnson's race were in the minority, and kept reasonably quiet until the bulletin for the 16th round said the "Smoke" had punched Moran in the nose six times. A "dusky" advocate gave vent to a feeble cheer, shouting, "Go it Jack!" However, no sooner had he uttered those words than he discovered himself to be in the hottest kind of an argument with a white hoper.

In New York there were some race riots and beatings in the wake of the fight bulletins. The *Herald* reported that there was a race battle between 200 whites and blacks. A black youth named Leon Earley, while riding a street car, uttered a cheer for Jack Johnson. This angered a crowd of white men, who attacked. They dragged him from the street car and gave him a severe beating, breaking his jaw. This brought a score of blacks to his rescue and a general fight took place. Many were beaten severely. It only ended when 50 policemen appeared.

A white man, James Walsh, charged Earley with slashing him with a razor. Earley was charged with felonious assault, while Walsh was taken into custody on a charge of disorderly conduct.

Another separate battle took place. For several days leading up to the fight, the Johnson–Moran bout had been the subject of bitter argument between white and black factions. Blacks' confidence in their champion and willingness to bet on him served to embitter the members of the white Gopher band, who had pinned their faith on Moran. Word was that the Gophers would wreak vengeance upon black folk if Moran lost. Hence, blacks were warned that if Johnson won, they should not appear in the streets unarmed.

When news of Johnson's victory reached the Gophers, a band of 15 of them appeared in the streets armed with heavy clubs. They gave battle to every black person they met. One of the whites, John Burns, wound up being slashed with a razor by a black man who was acting in self-defense.

[923] *New York Journal,* June 29, 1914.

Burns suffered a ten-inch gash to his shoulder, which required a tourniquet to save his life. He was taken unconscious to Bellevue Hospital.

Blacks were assaulted and badly beaten, overpowered by numbers. Four blacks were beaten into insensibility. Eventually, a dozen police appeared and quelled the riot. The police ordered all blacks off the streets. Several lesser riots took place.

In another incident, angered at Johnson's victory, a crowd of 15 men assaulted a black man. A policeman who came to his rescue was himself knocked down by the crowd, after which he used his nightstick freely. Several police soon appeared and the trouble was ended.[924]

Also in New York, a man named Michael Smith was followed down the street by a crowd of hooting children, for he was wearing a woman's dress. He was arrested and taken to the Night Court. He told the judge that he was paying a wager with his wife. If Moran had won, as he had predicted, his wife would have won a new dress. If Johnson won, he had to masquerade in an old dress. Smith was released on probation.

After the bout, Johnson was nursing a swollen right hand, which was almost twice its normal size. He attributed his injured fist to the fact that for the first time he wore four-once gloves instead of five-ounce gloves.

Johnson agreed to fight Sam Langford next, the fight to take place in mid-October for a guaranteed $30,000 plus 50% of the motion picture receipts. The articles were to be signed in London on July 1.

Gunboat Smith, the white heavyweight champion, issued a challenge to Johnson. It was opined that if Smith decisively defeated Carpentier in their scheduled July 16 bout that he would be the logical candidate for the next crack at Johnson, given that he had beaten Langford. "That he is a wonderful puncher there isn't the least doubt."

Unfortunately, the day after Johnson-Moran, on Sunday June 28, 1914 at Sarajevo, Bosnia, a young Bosnian-Serbian student, as part of a nationalist conspiracy, assassinated Archduke Francis-Ferdinand of Austria (who was the heir to the Austro-Hungarian throne and nephew of the Austrian emperor) and his wife, the Duchess of Hohenberg. The anarchist exploded a bomb that failed to kill them, but then he finished them off with a hail of bullets. Eleven others were injured by the bomb. This political assassination would trigger a series of events that led to the outbreak of World War I one month later. The war would serve to put big boxing in Europe on hiatus for quite a while.[925]

For whatever reason, within a couple days of the Moran bout, Jack Adams, one of Johnson's trainers, claimed that the Moran fight was faked for the benefit of the moving pictures and insiders who had bet that the fight would go the limit. He said the fight was framed eight weeks ago. McKetrick and others proposed Moran to Johnson as a man whom he

---

[924] *New York Herald*, June 28, 1914.
[925] *New York Herald*, June 29, 1914.

could handle with the utmost of ease. Moran would be built up in movies shown in America, they would fight, Johnson would carry him, and then they could make more for a rematch. Adams said Mrs. Johnson drew her husband's $30,000 the Saturday before the fight.

> I think the plot has been defeated by Johnson himself, who behaved in the ring with consummate folly, as he could have knocked Moran out in the fifth round.

> He didn't do so, on account of the movies. Later he spared the white hope in the most obvious way for money-making purposes.

> Tom Flanagan, who has been Johnson's adviser through thick and thin, knew the fight would go twenty rounds. Today he declared to me he was thoroughly disgusted and it was the last time he would have anything to do with such a contest.

> Johnson lied about his weight, as he entered the ring at 214 pounds, and not 208 or 206, as he told the newspapers.

> Johnson has now turned against himself the entire sporting public in the country, where he intends to make a permanent home, as the French won't credit him as being a great fighter again.

It was said that 30,000 people paid over $100,000 to watch the dullest and most wearisome bout that ever masqueraded as a championship fight. "Johnson could probably have won at any time, but he carefully avoided striking Moran in a killing place or with killing strength." Many left the building before the fight was over. Johnson allegedly promised the moving picture men to allow the fight to go at least 10 rounds.

Another claim was that Johnson stood to gain by carrying Moran because by failing to knock him out, Jack could earn big paydays against Smith and Carpentier, for the gullible public would think they now had a chance against him.[926]

Bill Brady described Jack Adams as a "well known Octoroon sportsman, who was one of the smoke's principal trainers in his last fight." Brady said Johnson was barred in America because of his "escapades with white women," and now, because of his fake fight with Moran, he had turned against himself the entire sporting public in France.

Brady still respected Johnson's ability. He said that even as badly out of condition as the "Smoke" was against Moran, he still could have secured a draw with Jeffries at Jeff's best. A fight with Corbett at Jim's best would have lasted forever and have been the most boring fight ever seen, for neither fighter would have cared the least about the crowd's booing. Brady said it was not fair to roast Moran, for he failed as others had.

Still, Brady believed there likely would be a new champion the next time Johnson fought a good man, for he was slipping. The concern was that the

---

[926] *New York Journal,* June 29, 1914.

man who defeated Johnson might be another black man, such as Langford, and the championship would not be restored to the white race.

Based on his boxing knowledge, wisdom, and experience, Brady believed that Jess Willard was the one man who had a good chance to whip Johnson. Willard was heavier at 235-240 pounds, much taller at 6'6 ½", had a longer reach, and had the punching power and strength to do it. Further, given his current condition and advanced age, Johnson would not be able to finish off a big man like Willard, and eventually would grow tired and vulnerable to a man of great strength.

Johnson vehemently denied the claims of a fake. "It's an absolute lie. Adams's statement is false from beginning to end."

Dan McKetrick and Wolff, Moran's two managers, also emphatically denied the charge.[927]

Battling Jim Johnson did not think the Moran bout was a fake. He thought the champ's poor showing was due to the fact that Jack was slipping and going back, rather than a deliberate attempt to prolong the bout or allow Moran to make a fair impression. "I was the last one to fight the champ before his battle with Moran, and I know he's about ready for the discard. He almost broke his left arm on me and didn't even jar me with a punch. I missed the chance of a lifetime in that I didn't knock him out."

Moran told Bill Brady that except for Brady, the newsmen had not been fair to him. Brady agreed. "Moran is a great deal bigger man, a better fighter and more deserving of respect and future consideration than anybody seemed to realize to date." Just because he lost to Johnson did not mean he was not a good fighter. He was the first challenger to last 20 rounds with Johnson, a man against whom it never was easy to look good.

Regarding the fight and the decision, Moran said,

> I've got no kick coming. The black completely surprised me. Everybody led me to believe all I had to do was to last ten or fifteen rounds, and I'd be sure to win solely on the bad condition and age of the negro. But Johnson's defense was as good in the nineteenth round as in the first, and when the twentieth round came I was too much all in to be able to notice.

Brady said Moran was as gritty a fighter as any that was in the ring. In the 4th round, Jack landed a straight left to the nose, which from that time on bled freely. Moran went through the remaining 16 rounds swallowing blood. To do that and have enough strength left to put up the fight that he did in the 18th and 19th rounds was worthy of anyone. He felt that Moran should feel no shame about his performance.

Brady opined that Moran was of the wrong build to defeat the champ. "His conqueror must be a giant who can do that hanging on and bearing

[927] *Denver Post, New York American,* June 29, 1914.

down in the clinches as well as the negro." Brady expected Johnson to be defeated before Moran garnered enough momentum for a return match.[928]

Several black-owned newspapers offered their perspectives on the fight. The *New York Age*'s Lester Walton said Johnson had humorously and easily defended the crown. Moran was sufficiently aggressive to make him perspire freely, but Johnson led all the way and was able to pull up. Moran did the "bunny hug" with the champ, and showed some new dance steps.

Responding to those who called the bout second rate, Walton said the fight was analogous to the recent "battle" at Vera Cruz, Mexico, waged between the American fleet and a handful of Mexicans. "The only difference lies in the fact that our American warriors are given medals of honor for marked bravery; while Johnson is disparaged for participating in the burlesque and dubbed by some American writers as a has-been." Sportswriters now were nearly unanimous in saying that Moran was the wrong man to go up against Johnson. "And yet many of them before the contest harbored a feeling that Moran was destined to come out victor." Johnson was the first pugilist of modern times to defend his title successfully at the age of 35 and over, and that deserved recognition.

Many were proclaiming loudly that Johnson was all-in because he did not knock out Moran. They said he no longer was the Johnson of old. "But did the champion really and truly want to knock out his opponent?"

Walton suspected that Johnson carried Moran. He noted William Rocap's statements that the bout was spoiled in the last 2 rounds because Johnson was not trying and "affected" being tired. On the other hand, William Brady said Moran's own fatigue saved Johnson from being knocked out. Hence, the two declarations varied. Walton opined, "Mr. Brady uncorked a sample of race prejudice which afflicts so many of our white Americans…and which renders one totally unable to size up a condition with an open mind and with any degree of fairness."

Walton noted several statements that correspondents sent to New York papers. For example, the *New York Sun* said, "It was not a fight. It was not even a near fight. Moran showed absolutely nothing. Johnson was never extended." The *New York Times* wrote, "In the final round Johnson stood still in the center of the ring. Moran circled about Johnson and called out, 'Come on, hit me!' Then the referee forced him to fight, and amid screams from the crowd Johnson landed a left uppercut and the fight was finished as Moran went reeling against the ropes."

Walton did not believe the champion was the high liver that the hostile press represented him to be. Jack was a cunning individual.

Walton opined that white hopes like Gunboat Smith and Jess Willard should first be made to obtain reputations. Moran should have been matched to meet Langford, McVea, or Jeannette to prove himself before getting a title shot. "It is not Johnson, but fight promoters, who hurt the

[928] *Denver Post*, June 30, 1914.

game." They promoted Johnson-Moran. Now Moran could make money in vaudeville, being touted as the man who went the distance with Johnson, and be hailed as a man of wonderful endurance.[929]

Writing for the *Chicago Defender*, Johnson's nephew Gus Rhodes, who had been in the champion's corner, said Johnson's victory set at rest any doubt as to his ability. His speed and power astonished fight followers. The bout's outcome never was in doubt, for Johnson was in a class of his own. The boasted white hope was punished at will. Anglo-Saxon supremacy received another crushing blow, as the crafty champion played with him just as cat does with a mouse. Both men were in fine condition. Owing to the ban on any fight films which traveled in interstate commerce, the motion pictures would not be shown in the United States.

According to Rhodes, it was the finest fistic encounter ever witnessed, with the greatest audience that ever attended a fight. Many French notables, aristocrats, and wealthy Americans who at home would be indignant if the champion's name was mentioned in their presence, all attended the fight.

Wearing the colors of France, Johnson defended the title in a manner that surprised even his greatest admirers. Despite the pre-fight belief that he had lost his speed; the lightning way he uppercut, jabbed the mouth and nose, countered and protected himself, showed the oldest follower of the game that he still was his old self.

From the beginning of the fight, Johnson saw that Moran was not his equal. He was the master of all champions, the pugilistic marvel of boxing. Anglo-Saxon supremacy was again trampled in the dust. There never was a second in which a Moran victory could have been said to be within the realm of possibility. Moran was outclassed as a boxer. Johnson was the master of boxing and his cleverness could not be equaled. Johnson's superb boxing was the same which characterized him in all of his encounters.

The *Defender's* Tony Langston lamented the fight stories published in some of the daily newspapers, which he called nauseating and the result of personal prejudice. William Rocap declared that Moran was entitled to 8 of the 20 rounds fought and that Johnson was hissed and hooted for holding and hitting in the clinches, yet in the same issue of the same newspaper was the description of the 20 rounds in detail, which accorded Jack all 20 rounds, with the exception of one which was called even, although the champ landed three to one during the session mentioned. "Can you beat it?" This writer said that if Moran was a sample of the best of the white hopes, then they were a "sorry bunch indeed."

Johnson fought a careful fight, and the reason Moran was there at the end was not only because Frank was trained to the minute, but because the champ was too wise to risk any chances of breaking his hands. Some claimed that Johnson allowed Moran to stay for the benefit of the pictures, in which he had a 50% interest.

---

[929] *New York Age*, July 2, 1914.

Now, if that were true, then why didn't the writer, knowing of it, expose the whole thing before the fight? He just naturally prevaricated, and his statement is just another sample of the rotten prejudice taken to Europe by a certain class of white people…who are using every means to instill race hatred among the nations who have always been the race's friends.

Langston said the best fighters in the world were Afro-Americans – Johnson, Langford, and Jeannette. "Such men as Ryan, Sullivan, Corbett, Fitzsimmons, Sharkey, or Jeffries in their best days would have been as putty in the hands of the champion."

The *Defender's* Frank Young reported that Johnson retained the title with ease, battering the white man and toying with him. It wasn't even a good fight, but more like a training bout for Johnson. Local sporting writers were peeved. Brady was another Corbett with his bitterness towards Johnson. Young said "the poor whites will never get over it." Johnson retained his title regardless of all the predictions that he was too old, out of form, had dissipated, had failed to train, and was overweight, as the authoritative Brady of the Hearst papers had told all of his readers. Instead, the greatest champ of them all toyed with Moran and smiled his golden smile. The only encouragement Moran received was from the Americans present.

Young said Brady had claimed that it would be the happiest day of his life, for Moran was going to win the crown. It must have been a bitter pill for him to swallow, and instead of giving Johnson credit, he and others slurred the fight.

From the 10th round on it plainly was Johnson's fight, for the white man was hanging on continually. Overall it was a clean fight, outside of Jack once hitting on the break.

Moran's punches failed to jar the champ, and in the 15th round, Johnson stood still in the middle of the ring, clapped his hands and grinned. He called to Moran to come on and wade in.

Some writers claimed that the victory was a signal for a celebration on State street (meaning the black neighborhood) and that the police were called in to quell the disturbance. "Now there was nothing of the sort."

The *Defender* lamented that for many years, every time three or four Afro-American boys and an equal number of white boys got into a row, the daily press termed the incident a race war. Not all friction between the races was a race war.

Some accused Johnson of being a disgrace to the race. "Johnson, it is true, may have had troubles and the ever-ready yellow journals that seek to create ill feeling between the two races took this as a matter to inflame the minds of its weak readers." These writers never overlooked any opportunity to slam one in on the dark race, and they went at it with vim.

Even racists like John L. Sullivan recognized Johnson's ability. "John L. Sullivan says that Johnson could lick any of the old fighters regardless of what they say themselves. He certainly ought to know."[930]

The *Freeman* wrote that Moran fought bravely, but had no show. The final rounds were tame. Billy Lewis said the bout was extremely important for the fight game, notwithstanding the effort by some to belittle it. It was treated like a national pageant in France, for that country was keyed up to the highest pitch.

Lewis sometimes thought that negroes pushed the race question too much. "Perhaps it is not wise to reprint all one sees. But why not since the white patrons of those publications who print daring things see them." His point was that blacks needed to counter what they saw as the biased white perspective.

Lewis noted that Johnson was a negro with a white wife, which basically was why he could not return to the U.S. Yet, he was in mighty high society on fight night, and gave an excellent account of himself.

It was Moran's gameness and wonderful stamina that enabled him to last the limit before the champion's terrible blows. Johnson was master of the fight from start to finish, and gave Moran a terrible beating. Although Frank was the gamest man he ever met, toward the end, the crowd jeered a good deal at some of the bleeding Moran's tactics, for he hung on frequently to save himself.

Lewis later said the Moran fight helped Johnson greatly in the world's estimation of him. He had proven so infinitely superior to his title challengers that even the most stubborn-hearted finally had given way to admiration. "And it would have been a most perverse generation had it not made an unconditional surrender to Mr. Johnson's greatness."

Johnson planned to tour Europe and visit places like London and Moscow.[931]

The *Freeman* published excerpts from several French publications in Paris regarding the Moran fight. The Paris edition of the *New York Herald* said, "It was an easy win for Johnson, the difference in the class of the two men being only too evident from the very beginning of the match." It went on to say the match was most disappointing.

> Moran, most of the time, was covering his face and trying to ward off the black's deadly uppercuts. Occasionally he attempted to land with a swing with his right.

> Johnson's stomach, indeed, seemed to be made of something harder than mere muscle. Several times when Moran, with a show of energy, tried punching his opponent's abdomen and ribs, the black raised his arms and let him do so without retaliating, turning his head toward

---

[930] *Chicago Defender*, July 4, 1914, August 15, 1914.
[931] *Freeman*, July 4, 11, 1914.

the public with a broad grin showing his white teeth, and seemed to say 'He can do that as long as he likes.'

To most of the spectators it seemed, after the first three rounds, that Johnson could have knocked out his opponent at any moment. Why he did not do so must be a matter of speculation. Certainly, Moran gave him no trouble.

All through the match Johnson never varied his tactics. Standing in the middle of the ring he waited for his opponent to come to him. When Moran got tired of walking round and round, he closed in and it was only then that the black did his fighting, which always turned to the other man's disadvantage.

The *Petit Parisien* was quoted as saying, "Must one conclude from this match that Jack Johnson no longer smites very hard…or else the white hope can take more punishment than any fighter of modern times?"

The *Matin* said, "The contest ended in the victory on points of Jack Johnson after a long-drawn out comedy, or rather, a pitiful exhibition by the champion of the world. For Johnson the match was merely the pretext for an excellent joke."

The *Gil Blas* said, "In beating Frank Moran on points after twenty somewhat monotonous rounds Johnson has certainly not in any way increased our admiration of him."

The *Journal* said, "But his tactical defence was superior almost from the outset to the attack of his challenger, and it seemed for a moment as if the fight would not last more than ten rounds. This was an error. Johnson never seemed sufficiently sure of himself to take the lead, and the battle lasted to the limit."[932]

The *Freeman* later said that there was not a minute of the fight in which Johnson was not the obvious master of the white man. He tried hard to do away with Moran, but Frank was in as perfect condition as a man could be. He could not beat Johnson because he could not hit him. Even the blows that did land, Johnson was going away from them, so they looked pleasant, but did no harm.[933]

On July 1, 1914 in New York, Joe Jeannette outpointed Battling Jim Johnson in a 10-round no-decision bout. Johnson was 33 pounds heavier, but Joe was never in danger. It was Jeannette's fourth victory over the sturdy Johnson.[934]

The *Defender* said the black race did not forget that Sam Langford viewed the Jeffries fight from Jeff's corner. It was rumored that if he defeated Johnson that Langford would then allow a white man to defeat him for the championship. This persistent rumor made Langford even less popular with

[932] *Freeman*, August 8, 1914.
[933] *Freeman*, August 29, 1914.
[934] *Freeman*, July 11, 1914.

some blacks, who saw him as a traitor. Not many believed that Langford could whip Jack, but they had "no particular love for him anyhow."

Johnson had gone to Russia. On July 9, he cabled the *Defender* from Moscow, saying that he planned to spend 10 days there. He then planned to visit Austria. He would fight Langford in October and then retire.[935]

On July 15, 1914 in New York, Joe Jeannette once again boxed Battling Jim Johnson to a 10-round no-decision. This one had had a split of opinion regarding who deserved to win or whether it was a draw.

On July 16, 1914 in London, Georges Carpentier won the white heavyweight championship when Gunboat Smith was disqualified in the 6th round for hitting Georges while he was on the canvas. In the 4th round, Carpentier landed a right on the kidneys that dropped Smith. In the 6th round, Carpentier dropped to his knees, either the result of a right to the jaw or from slipping down when off balance after throwing a blow. There was a mix of opinion. Smith then clearly hit him on the neck while he was down. Referee Eugene Corri immediately stopped the fight and disqualified Smith. Carpentier was on his feet almost at once. A storm of boos and hisses followed. Regardless, everyone agreed that Smith had hit him while he was down.[936]

The *Defender* said America had lost its latest white hope. It was a dying American newspaper effort to find a white man able to wrest the title from Johnson. Carpentier admitted that he was no match for Johnson. A Langford fight claimed attention, but Johnson's friends felt no concern over the outcome of that fight. Tom Flanagan said,

> Take it from me, Johnson can whip any man in the world today, black or white. Anyone sufficiently interested to learn can find out that Johnson is in the best condition and takes better care of himself than any other heavyweight does. Moran, a young husky giant was cut to pieces by Johnson, who hammered him at will, and it will be remembered that the fight lasted twenty rounds.[937]

On July 28, 1914, the Austrian-Hungarian government, backed by Germany, declared war on Serbia. Russia backed Serbia, and Germany declared war on Russia and its ally, France. Great Britain declared war on Germany when German troops invaded Belgium and Luxembourg, violating their official neutrality. Japan and Italy eventually also declared war on Germany. The Ottoman Empire and Bulgaria joined Germany and Austria-Hungary. The U.S. would not declare war on Germany until nearly three years later, on April 6, 1917. This brutal world war, in which over 9 million combatants would be killed, lasted more than four years, not ending until November 11, 1918. Naturally, a war which involved most all of Europe was going to affect Jack Johnson's boxing career.

---

[935] *Chicago Defender*, July 11, 1914.
[936] *Freeman*, July 25, 1914.
[937] *Chicago Defender*, July 25, 1914.

It was rumored that Johnson had offered to fight for France in the war. It was said that he would be made a colonel of a regiment and given a $500 pension.[938]

The *Freeman's* Billy Lewis reported that on July 31 in Chicago, the local federal court ruled that in light of the fact that the U.S. Circuit Court of Appeals had ordered that he be given a new trial on certain counts of the indictment and be re-sentenced on the counts for which he was found guilty, Johnson had to appear by the following Friday or his bond would be ordered forfeited.[939]

However, Federal Judge Geiger subsequently granted Johnson's attorney's request for a 20-day continuance on account of the war, and did not forfeit his bond. Johnson's attorney argued that the state of war which existed throughout Europe prevented Johnson from appearing.[940]

The *Freeman's* Billy Lewis said Jack Johnson was the most widely discussed man who had ever lived, outside of bible characters. Efforts to belittle his significance had failed. Of boxers, John L. Sullivan's name had lingered the longest, Fitz was loved, Corbett admired, Jeff lamented, and Burns regretted, but Sullivan was the most popularly remembered, perhaps because he was so transcendently superior up until the time he met his Waterloo. However, no one had received as much attention as Johnson.

On August 5, 1914 in New York, Joe Jeannette won another 10-round no-decision bout against Battling Jim Johnson.

One week later, on August 12, 1914 in New York, Sam Langford and Battling Jim Johnson boxed laboriously and perspiringly through 10 rounds of uninteresting milling, with Langford having the better of it. "It was a great exhibition for fat men." They rested upon each other at every opportunity. Langford weighed 205 pounds and Jim Johnson 224 pounds. Sam only showed flashes of the ability that once made him the most dangerous man in the ring.[941]

Some were saying that Johnson was the real promoter of the Moran fight, or a co-promoter. Given that he had a lot of outstanding debts, after the fight, pursuant to a court order, the French authorities seized the gate receipts, pending a decision on the debts owed.[942]

Startling revelations were made about the Johnson-Moran bout. A Paris newspaper, *L'Echo Des Sports*, printed a facsimile of a contract between Johnson and Moran in which Johnson offered to pay Moran more money if he agreed to lose inside of 8 rounds. Allegedly it read:

June 27, 1914

---

[938] *Chicago Defender*, August 8, 1914.
[939] *Freeman*, August 8, 1914.
[940] *Chicago Defender*, August 15, 1914.
[941] *Freeman*, August 29, 1914.
[942] *El Paso Herald*, August 3, 1914. Some later claimed that Johnson was not paid.

I hereby agree to divide my receipts with Frank Moran on June 27 on a basis of 40 per cent to Moran and 60 per cent to me provided that Frank Moran loses inside of eight rounds – Jack Johnson.

Johnson signed the typed document, and then wrote, "After fight must return this receipt."

Apparently, Moran double-crossed Johnson, during the fight deciding not to lie down. Some said that as a result of the revelations, Johnson would never again be allowed to box in France.[943]

Allegedly, Dan McKetrick confirmed that Moran had agreed to lie down in the 8th round.

Johnson declared that the fix claims were not true, but simultaneously alleged that he had agreed to allow Moran to last the limit of 20 rounds, and said that he did so in order to get Moran to take the bout. He said that he had lived up to his end of the bargain.

Folks wondered whether Johnson indeed had held back against Moran, or if he just made the claims to sting Moran and his backers. Many believed Johnson, because heavy money had been wagered on Moran to stay the limit. Once again, the press and public were not sure exactly what to make of or believe about Jack Johnson.[944]

---

[943] *Omaha Daily Bee*, August 9, 1914; *Daily Capital Journal*, August 11, 1914.
[944] *Daily Missoulian*, August 7, 1914.

CHAPTER 20

Jess Willard

In late 1914, Kansas cowboy Jess Willard was being called the best or most logical white hope to dislodge Johnson from his title. Those in the know felt that Johnson was just about ready to be beaten. He no longer was the invincible man who beat Jeffries. "In fact, it is the general belief that the first strong young aspirant with a hard punch and a little bit of cleverness to come along will upset him."

Sam Langford was said to be near the end and ripe for the plucking. Plus, Sam was the wrong color. Langford had been chasing Johnson for years. "Johnson was a wise bird and sidestepped so prettily that a lot of fans did not believe that Jack was evading the Tar Baby." However, recently, London promoters had agreed to Johnson's demand of $30,000, and Johnson had agreed verbally to meet Langford.

Willard was the only other battler conceded to have a good chance. Against Jess, it would not be a case of Jack towering over his foe. On the contrary, Jess would tower over him. Jess had greater height, reach, and weight. He was known for being game and durable, and could hit hard. He would be the toughest proposition Johnson had run up against in a long time, particularly since the champ was nearing the end of his rope. After all, Johnson already was past the age in which all other champions had lost their crowns. "Willard is just the type that should beat him. In fact he has a better chance by long odds than Gunboat Smith, who by the way happens to hold a twenty-round decision over the Kansas cowboy. Johnson likes to fight little men of the Smith type – not big ones like Willard." Jack Curley said he would back Willard against Johnson.[945]

Willard held victories over Arthur Pelkey, Sailor White, Soldier Kearns, Carl Morris, and George Rodel, and had a draw with Luther McCarty. Although Gunboat Smith held a decision victory over him, most felt that Willard matched up better with Johnson owing to his size, whereas the 180-pound Smith would be smaller than Johnson, who had proven that he could handle smaller men.

Johnson was doing a vaudeville stunt at a number of small halls on the outskirts of London, drawing big houses.

To some degree, the world war had broken up the fight game in Europe. Top black fighters who had been hoping to make good money fighting each other in Europe were no longer able to make fights; Johnson included.

Although the Langford fight had been agreed upon, no one knew when or where the bout would take place beyond the fact that it was supposed to

---

[945] *Freeman*, September 5, 1914.

take place in London. It seemed that Johnson was looking for one last big purse, and apparently he believed that Langford could supply it.

Yet, Langford allegedly also was scheduled to box Sam McVey 20 rounds at the Olympia in London in September, for a larger purse than what he was going to receive for fighting Johnson. Ultimately, neither fight would take place in London.[946]

The *Freeman's* Billy Lewis said that when the world was not talking war, it was talking about Jack Johnson. Lewis noted the bias against Johnson, observing how one writer introduced Jack this way:

> Dame Fortune is not only a fickle and flirtatious old girl, but she ain't at all particular on whom she smiles. Witness the case of her outrageous smirking at Jack Johnson, a vain, ignorant immoral negro, who was, 12 years ago, a levee roustabout at Galveston. ...

> It's small wonder that men seek fortune in the prize ring today, despite all the drawbacks connected with the game. One glance at the case of John Arthur Johnson and they sidestep the cotton bales and the harvest fields and run for the training camp.

Lewis responded that it was wicked and unjust to talk that way about a man because he happens to be a Negro. Thousands of whites came up from mean conditions to where they commanded thousands of dollars, yet one Negro was singled out, the only one whose financial success had been phenomenal. "This writer is envious of the 'nigger.' He doubtless is one of those white men who have decided that the world belongs to them and all that pertains thereto."

Regardless, Lewis also said that Johnson had obtained much consideration recently, owing to his long championship reign even at an advanced age. More whites were throwing down their prejudices and honestly giving him credit. He had not been allowed to fight for the title until he was 30 years old, already an advanced age for a fighter, and yet he still had retained the title for many years.

Regarding Johnson's condition at ringside for the Moran fight; one writer opined that he actually weighed more than 230 pounds. But still he was the master of his art. He picked off Moran's punches when Frank started them. He knew that Moran could not hurt him except by accident.

When Johnson was in Moscow filling a theatrical engagement, there was fear of a German bombardment. After he returned home to France, he reportedly was made a colonel in the French army. "The report has not been verified, and probably will not."

One white writer said that if Johnson and Willard were matched, once again the rumors of fake would go the rounds.

---

[946] *Freeman*, September 12, 1914. Langford agreed to $1,550 and 30% of the gate to fight Johnson, but he was fighting for a $10,000 purse against McVey.

Johnson has absolutely killed all possibility of believing his bouts now are on the level. His written agreement in the Moran affair, by which Moran was to receive a certain increased share of the receipts if he didn't go eight rounds, published in English and French papers, settled that. Johnson has passed his prime as a fighter. Dissipation and easy living have left him a far less effective fighting machine. His endurance has gone, and after boxing a few rounds he loses his strength and hitting power. ...

Personally I'd like to see Willard fight Johnson. He would probably beat the dusky champ. Willard is naturally a defensive fighter like Johnson, and he wouldn't run into anything through over eagerness. When hurt he hits a terrific punch or two before his natural caution returns. He uses a fast and hard left jab, and he has great advantages in height, reach, weight, and strength. Five years ago Willard would have had no chance with Johnson; today it's a different matter, as Johnson is all in.

But it isn't likely Johnson and Willard ever will fight. There'll be no boxing in Europe or England for some time. Even if there were Johnson would be barred because of the Moran agreement in his handwriting, so widely published. He can't fight any one in Australia, as he has been absolutely barred in that country. And he can't come back here and wouldn't be allowed to fight if he did come.

Hence, making a fight for Johnson would be difficult, for he could not box in the U.S. or Australia, big-time boxing was on a hiatus in Europe owing to the war, and even if it wasn't, many were soured by the Moran fight either because of its dullness or because they thought it was faked to some degree. Billy Lewis said, "Poor old Jack. And his only sin is being a successful Negro pugilist."

A Johnson-Carpentier fight could not take place even if Georges wanted it, because he had joined the French army for a four-year term of service. His pay was to be $20.40 per year, or 5.7 cents a day. It would be five years before Carpentier fought again.[947]

On September 15, 1914 in Boston, Sam Langford and Battling Jim Johnson fought to a 12-round draw.

Jack Johnson disputed the stories that he had applied for French naturalization. He visited the American embassy on September 18 to make it known that he was a United States citizen. He showed a passport obtained from the American ambassador in Paris six months earlier. A few weeks ago, he had been in Russia, then Berlin and Paris, after which he came to London. He was going back to Russia to fill more theatrical engagements. The only other black in Jack's party was his sparring partner.

---

[947] *Freeman*, September 19, 1914.

In London, because allegedly he used obscene language to a policeman after refusing to move his *legally* parked automobile, Johnson was called upon to appear before the magistrate. When he failed to appear for his hearing, a bench warrant was issued. However, Johnson returned from Liverpool to face his accuser.

The trouble arose when Jack's auto, parked outside a Leicester square barber shop where Johnson was being shaved, caused a crowd to collect, interfering with traffic. Instead of dispersing the people who were blocking the street, the policeman directed Johnson, who was parked legally, to move his car along, which he refused to do until his shave was finished, accompanying the refusal with a flow of derogatory words for the "ancestors of bobby." Jack told the judge that he could not keep people from staring at him. He was fined $10 for obstructing the street.

The *Freeman* said that newspapers continually printed falsehoods about Johnson, on the theory that Jack Johnson fiction was as good as any. All the talk about him becoming a French citizen or joining the French army was a matter of invention.

On October 1, 1914 in New York, Sam Langford and Joe Jeannette fought a close 10-round no-decision bout that had a split of opinion regarding who won. Many said it was a draw.

On October 5, 1914, Federal Judge George Carpenter declared Johnson's $30,000 bond forfeited when he failed to show up to stand re-trial on his white slave charges. The district attorney began a suit against the estate of Matthew Baldwin, the deceased professional bondsman, and Tiny Johnson, Jack's mother.[948]

During October, it was reported that Johnson might meet Jess Willard, the last of the old guard of white hopes. Many thought Johnson might lose as a result of father time. Johnson also was willing to fight Gunboat Smith.

Johnson told promoter Jim Coffroth that he would meet *any* man that Coffroth selected, as long as the financial terms were right. There was discussion of a potential bout in Mexico, perhaps in Tijuana.

Tom Jones, Willard's manager, said a Willard-Johnson match likely would be staged on March 7, 1915 in Juarez, Mexico. Authorities there had had authorized the bout. Cuba also wanted the fight, and officials there said that should any troubles arise in Mexico, the bout could be shifted to their island.[949]

On October 20, 1914 in Boston, Sam Langford knocked out Gunboat Smith in the 3rd round, avenging his prior 1913 decision loss to Smith. This eliminated Smith from consideration as the next Johnson challenger. Although many wanted to see Langford fight Johnson, "What the public wants now is a man to whip Johnson, and above all a white man."

---

[948] *Freeman*, October 3, 1914; *Chicago Day Book*, October 5, 14, 1914.
[949] *Freeman*, October 17, 24, 1914.

On October 26, 1914 in Joplin, Missouri, a black fighter named Jeff Clark won a 10-round decision verdict over Sam Langford.

One writer had said that Willard should fight Langford in order to convince the public that he could cope with Johnson. However, that was before Langford was beaten by Jeff Clark, and many were high on Willard regardless. "Jess is prominent among the heavyweights largely because of his size. He's a remarkably athletic giant. He is a fairly clever boxer. He is a heavy hitter. He is faster than any other big man we've seen during the past few years. ... When aroused he shows something."[950]

On November 10, 1914 in Boston, Joe Jeannette and Battling Jim Johnson fought to a 12-round draw.

On November 16, 1914, promoter Jack Curley (who had been involved with the Johnson-Flynn II promotion), who had traveled to London, secured Johnson's agreement to fight Jess Willard in March in a fight anywhere from 20 to 45 rounds, the bout's length to be at Curley's discretion. The location had not yet been set. The agreement further said the bout would be with 5-ounce gloves, and the parties were allowed to wear soft bandages and a cup to protect themselves from fouls. $30,000 was to be paid to Johnson before he entered the ring, plus $1,000 in expense money, plus 50% of the net motion picture proceeds. Curley would select the bout's location no later than February 1, 1915, for a contest to be held between March 15 and 30, 1915. Both agreed to train publicly and to submit to a medical examination. Each would deposit a $5,000 forfeit. Willard's end was not disclosed in the contract. Both agreed not to engage in any other boxing contest prior to the fight without Curley's written consent.

Johnson-Willard would be staged by a syndicate of New York sporting men who had agreed to give Johnson his demanded guarantee. The principal members of the syndicate were Harry Frazee, a theatrical promoter, James Butler, owner of both the Empire City race track of Yonkers, N.Y. and the Laurel, M.D. race track, Jack Curley, former manager of Russian wrestler George Hackenschmidt, and Harry Pollok, manager of Freddie Welsh, the world lightweight champ.[951]

The *Chicago Day Book* said there were rumors that if he fought in Mexico, the U.S. government might kidnap Johnson and bring him back to answer for his white slave violations. However, many whites wanted Johnson to remain at large. "This country is well rid of the black man. As long as a federal court conviction is held over him he will keep out of the United States, and that is all we want. If he returned, took his sentence and served it he would be free at its expiration to come and go as he pleased."

Regarding the upcoming Willard fight, the *Day Book* opined that Johnson was due to lose.

---

[950] *Freeman*, November 7, 1914. The *Freeman* reported that Clark outpointed Langford and was given the decision.
[951] *Freeman*, November 14, 1914; *Harrisburg Telegraph*, December 8, 1914.

Johnson is in no shape to fight. Willard is not of championship caliber, but he should be able to whip the dissipation-trained colored man. Johnson barely saved his title against Frank Moran, and the succeeding months have not improved him any.

Knowing that he is through, Johnson wants to make a final stake. He is not to be blamed. Single out the men who promote such fiascos to get the public money and the censure will be placed where it belongs.[952]

The *Rock Island Argus* also noted that the U.S. government was moving to try to capture Johnson, talking with the governments of Mexico and Cuba about his kidnapping, for formal extradition was impossible. One government official said he understood that Johnson was not going to fight in Juarez, Mexico as some suspected, but that he was heading to Cuba. "Department of justice officials have tried to tempt him back to this country, but the negro declined to bite." Not mentioned was what offer was made in order to tempt him back.[953]

Some said that Johnson stood to make more money if he lost to Willard. If he won, the films would not be worth much, but if he lost, everyone would want to pay to see the fight. In that case, the films would be worth over a million dollars, more than Johnson had made in his entire career combined. Prior to winning the championship, Johnson led a "hand-to-mouth existence, always in debt to his various managers, who succeeded each other in rapid succession." Since then, it was estimated that his fights and exhibitions had generated about $300,000 for him.

Early in his championship career, Johnson was content to fight for $5,000, from Burns through Kaufman. He made $12,000 for Ketchel. But after his huge purse against Jeffries, making $120,000 in all, he demanded a minimum of $30,000 to fight. Some said he actually made only $10,000 against Flynn, for few attended. He earned about $5,000 for an exhibition bout against Jim Johnson, his share of the receipts. Apparently, he had not collected his $35,000 from the Moran fight, for it was tied up in the French courts.[954]

On November 26, 1914 at Vernon, California, despite being dropped four times in the first 2 rounds, Sam Langford came back to score a KO14 over emerging 25-year-old black heavyweight Harry Wills.

On December 10, 1914 in New York, Sam McVey won a 10-round newspaper decision over Battling Jim Johnson. Ten days later, on December 20, 1914 in New Orleans, McVey won a 20-round decision over Harry Wills.

The *Ogden Standard* said the Willard contest was exciting fight fans. The four general predictions were either 1. Johnson would win in a real fight, 2.

[952] *Chicago Day Book*, November 24, 1914.
[953] *Rock Island Argus*, November 24, 1914.
[954] *Ogden Standard*, November 28, 1914.

Willard would whip Johnson in a real battle, 3. It would be a tame joke almost devoid of real result, as with the Moran fight, or 4. It would be a fake. Many of the younger generation felt that Willard was made to beat Johnson, given all of his physical advantages, as well as youth and stamina, plus they felt that his style was perfect to give an aging and less than best-conditioned Johnson trouble in a long fight. Willard fought cautiously and deliberately, and with his height and reach, could fight Johnson at long range, which would force Jack to attack more than he usually liked to do. In a long fight, at his age, Jack would wear down having to fight more aggressively. However, there were those who believed that if Willard was cautious, Johnson would remain cautious as well, and it would create a tame, slow fight that would not tire out Johnson.[955]

On December 19, 1914, California's new law went into effect, limiting all fights to 4 rounds. This law would last a decade.

Tom Flanagan said, "Jim Corbett once told me, 'Jack Johnson is the cleverest man that ever stepped into a ring.' … Corbett, Jackson, Mace, as the shiftiest men the ring ever knew, must stand down before Johnson, according to Corbett's estimate." Although Johnson was wonderfully clever, Flanagan also thought Willard might have a good chance to beat him in a long fight, for age was a more formidable rival than man.

> In all his fights it wouldn't take much trouble to count all the blows that have landed on him. Watching very closely in the Moran fight in Paris, I saw only one decent punch landed on him, except what he took for show sake.

> They don't get to him. He is fast on his feet and his style of fighting demands that his opponents carry the battle to him. Once they do they either leave themselves open or he makes an opening for himself. … Jack Johnson stands still enough until you think he has been caught, and then like lightning he either sidesteps to whip across a punishing uppercut or a terrific jolt, or smothers all leads with his powerful arms. …

> Johnson is no leader. … [H]e waits for the other fellow to walk into these ox-felling punches, and they all wade right into them. …He has…great speed and shiftiness…cleverness and ring generalship. …

> That is what strikes close followers of Johnson as making a fight with Jess Willard a problem. The big white giant is also a stand-offish battler, from all accounts. He is said to be shifty, too, and prefers to have his opponent bring the fight to him. And he can hit when they do, it is claimed.

> Perhaps Willard could force Johnson to the aggressive and solve the difficulty. … Jack Johnson's next fight will see him 37 years of age.

---

[955] *Ogden Standard*, December 12, 1914.

While no prizefighter in the history of the ring has ever taken as good care of himself as Jack Johnson, despite old stories to the contrary, all the same age is age, and there is no elixir for it.

At 37, Jack Johnson nor no other man can be expected to fight top speed for much over twenty rounds. Decidedly few of them could ever hope to go that distance at even a fair clip. ... If Willard or any other good big man with a punch can hold out for twenty rounds he has a great chance to win a long fight against Johnson.[956]

Jack Curley said Willard would defeat Johnson, especially if it was a long fight. Most of those who had fought Willard did not believe Johnson could last over 20 rounds with him. Jess had too many physical advantages - weight, height, reach, hitting power, and age. Willard would be 27 (listed birthdate of December 29, 1887) (although secondary sources say he actually was 33, born in 1881), whereas Johnson was approaching 37. Johnson had a lengthy 20-year career (that began in the mid-1890s), though he had been inactive and living leisurely in recent years, whereas Willard was fresh and frisky, having started his pro boxing career in early 1911, yet was sharp and active – with 29 fights under his belt in those four years. Jess had shown improvement in recent years, and led an exemplary life.[957]

During December 1914, Johnson left Great Britain and headed to Buenos Aires, Argentina to give some exhibitions there. Apparently, according to secondary sources, in one of his Buenos Aires exhibitions in either December 1914 or January 1915, Johnson knocked out sparring partner Jack Murray in the 3rd round, as well as some Argentinians.

In January 1915, Johnson said he enjoyed living in Buenos Aires. As soon as he completed his short exhibition tour, he would start formal training for the Willard fight.

Former Kansas cowpuncher Jess Willard revealed his racial motivations, saying that the reason he wanted to fight Johnson was to restore the championship back to the white race. "I believe a white heavyweight champion would do more to boost the boxing game than a negro. I believe I will bring the title back to the white race. ... If I never secured a penny for performing the feat, I would feel amply repaid for bringing the title back to the white race." Jack Curley said Willard would make at least $15,000.[958]

Although initially it was believed that the fight would be held in Juarez, Mexico on March 6, impediments arose. Mexico was a land of rebellion and revolution. General Francisco "Pancho" Villa was in favor of the fight. However, General Venustiano Carranza of the rival faction said he would prevent Johnson's entry into the country. He was in control of the ports, so it seemed it would be difficult for Johnson to enter Mexico.[959]

---

[956] *Chicago Defender*, December 26, 1914.
[957] *El Paso Herald*, December 29, 1914.
[958] *El Paso Herald*, January 1, 6, 9, 1915.
[959] *Day Book*, January 14, 1915.

On January 26, 1915, the 246-pound Willard started training at the Knaublack Ranch in El Paso, Texas, doing about 5 miles of roadwork. William Rocap said Willard's reach was more than 83.5 inches, which exceeded the champ's 78.5-inch reach by 5 inches. Willard was 6'6 ½" to Johnson's 6'1 ½".

Willard said he was confident that he could beat the "shine," for Johnson was not a knockout artist. He was certain that he could withstand any blow Johnson could throw, whereas he felt that he had sufficient power to take out the champ.

In late January and early February, Willard started sparring with Walter Monahan (white), a previous Johnson sparring partner, and Joe or Jack Thomas (black). He also worked with a man named Hemple or Hempel.[960]

Having left Buenos Aires on January 21, on February 8, Johnson arrived in Barbados, weighing 245 pounds. Shortly thereafter, he sailed for Cuba.[961]

Jack Curley said he picked Willard as Johnson's opponent because several highly respected experts such as Bill Brady and George Considine said Jess had the best chance of anyone to dethrone Johnson. He did not match Willard with Langford for fear that if Willard defeated him, Johnson's price would have gone up even further, up to a prohibitive figure.

When asked why Americans should support a Johnson fight at all, given that he was a fugitive from justice and charged with being a faker, Curley said he saw the Moran fight and it looked square to him. Furthermore,

It took 25 United States secret service men from the department of justice in Chicago, under the leadership of the chief investigator, five weeks to discover that Johnson, during three years of constant traveling previously, had committed the terrible crime of transporting a woman companion from Pittsburg to Chicago, for which he received one year under the Mann act.

Curley noted that folks were willing to pay Johnson $200,000 to lie down to Jeffries, but he refused and won the fight. He said both Johnson and Willard had too much pride to take a dive.[962]

On February 8, 1915, D. W. Griffith's film, *The Birth of a Nation*, was released. Based on Thomas Dixon, Jr.'s 1905 bestseller, *The Clansman*, it portrayed the

D·W·GRIFFITH'S MIGHTY SPECTACLE
THE BIRTH OF A NATION
FOUNDED ON THOMAS DIXON'S THE CLANSMAN

---

[960] *El Paso Herald*, January 23, 25, February 2, 1915.
[961] *Harrisburg Telegraph*, February 5, 1915; *Day Book*, February 8, 1915; *Star-Independent*, March 29, 1915.
[962] *El Paso Herald*, February 9, 1915. Ticket prices would sell from $5 up to $25.

Ku Klux Klan as heroes, and freed blacks as ignorant, rapists, sexually aggressive towards white women, unscrupulous politicians, and hapless idiots. It showed miscegenation as an evil that had to be prevented or avenged. The NAACP's attempts to ban the film only served to advertise it. The film was extremely popular and a huge financial success, generating millions of dollars. Democrat U.S. President Woodrow Wilson even had the film screened at the White House.

Jim Corbett said Jess Willard's chances would improve with every round, for as the fight progressed, Johnson would be growing more fatigued. Corbett believed that Willard was better than Moran, and noted that even Moran had lasted 20 rounds with the champ. Jim did not think a 37-year-old could last 45 rounds, especially not one who had been living easy during the past several years.

Willard trainer/sparring partner Tex O'Rourke said Jess was in great shape, and if Johnson did not take him seriously and failed to prepare properly, he would not be able to stand the pace for 45 rounds. For 6 - 7 miles, Willard was doing fast 200-yard sprints, and then walking between spurts. His sparring partners were utterly unable to hurt him at all.[963]

Frank Menke said Johnson would win with comparative ease if the fight was on the level. He said the negro race could grow old in years yet retain endurance, and could indulge in wild dissipation and not lose much physical power. He said most of those who thought Willard had a chance did not think so because they thought Willard was a wonder, but because Johnson had gone back so far that an ordinary fighter could beat him. It was true that Johnson had dissipated, but the extent had been exaggerated. When he fought Moran, folks had been saying the same thing, and yet he still won, toying with Moran. "He could have knocked out Moran in any round that he chose, but he elected that the white man should stay the limit." Johnson came out of the scrap without a mark.

Menke said Langford was the same way. Although he was getting older, living a careless life, and rarely trained for his fights, he still could knock out the best whites. Jeannette was 34 and still fighting well. Both Langford and Jeannette fought an average of once every three weeks for years, yet retained their powers. "And so in the face of what the negro fighters have done – and are doing – in spite of their added years and careless living, it seems to us that it is a bit unsafe to bet on Willard if you are banking on his meeting a physical wreck."

Willard manager Tom Jones said Jess was in top shape. Willard worked 2 rounds with chest weights, 2 at the punching bag, 9 rounds of sparring, 2 of wrestling, and 1 with the medicine ball, making 16 in all. He also did back and stomach exercises, in addition to his roadwork.[964]

---

[963] *El Paso Herald*, February 13, 15, 1915.
[964] *El Paso Herald*, February 17, 1915.

` The *Day Book* said that in condition, Johnson could lick a quartet of Willards in the same ring, but out of condition, he could be whipped by a good middleweight.[965]

Walter Monahan/Monaghan, who had been in the ring with both, said Willard would win. He figured the fight would last 20 rounds and that Jess would wear out Johnson with his left jab. Although Johnson was cleverer, he never saw the day that he could knock down the big Kansan.[966]

On February 22, Johnson arrived in Cuba. At that point, with only 12 days remaining before the supposed March 6 fight date in Mexico, some wondered whether Johnson could get to Juarez, Mexico, and whether he was in condition to last the limit. A postponement appeared likely.

Since the arrival of 220-pound sparring partner Jim Savage (who usually fought at 190), Willard had increased his sparring to 10 rounds, in addition to his usual use of chest weights, bag punching, wrestling, medicine ball throwing, and back and stomach exercises. His four sparring partners weighed from 187 to 220 pounds.

Willard was a Kansas cowboy and stock dealer. He was married and the father of four children. He did not drink or use tobacco. He could sprint 100 yards in 11 seconds.[967]

The *Daily Capital Journal* reported that it practically was certain that Johnson would not go to Juarez, for he could not secure permission from General Carranza, and he feared that he would be captured and deported to America. Hence, the likely fight location would be Cuba. That was what Johnson wanted.

Jack Curley said the bout would be postponed to late March or early April. He headed to Cuba to discuss matters with Johnson, hoping to keep the bout in Juarez.[968]

Johnson began exhibiting in Cuba. A wire from Jack Robinson, a former Battling Nelson manager but now a Havana promoter, said Johnson was in far better condition than most imagined, and was carrying little fat. He said the champ was concerned that he would not be able to get to Juarez.

With ease, Willard was handling 220-pound Jim Savage, 208-pound Walter Monahan, 196-pound Jack Hemple, and 220-pound Tex O'Rourke in 50 minutes of the hardest kind of sparring and wrestling. Savage said,

> He's the greatest big man I ever saw. Three rounds is my limit with him at any time. He's so strong, so hard to hit, so like a bear in the clinches that I can do nothing with him. I firmly believe he has an excellent chance of winning. If Johnson isn't in the best of shape Willard will win sure.[969]

---

[965] *Day Book*, February 19, 1915.
[966] *El Paso Herald*, February 19, 1915.
[967] *El Paso Herald*, February 22, 1915.
[968] *Daily Capital Journal*, February 24, 1915. *El Paso Herald*, February 25, 1915.
[969] *El Paso Herald*, February 27, 1915.

Hugh Fullerton, a Chicago sportswriter, was advising gamblers not to bet a cent on the fight. He said the conditions surrounding the fight were suspicious. There were rumors that a big job was being pulled off. "Jack Johnson is not now, has not been in the last two years and never will be again in condition to fight a good heavyweight. He has not fought 'on the level' in a long time." Fullerton said the champion's bouts with Jim Johnson and Frank Moran were crosses between a joke and a scandal.

> It is reported in Chicago among negroes and others who have been close to the big cotton-field coon that Jack is broke and needs the money. On that basis, reports have gone out that he has agreed to 'flop' to Willard.

> In justice (or rather, in reason) I must say I do not believe Johnson would lay down to anyone. He is an ignorant, conceited, spoiled negro. His vanity is beyond belief. If anyone could persuade him he would not lose his standing, he would be willing enough to lay down. No moral scruples would hold him.

> I doubt whether money, even, would tempt him to throw away his title.

> Nothing would be gained by arranging for Willard to lay down. Nine-tenths of the fight fans believe that Johnson, if he is even half way in condition, can whip Willard.

> From a sporting standpoint, the fight is a joke. Johnson, in the condition he was when he fought Jeffries, could beat four Willards in an evening. ... [Willard's only chance to win] is to avoid being massacred until the negro gets so weary he cannot hold up his arms or move his legs.[970]

Ed Smith, the well-known Chicago sportswriter, was enthusiastic over Willard's appearance in his workouts. He said if Johnson won, he would do it within 15 rounds, but if it went over that length, "Willard is a cinch."[971]

Willard said he would not make the same mistake that other white hopes had. He would not rush Johnson early on. He was cognizant of the fact that the champ was a master boxer who permitted his foes to wear themselves out trying to hit him so that they would be easy pickings for him later on.

As had been the case with Moran, the fight would not be the first time that Willard was in the ring with Johnson.

> I intend to make Johnson come to me at the beginning of the battle. I will wear him down with solid left jabs that will put him into a position for me to score easily with my right uppercut. I do not think he will last more than 25 rounds.

---

[970] *Tacoma Times*, February 27, 1915.
[971] *El Paso Herald*, February 27, 1915.

I have fought Johnson before, but only in exhibition bouts. He tried hard to knock me out, but failed utterly. If he couldn't put me away, or even knock me down when I was only a mere novice, it is quite unlikely that he is capable of turning the trick now, so many years after.[972]

Jim Flynn said Cuba had a rule against bouts between whites and blacks, the same as New York. Hence, the fight could not take place in Havana unless they obtained a special permit from the government.

Yet, as of March 8, it was announced that the fight would be held in Havana, Cuba during the first week of April, likely the 4th.[973]

Billy Murphy said the general criticism of Willard – that he was not aggressive and battled in a mild manner - was why he was picking him to beat Johnson. 45 rounds essentially was a finish fight. Willard was stronger, younger, and in better shape, and fighting cautiously was only going to help him in a long fight. He believed Johnson would be as fast as a bantamweight early on, but would be pumped out before an hour. Because Willard would not carry the fight to him, Johnson would have to assume the offensive, but would find that the Kansas chap could absorb a lot of punishment. Over time, Willard's superior condition would tell.

Murphy said the fight was not a fake. Many assumed a fake before the Jeffries fight and got fooled. "Johnson is not crazy. If he is beaten he is absolutely through. … He must win. Not all the money in Juarez could make him throw that fight. He'll lose, but it'll be on the square."

Murphy said Willard would re-draw the color line once he became champion. "Willard will never box another black man, if he can beat the present holder of the title."[974]

Jack Robinson said, "I have been watching Johnson work out and he doesn't look good to me. Whenever you see a heavyweight gathering beef around the knees and hips look out. Johnson is hog fat, and I am confident that the first good man who enters the ring against him will separate his ideas from his championship habits."[975]

Havana Governor Pedro Bustillo issued a statement that he would not prevent the battle. He saw no reason for interfering. He subsequently sent a letter to Colonel Jose D'Estrampes, chairman of the citizens' committee which invited Jack Curley to stage the battle there, saying that he would take no measures to prevent the bout. "Like you, I am of the opinion that there does not exist in Cuba such a thing as race hatred."

Cuban President Mario Menocal watched Johnson train, and like Governor Bustillo, declared that he would take no action to prevent the fight.

[972] *El Paso Herald*, March 1, 1915.
[973] *El Paso Herald*, March 3, 4, 8, 1915.
[974] *Ogden Standard*, March 9, 1915.
[975] *El Paso Herald*, March 12, 1915.

Johnson said that after the fight, he wanted to remain in Cuba, run a hotel business, and eventually become a citizen. "I've been in the ring nearly twenty years. I know the end must come soon. So this chance of engaging in a legitimate business appeals to me."[976]

On March 16, Willard reached Havana, along with Tom Jones, Walter Monahan, Jack Hemple, Jim Savage, and Tex O'Rourke.

Tommy Burns predicted a Willard victory, writing to the challenger,

> Jess, if you don't win from Johnson I will never try to pick another winner in the ring. I think you are absolutely sure to win. I fought Johnson wrong. I played into his hands, thinking I could outgame him. If I had boxed him I could have stayed the limit and won the decision. For Johnson, I think, is the poorest champion we ever had. On the defensive he is a great man, but he won't carry the fight. Sting him and he'll run. If he lands a blow or two, and doesn't hurt you, he gets discouraged. I don't see how he can hurt a big fellow like you, and if you play your cards right in this fight, you surely will be the next champion.[977]

The fight would take place at the Oriental Racetrack, Mariano, about five miles from the heart of Havana, with easy access by trolley, carriage, and auto. Tickets were priced from $3 up to $25.[978]

Johnson sent a letter to his mother telling her that he was intending to return to the U.S. "I am getting tired of knocking around. As soon as I have whipped Willard, I will come back to Chicago and take my medicine as the government has fixed it up for me." It is unclear what he meant by this.[979]

Battling Nelson said Johnson was in shape, even though he looked fat. He worked for 24 minutes in the gym without taking a long breath. He boxed, punched the bag, and skipped rope without an effort. Jack still seemed to be the perfect fighting machine.[980]

Johnson was expressing nothing but confidence. "I'm the best man in the world. No one stands a chance with me and Willard will go just like the rest." He was training very hard, with grim determination, resolved to be in perfect shape. Despite his work, he was fat. Regardless, in the early Havana wagering, Johnson was a 2 to 1 favorite.[981]

As of March 24, Johnson had reduced his weight from 240 down to 233 pounds, and was boxing in surprisingly good form. His training consisted of shadow boxing, work with dumb bells, and 8 rounds of sparring without intermission with Bob Armstrong, Dave Mills, Colin Bell, and Bill Scott, all heavy, fast men. His wind was excellent and his old cleverness in hitting,

---

[976] *Daily Gate City*, March 15, 1915; *Harrisburg Star-Independent*, March 17, 1915; *El Paso Herald*, March 26, 1915; *Richmond Times-Dispatch*, March 16, 1915.

[977] *El Paso Herald*, March 19, 1915.

[978] *New York Tribune*, March 20, 1915.

[979] *El Paso Herald*, March 20, 1915.

[980] *Bismark Daily Tribune*, March 21, 1915.

[981] *Daily Gate City*, March 21, 1915; *Washington Times*, March 23, 1915.

blocking, and clinching was evident. Only his judgment of distance was a bit off.[982]

On March 24, 500 spectators, a third of whom were women, saw Willard train at Miramar. His one-and-a-quarter hours of hard work consisted of pulley weights, punching the dummy, throwing the medicine ball, and boxing 12 rounds. He sparred John Pentz 3 rounds, Walter Monahan 4, Jim Savage 5, and then he wrestled with Tex O'Rourke. Willard hit terrific blows, demonstrating a good straight left. His defense was not the best, being hit often, though he took the punishment without showing discomfort. In the morning, he did 6 miles of roadwork.

JESS WILLARD AND SPARRING-PARTNERS

Four rounds a day with each of his training partners is the course which big JESS WILLARD, the cen ter figure, is pursuing in order to put himself in shape to wrest the championship from Jack Johnson, at Havana, one week from tomorrow. From left to right the above are: CHARLEY HENPIL, TEX O'ROURKE, JESS WILLARD, WALTER MONOHAM, and JIM SAVAGE.

Johnson also ran 6 miles. Unlike Willard, who took a minute rest between rounds, Johnson boxed 9 rounds with Armstrong, Bell, and Mills without intermission. Johnson's sparring partners were huskier and more experienced than Willard's.[983]

As of March 26, Jack Welch was chosen to referee the big fight.

Robert Edgren, who saw Johnson work, said he wanted to correct some mistaken impressions. Although Johnson was not as good as he was in Reno, he was anything but a dissipated physical wreck. Johnson was well trained and still had all of his old skill. He was thicker and burlier, but that was to be expected of a 37-year-old man. He appeared to be in better condition than he was against Moran.

Johnson's staff included Colin Bell of Australia, Dave Mills, who was with him at Reno, a scrapper they called "Steamboat Bill," and both Bob Armstrong and Sam McVey, the last two acting as massage artists. Sparring

[982] *El Paso Herald*, March 24, 1915; *Washington Times*, March 25, 1915.
[983] *Star Independent*, March 25, 1915.

8 rounds with Bell, Mills, and Steamboat Bill, the champion showed all of his skill, with his eye as quick and sure as ever. He smiled and talked as always. He even allowed Mills to pound away at his stomach for a minute, and then said, "I couldn't do that if I'd been doing the drinking they credit me with. If I drank a glass of beer they said I had a hundred." Johnson said he weighed 233, and two weeks ago had weighed 248.

Although the fight had been scheduled for Easter Sunday, April 4, because many folks did not like the idea of a fight occurring on the religious holiday, at President Menocal's request, the bout was moved to Monday April 5 at 12:30 p.m.[984]

$30,000 in American gold was deposited into a Havana bank, subject to the order of stakeholder Bob Vernon, the amount to be paid to Johnson upon his arrival at the fight. Jack demanded that payment be made before he entered the ring.

The *Day Book* said if Johnson was in condition he would polish off Willard easily. "Should Willard win he will have the black man's manner of life to thank, more than his own prowess."

On March 28, Cuban President Menocal was amongst a crowd of 2,000 that watched Willard train steadily for two hours. The president expressed admiration for Willard, though he confessed that previously he had wagered $100 on Johnson.

3,000 spectators watched Johnson, who pleased the crowd with his fast and heavy hitting and clever footwork. That morning, he did 6 miles of alternating jogging and sprinting.

Hugh Fullerton said two tipsters had told him that Johnson was going to lose, for he was badly in need of cash and had agreed to lose to clean up on the 2 to 1 odds. However, Fullerton said readers should not fall for such false tips, which he said were designed to affect the odds for gamblers. Gamblers spread such rumors as a way of dragging money out of their victims. "They know that the 'easiest marks' in the world are those fellows who are anxious to believe everything in sport is crooked." He said Johnson was too insanely egotistical and vain to flop, and even if he had agreed to do so, he would pull the double cross. If Johnson lost, it was because he was old, fat, out of shape, or drugged, not because he took a dive.[985]

Willard was weighing in the neighborhood of 235-240 pounds, while Johnson was about 225-230. The *Day Book* said Jess was crude, but he also was very big and powerful, and could take punishment. Moran stayed 20 rounds, and therefore Willard was likely to do so as well. And after 20 rounds, Willard would have better than an even chance. He was stronger, bigger, and more rugged than any man Johnson had ever faced.[986]

Ed Smith said Johnson was confident, strong, and quick, as always. He saw Jack work out, and although he was heavier than ever, 12 pounds more

[984] *New York World*, March 27, 1915.
[985] *El Paso Herald, Day Book, New York Tribune, Seattle Star*, March 29, 1915.
[986] *Day Book*, March 31, 1915.

even than when he fought Moran, he still was just as quick with his hands, feet, and defense as he ever was.

Johnson said,

> Win? You know I will. You know Willard will have to hit me and you know he can't. They say I must win in an hour or I won't last. Bosh! He can't last an hour and if he does he won't be worth much. Willard is too slow with his head, and size don't count against superior skill and speed. This is my climate, not his. We will fight during the hottest part of the day. Willard trains in the shade; I'm in the sun. It makes a big difference, he'll find.
>
> I need this extra weight against him. I won't be bothered by it as long as it don't hurt my speed. I was never more certain and will win unless some accident comes.[987]

Johnson said he was 217 for Moran and would be about 220 for Willard. On the 30th, Jack sparred 6 rounds.[988]

The *Washington Times* said Johnson had neglected to train hard. He tried to cover up his distaste for workouts and his heavy breathing by overindulgence in comedy, smiles, and conversation, but close observers could see that he was not the man who beat Jeffries. Experts felt that he was not in the type of condition that he needed to be for a lengthy bout. True, he still had all of his old-time speed and skill, but his punches were not as powerful. Conversely, Willard had not left anything undone in his training. Odds had dropped to 8 to 5, although the champ remained the favorite.[989]

As of April 1, Johnson was about 225 pounds, and said that was about what he would weigh against Willard. He would cut down on liquids starting April 2, three days before the fight.

Bob Edgren said Johnson was in as good a condition as a man of his age could be. That said, if the fight went over 10 rounds, he would tire more than Willard. Edgren also believed that Johnson could not take as much punishment as he could a few years ago.

The supremely confident Johnson said,

> I will win. I never saw Willard before and was surprised at his size, but I don't think he has a chance. All champions who fight long enough get theirs. I have been fighting over twenty years and my time is about due, but not in this fight. I will not fight again, as I won't risk losing the title. I will retire with it and any time in the next ten years when I want money I can go out and exhibit as the only undefeated champion and get plenty. I am satisfied with my condition and know I can fight forty-five rounds, but I won't have to.

[987] *Washington Herald*, March 31, 1915.
[988] *Star-Independent*, March 31, 1915.
[989] *Washington Times*, April 1, 1915.

Willard was confident that he would win by knockout. "The fight may not go a round and it may go twenty-five. I will get him when I hit him. ... If Johnson is willing to mix I will get him, and get him quick. If he uses his usual careful defense it will take more time."[990]

Johnson was advertised to engage in an exhibition bout with Sam McVey on Saturday April 3, just two days before the scheduled bout. Officials were trying to get him to call it off, fearing injury.

Battling Jim Johnson picked Willard to win by knockout, saying, "He had all he could do to get a draw with me in our fight in Paris. He was slow then, and puffing badly at the end of the ten rounds. I believe Willard's youth and his terrific punching powers will overcome Jack's experience."

The champ bet $1,000 at even odds that he would stop Willard within 25 rounds. His sparring partners said he was in great shape, and too fast and shifty for Willard. Naturally, Willard's sparring partners all picked him to win. Tex O'Rourke said Jess would win by knockout before the 20th round. "A powerful right-hand swing will do the trick."

As of April 1, Willard was weighing 238 pounds. On that day, before a crowd of 500 at the Hotel Miramar grounds, he boxed 7 rounds in the rain.

Johnson said, "I am in condition to fight the greatest battle of my life. I want my friends to bet on me and am telling them all to do so. I will win before the fight goes twenty rounds, probably before it goes thirteen."[991]

Various experts made their picks. Honest John Kelly said Johnson was too good and would make Jess look foolish. Charley White said Willard was the best white hope ever, and with his youth and strength would win. Harry Pollock said Johnson could win any time he wanted. Arnold Rothstein said he had a big bet down on Willard. Bob Fitzsimmons said Johnson would win unless Jess landed a lucky wallop. Billy Gibson picked Willard, saying that although Johnson was the greatest fighter ever, this time youth and strength would overcome cleverness and ring generalship. Joe Jeannette said Johnson would win quickly if he took the fight seriously. Frankie Erne said Willard would win because of youth, strength, and endurance, and because he fought just as carefully as Johnson. He expected a fight of more than 20 rounds. Jim Coffey picked Willard. Freddie Welsh predicted a Johnson victory in about 10 rounds. Dan McKetrick said, "It's a pipe for Johnson." Jack Curley said he was advising all of his friends to wager on Willard.

Mike Gibbons said,

> Johnson's great advantage over Willard is in boxing. Johnson is in much better condition than expected. Johnson will give Willard a hard beating at first, and will land often and block Willard's punches. If Willard lasts twelve rounds his chances of winning are good. After seeing both men I am up in the air and unable to predict the winner.

[990] *Evening World*, April 1, 1915.
[991] *El Paso Herald, New York Tribune, Evening Public Ledger, Washington Herald*, April 2, 1915.

832

Willard said he was fit to take anything Jack could give, and knew he would outlast him in a long contest.

Robert Edgren said that rumors of Johnson being broke were false, for he was quite wealthy. When Edgren asked him what he would do if beaten, Johnson said,

> Why, I don't think there's much chance of that, although we all get it some time. If Willard beats me he'll have to knock me cold to do it, and if he knocks me out the first thing I'll do when I get over it will be to congratulate him, because he'll be a mighty good man. If any man can beat me I won't hold a grudge against him. I'll show them I can be a sportsman even if they won't let me come home to my own country.

Tom Flanagan said a million dollars wouldn't induce Johnson to throw away his title. One of the promoters tried out Jack on that proposition, going to Johnson and saying, "Jack, you're in pretty soft. If you win you get $32,000 in cash and you make a few thousand more after the fight. If you lose you'll get two or three hundred thousand out of the moving pictures." Johnson replied, "Moving pictures – where'd I get all that money? There's no money in moving pictures now in Europe and they can't be shown in the United States. Don't talk pictures to me. I wouldn't give a nickel for them."[992]

Most believed the bout was on the square. Johnson remained the betting favorite, although there were many respected experts who were predicting a Willard victory.

Those who were trying to get an inside line on Johnson from his 6-round bout with Sam McVey on April 3 were disappointed. The champ simply fooled around with McVey, neither man trying to do anything. However, every now and then, Jack shot in a lightning quick jab to the face. He did not lead more than six times during the 6 rounds, but instead was content to block and clinch.

To dispel all rumors that he would quit to Willard to obtain a fortune from the moving pictures, Johnson put up $10,000 of his own money to bet on himself against $8,000 from Willard's backers. However, his money was not covered, for Willard supporters wanted even better odds. Jack said he would not take down his money until he entered the ring.[993]

The *World* said Johnson had trained well, out in the open, and the way he handled his sparring partners showed that he was anything but a "dead one." He had worked out day after day with a cheerful golden smile and was the picture of confidence.

Regardless, Willard had changed the minds of many who originally thought of him as a victim. Cubans were startled by his enormous size. He looked fit enough to have a chance with anyone. His work had been twice

[992] *Evening World*, April 3, 1915.
[993] *Washington Times*, April 4, 1915.

as hard as Johnson's. He had hammered his sparring partners and allowed them to hammer away at him. Not once did he show the slightest inclination to avoid work or punishment. He seemed impervious to punches. "In spite of the usual rumors in America, there is no indication here that anything else but a genuine fight is to be expected."[994]

Some experts advised Willard to follow Corbett's example against an old Sullivan – to fight on the defensive for several rounds, not throw too many punches, allowing the old man to get tired. Corbett did not care whether the crowd hooted him, for he used the methods necessary for his purpose.[995]

On April 5, 1915 in Havana, Cuba, 37-year-old Jack Johnson defended his world heavyweight championship against 33-year-old Jess Willard (who then was listed as 27) in a scheduled 45-round bout.[996]

At 6 a.m., vehicles of all descriptions started heading to the Miramar race track, the battleground, nine miles away from Havana. Few Americans spoke Spanish, but making fists like a fighter and pointing in the general direction of Miramar was enough for the rig drivers.

That morning, Johnson was in a playful mood, laughing and kidding with his companions. Willard was silent and serious. Jess said, "This is more than a personal matter with me. I want to restore the title to the white race."

Federal district Attorney Clyne had secret service agents at ringside. He said, "Look for sensational developments after the fight. On Jack Johnson's attitude after the fight will depend the actions of the Government's agents." It is unclear what he meant.

At 11 a.m., in accordance with the agreement, Johnson received his money.

As the crowd began to arrive, the sun broke through a darkly overcast sky.

A ring was erected on the race track in front of a big steel grandstand. The ring was 18 feet inside the ropes, on a 22-foot platform. Two hours before the fight, the heavy hemp ropes were wrapped twice with black tire tape. The floor beneath the red canvas covering had a score of red blankets for padding. However, another version said that under the canvas there was only one-sixteenth of an inch of felt. From two platforms, five moving picture machines worked. Three were used regularly, with two in reserve.

Already at 11:30 a.m., one hour before the fight was scheduled to start, several thousand spectators had arrived. Present was Havana's mayor/governor Pedro Bustillo, as well as the speaker of the Cuban House of Representatives. A number of well-armed soldiers guarded the ring and arena, keeping splendid order. They had rifles, bayonets, and revolvers. In fact, soldiers comprised a large portion of the crowd. A liberal percentage of

---

[994] *New York World*, April 5, 1915.

[995] *Washington Herald*, April 4, 1915.

[996] The following account is an amalgamation of ringside reports from the *El Paso Herald* and *New York Evening World*, April 5, 1915. Some additional information is from the *Washington Times*, April 5, 1915.

women were amongst the spectators, many Americans. At least 200 were well-dressed in striking colored dresses, which contrasted the duck-suited dandies of Havana or the black suits of American spectators.

Otto Floto and Sam Bennett kept time for the fighters, and they sat on either side of Bob Vernon, the official stakeholder and timekeeper.

At 11:45 a.m., Willard arrived at the battleground by auto. The crowd cheered him. He wore a heavy red sweater over his ring togs. He was rubbed down at his quarters, and was not the least bit excited.

Willard said he intended to go slow and expected to take a good deal of punishment during the first 10 rounds, hoping to wear down Johnson and get an opportunity to land a knockout blow.

The crowd around the ring helped stretch the red painted canvas covering. There was much laughter and good-natured bantering. The ring finally was finished at noon. Ben Rosenthal swept it. A carpenter put up steps at the corners. The reason why the ring construction took so long was that in the morning, the workers who were building the ring went on strike.

At noon, the heavy clouds began breaking up and the sun shone through patches of blue sky.

A few minutes after noon, Cuban president Mario Menocal arrived. The Cubans cheered him.

Willard walked around with his trainers, laughing at jokes. He said he was feeling great and more confident than ever.

The crowd was pouring through all of the entrances, many thousands standing on the hills outside the track from a half-mile to a mile away.

At 12:10 p.m. it was obvious that the fight would start late. All of the officials were at ringside, but the principals had not yet appeared. Nearly all of the seats were taken, but there was a never-ending stream of humanity still pressing forward from the entrances.

Johnson arrived at the track at 12:23 p.m., but did not emerge from his dressing room until later. Tom Flanagan accompanied Johnson's wife Lucille to the ringside. She said, "Jack told me he is confident of winning and surely will knock out Willard."

Referee Jack Welch/Welsh instructed the fighters in their dressing rooms.

The officials and middleweight champ Mike Gibbons were introduced from the ring.

At 12:30 p.m., announcer Jim Mace exhibited Johnson's signed receipt for $29,000, the remainder of the money that had been due him on the purse, announcing the facts through a megaphone. The meaning of these papers was explained to the crowd in both Spanish and English.

Johnson said, "I expect to win. If beaten I will congratulate the best man I ever fought. No one can beat me."

Johnson was the 10 to 6 betting favorite.

At 12:40 p.m., the sun was shining brightly.

There was a rush along the roads from Havana. There were no speed limits or rules of the road. As a result, there were several minor collisions. A large part of the crowd arriving by auto was charged as much as five times the usual taxi rates.

At least 17,000 people were in attendance. There were about 10,000 spectators inside the track, and many thousands more were in the stands. The aisles were packed. Americans were all around the ringside. Many boxes were filled with women and even some children. The surrounding palm-topped hills were crowded with people. Two military bands were playing in the grandstand and hundreds of Cuban army officers were grouped around the ring in full uniform. American and Cuban flags were flying everywhere.

For some reason, promoter Jack Curley had a row with announcer Mace and forcibly dragged him out of the ring. The crowd had been growing weary by the fighters' failure to appear, but hugely enjoyed this "preliminary" not on the card. Curley put in a substitute announcer.

At 1:05 or 1:11 p.m., led by Sam McVey, and accompanied by his full staff of trainers, Johnson appeared, and the enthusiastic Cubans applauded him. A minute later, he entered the ring through the ropes, clad in a long gray bathrobe, smiling. He walked around the ring before selecting his corner. In doing so, he looked for his wife's location. The moving picture cameras got very busy.

Johnson was seconded by George Munroe (a former bantam champ), Sam McVey, Dave Mills, Bob Armstrong, and Colin Bell.

Four or five minutes later, when Willard entered, he received prolonged yelling, cheering, and clapping by both Cubans and Americans. With him were Tom Jones, Tex O'Rourke, Jim Savage, and Walter Monahan.

Johnson objected to the presence of a woman in the press ringside stand named Cecilia Wright, who wrote for magazines and newspapers. He said he would not fight unless she left the ringside. She was moved to an adjacent box.

The fighters shook hands at ring center. Willard towered over Johnson.

The fighters stripped. Willard wore dark blue trunks and an American flag as a belt. Johnson wore bright blue trunks and a belt.

Scales were placed inside the ring, and both pugilists weighed in right then and there. According to the *El Paso Herald*, Willard was 238 pounds, while Johnson was 225. However, Robert Edgren said Willard was 247 and Johnson was 227. The *Sun* said Johnson's weight was announced as 227, while Willard's weight was 238 pounds, according to the announcer.

They put on the gloves in the ring. Jess was ready first, waiting in his corner. Jack talked to people around his corner, signed papers, and pulled on his gloves.

Ben Rosenthal received a hard call-down for walking in front of the moving pictures.

The hot sun began beating down on everyone.

Referee Jack Welch (or Welsh) introduced the principals.

At 1:23 or 1:28 p.m., the ring was cleared and time was called to start the fight.

1 - They began milling promptly. Johnson feinted and landed his left jab to the jaw. Jess feinted very deliberately. After a clinch Johnson landed his right uppercut and there was another clinch. Jack landed repeated right uppercuts to the jaw. Jess was very nervous. Jack was laughing. Willard drove three rights to the body and landed two jabs on the jaw. They fought hard up close, both landing body blows, Willard with his left and Johnson with his right. Jack landed a short right to the jaw, and Willard rushed into a mix-up. Robert Edgren claimed that Johnson was puffing badly already. Between rounds, he said to his seconds, "I'm going to box a little slow."

2 - Johnson easily blocked Willard's leads, feinting him out of position and scoring right and left to the jaw. Willard replied with a threshing right to the body. Johnson countered with a terrific right to the jaw. Jess jabbed, and Jack whipped a left hook into the pit of the stomach. He also landed three

jabs to the body. Willard laughed and forced the fighting. However, Johnson then rushed and drove Willard to the ropes, landing heavily with a tattoo of lefts to the face, body, and ear.

3 - After much feinting, Willard went for the body. Jess missed a right for the jaw and both laughed. Jack rushed him to the ropes, with one observer saying he missed three blows, while another said he scored a left on the body, right to the jaw, and another left on the body. Jess drove a hard right to the belly and Jack countered to the body and rocked Willard's head with a left to the jaw. The champ also landed a short left to the stomach, to which Willard asked something to the effect of, "Do you think that can do it?" A hard mix-up followed. Johnson appeared to be trying for a knockout, but Willard was blocking blows successfully.

4 - Willard sent five jabs towards the jaw. Johnson walked around the ring, laughing at his efforts. There was much feinting. Willard landed a left and right and they clinched. Johnson rushed in with fast swings, landing a left and right to the body and ribs, and a left to the face. Willard blocked and came out unhurt except for a small cut on the upper lip that bled. Jess scored a left to Jack's nose. Jack plunged in with a left hook to the jaw. Jess jabbed hard to the body and Johnson countered with a heavy right to the jaw. Both were fresh and cool.

5 - Willard jabbed twice. Johnson poked a light left and a right to Willard's face. In a clinch, Johnson tried to rough it, but Willard held him even in strength. The referee ordered them to break. Once inside again, Jack smashed hard to Willard's ribs and drove three blows to the stomach, with a left sinking into the pit of the stomach.

Johnson rushed Willard to the ropes, scoring punches with both hands to the head and body. Willard was rattled and distressed, holding his guard low as if hurt by the body shots.

Both fighters posed. Neither would be drawn in. Willard blocked some body blows. Johnson swung a right to the kidneys and a right to the jaw. Jess sent in right and left to the body and another left to the mouth. Jack's mouth was bleeding. A terrific Willard right to the jaw drove Johnson onto the ropes at the bell.

6 - Edgren said Johnson was puffing in his corner before the bell, while the *El Paso Herald* said Johnson was calm. Johnson beat Willard to the ropes with a fusillade of lefts. On the break, Johnson landed a smash to the jaw. Jess rubbed the cut on his upper lip at every opportunity. Jack landed three crashing blows to the unprotected body. Jess was taking punishment, but apparently was unhurt. He began forcing the fight and smashed a right into Jack's body. Johnson rushed him to the ropes, swinging furiously and landing his right on the cheek, cutting Willard's left cheek bone. At the bell, Johnson was hammering hard at Willard's body.

7 - Johnson was using every trick to force the fighting. He rushed Willard to the ropes, slugging with both hands repeatedly. A driving left to the ribs sounded hard, for it could be heard throughout the grandstand. Willard's body was covered with red marks. However, Willard's long left landed to the left eye, temporarily blinding Jack. His eye started closing a bit. Johnson came back with a series of swings to the body, though Jess blocked most of them. Edgren said Jack was breathing hard. He hit Willard with a hard left to the eye and drove his left to the body. He rushed, but Jess met the attack and drove him back.

8 - Willard was gaining confidence, blocking Johnson's leads, and he tried his hand at forcing the pace. Jack accepted his challenge. They battered each other across the ring, with Johnson having the better of it. Willard landed a fierce right to the jaw. Jack clutched and held. Another right sent Jack backwards. Jess also drove a left to the body. Jack landed an uppercut over the heart. Jess bounced off the ropes and landed a left to the jaw. Edgren said Johnson appeared desperate, for he was swinging furiously for the body. Jess jabbed him three times. Jack clinched, spitting blood. He swung two hard rights to the stomach. The round ended with Johnson swinging blows to the head.

9 - Willard assumed the aggressive. He landed three hard ones on the mouth and two hard lefts to the stomach. However, Jack landed his right to the jaw, and with another blow started one of the cowboy's ears bleeding. Willard jabbed Jack's head back and drove in a fierce right to the stomach. The champ landed frequently, but his blows seemed to lack their old-time power. Amidst the feinting, the crowd shouted, "Kill the black bear." Johnson immediately started a rally, driving three hard hooks to the stomach. A Willard left started Jack's mouth bleeding. Johnson then slugged him to the ropes.

Edgren said that around the ring, folks were calling out wagers of nearly even odds of $500 to $400 on Willard. Jess was taking Johnson's body blows successfully, while Jack was blowing hard in his corner. Jess was laughing at him.

10 - Johnson was slow in emerging from his corner. Still, he tried to force the fighting. Willard blocked easily and pushed him away. Jack, furious, re-attacked and drove Willard to the ropes without landing effectively. Willard scored two lefts to the face. Jess was blocking better as his nervousness wore off. Jack swung a left to the ribs and sent half a dozen blows to Willard's body and jaw. Jack then waited and countered with a hard left to the body as Jess jabbed. He knocked Jess to the ropes with right and left swings to the stomach. A hard right chop to the jaw rocked Willard.

11 - A bunch of folks around the ring began yelling at Johnson, calling him yellow. Jack replied loudly, "Wish I was, I could pass for white." Jack kidded, while Willard waited. The crowd derided Johnson, who was fighting and answering the witty remarks at the same time. Willard drove a left to

the mouth, but took a right hook to the body in return. Johnson attacked, landing a heavy left smash to the jaw. His left to the ear made Willard bleed. Jess blocked several swings and then drove two right smashes to the body. Jack stood off, sparring. A "yellow man" in a box seat said to Johnson, "You've got a real fighter in front of you." Jack then tried to rattle Willard by talking. Jess angrily replied in kind. At the bell, Jack tapped Jess' shoulder. Johnson sat down, talking to the spectators. He seemed to have found his second wind.

12 - Johnson opened by sinking both hands into the body and landing right and left to the jaw. In a clinch, he smashed Willard three times with his left. He then drove a right to the body and left to the head. However, Jack's blows appeared to have no effect. A furious Willard jabbed and drove a right to the body. Johnson rushed and held Willard's hands down with his right while he swung a left to the jaw. Jack seemed to have plenty of steam and all of his old skill. Jess jabbed a hard left to the jaw. He also drove a right to the body. Jack sent him to the ropes with terrific swings to the head. Jess was bleeding from both cheeks, but took the aggressive as the round ended. Although his ear and cheek were bleeding, at the bell, Willard spryly walked to his corner.

13 - Willard's body was red from the effects of the punishment. Undoubtedly, he was game. He had taken terrific blows without flinching and apparently was not hurt. Both men were breathing easily again, seeming as fresh as at the start. Jack, ducking under the leads, continued playing for the stomach. Jess drove him into a corner and landed a straight left to the

face. They feinted for half a minute, until Johnson rushed in with a jarring left hook to the jaw. He next hooked his left to the body, repeating the blow a moment later. There was plenty of snap to his punches. Jack feinted for the body, and as Willard's guard dropped low, Johnson rocked his head aside with a left to the jaw. He then straightened him up with a right to the jaw. However, at the bell, Willard went to his corner laughing.

14 - The round began with Willard firing a hard right uppercut, one observer saying it landed, while another said it missed. Johnson sank a left into the body. Jess was the aggressor and tried to force the fighting. Jack dove into a clinch. They fought at close quarters for half a minute. Johnson slammed him on the mouth with a left. Jess only laughed. When Jess jabbed, Jack returned the jab and roughed his face with the heel of his glove. Jess' jabs knocked Jack's head back. Jack was beginning to miss his leads. Willard drove a hard right to the ear. Johnson rushed, missing blows as Jess jumped away. Jack smashed a terrific hard left into the pit of the stomach at the bell.

15 - Both were very cautious. The crowd kidded Johnson, who then rushed Willard to the ropes with five heavy swings to the head. Johnson yelled, "I am a grand old man." Willard responded to the remark, driving a right to the body. Jack clinched. The champ was talking while fighting. He rushed Willard to the ropes again, but all of his blows were blocked. The bell found both fighting at ring center.

16 - Johnson feinted for a long time and then threw a right which Jess blocked. Jack attacked and Jess tangled his arms and held. Jack kept up a running conversation with the crowd. He said, "Willard is a good kid," and then rushed Jess to the ropes, scoring two hard punches to the body. Johnson then said, "I must be a great man if this fellow can't lick me." The

crowd retorted, "This is the only man you ever fought." Jack whipped a heavy left to the stomach that hurt Jess, who seemed a trifle unsteady as he went to his corner. Edgren said there was not much fighting in the round overall, for both were very careful.

17 - Willard landed a right to Johnson's body and left to the head. He again scored a right to the body and blocked the return. Johnson rocked Willard with a left hook to the jaw. Willard missed but afterward countered with a right to the jaw. He was angry again and kept up a hard attack, forcing Johnson to back away.

Jack rushed and drove Jess to a corner, pushing him to the ropes and swinging left and right squarely on the jaw. He again hooked a right to the body and followed it up with two punches to the head. It looked as if Willard had to show some effect from such blows, but instead he ripped into Johnson, forcing the fight. Willard landed a few rights to the body. Jack's mouth was open as the bell rang. Heavy blows had been exchanged in this round.

18 - Jess jabbed. Jack rushed him, landing blows to the chest and stomach. Johnson drove him to a corner, where he smashed Willard with an uppercut and right to the jaw. Jess missed an uppercut. The champ easily picked off Willard's leads. Jack swung a serious right uppercut to the jaw and furious left to the ear.

After several attempts, Willard landed a straight left jab very hard to the right eye and sent a right swing to the jaw, putting Johnson over the ropes. It was a terrific punch. Jack slowed up and Jess jabbed him almost at will. The crowd was delirious with excitement, jumping up and down, yelling Willard's name. Willard was much fresher than Johnson and looked as good as he did in the 1st round. At the bell, Jack landed a punch to the body and another to the jaw.

19 - Both pugilists slowed up a bit. Willard was now the aggressor. For a long while, Johnson stood in the middle of the ring and blocked blows, mostly jabs. During the first minute, not a single hard punch landed. Jack finally swung a left to Willard's eye. Johnson seemed able to divine Willard's every lead. The champ then started a rally, landing two lefts to the body and

a right to the jaw. Jess sank a right into the body, while Jack landed a hooking left uppercut to the chin. Johnson was scowling and feinting, looking for openings, when Jess jabbed and followed instantly with a heavy right onto the jaw. Edgren opined that Willard won the round.

20 - Willard opened the round with two light blows to the face. Jack laughed and said, "Lead again, kid." Willard did and smiled as well. The crowd at ringside yelled, "Hurry up, we want to see the races." Both were fighting very carefully. Willard stabbed and pawed the air until he landed a fearful right on Jack's jaw. Johnson immediately cut loose and mixed desperately, driving Willard back. They battled across the ring. Jess landed a smashing right in the stomach and Johnson tried to clinch. Jess chopped him on the back of the head with Gunboat Smith's occipital punch. Johnson seemed dazed and distressed. When Willard drove a hard right and left to the body at the bell, the crowd was frantic.

21 - Johnson waited a long time for the attack. Willard outwaited him. After a minute of posing and feinting, Johnson hooked his left to the body and sent a right swing to the head. Willard replied with a straight left to the face. When Johnson rushed, Willard blocked his blows well, laughing once they were clinched. The ringsiders were applauding Willard uproariously. Jack walked around the ring. Jess missed punches with both hands, and they both laughed. Jess jabbed and Johnson swung an overhand right to the jaw. Jess stepped away from Jack's rush. They were sparring for an opening at the bell.

22 - The fight had degenerated into a slow sparring and clinching battle, though neither appeared particularly tired or injured by the blows. Both feinted for a long time. Willard tried setting the pace. They went into a clinch, where Willard pounded the body. Johnson kept holding on while Willard punched and battered away at the stomach. Johnson only grinned at the shrieking crowd. Nevertheless, Johnson was showing the effects of the pace. He was slowing up. Jess did all of the forcing in this round.

23 - Willard rushed into a clinch and landed a left to the stomach. Jack held on until the referee ordered him to break. Willard walked steadily into Johnson, who retreated. Johnson blocked a dozen blows like a fencing master. Willard followed him constantly, but was unable to penetrate his guard. Eventually, the challenger shot two lefts to the face. They clinched and wrestled about the ring. The *El Paso Herald* said Johnson had not struck a blow in the round. Edgren said there had been almost no fighting in this round.

24 - Johnson blocked and wrestled, making Willard do all the work. The crowd yelled at the fighters to fight, but instead they clinched. Willard laid his weight on Johnson at every opportunity in the clinches. Johnson pushed him backward in the same manner that he did with Jeffries. Jack landed several light body blows, apparently trying to draw Willard in for a big smash. Jack missed two weak swings. He kept wrestling on the inside with the ex-cowboy. The crowd howled its disapproval. Willard smashed him with a left to the face at the bell. Edgren said Jack hippodromed all through the round, doing little actual fighting.

25 - Johnson had slowed down badly. His actions seemed to indicate that he did not think he could not knock out Willard and was trying to conserve energy and get the decision on points at the end of 45 rounds. Johnson was hitting lightly when Willard sunk a right to the heart that shook him. Cries went through the crowd, "Hundred even on Willard." Jess then clipped Johnson on the jaw with a fast left to the mouth, and started forcing the pace. Jack was conserving every bit of his energy. Willard again landed a left to the mouth, and then repeated it. Johnson blocked a right but Willard landed another heavy right to the mouth. Jess landed a heavy left to the

nose. Jack backed away along one side of the ring as the bell rang. He dropped heavily onto his seat.

26 - Between rounds, Flanagan jumped into Johnson's corner and spoke with him. When the bell rang, Johnson sat still until Referee Welsh called him from his chair. As they met, Willard sunk a right smash to the pit of the stomach and Jack nearly sat down. The referee forced them to break from a clinch. Willard rushed and slammed right and left to the body. In a clinch, Jack looked over his shoulder towards his wife's seat. Jess then smashed him.

On the outside again, Willard quickly stepped in and landed a terrific straight right to the jaw that knocked Johnson down. Jack remained down for the full ten-count, out cold. Jess Willard was the new heavyweight champion of the world.

A large portion of the great ringside crowd rushed into the ring. Several squads of soldiers then hurried onto the platform and cleared the crowd away to protect the fighters.

Summarizing, the *El Paso Herald* said Johnson led all the way up to the 22nd round, when his stamina failed as a result of the hard pace which he carried throughout the early rounds. When Johnson slowed down, Willard opened up his attack and carried the fighting to the champ. A terrific right to the jaw knocked out Johnson in the 26th round.

A U.S. district attorney revealed the purpose of having secret servicemen at ringside. They were following Johnson. He said if Johnson was to journey outside of the three-mile limit of Cuban waters he would be taken into custody.

Robert Edgren said it was the greatest heavyweight fight since Fitzsimmons-Corbett. During the first 20 rounds, Willard took punishment that would have knocked out any other man. However, he weathered it all and was as cool as Johnson. He even outwitted Johnson on many occasions, forcing him to lead and then outfighting him. Ultimately, though, youth won for Willard. After the 20th round, it was evident that nature had run its course, for Willard was still fresh, and growing more eager as he felt Johnson weakening. Jack attacked time and again, but there was no strength in his blows. Just before the knockout, Johnson glanced toward his white wife over Willard's shoulder. He didn't want her to see him knocked out. She was taken away from her box, but on her way out saw the end anyhow.

Edgren said the fight was legitimate, and that if it was a fix, Johnson was the greatest actor who ever lived. He said the end was inevitable, for Johnson's strength was gone and he was lasting on skill alone. When he went down, he was frozen, his arms stiffened rigidly over his head, absolutely out cold. When Johnson was helped to his corner, his legs and whole body quivered, and were still quivering when he stumbled from the ring ten minutes later. Two hours later, Johnson's quarters were an extremely gloomy place, like a funeral.

Some quoted Sam McVey as claiming that Johnson had laid down. However, Edgren's expert view was that Johnson fought his hardest to knock out Willard, but Jess wore him down and won fair and square.

The *Sun* said the fight disproved the stories about a frame-up and fake circulated before the bout. Nothing about the fight looked fake. It was an on the level, fair and square fight. In fact, Johnson had fought like never before, carrying the attack to Willard. Jess replied with counters and allowed Jack to tire himself out. "Johnson beat himself, said many, but it must not be forgotten that the fallen champion taxed his skill to the utmost before his strength began to ebb." His brain was as alert as ever, though his blows were not as powerful as they once were and his judgment of distance was bad at times. All that said, some were shocked and amazed that some of his blows did not deck Willard, for they landed flush on his jaw. Willard's knees sagged a score of times but he always managed to keep his feet. This had a dispiriting effect on Johnson as well.

The *Day Book* said, "Johnson's private life was not saintly, but there can be no doubt his head was turned from the adulation given him by white people after he had won the title. It is a good thing for the fight game that Willard has won." Still, it said that delirious blurbs that the white race had triumphed were all bunk. "A big white man, trained to the minute, beat a very fat and leg-weary colored man in a contest between individuals."[997]

The *Los Angeles Times* reported that the Associated Press hinted that Johnson quit. It said Johnson saw that he could not win, so when he was knocked down, he took the count rather than absorb further punishment. He sent his wife from the arena before the end, and then jumped up after the count was concluded.

For 20 rounds Johnson punched and pounded Willard at will, but Jess was able to absorb the punishment, and Johnson's blows grew perceptibly weaker as the fight progressed, until he was so tired that he seemed unable or unwilling to go on. Jack realized he could not stop Jess.

During the 25th round, Willard landed a right smash to the heart that was the beginning of the end. When the round ended, Jack sent word to his wife that he was all in, and told her to go home. She was on the way out when the fight ended.

However, another AP wire said that well before the end, Johnson was fading and his legs quivered. After he was decked, he never moved. His eyes were glassy and only the whites were visible. Johnson remained stretched on the floor even after the count of ten. The time of the round was 1 minute and 26 seconds.

The early rounds were filled with flashes of Johnson's former wonderful speed, raining rights and lefts to Willard's body and face, delivering ten blows to the challenger's one. Willard was on the defensive.

In many ways the fight went as Willard predicted. He said that if it lasted 20 rounds that Johnson could not win. This was based on the belief that Willard could withstand all of the punishment that Jack could inflict, and also the belief that Johnson's age and condition would be handicaps in a battle against a younger man with height, reach, weight, and strength advantages. Willard said he expected to take a beating for 10 to 15 rounds by a faster and more skilled opponent; had trained to withstand it, and that is just what he did.

Johnson's continual grin during the early rounds changed to a look of wonderment once the battle passed the 20th round. It was evident to the spectators that Johnson came to the conclusion that it was useless to try to knock out the giant. Johnson also seemed to know that he was in no condition to fight for 45 rounds. It seemed that he had believed that he would whip Willard within 20 rounds, was surprised that he had not done so, and realized that he could not do so. From the 20th round on he did little, and the fight became slow. Johnson was sparring for time and throwing few punches.

Afterwards, Willard said,

> The blow that brought the fight to a quick conclusion was a right-hand smash to Johnson's body early in the last round. I felt Johnson

[997] *Day Book*, April 6, 1915; *New York Sun*, April 6, 1915; *New York World*, April 10, 1915.

grow limp in the next clinch and knew I had the championship within reach. A left to the body and a right smash to the jaw put Johnson down for the count.

Mike Gibbons said it was no fluke. Johnson looked like the Johnson of old up to about the 17th round, but then grew tired. Willard's confidence grew in about the 19th round, and he made several rallies. Jack's downfall became evident in the 21st round. He became much more defensive and started stalling. It was plain that his blows lacked steam. The smile disappeared. He realized that he was up against a mighty hard proposition. Conversely, Willard grew more aggressive.

Jim Jeffries said he told Willard to stay away and let Johnson bring the fight to him, to wait for the old man to get tired.

The AP wire reports said Johnson had the best of the rounds, but he was not able to hurt Willard.

Jeffries balked at speculation of a fix. "This talk about it being a fake is ridiculous. The fact that it went twenty-six rounds proves that. If Johnson was going to quit on a frame-up he would have done it long before the twenty-sixth. It's nonsense to think of the fight as being crooked." Jeff said if it had been crooked, he would have been tipped off about it from some of his many friends. He didn't believe Jack would ever take a dive. "Jack Johnson would rather be champion of the world than President of the United States, I really believe, and no amount of money would induce him to part with that title."998

Jack Johnson said,

> At Reno, after I had beaten Jeffries, I asked you to let the Californian down easy, and you did, but accorded me all the credit I deserved. Now let me down easy.

> I was sure my experience and generalship would be too much for Willard, but I was mistaken. There is not another man in the world who could have stood twenty-six rounds with that youngster today. He gave me a beating, but I took his blows without wincing – and he can hit.999

Edgren quoted Johnson as saying, "I have met a younger and better man." The next day, Johnson said to Edgren, "He's an awfully big fellow, isn't he?" Johnson had tears in his eyes; he was so distraught over losing the title.

Jack Curley said the fight receipts were over $100,000, not the $70,000 originally reported.1000

The portions of the films that still exist reveal that at first, both were very cautious and deliberate, waiting on the outside, feinting, and being

998 *Los Angeles Daily Times*, April 6, 1915.
999 *New York Tribune*, April 6, 1915.
1000 *Washington Times*, April 10, 1915.

efficient and alert. The patient Willard primarily looked to land jabs to the head and rights to the body, but generally Johnson would jump back out of the way.

Willard presented a difficult stylistic dilemma for Johnson. Jack was used to having the superior height and reach, which forced his opponents to advance towards him, leaving them vulnerable to his counterattack. Also, Johnson typically could smother their shorter arms with his gloves and arms, utilizing his energy-sapping style while they attempted to hit him in futility.

However, against Willard, it was Jess who could stay on the outside and still hit Johnson from long range. Owing to the height and reach differences, when Willard attacked, it was more difficult for Johnson to time him or tie him up. Willard's long arms could shoot through Jack's defense more easily than other opponents could.

Willard also was cautious, not committing himself very much. Both would patiently wait on the outside, feinting and looking to set up their attack. When Willard stepped in, he did so briefly and quickly, throwing only one or two solid punches, and with his height and reach, he could do so from far away. His jab was strong, snapping Johnson's head a bit when it landed. Jess was very economical, carefully choosing when to punch, often landing when he did, either with his jab to the head or right to the body. Blows that fell short when others threw them would land when thrown by a man with arms as long as Willard's were. Johnson would duck, block, or step back from most blows, but still, more were landing for Willard than was the case with others.

Willard's ability to hit Johnson from far away led Johnson into more of an attacking style, one that was not as comfortable for him, and which required the use of more energy. Willard's height, reach, and ability to step back when attacked made him a difficult target. In order to hit Willard, Johnson had to step in and use his legs more and throw more punches to get to him. This caused Johnson, when he did throw, to work more and at a faster pace than was typical for him. Johnson threw some very impressive quick combinations over the course of the bout, but was unable to land effectively all that often on the huge Willard, who was able to step back, block with his arms, absorb some blows, and tie up. Willard actually was doing to Johnson what Jack had done to many others. Ironically, the very cautious defensive style which led to some criticism of Willard was the best way to fight Johnson in a long bout.

Johnson showed more offensive firepower and output than he did for several other fights, firing some very speedy combinations that were impressive, particularly for a man of 37 years of age. Ironically, the fight in which he was the most offensively active, and would lead one to believe that he still had a lot left as a fighter, would be the one in which he became separated from his crown. Even in a loss, Johnson was impressive.

In the 12th round, Johnson did some effective work when he quickly countered Willard's punches. However, quick combinations over the course of many rounds have more of a fatiguing effect on the boxer throwing them if they are not doing sufficient damage. Throughout the bout, Johnson threw more quick lengthy combinations that gave a good impression, but he was not able to do much damage. The huge Willard could take it, plus he knew how to roll, block, smother, pull away, step back, and clinch. Willard was much more efficient with his offense, carefully selecting his one or two heavy long punches at a time, utilizing a style that kept him relaxed and fresh. Conversely, Johnson was doing more work in order to hit Jess, and was not necessarily yielding sufficient dividends from his physical investment.

In the 14th round, each man took turns going on the attack. When they threw and attacked, the blows were fast and hard and the fight entertaining. Then they would clinch, break, and take their time to set up the attack again. There was tension and drama even in these moments. Sometimes they would exchange, sometimes one would step back as the other attacked, while at others Johnson would attempt fast counters and step in on the attack after Jess threw.

In the 15th round, Johnson attacked, got Jess on the ropes and landed a couple solid blows before being held. They feinted on the outside until Jack attacked again before the inevitable clinch. Johnson needed to charge in to find the range to land. Jess kept pumping his jab to the head and occasional right to the body from far away.

From the 17th through the 21st rounds, Johnson still occasionally was throwing very good quick combinations. Quite frankly, it is a testament to how good Johnson was to keep up that type of pace and throw that many quick combinations over so many rounds at age 37. However, in a 45-round bout, it wasn't about points and impression as much as it was about effective punches, pacing, and defense. Johnson was landing, but he was working hard, and Willard could take it and ensure that not very many effective blows got through.

The calm Willard kept a good pace himself, firing quick jabs to the head and solid rights to the body, and, beginning in the 18th round, he even began coming over with at least one solid right to the head in each round. Mostly, Willard's right went to the body, so when he threw it to the head, he likely caught Johnson off guard, surprising him. When stung by these blows, usually Johnson would attempt to get immediate payback, firing furious combinations of blows.

In the 21st round, Willard kept pumping in his metronome jabs to the head, while Johnson mostly played defense for a while. However, when Willard landed a right to the head, Johnson came back with a lengthy nonstop furious combination to the body and head, but because Willard was able to move back, block, and finally grab, the punches did not do much damage. What punches that did land well, Willard absorbed, and shortly thereafter, Jess came right back with his own attack. Nothing could discourage this behemoth of a man.

By the 25th round, Johnson had slowed up. He was moving back and holding more. The well-conditioned Willard still seemed fresh, outworking Johnson on the inside, digging many body shots as Johnson tried to hold. Johnson appeared to be taking more breaks on the outside as well, not throwing as much, while Willard seemed as frisky as ever. The aging Johnson had to be fatigued from the heat, dehydration, the fast pace, and the good body blows from a very big man.

In the 26th round, Jess threw a jab and right to the head and Jack clinched for a while. They feinted and posed at long range for a bit. Quickly stepping in off a jab, Willard immediately followed with a very good straight right to Johnson's jaw that caused Jack's body to go limp, falling towards the ground. Johnson tried to grab Jess as he was going down, but was unsuccessful. Johnson dropped backwards, with both his back and back of his head hitting the floor with a hard thud. At first Jack's knees are bent and his hands are above and over his face and eyes. Then his knees went limp and he remained motionless as he was counted out. Even after the count was concluded, Johnson remained still on his back. Jess Willard had become the heavyweight champion of the world in history's longest Marquis of Queensberry rules heavyweight championship bout, a record in heavyweight championship title fights which stands to this day.

It actually was a pretty good fight, one which should garner more respect for Johnson despite the loss. He certainly showed that he could outpoint a good big man in a shorter bout, the likes of which we have today and throughout most of the 20th century. He was very fast and reactive, and his defense still pretty good given how huge his foe was. Johnson showed more offense in this fight than he did in most other available fights on film for him. His performance is really amazing given his advanced age.

Ironically, the Congressional ban on interstate transportation of fight films also made it illegal to bring into the United States fight films for purposes of public exhibition. Few U.S citizens would be able to see the fight for many years to come. A law passed in part to prevent whites from seeing Johnson defeat whites also prevented whites from seeing a white man defeat Johnson.[1001]

In 1915, the Supreme Court of the United States upheld the constitutionality of the law barring the interstate transportation of fight films in *Weber v. Freed*, 239 U.S. 325 (1915), when the State of New Jersey refused to allow entry into the country the films of the Johnson vs. Willard fight. However, Johnson and the promoters could make money with the exhibition of the films throughout the rest of the world.

[1001] 18 U.S.C.A. section 405.

Although many blacks were sad that their champion had been defeated, some were happy, feeling that Johnson had been a menace to the race and had retarded their progress. Others still saw him as a symbol for what blacks could do when given a fair chance.[1002]

Despite the argument that Johnson had hurt the black race, from 1882 to 1908, there was an average of 88 black lynchings per year. There were 89 black lynchings in 1908, even before Jack Johnson won the title in late December. During his reign (1909-1915), there was an average of 59 black lynchings per year. Racism was present before Jack Johnson became champion, it continued during his reign, and after his defeat.

After winning the title, Jess Willard once again publicly re-drew the color line. The *Los Angeles Daily Times* wrote, "He already has announced that if he won he would not fight another negro." For whites, things went back to normal, the way they had been for decades before Johnson, and the way most whites felt things should be and should have been, with the heavyweight championship being a whites-only position.

For the next 22 years, no black man would be allowed to fight for the heavyweight championship. This was no coincidence. No black fighter was going to be allowed the chance that many believed Johnson never should have had in the first place. Many believed that Willard had "restored pugilistic supremacy to the white race." The caption underneath a photo of Willard in the *Los Angeles Daily Times* stated, "The cowboy pugilist, who yesterday knocked out Jack Johnson and restored the championship to the white race." One article stated that "the prevailing impression was that Johnson's defeat by the big Kansan would give a stimulus to boxing and make the sport more popular all over the United States. Now that the title is held by an American..."[1003] As a black

REDEEMER OF WHITE RACE

Jess Willard

WORLD'S HEAVYWEIGHT CHAMPION

Knocked out Jack Johnson—26 Rounds
Havana, Cuba, April 5, 1915

man, Johnson wasn't even seen as a true American. He most certainly was not going to be allowed to attempt to regain the title.

One of the more interesting issues surrounding the Willard bout was whether Johnson threw it. In July 1915, a London newspaper reported that Johnson allegedly had sent cables on June 9 (two months after the fight) to

---

[1002] *Broad Ax*, April 10, 1915.
[1003] *Los Angeles Daily Times*, April 6, 1915.

New York asking for $50,000 due under an agreement to lay down to Willard. Johnson said, "You signed contract to pay me $50,000 to lay down to Willard, which I did. You never kept your promise. I did. Now you must pay according to contract." Promoters Harry Frazee and Jack Curley vigorously denied any such agreement existed or that Johnson made any such statement. They said the only wires received by them from Johnson were asking for his end of the Canadian picture returns and a request to fight Willard again. Neither Johnson nor any newspaper ever produced any such alleged contract.[1004]

The following year, on February 3, 1916, the *New York World* reported an article published by the *People's Journal* in Glasgow, Scotland, with the headline, "Why Johnson 'Faked' His Fight with Willard." In that interview, Johnson said,

> I say now that there is not a man breathing whom I think I could not beat. These may be big words from the boxer who was beaten by Jess Willard at Havana, but those 'in the know' will be able to read between the lines. ...

> My fight with Willard was a financial proposition. But the story goes back some little way. ...

> Well, they promised me that if I would consent to be defeated by Willard I would no longer be molested and would enjoy the freedom any other man would. I would be allowed to see my old mother, who couldn't travel to see me. I would have my motor cars and other property restored to me. It sounded very attractive, but they played the double cross on me.

The *World*'s Robert Edgren did not believe Johnson's claims. "Jack Johnson didn't fake the Willard fight and didn't lie down unless he fooled every one around the ring. He surely fought desperately while he lasted and was well knocked out."

However, Edgren conceded that some promises of freedom had been made. The day before the Johnson-Willard fight, promoter Harry Frazee spoke with Edgren. "He said that he had been in communication with the legal authorities here, and that he had assured Johnson that everything had been fixed so that after the fight he could go to America without being arrested." Hence, apparently Johnson was under the belief that some sort of deal had been made.

However, Frazee also told Edgren the day before the fight that he had just received a message from the U.S. legal authorities saying that "it was impossible to square the Johnson matter, and that Johnson would be arrested the moment he set foot on American soil." Frazee and Edgren agreed not to tell Johnson anything about that recent message until after the fight. Hence, Johnson might possibly have been operating under the false

[1004] *Washington Times, New York Sun,* July 22, 23, 1915.

belief that a deal was in place. Exactly what deal Johnson had been told about was not revealed.[1005]

In March 1919, while he still was at large and had not yet returned to the United States, Johnson issued a statement saying that the Willard fight was fixed for Willard to win in the 10th round, but that Jess made such a poor showing and did so little that it was necessary to wait. Of course, that version is contradicted by Johnson's additional statement also claiming that he was waiting for a payment and a signal from his wife that it had been received. Once she signaled that the money had been received, he signaled back to her and then she left with the money.

Johnson also said he threw the fight to straighten out his Mann Act issues and to be able to visit his mother, but that the promise had not been fulfilled.

Some have speculated that perhaps Johnson's motivation for making the claim had to do with the fact that he felt swindled out of payment on the film rights and a copy of the films which had been promised to him, or he might have been trying to save face and generate interest in a rematch.

Willard and the promoters said Johnson made the claim because he was in need of money and wanted to garner momentum for a rematch.[1006]

In his 1927 autobiography, Johnson claimed to have told Mrs. Johnson a few moments before entering the ring that he was going to lose. Curley had paid him his percentage before he left his home. However, he also told Mrs. Johnson that there was more money due him, and that until the money was paid, he would not take a dive. He claimed that the reason why he did not take a dive sooner was that he was waiting to make sure his wife had been paid the remainder of the money owed, and that once she signaled to him that payment had been made, he then threw the fight.

> Mrs. Johnson was to signal me when she had received the additional money, and I was to signal her so that she might leave the ringside. … It was nearing the twenty-sixth round when the money was turned over to Mrs. Johnson. … After examining it she gave me the signal. I replied that everything was O.K. by a pre-arranged sign and she departed.

However, if he had been paid as claimed, it wouldn't make sense to be sending telegrams asking for the money after the fact. Of course, Johnson might say that he was owed additional payments even after the fight.

Johnson also claimed that he did no serious training, and hardly any at all for the fight, which is contradicted by the news reports and his performance.

Johnson said that when he went down he was conscious and was covering his eyes from the sun while on his back. He used the photo with bent knees and hands over his eyes to prove his contention. Some, who

---

[1005] New York World, February 3, 1916.
[1006] El Paso Herald, March 13, 1919; New York Tribune, March 14, 1919.

only saw that photo, and were not able to see the films, believed him. However, if you look at the films, you can clearly see that Jack threw his arms up over his face in a reflex action when he was dropped, but that his knees then went limp, and he did not move even after the count concluded. His arms appeared to be paralyzed and frozen in place. It even seemed as if Jack was trying to prevent himself from going down as he was falling, trying to grab Willard. If he was throwing the fight, he would not have tried to stop himself from going down by grabbing at Willard on the way down, nor would he have gone down as hard as he did.

Johnson also claimed to have thrown the fight in exchange for the ability to return to the United States with leniency for his Mann Act conviction. However, in an earlier part of his autobiography, he didn't exactly say there was a deal for him to throw the fight, but that it was suggested that if he did so that things might be easier on him.

> On the day of the fight, my condition was fair and I could have defeated Willard and retained the title, but temptation had come to me and as I was stirred by the irresistible desire to see my mother, I was trying to decide upon a course that would enable me to return to the United States. I still was hesitant about entering prison, but at times had decided that I would return and serve my sentence for the sake of seeing my mother, but never got quite to that point. … Preceding the Willard fight it was hinted to me in terms which I could not mistake, that if I permitted Willard to win, which would give him the title, much of the prejudice against me would be wiped out. Those who chafed under the disappointment of having a man of my race hold the championship, I was told, would be mollified, and it would be easier to have the charges against me dropped, and I could again be with my folks. …

> As matters turned out, I had cause to regret my action, for after I had permitted the title to pass to Willard, I found that such offers or hints of leniency as had been tendered me were without substantial foundation, and that immediate prospects for my return to my own country without going to prison were so slight that I could not give them serious thought.[1007]

In that same autobiography, Johnson also said Jack Curley "frankly told me that if I lost the fight to Willard I could return to the United States without being molested."

There is some limited primary source evidence of Johnson's claims. There were rumors of a fix before the fight. However, such rumors had floated around for many of Johnson's fights. Before the fight, some in Johnson's camp claimed that offers to Johnson to throw the fight were made by those associated with the promotion. It also was said that

---

[1007] Johnson, *In the Ring and Out*, at 100-102; 197-198, 201-203.

government officials had tried unsuccessfully to induce Johnson to return to the U.S. Sam McVey said Jack took a dive. Johnson did look at his wife shortly before the knockout, and she did leave the ringside. However, at the time, the belief was that a fatigued Johnson feared that his end was near, he did not want his wife to see him lose, and she did not want to see it either.

More likely than not, Jess Willard had been at the right place at the right time. Johnson was aging at 37, had fought only once per year for the last four years, and therefore likely was not at his sharpest, and naturally was fatigued by the 26th round. Johnson had been hitting Willard hard enough to knock him out, and did not appear to be holding back. Even if he had agreed to throw the fight, or even if representations had been made to him that the government might be lenient with him if he lost, which may well be true, the way he attacked Willard so ferociously certainly gives the impression that he was attempting to win. He was knocked out by a right to the jaw by a big 6'6" 238-pound man with a long reach stepping in quickly with full force. The fight and the knockout looked legitimate. The referee believed the fight was legitimate, and said that Johnson had bet on himself to win, he was so confident. Johnson's trainer also believed that the fight was on the level. Johnson fought confidently and punched ferociously for most of the fight, as if he expected to win via a knockout. However, fatigue set in against a younger, bigger, stronger, and better conditioned opponent.

It appears that like other champions before him, Johnson's ego did not allow him to concede defeat. He had tried to win, but after losing, used the offers made to him before the fight as an excuse. Years later, Gene Tunney said that Johnson preferred to have his fans believe he sold out rather than that he was washed up.[1008]

The fight-film ban helped Johnson make his representations of having thrown the fight without the public being able to develop its own opinion by watching the fight. However, Europeans, Canadians, and other foreigners were able to see the films and draw their own conclusions. Although the preponderance of the evidence does not support a fake, there always will be some lingering doubts, given Johnson's insistence that he threw the fight, combined with evidence that unethical offers and representations had been made to him.

[1008] Gene Tunney, *A Man Must Fight* (Boston: Houghton Mifflin Co., 1932), 180.

Afterword

Jack Johnson had reigned as champion for over six years, from December 26, 1908 to April 5, 1915. He held victories over fighters who were skilled, fast, strong, big, small, black, and white. He defeated the likes of Klondike John Haines, Joe Kennedy, Jack Jeffries, Frank Childs, George Gardner, Fred Russell, Ed Martin, Sam McVey, Jack Munroe, Sandy Ferguson, Joe Jeannette, Young Peter Jackson, Sam Langford, Bill Lang, Bob Fitzsimmons, Jim Flynn, Tommy Burns, Jack O'Brien, Tony Ross, Al Kaufman, Stanley Ketchel, James J. Jeffries, and Frank Moran. His long resume, with scores of lengthy bouts against the world's best, including 13 bouts that lasted 20 rounds, still stands out today as amongst the best ever career resumes of a heavyweight champion.

Just imagine if Johnson had been granted the title shot that he desired and deserved from 1903 to 1905, an opportunity which he would have obtained but for his race. If he would have won the title back then, he possibly could have been champion for ten or eleven years, which would put his reign's length on par with the likes of Joe Louis and Muhammad Ali. Even with having to wait until late 1908, when he was 30 years old, he still reigned for over six years, nearly as long as Larry Holmes.

Some quibble about the fact that he did not defend his title against the best black fighters of his era. However, he did defeat them all prior to becoming champion, and was willing to fight them all if his price was met. Economics and race combined were huge factors. When push came to shove, most promoters were willing to put up big money to see a white man attempt to defeat Johnson. Far fewer were willing to bankroll a black versus black championship bout. Also, promoters cancelled scheduled Johnson title bouts with both black and white fighters for a myriad of reasons. At various times, jurisdictions refused to allow Johnson to box for racial, moral, and legal reasons.

If Johnson had scheduled the Willard bout for 25 rounds, which was the greatest distance that James J. Jeffries had defended his title, or 15 rounds, as would be the case for most title bouts throughout the mid-20th century, or 12 rounds as is the case today, he would have successfully retained his title on points with ease. With shorter, limited-rounds bouts, he might very well have reigned for several more years. He quite possibly could have had the longest reign of all time. The fact that he could dominate a big man for so long even at age 37 is a testament to how good Jack Johnson really was.

In fact, Johnson did not lose another fight again for eleven years, until 1926, when he was 48 years old, having won anywhere from thirteen to twenty bouts in a row (depending on what record one consults), although he was not allowed to engage in championship or elite caliber bouts during those years. From 1916 through 1920, Johnson fought and resided in places like Spain and Mexico. He also lived in France and England.

One month after the Willard fight, on May 7, 1915, the RMS *Lusitania* was sunk off of the coast of Ireland. The Germans were behind the sinking of the ship, which had sailed out of New York. Rumor had it that there were ammunitions secretly stored on the boat, being sent to the British. The 1,924 passengers aboard the vessel had no knowledge of the cargo being transported. 1,119 passengers perished when the ship sank. However, the United States did not formally enter World War I until two years later.

On March 25, 1916 at New York's Madison Square Garden, just shy of a year after winning the title, Jess Willard defended his championship for the first time, winning a 10-round no-decision bout against Frank Moran. For a mere 10 rounds, Willard earned a guaranteed $47,500, and Moran $23,750. The gate receipts were $151,254. Willard did not fight or defend the title again for over three years.

On April 6, 1917, the U.S. declared war on the German Empire and joined the First World War. Under the command of General John J. Pershing, several million U.S. soldiers, including black regiments, fought on the battlefields of France and elsewhere on the side of the Allies (U.K., France, Russia, Italy, and Japan). World War I would end on November 11, 1918 with the defeat of the Central Powers, which in part consisted of Germany, Austria-Hungary, and Turkey. More than 70 million military personnel had been mobilized in the war, and more than 9 million combatants and 7 million civilians had perished.

On March 17, 1918, Jack Johnson's mother, Tiny Johnson, died.

On July 4, 1919 in Toledo, Ohio, Jack Dempsey defeated Jess Willard to win the world heavyweight championship. Willard was beaten so badly that he retired after the 3rd round.

The following year, on January 17, 1920, the 18th Amendment to the U.S. constitution went into effect, making the manufacture, sale, and transportation of intoxicating liquors illegal. The amendment would not be repealed until 1933.

On August 18, 1920, the 19th Amendment to the U.S. Constitution was ratified, guaranteeing all American women the right to vote.

Over five years after he lost his title to Jess Willard, on July 20, 1920, Jack Johnson returned to the U.S., surrendered to federal agents at the Mexican border, and was taken into custody. At his re-sentencing on September 14, 1920, Judge George A. Carpenter once again sentenced Johnson to serve a one year and a day prison sentence at Leavenworth Prison and pay a $1,000 fine.

In January 1921, the Leavenworth Prison's Parole Board (which included former Nevada Governor Denver Dickerson, who had hosted Jeffries-Johnson), held a parole hearing and unanimously recommended that Johnson be paroled.

However, on January 21, 1921, the Justice Department denied parole, and Johnson was required to serve his full one-year term, less any required credits for time previously served.

Interestingly enough, while he was in prison, Johnson applied for and was granted two patents – one for an improved automobile wrench and one for a theft-prevention device for vehicles.

As of May 31, 1921, the segregated Greenwood section of Tulsa, Oklahoma, a district known as Black Wall Street owing to its vibrant, wealthy, and prosperous black community, was one of the most successful flourishing black neighborhoods in the country. However, on that date, the *Tulsa Tribune* published an inflammatory story wherein a white 17-year-old female elevator operator named Sarah Page accused black 19-year-old shoeshiner Dick Rowland of attempting to rape or at least assault her the previous day. In fact, her allegations were that he grabbed her arm. Word quickly spread that a white lynch mob intended to take the law into its own hands and kill Rowland. A group of black men assembled outside the jail to protect Rowland from the approaching lynch mob. A white man attempted to take a gun from a black man, a shot was fired, and violence erupted.

Whites used this as an excuse to rampage into the Greenwood district and loot, destroy, and burn down the neighborhood, including black-owned businesses, homes, churches, grocery stores, restaurants, movie theaters, a hospital, bank, post office, libraries, schools, law offices, airplanes, and even buses. The white mob even used some of the black-owned airplanes to launch gasoline and dynamite bombs from the sky. During the riot, the mob, led by the Ku Klux Klan, which included policemen, killed black men, women, and children, shooting and burning them. It was a massacre.

By the time troops were deployed the next day, the town was virtually obliterated. Instead of arresting whites, the troops arrested thousands of blacks and held them in custody for several days before releasing them. No whites were ever arrested or charged.

Over 600 successful black businesses were ruined. Although the official death toll claimed 26 black deaths and 13 whites, the American Red Cross estimated over 300 deaths (many of whom were buried in mass graves), which is closer to the truth, 8,624 people in need of assistance, and over 1,000 homes and businesses destroyed. 35 square blocks had been torched. Eventually, the charges against Rowland were dismissed.

On July 9, 1921, a 43-year-old Jack Johnson was released from prison.

After his release, Johnson fought and exhibited in places like Cuba, Canada, and Mexico. Johnson later wrote, "I was sincere in challenging Dempsey, or any of the other heavyweights…but I realize that the private regulations and prejudices of boxing commissions prevent me from making a serious effort to arrange such a bout."[1009]

[1009] Johnson, *In the Ring and Out* at 249. Johnson sparred Luis Firpo prior to the 1923 Firpo-Dempsey fight and claimed to have mastered him. "Firpo made such a poor showing in the ring with me that Rickard, the promoter, fearing that publicity of this would injure the gate-receipts, stopped further boxing between Firpo and me." Johnson was willing to fight him. "Firpo would have presented no difficulties for me." Id. at 250.

Lucille Cameron divorced Johnson in 1924, owing to his infidelity. In 1925, Johnson married Irene Pineau, another white woman, to whom he remained married until his death.

It wasn't until he was 48 years old in 1926 that Jack Johnson again fought on a card in the U.S. (the previous time being in 1912 against Flynn). Some Americans would pay to see Johnson when he was a completely shot fighter and more likely to lose. He continued engaging in occasional bouts and exhibitions throughout the remainder of his life.

On June 10, 1946, Jack Johnson's driving finally caught up with him. He died in an automobile accident near Raleigh, North Carolina. He was 68 years old. He was buried next to Etta Duryea Johnson in Chicago.

It is befitting for Jack Johnson's story to end with some of Jack Johnson's own words:

> Although I have often encountered prejudice on account of my race...I have found no better way of avoiding racial prejudice than to act in my relations with people of other races as if prejudice did not exist. ...
>
> As I look back upon the life I have lived and compare it with the lives of my contemporaries I feel that mine has been a full life and above all a human life.[1010]

[1010] Johnson, *In the Ring and Out*, at 239, 256.

Appendix: Jack Johnson's World Championship Record

Born: March 31, 1878, Galveston, TX
Died: June 10, 1946, Franklinton, NC, age 68

1908

| Dec 26 | Tommy Burns | Sydney, NSW | W/TKO 14 |

Following another knockdown of Burns, at the request of the police, Referee Hugh McIntosh stopped the fight and rendered a decision, pursuant to prefight agreement.

1909

| Mar 10 | Victor McLaglen | Vancouver, CAN | EX 6 |

| May 19 | Jack O'Brien | Philadelphia, PA | W/D ND 6 |

There was a split of opinion regarding whether it was a Johnson victory or a draw, depending upon one's scoring criteria.

| June 30 | Tony Ross | Pittsburg, PA | W ND 6 |

| Sep 9 | Al Kaufman | Colma, CA | W ND 10 |

| Oct 16 | Stanley Ketchel | Colma, CA | KO 12 |

1910

| Jul 4 | James J. Jeffries | Reno, NV | DQ/TKO 15 |

Referee Tex Rickard's official ruling of a disqualification as a result of illegal assistance in rising after Jeffries went down for the second time in the round is at variance with the facts. He allowed the fight to continue until after Jeffries was knocked down for the third time in the round, and terminated the bout only once Sam Berger requested such.

1912

| Jul 4 | Jim Flynn | Las Vegas, NM | W 9 |

Police ordered the fight stopped as a result of Flynn's incessant and flagrant head butting. Pursuant to a pre-fight agreement which said that in the event of a police stoppage, a decision would be rendered for the man who had done the best work up to that point in time, Referee Ed W. Smith awarded a points decision victory to Johnson.

1913

| Dec 19 | Battling Jim Johnson | Paris, France | D 10 |

1914

| Jun 27 | Frank Moran | Paris, France | W 20 |

1915

| Apr 5 | Jess Willard | Havana, Cuba | L KO by 26 |

Bibliography

<u>Primary Sources</u>

Afro American Ledger
Albany Advertiser
Albuquerque Evening Herald
Albuquerque Morning Journal
Alexandria Gazette
Arizona Republican
Bennington Evening Banner
Billings Gazette
Bisbee Daily Review
Bismark Daily Tribune
Boston Globe
Boston Guardian
Boston Herald
Boston Post
Boxing
Chicago Broad Ax
Chicago Defender
Citizen (Honesdale, PA)
Daily Ardmoreite
Daily Capital Journal
Daily Gate City
Daily Missoulian
Daily Province
Day Book
Democratic Banner
Denver Post
Deseret Evening News
East Oregonian
Edgfield Advertiser
El Paso Herald
Evening Standard
Fort Worth Star-Telegram
Free Lance
Freeman
Goodwin's Weekly
Grey River Argus
Harlowton News
Harrisburg Star-Independent
Harrisburg Telegraph
Hawaiian Star

Herald and News
Honolulu Evening Bulletin
Honolulu Star-Bulletin
Kansas City Star
La Presse
Las Vegas Optic
La Vie Au Grand Air
Le Matin
Le Petit Parisien
Le Plein Air
Le Temps
L'Humanite
L'Intransigeant
Licking Valley Courier
London Daily Mail
London Times
Los Angeles Herald
Los Angeles Times
Mahoning Dispatch
Manchester Guardian
Mathews Journal
Marion Daily Mirror
Milwaukee Journal
Mirror of Life and Boxing World
Nashville Globe
Nevada State Journal
New York Age
New York American
New York Herald
New York Journal
New York Sun
New York Times
New York Tribune
New York World
Northern Star
Observer
Ogdensburg News
Ogden Standard
Omaha Daily Bee
Omaha World Herald

Philadelphia Evening Bulletin   San Francisco Evening Post
Philadelphia Inquirer   San Francisco Examiner
Philadelphia Press   Santa Fe New Mexican
Philadelphia Public Ledger   Saskatoon Star-Phoenix
Philadelphia Record   Seattle Republican
Pittsburg Press   Seattle Star
Pittsburg Dispatch   Spokane Press
Pittsburgh Post   Star-Independent
Reno Evening Gazette   Sydney Bulletin
Richmond Planet   Syracuse Journal
Richmond Times-Dispatch   Tacoma Times
Rock Island Argus   Thames Star
Salt Lake Herald   Times Dispatch
Salt Lake Herald-Republican   Wanganui Chronicle
Salt Lake Tribune   Washington Bee
San Francisco Bulletin   Washington Herald
San Francisco Call   Washington Post
San Francisco Chronicle   Washington Times

Secondary Sources

Gilmore, Al-Tony, *Bad Nigger!*, (Kennikat Press, New York, 1975).

Johnson, Jack, *In the Ring and Out*, (National Spots Publishing Co., Chicago, 1927).

Johnson, Jack, *My Life and Battles*, 1911-1914 French versions edited and translated by Christopher Rivers, (Praeger Publishers, Westport, CT, 2007).

Runstedtler, Theresa, *Jack Johnson: Rebel Sojourner*, (University of California Press, Oakland, 2012).

Sammons, Jeffrey T., *Beyond the Ring*, (University of Illinois Press, Chicago, 1988).

Tunney, Gene, *A Man Must Fight*, (Houghton Mifflin Co., Boston, 1932).

Ward, Geoffrey C., *Unforgivable Blackness*, (Alfred A. Knopf, New York, 2004).

A Note From the Author

My first boxing memory was watching Larry Holmes vs. Gerry Cooney in June 1982 with my father at a large gathering at a family friend's house. I was nearly 10 years old. I had no idea why it was such a big deal, but I enjoyed the fight. During my youth, I gradually grew to love and appreciate boxing's poetic skill, fluid kinetic motion, strategy, and yes, the controlled violence, the neutralization and dismantling of one's foe. Mike Tyson inspired awe in me. I also appreciated the skills and abilities of fighters like Chavez, Holyfield, Hearns, Duran, Hagler, Leonard, Foreman, and Holmes, etc. I started recording fights and watching them over and over and over again. Thanks to my parents for letting me use up all of those blank vhs tapes.

I purchased the documentary *The Legendary Champions*, which got me hooked on the oldies. I really wanted to learn more, and was fascinated by the idea that I actually could watch boxing history as far back as 1894. I read boxing magazines, which contained ads posted by collectors selling videos, and I started buying old fight videos. I watched anything and everything I could. The world of Louis, Ali, Marciano, Robinson, etc. opened up for me. Documentaries on the lives of Jack Johnson, Joe Louis, and Muhammad Ali added the additional intriguing layer of race and sociology, which deepened my interest in boxing.

I was fascinated by the fact that boxing was about so much more than just sport, but operated on so many different levels. It intertwined sport with history, race, sociology, film, personalities, business, law, politics, entertainment, journalism, and even religion. I always had a natural affinity for the underdog, and I appreciated and admired boxers and their struggles. The videos made me want to learn more.

I enjoyed reading and learning from boxing books. However, even as a teenager, I found that most books lacked the detail, thoroughness, authenticity, and multiple perspectives from primary sources that I wanted. There appeared to be a lot of holes, and I desired more. It was at this stage in my life that the kernel of the thought developed that one day I might write boxing books that would answer my unresolved questions. I still was in high school at the time.

I was so crazy for boxing that I immersed myself in it in many ways. I took boxing lessons. I tried to write about boxing in every high school class that I could. I wrote my English essays about boxers, Sociology essays about race in boxing, and even my Physics paper was about the physics of the punch. In college in the early to mid-1990s, for a Sociology class I wrote a piece called, "The Social Implications of the Black Heavyweight Champion in America." I read books like Gerald Early's *Culture of Bruising*, Nat Fleischer's *Black Dynamite*, Jeffrey Sammons' *Beyond the Ring*, and Al-Tony Gilmore's *Bad Nigger!*, as well as many others.

I did some boxing in college and even while in law school. I also participated in refereeing, judging, and coaching. My father and I often went to the Fight Nights at the Fabulous Forum in Inglewood, California, and I also traveled to see fights in Las Vegas and throughout Southern California. During law school, I was an intern at Top Rank Boxing. In subsequent years, I have run a boxing club, coached and managed boxers, and promoted both pro and amateur shows. I also was the chair of USA Boxing's Judicial Committee for a while. If it was boxing related, I was willing to try it.

All of those formative years in high school, college, and even law school sowed seeds in me which eventually led to and culminated in the boxing biographies I started writing and publishing in the mid-2000s. I feel that with my Jack Johnson biographies, my series has come full circle. I now realize that these are the books that I always was meant to write. I hope you feel that I have done Jack Johnson's story justice, and given you a fresh, new, unique, and more thorough perspective regarding his life, boxing career, and world in which he lived.

Adam J. Pollack

Acknowledgments

Thank you to all who have helped me in some way with this book, be it research, photographs, promotion, editing, French translation, advertising, or general support:

Tom Seemuth

Clay Moyle

Steve Compton

Corey Parker

Katy Klinefelter

Gregory Speciale

Steve Lott / Boxing Hall of Fame Las Vegas

Sergei Yurchenko

Thomas Hauser

Evan Grant

Kevin Smith

Robert Lancaster

Brandon Ogbunu

Tracy Callis

Paul Hindley

Tony Triem

Anna Bruno

Jayne Lady

Druet Klugh

Glenn Longacre / National Archives at Chicago

Natalie Allen

University of Iowa / Interlibrary Loan

Boxrec.com

Eastsideboxing.com

Cyberboxingzone.com

Trufanboxing.com

Index

Democrat, 484, 606, 679, 687, 751, 760, 824

Dempsey, Jack, 732, 861, 862

Densham, Jack, 409, 410, 411, 421

DeWoody, Charles, 689, 705, 722, 723

Dickerson, Denver, 295, 303, 327, 328, 331, 332, 368, 861

Dime, Jimmy, 89, 93, 94, 95, 99

Discrimination, 539

Disfranchisement, 553, 692

Dix, Governor John, 571, 658

Dixon, George, 75, 352, 669

Dixon, Jr., Thomas, 483, 823

Dorgan, Tad, 45, 60, 62, 68, 84, 100, 331, 346, 352, 362, 766, 767, 802

Douglas, Aimee, 23

Douglass, Frederick, 24, 363, 421

Drummond, Fred, 553, 574, 739, 762

Due process, 686

Duryea Johnson, Etta, 246, 305, 370, 436, 533, 542, 548, 612, 651, 662-664, 677, 695-697, 700-702, 704, 705, 707, 710, 711, 713, 720, 724, 758, 759, 777, 862, 863

Edgren, Robert, 103, 342, 352, 376, 416, 424, 659, 829, 831, 833, 837, 839, 840, 843, 844, 845, 849, 851, 856

Edwards, Harry, 32, 47

Emancipation, 461

Erbstein, Charles, 667, 671

Everett, Mexican Pete, 167, 242, 264, 338

Eyton, Charles, 246, 261, 264, 687

Ferguson, Sandy, 31, 73, 91, 92, 106, 171, 544, 859

Film, 15, 18, 27, 28, 30, 37, 42, 44, 45, 80, 102, 159, 161, 164, 172, 176, 177, 179-181, 184, 185, 196, 197, 199-202, 207-209, 212, 213, 215-217, 221, 222, 225, 226, 228, 234-236, 246, 274, 282, 285, 289, 298, 306, 308, 332, 335, 347, 348, 358, 366, 368, 369, 370, 417, 422, 425, 439, 453, 461, 463-471, 474, 478, 480, 482-485, 487, 490, 492, 494, 495,

500-502, 510, 527, 529, 533, 541, 544, 549, 550, 555, 557, 560, 562, 571, 578, 580, 591, 599, 606, 607, 612, 613, 616-619, 621, 622, 624, 625, 642, 645, 655-657, 664, 685, 686, 723, 749, 751, 754, 755, 768, 773, 778, 780, 782, 784, 786, 787, 789, 790, 804, 805, 808, 819, 820, 823, 824, 833, 834, 836, 851, 854, 856-858, 861, 866

Finnegan, Jack, 338

Fitzpatrick, Sam, 9, 10, 24, 25, 104, 177, 178, 255, 261, 410

Fitzsimmons, Bob, 14, 21, 23, 33, 44, 58, 70, 82, 108, 117, 162, 168, 170, 176, 224, 226, 237, 264, 297, 325, 326, 327, 337, 338, 339, 347, 348, 350, 369, 426, 427, 441, 444, 446, 511, 513, 517, 538, 552, 555, 604, 706, 802, 809, 813, 832, 849, 859, 883

Flanagan, Tom, 277, 278, 296, 315, 353, 354, 369, 435, 450, 550, 552, 586, 595, 598, 600, 602, 611-613, 636, 684, 689, 722, 752, 771, 777, 779, 805, 812, 821, 833, 835

Floto, Otto, 602, 610, 613, 633, 634, 764, 773, 835

Flynn, Jim, 3, 86, 90, 102, 106, 108, 112, 115, 121, 151, 160, 167, 177, 246, 251, 348, 422, 450, 544, 546, 550, 572, 575, 577, 579-650, 653, 661, 663, 665, 687, 692, 693, 726, 741, 749, 753, 761, 764, 768, 773, 774, 819, 820, 827, 859, 861, 863

Foley, Harry, 185, 315, 369

Fornoff, Captain Fred, 600, 612, 625, 626, 627, 630, 644

Frawley, James, 551, 571, 659

Frazee, Harry, 819, 856

Furey, Barney, 122, 147, 180, 185, 258, 262, 266, 305, 306, 369, 436, 697, 707, 710

Gallagher, Billy, 314, 360, 370

Gans, Joe, 201, 217, 229, 235, 240, 298, 352, 361, 490, 534, 729

Gardner, George, 90, 108, 144, 167, 323, 581, 859

Geyer, Jack, 265, 317, 354, 753

Gibson, Billy, 651, 652, 654, 832

London, Jack, 311, 313, 327, 340, 347, 357, 359, 375, 376, 378, 379, 382, 387, 389, 391, 392, 394, 397, 408, 409, 416, 420, 445, 452, 476, 515

Louis, Joe, 6, 751

Lynchings, 483, 854, 855, 861

Madden, Billy, 241, 251, 658

Magilligan, T. P., 319, 350, 512

Maher, Peter, 42, 739

Maitrot, Emile, 761

Malgan, Abdul, 592-594, 596, 598, 603, 604, 613

Mann Act, 667, 674, 676, 677, 681, 684, 691, 694, 699, 706, 712, 715, 716, 720, 722, 724, 731, 735, 754, 756, 759, 856, 857

Marriage, 9, 18, 19, 35, 473, 475, 527, 528, 530, 533, 536, 542, 662-666, 668, 670, 673, 675-677, 680, 682, 685, 686, 687, 691, 695-697, 702, 704, 710, 712, 713, 716, 717, 723, 731, 736, 759, 825, 861

Marshall, Ray, 588, 591, 592, 593, 594, 596, 598, 600, 604, 613

Martin, Denver Ed, 12, 13, 14, 167, 352, 859

Masterson, Bat, 100, 279, 660, 727, 734

McAuliffe, Jack, 50, 355, 369, 428

McCarey, Tom, 141, 142, 218, 234, 369

McCarney, Billy, 692

McCarthy, Charles, 751

McCarthy, Mayor P. H., 422, 443, 474

McCarthy, Tommy, 259, 531

McCarty, Luther, 585, 613, 649, 653, 654, 656-658, 665, 687-689, 692, 693, 717, 718, 730, 750, 762, 815

McClay, Hattie, 9, 19, 35, 237, 530, 532, 533, 696, 697, 700, 705, 706, 711-713, 720, 758

McCoy, Kid, 70, 279

McDonald, Governor William, 584, 587, 593, 597, 612, 627, 642, 643

McGovern, Terry, 50, 299

McGrath, Tim, 232, 313, 510

McGuigan, Jack, 36, 48, 49, 50, 71

McIntosh, Hugh, 4, 17, 18, 25, 29, 30, 148, 225, 234, 257, 327, 330, 342, 355, 369, 501, 514, 515, 533-535, 537, 539, 543, 544, 546, 553, 555, 571, 576, 579, 581, 598, 605, 606, 650, 651, 653, 657, 661, 665, 669, 688, 863

McKetrick, Dan, 539, 583, 650, 654, 656, 730, 731, 754, 761, 764, 771, 778, 779, 806, 814, 832

McLaglen, Victor, 13, 14, 15, 584, 863

McLean, Alec/Alex, 9, 79, 255

McLoughlin, William, 23, 48, 59

McMahon Brothers, 613, 656, 657, 659, 660

McReynolds, James C., 719

McVea/McVey, Sam, 7, 25, 26, 27, 92, 107, 116, 121, 144, 167, 236, 515, 534, 539, 540, 542, 543, 545, 546, 551, 553, 555, 572-574, 576- 581, 584, 605, 610, 614, 646, 647, 649-653, 655, 665, 669, 675, 688, 693, 725, 738, 739, 741, 752, 762, 807, 816, 820, 829, 832, 833, 836, 849, 859

Menocal, President Mario, 827, 830, 835

Meyer, Reverend F. B., 557, 558, 559, 560, 561, 565, 566

Miles Brothers, 161, 180, 212, 606, 645

Miller, Charles, 162, 165, 181, 185, 661

Miller, Charley, 153, 162, 173, 763

Millett, Joe, 107, 111, 153, 160, 181

Mills, Dave, 107, 110, 111, 114, 117, 122, 150, 151, 153, 156, 160, 161, 163, 165, 168, 175, 180, 185, 266, 278, 286, 287, 305, 306, 313, 323, 354, 369, 432, 763, 828, 829, 836

Miscegenation, 716, 824

Mixed-race, 18, 22, 145, 147, 291, 562, 563, 651, 658, 686, 727, 732, 765

Moir, Gunner, 77, 80, 542, 544, 556, 573

Monahan, Walter, 271, 279, 305, 316, 323, 354, 538, 542, 543, 582, 697, 823, 825, 828, 829, 836

Moran, Frank, 3, 28, 688, 693, 725, 730, 731, 737, 743, 745, 747, 748, 751, 753,

352, 355, 356, 357, 359, 360- 364, 370, 394, 397, 416, 418, 424, 426, 438, 441, 443, 444, 449, 451, 452, 455-459, 461-468, 470, 471, 473-501, 503, 504, 506, 507, 509, 519, 528, 530, 532, 533, 535, 538, 539, 542, 543, 546, 548, 549, 551, 552, 556, 557, 561-564, 575-577, 583, 585, 592-594, 600, 604, 610, 633, 642, 644, 653, 655, 658-663, 665, 668- 680, 682-684, 686, 690, 691, 695, 709, 716, 717, 719, 720, 723-725, 729, 749, 751, 752, 755, 760, 779, 803, 806, 807, 809-811, 819, 822, 824, 827, 834, 849, 854, 855, 857, 859, 862, 866

Race Riot, 274, 292, 363, 455, 456, 459, 460, 468, 528, 640, 672, 736, 803, 804, 862

Republican, 22, 72, 100, 246, 249, 252, 253, 256, 259, 537, 540, 676, 677, 678, 864, 865

Resspress, Kid Calvin Rastus, 588, 589, 590, 594, 596, 599, 602, 603, 604, 774

Rhodes, Gus, 724, 729, 778, 808

Rhodes, Jennie, 662

Rickard, Tex, 234, 235, 256, 260, 261, 265, 266, 267, 285, 289, 290, 291, 293, 295, 300, 303, 305, 308, 311, 327, 360, 365-368, 372, 379, 387, 402, 403, 415-418, 423, 428, 429, 433, 453, 474, 475, 506, 508, 509, 511, 514, 517, 574, 656, 860, 863

Rocap, William, 51, 53, 72, 779, 795, 801, 807, 808, 823

Roche, William, 261

Rock, William T., 289, 308, 347, 369

Roddenberry, Seaborn, 687

Roosevelt, President Franklin, 655

Roosevelt, President Theodore, 549, 665

Root, Jack, 323, 334, 357, 428, 506

Ross, Tony, 3, 17, 26, 88, 89, 90, 95, 108, 219, 536, 551, 552, 581, 661, 682, 730, 734, 739, 753, 762, 768, 773, 774, 859, 863

Rothstein, Arnold, 514, 832

Ruhlin, Gus, 70, 167, 338, 341, 429

Russell, Fred, 14, 92, 255, 610, 859

Ryan, Tommy, 33, 71, 158, 162, 252, 255, 585- 587, 590-597, 601, 605

Savage, Jim, 763, 825, 828, 829, 836

Scanlan, Jim, 90, 567

Schreck, Mike, 33, 90, 103, 108, 219, 234, 249, 542, 545, 572

Schreiber, Belle, 676, 677, 683, 695-711, 713, 714, 716, 717, 720, 725, 736, 756, 757

Sharkey, Tom, 28, 44, 50, 70, 77, 154, 160, 162, 167, 168, 226, 273, 296, 298, 319, 338, 350, 354, 357, 369, 373, 376, 425, 429, 555, 809

Shaughnessy, Mark, 111, 117, 122

Sims Act, 655

Sims, Thetus, 606, 655

Skelly, Kid, 589, 596, 613

Slattery, William, 351, 374, 415, 416, 421

Slavery, 224, 452, 484, 546, 671, 676, 680, 683, 684, 687, 689, 691, 693, 694, 725, 756, 818, 819

Slavin, Frank, 327

Smith, Denver Ed, 352

Smith, Ed, 78, 106, 112, 115, 118, 123, 139, 261, 265, 323, 332, 428, 592, 594, 600, 607, 609, 614, 625, 627, 630, 639, 663, 718, 763, 826, 830, 863

Smith, Gunboat, 153, 156, 174, 175, 177, 180, 184, 216, 217, 232, 237, 251, 544, 657, 688, 693, 718, 722, 724, 726, 730-734, 736, 738, 750, 752, 753, 754, 761, 762, 764, 767, 791, 800, 802, 804, 807, 812, 815, 818, 844

Smith, Hoke, 552, 553, 673

South, 47, 110, 185, 237, 292, 296, 302, 351, 352, 359, 364, 440, 461, 468-470, 473, 482, 483, 491, 493, 494, 497, 500, 501, 539, 541, 543, 553, 557, 560-565, 571, 575, 628, 652, 661, 672-676, 684-687, 691, 695, 729, 735, 750

Squires, Bill, 80, 237, 276, 447, 504, 551, 581

Stift, Billy, 33

Sullivan, Jack, 27, 33, 108, 146, 167, 171, 544, 579, 581

Sullivan, John L., 16, 75, 227, 245, 272, 295, 296, 305, 323, 335, 343, 344, 346, 369, 373, 378, 403, 408-, 412, 426, 446, 452, 474, 537, 540, 544, 583, 686, 775, 802, 810, 813, 883

Sullivan, Tim, 357, 368, 505, 581

Supreme Court of the United States, 18, 147, 470, 680, 681, 688, 691, 692, 719, 735, 759, 854

Sutton, Frank, 305, 306, 663, 706, 707

Taft, President William, 8, 163, 359, 655, 676, 751

Taupert, Mayor Robert, 597

Taylor, Ben, 77, 169

Taylor, Lew, 115, 117, 122

Temple, Larry, 33

Thompson, Jack, 602

Tillman, Senator Ben, 483, 497, 546, 735

Van Court, DeWitt, 241, 341, 370

Van Court, Eugene, 255

Van Loan, C. E., 250, 284, 326, 357, 378, 385, 391, 411, 415, 419, 420, 425, 448

Vancouver Athletic Club, 11, 12, 13

Vardaman, Governor James K., 483, 484, 497

Vienne, Theodore, 731, 737, 761, 762, 765, 778, 779

Villa, Francisco, 822

Vitagraph Company, 347, 471

Walcott, Joe, 171, 261, 599

Walton, Lester, 646, 658, 659, 661, 668, 679, 807

Washington, Booker T., 251, 310, 363, 487, 491, 669

Watkins, Bob, 599, 613

Welch, Jack, 17, 79, 155, 181, 186, 187, 196, 198, 200, 208, 261, 265, 306, 316, 504, 592, 829, 835, 837, 847

Wells, Billy, 3, 519, 536, 542, 544, 546, 547, 548, 550, 552, 556, 565, 573, 579, 600, 603, 693, 718, 753, 755

Wells-Barnett, Ida B., 683

White, Charlie, 57, 360, 372, 513, 832

White, James, 557, 559, 560, 565, 566, 576

Wilkerson, James, 667, 677, 695, 719, 721, 753, 759

Wilkins, Barron, 22, 242, 248, 528

Willard, Jess, 3, 655, 658, 692, 718, 727, 731, 737, 750, 751, 753, 754, 760, 761, 806, 807, 815-845, 847-861, 863

Williams, Al, 583, 585, 587, 588, 591, 593, 594, 596, 598, 600, 604, 613

Willie, John, 763

Willis, Joe, 107, 111, 544, 753

Wills, Harry, 596, 597, 724, 760, 762, 820

Wilson, President Woodrow, 719, 824

Woodman, Joe, 26, 109, 210, 234, 243, 276, 315, 335, 352, 518, 527, 528, 534, 539, 540, 550, 589, 688, 726, 731

Yellow streak, 18, 31, 85, 87, 117, 133, 149, 159, 220, 228, 242, 257, 264, 273, 289, 313, 344, 350, 361, 377, 382, 423, 424, 432, 433, 443, 446, 451, 476, 478, 480, 488, 492, 507, 508, 512, 523, 547, 636, 638

Young, Waldemar, 410

Other Books By Adam J. Pollack

John L. Sullivan: The Career of the First Gloved Heavyweight Champion

In the Ring With James J. Corbett

In the Ring With Bob Fitzsimmons

In the Ring With James J. Jeffries

In the Ring With Marvin Hart

In the Ring With Tommy Burns

In the Ring With Jack Johnson - Part I: The Rise

Adam J. Pollack is a professional and amateur boxing judge and referee, a publisher, and a member of the Boxing Writers Association of America. He also is an attorney practicing law in Iowa City, Iowa.

www.ingramcontent.com/pod-product-compliance
Lightning Source LLC
Chambersburg PA
CBHW020409100426

42812CB00001B/264